The SAGE
Handbook of

New Approaches in Management and Organization

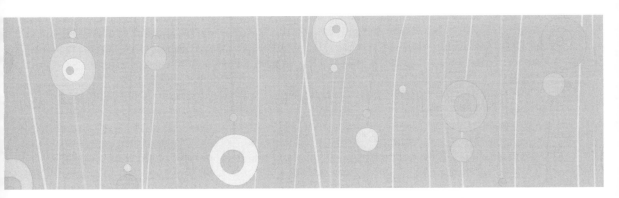

The SAGE
Handbook of

New Approaches in Management and Organization

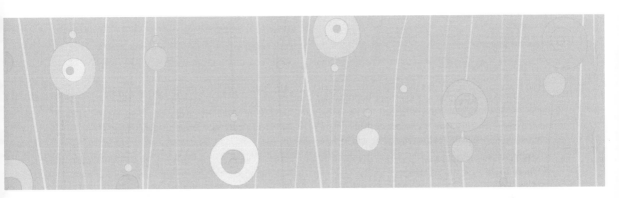

Edited by

Daved Barry and Hans Hansen

Los Angeles • London • New Delhi • Singapore

First published 2008

SAGE Publications Ltd
1 Oliver's Yard
55 City Road
London EC1Y 1SP

SAGE Publications Inc.
2455 Teller Road
Thousand Oaks, California 91320

SAGE Publications India Pvt Ltd
B 1/I 1 Mohan Cooperative Industrial Area
Mathura Road
New Delhi 110 044

SAGE Publications Asia-Pacific Pte Ltd
33 Pekin Street #02-01
Far East Square
Singapore 048763

Library of Congress Control Number: 2007935946

British Library Cataloguing in Publication data

A catalogue record for this book is available from the British Library

ISBN 978-1-4129-1218-1
ISBN 978-1-4129-1219-8 (pbk)

Typeset by CEPHA Imaging Pvt. Ltd., Bangalore, India
Printed in Great Britain by The Cromwell Press, Trowbridge, Wiltshire
Printed on paper from sustainable resources

Contents

List of Contributors   xiii

INTRODUCTION   1
The New and Emerging in Management and Organization: Gatherings,
    Trends, and Bets
Daved Barry and Hans Hansen

PART 1   LOOKING AT ORGANIZATIONS   **11**

1.1   The Future of Critical Management Studies   13
    Mats Alvesson

    Snapshot
    Theorizing the Future of Critical Organization Studies   27
    Dennis K. Mumby

    Snapshot
    Getting Critical About Sensemaking   29
    Albert J. Mills

1.2   The Art of . . .   31
    Daved Barry

1.3   How We Know What We Know: The Potentiality of Art and Aesthetics   42
    Ian W. King

1.4   Alterity/Identity Interplay in Image Construction   49
    Barbara Czarniawska

    Snapshot
    Organizational Identity as an Emerging Perennial Domain   63
    Dennis A. Gioia

    Snapshot
    Is Identity in and of Organizations Just a Passing Fad?   66
    Michael G. Pratt

1.5   Exploring Plato's Cave: Critical Realism in the Study of Organization and
    Management   68
    Mike Reed

Snapshot
Philosophy as Core Competence 79
Martin Kilduff and Ajay Mehra

Snapshot
For Informed Pluralism, Broad Relevance and Critical Reflexivity 82
Hugh Willmott

1.6 Revisualizing Images in Leadership and Organization Studies 84
Eric Guthey and Brad Jackson

Snapshot
Can a Leader be 'True to the Self' and Socially Skilled? 93
William L. Gardner and Claudia C. Cogliser

Snapshot
The Art of Global Leadership 95
Nancy J. Adler

1.7 Analyzing Artifacts: Material Methods for Understanding Identity, Status, and
Knowledge in Organizational Life 98
Beth A. Bechky

Snapshot
Risk and Organizations: Toward a Cultural-Symbolic Perspective 110
Robert P. Gephart, Jr., Cagri Topal and Michael Kulicki

1.8 On the Practise of Practice: In-tensions and Ex-tensions in the Ongoing
Reconfiguration of Practices 112
Elena P. Antonacopoulou

Snapshot
The Nature of Research Practice 132
Jean M. Bartunek

1.9 Statistico-organizational Theory: Creating Organizational Management Theory
from Methodological Principles 135
Lex Donaldson

Snapshot
Updating Organization Theory 146
Jerry Davis

Snapshot
Organization Studies is (and should be) Different from Economics 148
Jeffrey Pfeffer

Snapshot
A 'Neo-Carnegie' Perspective on Organizations 150
William Ocasio

Snapshot
The Frustrating Search for Interaction Effects 152
Herman Aguinis and Charles A. Pierce

Snapshot
From 20th Century Knowledge Management to 21st Century Challenges   154
Deborah Dougherty

1.10   Indigenous Perspectives on Restorying and Restoring Organizational Life   156
Laura Brearley, Treahna Hamm, Doris Paton and Mark Rose

Snapshot
Workplace Spirituality, Towards What Purpose?   167
Marjo Lips-Wiersma

1.11   Social Worlds Theory and the Power of Tension   170
Bente Elkjaer and Marleen Huysman

Snapshot
Learning about Networks from Terrorists   178
Margaret Wheatley

Snapshot
Musings on Current State of International Management Research   180
Rosalie L. Tung and Snejina Michailova

Snapshot
Globalization and Organization Studies   182
Mauro F. Guillén

1.12   Strategy: Past, Present, Future   184
Stephen Cummings

Snapshot
Toward the Ecological Ideal: Notes for a Complex Understanding of
Complex Organizations   195
Haridimos Tsoukas

Snapshot
New Problems for Strategy   199
Anita McGahan

PART 2   LIVING IN ORGANIZATIONS   **201**

2.1   Spin   203
David M. Boje

Snapshot
Schools for Organizing   213
Martin Parker

Snapshot
Empty Organizations   215
George Ritzer and Craig Lair

Snapshot
Organizational Defenses; Denials and Denials of the Denial   217
Chris Argyris

Snapshot
Making Research/Intervention in our Field: A Modest Proposal for
ASQ and AMJ   218
William R. Torbert

2.2   Technique and Practices from the Arts   220
Steven S. Taylor and Inga Carboni

2.3   Aesthetics in the Study of Organizational Life   229
Antonio Strati

Snapshot
Whither Emotion?   239
Stephen Fineman

2.4   The Social Life of Values: Cross-cultural Construction of Realities   241
Slawomir Magala

Snapshot
Nurturing the Divide: Toward Maximizing the Value of Management Research
from both Sides of the Atlantic   251
C. Marlena Fiol and Edward J. O'Connor

2.5   Humanist Organizational Studies: An Intersubjective Research Agenda
for Open (-plan) Fieldwork   255
Hugo Letiche

Snapshot
Feeding Marshmallows to Alligators: The Inherent Fragility of
Human Organization   266
Robert Chia

Snapshot
The Rise of Cartesian Dualism and Marketization in Academia   268
Mustafa F. Özbilgin and Myrtle P. Bell

2.6   Symbolic Value Creation   270
Davide Ravasi and Violina Rindova

Snapshot
Critically Constructing Constructionism   285
Dian Marie Hosking

2.7   The Role of Narrative Fiction and Semi-Fiction in Organizational
Studies   288
Gail Whiteman and Nelson Phillips

Snapshot
Towards a Critical Engagement with Metaphor in Organization Studies   300
Cliff Oswick

2.8   Routine Dynamics   302
Martha S. Feldman and Brian T. Pentland

Snapshot
'Enriching Research on Exploration and Exploitation'   316
Lori Rosenkopf

2.9   The Implications of Aristotle's *Phronēsis* for Organizational Inquiry   318
       George Cairns and Martyna Śliwa

       Snapshot
       Philosophy of Management: Instead of a Manifesto   329
       Ole Fogh Kirkeby

2.10   Wisdom: A Backdrop for Organizational Studies   332
       David A. Cowan and Lotte Darsoe

       Snapshot
       Knowledge in the Absence of Wisdom   344
       David Rooney, Bernard McKenna, Peter Liesch and Kim Boal

       Snapshot
       Organization and Management Studies: An End in Itself or a Means Towards
       a Better Social and Economic life?   347
       Tony Watson

2.11   Maternal Organization   349
       Heather Höpfl

       Snapshot
       Feminist Theorizing   359
       Marta B. Calás and Linda Smircich

       Snapshot
       Why Difference Matters in Organizations   362
       Martin N. Davidson

2.12   Strategy-as-Practice   364
       Paula Jarzabkowski

       Snapshot
       A New Focal Point: Interactions, Deliverables and Delivery   379
       Jeffrey D. Ford and Laurie W. Ford

       Snapshot
       Entrepreneurship and Competition at the Intersection: Maintaining
       Strategic Resilience   381
       Shaker A. Zahra and R. Isil Yavuz

       Snapshot
       Strategic Supply Chain Management   383
       David J. Ketchen, Jr. and G. Thomas M. Hult

2.13   Improvisation in Organizations   385
       Joao Cunha and Miguel Pina e Cunha

       Snapshot
       Researching the Private–Collective Innovation Model   396
       Georg von Krogh

PART 3   ACTING ON ORGANIZATIONS   **399**

3.1   Performing the Organization: Organization Theatre and Imaginative Life as
       Physical Presence   401
       Timothy Clark

3.2   This is Work, This is Play: Artful Interventions and Identity Dynamics   412
       Stefan Meisiek and Mary Jo Hatch

3.3   Aesthetic Play as an Organizing Principle   423
       Pierre Guillet de Monthoux and Matt Statler

3.4   If People are Strange, Does Organization Make Us Normal?   436
       Stewart Clegg

       Snapshot
       Identity Hijack   447
       Majken Schultz

       Snapshot
       The Tyranny of Theory   449
       Olav Sorenson

       Snapshot
       That's Important! Making a Difference with Organizational Research   451
       Adam M. Grant, Jane E. Dutton, and Brent D. Rosso

       Snapshot
       Some Thoughts About Trade-Offs   453
       Angelo S. DeNisi

3.5   Abduction   454
       Hans Hansen

       Snapshot
       The Dialectics of Propositional and Tacit Knowledge   464
       Daniel G. Spencer

       Snapshot
       700 Sage Words?   467
       Tom Keenoy

3.6   Corporeal Leaders   469
       Arja Ropo and Erika Sauer

       Snapshot
       The Future is Now   479
       James G. (Jerry) Hunt

       Snapshot
       Why Leaders Fail   481
       Robert J. Sternberg

Snapshot
How Can We Make Organizations More Ethical? 483
Edwin A. Locke

3.7 The Craft and Art of Narrative Inquiry in Organizations 485
Frances Hancock and David Epston

Snapshot
The Pragmatics of Resilience 498
Kathleen M. Sutcliffe and Timothy J. Vogus

Snapshot
A Note on 'The Future of Positive Organizational Scholarship' 501
Gretchen Spreitzer

3.8 Building Community 503
Natalia Nikolova and Timothy Devinney

Snapshot
Shifting Sands in Communities of Scholars 514
Greg Northcraft

3.9 Situated Knowledge and Situated Action 516
Silvia Gherardi

Snapshot
W(h)ither Knowledge Management? 526
Ulrike Schultze

3.10 Indigenous Organizing: Enacting and Updating Indigenous Knowledge 528
Steven J. Finlay

Snapshot
'Organizational' Behavior is Largely Tribal Behavior 538
Blake E. Ashforth

3.11 Un-gendering Organization 540
Stephen Linstead and Alison Pullen

Snapshot
Gender Inequity and the Need to Study Change 552
Joanne Martin and Debra Meyerson

3.12 Creating Better Understandings of Organizations While Building Better
Organizations 554
Roger L. M. Dunbar, A. Georges, L. Romme and William H. Starbuck

Snapshot
The Shape of Things to Come 565
Raymond E. Miles and Charles C. Snow

Snapshot
New Organization Forms – the Career of a Concept 567
Ian Palmer and Richard Dunford

Snapshot
Suppose We Took Organizational Performance Seriously   570
C. Chet Miller

3.13   Managers Who Can Transform Institutions in Their Firms: Activism and the
        Practices That Stick   572
        Robert Chapman Wood and Liisa Valikangas

        Snapshot
        Is Change on the Outside Like Change on the Inside?   583
        George Roth

3.14   Where Are You Going?   586
        Hans Hansen and Daved Barry

Index   589

Contributors

Nancy J. Adler is a Professor of International Management at McGill University in Montreal, Canada.

Herman Aguinis is the Mehalchin Term Professor of Management in the Business School at the University of Colorado at Denver and Health Sciences Center.

Mats Alvesson is at the Department of Business Administration, Lund University and also associated with the Universities of Queensland, St Andrews and Exeter.

Elena Antonacopoulou, is Professor of Organizational Behaviour at the University of Liverpool Management School and Director of GNOSIS, a dynamic management research initiative.

Chris Argyris is the James Conant Professor of Education and Organizational Behavior Emeritus at Harvard University.

Blake Ashforth is the Rusty Lyon Chair of Business in the W.P. Carey School of Business, Arizona State University.

Daved Barry holds the Banco BPI Chair of Creative Organization Studies at Universidade Nova de Lisboa's School of Economics and Management, and is Adjunct Professor of Creativity and Leadership at the Copenhagen Business School. Prior to this he was Visiting Professor at the Copenhagen Business School.

Jean M. Bartunek is the Robert A. and Evelyn J. Ferris chair and Professor of Organization Studies at Boston College.

Beth A. Bechky is an Associate Professor at the Graduate School of Management at the University of California, Davis.

Myrtle P. Bell is an Associate Professor of management at the University of Texas at Arlington.

Kimberly B. Boal (PhD, University of Wisconsin) is the Rawls Professor of Management at the Rawls College of Business, Texas Tech University.

David M. Boje holds the Bank of America Endowed Professorship of Management and the past Arthur Owens Professorship in Business Administration in the Management Department at New Mexico State University.

Laura Brearley is a based at the Schools of Education, Art, Creative Media and Architecture and Design at RMIT University, Australia.

George Cairns is Professor of Management at the University of Essex, UK.

Marta B. Calás is Professor of Organization Studies and International Management at the Department of Management, Isenberg School of Management, and adjunct professor of Women's Studies, at the Women's Studies Program, University of Massachusetts-Amherst.

Inga Carboni is an Assistant Professor of Organizational Behavior in the Mason School of Business at The College of William & Mary in Williamsburg, Virginia.

Robert Chia holds a Sixth Century Chair in Management at the University of Aberdeen Business School.

Timothy Clark is Professor of Organizational Behaviour at Durham Business School.

Stewart Clegg is Professor at the University of Technology, Sydney and Director of ICAN Research (www.ican.uts.edu.au); a Professor at the University of Aston Business School; a Visiting Professor of Organizational Change Management, Maastricht University Faculty of Business, as well as the Vrije University of Amsterdam, where he is Visiting Professor and International Fellow in Discourse and Management Theory, Centre of Comparative Social Studies, and also at Copenhagen Business School.

Claudia Cogliser received her Ph.D. from the University of Miami, with a focus on leadership and research methods.

David Cowan is Professor in the Management Department at Miami University.

Stephen Cummings is Professor of Strategic Management at Victoria Management School, New Zealand and Associate Fellow at Warwick Business School, United Kingdom.

Miguel Pina e Cunha is an Associate Professor at the Faculdade de Economia, Universidade Nova de Lisboa.

Joao Vieira da Cunha is a Professor at the School of Management and Economics at Universidade Nova de Lisboa.

Barbara Czarniawska is Malmsten Chair of Management Studies at Gothenburg Research Institute, School of Business, Economics and Law, Göteborg University, Sweden; a Titular Professor at the European Institute for Advanced Studies in Management, Brussels; Visiting Professor in the Management Centre, University of Leicester, UK, and University of Rome I 'La Sapienza', Italy.

Dr Lotte Darsø is Associate Professor at Learning Lab Denmark at the Danish University of Education.

Martin N. Davidson is Associate Professor of Leadership and Organizational Behaviour at the Darden Graduate School of Business, University of Virginia.

Gerald Davis is the Wilbur K. Pierpont Collegiate Professor of Management at the Ross School of Business and Professor of Sociology, The University of Michigan.

Angelo DeNisi is Dean of the A.B. Freeman School of Business at Tulane University.

Timothy Devinney (B.Sc. CMU; MA, MBA, Ph.D. Chicago) is Professorial Research Fellow at the Australian School of Business.

Lex Donaldson is a Professor in the Australian School of Business at the University of New South Wales.

Deborah Dougherty is a Professor at Rutgers University.

Roger L. M. Dunbar is a Professor of Management at the Stern School of Business, New York University.

Richard Dunford, BCA, BA (Hons) (VUW), PhD (ANU) is Professor of Management in the Macquarie Graduate School of Management, Macquarie University, Sydney.

Jane E. Dutton is the Robert L. Kahn Distinguished University Professor of Business Administration and Psychology at the University of Michigan.

Bente Elkjaer (BA, MA, PhD) is a Professor of Organizational and Workplace Learning at the University of Aarhus, Danish School of Education.

David Epston is Co-director of The Family Therapy Centre in Auckland. He is recognized internationally for his innovations (with Michael White and others) in narrative therapy ideas and practice. He is co-editor (with Dean Lobovits) of a website (http://www.narrativeapproaches. com).

Martha S. Feldman is a Professor in the Planning, Policy and Design Department and the Johnson Chair for Civic Governance and Public Management in the School of Social Ecology at the University of California, Irvine.

Stephen Fineman is Professor of Organizational Behaviour in the School of Management, University of Bath.

Steven Finlay runs his own agency (see www.src.ac.nz) and currently consults with many indigenous and newcomer groups to develop settlement strategy in a partnership between local and central government.

C. Marlena Fiol is currently Professor of Strategic Management at the University of Colorado at Denver and Health Sciences Center.

Jeffrey D. Ford is Associate Professor of Management in the Max M. Fisher College of Business at The Ohio State University in Columbus, Ohio.

Laurie W. Ford is the owner of Critical Path Consultants, a management consulting company specializing in organization design and change.

William L. Gardner (DBA, Florida State University) is the Jerry S. Rawls Professor in Organizational Behavior and Leadership and the Director of the Institute for Leadership Studies at the Rawls College of Business at Texas Tech University.

Robert P. Gephart, Jr. is Professor of Strategic Management and Organization at the University of Alberta in Edmonton, Canada.

Silvia Gherardi is full Professor of Sociology of Work and Organization at the University of Trento, Italy, where she is responsible for the Research Unit on Communication, Organizational Learning and Aesthetics (RUCOLA, www.unitn.it/rucola).

Dennis A. (Denny) Gioia is Professor of Organizational Behavior, and Chair of the Department of Management and Organization, Smeal College of Business at the Pennsylvania State University.

Adam M. Grant is Assistant Professor of Organizational Behavior at the University of North Carolina at Chapel Hill.

Mauro F. Guillén is Director of the Lauder and Zandman Professor of International Management at the Wharton School.

Pierre Guillet de Monthoux is Professor of General Management at Stockholm University, Stockholm, Sweden.

Eric Guthey is an Associate Professor in the Department of Intercultural Communication and Management at the Copenhagen Business School.

Treahna Hamm is a Yorta Yorta woman from the Murray River region. She is a high profile Aboriginal artist who has also worked in the field of Aboriginal education. Treahna in undertaking her PhD in the ways in which stories and artworks reveal individual and community identities.

Frances Hancock is a writer and practitioner, with over 20 years experience in community and organizational development. She has a Bachelor of Social Work with First Class Honours from Massey University (NZ) and a Master of Theological Studies from Harvard University (USA).

Hans Hansen is an Assistant Professor at Texas Tech University, where he teaches Organizational Theory, Organizational Creativity and Change, Organizational Behavior.

Mary Jo Hatch is the C. Coleman McGehee Eminent Scholars Research Professor of Banking and Commerce at the McIntire School of Commerce at the University of Virginia.

Heather Höpfl is Professor of Management and Director of the Essex Management Centre at the University of Essex, UK.

Dian Marie Hosking is Professor in Relational Processes at the Utrecht School of Governance (USBO).

G. Tomas M. Hult is Professor of International Business and Director of the Center for International Business Education and Research (MSU-CIBER) in The Eli Broad Graduate School of Management at Michigan State University.

James G. (Jerry) Hunt, PhD University of Illinois 1966 is Paul Whitfield Horn Professor of Management and Director Emeritus of the Institute for Leadership Research at Texas Tech University.

Marleen Huysman is Professor of Knowledge and Organization at the department of Economics and Business Administration of the VU University Amsterdam.

Brad Jackson is the Fletcher Building Education Trust Professor of Leadership at the University of Auckland Business School.

Paula Jarzabkowski is a Professor of Strategic Management at Aston Business School and an Advanced Institute of Management (AIM) Ghoshal Fellow.

Tom Keenoy is Professor of Management at the University of Leicester School of Management.

David J. Ketchen, Jr. serves as Lowder Eminent Scholar and Professor of Management at Auburn University and is Executive Director at the Lowder Center for Family Business and Entrepreneurship, Department of Management, College of Business, Auburn University.

Martin Kilduff (PhD, Cornell) is the Kleberg/King Ranch Centennial Professor of Management at the University of Texas at Austin.

Ian W. King co-founded the Essex Management Centre at the University of Essex, UK. He is a co-organizer and co-founder of the Art of Management conference series [London, 2002; Paris, 2004; Krakow, 2006; Banff, 2008] and is currently involved in the Aesthesis//CREATE project.

Ole Fogh Kirkeby, Professor at Copenhagen Business School, leads the Philosophy Group at the Department of Management, Politics and Philosophy.

Michael Kulicki is a PhD student in the Department of Political Science, University of Alberta, Edmonton, Canada.

Craig D. Lair is a lecturer at the University of Maryland.

Hugo Letiche is the Humanitas/ISCE Professor of 'Meaning in Organization' and Research Professor at the University for Humanistics, Utrecht, the Netherlands.

Peter Liesch is Professor of International Business at The University of Queensland Business School and Chair of the Enterprise and International Business Cluster.

Marjolein Lips-Wiersma is a Senior Lecturer at University of Canterbury, New Zealand.

Stephen Linstead is the head of the Critical Management Studies group at the York Management School. His research interests fall into five main areas – organization theory and philosophy; aesthetic approaches to organization; language based approaches to organization; gender and sexuality in organizations; qualitative methods, ethnography and culture.

Edwin A. Locke is Dean's Professor of Motivation and Leadership Emeritus at the R.H. Smith School of Business, University of Maryland.

Slawomir Magala is the Professor of Cross-cultural Management at the Rotterdam School of Management of the Erasmus University in Rotterdam, the Netherlands.

Joanne Martin is the Fred H. Merrill Professor of Organizational Behavior, Emerita, at the Graduate School of Business, Stanford University.

Anita M. McGahan is Professor of Strategic Management at the Rotman School of Management at the University of Toronto, a Senior Associate at the Institute for Strategy and Competitiveness at Harvard University, Senior Economist at the Massachusetts General Hospital Center for Global Health.

Bernard McKenna is Senior Lecturer at The University of Queensland Business School.

Ajay Mehra is an Associate Professor at the Gatton College of Business and Economics.

Stefan Meisiek is Assistant Professor of Management and Entrepreneurship at the School of Economics and Management, Universidade Nova de Lisboa.

Debra Meyerson is Associate Professor of Organizational Behavior at Stanford University's School of Education and (by courtesy) Graduate School of Business, and co-director of Stanford's Center on Philanthropy and Civil Society and Stanford Educational Leadership Institute.

Snejina Michailova is Professor of International Business at The University of Auckland Business School, New Zealand.

Raymond E. Miles is Professor Emeritus in the Haas School of Business at the University of California, Berkeley.

C. Chet Miller, PhD, is a member of the faculty and Farr Leadership Fellow at the Babcock Graduate School of Management, Wake Forest University.

Albert J. Mills, PhD, is Director of the PhD in Business Administration at Saint Mary's Sobey School of Business.

Dennis K. Mumby is Professor and Chair of the Department of Communication Studies at the University of North Carolina at Chapel Hill.

Natalia Nikolova is a Lecturer at the School of Management at University of Technology, Sydney.

Gregory B. Northcraft is the Harry J. Gray Professor of Executive Leadership and Director of Professional Education Development in the Department of Business Administration, and Institute of Labor and Industrial Relations, at the University of Illinois.

William Ocasio is the John L. and Helen Kellogg Professor of Management and Organizations at the Kellogg School of Management.

Edward J. O'Connor is currently a Professor of Management at the University of Colorado at Denver and Health Sciences Center.

Cliff Oswick is a Chair in Organization Theory and Discourse at Queen Mary, University of London.

Mustafa Ozbilgin is Professor of Human Resource Management at the Norwich Business School, University of East Anglia, UK.

Ian Palmer is a Professor of Management and Associate Dean, Research in the Faculty of Business, University of Technology, Sydney.

Martin Parker is Professor of Culture and Organization at the University of Leicester School of Management.

Doris Paton is an Aboriginal elder from the Gunnai Nation of South-Eastern Victoria and is currently undertaking her PhD in Aboroginal Eductaion.

Brian T. Pentland is a Professor in the Department of Accounting and Information Systems at Michigan State University.

Jeffrey Pfeffer is the Thomas D. Dee II Professor of Organizational Behavior at the Graduate School of Business, Stanford University.

Nelson Phillips is Professor of Strategy and Organizational Behaviour at Tanaka Business School, Imperial College London.

Charles A. Pierce is an Associate Professor of Management and a Suzanne D. Palmer Research Professor in the Department of Management, Fogelman College of Business and Economics, University of Memphis.

Michael G. Pratt (PhD, University of Michigan) is a James F. Towey Fellow and Professor of Organizational Behavior at the University of Illinois at Urbana-Champaign.

Dr Alison Pullen is based at The University of Technology, Sydney. Alison is also Visiting Fellow at the University of Bristol.

Davide Ravasi is an Associate Professor of Management at Bocconi University, Italy.

Michael I Reed is Professor of Organizational Analysis (Human Resource Management Section) and Associate Dean (Research), Cardiff Business School, Cardiff University.

Violina Rindova is an Associate Professor in Strategy and and the Ambassador Clark Centennial Fellow at the McCombs School of Business, University of Texas-Austin.

George Ritzer is Distinguished University Professor at the University of Maryland.

Georges Romme is Professor of Entrepreneurship and Innovation in the department of Technology Management, Eindhoven University of Technology (Netherlands).

David Rooney is Senior Lecturer in Knowledge Management, the University of Queensland's Business School.

Arja Ropo, University of Tampere, Finland. Professor of Management and Organization. Current research interests include leadership in creative organizations, aesthetics in leadership, corporeal leadership, processual and contextual leadership change.

Mark Rose is a Gunditjmara man from the South-West of Victoria and lectures in management.

Lori Rosenkopf is an Associate Professor at The Wharton School of the University of Pennsylvania.

Brent Rosso is a doctoral student in the departments of Organizational Psychology and Management & Organizations at the University of Michigan.

George Roth is a Principle Research Associate at the MIT Sloan School of Management.

Erika Sauer received her PhD in economics and business from University of Tampere, Finland. Current research interests include leadership in cultural organizations and leadership of creativity.

Majken Schultz is Professor at Copenhagen Business School.

Ulrike Schultze is Associate Professor in Information Technology and Operations Management at Southern Methodist University.

Martyna Sliwa is Lecturer in Management at the University of Essex, UK.

Linda Smircich is Professor of Organization Studies at the Department of Management, Isenberg School of Management University of Massachusetts-Amherst.

Charles C. Snow is the Mellon Foundation Professor of Business Administration in the Smeal College of Business at Penn State University.

Olav Sorenson is the Jeffrey S. Skoll Chair in Technical Innovation and Entrepreneurship and Professor of Strategy at the Rotman School of Management of the University of Toronto.

Daniel G. Spencer is an Associate Professor with the School of Business at the University of Kansas.

Gretchen Spreitzer is a Professor of Management and Organizations at the Ross School of Business at the University of Michigan (RSB) and a faculty affiliate of the Center For Effective Organizations (CEO) at the University of Southern California.

William H. Starbuck is Professor in residence at the Lundquist College of Business of the University of Oregon and Professor Emeritus at New York University.

Matt Statler is the Associate Director of New York University's International Center for Enterprise Preparedness.

Robert J. Sternberg is Dean of the School of Arts and Sciences, Professor of Psychology, and Adjunct Professor of Education at Tufts University. He is also Honorary Professor of Psychology at the University of Heidelberg.

Antonio Strati is Professor of Sociology of Organization and lectures at the Universities of Trento and Siena, Italy.

Kathleen M. Sutcliffe (PhD University of Texas at Austin) is the Gilbert and Ruth Professor of Business Administration at the University of Michigan Stephen M. Ross School of Business.

Steven S. Taylor is an Assistant Professor in the Department of Management at the Worcester Polytechnic Institute (WPI) in Worcester, Massachusetts, USA.

Cagri Topal is a doctoral student in the Business School of University of Alberta.

Bill Torbert is a Professor of Management at Boston College.

Haridimos Tsoukas is the George D. Mavros Research Professor of Organization Theory at ALBA, Greece, and Professor of Organization Studies at Warwick Business School, Warwick University, UK.

Rosalie L. Tung is a chaired Professor of International Business at Simon Fraser University.

Dr Liisa Välikangas is Professor of Innovation Management at Helsinki School of Economics.

Tim Vogus (PhD University of Michigan Ross School of Business) is an Assistant Professor of Management and Organization Studies at Vanderbilt University.

Georg von Krogh is Professor of Strategic Management and Innovation at the ETH Zurich's Department of Management, Technology, and Economics.

Tony Watson is Professor of Organizational Behaviour at Nottingham University Business School.

Margaret Wheatley is President Emerita of The Berkana Institute (www.berkana.org).

Dr Gail Whiteman is an Associate Professor at the Rotterdam School of Management (RSM) Erasmus University in the Netherlands.

Hugh Willmott is Research Professor in Organization Studies, Cardiff Business School.

Robert Chapman Wood is Associate Professor of strategic management and global management at San José State University in California.

R. Isil Yavuz is doctoral candidate in the Strategic Management and Organization department at Carlson School of Management, University of Minnesota, USA.

Shaker A. Zahra is Robert E. Buuck Chair of Entrepreneurship, Professor of Strategy and Director of the Gary S. Holmes Entrepreneurship Center at Carlson School, University of Minnesota.

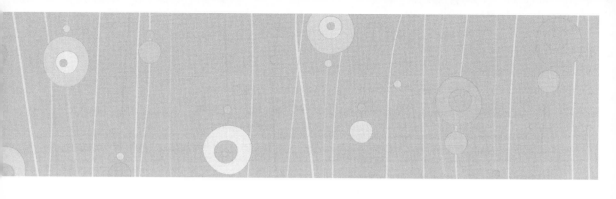

Introduction

The New and Emerging in Management and Organization: Gatherings, Trends, and Bets

Daved Barry and Hans Hansen

It was in the cafes of Wellington, New Zealand, where we first began to talk about assembling a text with all the theoretical and conceptual approaches that don't get coverage in mainstream texts or PhD-level courses. Our goal was to provide an alternative and fresh set of possibilities around management and organizations. We listed examples of newer topics like narrative theory; David Boje (2001) had recently produced a text on narrative theory, but there was no Handbook source for a collection of these and even more recent research streams. We envisioned a 20 chapter Handbook.

In addition to the classic Handbook models edited by March; Clegg, Hardy, and Nord; and Lincoln and Denzin, Sage Publications had begun a line of shorter Handbooks which focused on narrower topics. While the 'big' Handbooks had broad scopes, such as Organization Studies (Clegg et al., 1996) and Qualitative Research (Denzin and Lincoln, 1994), the shorter versions included more focused topics like Organizational Discourse (Grant et al., 2004). We pitched one of these shorter Handbooks, with topics related to a few emerging streams that we thought might potentially make a big impact.

Sage said yes, but soon our 'little' Handbook became a behemoth as the word went out and proposals and contributions came pouring in – people from many management and organization studies (MOS) disciplines wanted to discuss how their areas were developing, and even more importantly, how they should develop. Gradually, the book's position crystallized – it was to be a *prospective* guide to MOS, a provocative trend setter, a book of newness and freshness from leading edge MOS thinkers. As its position firmed up, we began combing the MOS seas, actively looking for new trends and ideas. We contacted all the editors, editorial board members, reviewers from the leading journals, major conference organizers, authors of prize-winning articles, and authors and topics whom others said were 'up and coming'. We had many discussions at many conferences and over the phone, always around the questions: 'What's the next big thing? What's coming? What should be coming? Where should we direct our attention?' While we knew highly recognized researchers would be invited, we also tried to find new topics through open calls for contributions, hoping to find new and emerging scholars both within but also beyond the walls of business schools. Finally, we travelled not only conceptually, but physically. Between the two of us, we had positions or visiting positions at the University of Victoria in Wellington, New Zealand, Copenhagen Business School, Kellogg School Management, Stanford, Universidade Nova de Lisboa, and Texas Tech University. We met or worked on this text in all of these places for weeks or months at a time, as well as going to many other cities to meet with various contributors. Through this we think we've managed to create a truly global perspective and set of voices.

Karl Weick said early on that we were making a 'betting book' – we're making wagers, and introducing new contenders as well. He's right. And undoubtedly, his point that only a few wagers ever win is equally right. With this, we think the long shots sometimes make a bigger impact, but there are too few of them. So we not only want to give some ideas a chance, but a push forward. We offer no word or speculation on which ones will make it, but we try to spot trends, combinations, and relations we hold hopes for.

A BRIEF AND TERSE HISTORY OF HANDBOOKS

James March (1965) edited the first handbook dedicated to organizational studies. The *Handbook of Organizations* had the straightforward aim of summarizing and reporting the present state of knowledge around organizations and organizing. During this time, business schools were being populated with economists, engineers, and a few sociologists. Organizational studies was still being formulated as a coherent field of study and March's first Handbook would

serve as a 'ready compendium of results, references, concepts, ideas, and theories' (March, 1965: ix). He did not attempt to summarize the present state of the field, as it was still coming together and in the process of assembling itself:

> No editor, and least of all a sympathetic one, should attempt to summarize that state. It is what it is; and what it is can best be discovered by reading the detailed chapters. (March, 1965: ix)

If March brought us all into the same field, we soon turned to uprooting and clod throwing. By the time the *Handbook of Organization Studies* and the *Handbook of Qualitative Research* came out 30 years later, the field was in the middle of a housing battle, if not a civil war. Those two texts came out well into the rise of post-positivism and more specifically, postmodernism within organization studies. Battle lines had been clearly drawn, often using language provided by Burrell and Morgan (1979) to demarcate functional and interpretive approaches. We divided up areas where we would contribute, with the burden of proof falling to the post-positivists, and interruption to the interpretivists. A polarization had occurred between positivism and post-positivism or modernist and postmodernists.

By the time the Clegg, Hardy, and Nord volume (1996) became the Handbook for the field, the lines had become even more clearly drawn and the division was a solid one. Fragmentation was complete. Their introduction (Clegg et al., 1996) discussed the incommensurability between the functional approaches of the 1960s and the interpretive paradigm. They suggested that incommensurability was helpful, that it allowed 'alternative' research to flourish because the protection of incommensurable status meant that these alternative approaches could not (and more importantly *did not have to*) explain themselves to other paradigms. They no longer had to answer to anyone. Clegg et al. note that the real battle was in *retaining*, not overcoming, incommensurability.

In some ways we've gone a long way unhampered by having to fight or justify our positions to the other side. There has been a lot of exploration on both sides and we've made wonderful discoveries. Yet, if our experiences in compiling this book are any indication, we might all be re-filing back into the same building for the first time in a long time. We suggest that, having had so much fragmentation and then pluralism, perhaps the time has come for the 'relational' – for combinations between those things that had been fragmented. Having broken up the field into a thousand pieces, we are now quite naturally making mosaics.

With this, old friends are meeting and instead of discussing the war, they are asking 'What have you been up to?' On the post-positivist side, they might explain that they've travelled thousands of miles and seen strange and amazing things the positivist could hardly imagine. The positivist might not care. 'We've been minding the store since you left!' they might exclaim, accusing interpretivists of a life of indulgence while they've done the hard work of keeping the lights on and serving customers (corporations, MBA students, and executives wanting to be 'updated'). Some of those who went on walkabout have ideas about remodelling, while some who stayed home have ideas about better maintenance. It seems everyone would like to live better. So our arguments now might be healthier – more about how to make a great new place to work rather than drawing uncrossable lines on the floor.

CHARACTER OF THE TEXT

Although our text is decidedly pluralistic, it also contains many relational threads. This means it is a patchwork in some sense; hardly a well-tended garden. What we wanted to do was create a space where these many ideas could compete and connect – a 'rhizomatic' mixture (Linstead and Pullen, this collection) that could give rise to many tendrils and offshoots. Making sense of them inevitably involves muddling, particularly as Hayek (1978) conceives the term. He compared two types of minds he found in his experience. One was a 'master of their subject' who had

all the rules, laws, and formulas committed to memory, and in much the same way, these researchers were committed to the rules and laws that made up their subject matter. On the other hand, there were 'puzzlers' or 'muddlers.' Muddle-headedness preceded independent thought. Hayek found himself to be of this breed, and characterized some advantages of muddling: '… it was because I did not remember the answers that to others may have been obvious that I was often forced to think out a solution to a problem which did not exist for those who had a more orderly mind' (Hayek, 1978: 53).

While muddle-headedness describes some individual researchers' approach to a field, terms like unification and pluralism describe the state of research fields themselves. We said that by the mid-1990s the state of organizational studies was decidedly pluralistic, but there were still calls for unification (cf. Pfeffer, 1993). There are arguments for each approach. Pfeffer (1993) implored us to follow a more unified paradigm approach in organizational studies. Cole (1983) warns us that if researchers accept any old unorthodox theory or method, the established consensus will be destroyed and the intellectual structure of science will become chaotic (see also Knudsen, 2003). Pfeffer tells us that fields with a more coherent paradigm will advance more rapidly, attract more resources and support, and have more journal hits.

But who cares for rapid advancement if we are going in the wrong direction? Ghoshal (2005) tried to warn us about the consequences of spreading bad management theories. They get enacted into being (Weick, 1995) and make themselves true. The problem is that at the very outset there's not much hope of telling the good ones from the bad ones. That being so, it is important we leave ourselves options to travel in many directions, as opposed to forming some kind of consensus to travel full speed ahead down any path wearing a pair of blinders, no matter how comfortable they are. What if we do not want to go fast? What if we see value in meandering and become reflexive consumers of our own path, adopting a sort of 'deliberate wandering' in hopes of discovering new ways? So our text leans toward muddle-headedness and pluralism. Pluralism is better for long-term advancement (Knudsen, 2003: 263), and muddle-headedness is the source of the rare new insights.

LANDSCAPE OF THE TEXT

The book consists of two types of contributions: full chapters and short notes. The traditional full-length chapters you see in most collections will be familiar. But we also sent out requests for what we've come to call 'notes'. We generated a list of potential contributors and then hand-picked a group whom we thought would provide an interesting assortment of views. Given that all of our noters are in positions to know 'what's what' and just as importantly, 'what should be', we asked them to go short on references to external material, and long on speculation and provocation. In their peppery ways they have created focused calls for new directions and declared a number of moratoriums. These are a bit like futuristic snapshots – brief but strongly considered opinion pieces about things that future generations should be thinking about. Importantly, they are not commentaries on individual chapters; rather, we placed them alongside chapters when they covered similar material or offered a different take on an idea or area.

With both types of contributions, we asked authors to either identify trends that might become major magnets for research and practice over the next 5–10 years, or create new domains that could do the same thing. Contributors were encouraged to talk with one another wherever possible, to share ideas and rough drafts, and to form works that spoke to one another. This happened in places, and many of the chapters have connecting threads. We also asked for fresh, engaging writing that would appeal to a broad audience: academics, 'pracademics', students, and practitioners. We have tried to make a conversational volume, one that is as conversation-provoking as it is trend-setting.

The text is organized around how we experience organizations, and at the same time around potential relations between the contributions and topics. We began to group the content by similar material, but felt we were missing something in doing that. It was in Portugal overlooking the sea that we asked ourselves, 'What if we present the text in a way that reflects how we experience organizations, rather than trying to group material in the usual 'clumps', by similarity?' Besides, in that our content really was really new and emerging, it was difficult to group things in any meaningful way based on content alone. In fact we found that in trying to do so, the uniqueness of the material prevented such groupings anyway. So we played with the idea of three large sections that reflect how we think about and work with organizations as both scholars and participants. The first entails new views and new ways of *Looking at* organizations. The next section is on *Living in* organizations; how we experience them and operate in their confines, and the new and emerging ways we are beginning to 'enliven' them. Finally, we have *Acting on* – how we push, prod, pull, and interact with organizations, how we change them and how they change us.

The way we organized the text then allowed us to do something else quite unique. While our table of contents is presented in the traditional fashion in the front of the book, we want to encourage you to think of approaching the text cross-sectionally, looking *across* the three sections, and yes … the relations across the content. To help you envision the content this way, we provide you with, quite literally, a table of contents that relates the chapters across the sections. We have never seen a text organized in this way, and thought a new and emerging text might be just the place to introduce this concept. In the *table of contents* below, we include only the full-length chapters to demonstrate how you might approach the text not only 'up and down' but also 'left to right' across the table. Take the first row for example, which actually consists of chapters 1.1, 2.1, and 3.1 in the traditional table of contents.

Here, those chapters make up a row of .1's. Looking across the text, this 'row' consists of three chapters that are all related to a more critical approach to organizational studies. Mats Alvesson's chapter looks at the future of critical management studies and how Critical Management Studies will view organizations moving forward. David Boje's chapter takes a critical look at spin, something we all encounter in the organizations we live in. And Timothy Clark shows how performances involve a critical approach to changing organizations. So we have three 'critical school' chapters looking across our text, but they are also grouped by whether they reflect how we *look at* organizations, how we *live in* organizations, and how we *act on* organizations. If you are interested in aesthetics, you can start with Ian King's chapter (1.3) on viewing organizations, then at what 'aesthetic life' entails by next reading

Antonio Strati's chapter (2.3), and finally at how we might actually organize by aesthetic principles by reading Matt Statler and Pierre Guillet de Monthoux's chapter (3.3) on aesthetic play. Interested in identity? You could read three chapters related to identity (look at row 4 of the table, or the row of '.4s'). Barbara Czarniawska presents a new way to think of identity and alterity. Slawek Magala describes the social life of values, and Stewart Clegg describes how we 'create strangers' and the consequences of those actions.

We think there are several benefits to approaching the text in this fashion. If you decide to read the text from cover to cover, you will be introduced to a variety of new approaches, some of which present new ways of looking at organizations, others about life inside organizations, and finally how we might change organizations. But we

Looking at organizations	Living in organizations	Acting on organizations
1.1 Future of critical management studies	2.1 Spin	3.1 Performing the organization: Organizational theatre
1.2 The art of …	2.2 Technique and practices from the arts	3.2 Artful interventions and identity dynamics
1.3 How we know what we know: the potentiality of art and aesthetics	2.3 Aesthetics in the study of organizational life	3.3 Aesthetic play as an organizing principle
1.4 Alterity/identity interplay in image construction	2.4 Social life of values	3.4 If people are strange, does organizing make us normal?
1.5 Exploring Plato's cave: Critical realism	2.5 Humanist organization studies	3.5 Abduction
1.6 Revisualizing images in leadership	2.6 Symbolic value creation	3.6 Corporeal Leaders
1.7 Analyzing Artifacts	2.7 Narrative fiction and semi-fiction	3.7 Craft and art of narrative inquiry
1.8 On the practice of practice	2.8 Routine Dynamics	3.8 Building Community
1.9 Statistico-organization theory	2.9 Implications of Aristotle's phronesis for organizational inquiry	3.9 Situated knowledge and situated action
1.10 Indigenous Perspectives on Restoring Organizational Life	2.10 Wisdom: A backdrop for organizational studies	3.10 Indigenous Organizing
1.11 Social worlds theory and the power of tension	2.11 Maternal organization	3.11 Un-gendering organization
1.12 A future of strategy	2.12 Strategy-as-practice	3.12 Creating better understanding while building better organizations
	2.13 Improvisation in organizations	3.13 Managers who can transform institutions: Practices that stick

think few people approach academic texts in this fashion. So you are not confined to approaching our text from top to bottom (though that is certainly fine), and you will encounter lots of new and emerging ideas this way. If some general topic particularly interests you, you can engage the material that way, updating yourself on a new way to look at organizations, at life inside organizations, and change. Also, it doesn't matter where you start in the text. Chapters don't progress from front to back; chapters 'near the end' of the table to contents are no less important, valuable, or insightful than earlier chapters.

TRENDS AND THEMES OF THE CONTRIBUTIONS

Beyond the groupings presented in the table of contents, are there any patterns here? Any meta-trends? This is a question we've often asked ourselves, peering into the book like a crystal ball. The answer is 'yes', though undoubtedly there are a number of things we've overlooked. We've grouped our observations around shifts toward agency, the lifeful, inversion, and continental changes in how management and organization studies are being conceived.

From made to making to makers making

Historically, much of the past MOS literature has focused on the *made*. We came to organizations and declared them constructed but knew little about how they were constructed and often less about the people who constructed them. We treated organizations as a 'found' society – 'discovering' them (a term borrowed from natural sciences), gazing at images of hierarchies and structures as though we were wandering around unearthed villages at an archaeological site. Looking at the various 'mades' in this way has also produced many recipes for *making* – analyzables, built-to-lasts, and we-shall-overcomes. This one stood longer than that one, so let's build with brick and leave the bamboo out of it.

The image of anthropologists crawling around on their hands and knees examining a thousand-year-old archaeological dig is ironic in a way. As management and organization scholars, we examine curiosities with monocles and pretend to dust off brand new objects and discuss the lives of 'ancient' inhabitants, even as they hustle and bustle around us. We meticulously scan the floor for any telltale droppings that might allow us to pontificate about the life that goes on around us. Perhaps organizations have been treated as long-dead societies because those are the societies we know how to attend to and measure with our methods. Everything is treated as a physical artifact because our borrowed scientific techniques apply to objects without meaning (or at least meaning has to be inferred from the object, but certainly not as constructed *in situ* or 'live'). So we go about speculating based on the remains we inspect after life has moved over the surface.

But now, we are interested in 'the making of' organizations. We are exploring construction sites instead of pouring over stale blue prints, which are often a poor reflection of what is actually built. We are concerned with how the making occurs in organizations, and how the makers go about making. This movement relates to a second trend, lifefulness.

Lifeful

Certainly we are seeing a trend toward more life-centred work. Many of the authors here are implicitly and explicitly calling for *lifeful* research methods and foci. *Who* is working in this place? Why are they doing what they're doing? How are *makers making* and *makers' makings* interrelated? How do the verbs and nouns move and change one another? Who is fun/exciting/interesting to talk with? Who's knocking on the door? Rather than stripping the mystery out, which has been such a part of past MOS work, our authors are arguing that we need to bring it back in, to not only edify our readers, but move them.

Consistent with the 'richness' special issue of the Academy of Management Review

(February, 2007, V50/1), we see a growing emphasis on aesthetics, both in the form different texts take, but also in how things are theorized and thought about. The language is more colourful, but the concepts also aim to stimulate and attract. Sometimes this revolves around attempts to invoke beauty, but we also see appeals around the comic, sublime, and even the grotesque. Our senses and emotions are being called on (we are frequently asked to 'feel' things here); numerous chapters focus on the body, not only noting where it's gone missing, but looking at ways to mainstream it. There is an emphasis on creating, of giving birth to, of noting and even embracing the messier parts of bringing new things into the world. Play – both in the gaming, imaginative sense and in the theatred one – is evident throughout, as is the lively.

This general direction calls more for homes than houses, life forms than built forms, country roads and paths than superhighways, and community relations rather than gated isolationism and soloism. Such paths lead several ways – forward and back as well as around. Thus, while we see our authors forming new paths to uncharted territory, we also find them exploring old ideas and well-travelled but forgotten paths that can take MOS to old haunts (i.e. 'back to' aesthetics and phronesis).

With this, we find that the certainties called for in past handbooks, certainties around descriptions, methods, moralities, logics, etc., have given way to questions: 'I'm not so sure', and 'Let's talk about this'. As you thumb through the pages, you will see far fewer absolutes put forth and far more lenses with which to look. Some of this comes with the new-and-emerging territory of course, but we also believe this portends how MOS will become as organizational complexities continue to rise and new organizational forms develop.

Inversions

While many of our contributions take an upending approach, very few are green field, start-from-scratch efforts. Rather, they work from pre-existing sites and materials. This is consistent with MOS's historical reliance on other fields, but we also think it points to a general tendency toward contextualization, localization, and embeddedness – part of the 'house to home' movement described above. That said, we also see different ways in which this is happening. One form of upending is through domain inversion – taking an existing area and deliberately contesting its basic assumptions. Dunbar, Romme, and Starbuck's chapter on organization design challenges much of what has been written in the design field and asks that we invert the usual way we approach things – to 'poke and prescribe' *before* we have analyzed things, given that some of the most important patterns can only be discerned when organizational stake-holders are uncomfortable. Other examples include Steve Linstead and Alison Pullen's chapter on ungendering, David Boje's work on organizational spin, Meg Wheatley's piece on learning from terrorism, Eric Guthey and Brad Jackson's work on CEO portraiture, Gail Whiteman and Nelson Phillips' essay on narrative fiction and semi-fiction, Jeff Pfeffer's points about organization studies, Bill Torbert's note on journal standards, and Stewart Clegg's work on strangeness and organization. Others contextually defamiliarize by bringing in the overlooked, the once familiar but now forgotten, and the generally sidelined into prominent view. Heather Hopfl's work on maternal organization asks that we bring back the messy acts of birthing and caring for to organization. George Cairns and Martina Sliwa's work on phronesis, Ole Fogh Kirkeby's note on the philosophy of management, David Cowan and Lotte Darso's work on wisdom, the chapters on indigeneity by Laura Brearley's group and Steve Finlay all fall into this group. Similarly, we have authors who give us new ways to see the old. David Epston and Francis Hancock's chapter on organizational questioning is a good example. As pioneers in the narrative psychology movement, they offer a compelling and refreshing example of how we might fundamentally change how we inquire about organizational life. Their work suggests ways in which the asking can alter both the answering and actioning. Likewise, the arts and aesthetics chapters (Barry, King, Meisiek and Hatch, Statler and Guillet de Monthoux, Strati, Taylor and Carboni) provide a multitude of ways to re-view and gain uncommon sense about work.

Continental Changes[1]

Historically, the U.S. set the standards for what constituted good and bad management research and practice. The rest of the world was expected to follow suit … and generally did. For many years the only globally recognized management texts used in Europe, Australasia, and Asia were American, and all the prominent business schools were founded as U.S. partnerships. This is rapidly changing. One of the more seismic trends in management and organization is toward different but equally legitimate conceptualizations of the field, particularly between North America and Europe, but also between North America and Australasia (especially New Zealand and Australia), and Asia. Europeans are no longer behind and on track to eventually catch up; they are taking a different path entirely. Whether this path eventually ends up co-mingling, re-merging, or completely separating from the North American traditions will be one of the things to watch for in the upcoming years.

A number of the basics are nicely captured in Marlena Fiol and Edward O'Connor's contribution to this handbook. Their research finds that the Atlantic divide between Europe and North America is a large and growing one, characterized by different research traditions, accreditation processes and valued, journal emphases, and general notions of what counts as worthwhile. Attempts by the Academy of Management to be more inclusive have generally failed, even as Europe's attempts to 'AoM-ize' are steadily lessening and more researchers and are leaving what has been dubbed 'NATO' (the North American Theory of Organizations) to form their own theoretical archipelagos. These observations parallel our own conclusions, both as we have lived

and worked in Europe and Australasia, and through assembling this volume. Although there have always been other management education traditions in Europe (e.g., Ecole Nacional de Administracion in France or Betriebswirtschaftslehre in Germany), we are finding that these various regional approaches are intermingling to form a distinctive European voice, replete with a host of state-based and independent business schools, integrated, cross-institutional business programs (via the Bologna Education Accord which emphasizes standard curricula and student exchanges), a large number of interrelated conferences, and a growing number of A-level journals, albeit ones that have a different notion of what 'A' means. This voice is leading to some productive differences and tensions.

One difference revolves around engagement with a research area. In North America, researchers are still largely concerned about their own work, focusing on ABI Informs and bibliographies to see who else has done or said something about it: 'Where am I relative to other academic works? If you are an institutional theorist, what does that make me?' Advancement, utility, and evidence ('I know this in a million ways') are centrally important themes. Frequently, data and analytical rigour stand for theory. Researchers first say 'Come and look at my funny data' and secondly ask 'What's going on here?' Comparatively, European researchers have tended to pursue what might fit, or whether there is convincing evidence. Theory stands for data as they say 'Come and look at my funny ideas … What shall we do with them?' In the past, this resulted in a quantity orientation – anything placed in any journal counted as good research regardless of its connection with other works. This is changing as Europe continues to anglify its writing and through this form a much larger and inter-connective internal market for MOS works, as European journals adopt high rejection and acceptance criteria, and European academic institutions discriminate between A, B, and C level outlets. With this, what counts as an 'A' is being increasingly contested. European journals and U.S. journals both ask the 'So

What?' question, but the implications of the questions, and thus the answers they seek, are different. In the U.S., the answer has to do with 'So what does this mean for a particular field?' or 'What does it do to fill a within-field gap that others have identified?' In Europe, the answers have more to do with 'So what is interesting about this?' and 'What does it reveal?' as opposed to 'What does it "fill"?'

At their cores, it seems North America prefers to answer questions, while Europe prefers to reflexively ask them. North American researchers like cumulative knowledge; they like to 'fill in' or puzzle solve, colouring in more and more blank space while staying within the lines. Ideally, one goes through all possible permutations to unearth universals and generalizables. Europe seems to be developing more of a puzzle-making culture, trying to blur lines or at least create crossovers. This can be seen in the European penchant for revisiting old knowledge (for them, management started with the Greeks rather than Frederick Taylor) and putting it into new contexts, as well as in the tendency to tie research to other 'haute' socio-cultural theorizing (e.g., Bourdieau, Giddens, Foucault, Habermas, Luhmann).

This links to considerations of the desirable. In Europe, life-work and work-life balance have long permeated the social structure. This translates into an emphasis on research that itself edifying and enjoyable. To be really good, research must have a certain emotional and aesthetic appeal, worthy of being accompanied by a good cup of coffee, chocolate, or glass of wine. A work might be humorous, wistful, melancholic, edgy, or sublime, but without any of these, it goes unread and ignored. If we consider the various European or European-influenced contributors in this volume, we also see that they value cultural depth; to be credible, a work must converse (even if only in allusional ways) with the philosophical, literary, and social traditions that underpin Western thought.

To the North American, all this can appear utterly messy – too many ideas, broad and seemingly unrelated references, too many balls bouncing about. Comparatively,

in North America the good entails 'getting somewhere', moving on, making things more efficient, or at least more workable. Rolled up sleeves, tenacity, and leanly muscled presentation – the Thomas Edison/Horatio Alger package – count for a lot. North America continues to sharpen what it has made such a reputation with – tightly reasoned, fast-paced, utilitarian, and ultimately profitable thinking. This isn't to say that the non-North Americans aren't working hard, or aren't concerned about worth; they most definitely are, but they do this toward very different ends.

Will they meet in the middle? Though Fiol and O'Connor suggest not, there are several forces which may foster some kind of blending. One is the rise of business school accreditation processes being used in around the world (e.g., AACSB, AMBA, EQUIS). These processes, with their tie-ins to the American quality assurance and standardization movement, are having a homogenizing effect – a school must have its courses in Organization Theory, Organizational Behaviour, Human Resources, Strategy, etc., and these end up having readings that look a lot like everyone else's. Another factor is the U.S. academic diaspora that's happened during the Bush era. Record numbers of Americans have taken up either visiting or permanent positions in non-U.S. schools, even as more highly skilled non-Americans have gone to U.S. schools for their PhD education and then returned to their home countries. Together, these two groups have created a surprisingly strong presence and uptake of North American research practices in non-North American settings. Finally, the ubiquitous Internet is resulting in far more transnational efforts. A quick 10-year survey of journal editorial boards on both sides of the Atlantic shows that memberships have become more mixed. Europeans, Australasians, and Asians are no longer 'tokens' in the AoM journals, and North Americans frequently appear in the non-North American outlets. Transnational research groups have always been around, but these days they seem to be forming less around data collection and generalizability purposes and more as means to create unusual and interesting thinking.

CONCLUSION

Will all these moves leave us somehow high and dry, or worse yet, deeply drowned? We suggest that while we may be amidst a rising tide of possibilities and complexity, we are not necessarily lost in this sea. We have ways to see where we are going. There are combinations, relations, and resonances between the denizens of this waterworld, some stickier than others, and while these may be tentative, temporal, momentary, interactive, and symbolic, they nevertheless can provide focus and direction. We can direct ourselves and our attention toward new areas without succumbing to a modernist anxiety that there is 'nothing to hold on to'. Thus we do not have this paradigmatic choice of all or nothing that postmodernism seems to have indicated. We may not have a place to stand, at least not in the sense of dry, unmoving land. But, but, but… we DO have a place to be. And with this conception of place comes much more space to move within and connect to.

NOTE

1 Many thanks to the many people who have contributed their opinions and observations here. Special thanks go to Stefan Meisiek, Joao Cunha, Miguel Cunha, mary Jo Hatch, Ken Friedman, Robert Austin, and Marlena Fiol for their thoughtful discussions on the topic.

REFERENCES

Boje, D.M. (2001) *Narrative Methods for Organizational and Communication Research*. London: Sage.

Burrell, G. and Morgan, G. (1979) *Sociological Paradigms and Organizational Analysis: Elements of the Sociology of Corporate Life*. London: Heinemann.

Clegg, S.R., Hardy, C. and Nord, W.R. (1996) *Handbook of Organizational Studies*. London: Sage.

Cole, S. (1983) 'The hierarchy of the sciences?' *American Journal of Sociology*, 89: 111–139.

Denzin, N.K. and Lincoln, Y.S. (1994) *Handbook of Qualitative Research*. Thousand Oaks, CA: Sage.

Ghoshal, S. (2005) 'Bad management theories are destroying good management practices', *Academy of Management Learning and Education*, 4 (1): 75–91.

Grant, D., Hardy, C., Oswick, C. and Putnam, L. (2004) *Handbook of Organizational Discourse*. London: Sage.

Hayek, F.A. (1978) *New Studies in Philosophy, Politics, Economics, and the History of Ideas*. Chicago: Chicago University Press.

Knudsen, C. (2003) 'Pluralism, scientific progress, and the structure of organizational theory', in H. Tsoukas and C. Knudsen (eds) *The Oxford Handbook of Organization Theory*. Oxford: Oxford University Press.

March, J.G. (1965) *Handbook of Organizations*. Chicago: Rand McNally and Company.

Pfeffer, J. (1993) 'AMR. Barrier to the advance of organizational science: Paradigm development as a dependable variable', *Academy of Management Review*, 18 (4): 599–620.

Weick, K. (1995) *Sensemaking in Organizations*. Thousand Oaks, CA: Sage.

PART 1

Looking at Organizations

The Future of Critical Management Studies

Mats Alvesson

Many researchers in management and organization studies hold the assumption that companies and other organizations are institutions working for 'the common good', that the outputs are making things better for customers, employees, owners and the general public. Organizational structures and practices are understood as functional for the accomplishment of organizational objectives, which then serve various stakeholders. Others, not as many though, look at organizations in a slightly more sceptical way. Organizational arrangements and objectives are viewed in the light of power and sectional interests (Pfeffer, 1981) or are viewed as reflecting popular societal myths or standard recipes for how things should look like, and for cognitive or normative reasons organizations mimic each other or follow fashionable trends in the structures and practices they develop (DiMaggio and Powell, 1983; Meyer and Rowan, 1977). Compared with these theories promoting modest scepticism to managerial and economic ideas on organizations, critical approaches to management and organization are more radically critical and intrinsically suspicious.

The word 'critical' has, of course, a number of meanings. All research is critical in the sense that the researcher is intolerant of weak argumentation, speculative statements, erroneous conclusions, etc. In this chapter, 'critical' is understood as the stimulation of a more extensive reflection upon established ideas, ideologies and institutions in order to eliminate or at least reduce repression, self-constraints or suffering. Critical research aims to stand on the weaker part's side when studying or commenting upon relations of dominance. Critical theory is referred to as a tradition of social science, including the Frankfurt School and related authors and lines of thought such as Foucault, critical post-structuralism, neo-Marxism, certain versions of feminism, etc.

A label that has been increasingly popular to use and, for many researchers, to associate themselves with, is critical management studies (CMS). This is a broad label, used in different ways, referring to somewhat varied constellations of approaches. CMS is interested in what is viewed as the negative aspects of organization and management. That there is a dark side of business and organizations should not come as a surprise to anybody. The existence of a large and expanding stream of work based in management schools, specializing in critical studies is perhaps something not many would have predicted a couple of decades ago.

Organizations do not merely contribute to people's needs through producing goods and services, but have many other implications on humans, nature and society, including the exercise of power, creating disciplinary effects on customers and subordinates but also on managers and professionals. They also include constructing 'needs', i.e. a focus on wants and orientations that various organizations claim to be able to satisfy. Companies operating on the market of consumer goods are, as indirect consequences of product promotion, often contributing to the creation of consumerist orientations, linking self-esteem to the purchase and consumption of goods, which often overlaps with or fuels egoism and envy (Pollay, 1986). Commercials are frequently emphasizing youth, beauty and perfection, which is creating feelings of insecurity, imperfection and frustration (Lasch, 1978). A general increase in consumption does not seem to increase the life satisfaction of a certain population, at least not in 'affluent societies' (Kasser, 2002). This of course raises doubts about the value and meaningfulness of a lot of organizational activities.

Within organizations, life is far from always positive. Of course, organizations contribute to material survival and affluence, job satisfaction and positive social relations, a sense of meaning and personal development. They also contribute to stress, bad health, they mean subordination and exploitation, they may encourage people to conformism, prevent them from 'free thinking' and free speech, erode moral standards, create or reinforce gender inequalities, etc. People working in organizations are subjected to, and formed by, administrative demand for adaptability, cooperation, predictability and conformity. We live in a thoroughly organized society and this creates particular kinds of subjects in a variety of subtle ways.

All areas of live – work, play, consumption, civil discourse, sex – are becoming more 'organized', that is subject to the dictates of regimes of instrumental rationality, whether originating from government, management, or craft standards. It is a measure of the pervasiveness of this ideology that it is difficult to describe in public discourse how 'becoming more organized' can be anything other than a good thing. (Batteau, 2001: 731)

There are thus good reasons to also encourage critical perspectives on management, organizations and working life and not assume, as in perhaps the majority of research and even more in textbooks, that organizations are mainly in the business of good-doing and that management only exceptionally deviates from the norm of fulfilling positive social functions in the interest of most stakeholders, or that problems can be resolved through 'better management'. Also, what is by gurus and media understood as better management may create harmful social effects.

Apart from looking at organizations as machines, organisms, brains, etc., it is fruitful to depict them as psychic prisons and instruments for the exercise of dominance (Morgan, 1997). Alvesson and Willmott (1996) suggest that management can be viewed as systematically distorted communication, the subordination of communication to an instrumental reason, mystification, selective creation of needs and conceptions, cultural doping or the company as an agent of socialization.

In this chapter, I will give a brief review of the development and contemporary versions of CMS, discuss its characteristics – and some of the debates around efforts to establish these – before pointing at some interesting tensions and debates within the area, and before finally suggesting some lines of development and possible futures.

THE DEVELOPMENT AND OVERVIEW OF CMS

There has, of course, always been critical work on business, management and organization, from leftist as well as right-wing positions (Fournier and Grey, 2000; Scarbrough and

Burrell, 1996). It was with the Marxist interest in labour process in the early 1970s that a high-profiled trend of critical studies of work organization, and by implication, management, started. The end of the 1970s and the 1980s saw a steady flow of work studying the relationships between labour and capital at the point of production, inspired by Braverman (1974). The seminal work of Clegg and Dunkerley (1980) took a broad look at organizations from a Marxist position. At the same time, the highly influential book by Burrell and Morgan (1979) explored organization studies in the light of sociological paradigms. They concluded that most work, despite considerable variation, was conducted within a functionalist paradigm, characterized by objectivist ideas and assumptions of consensus (or limited conflict) and social engineering. Burrell and Morgan argued that this was far too limited and encouraged the organizational research community to explore other paradigms. Two radical paradigms were formulated. One was radical humanism, and the Frankfurt School and Gramsci were the major high theorists, implying critical studies of ideologies and forms of consciousness. It tends to depict organizations as a psychic or cultural prison, where people tie themselves collectively to certain constraining versions of the world, turning ideology into reality. The other was radical structuralism, drawing upon objectivist Marxist ideas and emphasizing labour processes and structural features. One assumption is that organizations in important ways are more similar to real prisons, with forms of control, constraints, suppression and political struggles based on interest differences as key characteristics.

In the late 1980s and early 90s the trend within critical work on organizations and management moved from the earlier, Marxist-based focus on labour process, over to a stronger interest in culture, subjectivity and meanings. Organizational culture became a hot topic and it offered two important venues for people of a critical bent. One was targeting the great hope attached by business and management writers on control through corporate cultures, in the more extreme nightmare versions turning employees into corporate dopes or slaves (Willmott, 1993); the other was the anthropologically inspired cultural in-depth study of corporate life, which often revealed cracks, irrationalities and pecularities in organizations and also showed management control in action (Knights and Willmott, 1987; Rosen, 1985). Some semi-critical work, perhaps more ethnographic and interpretive than theoretically privileging a 'negative agenda', have been quite influential and offer rich and enjoyable readings of organizations from a middle level rather than a shopfloor point of view (Jackall, 1988; Kunda, 1992; Watson, 1994). In the 1980s and 90s also feminist work started to appear in management and organization studies in some quantities, much of it critically oriented (Alvesson and Billing, 1997; Calás and Smircich, 2006; Martin, 2003). An initial interest in mainly females was gradually supplemented by an interest in men and masculinities, although this was much more limited (e.g. Collinson and Hearn, 1996).

Poststructuralism and postmodernism reached organization studies in the late 1980s and attracted many people earlier interested in critical-interpretive approaches. During the first half of the 1990s postmodernist thinking characterized many who were enthusiastic for non- or anti-managerialist ideas, although with varying degrees of commitment to critical thinking, at least of the somewhat heavy nature indicated by the introduction to this chapter. With its, in some ways, quite extreme agenda and oppositional stance to other forms of thinking with an ambition of saying something and carrying out empirical studies, postmodernism evoked strong feelings and there were intensive debates (Parker, 1992; Thompson, 1993). Postmodernism has now passed its zenith, and there are probably relatively few people advocating the starker versions of it.

Today, the overall field of CMS is difficult to demarcate and what is to be counted as critical or not is seldom clear and sometimes contested. It is probably fair to say that the field is quite pluralistic and varied, though there are no dominant fashions or streams.

The amount of work that may be included in the CMS umbrella has increased rapidly. Of all the research products appearing in management and organization studies, CMS work has a high market share. So is the case in particular in the UK for various reasons, including close affinities between management departments and social sciences (Fournier and Grey, 2000; Grey and Willmott, 2005). The CMS conference in the UK attracts much attention and there are journals devoted specifically to critical work (e.g. *Critical Perspectives on Accounting and Organization*). It is (at least when this text was written) a successful institution (Grey and Willmott, 2005) and, as a somewhat less enthusiastic commentator expresses it, a popular brand (Thompson, 2005).

BRANCHES OF CMS

As said, it is very difficult to provide an overview of the field. The boundaries are very loose and it is quite arbitrary where to draw the line. Different groups perceive what is critical differently. As Fournier and Grey (2000) note, 'psychoanalytic, and humanistic work in general, may see itself as offering a basis for critique and reform which poststructuralists dismiss as disciplinary' (p. 16). Postmodernism is often seen as a subversive orientation but by some viewed as a conservative philosophy which leaves social reality intact and unquestioned and embraces a relativism that supports the use of various claims about how to represent the world that is well in line with contemporary capitalist institutions' preoccupations with, and exploitation of, representations, images and brands. Jackall (1988) sees strong parallels between PR specialists and postmodernists ('The truth?' 'Which truth?'). Further problems for the person interested in drawing a huge map of CMS includes that different authors and orientations can be divided up in various ways. As researchers change and move between positions – many are doing different kinds of work – it is better to talk about texts than authors in many cases. The following list of orientations is not intended to be exhaustive but to give a sense of the spectrum of approaches that could be incorporated or used in CMS projects. I start with orientations that are extremely non-objectivist and assuming the unknowability of the social world move over to approaches that assume that there is an objective world out there that we can develop robust (if imperfect) scientific knowledge about.

- Critical deconstructivists, marrying Derridaian ideas with a political agenda (such as feminism) like Martin (1990) and Calás and Smircich (1991).
- Foucauldians emphasizing knowledge/power in various management subfields (e.g. Knights, 1992; Knights and Morgan, 1991; Townley, 1993).
- Existentialist CMS people, studying subjectivity and how operations of power and human insecurity fuel various efforts of closure and compliance, although there always remain a space for uncertainty, anxiety and resistance (Collinson, 2003; Knights and Willmott, 1989).
- Critical theorists, drawing upon the Frankfurt School and/or Habermas and emphasizing the ideal and possibility of emancipation (Alvesson and Willmott, 1996, 2003; Forester, 2003; Willmott, 2003), possibly in combination with postmodernist inspiration (Alvesson and Deetz, 2000; Deetz, 1992).
- Critical interpretivists, working with an ethnographic approach in which an interest in culture and meaning has a critical slant (Jackall, 1988; Kunda, 1992; Watson, 1994).
- Gender studies people, emphasizing experiences of females and/or forms of domination of cultural ideas on masculinity. This camp thus includes both feminists and 'masculinists' (e.g. Alvesson and Billing, 1997; Calás and Smircich, 2006; Collinson and Hearn, 1996; Martin, 2003).
- Left Weberians, here the developments and mixed blessing of bureaucratic forms are being targeted, the oppressive and constraining organizational forms of hierarchy, division of labour and routines are critically assessed, but so is also presumably radical and progressive alternatives such as claims about post-bureaucracies (Adler, 1999; Perrow, 1986; Sennett, 1998).
- Labour process theorists (gradually with a less pronounced Marxist view), critically studying work organizations and employer/employee relations (e.g. Ackroyd and Thompson, 1999).

This list moves from extreme constructivist and language focused versions to more objectivist, materially interested and realist ontologies and epistemologies.

The mainstream or most typical CMS position is probably inspired by a kind of mix of Frankfurt School/Habermasian (or Gramscian) and Foucauldian ideas and some 'medium-radical' incorporation of general postmodernist thinking. Many people routinely camp Foucault with postmodernists against critical modernists like Habermas, but there are probably more similarities between Foucault and the Frankfurt School (Adorno, Horkheimer) than between Foucault and Derrida or Lyotard, at least according to Foucault himself (e.g. Foucault, 1983, 1995). Honneth (1995) draws attention to both Adorno and Foucault:

> ... see the process of technical rationalization as culminating in the 'totalitarian' organizations of domination of highly developed societies. Both theoreticians conceive its stability solely as the effect of the one-sided activity of administratively highly perfected organizations. (p. 178)

This CMS mainstream or middle position – which is my own stance – represents a moderate version of constructionism, some interest in 'reality out there', some in ideologies/discourses and subjectivity plus some interest in the specifics and details of language, but without driving it too far (a linguistic half-turn, perhaps). This could be seen as radical humanism with a clear postmodernist (poststructuralist) bent. This representation is a bit different from Thompson (2005) who thinks that postmodernists have hijacked the CMS label and reserved it for researchers with strong constructivist convictions.

Much work loosely associated with CMS, e.g. presented at conferences under this umbrella, is moderately non-managerial, interpretive, taking the views of non-elites seriously, pointing at some irrationalities in management/organization, wanting to be close to the empirical material and/or is playful, ironic, expresses 'esoteric' interests (like aesthetics, science fiction) and can perhaps be categorized as CMS light. It expresses a moderate to mild questioning or stirring up mainstream thinking, but does not embrace emancipation or resistance as the major goal, nor use the heavy CT thinkers or hard-core vocabulary such as power, domination, oppression, prisons, etc. to any great extent.

CHARACTERISTICS OF CMS

Having offered an overview of the different traditions and orientations of CMS, I will move over and try to give a suggestion for what are the core characteristics of this direction. A dilemma here is between wanting to police and monopolize the field versus to be so broadminded and open that the label tells us nothing and that the critical intent of CMS becomes blurred. Identifying characteristics is not easy: according to Fournier and Grey (2000), trying to find a minimalistic characterization, CMS has the following features:

- non-performativity
- denaturalization (constructivism)
- reflexivity

But this definition is controversial. Reflexivity is increasingly a standard feature of large parts of social research, some say of our entire culture (Giddens, 1991). Whether CMS can claim to score better or be more ambitious in this respect than others is hard to say. Denaturalization, in the sense of seriously considering the historical and socially produced nature of contemporary phenomena, is also common outside critical work. Large groups of researchers favour constructionist thinking – being open for the possibilities of constructions or representations of social reality in ways different from those being materialized and/or textualized at present. Performativity is defined as being about means-ends calculation and has the 'aim to contribute to the effectiveness of managerial practice' (p. 17). Non-performativity is again not unique for CMS but is characterizing many interpretivist researchers. It is also debatable within CMS.

I agree with Fournier and Grey that a prioritization of means-ends calculations and an emphasis on knowledge facilitating managerial effectiveness is anti-CMS, but on the other hand one can't say that there is something wrong with effectiveness *per se*, nor with knowledge wanting to facilitate it. I certainly appreciate the degree of managerial effectiveness that is behind the development, manufacturing and distribution of the computer I am using and making the writing of this text a (technically) smooth exercise. Sometimes there is a kind of hypocrisy or cynicism in critical research in the sense that people attack what they really enjoy and benefit from, like most examples of instrumental rationality creating material wealth and comfort. The problem is that performativity is too often the only significant criteria and that it frequently means the neglect of other values and is accomplished at the expense of other ideals, such as autonomy, democracy, gender equality, ecological balance, etc. Sometimes effectiveness is accomplished at the expense of other values and sometimes the outcome means something negative, e.g. far-reaching control over the minds of and preferences of customers or environmental problems. Bearing these negative features often associated with effectiveness closely in mind, and taking conflicts seriously, is not, however, the same as celebrating non-performativity as a guiding principle. Arguably, there are different ways of being performative and different relationships between (economical) effectiveness and other values. Most people in and around organizations probably often benefit from a higher degree of effectiveness of organizations. Within CMS, there may be a point in considering also the positive functions of management. In addition, critique can be seen as a means to facilitate emancipation (an end) – one can here talk about critical performativity as an ideal for CMS.

My own suggestion would be for a working definition of CMS to be about:

1 The critical questioning of ideologies, institutions, interests and identities (the four I's) that are assessed to be (a) dominant, (b) harmful and (c) underchallenged.
2 Through negations, deconstructions, revoicing or defamiliarizations.
3 With the aim of inspiring social reform in the presumed interest of the majority and/or those non-privileged, as well as emancipation and/or resistance from ideologies, institutions and identities that tend to fix people into unreflectively arrived at and reproduced ideas, intentions and practices.
4 With some degree of appreciation of the constraints of the work and life situations of people (including managers) in the contemporary organizational world, e.g. that a legitimate purpose for organizations is the production of services and goods.

Let me explore these four elements.

1 *Theme of study.* Critical questioning means that one carefully picks a theme or phenomenon that is assessed to deserve the whip of the CMS. Of course, life and society is full of negative things. The phenomena of most interest from a CMS perspective would be dominant and underchallenged, e.g. there is a degree of taken-for-grantedness guiding the common attitude to the phenomenon and/or how it is commonly being represented.
   This critical questioning is preferably non-reductionistic, which may mean to consider the 4 I's. Relating the links and overlaps between ideologies, institutions, interests and identities means that the interplay of idea systems, social forms, various human interests and the subjectivities of people are being explored. Sometimes this is over-packed under the over-exploited and often vaguely used label discourse, with the unfortunate consequence of obscuring the various elements involved (Alvesson and Kärreman, 2000). From a CMS point of view taking various elements into account along the structure/agent or culture-subjectivity dimensions is important.
2 *Methodological approach.* Doing fieldwork or other kinds of empirical inquiry within CMS can be done with all kinds of techniques, but some kind of denaturalization methodology marks the overall interpretive approach. This may mean radical deconstruction or just framing phenomena in such a language that their historically, societally and paradigmatically contingent character becomes clear. But rather than be dragged into conventional representations and accepting the reported views

and experiences of those being studied, some kind of alternative position is taken. This would mean some challenging to naturalize, reify or in other ways freeze culturally and theoretically dominant representations and understandings. More specifically, this may be conducted through methodological principles such as negations, deconstructions, revoicing or defamiliarizations (Alvesson and Deetz, 2000).

3 *Objective.* While being challenging, provocative and critical may be seen as values in themselves and means-ends reasoning may be problematic, the question of the purpose of all this seems motivated. Although social engineering and managerialism – involving a legitimation of expertise and the turning of subjects into objects of managerial intervention and control – is a justified favourite theme for critique, it should not exclude the idea of critical research trying to influence social and managerial practices.

Participation, dialogue, reduction of hierarchy and communicative action are key features in CMS oriented projects aiming at reformation of institutions. This would then mark a positive pole of CMS, different from critique based on fault-finding and the raising of the red flag. Emancipation means efforts to break away from structures and ideologies that tend to constrain values, objectives, forms of consciousness into prespecified routes and constrained imagination. For those of postmodernist convictions, autonomy and self-clarification may appear as old-fashioned and reflect the arrogance of the elitist-researcher, but the strive for a positive and less predefined space through the critical investigation of various traps and prisons can still be a possible route for CMS. Balancing the Foucauldian notion of persistent and ever-present micro-power, the idea of micro-emancipation (contra grandiose Marxist and other radical large-scale projects) has been proposed (Alvesson and Willmott, 1996). The third possible route for progressive politics is resistance, which tends to portray a much more defensive project. This is mainly reactive, fuelled by the ambiguities and multi-discursivity of the modes of power, at least in the postmodernistically inspired writings (e.g. Thomas and Linstead, 2002). (There are, of course, also more traditional and broader views on resistance, e.g. Ackroyd and Thompson, 1999; Prasad and Prasad, 1998.) The three versions of the very purpose of CMS – knowledge input to reform, emancipation and resistance – all target some social and managerial practices that are seen as repressive, socially disadvantageous or

dangerous and encourage some kind of movement away from this.

4 *Appreciation of the management and organizational context.* While all the gurus of CMS – from Marx, Gramsci, the Frankfurt School and Habermas to Foucault and Laclau and Mouffe – have been on a safe distance from business schools and management departments, most advocates of CMS are not. One possible definition of a CMS person would be a radical sociologist who could not get a job at a sociology department or who realized that resources and prospects for promotion are better in management than in a 'real' academic discipline. Arguably, being in a management discipline makes it reasonable to take management seriously and to recognize the legitimacy of values like productivity, quality, customer service and realize that some degree of coordination, control, division of labour, hierarchy and exercise of authority is often necessary and reasonable. Without some degree of these qualities social life may be characterized by the tyranny of structurelessness and be as impractical and unpleasant as some of the experiments in realizing the ideal of feminist organizations (Morgen, 1994). Some consideration of what organizations are supposed to accomplish is relevant, also for CMS. As Alvehus (2006) notes, in a lot of this literature organizations seem to produce (unhappy or imprisoned or normalized) subjects, but not much or many socially valuable products or services.

Critical ideas around social reform, emancipation and resistance should be produced bearing the societal and economic context and the social restrictions in mind. The more revolutionary and utopian ideas as well as radical versions of postmodernism and feminism may be less relevant for CMS than for critical research in general. A possible distinctive feature of CMS – as a specific branch of critical social science of some relevance for those engaged in or preparing for work in management and business – would thus be to relate ideas around reform, emancipation and resistance to production and results in contemporary organizations. This does not imply that all critical research should be 'realistic' or adapt to contemporary regimes and contexts, only that CMS acknowledges that the ideals of emancipation, autonomy, resistance, ecology, feminine values … may have drastic consequences on what firms, schools, hospitals and other organizations actually produce – apart from affecting the work and subjectivity of employees.

APPLYING CMS ON THE CMS COMMUNITY

On the flight between two conferences – one of these was a CMS one – I met a colleague and asked him about what he was working on. I had the intellectual project in mind, but he started by referring to names of the journals for which he was busy revising papers, then continued with referring to the UK Research Assessment Exercise, saying that he already had sufficient publications, but that he got extra rewards from the dean if he scored above what was needed. After all this he mentioned the content of the research work he was doing. Also talk with other UK and US academics, most in CMS (broadly defined) indicate that journal publication in the right journals with sufficient quantities is absolutely crucial. There is an emphasis on what counts, what one 'has to do'. People refer to 'the pressure to publish' as very strong. Suggesting less constrained forms of joint research without a predefined output does not seem to be positively received by many people. Strong instrumentality and adherence to the performativity principle appears to be very important for ambitious academics, perhaps not less so within CMS than in other fields. This seems to reduce the interest in, for example, rich empirical studies.

There are certainly signs of resistance in the sense of people distancing themselves from this – 'just a game', 'nonsense', etc. – but this does not reduce the grip of this emphasis on performativity. 'Resistance' in the form of such utterances probably legitimizes a self-view of oneself 'really' not being subjectively subordinated to the ideology and the regime. This positioning becomes a kind of excuse for action subordinated to a regime of performativity and a reproduction and strengthening of this ideology. Ideology is better seen as

located in people's actions than in what they occasionally espouse (Fleming and Spicer, 2003). Much 'resistance' is perhaps better seen as 'anti-resistance'.

There certainly are variations, but quite a lot of CMS people seem to adapt themselves and their work to the iron cage of high-performative Academia. Ideologies, institutions, interests and identities interplay in this development. There is perhaps some ambivalence about the ideology, but it is often acted upon in a strongly supportive way; institutional rules and loyalties are complied with, the interests in performing better than others and maximizing status and resources for one's own department are expressed and identities are supported by individual performances, appraisals and official rewards. There is here a strong ingredient of concertive control (Baker, 1993), where the CMS tribe, on a large scale but also at the level of the department, like other tribes in Academia, build up, reproduce and reinforce structures and norms that invoke strong pressure and strong inclinations to comply with.

We can thus note the following anti-CMS features of (significant parts of) CMS research practices:

- Research output performativity – a strong emphasis on means-ends calculation.
- Naturalization of the rules of the game – the acceptance of certain arrangements as close to social facts calling for compliance as a 'natural' attitude.
- Cynical false consciousness – where consciousness as expressed in the pub (and perhaps in one's self-conversations) indicates critical awareness and distance (resistance), but where action is based on and fuels a 'performativity-focused' consciousness, thus reproducing and reinforcing a particular regime.

All this does not mean that I am myself thinking that I am not caught in all this. I probably am as eager to publish in high-prestigious journals as other people in the field. Nor does it mean that I am against the rational element of putting pressure on people to engage in research and write good articles, to be accountable for their research time and to have quality control. I think this is legitimate – and journal publication and peer reviewing is not a bad system. The problem, from a CMS perspective, is the strong and one-sided emphasis on academic journal publication and instrumentality and the consequences in the form of quick fixes and fairly standardized forms and modes of doing research. Social and political relevance is reduced.

The heavy focus on journal output means that there is less emphasis on long-term, ambitious empirical work such as ethnographies and on books with a broader appeal, a shortage of more risky, innovative and unconventional research. CMS should, in my opinion, be in the forefront of research having these characteristics, but this does not seem to be the case. As an institution and social movement CMS strongly supports critical research, but it becomes fused with other institutionalized forces (careerism, want to maximize the inflow of resources and to increase departmental status) that partly work against the potential of delivering really interesting critical work.

DEVELOPING CMS: METHODOLOGIES

In order to change this situation and make CMS research of greater value and relevance one could consider the following suggestions for research:

1 Offer non-predictable empirical material and tell counter-intuitive or revealing stories, going to places not so well-trod before. A lot of research means getting access and then do one-hour long interviews with a number of managers (or other people) and then analysing this, perhaps in line with some kind of critical theory. This is seldom very imaginative. One would wish for CMS people to find examples of processes, activities and social practices that is less apparent. An excellent example of this is Jackall (1988), who studied ethical dilemmas in managers' lives in sharp, revealing and partly unexpected ways. A lot of stamina, imagination and hard work was called for. A general challenge of CMS is to get access to the backstage. I think CMS scholars have a lot to learn from critical journalists, suffering less from the inertia of academics and being more flexible, quick, socially active, opportunistic and creative in getting and using sources and digging out good empirical material (e.g. O'Shea and Madigan, 1998; Klein, 2000).

2 Investigate and relate the four I's. Arguably, a key feature of much CMS is the interest to relate 'subjectivity' to broader institutional and ideological arrangements. Through taking multi-level phenomena seriously and postponing integrating the various aspects (e.g. through an all-embracive concept of discourse) reductionism is avoided. Arguably, ideologies, institutions, interests and identities typically are connected, but not without tensions and unexpected relations. How institutions frame and bend ideologies (or discourses), how particular interests both shape and are shaped by institutions and how identities are guided by ideologies are worthy of study; but how people reframe and selectively construct identities also seem as interesting and challenging tasks.

3 Breaking out of CMS jargon and the standard format of writing, trying to find a less stiff-upper lip voice. There is a booming literature on ways of writing (e.g. Van Maanen, 1988), although a lot of experimental writing may not be so successful (Wolf, 1992). A greater problem than any lack of very bold and innovative ways of writing is the tendency for academic journal publications and conventions, even in CMS, to domesticate authors so that their texts sometimes contradict the espoused ideals of the orientation. Even in some research drawing upon Foucauldian and other poststructuralist ideas, the studies reported tend to produce conventional 'depersonalized third-person and apparently objective and authoritative representations' (Wray-Bliss, 2002: 20). Much of the critical terminology and style could perhaps be downplayed and a more engaging and lively style be used.

Two exemplars of studies illustrating these lines of development can be mentioned: Klein (2000) and Sennett (1998), both outside the group of those directly identifying with CMS, but very close in orientations with them. Both these studies sharply portray the overall ideological (and socio-economic) context and development, look carefully at specific social institutions within business and other organizations, take conflicts of interest formation seriously, and show the far-rearching and penetrating consequences of this on the personal level. The empirical material is created and used in innovative and flexible ways, the texts produced are personal, appealing and joyful (but also provocative) to read. The texts do something with the reader. In CMS work the texts of e.g. Kunda (1992), Rosen (1985), Van Maanen (1991) and Watson (1994) have qualities in this respect, but tend to be more narrowly focused on a specific empirical site and lack the broader connections and the covering of larger ground so prominent in Klein and Sennett.

I am certainly not denying that one may have reservations about some aspects of these books, but they have a very strong impact, and if CMS would be inspired by these examples, the future of the area would look more promising.

DEVELOPING CMS: TRAGIC, IRONIC AND PRAGMATIC STYLES

Another proposal for the development of CMS is to consider its possible linkages with less negative perspectives and genres.

The major narrative style of CMS is the tragedy (Jeffcutt, 1993): the dark and gloomy side of organizations dominate and there is not much joy to be found in organizational life. If there is, it reflects the operations of power exploiting emotions and pleasure.

Foucauldian, and to some extent Frankfurt School-style authors, portray 'subjects behaviouristically, as formless, conditionable creatures' (Honneth, 1995: 179). The counterviews are the resistance-person (e.g. Prasad and Prasad, 1998; Thomas and Davies, 2005). We thus have an interplay between the (Foucauldian) subject as an outcome of constant conditioning and the resistance responses. While the resistance person may show glimpses of heroism, this is within a basically tragic scene and main story of everything seemingly rational and good defining and constraining the subject and therefore worthy of suspicion. Both the dominance and resistance versions are, like all research, methodological artefacts. It may be images following from reading outcomes from plans, models, intentions and textbooks, respectively locating people in interview settings and asking them to give accounts of their situations – in which many people probably are eager to exhibit signs on having

a mind of their own and being in control. Small acts of (heroic) resistance in tragic story is still mainly in the genre of the tragedy.

But let us for a moment go outside this kind of narrative. A lot of research somewhat outside CMS produces interpretations of organizations as less in control, less rational and much more messy, confusing, fragmented and ambiguous. Organizations are pluralistic, decision-making is garbage can-like, symbolism, myths and conservative beliefs rule. Fashions and imitations put there imprints on managers and other people. The story line is here typically ironic (Jeffcutt, 1993).

This represents another form of questioning of organization and management, one of unpacking the claims of rationality, control, order and forms of power/ideologies dominating the scene. To put this into play with CMS ideas could be a way of making the latter less one-dimensional and less gloomy and better attuned with vital aspects of organization and management. It can be mobilized in various forms of questioning of management, but it is quite different and partly in opposition to heavy CMS. It should also be possible to combine tragedy with irony; Jackall (1988) is a good example.

Another form of genre is the pragmatic-realist one, trying to be down-to-earth and close to the practices and meanings as (easily) observable, type grounded theory qualitative inquiries. Here the intentions of the actors involved are taken seriously. A kind of bounded rational or try-to-make-things-work logic is typically prevalent. This is the genre that within an academic context (I am not referring to top-management at all in this chapter) is most relevant for practitioners. One could imagine links between this and CMS. One possibility would be for CMS to be more inclined to take the broader context than 'control of subjects' into account. It would relate discourses of masculinity, strategy, leadership or whatever to the specific work tasks and material situations people in organizations try to deal with and consider possibly socially productive (valuable) aspects associated with the former. Sometimes the idea of leadership may assist

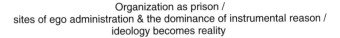

Organization as prison /
sites of ego administration & the dominance of instrumental reason /
ideology becomes reality

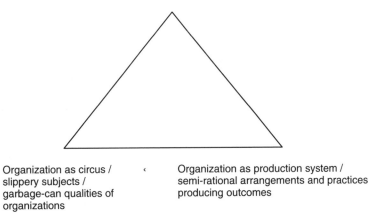

Organization as circus /   ‹   Organization as production system /
slippery subjects /   semi-rational arrangements and practices
garbage-can qualities of   producing outcomes
organizations

Figure 1.1.1   Possible metaphorical positions in organization studies

the formation of productive work relations and motivated authority in organizations; sometimes it creates and sustains unmotivated status differences and dependencies. The trick is to throw light on both. Advocates of critical and managerial thinking could have a shared interest, a bit different from the universal critique respectively in celebration of leadership that critics and managerialists tend to express. CMS ideas could also focus specifically on ideologies, practices and interests that are assessed to be harmful and negative in terms of constraints and unreflective thinking as well as being negative for production and business, e.g. certain instances of communicative distortions (group think), gender and race inequalities (keeping female and non-white talent down), uncritical following of fashion, careerism, subordination to experts with a shaky knowledge base, isomorphism, etc. Here CMS can perhaps offer a critical bite that can be seen as relevant also by people – practitioners, students and pro-management academics – that do not, as CMS authors tend to do, advocate ideals in organizations as the maximization of pleasure, gender equality, autonomy or resistance.

A somewhat expanded agenda for CMS would thus be to combine the critical-tragic metaphor(s) with a sceptical-ironic one and

possibly some appreciation of the production that still, after all, takes place in organizations, creating a surplus of resources financing, among other things, CMS research. This would bring us a combination of three aspects, of which the first is the key one for CMS (see Figure 1.1.1).

The three aspects or metaphors can be combined in studies in different ways. One possibility is to seek overlapping ground and a common focus. Circus and prison qualities can be combined, and one can imagine studies of management recipes and fashions that have questionable effects on autonomy as well as performances. Similarly the prison and production system images could be related, so that the trade-off between individual freedom and creativity and creation of material wealth is considered. In addition, one could draw attention to the many forms of managerial activity, e.g. a great deal of brand marketing, MBA's and many mergers and acquisitions that do not lead to much material well-being.

These routes would then complement 'hard-core' CMS with an appreciation of the often circus-like qualities of contemporary organizations – sometimes amusing rather than just motivating moral outrage – as well as productive and socially valuable features of many organizations. Various versions of prison-circus and respectively prison-factory metaphors are possible, with more or less emphasis on the critical element.

Another possibility is the use of multiple perspectives producing a multitude of results, combining heavy and light CMS. Going back and forth between critical and ironic or 'constructive' ideas is possible. Journal publication tends to give priority to narrowly focused presentations, often counterproductive to studies taking the ethos of critical research seriously.

CONCLUSION

CMS is a diverse and expanding research field. This triggers discussion around what it is and what it is not. There is always a dilemma between on the one hand trying to identify some key characteristics and suggest an agenda and, on the other, freeze and police an area. Negatively, such enterprises may be framed as leading to self-promotion of one's own favourite view and endless quarrelling of what is and what is not CMS and who is 'really' critical in the right way and who is not. Positively, this may be portrayed as triggering fruitful debate and clarification of alternatives and possibilities. At best it may enhance collective efforts strengthening a particular research paradigm that may have something vital to say in a world characterized by increasingly influential ideologies of managerialism, reinforced corporate power and the expansion of business schools, and management departments function as socialisation agencies for huge numbers of students and propaganda units for business in many countries. The risk of locking everybody into the same convention must be borne in mind.

In this chapter I have tried to account for the development and various subfields of CMS and discussed some of its key characteristics, acknowledging that this is a contested project. I have also indicated some problems with current CMS work – in particular that the strong tendencies that some of the ethos and social and political relevance of critical work is being contradicted and domesticated by the academic version of the performativity principle in the form of frequent publication in prestigious academic journals. Some CMS work then partly counteracts its very rationale. There are elements of cynicism here: seeing the organizational world as a supplier of negative features which one can exploit in critical articles, but not really doing something outside this career-facilitating space.

Two routes for more interesting, less reductionistic, more accessible and academically, socially and politically relevant CMS work are suggested. One concerns tactics for producing rich and engaging stories. This may involve being more creative, flexible and bold in getting access to interesting empirical sites and processes, broadening the focus compared to narrow studies of a strictly defined object (or theme) of study, to relate overall trends and institutions with identities and experiences (subjectivities) and to sidestep the standardized format and jargon of academic writing. The other is to produce stories that contain ingredients other than tragedy, i.e. are less one-dimensional in terms of negativity. Even if the very point of CMS should be that we don't live in a very good world – if we think we do we should realize that we don't – this gloomy main message can be combined with other messages. One possible bedfellow here is the ironic genre pointing at the confusions, ambiguities and irrationalities of organizational life, key qualities becoming significant when the sceptical author (often an ethnographer) moves behind the façade of rationality, order and control – possibly also moving beyond the beliefs of Foucauldians and others about Discourse being in control (apart from triggering a little resistance). Another possibility is to take also the production and outcome-related considerations and worries of organizational participants seriously, acknowledging their importance and legitimacy.

REFERENCES

Ackroyd, S. and Thompson, P. (1999) *Organizational Misbehaviour*. London: Sage.

Adler, P. (1999) 'Building better bureaucracies', *Academy of Management Executive*, 13 (4): 36–47.

Alvehus, J. (2006) *Paragrafer Och Profit.* Lund: Lund Business Press.

Alvesson, M. and Billing, Y. (1997) *Understanding Gender and Organization.* London: Sage.

Alvesson, M. and Deetz, S. (2000) *Doing Critical Management Research.* London: Sage.

Alvesson, M. and Kärreman, D. (2000) 'Varieties of discourse: on the study of organizations through discourse analysis', *Human Relations*, 53: 1125–1149.

Alvesson, M. and Willmott, H. (1996) *Making Sense of Management: A Critical Analysis.* London: Sage.

Alvesson, M. and Willmott, H. (eds) (2003) *Studying Management Critically.* London: Sage.

Baker, J. (1993) Tightening the iron cage: convertive control in self-managing teams, *Administrative Science Quarterly*, 38: 408–437.

Batteau, A. (2001) 'Negations and ambiguities in the cultures of organizations'. *American Anthropologist*, 102 (4): 726–740.

Braverman, H. (1974) *Labor and Monopoly Capital.* New York: Monthly Review Press.

Burrell, G. and Morgan, G. (1979) *Sociological Paradigms and Organizational Analysis.* Aldershot: Gower.

Calás, M. and Smircich, L. (1991) 'Voicing seduction to silence leadership', *Organization Studies*, 12: 567–602.

Calás, M. and Smircich, L. (2006) 'From the "woman's" point of view. Feminist approaches to organization studies', in S. Clegg, C. Hardy and W. Nord (eds), *Handbook of Organization Studies* (2nd edn). London: Sage.

Clegg, S. and Dunkerley, D. (1980) *Organization, Class and Control.* London: Routledge & Kegan Paul.

Collinson, D. (2003) 'Identities and insecurities'. *Organization*, 10 (3): 527–547.

Collinson, D. and Hearn, J. (1996) 'Breaking the silence: on men, masculinities and managements', in D. Collinson and J. Hearn (eds) *Men as Managers, Managers as Men.* London: Sage.

Deetz, S. (1992) *Democracy in the Age of Corporate Colonization: Developments in Communication and the Politics of Everyday Life.* Albany: State University of New York Press.

DiMaggio, P.J. and Powell, W.W. (1983) 'The iron cage revisited: institutional isomorphism and collective rationality in organizational fields'. *American Sociological Review*, 148: 147–160.

Fleming, P. and Spicer, A. (2003) 'Working at a cynical distance'. *Organization*, 10 (1): 157–159.

Forester, J. (2003) 'On fieldwork in a Habermasian way: critical ethnography and the extra-ordinary character of ordinary professional work', in M. Alvesson and H. Willmott (eds), *Studying Management Critically.* London: Sage, pp. 1–20.

Foucault, M. (1983) 'Structuralism and post-structuralism: an interview with Michel Foucault', by G. Raulet. *Telos*, 55: 195–211.

Foucault, M. (1995) 'The art of telling the truth', in M. Kelly (ed.) *Critique and Power.* Cambridge: MIT Press.

Fournier, V. and Grey, C. (2000) 'At the critical moment: conditions and prospects for critical management studies', *Human Relations*, 53 (1): 5–32.

Giddens, A. (1991) *Modernity and Self-Identity.* Cambridge: Polity Press.

Grey, C. and Willmott, H. (eds) (2005) *Critical Management Studies.* Oxford: Oxford University Press.

Honneth, A. (1995) 'Foucault's theory of society: a systems-theoretic dissolution of the dialectic of enlightenment', in M. Kelly (ed.) 1995 *Critique and Power.* Cambridge, MA: MIT Press.

Jackall, R. (1988) *Moral Mazes. The World of Corporate Managers.* Oxford: Oxford University Press.

Jeffcutt, P. (1993) 'From interpretation to representation', in J. Hassard and M. Parker (eds), *Postmodernism and Organizations.* London: Sage, pp. 25–48.

Kasser, T. (2002) *The High Price of Materialism.* Cambridge, MA: MIT Press.

Klein, N. (2000) *No Logo.* London: Flamingo.

Knights, D. (1992) 'Changing spaces: the disruptive impact of a new epistemological location for the study of management', *Academy of Management Review*, 17: 514–536.

Knights, D. and Morgan, G. (1991) 'Corporate strategy, organizations, and subjectivity: a critique', *Organization Studies*, 12: 251–273.

Knights, D. and Willmott, H. (1987) 'Organisational culture as management strategy', *International Studies of Management and Organization*, 17 (3): 40–63.

Knights, D. and Willmott, H. (1989) 'Power and subjectivity at work: from degradation to subjugation in social relation', *Sociology*, 23: 535–558.

Kunda, G. (1992) *Engineering Culture: Control and Commitment in a High-Tech Corporation.* Philadelphia: Temple University Press.

Lasch, C. (1978) *The Culture of Narcissism.* New York: Norton.

Martin, J. (1990) 'Deconstructing organizational taboos: the suppression of gender conflict in organizations', *Organization Science*, 11: 339–359.

Martin, J. (2003) 'Feminist theory and critical theory: unexplored synergies', in M. Alvesson and H. Willmott (eds), *Studying Management Critically.* London: Sage. pp. 66–91.

Meyer, J. and Rowan, B. (1977) 'Institutional-ized organizations: formal structure as myth and ceremony', *American Journal of Sociology*, 83: 340–363.

Morgan, G. (1997) *Images of Organization* (2nd edn). Thousand Oaks, CA: Sage.

Morgen, S. (1994) 'Personalizing personnel decisions in feminist organizational theory and practice', *Human Relations*, 47 (6): 665–684.

O'Shea, J. and Madigan, C. (1998) *Dangerous Company. The Consulting Powerhouses and the Businesses they Save and Ruin*. London: Nicholas Brealey.

Parker, M. (1992) 'Post-modern organizations or postmodern organization theory?', *Organization Studies*, 13: 1–17.

Pfeffer, J. (1981) *Power in Organizations*. Boston: Pitman.

Pollay, R. (1986) 'The distorted mirror: reflections on the unintended consequences of advertising', *Journal of Marketing*, 50 (April): 18–36.

Prasad, P. and Prasad, A. (1998) 'Everyday struggles at the workplace', in *Research in the Sociology of Organizations*, 15: 225–257. JAI Press.

Rosen, M. (1985) 'Breakfirst at Spiro's: dramaturgy and dominance', *Journal of Management*, 11 (2): 31–48.

Scarbrough, H. and G. Burrell (1996) 'The axeman cometh: the changing roles and knowledges of middle managers', in S. Clegg, and G. Palmer (eds), *The Politics of Management Knowledge*. London: Sage.

Sennett, R. (1998) The *Corrosion of Character*. New York: Norton.

Thomas, R. and Davies, A. (2005) 'Theorizing the micro-politics of resistance', *Organization Studies*, 26 (5): 683–706.

Thomas, R. and Linstead, A. (2002) 'Losing the plot? Middle managers and identity', *Organization*, 9 (1): 71–93.

Thompson, P. (1993) 'Post-modernism: fatal dis-traction', in J. Hassard and M. Parker (eds), *Postmodernism and Organizations*. London: Sage. pp. 183–203.

Thompson, P. (2005) 'Brands, boundaries and band-wagons. A critical reflection on Critical Management Studies', in S. Fleetwood and S. Ackroyd (eds), *Critical Realism in Action in Organisation and Management Studies*. London: Routledge.

Townley, B. (1993) 'Foucault, power/knowledge, and its relevance for human resource management', *Academy of Management Review*, 18: 518–545.

Van Maanen, J. (1988) 'The Smile Factory', in P. J. Frost et al. (eds), *Reframing Organizational Culture*. Beverly Hills: Sage.

Van Maanen, J. (1991) *Tales of the Field. On Writing Ethnography*. Chicago, IL, The University of Chicago Press.

Watson, T. (1994) *In Search of Management*. London: Routledge.

Willmott, H. (1993) 'Strength is ignorance; slavery is freedom: managing culture in modern organizations', *Journal of Management Studies*. 30 (4): 515–552.

Willmott, H. (2003) 'Organizational theory as a critical science', in H. Tsoukas and C. Knudsen (eds), *The Oxford Handbook of Organizational Theory*. Oxford: Oxford University Press. pp. 88–112.

Wolf, M. (1992) *A Thrice-Told Tale. Feminism, Postmodernism and Ethnographic Representation*. Stanford: Stanford University Press.

Wray-Bliss, E. (2002) 'Abstract ethics, embodied ethics: the strange marriage of Foucault and positivism in labour process theory', *Organization* 9 (1): 5–39.

Theorizing the Future of Critical Organization Studies

Dennis K. Mumby

I was a graduate student in the early 1980s when critical theory first entered the disciplinary discourse of organization studies. I didn't know it at that time, but the profound 'crisis of representation' that was wrought by the continental philosophical tradition out of which critical theory emerged would have far-reaching – indeed, transformative – effects on the ways that we theorize and study organizing processes. In its initial incarnation, critical studies was predominantly deconstructive, both in its analysis of organizational control processes and in its efforts to destabilize hegemonic theories of organizing. But a healthy body of research cannot live by deconstruction alone. As we head deeper into the twenty-first century, then, whither critical studies?

I'd like to suggest that critical studies' great insight that discourse brings organizing into being be taken both less and more seriously. In some ways it has become too easy to invoke (discursively construct?) the notion that organizations exist only through the everyday talk of members. I'd even suggest that critical organization studies has sometimes been guilty of a kind of 'text positivism'; one can easily get the impression in reading critical work that talking is pretty much all organization members do! There is certainly plenty in organizational life that exists 'outside of the text', and I think it's a mistake for critical researchers to ignore the non-discursive aspects of organizational life.

In taking discourse less seriously, then, critical organization studies need to contextualize discourse processes in terms of at least some of the following issues: work as an embodied, material experience; the political economy of work; the body as an object of organizational surveillance and control; and so forth.

To take discourse *more* seriously requires that it be more adequately problematized. For all our theoretical sophistication and appropriation of postmodern, poststructuralist, Foucauldian, etc. analytic tools, we still seem largely ill-equipped to get to grips with the nuances, complexities, and contradictions of organizational discourse. As much as we are happy to theorize about the discursive construction of identity, we seem less able to truly explore what that means in the practice of everyday organizational life (for an exception, see Kondo, 1990). Invoking the notion of organizations as discursive constructions is one thing; the real work of critical studies requires a careful exploration of how these discursive constructions function dynamically in the mundane work of everyday organizing.

Relatedly, while critical organization studies has broadened its ambit to include studies of gendered organizing, there is still a dearth of theory and research that has systematically addressed issues of race, sexuality, age, able-bodiedness, and so forth. For example, it has been 15 years since Stella Nkomo (1992) asserted that when it comes to the study of race and organizing, 'the emperor has no clothes'. Unfortunately, the emperor is still under-dressed. What critical organization studies really needs, I think, is for scholars to examine organizing dialectically and intersectionally, and produce rich and messy analyses of the ways that issues of race, class, gender, sexuality, etc., articulated together, are both medium and product of organizing processes. Critical studies has always been concerned with the possibilities for more emancipatory and democratic organizing forms. The critical

Continued

moment requires that we explore the barriers to such democratic possibilities as prefatory to re-imagining organizational life. Such re-imaginings cannot be adequately articulated if we continue to elide – through both theory and research – the subject positions of many organization members.

REFERENCES

Kondo, D.K. (1990) *Crafting Selves: Power, Gender, and Discourses of Identity in a Japanese Workplace.* Chicago: University of Chicago Press.

Nkomo, S.M. (1992) 'The emperor has no clothes: Rewriting "race in organizations"'. *Academy of Management Review*, 17, 487–513.

Getting Critical About Sensemaking

Albert J. Mills

It has been just over ten years since the publication of Karl Weick's *Sensemaking in Organizations* (Weick, 1995). Reaction has been mixed, to say the least. Those who are drawn to Weick's work – and there are many – are often glowing in their support, while others – particularly critical management scholars – simply ignore it. So what's the big problem? There really is no problem if we don't want to understand how structuration is structured; discourse is discursive; postcolonialism is posted; isomorphism morphs; techniques of the self are technically possible; gendering is gendered; local is localized; or praxis is practised. That is not to suggest that these foci lack theoretical robustness or that Weick's sensemaking is the answer to all known problems. It is to suggest that if we are to go some way to understanding the process of agency then Weick's sensemaking heuristic merits attention.

What can we learn from sensemaking and how can we overcome some of its apparent deficiencies? To begin with, it makes an important contribution to our understanding of everyday life in organizations by focusing attention on the social psychological processes through which organizing occurs and is made possible. In short, it provides an ethnomethodology of organizing. However, for critical scholars, this is problematic in its apparent focus on the reproduction of existing senses of organization rather than a way of understanding social change. Feminists, for example, could see this as yet another methodological reproduction of the gendered aspects of organizing through the normalization of the effects of sensemaking. Two things. First, this critique, although reasonable, underplays Weick's own attempts to argue for a revisiting of the concept and outcomes of organization as a sensemaking frame (Weick et al., 2005); he attempts to refocus us on organizing and, in the process, change the way we construct organizational life. Second, there is an important tradition within critical scholarship – from the work of the Frankfurt School through to Clegg's (1975) work on phenomenology – that has attempted to fuse psychologistic with critical theories: arguably, sensemaking, offers much as part of a more critical approach.

Here are a few thoughts on the type of insights that a more critical approach to sensemaking may provide. With its grounding in identity construction, critical sensemaking has much to offer research into identity-work by fusion, say, with poststructuralist notions of discursive practice. The fusion could allow us not only to understand the way that identity is embedded in and arises out of selected discourses but the hitherto underplayed (or ignored) socio-psychological processes through which those discourses operate. This may also contribute to issues of agency by allowing us to grasp the processes whereby people make sense of their realities by extracting cues, dealing with plausibility, meshing their sense of reality with their ongoing identity construction, before making retrospective sense that enacts the environment and thus alters it. This has enormous potential for feminists who seek to trace – in order to change – the psychological processes through which gendered sub-structures are made possible. Here Weick's notion of plausibility is rich in potential by focusing on the processes

Continued

through which discriminatory practices become acceptable. It is also an important focus for resistance in the notion that plausibility is relatively unstable and relies on constant maintenance. For example, a man may resist existing notions of gender discrimination without us knowing why he chose that course of action, and what we can learn from it. The answer could lie in the fact that gender discrimination has become less plausible owing to the use of inappropriate cues (e.g. references to a lack of women's physiological strength in a situation where everything is automated and requires little or no strength).

Attempts to develop critical sensemaking (i.e. an approach that takes account of power relationships and is focused on social change) are underway (Helms Mills, 2003; Mills and Helms Mills, 2004). We encourage others to take another, critical, look at the work of Weick and its potential for social change.

REFERENCES

Clegg, S. (1975) *Power, Rule and Domination*. London: Routledge and Kegan Paul.
Helms Mills, J. (2003) *Making Sense of Organizational Change*. London: Routledge.
Mills, A.J. and Helms Mills, J.C. (2004) 'When plausibility fails: Towards a critical sensemaking approach to resistance', in R. Thomas, A.J. Mills and J.C. Helms Mills (eds), *Identity Politics at Work: Resisting Gender and Gendered Resistance*. London: Routledge. pp. 141–159.
Weick, K.E. (1995) *Sensemaking in Organizations*. London: Sage.
Weick, K.E., Sutcliff, K.M. and Obstfeld, D. (2005) 'Organizing and the process of sensemaking', *Organization Science*, 16 (4): 409.

The Art of …

Daved Barry

We have had so many pushes, pulls, and turns in the field of management and organization: scientific ones, positivist and not-so-positive ones, cultural, discursive, critical, postmodern and post postmodern ones. Now I think we may be in for yet another – an artful one. Whether it will simply be a rounding of organizational corners or a seismic shift remains to be seen; much depends on whether the intriguing but far-distant concepts of the art world can find their way into organizational practice, or whether these ideas will simply prove too alien and insufficiently instrumental. Here I will be outlining some of the contours of the art and organization landscape, reviewing some of the current directions the field is taking, and making suggestions for those wanting to take things further. My views link to and complement a number of other art-related chapters and notes in this handbook, with a particular focus on how contemporary art thinking might inform the practice of management and organization.

OLD ART vs. CONTEMPORARY ART

In some ways, art in management and organization is not new at all. The 'art' word has been around in organizations a long time – at least since James Thompson mentioned it in the first pages of the first issue of *Administrative Science Quarterly*. Certainly we have seen many 'Art of' book titles over the decades: The Art of … leadership, strategy, work, innovation, management, etc. Yet a second look at these works tells us that art has often been used as a lure, something to give the work a bit of panache. In some cases, the only time the word art appears at all is in the title. More importantly, few, if any, of these works discuss art as professional artists do. They speak more about craft than art, where craft refers to the mastery of certain practices and traditions (Mintzberg, 1987). Thus, when we refer to leaders, strategists, managers, etc. as artists, we are usually saying that they are very competent, graceful, elegant, and perhaps aesthetically sophisticated as they push some standard to new highs. They create functionally beautiful compositions and performances.

An example is William Cohen's *The New Art of the Leader* (2002). The irony here is that despite its title, the book actually addresses the old art of the leader – leadership as craft. In it, we see chapter titles like 'The Combat Model: The Eight Universal Laws of Leadership', 'Secrets of Motivation', and 'Seven Steps to Taking Charge in Crisis Situations'. Each chapter mixes traditional research (e.g. Maslow's motivation theory) with personal anecdotes and popular cases; on the whole, it resembles today's popular cookbooks – a kind of Jamie Oliver of leadership where, if one follows the instructions closely, there is a pretty good chance one's mates will ask for more.

There is also a long tradition of organizational art purchasing – corporate art collections are common (Jacobson, 1993), and all large organizations have had some experience with some aspect of the artworld, even if it has been limited to dealings with architects. Finally, management practices have made inroads into artistic practices; art management has been a course of study since the 1960s and now art managers the world over have become familiar with concepts of human resource management, competitive strategy, operations management, and organization structure.

The art turn I am talking about, however, is much less connected to craft or investment, and much more to *fine art*, the term that developed as 19th-century artists tried to find their own, patronage-free forms of expression. Fine art's fundamentals, which revolve around contestation, meaning making, and aliveness, bear little resemblance to the ordered craft-arts of old. Rather than uphold given traditions, they seek to up-root and overturn commonly accepted truths and perspectives. They are distinctively contraire. At the same time, they attempt to *be usefully* contraire – they typically poke at the 'dead wood', seeking to challenge taken-for-granted sacred cows. By introducing doubt, play, and our senses, they create understandings that are lively

and generative. Even the ugliest and most disturbing contemporary arts have this as a goal – a different and better life.

This then, brings me to my working definition of art: art is that which is *unusually moving in tensional ways*.[1] From what I can tell, these three elements – the unusual, moving, and tensional – are always around when contemporary artists call something art, even if they don't always agree with or use these terms. First, it seems would-be art must be unusual; it must be distinctive, apart, recognizably different. This difference stands in a delicate relation to the known. If the work stands too far from the familiar, we no longer register it as different; we just think it odd. If it is too similar, we dismiss it with a 'been there, done that'. When this differencing is done well, the work seizes us.

Second, it appears that would-be art must move us to some new place – to new thoughts, new feelings, new sensations, new gestalts. 'Unusually moving' can and should happen in at least two ways – the work takes us to unusual places and it does this to an unusual degree. Rather than solve problems, it shifts them.

Third, it must do all this in contextually tensional ways; that is, persistent tensions between what we know and what we don't know are formed. A lively non-decidableness (in-decision?, known-unknown? same-new?) is established which nags, plays, tickles, and itches in attractive ways; we feel attracted and pulled in by the work even if it is repulsive. As such it foregrounds the possible, the unimaginable, and 'ways' rather than 'the way'. More specifically, art creates sensible tensions which challenge our sens/senses/sense of things. Both our physical senses and our sense of things (sense-as-understanding; Weick, 1993) are called upon and questioned. When these tensions dissipate, the work moves from active art to art-worked, unsettling to settlement, from 'dare we open the door?' to a comfortable pulsar and departure point. Picasso's work, for all of its earthquakes, has this quality now. We remember to look both ways at the same time, and go on.

With this, art addresses and challenges our aesthetic intelligence, causing us to widen, deepen, or change what counts for us as aesthetically good (Linstead and Höpfl, 2000; Strati, 1992; 1999; Taylor and Hansen, 2005). But this is not just aesthetics as the beautiful, sublime, or grotesque that is questioned. It is aesthetics *as sensus communis* (socially grounded common sense) – that collective, polyvocal, and constantly shifting sense of right and wrong, good and bad, desirable and undesirable – that is challenged (cf. Arendt and Beiner, 1989). Both personal and social truths are centre staged. Each partaker of the artwork must first have an experience and then evaluate that experience, comparing it with their past and with others' experiences in an attempt to negotiate its worth. If the work registers as 'high art', then one rearranges one's beliefs and feelings around it.

In today's economies of knowledge, experience and design, these personalizing fundamentals have become as important to organizational survival as the codification and solidification of assumptions were in the industrial age. As Henrik Schrat notes (personal communication), when art works, it brings about a newness that is different from engineering (where something becomes old as soon as something new comes along). Of course the successful artwork introduces new content and form, but at a more fundamental level it conveys that human beings are able to invent something new in general and that this ability to create something new *ex nihilo* is what makes them uniquely human. Extended to organizations, art calls attention to organizations as living cultures which develop rather than as things that require optimization (Ventura, 2005).

At the same time, organizational logics and artistic ones run in different directions, as Schrat humorously concludes:

An organisation is like a specialist: it continues to know more about less, until it knows everything about nothing. Logically on the other hand there is art: art always learns across wider fields, so keeps accumulating less knowledge about more, until it knows nothing about everything. (Schrat, 2005: 13)

Not surprisingly, confluences between the two can be variously conflicted and lively. There are several streams of influence going on: organizational stakeholders who are pulling art in, artists and artworlders who are pushing art in, and management and organization studies academics who are scribing art in, trying to nail it down even as the other two keep pulling and pushing the nails up.

ART PULLERS

The first group, the art-interested pullers, are often people who have historically enjoyed art and toyed with the idea that some of that enjoyment might be used to liven up the workplace. For them, 'unusually moving in tensional ways' means getting to a new view of things – trying to stretch employees' thinking, signalling that creativity is important, or perhaps taking the edges off an otherwise mechanized or industrialized setting. Thus we see Mads Øvlisen, former CEO of Novo Nordisk (Denmark's most respected pharmaceutical company), personally buying many 'difficult' works from young, unknown artists and putting them up throughout the company. The book *You Do Not Have to Like the Art You See at Novo Nordisk But I Hope it Makes You Stop and Ask a Few Questions* (Aunstrup et al., 2000) amply chronicles the discomfort this programme created, as well as Øvlisen's evolving thoughts about art's role in corporate life. The art collection functioned as a type of mediate (Barry, 2005), providing a ground where different art-and-business conversations and comments could emerge: 'Art should always challenge you. If it ends up being something you walk by, you could have bought some cheaper tapestry' (p. 16); or 'Art does not have to have likeness. What art is about is that you with as much care and accuracy and with as much tenderness as possible organize your feelings' (p. 105). I once spoke with him about it, asking if he had any practical intentions around the art collection – had he intentionally used it to stir up conversations for instance? 'No', he said with characteristic understatement,

'I just thought it might keep us a bit more awake.' I also talked with a number of Novo employees, asking them whether they would like to get rid of the works in the wake of Mads' retirement. They said 'No' as well. As one commented, 'I still really dislike some of the art, but it reminds us that we can and should do weird stuff here'.

In a variant of this, 'art pullers' seek to bring in not art pieces, but art processes and artists themselves. Companies like Siemens and Unilever spend large sums on arts-based training, assuming that taking painting, singing, poetry, and theatre classes will impart new ways of thinking – presumably creative ways that can then be leveraged to develop new products and structures (Darsø, 2004). Organization Theater (see the special issue of Organization Studies, V25(5), 2004; Clark, this volume; Meisiek and Barry, 2007) has become one of the fastest growing and most influential organizational art forms, although some versions are clearly more propagandistic than artful. With this have come other literary forms such as poetry (Adler, 2006), story (Boje, this volume) and fiction (Whiteman and Phillips, this volume). Musical practitioners and theorists such as Paul Robertson, Peter Hanke and Miha Pogacnik (Meisiek and Hatch, this volume) are using aspects of musical performance and composition to frame and inform corporate leadership. And arts-based design processes are increasingly finding their way into strategy and organizational design (Barry and Rerup, 2006; Dunbar et al., this volume; Liedtka and Mintzberg, 2006).

The various artist-business residencies that have arisen in the last 20 years (e.g., Harris, 1999) try to create the unusually moving by having an artist around. Here, there is a 'rub off' assumption, a metonymy where it is hoped that the artist's ways might inspire others to think out of the box. Finally, companies are increasingly hiring artists not only in a consulting capacity, but to work directly in HRM, marketing, public relations, and general management functions. As Daniel Pink, writing in that business bastion *The Harvard Business Review* notes: 'The MFA is the New MBA ... An arts degree is now perhaps the hottest credential in the world of business' (2004: 21, quoted in Adler, 2006: 486). Companies hire these people not to produce artworks, but to bring new languages and life to these all-too-familiar functions.

ART PUSHERS

Even as organizationalists are realizing that the 'art part' is a necessary complement to functionalist, rationalist, and scientific ways – that without rhyme, reason turns dull and senseless – artists and other denizens of the artworld are seeking to alter society via its most influential organizations. To them, 'unusually moving' means shifting our taken-for-granted understandings of work, capitalism, and corporatism to new, if not particularly benign or comfortable places. Sometimes this takes the form of activist art that uses parody or ridicule (e.g. the works of Etoy, which subvert many corporate stereotypes – see http://www.etoy.com), but increasingly we are seeing more 'dialogical' art forms, where professional artists not only use organizational phenomena as their subject matter, but seek quasi-insider encounters where organizational stakeholders and art communities can talk with one another. Henrik Schrat's 'Appearance of Fantasy' (Meisiek and Hatch, this volume) used bank customers' discarded candy wrappers to represent and question the flow of capital. Similarly, Lisa Autogena (2004) created a 'stock market planetarium' where the world's stock transactions were converted to shifting, star-like constellations and displayed in planetariums, thus contesting our usual and taken-for-granted representations of capital exchange. Kent Hansen, one of the first artists to work in this way, used a tree-house-like installation on an industrial factory floor to both highlight communication problems at the factory and to promote new thinking around these issues (Ferro-Thomsen, 2005).

In a landmark event in 2005, Mari Brellochs and Henrik Schrat brought in over 20 leading artists to use Cornelesen (Germany's leading educational publisher) as their subject matter – all with Cornelesen's blessing but without their financial sponsorship (Brellochs and Schrat, 2005a, 2005b; Guillet de Monthoux and Statler, this volume); funding was secured through a public art grant from the city of Berlin. Instead of the usual corporate art encounter where a lone artist confronts a large number of well-organized people, multiple artists organized themselves into a temporary 'art firm' (Guillet de Monthoux, 2004) using methods common to the art industry (Austin and Devin, 2003). Together they formed a large reflecting system where many facets of management, organization, and economy were questioned and transfigured. Much of the project's thinking and various experiences are captured in a comprehensive reader (Brellochs and Schrat, 2005a) and art catalogue (Brellochs and Schrat, 2005b). What is particularly notable is how art-informed organizing systems could create such widespread effects. As artist Enno Schmidt tellingly wrote on a 'reflecting mirror' at the end of the exhibition, 'I remember the power of artists coming together'.

ART SCRIBES

Working as a kind of bridge between the art pullers and pushers, a growing number of management and organization studies academics are recording, critiquing, theorizing, and teaching fine art perspectives using a variety of outlets and venues. For them, the focus is often on finding examples of the unusually moving and assembling/theorizing them in ways that can potentially address larger audiences – particularly through challenging today's business students and tomorrow's organizational leaders. Thus, Pierre Guillet de Monthoux's books *The Art Firm* (2004) and *Aesthetic Leadership* (Guillet de Monthoux et al., 2007) develop a number of philosophically and experientially grounded approaches to arts-based management and leadership, as do the works of Nancy Adler (2006), and Hatch et al. (2005). Rob Austin

and Lee Devin's book *Artful Making* (2003) theorizes and locates arts-based thinking alongside pre-industrial, industrial, and post-Fordist logics.

From a practice-based perspective, the theatre-centreed writings of Timothy Clark (this volume), Stefan Meisiek (2002, 2004; Meisiek and Barry, forthcoming), Nick Nissley (Nissley et al., 2004), Chris Steyaert and Daniel Hjorth (2002), and Steve Taylor (2000, 2003a, 2003b; 2008) offer different thoughts about why and when organizational theatre works (or doesn't) and use dramatistic writing to artistically theorize academia and other institutions. Some of my work (1994, 1996, 2005) attempts to account for when and how the use of traditional art mediums (e.g. paint, sculpture) by organizational members results in organizational development and change. Scholars such as Miguel Cunha and Joao Cunha (this volume), Karl Weick (1998), and Mary Jo Hatch (1999), have used jazz theory to develop 'how to' theories of organizational improvisation.

Finally, we are seeing a growing number of forums that join academics, managers, artists and students. Arts and aesthetics-based management conferences (e.g. The Art of Management Conference led by Ian King, Ceri Watkins, and Steve Linstead, the Organizational Aesthetics Conference led by Antonio Strati and Pierre Guillet de Monthoux, SCOS (Standing Conference on Organizational Symbolism), NUROPE (an arts and organization PhD programme – http://www.nurope.eu), and internet discussion forums such as AACORN (Arts, Aesthetics, Creativity, and Organization Research Network – http://www.aacorn.net) are creating new conversations between academics, artists, and managers. Arts-based management, leadership, and organization courses offered at universities such as McGill, Harvard, Copenhagen Business School, BI in Oslo, Universidade Nova de Lisboa, WPI in Massachusetts, and executive education centres such as the Banff Center and The Center for Creative Leadership, are experimenting with new ways to teach fine art thinking and methods. As Pierre Guillet de Monthoux has noted (personal communication), 'the Arts and Business Academy is becoming a reality'.

THE ART OF REVISITED

These many fine arts informed initiatives – which have now advanced to the point where they can be considered a formal field of study – collectively require that we revisit how we think about, discuss, and practise 'The Art of'. Craft, though still necessary, is no longer sufficient, especially if what we're after is the unusually moving, a/effective sensibilities, and lifeful work. The question is no longer whether artistic ways should be part of management and organization (clearly they already are) but when and how do they best fit in. When and how can traditional management and organization functions such as strategy, leadership, organization design, HRM, operations, and finance, be usefully informed by and possibly practised from an arts perspective?

Art When? The 'when' question is tied to what art is. If art is the unusually moving, then the 'art of' seems particularly appropriate when the status quo won't do anymore. Whereas traditional management speaks to ends and middles, art speaks to endings and beginnings. Instead of reproducing what we already know, it breaks up what we know and materializes what we don't know. It shifts rather than solves problems. But because it exists in a subjective, contextualized relationship with its users, art's effects are often very temporary, lasting only as long the understandings that were initially present are still about. Sometimes this can be a long time; for instance Calder's mobiles, which fundamentally challenge our beliefs about ground and mass, continue to attract record crowds (Barry and Rerup, 2006). But more often the effects quickly disappear unless there is some way of continually renewing the artwork's presence (e.g. Meisiek and Barry, 2007).

If we choose to view organizations as noun-based, relatively enduring goal-driven arrangements, then organizational art would appear necessary when an organization has become overly stiff and ossified, needing the equivalent of cardiac shock or plaque-reducing anticoagulants. It would also seem necessary in organizations prone towards 'sleepiness' – organizational forms that are so tightly coupled and routinized that they are on the verge of nodding off. The high reliability organizations that Karl Weick (Weick and Roberts, 1993) studies come to mind – nuclear power stations, public transport systems, aircraft carriers, etc. If organization is seen as a verb-based phenomenon of continual renewal, then a certain amount of ongoing artistry would also seem necessary, not so much to keep things loose or awake but to provide lifeful identity anchors. Historically we have thought of art in luxury terms, where artful approaches are only appropriate when there is sufficient organizational slack. But the art I am discussing here is 'survival art', where the artful is a fundamental part of how an organization 'stays alive'. In this sense it overlaps a great deal with narrative approaches to survival and change (Barry, 1997; Hancock and Epston, this volume). Narrative approaches revolve around artful reframings of intransigent problems; when they are successful, they lead to problem shifting – as much if not more so than problem solving.

Rob Austin's and Lee Devin's work (2003) suggests using more process specific criteria for choosing when and when not to go the artful route: the benefits and costs of novelty. If the projected benefits of novelty are high and the costs low, the iterative and non-linear approaches associated with art should predominate. Thus, software development, where novelty is both necessary and relatively low cost, is a good candidate for artful processes despite its historical use of factory-line methods. Conversely in the art glass industry, where novelty is costly and not especially beneficial, producers may be better off using linear organizational approaches.

Art Who? With the above comes a question that has been extensively debated in recent art-and-business conferences and AACORN forums: Who should (or can) practice in artistic ways? Can managers? Is managing, with its functionalisms of planning, organizing, directing, and controlling, at all compatible with art thinking and doing? Or can only artists create art? The fact that a number of successful artists are also competent at managing large collective projects (e.g. Christo – see Chernow, 2002)) suggests that coexistence of the two roles, manager and artist, is not only possible, but desirable (a view which is extensively developed in Hatch et al's *The Three Faces of Leadership: Manager, Artist, Priest*, 2005). Precisely because the role of manager and artist are so different, movement from one to the other has the potential to challenge and further both.

On the other hand, talking about the 'artist' may deflect us from more important questions about artistic practice. As Lucy Kimbell (2007) notes in an AACORN post:

> Sometimes when I read posts here, I sense something akin to a reification of the artist. It's as if artists have privileged access to creativity or a way of looking at the world that managers and organizations want and need. I understand the argument to go something like this: Good at working with uncertainty and ambiguity, having a vision, and making artifacts that people use to forge meaning, artists have something to offer to our understanding of leadership. Managers should be like/pay attention to artists.
>
> But it's hard to talk about what or who artists are and what they do without examples. As soon as we offer names of artists, we present historically situated artists and their practices. The names of Carvaggio, Beuys, Pollock and Latham have appeared in the last few posts, for example. For each of these artists, there is no singular or simple way of talking about their processes and their works. Art history, art criticism, and our own opportunities to see their works create these artists for us.
>
> So I do not find it convincing to invoke 'the artist'. I want to know which kinds of practices, what intentions, what context, which ways of working, what meanings, and – to avoid the instrumentalization of art by management – with what relation to the continually contested and shifting set of practices and artefacts which is art-making.

Similarly, Steve Taylor's work (see Taylor and Carboni, this volume) argues that practice is the more important consideration – artful

practice needs a lot of practice, just as management is a complex practice replete with dense contexts, tacit knowledges, and a distinct *sensus communis*. He comments:

> I think there are disciplines that we learn that we then embody. Perhaps not very consciously and perhaps not very well, but I know that there are disciplines I have learned in my training and practice as a playwright that are embodied in pretty much everything I do. And I think that you can bring disciplines from the arts to the act of managing. But you do have to learn them and learning embodied disciplines suggests different modes of education than you see in business schools. It suggests studios and practice based learning. It suggests doing and reflection on action and reflection in action. (Taylor, 2007)

In other words, it is naive to assume that one can simply pick up a 'twelve steps' artist's guide and hope to create organizational art; from a fine arts perspective, the 'Art of Management for Dummies' is a contradiction in terms (though I fully expect to see this book in an art show someday). It seems equally naive to assume that merely having art pieces around, even controversial ones, will result in different ways of doing things. Rather, it is the art practice that is necessary, and this practice must be something that is consciously done by organizational members and not just artwork (or artists) purchased at the latest art fair. From an organizational perspective, this means more than individual practice; it suggests taking a practising 'troupes' or ensemble perspective where individual art practices commingle to make larger ones.

Art How? An emphasis on art practice raises the question of how one achieves an artistic outcome. For Getzels and Czikszentmihalyi (1979), the way one approaches problems is important. The artistic approach emphasizes 'problem finding', where the artist searches out increasingly more interesting problems and grows 'ugly little problems' into intriguing opponents – not all problems of course, but enough to make things lively. For Austin and Devin (2003), a fundamental part of working artfully is taking an iterative and emergent approach to a problem. One doesn't know what the end product will be until it's there, and this requires having processes that allow a lot of back and forth; 'line management' must give way to 'curve management'. For example, in painting a picture one conducts hundreds of small experiments, putting an object here or there and then changing it depending on other elements that get added. The painter typically 'pulls the picture up' by bouncing back and forth from one area to another. Working for awhile on a 'weak area' suddenly makes more developed sections look inadequate, so the painter jumps to those areas and works on them until some other part of the canvas grabs his/her attention. The painter cannot know just what the final picture should look like (unless one's project is to create forgeries); rather, s/he feels whether the work has the necessary edge and itch and pulls the work up accordingly.

I would say inversion stands alongside iterativity as another basic facet of artistic work. As an example, Eirik Irgens (2000 and personal communication) tells of a manager who was asked to turn around one of Norway's dirtiest automotive facilities. The employees were looking for other work and there was no extra money for anything, salaries or otherwise. In what I consider an artful move, the manager asked the employees to paint the entire facility white – including the floors. They thought the whole idea was mad, and strenuously questioned his use of the little money they had left to buy white paint. This simple yet profound act ended up completely changing their world, and the facility went from 'dead dog' status to having new found life. Of course, as my various manager friends are quick to remind me, this could just as easily have gone completely wrong, ending up with the manager being fired, the plant shut down, and the road to other such approaches permanently closed. All this suggests that one may need to 'dose' organizational art projects (having smaller, easy-to-digest ones, as well as larger, more controversial ones). Depending on an organization's history, some forms, mediums, and content will be much easier to assimilate than others.

How does one think of such projects? The old view would have us think of muses and other out-of-the-blue, knock-on-the-head

things. A newer one stemming from social psychology (Amabile, 1996) would suggest that simply asking oneself (or others) to be creative can be enough. But I don't think either one of these can get us to artfully creative ideas. Too often the many creativity techniques that are around result in a mechanical otherness, something that is different, but not lifefully so. Instead, my observations suggest that the artfully creative results from sophisticated and well-informed play, both serious but also decidedly non-serious (see Pierre Guillet de Monthoux's 2004 discussions of Friedrich Schiller's concept of play; also see Barry, 2005; Kane, 2004; Schrage, 2000). All the artists I know seem to be on an almost constant lookout for the enjoyably odd, humorous, and ways to keep their 'funny bones' alive. At the same time, I never see them using creativity matrices, six or more hats, or even conventional brainstorming techniques – these don't seem to be sufficiently interesting or fun. This goes back to the idea of art as itchy, lively, and stimulating. Humour in this context can take many forms, ranging from the bitchy to the hilarious to the darkly gothic and subterranean.

Playing, making plays, putting things into play, and being a player also involves the willing suspension of beliefs, control by release, improvization, and making things up (Austin and Devin, 2003; Barry, 2005). Failure, or its equivalent, is an expected and necessary part of the play (Schrage, 2000) and certainly part of the development – if one 'gets it right' all the time, it is a sign that the work isn't experimental enough. As Steve Taylor (personal communication) notes:

> I am reminded of a talk Sr. Alessi gave about his company (the Italian design firm) at the Siena Organizational Aesthetics conference in 2000. He said that unless half of their designs failed they weren't pushing the edge of the envelope enough. I think artists and being artful means having a very different relationship with failure and risk.

In addition to the things one does, a practice involves the things and concepts one works with, one's materials. To create a viable 'art of' in management and organization,

I would argue that would-be organizational artists need to go beyond traditional art mediums (paint, poems, music, dance). Like the Norwegian hydroelectric manager, we must also work with organizational materials, palettes, and repertoires. Management and organization have their own peculiar properties, and it is through extensive interaction with them that the contours of organizational art can be fashioned. For example, choral director Peter Hanke (see Meisiek and Hatch, this volume) is especially sensitive to starting and stopping, to how a piece of music is begun and finished. In his work with executives he directly brings this to how they start and stop things in their work – their projects, directions, and communications. Their daily work processes form the material from which experiments in starting and stopping are fashioned. Another example is Carey Young's 'Disclaimer' project (Wood and Young, 2004), where she collects and contests the legal notices at the bottom of corporate emails to both challenge the idea of email as a 'free' form of communication and experiment with new models of negative space.

Art primarily works in associative ways – new meanings are developed by getting audiences to connect things that normally don't go together, and the worth of a work is often judged by the amount of associative resonance and tensional depth that it creates. This places a premium on one's associates – on the company one keeps. The company, associates, and associations that an artist collects end up informing the artist's style, taste, frames, and horizons. Whereas managers and business school students collect arrays of problem solutions, artists and art students typically collect lively, pleasurable reminders – instances of unusually moving tensions that keep their senses and imaginations enjoyably open (see Antonio Strati's ideas in this volume, as well as Taylor and Hansen, 2005). These often have a metaphoric, 'partly-this-is-partly-that' character rather than a 'this-is-the-tool-for-that'. Would-be organizational artists could do worse than to follow this example – to deliberately grow their collections and surroundings to include the provocatively pleasurable as well as the practically functional.

'Collections' leads to the idea of arts-informed project portfolios, arranged collections which are similar to but also different from business portfolios. Whereas business logics have led to diversified and unrelated portfolios as devices to reduce risk, art portfolios are diversified collections that become related in ways that promote risk. When I look at how artists collect and form their collections/associates/portfolios, I often get a sense of 'cultivated' relations; things are arranged to foster 'purposeful coincidences' rather than just being practically stacked; one thing feeds another which feeds another. There is an inter-play between little beauties, big excitements, lurking mysteries, brilliant blue days, and sublime/magnificent midnights and monsters – a consciously and unconsciously connected 'meshwork' (see Linstead and Pullen this volume) which leads to rich possibilities and creations. I would guess that an organizational art portfolio/collection would be similar, having a very few 'haute' or fine-as-rare art projects, a much larger group of 'smaller' artsies, art-likes, and artfuls – things that jiggle rather than moooove and which are eccentric rather than very unusual, and finally, a great number of 'pleasurables' ('aesthetic 'compost' if you will) – the enjoyables, the almost digested fine-as-granular experiences, and the not-quite-thrown-aways that form an organic base to grow from and rest on.

SOME ENDINGS AND BEGINNINGS

Pulling all of this together, we have the start of what an 'art of' might look like. The organizational artist will be someone who wants to create more lifeful outcomes, ones which are contextually connected to the immediate environment and the broader societal sphere. S/he will deliberately savour and extend key problems – excelling at problem finding and problem shifting, as well as problem solving. Iterativeness and sketchy ways of holding problems and possibilities will be processual hallmarks. Creating tensional frameworks that generate containable and enjoyable surprise will be another. And play and imagination, the fine artist's stock in trade, will undoubtedly constitute one more thread.

How these are to be woven together is another much larger question. To this end, we will require a great deal more study and experimentation. More close-up studies of artists and their collections, particularly of artists working with organizational art projects, will be needed. Studies of managers working with artists may provide an important complement. 'Dosing' and 'scaffolding' will be needed around the introduction of organizational art – 'simply bringing art in' will too likely 'boot art out'. Finally, we will also require new forms of scholarly inquiry, measurement, and framing, ones that respect the underlying assumptions of contemporary art, that keep and promote its lively qualities, and get the work done in delightful, imaginative ways.

ACKNOWLEDGEMENT

I owe a great debt of gratitude to the various reviewers of this chapter, particularly Hans Hansen, Stefan Meisiek, Henrik Schrat, Steve Taylor, and the many thought-provoking members of AACORN.

NOTE

1 Since attempts to define art are generally considered one of the most damning and hazardous things one can do, I hasten to add that I hold no one else responsible for this admittedly shaky and idiosyncratic definition.

REFERENCES

Adler, N. (2006) 'The arts and leadership: Now that we can do anything, what will we do?' *Academy of Management Learning and Education*, 5 (4): 486–499.

Amabile, T.M. (1996) *Creativity in Context*. Boulder, CO: Westview Press.

Arendt, H. and Beiner, R. (1989) *Lectures on Kant's Political Philosophy*. Chicago: University of Chicago Press.

Aunstrup, K., Rasmussen, M., Øvlisen, L. and Fisher, A. (eds) (2000) *You Do Not Have to Like the Art You See at Novo Nordisk, But I Hope it Makes You Stop and Ask a Few Questions*. Bagsvaerd, Denmark: Novo A/S.

Austin, R. and Devin, L. (2003) *Artful Making: What Managers Need to Know About How Artists Work*. New York: Prentice-Hall.

Autogena, L. (2004) *Black Shoals Stockmarket Planetarium*. Retrieved February 17, 2007 from http://www.blackshoals.net/description.html.

Barry, D. (1994) 'Making the invisible visible: Symbolic means for surfacing unconscious processes in organizations'. *Organizational Development Journal*, 12: 37–48.

Barry, D. (1996) 'Artful Inquiry: A symbolic constructionist framework for social science research'. *Qualitative Inquiry*, 2 (4): 411–438.

Barry, D. (1997) 'Telling changes: From narrative family therapy to organizational change & development'. *Journal of Organizational Change Management*, 10 (1): 32–48.

Barry, D. (2005) 'The play of the mediate', in M. Brellochs and H. Schrat (eds), *Sophisticated Survival Techniques: Strategies in Art and Economy*. Berlin: Kultureverlag Kadmos. pp. 57–77.

Barry, D. and Rerup, C. (2006) 'Going mobile: Aesthetic design considerations from Calder and the Constructivists', *Organization Science*, 17 (2): 262–276.

Brellochs, M. and Schrat, H. (eds) (2005a) *Sophisticated Survival Techniques: Strategies in Art and Economy*. Berlin: Kulturverlag Kadmos.

Brellochs, M. and Schrat, H. (eds) (2005b) *Product & Vision: An Experimental Set-up Between Art and Business*. Berlin: Kulturverlag Kadmos.

Chernow, B. (2002) *XTO + J-C: Christo and Jeanne-Claude*. New York: Saint Martin's Press.

Cohen, W. (2002) *The New Art of the Leader*. New York: Prentice-Hall.

Darsø, L. (2004) *Artful Creation. Learning-Tales of Arts-in-Business*. Copenhagen: Samfundsliteratur.

Ferro-Thomsen, M. (2005) 'Change through exchange: Organisational art and learning', in M. Brellochs and H. Schrat (eds), *Sophisticated Survival Techniques: Strategies in Art and Economy*. Berlin: Kultureverlag Kadmos. pp. 183–197.

Getzels J.W. and Czikszentmihalyi, M. (1979) *The Creative Vision*. New York: John Wiley and Sons.

Guillet de Monthoux, P. (2004) *The Art Firm: Aesthetic Management and Metaphysical Marketing*. Palo Alto: Stanford University Press.

Guillet de Monthoux, P., Gustafsson, C. and Sjöstrand, S. (eds) (2007) *Aesthetic Leadership: Managing Fields of Flow in Art and Business*. Houndsmills: Palgrave-Macmillan.

Harris, C. (ed.) (1999) *Art and Innovation: The Xerox PARC Artist-in-Residence Program*. Cambridge, MA: MIT Press.

Hatch, M.J. (1999) 'Exploring the empty spaces of organizing: How improvisational jazz helps redescribe organizational structure', *Organization Studies*, 20: 75–100.

Hatch, M.J., Kostera, M. and Kozminski, A.K. (2005) *The Three Faces of Leadership: Manager, Artist, Priest*. Oxford: Blackwell Publishing.

Irgens, E. (2000) *Den dynamiske organisasjon: Ledelse og utvikling i et arbeidsliv i forandring*. Oslo: Abstrakt.

Jacobson, M. (1993) *Art for Work: The New Renaissance in Corporate Collecting*. Boston, MA: Harvard Business School Press.

Kane, P. (2004) *The Play Ethic: A Manifesto for a ifferent Wzay of Living*. London: Macmillan.

Kimbell, L. (2007) *Art, Leadership + Design*. Retrieved February 16, 2007, from http://www.jiscmail.ac.uk/cgi bin/webadmin?A2=ind0702&L=aacorn&D= 1&T= 0&O=A&P=3814.

Liedtka, J. and Mintzberg, H. (2006) Time for design. *Design Management Review*, Spring: 10–18.

Linstead, S. and Höpfl, H. (eds) (2000) *The Aesthetics of Organization*. London: Sage.

Meisiek, S. (2002) 'Situation drama in change management: Types and effects of a new managerial tool'. *International Journal of Arts Management*, 4: 48–55.

Meisiek, S. (2004) 'Which catharsis do they mean? Aristotle, Moreno, Boal and Organization Theatre', *Organization Studies*, 25 (5): 797–816.

Meisiek, S. and Barry, D. (2007) 'Through the looking glass of organizational theatre: Analogically mediated inquiry in organizations'. *Organization Studies*, 28(12): 1805–1827.

Mintzberg, H. (1987) 'Crafting strategy', *Harvard Business Review*, 65 (4): 66–75.

Nissley, N., Taylor, S. and Houden, L. (2004) 'The politics of performance in organizational theatre-based training and interventions', *Organization Studies*, 25 (5): 817–839.

Pink, D.H. (2004) 'Breakthrough ideas for 2004', *Harvard Business Review*, February: 21–22.

Schrage, M. (2000) *Serious Play: How the World's Best Companies Simulate to Innovate*. Boston: Harvard Business School Press.

Schrat, H. (2005) 'Hotel concerto', in M. Brellochs and H. Schrat (eds), *Sophisticated Survival Techniques: Strategies in Art and Economy*. Berlin: Kultureverlag Kadmos. pp. 9–35.

Strati, A. (1992) 'Aesthetic understanding of organizational life', *Academy of Management Review*, 17 (3): 568–581.

Strati, A. (1999) *Organization and aesthetics*. London: Sage.

Steyaert, C. and Hjorth, D. (2002) 'Thou art a scholar, speak to it…' – on spaces of speech: A script. *Human Relations*, 55 (7): 767–797.

Taylor, S. S. (2000) 'Aesthetic knowledge in academia: Capitalist pigs at the Academy of Management', *Journal of Management Inquiry*, 9 (3): 304–328.

Taylor, S.S. (2003a) 'Ties that bind', *Management Communication Quarterly*, 17 (2): 280–300.

Taylor, S .(2003b) 'Knowing in your gut and in your head: Doing theater and my underlying epistemology of communication', *Management Communication Quarterly*, 17: 272–279.

Taylor, S.S. and Hansen, H. (2005) 'Finding form: Looking at the field of organizational aesthetics', *Journal of Management Studies*, 42 (6): 1210–1231.

Taylor, S. (2007) *Leader as artist literature*. Retrieved February 16, 2007 from http://www.jiscmail.ac.uk/cgi bin/webadmin?A2=ind0702&L=aacorn&T=0&O= A&P=2777.

Taylor, S.S. Forthcoming. 'Theatrical performance as unfreezing: Ties that bind at the Academy of Management', *Journal of Management Inquiry*.

Ventura, H.K. (2005) 'Organisation as art', in M. Brellochs and H. Schrat (eds), *Sophisticated Survival Techniques: Strategies in Art and Economy*. Berlin: Kultureverlag Kadmos. pp. 81–94.

Weick, K.E. (1993) 'The collapse of sensemaking in organizations: The Man Gulch disaster', *Administrative Science Quarterly*, 38: 628–652.

Weick, K.E. and Roberts, K.H. (1993) 'Collective mind in organizations: Heedful interrelating on flight decks', *Administrative Science Quarterly*, 38: 357–381.

Weick, K.E. (1998) 'Improvisation as a metaphor for organizing', *Organization Science*, 9: 543–555.

Wood, J. and Young, C. (2004) *Disclaimers*. Retrieved February 17, 2007 from http://www.careyyoung.com/essays/woodyoung.html.

How We Know What We Know: The Potentiality of Art and Aesthetics

Ian W. King

INTRODUCTION

The issue of how we know what we know in, and for, Management and Organization studies has been central to its development since its earliest days. Yet, it has only been relatively recently that our academic field has looked at its epistemological influences (see Burrell and Morgan, 1979; Clegg and Dunkerley, 1980) and reflected upon their significance in identifying the character of Management and Organization Knowledge (Orlikowski, 2002; Spender, 1994; Tsoukas, 2002; but see especially the editorial introduction of the special issue of *Organization Science*, 2002). Until this interest arose, assumptions regarding knowledge tended to associate its guise with the traditional influences gleaned from Science and Cartesian thought. The benefits of this tried and tested route of identification, collection and analysis would fulfil the ultimate aim of Management and Organizational educators – that of improved

performance. However, as the special issue identified (and has been reinforced by others such as Boland and Tenkasi, 1995; Tsoukas, 2002) such a view of knowledge provided only a part of the essential character of this field's knowledge (*Organization Science*, 2002). For me, it was Tsoukas's telling observation that knowing 'in' practice needs to be integrated into its definition that explicitly casts the need for the researcher to change their position with regard to the object of their research.

Tsoukas provides a rich discussion of his employment of Michel Polanyi's (1966) notion of 'tacit' knowing and consequently raises the potential of this more engaged form of knowing. This stance contrasts with the third-person Cartesian perspective which called for a distance between the beholder and the subject in order to create a distance for objective observation (see Descartes, reprinted 1985). Thus, Tsoukas's (2002) call for augmentation of the tacit with the objective created what Orlikoswki (2002) labelled as 'knowing in practice'. This label is reminiscent of a categorization of knowledge that had been developed by Gilbert Ryle (1949) that distinguished between 'knowing-how' and 'knowing-that' – in that 'knowing-how' is the particular ability of putting 'knowing-that' into practice (Brown and Duguid, 1998: 91).

Perception is the key to any characterization of the knowledge-making processes. In short, our perceptive lens selects and organizes the flood of signals that will emanate from any single event. Without some form of organization any of us would be overrun with information, and it is through our perceptive abilities to either select or conversely overlook certain aspects that our understanding of any event is characterized. Thus, what perception accomplishes, either explicitly or implicitly, is the reduction of this flood of information down to a manageable level. For some, the information received through the retinal image is sufficient to account for what we see around us (Gibson, 1950). For others, the retinal image is relatively poor and this requires our brains to supplement our vision with hypotheses as to what is most likely the actual nature of the external event given the information available to the retina (see Gregory, 1966).

We have now come to the crux of this chapter. Traditional science and the Cartesian approach argue that continuing to develop and refine our traditional approaches and tools within their framework will produce 'a cleaner cloth' in which to shine the Cartesian lens in order to produce more persuasive forms of knowing. Comparatively, rival epistemological approaches claim that the problem is the nature of the Cartesian lens itself. Their interpretation argues that no matter how long we gaze through it our perceptive capabilities are unlikely to produce the necessary forms of knowing that the followers of the Cartesian approach claim they are seeking. Of course, the followers of the Cartesian route disagree and continue to refine and cleanse their tools of scrutiny. The result is a fracture within the management and

organization field of scholars that continues to this day (see Grey and Willmott, 2005).

What I am trying to do here is raise our attention to the very real central role of the researcher within this process of investigation and the manner of their engagement with events, things and objects. Thus, I do acknowledge the contributions of the objective Cartesian approach and yet also appreciate its limitations in terms of the needs of individuals employing 'knowing-how'. A first-person engagement rather than a third-person inevitably casts the individual in a different role in terms of their perceptive abilities and as such should – and I stress 'should' rather than 'will' – privilege different features from an event. Nevertheless, to suggest such an engagement will open up the whole experience is of course erroneous. It is important to appreciate that to experience an event will always be partial – whether it be first or third person oriented. Furthermore, it should be clear that no matter which lens is employed our perceptive abilities will select and deselect factors in order to facilitate our understanding of any event. The problem is that the Cartesian lens conditions our perceptive lens according to a criteria which privileges only certain objective features of our knowing. On the other hand, a first-person perspective, by their very engagement, will often invoke very different layers and features. Thus, we are engaging with both ontological and empirical issues regarding the guise of knowledge. Our experience of art and aesthetics reveals quite different potential and draws on forms of contact that employ our senses – sight, touch, sound, smell and taste. I will concentrate on 'seeing' as a means of opening up the potential for the other senses to emerge.

ART AND AESTHETIC EXPERIENCE

There has been a rich interest in the potential of aesthetics as a means of examining and uncovering knowing in and for organizations (see for example Guillet de Monthoux, 2004; Linstead and Höpfl, 2000;

Organization, 1995; Strati, 1996, 1999). Each of these texts offers, to varying degrees, fascinating insights into the potential of each of the senses and their contribution to developing richer understandings of management and organizational life. The focus of this section of the chapter relates to my own utilization of art. Vickery argues that '… art revives our repressed or depleted powers of perceptual awareness, enlivening or transforming our basic perception of the natural world around us' (Vickery, 2006: 57). The centrality of our perceptive lens within a first-person engagement of the world requires a suitable stimulant that awakens and is able to display this potential – and for me paintings fulfil this promise.

At this stage I feel it is appropriate to introduce an example. I have sometimes turned to case studies at this point, but somehow – and perhaps this reflects the limitations of my own ability – these frequently fail to capture the layers of knowing I am seeking to reveal. This can also be true when I have tried to convey these issues to practising managers. Although I am seeking to fulfil the aim of relevance I find that utilizing examples from their own contexts incites defensive responses that inhibit the process. Accordingly, a few years ago I turned to art and in particular paintings. I find that careful selection of paintings can fulfil several functions. Firstly, painting(s) are often greeted with eagerness and openness – because they are so different from what would normally be expected. Secondly, selected paintings are good at de-familiarizing perceptions and therefore causing beholders to re-look at events, objects and things. Thirdly, it is possible to reveal, through guidance, the layers of meaning that can emerge from perceiving events at different levels in selected paintings. Of course, it should be noted, that paintings are merely images – and for that matter readers might suggest that as beholders our relationship in gazing at a painting is a third-person, one-way, engagement. My response to this charge is 'Yes' and 'No'. Yes, if the beholder restricts their layers of scrutiny to remain at a superficial level and yet 'No', if

Figure 1.3.1   Park bei Lu, 1938, 129 by Paul Klee © Estate of Rex Whistler/DACS London 2008.

the beholder is able to surpass this level and transcend to other levels of engagement.

Let me introduce you to this painting by Paul Klee (see Figure 1.3.1) by suggesting that you can engage with it on at least three levels. The first level, the most basic, is the unreflective visual and affective experience. That is, the initial experience of standing before it and taking into account that which lies before us within its frame. Thus, generally, we would note that it is a relatively small canvas (100 × 70 cms) painted in oils. What we do not capture here are the vibrant colours of the painting. Blue seems to be a predominant background colour but from this emerges other colours – each to varying degrees seemingly influencing the shade of the background colour. Through the different colours emerge a series of thickish sinuous lines decorating the face of the canvas in a seemingly haphazard fashion. Closer inspection reveals colours surrounding each of the lines and in the centre of the painting there is what resembles a line drawing of a tree bathed in orange. My description to this point is limited by my distance from the painting. This detached position has seemingly exhausted my description of that which lies on the canvas's surface. Nevertheless, I might transcend its surface and explore the second level: What does this painting mean?

The fact that the painting is mute raises a number of interesting issues. I am aware that post-modernists are often critical of privileging experience over the social/linguistic (see Alvesson and Deetz, 1996) and whilst I can appreciate these criticisms, to a point, I have written elsewhere of the persuasive relational aspects between painting and beholder that may overcome some of these concerns (see King, 2007a and 2007b). Nevertheless, despite Klee leaving considering notes regarding his output and approach, nothing can be found that relates specifically to the meaning of this painting. Perhaps in these circumstances we might infer that the painting possesses no meaning – therefore, should we view it as an abstract?

For me, and my choice of utilizing this painting for this chapter, is that I believe it does possess layers of meaning that are accessible to a beholder. Of course, what is interesting is that our respective perceptive engagements may reveal quite different interpretations of what the painting means.

The line drawing of the tree at the centre of the painting is crucial. For me, the shapes of the lines are significant in the sense that they would seem to capture the guise of the trees – yet without the detail. The absence of the detail is perhaps difficult – alternatively we might interpret their simplicity as being just about right? Certainly, I am aware that the artist Paul Klee had experimented with lines throughout his career. At first they were scratchy, thin lines, sometimes in pen and ink, often depicting child-like figures. But here on this canvas the lines are black and painterly bold, seemingly assured and clear as to their meaning. We can also remind ourselves of the title of this painting – Park Bei Luc(erne). Bal and Bryson (1991) argued that each of

the daubs of paint on a canvas are signs and that accordingly they can combine in such a way so as to suggest something which points beyond itself. We are aware from his own writings that Klee made his way through this park in Lucerne in Switzerland when visiting his sick wife in hospital. We must presume that Klee, for some reason, wanted to capture this experience.

Returning to the painting, if we look carefully we can see that the trees are represented by lines that seem to bulge, bend and interweave, both signifying the shape of the trees but also suggesting the swaying of the trees in the wind. The lines are not straight – they are not regularized – they are of different lengths, different heights, some bend to the left others to the right. Some lines suggest the trees are near whilst others imply the trees are broken or are short. The lines of the trees are stark, perhaps suggesting it is either late winter or early spring. But even more: they shape the pathways that we might travel in the park, the seat we might rest-a-while. We can also detect round painted dots – perhaps these are balls, possibly thrown in the air, being played with by children. This is the typical scene we would expect to experience in a park. Somehow, Klee is able to convey to me, with a few lines and colours, almost a feeling of being in that park on a bright, blustery, early-spring day. I am able to see, to feel, to smell, to walk, to sit on the bench. I can sense people playing and enjoying their day.

What I am doing here is both describing what I observe but also allowing my narrative to transcend descriptions of its appearance and speculate my engagement with its meaning(s). Furthermore, as exact meaning is not possible I analyse that the lines signify a relationship between my understanding of a tree's appearance and my interpretation of their essence. I have then, through this extension, included in my descriptions my interpretations based upon previous experiences of visits to municipal parks. For Merleau-Ponty (1961) noted that it was artist Henri Matisse who taught us not to look at these lines in a physical-optimal way, for the line need no longer represent an imitation of a thing but can cause within us, as beholders, the opportunity to surpass the line and bathe in its potentiality.

Thus, it is not necessary for Klee to have captured the exact likeness of the trees or other objects within the park but the context of my understanding in today's world has allowed me to appreciate Klee's goal – that of essence at the expense of mimetic accuracy – so that I might almost experience being there in the park with him. Thus, my own interpretation and engagement at this level no longer allows me to remain at a distance from the event, in the manner of the Cartesian. Instead I have by engaging at this level, adopted and acted in the first-person – by revealing my engagement and thus experience of things, events and objects.

The third level of engagement with the painting is when the beholder metaphorically takes a step back from their gaze and considers its place within context – perhaps within a gallery where it is displayed alongside other paintings or maybe within the context of political and economic change that was taking place in Switzerland and Germany in late 1938? Therefore this is a reflexive stage *on* (i.e. post-event) rather than a reflective stage *in* the (current) event and is an important and widely appreciated step that, at this point in our discussion, we can expand slightly further. For example, the rationale for this important step is to realize that any object, thing, or event possesses more presence than simply itself – thus, within every appearance there lies that which enables it. To use Merleau-Ponty's terminology, in order to appreciate the visible it is important to understand the vital role that the in-the-visible plays in its composition (Merleau-Ponty, 1968). Therefore, for a beholder engaging with this painting at this third level, they should be aware that that which lies within the frame has not materialized from nowhere but in fact is a product of a considerable number of processes of development and/or other influential factors that affected Klee and his actions in his composition and painting of this picture. We are not aware how important it was for Klee to spend time in this park – but it clearly inspired him. For us, the beholder, we

might look at this painting only at the first level and never seek to surpass this initial phase. At this initial phase we can still appreciate the vibrancy and colour of the painting – indeed its simplicity suggests it might be painted by a child (a criticism often labelled to Klee). But for me its simplicity belies its richness and layers of meaning. For my interpretation suggests that the painting's simplicity is an invitation by Klee to the beholder to surpass its initial appearance and engage with the layers that lie beneath its surface and as such, these layers of interpretation invite the viewer to add their own experiences to the form and meaning of the painting. Thus, there is not one meaning, but a collection. A collection gleaned from each and every beholder who brings, contributes, and shares their experiences with the painting. This does not have to be vocal and therefore necessarily shared with all beholders. Thus, depending on how far the beholder is prepared to engage with the painting the invitation offers the opportunity to surpass a one-way relationship and enter into a 'reversible' relationship that might extend to questions that Merleau-Ponty (1968) raised about knowing where seeing ends and being seen begins.

For Merleau-Ponty, then, perception is an encounter with 'meanings' and not a meaning – it is a tangible, dynamic, and inter-sensory journey. As Merleau-Ponty clarified: 'I perceive in a total way with my whole being: I grasp a unique structure of the thing, a unique way of being, which speaks to all my senses at once' (Merleau-Ponty, 1964: 50). Thus perception is creative; our presence in the world does not call up some pre-existent meaning. Rather, through our own activities and engagement with factors we develop our own sense of being in the world. This is a call for us to take up an uncontaminated position where we can truly grasp the natural raw exposure of events, an interpretation not reliant on man-made artificial structures, such as Science, but one that grasps the primordial characteristics that merge, clash, and overlap each other forming images often inaccessible within our scientific frame.

I might at this point return to exemplifying further examples from our examination of the

Klee painting, but instead let me return to one that is able to exercise more of our senses and in a context that is closer to this handbook. Let me discuss the example of being invited for a job interview.

Imagine the letter drops through the letter box and you (the applicant) have been waiting for a reply inviting you for interview. Let me now present you with two contrasting views of the same information leading up to the interview. Traditional prescriptions tend to focus on the informative elements regarding the interview process. The information provided in the letter is likely to contain such details as: date, time and location of interview, whom you are to meet on arrival, details of sender, response to invitation, i.e. confirming attendance, etc. Perhaps this, coupled with other advice you have managed to glean from books/Internet access, etc., helps you with issues such as dress code, timings and other forms of preparation for the interview, including specimen questions, etc. This description is typical of a third-person Cartesian-based approach. It remains, to use the terminology of layers introduced with regards to our discussion of the painting, entirely at the first level – that is, at its most basic, it limits itself with the detail of objective information. I now want to contrast this form of knowing with the other layers that we accessed through our close discussion of the Klee's Park Bei Luc(erne).

A first-person engagement appreciates the emotion that the arrival of the letter creates. You have been waiting for this moment, the letter is now here, and the experience of opening it and your initial impressions are likely to be very powerful. Of course, the same information is included but now the applicant (you) is touching the paper (what does it feel like – is it good or poor quality?); what is the experience of reading the letter – is it excitement or the opposite – apathy? If it is the latter – why? This leads to the question: 'do you really want the job?' Additionally, you may also consider such issues as the logo, the style and manner of writing – is it friendly, welcoming or perhaps overly formal or informal? Are these factors consistent with your expectations?

My point here is that for most people there is either an implicit or explicit series of engagements that cause the individual to form a collection of judgements. It is vitally important to appreciate the richness and extent of this set of experiences, for undoubtedly their effect will influence your response and approach in preparing for the interview. Let me move this scenario forward to the day of the interview. All of our senses are operating and will provide, in combination with each other, access to and understanding of this experience. For example, upon entering the foyer what is the overall impression? Is it formal, cold and grand, or is it warm, cosy and friendly? Perhaps the greeting and the way you are addressed at the reception desk is important, coupled with the manner of how you asked to wait (inevitably!). Are you offered refreshments and made to feel welcome and wanted, or are you largely ignored and called only by some impersonal communication system? Do you expect good or poor quality refreshments? Is it likely to have an effect on your perception of how you might be treated if you were to be offered the job? It is the accumulation of these factors that make a significant contribution to our knowing and undoubtedly impact on the final decision of whether to accept the job.

At the third level of engagement, the reflexive opportunities this layer allows might cause you (the applicant) to consider their effect in a non-linear manner. Thus, your own more general interpretation of being-in-the-world might either push you toward accepting the job or alternatively declining it based upon factors that largely are indirect to the process and yet still relevant. These factors might not be immediately apparent until you are actually in the situation, and thus this first-hand involvement reveals other indirect influences. For example, one's own personal needs (i.e. the need to move to a new job now), the quantity of comparable jobs being currently advertised, and other general issues such as economic climate or political change, etc.

Thus, the implications for this form of engagement are that a first-person sensual engagement will generate quite different forms of knowing about events, objects or things to that presented in traditional decision-making literature. But my experience is that once these levels of scrutiny are opened they can never again be closed.

CONCLUSION

In this chapter I have sought to expose the limitations of traditional influences on how we know what we know in and for organizations. The distance of the observer/researcher to these events on the one hand fulfils certain epistemological criteria and yet, on the other, fails ontologically to allow the individual(s) to grasp, to touch, to sense the richness of these events. In utilizing art and aesthetics this re-awakens this potential as inevitably individuals will seek to collapse their distance and seek a form of first-person engagement. Antonio Strati appreciated that '…only a tiny fraction of all knowable facts are of interest to scientists' (Strati, 1999: 51) – the danger is, if we ignore the remainder, then so much of that which is vital to what we need to know in organizations will be overlooked.

ACKNOWLEDGEMENT

Figure 1.3.1 reproduced with permission © Estate of Rex Whistler/DACS London 2008.

REFERENCES

Alvession, M. and S. Deetz, (1996) 'Critical theory and postmodernism approaches to organizational studies', in S. R. Clegg, C. Hardy, and W. Nord (eds) *Handbook of Organizational Studies*, London: Sage, 191–217.

Bal, M. and Bryson, N. (1991) 'Semiotics and art history', *The Art Bulletin*, June, Vol. LXXIII, No. 2: 174–208.

Boland, R.J. and Tenkasi, R.V. (1995) 'Perspective making and perspective taking: In communities of knowing', *Organization Science*, 9, 605–622.

Brown, J.S. and Duguid, P. (1998) *The Social Life of Information*, Boston: Harvard Business School Press.

Burrell, G. and Morgan, G. (1979) *Sociological Paradigms and Organizational Analysis: Elements of the Sociology of Corporate Life*. London: Heinemann.

Clegg, S.R. and Dunkerley, D. (1980) *Organization, Class and Control*. London: Routledge & Kegan Paul.

Descartes, Rene (1985) Discourse on Method; Passions of the Soul (1637; 1649) Vol.1 of the Philosophical Writings of Descartes (Trans. J. Cottingham et al.) 2 vols. Cambridge: Cambridge University Press.

Gibson, J.J. (1950) *The Perception of the Visual World*, Allen & Unwin: Houghton: Mifflin.

Gregory, R.L. (1966) *Eye and Brain*, London: Weidenfeld & Nicolson.

Grey, C. and Willmott, H. (2005) *Critical Management Studies, A Reader*. Oxford: Oxford University Press.

Guillet de Monthoux, P. (2004) *The Art Firm: Aesthetic Management and Metaphysical Marketing from Wagner to Wilson*. Stanford: Stanford University Press.

King, I.W. (2007a) 'Straightening our Perspective: The Logos of the Line'. *Organization*, 14 (2): 225–241.

King, I. W. (2007b) 'Engaging with listening, silence and noise: Peering-into the analytical/continental divide', *Culture and Organization*, 13 (1): 23–35.

Linstead S. and Höpfl, H. (2000) (eds) *The Aesthetics of Organizations*. London: Sage.

Merleau-Ponty, M. (1961) 'Eye and Mind' Reproduced in the Merleau-Ponty Aesthetics Reader: *Philosophy and Painting*. (ed. Galan A. Johnson). Evanston, IL: Northwestern University Press.

Merleau-Ponty, M. (1964) *Signs*. (trans. R.C. McCleary) Evanston, IL: Northwestern University Press.

Merleau-Ponty, M. (1968) *Visible and the Invisible*. Evanston, IL: Northwestern University Press.

Organization Science (2002) vol. 13 (3): May-June.

Orlikowski, W.J. (2002) 'Knowing in practice: Enacting a collective capability in distributed organizing', *Organization Science*, 13 (3), May-June, 249–273.

Polanyi, M. (1966) *The Tacit Dimension*. London: Routledge & Kegan Paul.

Ryle, G. (1949) *The Concept of Mind*. Hutcheson: London.

Spender, J.C. (1994) 'Knowing, managing and learning: A dynamic managerial epistemology', *Management Learning*, 25 (3): 387–412.

Strati, A (1996) 'Organization viewed through the lens of aesthetics', *Organization*, 3 (2) :209–218.

Strati, A. (1999) *Organizations and Aesthetics*. London: Sage.

Tsoukas, H. (2002) 'Do we really understand tacit knowledge?', in M. Easterby-Smith and M.A. Lyles (eds), *Handbook of Organizational Learning and Knowledge*. Oxford: Blackwell.

Vickery, J. (2006) *Organising Art: Constructing Aesthetic Value in Culture and Organization*. London: Routledge. pp. 51–64.

Alterity/Identity Interplay in Image Construction

Barbara Czarniawska

1. alterity n.
The state of being other or different.
(*The Concise Oxford English Dictionary*)

2. alterity
Term used in postmodern writings for the 'otherness' of others, or sometimes the otherness of the self. (*The Oxford Dictionary of Philosophy*)

Being different is hardly a postmodern invention, so why is that 'identity' is a part of our everyday vocabulary, while 'alterity' is reserved for esoteric writings, and even there only 'sometimes' related to the Self? I begin by sketching a historical process that might be an explanation of this development, and then argue that re-introducing alterity to the common vocabulary of organization studies might help us understand many of the interesting phenomena that we observe but obscure by dealing with them under the label of identity.

THE TYRANNY OF IDENTITY

The identity paradigm

> To exist is to differ; difference, in a sense, is the substantial side of things, is what they have only to themselves and what they have most in common. One has to start the explanation from here, including the explanation of identity, taken often, mistakenly, for a starting point. Identity is but a minimal difference, and hence a type of difference, and a very rare type at that, in the same way as rest is a type of movement and circle a peculiar type of ellipse. (Tarde, [1893]1999)

Why was identity taken as a starting point at the turn of the previous century, when Tarde wrote these words? Why does it continue to be taken as a starting point now? Peter Brooks (2005) explained this with the emergence of what he called an identity paradigm. Two phenomena were at the centre of attention in the nineteenth century, especially the attention of the young nation states. One was urbanization: the enormous movement from the countryside to the city. The previously content bourgeois became frightened; criminality was on the rise, and it was taking new, sophisticated forms. As Brooks pointed out, the picturesque figure of a 'master criminal' in a variety of disguises was not only a figment of the vivid imaginations of novelists, but existed in reality, to the exasperation of police forces. Another nineteenth century phenomenon had to do with the exigencies of running the colonies. How to tell the natives from one another if they all look alike to the eye of the colonialists? Also, how to tell working-class people from one another, if they not only wear the same clothes, but also imitate the bourgeoisie (or the other way around)? The problem, therefore, was too many differences and too few differences. A search for various technologies of identification was activated during this period: physiognomy, phrenology and then photography and finger-printing were put at the service of the police and the colonial authorities. Of course, says Brooks, the question of mistaken identities has always been a focus of interest of playwrights and novelists from Homer to Shakespeare, but the search for certain marks of identity became a non-fictional matter, and an especially acute one in the 1800s.

Whereas the issues of alterity and identity were born in relation to persons, they were transferred, by analogy, to the realm of abstract entities, such as legal persons (corporations; Lamoreaux, 2003) and nation states. Thus, the emergence of the identity paradigm in the nineteenth century was also most likely connected to the rise of nationalism (Anderson, 1983/1991). People grouped within the new borders desperately needed to know what they had in common, as the tendency was for them to see too many differences. This attempt was so successful that, in the opinion of Ian Buruma, 'identity' is behind most of the present world troubles:

> Identity is a bloody business. Religion, nationality or race may not be the primary causes of war and mass murder. These are more likely to be tyranny, or the greed for territory, wealth and power. But 'identity'

is what gets the blood boiling, what makes people do unspeakable things to their neighbors. (Buruma, 2002)

The situation in organizations might not be as drastic. Nevertheless, organization theory does not deviate from the current public discourse, with its focus on the phenomenon of identity construction (see e.g. Whetten and Godfrey, 1998; Schultz et al., 2000; Hatch and Schultz, 2003).

A corporate persona and its image

Although we have been saddled with the notion of 'organizations', thanks to the organization theorists' interest in system theory in the 1960s (Waldo, 1961), most of our reasoning circles, implicitly or explicitly, around the notion of a corporation – a legal person. This reasoning became even more valid in present times, when public administration units are encouraged or forced to assume shapes of 'real organizations': that is to say, corporations.

The history of corporations in the USA is a history of a competition, never concluded, between the school of thought that conceptualizes corporations as natural persons, and the one that sees them as artificial persons (Lamoreaux, 2003). According to the latter theory, a corporation is a person only to the degree bestowed on it by its legislator. Thus, an organization is a Super Person (Czarniawska, 1994), in the sense of being bigger in certain ways than all the individuals who contribute to its existence; yet also a Limited Person. Were Gabriel Tarde an organization theorist, he would say that each person employed in a company is much bigger and much more complex than the company itself, the latter being a collection of a repetition of one or few properties of its employees and machines (Czarniawska, 2004).

If one adopts a 'natural person' perspective, an organization can have a self. Within an 'artificial person' perspective, to which I subscribe, an organization cannot have a 'self', but can have, to borrow an expression from narratology, a Character (deducible and observable from its deeds and self-presentations). In corporate law, Naomi Lamoreaux tells us, the two theories tend to hybridize rather than clash. We can follow their example and agree on a common point: what is compared in order to establish an identity or an alterity relation is an organizational image. Whether this image reflects the essence of an organization or is an ongoing social construction may remain a point of discontent and personal belief. The fact remains that organizational images are constantly produced and reproduced by actors and observers within and outside organizations; they are used to control employees and the investors and to legitimate and to attract attention. Thus, two research questions arise. How are organizational images constructed (both in the sense of process and product)? and, How are they used?

Organization theorists had no problem in accepting and translating to their own use the constructivist view on the character of the self that would see it not as an essence to be located or expressed, but as an image of 'I' produced and reproduced in interactions (Mead, 1913). Such a self – individual or organizational – would be stable insofar there persists a memory of past interactions. The self is historical, and is both constituted by and constitutive of a community (Bruner, 1990; Rorty, 1991). If members of the community conceive of themselves as forming an abstract system, as it is the case of formal organizations, the image of this system will also be constructed in abstract terms.

It has also been accepted that '[i]dentities are performed in conversations. … what we achieve in conversations is positioning vis-à-vis other people' (Davies and Harré, 1990: 44), and against the background of a plot that is negotiated by those taking part in the conversation. Whether this background is the history of the community or one's life project may vary from one conversation to another. Thus, the self – individual and organizational – is produced, reproduced and maintained in discourses, past and present. It is community-constituted, as Rorty says,

in the sense of being created by those who take part in a conversation; it is historical because past conversations are evoked in the course of present ones.

While the idea that self is an image that is being constructed in and through discourses was taking root, the attention – including that of Davies and Harré – focused on identity construction as synonymous with the self. This fashionable focus of attention overshadows the simultaneous and unavoidable process of alterity construction, of constructing oneself as different. Indeed, whereas 'identity' entered everyday parlance, 'alterity' remains a precious concept limited to the circles of cultural studies. Yet there is no reason to suppose that the question 'Who am I like?' is more important than the question 'Who am I unlike?' and, even more poignant, 'How am I different?' Identity and alterity form the self, and their interplay results in an image – projected or received.

Alterity in social sciences

Both identity and alterity do appear in social studies – but usually in two versions, which can be situated on two extremes of the exclusion–inclusion dimension.

One version is typical for cultural studies, and is strongly influenced by Michel Foucault, who claimed that 'the forceful exclusion and exorcism of what is Other is an act of identity formation' (Corbey and Leerssen, 1991: xii).[1] The other end of the dimension is represented by post-Hegelians who see the interplay between identity and alterity as a dialectical move, resulting in 'increasing expansion and incorporation, assimilating or at least harmonizing all otherness in terms of expanding identity' (ibid., xi). Michael Taussig (1993) followed Benjamin in the belief that mimesis means yielding into the Other. Thus, in the discourse of and on identity, alterity is either attributed ('they are different and therefore not us') or incorporated ('they are actually very much like us'). The third possibility, the affirmation of difference ('we are different'), is omitted, with the exception of the work of Gilles Deleuze, who alone continued the Tardean tradition (Czarniawska, 2004).

The process of calling attention to distinctions has sometimes been called a negativity ('what we are not'), or a game of internal difference, as contrasted to 'true alterity', that of the Other (Zahavi, 1999: 196). For the Foucauldians, negativity is uninteresting in the face of the 'true', irremediable alterity, which, however, cannot concern oneself. For the post-Hegelians, it is but further proof of incorporation, of a harmonizing removal of differences in the process of identity formation. Deleuze's anti-Hegelian project suggests that negativity is the last point on the identity continuum constituted by The Same, The Similar, The Analogous and The Opposed, and needs to be distinguished from affirmation of difference (1968/1997: 265).

Although the simultaneous presence of exclusion-inclusion movements has been acknowledged before (Höpfl, 1992), the simultaneous construction of identity and alterity of such collective images as 'an organization' or 'management practice' requires attention. The need to distinguish between the two is justified by the different places they occupy in different attempts at construction of an image. Thus, following Deleuze's argument, identity and alterity can be seen as two dimensions (the alterity dimension being non-continuous).

Although The Same can be seen as an ideal on the identity continuum, it is not so. It is only The Primitive who returns to The Same, and therefore does not progress (de Certeau, 1975/1988). The Primitive Other imitates; The Moderns emulate (and do it better than the model). One can thus portray identity-alterity dimensions as a circle, the larger part of which the moderns have reserved for themselves. The Primitive Others are supposed to remain at the extremes; they repeat themselves, and they are unlike anybody else. The Moderns are free to engage in the identity-alterity interplay in many diverse fashions. (See Figure 1.4.1.)

The observation of actual practices tells a different story, however. The whole field is open to everybody, even if fashion might prefer some modes and some types of interplay. The Primitive Other is but an invention, a prop to be used in the interplay.

The analogy with corporations and 'corporate citizenship' is obvious. Actors and observers constantly produce and reproduce organizational images, which are used to control the employees and the investors, to legitimate, and to attract attention. Corporate leadership tries to convince employees that they have much in common, and convince the customers that the other corporations are different. The 'unsophisticated' organizations are either impossible to tell apart, or are unique and therefore irrelevant. But while practitioners construct the images playing on, both identity (Who are we like? and How?) and alterity (How are we different? and From whom?), scholars tend to concentrate only on the former part of this process.

The dominant conceptualization of 'identity free of alterity' has caused a significant semantic gliding in studies of corporate image construction. At one time merely denoting a relation (identity, like an alterity, is a judgement resulting from a comparison), identity has become an attribute – something that an organization can have or lack. A relational view of the identity/alterity interplay in organizational image construction promises a more nuanced understanding of these complex phenomena. I illustrate it here with the examples of three studies: city management (Czarniawska, 2000, 2002), business school management (Wedlin, 2006) and an IT company management (Strannegård and Friberg, 2001). In accordance with the logic of grounded theory, I present the first case in greater detail, whereas the other two serve as a test and extension of the theory of the interplay of identity and alterity in the construction of organizational images.

THE CONSTRUCTION OF CITY IMAGE AS AN INTERPLAY OF IDENTITY AND ALTERITY

City managers and politicians in Warsaw, Stockholm and Rome described to the researchers their cities and their own work in

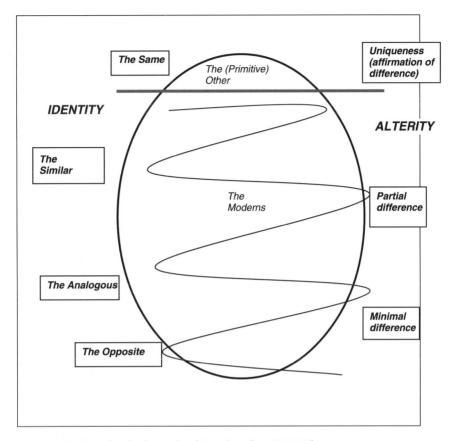

Figure 1.4.1   Identity-alterity interplay (Czarniawska, 2002: 35)

relation to an image of 'a modern European capital'. Although this notion had many topics in common, it also contained dramatically different visions of such a capital, given that the frame of reference differed from one city to another. These different frames included different constellations of European cities, but also local stories of specific developments in the three capitals. These accounts were intended to set the city apart – apart from all other cities and/or apart from specific cities. The ways of identification (same, similar, analogous), of negation (opposite), and of differentiation (unique or different) shifted in form and in content.

Images of 'a European capital' in Warsaw

There were three dominant elements of an image of a European capital that were common in Warsaw: such a national capital needed a metro, water treatment plants, and a centrally steered infrastructure.

The construction of the subway was the topic of the greatest controversy and the highest hopes at the time of my study in the late 1990s. I was continually asked whether I was aware that there were only two capitals in Europe without a subway – Warsaw and Tirana? Tirana, the capital of Albania, was Warsaw's Opposite, and not only in matters of transportation. My pointing out that Copenhagen had no subway had no effect; quite rightly, as it turned out (Copenhagen built a subway at the end of the 1990s). Everyone agreed that a subway would solve many problems connected with urban transportation.

The World Bank, however, comparing Warsaw to Johannesburg, had argued for a construction of an effective surface transport system, and was ready to help with that project. This position gained few supporters in Warsaw, and the alterity aspect of the image of the European capital became clear in this context. Such a capital cannot be in any place other than Europe, but one continent in which it most emphatically must not be located is Africa. Johannesburg was, at that time, an important prop in the alterity construction, and this construction revealed, among many other things, the untamed strength of racial prejudice. Western consultants were accused of trying to 'Africanize' Poland. This accusation had its root in the fact that many of the aid programmes had turned away from Africa and toward eastern Europe (Wedel, 2001). But while western liberals were despairing of the consequences for African countries, at least some eastern Europeans were annoyed that their situation could be seen as paralleling that of Africa. Johannesburg might be a more modern city than Warsaw; but, alas, it is in the wrong continent. Tirana may be a symbol of poverty and belatedness, but it is, at least, a European capital, The Opposite, not the Other.

The water quality problems were obvious as well. They were partly a result of shallow intakes, dirty water, and obsolete technology; but primarily due to the fact that Warsaw had only one water treatment plant, which collected wastewater from one side of the river. Warsaw had been classified by the Helsinki Convention documents and by the Baltic Water Protection Program as their most difficult case. A single-proprietorship city company, financed mainly with credit from the European Investment Bank, was created to build another wastewater treatment plant. It was considered appropriate that a European bank assisted in the Europeanization of Warsaw. What provoked my interest, was that the model for water management had been derived from the past – the 1930s in Warsaw – on the claim that although water quality and technology had both changed, the idea of effective management had not, and could be directly imported from the past. Warsaw was too different from other cities to rely on their experience.

There was also a strong conviction that the only effective management of infrastructure would be a centralized one. Some of my interlocutors pointed out that the idea of municipal corporations – an alternative to central control – had been borrowed from Germany, where it was being applied to small towns rather than major cities. The popular assumption of the incompatibility of democracy and efficiency revealed its sources in the memory of past emergency situations. Such a tendency to expect threat and emergency is typical of 'Mitteleuropa', and atypical of Sweden, where this historically induced sense of threat is unknown. This, among other factors, makes a tendency to imitate contemporary cities less pronounced in Warsaw than in Stockholm, as will be seen below.

The image of an 'ideal city' has had multifaceted role in managerial practice in Warsaw: it motivated and legitimated, focused discourse, guided action, and served as argument. Such an image was a composite of pictures, some of which could probably be traced back to some professional producers of images, but many of which seem to be produced by the actors evoking them. This composite used sameness ('Warsaw is a European city'), opposition ('Tirana is a European city but Warsaw must not be like it'), difference ('Warsaw is not an African city') and uniqueness ('Warsaw is different from all European cities'). This composite would be recognizable but not usable in Stockholm.

Images of a 'European big city' in Stockholm

By Warsaw standards, Stockholm fulfils all the requirements of 'the European capital': it has a subway and water treatment plants, and its infrastructure is centrally managed (in a company form). But these images were not those present in the minds of Stockholm politicians and managers. The 'big European city of the twenty-first century', as they called their image, had to fulfil quite another set of requirements. Because the big-but-not-capital cities like Milan, Stuttgart, Naples and

Gothenburg rebelled against the hegemony of capitals, the scope of identification could be extended. Stockholm was aware of being a not-so-big big city, and watched the agile moves of other not-so-big cities with interest. They also listened to what the 'field servicing' organizations (Hedmo et al., 2005) suggested. Opening one of many OECD conferences on 'The City and New Technologies' in 1992, Michel Delebarre said that information technology was the only way to increase the efficiency of municipal services, while attracting the computer industry to a big city that had disposed of its heavy and light industry. As a consequence, city managers began to market their cities within the frame of information technology: Osaka represented itself as City of Intelligence, Barcelona as City of Telematics, Amsterdam as City of Information, Manchester as Wired City and Stockholm as Internet Bay (Dobers and Strannegård, 2001).

Although the image of an IT-city did not originate in Stockholm, it was in Stockholm that it found a natural home. At the time of my study (1996–97), Stockholm City had put big money into CityNet, a new optic-fibre net connecting all municipal offices, a 'new city infrastructure'. Stockholm had created a home page early in the history of the Internet, and its politicians believed that computer education was the best way to deal with unemployment caused by a new immigration wave from the countryside to the city. The IT industries could not but agree.

Another image of a global character adopted in Stockholm was that of the city as a spectacle (Wilson, 1991). This is also an old idea: modern city as a spectacle and modern citizen as a spectator (flâneur) are images from the previous *fin-de-siècle*, which now seem to have reached their full expression. Allan Pred (1995) recounted the story of three spectacular spaces on which hang the history of modern Stockholm: the Stockholm Exhibition of 1897; the Stockholm Exhibition of 1930; and the multipurpose arena, the Globe, which opened in 1989. Thus Stockholm, intent as it is on following present development in other cities, also followed its own tradition.

The latest spectacle Stockholm offered the world was in 1998, in its role as Cultural Capital of Europe (Pipan and Porsander, 2000).

One image that is used forcefully for marketing purposes is that of Stockholm as Clean City, with fresh air and pure water (Adolfsson, 2005). The difficulty with this enterprise lies in providing the evidence. A modern city cannot rely on impressions of its tourists or its inhabitants, especially if these impressions are positive only in the negative statement, 'no pollution'. Thus an impressive apparatus for the measurement of air and water pollution, involving many people and machines, was constructed. An obelisk showing the level of pollution of air and water has been opened by the King.

Unfortunately, no dramatic results can be shown – the neon light indicators rarely darken. While 'dirty cities' (such as Rome and Warsaw) can show diminishing pollution levels, Stockholm's measurements lie almost constantly below the permissible EU norm. Although the city is truly clean, it is difficult to use it for either identity or alterity construction. As clean as … what other city? Cleaner than … any city?

There was a great supply of images of other cities in Stockholm as well as in Warsaw, but they were different (although in the debate about the traffic it has been said that, apart from Stockholm, only Tirana does not have an inner ring road). Gothenburg is usually seen as Stockholm's at-home opposite, while Copenhagen, Oslo and Helsinki as similar or analogous, which meant that any elements of managerial practice in these cities might be imitated – although Stockholm really wished to be imitated by others. Rome, on the other hand, wished to be placed on a different map entirely.

Images of the 'leading European capital' in Rome

There was a well-deserved grandiosity in city images present in Rome. Whereas Warsaw was painfully aware of its belatedness and Stockholm of its small size and Nordic location, Rome dreamed of joining the fashion leaders – Paris, Berlin and London. It shared with Warsaw the belief that rapid modernization was needed, with Stockholm an interest in the newest managerial fashion, and with Athens the pride of a unique past incorporated and preserved in the city. All these elements found expression in the images of the leading European capital that seemed to be guiding both political visions and managerial practices.

There were some palpable similarities between the traffic issues in Warsaw and Rome. One was the citizens' love of the automobile that results in a congestion of city traffic of which the citizens of Stockholm, with all their complaints about traffic problems, know little. Another similarity is the late arrival of the subway. By the time of the study, however, Rome already had two subway lines, and the subway construction problems were mostly primarily local and related to Rome's historical past. The uniquely Roman problem was that the city did not have a traffic system. There never was an urban transport plan, and neither the tariffs nor the networks were integrated. Rome is truly a palimpsest city, as Bauman (1998: 40) defined it.

Big European cities like Paris and Rome, with effective public transportation systems were seen as analogous. Berlin was especially attractive because its double networks of local trains and subway were close to the Roman programme 'to activate the iron' – the many unused railway lines that crisscross the city – and because of Berlin's recent experiences at joining its two parts again. There were, however, a great many difficulties involved in even partially imitating Berlin (Czarniawska, 2002). The sediments of the old regimes were residing not only under the ground as archeological monuments. It was, in many ways, a heroic enterprise to try to create a traffic system in a big city rather than merely extending or modernizing an existing system.

On the other hand, the idea of city as spectacle was obvious to Roman politicians, officials, and citizens. If anything, they were tired of it, as the relief at having lost the Olympics and the general wariness about

the Jubilee of the Third Millennium of Christianity clearly indicated. But with the approach of this last spectacle, forced onto Rome by the Vatican, the city was determined to make the best of it. The best had to be more durable than the event itself, and the past had to be turned into the main asset of the present. The Jubilee was to become a marketing opportunity: an excellent opportunity for spreading the image of Rome around the world. Rome was to become a city that offers its tourists all the modern comforts so they can better enjoy the beauty of the past (Pipan and Porsander, 2000).

Another managerial novelty in Rome – a more pervasive and far-reaching one – was the privatization of public services, which in Rome was perceived as a must for a modern European capital, inspired by the example of London. The first case in point was to be the privatization of Centrale di Latte, the city-owned dairy monopoly, which was probably seen as the easiest privatization target because it was such an obvious anachronism.[2] The process turned out to be far from easy. The citizens were against privatization, and union protests and street demonstrations followed. The subsequent privatization of ACEA, the conglomerate of water, sewer and city illumination proceeded slowly and cautiously. Mazza (2001) claims that Rome used Centrale di Latte as a learning case for further privatization. The outcome of this learning is still controversial in practice, but it has undoubtedly contributed to the legitimization of the privatization discourse in Rome. Such a legitimization permitted the city managers to follow a global fashion with the acceptance of its local audience. Privatization of public utilities in Rome can thus be seen as following a fashion in the world of public management, imitating those cities that are perceived as similar or analogous.

City management: Constructing identity and alterity

The interplay of identity and alterity work was visible in all the city image constructions: one could claim that such interplay was explicitly demanded by the audience. As Orvar Löfgren (1993) pointed out, contemporary norms prescribing how identities should be built – national, regional, local identities – include the paradoxical requirement that such an identity should be built around the image of uniqueness.

Thus Rome is comparable to Athens because of its cultural capital, but Athens is a city with many problems and no solutions, which Rome is not. London is the model of privatized municipal services, but its citizens do not enjoy the ancient cultural heritage of Rome. Berlin has a model traffic system with the railway at its centre, but German cities are over-organized, and the charm of Rome lies partly in its anarchy. Images of other cities become fragmented, and those fragments are used to construct both the similarity and the difference.

It was not always cities that supplied the images: in the case of preparations for the Jubilee and for the Cultural Capital year, the reference points were great events. Again, the Olympic Games in Atlanta were seen as opposite of what Rome wanted to achieve, and Stockholm saw itself as analogous to Glasgow and Copenhagen, but not to Antwerp. Thus, in many cases alterity construction was in fact subordinated to identity construction; in Deleuze's terms, the Opposite is the extreme end of the identity continuum, but remains within it. The cities (or actions within the management net) differ, but on the same dimension.

An interesting example of a combination of identity and alterity work was a frequent comparison between Rome and Barcelona. Barcelona was a model to imitate – not as a city, but as a case of transformation from a pre-modern to a late-modern city. The managers in Rome did not want Rome to become another Barcelona, but they wanted the same managerial success that their counterparts in Barcelona enjoyed. Guje Sevón (1996) called this phenomenon, after René Girard, the imitation of desire. Rome was different, but desired the same success.

But alterity was not only an aid in identity construction. In the case of Stockholm, there was also an affirmation of difference. Stockholm is the only truly Nordic and truly big city; Stockholm combines, in unique ways, Continental and Scandinavian traditions; Stockholm is the only capital situated both at the sea and on a lake; Stockholm is different. But in romantic terms, Stockholm is also the Venice of the North. In terms of management, Amsterdam, another city on water, was Stockholm's simile. The identity construction used The Similar (Amsterdam), The Analogous (Venice) and The Opposite (in the case of London's wrongly built 'city net') positions on the identity dimension.

The 'uniqueness of Warsaw' was a topic to which the interviewees often returned. Warsaw is different from all other cities in Poland, because it is a capital; because after the war it was dealt with by a special Decree; because in 1990 it was exempted from the Local Government Law. Warsaw is different from any western European capital because it has a different history; it is different from any eastern European capital because it has a different geopolitical position. Warsaw, in short, is different, and the affirmation of its difference dominated the city image. The identity moves were usually located on the Opposite point and consisted of such politically incorrect negations as 'unlike Tirana'. Warsaw's management had identity problems because a city unlike any other cannot legitimatize its actions by following the examples of others. An image built only on alterity is unclear. The 'decisive difference' – the one that supposedly determines the result of any market competition – must be positioned on a common dimension. Similar. Analogous. Opposite. But on the same scale.

This was exactly the idea behind the ranking of business schools, and example to which I now turn.

ALTERITY AND IDENTITY INTERPLAY IN BUSINESS SCHOOLS

Linda Wedlin (2006) studied the emergence of ranking lists and league tables as aids to the comparison and evaluation of higher education in the media. She focused on business schools, as the attempt to internationalize management education is one of the most prominent cases of the present globalization of university education. Her purpose was not to judge this activity, but to try to describe how and why the rankings were established, how they were met by business schools, and what were the observable consequences of their use. Limiting her interest to European business schools, she collected published material on rankings and media coverage of management education in Europe since the mid-1990s, conducted a survey of opinions of European business school deans and interviewed selected top administrators and media representatives. It is especially the interviews with the top administrators that are of interest to me, as they were summarized in two 'identity narratives' composed by Wedlin. While I concur with her analysis, I wish to show how the issues of affirmed alterity ('this is how we differ …') are subsumed under the identity heading. In producing the image of their schools, however, the deans are clearly (and skilfully) engaging in an identity/alterity interplay.

A University Business School

This 'academic' business school, as Wedlin chose to call it, is a relatively new (in existence since 1990) but a fast-growing one (60 research and teaching staff in 2002). Its specificity is the fact that it is part of a large and old university. One of the interviewees stated that the aim of the school was to be one of the leading international business schools, owing to a successful combination of teaching and research.

The identification was quite clear: the school wanted to be a 'true' business school. This meant, in the first place, an MBA programme ('… if you want to be a serious management/business school, you have to have an MBA course'; Wedlin, 2006: 49). The MBA credentials attract the interest of alumni, students, other business schools, and corporations all over the world. And the MBA's fees provide an important source

of income. Another trait common for business schools is the close link to practice: via inclusion of corporate representatives into the advisory board, via executive education, and via consulting undertaken by the faculty.

But the differences should not be overlooked. Unlike many other business schools, this was a school within 'an ancient, multi-faculty, inter-disciplinary university' (ibid., 47). The excellence of this university lies in the scholarly research that is closely connected to undergraduate and graduate teaching, and the business school had to be on the same level. This was a challenge, translated mainly into the high recruitment standards, but also a resource, consisting of easily formed links with other university departments.

Here, however, another differentiation occurred: in forging links with other university departments, the business school had to be careful to avoid becoming like (some of) them, that is 'ossified, backward-facing' (ibid., 47); it had to be vibrant and fast, like other international schools. Thus, the possibilities within the identity/alterity circle were fully exploited: the University Business School was to be like all international business schools through MBA and corporate contacts; unlike other business schools through scholarly research and tight links to the university tradition; but unlike other university departments and like business schools in terms of speed and vivacity.

A Business Business School

The other identity narrative that Wedlin presented was that of a business school without ties to a university, established partly outside of the national university system. It was established in the same year as the University Business School, and has the same faculty size. Being a 'true' business school did not mean that its alterity claims were non-existent; if anything, they were even stronger. The school represented 'a dramatically different model'; different from what? – 'the classical model you (Wedlin) will study' (p. 51). Further probing revealed that there were, in fact, two classical models from which a business school can differ. One was 'a typical university that knows best' (p. 53); the Business Business School was international (not parochial, like many universities), practical (no ivory towers here), and customer-oriented (rather than faculty-oriented). These differences meant in practice that there were no departmental divisions based on disciplines, no academic titles, and no tenure (the two latter measures intended to free time and energy from the usual academic power struggles, and divert it toward customer needs). The school also had a bonus system to attract and maintain high-level faculty.

Nevertheless, they claimed to be different from a typical business school: 'outstanding research, outstanding teaching, outstanding ratings, but doing everything differently …' (p. 53). The main difference from other business schools was the focus on research, and the interviewees claimed that the school managed to achieve what everybody dreams of: research that leads both to applicable results and to high-prestige academic publications. And, although they had an MBA programme, it was small and elitist, and it served primarily as a marketing device.

Different ways of braiding identity and alterity

The two narratives have in common the active interplay of alterity and identity features, but in differing proportions and with different results. The University Business School put relatively more weight on identity claims: they were like business schools in some aspects and like university in others. Their alterity was partly established by the attribution of difference to the others, the 'ossified departments'. In contrast, and similar to the city of Warsaw, the Business Business School built its narrative around a total alterity claim: it was dramatically different from everybody. A reader employed in academia might be sceptical about the degree of drama in such differences; yet at least one trait was unique – bonuses as rewards for research.

Both schools claimed to have good results, and their rankings support their claims. One can speculate, however, about a quicker faculty turnover at Business Business School, as it does not award tenure and its faculty members teach more than other business school teachers do (the University Business School faculty teach more than other university departments, but less than other business schools).

Wedlin interpreted the results similarly, although only in the vocabulary of identity (she spoke of similarities and differences, however). She pointed out that the props for constructing differences and similarities were truly effigies: 'the traditional university' (which probably does not exist anywhere anymore) and 'the real business school' (as to the character of which, opinions differ, depending on the contrast required).

AN ALTERITY ONLY?

Lars Strannegård conducted a prolonged direct observation of an IT company in Stockholm just before the 'IT-bubble' burst and during the crisis (October 1999–April 2001). His results are reported in the form of extensive quotes from field notes, discussed in theoretical terms, and illustrated by the work of an artist, Maria Friberg, who herself made a prolonged observation of young businessmen in Stockholm (Strannegård and Friberg, 2001).

The IT whiz kids (or rather young men and women) that Strannegård observed engaged often and spontaneously in self-image construction, both in words and in deeds. What struck me in this image was that it seemed to be constructed only upon alterity. They were different; and in order to be different, they needed to construct a monolithical identity of 'the Other', who were all alike and existed in order to differ from:

> They're not competitors. They're not innovative and they're still doing the same thing.
>   They're just a bunch of old dummies.
>   We're doing something totally new. We solve entire business problems and find new business possibilities. (p. 43)

Only one utterance was more conservative, but still in the same spirit: 'Internet companies don't do things all that differently. But it goes faster and is more dynamic' (p. 58).

Strannegård, inspired, among others, by my writings ('According to Czarniawska, the similarity dimension is the most important aspect of identity construction ...', p. 68), looked for the similarity dimension, and found none. Instead he found this web document describing the company's 'vision and values' (at least in that they were similar!):

> We were founded in Sweden, but we're not Swedish. We are a global company that provides global solutions for the global network economy.
> We are building a new model.
> There is no model for our business. Or for our kind of company. We have set our own standards. Created our own rules. And created our own success.

Until the 2000 stock market crash, 'they' were rather unspecified traditional industrial companies, and in the manifesto above, 'they' did not exist. The company was unique. After the crash, 'they' changed identity, and the company image moved towards negativity (The Opposite):

> But we're nothing like the traditional dot-com company. In most cases they have no business plan. They're not cohesive and in many cases not very serious about what they're doing, they're just out to make some quick money. They've been completely exaggerated (sic), spend huge amounts of money and haven't followed the way the Internet has actually developed. (p. 73)

The IT company is clearly an interesting case, difficult to analyse because of its claim to uniqueness. There are some elements resembling the colonial rhetoric in its contempt for 'the primitive' other – in this case, traditional industrial companies. There is the claim of being completely different, that resembles Warsaw's claims to uniqueness ('we are like no other city in Europe'). There are tones, especially in the last, more guarded description, similar to the Business Business School claim to be a real business school but dramatically different from all others. Observe, however, that the differences from 'the traditional

dot-com company' (how quickly do traditions form!) seem to make the IT company similar to the 'traditional industrial' one with its boring business plan, boring seriousness, and boring long-term planning. It is difficult to be different without at least somebody being similar.

THE IMAGE OF AN ORGANIZATION

The uses of an organizational image are as many as its users, but let me limit this reasoning to the ways that management can use an image of the organization they are managing. The cases described above allow us to discern the following ways that managers use the image of the city/the school/the company:

- to attract tourists/students/clients;
- to attract investors/sponsors;
- to manage the inhabitants/the employees/ themselves;
- to manage the legislators and the media;
- to compete with other organizations.

Therefore a specific identity/alterity interplay must be, intentionally or unintentionally, closely linked to strategy; it may become a part of it. As there are different ways of shaping this interplay, they must lead to different results. New institutionalists (Powell and DiMaggio, 1991) taught us that organizations in the same field of activity tend to acquire the same forms; this phenomenon was named 'isomorphism'. Isomorphism assumes strong identification mechanisms: managers imitate organization forms because they see their own organizations as similar to their models. Yet there is as clear a tendency to differentiation, at its peak becoming a quest for uniqueness. Therefore one could expect existence of allo-morphism (divergence of forms), but also of automorphism (Schwartz, 2006), an imitation of its own past (as in the case of Warsaw water management), or at least the past of the organization of which one is a part (University Business School). Figure 1.4.2 illustrates the

identification with others (identity dimension: similar or analogous)	**ISOMORPHISM** (organizational forms in the same field become alike: Stockholm, Rome, business schools)
identification with own past (identity dimension: the same)	**AUTOMORPHISM** (organizations handle the demands from their environment by using the strategies applied previously with some success: Stockholm, Rome, Warsaw, University Business School)
differentiation (alterity dimension: unique, identity dimension: opposite to)	**ALLOMORPHISM** (diversity of forms: Warsaw, Business Business School, IT company)

Figure 1.4.2   Consequences of different forms of alterity/identity interplay for an organization field

variety of mechanisms and their consequences for an organization field.

A dominance of a certain form might have far-ranging consequences for an organization field. As we live in an identity paradigm, it is usually assumed that the first form and the resulting isomorphism are most common. I would claim that the other two are equally frequent, but have not been studied enough. It would be interesting to make comparisons between different organization fields, between different regions of the world, between different periods. Many noteworthy things could be said about contemporary organizations by allowing alterity to take its place together with identity.

NOTES

1 The anthology edited by these two scholars, *Alterity, Identity, Image. Selves and Others in Society and Scholarship*, is an excellent example of this school of thought.

2 At the close of the nineteenth century and well into the Depression of the 1930s, many cities owned the production or distribution of such organizations as bakeries and dairies that were considered to be satisfying the basic needs of its citizens.

REFERENCES

Adolfsson, Petra (2005) 'The obelisks of Stockholm', in B. Latour and P. Weibel (eds) *Making Things Public.* *Atmospheres of Democracy.* Cambridge, MA: The MIT Press. pp. 396–397.

Anderson, Benedict (1983/1991) *Imagined Communities.* Chicago: University of Chicago Press.

Bauman, Zygmunt (1998) *Work, Consumerism and the New Poor.* Buckingham: Open University Press.

Brooks, Peter (2005) *The Identity Paradigm.* A talk at the Center for Cultural Sociology Spring Conference, 6-9 May, Yale University, Yale, CT.

Bruner, Jerome (1990) *Acts of Meaning.* Cambridge, MA: Harvard University Press.

Buruma, Ian (2002) 'The blood lust of identity', *New York Review of Books*, 49 (6): April 11.

de Certeau, Michel (1975/1988) *The Writing of History.* New York: Columbia University Press.

Corbey, Raymond and Leerssen, Joep (1991) 'Studying alterity: Backgrounds and perspectives', in R. Corbey and J. Leerssen (eds) *Alterity, Identity, Image.* Amsterdam: Rodopi. pp. vi–xviii.

Czarniawska, Barbara (1994) 'Narratives of individual and organizational identities', in S. Deetz (ed.) *Communication Yearbook 17.* Newbury Park: CA, Sage. pp. 193–221.

Czarniawska, Barbara (2000) 'The European Capital of the 2000s: On image construction and modelling', *Corporate Reputation Review*, 3 (3): 202–217.

Czarniawska, Barbara (2002) *A Tale of Three Cities, or the Globalization of City Management.* Oxford: Oxford University Press.

Czarniawska, Barbara (2004) 'Gabriel Tarde and big city management', *Distinktion*, 9: 81–95.

Davies, Bronwyn and Harré, Rom (1990) 'Positioning: The discursive production of selves', *Journal for the Theory of Social Behaviour*, 20 (1): 43–63.

Deleuze, Gilles (1968/1997) *Difference & Repetition*. London: Athlone.

Dobers, Peter and Strannegård, Lars (2001) 'Loveable networks. A story of affection, attraction and treachery', *Journal of Organizational Change Management*, 14 (1): 28–49.

Hatch, Mary Jo and Schultz, Majken (eds) (2003) *Organizational Identity. A Reader*. Oxford: Oxford University Press.

Hedmo, Tina, Sahlin-Andersson, Kerstin and Wedlin, Linda (2005) 'Fields of imitation. A global expansion of management education', in B. Czarniawska and G. Sevón (eds) *Global Ideas. How Ideas, Objects and Practices Travel in the Global Economy*. Malmö/Copenhagen: Liber/CBS. pp. 190–212.

Höpfl, Heather (1992) 'The making of the corporate acolyte', *Journal of Management Studies*, 29 (1): 23–34.

Lamoreaux, Naomi (2003) 'Partnerships, corporations, and the limits on contractual freedom in U.S. history', in K. Lipartito and D.B. Sicilia (eds) *Constructing Corporate America*. New York: Oxford University Press. pp. 29–65.

Löfgren, Orvar (1993) 'Materializing the nation in Sweden and America', *Ethnos*, 3–4: 161–196.

Mazza, Carmelo (2001) 'En milk-shake av ord och handlingar'. in R. Solli and B. Czarniawska (eds) *Modernisering av storstaden – marknad och management i stora städer vid sekelskiftet*. Malmö: Liber. pp. 128–158.

Mead, George Herbert (1913) 'The social self', *Journal of Philosophy, Psychology and Scientific Methods*, 10: 374–380.

Pipan, Tatiana and Porsander, Lena (2000) 'Imitating uniqueness: How big cities organise big events'. *Organization Studies*, 0: 1–27.

Powell, Walter W. and DiMaggio, Paul J. (1991) (eds) *The New Institutionalism in Organizational Analysis*. Chicago: The University of Chicago Press.

Pred, Allan (1995) *Recognizing European Modernities*. New York: Routledge.

Rorty, Richard (1991) 'Inquiry as recontextualization: An anti-dualist account of interpretation', in *Philosophical Papers 1*. New York: Cambridge University Press, 93–110.

Schultz, Majken, Hatch, Mary Jo and Larsen, Mogens Holten (eds) (2000) *The Expressive Organization*. Oxford: Oxford University Press.

Schwartz, Birgitta (2006) 'Environmental strategies as automorphic patterns of behaviour', *Business Strategy and the Environment*, in press, DOI: 10.1002/bse.567.

Sevón, Guje (1996) 'Organizational imitation in identity transformation', in Barbara Czarniawska and Guje Sevón (eds) *Translating Organizational Change*. Berlin: de Gruyter. pp. 49–68.

Strannegård, Lars and Friberg, Maria (2001) *Already Elsewhere. Play, Identity and Speed in the Business World*. Stockholm: Raster.

Tarde, Gabriel (1893/1999) Monadologie et sociologie. *(Monadology and Sociology)*. Paris: Institut Synthélabo.

Taussig, Michael (1993) *Mimesis and Alterity*. London: Routledge.

Waldo, Dwight (1961) 'Organization theory: An elephantine problem', *Public Administration Review*, 21: 210–225.

Wedel, Janine (2001) *Collision and Collusion: The Strange Case of Western Aid to Eastern Europe* (2nd edn). New York: Palgrave.

Wedlin, Linda (2006) *Ranking Business Schools. Forming Fields, Identities, and Boundaries in International Management Education*. Cheltenham: Edward Elgar.

Whetten, David A. and Godfrey, Paul C. (1998) *Identity in Organizations. Building Theory Through Conversations*. Thousand Oaks, CA: Sage.

Wilson, Elisabeth (1991) *The Sphinx in the City*. London: Virago Press.

Zahavi, Dan (1999) *Self-awareness and Identity: A Phenomenological Investigation*. Evanston, IL: Northwestern University Press.

Organizational Identity as an Emerging Perennial Domain

Dennis A. Gioia

Ours is a field full of fads. Little ideas pop up periodically, run through their 15 minutes of academic fame and fade from the scene. While they burn, they burn brightly, but then they burn out quickly, leaving barely a dying ember, even in the form of a footnote 15 years on. Even our good ideas or domains of work seem to have relatively short half-lives. They make an entrance, dominate the conversation for some period of time and then just sort of recede into the background – acknowledged as important, but exhausted (e.g. organizational culture). Others are deemed to be academically dead (motivation theory). Still others, however, seem to be perennials, that appear to regenerate interest because they are seen as pragmatically important and/or theoretically rejuvenated (leadership).

I confess that I have paid scant attention to 'what's hot' in trying to decide what to study. I'd rather lose myself in an engaging issue or problem, so intrinsic interest in a topic has always been my game (although, as a Renaissance idealist, I have an intrinsic interest in a lot of games – see Gioia, 2004). Nonetheless, I do try to read the glowing embers occasionally, so I can at least avoid working on a soon-to-be-dead area in which no one will care what I might have to say.

With that little proviso in mind, I serendipitously found myself interested in organizational identity in the early 1990s because it 'emerged' from one of my grounded studies. Tracking backwards, I found that Albert and Whetten (1985) had made a conceptual statement about identity, but then the notion languished until Dutton and Dukerich (1991) picked it up. That same year I published an identity study without overtly recognizing it as an identity study (Gioia and Chittipeddi, 1991). I pursued that line of work for some years (e.g. Gioia and Thomas, 1996), but by the latter 1990s my idea half-life sensors were screaming at me to 'Get Out Now!' because this domain was likely to flame out in interest right at about the turn of the millennium. I figured the field was ready for a culminating statement by that time (the special issue of *Academy of Management Review*, 2000), so I made what I thought was my swansong statement (Gioia, Schultz and Corley, 2000), and figured to get out while the getting was good – before the identity flame extinguished.

Boy, was I ever wrong!

Organizational identity theory and research has just continued to burgeon. More scholars are working in this area than ever before. Papers on identity have come to dominate the programmes of many of our conferences, and there is a steady stream of articles coming out in our best journals. The topic has seemed to fuel its own fire. Hmmm. Missing the end of a supposed trend cycle as badly as I missed this one has not only led me to have my half-life sensors re-calibrated, but also to muse on why interest in organizational identity is like the underground coal inferno in Pennsylvania that just keeps growing and spreading. Why is identity becoming an emerging perennial domain of interest?

Here's what I think: The idea of organizational identity simply resonates. It resonates with people in organizations, and it resonates with those of us who study organizations. It resonates because it constitutes the most meaningful, most intriguing, most relevant concept we deal with in both our personal and our organizational lives. Identity is

Continued

about us – as individuals and as organization members – and it inquires into the deepest level of our sensemaking and understanding. When you study identity you are delving into the inner reaches – of yourself and your subject of study. There is just something profound about the idea itself, as well as the scholarly effort to study it. Identity also has the requisite mystery that characterizes all the great domains of study. Furthermore, it harbours the multifaceted, multilevel character that is the hallmark of perennial domains. It is a 'built to last' concept, and I prophesy that it will continue to emerge and re-emerge in different guises over the coming years.

So, for a volume on emerging topics in organization study, why would I choose to focus on a concept already with us, rather than some demonstrably new concept? Well, it depends on how you construe what is 'new'. First of all, the study of organizational identity is a relatively young field. Empirical work is barely 15 years old. More importantly, though, the emergence of identity as a domain of interest is a fine exemplar of Durkheim's (1915) venerable and critical notion that 'new knowledge' is most often created by revising what we already know or think we know. In other words, transforming existing knowledge via new modes of understanding constitutes new knowledge. That's what I think is happening in the short history of identity study. What is perhaps most intriguing about the study of organizational identity, when viewed as a 'new' or 'emerging' area, despite its strong current presence in the field, is that it looks to be capable of regenerating and continuously re-emerging in new forms. It holds this potential because it represents one of the great themes in the human – and now organizational – experience and, therefore, is not only endlessly fascinating, but also endlessly reinterpretable. Picasso once noted that good artists borrow; great artists steal. What he meant is that the best artists reinterpret the great themes according to different tenets. Identity work will continue to be fresh mainly because it will attract the attention of some of our best scholars, who will work and rework the essence of the identity theme to generate new takes on it and make new sense of it.

Where, then, might organizational identity work be headed? I don't have a clue. But, I do have some preferences. I'd like to see some work on identity creation. To date, we've assumed away the genesis of organizational identity without doing a definitive study on how it actually forms in the first place. I'd also like to see more work on identity change (e.g. Corley and Gioia, 2004). Yes, identity is deep and close-to-the-bone and difficult to change – so much so that it often appears unchanging. Yet, there can be no bona fide deep change without identity change. How can an essential concept be both enduring by definition and yet also changeable? Oh, my! A real conundrum. As the bard in *Shakespeare in Love* put it, 'It's a mystery …!' Resolving this mysterious paradox is perhaps the future of work on organizational identity. Lastly, identity can be viewed as the centre of gravity of a nomological net. It's connected to every other important organizational concept. So, let's figure out what those connections look like – whether they be connections to learning, to knowledge, to practice, to culture, to whatever. Looks like a fantastically interesting set of curiosities that ought to keep this fire glowing incandescently for some time to come, as it continues to (re)emerge as a key organizational concept.

REFERENCES

Albert, S. and Whetten, D. (1985) 'Organizational identity', in L.L. Cummings and B.M. Staw (eds), *Research in Organizational Behavior*, vol. 7: 263–295. Greenwich, CT: JAI Press.

Corley, K.G. and Gioia, D.A. (2004) 'Identity ambiguity and change in the wake of a corporate spin-off', *Administrative Science Quarterly*, 49 (2): 173–208.

Durkheim, E. (1915) *The Elementary Forms of the Religious Life: A Study in Religious Sociology*. London: G. Allen and Unwin Ltd.

Dutton, J.E. and Dukerich, J.M. (1991) 'Keeping an eye on the mirror: Image and identity in organizational adaptation', *Academy of Management Journal*, 34: 517–554.

Gioia, D.A. 2004. 'A Renaissance self: Prompting personal and professional revitalization', in R.E. Stablein and P.J. Frost, (eds) *Renewing Research Practice*. Stanford, CA: Stanford Business Books. pp. 97–114.

Gioia, D.A. and Chittipeddi, K. (1991) 'Sensemaking and sensegiving in strategic change initiation', *Strategic Management Journal*, 12: 433–448.

Gioia, D.A. and Thomas, J.B. (1996) 'Identity, image, and issue interpretation: Sensemaking during strategic change in academia', *Administrative Science Quarterly*, 41 (3): 370–403.

Gioia, D.A., Schultz, M. and Corley, K.G. (2000) 'Organizational identity, image and adaptive instability', *Academy of Management Review*, 25: 63–81.

Is Identity in and of Organizations just a Passing Fad?

Michael G. Pratt

A colleague asked me a few years ago whether I thought the 'identity craze' in organizational studies was reaching its end. I was not sure then. However, even I – an admitted 'big fan' – am amazed at the growth in this concept: from new research on the inner workings of identity construction to the emergence of organizational identity in population ecology. But will this growth continue? Or will identity go the way of many other organizational constructs and become a passing fad?

Of course, in some ways, asking whether identity will become a fad is a trick question. Not only is identity ubiquitous across all of the social sciences – it can even be represented mathematically! It is also tied to fundamental concerns of human existence – such as 'Gnothi seauton' (know thyself). While newer to organizational studies and strongly articulated in Albert and Whetten's (1985) foundational piece on organizational identity, the history of identity in organizational research extends farther back. For example, Gouldner's (1957) classic work on cosmopolitans and locals is framed in terms of latent identities. But however deep its roots, it is hard to deny that identity is increasingly in vogue these days. This has led some to question whether identity is being over-used in organizational research, thus predisposing identity – or at least the label – towards becoming passé.

I think there are two conditions under which this might happen. The first is when a pre-occupation with capturing the term evolves into conceptual 'turf wars'. There has been a lot of energy (including my own) that has gone into defining what identity 'is' and 'is not' – which is either ironic, or highly fitting, for such a concept. However, if the conversation stays here – or worse, evolves into trying to prove that there is only one way to define identity – then the life and vitality of the concept is in peril. To begin, battles over definition dominance tend to exclude rather than invite constructive diversity into the conversation. Similarly, turf wars obscure the point that no one field or set of researchers owns the term. Identity is too big for any one theory or discipline to encapsulate. In organizational studies, we are, at best, humble caretakers in an ongoing conversation about 'who we are' and 'who I am'. Thus, while people should be clear about how they use the term, conceptual wars over the 'identity of identity' would appear to have severely diminishing returns.

Second, identity is in peril of becoming a fad when it can mean anything. Having a theoretical 'open dialogue' for conceptualizing identity does not mean that anything can and should be identity (or identity-related). In some ways, this is the flip side of turf wars. A net analogy may suffice. When one only allows one definition, it is hard to capture identity (or much else) because the net allows too little in – the holes are too small. By contrast, when anything can be identity, the net's holes are too big and can capture – and lose – almost anything. This leads one to wonder what the purpose of the net was in the first place.

Going too far down either extreme appears dangerous. But perhaps their common focus – capturing what identity is – is dangerous, too. For identity to continue to flourish and enliven our field, perhaps we should change our question from 'what is identity?' to 'what does identity do?' For example, I recently read March's (1994) work on how we make decisions and was surprised to find a fair amount there on identity. But his focus is not on identity, *per se*; rather he uses identity to open our eyes to logics of appropriateness. Similarly, Sen's (2006) book focuses on the role of identity – specifically the danger of ascribing singular identities to others – in fostering societal violence. This compelling analysis of identity-in-use raises several issues for organizational scholars. For example, if single identities (either ascribed or claimed) limit choice, then multiple identities may engender choice and freedom.

Even if the term, 'identity', went away, the question(s) that underlies it will continue to manifest itself in other guises. But to ensure its continued contribution to the organizational field, I would encourage all of us to spend more time looking at identity-in-use. This involves more than re-framing a paper as an identity story. Rather, it examines how individuals', groups', organizations', etc. self-construals influence how they think, feel, make choices, coordinate, organize, and otherwise act.

REFERENCES

Albert, S. and Whetten, D. (1985) 'Organizational identity', in Larry L. Cummings and Barry M. Staw (eds), *Research in Organizational Behavior*, vol. 7. Greenwich, CT: JAI Press. pp. 263–295.

Gouldner, A.W. (1957) 'Cosmopolitans and locals: Towards an analysis of latent social roles – I'. *Administrative Science Quarterly*, 2: 281–306.

March, J. (1994) *A Primer on Decision Making: How Decisions Happen*. New York: The Free Press.

Sen, A. (2006) *Identity and Violence: The Illusion of Destiny (Issues of our Time)*. New York: W.W. Norton.

Exploring Plato's Cave: Critical Realism in the Study of Organization and Management

Mike Reed

Plato's metaphor of the world of politics as a cave in which its dwellers were condemned to live permanently in a universe of shadows and illusions has become deeply embedded in the tradition of Western socio-political thought. As Wolin (2004: 39) remarks:

> As a kind of standing antithesis to the world of Forms, the world of politics testified to what life was like when it was unredeemed by that vision that 'sheds light on all things'. Without an illuminating vision of the Good, the members of a community were condemned to live in a cave of illusions, vainly following distorted images of reality and ceaselessly driven by irrational desires…. Far from being a 'real' world, political societies dwelt in a shadowy realm, a dream world 'where men live fighting one another about shadows and quarrelling for power, as if that were a great prize'.

Considered in this way, Plato treated the struggle for power, and the competitive advantages that it bestowed, as a symptom of an unhealthy society and polity – 'as the

problem against which political philosophy and the political had to contend' (Wolin 2004: 39). For him, political philosophy and ruling alike had as their overriding objectives the creation and maintenance of a good society: politics was, at best, distracting and, at worst, evil, and hence the task of philosophy and of ruling was to rid the community of politics. Thus, the Platonic conception of political philosophy and ruling was focused on a paradox: the science, as well as the art, of creating sustainable order was dedicated to an eternal hostility towards politics, towards the very phenomena that made such a science and art relevant and necessary.

Plato Wolin continues, overcame, or rather expunged, this paradox by imposing the world of Forms – that knew only regular, ordered motion – on the world of politics – that knew only random movement and capricious instability. He fashioned a philosophical solution to a moral and political problem by arguing that science had no choice but to become dedicated to the search for timeless and universal conceptual patterns that provided the ontological and epistemological basis for stamping society and politics in a definitive image. In this sense, for Plato, social and political order were generated and secured by imposing an 'informing vision which came from the outside, from the knowledge of the eternal patterns, to shape the community to a pre-existent form' (Wolin 2004: 41).

Plato's greatest pupil, Aristotle, develops a very different philosophical anthropology and political theory to that of his master. He stressed a socio-political ontology of growth, change, movement, instability, contradiction and tension in direct contrast to his teacher's insistence on purpose, order, stability and harmony. For Aristotle, this leads to a form of political, and hence social, science in which practical reason and judgement, rather than theoretical precision and mathematical certainty, become the driving force, intellectually and ethically, for political knowledge and analysis. Instead of timeless and universal conceptual forms – which are the only sure way of cutting through the shadow and illusion of a lived existence permanently condemned to see, at best, distorted visions of a 'reality' beyond the grasp of human beings literally 'grasping for' power and the material advantages that it can bestow – Aristotle offers a vision and technology of scientific understanding and explanation that are grounded in and generated from the socio-political practices and structures that make society and polity possible.

This underlying tension between a 'Platonic' conception of socio-political theory and science, focused on the totality of unity, order, equilibrium and stability, and an 'Aristotelian' vision (Cummings, 2003) grounded in mediated contingency, fragmentation, instability, competition and conflict, has been the dominant theme or narrative in the intellectual development of organization theory and analysis for much of the twentieth century. The former vision leads to a conception of 'the political', and hence 'the organizational', dominated by the search for systemic integration, order and control through extreme conceptual abstraction, simplification and generalization. The latter vision pragmatically accepts the real world as it is and generates and embeds its core analytical categories, conceptual models and theoretical frameworks in this inherently dynamic and unstable socio-political ontology. It asks us, indeed forces us, to engage with a conception of 'organization' as a highly complex social mechanism that generates and sustains collective action or 'corporate agency' within spatio-temporal contexts characterized by endemic power struggle, ideological disputation and moral controversy (Archer, 2000; Reed, 2003). As organizational researchers working within this 'Aristotelian tradition', we must focus on the ways in which corporate agency transforms itself in the very act of struggling to generate, elaborate and impose new organizational forms and practices – such as 'network-based' structures of political governance and management – on a stubbornly recalcitrant world.

The central theme and argument of this chapter is that critical realism (CR), considered as a philosophy of social science, offers a distinctive and coherent 'Aristotelian' social ontology and political anthropology that establish a very different set of domain assumptions for 'doing organization studies' to that proffered by either positivism or social constructionism – the dominant philosophies of (social) science in organization and management studies for much of the twentieth century (Reed, 1997, 2001, 2005). In this way, the chapter develops a set of core philosophical and theoretical arguments that position CR as an exemplification of 'Aristotelian' socio-political science in contemporary organization and management studies. These arguments also set CR apart from both positivism and social constructionism – as they have informed underlying conceptions of what 'doing organization studies' entails and how the activities related to the latter are to be understood and legitimated.

Six core arguments – that, taken together, provide a general characterization of CR as a meta-theory or philosophy of social science – will be developed in the rest of this chapter. First, the case for a stratified social ontology that lies at the philosophical heart of CR. Second, the logic and implications of retroductive analysis will be outlined. Third, the distinctive conception of causality and causal explanation that a commitment to retroductive analysis produces will be discussed. Fourth, the intensive research strategy and design that flow from the previously articulated arguments will be identified. Fifth, the 'transformational model' of social action underpinning CR will also be described. Finally, the way in which CR approaches the 'agency/structure' dilemma in socio-political analysis and explanation will be discussed. The wider significance of this CR position for the study of new forms of political governance and management will be reviewed in the penultimate section of the chapter. In this way, the chapter is intended to rediscover and revitalize organization theory's intellectual, historical and ideological roots in a tradition of political theorizing and historical analysis that stretches over more than two millennia that has major implications for debates about political governance and management in the present era (Wolin, 2004; Manicas, 2006).

STRATIFIED SOCIAL ONTOLOGY

As a philosophy of (social) science, CR attaches fundamental importance to the way in which the structure and content of the (social) world is defined and represented; that is, it prioritizes ontology (being) over epistemology (knowledge) because of its core assumption that the way the world is will fundamentally shape the various ways in which we will try to describe and understand it. As Lopez and Potter (2001) suggest, critical realist ontology is focused on objects or entities rather than events or processes. It insists that events and our experiences of them in no way exhaust the constitution of (social) reality. Indeed, it maintains that events and experiences are generated by underlying mechanisms or structures and that these are not directly accessible

to sense experience or reducible to events and activities. These underlying mechanisms or structures (the domain of 'the real', rather than 'the actual' or 'the empirical') possess inherent powers or tendencies that may or may not be mobilized and expressed in specific socio-historical contexts. Whether they are mobilized and expressed, and with what force or impact, depends very much on the situational contingencies that prevail within any particular socio-historical situation and the complex ways in which these interact with underlying structures and mechanisms. These situational contingencies may trigger or facilitate the articulation and impact of certain generative mechanisms but they may just as well prevent them from being expressed at all or at least substantially mitigate their effects.

Thus, critical realist ontology is focused on the underlying generative structures or mechanisms ('the real') as the dynamic source of change at the level of actually occurring events ('the actual') and the manifold ways in which these events are perceived and understood at the level of everyday sense experience ('the empirical'). But it is an anti-reductionist social ontology insofar as it contends that none of these 'levels of being' can be reduced or simplified to another, either lower or higher, level. Critical realist ontology is also anti-determinist in that it argues that the distinctive phenomena, objects or entities located at any one of these levels cannot be assumed to be programmed by or derived from those located at any other level. In this respect, critical realist social ontology is committed to the idea of 'emergence' (Sayer, 2000; Danermark et al., 2002); that is, that the complex interaction between entities or objects located at different levels of reality produces new, innovative or emergent phenomena that cannot be derived from phenomena located at any one level of reality. It is this complex interaction between phenomena located at different levels of reality, and the emergent phenomena that it produces, that provides critical realism with its unique focus on the interplay between 'necessity' and 'contingency' as the key to understanding and explaining how the social world works and why it works in the way that it does, and with what consequences for its inhabitants.

RETRODUCTIVE ANALYSIS

Given this stratified social ontology, in which the complex interaction or interplay between phenomena located at different levels of reality generates emergent phenomena in new and unpredictable ways, critical realism is committed to a form of retroductive analysis. As Lawson suggests (Lawson, 1997: 212), retroductive methodology and analysis aims to identify the underlying factors that, often in complex conjunction, produce a particular outcome or phenomenon. It achieves this by discovering the entities that generate certain tendencies or regularities under certain conditions through a process of model building, testing and evaluation. This process of retroductive analysis 'works backwards' from the particular substantive outcomes (e.g. changes to institutional forms and/or discursive regimes) that are of interest to the researcher to the preceding interplay between various mechanisms and contingencies that produced and sustained them. Consequently, retroductive analysis is necessarily committed to a form of analysis in which the complex temporal sequencing of the 'interactive chains' through which transitions to new institutional forms and organizational practices may be generated and sustained, or stunted and terminated as the case may be, becomes crucial to model building and theoretical explanation within a critical realist framework (Ackroyd and Fleetwood, 2000; Clark, 2000, 2003; Fleetwood and Ackroyd, 2004). The process of retroductive analysis is also 'likely to operate under a logic of analogy or metaphor and to draw heavily on the investigator's perspective, beliefs and experience' (Lawson, 1997: 156). Lawson (1997: 164–165) goes on to indicate that retroductive analysis, understood in this way, will require the combination of two forms of explanation: 'theoretical explanation', in

which the identification of underlying structures and their powers is the primary concern, and 'applied explanation', in which relatively unique or novel phenomena generated by conjunctures of numerous countervailing tendencies are the major interest for the researcher. While the former is focused on general trends and trajectories – such as the putative shift towards more indirect and internalized modes of organizational control (Reed, 1999) – the latter is more concerned with providing nuanced readings of specific and localized situations – such as the emergence of new control regimes in call centres (Taylor and Bain, 1998). The combination of these two logics or forms of critical realist explanation is dependent on a particular conception of 'causality' and the model of causal explanation that it legitimates.

CAUSAL EXPLANATION

So far, it has been suggested that CR, as a philosophy of social science, is focused on the underlying structures and mechanisms that generate events and experiences rather than, as claimed by positivists, the events or regularities in their own right. It further claims that these underlying structures or mechanisms are not amenable to direct observation, in the sense that they are located at a deeper ontological level than actual events and/or sense experience, and that their existence and 'causal powers' have to be inferred from their complex effects on the outcomes in which social scientists are interested. These 'causal powers' have to be accounted for within a model and logic of explanation that rejects the conventional 'Humean' conception of causation involving regularities among sequences of events. Sayer (2000: 14) summarizes the CR 'take' on causality and causal explanation in the following terms:

> Objects are, or are part of, structures. 'Structure' suggests a set of internally related elements whose causal powers, when combined, are emergent from those of their constituents.... Whether these powers are ever exercised depends on

other conditions.... Consequently, for realists, causation is not understood on the model of regular succession of events, and hence explanation need not depend on finding them, or searching for putative social laws. The conventional impulse to prove causation by gathering data or regularities, repeated occurrences, is therefore misguided; at best these might suggest where to look for candidates for causal mechanisms. What causes something to happen has nothing to do with the number of times we have observed it happening. Explanation depends instead on identifying causal mechanisms and how they work, and discovering if they have been activated and under what conditions ... explaining why a certain mechanism exists involves discovering the nature of the structure or object which possesses that mechanism or power.

As Sayer (2000: 16–17) also goes on to note, this critical realist conception of causality and causal explanation predisposes the social scientist to 'counterfactual', rather than 'associational', thinking and reasoning; that is, the explanatory focus shifts from 'what happens to be associated with what' towards 'could these associations have been otherwise'? In turn, this counterfactual mode of reasoning and analysis gives a central explanatory role to the ways in which we conceptualize the objects of our study as social scientists. The nature of this original conceptualization will drive our intellectual efforts to identify, much more precisely, those internal aspects of the phenomena and the status of the relations between them that we are interested in and how we will formulate our attempts to account for them. But the commitment to a 'generative', rather than 'successionist', conception of causality will necessarily lead critical realist research explanation to focus on the 'relatively enduring' nature of institutional structures and the complex interplay between the various mechanisms that produce and reproduce them across a range of spatio-temporal relations.

INTENSIVE RESEARCH STRATEGY/DESIGN

Critical realist research strategy and design tends to favour what Sayer (1992; 2000)

calls an 'intensive', rather than 'extensive', approach to formulating research questions and developing ways of trying to answer them (see also Blaikie, 1993, 2000; Danermark et al., 2002). As we have already seen, CR rejects the idea that causal explanation consists of identifying statistical generalizations of empirically observed covariance of constant conjunctions of events and accounting for these in terms of general hypotheses derived from higher level theoretical principles or laws. Instead, it focuses its explanatory efforts around the internal causal powers or tendencies of the objects or entities in which it is interested – such as discourses, institutions, organizations and networks – and the complex ways in which these internal powers and relations interact and combine with other mechanisms to generate specific outcomes in particular socio-historical contexts. While extensive research strategies and designs are geared to the search for empirical regularities that will statistically demonstrate how prevalent and generalizable certain phenomena and patterns are within a particular population (of people, or organizations or institutions), intensive research strategy and design is much more concerned with what makes certain things, rather than others, happen in particular socio-historical contexts. Usually, the latter requires a combination of ethnographic, historical and structural research methods that are geared to the identification and explanation of specific phenomena or entities and the complex interactions between underlying causal mechanisms and situational conditions that brought them into existence. Thus, critical realists are much less interested in finding quantitative regularities between 'independent' and 'dependent' variables and explaining them in terms of the formal relations of association and statistical representation specified by higher level general principles or laws. Their research focus and activity is driven by a concern to specify and account for various combinations of situations, mechanisms and outcomes in particular spatio-temporal contexts and to assess what this might tell us about similar combinations in other contexts.

Usually, this takes the form of producing and evaluating different analytical and historical narratives about the underlying dynamics of social, institutional and organizational change in terms of the complex combinations of situational contingencies and underlying structures or mechanisms that generated certain developmental trajectories and outcomes rather than others (Clark, 2000, 2003; Reed, 2001, 2003, 2005).

TRANSFORMATIONAL MODEL OF SOCIAL ACTION

Underpinning the various elements or aspects of CR that have been outlined so far, is what Bhaskar (1989) has called the 'transformational model of social action' (see also Archer, 1995, 2003). The transformational model of social action (TMSA) argues that the causal powers or tendencies inherent in existing structural forms or mechanisms are always and everywhere mediated through human agency. While social structures or forms pre-date and constrain the sequences of social action that subsequently reshapes and transforms them, they are also the emergent outcomes of historical interventions on the part of previous generations of individual actors and corporate agents that originally produced them. Thus, the TMSA is based on a core proposition concerning the ways in which social structures are established, reproduced and transformed; this argues that, within any spatio-temporal context, human agents, individually and/or collectively, will be faced with a pre-existing set of social structures and the complex network of social relations in which they are embedded. These agents will then elaborate, reproduce and/or transform the structural context and conditions under and within which they operate so as to generate new forms of institutional association and organizational practice that will selectively inherent and embody material, social and cultural resources taken from previous social forms.

The socio-historical contexts in which human agents are located and operate will already be structured and organized in various ways before they enter them. This 'pre-structuring' process and its outcome will generate pressures for elaboration, reproduction and transformation that will impinge on human agents differentially located within and rewarded by the allocations of power, authority and position that such social structures bestow. These pressures will in turn generate underlying tensions between the existing authorizations of socio-political power and allocations of material reward legitimated by the 'structural status quo' and the everyday experiences of social actors that are differentially located within and rewarded by the existing structural arrangements. It is out of these pressures and tensions that the search for new forms of organization and new strategies of organizing are likely to emerge as human agents, acting in isolation and/or together, creatively respond to their existing conditions and strive to improve their 'lot' by whatever means are available to them in that particular place and at that particular time. However, their creative response to the conditions that they face and the pressures for change that they generate will have all sorts of intended and unintended consequences that will structure the socio-historical contexts inhabited by future generations of human agents. Thus, from the perspective of the TMSA, social action always possesses the inherent potential causal power to change and transform pre-existing social structures and the material conditions in which they are anchored. But whether and how the potential 'transformational power' that inheres in human agency and social action is actualized in any particular context depends upon a complex series of interactions between structural constraints and 'agentic interventions' played out under changing socio-material conditions.

THE AGENCY/STRUCTURE DILEMMA

Each of the preceding components of CR holds major implications for the way in which the 'agency/structure' dilemma that has shaped the intellectual development of organization theory and analysis is framed and debated. The 'agency/structure' dilemma has been a recurring theme in the intellectual development of social and organization theory for more than a century and its philosophical and analytical roots, as conveyed in the opening section of this chapter, can be traced much further back to classical social and political thought (Reed, 1988, 1997, 2003, 2005, 2006; Dawe, 1979; Wolin, 2004). As indicated in the previous section of this chapter, CR develops a distinctive line of argument on this issue, which revolves around the key question of 'how creativity and constraint are related through social activity – how can we explain their co-existence?' (Layder, 1994: 4). The answers that we give to this question are pivotal to the way in which we construct and evaluate theoretical explanations of social phenomena, such as organization and management, because they define the 'ontological terrain' on which these explanations are to be constructed and assessed. In other words, the answers we give to this question map out the philosophical and conceptual ground on which our explanatory theories about social/organizational reproduction and transformation are constructed and defended. As Archer (2000) has recently insisted, we need to develop a philosophical and analytical framework that coherently links 'agency and structure' in a way that makes it possible for researchers to specify 'the conditions under which agents have greater degrees of freedom or, conversely, work under a considerable stringency of constraint' (Archer, 2000: 6).

Critical realism develops an approach to the 'agency/structure' dilemma that is adequately equipped to deal with what Emirbayer and Mische (1998) call the 'double constitution of agency and structure'. The latter requires an ontological commitment and a methodological position which are attuned to the fact that 'temporal-relational contexts support particular agentic orientations, which in turn constitute different structuring relationships of actors to their environments. It is the constitution of such orientations within

particular structural contexts that gives form to effort and allows actors to assume greater or lesser degrees of transformative leverage in relation to the structuring contexts of action' (Emirbayer and Mische, 1998: 1004). Both the creative and constraining aspects of both agency and structure have to be simultaneously incorporated into analytical frameworks that are focused on 'how temporal-relational contexts constitute the patterns of response that shape agentic orientations, which go on to constitute different mediating relationships of actors toward those contexts' (Emirbayer and Mische, 1998: 1004).

This reading of the 'agency/structure dilemma' is consistent with Bhaskar's 'transformative model of social action' (TMSA) insofar as they both argue that agency and structure need to be ontologically and analytically separated if we are to understand how they interact and combine with each other to generate institutional forms and organizational practices that inherent much from the past but also break with it in crucial respects. Social structures are conceived as embodying relatively enduring relations between social agents in virtue of the social positions that such structured relations make available to them and the ways in which these same social agents creatively engage in various forms of social action with a view to changing the conditions under which they are placed. It is in this complex and unpredictable interplay of and combination between 'constraint' and 'creativity' that the key 'generative mechanisms' which provide the initial impetus and dynamic driving attempted social change are to be located. How the initial energy, drive and potential released by these 'generative mechanisms' subsequently becomes translated into sustainable forms of 'agentic intervention' that will have a demonstrable and relatively enduring impact on subsequent phases of 'institution building' remains to be seen and cannot be predicted. But critical realism is sufficiently sensitive to the fact, to the reality, that human agency, at a multiplicity of levels and through a range of institutional forms and organizational practices, can be powerful enough to break through pre-existing constraints in a way that actualizes the potential transformative power that it innately possesses. It is only by understanding and appreciating this complex 'dialectic between constraint and creativity' that social scientists can begin to formulate and test 'trial explanations' of social change that give proper explanatory weight to the 'double constitution' of agency and structure (Manicas, 2006).

IMPLICATIONS: CR IN THE STUDY OF ORGANIZATION AND MANAGEMENT

How can CR help us to illuminate the recesses of Plato's cave that would otherwise remain shrouded in darkness and cloaked in obscurity? What does CR do for us that helps us to understand the layers of complexity that lie within our 'cave of being'? More ambitiously, how does CR help us to get outside the cave and into the much wider ecology and context in which it is embedded?

At its most basic level, CR insists that 'politics', in its widest sense of fundamental contestation over the values and interests that shape our lives and the institutional framework within which it is lived, plays a central and irreducible role in framing, indeed constituting, human existence. In turn, this forces us, as organisational researchers and participants, to focus on 'the political' as that complex mosaic of relations, practices and structures through which we order and disorder our lives as irrevocably political beings and agents. As such, we necessarily operate within dynamic socio-temporal contexts that are structured and constrained by 'past inheritances' that have been left to us by previous generations.

In turn, this leads to an explanatory focus on the complex and diverse way in which 'corporate agency' (Archer, 2000) – that is, a form of collective agency with 'strategic intent' and the organizational mechanisms required for its mobilization – is continually redefined and reconstituted in response to changing socio-material conditions. The consequence of this process of 'remaking' corporate agency for the subsequent elaboration and transformation of pre-existing social structures and organizational forms also emerges as a pivotal explanatory concern for critical realist scholars in organization studies (Delbridge et al., 2006). At the substantive core of this process lies the power relations and political practices through which corporate agency becomes articulated and enacted as a distinctive, if contestable and contradictory, collective entity and the, similarly contested and contradictory, organizational logics and forms through which it is reproduced and transformed.

One, highly relevant, example of this process of the 'remaking of corporate agency' is the matrix of ideological and structural changes associated with the rise of 'new managerialism' or 'new public management' and the various ways in which it has been mobilized to legitimate and transform established notions of 'public services' in Anglo-American welfare systems (Reed, 2002, 2006; McLaughlin et al., 2002). Another example, directly linked to the rise of 'new managerialism/new public management', is the emergence of new modes of organizational governance and control associated with the longer-term development of 'network-based' political economies and societies (Reed, 2005a). In both of these, interrelated, cases, ideological, discursive and organizational resources have been mobilized by various groups, particularly by political and economic elites located in strategic institutional locations, to redefine and reconstitute the logics and forms of collective action through which 'the public domain' is identified and legitimated (Marquand, 2004; Fairclough, 2005).

TOWARDS A HISTORICAL SCIENCE OF ORGANIZATIONAL GOVERNANCE

All the previous discussion has indicated that critical realist-inspired research, analysis and explanation are irredeemably historical, contingent, dynamic, and open to critique and revision. CR has the clear potential to revitalize organization theory and analysis as a historical science geared to the explanatory problem of identifying key mechanisms of organizational elaboration, reproduction and transformation. Such a historical science will be focused on 'the view that some structures (mechanisms, objects or whatever we care to call them) are more important than others in shaping particular outcomes … what is central or most important depends on what objects we are dealing with and what we are trying to explain' (Sayer, 2000: 74). It will also contend that it is within the dynamic interplay between structure and agency where the key 'generative mechanisms' are to be located, documented and deployed in order to account for particular outcomes in specific socio-historical contexts. There is an undeniable risk that CR will overstate the explanatory role and status of 'structure' at the expense of 'agency' because of the emphasis that it consistently gives to the manifold ways in which social structures shape and constrain the opportunities for agency. But this implicit risk can be counteracted if the dynamic and creative tension between them, over a broad range of spatio-temporal contexts, is kept at the very centre of our organizational research and analysis as critical realists.

A conception of organization theory and analysis as a historical science, focused on multiple, interactive causation between generative mechanisms located at different levels of social reality and analysis, would open up new possibilities for the study of a phenomenon at the core of any 'Aristotelian social science' – that is, the governance paradigms, structures and practices emerging in modern political economies in the early years of the twenty-first century (Ezzamel and Reed, 2008, forthcoming). Debate over the logics, forms and practices of governance emerging in the 'knowledge-based economies and societies' has dominated social science research and analysis for over two decades or more. These debates have coalesced around the complex interplay between a series of 'disjunctive' economic, technological, cultural, political and social changes

that putatively have transformed established governance structures and practices through which socio-political power has been institutionalized and mobilized in the post-Second World War era (Sennett, 2006). A deepening 'legitimation crisis' in 'state-centred' forms of political representation and administrative co-ordination is seen to be paralleled by a 'managerial crisis' in 'corporate-centred' forms of economic organization and political control (Jessop, 2002; Harvey, 2003; Reed, 2005a). In conjunction, these emerging crises in established forms of governance seem to promise radical innovation and change in the ways in which we are ruled and the manner in which such rule is legitimated. New forms of governance, usually theorized in relation to the key concept of 'network-based' structures of political rule and administrative management (Reed, 2005a), are seen to be emerging out of the complex interaction between the weakening power of 'state-centred' authority and the implosion of 'corporatist-based' systems of bureaucratic control (Castells, 2000; Jessop, 2002; Wolin, 2004).

A critical realist-inspired historical science of organizational forms and managerial practices would seem to be ideally placed to make a vital contribution to these contemporary 'governance debates' and their longer-term implications for policy development and implementation (Whitley, 2000; Clark, 2000, 2003; Reed, 2004). This is so to the extent that it would help us to understand and explain the complex chains of interaction between underlying causal mechanisms that are generating the dynamic tensions and pressures for radical changes in governance regimes, at different levels of political rule and analysis, and the responses being made by corporate elites and organizational stakeholder groups to these, potentially destabilizing, transformations. These collective responses to developing 'governance crises and instabilities' in the contemporary era will generate new forms and practices of governance that will, in time, shape the 'institutional legacies' inherited by future generations of social actors and corporate agents.

In this way, we may begin to bring a little more light into Plato's darkened cave and to see a little more clearly as to what is actually going on and why it is going on in this way rather than in any other way. We may begin, in other words, to see 'the political', and hence 'the organizational', as a necessary and vital feature of social life at any time and in any place when and where human beings come together to fashion the institutional arrangements through which they attempt to align collective needs and individual interests.

REFERENCES

Ackroyd, S. and Fleetwood, S. (eds) (2000) *Realist Perspectives on Management and Organization.* London: Routledge.

Archer, M. (1995) *Realist Social Theory: The Morphogenetic Approach.* Cambridge: Cambridge University Press.

Archer, M. (2000) *Being Human: The Problem of Human Agency.* Cambridge: Cambridge University Press.

Archer, M. (2003) *Structure, Agency and the Internal Conversation.* Cambridge: Cambridge University Press.

Bhaskar, R. (1989) *Reclaiming Reality.* London: Verso.

Blaikie, N. (1993) *Approaches to Social Inquiry.* Oxford: Polity Press.

Blaikie, N. (2000) *Designing Social Research.* Oxford: Polity Press.

Castells, E. (2000) *The Rise of Network Society.* Oxford: Blackwell.

Clark, P. (2000) *Organizations in Action: Competition Between Contexts.* London: Routledge.

Clark, P. (2003) *Organizational Innovations.* London: Sage.

Cummings, S. (2003) 'Strategy as ethos', in S. Cummings and D. Wilson (eds), *Images of Strategy.* Oxford: Blackwell. pp. 41–73.

Danermark, B., Ekstrom, M., Jakobsen, L. and Karlssson, J. (2002) *Explaining Society: Critical Realism in the Social Sciences.* London: Routledge.

Dawe, A. (1979) 'Theories of social action', in T. Bottmore and R. Nisbet (eds), *A History of Sociological Analysis.* London: Heinemann Educational. pp. 362–364.

Delbridge, R., Mutch, A. and Ventresca, M. (eds) (2006) 'Situating institutional analysis of organizations', *Organization* 13 (5), Special Issue.

Emirbayer, M. and Mische, A. (1998) 'What is agency?', *American Journal of Sociology,* 103(4): 962–1023.

Ezzamel, M. and Reed, M. (2008 forthcoming) 'Governance in transition?: emerging paradigms and practices in the twenty-first century', *Human Relations,* Special Issue.

Fairclough, N. (2005) 'Discourse analysis in organization studies: the case for critical realism', *Organization Studies,* 26 (6): 915–939.

Fleetwood, S. and Ackroyd, S. (eds) (2004) *Critical Realist Applications in Organization and Management Studies.* London: Routledge.

Jessop, R. (2002) *The Future of the Capitalist State.* Cambridge: Polite Press.

Harvey, D. (2003) *The New Imperialism.* Oxford: Oxford University Press.

Lawson, T. (1997) *Economics and Reality.* London: Routledge.

Layder, D. (1994) *Understanding Social Theory.* London: Sage.

Lopez, J. and Potter, G. (eds) (2001) *After Postmodernism: An Introduction to Critical Realism.* London: Athlone Press.

Manicas, P. (2006) *A Realist Philosophy of Social Science: Explanation and Understanding.* Cambridge: Cambridge University Press.

Marquand, D. (2004) *Decline of the Public.* Cambridge: Polity Press.

McLaughlin, K., Osborne, S. and Ferlie, E. (eds) (2002) *New Public Management: Current Trends and Future Prospects.* London: Routledge.

Reed, M. (1988) 'The problem of human agency in organizational analysis', *Organization Studies,* 9 (1): 33–46, Special Issue on Current trends in Organization Studies.

Reed, M. (2002) 'New managerialism, professional power and organizational governance', in A. Amaral, G. Jones and B. karseth (eds), *National Perspectives on Institutional Governance.* Dordrecht: Kluwer Academic Publications. pp. 181–203.

Reed, M. (1997) 'In praise of duality and dualism: rethinking structure and agency in organizational analysis', *Organization Studies,* 18 (1): 21–42.

Reed, M. (1999) 'From the cage to the gaze?: the dynamics of organizational control in late modernity', in G. Morgan and L. Engwall (eds), *Regulation and Organizations: International Perspectives.* London: Routledge. pp. 50–68.

Reed, M. (2001) 'Organization, trust and control: a realist analysis', *Organization Studies,* 22 (2): 201–203.

Reed, M. (2003) 'The agency/structure dilemma in organization theory: open doors and brick walls', in H. Tsoukas and C. Knudsen (eds), *The Oxford Handbook of Organization Theory.* Oxford: Oxford University Press. pp. 289–309.

Reed, M. (2004) 'New managerialism and changing forms of organizational governance', in H. Dumez (ed.), *Gouverner les Organizations*. Paris: L'Harmattan Ecole Polytechnique. pp. 287–312.

Reed, M. (2005) 'Reflections on the realist turn in organization and management studies', *Journal of Management Studies*, 42 (8): 1621–1644.

Reed, M. (2005a) 'Beyond the iron cage?: bureaucracy and democracy in the knowledge economy and society', in P. Dugay (ed.), *The Values of Bureaucracy*. Oxford: Oxford University Press. pp. 115–140.

Reed, M. (2006) 'Organizational theorizing: a historically contested terrain', in S. Clegg, C. Hardy and W. Nord (eds), *The Handbook of Organizational Studies*, 2nd edn. London: Sage.

Sayer, A. (1992) *Method in Social Science*. London: Routledge.

Sayer, A. (2000) *Realism and Social Science*. London: Sage.

Sennett, R. (2006) *The Culture of the New Capitalism*. New Haven: Yale University Press.

Taylor, P. and Bain, P. (1998) 'An assembly line in the head: the call centre labour process', *Industrial Relations Journal*, 30 (2): 101–117.

Whitley, R. (2000) *Divergent Capitalisms: The Social Structuring and Change of Business Systems*. Oxford: Oxford University Press.

Wolin, S. (2004) *Politics and Vision*, (Expanded edition). Princeton: University of Princeton Press.

Philosophy as Core Competence

Martin Kilduff and Ajay Mehra

Organizations are knowledge creating entities, exploiting core competencies to produce new ideas, and creating new systems to test those ideas in terms of actual services and products. But the field of organizational studies has failed to recognize the importance of a set of theoretical discourses especially tailored to the analysis of how knowledge is systematically produced. The philosophy of science focuses on how knowledge about the world is discovered and articulated, with especial emphasis on the progress of scientific knowledge over time. In positing different lenses with which to understand organizations, organizational studies has reached for metaphorical understanding of sociological processes of power and influence, but has neglected philosophical theories of scientific progress. In viewing organizations from the perspective of a contrasting set of philosophy of science theories, we illuminate unexpected aspects of organizational theorizing and functioning.

THE CYBERNETIC ORGANIZATION

From a logical positive perspective (Blumberg and Feigl, 1931), the success or failure of a knowledge-producing organization is directly related to the extent to which its guiding theory (core principles, strategy) can be progressively reduced to a set of operating routines directing inquiry to the world of individual experience. To the extent that the 'vision' of the organization remains untranslatable into operating routines, then knowledge production will be limited. These ideas have been vastly influential in organization theory in such diverse areas as the management-by-objectives movement and the Carnegie school emphasis on production through hierarchically arranged and carefully specified routines. As a theory of scientific progress, logical positivism separates theory from observation, and posits a correspondence between linguistic statements and facts in the world. A logical positivist lens highlights the organization as a computer program simulating reality, with employees and machines interchangeable implementers of logical routines.

THE PARLIAMENTARY DEMOCRACY

An alternative to this cybernization of knowledge production was offered by Karl Popper's (1935/1959) emphasis on three-cornered fights between rival theories and evidence. The successful knowledge-producing and learning organization, from this perspective, resembles a parliamentary democracy – Italian style – in which an endless cycle of competing top management teams put forward differing bold, specific and falsifiable visions of the way forward. Governing coalitions are replaced on the basis of actual or potential success in predicting and controlling events. The organization is always

Continued

provisional in its adherence to theories that can be falsified by severe market tests, and is open to bold challenges to accepted wisdom.

THE DARWINIAN ORGANIZATION

Imre Lakatos (1970) built upon this Popperian/Darwinian argument, to articulate more clearly the basis upon which organizational members could rationally choose between competing claims for how the core competencies of the organization (its 'DNA') could be exploited and renewed. As the organizational ecologists have reminded us, the organization is founded around a core set of taken-for-granted assumptions (termed the 'hard core' by Lakatos). From these core assumptions, new ideas and theories of the world are extrapolated. To maximize its production of knowledge, the organization must differentiate between its hard-core assumptions and the less fundamental ideas that make up the periphery. Lakatos states that the members of the organization should judge the way forward based on the extent to which new ideas signal new empirical phenomena unnoticed or neglected before, and the extent to which these new phenomena find corroboration in the empirical research performed.

THE ORWELLIAN ORGANIZATION

A different picture is painted by Thomas Kuhn (1970) in his emphasis on the importance of a reigning paradigm for the successful production of knowledge. It is the strong culture organization (within which members are united by their adherence to an ideology) that will successfully grind nature down into its components and reveal its secrets, according to Kuhn. The organization has a set of core assumptions – about this both Lakatos and Kuhn agree. But in Kuhn's version there is no competing set of derivations from these core assumptions vying for the attention of members; nor is there any alternative paradigm to which organizational members can switch. The success of the organization in its pursuit of knowledge depends upon focusing relentlessly on the puzzles to be solved as articulated by the paradigm. Ironically, it is this very puzzle-solving activity that identifies stubborn anomalies and prepares the way for the demise of the organization, and its replacement by a totally different challenger. The successful organization is Orwellian, inertial, and incapable of learning radically different ideas or operations.

THE ORGANIZATION AS MARKET

As a contrast to this one-party state version of organizational success, Paul Feyerabend (1970) put forward an organization-as-market view of knowledge production: to succeed in the production of knowledge, nothing must be placed in the way of the imaginative activities of organizational members. Individual freedom to think and imagine is preferable over any systematic, bureaucratic method that could be devised for knowledge production. The Darwinian approach is here taken to an extreme in Feyerabend's emphasis on the importance of knowledge producers relentlessly pursuing their own initiatives – many mutually exclusive – in competition for resources. The high-tech world of Silicon Valley is prefigured in this competitive free-for-all description of how knowledge can be produced in the absence of shared assumptions, systematic control over decision premises or shared rules of operation.

Thus, the discourses of the philosophy of science, to the extent that they model the rational production of knowledge, offer theories of organization. Clearly, logical positivism has been vastly influential as a theory of knowledge production, especially in its instantiation in the work of the Carnegie school. It is time to examine discursive alternatives to this powerful approach. If organizations are knowledge-producing entities and if organizational members are personal scientists busy testing their theories against experience, then the discourse of the philosophy of science may provide both macro and micro implications for organizational theory and research.

REFERENCES

Blumberg, A.E., and Feigl, H. (1931) 'Logical positivism'. *The Journal of Philosophy*, 28: 281–296.
Feyerabend, P. (1970) 'Consolations for the specialist' in Imre Lakatos and Alan Musgrave (eds), *Criticism and the Growth of Knowledge*. New York: Cambridge University Press. pp. 197–230.
Kuhn, T.S. (1970) *The Structure of Scientific Revolutions*, 2nd edn. Chicago: University of Chicago Press.
Lakatos, I. (1970) 'Falsification and the methodology of scientific research programs', in Imre Lakatos and Alan Musgrave (eds), *Criticism and the Growth of Knowledge*. New York: Cambridge University Press. pp. 132–196.
Popper, K. (1959) *The Logic of Scientific Discovery*. London: Routledge.

For Informed Pluralism, Broad Relevance and Critical Reflexivity

Hugh Willmott

The future of management and organization studies (MOS) will be sealed by developments in the wider social, political and intellectual milieu in which it evolves, and to which it contributes. Whatever the course of its future development, however, it seems likely that MOS will continue to be buffeted by demands for academic rigour and applicability to practice. When subjected to these pressures, the recurrent risk is not that the field will buckle or disintegrate, but rather that it will bring about a reactionary return to some mythical, apparently authoritative notion of rigour and a narrow sense of relevance in which the particular demands of privileged groups, such as managers, policy makers and academics, are represented as universally valued.

My hope is that this reactionary scenario will not unfold, and that, instead, a flourishing of informed pluralism will characterize the future development of the field. Pluralism is a powerful antidote to the prospect of a regressive trajectory. Pluralism is 'healthy' not just because it fosters diversity but because, in principle, it helps to problematize and temper knowledges that claim sole authority, and thereby underwrite dogma and tyranny. Informed pluralism is distinguished by an incorporation within each knowledge claim, or contribution, of a critical awareness of its own limits. The basis of this awareness is an in-depth appreciation of, and not just a passing acquaintance with, the nature and value of alternative methodological strategies for constructing our studies, and associated knowledges, of management and organization.

Informed pluralism is also 'healthy' when it challenges an easy, repressively tolerant, assumption that each contribution to, or 'image' of, organization and management provides a unique and necessary part of a larger picture. What might be termed the jigsaw concept of MOS slides past a close examination of how approaches may be in opposition, rather than complementary, to each other. Some pieces may fit together but others form parts of very different puzzles. The jigsaw notion of pluralism simply ignores the divergent epistemological and ontological assumptions upon which the distinctiveness of the different puzzles and associated 'pieces' is founded. And it also slides past consideration of the practical outcome, or relevance, of giving much greater attention to some of these puzzles and pieces than to others.

So, I would hope to see the flourishing of an informed, radical pluralism where there is an inquisitiveness about, and reflection upon, the value-basis and the likely outcomes, intended and unanticipated, of different ways of constructing knowledges of management and organization. Associated with this hope for the future is a balancing of knowledge being evaluated in relation to conceptions of epistemological correctness or ontological credibility by giving greater weight to an assessment of its practical effects. This emphasis is informed by a belief that the value of knowledge ultimately resides in its broad relevance notably, its capacity to enrich collective self-understanding and thereby provide the basis for sustaining and improving the quality of life – ecologically as well as socially – for all sensuous beings. It seems to me that many different kinds of power-knowledge – from the instrumental to the meditative – can contribute to this capability; and hence my emphasis upon pluralism in order to counter contemporary vulnerabilities to the effects of a monist conception of scientific enquiry which is corrosive of collective self-determination.

With this, we require critical reflexivity. By this, I mean a capacity to recognize the inescapably partial and constructed foundation of all knowledge claims about management and/or organization. It involves an awareness of the contingencies of knowledge production, embedded as knowledge inescapably is in particular traditions, disciplines, methodological protocols, temporal contexts, etc. In addition to reminding us particularity of what counts as knowledge – for example, in its dependence upon the privileging of particular epistemological and ontological assumptions – critical reflexivity heightens attentiveness to its (unavoidable) ethical significance with regard to the consequences of taking knowledge claims to be true. So, when practising an informed pluralism, critical reflexivity would be incorporated in assessing the value and validity of diverse forms of analyses in relation to ethical criteria, and not predominantly in relation to its degree of compliance or correspondence with a projected ontology, whether 'realist' or 'constructionist' in formulation; or its adherence to a favoured set of methodological protocols, whether 'quantitative' or 'qualitative' in attribution. Of course, ethical criteria are themselves diverse, contested and open to debate; and it is in the explication of currently unacknowledged ethical implications of knowledge production as well as in the debating of relevant ethical criteria that MOS, guided by informed pluralism, can make a useful contribution.

The interrelationship of informed pluralism, broad relevance and critical reflexivity is at the core of my hopes for the future of MOS. A key resource and inspiration for this possible future has been, and is likely to continue to be, the strands of knowledge production that comprise the rich and contested traditions of critical thinking as applied to, and developed within, MOS: critical hermeneutics, Critical Theory, radical feminism, poststructuralism, critical realism, post-Marxism, postcolonialism, etc. Such critical thinking has taken MOS in a pluralist direction that is more informed about the differences and limitations of varied forms of analysis; it has promoted a broader conception of relevance; and it has stimulated a critical reflexivity about knowledge-claims. By valuing and nurturing a plurality of traditions, MOS is more likely to interrogate topics and to engage with diverse audiences in ways that are attentive to its broader social and ecological relevance and consequences. But, to return to the historical embeddedness of MOS, the extent to which such a future is realized will depend, above all else, upon the conduciveness and receptivity of the broader milieu in which MOS develops; and, more specifically, the extent to which this milieu is supportive of an informed pluralism wherein the diverse strands of critical management studies can be expected to play a key role.

REFERENCES

Alvesson, M. and Willmott, H.C. (1996) *Making Sense of Management: A Critical Introduction*. London: Sage.

Willmott, H.C. (2003) 'Organizational theory as critical science: The case of 'New Organizational Forms', in C. Knudsen and H. Tsoukas (eds), *Organization Theory as Science: Prospects and Limitations*. Oxford: Oxford University Press. pp. 88–112.

Willmott, H.C. (2005) 'Theorizing contemporary control: Some poststructuralist responses to some critical realist questions', *Organization*, 12 (5): 747–780.

Revisualizing Images in Leadership and Organization Studies

Eric Guthey and Brad Jackson

We argue that visual images function as complex sites of social interaction and struggle over meaning. On the basis of this argument, we propose to re-visualize the concept of image in leadership and organization studies. These fields have produced important research on leadership images (Chen and Meindl, 1991); on construed external image (Dutton and Dukerich, 1991); on organizational identity and image (Gioia et al., 2000); and on professional image (Roberts, 2005). Such approaches invoke many visual metaphors – mirrors, eyes, pictures, and so on – but define image as an abstract, collective mental impression or schema. None of this work analyses an actual visual image or explores the centrality of visual images to the construction of 'image' in the abstract. Studies of visual evidence in organizational research do not engage the image literature (Dougherty and Kunda, 1990; Anderson and Imperia, 1992; Larsen and Schultz, 1992; Preston et al., 1996). Leadership and organization scholars have employed the term 'image' metaphorically to refer to 'the pictures in our heads'. It is time to look at the pictures in front of our eyes as well.

Visual images saturate contemporary society via ever proliferating media channels. Photographs construct and certify who we are to the point where identity has become 'inconceivable without photography' (Schroeder, 2002: 14). Photographs of top management figures often represent their organizations in an explicitly visual, even iconic sense. The corporate quest for a human face and the voracious appetite of the business media drive the production and circulation of visual images of business leaders. By investigating such images, we call into question key assumptions behind the concept of image itself (Guthey and Jackson, 2005). We outline here empirical, methodological, and theoretical aspects of this contribution, and develop an approach for analysing CEO portraits as complex forms of visual communication, interaction, and conflict over the representation of individual leaders and business leadership writ large.

With respect to the empirical contributions, we can't literally 'see' the pictures in anyone's head. From this perspective the image literature pursues an elusive and aggregate construct, pieced together by researchers from multiple texts or survey questionnaires. But visual images are tangible objects – they are 'sights' or 'sets of appearances' reproduced in material form (Berger, 1972). They are physically present and directly accessible. They are produced and consumed by many actors under diverse constraints in specific contexts. They are multiple, because many images compete for attention and predominance, and multivalent, because individual images contain within themselves multiple levels of meaning that interact and often conflict with each other.

In methodological terms, the complexity of visual representation encourages scholars of organization to look to other disciplines for new ways to understand images. Schroeder's work (2002, 2006) on visual issues in marketing and consumption demonstrates how such cross-fertilization can proceed. The effort requires getting used to the fact that other disciplines make different claims to insight and objectivity (Daft, 1980; Taylor and Hansen, 2005). A focus on visual images also makes clear that all approaches to image involve interpretation, and that no interpretation enjoys a monopoly on meaning. Not only the content of visual images, but their aesthetic and stylistic aspects can be understood productively as forms of social process and interaction (Rosenblum, 1978).

To exemplify these points, we draw together concepts from photography criticism, film studies, and art history to analyse two photo illustrations of Carly Fiorina that appeared in *The New York Times* after her ouster as CEO of Hewlett Packard (HP) in February of 2005. We describe these illustrations as metapictures, a special class of images that foreground the very representational conventions according to which they produce meaning. We investigate these conventions through the analytical categories of frame, gaze, and period eye. The concept of frame foregrounds the multiple ways in which images can be viewed. The concept of gaze highlights the interaction of multiple viewing subjects within any given image. The notion of the period eye places limits on the potential meanings these active subjects can produce by specifying the context-bound habits, skills and predispositions that influence image production and consumption. Together, these concepts help foreground the social and relational nature of image production and interpretation. We conclude with a discussion of how the study of visual images can help cultivate within organization studies a cultural materialist perspective and social theory of practice that can enhance not only the image literature, but other research streams as well.

METAPICTURES

The forced resignation of Carly Fiorina was a remarkably visual event. Within hours HP had removed her portrait from its place of prominence on its website. By the next day, several news outlets had produced pictorial essays about her career, highlighting the staggering volume of visual images of Fiorina already in circulation (*Business Week*, 2005; *Forbes*, 2005; *Fortune*, 2005). 'Carleton S. Fiorina has been to business magazines what Diana was to their general-interest counterparts: a princess', declared *The New York Times*. 'Put her on the cover and copies fly off the rack' (Seelye, 2005). Others argued that Fiorina's high profile cover girl of the computer industry had contributed to her downfall by creating a gulf between the carefully managed images and HP's performance under her leadership.

Amidst this swirl of images and arguments about them, *The New York Times* published two intriguing photo illustrations. In the first, several hands hold up three picture frames for display (Fig. 1.6.1). The far left frame contains a photo of Fiorina smiling in front of a backdrop plastered with HP and Compaq

Figure 1.6.1   (Bilton, 2005) Reprinted with permission from Nick Bilton/New York Times.

company logos. The middle frame shows Fiorina at the World Economic Forum in Davos, just weeks before her ouster, positioned as if she were glancing over her shoulder at the third frame. This last frame contains nothing but empty white space, ostensibly signifying Fiorina's removal from the company and the field of vision. Another illustration, which appeared a few days later, also contains multiple portraits of Fiorina. These were printed out, crumpled up, and tossed into a waste basket (see http://www.nytimes.com/2005/02/14/technology/14HP.html).

At first glance, both images function as straightforward reinforcement for the articles they accompanied. The first noted that Fiorina had been 'the subject of frequent and flattering magazine cover stories', that 'her status (had) blossomed to that of a rock star in the computer world', but that 'in the end, her superstar status was also her undoing' (Markoff, 2005). The second bore the title 'Tossing Out a Chief Executive' (Rivlin and Markoff, 2005). From this perspective the illustrations reinforced speculation about how Fiorina's high-profile celebrity and failure to fit into HP's egalitarian corporate culture had precipitated her downfall.

But compositional aspects of these illustrations make possible several alternative interpretations. On second glance, they are not just photographs of Fiorina, but photographs of photographs of Fiorina. As such,

they function as pictures about pictures, or 'metapictures' – self-referential images that represent in visual form the phenomenon of visual representation itself (Mitchell, 1995). Metapictures foreground the possibility of multiple, conflicting interpretations, and call into question visual and referential conventions that influence their own construction and the ways we go about understanding them. We can use these two metapictures to talk about some central visual conventions behind top executive portraits in the media.

FRAME

The most striking aspect of the first illustration is the many frames within the frame. The simple notion of a frame as the edge or border of an image conceals behind it a wealth of representational complexity. Paraphrasing Saussure, Heath points out that the presence of the frame transforms the 'scene' into the 'seen' – it mediates the viewer's experience of the image by explicitly marking what is contained within its borders as a bounded representation (Heath, 1981; Pickett, 2003). Frames imply the exercise of choices about what to put inside them, even though convention diverts attention away from these choices and towards the content within.

In the first *Times* illustration, the succession of frames from left to right may appear to tell a linear story of an individual moving from triumph, to overreaching pride, to downfall. The third frame represents not Fiorina's replacement, but her erasure as a visible presence. The worst thing that can happen to celebrity CEOs like Fiorina is to be removed from the frame, because they depend for their existence on their visibility and visual association with their company. In this interpretation, ultimate power belongs not to the CEO, but to the board of directors who remove Fiorina from her post.

But the framing also works against this straightforward interpretation by referring to itself and to the entire phenomenon of media representation. The empty frame, and the artificial drawings of a frame around each picture, highlight the fact that the whole illustration is carefully framed. The 'unframed' space in between represents the world outside the artificially framed media images. Of course, this space is contained within the frame of the illustration itself, within the pages of the *Times*, and so on. These frames within frames suggest that there is no unmediated space outside the media spectacle. Four sets of hands hold up these frames for display, implying that a number of different people maintain different views of Fiorina. Two of the sets of hands criss-cross to hold up two different photos each, suggesting that individual viewers don't share one image of Fiorina, but entertain multiple, even conflicting views at the same time.

Multiple frames and meanings also dominate the second illustration, which contains five different images of Fiorina, and implies that there are many more. The fact that all of these images are thrown into a trash can implies heavily that such celebrity CEO images are fleeting, disposable, and, literally, worthless. This could imply a criticism of the arrogance of CEO celebrities themselves, an assertion of the power of the business media to create and destroy celebrities, or a criticism of the role the media has to play in hyping and circulating such 'trash'.

Fiorina's ouster occurred behind closed doors and provided no new photo opportunities. Instead, recycled images gained new meanings from the ways they were framed to serve the new situation. This process foregrounded a high degree of self-consciousness about the multiple, constructed meanings and identities in the photographs. A focus on frames highlights the social and interactive nature of visual images – because the framing of any image is not a natural occurrence but a conscious choice; because there are multiple visible or implicit instances of such choices in any image; and because these various choices can interact and conflict with each other.

GAZE

Frames objectify, gazes subjectify – the concept emphasizes the active looking that must occur in and around an image to produce meaning. As Berger puts it, 'every image embodies a way of seeing' (1972: 10). Or as Lutz and Collins state, 'All stories about looking' (1993: 187). Scholars of visual media have turned the word 'gaze' into a technical term to explore these acts of looking and the ways they constitute viewing subjects. Much of this work emphasizes that the gaze exerts power over others within the visual frame.

Feminist film scholars in the 1970s employed psychoanalytic concepts to argue that the cinematic gaze reinforces male domination over women. Building on Lacan's work equating the gaze with desire, and on Freud's discussions of the 'scopophilic' pleasures men derive from gazing at female bodies, Mulvey argued that women on screen most often play an exhibitionist role in the service of the determining male gaze, and that their visual function is primarily to connote 'to-be-looked-at-ness' (Mulvey, 1975). 'Men look at women. Women watch themselves being looked at', says Berger. 'This determines not only most relations and women, but also the relations of women to themselves' (1972: 47).

The many images of Fiorina seem to connote just this kind of 'to-be-looked-at-ness'. Several sources speculated that Fiorina became such a visible business icon precisely because she is a woman. 'She was a she', noted *USA Today*. 'An attractive woman, at that' (Horovitz, 2005). *Fast Company* magazine asked 'What if Carly were a Man?' and pointed out that 'even the most routine aspects of her life were put on display. Her travel schedule, her husband's decision to slow down his career, even impudent questions like, "Who cooks?" seemed to be fair game and kept attracting attention'. One Internet chat room frequented by HP employees featured a post titled 'Back to the kitchen, Carly', while a columnist for the *New York Observer* quipped, 'Pack it in, babe. You stink' (Anders, 2002). Articles that did not indulge in such derision still used visual images to highlight the gender issue. 'The pictures seem to emphasize (or criticize) Fiorina's excess vanity', observed one commentator. 'The words, on the other hand, seem anxious to reassure that the firing was gender-blind' (Shaw, 2005).

We cannot reduce these complex gender politics to the domination of the passive female image by the active male gaze, and many media theorists have moved beyond such blunt formulations. To appropriate the conclusion that Modleski draws from her study of gender dynamics in the Hitchcock's films, Carly gazes back (Modleski, 1988). Her sideward, perhaps knowing glance in the middle frame of the illustration suggests that the gaze not only constitutes subjects and power relations, but also complicates them. The dominating male gaze cannot fully objectify women within the frame because women often establish their own agency through the act of gazing themselves. Photographs are not the exclusive province of the dominating male gaze, but domains where power and gender relations play themselves out in visual form.

Lutz and Collins make this point in their analysis of *National Geographic* magazine's trademark photographs. They argue that such photographs function as sites where many gazes intersect – including the photographer's; the magazine editors'; the readers'; the non-Western subjects'; the gaze of Westerners portrayed within the frame looking at non-Westerners; and the academic gaze (Lutz and Collins, 2003; also Elkins, 1996). These authors conclude that meanings and power relations are constantly renegotiated at those points where gazes intersect – including where they intersect with the gaze of the academic researcher.

Although the lines of sight and the cultural contexts in question are different, CEO portraits also function as sites where gazes intersect, including those of media consumers, board members, employees, investors, competitors, regulators, and other media outlets. Because these viewing agents have different interests and preconceptions, they can frame the image in overlapping, divergent, or even conflicting ways, thus precluding a monolithic or collective interpretation of their significance. An image does not merely embody a certain way of seeing. Even an individual image embodies multiple ways of seeing, and constant interaction between them.

PERIOD EYE

The social and multivalent nature of visual images does not imply that they can mean anything at all. There are limits and pressures on the interpretation of any image. Visual style and composition exert some of these pressures. Social and historical contexts exert others. The challenge is to articulate these constraints and pressures without lapsing into a visual determinism whereby the image must mean this or that, thereby denying the multivalent and interactive nature of image production and interpretation.

Baxandall treads this fine line with his notion of the period eye – a set of socially embedded visual habits and predispositions – which he developed to connect the style of Italian Renaissance paintings to their historical and social context. By analysing contracts between art patrons and painters during this period, Baxandall details a shift away from the desirability and value of 'rich', high grade blues and golds and towards an emphasis on the skill of the master painter. He connects this shift to the rise of a new class of merchants eager to secure cultural status by establishing themselves as the arbiters of artistic merit. These dynamics contributed to the development of a set of 'distinctive visual skills and habits' that informed the production and reception of Renaissance painting. By looking at images through this 'period eye', the mind brings three kinds of culturally relative resources to the interpretation of an image – 'a stock of patterns, categories and methods of inference; training in a range of representational conventions; and experience, drawn from the environment, in what are plausible ways of visualizing what we have incomplete information about' (Baxandall, 1988: 32).

In this view contextual information is crucial to understanding the pictorial style of visual images. Conversely, visual images provide important clues for reconstructing the 'distinctive social experiences' out of which pictorial styles and visual habits evolve. Both of these points are relevant to the analysis of CEO portraits, for which task we might develop the notion of the 'corporate capitalist eye' or the 'business media eye'. This term implies that the analysis of CEO portraits requires familiarity with a stock of props, poses and visual cues associated with the representation of business leaders; facility with stylistic conventions common to media portrayals of not only business leaders but also celebrities and other important persons; and experience with the now widespread practice of representing what is essentially impossible to photograph – the complexity of corporate agency – primarily by means of portraits of individuals who come and go as their titular leaders. Without a sense for the business media eye, an official portrait of a CEO like Fiorina could look like 'just another tart with too much makeup on', as one Oxford don characterized an image we highlighted during a presentation of this research at the Said Business School in December 2004.

Analysing images of business leadership therefore requires the practice of visual genealogy to place them in their proper context (Schroeder, 2006), and despite the influence of the period eye, Baxandall insists, 'each of us has had different experiences, and so each of us has slightly different knowledge and skills of interpretation' (1988: 29). Baxandall argues that visual images are 'a distinct kind of fact' that can function as historical documents that are 'as valid as any charter or parish roll' (1988: 152). He does not mean that visual images understood in the proper context can mean only one thing. CEO portraits, for example, provide important information about the social and aesthetic experience of living under turn-of-the-21st-century corporate capitalism. The sheer volume of CEO portraits in the media constantly shouts out the importance of leaders and leadership. Individually, every next CEO portrait reinforces the anti-determinist bias of business media coverage (Chen and Meindl, 1991) by carving individuals out from the organizational background, prioritizing their causal significance above structural factors, and committing a sort of visual version of the fundamental attribution error. Many CEO portraits appear to project the visible presence and authenticity considered crucial for organizations and their top executives. But these same photos can undercut the artificially constructed nature of photographic representation, corporate self-promotion, and CEO image (Guthey and Jackson, 2005).

Neither of these interpretations is more correct. That they can co-exist within an individual image means that CEO portraits are complex social facts. Previous work on leadership images takes this phrase to mean that they reflect the views of the business community, the commercial and organizational imperatives of the media, or the collective conceptions of organization and leadership dominant in the national culture at large (Chen and Meindl, 1991; Meindl and Thompson, Forthcoming). By contrast, a visual focus makes clear that leadership images contain within themselves a number of potential meanings that interact and often conflict with each other. CEO portraits play an active role in ongoing debates over the authority and legitimacy of individual business leaders and business leadership as an institution.

CONCLUSION

Visual images of business leaders and leadership are concrete, embedded, multiple, and multivalent. They do not exist in the abstract, and do not merely reflect collective agreement about the ways that business leaders get represented. Even individual images constitute complex forms of social interaction and often struggle over meaning. To understand these dynamics, scholars of organization must loosen their dependence on the certainty of empirical data and draw upon insights and methodologies from the humanities, art history, and visual culture studies. These efforts can draw from research on the aesthetic aspects of organizations (Strati, 1992; Strati and De Monteux, 2002; Taylor and Hansen, 2005). But care should be taken to avoid reifying or romanticizing aesthetic issues. Visual images of leadership are not merely aesthetic phenomena; they are products of interaction between a variety of corporate and cultural intermediaries pursuing different interests. Future research can build on the strengths of organization studies to explore the social and organizational dynamics behind the production and distribution of top executive portraits, and other visual images of leadership and organization, drawing inspiration from the production of culture perspective (Peterson and Anand, 2004; Battani, 1999).

Social interaction also characterizes the pictorial style of CEO portraits. We have employed the concepts of frame, gaze, and period eye to exemplify this point, but we do not mean to reify these particular analytic tools. Future research should explore how these and other conventions get mobilized and interpreted in different types of CEO photographs – from elaborately staged publicity stills of businessman heroes (and a few heroines) that dominate annual reports,

company websites, and glossy business magazines, to less flattering tabloid candids of indicted CEOs in handcuffs; from grip-and-grin snapshots that litter newsletters and press releases, to idiosyncratic photographic portraits produced by recognized artists that sometimes hang in museums and galleries. Research into the historical lineage of these genres can help explain developments in the representation of business leadership over time. It will be important also to examine differences in the construction of CEO images across borders and cultures, and to investigate how executive photographs mobilize or suppress not only gender but also a variety of other markers of status, difference and identity.

Research into the production and style of leadership images is important, but we also need to investigate how different audiences view them. To understand the period eye for CEO portraits, we need to find out how they are consumed. Building on methods developed to explore reputation and image in the non-visual sense, future research should include photo elicitation and viewer response surveys, supplemented by intensive interviews with focus groups, in a variety of different contexts. The resulting data need not be aggregated into one image of a given business leader. It can provide instead a deeper, more contextual understanding of the social nature of CEO portraits as the intersection of multiple and even conflicting visions of corporate and executive identity.

The point of this research would be to re-visualize existing perspectives on image in leadership and organization studies. For example, research on the social construction of leadership images questions conventional assumptions about charismatic business leadership by investigating the processes that produce leadership images in the media (Meindl et al., 1985; Chen and Meindl, 1991; Hayward et al., 2004). A re-visualization of the concept of image can extend the most promising aspects of this work by correcting its tendency towards an abstract, collective understanding of image as a mental construct or 'social representation' (Meindl and Thompson, Forthcoming) – in short, by rendering the concept of image more truly social (Jackson and Guthey, Forthcoming). An emphasis on multivalence, context, interaction, and conflict takes significant steps in this direction. We propose further that a visual focus can introduce to the study of image a social theory of practice predicated on the insistence that the cultural and symbolic realms are inextricable from material activities.

Approaches to image in organization studies and the social sciences reproduce the Kantian distinction between empirical reality and human consciousness as well as the classical Marxist distinction between base and superstructure. Future research can draw on the work of Baxandall, Bourdieu and Williams to critique such distinctions, and to approach images not as secondary reflections or symbolic by-products but as central practices in the production of social and organizational experience itself. For example, Bourdieu's concept of the habitus sought to reorient cultural analysis towards material practices and class distinctions rather than aesthetic forms or abstract ideas (Bourdieu, 1984). He published an introduction and French translation of the second chapter of *Painting and Experience in Fifteenth Century Italy* because Baxandall used the concept to reconceive of painting as a concrete practice embedded in historical and economic circumstances and ongoing struggles for class domination (Bourdieu and Desault, 1981). Langdale (1998) points out that the shift Baxandall describes from an esteem for rich colors to an esteem for painters' skills can be described in Bourdieu's terms as a shift from material to symbolic capital. Langdale also draws strong parallels to the work of Williams, who sought to critique the separation of base from superstructure as a misreading of Marx himself, and to propose in its place an understanding of cultural products and specifically visual images as active forms of mediated social practice and interaction (Williams, 1977). Because of the many obvious connections between CEO portraits and these issues of economic power, capitalist modes of production, and class dynamics, Bourdieu's social theory of practice and Williams' cultural materialism provide a solid foundation upon which to pursue research on the visual construction of business leadership and corporate organization into the future.

REFERENCES

Anders, G. (2002) 'What if carly were a man?' *Fast Company* 57 (April): 114.

Anderson, C.J. and Imperia, G. (1992) 'The Corporate Annual Report: A photo analysis of male and female portrayals', *The Journal of Business Communication*, 29 (2): 113–128.

Battani, M. (1999) 'Organization fields, cultural fields, and art worlds: early efforts to make photographs and photographers', *Media, Culture and Society*, 21: 601–626.

Berger, J. (1972) *Ways of Seeing*. London: Penguin.

Baxandall, M. (1988) *Painting and Experience in Fifteenth Century Italy*. Oxford: Oxford University Press.

Bilton, N. (2005) 'Untitled Photo Illustration', *The New York Times*. (February 10): C1.

Bourdieu, P. and Desault, Y. (1981) 'Pour un sociologie de la perception', *Actes de la Recherche en Sciences Sociales*, 4: 3–9.

Bourdieu, P. (1984) *Distinction: A Social Critique of the Judgment of Taste*. Cambridge, MA: Harvard University Press.

Cenicola, T. and Best, J.C. Jr. (2005) 'Untitled Photo Illustration', *The New York Times*, (February 13): C1.

Chen, C.C. and Meindl, J.R. (1991) 'The construction of leadership images in the popular press: The case of Donald Burr and People Express', *Administrative Science Quarterly*, 36 (4): 521–551.

Daft, R. (1980) 'The Evolution of Organizational Analysis in ASQ, 1959–1979,' *Administrative Science Quarterly*, 25: 623–636.

Dougherty, D. and Kunda, G. (1990) 'Photograph analysis: A method to capture organizational belief systems', in P. Pasquale (ed.), *Symbols and Artifacts: Views of the Corporate Landscape*. Berlin: Walter de Gruyter. pp. 185–206.

Dutton, J. and Dukerich, J. (1991) 'Keeping an eye on the mirror: image and identity in organizational adaptation', *Academy of Management Review*, 34: 517–554.

Elkins, J. (1996) *The Object Stares Back: On the Nature of Seeing*. New York: Simon & Schuster.

Fortune (2005) 'What *Fortune* said about Carly', *Fortune*. Retrieved on February 10 from http://money.cnn.com/magazines/fortune/.

Gioia, D., Schultz, M. and Corley, K. (2000) 'Organizational identity, image, and adaptive instability', *Academy of Management Review*, 25 (1): 63–81.

Guthey, E. and Jackson, B. (2005) 'CEO portraits and the authenticity paradox', *The Journal of Management Studies*, 42/5 (July 2005): 1057–1082.

Hayward M.L.A., Rindova V.P. and Pollock, T.G. (2004) 'Believing one's own press: The causes and consequences of CEO celebrity', *Strategic Management Journal*, 25(7): 637–653.

Heath, Stephen (1981) *Questions of Cinema*. Bloomington, IN: Indiana UP.

Horovitz, B. (2005) 'Media always fascinated with Fiorina', *USA Today*, (February 10): B3.

Jackson, B. and Guthey, E. Forthcoming. 'Putting the visual into the social construction of leadership', in Shamir, Pillai, Bligh and Uhl-Bien (eds), *Follower-Centred Perspectives on Leadership: A Tribute to the Memory of James R. Meindl*. Greenwich, CT: Information Age Publishing.

Langdale, A. (1998) 'Aspects of the critical reception and intellectual history of baxandall's concept of the period eye', *Art History* 21 (4): 479–497.

Larsen, J. and Schultz, M. (1992) 'Artefacts in a bureaucratic monastery', in P. Gagliardi (ed.), *Symbols and Artefacts: Views of the Corporate Landscape*. Berlin: Walter de Gruyter. pp. 281–302.

Lutz, C. and Collins, J. (1993) *Reading National Geographic*. Chicago: The University of Chicago Press.

Markoff, J. (2005) 'Shake up at Hewlett: The departing chief: When + adds up to minus'. *The New York Times*. (February 10): C1.

Meindl, J.R., Ehrlich, S.B. and Dukerich, J.M. (1985) 'The romance of leadership', *Administrative Science Quarterly*, 30 (1): 78–102.

Meindl, J.R. and Thompson, K. Forthcoming. 'The celebrated CEO: Notes on the dynamic ecology of Charisma Constructions', in M. Ventresca and J. Porac (eds), *Constructing, Industries and Markets*. London: Elsevier.

Mitchell, W.J.T. (1995) *Picture Theory: Essays on Verbal and Visual Representation*. University of Chicago Press.

Modleski, T. (1988) *The Women Who Knew Too Much: Hitchcock and Feminist Theory*. London: Routledge.

Mulvey, L. (1975) 'Visual pleasure and narrative cinema'. *Screen*, 16 (3): 6–18.

Peterson, R.A. and Anand, N. (2004) 'The production of culture perspective', Annual Review of Sociology, 30: 311–334.

Pickett, K. (2003) 'Frame', from 'The University of Chicago, Theories of Media Keywords Glossary', retrieved on February 20, 2006 from http://humanities.uchicago.edu/faculty/mitchell/glossary2004/frame.htm.

Preston, A.M., Wright, C. and Young, J.J. (1996) 'Imag(in)ing annual reports', *Accounting, Organizations and Society*, 21 (1): 113–137.

Rivlin, G. and Markoff, J. (2005) 'Tossing out a chief executive', *The New York Times*. (February 14): C1.

Roberts, L. (2005) Changing faces: Professional image construction in diverse organizational settings', *Academy of Management Review*, 30 (4): 685–711.

Rosenblum, B. (1978) 'Style as social process', *American Sociological Review*, 43, June: 422–438.

Schroeder, J. (2006) 'Critical visual analysis, in J. Belk (ed.), *Handbook of Qualitative Research Methods in Marketing*. Aldershot: Edward Elgar.

Schroeder, J. (2002) *Visual Consumption*. London: Routledge.

Seelye, K. (2005) 'Carly's nemesis: fate or fortune', *The New York Times*. (February 13): Section 3, 2.

Shaw, M. (2005) 'Parting (head) shots'. Posted and downloaded on February 14, 2005, at www.bagnewsnotes.com.

Strati, A. and Guillet de Monthoux, P. (eds) (2002) 'Organizing aesthetics'. Special Issue of *Human Relations*. Volume 7.

Strati, A. (1992) 'Aesthetic understanding of organizational life', *The Academy of Management Review*. 17 (3): 568–581.

Taylor, S. and Hansen, H. (2005) 'Finding from: Looking at the field of organizational aesthetics'. *Journal of Management Studies*. 42 (6): 1211–1231.

Williams, R. (1977) *Marxism and Literature*. Oxford: Oxford University Press.

Can a Leader be 'True to the Self' and Socially Skilled?: The Paradox of Leader Authenticity and Behavioral Flexibility

William L. Gardner and Claudia C. Cogliser

Keys to effective leadership include sensitivity to followers' needs and values and an ability to align followers' interests with the interests of the collective. Given these requirements for effective leadership, one would expect skilled leaders to be adept at ascertaining contextual demands and adjusting their self-presentations to meet – or at least appear to meet – follower expectations. Indeed, there is ample conceptual and empirical evidence that leaders who are high self-monitors, behaviorally flexible, emotionally intelligent, and socially and politically skilled are highly successful in rallying followers to support, pursue and achieve desired outcomes (Yukl, 2006).

Another common assumption about leadership that is gaining increased attention is the notion that leaders who are both self-aware and authentic are especially effective. The philosophical foundations for the construct of authenticity date back to the ancient Greeks, as reflected in Socrates' admonition, 'Know yourself', and Shakespeare's adaptation in Hamlet, 'To thine own self be true'. An authentic person is one who remains true to his or her values and beliefs, even in the face of situational pressures to do otherwise. While other persons play a key role in developing the attributes, values, motives, and beliefs that constitute one's 'self', to demonstrate authenticity at a given point in time involves abiding by one's internal principles, as opposed to the wishes and expectations of others.

These concepts reveal a fundamental paradox for proponents of authentic leadership. How does one reconcile the notion that authentic and behaviorally consistent leadership produces sustainable gains in performance in the face of evidence that the most effective leaders are high self-monitors who display behavioral flexibility? Answering this question requires a more thorough understanding of the construct of 'self'. Rather than viewing the self-concept as a singular and static entity, modern conceptions of the self describe it as a multi-faceted and dynamic cognitive system composed of an assortment of schemata that encode and store self-relevant information (Leary and Tangney, 2003). Indeed, we have many selves, and at any given moment, environmental cues may elicit a self that produces behavior that is both authentic and in tune with situational demands.

While it is possible for a leader to respond to contextual forces by adjusting his or her self-presentation to reflect salient features of the self without being inauthentic, one would still expect the leader's behavior to be aligned with core values that permeate the self-system. That is, authentic leaders are persons who exhibit behavioral flexibility to fulfill situational requirements without compromising their core beliefs and values (Gardner, et al., 2005).

Here, it is useful to consider Snyder's (1979) construct of self-monitoring which he defines as the ability to ascertain situational demands and audience expectations, making appropriate adjustments in one's self-presentations to secure desired impressions. To Snyder, the high self-monitor is a person with a multi-faceted self-concept who asks the question, 'What me does this situation require me to be?' In contrast, the low self-monitor has a stable and less complex self-system who asks 'How can I be me in this situation?'

Continued

Hence, the low self-monitor displays much greater cross-situational consistency than the high self-monitor, who tailors his or her behavior to secure desired impressions. While it is likely that high versus low self-monitoring leaders may be more inclined to present themselves in an inauthentic fashion (i.e. misrepresent their true identity, values and beliefs), there is no inherent necessity for them to do so (Bedian and Day, 2004).

If one accepts this resolution of the aforementioned paradox, a series of related questions emerge. To what extent are leader self-presentations in everyday life authentic? Does authenticity vary across modes of self-presentation (e.g. narratives, aesthetics, actions, symbols)? To what extent do high self-monitoring leaders who successfully adapt their behaviors to fulfill follower expectations and situational requirements do so without compromising their authenticity? Are leaders who exhibit self-presentations that are simultaneously authentic and responsive to contextual forces and follower needs more effective at achieving and sustaining high performance outcomes?

As proponents of authentic leadership, we believe the answer to the latter question is 'yes'. At present, however, this is an open question that can only be answered through a systematic program of empirical research incorporating multiple perspectives (e.g. cognitive psychology, sociology, organizational theory), methods (e.g. quantitative and qualitative), and levels of analysis (e.g. individual and collective). Posited benefits that can accrue from the development of authentic leaders who model exemplary ethical conduct include: (a) the development of authentic followers who experience elevated levels of task engagement, personal growth, and well-being; (b) the creation and maintenance of positive organizational cultures that promote and reward high ethical standards and behavior; and (c) the attainment of veritable and sustained improvements in organizational performance (Avolio and Luthans, 2006; Gardner et al., 2005). In short, there is much that may be gained by exploring ways to help leaders and their followers identify core values and remain true to their selves.

REFERENCES

Avolio, B.J. and Luthans, F. (2006) *The High Impact Leader*. New York: McGraw-Hill.

Bedian, A.G. and Day, D.V. (2004) 'Can chamelians lead?' *The Leadership Quarterly*, 15 (5): 687–718.

Gardner, W.L., Avolio, B.J. Luthans, F., May, D.R., and Walumba, F.O. (2005) 'Can you see the real me?' A self-based model of authentic leader and follower development. *The Leadership Quarterly*, 16 (3): 343–372.

Leary, M.R. and Tangney, J.P. (2003) *Handbook of self and identity*. New York: Guilford Publications.

Snyder, M. (1979) 'Self-monitoring processes', in L. Berkowitz (ed.), *Advances in Experimental Social Psychology*, Vol. 12: 85–128. New York: Academic Press.

Yukl, G. (2006) *Leadership in Organizations* (6th edn). Upper Saddle Creek, N.J: Prentice-Hall.

The Art of Global Leadership: Designing Options Worthy of Choosing

Nancy J. Adler

'The MFA is the New MBA ...'

Harvard Business Review (Pink, 2003)

Twenty-first century society yearns for a leadership of possibility, a leadership based more on hope, aspiration, and innovation than on the replication of historical patterns of constrained pragmatism (Adler, 2006). Luckily, such a leadership is possible today. For the first time in history, companies can work backward from their aspirations and imagination rather than forward from their past (Hamel, 2000: 10). The defining question – and opportunity – for the 21st century is that of Canadian designer Bruce Mau, 'Now that we can do anything, what do we want to do? (Mau et al, 2004)'

Designing options worthy of implementation calls for levels of inspiration and passionate creativity that have been the domain of artists and artistic processes more than that of most managers. As Harvard business Professor Rob Austin well understands, 'The economy of the future will be about creating value and appropriate forms, and no one knows more about the processes for doing that than artists.'

The time is right, as we enter the 21st century, for the cross-fertilization of the arts and leadership. 'It seems that all the overripe hierarchies of the world, from corporations to nation states, are in trouble and are calling, however reluctantly, on their people for more creativity, [more] commitment, and [more] innovation (Whyte, 1994: 21)' Why else, as we enter the 21st century, would we be seeing increasing numbers of corporate leaders bringing artists and artistic processes into their companies? Consider what has transpired in just the first few years of the 21st century:

- Major corporations worldwide are inviting a poet, David Whyte, to address their senior executives, including heavy-manufacturing companies that are not by-any-definition arts-based.
- A Harvard Business School professor chose to collaborate with a theatre director to author the book *Artful Making: What Managers Need to Know about How Artists Work* (Austin and Devin, 2003).
- The 2004 Davos World Economic Forum offered a workshop entitled 'If an Artist Ran Your Business.'
- Denmark opened the world's first business-school-based Center for Art and Leadership – housed in Copenhagen Business School's Law, Politics, and Philosophy Dept. The graduates are now among the most highly sought after job candidates on the European employment market.
- North American recruiters are increasingly visiting top art and design schools in search of corporate talent. According to *Harvard Business Review*, not only is an arts degree the new hot credential; the MFA (Master of Fine Arts) is becoming the new business degree (Pink, 2003). Consulting firm McKinsey explains that the scarce resource today is innovative designers, not financial analysts (Pink, 2003).
- Leading business schools worldwide are adding arts-based courses to their curriculum, including Wharton's compulsory MBA workshop entitled 'Leadership through the Arts' facilitated by the world renowned dance company Pilobolus. At MIT, three Sloan Leadership courses have had arts-based components, including 'Unconventional Leadership: A Performing Advantage' and 'Leadership as

Continued

Acting: Performing Henry V.' The University of Chicago's leadership course requires MBAs to write, produce, and showcase a film.

According to management consultant and opera singer David Pearl, '…business and the arts [are] not …different fields, but …different aspects of the creative process.'

The 21st century is already anything but business as usual, and most managers already know it. Options and approaches that worked well in the 20th century no longer work as well, if at all, today. Leaders today know that we can't get to where we want to go by simply using what we already know. Strategies unimaginable even a few years ago are realized daily, if not by one's own company then by competitors half a world away. The challenge facing business is to design strategies worthy of implementation, not simply to select from among approaches that have succeeded in the past (see Boland and Collopy, 2004).

The new coveted degree might become the MBD (Masters of Business Design), or the MBArts (Masters of Business Arts), rather than the traditional MBA. Why? Because the challenges we face cannot be solved with our current level of knowledge. We can't get from where we are to where we want to go by using what we already know. The 21st-century challenge is to create options worthy of choosing; and that type of creativity calls for innovative design skills, not merely the continued application of increasingly sophisticated analytical skills that have until defined most MBAs and their approaches to management.

ACKNOWLEDGMENT

Academy of Management Learning and Education by Nancy Adler. Copyright 2006 by Academy of Management (NY). Reproduced with permission of Academy of Management (NY) in the format Textbook via Copyright Clearance Center.

REFERENCES

Adler, Nancy J. 2006 'The Art of Leadership: Now that we can do anything, what will we do?' *Academy of Management Learning and Education Journal*, (in press).
Austin, Rob and Devin, Lee 2003. *Artful Making*. Upper Saddler River, New Jersey: FT Prentice Hall.
Boland, Richard and Collopy, Fred (eds) 2004. *Managing as designing*. Palo Alto, California: Stanford University Press.
Hamel, Gary 2000. *Leading the revolution*. Boston, Mass.: Harvard Business School Press.
Mau, Bruce and the Institute without Boundaries 2004. *Massive change*. London: Phaidon Press Ltd.
Pink, Daniel H. 2003. Breakthrough ideas for 2004. *Harvard Business Review*, December.
Whyte, David 1994. *The heart aroused*. New York: Currency Doubleday.

Analyzing Artifacts: Material Methods for Understanding Identity, Status, and Knowledge in Organizational Life

Beth A. Bechky

Recently, I visited my sister Stephanie in the New York suburbs, where she works as a bank teller. A few months earlier, the bank had been acquired and Stephanie got a new branch manager. Every morning when the manager first arrived, he walked behind the teller counter and neatened their work spaces. 'He is driving me up a wall!' Stephanie said, 'He keeps moving my envelopes and I can't reach them!' Stephanie kept her drive-through envelopes on the left side of the counter, where she can grab them easily when she had to turn around to the drive-through window. Stephanie told her manager repeatedly that she is left-handed so the left side works best for her. Still, he popped up behind her every

morning and moved the envelopes to the right side.

Listening to Stephanie complain about her manager disturbing her work setup substantiated my conviction that focusing on artifacts is an important way to learn more about organizational dynamics. When I pursued the tale of the envelopes further, I learned how meaningful the objects in her work space were to Stephanie – she could tell me precisely what type of inbox arrangement she and each of her colleagues constructed from the odds and ends they hoarded when the bank was bought and the supplies changed.

I already knew that Stephanie was frustrated with the minimal latitude she had in her job – everything she did as a teller was checked and cross-checked. Tellers were called onto the carpet every time their drawers do not 'proof' and Stephanie felt shamed by the managers when she made an honest mistake and came up short. However, Stephanie's artifact tales brought her frustration and lack of autonomy into focus, materially demonstrating how little control tellers have over their work. When her branch manager moved her envelopes, he not only intruded on her work, signaling his status and wielding power over her, but he also challenged her identity as a teller, infuriating her by messing with the objects that allowed her to work efficiently and were central to her work identity.

Stories such as Stephanie's suggest that there is significant value in studying artifacts in organizations. In organization theory we don't pay as much attention to artifacts as we should – objects are central to the work of organizations and our theories of organization would therefore be greatly enriched by adopting the study of artifacts as an analytic method. In organizations, we produce artifacts and use them as tools; objects provide points of contact for people and are imbued with meaning. By looking at how objects are used in organizations researchers will be enmeshed in the work of organizations, and by getting closer to what actually goes on in organizations we will consequently draw analytic attention to work, process and the social and material construction of organizational life.

As Lynch suggests,

> things become integral to attributions of blame; they embody norms and sanctions; they become (or become subject to) social control mechanisms; they enact social roles; they facilitate and defeat rational expectations; and they become material features of our interactional repertoires. (1996: 246, emphasis his)

As material manifestations encoding social meanings, artifacts have great potential as a tool for teasing out organizational dynamics that might otherwise be hard to trace. In a classic example, Cyert and March (1963) used artifacts such as reports to describe the process of decision-making; more recently

Fine (1996) has illustrated how kitchen artifacts contribute to the aesthetic work of cooks. Moreover, artifacts have played a central role in our understanding of organizational culture – because studies of culture focus on the meaning of the organization to its members, they require a thorough examination of the symbolic elements of organizations (see Gagliardi, 1990 for a broad-ranging survey of symbolic organizational artifacts).

However, in the past decade or so, researchers have begun to reach beyond symbolic interpretations, incorporating artifacts into their analyses of organizational processes at the individual, intergroup, and interorganizational levels. Specifically, researchers have used artifacts to help us understand how people maintain and legitimize identities, how groups enact membership and status, and how organizations transform and manage knowledge. These processes are critical to our theories of organizations, and using artifacts allows researchers to delve into the social and material aspects of these processes simultaneously.

In this chapter, I argue that analyzing artifacts and their use by organization members can expand our theorizing because artifacts are material representations that draw attention to the social construction of organizations, the influence of work processes, and the multiple interpretations held by organization members. I draw on recent developments in organizational theory at three levels of analysis – individual identity processes within organizations, intergroup status and conflict, and cross-organizational knowledge management – to offer illustrations of how we might use artifacts as a means for illuminating the social and material construction of organizational life. In some of these studies, artifacts appear on the periphery of the findings, but I suggest several ways that featuring the role of artifacts in work processes will open up these areas of organization theory even further. Finally, I explore some of the methodological implications for research featuring artifacts in organizations.

ARTIFACTS SIGNIFY AND INFLUENCE IDENTITY IN ORGANIZATIONS

Artifacts play an important role in the construction of identity. Mead (1934) theorized that one's identity as a body was confirmed through interactions with the objects one encounters, grasps, and uses. Further, Csikszentmihalyi and Rochberg-Halton (1981: 53) suggested that 'objects affect what a person can do, either by expanding or restricting the scope of that person's actions and thoughts. And because what a person does is largely what he or she is, objects have a determining effect on the development of the self'. Artifacts construct identity through individual contact, and through a sense of what Knorr Cetina (1997: 20) called solidarity: 'a sense of bondedness or unity … a moral sense and states of excitement reaffirming the bondedness.' These conceptions stress the identity that emerges as one uses and gains knowledge of particular objects. This identity is continually reaffirmed (to both others and ourselves) because objects are material, ever-present reminders that can be employed repeatedly to remind us who we are (McCarthy and Doyle, 1984).

Because the workplace is a locale in which people's many identities intersect, the study of organizational identity has burgeoned in the past decade. Moreover, the analysis of artifacts has engendered significant progress in our theoretical conception of how identity is represented in organizations. For instance, recent research in organizational identity suggests that people draw on objects such as clothing or personal possessions to symbolize and legitimize both professional and personal identities in the workplace (Pratt and Rafaeli, 1997; Rafaeli and Pratt, 2006; Rafaeli et al., 1997).

One set of identity studies that stands out for its emphasis on artifacts is Kim Elsbach's research on workplace objects as markers of identity (Elsbach, 2003, 2004, 2006). Elsbach shows how physical artifacts, such as office décor, layout, or dress, represent group and personal identity in organizations. She argues that identity objects are most often used

in the workplace to signify distinctiveness, satisfying our need to differentiate ourselves and the groups to which we belong. They also symbolize status, indicating prestige, achievement, or social rank (Elsbach, 2003, 2004).

Beyond the symbolic, Elsbach's research addresses the processes by which identities are both categorized and legitimized. For instance, she finds that people use different processes to categorize the workplace identities of others – those that categorize others through a detailed bottom-up process encompassing many cues have a complex sense of others' identities, while those who categorize via a top-down theoretical process based on visually salient objects develop more stereotyped assessments of others' identities (Elsbach, 2004). Elsbach therefore extends theory about identity processes by identifying the role of physical objects in people's perceptions of the identities of others. Furthermore, she demonstrates that artifacts are so important for signaling workplace identity that people feel threatened when their ability to display such material markers is lost. The employees in her study of an office that shifted to a non-territorial 'hoteling' arrangement went to great lengths to reaffirm and legitimize their identities, 'squatting' in their assigned cubicles, moving furniture and posting work plans and drawings on the walls of common areas, and bringing in portable personal items such as magnetized pictures of their children to mark their space in distinctive ways (Elsbach, 2003).

Studies of the role of artifacts in organizational identity have not only contributed to our understanding of how the display of objects such as décor or clothing symbolize identity, but Elsbach's work (2004, 2005) also helps explain the processes of enacting identity in organizations. By using artifacts, this work draws on material manifestations of identity to enable a closer examination of the process by which identity is projected and legitimated in the workplace.

Theories of organizational identity could be developed even further by considering the ways that people use work-related artifacts to construct identity in organizations, as objects are not merely symbolic but also have material effects on identity (Mead, 1934; Knorr Cetina, 1997). Because artifacts influence action and constrain and enable workplace behavior, our understanding of organizational identity would be enhanced by pursuing studies of how workplace objects act on individuals' identities. For instance, in addition to exploring the objects that people display, researchers should also explore the objects they use in the course of their work. Elsbach's work on non-territorial workplace objects is suggestive of this, as some of her informants used work objects such as drawings as markers of group identity.

Workplace objects are not merely markers of identity, but they can be integral to the development of identity itself: when a doctor dons a white coat and stethoscope, she not only represents her identity to others, but her identity as a doctor is formed in relation to those objects. Thus, identity research might similarly consider not only how a drawing marks someone's identity, but how the creation of that drawing contributes to the informants' conceptions of themselves as engineers, for example. Or, to return to the example of my sister, how does the way that Stephanie uses her cash drawer influence her identity as a teller? Her interactions with her managers around the process of 'proofing' the drawer seem to play a large part in the construction of her workplace identity, as this process links making mistakes, learning the teller's craft, and developing pride in her work. Considering how the use of workplace artifacts constructs identity would orient identity research toward elements of work, process, and social construction that have not yet been explored.

ARTIFACTS ENACT GROUP MEMBERSHIP AND STATUS IN ORGANIZATIONS

The display and use of objects is a key mechanism for signaling and representation of social membership. Anthropologists have examined how the flow of objects influences and constructs social relations; for instance, gift giving (Mauss, 1976) and commodity exchange practices signal kinship and social integration (Douglas and Isherwood, 1979). Studies of taste and consumption also point to the function of artifacts, and people's stance toward them, for signaling membership in a particular class (Veblen, 1899; Bourdieu, 1984), expressing cultural categories and ideals, and maintaining lifestyles (McCracken, 1988; Appadurai, 1986). Thus, in organizations, artifacts can be used to symbolize an individual's membership in a particular social milieu, such as an organizational subculture or occupational community. Further, such objects are not only indicators of social status (Simmel, 1957; Riggins, 1984) but also can be used to reproduce and protect status systems, maintaining a differentiated social order (Appadurai, 1986; Csikszentmihalyi and Rochberg-Halton, 1981).

Because artifacts are socially constructed, an artifact has as many meanings as there are different social worlds (Mulkay, 1979) and social groups will differ in their understanding and use of such objects (Pinch and Bijker, 1984). Organization theorists taking a grounded approach to the social construction of objects have shown, for example, how people's perceptions of a technology shape and are shaped by interactions with that technology within their organizational context (Barley, 1986, 1988; Orlikowski, 1992). Different subgroups in organizations may therefore develop their own 'technological frames' (Orlikowski, 1993) around particular objects, using such objects to enact group membership and status.

Because objects are not only symbolic, but are constitutive of status in organizations, studying the intergroup dynamics around them yields interesting and fruitful data about intergroup relations. For instance, my own research on the social construction of objects within groups in organizations explored the negotiation of occupational jurisdiction through the use of artifacts (Bechky, 2003a, b). In this work I found that the interactions of engineers, technicians, and assemblers around the drawings and machines at a manufacturing plant could be characterized as three analytically distinct but interrelated dynamics of jurisdictional conflict: knowledge, authority, and legitimacy (Bechky, 2003b). As representations of knowledge, objects such as drawings and machines were both useful for solving problems and for reflecting the status of each occupation's knowledge. The occupational groups also enacted claims of authority around drawings and machines by asserting their physical control over these objects and the processes used to create them. Finally, the objects represented occupational legitimacy: because they transmitted reputations, objects were used by people to claim standing as valid practitioners of a particular occupation.

Studying how occupational jurisdiction was contested through the use of objects enabled me to place the focus of my analysis squarely on the work process. The research on occupational jurisdiction (Abbott, 1988) already provided a thorough analysis of how professions compete at the field level through activities such as lobbying, influencing public opinion, and educating members. But this literature was silent with respect to how this competition happens at the level where the work is carried out. Analyzing artifacts gave me the leverage I needed to demonstrate the significance of the patterns of occupational negotiation that occurred at the workplace level.

A related domain for intergroup relationships in organization theory that could benefit from similar object-oriented analysis is the study of distributed work. Research on these teams investigates how to ameliorate the conflict and problems in intergroup communication that result from geographic and temporal dispersion. Several recent studies in this area hint that objects influence intergroup dynamics in virtual team settings. For instance, Hinds and Mortensen (2005) found that shared context is an important factor in moderating conflict in distributed teams. One factor comprising shared context in these teams was the use of the same work tools and processes. Further, Metiu's (2006) study of a distributed

software team in the U.S. and India suggested that elements of their intergroup conflict were reflected in the way group members used (or ignored) work objects. For example, some of the developers in the dominant U.S. half of the team refused to read the software code and documentation created by the Indian team members, asserting that it was poor quality code without even examining it. These studies point to the role of work objects in reflecting and constructing intergroup conflict and status in virtual organizations.

Given the influence of such artifacts in studies where they appear in the background, imagine what research methods that bring artifacts to the foreground might tell us about the dynamics of distributed work. Asking specific questions about software documentation, or tracking the changes that different groups make in particular, work tools would focus closer attention on the processes by which membership in subgroups influences the dynamics of virtual teams. For example, Hinds and Mortensen (2005) asked their informants questions about elements of shared context that included how frequently they encountered incompatibility between team members' tools and the differences in information held by team members. An object-based analysis of shared context could more concretely map these differences by either observing the teams' use of tools or asking more specific questions about how differences in the use of objects influenced the team dynamics.

Moreover, since we know that social groups use and understand objects differently, focusing on aspects of use and meaning with respect to objects would probably unearth new ideas about the basis of the conflicts across these distributed teams. The literature on distributed team dynamics encourages face-to-face interaction among team members, particularly in situations of ambiguity or uncertainty (Nohria and Eccles, 1992; Daft and Lengel, 1984; Trevino et al., 1987), because such interaction provides social cues such as facial reaction and body language to guide understanding and engender trust. However, one point not developed in this literature is that such interaction also allows group members to develop a shared point of reference with respect to work objects. For instance, in the teams Hinds and Mortensen (2005) studied, it is quite possible that the members of these teams that did not interact face-to-face used the same work tools in different ways, which detracted from their compatibility. By bringing objects into the analysis, the ways in which the work of these teams figures into intergroup conflict might be more clearly articulated and could therefore enrich our understanding of the process of intergroup conflict in distributed teams.

ARTIFACTS CONSTRUCT AND EMBODY ORGANIZATIONAL KNOWLEDGE

Objects play a significant role in the knowledge processes of organizations. In science studies, for example, knowledge objects are treated as social facts, and the relationships between such objects and the people who encounter them are important for revealing the social organization of science work (Lynch and Woolgar, 1988). Because social dynamics can inhere in material objects, their function is not only technical, but social (Latour, 1988; Winner, 1980; Foucault, 1979; Knorr Cetina, 1999). Also, because artifacts embed the knowledge of their creators, they can operate as boundary objects between groups, conveying information and mobilizing action (Star and Griesemer, 1989; Henderson, 1999).

Recent research in knowledge management has adopted some of these notions to explore the role of objects in knowledge-related work in organizations. This work draws on ideas about boundary objects and inscriptions (Star and Griesemer, 1989; Latour, 1986), as well as the communities of practice literature (Lave and Wenger, 1991; Brown and Duguid, 1991), to argue that artifacts are an important mechanism for boundary crossing between groups in organizations. Because such objects can be understood in more than one community, they can help solve problems

(particularly technical problems) across such groups.

In this area, Paul Carlile's work (2002, 2004; Carlile and Rebentisch, 2003) is notable both for the integration of objects into his analysis and his theoretical stance toward the groups that use such objects. He focuses on the dependencies between groups as they go about solving everyday dilemmas in product development. Carlile provides a framework for managing knowledge at group boundaries in organizations, arguing that different types of capabilities are needed to manage different types of boundaries. For instance, syntactic boundaries are those in which the differences and dependencies between groups are known. These can be managed through the transfer of knowledge via a common lexicon, and thus the objects used at this boundary are stable and their meaning is shared by all. In contrast, as problems increase in novelty, groups have different interests as well as different knowledge and understanding of objects, and therefore these pragmatic boundaries require changing the knowledge that is at stake between groups through practical effort (Carlile, 2004).

By taking an artifact-related approach, Carlile has extended the knowledge and technology management literature beyond the information processing metaphor. With this metaphor, knowledge management had been represented as a simplified process of 'knowledge transfer' across groups: for instance, turning tacit knowledge into explicit knowledge through codification (Nonaka, 1994). Carlile's studies of managing knowledge at organizational boundaries, in contrast, incorporate an understanding of the practical action, interests, and dependencies inherent in processes of knowledge exchange. Much of the boundary spanning work involved in knowledge management activities entails interactions around work objects, and the groups involved have different levels of vested interests in these objects. It is through studying artifacts that such practical actions and interests are made evident.

Jason Owen-Smith's research also illustrates the analytical impact of exploring the use of objects in knowledge work. His study of a university technology licensing office (Owen-Smith, 2005) demonstrates how associates in the office orient their work and problem-solving activities around dockets, which are artifacts that bundle the disclosures, intellectual property information, markets, articles about the inventors, and opinions of the associates about particular deals. In breaking down dockets into their socio-technical components, Owen-Smith (2005) showed that in this office, dockets enabled commensuration of deals, providing a common metric that associates drew on for their negotiations around deals. Further, he demonstrated how this local negotiation resulted in organizational learning through the institutionalization of stable rules, procedures and language that emerged. By examining the material and social features of dockets, Owen-Smith linked local negotiation of knowledge with organizational and institutional change.

These types of analysis could also help us further understand the relationship between the material and the social in knowledge transfer and learning that crosses organizations. While Owen-Smith's (2005) study of negotiations of dockets focused on local institutionalization of rules, the process of commensuration and organizational learning is also likely to take place across organizations in the same field. He noted, for instance, that the associates in the technology licensing office often conducted seminars and outreach activities to offices in other universities (Owen-Smith, 2005). We would expect the artifacts they used to accompany them during such activities, and to be useful in cross-organizational interactions.

In particular, knowing how knowledge artifacts move across organizations, and how they change or become stabilized at a field-level, would further our understanding of how knowledge filters across organizations through the work processes and interpretations of organization members. One branch of the knowledge management literature has concentrated on the factors that influence knowledge transfer across organizational units – in particular,

motivation and trustworthiness (Szulanski et al., 2004; Osterloh and Frey, 2000). Tracing the movement of artifacts would allow researchers to more directly examine such cross-organizational processes, incorporating the work and interaction around artifacts that accompanies such learning.

For instance, Szulanski et al. (2004) found that trustworthiness may impede successful implementation of knowledge transfer in situations that are ambiguous (which they define as situations in which the knowledge being transferred is not fully observable), because trust can lead to lower levels of vigilance and monitoring. However, this survey-based research presents a retrospective snapshot of the factors affecting such transfer. Incorporating an analysis that followed the artifacts involved in transferring the knowledge would provide a more complete and accurate picture of the processes by which these transfers happened. Because objects have different meanings in different social worlds (Pinch and Bijker, 1984) and because they are used by people to construct knowledge (Carlile, 2002), tracing these objects could turn up patterns of use or adoption that explain why groups that trust one another have implementation problems. A lack of vigilance or monitoring may not be the root cause of such problems; analyzing the artifacts used in cross-organizational knowledge diffusion would help us understand more about the source and nature of knowledge asymmetries.

Future research could investigate questions such as: Which particular elements of knowledge or aspects of knowledge objects were adopted, and why? How did the dependencies between the organizations influence their understanding and consequently, their adoption? By examining the use of artifacts during this process, researchers could raise questions about what happened when such objects were not universally understood by the other organizations or had completely different meanings. Tracing these discrepancies and being attentive to any disagreements that emerged would provide interesting new data on the knowledge transfer process. Doing so would extend the line of research on cross-organizational knowledge transfer beyond motivation and trust to an understanding of the power and negotiation dynamics inherent in transferring knowledge across groups and organizations.

METHODOLOGICAL APPROACHES TO ARTIFACTS IN ORGANIZATIONS

As Rafaeli and Pratt note, the recent spate of studies in organization theory that incorporate artifacts into their analyses have pushed our conceptualization of objects beyond symbolic representations of organizational culture, which hopefully will 'lead students of organizations to embrace the full complexity and richness of artifacts' (2006: 2). I believe that by being creative in our approach to using artifacts analytically, we can capitalize on that complexity in order to generate new understandings about organizational processes.

The studies in the three areas I touched on above used a variety of strategies to uncover the meaning of the use of artifacts in organizations, and each suggests particular methodological issues and opportunities. For instance, in her research exploring workplace identity, Elsbach (2004) started with questionnaires, asking some informants for descriptions of their own displays of physical identity objects and others for descriptions of what they noticed about their colleagues' displays. She followed these questionnaires with interviews about times when people felt these objects mattered to managerial decisions such as promotions. For the study of the non-territorial office space, Elsbach (2003) conducted open-ended interviews of informants. She also observed her informants in their work spaces, and took digital photographs of the identity objects in people's cubicles.

Interestingly, Elsbach's use of digital photographs does not appear in the sections of her published studies. Photographs figure prominently in the studies of culture and artifacts (Dougherty and Kunda, 1990; Riggins, 1984) – authors analyze the features of

the objects in the pictures and use them to enhance the reader's experience of the meaning. In contrast, Elsbach mentioned to me that she had a difficult time persuading reviewers in organization theory journals that her interpretations of the photographic evidence were valid and representative of her informants' interpretations. Because photographic analysis is not an established method in organization theory, it may elicit a higher standard for support than what is required for more traditional textual evidence.

Despite this potential obstacle, photographs present a valuable opportunity to delve into the meaning of objects without their actual presence. The use of digital photography to capture identity objects, for instance, could potentially aid the researcher's recall and analysis, particularly in settings with mobile or distributed work, where workers move such objects as they frequently change and reconstruct their workspaces. Another way pictures could further analysis is by showing them to informants and asking them for additional detail with respect to the meaning of the items. Alternately, the researcher could ask others what they would think of the particular set of objects if a colleague displayed them. This might stimulate thinking and emotion among informants in the absence of the artifacts themselves. It would also allow researchers to thoroughly compare the messages people believe they are sending with those that are actually perceived by others, and explore these differences fully.

Studies of artifacts with a significant observational component present different challenges. Both Carlile and Owen-Smith used observational methods in combination with interviews to capture the interaction around artifacts in organizations. Carlile (2002, 2004) used vignettes describing cross-functional groups interacting around objects such as models and plans. He gathered data for these vignettes through observation of cross-functional events as well as interviews of participants to clarify the details of such events. Owen-Smith (2005) observed the meetings of associates in the technology licensing office where dockets were discussed, and also followed up with participant interviews.

The challenge with observational methods, of course, is that you cannot always be sure that the event of interest (interaction using an artifact) is going to happen. I do not think it is coincidence that much of the research that examines knowledge work is set in manufacturing plants – the ready availability of work featuring artifacts makes the processes and dynamics of knowledge work more accessible to researchers. My own preference for studying occupations with a strong material component to their work reflects my belief that analyzing the use of objects helps me pinpoint the central elements of the work that contribute to occupational status dynamics.

A related concern with observational methods is that the researcher must be aware of the different interests and meanings that cohere in artifacts. For instance, my study of occupational jurisdiction also depended primarily on participant observation, including informal interviews with my informants. It took many hours of such observation and interviewing before I understood the different perspectives my informants held about the machines and drawings they created, and I never felt I completely captured all the nuances of meaning that existed for the different groups.

Also, sometimes artifacts do not present themselves neatly for analysis. I initially had hoped that I could trace the movement of an engineering drawing as it was created by engineers, altered by technicians as they built the prototypes, and finally, used by assemblers to build the machine in final assembly. It turned out to be impossible for me to follow a single drawing – there were too many handoffs. Many groups outside of those involved in production, such as document control and scheduling, seemed to have their hands on the drawings. While asking questions about how I might accomplish this, it became clear that following a single drawing would actually draw my attention away from the specific interactions that interested me (that of technical workers involved in

production). It would also take a really long time, and I was only going to be a participant observer in the setting for about a year.

Instead, I complemented a traditional ethnographic approach with a targeted set of interviews. I analyzed the use of many different drawings and machines over the course of my time in the field, and I developed an understanding of the patterns of occupational jurisdiction as a result of observing interactions between groups around these different objects. Further, because I wanted more information about the way people interpreted and used artifacts in the setting, I brought one particular set of engineering drawings to interviews with a variety of informants from different occupational groups and asked them to explain how they would use such drawings in the course of their daily work either designing or building a machine. This approach helped me to achieve my goal of figuring out the different meanings and uses of drawings without requiring me to track just one set of drawings over time. What I lost in continuity, I made up for in variability through observation. And by creating some continuity through the interviews around the same set of drawings, I was able to fill the gaps in my understanding of the interpretation differences across occupational groups.

In other settings, tracing the use of a particular object might make analytic sense and also be more feasible. For instance, in a distributed software team like the one described earlier (Metiu, 2006), one could examine the changes in the code over time. Because software developers are not always religious about notating these changes, the researcher might try a small intervention requiring them to do so. This would provide a detailed object for study through several approaches: observation, interviews, and network analysis. The artifact itself could be analyzed using a social network approach to trace the changes and see whose changes 'stick' over time. Further, while the code is being changed, the researcher could observe how the members of the group choose to make changes and interact with one another with respect to the code. Finally, the code could also be used in interviews to elicit additional data about instances that the researcher did not observe, or to further understand the process the researcher observed.

To return to my initial story, what do these ideas suggest about how to design an object-oriented study of my sister Stephanie's bank? If the research question was occupational in nature, I would start with some ethnographic observation of what tellers do every day, explicitly noting the setup of each teller's counter space and paying careful attention to the cash drawer. It would be ideal to see the changeover to new management, as the teller's work spaces were physically altered at that point, so if I knew about the acquisition in advance I would try to schedule the observation period to overlap such change.

Additionally, since proofing the cash drawer happens as the shift wraps up, I would schedule visits to allow me to observe that process. Given what I know about Stephanie's issues with proofing, I would also interview the tellers about their experiences, leading off with questions such as 'What happens when your drawer doesn't proof?' or 'What happens when the other tellers' drawers don't proof?' This hopefully would generate data related both to how the use of the drawers influences the tellers' identities and to their feelings about group membership and status in the bank. I suspect such an analysis would also provide data for understanding how tellers learn as well.

Given the way that object-oriented analyses have expanded our thinking about identity, knowledge, and status dynamics in organizations in the past few years, I believe organization theory at all levels – individual, group, and organizational – would benefit from additional studies of this type. Analyzing artifacts draws researchers in more closely to organizations – artifacts establish a sense of presence in the life of organizations because much of the work that is done in organizations is rooted in the use, display, and creation of things. Moreover, as organizations have become more dynamic and flexible, their boundaries have changed in 'scope, composition, duration and enforcement mechanisms'

(Scott, 2004). With such changes, the work itself becomes an even more defining feature of organizations. It therefore makes sense to follow the work in organizations, and artifacts can help us to do this. By steeping us in the things that matter in organizations, such an approach can ground our explanations of organizational life in the work, the social dynamics, and the meaning of such artifacts for organization members.

REFERENCES

Abbott, Andrew (1988) *The System of Professions: An Essay on the Division of Expert Labor.* Chicago: University of Chicago Press.

Appadurai, Arjun (ed.) (1986) *The Social Life of Things: Commodities in Cultural Perspective.* Cambridge: Cambridge University Press.

Barley, Stephen R. (1986) 'Technology as an occasion for structuring: Evidence from observations of CT scanners and the social order of radiology departments', *Administrative Science Quarterly*, 31: 78–108.

Barley, Stephen R. (1988) 'The social construction of a machine: Ritual, superstition, magical thinking and other pragmatic responses to running a CT scanner', in M. Lock and D. Gordon (eds), *Biomedicine Examined.* Kluwer Academic Publishers.

Bechky, Beth A. (2003a) 'Sharing meaning across occupational communities: The transformation of knowledge on a production floor', *Organization Science*, 14: 312–330.

Bechky, Beth A. (2003b) 'Object lessons: Workplace artifacts as representations of occupational jurisdiction', *American Journal of Sociology*, 109: 720–752.

Bourdieu, Pierre (1984) *Distinction: A Social Critique of the Judgment of Taste.* Cambridge, MA: Harvard University Press.

Brown, John S. and Duguid, Paul (1991) 'Organizational learning and communities of practice', *Organization Science*, 2: 40–57.

Carlile, Paul R. (2002) 'A pragmatic view of knowledge and boundaries: Boundary objects in new product development', *Organization Science*, 13: 442–455.

Carlile, Paul R. (2004) 'Transferring, translating, and transforming: An integrative framework for managing knowledge across boundaries', *Organization Science*, 15: 555–568.

Carlile, Paul R. and Rebentisch, E. (2003) 'Into the black box: The knowledge transformation cycle', *Management Science*, 49: 1180–1195.

Csikszentmihalyi, Mihaly and Rochberg-Halton, Eugene (1981) *The Meaning of Things: Domestic Symbols and the Self.* Cambridge: Cambridge University Press.

Cyert, Richard and March, James (1963) *A Behavioral Theory of the Firm.* Englewood Cliffs, NJ: Prentice-Hall.

Daft, Richard L. and Lengel, Robert H. (1984) 'Information richness: A new approach to managerial behavior and organization design', *Research in Organizational Behavior*, 6: 191–233.

Dougherty, Deborah and Kunda, Gideon (1990) 'Photograph analysis: A method to capture organizational belief systems', in Pasquale Gagliardi (ed.), *Symbols and Artifacts: Views of the Corporate Landscape.* Berlin: Walter de Gruyter. pp. 185–206.

Douglas, Mary, and Isherwood, Baron (1979) *The World of Goods: Toward an Anthropology of Consumption.* New York, NY: Basic Books.

Elsbach, Kimberly D. (2003) 'Relating physical environment to self-categorizations: Identity threat and affirmation in a non-territorial work space', *Administrative Science Quarterly*, 48: 622–654.

Elsbach, Kimberly D. (2004) 'Interpreting workplace identities: The role of office décor', *Journal of Organizational Behavior*, 25: 99–128.

Elsbach, Kimberly D. (2006) '"Mis-interpretation" of physical identity markers: Relating physical artifacts to perceptual biases', in A. Rafaeli and M. Pratt (eds), *Artifacts in Organizations*, Mahwah, NJ: Lawrence Erlbaum.

Gagliardi, Pasquale (1990) (ed.) *Symbols and Artifacts: Views of the Corporate Landscape.* Berlin: Walter de Gruyter.

Fine, Gary Alan (1996) *Kitchens: The Culture of Restaurant Work.* Berkeley, CA: University of California Press.

Foucault, Michel (1979) *Discipline and Punish: The Birth of the Prison.* New York: Vintage Books.

Henderson, Kathryn (1999) *On Line and on Paper: Visual Representations, Visual Culture, and Computer Graphics in Design Engineering.* Cambridge, MA: The MIT Press.

Hinds, Pamela J. and Mortensen, Mark (2005) 'Understanding conflict in geographically distributed teams: The moderating effects of shared identity, shared context, and spontaneous communication', *Organization Science*, 16: 290–307.

Knorr Cetina, Karin (1997) 'Sociality with objects: Social relations in postsocial knowledge societies', *Theory, Culture and Society*, 14: 1–30.

Knorr Cetina, Karin (1999) *Epistemic Cultures: How the Sciences Make Knowledge.* Cambridge, MA: Harvard University Press.

Latour, Bruno (1986) 'Visualization and cognition: Thinking with eyes and hands', *Knowledge and Society*, 6: 1–40.

Latour, Bruno (1988) 'Mixing humans and non-humans together: Sociology of a door-closer', *Social Problems*, 35: 298–310.

Lave, Jean and Wenger, Etienne (1991) *Situated Learning: Legitimate Peripheral Participation*, Cambridge: Cambridge University Press.

Lynch, Michael (1996) 'DeKanting agency: Comments on Bruno Latour's "On interobjectivity"', *Mind, Culture and Activity* 3: 246–251.

Lynch, Michael and Woolgar, Steve (1988) 'Introduction: Sociological orientations to representational practice in science', *Human Studies*, 11: 99–116.

Mauss, Marcel (1976) *The Gift: Focus and Functions of Exchange in Archaic Societies.* New York: Norton.

McCarthy and Doyle, E. (1984) 'Toward a sociology of the physical world: George Herbert Mead on physical objects', *Studies in Symbolic Interaction*, 5: 105–121.

McCracken, Grant (1988) *Culture and Consumption.* Bloomington, IN: Indiana University Press.

Mead, George Herbert (1934) *Mind, Self and Society.* Chicago: University of Chicago Press.

Metiu, Anca (2006) 'Owning the Code: Status Closure in Distributed Groups', Forthcoming, *Organization Science.*

Mulkay, Michael (1979) *Science and the Sociology of Knowledge.* London: Allen & Unwin.

Nohria, Nitin and Eccles, Robert G. (1992) 'Face-to-face: Making network organizations work', in Nitin Nohria and Robert G. Eccles (eds), *Networks and Organizations: Structure, Form, and Action.* Boston, MA: Harvard Business School Press. pp. 288–308.

Nonaka, I. (1994) 'A dynamic theory of organizational knowledge creation', *Organization Science*, 5: 14–37.

Orlikowski, Wanda (1992) 'The duality of technology: Rethinking the concept of technology in organizations', *Organization Science*, 3: 398–427.

Orlikowski, Wanda (1993) 'Learning from Notes: Organizational issues in groupware implementation', *Information Society*, 9: 237–250.

Osterloh, Margit and Frey, Bruno S. (2000) 'Motivation, knowledge transfer, and organizational forms', *Organization Science*, 11: 538–550.

Owen-Smith, Jason (2005) 'Dockets, deals, and sagas: Commensuration and the rationalization of experience in university licensing', *Social Studies of Science*, 35: 69–97.

Pinch, Trevor J. and Bijker, Wiebe E. (1984) 'The social construction of facts and artifacts: Or how the sociology of science and the sociology of technology might benefit each other', *Social Studies of Science*, 14: 399–441.

Pratt, Michael G. and Rafaeli, Anat (1997) 'Organizational dress as a symbol of multilayered social identities', *Academy of Management Journal*, 40: 862–898.

Rafaeli, Anat and Pratt, Michael G. (2006) *Artifacts and Organizations: Beyond Mere Symbolism*. Mahwah, NJ: Lawrence Erlbaum Associates.

Rafaeli, Anat, Dutton, Jane, Harquail, C.V. and Mackie-Lewis, S. (1997) 'Navigating by attire: The use of dress by female administrative employees', *Academy of Management Journal*, 40: 9–45.

Riggins, Stephen H. (1984) 'Introduction', in *The Socialness of Things: Essays on the Socio-semiotics of Objects*, Stephen H. Riggins (ed.), Berlin: Mouton de Gruyter. pp. 1–5.

Scott, W. Richard (2004) 'Reflections on a Half-century of Organizational Sociology', *Annual Review of Sociology*, 30: 1–21.

Simmel, Georg (1957) 'Fashion,' *American Journal of Sociology*, 62: 541–558.

Star, Susan Leigh and Griesemer, James R. (1989) 'Institutional ecology, "translations" and boundary objects: Amateurs and professionals in Berkeley's Museum of Vertebrate Zoology, 1907–39', *Social Studies of Science*, 19: 387–420.

Szulanski, Gabriel, Cappetta, Rossella and Jensen, Robert J. (2004) 'When and how trustworthiness matters: Knowledge transfer and the moderating effects of causal ambiguity', *Organization Science*, 15: 600–613.

Trevino, Linda K., Lengel, Richard H. and Daft, Richard L. (1987) 'Media symbolism, media richness, and media choice in organizations: A symbolic interactionist perspective', *Communication Research*, 14: 553–574.

Veblen, Thorstein (1979 [1899]) *Theory of the Leisure Class*. New York: Viking Penguin.

Winner, Langdon (1980) 'Do artifacts have politics?', *Daedalus*, 109: 121–136.

Risk and Organizations: Toward a Cultural-Symbolic Perspective

Robert P. Gephart, Jr., Cagri Topal and Michael Kulicki

The study of risk in contemporary social life has become 'one of the most lively areas of theoretical debate in social and cultural theories in recent times' (Lupton, 1999a: 1). Although some organizational scholars have addressed risks relevant to organizations (e.g. Gephart, 1997), the field of organizational scholarship has not accorded the topic of risk, the centrality or concern that it has achieved in social theory. Further, where risk has been explicitly addressed in organizational research, the cognitive science approach has often been adopted. The cognitive science approach presumes risk is an objective phenomenon subject to quantification. Socio-cultural theories of risk contrast with prevailing cognitive science models of risk and emphasize the social and cultural contexts in which risk is understood, negotiated and interpreted (Lupton, 1999b).

Socio-cultural theories of risk hold promise for informing organization studies and providing alternative and new insights into organizational and social phenomena. The cultural-symbolic approach to risk is evidenced by the work of Mary Douglas (e.g. 1966). According to this view, risk is never fully objective or knowable outside of belief systems and moral positions. Risks are always embedded in cultures which give them meaning. The meaning of risk is neither static nor objective, but is constantly constructed and negotiated.

Following this reasoning, risks which are noticed and addressed are those risks connected with legitimating moral principles in culture which transgress moral-cultural boundaries and threaten social disorder. Douglas' work suggests that in individualistic societies or organizations, individuals are held responsible for risks and dangers since social logics impute agency to individuals for untoward events or for failure to respond effectively to such events (Lupton, 1999b). Individuals are not only the building blocks of social order but also the main threat to the same order. Thus, considerable risk sensemaking is directed at locating individuals as sources of risks and blaming individuals for risks.

From an organizational perspective, the cultural-symbolic approach suggests we need to understand risks as these are conceived by local actors and to understand whether and how these risks produce fear and anxiety. One would expect that events or actions which are likely to transgress social boundaries and disrupt social order will be conceived as risky and stressful. In individualistic societies, considerable sensemaking would be expected to be oriented to individuals as sources of risks or individuals' failure to manage risk.

A cultural-symbolic approach to risk would thus examine the organizational phenomena conceived as risky and the meanings given to risky events. Different groups would be expected to hold different views of risks. Social interaction and conversation would be expected to address the meaning and validity of risks. In addition, sensemaking would be expected to address how one can manage these risks to restore a sense of social order that has been disrupted.

The events of September 11, 2001, addressed by Byron and Peterson (2002) in terms of work and life stress, can be examined using the cultural-symbolic perspective on risk. The terror and widespread sense of strain which people experienced from the events (Byron and Peterson, 2002) arose because the actions breached social boundaries that many persons rely on for safety at home and work. The attacks threatened widely held beliefs about the safety of air travel and life in society in general.

In the aftermath of the events, people struggled in a wide range of social settings to interpret and make sense of the events which were uncommon and unexpected in their culture. This intense sensemaking may have contributed to the enhanced strain in individuals that Byron and Peterson found, rather than reducing strain as anticipated by theory, since the implications of the actions were widely discussed. The transgression was so shocking that any sensemaking attempt failed to normalize it and intensified stress, further highlighting the extraordinary nature of the event within the existing cultural context. The risk of terrorism became an important concern in societal discourse. Terrorism has become a political issue and the response to terrorism has become conditioned and mediated by cultural beliefs and values. Terrorism thus emerged from the events as a form of social pollution that threatens external boundaries of organizations and nations. It transgresses internal boundaries which demarcate safe places and persons and shows limits and contradictions in culture such as those related to risk preparedness. Stress and strong moral indignation emerged. Consistent with individualistic norms, considerable effort has been directed at locating, blaming, and punishing terrorists and their leaders who are conceived as adversaries to prevailing Western cultural values.

The risky social context that has nourished terrorism has largely been ignored. Socio-cultural perspectives suggest that the meaning of risk varies culturally, which is an important feature of risk that cognitive science approaches, with their assumptions of objectivity and emphasis on quantification, cannot bring to light. These meanings need to be understood and they can be recovered using qualitative research.

REFERENCES

Byron, K. and Peterson, S. (2002) 'The impact of a large-scale traumatic event on individual and organizational outcomes: exploring employee and company reactions to September 11, 2001', *Journal of Organizational Behavior*, 23: 895–910.

Douglas, M. (1966) *Purity and Danger*. London: Ark Paperbacks.

Gephart, R.P. (1997) 'Hazardous measures: an interpretive textual analysis of quantitative sensemaking during crises', *Journal of Organizational Behavior*, 18: 583–622.

Lupton, D. (1999a) 'Introduction: risk and sociocultural theory', in *Risk and Sociocultural Theory: New Directions and Perspectives*, Lupton, D. (ed.), Cambridge: Cambridge University Press. pp. 1–11.

Lupton, D. (1999b) *Risk*. London: Routledge.

On the Practise of Practice: In-tensions and Ex-tensions in the Ongoing Reconfiguration of Practices

Elena P. Antonacopoulou

INTRODUCTION

Understanding and engaging with the social complexity of organizing remains a fundamental challenge in management and organization studies. New and emerging approaches to management and organization research need to fundamentally engage with such complexity in its own terms. Instead of seeking simplifications and classifications of the complex into substances and variables to be isolated, measured and tested, we need to learn to work with complexity in the relational, interconnected, nested and perplexed ways in which it constitutes and defines the social.

In this chapter this view is applied in rethinking the current dominant logic and approach that governs research on practice in management and organization studies.

In recent years we have witnessed a return to practice as a fundamental aspect of organization (Schatzki et al., 2001). In management studies alone the focus on practice has been explored in relation to topics such as communities of practice (e.g. Brown and Duguid, 2000; Wenger, 1998; see also Elkjaer and Huysman, Chapter 1.11 this volume), knowing in practice (e.g. Cook and Brown, 1999; Gherardi, Chapter 3.9 this volume), strategy as practice (e.g. Hendry, 2000; Johnson et al., 2003) and learning as practice (e.g. Gherardi and Nicolini, 2002). It has also been a lens through which a number of phenomena have been re-examined. For example, Seo and Creed (2002) use a practice lens to re-examine institutional change, while Dougherty (1992, 2004) and Orlikowski (2000) rethink technology through a practice perspective.

The emergent body of work now referred to as practice-based studies (PBS, see Gherardi, 2006 for overview) focuses predominantly on the situated nature of action as this is enacted by actors and manifested in language, the physical environment and the interactions between actors. This is consistent with the view of the dynamic nature of routines articulated by Feldman and Pentland (2003; Chapter 2.8 this volume) as well.

Both practice-based studies and re-conceptualizations of routines draw heavily from actor-network theory (Law, 1999) and concentrate on the 'power of association' as Latour (1986) puts it, to account for the importance of connections between actants in the process of creating and recreating both agency and structure. This perspective has proven most valuable because it sensitizes us to the importance of the interactions between agency and structure, a point that has been central to both Bourdieu's (1990) analysis of practice and Giddens' (1984) structuration theory. Yet, we have not identified ways of capturing not only multiple associations, but the forces that underpin the interconnections that drive these associations. If we are to understand the dynamic nature of social phenomena, we need to make interconnections as the focus of our attention and the conditions that underpin the interrelationships between different forces or actants as the core of our inquiry (Antonacopoulou, 1996, 2008).

This view is consistent with wider calls in social sciences in general (see Emirbayer, 1997), for a relational analysis of action as not the product of inter-actions, but action as emanating from trans-action where the relations and the entities creating these actions are not isolated but are seen to co-evolve in ongoing negotiation as constitutive of each other and of the possibilities their interrelationships can productively create. This call echoes many of the insights of pragmatism (Dewey, 1927), critical realism (Sayer, 1992; Archer, 1995) and various branches of phenomenology – from Husserl's (1936) transcendental phenomenology to Heidegger's (1927) hermeneutic phenomenology, to Schutz's (1932) phenomenology of the social, and not least Merleau-Ponty's (1945) phenomenology of perception.

These ideas are experiencing a revival in what is emerging as a new science of complexity (Kauffman, 1995). Complexity science has penetrated management debates and some scholars are employing complexity to better understand organizational and managerial issues, such as strategic management (Stacey, 2003), strategic change (Stacey, 1995; Brown and Eisenhardt, 1997) innovation management (Cheng and Van de Ven, 1996) and design management (Chiva, 2004). One of the resulting conceptualizations emanating from the use of complexity science is the view of organizations as complex adaptive systems (Gell-Mann, 1994; Stacey, 1996; Anderson, 1999; Axelrod and Cohen, 1999) with a capacity to learn as one of the most important characteristics of these systems (Gell-Mann, 1994; Stacey, 1995, 1996; Sherman and Schultz, 1998).

One of the main tenets of complexity theory is the focus on self-organization and emergence, or what could otherwise be called the science of interconnectivity. The attention is not only on the dynamic nature of systems as holistic containers of social activity. Complexity focuses on the interrelationships between systems and treats systems as holons (Koestler, 1969), i.e. parts and wholes at the same time. Complexity also embraces the elements of surprise and serendipity and emphasizes the multiplicity of possibilities that connections within and between systems create as order emerges from chaos and chaos emerges from order.

This chapter draws on some of the principles of complexity theory to articulate and represent the social complexity of organizing through the dynamic and emergent nature of practice. In doing so the analysis will highlight some of the neglected aspects in current practice research and provide an integrative account of how hitherto dispersed aspects of practice can be connected to reveal the richness of the phenomenon. The discussion will also outline a new methodological approach for extending practice-based studies drawing attention to the ways in which the emergent and fluid nature of practice can be studied.

The discussion is organized in three main sections. Firstly, a review and critique of current conceptualizations of practice is offered. This review shows the different conceptualizations of practice in the way specific aspects of practice have formed the focus of attention at different points in time. The discussion seeks to illustrate how these various aspects of practice when combined can provide a richer conceptualization of practice. This richer conceptualization also makes the relationship between practices, routines and rules more clear. The second section extends the analysis of practice by addressing three hitherto neglected aspects of practice: the embodiment of practice, the role of internal and external goods, the connections between the intensity, integrity and intentionality underpinning practice. These three aspects of practice provide a basis for re-conceptualizing practice more dynamically focusing on the role of tensions as a reflection of the social complexity it reflects. The third section develops the idea of tensions to advance theoretically a dynamic logic of practice drawing on principles of complexity science. By focusing on the emergent and self-organizing nature of practice the focus shifts to practise and practising. This new perspective on practice marks a clear departure from existing conceptualizations of practice which focus on the process of institutionalization. Instead, the analysis shows that practising attempts are founded on repetition which itself is founded on reflexivity and ongoing transformation. The chapter concludes with a review of the implications of the emergent view of practice for future practice research and research in organization and management studies.

SOCIAL COMPLEXITY: DOMAINS OF THE SOCIAL LIFE OF ORGANIZING

Social complexity does not only imply the messy interactions between social actors (human and non-human) and the governing structures that shape different forms of organization. Social complexity also reflects the powerful dynamics as social forces transact with each other negotiating order in the midst of chaos. In this section I explore what practice may mean by extending the analysis of practice not only to a review of the limited definitions currently available in the existing practice literature. I also examine what the relationship between practice, routines and rules may be. I focus on these relationships as means of unpacking the social complexity that constitutes the self-organizing and emergent nature of practice.

WHAT IS PRACTICE?

Despite the widespread interest on practice there is limited agreement as to what practice is. A review of the practice literature suggests that currently there are at least five different conceptualizations of practice: practice as action (Bourdieu, 1990); as structure – language, symbols, tools (Turner, 1994); as activity system (Engeström et al., 1999); as social context (Lave and Wenger, 1990); and as knowing (Nicolini et al., 2003). Whilst each of these perspectives provides a useful dimension of practice and extends our understanding of the domains of social life that practices reflect, there is hardly any consistent conceptualization that guides the way practice is understood or defined. There appears to be a tendency to employ notions of practice to provide all encompassing descriptions of cultural characteristics on a macro level or specific activities on a micro level.

Recent attempts by some scholars (see Rechwitz, 2002; Warde, 2005) to consolidate the main debates in practice theory tend to account for the philosophical and sociological underpinnings of practice (see also Gherardi, 2006) and reveal a number of different perspectives drawing attention to the economic, social or cultural dimensions of practice. These dimensions, with the cultural being the most dominant, inform some of the current definitions of practice. Below four different definitions of practice are presented chronologically.

1 Schatzki (1996: 89) defines practice as '... a temporary unfolding and spatially dispersed nexus of doings and sayings ...'.

   Schatzki (1996: 91–98) distinguishes also between 'dispersed' and 'integrated' practices to draw attention to different levels at which practices can be understood. Dispersed practices are concerned with understanding how to carry out an appropriate act, whereas integrated practices emphasize the complex aspects of social life such as the core principles that govern a practice.

2 Rechwitz (2002: 249–250) defines practice as '... the whole of human action ... a routinized type of behaviour which consists of several elements, interconnected to one another: bodily activities; forms of mental activities, 'things' and their use, a background knowledge in the form of understanding, know-how, states of emotion and motivational knowledge. A practice ... forms so to speak a 'block' whose existence necessarily depends on the existence and specific interconnectedness of these elements'.

3 Warde (2005: 134) defines practices as 'coordinated entities [which] require performance for their existence. A performance presupposes a practice and a practice presupposes performances'. Warde identifies three components of practice '... (1) understandings, (2) procedures and (3) engagements' which form a 'nexus ... through which doings and sayings hang together and can be said to be coordinated'.

4 Gherardi (2006: 34) defines practice as 'a mode, relatively stable in time and socially recognized, of ordering heterogeneous items into a coherent set'.

The above definitions reflect efforts to engage with the holistic and temporal nature of practice, as well as their role in supporting social order and institutional structures in communities of practitioners. Despite some commonalities among these definitions, they do reflect a different epistemological and ontological stance on what practice may be. Whilst these definitions seek to provide as complete and encompassing a description of practice as possible, they have difficulty articulating the dynamic nature of practice. Moreover, currently we have limited explanations as to how practices emerge and evolve over time.

One notes that some descriptions of what constitutes practice tend to favour the observable and reportable aspects of practice (e.g. activities, ordering principles, procedures, discourse) often at the expense of unconscious, inactive and 'un-thought' aspects of the phenomenon (Swidler, 2001: 74). There is a tendency to assume that to give practice presence it must have substance, however temporary or dispersed these substances may be. Therefore, a current preoccupation that dominates the practice field is the ontology of substance (see Emirbayer, 1997), which focuses on the aspects of practice that are 'tangible' and observable. It is not surprising, therefore, that practice has come to be equated with action and what people do.

This observation is much in evidence in the perspective that dominates the debate in strategy research where the dominant strategy-as-practice (see Jarzabkowski, 2005; Johnson et al., 2003) perspective adopts predominantly a focus on activities and actions as a basis of understanding how strategy happens when managers strategize. Whittington (2006) adopts a wider view of practice as distinct from praxis and acknowledges the role of practitioners in enacting practices through activities but also through 'shared routines of behaviour, including traditions, norms and procedures for thinking, acting and using "things"'. He draws particular attention to the relationships between practices, praxis and practitioners as an important aspect of understanding practices holistically. This conceptualization however, still fails to provide a clear understanding of how soft and hard aspects of practice combine to create that which is referred to as practice. The confusion seems to be exacerbated by the lack of clarity regarding the relationship between practices, routines and rules as domains in the social life of organizing.

PRACTICE, ROUTINES AND RULES

Reflecting on the current debate in practice theory, one cannot help notice that there is a general tendency to describe practice in relation to routines and rules. Practices are seen as 'routinized activities' (Rechwitz, 2002) or 'behavioural routines' (Whittington, 2006). The notion of routine is often used to capture repetition as an integral characteristic of practice, to the extent that it is possible to recognize practice by virtue of the predictable cycles (routine) it goes through when performed. Practices are also seen to have governing structures in the rules that define and distinguish one practice from another, dispersed from integrated practices (Schatzki, 1996) but also as shared and common particularly due to the coherence they provide to the functioning of social groups (Lave and Wenger, 1990).

Practices, however, are not simply a set of routines, nor are they only governed by rules. They are not simply a set of standard operating procedures that are reproduced by obeying a particular set of rules. And we cannot assume either that rules and routines are fixed and standard ways of doing things. As Feldman and Pentland (2003) remind us, routines are dynamic and flexible, not least because every time they are performed some of their ostensive aspects are being redefined. A similar conceptualization may be more suited to our understanding of rules as well; for every time a rule is applied another one is broken. Rules are not only repositories of knowledge, they are also means of socialization providing the grammar for social action (Pentland and Rueter, 1994; March et al., 2000; Reynaud, 2005). Therefore, rules are both written and unwritten, tacit and explicit. They are also, as Beck and Kieser (2003) remind us, complex and ever-changing subject to the systems of innovation that operate as mechanisms renewing the focus and orientation of rules. Similarly, Howard-Grenville (2006) provides a thorough analysis of the forces that can usefully account for the persistence of routines which shows that power shapes the interaction between agency and context and contributes to either the change or persistence of routines over time. Hence, even when routines persist they are changing and vice versa.

We therefore cannot simply equate practice to a set of routines, nor a set of rules. Both routines and rules are constitutive of the dynamics that shape how a practice emerges. As part of the sub-cultural and often counter-cultural terrain of organizing, routines and rules may be one way we can explore how different actants within and between practices interact and create connections that then renew practices. The routines within any practice self-organize to create new rules and new routines as a practice co-evolves with other practices. Therefore, routines and rules may well shape how a practice unfolds. Routines and rules, however, are only one of the many aspects of any dynamic practice.

Engaging with the dynamic nature of practices, it is not enough to argue that practices are temporal and holistic when their performances are only seen through the eye of institutionalization. Practices must not be confused with institutions (McIntyre, 1985; Giddens, 1984). Given their fluid nature practices, routines and rules reproduce themselves not only in the process of institutionalization, but also in the process of improvization. Institutionalization has no end; it is itself an unfolding process and the 'institution' of practices, routines and rules in the realm of organizing is itself an arena of negotiated order (Maines and Charlton, 1985; Strauss, 1978).

Equally, it is not sufficient that we identify the various elements of practice and draw attention to their interconnectedness (Rechwitz, 2002; Whittington, 2006). For example, Rechwitz's (2002: 250) emphasis on both bodily and mental routines is not sufficient to help us understand how practices are embodied as social forces transact to define and redefine practice. If we are to more fully account for practice as embodied and not only enacted by practitioners, we need to explain how the interconnectedness between various aspects of practice are to be studied empirically. Figure 1.8.1 provides an integrated model of the various aspects of practice articulated by various practice theories. By exploring the various aspects of practice across different theoretical

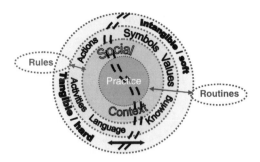

Figure 1.8.1 Connecting different perspectives on practice

contributions, this model seeks to illustrate the complex character of practice as a social phenomenon.

Focusing on tensions is one possible approach for articulating and empirically engaging with the self-organizing processes that shape practice as a mode of organizing. Tensions not only underpin the interconnections within and between practices, they also define the emerging character of a practice and provide scope for dynamic 'ways of seeing' practice. I explore this avenue of rethinking practice in the next section.

EMBODIED PRACTICE: INTERNAL AND EXTERNAL GOODS IN-TENSION

The preceding analysis sought to highlight the need for practice theory to adopt a more fluid approach to understanding the dynamic and emergent nature of practice. In this section I pursue further the analysis of the dynamic nature of practice by addressing three issues that hitherto have not received sufficient attention in the Management and Organization studies literature on practice. Firstly, I examine the embodied nature of practice, and secondly, explore how this embodiment gives rise to the internal and external goods of practice. Drawing on McIntyre (1985), a richer conceptualization of practice is presented bringing attention to ways in which the external and internal 'goods' of practice can be better understood in relation to the underlying intention of practice.

This draws attention to the third dimension which unpacks the intentionality of practice in relation to its intensity and integrity. The latter point uncovers powerfully some of the inter-connections between the internal and external goods of practice and highlights the importance of understanding tensions as a valuable way of unveiling the conditions that shape the emergence of practice.

EMBODIMENT

In a recent exposition of the social nature of computing, Dourish (2001) makes a valuable observation about the relationship between the physical (tangible) and the social (intangible). He draws attention to the intertwined and inescapable connection of the social and the physical as aspects of our everyday experiences. He makes a useful connection between the tangible and the intangible in our everyday life by emphasizing their embodied nature. He argues that we and our actions are embodied elements of the everyday world (p. 100). Therefore, embodiment is a way of being, a participative status that emphasizes the interactions between meaning (intangible) and action (tangible). He defines embodiment as 'the property of our engagement with the world that allows us to make it meaningful' (p. 126).

The reason why embodiment is so important to our analysis here is that as Dourish (2001: 108) points out the most important aspect about the way in which we encounter the world is that 'we encounter it practically' (original emphasis). Practice in this context is 'the everyday engagement with the world directed towards the accomplishment of practical tasks' (p. 125). We come to understand and live in the world by shaping it through our engagements with it. We find the world meaningful primarily with respect to the ways in which we act within it. Embodiment, therefore, is a source for intentionality as it allows meaning and action to connect in ways that provide purposefulness to practice. This perspective on practice is consistent with many of the current philosophical under-pinnings of practice in Heidegger's Dasein (1927), Schutz's (1932) Lebenswelt, and Merleau-Ponty's (1945) 'phenomenological presence' – theory of the body and perception, to name but a few.

Therefore, it is not only the meanings and actions that constitute the embodiment of practice. It is also the way the practice is performed to derive new meaning and to achieve the purposeful intentions that have driven the need to act in the first place. There are, therefore, a number of other qualities to practice that need to be understood over and beyond the reportable aspects of action, language and experience. We cannot afford to limit our understanding of practice only as 'praxis' (action/activity); we also need to understand practice as 'phronesis' (virtuous modes of knowing; practical judgement), in relation to the 'telos' (objective/purpose/excellence) to which it is orientated. This Aristotelian view reminds us of the need to understand the dynamic nature of practice through the ethos that constitutes a practice. The ethos of a practice is what ultimately defines its character in the way it is also performed – embodied by the practitioners who constitute the core of a practice alongside the purpose that drives their pursuit of a practice. The ethos of a practice, therefore, provides scope for thinking about practice more holistically by bringing closer to focus both the practitioner and the purpose within a practice. This view extends current conceptualizations of practice reviewed in the previous section. It provides a new platform for re-conceptualizing practice and its dynamics.

Practice, therefore, is not only what practitioners do, but also how they do what they do. An important dimension that does not feature prominently in much current practice theory – why practitioners perform practices the way they do, in other words, the telos – the purpose of a practice is redefined in relation to what is done and how it is done.

Figure 1.8.2 represents diagrammatically the relationships between the what, how and why of practice by drawing attention

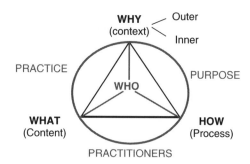

Figure 1.8.2   The dynamic nature of practice

to the embodiment of practice in the way practitioners, practice and purpose meet. The dynamism of practice is symbolized by the triangle which also extends the traditional view of change (see Pettigrew, 1987) as the content (what), process (how) and context (why) by reminding us of the power of the practitioner (who) driving the change.

An illustrative example would be to consider a professional car racing driver who participates in Formula 1 car racing. The practice of car racing can lead to the driver earning a medal at the end of a race or the championship title at the end of a tournament/season. How the driver runs each race and how he seeks to perform without injuring himself and the other drivers, how he engages in each race not only in terms of physical fitness but also psychological and emotional state, are aspects of the practice of car racing. In short, how the driver competes, the distinctive qualities he brings to every race as he performs in a race, includes not only technical competence but also a set of virtues as well. This is particularly evident when a driver fails to complete the race they prepared so hard for.

INTERNAL AND EXTERNAL GOODS

Influenced by Aristotle's philosophical orien-tation, McIntyre (1985: 188–191) emphasizes the need to understand practice as a dynamic between the goods internal and external to a practice. He describes as external, those 'goods' like wealth, social status, prestige, fame, power and influence. They are 'goods' which one possesses in competition with others who may not own them. Internal goods, on the other hand, are the virtues that create good for the community one is part of. Internal goods are not 'goods' as they are not possessions. They are the kind of 'qualities' however, that can only be identified through participation in a practice. Such distinctive qualities include virtues like justice, trustworthiness, courage and honesty. In other words, they are internal to the character of the practice in the way practitioners choose to perform a practice.

It could be argued therefore, that practice provides an arena in which the internal goods of a practice can be exhibited, while external goods may be potentially earned. A practice, therefore, may have external goods as those 'hard' and measurable aspects that give a practice competitiveness over other practices. Internal goods, on the other hand, are the virtues of justice, courage and honesty to excel in competition with others and with one's self. They are the 'soft' aspects that distinguish one practice from another by virtue of their achievement of good for the whole community who participates in a practice.

Internal goods, therefore, are constitutive of the social context created by ostensive values, symbols, meanings and principles (core assumptions) that reflect (often unarticulated) images of practice as different modes of knowing not only enact but also embody a practice (see Antonacopoulou, 2006a). Internal goods would also include the human capital of a practice in the way practitioners and their unique capabilities, identity, emotions and core values shape a practice and become socialized into a practice. External goods, on the other hand, would include the hard and performative aspect of practice reflected in actions, activities, governing structures and procedures, artefacts and tools including the language used to spell out the specifics of practice. They would also comprise the projected end results and expected rewards that often drive the actions taken. Table 1.8.1 summarizes the possible internal and external goods of a practice.

Table 1.8.1 The internal and external goods of practice

External goods	Internal goods
Actions	Virtues – justice, trustworthiness, courage, honesty
Activities	Social context
Governing structures	Ostensive values
Procedures	Symbols
Artefacts	Meanings
Wealth/social status	Principles (core assumptions)
Prestige/fame	Images of practice
Power and influence	Modes of knowing
Tools – language, projected end results and expected rewards	Human capital – practitioners' unique capabilities, identity, emotions

Returning to the example of car racing driver it could be argued that to better understand car racing as a practice we need to account for both the external and internal goods. External goods like the championship title may provide a motivation, a guidance and even infrastructure of boundaries around which the activities constitutive of expressing a practice are built. However, it is the internal goods that also provide the distinctive qualities of car racing practice as a lived experience (see also De Certeau, 1984). The internal goods operate at the conscious and unconscious level and beyond, providing meaning and significance to the various external goods; they also build the strength to overcome the obstacles along the way. Therefore, the internal and external goods of car racing as a practice are not simply interacting; they are transacting. This means that they are consistently re-negotiating their role and significance in relation to the intentions that guide how, why and with what means the practice is performed.

McIntyre's account of the internal and external goods of practice provides us with a way of rethinking the relationship between the tangible (hard, formal) and intangible (soft, informal) aspects of practice. By using the notion of 'good' McIntyre accounts for both hard and soft aspects of practice. In other words, any practice comprises the tangible evidence of excellence as well as the intangible elements of the pursuit of excellence. Based on this integration of tangible and intangible aspects of practice McIntyre (1985: 187) reinforces the embodied nature of practice and introduces a strong moral dimension to his account of practice which he defines as:

> ... any coherent and complex form of socially established cooperative human activity through which goods internal to that form of activity are realized in the course of trying to achieve, those standards of excellence which are appropriate to, and partially definitive of, that form of activity, with the result that human powers to achieve excellence, and human conceptions of the ends and goods involved, are systematically extended.

Internal and external goods, therefore, are not sets of predefined elements but possibilities that may be created when different dimensions they entail connect. This view is compatible with what Gibson (1979: 222) refers to as 'affordance', a three-way relationship between the environment, the organisms and an activity. An embodied view of practice can only account for the affordances as internal and external goods interact with the emerging intentions.

INTEGRITY, INTENSITY AND INTENTIONALITY

To understand the complex nature of practice it is not simply a matter of examining the connections between internal and external goods. There is a much more unpredictable force at play which draws attention to the conditions that underline the way internal and external goods may be interconnected. There is every possibility that what one does and how one goes about doing it may be governed by a different set of intentions which themselves change in the process of performing a practice. Integrity as a force affecting the interconnectivity of internal and external goods can be illustrated in the example of the car racing practice by considering the way a race can be transformed as a driver drives in the race.

The car racing driver's intention may be to complete the race to earn more championship points. He may also be motivated to win over another driver or racing team to improve the overall team performance. A car racing driver may be driving parts of the race by testing different techniques or trying new technical equipment, e.g. new tyres. At the same time, he may run the race with all these possibilities in mind but may change entirely his course of action if the weather changes, or if an engine failure forces him to retire. An error by another driver in the race may unintentionally push him off course or challenge him to change his pace and his racing strategy. The driver may race different parts of the race with different intentions. All-in-all no one really knows what the outcome of any race will be, not even the driver themselves, however well prepared they may be for the race.

Therefore, central to a practice is not only the integrity that internal and external goods provide. The intensity with which internal and external goods interconnect affects significantly the intention of a practice. Therefore, the interrelationship between internal and external goods is affected by the changing intentions that govern the importance attached to different internal and external goods at different points in time and space. By drawing attention to the way internal and external goods, when interconnected, give integrity and intensity to a practice when performed, we enrich our understanding of the intention – telos of practice. We also become more mindful that the social complexity of practice does not only entail a context, process and content in relation to the practitioner, it also entails time and space. This point introduces beyond the what, how and why of practice, the when and where of practice. Figure 1.8.3 represents the interconnections between the what, how, why, when and where of practice diagrammatically, as a compass guiding the changing direction of a practice towards the multiple purposes/telos to which it is intended.

Intentions, therefore, can be seen as a driving force helping us understand how and why internal and external goods of a practice interconnect. Intention can act as

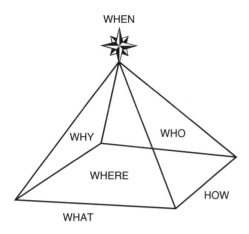

Figure 1.8.3 The compass of reconfiguring practices

a 'torch throwing light' (Hampshire, 1965: 125) to the various potential obstacles in the course of action. Therefore, intention as a source of meaningful action can provide a sense of continuity between the past, the present and the future. It also highlights that unconsciously intentions transform meanings and actions and change the course of performing a practice. External and internal goods are therefore, in-tension.

TENSIONS: INTER-PRACTICE, INTRA-PRACTICE, INTER-TEMPORAL

In management research tensions have been a topic of some debate (see Huxham and Beech, 2003; Johnson, 1996; Quinn, 1988). For example, Argyris and Schön (1978) have articulated the inconsistencies in relation to learning practices as 'espoused theory' and 'theory in use', while March (1991) positioned the tension between 'exploration' and 'exploitation'. Legge (1995) in her analysis of Human Resource Management (HRM) practices describes tension as the chasm between 'rhetoric' and 'reality' and the 'hard' and 'soft' aspects of HRM. Feldman and Pentland (2003) reveal the tensions between 'ostensive' and 'performative' routines. They effectively suggest that practices exist at the

same time as ideal-types in the minds of actors (ostensive – which share some characteristics with the habitus of Bourdieu) and as real-life performances, adaptation of these ideal models to the circumstances and constraints present in the here and now. The discrepancy clearly generates tension, as actors aspire to the ostensive practice and need to make do with the performative version. To this tension, I would add a historical perspective – tension is not just between performance today and ostensive, but also between performance today versus performance yesterday.

Therefore, tensions are generally intended to present conflict, internal contradictions, the difficulty of balancing competing priorities, inequalities of power and control and generally paradoxes that cannot be resolved (see Antonacopoulou, 2000, 2001). Tensions tend to be presented as problematic mostly because a dialectic logic governs the way tensions are represented. Within a practice tensions would reveal the range of internal contradictions between intentions and actions and highlight the difficulties of balancing competing priorities in the internal and external goods that constitute a practice. Therefore, tensions, on the one hand, may reflect instances when a practice seeks to address many equally viable intentions at the same time, but potentially resulting in confusion and inertia. On the other hand, tensions may be created when a practice seeks to address potentially conflicting agendas or when there may be internal contradictions within a practice. This would be the case when the internal goods of a practice may be driving one set of intentions and the external goods may be driving another set of intentions.

Returning to the example of the car racing driver, we can suggest that running a race is full of tensions, including the need to excel in one's race and winning a medal and trying new techniques in the course of the race and following the well-tried strategies that deliver results. There would be other tensions when the drive to achieve maximum performance may lead to an attempt to bend the rules. Another tension would be when there is a conflict between one's own ambitions and the need to contribute to a collective team effort. It is therefore, not uncommon for a race to be driven by a team strategy that may demand that one of the two drivers change their race in the interest of a team result. Equally, during pit stops the efficiency of the team effort can be the key to winning a race.

The tensions between internal and external goods of a practice provide only one part of the dynamic nature of practice. The dynamic nature of practice is not only subject to the tensions within a practice, i.e. intra-practice – endogenous forces. Equally powerful are the exogenous dynamics in the tensions between practices within an organizational field. The inter-practice dynamics reflect the multiple and often conflicting values promoted by different practices. The inter-practice dynamics are likely to generate pushes towards homogeneity and heterogeneity at the same time. As different practices interact, they are likely to develop new language and understanding, which is the antecedent to knowledge transfer or translation (Szulanski, 1996; Bechky, 2003). In other words, as practices become more and more institutionalized they diffuse in the social group at hand (Gherardi and Nicolini, 2002). At the same time, these interactions are likely to generate as much new knowledge and understanding in all participants (Carlile, 2002), thus increasing (through path dependency) the differences between different instances of the same practice.

Moreover, what tensions between practices also reveal is how malpractice may be created. The political forces underlying the transaction between practices may well lead to power differentials that may redirect the intentions of collective practices in the pursuit of internal and external goods which may be less than ethical.

Therefore, the nested and interlocked nature of bundles of practices may create inconsistencies between practices as different economic, social, political and ethical forces shape individual practices and in turn the relationships between practices in an organizational field. This point reminds us

that bundles (collectivities or communities) do not consist of homogeneous agents. There is a great deal of diversity both in the characteristics of practitioners forming the community, as well as their interpretations of what the practice is and how they are to perform it (Antonacopoulou et al., 2006). This diversity invites us to rethink critically the relationship between community and practice. Issues of power, differentials of knowledge and information are among the forces acknowledged as underpinning the diversity of communities of practice (Contu and Wilmott, 2003; Roberts, 2006). We have yet, however, to fully capture how and why homogeneity (that governs much current thinking in the communities of practice literature, Lave and Wenger, 1990; Wenger, 1998; Wenger and Snyder, 2000) coexists alongside heterogeneity (Brown and Duguid, 1991; Handley et al., 2006). Practitioners within a practice experience a number of competing priorities that alongside the ongoing negotiation of values, assumptions, behaviours and actions constantly reinterpret the rules of engagement in a practice and have a significant bearing on the unfolding character of a practice. The diversity and heterogeneity of multiple and competing practices constantly redefine each practice and by implication the field to which a practice is embedded. Therefore, to suggest that practices are interlocked and nested is to imply the possibilities that their dynamic interconnections can create, mindful of the power and political dynamics that drive the relationships between practices.

Formula 1 car racing as a practice is only one of many other practices in the motor sports field; NASCAR and the promising new A1 motor sports racing are at least two other kinds of car racing practices. Each of these practices, although they broadly belong to the same field, are governed in some instances by very different regulations. Moreover, within any one of these communities of practice one can identify multiple communities focusing on specific sub-practices of Formula 1 motor racing. For example, the community of technical experts and engineers would work very differently from the community of sales people and public relationship experts. Each would focus on a different part of car racing often in ways that could create competing and often contradictory priorities. For example, the design of F1 cars needs to accommodate both the requirements of technical efficiency to provide maximum performance alongside the requirements for style and advertising space that can be sold.

The tensions within and between practices are therefore, critical to the way a practice is formed and the way it unfolds over time and across multiple contexts. However, it is when we combine the intra- and inter-practice tensions that we begin to reveal that tensions are also a reflection of elasticity and inter-temporality. Tension is not only a matter of negative or positive possibilities but it is also about the ways in which the space of possibilities is created as elastic (flexible and ever changing) practices create a space where meanings, actions and intentions can co-evolve. Tensions therefore, also reflect the elasticity embedded in a practice when it stretches, as an elastic band would do, in multiple directions. Tensions can extend the elasticity of a practice to bend, adapt and be constantly transformed in the way endogenous and exogenous dynamics interact to define and redefine the practice. In short, it is in the inter-connectivity that possibilities are created and tensions within a practice are transformed from in-tensions into ex-tensions.

The preceding paragraphs have exposed various layers of richness in our re-conceptualization of practice. I have made the case for the embodied nature of practice, the role of internal and external goods, the interconnectivity between internal and external goods and the resulting integrity, intensity and intentionality of a practice as inter-practice and intra-practice tensions are exposed inter-temporally. I have also repositioned tensions to reflect the elasticity of practices due to all the endogenous and exogenous forces that underpin them

and affect the interconnectivity between the various aspects of practice and across practices in time and space. Based on this analysis a new definition of practice can be proposed.

In the context of this analysis practice is defined as inter-connectivity, between endogenous (intra-practice) and exogenous (inter-practice) forces, with intentionality, to expand the space of possibility in the emerging internal and external goods.

Unlike previous definitions of practice, this definition does not apply an ontology of substance in understanding practice. Instead, an ontology of embeddedness and an epistemology of connectivity informs the understanding of practice promoted here (see also Antonacopoulou, 2006b, 2008). By drawing attention to relationality and interconnectivity, the focus moves beyond the powers of association or systemic conceptualizations. The focus is on the conditions that underpin the relationships between different aspects of practice. This relational view also focuses more on the fluid nature of practice as a reflection of its dynamic nature. The space of possibility that tensions within and between practices create reveal another powerful aspect of practice that is not often accounted for; its practise (i.e. the ongoing reconfiguration of practice). These ideas are explored further in the next section as part of developing a dynamic logic of practice.

PRACTISE AND PRACTISING: A NEW DYNAMIC LOGIC OF PRACTICE

The analysis in the previous section has painted a more complex picture around the emerging character of a practice. Focusing on this richness and seeking to extend our understanding of the dynamic nature of practice, this section will present a new logic of practice. The focus in the previous section was to unpack the complex dynamics that constitute practice. In this section I will explore how practice as a complex social system remains viable (Axelrod and Cohen, 1999; Beer, 1972). I will argue that a new logic of practice needs to focus on the practise[1] of practice. Practise and practising attempts are reflective of the fluidity of a practice. They draw attention to the deliberate, habitual and spontaneous repetition as reflective of the dynamic and emergent nature of practice (Antonacopoulou, 2004a; 2006b). These hitherto neglected aspects of practice also reflect the generative dance between formal and informal, tangible and intangible aspects of a practice as these are re-orchestrated (interconnected) to create different experiences and possible outcomes every time a practice is performed. In other words, practise and practising reflect a process of becoming based on trying things out, rehearsing, refining, and changing different aspects of practice and the relationships between them. Practising, therefore, in relation to becoming is tentative and ongoing. It is not merely a process punctuated by events and activities, it is a movement that develops and unfolds through the intensity of connections that drive the process of becoming (see Clegg et al., 2005; Tsoukas and Chia, 2002).

Practising, therefore, is as much a process of repetition as it is a space embracing the multiplicity of possibilities as different (new) dimensions are (re)discovered in a moving horizon where past, present and future meet. Repetition, therefore, in the context of practising, is not a mechanistic process of replication. Replication implies institutionalization in the process of re-presentation and re-production. Repetition, on the other hand, implies re-hearsing, re-viewing aspects of practice.

Practising as repetition embraces learning and changing as part of reflexive critique (Antonacopoulou, 2004b). This means that at the core of practising a practice is actively learning and unlearning different aspects of a practice in a proactive way that does not only rely on routines of habit but different ways of embodying a practice. Learning and practising therefore are not outcomes nor accomplishments but a flow through order and chaos in the endless journey of becoming. This point is not to equate learning with practising, but to account for practising as a central aspect of learning and learning as a central aspect of practising (see also Antonacopoulou and Bento, 2003; Antonacopoulou, 2006b). As Deleuze (1994: 5–14) points out, repetition is perfection and integration. Repetition is transgression. It forms a condition of movement, a means of producing something new in history. Repetition also allows for spontaneity in the way practitioners respond to intended and unintended conditions that shape their practice.

Practise can be defined as the process of repetition where deliberate, habitual or spontaneous performances of a practice enable different dimensions of a practice to emerge or be re-discovered. Practice therefore, exists because it is in practise, not simply performed, but formed and transformed as practising attempts reveal different aspects that configure and reconfigure a practice on an ongoing basis. Practising must not be confused for improvising. Researchers who have studied improvisation and its application in a range of contexts (Crossan et al., 1996; Hatch, 1998; Moorman and Miner, 1998) explain that improvisation is about the engagement of a practitioner in the practice through active participation and listening as well as openness to ideas and possibilities. Whilst all these qualities are important in practising they are not sufficient. Practising also entails visualization and immence concentration in rehearsing again and again parts of a practice differently. It also involves a process of losing the structure once in the act. This means that the practice becomes a second nature for the practitioner to the extent that they are their practice. Practising therefore, does not only require engaged participation, it demands embodied participation. The latter includes over and beyond engagement the identification and unity of the practitioner with the practice in the course of enacting it. This is why the practice and its practise emerge through the undivided unique and individual contributions generated by the practitioners who perform it. They define the ethos of the practice by reflecting different aspects of practice in their practising attempts.

The ongoing permutations of practice in practising attempts help to explain why no practice is ever the same. It helps explain why the same practitioner can perform the same practice very differently at different times and across space. Moreover, different practitioners in the same context can perform the same practice very differently. These variations in practice and its delivery are all reflecting the reconfiguring dynamics – practising – embedded in practice. Reconfiguring is not only a changing routine; it is also a perennial flow, a flexible, ever-changing structure that connects practice, practitioners and purpose together.

It is in different forms of practising where we can begin to locate one of the most powerful consequences of practice; namely the emerging promise they hold to make a difference to organizing. Promising therefore are the practices which emerge out of the possible connections that can be fostered within a practice and across practices. Promising practices[2] would have the dynamic capability (Zollo and Winter, 2002) to renew themselves as part of their ongoing, proactive and dynamic process of reconfiguration. The practising attempts that are central to promising practices enables them to maintain their natural fluidity as they take account of and respond to the multitude of endogenous and exogenous forces. In other words, promising practices are those practices that enable organizations to change their routines and to proactively reconfigure their existing practices. The patchworks of practices reveal that practising and learning keep the organization in tension. This point would suggest also that by definition there is no end to this process of practising and the promise of any practice can be an ideal pursuit in the process of becoming rather than an end in itself.

These ideas are noticeably absent in current practice research and could usefully act as new platforms on which the promise of practice as a powerful concept for future research in management and organization studies can be realized. The focus on practise in particular raises a number of implications for future practice research. These issues are discussed next.

REALISING THE PROMISE OF PRACTICE: PRACTISE-CENTRED RESEARCH

Throughout the analysis presented in this chapter, the case has been made that practice may be an idea whose time has come. The promise of the concept of practice for the study of organization is varied and rich. It allows us to move beyond current metaphors of organization (Morgan, 1980). It provides us with the analytical and explanatory power to reveal the co-existence and interdependency between seemingly paradoxical or contradictory perspectives. Ironically, so powerful is the concept of practice that we are in great danger of reading all aspects of organization as practice. To paraphrase Smircich (1983) we could be on the verge of developing a view that practice is something an organization has as well as something an organization is. Yet, if the development of the culture concept is anything to go by, and Smircich (1983) provides a useful exposition of the development of culture research in relation to organizational analysis, we need to critically reflect what may be the added value of the concept of practice in understanding organization. We need to rethink carefully what aspects of organization does the practice concept reveal that other aspects fail to bring to our attention. We also need to take some of the very medicine practice research suggests and take stock of our responsibility as organization studies researchers regarding the ethical implications of the practice concept in researching organizations.

The analysis of the practice concept in this chapter has been very much guided by these questions. In this section I seek to provide further reflections on the implications the analysis presented, that raises for both future practice research and management and organization research more generally.

By drawing attention to the practitioner, their intentions and the tensions that they experience in the course of coming to know their world (Lakoff and Johnson, 1980), we come to understand why practice is always open ended.

Put simply, the practice concept provides a new lens for engaging with the fluidity of organizing. It embraces ambiguity, uncertainty and discontinuity as the realm of the unknown and the foundation of emerging/becoming/organizing. Practice therefore, exists in practise. Practise provides not only another word for processual studies of organization (Pettigrew, 1997; Langley, 1999). More importantly, it provides a space where the process under examination becomes the force helping us understand the process itself. This perspective overcomes dualities of structure and agency, stability and change and other natural paradoxes that tend to be presented as irreconcilable positions of 'either/or'. Instead, the practise concept creates a space where practising attempts allow a practice to emerge. All these principles are constitutive of the practise-centred research approach (Antonacopoulou, 2008).

The practise-centred approach to researching practice does not only focus on what is practice and how practice is performed, which is central to practice-based studies. It also asks who are the practitioners, why they perform the practice the ways they do in relation to where and when the practice is performed. Practise-centred research also seeks to understand the role and power of practitioners in shaping their practice by virtue of the choices they make through their practical judgements and modes of knowing (phronesis). Practitioners' phronesis reflects their insights, their identity and identification with the practice, their passion and personality. This provides us with a richer understanding of human nature. Practise-centred research also draws attention to *re-search* as a practice. It invites us as practice researchers and organizational analysts more generally to enrich our research practices by rethinking not only the questions we ask and our roles as researcher practitioners but also the tools we employ and the purpose which our research seeks to serve.

CONCLUSIONS

The analysis of the dynamic and emergent nature of practice presented in this chapter has provided access to important aspects of the social complexity of managing and organizing. It reveals how tensions within and between internal and external goods of a practice form conditions that shape how practices inter-connect. The inter-connectivity that governs the emergent configuration of a practice defines not only its nature but also its character. Connections within and between practices can help explain the micro foundations of organization, and thus contribute to our understanding of how organizing emerges from the ongoing practising attempts of organizational members. In other words, focusing on practice and practising provides us with a means to understand more clearly key processes such as emergence and self-organization, which are essential to understanding social complexity.

The practice concept, therefore, captures the social complexity of organizing by shifting the focus beyond the interactional dynamics that bring about organization. The practice concept ontologically places the focus on the flow of connections between multiple dimensions that define the workings of a social group in relation to wider contextual forces that shape interpretations and constructions of reality. Epistemologically we can come to know practice in practise and through practitioners, for both practise and practitioners reveal some of the conditions that feed social complexity and drive the emerging modes of organization that we come to acknowledge and refer to as collective activity, coherent set of values and actions, community and culture. Thus the analysis looks at practice as a complex, dynamic, social process that emerges over time as practising attempts seek to accommodate endogenous and exogenous forces, brought about by economic, social and political dynamics.

A practise-centred approach for developing future practice research focuses on the emergence of practice. It draws particular attention to the repeated enactments and emerging embodiments of practice which configure multiple arenas for negotiations of order. By focusing on practice and its emergence, attention is drawn to ways in which multiple levels impact on the way practice is orchestrated, through different structuration activities (Giddens, 1984). At the same time, this approach to practice research contributes to this body of literature by literally putting practise at the centre of our investigation, thus pushing practice-based theorizing forward. In doing so, the practise-centred approach seeks to account more fully for the (diverse interests) political forces underpinning organizing at different levels, in time and space. In advancing a practise-centred approach to practice research, the objective is also to develop further theories and methodologies that could help us understand better how fluidity can be studied in inter-connectivity. All these issues taken together fundamentally reframe our engagement with practice and challenge management and organizational researchers generally and practice researchers specifically to critically review their re-search practices.

Acknowledgements

The ideas in this chapter are central to the AIM International Project 'Practice and Practising: A Comparison across Organizations, Industries and Countries' under grant number RES-331-25-0024, financially supported by the ESRC/EPSRC Advanced Institute of Management Research. I have been practising and developing the ideas presented in this chapter over a significant period of time and have benefited greatly from my discussions with a number of AIM International Visiting Fellows, including Susan Taylor, Georges Rommes, Yvon Pesqeaux, Martha Feldman, Silvia Gherardi, and junior researchers involved in this project. The comments provided by Celest Wilderome, Paul Edwards, Robin Wensley and Gerard Hodgkinson to earlier versions of this chapter were also of great help. My special thanks are due to members of my research team Manolis Gheredakis, Ketu Patnaik, Daniel Geiger, and other GNOSIS collaborators Paul Oliver, Barry Cooke, Susanne Broekhuizen, Diego Ponte and Nicolas Dragonnetti, who have contributed in their own and very different ways to the sharpening of some of the ideas in this chapter. A special note of thanks is due to Alexandros Antonacopoulos who at five years old constantly refers to the importance of practising every time he tries things out as he discovers his world.

NOTES

1 The Oxford Dictionary (2001) defines *practice* as 'the action of doing of something' or 'a way of doing something that is common, habitual or expected' such as the work of a doctor working in general practice or the car racing driver running a race. *Practise* on the other hand, is defined as 'to do something repeatedly or regularly in order to improve one's skill' or 'to do something regularly as part of one's normal behaviour' e.g. to work as a doctor is to be in practise or a driver planning the next race as soon as he has completed one is also in practise. The dictionary cautions the possible confusion between practice and practise and clearly points out that the former should be used when referring to the noun and the latter should be used when referring to the verb. It should be noted that in the US language there is no distinction between the *c* and *s*. Both practice and its practice are spelled with c, hence, making the distinction more difficult.

2 A distinction is made here between notions of 'best' practice and 'promising' practice. While the former are contextually specific and not possible to transfer, the latter provide scope for wider adaptability to local conditions. The reason that promising practices transfer better than best practices is because they are founded on the principle of transience and adaptability rather than benchmarking and copying which dominates the way best practices are understood.

REFERENCES

Anderson, P. (1999) 'Complexity theory and organization science', *Organization Science*, 10 (3): 216–232.

Antonacopoulou, E.P. (1996) 'A study of interrelationships: The way individual managers learn and adapt and the contribution of training towards this process'. Unpublished PhD Thesis, Warwick Business School, University of Warwick.

Antonacopoulou, E.P. (2000) 'Employee development through self-development in three retail banks', *Personnel Review*, Special Issue on 'New Employee Development: Successful Innovations or Token Gestures?' 29 (4): 491–508.

Antonacopoulou, E.P. (2001) 'The paradoxical nature of the relationship between training and learning', *Journal of Management Studies*, 38 (3): 327–350.

Antonacopoulou, E.P. and Bento, R. (2003) 'Methods of "Learning Leadership": Taught and Experiential', in J. Storey (ed), *Current Issues in Leadership and Management Development*. Oxford: Blackwell. pp. 81–102.

Antonacopoulou, E.P. (2004a) 'On the virtues of practising scholarship: A tribute to Chris Argyris a timeless learner', *Management Learning*, 35 (4): 381–395.

Antonacopoulou, E.P. (2004b) 'The dynamics of reflexive practice: The relationship between learning and changing', in M. Reynolds and R. Vince (eds), *Organizing Reflection*. London: Ashgate. pp. 47–64.

Antonacopoulou, E.P. (2006a) 'Modes of knowing in practice: The relationship between learning and knowledge revisited', in B. Renzl, K. Matzler and H.H. Hinterhuber (eds), *The Future of Knowledge Management*. London: Palgrave. pp. 7–28.

Antonacopoulou, E.P. (2006b) 'Working life learning: Learning-in-practise', in E.P. Antonacopoulou, P. Jarvis, V. Andersen, B. Elkjaer and S. Hoeyrup (eds), *Learning, Working and Living: Mapping the Terrain of Working Life Learning*. London: Palgrave. pp. 234–254.

Antonacopoulou, E.P. (2008) 'Practise-centred research: The study of inter-connectivity and fluidity', in R. Thorpe and R. Holt (eds), *Dictionary of Qualitative Management Research*, London: Sage. pp. 165–169.

Archer, M.S. (1995) *Realist Social Theory: The Morphogenetic Approach*, Cambridge: Cambridge University Press.

Argyris, C. and Schön, D. (1978) *Organizational Learning: A Theory-in-action Perspective*. Reading, MA: Addison-Wesley.

Axelrod, R. and Cohen, M.D. (1999) *Harnessing complexity*. New York: The Free Press.

Bechky, B. (2003) 'Sharing meaning across occupational communities: The transformation of understanding on a production floor', *Organization Science*, 14: 312–330.

Beck, N. and Kieser, A. (2003) 'The complexity of rule systems, experience and organizational learning', *Organization Studies*, 24: 793–814.

Beer, S. (1972) *Brain of the Firm*. London: Penguin.

Bourdieu, P. (1990) *The Logic of Practice*. Cambridge: Polity.

Brown, J.S. and Duguid, P. (1991) 'Organizational learning and communities of practice: Toward a unified view of working, learning and innovation', *Organization Science*, 2 (1): 40–57.

Brown J.S. and Duguid, P. (2000) *The Social Life of Information*. Boston, MA: Harvard Business School Press.

Brown, S.L. and Eisenhardt, K.M. (1997) 'The art of continuous change: Linking complexity theory and time-paced evolution in relentlessly shifting organizations', *Administrative Science Quarterly*, 42: 1–34.

Carlile, P.R. (2002) 'A pragmatic view of knowledge and boundaries: Boundary objects in new product development', *Organization Science*, 13: 442–455.

Cheng, Y.T. and Van de Ven, A.H. (1996) 'Learning the innovation journey: Order out of chaos?, *Organization Science*, 7: 593–614.

Chiva, R. (2004) 'Repercussions of complex adaptive systems on product design management'. *Technovation*, 24: 707–711.

Clegg, S.R., Kornberger, M. and Rhodes, C. (2005) 'Learning/becoming/organizing', *Organization*, 12 (2): 147–167.

Contu, A. and Willmott, H. (2003) 'Re-embedding situatedness: The importance of power relations in learning theory', *Organization Science*, vol. 14, no. 3: pp. 283–296.

Cook, S.D.N. and Brown, J.S. (1999) 'Bridging epistemologies: The generative dance between organizational knowledge and organizational knowing', *Organization Science*, 10 (4): 381–400.

Crossan, M., Lane, H., White, R. and Klus, L. (1996) 'The improvising organization: Where planning meets opportunity'. *Organizational Dynamics*, 24 (4): 20–35.

De Certeau, M. (1984) *The Practice of Everyday Life*. Berkeley: University of California Press.

Deleuze, G. (1994) *Difference and Repetition*. London: Continuum.

Dewey, J. (1927) 'The public and its problems', in J.A. Boydston (1988) *The Later Works of John Dewey, 1925–1953*, vol. 2. Carbondale and Edwardsville: Southern Illinois University Press. pp. 235–372.

Dougherty, D. (1992) 'A practice-centred model of organizational renewal through product innovation', *Strategic Management Journal*, 13, Summer Special Issue: 77–96.

Dougherty, D. (2004) 'Organizing practices in services: Capturing practice based knowledge for innovation', *Strategic Organization*, 2 (1): 35–64.

Dourish, P. (2001) *Where the Action is: The Foundations of Embodied Interaction*. Cambridge: MIT Press.

Elkjaer, B. and Huysman, M. (this volume) 'Organizational learning and social worlds theory', in D. Barry and H. Hansen (eds), *Handbook of New and Emerging Approaches to Management and Organization*. London: Sage.

Emirbayer, M. (1997) 'Manifesto for a relational sociology', *American Journal of Sociology*, 103 (2): 281–317.

Engeström, Y., Miettinen, R. and Punamäki, R.-L. (1999) *Perspectives on Activity Theory*. Cambridge: Cambridge University Press.

Feldman, M.S. and Pentland, B.T. (2003) 'Reconceptualizing organizational routines as a source of flexibility and change', *Administrative Science Quarterly*, 48 (March): 94–118.

Feldman, M.S. and Pentland, B.T. (this volume) 'Routine dynamics', in D. Barry and H. Hansen (eds), *Handbook of New and Emerging Approaches to Management and Organization*. London: Sage.

Gell-Mann, M. (1994) *The Quark and the Jaguar. Adventures in the Simple and the Complex*. New York: W.H. Freeman.

Gherardi, S. (2006) *Organizational Knowledge: The Texture of Organizing*. London: Blackwells.

Gherardi, S. (this volume) 'Organizational Knowledge', in D. Barry and H. Hansen (eds), *Handbook of New and Emerging Approaches to Management and Organization*. London: Sage.

Gherardi, S. and Nicolini, D. (2002) 'Learning in a constellation of interconnected practices: canon or dissonance?', *Journal of Management Studies*, 39 (4): 419–436.

Gibson, J. (1979) *The Ecological Approach to Visual Perception*. New York: Houghton-Mifflin.

Giddens, A. (1984) *The Constitution of Society*. Cambridge: Cambridge University Press.

Hampshire, S. (1965) *Thought and Action*. London: Chatto and Windus.

Handley, K., Sturdy, A., Fincham, R. and Clark, T. (2006) 'Within and beyond communities of practice: Making sense of learning through participation, identity and practice', *Journal of Management Studies*, 43 (3): 641–653.

Hatch, M.J. (1998) 'Jazz as a metaphor for organizing in the 21st century', *Organization Science*, 9 (5): 556–557.

Heidegger, M. (1927) *Being and Time*. English translation 1962. New York: Harper and Row.

Hendry, J. (2000) 'Strategic decision-making, Discourse and strategy as social practice', *Journal of Management Studies*, 37 (7): 955–977.

Howard-Grenville, J.A. (2006) 'The persistence of flexible organizational routines: The role of agency and organizational context', *Organization Science*, 16(6): 618–636.

Husserl, E. (1936) *Die Krisis der europäischen Wissenshaften und die transzendentale Phänomenologie: Eine Einleitung in de phänomenologische Philosophie*. The Hague: Martinus Nijhoff. (Tr. D. Carr. 1970) *The Crisis of European Sciences and Transcendental Phenomenology*. Evanston, IL: Northwestern University Press.

Huxham, C. and Beech, N. (2003) 'Contrary prescriptions: Recognizing good practice tensions in management', *Organization Studies*, 24 (1): 69–93.

Jarzabkowski, P. (2005) *Strategy as Practice: An Activity Perspective*. London: Sage.

Johnson, B. (1996) *Polarity Management: Identifying and Managing Unsolvable Problems*. Amherst, MA: HRD Press.

Johnson, G., Melin, L. and Whittington, R. (2003) 'Micro-strategy and strategising', *Journal of Management Studies*, Special Issue, 40 (1): 3–20.

Kauffman, S.A. (1995) *At Home in the Universe*. Oxford: Oxford University Press.

Koestler, A. (1969) 'Beyond atomism and holism: The concept of the holon', in A. Koestler and J.R. Smythies (eds), *Beyond Reductionism*. Hutchinson: London. pp. 192–232.

Lakoff, G. and Johnson, M. (1980) *Metaphors We Live By*. Chicago: University of Chicago Press.

Langley, A. (1999) 'Strategies for theorizing from process data', *Academy of Management Review*, 24 (4): 691–710.

Latour, B. (1986) 'The powers of association', in J. Law (ed.), *Power, Action and Belief*. London: Routledge and Kegan Paul. pp. 261–277.

Lave, J. and Wenger, E.C. (1990) *Situated Learning: Legitimate Peripheral Participation*. Cambridge: Cambridge University Press.

Law, J. (1999) 'After ANT: complexity, naming and topology', in J. Law and J. Hassard (eds), *Actor Network Theory and After*. Oxford: Blackwell Publishers. pp. 1–14.

Legge, K. (1995) *Human Resource Management, Rhetorics and Realities*. Macmillan Business.

Maines, D.R. and Charlton, J.C. (1985) 'The negotiated order approach to the analysis of social organization', in H.A. Farberman and R.S. Perinbanayagan (eds), *Foundations of Interpretative Sociology: Original Essays in Symbolic Interaction* – Supplement 1. Greenwitch, CT: JAI Press. pp. 272–308.

March, J. (1991) 'Exploration and exploitation in organizational learning', *Organization Science*, 2 (1): 71–87.

March, J.G., Schulz, M. and Zhou, X. (2000) *The Dynamics of Rules: Change in Written Organizational Codes*. Stanford: Stanford University Press.

McIntyre, A. (1985) *After Virtue: A Study in Moral Theory*. London: Duckworth.

Merleau-Ponty, M. (1945) *The Phenomenology of Perception*. English translation, 1962. London: Routledge.

Moorman, C. and Miner, A. (1998) 'Organizational improvisation and organizational memory', *Academy of Management Review*, 23 (4): 698–724.

Morgan, G. (1980) 'Paradigms, metaphors and puzzle solving in organization theory', *Administrative Science Quarterly*, 25: 605–622.

Nicolini, D., Gherardi, S. and Yanow, D. (eds) (2003) *Knowing in Organizations: A Practice-Based Approach*. Armonk, NY: M.E. Sharpe.

Orlikowski, W. (2000) 'Using technology and constituting structures: A practice lens for studying technology in organizations', *Organization Science*, 12 (4): 404–428.

Oxford Dictionary (2001) *Practice, Practise, Practising*. Oxford: Oxford University Press. p. 702.

Pentland, B.T. and Rueter, H.H. (1994) 'Organizational routines as grammars of action', *Administrative Science Quarterly*, 39 (3): 484–510.

Pettigrew, A.M. (1987). 'Context and action in the transformation of the firm', *Journal of Management Studies*, 24 (6): 649–670.

Pettigrew, A.M. (1997) 'What is a processual analysis?', *Scandinavian Journal of Management*, 13 (4): 337–348.

Quinn, R. (1988) *Beyond Rational Management: Mastering the Paradoxes and Competing Demands of High Performance*. San Francisco: Jossey-Bass.

Rechwitz, A. (2002) 'Toward a theory of social practices: A development in cultural theorizing', *European Journal of Social Theory*, 5 (2): 243–263.

Reynaud, B. (2005) 'The void at the heart of rules: Routines in the context of rule-following. The case of the Paris Metro workshop', *Industrial and Corporate Change*, 14: 847–871.

Roberts, J. (2006) 'Limits to communities of practice', *Journal of Management Studies*, 43 (3): 623–639.

Sayer, A. (1992) *Method in Social Science: A Realist Approach*, 2nd edn. London: Routledge.

Schatzki, T.R., Knorr-Cetina, K. and von Savigny, E. (2001) *The Practice Turn in Contemporary Theory*. London: Routledge.

Schatzki, T.R. (1996) *Social Practices: A Wittgensteinian Approach to Human Activity and the Social*. Cambridge: Cambridge University Press.

Schutz, A. (1932) *The Phenomenology of the Social World*. Evanston, IL: Northwestern University Press.

Seo, M-G. and Creed, W.E.D. (2002) 'Institutional contradictions, praxis and institutional change: A dialectical perspective', *Academy of Management Review*, 27.

Sherman, H. and Schultz, R. (1998) *Open Boundaries*. New York: Perseus Books.

Smircich, L. (1983) 'Concepts of culture and organizational analysis', *Administrative Science Quarterly*, 28 (3): 339–358.

Stacey, R.D. (1995) 'The science of complexity: An alternative perspective for strategic change processes', *Strategic Management Journal*, 16: 477–495.

Stacey, R.D. (1996) *Complexity and Creativity In Organizations*. San Francisco: Berret-Koehler Publishers.

Stacey, R.D. (2003) *Strategic Management and Organizational Dynamics: The Challenge of Complexity*. Essex: Prentice-Hall.

Strauss, A. (1978) *Negotiation: Varieties, Processes, Contexts and Social Order*. San Francisco: Jossey-Bass.

Swidler, A. (2001) 'What anchors cultural practices', in T. Schatzki, K. Knorr Cetina and E. von Savigny (eds), *The Practice Turn in Contemporary Theory*. London: Routledge. pp. 74–92.

Szulanski, G. (1996) 'Exploring internal stickiness: impediments to the transfer of best practice within the firm', *Strategic Management Journal*, 17 (Winter Special Issue): 27–43.

Tsoukas, H. and Chia, R. (2002) 'On organizational becoming: Rethinking organizational change', *Organization Science*, 13 (5): 567–582.

Turner, S. (1994) *The Social Theory of Practices: Tradition, Tacit Knowledge and Presuppositions*. Cambridge: Polity.

Warde, A. (2005) 'Consumption and theories of practice', *Journal of Consumer Culture*, 5: 131–153.

Wenger, E. (1998) *Communities-of-Practice: Learning, Meaning and Identity*. Cambridge: Cambridge University Press.

Wenger, E.C. and Snyder, W.M. (2000) 'Communities of practice: The organizational frontier', *Harvard Business Review*, 78 (1): 139–145.

Whittington, R. (2006) 'Completing the practice turn in strategy research', *Organization Studies*, 27 (5): 613–634.

Zollo, M. and Winter, S.G. (2002) 'Deliberate learning and the evolution of dynamic capabilities', *Organization Science*, 13 (3): 339–351.

The Nature of Research Practice

Jean M. Bartunek

Please conduct a thought experiment.

Imagine someone who has a doctorate in management or organization studies and substantial research training in both quantitative and qualitative methods. Imagine that she has been working in a corporate setting and conducting research there.

Now imagine that, for a diversion from her normal fast-paced and time-pressured work, she is studying you, an academic, as you go about researching and writing a scholarly article. She might watch you plan the article carefully in advance or she might see that you initiate it because of a kind of serendipity (a book falls off your bookshelf). She might see you working in a very messy office, and see that you are interrupted regularly while you work. She might interview you about why you take breaks to surf the Internet or eat snacks while you're working. She might see you go through drafts and drafts, first of a proposal, and then, eventually, of the whole paper. She might see you collect data and watch the complications you encounter as you do so. She might talk with you about all your other activities, the teaching, the committee work, and your family life, that provide the context in which your research takes place. She might see your happiness when you are finally ready to 'get the article off your desk' by submitting it. She might hear your anger when your article is rejected or gets an unfair review. She might, if she has sufficient patience, observe what happens to you and your article for several years until it (hopefully) appears in print.

These particular events are, of course, only a small part of what someone studying you would see, only a small part of what goes into carrying out a research project from beginning to end. What would be the value of such a thought experiment?

When we as academics conduct studies, especially those that rely on observation or an equivalent methodology, the processes of the people and/or organizational units we study are open to view. We explore their cognitive maps, their aims and how they hope to accomplish these aims. We see them struggle to reach decisions. We see differences and disagreements among members of an organizational group or between groups. We see wrong paths they go down, ways they get back on track (or not), and factors that affect their success. Features like these are often key to understanding organizations and the actions within them.

But what about our own research processes as academics? Our own cognitive maps about our work, or, as Argyris and Schön (1974) more properly refer to them, our theories of action, play central roles in the conduct of our research. Our initial and evolving aims for our work, the ways we expect to achieve these aims, and the processes through which organizational research takes place are important in determining how our initial ideas become expanded, modified, and/or discarded all together and eventually lead to a scholarly product. But, as Weick (1989) notes, they are not often salient to us as academics.

For example, I began to write the first draft of this short essay while I was sitting in an airplane as we flew over the Midwest U.S. I chose that setting because I was having difficulty getting started, and I figured that sitting in a plane would provide relatively few distractions.

This is not the kind of description that is typically included in depictions of how scholarly products are presented. But it helps to make explicit two important pieces of information.

The first is my theory of action. Argyris and Schön (1974) argued that all human beings, researchers included, have theories of action about how to behave effectively with others, to accomplish particular intended consequences. These may not be fully explicit and may not look like the types of propositions or hypotheses that are easily assessed by structural equation modelling, but they are hypotheses nonetheless.

My hypothesis, implicit at the time, was something like the following: I'm much more likely to begin a somewhat ambiguous task that I'm interested in but don't quite know how to do if I can play with it in a setting where I will have very few other options for behaviour and where I have a finite amount of time, so I won't feel as if I have to complete anything. An airplane might provide such a setting. I tested the hypothesis by bringing the invitation letter and a small laptop computer with me and by typing whatever came to my mind. Fortunately, my hypothesis was supported; I did get started with this article.

The second piece of information this description contributes is observation of what I actually did. More than three decades ago Henry Mintzberg (1973) conducted an observational study and then wrote a book that detailed how managers actually acted. This book showed that the functions of managers that had been assumed by classical management theorists bore only sketchy correspondence with the ways that managers actually spend their time. His work opened up completely new understandings of and approaches to studying management.

What did I actually do? I thought a bit. I typed on a laptop sitting on a plane. I looked no different from the other passengers typing on their laptops. My 'practice' appeared to be very ordinary activity, just as the other passengers' typing appeared to be.

There are an increasing number of occasions being provided in which a select group of accomplished management scholars have been invited to write about how they work. Peter Frost co-edited multiple volumes in which scholars were invited to reflect on this. Arthur Bedeian has edited an autobiography series. Hari Tsoukas, as editor of *Organization Studies*, has begun a new section of that journal called 'Vita Contemplativa' in which he has invited some scholars to describe their intellectual careers. Kenneth Smith and Michael Hitt edited a book in which scholars told how their influential theories came to be developed.

But on the whole, little is known, in any systematic way, about how individual scholarly works on organizational behaviour and management are actually produced, the ways through which articles (the ones with high impact and the ones without any impact) are conceived, designed, carried to fruition and then published. Or not.

But this is very important. This is the practice of research, the way that causal models, questionnaire numbers, interviews, observations, archival data, and so forth get imagined, carried out, collected, conducted, written about, and translated into scholarly contributions. Similar to what Mintzberg found about managing, these processes are likely best described in different categories than those typically used in teaching research methods. Attention to these processes may help develop much greater understanding of what scholarly work really entails than do standard emphases on what theorizing and research processes ought to be. Weick (1989: 519) noted, for example, that most discussions of theory building are mechanistic, with 'little appreciation of the often intuitive, blind, wasteful, serendipitous, creative quality of the process'.

Continued

Why might it be best to have a practitioner, albeit one trained in social science research methods, conduct such a study? It is unlikely that if Mintzberg's managers had studied themselves they would have seen anywhere near what Mintzberg did; too many of their actions would not stand out for them as worthy of attention. It seems likely that people who work in settings other than academia, who bring different norms, concerns and questions with them than academics do, would be more likely to view what we are doing from different frameworks than our standard ones, and thus help to make much that is tacit about scholarly processes much more explicit.

For example, a manager told me recently that in his job having two months to write a paper was a luxury; he was used to a few days at most. For me, and for many academics, two months to write a paper is barely enough time to start thinking about it. This conversation made me aware of a norm about time in academia that I had not thought of before. There are undoubtedly many other norms that we are unaware of, but that might be obvious to others.

In addition, those in other occupations might help surface our theories of action more effectively. What are our aims when we are writing a scholarly article? Contribute to theory? Get an 'A' hit? Get tenure? Help our doctoral students get jobs? Get into print faster than a competitor? How do both the macro (developing elegant theory) and micro (waiting to write until we're on an airplane) processes of our working on the article contribute to these explicit and implicit aims?

Perhaps joint insider-outsider studies (Bartunek and Louis, 1996) in which both the researchers (those who work outside academia) and research participants (academic researchers) attend to processes and work together to interpret what's going on might be valuable. Outsiders can help to surface our aims, practices and norms, while academics can help explore cognitions and feelings about them. Such joint work and reflection are likely to lead to more heterogeneous conjectures, and thus more creative understandings (Weick, 1989) of what doing scholarly research is and means in practice for academics than reflections carried out solely by academics.

Regardless of whether an experiment such as I have described remains in our thoughts or is actually conducted, it might heighten academic researchers' attention to the theories that guide our action, to our practice, to the norms of our profession, and how integral these are for our research practice.

REFERENCES

Argyris, C. and Schön, D. (1974) *Theory in Practice*. San Francisco: Jossey-Bass.
Bartunek, J.M. and Louis, M.R. (1996) *Insider-Outsider Team Research*. Thousand Oaks, CA: Sage.
Mintzberg, H. (1973) *The Nature of Managerial Work*. New York: Harper and Row.
Weick, K.E. (1989) 'Theory construction as disciplined imagination', *Academy of Management Review*, 14: 516–531.

1.9

Statistico-organizational Theory: Creating Organizational Management Theory from Methodological Principles

Lex Donaldson

This chapter briefly presents a new organizational management theory: statistico-organizational theory. Its central idea is to use methodological principles to drive substantive theory about organizations and managers. Thus, the theory attempts a highly unusual crossover between the domains of methodology and theory, in which methodology becomes the theory. In this way, statistico-organizational theory is a high-water mark in the positivist agenda. Methodology offers a highly developed intellectual apparatus that compares favourably with existing substantive theories of organization and management. Many working organizational and management researchers are committed to these principles, using them as the arbiters to

accept or reject substantive theories as being true or false. Thus, given the foundational commitment to methodology in the belief systems of organizational research, it suggests that using methodology principles to derive substantive theory would be fruitful.

Methodological principles stipulate pitfalls that researchers can make in drawing inferences from numerical data. The key idea of statistico-organizational theory is that these pitfalls must apply also to managers when they are looking at data in their organizations. Thus, methodological principles enable us to predict what errors managers will make and in what situations errors will be most egregious. These data inference errors flow through to managerial decision-making, degrading it and leading to loss of organizational performance. The theory has implications for strategy, structure, human resource management, franchising and other topics in organizational management. The theory leads to a series of theoretical propositions that can be tested in future empirical work. The primary thrust of theory is positive in that its aim is to explain existing patterns of behaviour, rather than to prescribe error elimination.

The methodological principles used here are sampling error and measurement error (unreliability), though these two principles are merely illustrative rather than exhaustive. Once introduced to the concept of deriving theory from methodology, organizational researchers can readily use the methodological principles with which they are familiar to come up with new statistico-organizational theory propositions. In that sense, the theory is inclusionary and has a facilitative, open architecture.

The purpose of this chapter is to offer a new organizational theory: statistico-organizational theory. This is a wholly new class of organizational theory. Unlike previous organizational theories, statistico-organizational theory utilizes ideas from statistics to generate a theory of organizations.

Organizational theory is presently composed of many different theories that draw from various base disciplines. Some organizational theories, such as institutional theory (Scott, 1995), draw upon ideas from sociology. Organizational ecology (Hannan and Freeman, 1989) draws upon ideas from biology. Other organizational theories, such as transaction cost economics (Williamson, 1975), draw upon ideas from economics. Yet, it is possible that productive ideas to build organization theory may be drawn from academic disciplines other than these traditional source disciplines. Previously, we suggested that the finance discipline might be drawn upon, to yield the new organizational theory of organizational portfolio theory (Donaldson, 1999). Herein, we are suggesting that it may be fruitful to draw organizational theory ideas from statistics and the related area of social science methodology. Thus, the present work

is part of a larger programme intended to try to enrich organizational theory by drawing ideas from other than the conventional disciplines.

Statistico-organizational theory is a radical departure from conventional organizational theories and so potentially offers previously unavailable insights. Moreover, it draws on ideas from statistics that enjoy a high degree of validity and coherence. Many of these ideas are already familiar to social scientists versed in modern methodology. The key cross-over attempted by this theory is to take principles of methodology that are already widely believed by researchers, and use them to generate substantive theory about organizations (a brief introduction has been made available in Donaldson, 2007).

The central idea of statistico-organizational theory is that the pitfalls that exist whenever a social scientist examines research data are also present whenever a manager examines data in his or her organization. Therefore, the principles of social science methodology can be used to predict errors of managers in making inferences from numerical data. Statistico-organizational theory analyzes how the data that organizations make available to their managers shape the inferences managers make, thereby influencing managerial decision-making. The theory seeks to develop a series of propositions about when errors will be made by managers who are using numerical data. The theory also seeks to specify the conditions under which those errors are likely to be most egregious. In this way, statistico-organizational theory seeks to reverse a neglect that has characterized organizational theory to date, namely, neglect of the informational content of organizational control systems. The propositions of statistico-organizational theory offer illumination on a broad range of organizational issues, such as strategy, structure, human resource management, franchising and other aspects of the organization. The discussion will be presented in a non-technical way, because the emphasis is upon the concept of deriving theory from methodological principles and its potential broad applications to understanding organizational management.

INFERENCES FROM DATA BY RESEARCHERS AND MANAGERS

Social science researchers spend long hours poring over quantitative data. They use statistical tools, such as significance tests, to try to help them avoid making erroneous inferences. They use statistical tools to separate information from noise. A core premise of the present work is that managers face the same task when they look at quantitative data in their organization. The researcher looks at the study data to try to better understand how the world works. Likewise, the manager looks at data inside their organization to try to understand how their organization is working and what is happening in its environment. The manager tries to make valid inferences from the data and tries to separate information from noise. This managerial problem is not merely an analogy of the researcher's problem. Managers face the *same* problems as researchers in many respects, and both face the problems that inhere in making inferences from numerical data. The potential traps, such as errors from looking at unreliable data, are present in any numerical data, whether in the hands of researchers or managers. The statistical properties of data give rise to problems that are inherent in numerical data. Thus, considerations that apply to research also apply to managers. The methodological principles that apply when a researcher looks at data in their study also apply when a manager looks at data about their organization and its environment. Hence, methodological principles in social science must have implications also for managerial decision-making.

Statistical theory has been used by researchers over the years to create a set of methodological principles that help the researcher to make valid inferences. These are statistical theories such as the law of large numbers, and methodological issues such as the sources of error in measurement. These issues must hold also when managers look at organizational data. Therefore, to better understand managerial decision-making, we must theorize the processes that govern managers when they make inferences from organizational data. This involves an analysis of many facets of the data in organizations, such as the number of observations, the reliability of measurement and so on. It also leads to an analysis of how the data presented to managers are shaped by the organizational structure. Again, it leads to an analysis of how the data in an organization are shaped by other characteristics of the organization, such as its size, and by characteristics of the environment of the organization, such as the size of the national population.

A core idea of statistical inference is that what appears to be true may be false. This can be a trap for a manager looking at data, and can lead to the manager making a false inference from the data. This wrong message, in turn, feeds into managerial decision-making. Thus, knowledge of statistical, and other methodological principles, enables prediction of when managerial inference errors will be made and when they will be most egregious. This in turn allows prediction of when data-based inferences will produce mistaken managerial decisions.

FOUNDATIONS OF THE KUHNIAN RESEARCH PARADIGM

A fundamental issue in social science is the search for foundations of knowledge, that is, for valid premises from which to generate theoretical propositions. The argument of statistico-organizational theory is that the principles of social science methodology provide a secure foundation from which to develop valid theory about social organization.

Statistics is much involved in helping scientists make the soundest inferences possible from their data. For example, estimates of parameters are more valid, the larger is the number of cases in the sample. Also, estimates of parameters are more accurate if the data are reliable through having little measurement error. These foundational statistical theoretical ideas are used in established social science methods to deduce many statistical procedures, which form a coherent intellectual structure. This structure allows reasoning involving mathematical formulae and precise quantity estimates. The structure displays a degree of rigour that social theory can only envy. Social scientists are trained in these quantitative techniques, such as statistical testing, and become familiar with the underlying statistical theoretical ideas. These ideas (such as the importance of large numbers in sampling) function as accepted principles on which methodological practices are based. Thus, much of the day-to-day work conducted by social scientific researchers, when devising studies or processing data, takes these statistical ideas as axiomatic.

In contrast, the propositions derived from organizational theories are treated by academic researchers as mere hypotheses, to be tested through the methodological principles. The theories are fallible and, indeed, may be shown to be false, when the methodological principles are applied. Thus, the truth or falsity of substantive theories is ascertained against the methodological principles that are the criteria for validity. Kuhn (1970) argues that scientists normally work in a paradigm, which is a set of assumptions about what constitutes valid knowledge, which they adhere to without challenging these assumptions. For many social scientists in organizational research, this unquestioned paradigm is not a theory, but, rather, is the set methodological principles that are used to test the theories. Thus, for many organizational researchers, the Kuhnian paradigm is the set of methodological principles. When Burrell and Morgan (1979) sought to identify the fundamental paradigms in organizational theory, they over-looked the methodological principles that constitute the real paradigm of much empirical organizational research. Indeed, many working social scientists entertain a degree of scepticism about substantive organizational theory, while believing in the methodological principles. These methodological principles are respected, and are treated as being fundamental truths. If methodological principles are so strong,

and substantive theories are relatively frail, why not construct substantive theories from methodological principles?

Statistico-organizational theory focuses attention upon the statistical phenomena, such as how the numbers of observations shape errors of inference, which are integral to the organization. Thus, the statistical properties of the situation confronting the organization are a new class of determinants. These statistical phenomena are located in data about the organization and its environment, which are visible to organizational managers inside the organization; and these statistical phenomena in organizational data are objective facts that constrain the managers who are making inferences from them. In that sense, the present analysis continues the tradition of positivist theorizing in organizational science (Hannan and Freeman, 1989; Donaldson, 1996).

It is a particularly opportune time to be applying methodological principles in the new way stated here, because recent advances in methodology have led to the crystallization of a philosophy that 'data have a deep structure'. This philosophy implies a strong form of the argument that an analyst can be misled by the initial impression given by data (Hunter and Schmidt, 2004). This awareness leads to the adoption of the methodological techniques of meta-analysis, in order to reveal the true, underlying picture (Hunter and Schmidt, 2004). There are implications of all this for management. In order for managers to see the true picture, certain conditions would need to be met. Yet, some organizations are unlikely to readily meet these conditions because of inherent situational limitations, such as small organizational size. Again, some organizations could meet these conditions but fail to do so because of managerial practices, such as the way the organization is structured or how performance is measured, so that managerial inferences are infected with error.

We seek to construct a theory of how the properties of organizational data affect the validity of managerial inference and their consequences. That is to say, we are interested in the pattern of managerial and organizational behaviour that results from organizational data. And we are also interested in antecedents of the organizational data, that is, in the causal variables that shape organizational data, such as the organization and its environment. Thus, we wish to better understand how decision-making and managerial action are formed by data, whose properties and pitfalls are specifiable by statistical theory. In this way, we can create a statistical theory of organizations, which can shed light on important aspects of organizational life and death, beyond that available from existing organizational theories.

WHAT THE THEORY IS NOT

Inductivist, or grounded, research seeks to develop theory from data, by finding patterns in empirical evidence and then devising a theory from them. The present enterprise is completely different. Statistico-organizational theory derives theory from methodological principles. Thus, it works deductively, and is theory-driven. Statistico-organizational theory is not empirically-driven nor inductive. Neither is statistico-organizational theory a methodology; rather, it uses methodological principles to construct a theory. The role of statistics in statistico-organizational theory is not to provide a method for analysing data. Instead, statistical (and other methodological) ideas are used as the premises of a theory of organizational management.

There is no presumption in statistico-organizational theory that managers do, or should, base all their decision-making on quantitative data; rather, the argument is that when they do so, certain errors are liable to arise.

Prescriptively, managers may sometimes be advised to follow statistical procedures to reduce errors of inference, so that statistics is being used normatively. In contrast, the intent of the present work is positive, to use statistics to explain where managers will make erroneous inferences from data.

There has been a tradition of empirical study of biases in human decision-making. In particular, it has been shown that human beings have cognitive biases and often fail to grasp fundamental statistical ideas or fail to use them in a logical way (e.g. Kahneman and Riepe, 1998; Vecchio et al., 1996; Staw, 1981; Janis, 1972; Whyte, 1989). There is also a literature about managerial decision-making as being affected by political processes, such as the pursuit of self-interest (e.g. Pettigrew, 1973), and about how structural position in the organization can affect perceptions. Accepting that these processes occur, our concern is different. Our concern is to examine the role of another set of factors that bias managerial judgements. Our focus is upon the data that are presented to managers by the organization and its environment and the resulting statistical properties of that data that then influence managerial decisions. Thus, the central issue is the factual properties of organizational data and the inferences managers make from them. Hence, even if the manager is completely rational, he or she will still make the errors being discussed here. Thus, without invoking inherent human biases, inability to be a natural statistician, or political self-interest, managerial decision-making is still subject to the problems that are identified by statistico-organizational theory.

INFORMATION-PROCESSING AND DATA

The theory of organizational structure has been dominated by the information-processing and administrative decision-making school. From the foundational writings of Simon (1957) in 1950s onwards, the major paradigm for much of organizational theory has been the organization as a decision-making engine. Following Simon (1957), an organization is conceived of as a system for processing information and making decisions. Within this paradigm, Galbraith (1973) has articulated the central role of information-processing and this has been pursued by subsequent organizational theorists (e.g. Egelhoff, 1982, 1988). The Galbraithian model focuses upon the need to efficiently schedule operations throughout an organization that contains several interdependent parts and thereby the need to coordinate the parts. This is achieved through mechanisms such as plans and may be affected by inventory buffers.

Organization theorists have been much concerned with the effects of uncertainty in such a system. Uncertainty reduces the ability to predict and to make estimates accurately. This prevents clear choices between options, and reduces the effectiveness of planning. The main solution strategy, under uncertainty, is to obtain more information. The central idea of Galbraith (1973) is that when a decision is uncertain, more information must be processed to resolve the uncertainty. This insight leads to an emphasis on how much information is available in each part of the organization, through hierarchy, vertical information systems, and the like.

The discussion embraces enhanced mechanisms for processing information, such as investment in vertical integration systems, e.g. computers to process more information, and more quickly transmit it into a central planning office (Galbraith, 1973). The obverse of reducing uncertainity is taking steps to cope with substantial uncertainly, through carrying inventories and dividing operations into autonomous sub-units, thus sealing them from each others' fluctuations.

While this discussion of uncertainty and organization design by Simon (1957) and then Galbraith (1973) is seminal, it has focused mainly on the amount and location of information. In so doing, the theory overlooks certain implications of its own insights. Uncertainty does indeed require more information for its reduction. However, for data to reduce uncertainty, the data must allow people to extract valid information from them. But the data obtained provide an increase in certainty only if they yield accurate estimates of the underlying variables. That is, the parameter estimates, such as mean values, need to be accurate. Otherwise, extensive

data collection by the organization only yields noisy data that cannot reduce the uncertainty. Therefore, our concern, in a sense, goes back a step, to ask how information is extracted from data. The approach taken here focuses on how the properties of data affect the inferences drawn from them by managers.

Much of the way organizational data are collected and fed to organizational managers is in the control systems. For examples, sales performance reports generate sales data, accounting systems generate cost data, and human resource management systems create appraisals of managerial performance. In his seminal case histories of the development of the modern corporation, Chandler (1977) charts the crucial role played by control systems, such as accounting and forecasting systems. He shows how these control systems were developed as part of the changes in scale, strategy, and structure that brought into being the modern corporation. Thus, the vertical integration of specialist function firms into the multi-function firm was premised in part on the development of statistical flows of data that allowed sales forecasts to form the basis for production (Chandler, 1977). Subsequently, the integration of multiple businesses into the diversified multi-divisional structure was facilitated by the measurement of the profitability of each division as the main accountability structure, in place of cost centres (Chandler, 1962). Organizational theory has followed Chandler in being much concerned with organizational strategy and structure. However, organizational theory has mostly neglected to theorize about how the informational content of control systems shapes managerial decision-making. We seek to try to fill that lacuna.

OVERVIEW OF STATISTICO-ORGANIZATIONAL THEORY

The central idea of statistico-organizational theory is that organizations are statistical machines. Their workings are governed by the universal principles of statistics that pervade all of their operating processes.

Thus, statistico-organizational theory takes ideas from statistics and social science methodology, and uses these as the axioms from which to develop substantive theory about organizations.

We shall focus in this chapter on two principles, each pinpointing a factor, or class of factors, that determine whether numerical data give managers correct signals about the true state of their organization and its environment. These principles are the Law of Small Numbers and measurement error (i.e. unreliability).

The Law of Small Numbers

From the Law of Large Numbers in statistics is taken the idea that estimates of parameters by managers in organizations are more valid where the data consist of a large number of observations. Conversely, where inferences are made from few cases, then errors are introduced. Since we are interested in errors that occur from data, we will call this the Law of Small Numbers. Managerial decision-making about marketing and production strategies, as examples, will be more erroneous, the smaller the number of cases, because the inferences on which they are based are more likely to be incorrect.

The Law of Large Numbers states that, the larger the number in a sample from a population, the closer the sample parameter (e.g. the sample mean) approximates to the population parameter (e.g. the population mean). There is less random variation of sample parameters around the population parameter in large samples than in small samples. The larger the samples, the more the mean obtained in the first sample is approximated in the second sample.

Conversely, the Law of Small Numbers states that the smaller the number of observations in the sample from a population, the more the sample parameter tends to vary from the population parameter. The variation of sample parameter around the population parameter is random, so that some samples have a parameter that is below the population parameter and some have a parameter that

is above it. The population parameter is the true value, so the smaller the sample, the more it tends to vary randomly below or above the true value. Therefore, the smaller the number of observations in a sample, the higher the probability that the inferences from that sample will be erroneous. This statistical principle applies to any quanta in organizations: pencils, gaskets, sales, books, people, etc. Thus, every time a manager uses a parameter based on a small number of observations to estimate the true value, random error intrudes. The implications for organizations are pervasive, as will be seen.

Moreover, there is more random variation from sample to sample in small samples than in large samples. The smaller the sample, the less one can rely on the parameter value (e.g. mean) obtained in the first sample being approximated in the second sample. Therefore, the smaller the samples, the more that they appear to come from different populations, when they really come from the same population. Therefore, small samples are liable to give the appearance that there is real variation when truly there is none.

This problem of small numbers can arise in many ways. Countries with smaller populations tend to have smaller sized organizations. Smaller organizations have fewer sales and fewer customers or clients (Blau and Schoenherr, 1971). But even larger organizations may unwittingly decimate the data they present their managers, through decentralization into small branches. Also, over-enthusiasm for very recent data can throw away useful observations from prior periods. In these, and many other ways, managers, sometimes unknowingly, find themselves facing data from too few observations so that their inferences are erroneous and lead to wrong decisions.

Meta-analysis has shown that small numbers are a particularly major source of errors in social science (Hunter and Schmidt, 2004) and so statistico-organizational theory emphasizes small numbers as a potential source of error for managers. In meta-analysis, each individual study of a topic is combined with others, so that parameter estimates can be based on a larger number of observations. Thereby, these estimates are sounder than those from any individual study, which are based on a smaller number of observations (Hunter and Schmidt, 2004). In meta-analysis, the variations in parameter values from study to study can be shown to result from the random variation due to the small number of observations in the individual studies, rather than to real variation (Hunter and Schmidt, 2004). Therefore, the aggregate value is the truer value (Hunter and Schmidt, 2004). Thus, meta-analysis leads to the philosophy that data should be combined to produce a larger number of observations. It leads also to distrust of variations that may appear to reflect some real difference in individual studies, such as their locales, but are often just random variation. Whether apparent variation between locales is genuine can only be ascertained by an analysis of the aggregate data.

Large organizations are like meta-analytic machines. Their managers sit atop a vast pyramid that produces at its top data with large sample sizes, from which most of the random variation have already been extinguished, simply through aggregation. In contrast, managers of smaller organizations are faced with small-scale data-sets, consequently full of puzzles and apparent trends, many of which are illusions, that is, are simply artefacts produced through small numbers. The task of these managers of small organizations is akin to the social scientist trying to infer causal relations from a small sample of, say, 20 subjects – in fact it is the same task. Thus, large organizations are meta-machines and therefore are inherently superior to smaller organizations in the informational aspects of organizational learning, adaption, and management.

Thus, small organizations are closer to their customers, but so close that they cannot tell the wood from the trees. The manager of a small organization receives up-to-the-minute data on a rich variety of aspects, more so than any one manager in a large organization. The problem for the manager of the small organization is making sense out of all the jumble of facts that are based on small numbers. In contrast, the senior manager in the large organization reviews tables of statistics that aggregate thousands of data, in standardized format, allowing comparison. From these data, clear, meaningful patterns and trends can be identified, allowing causal inference, prediction, and planning. For this reason alone, other things being equal, large organizations will tend to be the trendsetters in reacting to environmental changes. Smaller organizations may then match their larger competitors and so follow their lead. Hence some part of the leadership role of large organizations in an industry – sometimes ascribed to oligopoly dominance or professionalized management – inheres in the large organizations' inherent ability to make better numerical analyses, a capacity which their smaller competitor organizations cannot have.

While a large organization starts with the inherent advantage of having a large number of observations, it may dissipate this advantage by disaggregating its data. This can occur through aggregating data only within organizational sub-units, such as divisions or departments or branches, so that the number of observations is only for that sub-unit. Therefore, the base for any parameter calculated from the data is not that of the whole organization but only for the sub-unit. This means that there will be more random variation in the parameters of a sub-unit than the whole organization, so that the figures are more likely to mislead managers into making the wrong decision.

Therefore, the organization needs to have a structure in which data are aggregated at the centre. These aggregate data can then be used to validly determine which factors really vary by organizational sub-unit, e.g. locale, so that decisions about them may be decentralized down to those organizational sub-units. In that sense, the organizational structure has to centralize before it decentralizes.

A conventional human resource management development practice, for instance in a multi-branch bank, is to appoint an individual to be the manager in charge of a small branch. If that branch's performance over a period (e.g. two years) is good, then the individual is judged to be an effective manager and is promoted to manage successively larger branches. If, however, that branch's performance over the period is bad, then the individual is judged to be an ineffective manager, possibly leading to out-placement. However, the smaller numbers of business operations (e.g. commercial loans) that occur in a small branch mean that there is more random variation in the performance of the small branch. Thus, the attribution that the manager is effective or ineffective is contaminated by the luck of the small branch. Hence, the subsequent decision to promote has elements of a lottery. If they ascend the hierarchy their performance will be that of larger units and so luck will decline as arbiter of their fate – if they survived the early trials.

There is an implication of all this for organizational control. Upper level managers tend to intervene if they see a problem of poor performance. Yet, at each lower level of the hierarchy, the number of observations, e.g. sales, is smaller and therefore has more random noise. Therefore, there is more likelihood that, by chance alone, performance will appear poor. Thus, any analysis of overall organizational data may reveal to upper managers spurious cases of poor performance, leading them to intervene. They may then intervene and blame lower-level managers, upsetting trust and the smooth working of the organization. However, this perception of poor performance, and of rectification being required, is an illusion, created by disaggregating the organization's data.

Some decisions are taken by having each sub-unit, e.g. franchise, decide whether a new approach works or not. Then each franchise essentially 'votes', by saying whether it worked for them or not, and the 'votes' determine the organization's decision. But each franchise is much smaller than the whole organization, and so there is much random variation in their results. Thus, some franchises find that the new approach did not work, but this may be spurious, caused by chance, when actually the new approach is working across all the franchises. Hence

voting distorts the true picture. In contrast, aggregating all the data across the whole organization yields a much accurate picture, leading to better decisions.

Measurement error

Again, from social science methodology, we can take the concept of measurement error (Hunter and Schmidt, 2004). Measurement error is the error of the value of the measured variable differing from the value of the true variable and is also referred to as the problem of unreliability (Hunter and Schmidt, 2004). This has several origins, and one in particular will be discussed here: difference scores – because of the likelihood of its occurrence in organizations and its potentially severe impact on managerial decision-making.

Difference scores are a major source of measurement error. A difference score is produced by subtracting one score on a variable from another score on another variable (or that same variable). This difference score can have lower, often much lower, reliability than the variables from which it is derived (Johns, 1981). Therefore, estimates of parameters of difference scores are (often much) less reliable than the original variables, so that inferring the true parameter from difference score data is hazardous and error prone. However, organizations sometimes generate data that are difference scores. Indeed, organizations may use difference scores as mainstays of their control systems, oblivious to the errors in inference that this introduces. For instance, profit is a difference score (the difference between sales revenue and costs) and is therefore subject to inherent unreliability, so that it is error prone. Nevertheless, profit is widely used in internal organizational control systems, as a basis for performance measurement, accountability, reward, managerial succession, investment, and strategy setting – despite the fact that its unreliability makes it a hazardous measure on which to base such decisions.

Not only profit, but other measures, often used by managers and directors of organizations to measure organizational performance, can suffer from low reliability. Again, much of this lower reliability stems from these measures being difference scores. Profitability measures, that is, ratios of profit to other financial variables such as assets or sales, are as unreliable as profit. Similar problems inhere in sales growth and other rates of change over time. Again, analysing a performance measure relative to a control variable or a target, also leads to lower reliability.

Both of these sources of error (small numbers and measurement error) may be operating to produce error in the organizational data being used by managers to make a decision. Hence, both sources can add to the error in the data. For example, divisional profitability compounds the unreliability of the profitability measures with the problems from smaller sample size, in that profitability is calculated for each division, which disaggregates the organization's performance. As another example, niche analyses suffer likewise, being the inherently unreliable profit measure calculated separately for each different product-market of the organization, thereby disaggregating the organization's data. Therefore, the finer-grained the niche analysis, the more unreliable it is, and so the more erroneous are the resulting managerial decisions about strategy. The spuriously low performance of a niche may cause management to eliminate that product-market, whereas in actuality it is beneficial to the organization. Thus, the possible reinforcing of small numbers errors by measurement errors means that managerial inferences from data are potentially prone to considerable error.

CONCLUDING COMMENT

The present chapter is simply a preliminary statement of statistico-organizational theory that puts forward the main concept – using methodological principles to generate substantive theory – and illustrates this for certain methodological principles. There are methodological principles, other than the Law of Small Numbers and measurement error, which can be used to generate

theoretical propositions about organizations and their managers (see Donaldson, 2009). Yet other methodological principles may be used in the future, to produce a more comprehensive statistico-organizational theory. Since many social scientists are well versed in methodological principles, it is likely that many of them can not only help refine statistico-organizational theory, but also greatly add to it.

For instance, restriction in the range of a variable will lead to its correlation with other variables being under-stated. As an example, in an organization, training its members improves their performance. Initially, the amount of training received by organizational members varied widely, producing a strong correlation between training and performance. This led management to the correct inference that was important and to be encouraged. Thus, subsequently, all members received training. However, this restricted the range on amount of training, with everyone high and nobody low, so producing only a weak correlation between training and performance. This then led management to wrongly infer that training was now ineffectual, so they ceased training new members, whose performances consequently failed to attain those of existing members.

REFERENCES

Blau, Peter M. and Schoenherr, P.A. (1971) *The Structure of Organizations.* New York: Basic Books.

Burrell, Gibson and Morgan, Gareth (1979) *Sociological Paradigms and Organisational Analysis: Elements of the Sociology of Corporate Life.* London: Heinemann.

Chandler, Alfred D. Jr. (1962) *Strategy and Structure: Chapters in the History of the Industrial Enterprise.* Cambridge, MA: MIT Press.

Chandler, Alfred D. Jr. (1977) *The Visible Hand: The Managerial Revolution in American Business.* Cambridge, MA: Harvard University Belknap Press.

Donaldson, Lex (1996) *For Positivist Organization Theory: Proving the Hard Core.* London: Sage.

Donaldson, Lex (1999) *Performance-Driven Organizational Change: The Organizational Portfolio.* Thousand Oaks, CA: Sage.

Donaldson, Lex (2007) 'Statistico-organizational theory: A new theory of organizations', in Gavin M. Schwarz, Stewart Clegg, Thomas G. Cummings, Lex Donaldson and John B. Miner: 'We See Dead People? The State of Organization Science', *Journal of Management Inquiry*, 2007, 16, 4 (forthcoming).

Donaldson, Lex (2009) *Statistico-Organizational Theory: Using Methodological Principles to Create a New Theory of Organizational Management*, Irvine, CA: ME Sharpe, Inc.

Egelhoff, William G. (1982) 'Strategy and structure in multinational corporations: an information-processing approach', *Administrative Science Quarterly*, 27: 435–458.

Egelhoff, William G. (1988) *Organizing the Multinational Enterprise: An Information Processing Perspective*. Cambridge, MA: Ballinger.

Galbraith, Jay R. (1973) *Designing Complex Organizations*. Reading, MA: Addison-Wesley.

Hannan, Michael T. and Freeman, John (1989) *Organizational Ecology*. Cambridge, MA: Harvard University Press.

Hunter, John E. and Schmidt, Frank L. (2004) *Methods of Meta-Analysis: Correcting Error and Bias in Research Findings*. 2nd edn. Thousand Oaks, CA: Sage.

Janis, I.L. (1972) *Victims of Groupthink*. Boston, MA: Houghton-Mifflin.

Johns, Gary (1981) 'Difference score measures of organizational behavior variables: a critique', *Organizational Behavior and Human Performance*, 27: 443–463.

Kahneman, D. and Riepe, M.W. (1998) 'Aspects of investor psychology: beliefs, preferences and biases investment advisors should know', *The Journal of Portfolio Management*, Summer: 52–65.

Kuhn, Thomas S. (1970) *The Structure of Scientific Revolutions* (2nd enlarged edn). Chicago: University of Chicago Press.

Pettigrew, A.M. (1973) *The Politics of Organizational Decision-Making*. London: Tavistock.

Scott, W. Richard (1995) *Institutions and Organizations*. Thousand Oaks, CA: Sage.

Simon, Herbert A. (1957) *Administrative Behavior: A Study of Decision-Making Processes in Administrative Organization*. New York: Free Press.

Staw, B.M. (1981) 'The escalation of commitment to a course of action', *Academy of Management Review*, 6: 577–587.

Vecchio, R.P., Hearn, G. and Southey, G. (1996) *Organisational Behaviour* (2nd edn). Sydney: Harcourt Brace.

Whyte, G. (1989) 'Groupthink reconsidered', *Academy of Management Review*, 14: 40–56.

Williamson, Oliver E. (1975) *Markets and Hierarchies: Analysis and Antitrust Implications*. New York: Free Press.

Updating Organization Theory

Jerry Davis

The field of organization studies in North America incubated during the post-World War II era when economic life was becoming increasingly 'organized' – that is, housed within organizations. March and Simon's influential 1958 synthesis *Organizations* provided a framework suitable for studying behavior within organizations as well as the behavior of organizations, understood as discrete units of social structure. Their mid-century academic contemporaries described an emerging social order that was, as Perrow would later describe, a 'society of organizations,' particularly within the US. A consensus developed about the predominant place of the mass production corporation. Peter Drucker wrote that 'The big enterprise is the true symbol of our social order... In the industrial enterprise, the structure which actually underlies all our society can be seen ...'. and that 'the representative, the decisive, industrial unit is the large, mass production plant'. For more than two decades, the biggest organizations kept getting bigger, as the share of assets and employment controlled by the largest few hundred corporations became ever greater. And the expansion of large organizations, particularly manufacturers, was matched by the expansion of theories about organizations. By the late 1970s, perhaps a dozen theories contended to explain the dynamics of the large organizations that dominated industrial society.

But since the early 1980s, corporate assets and employment have become more dispersed in the US, and the practices of the large manufacturers that once occupied the core of the economy are increasingly irrelevant to the bulk of the population. The share of the labor force employed by the 500 largest firms shrank from 21% in 1980 to 16% in 2000. The average US worker is far more likely to be employed in retail than manufacturing, in 2007 there were more mortgage brokers than textile mill workers. Wal-Mart alone employs more people than the eight largest US manufacturers combined. The transition to post-industrialism is nearly complete in the US, and the organizations that shape our lives and careers look little like those described in our most beloved paradigms of the industrial era (reviewed in Scott and Davis, 2007).

Yet organizational research continues to operate under an overhang of theory rooted in an era that has passed. Consider transaction cost economics, a theory whose early empirical base was rooted almost entirely in the study of General Motors as it was in the 1920s (its development of the multi-divisional form and its vertical integration of Fisher Body) and the 1970s (its make-or-buy choices for various parts). The availability of comparable industry concentration and input-output data limited the study of resource dependence tactics, such as mergers, joint ventures, and board interlocks, to manufacturing – a sector accounting for less than 10% of US employment today. Our vocabulary for post-industrial organization is limited by our need to translate back to prior theory.

Organization theory needs to adjust to three things: the transition to post-industrialism, in which the vast majority of the workforce is not engaged in the production of tangible things (agriculture, mining, manufacturing, or construction); the globalization of trade and finance and the changing relations of organizations to states; and the increasing centralty of financial markets to decision making by firms, states, and households. Two industries are particularly apt places for future work. First, the utter centrality of finance to the contemporary world economy has not been matched by the study of financial institutions and markets by organizational scholars. As a field, we know much less than we should about investment banks, mutual funds, commercial banks, hedge funds, and insurance companies. Both ethnographic research and archival studies of industry evolution are highly appropriate. There is some excellent contemporary work on financial firms, but there is room for much more.

Second, shipping may be the industry most under-appreciated by organizational scholars. Ninety percent of the world's exports travel by ship, and more than half the retail goods sold in the US arrive by ship. Moreover, commercial ships are among the most institutionally unconstrained organizations, able to choose their nationality and legal framework with ease (Panama and Liberia being the most popular flags of convenience). As such, shippers represent a vanguard of post-industrial, post-state organizations, and a compelling (and under-studied) industry.

REFERENCES

Drucker, Peter F. (1949) 'The new society, 1: Revolution by mass production', *Harper's Magazine*, September: 21–30.

March, James G. and Herbert A. Simon (1958) *Organizations*. New York: Wiley.

Scott, W. Richard and Gerald F. Davis (2007) *Organizations and Organizing: Rational, Natural, and Open Systems Perspectives*. Upper Saddle River, NJ: Prentice-Hall.

Organization Studies is (and should be) Different from Economics

Jeffrey Pfeffer

Organization studies suffers from economics envy. In subfields ranging from the study of organizational strategy, where transaction costs and industrial organization economics hold sway to the study of managing people where, in the domain of human resource management, the only outcomes that seem to matter are some version of productivity, quality, profitability, or stock market return, to the exploration of individual decision making and motivation where the assumptions of individual rationality and the pursuit of self-interest tend to dominate, and in many other topic domains as well, organization studies not only cites the economics literature at an increasing rate but has bought in many of the behavioral assumptions that underlie economics. This economics dominance is the case even though, as Ghoshal (2005) has argued, many of these economic assumptions are harmful for our students and for practice, and even though, as Bazerman (2005) has noted, many of these economic assumptions and theories have been shown to be wrong.

There are numerous problems with the fascination with economics logic, language, and assumptions. The first is that, as documented in many places, this interest is not reciprocated – economics is almost exclusively a field that cites itself and where there seems to be little interest in incorporating the insights or ideas of related fields, such as organization studies (e.g. Ferraro et al., 2005). Second, it is not the case that in the end, 'truth triumphs'. As has been shown, there are many mechanisms that make theories become self-fulfilling (Ferraro et al., 2005), so that the theories that are believed and advocated most strongly may win in the marketplace of ideas, regardless of either their utility or empirical validity.

Third, and perhaps most importantly, organization studies runs the risk of leaving some important questions unasked, and some important insights unexplored to the extent it becomes too much a step-cousin of economics. As the critical theorists note, much of organization theory is written from the point of view of the interests of those in power. Performance, for the most part, is company profitability or return to shareholders, not how many people have a comfortable retirement or the levels of alienation and distrust in the workplace. Strategy is about achieving sustainable competitive advantage, not whether or not such competitive advantage has any implication for sustainability (in terms of resource use) or for the production or diminution of inequality in a society. The various control regimes and strategies to which people are subjected, ranging from strong cultures to financial incentives, are seldom investigated in terms of their effects on the people themselves as contrasted with their effects on compliance with organizational requests. Many more examples, I am sure, come to your mind.

Because economics and its methodology is primarily premised on individual rationality and methodological individualism, many important topics fade into the background to the extent organization studies adopts economics thinking. For instance, as my colleague James March has often lamented, seeing organizations and institutions as simply a nexus of contracts or as a place where individual preferences come together denies a lot of the fundamental reality and explanatory power that derives from seeing organizations as having a life and an existence and power of their own, separate from their members and different from the idea that 'the people make the place.' Organizations not only reflect individual deals and inducements-contributions calculations and the preferences that people bring to the workplace, but they also are powerful shapers of attitudes and preference, what people believe to be fair and just, how people see their work and even their time, and how people make sense of the world in which they exist. Emotions is another topic that fades into the background with too much emphasis on rational choice. Moreover, even the very phrase 'decision biases', used to describe phenomena such as the availability heuristic or anchoring and adjustment, presumes a normative correctness to some forms of decision logic over others, with little consideration of their relative frequency or of their consequences for people. The 'norms' are set against a theoretical conception of judgment and choice, not against a base rate of what people actually do, nor against some standards of appropriateness derived from alternative theoretical conceptions.

'Interdisciplinary' is a term that seems to evoke unquestioned positive approval, and the idea that organization studies should borrow from economics has assumed a taken-for-granted quality. But there is much to be gained from proposing incompatible theoretical views and then confronting alternative predictions and explanations with data. As Thomas Kuhn reminded us, that is how scientific progress occurs. So, 'paradigm wars' may actually be healthy for the organization sciences, and not being coopted by economics is crucial for maintaining a set of topics, assumptions, and methods that otherwise will be lost.

REFERENCES

Bazerman, Max, H. (2005) 'Conducting influential research: The need for prescriptive implications', *Academy of Management Review*, 30 (1), January: 25–31.

Ferraro, Fabrizio, Pfeffer, Jeffrey and Sutlon, Robert, I. (2005) 'Economics language and assumptions: How theories can become self-fulfilling', *Academy of Management Review*, 30 (1), January: 8–24.

Ghoshal, Sumantra (2005) Bad management theories are destroying good management practices', *Academy of Management Learning and Education*, 4 (1), March: 75–91.

A 'Neo-Carnegie' Perspective on Organizations

William Ocasio

With all the focus on the new and emerging in this wonderful volume on organization studies, it behooves us also to consider what remains practical and desirable about old theories and old perspectives on organizations and management and bring this knowledge back to life. For me no perspective remains as relevant and informative about real-world organizations as the 'Carnegie School', with its three foundational volumes *Administrative Behavior* (Simon, 1947), *Organizations* (March and Simon, 1958), and *A Behavioral Theory of the Firm* (Cyert and March, 1963).

Understanding and studying organizations requires us to distinguish formal organizations from other social systems and forms of informal organizing. The Carnegie School tradition provides an important answer: organizations are social systems for structuring decision making, where the organization – with its formal and informal structures and processes – provides individuals and groups with decision premises and decision rules. One thing that is missing from many new and emerging perspectives on organizations is the recognition of the importance of formal structures and processes. Organizations and organizational decision making must be understood as being shaped not only by formal rules and procedures but by informal relations and processes guided by both the psychology and sociology of social systems.

What is remarkable about the Carnegie School is that it incorporates a myriad of both formal and informal dimensions into a theory of organizations – many clearly understood as part of the Carnegie tradition such as bounded rationality, organizational learning, standard operating procedures, selective attentional focus, and political coalitions. Yet upon re-reading the classic texts of the Carnegie School one also finds the centrality of critical dimensions not typically associated with the Carnegie tradition such as formal authority, hierarchy, identification, language, conflict, and communication processes.

Organizations are clearly multi-dimensional and a common research approach is to focus on one aspect of organizations or organizing (e.g., social relationships), while ignoring others. I suggest instead that the future of organization theory lies in integrating new learning about organizations into existing foundations that incorporate both formal and informal structures and processes. Here is where the Carnegie School perspective provides a foundation and the Neo-Carnegie view represents the future. The foundational pillars of the Carnegie School: (1) bounded rationality; (2) the structure of authority, attention, and communication; (3) the interplay of politics, interests, and identity in maintaining organizational coalitions; and (4) routine-based behavior and performance feedback, provide the building blocks for a comprehensive, multi-dimensional theory of organizations and management. But the Carnegie School is missing key understandings about organizations that were not available in the 1940s, 1950s, and early 1960s. Bridging the gaps is where a Neo-Carnegie perspective provides new and added value to organization theory while valuing the old foundations.

My collaborators and I are developing this Neo-Carnegie view (Gavetti et al., 2006). We propose a 'Reconstructionist' sensibility. The Reconstructionists share with Orthodoxy a reverence and respect for the original source texts but attempt to understand these original source materials in a contemporary light. Our Neo-Carnegie reconstruction incorporates three important dimensions missing from the original Carnegie foundation. First, a more developed view of the micro foundations of organizational behavior, with a more expanded role for emotions, a new view of cognition including the role of analogy and metaphor, and a sensibility for the role of both intuition and analysis in decision making. Second, a more flexible view of decision making than in the original formulation, with greater attention to ambiguity and loose coupling, as reflected in post-Carnegie theories of ambiguity and choice (March and Olsen, 1976). Finally, a more developed view of the effect of the environment on organizations. A central learning of organizations theory since the 1970s is the importance of the environment in shaping organizational structures and outcomes. Here the Neo-Carnegie view treats behavior and decision making in organizations as embedded in multiple social, cultural, institutional, and market environments.

Linking together the foundational pillars of the Carnegie School with the three new dimensions: revised micro-foundations, loose coupling, and embeddedness provides with an integrative theoretical perspective for the future of organization, which builds on and reconstructs established orthodoxy.

REFERENCES

Cyert, R.M. and J.G. March (1963) *A Behavioral Theory of the Firm.* Englewood Cliffs, NJ: Prentice-Hall.

March, J.G. and J.P. Olsen (1976) *Ambiguity and Choice in Organizations.* Universites forlaget Bergen: Norway.

March, J.G. and H.A. Simon (1958) *Organizations.* New York: Wiley.

Simon, H.A. (1947) *Administrative Behavior: A Study of Decision-making Processes in Administrative Organizations.* Chicago: Macmillan.

The Frustrating Search for Interaction Effects

Herman Aguinis and Charles A. Pierce

An interaction effect occurs when the relationship between two variables depends on the value of a third variable. For example, if the relationship between individual skills and job performance depends on the level of employee motivation, then there is an interaction (also labeled a moderating effect) between skills and motivation (e.g. Aguinis, 2007).

Interaction effects have been hypothesized in such diverse research domains as job satisfaction, job stress, pre-employment testing, career management, perceived fairness of organizational practices, leadership, organizational performance, and international business (Aguinis, 2004). In spite of strong theory-based rationale for such hypotheses, researchers often lament the fact that hypotheses about interaction effects are not supported and, if they are, the observed size of interaction effects is quite small. For example, we reviewed 30 years of published articles in *Academy of Management Journal, Journal of Applied Psychology*, and *Personnel Psychology* and found that the median effect size for interaction effects involving a categorical moderator (e.g. gender, nationality, organizational unit, ownership control) was only $f^2 = .002$ (Aguinis et al., 2005). This means that the ratio of systematic variance accounted for by the moderator variable relative to unexplained variance in the criterion or dependent variable is only .02%. Given that variance explained could potentially range from 0 to 100%, this observed median effect size may be considered miniscule by any standards we use.

Why is it that the search for interaction effects in management and organization studies is such a frustrating endeavor? Is it possible that most hypothesized interaction effects do not actually exist? Is it possible that management and organization studies theories including hypothesized moderators such as gender, ethnicity, goal difficulty, organizational unit, type of feedback, task control, training method, employment status, type of compensation, leadership style, nationality, ownership control, pay plan, and so forth, are simply wrong? Of course, we cannot discard this possibility with complete certainty. However, a more likely explanation is that, assuming many of these theories are correct, measurement and design issues are the culprits.

Aguinis (2004) reviewed the numerous measurement and design issues that often prevent researchers from detecting interaction effects that exist in the population. These often-referred-to as statistical and methodological artifacts include issues related to the distributions of the variables (e.g., error variance heterogeneity, predictor variable truncation), the way in which the variables are operationalized (e.g., measurement error, scale coarseness), sample size (i.e., total sample size as well as subgroup-based sample size when the moderator is categorical), and characteristics of the predictor variables (e.g., multicollinearity between the predictors, relationship between the predictors and the criterion). Strategies aimed at improving the estimation of interaction effects that rely on one or two sources of the problems only are not likely to lead to substantial improvements in the accuracy of estimation of interaction effects (Aguinis and Stone-Romero, 1997).

So, what can researchers in management and organization studies do to improve their chances of estimating interaction effects accurately? First, researchers need to become aware of the numerous artifacts that are likely to render interaction effect hypothesis testing invalid (see Aguinis, 2004, for a thorough description of these artifacts). Second, precautions must be taken at the research design stage so that, prior to collecting data, researchers minimize the negative impact of artifacts. For example, these include not dichotomizing truly continuous variables, avoiding variable truncation, using scales with proven psychometric properties, and so forth. Third, computer programs should be used prior to collecting data to estimate statistical power (Aguinis, 2004, provides a description of such programs, which are available online at http://carbon.cudenver.edu/~ haguinis/mmr/index.html). Estimating power a priori will provide researchers with information on the type of research design that will be conducive to detecting an existing interaction effect. Fourth, after the study is completed, results should be reported not only in terms of statistical significance but also in terms of practical significance.

In short, every time a researcher describes anticipated results in terms of contingencies or uses the phrase 'it depends', he or she is referring to an interaction effect. Interaction effects are pervasive in management and organization studies and their presence in our theories will become even more pervasive as our models become more complex. Researchers should be aware of the latest methodological advances if they want their attempts to estimate interaction effects to be less frustrating and more rewarding.

REFERENCES

Aguinis, H. (2004) *Regression Analysis for Categorical Moderators*. New York: Guilford.

Aguinis, H. (2007) *Performance Management*. Upper Saddle River, NJ: Pearson Prentice-Hall.

Aguinis, H., Beaty, J.C., Boik, R.J. and Pierce, C.A. (2005) 'Effect size and power in assessing moderating effects of categorical variables using multiple regression: A 30-year review', *Journal of Applied Psychology*, 90, 94–107.

Aguinis, H. and Stone-Romero, E.F. (1997) 'Methodological artifacts in moderated multiple regression and their effects on statistical power', *Journal of Applied Psychology*, 82, 192–206.

From 20th Century Knowledge Management to 21st Century Challenges

Deborah Dougherty

Models for knowledge management developed during the 20th century are, I suggest, based on linear, scalable, path dependent processes that obey the laws of physics, and emphasize engineering. These models provide enormous insight—we have nailed the managerial principles of: (1) high volume, high quality manufacturing; (2) trajectories and learning curves for technological emergence; and (3) platforms and architectures underlying product innovation. But many 21st century challenges involve non-linear, non-scalable, profoundly ambiguous activities that obey the 'laws' of life and social sciences, and emphasize sciences along with engineering. These challenges include bio-pharmaceuticals, where the functioning of the human body is largely unknown; health care more generally, where socio-economic forces combine with massive redundancies to create real messes; various combinations of 'bio' and 'nano' with whatever else; ecologies and climate changes; and terrorist and intelligence systems.

Our existing models are limited instances of knowledge and innovation management. My current work suggests three avenues into the unknown future. The first is to acknowledge that 'techno-hype,' or the privileging of technology *per se*, dominates both popular and academic thinking. While technologies are important, it is more important to dig into the complex human and social processes of knowing that underlie 21st century challenges, so we can appreciate how, when, and why technologies can be woven into those processes more effectively.

A second avenue into the unknown is to understand the differences across diverse 'knowledge workers', rather than treat them all as a monolithic entity. We know that different thought worlds, knowledge regimes, and epistemic communities exist, but we do not know how these differences might affect sector-wide inter-weavings of knowledge necessary for innovation. Dunne and Dougherty (2006) suggest that engineers working on paradigmatic technologies (the basis for 20th century models) search for answers to defined problems using clear, measurable criteria, while life scientists search for clues to define the problem in the first place, in a very emergent, stepwise fashion. Engineers integrate by pulling together existing solutions into a new package within a defined framework such as an architecture or product concept. Life scientists integrate by iterating among specialties, or rounding up clues into partial patterns rather than defined frameworks. Engineers make sense by learning by doing, a concrete process with immediate feedback. Life scientists make sense using all senses, in a cerebral and unconscious rather than concrete fashion, although experience and the situation are vital too. If technology based management templates are imposed on the whole process, scientific learning could be seriously inhibited.

A third avenue into the unknown is just that – for many 21st century challenges people are managing what they do not know. Rather than concentrate on plans, answers, or solutions, attention shifts to the questions: are we asking the right questions in the right way? How many questions of which kind should we explore? In addition, people need a 'total answer' rather than a single result that something did or did not work. People need to know why and how something did or did not work, what are the conditions under which problems arose, and are there places where it did not? Managing the unknown highlights the social and technological knowing, deciding, and interpreting, and calls into question the material application contexts (production, users) that convey so much of the 20th type of knowledge.

Managing knowledge in the 21st century may not have the simple frames that we now understand so well. There may be no paths along which learning accumulates, no architectures that enable modularity or 'chunking' of complex problems into smaller bits, no scalability, and no feedback (e.g. it takes up to 16 years to develop a new drug). But without some 'frames', learning might be idiosyncratic, fragmented, and easily disrupted, so one research agenda is to develop new kinds of frames for knowing. Synchronous intertwining of science and technology clues of scientific learning may be a frame, but we must first identify the unique contributions of each to innovation. Differentiating the overall processes of inquiry, iteration, and sensemaking into separate levels (e.g., sector, strategic, disease pathway, project team) may also help capture knowledge and provide a fluid framing process for choices. In any case, it seems that organizing will be a primary organ of intelligence for 21st century knowledge and innovation.

REFERENCE

Dunne, Danielle and Dougherty, Deborah (2006) 'Learning for innovation in science-based industries: The case of bio-pharmaceuticals', Working paper. Rutgers University.

Indigenous Perspectives on Restorying and Restoring Organizational Life

Laura Brearley, Treahna Hamm,
Doris Paton and Mark Rose

INTRODUCTION

The Indigenous peoples of Australia have been living and working together in clans and tribes for over 40,000 years. Over this time they have developed a depth of wisdom about sustainable ways of being together in community. We have created this chapter to reveal some of these ancient practices and to explore how they may illuminate some pathways into the future of organizational life.

We are a group of Indigenous and non-Indigenous researchers. In this chapter we are exploring how the Australian Aboriginal concept of Dadirri can be applied within organizations. Dadirri is an Aboriginal word from the Ngangikurungkurr people of the Daly River in the Northern Territory of Australia (Ungunmerr, 2005). There is no equivalent word in English. The closest we can get to describing it in English is a deep and respectful listening which builds community.

Within this chapter we explore the application of this concept to organizational life, looking particularly at how we might restore and restory our organizations through listening deeply and respectfully, building community and connection and reframing our concept of time.

Much of the text in this chapter has been developed through a series of conversations that have been recorded, transcribed and then edited. When the experience of an individual is being described, we identify whose voice it is.

In keeping with the Indigenous Standpoint Theory of Professor Errol West (Japanangka), the chapter incorporates multiple ways of knowing, including stories, poetic text and images. Japanangka's model describes the multi-dimensional nature of experience through an integrated model of eight voices: cultural, spiritual, secular, intellectual, political, practical, personal and public

(West, 2002). Japanangka's model is congruent with the multi-perspectival and poly-vocal approaches of Richardson (2007, 2001, 2000, 1997); Ellis (2004, 2000, 1997) and Lather and Smithies (1997).

THE SPACES BETWEEN

Working in the space between Indigenous and non-Indigenous ways of knowing is a fertile and fragile place to be. The fears of repeating patterns of appropriation and colonization are real for everyone involved. We are continually questioning the possibilities and complexities of Indigenous knowledge and its relationship to the non-Indigenous world. One of our core questions is: How might the non-Indigenous world learn from Indigenous wisdom in a way that is respectful and cognisant of the 'integral relationship of power with Indigenous knowledge'? (Agrawal, 2005)

Alfred Wunbaya, Deputy Chair of the Galiwinku Community, contends that knowledge lives in the head, but it is not made real until it is transferred to the hand and applied in action (Richmond, 2005). As a group of Indigenous and non-Indigenous researchers, we are exploring the possibilities of reframing Indigenous narratives of loss and marginalization into ones in which Indigenous people have agency in their knowledge and in the way in which it is applied.

We are keenly aware of the power dimensions of knowledge that post-colonial researchers describe (Smith, 2005, 2001; Bishop, 2005; Langton and Rhea, 2005; Agrawal, 2005; Anderson, 2005; Banerjee and Linstead, 2004). Emerging from this doubt is Patti Lather's concept that constructive turmoil 'allows for a search of different possibilities of making sense of human life, for other ways of knowing which do justice to the complexity, tenuity and indeterminancy of most of human experience' (Lather, 1991: 52). In discussing Martin Luther's construct of 'paralysis of analysis', Lather writes that 'just getting on with it may be the most radical action one can make' (Lather, 1991: 20).

It is an Indigenous practice in Australia, when a community comes together, to acknowledge the traditional landowners, to welcome people to the country and to wish the community a fruitful meeting. In keeping with this tradition, as we come together around the ideas presented here, we would like to acknowledge the traditional Indigenous landowners throughout the world, and pay our deep respect to the elders, past, present and future.

HISTORICAL CONTEXT

Indigenous management systems in Australia existed thousands of years before Western management theory and practice. The Gunditjmara people live in Australia's South-east in what is now known as Victoria. On the dried-up bed of Lake Condah, rock constructions still stand that were once part of a massive fish and eel trapping system built by Gunditjmara people. These constructions are over 8000 years old. The elaborate fish traps caught fish and eels and they were then processed by a smoking procedure that preserved them. The produce was then traded with neighbouring clans. The Lake Condah clan also built permanent stone cottages prior to white contact.

Two thousand kilometres away from Lake Condah, on the land of the Jali people, in what is today called the 'Northern Rivers' of New South Wales, is a traditional market site. Jali Elders tell of how Aboriginals travelled as far as from 'the Centre' to trade with Chinese merchants, years before Captain Cook arrived in Australia. International trade, enterprise and commerce were traditional activities as opposed to the imposed mythologies of nomadic noble savages that wandered aimlessly about on 'walkabout'.

Bedeian and Zammuto (1991) contend that for thousands of years, collectives of individuals managed and organized themselves in organizations that revolved around tribal or village constructs. These constructs survived, developed and evolved over this time until their existence was threatened by the invention of steam. The Industrial Revolution intruded on both social and economic domains. As a consequence, people were forced to move away from these natural collectives to newer ones represented by large factories, the forerunner of today's corporations.

While the issues of control and conformity were being played out in sociological and organizational terms, a tandem process of colonization emerged as yet another product of the Industrial Revolution. Greater production meant increased reliance upon raw materials as well as new markets, and this meant territorial expansion and the consequent invasion of countries such as Australia. Indigenous knowledge about living and working in communities has a long history.

Applying Dadirri in organizational life

We live in times of escalating pace and pressure on our systems and structures. The cracks have been appearing for a while. Cracks destabilize but also bring with them new possibilities. In paying attention to different ways of knowing and being, new sensibilities can emerge. The concept of Dadirri offers a different way of knowing and being. Dadirri is about being profoundly aware and respectful. It is about being patient and taking the time that is needed. Dadirri builds community (Ungunmerr, 1999).

There are more than 400 Aboriginal languages in Australia. The word for it changes, but the concept of Dadirri appears in many Aboriginal languages (Atkinson, 2001). Miriam-Rose Ungunmerr describes Dadirri like this:

> Dadirri is inner deep listening and quiet still awareness. In our Aboriginal way we learnt to listen from our earliest times. We could not live good and useful lives unless we listened. We learnt by watching and listening, waiting and then acting. Our people have passed on this way of listening for over 40,000 years. Through the years, we have listened to our stories. (Ungunmerr, 2005)

Professor Judy Atkinson, an Australian Indigenous scholar, incorporated the concept

of Dadirri into the research methodology of her doctorate. She writes:

> The result of Dadirri's profound, non-judgemental watching and listening is insight and recognition of the responsibility to act with fidelity in relationship to what has been heard, observed and learnt. Dadirri at its deepest level is the search for understanding and meaning. (Atkinson, 2001: 8)

In this chapter, we will examine three inter-related ideas within the concept of Dadirri that can enrich the nature of our experience in organizational life. The first is the concept of deep listening with respect, the second is building community and connection and the third is re-examining our relationship with time.

Listening deeply with respect

Listening deeply with respect is a central idea within the construct of Dadirri. Listening with respect raises the issue of power in organizational life, taking us beyond positional power to a perception of authority that may transcend assigned leadership roles.

Dadirri asks us to pay attention to stories and to silence and to the spaces that lie between. It sensitizes us to the aesthetics of an organization. It awakens that which may not be overtly stated but which is palpable in the corridors.

Treahna

Dadirri opens up a space to think about inner experience
Dadirri is deep listening not only with your ears
It's deep listening with your eyes
It's deep listening with all the senses
It's connected to a spiritual realm

Doris

When I was working in policy in Canberra, I worked with a man who needed to come down and see some Aboriginal people on educational business. I knew the community. We got off the plane in Melbourne and we drove to the place. The man from the government paced up and down impatiently for about an hour, and I said, 'We aren't going to do business yet. We'll do business when we've talked about family, community, and had a cup of tea, and they feel relaxed with you. Then we'll sit down and do business.'

We took some people from a government department down to Wilson's Promontory for the day. The old man began talking from the minute we got on the bus, until we arrived, and on the way we visited a few of his friends. When we arrived, the government people said, 'Have we started? When are we starting?' And we said: 'Have you been listening? We started a long time ago. You need to listen to what is being said by this old man. You need to listen and follow the cues, and not expect to have a big piece of paper with dot points put up in front of you. We're doing it our way'.

Sometimes our people just talk and they don't necessarily go straight to the point of the issue. My old Aunties sit there for ages and talk and talk and talk. They don't like to be interrupted. As an Indigenous person, you learn that respect for other people.

Talk family
Talk community
Talk country

Let them know you're interested in her as a
    person

When she wants to tell you
Then she will tell you

Treahna

Life has many meanings to me. I am a member of the Stolen Generation. I'm an Aboriginal woman, I've got German heritage in my adopted family, English heritage in my adopted family and I've got a Celtic name. There are many dimensions to me as a person.

As Indigenous people we see and read signs, from the landscape, animals, birds and other people. We have learned to practice Dadirri and to listen deeply to the internal and external guidance that we receive and to respect the signs and symbols that sometimes go beyond rational understanding.

When I make art, I delve deeply into who I am. I get inside the questions which reflect individual narratives as well as total community experience. Whatever I learn through historical or cultural knowledge, reveals something to me about myself. In my artwork and in my research, I have had some profound and affirming experiences which have led me to trust my intuition and my inner knowing. As Indigenous people we see and read signs, from the landscape, animals, birds and other people. I have learned to practice Dadirri and to listen deeply to the internal and external guidance that I receive and to respect the signs and symbols that sometimes go beyond rational understanding.

In Indigenous culture there is knowing on many different levels. We know the spirits of the ancestors and the spirits of the land are around us. We can feel them. It goes unsaid a lot of the time but there are deep connections and they are always there. They reinforce the stories that the old ones tell us. They reinforce our beliefs, our culture and our identity.

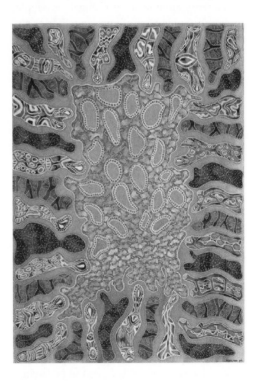

We look up at the sky and we see the clouds
We see the blue gaps in between

The gaps matter
They link the clouds together

The shapes we see in the clouds may differ
But the sky and the clouds connect us all

In our work we make meaning in different
* ways*
But our relationships bring us together

We give of ourselves
We come to know what we value and share

The demands of control and compliance
Stifle our connections and suppress our
* creativity*

When we limit creativity and compassion
And replace it with control

We are working only with bones
the meat has been stripped away

Mark

When we communicate as Indigenous people, we use different ways of knowing. Stories and symbols are common in our communication. We can turn something complex into a bird, or a movement of animals, or a tree, and use that to explore an issue. You can actually reveal complex ideas in beautiful, immediately known symbols or stories. Silence is also a communication. If we are constantly talking, we are locked into a tennis match of logic against logic, point against point, one wins and one loses.

Sometimes our meetings begin with a massive belly laugh. Given the amount of trauma we have in our life, it might seem strange to be laughing. But it comes from the deepest residual enclave of our belly. The laughter comes from our inner spirit. It's loud and deep. It's a sign that people are getting in touch with themselves. Communal laughing brings us back to the essence of who we are as Indigenous people.

When I communicate with a group, my spiritual voice tells me what I need to be saying. I tune in to what the group needs. Their spirits communicate with me and they tell me what they need to hear. The Elders and the ancestors will talk through me. Our intelligence is not actually our intelligence. I believe there is a

deeper wisdom accessible to everybody if you open up to multiple ways of knowing.

BUILDING COMMUNITY AND CONNECTION

'We must have genuinely reciprocal relationships in all dealings. Anangu says "Ngapartji-ngapartji": we give, each to the other.' These are the words of Aboriginal elder Lowitja O'Donoghue (O'Donoghue, 2001). Organizational development literature also stresses the importance of reciprocity and co-creative relationships. According to Meg Wheatley, our capacity to engage with each other and to connect is what generates power in organizations. To make a system stronger, relationships need to be strengthened (Wheatley, 1999).

The building of community through deep and respectful listening in Dadirri links to Wheatley's concept of networks of interdependent relationships within organizations. If we frame an organization as a living organic system (Morgan, 1986, 1996), we can create spaces within them in which to build networks based on trust. When we make connections across formal structures and boundaries, we are able to work creatively with the juice that lies in the cracks of an organization. Building relationships between and beyond formal structures is a creative and potentially subversive act.

A community that is built on trust and respect within an organization can generate a sense of belonging that links inner and outer worlds, reflecting Thich Nhat Hanh's notion of dependent co-arising (Hanh, 1991).

Doris

In our Indigenous communities, we work together in cooperative, collaborative ways. What we value is the human element of doing business through trust, relationships and listening to people. In our community, if people don't want to talk to you, they will disappear. And if they don't have that relationship with you, or if they think you're pushy, or if they think that you're not listening, they will disappear. Aboriginal people are really tuned in to whether somebody's actually listening to them, and whether they're showing that by the respectful way of interacting with them.

The process of working with people in the community is to build the relationship, to build the trust and to trust that you have the same vision in the long run. There are ways of doing things and we need to sit down and work out these things. That's the way Indigenous people do business. We sit and we listen and we talk. We wait and we learn and then we decide how to move forward.

Mark

The kinaesthetic fleshy stuff matters enormously. If we've got a hot issue at work, we can call a 'brief scrum'. Everyone stops what they're doing and comes to my office. I say: 'We've got ten minutes, this is the hot issue, let's use our collective minds'. People stop what they are doing and like a clan or a tribe, we come together. It is a deeply physical act, watching people leave their desks to come together, to stand shoulder to shoulder, to focus on a shared problem that needs solving.

Standing shoulder to shoulder is about being part of a tribe or a clan. For tens of thousands of years, Indigenous people have come together to sing, tell stories and dance. Our organizations are modern day tribes. Organizations can be framed as sausage factories, getting product to market and keeping costs down. Another frame is seeing an organization as the spiritual, structural and emotional aspects of a tribe. No one is saying, 'That person is doing my job' because that job is everyone's job.

Doris

We need a collaborative and cooperative way of working and decision making. The holistic way of doing things is about the environment, the people and the business. Shared values and the respect, that's the way we see things.

In doing business, body language is really important. Aboriginal people are very tuned in to body language and they can pick up straight

away what sort of a person you are. There are all sorts of things that are culturally relevant in doing business.

The top-down management stuff isn't appealing at all. From our point of view it's very much the missionary type approach. The businesses that do really well are where people feel they belong in that business and that their input is valued. Big business has got a lot to learn. The racy, pacy stuff stresses people and burns them out. In the end, people jump off the ship.

Laura

We listen to silence and stories
And spaces that lie in between

We open to new ways of knowing
Of sensing and feeling and thought

Our relationships weave us together
We link the parts with the whole

We work with the muddy, the complex, the grey
In content and context and form

We sit and we listen, we watch and we wait
When the time is right we connect and create

Treahna

When we are with the Elders, there's a strengthening of the bond that we share. There's a sharing of stories. When we are weaving together, even though the stitches are the same, there's an element of self that goes into the stitches. No matter what we create, and whether we remember the conversation or not, the main thing is to be creating and learning at the same time.

We don't ever really know how deep the water is that we're wading in.

The river is a body
The meaning of life is in the river
The billabong stagnates and dies if there is no
   life flow
If it is not in touch with the river

If the shell limits and blocks
We are cut off from the source of life

We are part of the landscape
When the water is sick, the people get sick

When our work is creative the water filters
  through the trees
And we are connected to the river

REFRAMING OUR CONCEPT OF TIME

Dadirri asks us to take time. Continually feeding relationships takes time. The investment in
relationships and the need to take time are integrally connected. It leads us into paradoxical
terrain in the time-poor atmospheres that exist
in so many organizations. It seems we can't
afford the time, and yet we must. Sometimes,
it helps to think about time differently.

If we re-imagine time beyond a linear, mono-directional construct of past,
present and future, we become more open
to experience a malleable and fluid sense
of time. A re-imagining of time in this
way resonates with some Indigenous conceptions of time. The Hawaiian epistemologist,
Manulani Meyer, advocates that we remember
our future (Meyer, 2005). A related idea is
reflected in the Maori concept of walking
backwards into the future looking at our past
receding in front of us.

How we choose to prioritize our activities
is another aspect of how we frame time.
The deeply embedded sense of service to
family and community that is a core value
in Indigenous communities is often at odds
with the demands of economic imperatives
and the intense pace of organizational life.
Plans may suddenly change if a member of
the community has needs or if there is 'sorry
business' to attend to.

We find ourselves facing a central paradox.
Building communities in organizations takes
time. Deep and respectful listening takes time.
The frenetic pace of our lives reinforces the
notion that there is no time. At the deepest
of levels, Dadirri functions beyond time. It
invites us to transcend what we understand
time to mean.

Doris

Time is a real issue in today's world and
there's a paradox there. There are creative
ways of working where time and space can
be approached differently. People need a work
space that they feel comfortable in, that they
can create in and that they can feel positive
about. It's helpful to have time-out places,
where you could move away from your desk,
move over to the window or lie on a couch
and take a phone call.

> We still have to teach the non-Indigenous people
>   many things, things like:
>
>> It's not the right time to do this
>> These things happen for a reason

We clue in to when it feels right,
We don't tend to say.

>> This has got to happen now, now, now
>> It doesn't work like that
>>
>> It might take a long time and you might
>>   only get so far
>> But then when things are realised
>> Then you know that people have been
>>   really listening
>> We sit and we listen
>> And we wait
>>
>> Until the time is right

What matters most is respect, relationship
and trust.

AN EXAMPLE OF DADIRRI IN PRACTICE

So far, we have been speaking in general terms about the application of Dadirri to organizational life. Here, we will give an example of how we are applying this practice within our own organization.

We are part of a project involving 17 Indigenous research students who are undertaking Masters degrees and Doctorates. Some of us are research supervisors and some of us are students. The group of students is known as the Koori Cohort of Researchers. (Koori is the generic name for Aboriginal people of the South-Eastern region of Australia.)

Many of the students are using the concepts of Dadirri as a methodology within their research projects. As a group, we are also using these concepts as a way of working together as a research community within a university system.

We have invested considerable time in building this community of scholarship and exploring what Dadirri means in this context. Our work in this community is underpinned by an educational philosophy which recognizes Indigenous wisdom and encourages multiple ways of knowing. The Indigenous students and their ancestors have known since ancient times that wisdom does not have to be written down to endure, that you can dance a story and that you can sing a land into existence.

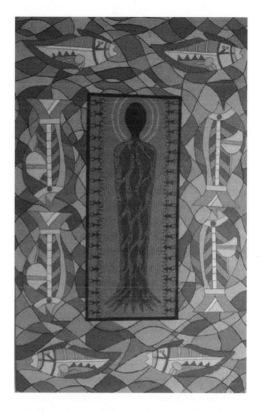

Treahna

We are stabilized
And linked to our stories

If we are disconnected
We are cut off from love and life
In our work we need to value our shared humanity
Before any real connection can begin

Story-telling builds trust and deepens meaning
It creates a focal point for understanding

In our stories
We come to know ourselves

Laura

I think it was a mixture of naivety and courage
That led me to working with Indigenous research students

I was asked to take on an Indigenous doctoral student
He was almost out of time

We found a way of working together
That felt like a partnership

We both bent and stretched
And trust between us grew

His work was strong and important
And immediately relevant to the needs of the community

There was a big celebration
On the night of his graduation

An Elder said she could feel the ancestors very close
They were dancing

Word got around of the successful completion
The Koori grapevine is an amazing thing

Other Indigenous students wanted to join the research program
They had heard there was a way of doing research

In which there was room for Indigenous voices
And multiple ways of knowing

They were artists, musicians and educators
Well-known in their community

The project attracted some willing staff
Who were keen to work at the boundaries of
knowledge and wisdom

To challenge the system to stretch its edges
To reframe, rethink and include

To question at the deepest of levels
What a university is and what it might become

One of the students introduced us to the concept
of Dadirri
A way of being with others which encouraged
an inner, deep listening

An approach to research based on respect
Involving the head, the heart and the spirit

The practice of Dadirri in our work has made a
space where
Creativity, research and reconciliation
interconnect

I have come to see that trust is everything
It is slowly gained and easily lost

Trust is what keeps the conversation alive
Through the painful mistakes and unchallenged
assumptions

There are so many reasons not to trust in this
world
And yet it is all we have

It is the essence of our work together
It is what the bridges are made of

A group of staff and students called Friends
of the Cohort has been attracted to the work
that is being done in the group. The Friends
form part of an extended community who
are interested in the concept of Dadirri.
Some of the Friends of the Cohort are jazz
musicians who for the last two years have
been improvising in public performances with
the artwork, music and stories being generated
from the research projects of the Koori Cohort
members.

Mike Jordan is a jazz drummer who has
done a number of collaborative performances
projects with the Koori researchers. Dadirri is
at the heart of this work.

You have to respond as a musician and as an
improvisor

You have to respond
You have to be as faithful as you can to your own
feelings
You have to listen very carefully and listen
within
Allowing your feelings to rise
And then responding to those feelings

In improvisation, I find critical points where
I have to make a decision
I travel along a certain path and then I come to
a point
It's at those points that your listening has to be
heightened
You have to very aware

It's good to listen to silence and then be aware
When that silence is broken

Silence plays an essential part

(Mike Jordan, 2005)

Mike is Kipps Horn's research student. Kipps
is a research supervisor in the Koori Cohort.
He writes:

Dadirri involves entering people's silence
And entering my own silence
And letting ideas and feelings emerge
Within those spaces and silences
Being in that silence and space
And listening and feeling the spaces and silence
Is not always an easy thing to do
When it happens deeper things emerge

(Kipps Horn, 2005)

CONCLUSION

The practice of Dadirri has a great deal to
teach us about how we communicate and
co-exist with each other in organizations. It
describes a way of heightening awareness
and building relationships in creative and
respectful ways. A consciousness of Dadirri
enables us to question our organizational
story-telling, 'What do we listen to? What
stories do we value?' The practice of 'Dadirri'
also invites us to question who is deserving of
respect. According respect where it is due is a
subversive act which can reveal new sources
of knowledge and wisdom. Deep listening and
respect are closely intertwined.

Dadirri is a radical shift from the trajectory of increasing intensification of the workplace. It asks us to consider both process and outcome and the relationship between them. The capabilities that are needed to apply the concept of Dadirri in organizations are a capacity to work with paradox and a willingness to take risks. Certainly courage is needed, intuition and patience.

The concept of Dadirri is particularly helpful for organizations in transition where systems may be crumbling or being re-organized. Application of these concepts during periods of transition reframes cracks in the system as an advantage rather than a threat. Building relationships across formal structures opens opportunities for the marginalized or overlooked to have a voice. Trust and respect can emerge in organic ways rather than where they are structurally implied.

The application of Dadirri in an organizational context is a call to different ways of knowing and more human ways of being. The issues of how we prioritize and what we regard as a valuable use of our time lead us to questions of an existential nature:

Who can I trust?
Who do I respect?
Where is it safe?
What is sustainable?
What matters?
What matters most?

At the heart of the restorying and restoring of our organizations is the willingness to take the time to deeply listen and truly connect.

Beyond the crisp and certain
And the recipes of one minute management and seven steps to somewhere
Beneath the longing to keep ambiguity and anxiety at bay
Lies the doubtful, the liminal, the possible

A fumbling search to be authentic, not for greater productivity or power
But for something that might help us to be and become more human together

To help us reveal what lies below and beyond

And between the worlds we create together in our organizations

Against the backdrop of the time constraints and by profit-driven imperatives, Dadirri presents us with an alternative narrative of organizational life.

Acknowledgement

Artwork and associated poems reproduced by permission of Treahna Hamm. She wishes to acknowledge the Elders who have supported her in her academic and cultural studies.

REFERENCES

Agrawal, A. (2005) 'The politics of Indigenous knowledge', *Australian Academic and Research Libraries*, 36(2): 73–85.

Atkinson, J. (2001) *Privileging Indigenous Research Methodologies*, Paper presented at the National Indigenous Researchers Forum, University of Melbourne, Sept 2001.

Anderson, J. (2005) 'Indigenous knowledge, intellectual property, libraries and archives: crises of access, control and future utility', *Australian Academic and Research Libraries*, 36(2): 85(13).

Banerjee, B. and Linstead, S. (2004) 'Masking subversion: Neocolonial embeddedness in anthropological accounts of Indigenous management. *Human Relations*, 57(2): 221–247.

Bedeian, A. and Zammuto, R. (1991) *Organisations: Theory and Design*, Chicago: Dryden.

Bishop, R. (2005) 'Freeing ourselves from neo-colonial domination in research: A Kaupapa Maori approach to creating knowledge, in Norman Denzin and Yvonna Lincoln (eds) *The Sage Handbook of Qualitative Research* (3rd edn). Thousand Oaks, CA. pp. 109–138.

Ellis, C. (1997) 'Evocative autoethnography: writing emotionally about our lives', in W. Tierney and T. Lincoln (eds) *Representation and the Text: Reframing the Narrative Voice*. Albany, NY: State University of New York Press.

Ellis, C. (2000) 'Creating criteria: An ethnographic short story', *Qualitative Inquiry*, 6: 273–277.

Ellis, C. (2004) *The Ethnographic I: A methodological Novel about Autoethnography*, Walnut Creek, CA: Alta Mira Press.

Hanh, T.N. (1991) *Old Path White Clouds: Walking in the Footsteps of the Buddha.* Berkeley, California: Parallax.

Meyer, M. (2005) 'Remembering our future: Hawaiian epistemology and the specifics of universality', *International Journal of Entrepreneurship, Advancement, Strategy and Education*, 1(1): 49–56.

Morgan, G. (1986) *Images of Organisation*, Beverly Hills, CA: Sage Publications.

Morgan, G. (1996) 'An afterword: Is there anything more to be said about metaphor?', D. Grant and C. Oswick (eds), 1996, *Metaphor and Organizations*, London: Sage Publications, pp. 227–240.

Lather, P. (1991) *Getting Smart: Feminist Research and Pedagogy with/in the Postmodern.* New York: Routledge.

Lather, P. and Smithies, C. (1997) *Troubling the Angels: Women Living with HIV/AIDS.* USA: Westview Press.

Langton, M. and Rhea, Z.M. (2005) 'Traditional indigenous biodiversity-related knowledge', *Australian Academic and Research Libraries*, 36(2): 47(26).

O'Donoghue, Lowitja, in Kirstie Parker and Katrina Power (eds) 2001, *Kaltja Now: Indigenous Arts Australia.* Wakefield Press in a association with the National Aboriginal Cultural Institute – Tandanya.

Richardson, L. (1997) *Fields of Play: Constructing an Academic Life.* New Jersey: Rutgers University Press.

Richardson, L. (2000) 'Writing as a method of enquiry', in N.K. Denzin and Y. Lincoln, (eds) *Handbook of Qualitative Research* (2nd edn). Thousand Oaks, CA: Sage Publications.

Richardson, L. (2001) Poetic representation in interviews, in J.F. Gubrium and J.A. Holstein (eds), *Handbook of Interview Research.* Thousand Oaks, CA: Sage Publications. pp. 877–891.

Richardson, L. (2007) 'Reading for another: A method for addressing some feminist research dilemmas', In S.N. Hesse-Biber (ed.) *Handbook of Feminist Research.* Thousand Oaks, CA: Sage Publications. pp. 459–467.

Richmond, C. (2005) 'Libraries and knowledge centres in the Northern Territory', *Australian Academic and Research Libraries*, 36(2): 29(10).

Smith, L.T. (2001) *Decolonising Methodololgies: Research and Indigenous Peoples.* Denedin, New Zealand: Zed Books, Room 400 and University of Otago Press.

Smith L.T. (2005) 'On tricky ground: Researching the native in the age of uncertainity', in Norman Denzin and Yvonna Lincoln (eds) *The Sage Handbook of Qualitative Research* (3rd edn). Thousand Oaks, CA, pp. 85–107.

Ungunmerr, M.R. in Jennifer Isaacs, (1999), *Spirit Country: Contemporary Australian Aboriginal Art.* San Francisco: Hardie Grant Books.

Ungunmerr, M.R. (2005) http://www.heartlanddidgeridoos.com.au/Cultural/dadirri.htm Accessed 12/07/05.

West, E. in D. Foley, (2002) 'An indigenous standpoint theory', *Journal of Australian Indigenous Issues*, 5(3): 3–14.

Wheatley, M. (1999) *Leadership and the New Science: Discovering Order in a Chaotic World*, (2nd edn). San Francisco: Berrett-Koehler Publishers.

Workplace Spirituality, Towards What Purpose?

Marjo Lips-Wiersma

In the past decade over 400 books on workplace spirituality have appeared in print, special journal issues have been dedicated to the topic, handbooks have been published and an Academy of Management interest group has been established. In this note I consider the contribution of this field of inquiry. Matthew Fox tells us that the questions we address in our practice tell us what matters (Fox, 1991). To date the questions we ask in the workplace spirituality field tell us that the following purposes matter: increasing the bottom line, meaningful living / self-realization, enacting our interdependent reality and moving beyond self-interest to serve the real needs of humanity. Below I review the contributions and pitfalls of each of these.

Typically the field of inquiry that aims to contribute to increasing the bottom line has the following line of reasoning: 'Spirituality makes people want to work together, gives them greater clarity in their values, or makes them happier, hence they are more loyal or innovative, hence the organization benefits, hence it should implement practices that enable the individual to work from her spiritual self'. Implicit in this body of work is that the purpose of spirituality is to be an instrument to further the higher priority goals of growth, market capitalization and shareholder value. The benefit of this approach is that it is practical, which is helpful in a field that has the potential to begin and end with words. It recognizes that organizations have survival needs, and does not make spirituality the moral high ground and material concerns unworthy of consideration. Spirituality as an instrument to increase the bottom line does, however, raise significant ethical questions, given that the harnessing of hearts and souls for the sole purpose of increasing the bottom line will diminish rather than enhance meaningful living. From a spiritual perspective, business is something that we do, but it is not the ultimate purpose of existence, nor the place where we seek guidance as to how to live a spiritual life. Rather than attempting to justify workplace spirituality economically, a more pertinent question is therefore how business can serve our individual and collective spiritual well-being. We currently see many examples such as the Body Shop and Ben and Jerry (which have a purpose beyond profit, and in which the owners have tried to express a series of spiritual principles), that struggle in finding the right capital and ownership models. I therefore suggest a future research agenda on the bottom line that does not make spirituality secondary to profit and where questions focus on the material conditions under which organizations that want to enact spiritual principles and be socially activist can remain viable without having to succumb principles to market forces.

Typically the field of inquiry that aims to contribute to meaningful living states that we have a crisis of meaning as a result of the diminishing influence of the church and community as our main systems of guidance and support. As a result, it is argued, we are increasingly looking at our paid work to experience a sense of meaningfulness. The contribution of this field of study is that it consistently acknowledges that a significant proportion of our behaviour in organizations is based on our desire to fulfil emotional and existential needs. Given that the search for 'who I am' and 'why I am here' has traditionally

Continued

been strongly embedded in various forms of spirituality, this is a legitimate place for workplace spirituality to contribute.

There are also potential risks to this approach. The original purpose can easily become derailed as leaders or organizations are 'providing' meaning which results in diminishing rather than supporting our sense of self. Another danger is in leaders achieving guru-like status or that the organization itself becomes an invisible religion. Because this religion is invisible there is no rigorous questioning and this can lead to dogmatism or cultism with its subsequent pressures and infringements on individual rights. An unbalanced drive for self-realization can also lead to increased individualism and an unmitigated self-help culture that does not recognize the long-standing argument of critical theorists that organizations can trample personal freedom and individual fulfilment (Stern and Barley, 1996). To rigorously examine the spirituality – meaningful work relationship, we need to increase our understanding of whether and how well-established spiritual practices such as discernment and dialogue translate into commercial organizations; to distinguish between 'managing meaning' and 'enabling meaningful work'; to study not only the factors that make work meaningful, but also those that make work meaningless and to study the combined meaning of various life roles rather than assuming that paid work will be the primary avenue for meaningful living.

Typically the rationale for acting out of a sense of relatedness is that we are all interdependent and that spirit, as Thomas Aquinas said, is the capacity to relate to the totality of things. Given that it is broadly acknowledged that moral solidarity, sacrifice and generosity are not a product of the intellect but a creation of the human spirit, workplace spirituality may, from this perspective, meaningfully contribute to business ethics and team work beyond empty ritual. In this approach too, there are some possible pitfalls. At a micro level religious diversity is often not acknowledged. The argument is that when we work from a spiritual paradigm we are more unified. However, the tenets of religious traditions individuals bring to workplace are often not compatible. Another risk at both micro and macro level is that some new age perspectives such as 'cosmic energies' become politically illiterate platitudes that do nothing to change conditions in the world. An important question is whether we can meaningfully pose a return of the subject-actor as a social force, or whether these stirrings of disaffection of the soul remain merely a private retreat, another iteration of quietism (Casey, 2002) in which case a return to personal meaning-making and a sense of belonging may be encouraged by organizations to keep unrest at bay.

The final purpose of workplace spirituality literature and research is to aid business in serving a healthy and just global society. Typically it is based on the premise that human beings are intrinsically motivated to realize their spiritual nature and purpose which is naturally exercised in service beyond self-interest. Hence the overall priority goal or existential foundation of business that wants to work with the hearts and souls of its employees becomes to directly or indirectly serve the real needs of humanity. Another premise is that business is not at the centre of society, but that our collective spiritual and material well-being is. From this perspective spirituality is viewed to be not just another slice in the pie of our work and life priorities, but the foundation to all human life. Here we would focus on the question of 'What are the consequences of the existence of organizations?' (Hinings and Greenwood, 2002). Given that management is becoming an increasingly universal framework for negotiating the myriad of human experiences and interactions (Grey, 1999), spirituality can provide one alternative framework through which to discern possible futures that we may want to create through our work and organizations. From this perspective we would ask more questions about the micro and macro conditions under which we can best create a better future for all of humanity. Rather than measuring the contribution of spirituality by traditional performance measurements we would focus on such concepts as dignity, equity and justice. We would further our understanding of the conditions under which 'doing good' would be given priority over 'doing well' where these are (as is so often the case) in conflict. This, to me, is the most challenging but also most promising contribution of workplace spirituality literature and research.

REFERENCES

Casey, C. (2002) *Critical Analysis of Organizations: Theory, Practice, Revitalization.* London: Sage Publications.

Fox, M. (1991) *Creation Spirituality: Liberating Gifts for the Peoples of the Earth.* New York: HarperCollins.

Grey, C. (1999) '"We are all managers now"; "We always were": On the development and demise of management'. *Journal of Management Studies,* 36: 561–585.

Hinings, C.R. and Greenwood, R. (2002) 'Disconnects and Consequences in Organizational Theory?' *Administrative Science Quarterly,* 47(3): 411–421.

Stern, R.N. and Barley, S.R. (1996) 'Organizations and social systems: Organization Theory's Neglected Mandate', *Administrative Science Quarterly,* 41(1): 146–162.

Social Worlds Theory and the Power of Tension

Bente Elkjaer and Marleen Huysman

INTRODUCTION

The contemporary 'practice-turn' (Schatzki et al., 2001) of organization studies and the focus upon organizations as both actions or 'doings' as well as fields of practices (Gherardi, 2006; Nicolini et al., 2003) has introduced a radically new way of approaching the issue of organizational learning. This perspective can be traced back to Jean Lave and Etienne Wenger's work on learning as legitimate peripheral participation in communities of practice (1991). The practice-based take on organizational learning has been helpful in bringing our attention to learning as collective endeavours rather than viewing individuals as representatives for organizational learning, and it has alluded us to learning which is not connected to any kind of teaching, instruction, intervention, or supervision.

Before the introduction of the practice-based understanding of organizational learning, learning was mostly conceived as information processing and communication, which relies heavily on the image of organizations as cognitive systems or 'brains' (see e.g. Cook and Yanow, 1993; Morgan, 1986). These perspectives on learning focus on adaptation to feedback signals and on changing mental models, communicative patterns, as well as behavioural routines. This kind of organizational learning with its focus mainly upon individual learning has been prominent for several decades, but has been criticized for failing to explain how learning at a collective level may occur. Moreover, the adaptive learning literature is mainly directed towards planned and goal-oriented learning processes and as such is not able to encompass that learning which often takes place as part of the lived day-to-day organizational activities (Huysman, 2000). With the danger of constructing history, we might say that the work of Lave and Wenger, introduced to a larger audience by Brown and Duguid (Brown and Duguid, 1991), came as a welcome alternative as it provided an avenue for spotting the individual learning bias in the organizational learning literature as well as the bias towards planned and goal-oriented learning. Lave and Wenger's practice orientation enabled organization scholars to see learning as part of everyday organizational life and work, as a 'side-effect' of participation in work activities – sometimes termed 'informal learning' (see also Marsick and Watkins, 1990) taking place in and by communities of practice.

Although we regard the practice-turn within organization studies – and particularly within organizational learning – as an eye-opener for the field and as such pointing to new directions for actions and understandings, the practice-based perspective has its shortcomings. First of all, learning as participation is oriented towards the inclusion of newcomers into communities of practice rather than the disruptive and confusing elements of admitting membership to newcomers. This means that the gaze is directed towards processes of adoption and adaptation rather than the tensions that may arise from newcomers' (and others) participation in organizational life and work. We propose an understanding of organizational learning in which it is the production of tensions that is interesting to look at, as they may (or may not) act as a potential trigger for learning in organizations (see also Contu and Willmott, 2003; Roberts, 2006). Secondly, from the practice-based literature on organizational learning, it is difficult to see how communities are formed and reformed. In order to understand the organizing patterns in organizations, it is important to include agency in the analysis. With agency we refer to a view on active construction of 'reality'. This approach to agency should not be confounded with individual or human agency; agency might very well be played out by collectives or artefacts. Thus, we are not embarking on a rationalist discussion on the need for e.g. 'change agents' (see also Caldwell, 2005). We use the term for identifying what makes it possible to understand various organizational actions and learning and how these are enacted by different kinds of agencies (see also Chia, 2003). We propose to apply the

term 'commitment' with its double meaning of 'have to' and 'want to' (obligations and wishful actions) as an organizing principle for how these organizational collectives are formed and reformed. It is through the notion of commitment that we bring in agency by way of the power to act or not to act. Looking at different kinds of agencies and their diverse commitments will open up the concept of community of practice to both internal differentiations, i.e. to different forms of participation among its members and to differences between communities of practice.

To develop a perspective on organizational learning that includes both tension as a trigger for learning as well as agency, we have turned to pragmatism and especially the sociological version hereof – Symbolic Interactionism. In particular, we believe that 'social worlds theory' which stems from this sociological tradition offers a way of focusing on agency and tension simultaneously as major triggers for learning (Clarke, 1991; Elkjaer, 2004; Strauss, 1978b, 1993). Symbolic Interactionism perceives organizations as arenas in which social worlds and subworlds emerge as a result of commitment to organizational actions, activities and values. It is the different commitments that create tensions, which in turn may act as a potential trigger for learning. By including commitment to organizational actions and values as the organizing principle played out in social worlds and emerging subworlds, agency is introduced at the collective level. This makes it possible to see variation in outcome of participation in organizational practices as part of collective acting and reasoning and not just as individual deliberation. Thus, following social worlds theory in relation to organizational learning, we will focus on learning as a result of tensions. It provides the image of organizations as negotiated orders and organizational learning as processes of negotiation (including tensions) between different voices and social (sub) worlds.

We will discuss in more detail what the theory of social worlds has to offer to organization studies and in particular to organizational learning. We will identify this conceptually, and through a case story we will show how tensions between social worlds both further (within the existing social worlds) and hinder (between the existing social worlds) organizational learning in terms of potential or actual development of habitual actions.

SOCIAL WORLDS THEORY

The notion of 'social worlds' has been available in the sociological literature for many years (see e.g. Park, 1952; Shibutani, 1955). It has its roots in pragmatism – especially the social-psychological version (see e.g. Dewey, 1922 [1988]) and Symbolic Interactionism (Mead, 1934 [1967]). In accordance with the Chicago school of sociology (Fisher and Strauss, 1978; Strauss, 1991: 3–32), the term 'social worlds' is applied to organizational life as it unfolds among members of and in the context of organizations. As part of the Chicago School's Interactionism and oriented towards understanding change and changes, social worlds theory is a conflict theory. The generic social process is assumed to be intergroup conflict unless and until the data has proven otherwise (Strauss, 1978a). Social worlds theory looks at organizations as arenas of negotiated orders. It is the arenas that are usually taken as the locus of analysis because, according to Strauss, one cannot understand an individual social world in isolation (Clarke, 1991) but instead need to look at its embeddedness in a larger negotiated order, e.g. an organization.

Social worlds are not social units or structures, but make up a recognizable form of collective actions and interactions shaped by 'commitment' to organizational activities (see also Becker, 1970). Important features of social worlds are that they are not bounded by geography or formal membership but by 'the limits of effective communication'. Thus, a social world is an interactive unit, a 'universe of regularized mutual response, communication or discourse' (Shibutani, 1955: 566).

As a result, social worlds influence the meaning that people impute on events. Social worlds, consciously or unconsciously, inform members about what knowledge is important or not. One can think of social worlds as, for example, the world of the deaf, the advertisement world, the gay world, etc., but also as groupings within organizations. Social worlds may first emerge as subworlds created and maintained by new and emerging commitments to organizational actions, activities and values (Clarke, 1991; Strauss, 1978b; Strauss, 1993).

The notion of organizations as arenas of social worlds resembles the understanding of organizations as communities of practice. Both are highly fluid and emergent structures consisting of individuals with a shared collective interests. Social worlds just as communities of practice stress the importance of going beyond thinking in social structures, i.e. classes, gender, ethnic groups, institutions, etc. as determining and significant variables. Note the resemblance between communities of practice and the definition of social worlds given by Clarke:

> Groups with shared commitments to certain activities, sharing resources of many kinds to achieve their goals, and building shared ideologies about how to go about their business. (Clarke, 1991: 131)

Within the communities of practice perspective, however, the focus is upon joint efforts, social cohesion and mutual identity (Wenger, 1998). In a social world's perspective, on the other hand, the processes of tension, competition, negotiation and exchange are stressed. These processes unfold within and between social worlds, creating arenas of social worlds and subworlds in potential creative tensions. In arenas 'various issues are debated, negotiated, fought out, forced and manipulated by representatives' of the participating social worlds and subworlds (Strauss, 1978b: 124). Thus, the use of the social worlds concept lets us see that participation not only involves striving for harmony but also calls attention to tensions, conflicts and emotions reflected in the different commitments to organizational actions and values (Handley et al., 2006).

An important feature of social worlds is their differentiation into subworlds, which are segments of social worlds that emerge out of tensions as a result of a conflict in commitments between various social worlds (Strauss, 1984). This segmentation process has been ignored so far in the literature on organizational learning and in literature on communities of practice. Strauss mentions several steps that this segmentation process may follow and identifies various sources of segmentation such as space, objects, technology and skills, ideology and intersections with other social worlds, all related to variation in commitment. According to Strauss, most organizations can be viewed as 'arenas wherein members of various subworlds take differential claims, seek differential ends, engage in contest and make or break alliances in order to do the things they wish to do' (Strauss, 1978b: 125). Looking at formation of subworlds as a consequence of mutual learning processes by groups emerging from different social worlds, also stresses the role of emotion as key to organizational learning (see also Vince and Saleem, 2004). Groups converge into social worlds and diverge into subworlds as a result of shared or opposing emotions. Learning is influenced by feelings of liking and disliking, trusting and distrusting. This in turn is influenced by what people, according to their reference groups, are supposed to see and to like (March and Olsen, 1976). In other words, people learn to become member of a social (sub) world to which they want to or have to be committed to.

To illustrate the value of a social world's perspective on organizational learning we present a case story in which the notions of social worlds, subworlds, and tensions are used to understand organizational learning dynamics that unfolded during the research period. By looking at the groups as being part of conflicting social worlds, we illustrate how agency and power influence organizational learning and redefine organizational knowledge.

TENSION AS A POTENTIAL AVENUE FOR ORGANIZATIONAL LEARNING – AN ILLUSTRATION

The point of departure for our case story was an information systems design department of a large organization that was experiencing the transition from a public to a private company. Until recently, the organization belonged to one of the largest non-profit service providers in The Netherlands. During its 150 years of existence it provided job-security for its many employees, which was perceived as an important reason to work for the company. The information systems design department emerged out of a division of a highly technical computer department into a programming and a design department – the latter became the information systems design department. With this division a group of about 25 computer engineers were selected to become information systems designers. Although in-house training courses in information systems design were offered, most of the designers continued relying on their technical routines that they used during their previous job as computer programmers.

Over the years, the demand for and supply of information systems grew steadily, and the existing group of former-programmers was extended with a new group of about 20 system designers. Most of these newcomers were hired from outside the company. As a result of their institutional (educational and professional) background, these newcomers were in some aspects significantly different from the old-timers. Besides being younger, newcomers had received a professional training in information systems design and had gained professional experience at other organizations. This meant that the new group of information systems designers had other occupational routines that contrasted with those used by the old-timers. While old-timers mainly perceived their tasks from an engineering perspective, newcomers believed that system design involved close interaction with customers, i.e. users. Formal documentation of the functional designs, the use of a standard methodology and the exchange of experiences (e.g. 'walkthroughs') were also considered important professional routines by the newcomers. Newcomers also knew more about complaints of the users than did the old-timers because of their close client-contacts. Users, for example, complained about the quality of the systems and the time it took to deliver them. Attempts of the newcomers to convince the old-timers that the department needed a change, for example by proposing to introduce walkthroughs, mostly ended up in newcomers' frustration and confirmation of their understanding of old-timers' conservatism.

Two reasons can be given for the absence of change. First, there were more old-timers than newcomers. More importantly perhaps is that a representative from the 'old school' managed the department. Like many old-timers, this manager had received an engineering education, was a former programmer and worked for more than 20 years at the same company. According to this manager, things did not need to change; after all, the demand for designing information systems only grew. Consequently, without being inhibited by management, the old-timers continued to do what they always had done. While some of the newcomers gradually adapted to the work-practices that were valued by the dominant coalition, other newcomers became more and more discouraged.

This continued until the strategic decision was made to privatize the company. All units, including the IS department, were assessed on their potential commercial viability. As a result, inquiries were held among users of the IS systems. The results were dramatic; the IS department was often too relaxed in delivering systems, the products were evaluated as having a low-quality and designers hardly ever visited the potential users of the systems. Informed by these negative results, top management replaced the department manager with a much younger and highly career minded manager who belonged to the more professional world of information systems. He identified himself with the world of information systems designers and commercial software houses. He propagated

the necessity to become more 'cost-aware, client-friendly, and commercially minded' and asked for the active involvement of the department members in this change-process. While many newcomers welcomed the efforts of the new manager and actively engaged in the Total Quality Management initiative, others showed a general lack of interest.

The many years of employment at the organization had taught the old-timers that managers primarily command and control their subordinates. They had learned not to communicate informally with managers and not to run the risk of being perceived as deviating from the norm. Consequently, the new manager's request for active participation in the change process was answered by passivity. The behaviour and attitude of the old-timers frustrated the new manager who considered the passivity of the old-timers as a sign of severe conservatism and aversion to change. As a result, he became more and more authoritative and oppressive, announcing that lay-offs would be considered if people did not change their current behaviour. This only reinforced the ongoing negative learning spiral.

Next to the old-timers and the newcomers, another subgroup emerged as a result of the confrontation with the two groups. This hybrid group consisted of newcomers and old-timers who had learned from each other and over time converged to one another. While most of the old-timers and newcomers diverged from each other, becoming even more conservative (old-timers) or revolutionary (new-comers), this new subgroup converged through mutual learning. Newcomers who felt more committed to the organization than to their profession and to the active spirit of the other newcomers, learned from the old-timers how to act according to the group and organizational culture. Likewise, a group of old-timers felt more committed to the new way of designing systems and learned this know-how from working together with newcomers.

Frustrated about his inability to make a difference, the department manager moved to a commercial consultancy firm and was succeeded by one of the newcomers who 'belonged' to this new subgroup. He reorganized the department into a small commercial business unit. Most of the designers that belonged to the group of newcomers had already found a job elsewhere while most of the old-timers had been appointed to another job within the company or had taken early retirement. Almost all of the people that belonged to the third subgroup of professional IS designers who adapted to the company's culture were appointed at this commercial IS business unit.

CONCLUSION AND DISCUSSION

We began our chapter by applauding the practice-turn within organization studies and especially within the field of organizational learning. This turn is considered an adequate alternative to seeing learning as primarily a matter of individual information-processing in organizations understood as cognitive systems. We welcome an understanding of learning as participation in communities of practice because it takes away the individual and cognitive biases in the field of organizational learning and brings in collectivity and practice. However, the practice-turn also has its problems because learning as participation in communities of practice put too much stress on harmony at the expense of conflict and tensions. This is problematic as we regard tensions to be at the heart of learning, i.e. to be the potential trigger for organizational learning.

This was our background for turning to pragmatism, especially the sociological version: Symbolic Interactionism that helps us identify organizations as arenas of social worlds and emerging subworlds, which are produced by commitments to organizational actions, activities and values. This means that the compositions of the social worlds are grounded in agency, which should not be seen as solely individual but as composed by a variety of issues at stake. What is important in this understanding of organizations is that commitments are continuously negotiated and

renegotiated and as such creates continuous tensions and conflict, which in turn are potential triggers for organizational learning.

We illustrated our theoretical proposal with a case story in order to show how social worlds theory may be applied to open up our understanding of organizational learning by including commitment, i.e. agency as well as tensions. We saw how the two social worlds of the newcomers and old-timers existed within the organization with each having its own institutional background created and maintained over a period of time. Their commitment to different frames of understanding and specific actions, activities and values of each social world seriously impeded organizational learning. What we saw was the reinforcing of boundaries between the social worlds in order to gain social legitimacy for the actions and values of their own social world. We described how old-timers and newcomers maintained a relationship over a number of years full of tensions making it in this case impossible to change routines as they stuck to their own internal identity. However, the perspective on agency and tension also enabled us to see how over time a new social subworld emerged out of mutual learning processes.

The case thus illustrates the importance of tensions in the sense that it provides anxiety and might impede learning across social worlds but at the same time enhances learning within social worlds and creates the emergence of subworlds. Tensions are occasions for organizational learning. It is therefore important to be on the lookout for different commitments and the tensions they produce rather than to see learning as a more or less harmonious process of inclusion, joint enterprise, mutual agency and a shared repertoire. It is through directing the gaze towards commitments and tensions that we can see the possibilities for productive negotiations and renegotiations of actions and values.

While the concept of communities of practice makes us focus upon learning to become an insider of a community, it does not provide conceptual tools instrumental to study the tensions that to us inevitably are connected to organizational learning within (and between) organizations. The concepts of social worlds and emergent subworlds that are introduced in this chapter provide an alternative methodology for studying organizational learning as they point to the value of organizational tensions derived from different commitments to actions, activities and values. Social worlds theory offers, in other words, an ecology of an organizational learning perspective in which social worlds mutually influence each other – both in conservative and detrimental as well as in potential constructive ways.

We have argued that the Symbolic Interactionist approach to social worlds, negotiated order and organizations as arenas will provide the necessary conflict and agency lens that organizational learning theories need. It is obvious that this understanding of organizational learning needs more empirical grounding. We, however, hope that this chapter will contribute to the current debate among scholars within the field of organizational learning who realize the shortcomings of the practice-turn in the literature and who may want to take a closer look at what pragmatism can offer in terms of an understanding of organizational learning.

REFERENCES

Becker, H.S. (1970) 'Notes on the concept of commitment', in H.S. Becker (ed.), *Sociological Work. Method and Substance.* Chicago: Allen Lane The Penguin Press. pp. 261–273.

Brown, J.S. and Duguid, P. (1991) 'Organizational learning and communities-of-practice: Toward a unified view of working, learning, and innovation', *Organization Science*, 2 (1): 40–57.

Caldwell, R. (2005) 'Things fall apart? Discourses on agency and change in organizations', *Human Relations*, 58 (1): 83–114.

Chia, R. (2003) 'From knowledge-creation to the perfection of action: Tao, basho and pure experience as the ultimate ground of knowing', *Human Relations*, 56 (8): 953–981.

Clarke, A.E. (1991) 'Social worlds/arenas theory as organizational theory', in D.R. Maines (ed.), *Social Organization and Social Process. Essays in the Honor of Anselm Strauss.* New York: Aldine de Gruyter. pp. 119–158.

Contu, A. and Willmott, H. (2003) 'Re-embedding situatedness: The importance of power relations in learning theory', *Organization Science*, 14 (3): 283–296.

Cook, S.D.N. and Yanow, D. (1993) 'Culture and organizational learning', *Journal of Management Inquiry*, 2 (4): 373–390.

Dewey, J. (1922 [1988]) 'Human nature and conduct', in J.A. Boydston (ed.), *Middle works 14*. Carbondale and Edwardsville: Southern Illinois University Press.

Elkjaer, B. (2004) 'Organizational learning: The "third way". Management Learning', 35 (4): 419–434.

Fisher, B. and Strauss, A.L. (1978) 'The Chicago tradition and social change: Thomas, Park and their successors', *Symbolic Interaction*, 1 (2): 5–23.

Gherardi, S. (2006) *Organizational Knowledge: The Texture of Workplace Learning.* Malden, Oxford, Carlton: Blackwell Publishing.

Handley, K., Sturdy, A., Fincham, R. and Clark, T. (2006) 'Within and beyond communities of practice: Making sense of learning through participation, identity and practice', *The Journal of Management Studies*, 43 (3); 641–653.

Huysman, M. (2000) 'Rethinking organizational learning: Analyzing learning processes of information system designers', *Accounting, Management, and Information Technologies*, 10 (2): 81–99.

Lave, J. and Wenger, E. (1991) *Situated Learning. Legitimate Peripheral Participation.* Cambridge: Cambridge University Press.

March, J.G. and Olsen, J.P. (1976) *Ambiguity and Choice in Organizations.* Bergen: Universitetsforlaget.

Marsick, V.J. and Watkins, K.E. (1990) *Informal and Incidental Learning in the Workplace.* London: Routledge.

Mead, G.H. (1934 [1967]) *Mind, Self, and Society: From the Standpoint of a Social Behaviorist.* Chicago and London: The University of Chicago Press.

Morgan, G. (1986) *Images of Organization.* London: Sage Publications.

Nicolini, D. and Meznar, M.B. (1995) 'The social construction of organizational learning: Conceptual and practical issues in the field', *Human Relations*, 48 (7): 727–746.

Park, R.E. (1952) *Human Communities. The City and Human Ecology.* Glencoe, IL: The Free Press.

Roberts, J. (2006) 'Limits to communities of practice', *Journal of Management Studies*, 43 (3): 623–639.

Schatzki, T.R., Cetina, K.K. and Savigny, E.V. (eds). (2001) *The Practice Turn in Contemporary Theory.* London & New York: Routledge.

Shibutani, T. (1955) 'Reference groups as perspectives', *The American Journal of Sociology*, 60 (6): 562–569.

Strauss, A. (1978a) *Negotiations. Varieties, Contexts, Processes, and Social Order*. San Francisco: Jossey-Bass.

Strauss, A. (1978b) 'A social world perspective', *Studies in Symbolic Interaction*, 1: 119–128.

Strauss, A. (1984) 'Social worlds and their segmentation processes', in N. Denzin (ed.), *Studies in Symbolic Interaction* (Vol. 5). Greenwich, CT: JAI Press. pp. 123–139.

Strauss, A.L. (1991) *Creating Sociological Awareness. Collective Images and Symbolic Representations*. New Brunswick and London: Transaction Publishers.

Strauss, A.L. (1993) *Continual Permutations of Action*. New York: Aldine de Gruyter.

Vince, R. and Saleem, T. (2004) 'The impact of caution and blame on organizational learning', *Management Learning*, 35 (2): 133–154.

Wenger, E. (1998) *Communities of Practice. Learning, Meaning, and Identity*. Cambridge: Cambridge University Press.

Learning about Networks from Terrorists

Margaret Wheatley

People often comment that the leadership I describe based on living systems doesn't work in 'the real world'. I assume they are referring to life in their organizations. Yet this is not the real world; rather it is a dangerous fiction that blinds us to current realities. The real world demands that we learn to cope with chaos, that we understand human motivation, and that we adopt strategies and behaviours that lead to order, not more chaos.

In this historic moment, we live caught between a worldview that no longer works and a new one that seems too bizarre to contemplate. To expose this situation, I want to apply the lens of new science to free societies' real world challenge: global terror. This new lens reveals dynamics that are crucial to understand, yet are obscured by the mechanical paradigm.

How is it possible that a few thousand enraged people can threaten the stability of the world? How is it possible that the most powerful governments on earth find themselves locked in a costly and fearsome struggle, diverting large amounts of resources and attention to suppress the actions of a small group of fanatics? Global terror networks are among the most effective and powerful organizations in the world today, capable of changing the course of history. They do this without formal power, advanced technology, large budgets, or great numbers of followers.

We are dangerously blind to their strength because we use factors that apply to the behaviour of hierarchical organizations, not to networks. We assume that Bin Laden is a weaker leader now that he is on the run, without sophisticated communications, unable to give orders directly. We focus on finding the top leaders, and decapitating their organization so that young terrorists will slink away from this leaderless group.

These groups are not leaderless; they are well-led by their passion and rage. An ideal or purpose gives them a group identity which compels them to act. They are geographically separate, but 'all of one mind' (Arquilla, 2001: 9). They are encouraged to do 'what they think best' to further the cause. This combination of shared meaning with freedom to determine one's actions is how living systems grow more effective over time. People with a cause don't need directives, rewards, or leaders to tell them what to do. They invent increasingly extreme means to support their cause. Network analyst Albert-László Barabási notes: 'Bin Laden and his lieutenants did not invent terrorist networks. They only rode the rage of Islamic militants, exploiting the laws of self-organization along their journey (2002: 224)'. In this way, movements that begin as reasonable often migrate to more extremist measures, propelled there by their members' zealousness.

As networks mature, they are fuelled more by passion than by information. We play into the growth of terrorism right now because our actions incite more rage. As their anger grows, they become more innovative, not waiting for any leader to tell them how to respond.

These descriptions and dynamics do not surprise anyone familiar with new science and its networks. Networks possess amazing resiliency. They are filled with redundant nodes, so that one picks up if another goes down. Human networks always organize around shared meaning. Meaning is a 'strange attractor' – a coherent force that holds seemingly random behaviours within a boundary. What emerges is coordinated behaviours without control, and leaderless organizations that are far more effective in accomplishing their goals.

When we think of organizations as machines, we are blind to the power of self-organized networks. We keep looking for the leader. We assess an insurgency by whether its leader is visible, available, and able to communicate easily with the forces. This is a profound and dangerous misperception of the leader's role. Barabási warns that: 'Because of its distributed self-organized topology, Al Qaeda is so scattered and self-sustaining that even the elimination of Osama bin Laden and his closest deputies might not eradicate the threat they created. It is a web without a true spider' (2002, 223).

If Al Qaeda 'rides the rage' of angry Islamic militants, then the best strategy for immobilizing terrorist networks is not to kill their leaders, but to defuse the sources of their anger. Many analysts arrive at a similar conclusion – we can only win the war on terror by eliminating the causes of rage. Barabási states: 'If we ever want to win the war, our only hope is to tackle the underlying social, economic, and political roots that fuel the network's growth.' We might win small and discrete battles, we might break up different cell groups, but if we do nothing to eliminate their rage, people will continue to form these deadly networks and 'the netwar will never end' (2002: 224).

This is the real world. If we continue to seek to control it by exerting ever more pressure on those who hate us, those who are disconnected and impoverished, we only create a future of increasing disorder. To see a way out of this terrifying future, we must learn to understand and see the world differently. We must understand the behaviour of networks in this densely interconnected world. We must understand human motivation and our astonishing capacity to self-organize when we care about something. We must understand that we lose capacity and in fact create more chaos when we insist on hierarchy, roles, and command and control leadership.

REFERENCES

Arquilla, John and Ronfeldt, David (2001) *Networks and Netwars: The Future of Terror, Crime, and Militancy.* National Defense Research Institute RAND.

Barabási, Albert-László (2002) *Linked: The New Science of Networks.* Cambridge, MA: Perseus Publishing.

Musings on Current State of International Management Research

Rosalie L. Tung and Snejina Michailova

Being based on both the disciplines of management and international business, the field of international management (IM) pertains to the theory, research and practice of management with a cross-border or cross-cultural dimension. Since its emergence as a distinct field of inquiry some 50 years ago, it has progressed beyond its infancy and has now embarked on its growth phase, attracting interest and attention among management scholars from around the world. In this chapter we present some important challenges that the field has to contend with in its growth phase.

NEED TO LEAD, RATHER THAN LAG, CUTTING-EDGE MANAGEMENT PRACTICES

Thus far, IM scholars are preoccupied with studying phenomena that have already occurred rather than develop new ideas that could shape IM practice. Because we deal with dissimilar processes, phenomena and contexts that occur across countries and because we take managers as an audience seriously, we should be better positioned to detect new trends as they emerge, and hence anticipate these changes rather than merely trail them. In so doing, we can influence and shape practice. Perhaps, we should emulate the experience of our counterparts in the pure and physical sciences and be more receptive to hypothesis generation, rather than focusing mainly on hypothesis testing. In this way, we do not have to lag behind practice most of the time, but rather lead and truly influence practice for a change.

IMBALANCE BETWEEN INSTRUMENTALITIES AND MENTALITIES

Much of IM research has been preoccupied with techniques and instrumentalities, with less focus on mentalities and ideologies that explain the rationale and meanings of techniques and instrumentalities used. This approach is characteristic of North American conceptualizations that have dominated the field thus far. Interestingly, however, the domination by North American approaches has been challenged more often than the conceptualizations themselves. While rational purposive thinking is characteristic of the North American-based IM research approach, it might not be valid or appropriate for other contexts because the meaning of management and its fundamental purpose, with its accompanying implications, vary across countries. The term 'comparative management', for example, has dominated IM inquiry because it attempts to understand management in other locations in comparison with US management – while unstated, it is generally assumed that the latter is superior. We contend that IM inquiry needs to seriously consider both instrumentalities and mentalities, similar to the term 'managerial practices' which refers to both managerial techniques and managerial ideologies.

INABILITY TO ENGAGE IN TRUE INTERDISCIPLINARITY

While the practice of IM is, by its very nature, interdisciplinary, multi-contextual, multi-layered and multi-functional, as IM researchers we seldom engage in studying phenomena with a broader and multi-faceted vision. For instance, comparative sociology has seldom occupied a central place in IM studies although the impact of sociology on the field of management has been far-reaching. Neither has the IM research field paid sufficient attention to economic geography. The failure to engage in truly interdisciplinary research will likely widen the gap between what Martínez and Toyne (2000) called 'internationalized management' and 'IM'. Furthermore, it can perpetuate the focus on research that merely seeks to replicate, verify and extend culture-bound management theories rather than to generate truly distinctive management knowledge.

ARTICULATION OF IDEAS AND FINDINGS AS IF THEY EMERGED IN A VACUUM

It has been postulated that all theories are a fragment of some autobiography (Valery, 1938, 1958, cited in Bedeian, 2004). As such, it is important for theorists to assert who they are. We contend that it is imperative for IM scholars to reveal their biases and assumptions because of the nature of their research inquiries. Despite repeated exhortations by influential IM scholars to this effect, disclosure of self-reflection on the topic under investigation is rare in our publications and perhaps discouraged. Our writings are often presented as depersonalized undertakings, devoid of the writers' predispositions, beliefs and convictions. Thus, readers can only extrapolate or conjecture what has shaped these perspectives and approaches. By and large, we have ignored the exhortation to '… prolong and deepen those moments [of reflexivity] so that [we can] see just how situated and constructed [our] universals are and how few voices [our] situated assertions incorporate' (Weick, 1999: 802).

To further advance IM research, we need to engage more openly in dialog of these critical issues that might constrain the continued growth and development of the field.

REFERENCES

Martínez, Z.L. and Toyne, B. (2000) 'What is international management, and what is its domain?, *Journal of International Management*', 6: 11–28.

Bedeian, A.G. (2004) 'The gift of professional maturity', *Academy of Management Learning and Education*, 3(1): 92–98.

Weick, K.E. (1999) 'Theory construction as disciplined reflexivity: Tradeoffs in the 90s', *Academy of Management Review*, 24 (4): 797–806.

Globalization and Organization Studies

Mauro F. Guillén

It may not surprise anyone if I were to point out that perhaps the biggest challenge facing the field today involves what to make of the momentous changes taking place in the global economy. To some, globalization means that local peculiarities are less relevant than in the past. Hence, our theories (which tend to harbor ambitions of universal applicability) ought to serve us as well when it comes to analyzing group performance in, say, Kenya, as in the more familiar setting of Cicero, Chicago, where the Hawthorne investigations took place almost a century ago. To others, however, globalization represents a reminder that we continue to be very parochial and short-sighted, that there is a world out there waiting to be comprehended and studied.

In my view, globalization has generated three processes that should be of general interest to organizational scholars, changes that provide unique opportunities to advance organizational theory. The first has to do with the highly selective process by which organizations are splitting up their value chain of activities and locating each of them in a different country, depending on circumstances such as labor costs, availability of raw materials, government incentives and transportation costs, to name but a few. This process is sometimes undertaken by the firm itself, sometimes 'outsourced'. The ubiquitous iPod, for instance, is designed in California, assembled in China of components made in at least ten different countries, and marketed from the United States to countries around the world. While economics and strategic management have devoted a considerable amount of attention to this process, few organizational scholars seem to bother with it. Yet, it is transforming the way in which companies operate and the way in which work takes place.

The second major change brought about by globalization is cultural in nature. Paradoxical as it may be, the increasing interconnection among communities and individuals around the world has developed in parallel with a reaffirmation of local identities, traditional values and nationalism in practically every corner of the planet. Some scholars argue that the revival of particularistic and local cultural identities represents a reaction against the homogenizing pressures of globalization. Intriguingly, technology has encouraged cultural fragmentation by lowering the cost of producing and distributing music, text, political and religious discourse and visual representations. Again, all sorts of social scientists have devoted time and effort to understanding this process of cultural fragmentation. Meanwhile, organizational scholars continue to miss the opportunity to study the role that organizations are playing in this massive cultural reconfiguration.

The third process of change associated with globalization involves the shifting balance of power in the world between the haves and the have-nots, the skilled and the unskilled and the rich countries and the poor. Once again, there is an organizational story to be told about this process of change. Organizations often exacerbate individual dynamics. For instance, a well-qualified worker can be more productive if he or she works in the same organization together with other highly skilled workers.

I hope that these remarks stimulate organizational scholars to join economists, sociologists, anthropologists and political scientists in the study of globalization. Unless we show how organizations are shaping this cardinal process of change, nobody else will. It would be a pity if the narrative of globalization, the way in which future generations will learn about this process, did not include a story about organizations.

Strategy: Past, Present, Future

Stephen Cummings

This chapter describes where strategic management has come from, where it has got to, and what should happen in the future. Table 1.12.1 outlines this chapter's structure. It describes 12 movements that are grouped according to the categories invoked previously: practice, processes, people. But they all connect to one fundamental shift: a move away from a belief in their being one definition of, and approach to, strategic management; a shift toward a plurality of views and the need for individualized practices. If we were to theorize, we might describe this as a move away from strategy's modernist foundations toward a 'postmodern' or 'after-modern' phase (Pettigrew et al., 2002; Cummings and Wilson, 2003; Whittington, 2003; Cummings, 2004).

THE PRACTICE OF STRATEGY

1   Strategy is about …

Chandler's Strategy and Structure (1962) is credited with providing the classic definition of strategic management: 'the determination of the basic long-term goals and objectives of an enterprise, and the adoption of courses of action and the allocation of resources necessary for carrying out these goals'. In this, and other works considered foundational (e.g. Ansoff, 1965; Learned et al.'s, 1969; Andrews, 1971), strategy is about those at the top developing long-term objectives and plans based on an articulation of the company's desired position in the market.

However, we have witnessed increasing scepticism with regard to this view. Famous debates about 'what strategy really is' took place in the 1990s between Mintzberg (1991, 1994a) and Ansoff (1991, 1994). Prefiguring the view of strategy as practice outlined in an earlier chapter, Mintzberg argued that the classical view was dependent on the 'fallacy': that strategic 'thinking' and operational 'doing' are separate and distinct. Managers were not rational, logical, directors, Mintzberg argued, they (and thus their strategies) were influenced by what they were embedded in: politics and history, and patterns of behaviour that emerged over time. Ansoff, was backed up by heavyweights like Porter (1996), who argued that we were in danger of being misled by the 'emergent' school's 'dangerous half-truths' that confused operational activities with strategy. By the late 1990s, this battle over

Table 1.12.1   Future trends in strategy

Strategy	Was about...	Will also be about...
Practice		
1. Strategy is about ...	long-term plans and objectives	intent and agility, orientation and animation
2. Strategy comes from ...	rational analysis and top-down	emergent activities and micro-planning practices from anywhere
3. Strategic choice is ...	generic, either/or, e.g. cost or individual paradox resolutions, differentiation, global or local	'both/and' thinking
4. Margins enhanced by ...	'best-practice' benchmarking developing organizational specific	'next practice'
Processes		
5. Organization should be ...	hierarchical, generic, depicted by distinctive, individualized standard organization charts	depicted by unique 'organigraphs'
6. Value-added depicted ...	through generic value chain	through fluid and flexible value webs
7. Underlying assumption is ...	increasing efficiency	promoting knowledge, which requires slack
8. Vision and values are ...	about creating the future	about remembering and utilizing the past
People		
9. Key personnel are ...	senior execs and consultant advisors	a broader band including people at all levels
10. Strategy makers are ...	increasingly professional	increasingly amateur
11. Employees/managers/students ...	consume strategy	produce strategy
12. Strategy research is ...	increasingly empirical	increasingly idealist or intuitive

the correct definition of strategy caused one prominent journal editorial to lament: 'Were the many decades of vigorous development wasted? Does anybody at least know what strategy is?' (Zeleny, 1997; see also Markides, 2004).

Something of an accord has emerged in recent times, however. This may be traced back to a 1996 forum that took interpretations of Honda's strategy for entering into the US motorcycle market as its starting point. Honda's plans did not work out in practice (their rational analysis suggested big bikes were what Americans wanted, but they ended up selling small bikes – something this market had not considered before). But their plans gave them the intent and impetus to move forward, and from there their agility enabled them to reorganize resources and capabilities to seize emergent unforeseen opportunities. The forum concluded that we should acknowledge the strengths of both the classical and emergent perspectives, and that companies should aim to exhibit 'strategic

agility': the ability to move quickly to, and away from, set plans (California Management Review, 1996).

This debate and subsequent accord is characteristic of a shift from a modernist ontology, an increasing pragmatism in the light of environmental changes, and a recognition of the classical view's limitations. The debate over 'what strategy really is?', and the assumption that this question should have one true or representative answer, shows an adherence to a modernist set of beliefs about the nature of the world, scientific inquiry or the advance of knowledge. The recognition that strategy could be about more than one thing – paradoxically planning and emergence (and much more besides) – indicates a postmodern turn (Harvey, 1990). Associated with this is a pragmatism that recognized the limitations of the classical theory of strategy in light of practical reality, particularly in increasingly complex and turbulent environments. A top-down planning and positioning approach tends to make a firm slow, rigid and unresponsive to unforeseen opportunities and threats. It also disengages 'lower level' employees who may have much to add. These recognitions have led to more emphasis being placed on strategy being about setting a general sense of intent that can be filled in, added too and subtracted from by employees as situations unfold. In addition, the idea that there should be one view of what strategy is leads to diminishing returns in terms of innovation and creativity. If we take seriously Koestler's (1976) definition of creativity as 'connecting previously unrelated dimensions of experience' and a subsequent 'defeat of habit by originality', then a homogenized view of strategic practices and processes works against successful strategizing (Christensen, 2000).

Subsequently, a more open, flexible and pragmatic mindset should shape future perspectives on what strategy is or could be. This can already be detected in a number of works: in Mintzberg et al.'s (2001) argument that there are many schools of thought about strategy and all have merit; in De Wit and Meyer's (2004) approach that strategy is about living with and making the most of paradox and embracing both/and rather than either/or thinking (e.g. seeking cost reduction and differentiation rather than seeing an either/or choice); or in Cummings and Wilson's (2003) argument that we should focus less on finding a singular definition of what a good strategy is and more on what good strategies actually do in practice: they *orient, animate* and *integrate*; and these outcomes may stem from top-down planning, and/or emergent ideas, and/or a strong brand and/or a particular process, depending on the nature of a particular organization.

2   Strategy comes from …

The classical definition of strategy was matched with a triangular, layered and divisionalized view of organization and, subsequently, the notion that strategy came from the rational analysis carried out at the top or highest levels of the triangle. Hence, strategy was seen as distinct from shorter-term tactical or operational decisions (which

happen at lower levels). Indeed, Ansoff's (1965) model of organization simply took the micro-economic theory of the firm (a function that sought to turn inputs into outputs according to a criterion of maximizing efficiency), and added a strategic decision making level over this function where decisions about how resources might be best deployed were made. The influence of this shape can still be seen in textbooks that present a hierarchy of strategy from separate corporate to business to functional levels and depict a strategy process beginning with vision at the top and ending with implementation at the bottom.

This perspective was compounded by the concurrent setting of the conventional business curriculum and establishment of management as a worthy university subject compounded by emerging conventions. In 1959, the Ford and Carnegie reports concluded that business programmes should follow a generic form with economics as the central stem and finish with a 'capstone course' that would 'pull together what was learned in the separate business fields' (Gordon and Howell, 1959; Pierson, 1959). This capstone became 'strategic management'. And, around this time, management was becoming an accepted university subject. Supporting this acceptance, grand histories of management were written that defined management as about 'planning, directing, organizing and controlling' (George, 1968; Wren, 1972), and that subsequently saw strategic management as the development of these things at a higher level for the organization as a whole for the long term (Cummings, 2004).

But critics also questioned this view of where strategy comes from. In 1973, Mintzberg's *The Nature of Managerial Work* purported to look not at what managers should be (rational, analytical) and should do (plan, direct and design) but what they actually did. He found that strategies were likely to emerge from chance events, interactions and patterns of behaviour, rather than from a detached and logical planning process. Thus, day-to-day operational activities can be, or become, strategic.

In later work, Mintzberg (1994b) found that the interaction crucial to strategy does not happen between top executives and the environment. It occurs where employees at the operational base of the organization interact with one another and react to or anticipate customer needs and wants. Over time, what goes on here may create patterns of behaviour that filter up to be formalized in plans; but strategy is not really about what happens at the top. A nice illustration is Post-it Notes, which did not come from the rational analysis of 3M's senior management team but from a research scientist who produced an experimental adhesive that failed. A happy accident from the bottom of an organization that was shaped and adapted as it moved up the organization to eventually drive a good part of 3M's strategy and success.

Others have added to Mintzberg's critique. Whittington's (1996, 2006) view of 'strategy as practice', for example, has sought to keep a focus on what managers actually do when creating strategy, and to see strategy as emerging from small or 'micro' actions rather than big 'macro' thinking.

As these criticisms gain credence our view of where strategy comes from will get broader. Strategy can come from the top down, but also from the 'bottom-up', or maybe from the middle; from senior executives to scientists to sales people to customers; from rational analysis to unforeseen environmental changes to changing societal norms – depending on the particular nature of the organization in focus.

This broad range of possibilities would indicate that the content of each firm's strategy, indeed each particular strategy within a firm, could be seen to come from a unique set of influences. This adds weight to the 'resource-based view of the firm' and associated frameworks that focus on a strategic advantage stemming from unique constellations of tangible and intangible resources, and the relationships between these resources that have emerged over time (Wernerfelt, 1984; Rumelt, 1984; Barney, 1991; Van Witteloostuijn and Boone, 2006). The fact that such constellations are organic,

embedded, unique and thus rare and difficult (or costly) to replicate, contributes to the next two future trends in strategic practice: that strategic choice will become less generic; and that greater gains in margins will come from a 'next practice' approach rather than replicating 'best practice'.

3   Strategic choice is …

The future will see strategic choice as less about generic categories and either/or decisions and more about individualized and often paradoxical attempts to gain the best of many worlds. The classical approach to strategy spawned a range of generic frameworks developed to guide best strategic practices. Generally, these frameworks encouraged either/or choices, between, for example, a focus on cost reduction or differentiation, or divestment or acquisition; or they offered a discrete range of elements that could be applied to analyse any environment, industry or company.

Porter's (1985) Generic Strategy Matrix, for example, with its combination of two axes: competitive advantage (two choices: a cost focus or a differentiation focus) and competitive scope (two choices again: either a broad scope or a narrower focus), created four generic strategic positions that made it easy to plot a company relative to the competition. It made knowing where you stand and not getting dragged in opposing directions by trying to do two things at once an imperative. However, as markets have globalized, as companies have become more mobile and networked and as competition has intensified, it had become clear that strategic choice is not so simple. Bartlett and Ghoshal (1989) were the first to outline why firms will no longer be able to survive unless they are able to *both* reduce costs and differentiate, globalize and localize, centralize and decentralize.

How might such a 'both/and' approach to strategic thinking be manifested? The desire to act big in some ways (e.g. access to capital, reducing supplier power) and be nimble and niche oriented in others, will see a continued increase in network or alliance based strategies and growth through acquisition whereby the independence and differentiation of the acquired or smaller companies is maintained in some areas while costs are trimmed through greater economies of scale and bargaining power in others. As a general rule, we might expect that differentiation, independence and strategic influence on the firm will be maintained in such corporations in areas that relate to the 20 per cent of a product or service that makes 80 per cent of the difference when it comes to the purchase decision. In a high-end car, this 20 per cent might be design or where the engine is manufactured. In a bank or an airline, this might relate to service style or quality. In low-end electronics, it might be manufacturing (Cummings and Angwin, 2004). Other elements might be shared or bundled or outsourced to achieve economies. As firms converge while promoting the independence of some of their elements it will become hard to determine a firm's strategy without contradiction (Jarzabkowski, 2005).

We can refer back to the GSM and wonder what might become of the classical frameworks. Thinking of the auto industry, how might one use the GSM to think through the strategy of the Ford Motor Group with its many brands: Ford, Volvo, Jaguar, Aston Martin and Land Rover, in addition to its interest in brands such as Mazda? In fact, the GSM is a good starting point to begin to think through the mix, whether they complement or compete with one another, and how resources might be shared and where independence should be protected to protect and grow a brand's market share. However, Ford or VW's or DaimlerChrysler's strategy is now more complex than picking a box or an emphasis, it depends on a range of subtle relationships and balances. While conventional strategy frameworks built on assumptions of either/or choices are still good places to begin to spark debate, they may no longer be good places to end. They will need active customization.

4   Margins can best be enhanced by …

The success of any business strategy is generally measured by its ability to create a competitive advantage that garners healthy margins over time. While some strategies may defer margins (e.g. companies like Google and Amazon realized that securing market share was initially more important), or some brands may lose money so long as they promote the business in other ways, corporate margins must eventually accrue.

At present there is growing interest in how to protect, maintain and grow the intangible components of a firm's capabilities or competitive advantages that lead to healthy margins. This is largely due to the fact that the process of copying tangible hard systems and technology is becoming easier and faster: a fact that can be related to the rise and fall of best practice benchmarking as a strategy aid. It leads to increasing iso-morphism, homogenization and subsequently declining margins as firms have little between them to compete on but price (Nattermann, 2000). While copying best practice can help reduce costs, additional focus will be placed on developing organizational specific 'next practice' as a means of enhancing a firm's inimitable differentiation (Cummings, 2004).

THE PROCESSES THAT SHAPE THE PRACTICE OF STRATEGY

5   Organization should be …

Chandler's thesis in Strategy and Structure was that the expansion strategies followed by growing pan-American organizations created a need for a new configuration that could enable effective control across large terri-tories where communication was imperfect. Given this, the M-form became *the form* of modern organization. Chandler's work gave rise to the dictum that 'structure follows strategy'. Others have since questioned this, arguing instead that 'structure shapes strategy' (Pettigrew, 1979, 1985; Peters and Waterman, 1982). Whatever one's view of what comes first, it is clear that the processes encouraged by a particular way of structuring an organi-zation influences the content of a strategy or the practice of strategy-making. The M-form clearly supported seeing strategy in classical terms.

As the geographical spread of companies continued, new organizational strategy challenges arose. The need for coordinating and controlling to achieve economies of scale and reduce risk, as well as adapting to different local demands to meet customers' needs, strained M-form organizations. Where the need for global standardization, and so centralized control, was dominant, a centralized hub form controlling different regional divisions was still useful. But where strategies of local responsiveness came to be more important than global standardization, a decentralized federation (joined as needed) became a better fit.

Consequently, organizational structures have confronted the dualisms characteristic of a shift from modernism. In order to reflect a strategic emphasis on being global and local, a hybrid form called a 'matrix' crossing divisions with functions or product lines became popular. However, the matrix's complexity led to confusion over responsibilities, absorbed a great deal of time and made quick strategic decisions difficult. Bartlett and Ghoshal (1989) subsequently proposed a 'transnational' design combining functional, product, geographic designs into networks of linked subsidiaries held together by nodes for coordination. Perhaps its most important feature is that it focuses less on hard structure and financial controls and more on management processes and culture, things that provide a general strategic intent to ensure coordination while leaving the detail to emerge or be adapted closer to the customer. This coincided with the findings of others (e.g. Peters and Waterman, 1982; Hedland, 1986) who saw the advantages of 'simultaneously loose-tight properties', or organizations as coalitions of individuals held together by a 'corporate glue' of shared values rather than tightly controlled hierarchies.

This thinking has been developed under a number of different banners: flexible hub and spoke arrangements (Leifer et al., 2001; De Sanctis et al., 2002); fluid corporate 'hyperarchies' (Evans and Wurster, 1997); 'value constellations' (Normann and Ramirez, 1993); 'multi-centred firms' (Forsgren, 1990); 'heterarchies' (Hedlund, 1986) and 'multifocal corporations' (Doz and Prahalad, 1987). John McGee (2003) sees organizations disintegrating into webs of knowledge where the strategist is less a 'planner', 'director' or 'controller' and more an orchestrator. But perhaps the best way to capture the shift is by describing a move from an M-form to an N or 'network' form of organization.

A major implication of an emphasis on individualized networks rather than a generic organizational form will be the continued diminution in the belief in there being 'one-best' organizational structure. Each organization should be seen as a one-off and treated as such (Bartlett and Ghoshal, 1997). And, given that structure shapes strategy, to promote individualized strategies we must promote seeing and thinking about strategy in terms of individualized organizational configurations or 'organigraphs' (Mintzberg and Van der Heyden, 1999).

6   Value-added depicted …

The most popular means for depicting the processes by which firms add value has been Porter's (1980) 'Generic Value Chain'. The value chain's geometry and categorization of space follows the classical view of organization. Its linear chain of operational functions with 'tactical' and 'strategic' aspects layered on top, provides an ordered framework with which to consider how the various processes within the firm are adding value to the outputted product or service. If, upon analysis, certain things are found not to be adding value above what they cost to perform, they should be 'addressed' or eliminated.

That the Value Chain is still widely used is testament to its value as a thinking framework. But it has become increasingly difficult to capture how individual organizations are adding value within its lines. Three main factors will continue to strain the assumptions upon which it is based.

Fragmentation: Large chunks of production chains have been 'outsourced' or taken on by alliance partners as firms take advantage of diminishing boundaries, diminishing contracting costs, and advances in information technology. The idea that all of the processes that go toward delivering a product or service can exist under one roof or in one organization's 'chain' will become rare as firms 'externalize' and become more like constellations (Malone et al., 2003).

Relationality: As organizational fragmentation and externalization takes place, and organizations are seen as more about relationships than functions, the placement of stakeholders like suppliers and customers outside of a company's chain will seem an oversight. Relatedly, while the externalization of some organizational processes will continue, others once seen as external will be embraced or increasingly internalized. Key customers, suppliers and other stakeholders will come to form a part of most organizations' understanding of themselves. Pictures of the processes by which organizations add value will look more like ecosystems than input-process-output functions.

Multiplicity: As strategies become increasingly multiple, it will be difficult to fit an organization's business model into one unitary chain. In response to this, new forms of depicting strategic processes are emerging. Cummings and Angwin (2004) outline what they call a 'value chimera' as an attempt to accommodate future imperatives in organizational strategy while retaining many of the characteristics of Porter's value chain. They claim that successful strategies cannot afford to leave past imperatives behind: financial control, efficiency and cost and risk reduction are still, and will always be, important. However, new necessities, responding to particular customer needs in a world characterized by 'long-tail economics' (Anderson, 2006), agility, multiplicity, differentiation and innovation, must also be achieved. Rather than a generic input-process-output chain with a single point of contact with customers, the value chimera can be drawn with any number of differentiated 'heads' targeted at different markets stemming from a single body of shared resources and core competencies.

7   Underlying assumption is …

Despite the classical views' separation of strategy as above and beyond the input→ process→ output system of operations management, modelling generally rested upon the language of efficiency that was seen to underpin the management of operations. When finalizing his model of the firm Ansoff (1965) concluded that since: 'there is no general agreement on a proper philosophical basis for business objectives … our framework for formulating objectives was made adaptable to a variety of different management attitudes, so long as the underlying concept of the firm is that of an efficiency-seeking organization'.

While there was much to be gained by improving the efficiency of organizations as increasing global competition and reduced trade protection eliminates inefficient competitors, as the ease with which firms can reduce costs by producing in economies with low factor costs, and as expertise on logistics and supply-chain management becomes easier to 'buy in', efficiency becomes a 'hygiene factor'. This will lead to more emphasis on strategy as about differentiation through other, more inimitable, means. Indeed, there will be an increasing emphasis on building strategic advantage out of the unique forms of explicit and tacit knowledge than an organization's particular network of employees engenders. This sort of knowledge comes from having time to reflect and think and develop. And this requires encouraging 'slack' instead of a focus on reducing the ratio of inputs over outputs (Lawson, 2001).

8   Vision and values are …

Given what has been said above, it may be that strategy in the future is as much about remembering, reconstructing and utilizing the past as it is about a design toward something new. Again we may relate this phenomenon to a 'postmodern turn'.

As thinkers like Nietzsche, Foucault, Lyotard and Deleuze have expressed, the diminution of a belief in the power of grand designers and grand designs for the future, and the decline of the idea that there are objective or essential categories that can be appealed to, leads to a scenario where an individual history, rather than being taken as given or seen as no longer relevant, can be treated aesthetically: as a work of art to be restored, worked upon, promoted and used to give meaning in the present. Hence, we may see greater emphasis on the articulation of strategic visions, missions and values moving something like a 'catchstith', with a thread drawn backwards to reconnect with aspects of an organization's past and consolidate its understanding of itself in the present before following this trajectory into the future.

THE PEOPLE THAT ENACT STRATEGY PROCESSES AND PRACTICES

9   The key personnel in strategy are …

Traditionally, the key players in strategy formulation are senior executives and their consultant advisors. While these people will continue to be important, strategy should evolve to incorporate a broader band of influences, including people at all levels, strategic suppliers and key customers. In the future, we should see more discussion about, and research into, how different people can effectively bring their perspectives and insights into the practice of strategy and strategy processes, and how organizations might manage this multiplicity of influences to best effect.

Already the 'emergence school' (Mintzberg, 1994b), the 'process school' (Pettigrew et al., 2002) and the 'practice school' (Whittington, 2003) have highlighted the strategic importance of what happens at lower levels of organization. Earlier sections of this chapter have spoken of the need to bring suppliers inside an organization's strategic 'tent'. Other research has suggested ways of seeing strategy differently, in order to better organize according to customers' motivations

and needs (Pugh et al., 2002; Eddleston et al., 2002; Gutek et al., 2002). And others still have highlighted the pivotal role that middle managers, previously maligned as an unnecessary layer, play in strategy development as 'wind-readers', 'mid-wives' and 'amplifiers of knowledge' (Nonaka et al., 1995; Floyd and Wooldridge, 2000; Dutton et al., 1997; Huy, 2001).

10   Strategy makers are …

The first business schools were variable in both substance and quality. The standardization of how managers and subsequently strategy makers were educated which stemmed from investigations that began in the 1950s, and the development of national and international bodies and standards led to efficiency gains in respect to the rate at which a particular type of strategist was produced; efficiency gains in the sense that more managers could communicate using a shared language provided by common frameworks; and an increase in what we might call 'professionalism'. For example, the MBA degree now provides a universal language to its students – wherever they may be in the world. But it is also true that criticisms of the spread and influence of the particular type of knowledge and 'lingua franca' granted by this universal education are beginning to mount (Mintzberg, 2004; Bennis and O'Toole, 2005). The benefits of this standardization and narrowing of educational influences on strategy makers may soon be outweighed by the costs.

One development that may emerge out of this is that strategy makers, or at least some strategy makers, will become more 'amateur'. What has happened in the past decade in the field of journalism may be salient. New communication technology means that people other than professional journalists have the potential to observe and broadcast more immediately than traditional media outlets, adding a 'grassroots' dimension to the media terrain. Subsequently, amateur journalists are scooping mainstream news outlets as well as critiquing or pointing out errors in mainstream articles. Their strengths generally include a real passion for their subject material, deep or specialist domain knowledge, excellent industry contacts, and the fact that they are close to the action and close to those directly affected by the action – if not directly affected. Washington University's Centre for Communication and Civic Engagement describes the changing landscape as shifting 'away from the broadcast model where the few communicate to the many, toward a more inclusive model in which publics and audiences also have voices'. Were we to view an organization as a society in microcosm, it is interesting to reflect on how a firm might benefit from bringing grassroots 'bloggers' into the ranks of those who contribute to strategy or from making strategists more like bloggers.

11   Employees/managers/students …

All of the above should lead to changes in the way we teach strategy. Whereas we may have viewed students, and also employees, as 'consumers' of strategy, in the future they will need to be regarded as 'producers'. Indeed, strategy might be better learnt less like a degree and more like an apprenticeship that requires people to learn by doing.

Paula Jarzabkowski's chapter raises the mismatch between the conventional Harvard Business School business case method of teaching and how strategy actually happens in practice. Harvard cases are typically 20 to 30 pages long with all the 'relevant' information synthesized and contained within its pages, so that the student need look no further, and they generally come with case notes available for the instructor and outline for them the best types of analysis and solutions in the light of 'what actually happened' (Contardo and Wensley, 2004). In the future, attempts should be made to guide students by means that actually engage them in running a business venture (Bennis and O'Toole, 2005), or through cases that are simply a brief statement of an issue or a problem which then requires the student to 'build the case' themselves, as they would need to do in the workplace (Angwin et al., 2007).

12   Strategy research is …

As strategic management has become more professionalized, the academic field of strategy has sought to taken on the appearance of a 'science' with its foundations and propositions based on solid empirical research. While there have been many benefits, including increasing 'rigor', we may reach the point where associating seriousness or worthiness with 'proper' empirical research, and seeing anything other than this as less than worthy or worth taking heed of, is seen to be limiting the field's development.

While much of what is seen as the leading research published in the sciences is based on empiricism, the need to think differently from what has gone before in competitive industries or markets in order to capture higher margins in the future may require effective strategic management research to (re)embrace intuition and idealism. While this chapter has explained the limitations of the conventional approaches to strategy that emerged in the 1960s and 1970s, one advantage that was exhibited there was more 'free-thinking'. For example, the Boston Box did not emerge from exhaustive research on what firms actually did, but from a doodle to help the Mead Paper Corporation view their diversified business units in cash usage terms (Smith, 2007). Whereas it is easy to see the limitations of such frameworks 40 years on, there is no doubt that they provided helpful advances when they were developed. If strategic management in the 21st century is to make quantum leaps in addition to incremental steps, it may be that we need to recapture the sort of bold untrammelled 'green-field' or 'blue ocean' idealism that inspired the field's pioneers.

REFERENCES

Anderson, C. (2006) *The Long Tail: Why the Future of Business is Selling Less of More.* New York: Hyperion.

Andrews, K. (1971) *The Concept of Corporate Strategy.* Homewood, IL: Irwin.

Angwin, D., Cummings, S. and Smith, C. (2007) *The Strategy Pathfinder.* Oxford: Blackwell.

Ansoff, I. (1965) *Corporate Strategy: An Analytical Approach to Business Policy for Growth and Expansion.* New York: McGraw-Hill.

Ansoff, I. (1991) 'Critique of Henry Mintzberg's "The design school: Reconsidering the basic premises of strategic management" '. *Strategic Management Journal,* 12, 449–461.

Ansoff, I. (1994) 'Comment on Henry Mintzberg's "Rethinking strategic planning" '. *Long Range Planning,* 27 (3): 31–33.

Barney, J. (1991) 'Firm resources and sustained competitive advantage', *Journal of Management,* 7 (1): 99–120.

Bartlett, C.A. and Ghoshal, S. (1989) *Managing Across Borders: The Transnational Solution.* Boston, MA: Harvard Business School Press.

Bartlett, C. and Ghoshal, S. (1997) *The Individualized Organization.* New York: HarperBusiness.

Bennis, W. and O'Toole, J. (2005) 'How business schools lost their way', *Harvard Business Review,* May: 96–104.

California Management Review (1996) 'CMR Forum: The "Honda Effect" revisited', *California Management Review,* 38 (4): 78–117.

Chandler, A.D. (1962) *Strategy and Structure: Chapters in the History of the Industrial Enterprise.* Cambridge, MA: MIT Press.

Christensen, C. (2000) *The Innovator's Dilemma.* Harvard Business School Press.

Contardo, I. and Wensley, R. (2004) 'The Harvard Business School story: Avoiding knowledge by being relevant', *Organization,* 11 (2): 211–231.

Cummings, S. (2004) *Recreating Strategy.* London: Sage.

Cummings, S. and Angwin, D. (2004) 'The future shape of strategy', *Academy of Management Executive,* 18 (2): 21–36.

Cummings, S. and Wilson, D. (2003) *Images of Strategy.* Oxford: Blackwell.

De Sanctis, G., Glass, J.T. and Morris Ensing, I. (2002) 'Organization designs for R&D', *Academy of Management Executive,* 16 (3): 55–67.

De Wit, B. and Meyer, R. (2004) *Strategy: Process, Content, Context.* London: International Thompson.

Doz, Y. and Prahalad, C.K. (1987) 'A process model of strategic redirection in large complex firms: The case of multinational corporations', in A. Pettigrew (ed.), *The Management of Strategic Change.* Oxford: Basil Blackwell. pp. 63–83.

Dutton, J.E., Ashford, S.J., O'Neill, R.M., Hayes, E. and Wierba, E.E. (1997) 'Reading the wind: How middle managers assess the context for selling issues to top managers', *Strategic Management Journal,* 18 (5): 407–423.

Eddleston, K.A., Kidder, D.L. and Litzky, B.E. (2002) 'Who's the boss? Contending with competing expectations from customers and management', *Academy of Management Executive,* 16 (4): 85–95.

Evans, P. and Wurster, T. (1997) 'Strategy and the new economics of information', *Harvard Business Review,* Sept-Oct: 70–82.

Floyd, S.W. and Wooldridge, B. (2000) *Building Strategy From the Middle: Reconceptualizing Strategy Process.* London: Sage Publications.

Forsgren, M. (1990) 'Managing the international multi-center firm', *European Management Journal,* 8 (2): 261–267.

George, C.S. (1968). *The History of Management Thought.* Englewood Cliffs, NJ: Prentice-Hall.

Gordon, R.A. and Howell, J. (1959) *Higher Education for Business.* New York: Columbia University Press.

Gutek, B.A., Groth, M. and Cherry, B. (2002) 'Achieving service success through relationships and enhanced encounters', *Academy of Management Executive,* 16 (4): 132–144.

Harvey, D. (1990) *The Condition of Postmodernity.* Oxford: Blackwell.

Hedland, G. (1986) 'The hypermodern MNC: A hierarchy?', *Human Resource Management,* (Spring): 9–35.

Huy, Q.N. (2001) 'In praise of middle managers', *Harvard Business Review,* 79 (Sept-Oct): 72–81.

Jarzabkoski, P. (2005) *Strategy as Practice.* London: Sage.

Koestler, A. (1976) *The Act of Creation.* London: Hutchinson.

Lawson, M.B. (2001) 'In praise of slack: time is of the essence', *Academy of Management Executive,* 15 (3): 125–135.

Learned, E.P., Christensen, C.R., Andrews, K.R. and Guth, W.D. (1969) *Business Policy.* Homewood, IL: Irwin.

Leifer, R., Colarelli O'Connor, G. and Rice, M. (2001) 'Implementing radical innovation in mature firms: The role of hubs', *Academy of Management Executive,* 15 (3): 102–113.

Lieberman, M.B. and Asaba, S. (2006) 'Why do firms imitate each other?', *Academy of Management Review,* 31 (2): 366–385.

McGee, J. (2003) 'Strategy as orchestrating knowledge', in Cummings, S. and Wilson, D. (eds), *Images of Strategy,* Blackwell: 136–163.

Malone, T.W., Laubacher, R. and Scott Morton, M.S. (eds) (2003) *Inventing the Organizations of the 21st Century.* Cambridge, MA: MIT Press.

Markides, C. (2004) 'What is strategy and how do you know if you have one?' *Business Strategy Review,* 15 (2): 5–12.

Mintzberg, H. (1973) *The Nature of Managerial Work.* New York: Harper & Row.

Mintzberg, H. (1991) 'Learning 1, planning 0: Reply to Igor Ansoff', *Strategic Management Journal,* 12, 463–466.

Mintzberg, H. (1994a) 'Rethinking strategic planning – Part one: pitfalls and fallacies', *Long Range Planning,* 27 (3): 12–21.

Mintzberg, H. (1994b) *The Rise and Fall of Strategic Planning.* New York: Free Press.

Mintzberg, H. (2004) *Managers not MBAs.* Berrett-Koehler.

Mintzberg, H. and Van der Heyden, L. (1999) 'Organigraphs: Drawing how organizations really work', *Harvard Business Review,* 77 (Sept-Oct): 87–94.

Mintzberg, H., Ahlstrand, B. and Lampel, J. (2001) *Strategy Safari: A Guided Tour Through the Wilds of Strategic Management. Financial Times,* Prentice-Hall.

Nattermann, P. (2000) 'Best practice does not equal best strategy', *The McKinsey Quarterly,* vol. 2: 22–31.

Nonaka, I., Takeuchi, H. and Takeuchi, H. (1995) *The Knowledge–creating Company: How Japanese Companies Create the Dynamics of Innovation.* Oxford: OUP.

Normann, R. and Ramirez, R. (1993) 'From value chain to value constellation: Designing interactive strategy', *Harvard Business Review,* July-August: 65–77.

Peters, T.J. and Waterman, R.H. (1982) *In Search of Excellence.* New York: Warners.

Pettigrew, A. (1979) 'On studying organizational cultures', *Administrative Science Quarterly,* Vol. 24: 570–580.

Pettigrew, A. (1985) *The Awakening Giant: Continuity and Change in ICI,* Oxford: Blackwell.

Pettigrew, A. (2003) 'Strategy as process, power and change', in S. Cummings and D. Wilson (eds), *Images of Strategy.* Oxford: Blackwell.

Pettigrew, A., Thomas, H. and Whittington, R. (2002) *Handbook of Strategy and Management.* London: Sage.

Pierson, F.C. (1959) *The Education of the American Businessman,* New York: McGraw-Hill.

Porter, M.E. (1980) *Competitive Strategy.* New York: Free Press.

Porter, M.E. (1985) *Competitive Advantage.* New York: Free Press.

Porter, M.E. (1996) 'What is strategy?' *Harvard Business Review,* 74 (Nov/Dec), 61–78.

Pugh, D., Dietz, J., Wiley, J.W. and Brooks, S.M. (2002) 'Driving service effectiveness through employee-customer linkages', *Academy of Management Executive,* 16 (4): 73–84.

Rumelt, R. (1984) 'Toward a strategic theory of the firm' in R. Lamb (ed.), *Competitive Strategic Management.* Englewood, Cliffs, NJ: Prentice-Hall. pp. 556–570.

Smith, C. (2007) 'The big picture', in D. Angwin et al. (eds), *The Strategy Pathfinder.* Oxford: Blackwell.

Wernerfelt, B. (1984) 'A resource-based view of the firm', *Strategic Management Journal,* vol. 5: 171–180.

Whittington, R. (1996) 'Strategy as practice', *Long Range Planning,* 29 (5): 731–735.

Whittington, R. (2003) 'The work of strategizing and organizing: For a practice perspective', *Strategic Organization,* 1 (1): 119–127.

Whittington, R. (2006) 'Completing the practice turn on strategy research', *Organization Studies* (forthcoming).

Van Witteloostuijn, A. and Boone, C. (2006) 'A resource-based theory of market structure and organizational form', *Academy of Management Review,* 31 (2): 409–426.

Wren, D.A. (1972) *The Evolution of Management Thought.* New York: Wiley.

Zeleny, M. (1997) 'The fall of strategic planning', *Human Systems Management,* 16, 77–79.

Toward the Ecological Ideal: Notes for a Complex Understanding of Complex Organizations

Haridimos Tsoukas

Two important intellectual trends have arisen in organization studies in the past 15 or so years. They are promising and, with the passage of time, I anticipate they will become stronger, since they reflect broader and deeper social and intellectual changes. One is the effort to overcome 'the Newtonian ideal' – the mechanistic approaches to organizational phenomena. In its place, an 'ecological' view is emerging whose main feature is the acceptance of complexity. The other important trend is the knowledge-based perspective on organizations – the view that organizations are constituted by knowledge (Tsoukas, 2005).

The two trends are inter-connected to some extent. One of the reasons why we tend to think that social life at large has become more complex in late modernity is because of the continuous feedback of information about the functioning of social practices into the social practices themselves. Important changes in the nature of economic activities in late modern societies have led toward the increasing dematerialization of such activities, the increasing importance of information and mediated communication and the emergence of generalized social reflexivity. These changes make social practices more prone to change and, to the extent this is the case, they increase uncertainty.

If complexity is defined as the number of distinguishable states a system is capable of having, organizations become, in conditions of late modernity, ever more complex as they abstract and uncouple time and space, and recombine them, making action at a distance possible. More components, across time and space, are included in an organized social system; and more information about how they interact and about the outcomes of their interaction, entailing the chronic re-constitution of those social systems, help make social systems more complex by multiplying the number of possible states they may have.

A complex system is capable of surprising us since the interaction of its components cannot be exhaustively mapped out – it will always have emergent properties. At the same time, if we have developed today a more subtle understanding of organizational life than in the past, this is because we, as organizational researchers, have complexified our language. The complexification of the language of organization studies has occurred, to a large extent, through acknowledging the centrality of human agency in the constitution and functioning of organizations. Changing reality and ideas about how reality may be dealt with constitute a loop: conditions in late modernity have given rise to more complex social and organizational phenomena, while a more sophisticated intellectual discourse has made it possible to recognize complexity in the phenomena of interest.

We have increasingly come to appreciate that social scientific language is not merely representational – representing organizational phenomena as they are – but also partly constitutive of the phenomena it deals with. This has been a major recognition because, on the one hand, it makes organizational theorists more reflexive about the categories they use and the assumptions they make, while, on the other hand, it has helped shift the emphasis from a more objectivist or entitarian approach to an enactivist or performative one.

Continued

If organizations do have emergent properties, then human agents in organizations need to be seen in performative terms, since how human agents interact gives organizations the emergent properties they have. In turn, this implies that human agents' capacity for action cannot be fully described in advance, since a performance is always situated in circumstances and grounded in practices that cannot be exhaustively known ex ante.

Whereas in representational terms the partial ignorance that emergent organizational properties generate can be offset with better techniques for describing and predicting organizational behaviour; in performative terms such a task is futile: one needs to learn to live with such ignorance and try instead to enhance agents' capabilities for undertaking effective action in ever-changing circumstances. Thus, appreciating the emergent texture of organizations – namely treating them not so much as collections of routines, structures and rules but as interactive accomplishments – leads us to appreciate also the inherently creative role individuals play.

A performative perspective on organizations highlights the inescapably situated and ever unfolding nature of organizational reality, since the latter is not a *fait accompli* but is (re)created through practice – through what agents do. Individuals are able to act by virtue of being embedded in a discursive practice – an unarticulated background which they take for granted. The unarticulated background consists of certain evaluative distinctions individuals learn to internalize and through which they relate spontaneously to their surroundings. To be embedded into an unarticulated background is to experience one's situation in terms of already constituted meanings and proto-interpretations. The background provides the frame that makes individuals' explicit representations possible and comprehensible. However, individuals are implicitly aware of the background; their awareness is largely inarticulate. The more able individuals are to articulate aspects of their background, namely to obtain a focal awareness of it, the clearer the understanding of their action will be. In other words, the non-focal (inarticulate) awareness of the background and the effort to articulate it, as well as the inescapably local (situated) character of human action make the latter inherently creative.

Creative action cannot be adequately theorized in the traditional manner of efficient causality, since if we could specify in advance what would count as creative it would cease to be so. However, processes can be theoretically described which make creative action possible. To recognize the importance of human agency means one needs to accept the specific human capacities for action while acknowledging the inherent incompleteness in knowing how such action might unfold. Moreover, since theories do not just represent the world but help constitute it, complex theorizing provides also a template for action. To the extent this is the case, assumptions about what it is to be and act like a human agent are crucial. A complex way to think about human agents is to view them not in atomistic but in social terms. Human agents act the way they do by virtue of their membership in certain social practices. Seeing both the individual and the broader collective domain within which individual action is undertaken, without reducing one to the other, is crucial for understanding human action.

Taking the emergent properties of organizations seriously entails a number of things related to how organizations might be theorized. In conditions of late modernity, the fundamental challenge for an organized system is to ensure the responsible and spontaneous cooperation of its members under authority relations. This was always important but the Newtonian ideal has obscured it from view, emphasizing mainly the authority relations in an organization. Spontaneous cooperation is important as it not only reduces coordination costs and enhances responsiveness in conditions of uncertainty, but helps secure human dignity (since it explicitly acknowledges agency) and highlights the potentially creative character of human action. An organized system that aims at securing the responsible and spontaneous cooperation of its members under authority relations is more complex than one that is based on the traditional principles of formal organization. Organizational complexification is a continuous process which is achieved through self-generated initiatives in response to local conditions, and institutionalized processes of learning and reflexivity. The more complexly idiosyncratic an organized system is, the less imitable it is.

Spontaneous cooperation under authority conditions is responsible when individuals aim at enacting the common organizational good, for which they cultivate their phronesis, namely the ability to act prudently by adapting generic rules to local circumstances in a way that enhances the common good. For this to be possible, organized social systems need to develop a *sensus communis*, which is possible when authority is bound by rules, and leaders become exemplars of behaviours that enhance the organizational common good. The latter cannot be seen separately from broader conceptions of the social good at large. Just as organizational members act in the service of the common organizational good, organized systems act in the service of the broader social good, namely for the fulfilment of ever-changing social needs. Organized systems operate increasingly within a public sphere – an agora – within which expectations are shaped, their practices are visible and discussable and within which they strive to earn reputation and legitimacy.

Complex forms of theorizing organizations in late modernity need to be grounded on an open-world ontology, an enactivist epistemology and a poetic praxeology. An open-world ontology assumes that the world is always in a process of becoming, of turning to something different. Flow, flux and change are the fundamental processes of the world. The future is open, unknowable in principle, and it always holds the possibility of surprise. An enactivist epistemology assumes that knowing is action. Human agents bring the world forward by making distinctions and giving form to an unarticulated background of understanding. Knowledge is the outcome of an active knower who follows certain historically shaped cognitive practices and is rooted within a socio-cultural practice. A poetic praxeology sees the practitioner as an active being who, while being inevitably shaped by the socio-cultural practices in which he/she is rooted in, also necessarily shapes them back by undertaking action that is relatively opaque in its consequences and unclear in its motives and desires, unreflective and situated in its mode of operation, but which is inherently capable of self-observation and reflexivity, and thus susceptible to chronic change. A poetic praxeology acknowledges the complicated motives of human action, makes room for the influence of the past and its transmutation into new forms in the present, understands the relatively opaque nature of human intentionality, allows for chance events, influences and feedback loops and accepts the inescapable contextuality and temporality of all human action.

Finally, seeing organizations as constituted by knowledge enables researchers to show the recursive loop between ways of knowing and knowledge produced. The Newtonian ideal generated mechanistic knowledge, which acted as a template for constructing mechanistic organizations and for conceiving human action in instrumental terms. The ecological ideal, with its emphasis on inter-connectedness, situatedness and creative

Continued

action, helps generate knowledge that is more organic, notices the emergent properties of organizations and the processes through which they are generated and views human agency in poetic (making/creative) terms. To think complexly about organizations is to place processes at the centre of inquiry; to recognize the recursive loop that connects knowing and knowledge; and to privilege socially embedded human agency.

REFERENCE

Tsoukas, H. (2005) *Complex Knowledge: Studies in Organizational Epistemology.* Oxford: Oxford University Press.

New Problems for Strategy

Anita McGahan

A few years ago, a friend at NYU's Stern School of Business asked me whether I felt that Strategy had emerged as an independent discipline. We easily agreed that it had, with its own theory, methods and empirical traditions. Most of us agree that Strategy has its roots in the fields of Administrative Sciences (including Operations Management, Business Policy and Organizational Behavior), Economics and Sociology. We can legitimately and proudly declare ourselves as strategists rather than as only administrative scientists, economists and sociologists. We've generated knowledge about alliances, resources, capability development, management cognition, and several other important facets of business problems. We know a great deal about topics that could not have been understood fully from the perspectives of our root disciplines. This is the good news.

There are also significant challenges in the field. Their genesis lies in the fact that we are having trouble in launching new streams of ideas in which the insights of multiple researchers can accumulate. We have pressed forward on a relatively small set of important topics to the point of diminishing returns.

Unless we can fix this problem, and fix it quickly, we're at risk of losing our relevance. I'm worried that we're not fully deploying our analytical powers to address the world's most pressing strategic problems and opportunities. Here's my short list of the issues that I wish we studied more fully: Oil will become quite expensive over the next few decades and then run out. Infectious disease is rampant in settings of poverty and threatens the social, economic and political stability of institutions around the world. Inequality is increasing. Conflicts of interest in business abound. The explosion of world trade has made some companies larger than some national governments. The secular institutions of business provoke non-secular responses in some parts of the world. The productivity benefits of new-technology development are not widely accessible and hence the technologies themselves are developing too narrowly.

Another challenge that has emerged in our young field is that we focus a great deal on value-capture challenges rather than value-creation challenges. We typically define the field of Strategy as the study of organizational performance. In practice, this often means that we investigate the drivers and consequences of firm profitability, rather than the creative processes that stimulate new value creation. We leave to our colleagues in Entrepreneurship and Operations the messy tasks of sorting out the qualitative processes that make some firms better than others at innovation. This is a mistake.

If we're up to the challenge, then there is a lot we can do to prevent the field of Strategy from staying too narrow. We can consolidate our thinking about new topical areas in special issues of journals. Today, many special issues focus on well-baked topics. I hope that, in the future, the editors of our major journals will also sponsor special issues that can serve as platforms for launching new areas of inquiry in our field. We should expand our theoretical base and implement new reviewing standards that reflect the potential significance of burgeoning research streams. The field of Strategy is only beginning to lock down its major theoretical precepts, yet we need to accept eclectic theory that can

Continued

support inquiry into new problems. It is difficult to simultaneously broaden our theoretical base and implement standards for evaluating new theory, but it is also essential to the health of the field. A strength of the field of Strategy is in the methods that we have inherited from our root disciplines in the social and administrative sciences. I hope that, as Strategy evolves, we find a way to incorporate the methods of Business History and Anthropology to complement our established approaches. Finally, we can accept a range of empirical approaches. One of the most satisfying methodological developments in Strategy over the last few years has been the resurgence of rigorous field research. We can work better with practitioners on field research sites, databases and feedback on the usefulness of our ideas. In particular, we could use help from practitioners in developing better data on innovation and performance. As our areas of inquiry expand, we must be open to new empirical methods such as controlled experimentation, oral history and behavioral investigation.

Our young field of Strategy will become more secure when we find ways of enhancing our relevance by spawning new areas of inquiry. I hope we take on the challenge sooner rather than later.

PART 2

Living in Organizations

Spin

David M. Boje

Spin is the most neglected aspect of story research. Spin, though unstudied, is powerful in *storytelling organizations* such as Nike, Disney, McDonald's, and Wal-Mart. *Storytelling organization* is defined as 'a collective system in which the performance of stories is a key part of members' sensemaking and a means to allow them to supplement individual memories with institutional memory' (Boje, 1991: 106). Each has its war room, orchestrates spin campaigns, and answers activist story campaigns with strategic spin. Why study spin? *Storytelling organizations* spend billions on story technology, hiring spin talent, increasingly appropriating our *living stories* (stories we live), consummating *spin* we are socialized to live, then selling them back to us to shape the very 'reality' we story researchers study, robbing story magic.

When was story magical you ask? Well, that was long, long ago, before Hans Christian Andersen and brothers Grimm would steal story from the folk, and create, with flourish mind you, quite fantastic collections that were popular not just with common folk, but with royalty. François Rabelais was the last collector who chronicled the power of story when it belonged to the folk, when

a peasant could speak back to power (within limits). As Bakhtin's (1940/1968) dissertation thesis claims, during carnival time of early Renaissance, leaders of church and state put on their masks, mingling with the folk, listening to critiques of themselves that were often quite vulgar, I mean like tossing dung and revealing a bit of nudity. Speaking with profanity to power was a dialogic manner of story, not repressed narrative. You are right; those days are gone. Modernity turned to science. The powerful no longer attend carnival.

Appropriation began with old-time folklorists, anthropologists and ship captains collecting story to enable colonization. Folklorists built huge collections of indigenous tales while mapping the territories for invasion. Anthropologists lifted cultural knowledge from the folk. Neither folklorist nor anthropologist shared authorship. Yes, both fields have scholars now quite critical of their forebears, and go about research differently now. I best end this introduction by telling you a story (as If I had not already).

Story: It was March 10th, 1983, and we did assemble the new breed of folklorist and anthropologist to meet up with management researchers and a hoard of corporate and government executives for what we called '*Myth, Symbols & Folklore: Expanding the Analysis of Organizations*' (Jones et al., 1983). I am looking at a program listing these management scholars (to drop a few names): Olaf Berg, Janice Beyer, Tom Cummings, Tom Dandridge, Peter Frost, Mary Jo Hatch, Craig Lundberg, Joanne Martin, Fred Massarik, Ian Mitroff, Karen Vinten, J.C. Spender, Harrison Trice, and William Wolf. And the who's who from a fledgling field called 'organizational folklore': Gary Allen Fine, Robert Georges, Michael Owen Jones, Yvonne Lockwood, Elliott Oring, and William Wilson. Organization Folklore is not the same as traditional folklore done by Alan Dundes' (1963) 'diffusion models' of tale-types migrating from counry to country, or Stith Thompson's (1946) 'motif-index' scheme to classify symbol and plot. Management studies adopted some of this, but left out the bottom-up-view and story-behaviors, so critical to 'organization folklore'. Management research found motif-indexing too confusing, finally jilting folklore for narratology.

And we invited executives from the Aerospace Corporation Anheuser-Bush, Hughes Aircraft, Mattel Toy, Max Factor Southern California Edison, Standard Brands Paint, and Wyle Labs.

Guess what happened? You got it. Like some school dance, folklorists went to one side of the hall, and management scholars to the other. Here is the punch line. And believe it, for I would not make up such a thing, it was the executives who danced with the folklorists; they had already heard what management researchers had to say; they glimpsed the holy grail; *story control.*

How do I put this politely? Management researchers tended to look at story from the *managerialist* viewpoint (top makes the story)! Organization folklorists were opposite, looked at story from the *workers'* viewpoint (bottom up).[1] Folklorists (given their history with colonizing) were very distrustful of management-types.

What about executives? Oh, you know this story! They stole the show. They saddled

right up to the folklorists, to steal story magic powers. *Folk* 'spun' yarns, stitched a weave of threads of fact and fiction. But management turned the magic to spinning, stretching, turning, shaping, twisting, and exploiting story.

It takes a critical approach to study spin. For me, that is 'critical antenarratology'.

What is Critical Antenarratology? It's the study of hegemonic processes of collective story-spin practices that privilege some tellings over others; such as, creating a heroic façade in the face of activists, exposé journalists and critical scholars. *Antenarrative* is defined as 'the fragmented, non-linear, incoherent, collective, unplotted, and pre-narrative speculation, a bet … a proper narrative can be constituted' (Boje, 2001: 1). 'Stories are "antenarrative" when told without the proper plot sequence and mediated coherence preferred in narrative theory' (2001: 3).

Antenarratives are dialogically pluralistic, emergent, fragmented, simultaneous, and collectively realized. Antenarratives self-deconstruct and reconstruct, picking up and discarding content and reference in trajectories between times and places, as people shape story differently in acts of co-construction.

Critical antenarratology research is skeptical of *spin*, holding out the possibility that *storytelling organizations* are dialogically-complex systemicities, more than fiction, they realized in, and shape, material conditions, with material consequence (Boje, 2001, 2005b, c, 2008). I define systemicity as unmerged agents (each different), unfinalized and unfinishable wholeness.[2]

My thesis is that dialogized-story has been appropriated by corporate power, harnessed to technology to control story in ways we have not begun to research. I envision two directions for storytelling organization research: spin *consummation* and spin *answerability*. These are important because organizations are consummating stories in more sophisticated ways than ever before, and people around the world are demanding answerability for those stories. Bakhtin (1990: 11), in his first published essay (dated September 13, 1919), asserts, 'I have to answer with my own life for what I have experienced and understood.' Bakhtin (1990) did not buy into the assumption that the author is dead, and asked, how systemicity gets *consummated*, that is whom is '*authoring*' stories and when does *answerability* inquiry commence?

Answerability has been defined by Bakhtin (1993: 42): 'An answerable act or deed is precisely that act which is performed on the basis of an acknowledgment of my obligative (ought-to-be) uniqueness.'

Story consummation is the study of the problem of story co-construction, how stories emerge as less-than-coherent antenarratives, are shaped collectively into wholes (cohesive, plots, sometimes petrified), transform, and can spin out of organizational control, disassociate, and destabilize into nothing.

Story answerability is the study of the problem of who is doing the storying, and who is listening, and are they aware of their answerability for stories being consummated. Each storytelling organization is a labyrinth of stories being produced, consumed, and distributed collectively that has *answerability*. *Living story* is the story we live, that comes out of our community and family life experience; it is no longer separate from storytelling organization.

CONCEPTUAL DEBATES IN STORY THEORY

1. *Story is restricted by narrative to be a cohesive plot of beginning, middle, and end (hereafter, BME).*[3] According to Aristotle (350 BCE 1450b: 25: 233), narrative requires story to be a *proper* 'imitation of an action that is complete in itself, as a whole of some magnitude ... Now a whole is that which has beginning, middle, and end' the definition of coherent narrative (233). For my colleague Gabriel (2000) a 'proper' story must have Aristotelian narrative BME coherence. As well for my colleague Czarniawska's early work (1997, 1998), narratives must have a casual sequence, a plot. Plot is grasped in retrospective sensemaking. prefer a broader definition, *story* defined 'as an exchange between two or more persons during which a past or anticipated experience was being referenced, recounted, interpreted, or challenged' (Boje, 1991: 111).

Recently, Czarniawska (2004: 38) relaxed the 'proper story' restriction of narrative plot on story, allowing wider variety of forms: 'storytelling in contemporary organizations hardly follows the traditional pattern of a narrator telling a story from the beginning to end in front of an enchanted and attentive audience.'[4]

2. Story is restricted to reflecting upon experience as retrospective sensemaking while ignoring 'spin'. Weick (1995: 129), for example, argues that narrative control is accomplished retrospectively by 'a repertoire of stories ... important for sensemaking' Retrospective sense-making is important. So is *prospective sense-spinning*, the ongoing antenarrative construction of spin, as the movie title put it, to '*Wag the Dog!*'[5]

McDonald's is critiqued for its packaging and environmental waste, so it makes a strategic alliance *Environmental Defense Fund* (EDF), in a flurry of press releases, a green-spin story is created: McDonald's is environmentally sustainable (Starkey and Crane, 2003). McDonald's forms a strategic alliance with *People for Ethical Treatment of Animals* (PETA); there are more press releases, and a new spin: McDonald's has seen the light, and has humane animal-slaughter practices. McDonald's succeeded in parrying several, 'my child is getting fat at McDonald's' lawsuits.

McDonald's sees 2004 *Supersize Me* documentary by Morgan Spurlock is garnering film awards, and headed into theatres everywhere; the story is about a young man eating at McDonald's and he keeps getting fatter, and doctors are saying he is ruining his health. McDonald's changes its 'story strategy' (Barry and Elmes, 1997) by ceasing its Supersize options, redoing its tray liners, putting out new salads (Boje et al., 2005). McDonald's global story strategy is respun: *Go Active!* 'To be the leading restaurant promoting healthy, happy, active lifestyles everywhere we do business' (Kapica, 2004: slide 17).

Spin: eating fast food is compatible with active, fitness, and balanced nutrition lifestyle. Ronald McDonald gets a new show, does fitness work out exercises; other fitness coaches, such as Bob Greene (Oprah Winfrey's trainer) are recruited to sell the new spin strategy; trayliners are printed with references to Greene and Oprah, including nutrition charts; Adult Happy Meals include step-o-meters; stores gave out brochures instructing parents how many hours of exercise children required to keep them healthy on their fast food diet (Boje et al., 2005).

It is unlikely that Oprah agrees to Mickey D's spin since she made such a disparaging remark on her April 15, 1996 show, when guest Howard Lyman spoke out about Mad Cow disease, Oprha exclaimed, 'It has just stopped me cold from eating another burger!'(Boje et al., 2005). Millions of fans stopped eating burgers; sales plummeted; she was sued by Texas cattle barons, because in Texas it's illegal to disparage the meat industry.

My point is that there is a lot of corporate investment in spin, some based on changing reality to fit spin, such as removing *Supersize* portions, creating strategic alliances with fitness/nutrition experts; this way the story has many grains of truth; other times spin is just the triumph of fiction over reality, such as with Enron. There is story research opportunity studying spin.

Things that disturb me

1. *I find managerialist linear story of progress to be particularly disturbing.* Managerialist means to tell just management's side of the story, as if it were not dialogic to counterstories. The challenge to story research is to move from managerialist (monophonic and monologic) story to polyphonic (many voices) and polylogic (many logics) story, what Bakhtin (1981: 25) calls 'dialogized story' (Bakhtin, 1981: 25; Boje, 2005a, 2008; Boje and Kadija, 2005). Rather than just abandon managerialist story, researchers could investigate multiple counterstories. My colleagues and I have been studying dialogic story, how

McDonald's corporation narrates through other narrators (Boje, 2005a; Boje et al., 2005; Boje and Rhodes, 2005, a, b; Boje et al., 2005).

Story advice books (Boje, 2006b) bother me, such as Denning's (2001) 'springboard' story, 'a story that enables a leap in understanding by the audience so as to grasp how an organization or community or complex system may change' (xviii). The executive gets to spring such stories, but they have decidedly linear and managerialist characteristics: (1) story from perspective of single protagonist (i.e. the manager/leader) in prototypical business predicament; (2) explicit story familiar to the audience; (3) stimulates their imagination; (4) must have a positive or happy ending (Denning, 2001: xix, 124, 126, 198). It is ironic for Denning (p. xvi, footnote 5) to invoke Bakhtin's (1973) polyphonic dialogism, since springboard story is not dialogic; it is a linear managerialist-narrative!

Bakhtin (1973: 4), for example, explored how Dostoyevsky's novels were marked by 'the plurality of independent and unmerged voices and consciousnesses and the genuine polyphony of full-valued voices', a *systematicity* that is 'unfinalizedness [in] its openendedness and indeterminacy' (p. 43) and gives rise to 'the polyphonic manner of the story' (p. 60).

2. *I find the concept of 'positive' story in Appreciative Inquiry and story advice books to be particularly disturbing.* Cooperrider and Srivastra (1987) first developed *Appreciative Inquiry* (AI) as a positive science, to focus on the positive while facilitating the co-construction of new organization-story; four Ds: Discovery (Appreciating), Dream (Envisioning results), Design (co-constructing), and Delivery (Sustaining) form a cycle (Cooperrider et al., 2000). AI devotees are against deconstruction, since that would be negative, not positive science; story work at that time focused on telling only positive stories. Ludema et al. (1996: 6) say deconstructionists have 'failed to become catalysts for positive organizational transformation because they rely on methodologies that by design are meant to de-legitimate existing organizational theories

rather than create new constructs that hold positive possibilities for future.' My colleague from the UK, Cliff Oswick, says 'it is time for a *Depreciative Inquiry*' (DI) so that AI can learn the value of being critical (Oswick, personal communication, 1999). Two AI experts, Spicochi and Tyran (2002), have done pioneering story research by looking at how to use AI after assessing the more hegemonic story domination processes of organizations; they do not, however mention the word 'deconstruction'.

3. *Most story research is about textuality instead of intertextuality.* There are exceptions: Fairclough (1992) studied intertextuality and hegemony in newspaper stories; O'Connor (2002) studied intertextuality in entrepreneurial narratives; and I deconstructed the intertextuality of Nike's press releases, to illustrate how the official Nike story, here and there an answer to an activist story (Boje, 2001: 79–92); and my colleagues and I analyzed the intertextuality of antenarratives in over 5,000 Enron stories (Boje and Rosile, 2002, 2003; Boje et al., 2004).

One reason story-intertextual research is not progressing is an over-reliance upon qualitative research software, such as Ethnograph and NUDIST (renamed to more politically correct, NVIVO). Story research has become a matter of collecting story-text (from interview, observation, or documents) then developing a codebook of variables to facilitate text classification and model building, Yet, once entered into story databases, the context of the story is lost. It is not impossible to do intertextual work with software, just difficult. While reviewers seem to like text software, to give the article that empirical feel, I still prefer highlighting a transcript (or document), and then making margin notes how various words and phrases, and sometimes a story, are intertextual to other texts and other stories.

What we could be doing and questions we could be asking

1. *Stop placing story research emphasis on written and verbal story; we miss the multiple*
stylistic modes of telling that are very telling. It's time to look at visual and gestural and ways people move bureaucratically (or not) was modes of telling.

When I enter a Disney place, a McDonald's, Wal-Mart, or a NikeTown, I am assaulted by visual storying that is more than the words spoken or written. There are visual displays arranged in storyboard, portraits of stars and customers covered in brand images, ways of storying products in juxtaposition with architecture and décor that is to some a feast for the eyes, or to others, a visual nightmare. I am under the influence of not only visual story, but smells, and invitations to touch the merchandise, to enter into the experience of story that involves all five senses.

One avenue of research would be to look at how all five senses are being engaged in the storytelling that organizations erect and orchestrate for us to participate within. Bakhtin (1981) provides a way to proceed, by suggesting there are at the very least five stylistic modes of expression. Stylistics is defined as the interaction of various modes of communication. There are five styles Bakhtin (1981: 262) imagines, and these are in a special kind of relationship, one where by various modes of style, a storytelling occurs (in spoken, architectural, and several modes of writing, some scientific, others more everyday speech or 'skaz' such as 'Just Do It' or all those 'Mc' accented words). *Multi-Stylistic Dialogism* is a manner of story told through a juxtaposition of pictures of characters that invite the reader into the pictures, stars using narrated words (skaz and direct speech), numbers in scientific charts followed by names of institutions, workers buzzing about in uniforms, will customers queue up, and so forth.

Some potential research questions: How story is told with multiple modes of telling? Does one stylistic mode dominate other story expression? How do the styles juxtapose to constitute story that appeals to each of our senses? How does multi-mode stylistics influence customer, worker, or activist behavior? What does it mean when one style of telling is mismatched with a style telling a counter-story?

2.   *In placing emphasis on story told to all in one room, we may miss the obvious point: You can not be in every room at once.* In my story research on Disney, I proposed a new model of *storytelling organization*; I called *Tamara* (Boje, 1995). *Tamara* is defined as the landscape of story co-production, distributed across simultaneous performance sites, where chasing storylines means networking with others, and people in the same time and place can experience story differently because they arrive from different telling in other places; and no one is everywhere at once. *Tamara* is a postmodern play, where characters unfold their story, before a running, often running, fragmenting audience chasing story from room to room instead of the fixed seating and elevated stage of modern theatre. I think many story researchers agree that it is virtually 'impossible to sustain monological accounts of social reality' under conditions of simultaneous storytelling and story network-ing going on between tellers and listeners in organizations (Bryant and Cox, 2004: 580, citing Oswick and Keenoy, 2001: 224).

3.   *Do storytelling organizations have lots of story power?* I mean the ability to command resources (talent and technology), to make one's way of telling a story ready-to-hand to millions of people. Part of managing and controlling a *storytelling organization*, is deploying storytellers to offset damage from counterstories activists disseminate in their campaigns. For example, Nike has followed Monsanto's tactic of sending staff members to academic conference to counter activist accounts. McDonald's spends a billion a year on its advertising to children and parents that fast food is healthy for you. Nike spent more advertising dollars on Michael Jordan annually than the entire workforce of Indonesia earned making Nike sneakers and garments (Ballinger and Olsson, 1997); Tiger Woods makes more in a year than all the Nike workers in Asia. Advertising budgets of these and other multi-national and global corporations produce story leverage.

The activist strategy can also be studied; putting a human face on the plight of sweat-shop workers, since consumers often have no idea who makes their clothing, sneakers, toys, computers, etc. Research can indicate whether such tactics make any difference.

How story is orchestrated in war rooms is a topic of study. Ray Kroc formed a 'war room' to keep track of 'agitators' and to strategize 'campaigns' that included managing the stories being told; taking out full page ads in newspapers, getting positive stories told in the press. McDonald's counters activist claims by wrapping the 'M' in patriotism (US flags flown over most stores US), community charity (Ronald McDonald House), green ways of packaging, etc. Nike's *war room* staff is very aggressive about discouraging authors and activists from pursuing stories that might negatively affect the bottom line. I should know. Nike blocked my publishing activist stories, rattling its Swoosh saber at a UK book publisher, and *Journal of Organizational Change Management*. MCB (publishers of JOCM) were terrified, and decided never again to allow me to write any article using the word 'Nike'. Nike said they'd sue me and the publisher if a certain chapter I wrote was published, and sue me if I divulge their critique. The irony is that this chapter had already been published as a JOCM article (Boje, 1999). And the article I had in production at JOCM on Nike was pulled, and in its place I did the same radical critique, but on Disney (Boje, 2000a), then wrote an exposé story in *Management Communication Quarterly* Boje, 2000b).

4.   *What happens when the wagons circle and corporations have to change their ways?* I suspect that given the resources that organizations are investing in telling a story-image-management, that change is partly due to the growing legion of activists. There are also calls for more dialogically polylogical organizations (Boje, 1995, 2008) with more polyphonic (multi-voiced) story strategy have been issued (Barry and Elmes, 1997).

Wal-Mart is the biggest corporation in the world, 1.2 million employees worldwide and $256 billion in global revenue fiscal year 2005. Research can look at how aggressively a corporation stories itself in reaction to activism. As CEO Lee Scott puts it, 'For me personally, you can expect to see me continue to tell the Wal-Mart story more aggressively' (Wal-Mart, 2005 Annual Report, p. 13).[7] Aggressive storytelling includes the work of consulting firms; PSG consulting, for example creates and implements 'managed grassroots campaigns' to win both public and political support toward Wal-Mart store construction.[8] Other consulting firms such as, Global Insight Inc. host economic summits for Wal-Mart, such as one on November 4, 2005 to deal aggressively with negative press expected from a new film, '*Wal-Mart: The High Cost of Low Price*', by Robert Greenwald.

Quinn (1998) asserts that Wal-Mart managers, in some locations, keep a full-time associate busy collecting prices from any business selling competitive goods at the same or lower prices; Wal-Mart then undercut those prices. By contrast, Wal-Mart stories itself as the engine of economic progress, as the kindest of employers to its 'associates'.

Attorneys for six lead plaintiffs have won the largest certified civil-rights class-action (filed 2001) in US history, and it's against Wal-Mart; it could results in billions in added economic losses. The suit alleges Wal-Mart discriminated against female employees in pay, promotion and training, and retaliated against women who complained about any alleged abuse. Wal-Mart is now appealing the verdict and award to a higher court. Earlier in 2005, Wal-Mart agreed to pay a record $11 million to settle civil charges that it knowingly hired floor-cleaning contractors who employed illegal aliens.

Wal-Mart has updated its web sites, setting off the kinds of answers to tough questions one sees at Nike's site. It is managing its story, doing its best to put its most positive image in play. Activist groups such as Wake Up Wal-Mart, Wal-Mart Watch have initiated their own war rooms that now counter strategies of Wal-Mart's war room.

CONCLUSIONS

There is no such thing as story neutrality, or an unbiased storyteller, in the dialogized story arena. I take the position that researchers, executives, employees, journalists, and activists hold organizations *answerable* for stories they *consummate*.

It is time to throw off narrative shackles placed onto 'proper' story. The debate between story and narrative scholars centers on whether 'story' is in the collective mind of tellers and spectators (readers) or is it in-between tellers and spectators, in intertextuality?

The story you are able to spin or create resides in the mind of the other; reassembling (spinning) material that resides in someone else's head amounts to long-distance brain surgery. Stein anticipated my focus on 'antenarrative story', by being flat-against confining story to just coherent narrative, a developmentally-plotted (linear) story complete with beginning, middle, and end.

It is time to research story power, address story answerability and how story is consummated in storytelling organizations. It is too reductionist to focus on the positive narrative; storytelling is dialectic and dialogic. Story is crafted in war rooms.

NOTES

1 There were exceptions, e.g. Martin and Powers (1983) critique of corporate story as propaganda.
2 Bakhtin (1981: 152) uses the term 'systematicalness' to denote unmerged parts, and unfinalized wholeness of systems; I abbreviated this to 'systemicity'.
3 There were exceptions, e.g. Martin and Powers (1983) critique of corporate story as propaganda.
4 It should be noted that in 1970s, organizational folklore departed from motif-index analysis of collections of tales; and instead looked at behavior of storytellers *in situ*. I learned this at UCLA (1978–1986).
5 1997 New Line Cinema, a Barry Levinson film starring Dustin Hoffman and Robert De Niro; war is fabricated to distract public attention from a sex scandal.
6 If you perceive a style of story that is much like Pondy (1978), then you are correct; Pondy was my

mentor, and taught me how to get to the point, exaggerate for effect, and did make the mistake of encouraging me to tell stories and research them.

7 Wal-Mart 2005 Annual Report accessed August 9, 2005. http://www.walmartstores.com/Files/2005AnnualReport.pdf

8 Don't let Wal-Mart's consultants fool you, Paul Johnson, Nashua Published: Monday, Aug. 8, 2005, accessed August 9, 2005 http://nsnlb.us.publicus.com/apps/pbcs.dll/article?AID=/20050808/OPINION02/108080135/-1/business

REFERENCES

Bakhtin, M.M. (1940/1968) *Rabelais and His World*. Translated by Hélène Iswolsky. Cambridge/London: The M.I.T. Press. 1940 date dissertation 1st submitted; 1968 English publication.

Bakhtin, M. (1973) *Problems of Dostoevsky's Poetics* (C. Emerson, ed. and trans.). Manchester: Manchester University Press.

Bakhtin, M.M. (1981) *The Dialogic Imagination*. Four Essays by M.M. Bakhtin (ed. M. Holquist). Austin, TX: University of Texas Press.

Bakhtin, M.M. (1990) *Art and Answerability*. Edited by Michael Holquist and Vadim Liapunov. Translation and Notes by Vadim Liapunov; supplement translated by Kenneth Brostrom. Austin, TX: University of Texas Press. From Bakhtin's first published article and his early 1920s notebooks.

Bakhtin, Mikhail, (1993) *Toward a Philosophy of the Act*. Translation and notes by Vidim Liapunov. Edited by Michael Holquist and Vadim Liapunov. Austin, TX: Univeristy of Texas Press.

Ballinger, J. and Olsson, C. (eds). (1997) *Behind the Swoosh: The Struggle of Indonesians Making Nike Shoes*. Uppsala Sweden: Global Publications Foundation and International Coalition for Development Action.

Barry, D. and Elmes, M. (1997) 'Strategy retold: Toward a narrative view of strategic discourse'. *Academy of Management Review*, 22 (2): 429–452.

Boje, D.M. (1991) 'The storytelling organization: A study of storytelling performance in an office supply firm'. *Administrative Science Quarterly*, 36: 106–126.

Boje, D.M. (1995) 'Stories of the storytelling organization: A postmodern analysis of Disney as "Tamara-land"' *Academy of Management Journal*. 38 (4): 997–1035.

Boje, D.M. (1999) 'Nike, Greek goddess of victory or cruelty? Women's stories of Asian factory life'. *Journal of Organizational Change Management*, 11 (8): 461–480.

Boje, D.M. (2000a) 'Phenomenal complexity theory and change at Disney'. *Journal of Organizational Change Management*, 13 (6): 558–566.

Boje, D.M. (2000b) 'Nike corporate writing of academic, business, and cultural Practices'. *Management Communication Quarterly*, issue on Essays for the Popular Management Forum, 4 (3): 507–516.

Boje, D.M. (2000c) 'Nike is Just in Time' presentation in 'Time and Nike,' an All Academy Showcase Session of the Academy of Management Meetings in Toronto Canada. Session #170 Wednesday 8:30–10:20 Royal York Room, August 9th, Nancy E. Landrum and David M. Boje co-chairs.

Boje, D.M. (2001) *Narrative Methods for Organizaitonal and Communication Research*. London: Sage.

Boje, D.M. (2003) 'The antenarrative cultural turn in narrative studies'. To appear in book edited by Mark Zachry and Charlotte Thralls *The Cultural Turn Communicative Practices in Workplaces and the Professions*; chapter revised Sept 16.

Boje, D.M. (2005a) *Dialogism in Management Research*. Sage Dictionary, forthcoming.

Boje, D.M. (2005b) 'Antenarration Inquiry: The Utrecht lecture on exposition'. Utrecht University, 16 Mar 05, published in 2005 *Annual Review of Management and Organization Inquiry* (sc'MOI). Copy available at http://scmoi.org

Boje, D.M. (2005c) 'From Wilda to Disney: Living Stories in Family and Organization Research'. Chapter accepted for Jean Clandinin (ed.), *Handbook of Narrative Inquiry*. London: Sage.

Boje, D.M. (2006) 'Pitfalls in storytelling advice and praxis', *Academy of Management Review*, 31 (1): 218–224.

Boje, D.M. (2008) *Storytelling Organization: Releasing Story from Narrative Prison*. London: Sage; pre-publication version at http://business.nmsu.edu/~edu/690

Boje, D.M. Driver, M. and Cai, Y. (2005) 'Fiction and humor in transforming McDonald's narrative strategies', *Culture and Organization*, 11 (3): 195–208.

Boje, D.M. and Khadija, A.A. (2005) *Toward a Dialogic System Theory*. Paper presented to Standing Conference of Management and Organization Inquiry (sc'MOI). Available in proceeding archive online http://scmoi.org

Boje, D.M. and Luhman, J. (1997) 'The deconstruction-affirmative inquiry debate', *Academy of Management Meetings*, Boston.

Boje, D.M., Luhman, J. and Baack, D. (1999) 'Hegemonic tales of the field: A telling research encounter between storytelling organizations'. October issue of *Journal of Management Inquiry*, 8 (4): 340–360.

Boje, D.M. and Rhodes, C. (2005a) 'The leadership of Ronald McDonald: Double narration and stylistic lines of transformation'. Accepted for publication in *Leadership Quarterly Journal* on April 9, 2005.

Boje, D.M. and Rhodes, C. (2005b) 'The virtual leader construct: The mass mediatization and simulation of transformational leadership'. Accepted for publication in *Leadership Journal*.

Boje, D.M. and Rosile, G.A. (2002) 'Enron Whodunit?' *Ephemera*, 2 (4): 315–327.

Boje, D.M. and Rosile, G.A. (2003) 'Life imitates art: enron's epic and tragic narration', *Management Communication Quarterly*, 17 (1): 85–125.

Boje, D.M., Rosile, G.A., Durant, R.A. and Luhman, J.T. (2004) 'Enron spectacles: A critical dramaturgical analysis. Special Issue on Theatre and Organizations edited by Georg Schreyögg and Heather Höpfl, *Organization Studies*, 25 (5): 751–774.

Boje, D.M., Enríquez, E., González, M.T. and Macías, E. (2005) 'Architectonics of McDonald's cohabitation with Wal-Mart: An exploratory study of ethnocentricity', *Critical Perspectives on International Business Journal*, 1 (4): 241–262.

Bryant, M. and Cox, J.W. (2004) 'Conversion stories as shifting narratives of organizational change', *Journal of Organizaitonal Change Management*, 17 (6): 578–592.

Collins, D. and Rainwater, K. (2005) 'Managing change at sears: A sideways look at a tale of corporate transformation', *Journal of Organizational Change Management*, 18 (1): 16–30.

Cooperrider, D.L., and Srivastra, S. (1987) 'Appreciative inquiry in organizational life', *Research in Organizational Change and Development*, 1: 129–169.

Cooperrider, D.L., Sorenson, P.F. Jr., Whitney, D. and Yaeger, T.F. (2000) *Appreciative Inquiry: Rethinking Human Organization Toward a Positive Theory of Change*. Champaign, Stipes.

Czarniawska, B. (1997) *Narrating the Organization: Dramas of Institutional Identity*. Chicago: University of Chicago Press.

Czarniawska, B. (1998) *A Narrative Approach to Organization Studies*. Qualitative Research Methods Series, Vol. 43. Thousand Oaks, CA: Sage Publications.

Czarniawska, B. (2004) *Narratives in Social Science Research*. London: Sage.

Dalcher, D. and Drevin, L. (2003) 'Learning from information systems failures by using narrative and antenarrative methods'. Proceedings of SAICSIT, pp. 137–142.

Denning, S. (2001) *The Springboard: How Storytelling Ignites Action in Knowledge-Era Organizations*. Boston/Oxford: Butterworth-Heinemann.

Dundes, A. (1963) 'Structural typology in North American Indian folktales', in A. Dundes (ed.), *The Study of Folklore*. New Jersey: Prentice-Hall, pp. 206–217.

Emerson, T. (2001) 'Swoosh Wars' *Newsweek International*. March 12 issue. MNBC.com copy (accessed August 8, 2005). http://www.1worldcommunication.org/swooshwars.htm

Fairclough, N. (1992) *Discourse and Social Change*. Cambridge: Polity Press.

Gabriel, Y.A. (1991) 'Turning facts into stories and stories into facts: A hermeneutic exploration of organizational folklore', *Human Relations*, 44, 857–871.

Gabriel, Y.A. (2000) *Storytelling in Organizations: Facts, Fictions, and Fantasies*. London: Oxford University Press.

Gardner, C. (2002) 'An exploratory study of bureaucratic, heroic, chaos, postmodern and hybrid story typologies of the expatriate journey'. Dissertation in Management Department of College of Business Administration and Economics.

Jones, M.O. Boje, D.M. and Guiliano, B.S. (1983) 'Myth, Symbols and Folklore: Expanding the Analysis of Organizations'. The first and last 'Organizational Folklore Conference' took place Mar 10–12, Santa Monica, California. It was partially funded by Skaggs Foundation and National Endowment for the Humanities.

Kapica, C. (2004) 'The role of quick serve restaurants in wellness: Can we get people to eat smart and be active?' Kapica is director of global nutrition for McDonald's. This is a presentation of global corporate strategy to the American Overseas Dietetic conference, Nicosia, Cyprus, March 27. http://www.cydadiet.org/april2004/cathyKapica.pdf

Landrum, N.E. (2000) 'A quantitative and qualitative examination of the dynamics of Nike and Reebok storytelling as strategy'. Dissertation, New Mexico State University, Management Department.

Ludema, J.D., Wilmot, T.B. and Srivastva, S. (1996) 'Organizational hope and textured vocabularies of possibility: Reaffirming the constructive task of social and organizational inquiry'. Weatherhead School of Management, Case Western Reserve University (July).

Martin, J. and Powers, M.E. (1983) 'Truth or corporate propaganda: The value of a good war story', in L.R. Pondy, P. Frost, G. Morgan, and T. Dandridge (eds), *Organizational Symbolism*. Greenwich, CT: JAI. pp. 93–107.

O'Connor, E. (2002) 'Storied business: Typology, intertextuality, and traffic in entrepreneurial narrative', *The Journal of Business Communication*. 39 (1): 36–54.

Oswick, C. and Keenoy, T. (2001) 'Cinematic re-presentation of Las Vegas: Reality, fiction and compulsive consumption', *Management Journal*, 4 (3): 217–227.

Pondy L.R. (1978) 'Leadership as a language game', 87–99 in McCall, M.W. and Lombardo, M.M. (eds), *Leadership: Where Else Can We Go?* Durham, Duke University, NC: Press.

Quinn, B. (1998) *How Wal-Mart Is Destroying America: And What You Can Do About It.* Berkeley, CA: Ten Speed Press.

Ritzer, G. (1993/2002) *The McDonaldization of Society.* Newbury Park, CA: Pine Forge. First edition 1993; Second edition 2002.

Schlosser, E. (2001) *Fast Food Nation: The Dark Side of the All-American Meal.* Boston: Houghton Mifflin.

Spicochi, R. and Tyran, K.L. (2002) 'A tale of two leaders'. Exploring the role of leader storytelling and follower sensemaking in transformational change. An Organizational Development and Change (ODC) paper presented to Special Interest Topics session # 1022 'Storytelling and Narrative' at Denver meeting of Academy of Management on Wednesday August 14 2002.

Starkey, K. and Crane, A. (2003) 'Toward green narrative: Management and the evolutionary epic', *Academy of Management Review*, 28 (2): 220–243.

Thompson, S. (1946) *The Folktale.* New York: Dryden Press. Revised 1951, in 1955 it became a 6 volume edition.

Vickers, M.H. (2002) 'Illness, work and organization: Postmodernism and antenarratives for the reinstatement of voice'. Working paper, University of Western Sydney. Accepted for publication at *Tamara: Journal of Critical Postmodern Organizational Science.*

Weick, K.E. (1995) *Sensemaking in Organizations.* Thousand Oaks, CA: Sage.

White, M. and Epston, D. (1990) *Narrative Means to Therapeutic Ends.* New York/London: W.W. Norton and Company.

Schools for Organizing

Martin Parker

The kings and bishops who endowed mediaeval universities were not doing so in order to educate the common people. These weighty masses of stone solidified a relation between hierarchy and cultural capital, naturalized as the ivy grew over the scholars' windows. Nowadays, the soaring spires may have been replaced by the glass atrium of the Management School, but the same relation still holds. These are places that ingratiate themselves with the powerful, or those who wish to become powerful, and common people only enter in order to empty dustbins and serve cappuccino. Nonetheless, there have always been well-paid malcontents who like to deny their tutelage, and even some people who find in universities spaces to move and think and laugh. Despite their foundations being deep in the moist soil of power, sometimes universities can encourage some thinking. And once there is thinking, who knows what else might follow?

Think about this. On the wall of one of the buildings of your local university will be a grand sign that proclaims that this building houses the 'University of X Department of Management', or 'The X University Business School', or 'The (Insert Rich Man's Name Here) Institute of Commerce'. Or whatever. And within that building, people will be teaching about organizations. Organization is an odd word because, like ivy, it gets everywhere. Organization is the noun that refers to the outcomes of organizing. Major examples of organizing include families, worker self-management, queues, communes, co-operatives, social movements, pressure groups, tribes, communities, mobs, gangs, cities, clubs, schools, utopias, segmentary lineage systems, piracy, angelic choirs, the mafia, the Zapatista, and the landing of Apollo 11 on the moon at 8:17 GMT in the evening of Sunday July 20th 1969. Other (minor) examples include management, business and commerce (Parker et al., 2007).

It seems clear enough what is going here, but most of us don't see it because we are walking quickly past the sign. Human beings have organized themselves in a vast variety of patterns which vary historically, geographically, culturally, politically and so on. In fact, the multiplicity of differences seems to far exceed any similarities, unless we remain at the highest level of generalization. Faced with such a dizzying range of specific procedures, we might stop for a moment, enjoying the view, and then start to begin to learn from this multiplicity. If we want to learn how to produce forms of organizing that provide us with nice things to eat and do, interesting people to talk to, and interesting places to go, then we have a rich range of successes and failures to look at. It would be sensible to learn from what other people have already tried, unless we really think that we are the cleverest people who have ever lived.

Because if we did think that we were the cleverest people who had ever lived (or were working for people who seemed to think that of themselves) we might believe that we have already found the best way to organize, and that the words that are currently used to describe this form of organization (management, business, commerce) should become synonyms for organization. The fact that the people who are fond of 'management' words are also powerful, and can provide universities with chairs, tables, and atriums, might

Continued

also help us with our amnesia. It might help us forget that we are schooling people to reproduce market managerialism, and to dismiss all these other organizings to other departments where they can become other people's problems. We can only see the ivy from our windows, and so all plants must be ivy.

> The plant world exhibits astonishing diversity. Plants vary from microscopic, one celled algae to huge trees such as the Giant Redwoods of California, towering some 300 feet or more into the sky. In between these two extremes is a bewildering array of more than a quarter of a million naturally occurring species and uncounted numbers of cultivars developed by man during more than 2000 years of cultivation and selection. (Brickell, 1993: 5).

Would you study somewhere that taught you about only one plant? Would you listen to a gardener who appeared to believe that plants from other places and times were irrelevant? Who cultivated only one plant and regarded everything else as weeds (Bauman, 1991)?

I would like to imagine a new and emerging school for organizing, and for organizers. It would teach everything from Angels to Zapatismo, and would certainly not restrict itself to interbreeding varieties of management. This will be a school for people who want to learn from multiplicity, and to apply these lessons to their own attempts to organize. It will not be a finishing school for global leaders, or an exercise in legitimating inequality. Of course, to build such an institution will take time, but here's a quick fix. Take a spray can and go to the front of your local Business School. Notice any ivy, or flowers, or weeds. Turn to the sign and then erase its arrogant demands for hierarchy, leadership and capitalism with a generous invitation to learn about organizing. All of it, not just management.

REFERENCES

Bauman, Z. (1991) *Modernity and the Holocaust.* Oxford: Polity.
Brickell, C. (ed.) (1993) *The Royal Horticultural Society Gardener's Encyclopedia of Plants and Flowers.* London: Dorling Kindersley.
Parker, M. Fournier, V. and Reedy, C. (2007) *The Dictionary of Alternatives: Utopianism and Organization.* London: Zed Books.

Empty Organizations

George Ritzer and Craig Lair

Three trends, each leading in different ways to 'emptiness', are affecting the organizational structures of major multi-national corporations. The first relates to the fact that such corporations are increasingly defined by 'nothing'. While this means several things, above all else nothingness involves the global production and spread of (largely) empty forms devoid of distinctive content. The centralized conception and control associated with these forms means that they are diffused globally in such a way that they reflect little of the character of the geographic locales in which they come to be found. Thus, the principles by which McDonald's fast-food restaurants around the world operate – efficiency, predictability, calculability, and increasing control through non-human technologies – define such restaurants everywhere in the world (Ritzer, 2004b). One could say that they all have essentially the same structure in that they operate according to the same system. In this sense, McDonald's restaurants across the globe are 'empty'; they are lacking much in the way of distinctive local content.

The second trend in the direction of emptiness involves the effort by many different entities, especially organizations, to *outsource* seemingly everything they can (Ritzer and Lair, 2007). Those actively and aggressively involved in this process can end up with something approaching an 'empty organization'. While the trend toward nothingness leads to organizations that are empty in the sense they end up with content-less structures, outsourcing can lead to organizations with structures that have been emptied of their operations.

The third trend is in the direction of what has been called 'virtual companies'. These are companies that conduct their operations through a network that is connected largely through various information technologies and it is only if and/or when employees are required to be in one another's physical presence or to meet with clients that the organization takes on a more material form. However, even such meetings are likely to take place in transitory and temporary locations such as hotel rooms, airports, leased office space where desks are given on a first come, first serve basis). For example, Accenture has no operational headquarters or formal branches; its employees and managers, including its executives, are spread around throughout the world, though constantly on the move either to meet clients or to have meetings in various (temporary) locations; the office space that the company does have it leases on a temporary basis (Hymowitz, 2006). Even managers must manage on the move coordinating the activities of their subordinates virtually via the web, phone calls, videoconferencing, and the like. Virtual companies are empty in the sense that they lack a material base and material structures in which they operate.

Taken together these developments clearly indicate that a dramatic change is taking place in organizations that not too long ago generally sought to be as 'full' as possible – to have distinctive content that served to define them everywhere in the world, that performed as many of their operations as they could themselves, and that were dominated by material structures and face-to-face relationships.

Continued

This discussion raises several interesting issues. First, are there other forms of organizational emptiness that we have left out? Or are going to see in the future? Second, while these three types have all been included under the heading of emptiness, there are important differences among and between them that need to be teased out. For example, does outsourcing necessarily lead to nothing? Or to the material emptiness of a virtual organization?

Another set of issues, especially for those who work in empty organizations, revolves around whether these trends will also lead to personal emptiness? Or to new, and perhaps even greater, personal fulfilment? This is a ripe area for an ethnographic study exploring the relationship between an empty organizational structure and the effects that it has on its workers.

These questions will be answered as these new organizational forms, and others like them, develop. One thing seems sure, though, and that is that we will see an ever-increasing number of empty organizations, in various senses of the term, in the future.

REFERENCES

Hymowitz, Carol. (5 Jun 2006) 'Accenture's Executives Run "Virtual" Company'. *Wall Street Journal.*
Ritzer, George. (2004a) *The Globalization of Nothing.* Thousand Oaks, CA: Pine Forge Press.
Ritzer, George. (2004b) *The McDonaldization of Society: Revised New Century Edition.* Thousand Oaks, CA: Pine Forge Press.
Ritzer, George and Craig D. Lair. (2007) 'Outsourcing: Globalization and Beyond'. *Blackwell Companion to Globalization*, G. Ritzer, (ed.). Oxford: Blackwell.

Organizational Defenses; Denials and Denials of the Denial Suggestions for Future Research

Chris Argyris

The literature is full of examples of factors that inhibit organizational effectiveness in detecting and correcting errors especially about problems that are embarrassing or threatening to the participants. Examples of these factors are spinning, cover-ups, undiscussables, denial of responsibility, victim mentality, blaming others and organizational culture. A review of the literature of practice (Argyris, 2000) leads to several intriguing questions. Why do these practices that inhibit learning and effectiveness persist? Why are they supported by the very individuals and groups that condemn them? Why do the participants answer these questions by asserting they are victims and they are helpless to make changes that they acknowledge are necessary?

I suggest that researchers and consultants pay more attention to these questions in the future. In doing so, they may wish to focus on the following types of claims. First, when dealing with problems that may be embarrassing or threatening, participants activate a defensive reasoning mindset. The purpose of such a mindset is primarily to protect individuals, groups, organizations from the embarrassment or threat. Whenever the defensive reasoning mindset is activated it produces actions such as denials, denials of denials, a rejection of personal responsibility, spinning and designed lying. This mentality is maintained by the counterproductive features just described. Participants also have micro theories of effective action. The behavioral values include unilateral control, win, do not lose and suppress negative feelings. The result is escalating errors, self-fulfilling prophecies, and self-sealing processes. The result is that an underground organization is created that sanctions and protects a designed lack of transparency of its existence. Lastly, researchers who describe features of the underground organization and how they inhibit the detection and correction of errors do not design and implement interventions to change the counterproductive features that they describe. When, queried about this puzzle, researchers place the blame on their communities' rules for rigorous research and the interpersonal skills required to get along with their colleagues (Argyris, 2004).

REFERENCES

Argyris, C. (2000) *Flawed Advice* New York: Oxford University Press.

Argyris, C. (2004) *Reason and Rationalizations.* Oxford: Oxford University Press.

Argyris, C. (2005) 'On the demise of organizational development', (eds Bradford, D., Bŭrke, W. W.) *Reinventing Organizational Development.* San Francisco: Pfeiffer. pp. 113–130.

Making Research/Intervention in our Field: A Modest Proposal for ASQ and AMJ

William R. Torbert

This modest proposal about the guidelines that all article submissions for *ASQ* and *AMJ* will be asked to follow during the years between 2015 and 2018 is itself framed as a form of research on the future. In research on the future (Ogilvy, 2002), the initial article (e.g. this one) may be conceived primarily as an active intervention intended to influence readers' imaginations and further inquiries by portraying a radically alternative future to current trends in their field. In other words, the future scenario portrayed will show, not just incremental accumulation and single-loop correction to current-paradigm work, but rather double-loop transformations of the norms and institutions of the field.

Later steps in this research/intervention process can document the degree to which this initial article and later related initiatives and dialogues influence practitioners and institutions in the field (in this case AoM academics and their top empirical journals) to change their paradigms, theories, methods, practices, and products, For example, in this particular case one can later compare how many articles in *ASQ* and *AMJ* included the properties recommended below in the 2002–2005 period (0) with the number that come to include the recommended properties in 2015–2018?

In this case, the projected future scenario involves the Academy of Management changing its election system so as to elect a fulltime CEO of AoM from among its academic members for a non-renewable three-year-period, starting in 2009. Each such CEO implements the pre-existing strategy, but also runs for the office on his or her distinctive strategic priorities, which are given preference insofar as they are not in conflict with the pre-existing strategies during his or her period of office, and then become the governing strategy for the following three years. For example, one of the initiatives of the 2009 AoM CEO is to create an annual poll that rank orders what members consider the most important questions in the field, with sufficient attendant demographic data (e.g. age, gender, academic rank, university type, etc.) to permit analyses of how different subgroups' ranks differ.

Within this future scenario frame, the AoM CEO elected in 2012 has run for office on a vision of integrating quantitative, qualitative, and action research, with strategic priorities that include the following broad guidelines for *ASQ* and *AMJ* article-submissions:

1 Each article will include explicit commentary on the ways in which its reported research interweaves quantitative, qualitative, and action research methods, engaging Alain Badiou's thesis about the relationship of mathematics, time, and action (Hallward, 2003).

2 Insofar as the article is quantitative in nature, its findings will not only achieve currently normative degrees of statistical significance, but will not be considered for publication unless its principle independent variable accounts for at least 20% of the variance in the principle dependent variable (although this guideline alone may panic current empirical researchers, it is hypothesized to become easier to attain as the following guidelines are also met).

3 Insofar as the article is qualitative in nature, its findings will not only meet current best practices in qualitative validity and reliability testing, but also will be considered for publications only if it includes a '1st person' research section in which the researchers describe in their own 'critically subjective'

voices how the experience of the research has influenced their views of the topic, of their methods, and of themselves(Ellis and Bochner, 2000; Foldy, 2005).

4 Insofar as the article is intervention-research-oriented, its findings will include a '2nd person' research section that represents the distinctive voices of non-authorial participants in the research (Reason and Bradbury, 2007), as well as a description of the ethical safeguards exercised among the participating research/practitioners during the course of the action/study (Institutional Review Board approval of research will, of course, not be necessary for research that is paid for by the client system and incorporates these '2nd-person ' research characteristics).

5 Studies focusing primarily on the present and the future will be given equal consideration with studies focusing primarily on the past (Senge et al., 2004).

6 Studies focusing primarily on double-loop transformation and triple-loop realignments among mission/paradigm, strategy/theory, performance/method, and outcomes/data will be given preference over mere single-loop hypothesis testing (Torbert and Associates, 2004).

It will obviously be in the interest of PhD programs seeking to prepare their students for such guidelines to require quantitative, qualitative, and action research courses (as only one major U.S doctoral program in the organization sciences currently does). They will also want to highlight how 1st-, 2nd-, and 3rd-person intervention/research methods triangulate with one another, and how increasing the number of methods used in given study increase the likelihood of successfully accounting for larger proportions of the variance in critical relationships.[1]

NOTE

1 To be precise, 81 different types of methods ($3\times3\times3\times3$) become available when one investigates the full spectrum of 1st-, 2nd-, and 3rd-person voice 1st-, 2nd-, and 3rd-person practice, single-, double-, and triple-loop awareness and change, in the past, present, and feature (*ibid*, 220–224).

REFERENCES

Ellis, C. and Bochner, A. (2000) 'Autoethnography, personal narrative, reflexivity', in N. Denzin and Y. Lincoln, *The Handbook of Qualitative Research*. Thousand Oaks, CA: Sage. pp. 733–768.

Foldy, E. (2005) 'Claiming a voice on race (and response)', *Journal of Action Research*, 3 (1): 33–54.

Hallward, P.(2003) *Badiou: A Subject to Truth*. Minneapolis: University of Minnesota Press.

Ogilvy, J. (2002) *Creating Better Futures: Scenario Planning as a Tool a Better Tomorrow*. Oxford: Oxford University Press.

Reason, P. and Bradbury, H. (eds) (2007) *Handbook of Action Research*. London; Sage.

Senge. P., Scharmer, C., Jaworski, J. and Flowers, B. (2004) *Presence: Human purpose and the field of the future*. Cambridge, MA: SoL (The Society for Organizational Learning).

Torbert. B. and Associates (2004) *Action Inquiry: The Secret of Timely and Transforming Leadership*. San Francisco: Berrett-Koehler.

Technique and Practices from the Arts: Expressive Verbs, Feelings, and Action

Steven S. Taylor and Inga Carboni

There is a long tradition of using the arts as a metaphor to describe organizations. Perhaps the best known example is the organization as theater, which started with Goffman (1959), was more fully developed by Mangham and Overington (1987) and continues to surface in works such as Vaill's (1989), *Managing as a Performing Art*. The hottest metaphor in recent times is the organization as jazz (e.g. DePree, 1992; Hatch, 1998; Mirvis, 1998; Montuori, 2003; Weick, 1998). And of course the metaphor of organizational action as storytelling is so strong that it has permeated all aspects of organizational theory and management (see Taylor et al., 2002 for a review). These metaphors have provided new and useful ways of understanding organizations.

In recent years there has been some effort to move beyond metaphor and learn more directly from the arts. Typical of this movement is the interest in management and leadership lessons based in Shakespeare's work (Augustine and Adelman, 1999; Burnham et al., 2001; Corrigan, 1999; Shafritz, 1999; Whitney and Packer, 2000) in which we look to the arts for wisdom. Other work looks at using arts-based practices within organizations. Practices considered include the variety of theater-based training that occurs within organizations (Nissley et al., 2004), and the arts-based practices within management education (Nissley, 2002). There is also a small and emerging stream of work that applies techniques from the arts to the problems and practices within organizations (e.g. Austin and Devin, 2003; Ferris, 2002). It is this approach of applying practices from the arts to organizations that we will discuss in this chapter. We start by considering the aesthetic nature of organizations and the implications of that nature for practice. We then offer a detailed description of an adaptation of Stanislavski's (1936a, b, 1961) method of acting to analyze organizational actions in which we use expressive verbs.

THE AESTHETIC NATURE OF ORGANIZATIONS

At the dawn of the enlightenment, Descartes privileged intellectual thought and ways of knowing with his famous dictum, *cogito ergo sum*. In response to this, Baumgarten (1750 (reprinted in 1936)) and Vico (1744 (reprinted in 1948)) argued for the importance of feeling and founded modern aesthetics. At the heart of aesthetics is *knowing* gained directly from our sensory experience. This sensory experience is our primary experience of organizations and the basis for all other forms of knowing (Dewey, 1958; Gagliardi, 1996; Welsch, 1997). Thus, 'aesthetics is an undeniable part of the fabric of organizational experience and organizational reality (Ottensmeyer, 1996: 189).' Yet, even though aesthetic experience is the basis of all other experiences in organizations it has received comparatively little attention (see Taylor and Hansen, 2005 for a review of organizational aesthetics).

One of the reasons that the aesthetic nature of organizations has not received much attention may be ontological. Organizational research that is based in social positivism focuses on finding objective knowledge and causal theories that can be applied across multiple contexts. Aesthetics embraces its subjectivity and thus leaves little room for theories of organization that claim generalizable knowledge that can lead to prediction and control of organizational phenomena. Giving up explanatory approaches to studying organizational action is anathema to a social science that is dominated by positivism.

But the conflict is deeper than objectivity versus subjectivity. As Gibb says, 'a concern, even in passing, with the aesthetic, where the language, concepts, and philosophy of beauty exist and prevail is to overturn all that is grounded in social positivism' (Gibb, 2004: 69). This is because a concern with aesthetics suggests that we should also be concerned with beauty and that implicitly beauty is a higher goal than the implied goals of efficiency and effectiveness that are the underpinnings of social positivism. We see this bias toward positivism in organizational studies as the predominant research questions of the twentieth century are tied to increasing efficiency and effectiveness and the methods sought objective data and theory (Van de Ven and Poole, 2005). More usually, when the Academy engages with aesthetic subjects we produce criticism.

By criticism, we mean art criticism, not the criticism of Critical Theory and the Frankfurt School. We mean the sort of criticism that your local theater critic engages in when they write a review of the latest production. The purpose of criticism is not to claim generalizeable knowledge, but rather to interpret art and evaluate its quality (Barrett, 1994; Feldman, 1994). For example, when Hatch et al. (2004) critique the stories that Chief Executive Officers tell in *Harvard Business Review* interviews, they interpret the stories and analytically group them into four genres: epic, comic, romantic, and tragic stories; describing the different protagonists, emotions, plot, and predicament for each genre of story. There are certainly many benefits to this sort of critical engagement with art and by extension critical engagement of organizational phenomena as art, such as deeper understanding and an ability to better appreciate quality (Anderson, 2005).

However, as much as the critical analysis offers understanding and allows audience members to engage more deeply with the object of criticism, it is less useful in producing art. In one of the few works that has taken seriously the concept that organizational phenomena are fundamentally aesthetic, Hatch et al. (2004) take an aesthetic approach to leadership. They approach leadership as critics and analyze it as storytelling, drama, and mythology, offering different genres of stories, types of drama, and a pantheon of gods that appear in leaders' stories. The Hatch et al.'s (2004) analysis helps us understand and appreciate what leaders do when they tell stories and even helps us make judgments as to the quality of leadership when we encounter it. But it is much less useful in helping us become leaders ourselves because it does not develop our leadership or even our storytelling skills.

It does not show us how to produce artful leadership.

A different approach to the organization-as-work-of-art is to explore organizational aesthetics with the goal of producing art. In other words, if there are lessons to be learned for organizations from the arts and if those lessons are to be helpful in enacting organizational phenomena rather than in appreciating those phenomena, then those lessons should come from the practice of art rather than from art criticism. We shall offer one such example, the use of expressive verbs from acting, later in this chapter.

One of the difficulties with drawing upon arts practices rather than art theory and criticism is that much more art theory and criticism has been consigned to text and text, especially written text, is the primary medium of knowledge transfer in academia. The relative paucity of arts practice text is due to a fundamental difference between two ways of knowing. On the one hand, art theory and criticism is based on propositional knowledge which is easily translated into text. Art practices, on the other hand, represent pragmatic knowledge which is not easily translated into text. Practice, in the arts as elsewhere, is historically learned through 'practical' hands-on experiences such as apprenticeships and studio models. Practice is learned through practice. Thus, the aesthetic approach changes the focus of study from 'knowing that' to 'knowing how' (Brady, 1986) by acknowledging both the value of tacit, embodied knowledge and the experiential medium through which such knowledge transfer takes place. In our own extended example, presented later in the chapter, we reference Stanislavski's books, but we freely admit that the actual knowledge really came from studio-type acting and directing classes.

As an example of what we mean by drawing on art practice rather than on critical techniques, let us turn to storytelling. There is a large 'how to' literature on storytelling which discusses the practice, or technique of the craft (e.g. Cassady, 1990, 1994). Twain notes that in delivering a good story, 'you *must* get the pause right; and you will find it the most troublesome and aggravating and uncertain thing you ever undertook' (Twain, 1996 (originally published in 1897)). But there is no theory of the pause; it is a 'knowing how' that can only be gained through practice and technique. The successful storyteller will vary the volume of his or her voice, pitch, rhythm, emphasis, pacing, and enunciate clearly (Chapey, 1989; Dubrovin, 1995; Plotnick, 1996; Roesch, 1989) – although, too distinct an enunciation is fatal to success (Burrell, 1926) – when conveying meaning and mood to an audience. Such technique can only be learned through practice with a master storyteller who can say, 'no, that's too much variation' or 'yes, that's just the right level of enunciation.' Moreover, the guidance of a master storyteller must be fitted to the abilities and talents of the apprentice. A pause that is too long for one storyteller may be just right for another. We suggest that real insights for better enacting of organizations come from delving deeper into these fundamentally aesthetic practices.

The performing arts provide some of the best practices for organizations because organizations exist in three dimensional space and are enacted over time. Thus we look to performing arts practices, such as storytelling, jazz, and the theater for insights from practice. In the following section we offer one such example in detail: the actor's practice of using expressive verbs to re-create believable behavior.

EXPRESSIVE VERBS

Understanding and addressing the emotional currents that underlie all that we say and do can be a difficult task. The problem has to do with recognizing feelings when 'we often don't know how we feel' (Stone et al., 2000: 91) and

> feelings are more complex and nuanced than we usually imagine. What's more, feelings are very good at disguising themselves. Feelings we are uncomfortable with disguise themselves as emotions we are better able to handle, bundles

of contradictory feelings masquerade as a single emotion; and most important, feelings transform themselves into judgments, accusations, and attributions. (Stone et al., 2000: 91)

Within organization studies, the importance and difficulty of working with feelings has long been recognized. At an individual level, therapy methods focus on helping individuals surface and analyze their own feelings, often with the help of a therapist or counselor who is trained to interpret utterances in terms of existent theory. In non-therapy settings, the therapist or counselor is replaced by one or more consultants, coaches, or facilitators who help the individual identify feelings by asking leading questions and relating the individual's responses to typical or previous responses.

Organizations have also attempted to embrace feelings, although in a limited and, in the long run, not very successful way. For example, the human relations school of the 1950s and 60s set out to help members discover and utilize methods of scientific inquiry (i.e. observation, feedback, analysis, experimentation) as a way to increase relationship development and individual growth (Bradford, 1964). Methods included sensitivity training groups (or t-groups), clarification groups, and Tavistock groups. In the action science tradition (Argyris et al., 1985) feelings are represented in the left-hand column of the two column case, which lists thoughts and feelings that were not expressed in the conversation. These unexpressed thoughts and feelings are then treated as data along with the actual utterances.

All of these methods for understanding emotions have merits as well as limitations for working with feelings. Most depend to a large degree on the skill and insight of the analysts, which not only vary considerably but are extremely difficult to measure, assess, and (most importantly) transfer (Yalom, 1995). To avoid these difficulties and, in the ultimate assertion of objectivity, the emerging field of organizational emotion treats emotions as variables to be dissected, analyzed, and captured in text (e.g. Seo et al., 2004). This clearly shows the science-based idea that we can best help practitioners by offering them decontextualized, generalizable theory that they can apply to their specific situation. The arts take a different approach, offering instead methods and approaches that always context dependent and sensitively value subjective knowing. One useful example is that of theater.

Theater has approached feelings by linking feelings to action. The fundamental task of an actor is to create life on stage that seems real. The practical problem is how to create the complex, nuanced, and often unconscious feelings that an audience would find believable. This is doubly difficult in that humans are very difficult to convince. Indeed, 'studies show that while few people are good at detecting factual lies, most of us can determine when someone is distorting, manufacturing, or withholding an emotion' (Stone et al., 2000: 88). As a director, Stanislavski (1936a) realized that actors can create realistic life on stage, including the appropriate real feelings, by focusing on concrete objectives, which are expressed as verbs or actions. For example, rather than try to play emotions such as happy and nervous, or feelings such as lust for the other character, an actor can focus on the objective of *seducing* the other character. Stanislavski's (1936a, b, 1961) technique is generally called *method acting* and it revolutionized the modern theater. We argue that this same technique can be fruitfully applied to organizational action.

A key aspect of method acting is breaking a play down into smaller and smaller units and identifying the objective for each unit. The smallest unit is an individual line. The objective is what the actor is trying to achieve, what they are doing within that unit of the play. Stanislavski notes, 'the objective must always be a *verb*.' (1936a: 134, italics in original). For example, in the script an actor enters and says, 'It's nice to see you.' The actor could choose the objective, *to greet*. Alternatively, they could choose the objective *to chastise for standing me up yesterday*. The two objectives would produce very different performances and feelings.

This idea of thinking of a line in terms of the verb is the same as approaching an utterance in terms of the speech act (Austin, 1962; Searle, 1969). The speech act is the illocutionary force behind the utterance, or in Austin's terms, what we do with words. Thus, in the same way that an actor chooses a verb in order to create real life on the stage, we can reverse the process by looking at real life and finding the verbs. In fact, we would argue that this is something we do unconsciously all the time.

We now offer a detailed example of how we might gain insight into actions by looking at the expressive verbs. This conversation is presented in a two column case format (Argyris et al., 1985) and was analyzed using the learning pathways grid (developed by Action Design, see Rudolph et al., 2001; Taylor, 2004 for a detailed description) as part of a graduate class in interpersonal and leadership skills (Taylor et al., 2008). In the case, Mia overhears her team leader, Cal, telling the training coordinator that he must focus on three of her colleagues (Ralph, Donnie, and Chris) in an upcoming training session that she is also scheduled to attend. As a result, Mia initiates the conversation as shown in Table 2.2.1.

We can see from her left-hand column that this is a very emotional conversation for Mia. When asked what she wanted from the conversation, she said that she wanted to be released from having to go to the training class. She did not achieve this outcome. Further probing suggested she also wanted to get to use the material from the class and that she wanted to feel good about the decision to attend the class. By the end of the conversation she was frustrated and had achieved none of the outcomes she had hoped for going into the conversation. This raises the question, what went wrong? What happened in this conversation and how could Mia have acted differently?

We are sure that everyone who reads this has an answer to these questions. Many will look at the content of the conversation and suggest that Mia did a poor job of arguing her position and suggest ways that she could have made her case more convincingly. Others might suggest that she failed to inquire into Cal's thinking. Others might suggest that she would have done well to use active listening and paraphrase Cal's position back to him. We would suggest that all of these are focusing on the presenting, instrumental content of the

Table 2.2.1

What Mia thought and felt	What was said
I am so frustrated. Sometimes I feel that some of the newer guys are being given opportunities that haven't been given to me, and I have been in this group longer. Is it because they are engineers and technically I am not?	Mia: So we are all attending this course next week? Cal: Yes. Mia: Why do I have to be trained on something I will never use? I could much rather utilize the time doing my scheduled work next week.
Right. Eventually. He is just blowing me off.	Cal: This is information that everyone needs to learn. And you will use it eventually.
What?! I cannot believe he told you I said that. We spoke about that during my review when he asked me what else I was looking at getting in to.	Mia: But you told Edward to focus specifically on Ralph, Donnie, and Chris. Cal: I heard you told Bob that you wanted to be included in the Network Applications.
I feel very angry and I just want to end this conversation.	Mia: He told you that? All I said was that I was more than willing to learn it when you were teaching them but the opportunity was not extended to me at the time.
I WILL NEVER EVER TELL HIM ANYTHING EVER AGAIN!	
I am frustrated! If I will never get the opportunity to work on this stuff, let me work on the things that I am doing now. Training is expensive and you are wasting money sending me if I won't use it!	Cal: Of course he tells me these things, but he would never tell me anything you say to him in confidence. What's up, you seem really frustrated? Mia: I would just rather not spend five days in a training class learning material that I will never apply when I have other work piling up on my desk!
Blowing me off again. I am so done with this conversation.	Cal: We will get you working on this stuff eventually.

conversation. That is, in the classic conduit model of communication (Axley, 1984) the focus is on the message contained in the utterances.

Drawing upon the idea of communication as action from the theater, we start to answer the question of what is going in the conversation by identifying the expressive verbs. We do this by asking Mia and others what action they think was being taken with each utterance. Bearing in mind that naming the action always requires some level of interpretation and there can be no single definitive naming of the action (Taylor, 2005), we look for a consensus around what the action is, with Mia's sense of what the action was having somewhat more weight. We offer the conversation again, this time with the actions for each utterance identified (see Table 2.2.2).

The expressive verbs make it very clear that this conversation is not primarily about the instrumental content. Mia has heard Cal tell the training coordinator to focus on three of her co-workers and not her, so she is angry and wants to fight Cal. Even more importantly, as we talk about the dynamic of the fight, she realizes that she attacks Cal because this is her way of letting Cal know that she is upset and that this is an important issue for her.

We believe that Cal 'gets' that Mia is upset, but we are not sure that Cal really knows why or is left in a place where he can help Mia. We suspect that Cal is instead left wondering what's going on with Mia and is perhaps somewhat angry at Mia for attacking him.

This in turn leads to a discussion with Mia about how she might best handle herself when she is frustrated and angry. We suggest that she work on being able to recognize and then 'own her feelings' (Stone et al., 2000) in conversations. The expressive verbs have moved us from a focus on the instrumental content to the conversational dynamic, from the outcomes to the actions. It is in those actions that the real heat of the conversation makes sense.

DISCUSSION AND CONCLUSIONS

The foregoing case illustrates the power of expressive verbs. In the case, the 'attack, defend, counter attack' fight dynamic captured the emotions underlying the actions and revealed significant insights into the unexpressed (and unacknowledged) objectives driving the interaction.

This can be contrasted with other possible ways of analyzing the actions in a

Table 2.2.2

Action / Expressive verb	What was said
Mia: Pick a Fight	Mia: So we are all attending this course next week?
Cal: Humor Mia	Cal: Yes.
Mia: Attack Cal	Mia: Why do I have to be trained on something I will never use? I could much rather utilize the time doing my scheduled work next week.
Cal: Defend (with rational explanation)	Cal: This is information that everyone needs to learn. And you will use it eventually.
Mia: Attack Cal	Mia: But you told Edward to focus specifically on Ralph, Donnie, and Chris.
Cal: Counter attack Mia	Cal: I heard you told Bob that you wanted to be included in the Network Applications.
Mia: Retreat in defeat	Mia: He told you that? All I said was that I was more than willing to learn it when you were teaching them but the opportunity was not extended to me at the time.
Cal: Claim victory and offer a way out	Cal: Of course he tells me these things, but he would never tell me anything you say to him in confidence. What's up, you seem really frustrated?
Mia: Try to reclaim her opening position.	Mia: I would just rather not spend five days in a training class learning material that I will never apply when I have other work piling up on my desk!
Cal: Assert his position and victory.	Cal: We will get you working on this stuff eventually.

conversation, such as Torbert's (Torbert and Associates, 2004) parts of speech (which are the verbs: frame, advocate, illustrate, and inquire). For example, if we apply Torbert's verbs to our case, we would see a pattern where Mia and Cal take turns advocating but do little inquiry or framing (we see Mia's questions as advocacies in the form of a question rather than as true inquiry). The verb set would imply the prescription that Mia frame and inquire more, which is useful, but hasn't provided the insight into what the core emotional issues are for Mia. Key to this emotional insight was access to the feelings underlying the intellectual analysis of the case.

To broaden the discussion we see a great potential in drawing upon arts practices and techniques to understand and enhance the enactment of organizational actions. Expressive verbs are just one of many techniques from the theater that can be effectively applied to organizations. We can just as easily imagine Johnstone's (1979) seminal work on status being applied within organizations (and in fact have done so on a personal level on many occasions). Mary Jo Hatch tells us that when she uses the metaphor of jazz with senior managers, it is the specific techniques such as the way in which a musician who is comping behind a soloist offers background riffs as a suggestion that the soloist can take or ignore, that the managers resonate most strongly with.

The problem with applying techniques and practices from the arts is that it requires skill in the practice of the techniques. We would have difficulty working with the idea of how to comp behind a soloist as neither of us is a jazz musician. Reading books about comping for jazz guitar would be of little help as we just don't have the experiential base, the feel for what comping is. In simplest terms, drawing upon techniques and practices from the arts requires us to be both an artist and a scholar (Taylor et al., 2005). That is to say, it requires both the mastery of the arts based skills set and the deep knowledge of organizations to see how the skill may be applied to organizational settings. Having said that, we have encountered many organizational scholars who are also artists

(particularly working in the area of organizational aesthetics) and many artists who have spent years working within organizations. We look forward to seeing more arts-based methods applied to organizational phenomena as the field of organizational aesthetics grows. We imagine such methods being the core of what Pierre Guillet de Monthoux calls a 'Master of Business Arts (MBA)', and the heart of the real practice of the art of management.

REFERENCES

Anderson, M. (2005) 'The quality instinct: how an eye for art can save your business', *Journal of Business Stratgey*, 26 (5): 29–32.

Argyris, C., Putnam, R. and Smith, D. (1985) *Action Science: Concepts, Methods, and Skills for Research and Intervention*. San Francisco: Jossey-Bass.

Augustine, N. and Adelman, K. (1999) *Shakespeare in Charge: The Bard's Guide to Leading and Succeeding on the Business Stage*. New York: Hyperion.

Austin, J.L. (1962) *How to Do Things with Words*. Oxford: Clarendon Press.

Austin, R. and Devin, L. (2003) *Artful Making: What Managers Need to Know About How Artists Work*. New York: Financial Times Prentice Hall.

Axley, S.R. (1984) 'Managerial and organizational communication in terms of the conduit metaphor', *Academy of Management Review*, 9 (3): 428–437.

Barrett, T. (1994) *Criticizing Art: Understanding the Contemporary*. Mountain View, CA: Mayfield Publishing Company.

Baumgarten, A.G. (1750) (reprinted in 1936). *Aesthetica*. Bari: Laterza.

Bradford, L. (1964) 'Membership and the learning process', in L. Bradford, J.R Gibb and K. Benne (eds), *T-group Theory and the Laboratory Method*. New York: John Wiley & Sons. pp. 190–215.

Brady, F.N. (1986) 'Aesthetic components of management ethics', *Academy of Management Review*, 11 (2): 337–344.

Burnham, J., Augustine, N. and Adelman, K. (2001) *Shakespeare in Charge: The Bard's Guide to Learning and Succeeding on the Business Stage*. New York: Hyperion.

Burrell, A. (1926) *A Guide to Story Telling*. London: Sir Isaac Pitman & Sons, Ltd.

Cassady, M. (1990) *Storytelling Step by Step*. San Jose, CA: Resource Publications, Inc.

Cassady, M. (1994) *The Art of Storytelling: Creative Ideas for Preparation and Performance*. Colorado Springs, CO: Meriwether Publishing.

Chapey, G. (1989) *Developing Speaking Skills*. New York: McGraw-Hill Book Company.

Corrigan, P. (1999) *Shakespeare on Management: Leadership Lessons for Today's Managers*. London: Kogan Page.

DePree, M. (1992) *Leadership Jazz*. New York: Dell.

Dewey, J. (1958) *Art as Experience*. New York: Capricorn.

Dubrovin, V. (1995) *Create Your own Storytelling Stories*. Masonville, CO: Storycraft Publishing.

Feldman, E.B. (1994) *Practical Art Criticism*. Englewood Cliffs, NJ: Prentice-Hall.

Ferris, W.P. (2002) 'Theater tools for team building: How an improvisational play got one software team back on track', *Harvard Business Review*, 80 (12): 24–25.

Gagliardi, P. (1996) 'Exploring the aesthetic side of organizational life', in S.R. Clegg, C. Hardy, and W.R. Nord (eds), *Handbook of Organization Studies*. London: Sage. pp. 565–580.

Gibb, S. (2004) 'Imagination, creativity, and HRD: An aesthetic perspective', *Human Resource Development Review*, 3 (1): 53–74.

Goffman, E. (1959) *The Presentation of Self in Everyday Life*. New York: Doubleday.

Hatch, M.J. (1998) 'Jazz as a metaphor for organizing in the 21st century', *Organization Science*, 9 (5): 556–557.

Hatch, M.J., Kostera, M. and Kozminski, A.K. (2004) *The Three Faces of Leadership: Artist, Manager, Priest*. London: Blackwell.

Johnstone, K. (1979) *Impro: Improvisation and the Theatre*. London: Faber & Faber.

Mangham, I.L. and Overington, M.A. (1987) *Organizations as Theatre: A Social Psychology of Dramatic Appearances*. Chichester: Wiley.

Mirvis, P.H. (1998) 'Practice improvisation', *Organization Science*, 9 (5): 586–592.

Montuori, A. (2003) 'The complexity of improvisation and the improvisation of complexity: Social science, art and creativity', *Human Relations*, 56 (2): 237–255.

Nissley, N. (2002) 'Arts-based learning in management education', in C. Wankel and R. Defillippi (eds), *Rethinking Management Education for the 21st Century*. Greenwich, CT: Information Age Publishing.

Nissley, N., Taylor, S.S. and Houden, L. (2004) 'The politics of performance in organizational theatre-based training and interventions', *Organization Studies*, 25 (5): 817–840.

Ottensmeyer, E.J. (1996) 'Too strong to stop, too sweet to lose: Aesthetics as a way to know organizations', *Organization*, 3 (2): 189–194.

Plotnick, A. (1996) *The Elements of Expression: Putting Thoughts into Words*. New York: Henry Holt & Company.

Roesch, R. (1989) *Smart Talk: The Art of Savvy Business Conversation*. New York: American Management Association.

Rudolph, J.W., Taylor, S.S., and Foldy, E.G. (2001) 'Collaborative off-line reflection: A way to develop skill in action science and action inquiry', in P. Reason and H. Bradbury (eds), *Handbook of Action Research: Participative Inquiry and Practice*. London: Sage. pp. 405–412.

Searle, J.R. (1969) *Speech Acts*. Cambridge: Cambridge University Press.

Seo, M.-G., Feldman-Barrett, L. and Bartunek, J.M. (2004) 'The role of affective experience in work motivation', *Academy of Management Review*, 29: 423–439.

Shafritz, J. (1999) *Shakespeare on Management: Wise Business Counsel from the Bard*. New York: HarperCollins.

Stanislavski, C. (1936a) *An Actor Prepares* (E.R. Hapgood, trans.). New York: Routledge.

Stanislavski, C. (1936b) *Building a Character* (E.R. Hapgood, trans.). New York: Routledge.

Stanislavski, C. (1961) *Creating a Role* (E.R. Hapgood, trans.). New York: Routledge.

Stone, D., Patton, B. and Heen, S. (2000) *Difficult Conversations: How to Discuss What Matters Most*. London: Penguin Books.

Taylor, S.S. (2004) 'Presentational form in first person research: Off-line collaborative reflection using art', *Action Research*, 2 (1): 71–88.

Taylor, S.S. (2005) 'My mother, my sweater: An aesthetics of action perspective for teaching communication', *Journal of Organizational Behavior Education*, 1 (1): 57–72.

Taylor, S.S., Fisher, D. and Dufresne, R.L. (2002) 'The aesthetics of management storytelling: A key to organizational learning', *Management Learning*, 33 (3): 313–330.

Taylor, S.S. and Hansen, H. (2005) 'Finding form: Looking at the field of organizational aesthetics', *Journal of Management Studies*, 42 (6): 1211–1232.

Taylor, S.S., Rudolph, J.W. and Foldy, E.G. (2008) 'Teaching reflective practice in the action science/action inquiry tradition: Key stages, concepts and practices', in P. Reason and H. Bradbury (eds), *Handbook of Action Research*, 2nd edn. London: Sage. pp. 656–668.

Torbert, B. and Associates. (2004) *Action Inquiry: The Secret of Timely and Transforming Leadership*. San Francisco: Berrett-Koehler.

Twain, M. (1996) (originally published in 1897) *How to Tell a Story and Other Essays*. New York: Oxford University Press.

Vaill, P.B. (1989) *Managing as a Performing Art*. San Francisco: Jossey-Bass.

Van de Ven, A.H. and Poole, M.S. (2005) 'Alternate approaches for studying organizational change', *Organization Studies*, 26 (9): 1377–1404.

Vico, G. (1744) (reprinted in 1948) *The New Science of Giambattista Vico* (T.G. Bergin, and M.H. Fisch, trans.). Ithica, NY: Cornell University Press.

Weick, K.E. (1998) 'Improvisation as a mindset for organizational analysis', *Organization Science*, 9 (5): 543–555.

Welsch, W. (1997) *Undoing Aesthetics* (A. Inkpin, trans.). London: Sage Publications.

Whitney, J. and Packer, T. (2000) *Power Plays: Shakespeare's Lessons in Leadership and Management*. New York: Simon & Schuster.

Yalom, I. (1995) *The Theory and Practice of Group Psychotherapy* (4th edn). New York: Basic Books.

Aesthetics in the Study of Organizational Life

Antonio Strati

INTRODUCTION

The strand of inquiry which concerns itself with organization and aesthetics is rooted in the culturalist turn in organization studies that came about during the 1980s, and in particular in those studies which analysed the organization in terms of every-day life experience and symbolic and aesthetic construction. These two aspects have mainly distinguished the aesthetic approach to organizations (Strati, 1992) among the various styles of inquiry into the aesthetic dimension of organizations developed since the early 1990s (Benghozi, 1987; Carr and Hancock, 2003; Gagliardi, 1990; Linstead and Höpfl, 2000; Guillet de Monthoux, 2004; Jones et al., 1988; Ottensmeyer, 1996; Rafaeli and Pratt, 2005; Ramírez, 1991; Schroeder, 2006; Strati, 1999; Strati and Guillet de Monthoux, 2002; Watkins et al., 2006). But what is the significance of this strand of organization studies for empirical research and organizational theory? What are its implications for the future of organizational analysis?

Answering these two questions requires us first to look at the origin of this strand of inquiry. This I shall do in the first part of the chapter, where I describe how my study on the aesthetic dimension of organizational life took shape, and then frame it in the context of other studies which, together with mine, gave life and social legitimacy to the study of the aesthetic dimension of organization. This was largely academic research which began and developed within the mainstream of symbolic-cultural studies on organizations. It addressed a wide range of classic topics in organization studies but shifted them to unexplored and experimental terrain where they were theoretically and methodologically renewed. The second part of the chapter consists of five 'fragments of organizational discourse' which I feel are crucial for re-invigorating the desire for knowledge and the passion for organizational research.

AESTHETICS AS 'ART OF ORGANIZATIONAL SIN'

My reflections on the aesthetic dimension of organizational life began to take shape during research conducted in the departments of mathematics, education, and visual arts of one of the oldest universities in Europe. This research brought me to realize that aesthetics pervades everyday life in workplaces; that it is a component of organizational cultures; and that it does not always 'act' in the same way in different organizations. These findings prompted my first work on organizational aesthetics (1990) and formed the basis for the reflections put forward shortly afterwards in my publications (1992, 1999) proposing an aesthetic approach to organization study.

It should be borne in mind that the same period saw other works on organizational aesthetics. Indeed, never since has there been a collective scientific endeavour, neither organized, nor even less coordinated, on this topic with such impact and importance. Art and aesthetics and the notions of beauty and *pathos* became part of the vocabulary of organizational discourse in:

- works which argued that the management of organizational processes should be grasped in its nature as an aesthetic phenomenon, because its participants are 'craftpersons and aesthetes' (Jones et al., 1988: 160), and that the organizational metaphor of the 'manager as artist' can be used to make sense of the plurality of organizational forms (Dégot, 1987);
- works which addressed the theoretical-methodological issue of how empirical research can grasp the beauty of the organization as a whole (Ramírez, 1991; Strati, 1990) for the actors involved in organizational dynamics;
- works which stressed the *pathos* of the artifacts (Gagliardi, 1990) that constitute the organization's symbolic landscape by virtue of their influence on the basic assumptions of people at work, and which are consequently a form of organizational control exercised at the emotional and aesthetic level rather than the normative and cognitive one.

Art and aesthetics became *constitutive items in the definition of both* 'organizational actor' and 'organization'. They connoted as much the materiality of everyday organizational life – asserting the corporeality of people's knowledge and interactions, and the physicality of non-human objects – as the immateriality of fantasizing with organizational metaphors (the manager as artist) and aesthetic sentiments on theoretical abstractions like the organization *tout court*.

This was akin to a Copernican revolution in organizational theories, although it did not have the same impact. The dispute with positivist and rationalist studies centred on a *theoretical proposal which questioned the definitional bases of what was meant by not only 'human being' and 'organization' but also 'organizational study'*, because aesthetics, sentiment, and pathos restored theoretical value and scientific significance to the knowledge-evoking process – then overshadowed by the predominant logical-analytical procedures – and art acquired theoretical-methodological legitimacy rather than delimiting one type of social world.

What was the outcome of studying the aesthetic dimension of the three university departments mentioned above? That *aesthetic difference is a distinctive feature of organizations*.

Aesthetics, as we know, affirms that individuals differ in their sensory perceptions, and in the judgements that they make using their taste and senses. If we have to choose a perfume or an aftershave, we do not usually just read the chemical ingredients listed on the label – that is, the scientific definition of the product's ontology; nor do we rely solely on the corporate *ethos* symbolized by the brand. What we do is sprinkle some drops on our skin and sniff them: 'it's too sweet; it's too spicy; it doesn't suit me; it's good (in the aesthetic, not ethical, sense); it's right for an evening at a discotheque or at the theatre; it's different, so I can change my image'.

Hence we rely on our taste, as constructed by our social interactions, and on our sense of smell, which though absolutely personal, has likewise undergone social processes that have refined or blunted it: for example, the possible choices provided by the number of the varieties of the product. However large this number may be, it signals to us that among users of perfumes and aftershaves, there are many who make the same choices as ours, even if they may not smell exactly as we do because perfumes or aftershaves merge and react with other skin odours. But what essences are we able to identify in the perfume or aftershave which we are examining with our sense of smell? Theoretically, a human being is able to distinguish ten thousand different odours. How many can our own sense of smell identify? What happens if the person with us says: 'Oh no, don't tell me you like this one! Can't you feel that it's not right for you?' Does there not now begin the negotiating dynamic whereby, overwhelmed by a medley of perfumes, we eventually settle for a particular product, only to find that it smells differently when we put it on at home? This example from everyday life serves two purposes. First, it highlights an organizational phenomenon which consists of perfume houses, perfume shops, and the organized social settings in which perfumes are used. Second, it gives us an experiential (albeit imaginary) answer to the following question: how does the 'nose' – the term for the in-company expert who invents new perfumes – avoid the anaesthetizing of his perceptive-sensory faculties, and create products that may or may not be to the taste of customers only imagined or potential until the perfume or aftershave is placed on the market?

Aesthetics therefore highlights the individual differences due to our perceptive-sensory faculties and sensitive-aesthetic judgement. What my study on the three university departments showed was that aesthetic difference pertains to collectives and organizations as well. Each of the three departments – visual arts, education, and mathematics – had its own relation between aesthetics and organization. This I shall now illustrate, beginning with the department institutionally most concerned with aesthetics, and concluding with the one least so concerned.

The department of visual arts

In the department of visual arts, the aesthetic dimension of organizational practices was deep and pervasive; but it related more to the beauty, allure, and sacredness of materials and workplaces than it did to the manner in which research, documentation and teaching was conducted. The beauty of work in the department was constituted above all by materials, and the appreciation of such beauty was both the motive and meaning of the work choices of the teaching staff, research staff and, in many respects, the technical staff as well. The study of beautiful materials and frequent contact with 'art' works constituted the fundamental aesthetic dimension of working and organizational practices in the department, where the aesthetics of materials and places influenced various of its organizational features.

The question 'Do you make beautiful things?' further highlighted this feature. All replies to it stressed that the department's academic and technical-administrative staff produced not beautiful things but 'useful' ones. One interviewee commented that the department produced things which were:

> beautiful in the sense of good. But, you know, all those words … beautiful, good, valid … if by beautiful you mean valid then yes, I believe in what I say, in the method that I propose, and so I believe it is valid, positive, 'beautiful' if you want to use – though very improperly – the adjective 'beautiful', but beautiful means valid, efficient … Yes, it gratifies me … there's also gratification … but, I mean to say, I'm not a creator, I'm a scholar, I don't do art, I study the art done by others, so let's leave beauty to those who actually produce it.

The department's members were able to spend their working lives producing *a 'beauty' which belongs to ethics rather than to the aesthetics.* Ethical beauty characterized their symbolic construction of the organizational life of the visual arts department, within a setting – or an organizational landscape (Gagliardi, 1990) – largely made up of artifacts with considerable beauty, yet also of artifacts that were ugly, repellent and kitsch. This organizational landscape, of course, did not coincide with the department's front desk and the sheets of paper, books, slides and photocopies temporarily placed upon it. Rather, it was an 'imaginary workplace' constructed on the basis of both the departmental work settings and the other places where the department members were conducting their study and research, such as an art gallery, a library, a sacristy, or a private house where family portraits were collected and eventually displayed.

The education department

In the education department, by contrast, the aesthetic resided neither in the materials on which research was conducted nor in the imaginary workplace described above. Instead, the aesthetic dimension emerged in relation to (a) academic teaching and (b) university management. This is apparent from the following remarks by a researcher and a lecturer in the department:

> We'd been working here for a year and we did something really beautiful, all the researchers … and I think it was extremely important. We held a seminar and all the students for all three years of Education could attend […] We organized everything, we got everything ready … and it was really beautiful … it all went well, with the exams, everything. But it was never repeated. And every so often when we get together for a chat, etcetera, we feel nostalgic for that time, because I believe it was a beautiful event. The university really came alive.
>
> I believe that these people should have a minimum of aesthetic taste […] if you teach education you have to enjoy yourself, otherwise you do it very badly! So I said that, according to me, the character of the staff is very important. I must say that when I was dean, I got into loads of shouting matches, and in the end I had a heart attack […] but I enjoyed myself, how I enjoyed teaching!

Besides the enjoyment of teaching or organizing a seminar described as 'beautiful', these interview extracts also highlight the aesthetic taste for 'managing these things', the 'taste for power' of those who assumed official responsibilities as the head of a department, of a master programme, or the dean of a faculty. The above comments show that the aesthetic dimension of the education department became manifest when it interwove with an organizational culture inspired by

civic commitment and social utility. Once again, *aesthetics was linked to ethics*, almost depending upon the latter, which provided the frame for its organizational approval. Otherwise, aesthetics was an organizational 'sin' and remained hidden, seen and unseen, and inexpressible, as in the case of the relation between aesthetics and research stressed by one of the lecturers:

> Instinctively, I'd say no, because ethically I've come to consider the presence of aesthetics … as sin! It must be accomplished with time, but in an underhanded way, in the sense that it is camouflaged … sometimes the scientific dimension is not evidently aesthetic but I know that it is aesthetic … a beautiful table [of statistics] has every reason to be aesthetic, but the others don't know it.

One notes *the conflict between ethics and aesthetics* here, and also the fact that this conflict characterized the symbols and culture of the education department. Indeed, as the following extract illustrates, its members were confronted by contrasts:

> … then, I like doing research … I mean, working regardless of social utility. This is one of the jobs that allow you to do that … I mean, the self-directedness of the work … independently of external ends …

Here the aesthetic dimension of knowledge creation and learning management lay concealed behind a veil of modesty. It thus constituted *an organizational paradox: aesthetics as civic and social commitment, and aesthetics as liberation* from the constraint that work in the department should be socially useful.

The mathematics department

Matters were different in the mathematics department. There, it was the mathematicians themselves who made beautiful things by creating knowledge; who produced mathematics as an artifact with aesthetic appeal; who constructed a research practice symbolically connected to aesthetics:

> the most beautiful result is one where the author has been able to identify fundamental ideas, after which he works out his theory following a line of reasoning and a generally geometric intuition, and the thing acquires a particular significance, it

becomes clearer, it's easier to understand ... A beautiful result is often one in which the author demonstrates more than he says.

Another member of the department clarified the organizational character of engaging directly in a discourse carried forward at both the mathematical and the aesthetic levels. He recounted how an eminent Italian mathematician had decided to publish a theorem even though its proof did not work because 'it was beautiful all the same':

> ... he could do that because it was at such a level that it was acceptable even without a proof. He'd done a great deal in any case, because he'd made [...] you feel that the thing held together. After which, proving it was another matter.

This account also highlights the beauty of the eminent mathematician's gesture, namely his organizational practice of creating an idea to appreciate, an intuition upon which to reflect, a problem to study, and which was available to other scholars. Here, as often happens in organizations, aesthetics and ethics interwove so that it was often very difficult to determine whether or not 'beautiful' was being used as a synonym for 'good'. In this case, however, one is struck by how closely a beautiful idea was bound up with the values that inspire the beauty of the organizational practices of mathematicians in creating both knowledge and learning – as the following comment by another member of the department illustrates:

> The wonder you feel at this type of proof is like having a sensation of the beautiful ... you understand that it's a mathematical, logical, philosophical type of beauty which perhaps can't be compared with the artistically beautiful, but the fact that simple propositions have been proved with profound ideas is something whose beauty even a non-specialist is able to understand.

In the mathematics department, we may therefore conclude *aesthetics was collective life*: it underpinned the intellectual production and transmission of scientific knowledge, and it was one of the central pillars for the work identity of the organization's members. Seen from afar, mathematicians resemble scientists. But they describe themselves as

if the cleavage between art and science, and the dominance of scientific discourse in the organization of academic knowledge, had never happened. Compared with their colleagues in the other two departments, they seemed obsolete in the age of modernity, where science has very little to do with art.

To recapitulate

What was the result of this study on organizational aesthetics? On the one hand it brought out distinctive features of the organizational cultures studied, and demonstrated that the aesthetic is socially constructed in organizations on the other. These are two closely interconnected organizational themes, but in certain respects they are very distinct. The former finds in the aesthetic dimension *a way to study organizations*; the latter finds in organizational experiences the *negotiative processes that give shape to the aesthetic* and to its relations with the classic issues of ethics and truth.

Beauty was truth in itself – organizational truth, we would say – in the mathematics department: the mathematicians invented, described, cooperated and organized by weaving the aesthetic, the ethical, and the truth dimensions together. But this was not so in the other two departments, where ethics was socially instituted as the theoretical framework within which the meanings and organizational valences of aesthetics were determined. The visual arts scholars sharply separated their historical/scientific output from the aesthetic dimension underpinning their choice of work, the network of scholars with whom they collaborated, and the organization that they had decided to join. Although those who worked in the education department appreciated the aesthetic dimension of teaching and of running the university, they tended to downplay it and keep it under control, emphasizing the ethic of social utility instead. Consequently, in both these departments the aesthetic dimension did not possess organizational truth in and of itself; rather, it depended on the ethical dimension. Aesthetics was the *art of organizational sin*, and although it was intrinsic to the organization's practices, it lay at a lower level than ethics and was regulated by the latter. Thus aesthetics was sterilized by the organization's ethics: the aesthetics were silenced and concealed, seen and not seen, while ethics dictated the content of organizational discourse.

Such were the beginnings of my aesthetic approach to the study of organizational life. The next section discusses the issues raised for future research by current developments in the aesthetic strand of organization studies.

FRAGMENTS FOR A DIALOGUE IN ORGANIZATION STUDIES

It seems that the empirical and theoretical analysis of the relations between aesthetics and organization is now well-established: witness the several texts that seek to systematize the organizational literature on aesthetics (Dean et al., 1997; Gagliardi, 1996; Ramírez, 2005; Strati, 1999, 2007; Taylor and Hansen, 2005), the work of virtual communities – in particular, the Art, Aesthetics, Creativity, and Organisations Research Network (AACORN), and the increasingly frequent discussions on the topic at conferences, conference sections, and workshops. Recent years have seen mounting intellectual interest in organizational aesthetics, a flourishing of cultural initiatives in its regard, and a fierce polemic against the organizational theories that still divide art from science so that the logical-analytical dimension of intellectual inquiry may maintain its dominance.

All this has happened amidst a severe crisis of faith in scientific beliefs and the myth of rationality which, during the last century, presided over the social construction of organizational discourse until the culturalist turn in the social sciences at the end of the 1980s. A turn, moreover, which occurred in aesthetics as well (Jimenez, 1997: 397–432), both in philosophical debate and in art production and art criticism.

What are the implications of these developments for organizational theory in general, and management studies in particular? Certainly not the likelihood of any predominance of aesthetic understanding in organization studies; but rather, a new register somewhat like a new musical note used as the benchmark to tune a musical instrument. Consequently, instead of conducting systematic treatment, I shall use 'fragments' from the aesthetic discourse on organizations to develop a dialogue – also based on conflict and controversy – with other approaches.

Why fragments? Because I find fragments particularly appealing, as will be apparent from the following image based on a story about Gaudì's architecture. The story which I am about to recount – its authenticity is of little relevance here – describes the interactions among Gaudì, a master craftsman, the great sheet of glass produced by the craftsman for the main door of Gaudì's building, and the ground. When Gaudì was shown the beautifully prepared sheet of glass, he said to the craftsman something like: 'It's perfect. Now drop it on the ground!' And when the glass had shattered into pieces of various sizes, he said, accompanying his words with hand gestures, 'Right, now assemble these fragments with wrought iron and make the building's front door'.

A fragment has (intuitively) very little to do with the systematic information yielded by an excerpt made *ad hoc*. The fragment from the story about Gaudì acquires form in the interaction between different competences, and between humans and artifacts. 'How' the glass shattered is just as important as 'how' the craftsman dropped it or 'how' the latter obeyed the architect's instructions. Conflict between feelings and aesthetic judgement, hierarchical power and expert knowledge, processes of organizational destruction and construction connote this organizational interaction performed on the aesthetic dimension, and in which the glass fragments demonstrate 'that the situation of creative invention is that of striving to an end that, even if it is impossible to specify and plan, is in a sense directing the process' (Menger, 2006: 63). There are some fragments of aesthetic discourse on organizations that strike me as especially significant, viz.:

1 Embedding the study of organizational aesthetics in the context of *paradigmatic controversies* in organizational theory. The latter has rarely concerned itself with aesthetic-sensory knowledge, taste, the aesthetic judgement, or art; in short, it has neglected numerous dimensions of 'practice' in organizations (Nicolini et al., 2003). By contrast, study of the aesthetic dimension emphasizes the practical knowledge, passion, and taste – all socially constructed – which give difference and specificity to every individual and every collectivity (community of practices, occupational or professional community, organizational culture). An organization is therefore an artifact configured within post-social relations. It does not exist independently of the symbolic interactions between humans and artifacts. It is these features that distinguish the interpretative theoretical paradigm in organization studies from the functionalist paradigm. Within the former, the study of organizational aesthetics privileges critical analysis of the factors impeding organizational actors from full self-realization through their creativity and difference. Principal among these factors is the social aesthetization which anaesthetizes (Marquard, 1989) rather than activates their aesthetic-sensory sensibilities.

2 The qualitative methodology used by empirical research on the aesthetic dimension in organizations. This methodology draws on research styles which conventionally distinguish between qualitative and quantitative analysis: ethnography, non-structured methods of empirical inquiry, and techniques which let the theory emerge from the data, as in constructionist and phenomenological grounded theory. It explores other avenues as well, drawing on visual anthropology and interactionist visual anthropology to do so, as well as on artistic experience (Barry, 1996; Brearley, 2001; Guillet de Monthoux, 2004; Steyaert and Hjorth, 2002; Strati, 2005; Taylor, 2004; Warren, 2002). The *methodological novelty of this mixing and hybridization of art and science is primarily theoretical*, in that it conducts an epistemological critique of the cleavage that has logical-analytical understanding predominate over empathic-evocative understanding. It is also innovative in regard to everyday research practice – its styles and rituals – because it mixes and merges actions with different time frames (consider the ephemerality of artistic performance and the open-ended time horizon of research) and distinct professional competences, namely those of the art world and academe. Third, it is innovative by virtue of the *ethos* – 'comprehension-cum-action' – that inspires research, given that this requires activation of the sensory faculties, the aesthetic judgement, and the cognitive and ratiocinative capacities of both the researcher and the participants in the research.

3 *Organizational power for the emancipation* of actors – individual and collective – *and also for their subjection* to organizational cultures. Aesthetics is individual difference first and foremost; but it is also what aggregates or disperses collectives in organizational settings through both personal commitment and organizational manipulation of individual feelings. Tastes, professional lifestyles, missions, talents, inventiveness, and ability are all sources of aesthetics-based organizational power, although they are seldom examined together with those based on norms, economic, or technological position and investigated relative to their emancipatory or subjugatory ambivalence. Aesthetics is organizational power that operates both reactively, as testified by the expression 'I/we don't like it', and proactively through the assertion of an operational style, a product design, or a sense of humour. This can be well understood if one considers the control over the organization's zones of uncertainty (Crozier and Friedberg, 1977) exercised by complex organizational actors consisting of inter-related people and artifacts. These are areas of interaction that the organization regards as important, if not crucial: for example, the area controlled by someone with a good sense of smell, the 'nose', in a perfume house, or someone with a good eye who directs an international photography collection, or again, someone with a passion for writing software programs and who creates a virtual community. The power of aesthetics therefore has its main root in the tacit dimension of knowledge (Polanyi, 1958) essential for organizational practices and the formation of communities of practice in organizations. In other words, it is rooted in that form of organizational knowledge whereby actors know how to do things and are able to describe their ability in the evocative terms of the metaphorical language pertaining to aesthetic understanding, but not in logical-analytical terms. It has another root as well: the organizational control exerted through the *pathos* of the organizational artifacts making up the organization's symbolic landscape

(Gagliardi, 1990), and through the disciplining of corporeality (Hancock and Tyler, 2000) and the anaesthetizing aesthetization (Marquard, 1989) mentioned above.

4 The *dynamic between the semiotization of working and organizational practices and sensible knowledge*. The semiotization of activities in organizational settings followed the advent of mass education and the diffusion of written texts in the industrialized societies. Now supported by information and telecommunications technologies, it has allegedly reduced the range of the sensory perceptions and aesthetic judgements activated as people work in organizations. But this is not the case, for if one observes software programmers at work, one notes their evident private relationship with the code being written, a relationship based on personal taste and affect which gives rise to 'quarrels about which are the most beautiful programs, which are the best programming languages and who is entitled to have a say in those discussions' (Piñeiro, 2004). In this case, too, art is valuable because it reminds us that reading a poem 'is equivalent to entering into *contact*: experiencing its sense as inseparable from its verbality. Reading a poem is to verify it tactilely; it is a sensual experience. It involves a *physics of sense*' (Cortellessa, 2006: XXII). Awareness is particularly significant for the aesthetics of the organizational discourse, since the semiotization is dominant in the practices of organizational research and its representation.

5 *Challenging logico-analytical knowledge* in order to create metaphorical spaces for dialogue. Aesthetic understanding and logical-analytical understanding alternate with each other: they overlap, they merge, they cancel each other out. They exist, not in spite of each other, but in a reciprocal challenge in which aesthetic understanding has numerous strengths. I shall dwell on two of them in particular. The first highlights areas where aesthetic understanding is particularly appropriate but analytical understanding is not. The second is the case in which aesthetic inquiry reveals organizational phenomena of particular importance for organizational theory – phenomena which analytical inquiry also appropriately investigates in its own fashion. The former case is exemplified by the forms of organizational knowledge that aesthetics equips with language for their expression, as happens apropos the tacit dimension of knowledge in organizations: by virtue of the evocative process of which it is capable, aesthetic understanding

does not violate the tacitness of such knowledge, while logical-analytical understanding instead does. The second case can be exemplified by the materiality of organizations and by the post-social relations that weave their everyday lives together. This is the study of the 'symbolic artifacts' (Gagliardi, 1990; Rafaeli and Pratt, 2005) to which aesthetic understanding attributes a capacity for action in many respects like that ascribed to 'non-human elements' in logical-analytical understanding (Latour, 2005). Of course, organizational discourse operates at several levels; but it is remarkable that in these very same years the 'object' has changed theoretical status in both analytical and aesthetic studies, becoming in the former an actant, or an intermediary able to activate courses of organizational action, and in the latter, the symbolic artifact whose *pathos* activates organizational knowledge.

CONCLUSIONS

In this chapter, I have sought to illustrate the rationale for studying the relations between organization and aesthetics. In these conclusions I would add a final consideration prompted by the following theoretical-methodological question: Why should we continue to study aesthetics in the everyday lives of organizations? My answer is not scientific but aesthetic: 'because it is pleasurable'. As long as it is so, and as long as aesthetic and emotional pleasure is the principal purpose of this strand of organization studies, analysis of the relationships among art, aesthetics and everyday life in organizations will maintain its roots in, and derive its features from, aesthetics. Studying organizational aesthetics *for the pleasure of doing so* is not to attribute such inquiry with the teleological purpose of determining which form of organizational understanding is better, more profound, more complete or more useful – that pertains to endeavours with knowledge objectives inspired by the principles of the good and the true, but not the beautiful.

The chapter has proposed some 'fragments' of the aesthetic organizational discourse in order to develop dialogical knowledge and learning in organization studies. They are not intended to provide the basis for a systematic, exhaustive and complete discourse furnishing emotional reassurance and scientific support for organizational scholars and students of organizational life. They are only fragments, and to grasp them fully we must rely on art and on what we have learnt from studies on art. The organizational discourse on art and aesthetics in the everyday lives of organizations is a collective symbolic construct accomplished socially by moving 'towards an unspecified end' (Menger, 2006: 62), but doing so purposefully, selecting among the many opportunities that we see and those that we intuit without really understanding them.

REFERENCES

Barry, Daved (1996) 'Artful inquiry: A symbolic constructivist approach to social science research', *Qualitative Inquiry*, 2 (4): 411–438.

Benghozi, Pierre-Jean (ed.) (1987) 'Art and organization', Special Issue of *Dragon*, 2 (4).

Brearley, Linda (2001) 'Exploring creative forms within phenomenological research', in R. Barnacle (ed.), *Phenomenology*. Melbourne: RMIT University Press. pp. 74–87.

Carr, Adrian and Philip Hancock (eds) (2003) *Art and Aesthetics at Work*. Basingstoke: Palgrave Macmillan.

Cortellessa, Andrea (2006) *La fisica del senso. Saggi e interventi su poeti italiani dal 1940 a oggi (The Physics of Sense: Essays on Italian Poets since 1940)*. Rome: Fazi.

Crozier, Michel and Erhard Friedberg (1977) *L'acteur et le système. Les contraintes de l'action collective*. Paris: Seuil. (Eng. trans.: *Actors and Systems: The Politics of Collective Action*. Chicago: University of Chicago Press, 1980.)

Dean, James W. Jr, Ottensmeyer, Edward and Rafael Ramírez (1997) 'An aesthetic perspective on organizations', in C. Cooper and S. Jackson (eds), *Creating Tomorrow's Organizations: A Handbook for Future Research in Organizational Behavior*. Chichester: Wiley. pp. 419–437.

Dégot, Vincent (1987) 'Portrait of the manager as an artist', *Dragon*, 2 (4): 13–50.

Gagliardi, Pasquale (ed.) (1990) *Symbols and Artifacts: Views of the Corporate Landscape*. Berlin: de Gruyter.

Gagliardi, Pasquale (1996) 'Exploring the aesthetic side of organizational life', in S.R. Clegg, C. Hardy and W.R. Nord (eds), *Handbook of Organization Studies*. London: Sage. pp. 565–580.

Guillet de Monthoux, Pierre (2004) *The Art Firm. Aesthetic Management and Metaphysical Marketing*. Stanford: Stanford University Press.

Hancock, Philip and Melissa (2000) '"The look of love": Gender and the organization of aesthetics', in J. Hassard, R. Holliday and H. Willmott (eds), *Body and Organization*. London: Sage. pp. 108–129.

Jimenez, Marc (1997) *Qu'est-ce que l'esthétique*. Paris: Gallimard.

Jones, Michael Owen, Moore, Michael D. and Richard C. Snyder (eds) (1988) *Inside Organizations. Understanding the Human Dimension*. Newbury Park, CA: Sage.

Latour, Bruno (2005) *Reassembling the Social. An Introduction to Actor-Network-Theory*. Oxford: Oxford University Press.

Linstead, Stephen and Heather Höpfl (eds) (2000) *The Aesthetic of Organization*. London: Sage.

Marquard, Odo (1989) *Aesthetica und Anaesthetica. Philosophische Uberlegungen*. Paderborn: Schoningh.

Menger, Pierre-Michel (2006) 'Profiles of the unfinished: Rodin's work and the varieties of incompleteness', in H.S. Becker, R.R. Faulkner and B. Kirshenblatt-Gimblett (eds), *Art from Start to Finish. Jazz, Painting, Writing, and Other Improvisations*. Chicago: The University of Chicago Press. pp. 31–68.

Nicolini, Davide, Gherardi, Silvia and Dvora Yanow (eds) (2003) *Knowing in Organizations: A Practice-Based Approach*. Armonk, New York: M.E. Sharpe.

Ottensmeyer, Edward (ed.) (1996) 'Essays on aesthetics and organization', *Organization*, 3 (2).

Piñeiro, Erik (2004) *The Aesthetics of Code. On Excellence in Instrumental Action*. Stockholm: Fields of Flow Series.

Polanyi, Michael (1958) *Personal Knowledge*. London: Routledge & Kegan Paul.

Rafaeli, Anat and Michael G. Pratt (eds) (2005) *Artifacts and Organizations: Beyond Mere Symbolism*. Mahwah, NJ: Lawrence Erlbaum Associates Inc.

Ramírez, Rafael (1991) *The Beauty of Social Organization*. Munich: Accedo.

Ramírez, Rafael (2005) 'The aesthetics of cooperation', *European Management Review*, 2: 28–35.

Schroeder, Jonathan (ed.) (2006) 'Aesthetics, images and vision', Special Issue of *Marketing Theory*, 6 (1).

Steyaert, Chris and Daniel Hjorth (2002) '"Thou art a scholar, speak to it …" – on spaces of speech: A script', *Human Relations*, 55 (7): 767–797.

Strati, Antonio (1990) 'Aesthetics and organizational skill', in B.A. Turner (ed.), *Organizational Symbolism*. Berlin: De Gruyter. pp. 207–222.

Strati, Antonio (1992) 'Aesthetic understanding of organizational life', *Academy of Management Review*, 17 (3): 568–581.

Strati, Antonio (1999) *Organization and Aesthetics*. London: Sage.

Strati, Antonio (2005) 'Organizational artifacts and the aesthetic approach', in A. Rafaeli and M. Pratt (eds), *Artifacts and Organizations*. Mahwah, NJ: Lawrence Erlbaum Associates Inc. pp. 23–39.

Strati, Antonio (2007) 'Sensations, impressions and reflections on the configuring of the aesthetic discourse in organizations', *Aesthesis. International Journal of Art and Aesthetics in Management and Organizational Life*, 1 (1): 14–22.

Strati, Antonio and Pierre, Guillet de Monthoux (eds) (2002) 'Organizing aesthetics', Special Issue of *Human Relations*, 55 (7).

Taylor, Steven (2004) 'Presentational form in first person research: Off-line collaborative reflection using art', *Action Research*, 2 (1): 71–88.

Taylor, Steven and Hans Hansen (2005) 'Finding form: Looking at the field of organizational aesthetics', *Journal of Management Studies*, 42 (6): 1210–1231.

Warren, Samantha (2002) 'Show me how it feels to work here': Using photography to research organizational aesthetics', *Ephemera. Critical Dialogues on Organization*, 2 (3): 224–245.

Watkins, Ceri, King, Ian and Stephen, Linstead (eds) (2006) 'Art of Management and Organization Conference series', Special Issue of *Culture and Organization*, 12 (1).

Whither Emotion?

Stephen Fineman

In the past decade or so emotion has moved from being a marginalized, even silenced, discourse in organizational and management studies to being something of a 'must'. The image of the dispassionate organization has at last given way to the sentient organization where our gripes, loves, jealousies, despairs, excitements, angers and so forth shape, and are shaped by, our workplace actions and experiences. From a distance the organization resembles a meteorological map of emotion fronts, pressures, contours and zones. So-called 'structures', 'relationships', 'decisions', 'deals', 'rewards', 'downsizings', 'leadership', 'trust', and the like are fluid states where the trading and representation of feeling are axiomatic to created meanings. Emotion is no incidental fuzz to 'proper' business, but a substantive feature of what happens and what matters.

This is exciting territory for organizational researchers and reflective practitioners. It holds promise of rich, culturally contextualized studies where different symbols of feeling – verbal, written, pictorial, material – are the subjects of interpretation and reinterpretation. It also takes emotion beyond the realm of individual, intrapsychic, impulses into social/political arenas where the nuances of lived emotion underscore or destabilize power relationships. Here is fertile territory for critical inquiry. By this I mean the way emotion is appropriated, used and abused in organizations, such as in the suppression of particular voices (gender, age, ethnic) and the privileging of others; in the emotional and political architecture of discrimination, harassment and bullying; and in the erosion of dignity in the workplace.

New organizational forms raise challenging questions for the student of emotion. Virtuality could be placed near the top of the list. Virtual organizations, by their very design, obviate most or all of the corporeal presence that we have come to regard as fundamental to the learning and social construction of emotion. In its place are virtual links across various forms of computer mediated communication – ranging from the PC to the multi-facility mobile phone. Is this a pathway to emotional atrophy? Or should we see virtual organizations as evolving contexts where we invent, share and test different protocols for emotional expression, bonding and trust?

All these questions lend themselves admirably to qualitative approaches, such as tried and tested modes of ethnography, participant observation, narrative analysis, storytelling, and phenomenology. There is much potential in combinations of such methods, especially if augmented by less conventional (in the social sciences) visual representations of emotion, such as photographs and video.

The picture I have portrayed offers promise of a special contribution to our understanding and wisdom about organizing and organizations. It 'writes in' emotion as a relational phenomenon of many shades and guises, and resists trivializing or oversimplifying affectivity.

The kind of *in situ* studies that I envisage would aim at engagement with both workaday and 'heightened' organizational events. The latter (e.g. crises, inspections, radical change, downsizing, mergers, relocations) are where emotions are likely to be

Continued

sharpest in labour and management processes. One could, for example, focus on the way resistance, conformity and discipline are enacted against a shifting background of uncertainty, fear, excitement and suspicion. Major, morally contentious matters are especially intriguing in that morality acquires its affective edge through shifting contours of shame, guilt, embarrassment, and anger.

Yet, ironically, it is the emotions of the 'everyday' that we understand least well. We lack portraits of the minutiae of emotionality that constitutes the warp and weft of daily organizational life, determining the character and direction of relationships. It is where life with colleagues, clients, customers, superiors and subordinates is shaped and reshaped, reinforced or fractured – in corridor meetings, around the water cooler, across the lunch table, in the formal conferences, in e-mails. This scenario awaits the attention of embedded organizational researchers with access to off-stage and on-stage encounters, and to the stories and reminiscences that frame them.

REFERENCES

Fineman, S. (2004) 'Getting the measure of emotion – and the cautionary tale of emotional intelligence', *Human Relations*, 57 (6): 719–740.

Fineman, S. (2005) 'Appreciating emotion at work: paradigm tensions', *International Journal of Work, Organization and Emotion*, 1 (1): 4–19.

Fineman, S. (2006) 'On being positive: concerns and counterpoints', *Academy of Management Review*, 31 (2): 270–291.

Fineman, S. (2006) 'Emotion and organizing', in S. Clegg, C. Hardy, W. Nord, and T. Lawrence (eds). *The Sage Handbook of Organization Studies, Second Edition*. London: Sage.

Fineman, S. (ed) (2008) *The Emotional Organization: Passions and Power*. Oxford: Blackwell.

Fineman, S., Mailtis, S. and Panteli, N. (2007) 'Virtuality and emotion', *Human Relations*, 60 (4): 555–560.

The Social Life of Values: Cross-cultural Construction of Realities

Slawomir Magala

The undermining of standards of seriousness is almost complete, with the ascendancy of a culture whose most intelligible, persuasive values are drawn from the entertainment industries. (Sontag, 2001: 273).

Contemporary complex societies and their increasingly complex processes of knowledge production and dissemination are imagined under the powerful shadow cast by the biological theories of evolution. While we do not believe in linear and inevitable Progress along the Enlightenment lines (having discovered empirical falsification of 'grand narratives' in Soviet Russia and Nazi Germany and having traced religious roots of secularized bureaucracies to the perseverance of professional corporate bureaucracies), we do tacitly believe that development and changes in our societies can ultimately be explained and brought under human control, at least to a certain – manageable – extent. Popper's vision of 'piecemeal social engineering' of an open society opposed to the utopian ideology

of the closed ones remains philosophically attractive, but calls for a new defence in view of the relativistic uses of Kuhn's concept of 'Gestalt switch'. Imagining our societies and our knowledge about them, we tend to accept tacitly or explicitly that even the most random changes ultimately can find meaningful interpretation according to a variant of causal explanation, perhaps at the price of accepting its sophisticated functional form.

These evolutionary and biological explanations and analogies are resisted in social sciences, where ideas of 'sociobiology' had been discredited as an updated version of 'social darwinism' a la E.O. Wilson, but continue to re-emerge as neo-sociobiologies under various guises of 'holistic darwinism' (Corning, 2005) or 'machiavellian intelligence' (Byrne and Whiten, 1988; Whiten and Byrne, 1997). While they merit attention, they should be vigorously opposed, since their simplified and popularized versions disseminate a mistaken belief in the profoundly false and potentially dangerous analogy between biological 'genes' and sociocultural 'memes' (both of which presumably can be controlled by specific gatekeepers, for instance peer control, performing a role of artificial 'natural selection'). This tacitly accepted analogy is misleading. The history of human societies, the sociocultural history of growing complexity and the intensity of human cooperation and conflicts is not carried by 'hidden core memes' of sociobiological, holistic evolution (no matter whether we call this hidden 'core' meme a divine Revelation or a secular Reason and no matter how we explain the opening of the path of rational development of complex societies towards a more 'perfect union' with itself or higher being).

'Memes' – or what could possibly pass for their rough equivalents – are sociocultural constructs, which are continuously renegotiated, translated, reinterpreted, re-communicated and reconstructed throughout history. Sociocultural imagination – which stores and re-engineers such constructs for future uses – is fuelled by core values (embedded in social and individual memories as bourgeois virtues and as multiple types of alternative or counter-values: bohemian, heretic, subversive, protestant, etc.) which prompt multiple communities to redefine, retranslate and re-communicate speeches, texts and other cultural units, using them as resources in political, economic and cultural struggles. In the course of these multiple interactions, transmissions and translations – old and new inequalities generate both a 'renaissance' of interest in inherited 'memes' and organized 'deletion' of other memes (or of their former custodians). Growth of knowledge requires some growth of social amnesia about selected ('revived', revised and subsequently forgotten) aspects of sociocultural memes.

The forgotten role of the Islamic centres of learning in transmitting the ancient Greek and Roman heritage to Latin Europe may serve as an illustration of the process of re-engineering of stored 'memes' of the 'classical Greek and Roman heritage'. Historical deletion of the Arab and Muslim contribution to the recovery, preservation, refinement and transition of the ancient Greek and Roman texts for Christian Europeans before the outbreak of the Italian Renaissance is the first case in point ('The arabization of European Renaissance'). Had this deleting been prevented, we might have gained a better insight into the crucial role of communities of interpretive practice, into multilinguistic and multicultural process of transmitting 'memes' and into emergent regularities of apparently random 'memic' drift of meaning through translations and retranslations in the process of sociocultural evolution. Incommensurability does not emerge with the scientific research communities pursuing methodological puzzle-solving à la Kuhn. It puzzled the first translators of Aristotle from Greek into Syriac, from Syriac into Arabic, from Arabic into Latin and from Latin into Italian, German or Polish. However, we are often prevented by our narrow-minded defence of existing political and cultural inequalities and parochial philosophy of knowledge (scientific, religious, political, moral, economic, etc.) from defusing potential growth of conflicts out of control.

In order to avoid triggering a potential spiral of violence and destruction one has to preserve the minimal consensus for the ongoing negotiations at the partially virtual agoras of the future – and the minimal consensus of a professional research community is precisely the type of a community of scientific knowledge presupposed by the falsificationist and evolutionary epistemology of intersubjective scientific knowledge suggested by K.R. Popper. Popper's falsificationist and evolutionary epistemology has to be recovered from behind the smokescreen of T. Kuhn's crudely sociobiological and Cold War-driven theory of scientific revolutions imagined as a sequence of paradigmatic dictatorships separated by sudden 'Gestalt switches'. The resuscitation of Popper's philosophy of science could help in developing more mature, moral, democratic and liberal communities of knowledge. The latter could turn out to tread a superior 'third way' between communities led by two rival visions. Popperian vision is opposed to tacit acceptance of either the neopositivist dogmatism (cf. Wilson, 1998), as is usually the case in mainstream academic establishments, or to tacit acceptance of the relativist Kuhn, as tends to be the case in social sciences and the humanities, where postmodernists 'adopted' Kuhn in their struggles against neopositivism as the dominant ideology of academic institutions ('Emergent cross-cultural competence: interdisciplinary, inter-paradigmatic, intermediating'). In their quest for defence weapons against neopositivism, these postmodern social constructivists had embraced radical incommensurability thesis (pronounced by Kuhn about two successive paradigms which cannot be compared along the single line) and applied it to their footholds in academia, which they wanted to defend against the neopositivist onslaught. They pronounced Kuhn's theory of Gestalt switch (scientific revolution) to be a defensive doctrine preventing different paradigmatic communities of learning from clashing while functioning within the same academic institutional environment: 'What we call progress in science, for Kuhn, is not then movement from a less to a more objectively accurate paradigm.(…) No longer was it possible to justify science as a quest for *truth* (Gergen, 1999: 54). In the following section, I develop these themes further through an examination of the international crisis caused by Danish cartoons.

CLASH OF INEQUALITIES: BOURGEOIS VIRTUES AND GLOBAL IMMIGRANTS

On September 30, cartoons by 12 artists appeared in *Jyllands Posten* (a conservative Danish daily). One of the cartoons presented the turbaned head of the Prophet, with a burning fuse protruding from it as if Muhammad was carrying a bomb on his head. Another showed the Prophet trying to stop the crowd of martyrs from queuing before the gates of paradise by exclaiming that he had run out of virgins. Cartoons might

have remained unnoticed by the Islamic population of Danish capital (ca. 5000), but their religious leaders made a case against what they perceived as *de facto* discrimination on educational and job markets.

These local religious leaders of Danish Muslims were presiding over a marginalized and discriminated segment of Danish population, which does not feel embedded in broader civil society nor is adequately represented by local political parties. When their protests failed to elicit responses they had initially counted on (on the part of local authorities, job agencies, employers' organizations, trade unions, Christian communities and organizations and state authorities), they lodged a formal complaint against a blasphemy intended to hurt their religious feelings, asking the regional public persecutor in Viborg to investigate the case and to punish the perpetrators. On January 6, 2006, the regional public persecutor in Viborg announced that investigations into cartoons have been terminated since no evidence of illegal activity, i.e. punishable offence, has been found.

Meanwhile, the Egyptian foreign minister, Ahmed Abul-Gheit, had publicly criticized anti-Islamic cartoons published in Denmark (November 2005) and made use of the Future Forum (a conference of the ministers of foreign affairs of Muslim countries of the Middle East) in Bahrain, calling for joint diplomatic action. Their declarations had no immediate influence upon the course of Danish justice or European Union's media policy, but they managed to mobilize shop owners and food retail chains in their own countries. Shop owners started boycotting Danish dairy products and symbolically trampled upon Danish flags spread on pavements outside of boycotting shops (which increased media visibility of the protests). Very soon crowds of fanatics, sometimes with governments' approval (in Syria, Iran) and sometimes without (Libya, Pakistan and Afghanistan) attacked Danish diplomatic buildings, setting some of them on fire. People died. Could this have been avoided, if local Danish authorities had paid attention to the original declaration of Danish imams? In this declaration, we read, among others:

'We urge you – on behalf of thousands of believing Muslims – to give us an opportunity of having constructive contact with the press and particularly with the relevant decision-makers, not briefly, but with a scientific methodology and planned and long-term program seeking to make views approach each other and remove misunderstandings between the two parties involved. Since we do not wish for Muslims to be accused of being backward and narrow, likewise we do not wish for Danes to be accused of ideological arrogance either. When this relationship is back on the track, the result will bring satisfaction, an underpinning of security and stable relations, and a flourishing Denmark for all that live here.

We call your attention to this case, and place it in your hands, in such a way that we together may think and have an objective dialogue regarding how an appropriate exit can be found for these crises in a way which does not violate the freedom of speech, but which at the same time does not offend the feelings of Muslims either. (*Jyllands*, 2006: 6)

Since the only response was the prime minister's stern reminder that they are free to turn to the courts, the imams started lobbying in the Middle East, where events soon got out of control. Fundamentalist newspapers in the Arab world (e.g. *Al-Najaf al Balagh* published by Shiites in Iraq or *Jama'at-i Islami* published by fundamentalists in Pakistan) supported the demand for a public acknowledgement of wrongdoing on the part of the Danes and for a public apology. The Pakistani newspapers mentioned above went further and offered financial reward for any true Muslim who would kill the cartoon artists, defending the honour of the entire community of the faithful. On November 14, 2005, a radical fundamentalist leader of Islamic youth in Pakistan, Shahid Pervez Gilani, allegedly promised half a million rupees for accomplishing this murder. His press spokesman had later denied those allegations, claiming that his party embraced democracy and rejected violence, but the media managed to carry this message around the Islamic world.

At this point – from mid-January to mid-February 2006 – Muslim crowds turned

violent during street manifestations, destroying not only Danish diplomatic buildings (which had been burnt in Damascus and Beirut), but turning their wrath against symbols of 'the West' in general and the United States and the European Union in particular (young Palestinians torched the seat of the EU representative to the Palestinian Authority). Street demonstrations, most of them violent, some involving loss of life, took place in Iraq, Lebanon, Kashmir, Malaysia and Indonesia. However, the cartoon crisis turned out to be short-lived. The Egyptian government threatened boycotting of Danish products but failed to implement the threat, while Saudi Arabia recalled their ambassador from Denmark. At the end of February demonstrations died down.

Meanwhile, responses on both sides of the Christian–Muslim divide became more differentiated and less clear-cut. On the one hand, the responses of the Arab societies have not been as one-sided and fundamentalist as TV images of arsonist crowds throwing Danish products out of supermarkets and fighting riot police would suggest. Although it was hard to find this information in Europe's main dailies, there were brave Arab journalists – in Algeria, Yemen, Jordan and Egypt – who did reprint Danish cartoons in their newspapers and weeklies. In spite of the fact that the cartoons were reproduced fuzzily in order to diminish their impact, and in spite of the fact that they had been provided with condemning comments, some of these journalists were arrested, although all of them were eventually set free on bail. The list of courageous Arab journalists includes Mohammad al-Asaadi (editor of '*Yemen Observer*'), Akram Sabra and Kamal al-Aalafi (editors of, respectively, '*Al Hurryia*' and '*Al-Rai al-Aam*', both in Yemen) and Kahel Bousaad and Berkane Bouderbala (editors of, respectively '*Errisala*' and '*Iqraa*', both of which are Algerian weeklies). One should stress the fact that these arrests and the accompanying closure of publications happened in 2006, after street riots had spread. Originally, in October 2005, when two Jordanian weeklies ('*Al-Mehwar*' edited by Hisham Khalidi and

'*The Star*'), and two newspapers – Jordan's '*Al Ghad*' and Egypt's '*Al Fagr*' reprinted the Danish cartoons, the reprints attracted little attention and have not yet been seized by any party framing them as a *casus belli*. However, when Jihad Momani reprinted the very same cartoons in Jordanian weekly '*al-Shihan*' on February 2, 2006, he was immediately arrested and had his weekly closed down by alarmed authorities.

On the other hand, the 'Western' world had also been far from uniform in its response to the 'Danish cartoon crisis'. The US media refused to reproduce the cartoons and so did the media in the UK. On February 15, 2006, the European Parliament accepted a resolution condemning acts of violence against Danish diplomatic buildings and expressed solidarity with Danes and other attacked Europeans. The European Union upheld the rights of Danish press to exercise its right for free expression of opinion on all topics, including religion, but originally expressed concern with the 'Danish satirical and offensive cartoons' (Xavier Solana). Gradually, the official position of the EU became more pro-Danish and less pro-Muslim and on February 26 ministers of foreign affairs issued a declaration after their meeting in Brussels. They regretted that Arab audiences had perceived these cartoons as offensive, but did not describe them as offensive themselves and offered no apologies.

Meanwhile, on February 25, the Dutch minister of developmental aid and cooperation, Agnes van Ardenne – van der Hoeven, published an article in the London-based Arab newspaper '*Asharq Al-Awsat*' (reprinted later by '*Yemen Times*') under the title 'The cartoon crisis, a distorted picture'. According to her, the secular point of view, upheld by the Danish authors and publishers of Muhammad cartoons, is based on an assumption that religion is outdated and had been historically superseded by a superior – rational and secular – culture. Secular fundamentalists pocket religion in marginal areas of individual social life, closer to personal hobbies than social and civil virtues. This is wrong, because it focuses the on wrong aspect of

the conflict. The Arab world is suffering not because it is predominantly Muslim, but because it is predominantly ruled by undemocratic regimes, which waste chances for improvement. Agnes van Ardenne quoted president Roosevelt's famous war speech (State of the Union address of 1941), in which the US president mentioned four basic liberties (which subsequently contributed to the creation of the Declaration on Universal Rights of Man); the first of them was indeed freedom of expression, but it was closely followed by freedom of religious worship. Exercising our rights according to the former we should not take undue liberties with the latter, since our enemy is not a 'religious superstition' but 'political tyranny' (no matter whether it is justified with a secular ideology or religious doctrine). Both her article and reprints of cartoons by Muslim journalists create a potential agora for discussing future 'cartoon crises' by demonstrating that there is a space for a re-negotiation of meaning of religious values in contemporary social life, even during a growing crisis. Such re-negotiation would require a comparative analysis of the role of religious values in social life and an analysis of the conflicting values (Danish choice of freedom of expression at the expense of stigmatized immigrants). Not many Western or Muslim intellectuals offer guidance in this respect. Rare positive cases in point include, for instance, a critical reconstruction of the role of Christianity and of the Catholic Church in shaping Western political institutions (cf. Mouffe, 1999), the role of organized religion in shaping contemporary political philosophy and managerial ideology of institutional science (cf. Fuller, 2003) and analyses of the dismantling of ideological walls (Said, 2000; Hussein, 2002). Mouffe edited a volume of critical essays on Carl Schmitt, Schmitt's studies of 'Political Theology' and 'Roman Catholicism and Political Form' from the 1920s. He reconstructed the 'rationalism' of the Catholic Church and traced institutional logic of bureaucratic politics (which offers an institutional demonstration of this rationality) to contemporary political systems and especially to the uneasy relationship between the executive and legislative branch of government. According to his leftist commentators, he had recognized the crucial role of 'political management' in overcoming parliamentary crises and opposed the 'objective-economic' approach, which dominated both Marxist and neoliberal thinking, condemning them to either subversive conspiracy of a single party (Marxist core values of building a classless society at any cost) or to alienating parliamentary deal-making (liberal core values of continuing coercion-free dialogue no matter how coercive are the experienced constraints of inequalities by scapegoated groups):

> Schmitt takes up a position against what he sees as the dominant tendencies of Catholicism at the time; he criticizes its bending towards a private and subjective belief (…), he maintains Catholicism loses its way when it seeks only to bring another soul to a world condemned to the grip of economic and technical rationality. (…) He seeks (…) a model which makes it possible to affirm the primacy of the political over economics, of decision over impersonal structural constraints, of the Idea over matter. (Colliot-Thélène, 1999, 146–147)

Schmitt's idea of a political democracy involved an assumed homogeneity of members of an imagined political community. It was very restrictive :

> For him democracy requires the exclusion and 'if the need arises – the elimination or eradication of heterogeneity'. (Preuss, 1999, 171)

This question of homogeneity and eliminated heterogeneity arose at the core of the Danish cartoon crisis. Global flows brought Muslim immigrants into an environment, where they stood out as 'heterogeneous'. Persistent social inequalities forced immigrant Muslim communities into a defensive fold of imagined religious community. While discriminated against in housing, jobs and education, they could feel different but equal to their Danish hosts in their religious worship (which also legitimized their traditional family roles thus providing a buffer against secularization of the youth). When cartoons ridiculed even their religious community, without at the same time offering a consolation of increased

care for them as 'underdogs' and without genuine will to redress some of the other inequalities – Danish imams realized they were losing the only trump they still had in their social game for recognition and acceptance. Can we organize a game, in which consequences of playing trump cards by imagined or real 'underdogs' on a global scale will be less dangerous? In order to answer this question, let us examine knowledge communities, which are responsible for producing socially acceptable knowledge, which, in turn, influences our behavior in crises.

EMERGENT CROSS-CULTURAL COMPETENCE: INTERDISCIPLINARY, INTERPARADIGMATIC AND INTERMEDIATING

Not all religious values are lost in an interdisciplinary translation from principles of conduct for a religious sect in an originally hostile environment to universal principles of research community devoted to a scientific paradigm competing against other paradigms and other professional communities. Some of them survive in philosophies or historical reconstructions of ways and means of generating socially acceptable scientific knowledge. Commenting on the Popper–Kuhn debate, which had taken place in the early 1970s and decided about further development of contemporary philosophy of science, Steve Fuller points out that the construction and maintenance of moral, legal and institutional preconditions for free inquiry and ongoing criticism depends on a generalized loyalty to this free inquiry but without blind commitment to any particular theory of paradigm. Upholding standards of criticism is more important than having one's theory defended at their expense and these standards (linked to falsifiability, crucial experiments and the like) are maintained independently of theories, in the defence of which they are, with varying luck, evoked and applied. However, this Popperian 'virtue' of a rational member of

Western research community (who remains faithful to the spirit of critical inquiry, even if his own theories suffer as a result of acting in this spirit), has eroded under the influence of both contradictions in Popper's own philosophy of science (expressed in a number of publications, of which the evolutionary epistemology presented in 'Objective Knowledge' is the case in point) and under the influence of Thomas Kuhn's cold war ideology of mobilization of the scientific elites disguised as a 'theory of scientific revolutions', which justifies defence of status quo by members of 'normal science' (established professional communities in hierarchic academic bureaucracies) and unwillingness to subject one's own and one's colleagues' theories to too much criticism (especially from the point of rival paradigms, which are stigmatized as 'unscientific' and ignored):

> Science policy has regressed from a struggle for recognition to a struggle for survival. As universities increasingly abandon, or attenuate, the institution of tenure, and researchers are forced to depend on external grants, scientists have become all too keenly aware that one bad decision can ruin the material basis of their entire career. (...) To Popper and his students, this strategic mentality, characteristic of Kuhnian normal science, revealed science's captivity to its social and material conditions. Kierkegaard helped Popper forge the link between the critical spirit of classical Athens and the Protestant Reformation by making decision making central to his thought. Indeed, Popper has not unfairly been treated as a scientific existentialist. (Fuller, 2003, 108–109)

Fuller's use of religious analogy merits attention, because it continues some intuitions expressed by Feyerabend (who traced analogies between 'progress' in arts and sciences of the eighteenth century trying to demonstrate their shared underlying 'mechanism' for ensuring professional peer control and creating impression of 'progress') and compares directly episodes from institutional history of Christianity and cases from institutional history of Western academic establishments. Fuller believes that Popper's 'Catholic' approach (falsificationism being the tacit 'dogma' of anti-dogmatic academic bureaucracies) with 'Protestant' rebellions of

his students (Paul Feyerabend springs to mind, as an anarchist, and as a true heir to Rousseau's comparison of arts, sciences and morality) has been a much more fortunate translation of the religious message into a philosophical guide for methodology of scientific inquiry than Kuhnian 'sectarian' vision of paradigmatic and generational plots disturbing the continuity of 'normal science's' historical development. Kuhn's theory of rival paradigms succeeding each other for periods of domination over rival paradigms in fact turned out to be a convenient ideological alibi both for the established neopositivists unwilling to rock the academic boat (and willing to freeze too much interparadigmatic rivalry) and for the representatives of the postmodernist coalitions fighting for survival within these academic bureaucracies (willing to protect themselves from the dominant neopositivist orthodoxy in feminist, multicultural, postcolonial and other niches). Fuller reconstructs Popper's philosophy of science as a variant of 'scientific existentialism' and attributes the origins of this philosophical doctrine to the attempted synthesis between the critical spirit of the ancient Greeks ('classical Athens') and the Protestant Reformation (as the reform of an organized religion, which gave individual more chances than a professional bureaucracy of a Catholic church would be willing to concede). This is the genesis of the Kierkegaard connection:

> Kierkegaard characterized Christianity as a 'hypothesis' that one voluntarily undertakes in the full knowledge that the consequences are solely one's own – not God's – responsibility. (...) Similarly, for Popper, when a scientific knowledge claim is falsified, the responsibility lies solely with the scientist who proposed it – and not nature's failure to act in some desired fashion. The appropriate response is to hypothesise and test anew, not to rationalize the situation by claiming that the old hypothesis was 'really' true, but somehow the test fell victim to factors beyond the scientist's control. (...) If this appears too high a standard, then science is in *stasis*. For Popper, science is indeed in *stasis* – a 'fallen' state, a closed society, much as the Roman Catholic Church was when Martin Luther launched what became the protestant Reformation. (Fuller, 2003, 110)

Feyerabend's call against this '*stasis*', this 'fallen' state of scientific establishment, which arrogantly imposes a monopoly of academically produced knowledge on contemporary complex societies to the exclusion of all other types of knowledge (expressed in 'Against Method' and discussed in the 1970s, but forgotten shortly afterwards, cf. Feyerabend, 1975, 1979) should thus, according to Fuller, be seen as the call for Protestant-like decentralization of scientific corporations (including universities, research institutes, think-tanks and educational institutions), a passionate plea for 'devolution' of support for scientific projects to local communities and authorities, away from centralized megabureaucracies. No wonder that Fuller appeared as a witness in a recent trial in Pennsylvania, in which the claim of a board of education to equal treatment of intelligent design theory and theory of biological evolution during biology lessons in a public school (demanded by parents making use of their democratic rights) has been challenged by those who believe that public education should be limited to the theories approved of by academic establishments (and theory of intelligent design is not).

There are limits to analogy between religious movement of Protestantism within Christianity dominated institutionally by the Catholic Church in Western Europe of the sixteenth century and schools and polemics in contemporary philosophy of science (although the present revival of interest among scholars and scientists in the Popper–Kuhn, Lakatos–Feyerabend debates is fairly symptomatic for a renewed interest in 'criticism and the growth of knowledge'). These limits can best be summarized as a debate on relativism and are closely connected to social life of values. From the point of epistemological and methodological criticism of Popper's philosophy of science two charges brought by philosophers of science stand out and will continue to stand out even if Kuhn's theory of scientific revolutions is refuted and loses its popularity. The first is that Popper embraced evolutionary epistemology, which tacitly identifies an ability of an amoeba

or of an Einstein to (biological) survival with this agent's (Einstein's or amoeba's) rationality. Thus one assumes what should become known only after we understand evolutionary processes – rationality of carriers of ability to survive is measured with their survival and survival is then explained as a manifestation of their (superior) rationality' (cf. Chmielewski, 1995). A vicious circle becomes a real threat to our explanation: why do agents survive? Because they are rational. Why are they rational? Because they survive. The second charge is that theory of evolutionary epistemology with elements of falsificationism may be granted a status, which makes it immune to the very criticism it advocates with respect to every other theory:

> There are no reasons to believe that Popper's critical theory is criticizable, from which it follows that Popper's theory of rationality, that made criticizability a condition of rational acceptance of a theory in science, and which denied such status to Marxism and psychoanalytical theories, turns out to be guilty of the same sin, is not distinguishable from them in this regard, and as a result, according to its own requirements, has to be – like them – rejected. (Chmielewski, 1995: 229)

This double trouble with relativism has been a permanent companion of contemporary philosophy of science. Apparent incompatibility of a theory of scientific rationality (the logic of scientific discovery based on falsificationism) and of a theory of sociocultural evolution (objective, or rather intersubjective knowledge based on evolutionary epistemology) is one of the more recent, Popperian, cases in point. One of the Polish critics of Popper, Adam Chmielewski, elegantly expresses his view on this incompatibility by defining it as Popperian attempt to harmonize Platonic vision of superior methodology of acquiring (scientific) knowledge with Darwinian vision of a superior reconstruction of the origins of evolving life, changing societies and developing knowledge. Complex societies deal with this danger of relativism by establishing formal procedures rather than imposing content-bound core dogmas. Some of the ambiguities can, indeed, be procedurally decided upon in a formal way. On December 20, 2005, the US court decided that the theory of intelligent design does not have a scientific status and should not be part of a biological curriculum in public schools. Religious motivation of the followers of the theory of intelligent design had been quoted in justification of the ruling. What would have been the outcome if Muslim complaint about Danish cartoons did result in the court case in Viborg?

Pursuing the flawed rationalism of scientific communities (scientific rationality is supposedly based on logic, empiricism and falsificationism, but their clustering and applications evolve), one wonders what would be the community of knowledge, which could discuss the Danish cartoon incident as a relatively impartial third party equally acceptable to the Danish imams and Danish cartoon artists, Irish Catholics and Arab Muslims alike? Fuller quotes Popper as trying to persuade scientists to sign a version of the Hippocratic Oath in order to diminish harm they could inflict on mankind (as suppliers of military industrial complexes) and Feyerabend as suggesting 'devolution of science funding from nation-states to local communities' (Fuller, 2003: 213). These suggestions would indicate a necessity to search for methods of influencing, managing and embedding academic communities. However, followers of Popper and Feyerabend, or of Lakatos and Toulmin (to mention just some of the authors, who had contributed to the growing literature on principled behaviour in spite of relativist shadow) do not seem to share their masters' ambitions to act as public intellectuals. Kuhn had been conspicuously silent after the Popper–Kuhn debate and stayed away from public intellectual's platforms and media. Feyerabend did not, but remained an *enfant terrible* of a relatively narrow academic circle of post-Popperian philosophers of science and some postmodernists. Perhaps politicians and human rights activists could form a panel for cases like the one involving cartoons to defuse its latent terrorist potential? Agnes van Ardenne quotes actually existing networks of entrepreneurs, human rights activists,

politicians, business people, intellectuals and media people, who come together in temporary projects (she quotes an anti-HIV virus campaign launched in Yemen's capital Sana) or who are selected as laureates of an annual 'freedom award' (she mentions the one granted by the Dutch city of Middleburg). Would a panel composed of people from diverse religious, ethnic, professional, gender and age groups offer sufficient neutrality and command sufficient authority to be considered binding by the involved parties? These are pragmatic questions, but answers to both political (how to manage reconciliation of offences and neutralization of inequalities) and cognitive (how to arrive at acceptable and critically legitimized knowledge about cross-cultural construction of social realities) questions depend on our ability to extend our cross-cultural competence to embrace 'otherness' and heterogeneity, which had been doomed to exclusion in previous rounds of conflicts, clashes and incidents. In networking social spaces one has to remember about including those which had been systematically neglected. The latter include predominantly ethnically and religiously 'different' (different, that is, from the former working classes, which consisted mostly of peasants migrating to industrial cities) underclasses of EU urban centres. Immigrant labour filled the gaps in urban spaces and the social care system left by upwardly mobile working class; but cannot fit into the same channels of upward mobility and does not have the resources to oppose dismantling of welfare state (whose former beneficiaries, working classes, moved up to the middle class and do not oppose it strongly enough either). Can management of secular and religious identities facilitate integration by a promise of palpable upward mobility? Tracing social life of political values we should not forget those values, which may lead clandestine existence as religious ones and thus remain in need of cultural, political and managerial translation, or do so in ways we do not 'officially' acknowledge or respond to. In both cases, we need a new approach to the interparadigmatic, intercultural and interdisciplinary translation, which can be accomplished:

> by stretching the idea of 'translation' from the merely linguistic to the broader cultural level. This is a decisive but still enigmatic task, one that involves acknowledging certain impossibilities ('nontranslatable' ideas and forms) and looking for equivalences; scientific, literary, legal and religious 'universals'. (Balibar, 2004: 235)

Thus having started with the idea of translation as a crucial 'link' in the socio-cultural evolution (the Arab input into the European Renaissance), which transmits 'memes' through time and space, we arrive at the idea of intercultural translation (which goes beyond linguistic equivalents) and a plea to embrace the Popperian search for universals in spite of empirical failure to rescue them from the shadow of relativism, as a much more ambitious and promising alternative to Kuhn's facile paradigmatic sectarianism. Let us repeat it once again. Social life of values is better served by Popperian ambiguities and incommensurabilities (which beg the question, but allow begging) than by Kuhnian enclosures (which question the beggars, but limit questioning). The threat of relativism looms large, but the agenda is less restrictive. Are our professional communities able to face this challenge of revived Popper and Feyerabend or will they fall back upon Kuhnian alibis?

REFERENCES

Balibar, Étienne (2004) *We, the People of Europe? Reflections on Transnational Citizenship*, Princeton: Princeton University Press.

Boje, David (2002) *Narrative Methods for Organizational and Communication Research*. London: Sage.

Byrne, R.W., Whiten, A. (eds) (1988) *Machiavellian Intelligence: Social Expertise and the Evolution of Intellect in Monkeys, Apes, and Humans*. Oxford: Oxford University Press.

Chmielewski, Adam (1995) *The Philosophy of Karl Popper. A Critical Analysis*, Acta Universitatis Wratislaviensis no. 1639, Wroclaw.

Colliot-Thélène, Catherine (1999) 'Carl Schmitt versus Max Weber: Juridical Rationality and Economic Rationality', in Chantal, Mouffe (ed.) *The Challenge of Carl Schmitt*, London: Verso.

Corning, Peter A. (2005) *Holistic Darwinism. Synergy, Cybernetics, and the Bioeconomics of Evolution*. Chicago: The University of Chicago Press.

Feyerabend, Paul (1975) *Against Method*. London: New Left Books.

Feyerabend, Paul (1979) *Science in a Free Society*. London: Verso.

Fuller, Steven (2000) *Thomas Kuhn. A Philosophical History for our Times*. Chicago: The University of Chicago Press.

Fuller, Steven (2003) *Kuhn vs. Popper. The Struggle for the Soul of Science*. Cambridge: Icon Books.

Gergen, Kenneth (1999) *An Invitation to Social Construction*. London: Sage.

Hussein, Abdirahman A. (2002) *Edwards Said. Criticism and Society*. London: Verso.

Jyllands Posten (February 18, 2006) in http://en.vikipedia.org/wiki/Jyllands-Posten_Muhammad_cartoons

Kunitzsch, P. (1974) *Der Almagest; die Syntaxis Mathematica des Claudius Ptolemaus in Arabisch-Lateinischer Überlieferung*. Wiesbaden: Otto Harrasowitz.

Magala, Slawomir (2005) *Cross Cultural Competence*. London: Routledge.

McCloskey, Deirdre (2006) *The Bourgeois Virtues. Ethics for an Age of Commerce*. Chicago: Chicago University Press.

Montgomery, Scott L. (2000) *Science in Translation. Movements of Knowledge Through Cultures and Time*. Chicago: Chicago University Press.

Mouffe, Chantal (ed.) (1999) *The Challenge of Carl Schmitt*. London: Verso.

Preuss, Ulrich K. (1999) 'Political order and democracy: Carl Schmitt and his influence', in Chantal, Mouffe (ed.) *The Challenge of Carl Schmitt*. London: Verso.

Rosenthal, F. (1975) *The Classical Heritage in Islam*. London: Routledge & Kegan Paul.

Said, Edward W. (2000) 'Opponents, audiences, constituencies and communities', in: Edward W. Said, *Reflections on Exile and Other Essays*. Cambridge, MA: Harvard University Press.

Sennett, Richard (2006) *The Culture of the New Capitalism*. New Haven: Princeton University Press.

Sontag, Susan (2001) *Where the Stress Falls. Essays*. New York: Farrar, Straus and Giroux.

Whiten, A., Byrne, R.W. (eds) (1997) *Machiavellian Intelligence II: Extensions and Evaluations*. Cambridge: Cambridge University Press.

Wilson, Edward O. (1998) *Consilience. The Unity of Knowledge*. London: Abacus.

Nurturing the Divide: Toward Maximizing the Value of Management Research from both Sides of the Atlantic

C. Marlena Fiol and Edward J. O'Connor

THE DIVIDE

The push-pull dynamic that seems to characterize the relations between N. American and European management scholars is fascinating – and dysfunctional. The Academy of Management (AoM) has attempted to be inclusive of non-N. American (e.g. European, the focus of this note) traditions by claiming to 'internationalize', while simultaneously holding tightly onto N. American research standards and norms. Europeans have responded on the one hand by increasing their membership in the AoM and linking their associations to the AoM, and on the other hand, by increasingly emphasizing in their associations all of the ways that their research is *not* like N. American research. On both sides, there is both a pull toward integration and a push for separation. We seem to be enmeshed in a no-win situation.

The Pull to internationalize the AoM and the Push against changing standards and norms

In his 1998 Presidential address to the AoM, Bill Starbuck projected (based on trends at the time) that more than half of the Academy's members would be living outside the United States within just a few years. To address this trend, the AoM leadership has attempted to become a global society by broadening participation in governance and editorial processes and by expanding its family of associations. For example, it belongs to the International Federation of Scholarly Associations of Management (IFSAM), a global organization explicitly aimed at fostering international cooperation. And the European Group for Organizational Studies (EGOS) and the European Academy of Management (EURAM) are a part of the AoM's 'family' of Associated Societies.

At its core, however, few doubt that the AoM remains solidly North American. The officers and the power structure of the academy and its journals are decidedly N. American. Twelve of the 15 Board members, all editors of the AoM's journals, and 72 of the 79 AoM Fellows are N. American! Many N. Americans view European management research as 'sloppy' café conversations, based on very little systematic data of any kind, which provides a strong motivation to push to keep United States standards firmly in place. Here's an example: Members of one of the divisions of the AoM recently received a questionnaire on the quality of journals that did not even include a European journal on the list!

It is hardly surprising that the number of new international members has not reached the 50% level Starbuck predicted in his 1998 address; out of the 16,151 AoM members in April of 2006, only about one-third live outside the United States. According to one informant, many members of the associated European conferences 'hate the AoM', but the AoM doesn't seem to notice, continuing to believe that it is, in fact, successfully 'internationalizing'.

Continued

The Push to differentiate European research and the Pull to legitimize it through N. American affiliations

At the same time, European scholars are pushing to differentiate their work from N. American research. According to informants, Europe's largest management associations were explicitly formed as a counterbalance to the AoM. As early as 1973, EGOS was founded as an intellectual antidote to N. American management theory and research, regarded by one EGOSian as 'second rate, managerialist, highly reductionist and with little grounding in the social sciences'.

More recently (2000), EURAM was formed, again explicitly to counter AoM's positivist perspective, and to foster a more eclectic European approach to research. Its journal, the *European Management Review*, has the ambition of being the journal of first choice for management scholars, especially drawing on untapped intellectual resources from outside of N.A. The *EMR-AMR* ('*European*' rather than what is often referred to as the '*American*' *Management Review*) contrarian symbolism is hard to miss!

The push for European differentiation has been as schizophrenic as AoM's pull for internationalization, however. There is no doubt that many would like Europe to develop its own distinctive orientation and research products – e.g. a distinct accreditation standard. At the same time, however, the European accreditation organization has recently negotiated a cooperative agreement with the N. American accreditation board (AACSB). And despite the desire to be different than the AoM and its standards, many seem pleased with the legitimacy that European associations may gain by attracting N. American participants.

ALL OF THIS IS NOT SURPRISING

In his research on the deep-rooted Israeli-Palestinian conflicts, Kelman (2001) described a negative interdependence between the identities of the groups, such that asserting one group's identity requires opposing the identity of the other. We have found a similar pattern of negative interdependence in other arenas of conflict (Fiol et al., 2006): In many cases each group's identity is actually defined by the fact that they are *not* the 'other'. Does this sound familiar?

Attempting to integrate conflicting groups into a single transcendent whole without first developing within each group a respected and secure sense of separateness will have predictable consequences: (1) Each group's own identity will be too threatened to acknowledge the value of the 'other', and (2) the potentially valuable unique contributions of each group are watered down through necessary compromises. In other words, premature integration will violate the core of both sides, leading to the schizophrenic push-pull dynamics we have described.

MUTUAL EXCHANGE AND COOPERATION RATHER THAN INTEGRATION

Integration is an over-rated concept that is not likely to get us what we want even if European and N. American associations were to become much more 'international'. Not surprisingly, dual-identity researchers (e.g. Gaertner et al., 1999) are beginning to provide empirical evidence that relations among groups with conflicting identities are likely to be more cooperative when each group maintains a strong and distinctive sense of its differentiated self along with a feeling of togetherness with the 'other', than when only the togetherness is emphasized.

This implies a way out of our push-pull dynamic that entails nurturing the distinctive differences of each group. It implies a celebration of what is uniquely American about the AoM, and a celebration of what is uniquely European about European associations. Most important, it requires a shift from a group identity based on 'who we are *not*', to a deep appreciation within each group of 'who we are' to successfully move down this path. European associations, such as EURAM, which were originally formed partially in opposition to the AoM, are beginning to establish their identity as unique and distinctive societies. From the perspective of dual identity theory, it is important for them to continue to nurture their own separateness and to fulfill their own distinctive needs before attempting to associate too closely with other groups.

We were told that when EGOS began, it was expressly intended to be an upscale management association for Europeans. N. Americans were allowed to present, but not to chair their sessions/tracks. According to some EGOSians, it is becoming more AoM-like with more Americans running tracks. From the perspective of dual identity theory, this is an unfortunate trend that does not nurture the differences that make each group unique.

Complete and lasting separation among the scholarly groups from both sides of the Atlantic is certainly not the desired end. However, to bring incompatible groups such as these together, they must first be pulled apart and strengthened separately. Steps leading to the needed separation and strengthening include:

1 Identify and loosen the schizophrenic connections that keep each group negatively tethered to the other (e.g. discourage self-definitions based on *not* being like 'them').
2 Promote and nourish the differentiated identity of each separate group (e.g. communicate and celebrate the impact on the field of the group's work; develop a clear and relevant measurement system for documenting the value of the work).
3 Promote a sense of belonging within each group (e.g. instill pride in belonging to one's own group; establish frequent meaningful contact among ingroup members; make membership in the group highly visible).

The ultimate objective is for European and N. American (as well as other) research communities to feel strength in their separate and distinct identities in order to then, simultaneously, feel a bond of commitment to a common research cause. To attempt integration and commonality before separating and strengthening is only likely to lead to more schizophrenic and highly dysfunctional behaviors. Only after finding our own separate and unique sources of strength can we honestly ask what it is that we can accomplish as a global research community that we cannot accomplish separately, and how those outcomes may be valuable for both (all) groups.

REFERENCES

Fiol, C.M., Pratt, M.G. and O'Connor, E.J. (2006) 'Towards a model of managing entrenched identity conflicts'. Working paper, University of Colorado-Denver.

Continued

Gaertner, S.L., Dovidio, J.F., Nier, J.A., Ward, C.M. and Banker, B.S. (1999) 'Across cultural divides: The value of a superordinate identity', in D.A. Prentice and D.T. Miller (eds) *Cultural Divides: Understanding and Overcoming Group Conflict*, New York: Russell Sage Foundation. pp. 173–212.

Kelman, H.C. (2001) 'The role of national identity in conflict resolution', in R.D. Ashmore, L. Jussim and D. Wilder (eds), *Social Identity, Intergroup Conflict, and Conflict Reduction* New York: Oxford University Press. pp. 187–212.

Humanist Organizational Studies: An Intersubjective Research Agenda for Open(-plan) Fieldwork

Hugo Letiche

An organizational studies that methodologically favors disengagement (in pursuit of objectivity), assumes instrumental reason (for instance via rational choice theory) and leads to an atomistic view of society (by focusing on the behavior of discrete agents), is anti-humanist because it makes human experiencing unthinkable. Organizational members and researchers surely have a measure of self-autonomy. Judgment, responsibility and purpose enter into their choices. An organizational studies that alienates the researcher, the researched, and the reader, from disclosure of their shared being-in-the-world does a fundamental disservice to co-operative co-evolution – that is, to organizing and organization. In this chapter I will focus on the complex social (human) constitution of meaning.

Humanism in the second half of the twentieth century was the bane of many critical thinkers because it had been a source of unearned claims and false optimism, and because it had often been used to avoid responsibility as well as to silence claims for justice. One of the most prominent of these critics, Julia Kristeva, has recently embraced the 'other concept of the human that is self-constituting, wherein transcendence is immanent ... [which] appeals to desire for sense(-making), is inseparable from pleasure ... and draws as well on the sublimity of culture as the brutality of passing to action'. She asserts that it is now the time for a re-new(ing) humanism, producing 'a new type of knowledge' (Kristeva, *Le Monde*, 18.11.2005). My effort will be to indicate – with Tzvetan Todorov and with mention of Avishai Margalit and Axel Honneth as key resources, what this could mean for organizational studies.

The goal is not to deny Deleuze's metaphysics and/or Luhamann's systemic autopoesis, but to explore a consciousness-based, research alternative.

Humanism, in effect, grounds its claims in the 'real' or 'bare life' of existence – that is, in the interaction between identity and action. This is currently framed in two very different ways: (i) as a dialectic between autonomy and structure, and (ii) as a product of incompleteness and indeterminacy. Humanism claims that nothing is more important than the 'real' or actual life. Experience and relationships are the primary stuff of existence and of consciousness. Anti-humanism supposedly replaces the existent with the ideal, thereby betraying concrete existence, diversity and emergent possibility. I will further enunciate each of the two humanist strategies, indicating what its answers to anti-humanist attack are and will work out what impetus is (potentially), thus to be given to organizational thought.

CIVIC HUMANISM, ETHICS AND ORGANIZATION

At the end of the twentieth century, we experienced in critical organizational studies an attitude of: 'If the answer is ethics, the question is wrong.' Corporate Social Responsibility flourished as national governmental irresponsibility grew. The state abandoned as much as it could: responsibility for welfare, healthcare, education and full-employment. CSR developed in response to the social ethical vacuum, which threatened to leave society with too few motivated and committed citizens. A neo-liberal politics, attacking workers' rights and the position of the middle class, supposedly needed to be monitored by business ethics. But business ethics was long in rhetoric and check-lists, and short in results. Recall that a model business ethics case, meant to spotlight good practice, was written and taught based on Enron. Business ethics seems to inure employees to all real considerations of personal responsibility. Rules replace awareness, authority overmasters situational response and black-white thinking predominates. CSR's dubious relationship to social or political justice has made its role highly ambiguous. But, as belief in history, social truth, or progress has receded, ethics has remained as a (lonely) potential critical resource.

Twentieth-century humanism created an epistemic space for the absolute, the good and the ideal – in effect, the reign of profane metaphysics. In the place of the Christian God, there was the 'new man'. But this sort of idealistic humanism did not survive the twentieth century; it died in the concentration camps and the gulag. Humanity as its own absolute, which could and ought to transcend the real into the ideal, was renounced once the terror was understood. But, twenty-first century humanism threatens to offer little more than bodily survival – or a minimalist agenda of eking out a livelihood and of conformist 'pleasures'. Humanity no longer dares to claim to want to invent itself. Past historical failures have led to a loss of will. Human uniqueness no longer drives artists or politicians to self-flourishing, transcendence, or the embrace of the *surhomme*. The space of humanist volunteerism has been contaminated by totalitarianism. Humanism no longer dares to have a program of its own. For some, humanism has become an escape into the mediocrity, complacency and fear of consumerist society (Badiou, 2005a). It is claimed that a reductionist humanism has taken over and has prevailed – one that destroys ambition and purpose. This pseudo-humanism is – for idealists – ethically abhorrent; a mirror image of disenchanted consumerism and performative rationality. But are not 'cathedrals of consumption' better than the goulag (Ritzer, 1999)?

Civic humanism was not strong enough during the twentieth century to prevent exploitation, humiliation and warfare. Civic humanism is grounded in the assumption that everyone 'has the right to rights', or ought to belong to a community capable of providing him or her with citizenship (Arendt, 1973). The right of belonging to a human collectivity is posited to be inherent and equated with one's very humanness. But while civic humanism may be grounded in a universal quality of the human, it can only manifest itself in specific collectivities, organizations and/or states. Between the universal and the specific, there has been an historical chasm (Benhabib, 2004). Organized human community supposedly protects persons from barbarism by insuring a minimum level of civility. The assumption is that 'we can produce equality (of rights) through organization' (Arendt, in Benhabib, 2000). The person is protected from injustice, violence and wanton injury by the collectivity or nation. Basic respect for the human other is supposedly organized by the state and its institutions. But during the twentieth century, this assumption repeatedly broke down. Civic humanism unto itself proved no match for racism, extreme nationalism or totalitarianism. Other sources of humanism may be stronger and they may lead to civic humanism. Self-conscious particular involvement, in shared commitment and relationship as found in the poetic (love) and ethical (civic), comes to mind.

HUMANISM, *TECHNIK* AND EXISTENCE

There are, I am arguing, two strands to contemporary humanism: (i) one grounded in the assumed autonomy of the subject, and (ii) one fashioned around intersubjectivity and the experience of (an)other. Both aim at civic humanism, meaning thereby a (liberal) democratic effort at civility. For the first stream, the relationship to organization is paradoxical – organization is thought of as an 'iron cage' that endangers independence and self-sufficiency. But autonomy of choice-making and the freedom to define one's own life project require a complex, differentiated and wealthy society made possible by organizational (hyper)performativity. The argument for autonomy often tries to put its dependence on highly developed social and economic organization into abjection.

A polarity is assumed between 'autonomy' and 'social technology' while contemporary 'autonomy' really assumes very complex 'social technology' to be able to exist. 'Technik' forms the aporia of such autonomy thinking. For the second stream, the fear of repressive conformism, hyper-consumerism and authoritarian essentialism, all feed into the mistrust of organization. But the polyphony, dialogism and intersubjectivity it celebrates, is also a form of organization. Humanist intersubjectivity is most often (see below) not grounded in universal principles of the social, or in an ethics of political rights, but in 'one-on-one' relationship(s). Humanist intersubjectivity is conceived to be a consequence of successful self/other relationship(s). Such a humanism entails a theory of (anti)organization – that is, it entails fundamental assumptions about the possibilities of self and (an)other wherein 'organization' is mostly defined as the anti-pole of those possibilities.

Humanism, in effect, entails philosophical anthropology. Humanism assumes that we are capable of knowing about our own nature, and that this knowledge can and/or ought to be crucial for our actions. But assertions that we cannot jump over our own shadow (Arendt, 1958; Heidegger, 1980), or that the part cannot be the master of the whole (Capra, 1984), or that ideas must not be allowed to overwhelm experience (Husserl, 1970), point to the limits of such humanist knowing. Organization as blueprinted and implemented structure, wherein people are identified with shared interests or purposes, supposedly threatens to replace lived interaction with (pseudo-)rational goals and (oppressive) controls. Supplanting free or indeterminate intersubjectivity with rule-governed structure may be economically efficient, but it does not further one's experience of being-with-the-other. The opposition of phenomenal awareness versus critical reason is unsolvable. Making existential awareness into a counter-move for *technik* wherein what organization (or society) calls 'freedom' is really 'exploitation', and 'justice' is mostly 'privilege' and 'welfare' is a synonym for 'bureaucracy', imprisons daily existence in an unending conflict (Heidegger, 1982). But admittedly, Heidegger's fear of *technik*, and specifically that human being or *dasein* can become lost or endangered in it, may be quite accurate. *Technik*, translated into organizational terms, produces the image of the organization organizing organization, in a closed rational system that makes shared human existence irrelevant. Organization is then thought of as uninhabited by flesh and blood individuals and as anonymous and predictable. Supposedly there is no authentic self in *technik* – no existential awareness, no critical reflexivity, no space for emergence. But can a hegemony of *technik* really exist – isn't it a (anti-)chimera of materialist and mechanistic metaphysics? If it is to honor intersubjectivity and openness in practice, humanism must not become the anti-*technik* pole of a dualist metaphysics.

Humanism asserts the criticality of consciousness. But is it a consciousness that stresses individual choice at the cost of collective values, or one of intersubjectivity, co-authorship and co-evolution? While Hegel could believe that self and world, or reason and culture, could be profoundly complementary, contemporary thought stresses conflict, disputed territory and conceptual disconnects. These schisms are political – they lead to separate universes of the private and public, authentic and performative, intersubjective and autonomous. And they inevitably determine differing theories of organization.

The two competing humanisms strive for hegemony. One is the humanism of individual autonomy leading to neo-liberal hyper-competitivity; and the other is the humanism of the social constitution of relationships. Both claim to lead to (liberal) democracy; but in the one, individualism reigns and in the other, shared-community. Qua organizational studies, the primacy of autonomy leads (perhaps paradoxically) to the 'audit culture' wherein individual achievement is measured, controlled and rewarded (Strathern, 2000). Constitutive or co-evolutionary humanism leads to 'emergent organization' wherein sense-making,

creativity and innovation (re)define action. The 'audit culture' measures achievement in terms of pre-set criteria, which are determined and unwavering. Contrastingly, emergent organization follows the logic of constant change, technological as well as social, wherein renewal and coherence are continuous and ongoing processes. Organizational studies is increasingly forced, in theory and in practice, to choose between these two. Mainstream management studies celebrates strategy, choice and decision making – the rational autonomy of management is emphasized. Critical management studies stresses relationship, ethics and indeterminacy – emergence, coherence and connection are attended to.

RELATIONSHIP AND HUMANISM

Within humanism, the balance between autonomy or self-design and openness-to-the-other, is hotly debated. There are two very different humanistic logics in circulation. One is defined in terms of 'negative freedom' or freedom 'from', and the other is defined in terms of 'positive freedom' or freedom 'to'. The classical text identified with the first is *On Liberty* by John Stuart Mill; Nietzsche is the outspoken source for the second. The two strands are more oppositional than complementary. The first is more Anglo-Saxon and the second (continental) European. Kwame Anthony Appiah and Arthur Kleinman represent the first; Tzvetan Todorov and Axel Honneth, the second (Appiah, 2005; Kleinman, 2006; Tordorov, 2002; Honneth, 1991, 1995). Autonomy in the first tradition is an 'empty concept' – it is a space to be filled-in by the individual. In the second approach, the self is constitutive and grounded in social ethical event(s).

Appiah assumes that how the person gives meaning to circumstance, and takes action in the world, defines autonomy. Individual choice and sense-making are the crux of the matter. Humanism is a form of individualism. In *What Really Matters,* Kleinman investigates basic human decency

(Kleinman, 2006). For instance, he describes betrayal, humiliation and opportunism as characteristics of modern Chinese society and focuses on how an individual can resist, persist and retain, dignity. In another chapter, he explores the personal integrity and decency of an aid worker in Africa. And, he also reflects on a Protestant minister whose repeated experiences of intense pain help him to blot out (unwanted) sexual fantasies. Thus, individuals can make human moral statements in their thoughts and actions, but no group, organization or society is influenced. Kleinman celebrates individual worth and autonomy in a world wherein organization is at best neutral and more often destructive. Likewise, much 'critical management studies' celebrates autonomy and chastises organization in the tradition of Michels (organizational logic inevitably perverts 'ideals'), and Weber (organization is identified with the 'iron cage' of bureaucracy) (Parker, 2002). In contrast, Todorov maintains that humanism is not an individualism but an intersubjective theory, wherein co-evolution (organization) is a positive value. Ideas influence societies; personal choices organize (present and future) events. It is this tradition, wherein self and organization are not opposed, which I will explore further.

In both the autonomy and intersubjective tradition of humanism, relationships between circumstance and awareness, event and self, action and reflection, play a key role. Humanism refers to the experiencing subject and to (her or his) consciousness. In the intersubjective tradition, relationships between self, other and culture are explored as constitutive of knowledge, identity and organization. All awareness of the world presents itself (and/or has presented itself) to consciousness. Knowledge inherently entails at least two elements – (i) that which presents itself (world), and (ii) that to which it has been presented (or consciousness). Human consciousness has no third external position from which it can observe this process – it remains consciousness attempting to be conscious of world, and (perhaps also) of consciousness. Philosophy and other self-reflexive cultural

products come as close to defining a third position as is possible. It is inherent to the human – that is to consciousness, that it cannot know about the 'world' and about itself all at once. Heidegger's insight was that it is much more 'natural' for consciousnesses to know the 'world' than to seize upon itself. Thus humanism is counter-intuitive when it focuses on the (social) processes of the knowing subject, rather than on the world to be known and/or acted upon. Prioritizing the knower rather than the known, emphasizes human consciousness rather than activity. And contemporary economic (hyper-) performativity wants no truck with consciousness or shared social processes; it emphasizes (the rewards of) business or organizational success. By emphasizing consciousness and human knowing, one pursues the humanist argument against *technik* and scientism. Thus, I must balance being ambivalently critical of, but deeply influenced by, the Heideggerian tradition. Humanism is a being-in-the-world where being-with-others has a fundamentally positive role to play. Heidegger's emphasis on existential experiencing is embraced, but his overwhelming fear of chatter and the other, as a source of inauthenticity, is not.

INTERSUBJECTIVE HUMANISM

Crucial contemporary resources for an intersubjective theory of humanism include Tzvetan Todorov, Axel Honneth and Avishai Margalit. Qua organizational studies, they define what I will call *open(-plan) fieldwork* (Spivak, 2003). 'Fieldwork' because experience, circumstance and interaction are crucial. 'Open-plan' because the research is open to the other, and is intended to open rationality (and research planning) to criticism. Todorov bases his description of humanism on a triptych: the autonomy of the *I*, the finality of the *You* and the universality of the *They* (Todorov, 2002). Herein an anthropology of sociability, a morality of cherishing others for themselves and a politics directed to autonomy and rights, are combined. 'Autonomy' here is a quality of relatedness and not of individualism.

The self, according to Todorov, is fluid, multiple and instable – the *I* is characterized by its social and communicative motility (Todorov, 1999a). The human is to be discovered in the particular – 'autonomy' characterizes quotidian concrete existence. Todorov's *I* owes a great deal to Heidegger – the self is 'thrown' – it discovers itself in world, relationship and event. A self in- and for-itself, makes little or no sense – there is a self, in so far as there is event, circumstance and interaction. Heidegger in *Being and Time* developed *dasein* (or the quality of throwness or being-in-the-world) as an existential and ultimately ontological investigation (Heidegger, 1962). On the existential (or ontic) level, Heidegger attended to the concept of care and to *mitsein*. *Mitsein*, or being-with-the-other, is Todorov's focus. The *I* or self, according to Todorov, has several crucial characteristics, all of which are developed, expressed and realized, in *mitsein*. The *I* is characterized by: (i) the capacity to change, (ii) the necessity to assume some situation or context, and (iii) the stream of consciousness. The individual alone, solitary and autarchic, is a myth. All three of the self's characteristics are developed, manifested and expressed in (social) relationship(s). But there is an independence of the self – that is, an 'autonomy' of experience, choice and awareness. The individual with a culturally, socially and circumstantially formed identity, is (partially) autonomous. No matter what one has done, one can (to some degree) change. Human existence is not pre-determined. The person can (re-)interpret her or his past, and undertake action. The human is born incomplete, partially unformed and inherently able to recast her or his fate. The person can act differently from what has been, or seems to be the most logical, or what was to be expected.

Todorov stresses the double identity of the human: individual and social; 'man has a double and contradictory ideal. Yet he can be happy only as unity' (Todorov, 2001b: 21). On the one hand, there is the noxious character of chatter and conformity, which all too often dominate communal life; and on the other hand, there is the will-to-exist, an energy and awareness that can make life deeply worthwhile. From Rousseau, Todorov borrows the distinction between *amour-propre* and *amour de soi* (Todorov, 2001b: 7). *Amour de soi* entails the will to exist or the innate passion for becoming, and the life-energy to take action. It is 'the sole passion natural to man … a primitive innate passion, which is anterior to every other and of which all others are in a sense only modifications' (Rouseau *Emile* quoted in Todorov, 2001: 8). But it is a passion that can only be fully realized in positive relationship to others. *Amour-propre* is a negative impulse of vanity, jealousy and consumerism – an *I* lost in social alienation. The *I* or *self* has existential resources (*amour de soi*) with which it relates to circumstances; but it always exists within a context. The *I* possesses relative and not absolute autonomy. Consciousness is consciousness of self and world, of I and other, and of circumstance and choice. This is the nature of the *autonomy of the I.*

The I <> You (or thou) relationship forms the crux of Todorov's analysis. As he makes clear in *Life in Common*, this is a formative and constitutive social-psychological relationship (Todorov, 2001a). In addition to the *amour-propre* and *amour de soi* there is a third factor, i.e. *consideration* (or recognition) – which is what Heidegger called 'care'. It gives rise to innate human sociability. Humans owe their very existence to others, as they are born in a condition of inborn insufficiency. Of course the baby depends on feeding and physical attention, but from the youngest of ages, babies seek the gaze of the other. The baby wants to be recognized, acknowledged and seen. The human *I* exists from the beginning outside of the self, in relationship(s) of see-er and seen. Recognition, as (the young) Hegel understood, is existentially fundamental. The human is always at least two in number. But the *I/other* relationship is structured according to Todorov in a polymorphic dyad of love, and not in one of (master/slave) conflict (Todorov, 2001a). There are no isolated individuals. First there is sociability, interaction and development; then there is self-awareness and self(-identity). The psychology – for instance, of Freud – that departs from basic innate drives that precede sociability, is ideologically individualistic and empirically inaccurate. Being-with-the-other or *mistein,* is prior to self(-consciousness).

Todorov thus assumes an intersubjective anthropology in the tradition(s) of René Girard, Ludwig Feuerbach, Martin Buber, Mikhail Bakhtin, Emmanuel Levinas and Jürgen Habermas (Todorov, 2001a: 38). The self internalizes dealings and interactions; the self becomes subject in inter-relationship. Todorov stresses the crucial import herein of love – human identity is constituted in the meeting of concrete, specific and particular voices. The *I* does not exist without the *You* – and it is a *You* that is an actual tangible other (Todorov, 2001a).

Todorov differentiates between the generalized *You* of citizenship, the marketplace or of politics, and the specific *You* of formative personal relationship. Love entails singular beings who are not interchangeable; one cannot simply replace one love object with another. The unicity of the care relationship, in the regard of love, is essential. In the *I <> You* relationship there is human existential specificity. Love is not about equality, rights, welfare or other generalizable things. In love the other is the ultimate end. Love involves a gaze of attachment and of care. In love – that is, in intimacy, fellowship and friendship – the human relationship is valued for itself. Thus, the 'finality of the you'. The *You* is, unique, distinctive, inimitable and irreplaceable (Todorov, 2002: 137). And, the *You* is formative – care, engagement and involvement create the interaction necessary for the self to exist. The self is a product of relationship and without the relationship there would be no self. The self sees itself thanks to and through the other; the self reflects on events and its role therein, because it is involved with others. The *I* is a possible foreground to the self-other relationship; without the relationship, there is no foreground. Love is the positive name for the constitutive relationship of the self. Without love there will be embittered egotistical behavior, autism and violent repression.

Thirdly, in Todorov's social anthropology there is the *universality of the they*. The *they* is the community – everything sedimented in language, culture and structure. The *they* is universal – it is the realm of generalizability, cosmopolitanism and knowledge. For Todorov the *autonomy of the I* and the *finality of the You* (Other) form the most important qualities to what is universal. The *they* of citizenship, science and public existence, must not be allowed to overshadow the private self, grounded in the *I <> You* relationship. Todorov's humanism focuses on horizontal transcendence. It is a theory of immediate relationship and of how the *I <> You* relationship is constitutive. Ethics as a force for respect, care and the enjoyment of existence, is grounded in immediate relationships in the gaze of *self <> other* recognition. Todorov aims to refute theories of *self <> world* dichotomy, wherein presumed conflict between the *I* and the *They* are the point of departure. He aims to replace the dualities of labor/capital, master/slave, individual/society, with a developmental model wherein the *self <> other* gaze of, relationship and mitsein, is constitutive of ethical relationship(s).

RECOGNITION AND ORGANIZATION(AL) RESEARCH

Todorov's humanism of the *I <> You <> They* relationship is obviously a theory of recognition. Axel Honneth has more explicitly than Todorov developed a social theoretical or critical theory of recognition (Honneth, 1991, 1995). Todorov has worked out a developmental framework of recognition; Honneth has attempted to define a conceptual framework in reaction to non-recognition or injustice. While Todorov traces how the self comes to horizontal transcendence, Honneth focuses on what is needed to achieve a critique of humiliation and disrespect. The two are obviously complementary, but Honneth develops a public theory of humanism grounded in the *They,* while Todorov's focus is on the generative quality of the *I <> You* relationship. To shed more light on organizational studies, let us assume Todorov and now focus on Honneth.

Honneth in his anthropology focuses on three principles: love, law and achievement. On the personal aggregation level, recognition is about care, respect, affection and mutuality. On the socio-moral level of singular subjects and their ethical constitution, the affective quality of experience is crucial. Here we find the power of intersubjective affirmation. In the relationship between persons and institutions, principles of political equality are crucial. The autonomous person wants to be recognized as possessing equal rights to all others. These rights include the legal procedural dimension, but also social-economic and cultural dimensions. The just distribution of full social and cultural membership is at issue.

Specifically we are confronted with the issue of achievement. Recognizing that human well-being is grounded in intersubjective recognition, how does one collectively, justly, organize acknowledgement? The value of the contribution of individuals to social welfare and well-being is hotly disputed. Who is under- or over- rewarded for her or his efforts and what should be done about it? Can we achieve participatory parity and should it be our goal? With many (for instance of immigrant background) poorly integrated, in (my Dutch or Honneth's German) society, is just recognition achievable, and if so how? While Todorov stays at a safe distance from concrete issues of (in-)justice, Honneth weighs in very close to the current social raw nerves. He asserts that the traditional metaphysics of political relationships – for instance, cast in terms of the proletariat versus capital – have become entirely inappropriate. Political ethics prioritizes what is collectively channeled and publicly organized, making private suffering invisible. The actual subjects of injustice are made faceless, expressionless and invisible. A public façade is created, which makes experienced anguish imperceptible. Injustice has come to exist only insofar as it can be collectivized and organized, bureaucratically addressed and

politically exploited. Social discourses of integrity and dignity are acknowledged; private ones are relentlessly repressed. Honneth questions what moral expectations are appropriate, irrespective of whether they are privately or publicly defined.

While Honneth's agenda is programatically radical, trying to open critical studies to attend to phenomenal social suffering and moral discontent wherever they may be found, he has not actually taken the next step and brought his work closer to experience. Undergone injustice, underlying normative expectations and (non-) recognition of identity claims, certainly requires portraying. Honneth's 'initial premise that the experience of a withdrawal of social recognition – of degradation and disrespect – must be at the center of a meaningful concept of socially caused suffering', is very persuasive (Fraser and Honneth, 2003: 132). It logically leads to studies of reification and domination that investigate the moral content of social interaction. Such a research agenda could be very powerful, just because it would work inductively, starting out with concrete feelings of humiliation and disrespect. The ethics would be immanent – that is, construing 'transcendence as a property of immanence itself' – staying, in the realm of 'horizontal transcendence' (Fraser and Honneth, 2003: 144). The (ill-)legitimacy of withheld recognition is a very compelling theme. Lacks in affirmation are enormously powerful. Put positively, networks of recognition require dialogic exchange and joint understanding to operate. Experiences of (social) (in-)justice always involve shared discourse, mutual visibility and communicative processes, all of which need to be studied.

Organizational studies can bring a new *différance* to its subject matter: by attending to the ethics of how self-representation is organized and by exploring the normativity of discursive relationships, while trying to open organization to alternative spaces of 'autonomy'. But the idea of research that predominates, avoids such fundamental issues and honors technocratic performativity and market success (Readings, 1996). Exploration of the immanent relations of alterity with their potential for (dis-)respect could renew the field. Beginning with Margalit's impassioned exploration of humiliation, one could study 'recognition' in more depth (Margalit, 1996). Following that on with Agamben's *homo sacer* – or the human reduced to raw physicality without rights, possessions or civil liberties, which further illuminates what is at issue here (Agamben, 1998). Denying the other's capacity to be free is very much with us – in terms of contemporary production processes, consumption practices and organizational principles. Humiliation rejects human beings as human and absolutely denies the *I <> You* relationship, wherein the seeing of human beings, as human, is immanent.

All too often leadership in contemporary society manifests itself as the bully who tries to obliterate the other's self-respect via an attack on his or her very possibility of self-identity. Humiliation tries to paralyze relationship by existentially threatening autonomy. Organizations and institutions do not love and they cannot become the antidotes to humiliation. But organizational norms of decency can try to prevent abuse: 'Humiliation is the extension of cruelty from the physical to the psychological realm of suffering. Humiliation is mental cruelty. A decent society must be committed not only to the eradication of physical cruelty in its institutions but also to the elimination of mental cruelty caused by those institutions' (Margalit, 1996: 85). The dynamic of mitsein grounded in the gaze of (mutual) recognition and the constitutive role of love, has the power to oppose humiliation. The humanist research agenda for organizational studies needs to attend to the dialectic of humiliation; that is to study the forces that initiate and support degradation, and those that prevent and oppose it. Such research is phenomenological – that is, close to events, persons and their relationships; and it is focused on horizontal transcendence – that is, on how relationships can construct meaningful identity and even joyful moments.

OPEN(-PLAN) FIELDWORK

Humanist organizational studies involves *open(-plan)field* studies and open(plan)*field-studies* – that is, *open-field* work (i.e. research that opens up a field of observation and reflection) and open *fieldwork* (i.e. ethnography undertaken without an hypothesis or 'openly'). On the one hand, it is dedicated to exploring *open-field* (versus closed-field) phenomena; and on the other, it is focused on *field-studies* (versus experimental or analytical-deductive research). Qua form, humanist organizational studies needs to be *essayist* ('essay/assay' or *essai*) which involves trial or try-out, and interpretative work in the critical examination of organizing. Research is *open-field,* in the sense that the researcher chooses for phenomenological and existential openness in the study of (an-)other. The *I <> You (thou)* engagement is *open-field* because researcher and researched are intersubjectively committed to (re-)defining their identity in relationship to one another. Who studies and what is studied are inherently (re-)interpreted, (re-)discovered and (re-)described in the *I <> thou* relationship. Neither the identity of the researcher nor of the researched can be pre-defined, pre-established or pre-determined in *I <> thou* relationship. Thus research is literally a process of (re-)searching relationships of identity, meaning and order. Such research entails planning to engage in *open-field* involvement, exploration and writing. In normal research, the research question stands central; in *open-field* research, the relationship(s) stand central.

Organizational research requires *fieldwork.* Organization happens in a shared (quasi-)open space wherein *I <> thou* and *they* are juxtaposed. Organization as *they* is a reification, but organizing only as *I <> thou* dyads underestimates the force of collective and historical structure(s). In fieldwork, situations or circumstances are studied wherein persons and their ideas count. As Todorov indicated, writers can voice the deep paradoxes between sociability and involvement, freedom and personal limits, the self and the other. Voice is possible, in the sense that persons in relationship to others (for instance, listeners, discussants and readers), can actually say things that are memorable, important and deeply worth thinking about. The unicity of the *I <> other* relationship is at its most powerful when it expresses lived dilemmas and does not lead to relativism. Unique events or moments of relationship retain the possibility of voicing the ideas and sentiments involved, and of revealing shared import. Fieldwork involves the exploration of a concrete situation and circumstance; any (adequate) account of an *I <> thou* relationship, describes the immanence or place and time of the interaction. Such places and times of relationship are instances of organization. Organization can thus be equated with instances of the *I <> thou* relationship.

Humanist organizational studies needs to reveal the foreground of the interaction and inter-relationship, as well as the background of its assumptions and pre-structures. In organizing there are always *I <> thou*'s, but they can be disrespectful, humiliating and destructive. Todorov examined the humanizing force of the I <> thou and not its destructive possibilities. Organizational studies needs to focus on the humanizing as well as dehumanizing dimensions of interaction and thus the need for Honneth and Margalit. A humanist organizational studies would make an ethical choice to further the potential(s) of the *I <> thou* relationship, which entails a very difficult philosophical and reflective process of defining just what 'positive potential(s)' might be possible. Given the prioritization of the *I <> thou* relationship, definitional exploration needs to reflect dialogic, polyphonic and inter-relational process(es).

The essay embodies the tentativeness and exploratory openness required by humanist organizational studies. Essayism invites open, discursive and heterogeneous reflection. Not only the content of the thought, but the social interaction of the thinking needs to be crucial to the research agenda. As Todorov has argued (in his analysis of Constant the theoretician of liberal democracy), the most radical and democratic openness to the other,

can threaten to paralyze the authorial 'I' in other-directedness, doubt and ambivalence. The commitment to another commits the researcher to serendipity, because one can not know where the process of investigation will lead. Fundamental openness leads to an open research plan, wherein thematization is a shared process. Such research strives for immanent mutual exploration, wherein the organization of the research epitomizes the assumptions made about organization. The research form thus illustrates the intended content, and the research process intends to exemplif the ethics adhered to.

REFERENCES

Agamben, G. (1998) *Homo Sacer*. Stanford: Stanford University Press.

Appiah, K.A. (2005) *The Ethics of Identity*. Princeton: Princeton University Press.

Arendt, H. (1958) *The Human Condition*. Chicago: University of Chicago Press.

Arendt, H. (1973) *The Origins of Totalitarianism*. New York: Harvest Books.

Badiou, A. (2005a) Le siècle Paris: Senil.

Badiou, A. (2005b) 'L'humiliation ordinaire' in *Le Monde*, 16.11.2005, p. 21.

Benhabib, S. (2000) *The Reluctant Modernism of Hannah Arendt*. Walnut Creek: Rowman & Littlefield.

Benhabib, S. (2004) *The Rights of Others*. Cambridge: Cambridge University Press.

Capra, Fritjof (1984) *The Turning Point*. New York: Bantam Books.

Faser, Nancy and Axrel Honneth (2003) *Redistribution or Recognition?* London: Verso.

Foucault, M. (1973) *The Order of Things*. New York: Vintage.

Foucault, M. (1977) *Language, Counter-Memory. Practice* Cornell: Cornell University Press.

Heidegger, M. (1962) *Being and Time*. New York: Harper Bros.

Heidegger, M. (1980) *An Introduction to Metaphysics*. New Haven, CT: Yale University Press.

Heidegger, M. (1982) *The Question Concerning Technology*. New York: Harper.

Honneth, A. (1991) *The Critique of Power*. Cambridge, MA: MIT Press.

Honneth, A. (1995) *The Struggle for Recognition*. Cambridge, MA: MIT Press.

Husserl, E. (1970) *Crisis of European Sciences*. Evanston, IL: Northwestern University Press.

Kleinman, A. (2006) *What Really Matters.* Oxford: Oxford University Press.

Kristeva, J. (1984) *Desire in Language: A Semiotic Approach to Literature and Art.* London: Blackwell.

Kristeva, J. (2005) 'Je vis avec ce désir de sortir de moi', *Le Monde*, Vendredi 18 November 2005. p. 12.

Kristeva, J. (1984) 'Place Names'. Trans. T. Gora, A. Jardine and L.S. Roudiez, in J. Kristeva, *Desire in Language: A Semiotic Approach to Literature and Art.* London: Blackwell.

Letiche, H. (2005) 'Ethics of Recognition: I <> you (thou) <> they' Paper presented at *ADERSE* 18–19 November Lyon France.

Lyotard, Jean-François (1979) *La Condition Postmodern.* Paris: Les Éditions de Minuit.

Margalit, A. (1996) *The Decent Society.* Cambridge, MA: Harvard University Press.

Margalit, A. (2002) *The Ethics of Memory.* Cambridge, MA: Harvard University Press.

Parker, M. (2002) *Against Management.* Cambridge: Polity Press.

Readings, B. (1996) *The University in Ruins.* Cambridge, MA: Harvard University Press.

Ritzer, G. (1999) *Enchanting a Disenchanted World.* Thousand Oaks, CA: Pine Forge Press.

Spivak, G.C. (2003) *Death of a Discipline.* New York: Columbia University Press.

Strathern, M. (2000) *Audit Cultures.* London: Routledge.

Todorov, T. (1977) *The Poetics of Prose.* Oxford: Basil Blackwell.

Todorov, T. (1982) *La Conquête de l'Amèrique.* Paris: Seuil. (*The Conquest of America,*1992, New York: HarperPerennial).

Todorov, T. (1993) *On Human Diversity.* Cambridge, MA: Harvard University Press.

Todorov, T. (1999a) *A Passion for Democracy.* New York: Algora.

Todorov, T. (1999b) *Facing the Extreme.* New York: Phoenix.

Todorov, T. (2001a) *Life in Common.* Lincoln: University of Nebraska Press.

Todorov, T. (2001b) *Frail Happiness.* University Park, PA: Pennsylvania State University Press.

Todorov, T. (2002) *The Imperfect Garden.* Princeton, NJ: Princeton University Press.

Todorov, T. (2003) *Hope and Memory.* London: Atlantic Books.

Todorov, T. (2005) *The New World Disorder.* Cambridge: Polity.

Feeding Marshmallows to Alligators: The Inherent Fragility of Human Organization

Robert Chia

This essay is prompted by reflections on the fragility and vulnerability of human organizational accomplishments in the face of nature as vividly illustrated by the devastation caused by Hurricane Katrina in 2005. Almost exactly a year before the Academy of Management (AOM) had held its annual conference in New Orleans, and this provided a serendipitous opportunity for the author to take off from the chandelier-lit hotel conference rooms of downtown New Orleans to the swampy wilds of the Mississippi delta in search of alligators: a respite from the increasing tedium of grand theorizing.

The watery emergence of primitive life forms from their natural and oftentimes inhospitable habitat tells an intriguing story of the triumph of organization far removed from the sanitized accounts often presented at prestigious management conferences: it documents the ongoing struggles of organisms to extricate themselves, adapt to, co-opt and occasionally break free (if only temporarily) from the material constraints of their immediate surroundings. The drama of life that unfolds in the wilds encapsulates well the inherent fragility of human organizational endeavours when confronted with extra-organizational forces like Hurricane Katrina. The artificiality and manifest feebleness of human forms of organization exemplified by the 'levees' used to protect the city of New Orleans, when confronted with the immanent forces of nature, is flippantly captured in the almost absurd imagery of *feeding marshmallows to alligators*: a bizarre and unforgettable experience for the author. Yet, this unlikely image captures succinctly the ever-present vulnerability of human accomplishments, and the enormous gulf that separates our feeble theoretical efforts from the stark reality of the ceaseless struggle required to shield our artificially created organizational order from the ever-present disruptive forces of nature.

One can study organization as a *fait accompli*, in its sanitized stable state, in the luxurious settings of downtown hotels in New Orleans: describing their attributes, analysing their characteristics, identifying their causal origins and speculating on their functional consequences. Alternatively one can up the ante: examine organization as a quintessentially human cultural achievement: a symbolic artefact sustained through language, discourse, actor meanings, social interactions and power relations. In both cases one studies the phenomenon of organization from the 'outside': from a detached researcher's point of view. One adopts an observer-led mode of explanation with its implied methodological individualism, its vocabulary of intentions, representations, rules, plans and laws that constitutes the operating discourse of the academic. This 'intellectualocentrism' (Bourdieu, 1990: 29) of the phenomenon of organization detracts from an intimate understanding of the ongoing practical struggles and the everyday coping strategies involved in wresting order and organization from the constant entropic tendencies of the natural environment. It obscures the problem of organizational emergence in the very movement in which it tries to offer it because it privileges the researcher's own desire for explanatory coherence over the immediate 'mindless'

(Dreyfus, 1991: 3) practical coping concerns of the organism/organization itself. Organizations like organisms *become* what they are.

To recover understanding of the latter, one must strive to abandon academic distance, immerse oneself in the organism's/organization's preoccupations and attempt to understand organizational emergence from within as it strives to survive by bootstrapping itself into independent existence from the oftentimes debilitating effects of its immediate circumstance: lifting itself up from the muck it finds itself in, enhancing its life chances, expanding its available degrees of freedom and its autonomy and ultimately securing its stability and identity. Economy and efficiency are thus built into the very fabric of organizational survival and not just a specific concern of modern organizations: organizational evolution is that process in which the utilization of the earth's resources by living matter is rendered progressively more efficient.

Human organization is a technology for appropriating nature's energy and putting it to service to enhance life chances and to expand our degrees of freedom. The taming of fire, the development of tools, oral language and then written inscriptions constitute the gradual progression of humans' systematic overcoming of their immediate environment. Whilst the history of civilizations is often presented as a tallying of the dynasties, governments, wars and cultural transformations that have taken place over this brief period, this is not the whole picture of human progress. Instead, the attainment of modern organizational life is fundamentally a story of how humans have slowly extricated themselves from a slaved-like dependence on their immediate environment by developing more and more sophisticated tools and systems in order to more efficiently exploit the latter for our benefit. *It is this human ingenuity for devising techniques and mechanisms for trapping, conserving, retrieving and productively utilising energy and resources to secure and enhance our own level of existence* (Sahlins, 1960) that constitutes what we mean here by the phenomenon of ORGANIZATION. Yet, as we have been starkly reminded by catastrophes such as Hurricane Katrina, such human organizational accomplishments are never totally secure: they remain precariously balanced, perpetually in tension and irretrievably incomplete.

REFERENCES

Bourdieu, P. (1990) *The Logic of Practice*. Stanford, CA: Stanford University Press.
Dreyfus, H. (1991) *Being-in-the-World*. Cambridge, MA: MIT Press.
Sahlins, M.D. (1960) 'Evolution: Specific and general', in Sahlins, M.D. and Service E.R. (eds), Evolution and Culture. Ann Arbor, MI: University of Michigan Press.

The Rise of Cartesian Dualism and Marketization in Academia

Mustafa F. Özbilgin and Myrtle P. Bell

Processes of academic employment and production appear at first sight to be characterized by Cartesian dualism, the separation of body and mind. The traditional image of the scholar, one whose work processes are shrouded in science, whose body is draped in an institutional gown, posing seated in close proximity to his or her own works of scholarship is no longer. This image is now replaced by a disembodied figure whose physical appearance (body) is no longer strongly regulated, but whose academic work (mind) is dissected to its bare elements, crudely categorized along lines of Research, Administration, Teaching and Supervision.

Through several decades, economic liberalization of education has allowed for market logics to enter into processes of academic work, where such work is distilled into its basic components, graded, performance assessed and essentially me(r)chan(d)ized. The introduction of stakeholder perspectives, which meant that students, parents and prospective employers' views are invited to shape the processes of employment and production in academia, increased the marketization of its processes and products. This has brought about a sense of vulgarization as the barrier between the scholarly and the folk ways of knowing has eroded, in efforts to make 'scholarship' accessible to more people. This marketization has surreptitiously crept in and taken root in academic establishments without facing significant resistance.

In another paradox, the sense of hierarchical organization is also entrenched in the inter-generational and inter-sectional organization of work: while senior academics are over-stretched in holding key academic posts, aspiring junior scholars are kept at arm's length. Although women, racial and ethnic minorities, people with disabilities and sexual minorities have sought access and have been allowed in increasing numbers to academic posts (partly due to the decline in pay and conditions) these groups are still afforded limited access and remain under-represented in prized posts and in highly rated academic institutions. In the absence of effective mechanisms to challenge overt and subtle forms of discrimination and exclusion in the ambivalent processes of academia, these groups remain outside the inner circle. 'Mainstream' work in carefully proscribed and highly rated outlets is required in order for a scholar to obtain key positions and earn tenure, effectively silencing marginal interests and inquiry of 'non-traditional' academics and further compromising scientific inquiry. Multiple, lengthy revisions and long time to press in the frenetic pace of obtaining tenure often shift focus from scientific inquiry and pursuit of knowledge to obtaining acceptance of an article.

We argue that this apparent division of body and mind and its allied processes of marketization in academic employment are neither sustainable nor desirable developments. Indeed, they crudely commodify knowledge and constrain academic bodies through intensified work processes. Academic workers are alienated from traditional pursuits of scientific knowledge and of developing individuals and their faculties of scientific inquiry. These critical pursuits have been replaced with mass production of graduates whose key gain in the process of academic education is stunted at the level of mere vocational skills.

Universities have a history and assumed role in liberating individuals from common wisdom, and in upholding ideas of equality, justice and fairness in pursuit of better social and economic futures. However, the academic establishment has not been very successful in protecting its own interests. Only by recourse to the self-reflective, autonomous, transformative and revolutionary character of universities and of scholarship will it be possible to challenge the insidious patterns of marketization, intensification and vulgarization of work and production in academia.

Symbolic Value Creation

Davide Ravasi and Violina Rindova

INTRODUCTION

Scholars working in areas as diverse as business history (e.g. McKendrick, et al., 1982; Williams, 1982), sociology (e.g. Bourdieu, 1984; du Gay, 1997), anthropology (e.g. Belk, 1985; McCracken, 1988), and consumer behavior (e.g. Holbrook and Hirschman, 1982; Holt, 1998) have documented that consumers are increasingly purchasing goods not only for their practical functions, but also for their meanings. Acts of purchase and consumption reflect proactive efforts to claim a position in the system of social relationships by changing the characteristics of the artifacts that surround, support and often mediate human interactions. In other words, for consumers goods are symbols, the possession and use of which reflect, express, and reconstitute the system of social relationships and their perceived place in it.

Strategy researchers, however, remain inattentive to the symbolic side of exchanges. Extant theories advise firms to create value by improving product performance often along pre-determined dimensions of functionality, such as speed, precision, size, or endurance. They remain silent about how firms can produce goods that consumers desire for their symbolic value. In other words, extant theories tend to advise firms how to make better widgets – insert your favorite industrial age product here – while consumers are increasingly buying dreams, hopes, fantasies … and symbols.

The symbolic value of a product is *determined by the social and cultural meanings associated with it that enable consumers to express individual and social identity through the product's purchase and use.* When a firm produces an object that carries a set of cultural meanings that consumers want to be associated with, symbolic value is created. To create such objects a firm must be able to understand the cultural meanings associated with different objects, to identify and select those that consumers may find attractive, and to embody them in a new object. Whether symbolic value is created, however, ultimately depends on the inclusion of products in patterns of consumption and use. In other words, while firms may actively *try* to endow their products with attractive cultural meanings, there is no guarantee that their efforts will eventually produce the intended results.

To address the question of how firms can get better at performing their part in this delicate and unpredictable process, we draw on research in the sociology and anthropology of consumption, cultural studies, and semiotics, as well as on evidence collected in our own research. Our goal is to offer a cultural perspective on production that envisions firms as producers of culture. As such, firms have to become adept at locating their products in the web of meanings that defines a culture (Geertz, 1973).

SYMBOLIC CONSUMPTION

Consumer behaviorists use the term 'symbolic consumption' to describe the purchase and consumption of products for the purposes of social and self-expression defined as the communication of social and individual identity (McCracken, 1988; Hirschman and Holbrook, 1980). While they track early signs of symbolic consumption back to fifteenth-century England (Mukerji, 1983; McCracken, 1988), they locate the dramatic increase in symbolic consumption some time between the mid-eighteenth and mid-nineteenth century, as a result of 'the commercialization of fashion' (McKendrick et al., 1982). Josiah Wedgwood is credited with introduced marketing techniques to accelerate obsolescence and stimulate unprecedented growth in consumption. As a result, patterns in consumption changed, and

'what were once bought at the dictate of need, were now bought at the dictate of fashion. What were once bought for life, might now be bought several times over (McKendrick et al., 1982: i).

In today's affluent societies, consumption increasingly performs a communication function, and an expanding range of products including clothing (Hedbige, 1979; Crane, 2000), transportation, food and beverages (Bourdieu, 1984), house furnishings (Csikszentmihalyi and Rochberg-Halton, 1981), adornment and pets (Belk, 1988), and, more recently, even sports events (Hopkinson and Pujari, 1999) and consumer electronics

(du Gay et al., 1997), are consumed as means for expressing personal and social identity. According to anthropologist of consumption Grant McCracken:

consumption is shaped, driven, and constrained at every point by cultural considerations. The system of design and production that creates consumer goods is an entirely cultural enterprise. The consumer goods on which the consumer lavishes time, attention, and income are charged with cultural meaning. Consumers use this meaning to entirely cultural purposes. They use the meaning of consumer goods to express cultural categories and principles, cultivate ideals, create and sustain lifestyles, construct notions of the self, and create (and survive) social change. Consumption is thoroughly cultural in character (McCracken, 1988: xi).

'SYMBOLIC PRODUCTION': A NEW MARKET TREND?

The growing importance of symbolic consumption in modern consumer culture has led to an impressive growth in the number and size of companies that produce products with a highly expressive content, which we refer to as 'symbolic production'. Symbolic production has obviously always been central to the success of manufacturers of clothes and accessories, such as Armani, Diesel, Levi's, Swatch, or Swarovski, because clothing has always been used to decorate one's body and to express social identity (McCracken, 1988: 57–70; Davis, 1992: 15–17; Crane, 2000) and signal social status (Veblen, 1899; König, 1973).

In recent years, however, issues of expressive potential of products have gained increasing relevance also in industries where firms have traditionally competed on technological performance, price, or convenience. For example, while the value of electric and electronic appliances, such as refrigerators, toasters, computers, phones, and music players, has traditionally been viewed as based almost entirely on the quality and innovativeness of the underlying technologies, in recent times, changes in cultural values and patterns of consumption seem to have created opportunities for rethinking about the role of technological objects in people's lives in affluent societies. Apple, Nokia, and Philips, among others, have built or reinforced their strategic positions in both niche and mass markets by altering the form, look, and feel of conventional electronics and household appliances, thereby changing the way consumers experience them and the associations they evoke (Ravasi and Lojacono, 2005). In doing so, these companies have converted products that are conventionally viewed as tools into personally meaningful objects – objects that consumers find interesting, engaging, and attractive, objects that consumers like to surround themselves with and to show off to others. In other words, they have created objects that enable consumers to make statements about identity, status, and their varied 'selves'. The case of Dutch conglomerate Philips illustrates this trend. Stefano Marzano, Chief Designer at Philips, explains the new philosophy guiding such design choices:

> In the past emphasis was on quantity: products were impressive for the number of functions, the number of gears or the number of programs. The car was judged on its speed, the stereo system for its volume, and so on. Perhaps because of this quantitative materialist approach, we have now reached the limits to growth (…) We should therefore make sure we create *relevant* objects (…) meaningful objects that represent memories, actualities and culture. (Marzano, 1998: 12–13)

Following this new design philosophy, in the last decade, Philips has introduced domestic and medical appliances, characterized by soft rounded lines, pastel colors, and velvet textured finishes. The new design communicates meanings of affection and domesticity, which enable consumers to engage in new interactions around the concept of 'home'. As a result, consumer perceptions of the company have changed and Philips is now seen as a producer of artful and meaningful objects, a trend-setter, and style maker. By providing consumers with new means for communication, companies like Philips create symbolic value and charge price premiums that reflect this different type of value-created.

Specialty retailers, such as Starbucks, The Body Shop, and Ben & Jerry use the design of the retail space to imbue their products with meanings that become part of the overall consumption experience, including subsequent product use. At Swedish furniture dealer Ikea, for instance, retail design is carefully used in order to enrich the experience of international customers and to influence their perceptions of the products. Everything in an Ikea store – from the yellow and blue corporate colors to the large wall pictures of the Swedish countryside, from the baby care centre to the internal cafeteria serving Swedish delicatessen – is carefully designed in order to emphasize the 'Swedishness' of the products and to embed them in a collective imagery of Nordic functionality and modesty, sober elegance and essentiality, ultimately increasing the symbolic appeal of what are often low-cost imitations of classics of Nordic industrial design. Relying on product design and labeling, on store ambiance and advertising, as well as on the social identity and interpersonal interaction styles of their employees, large retailers like Ikea increase the attractiveness of their products by providing consumers with opportunities to use consumption as means for self-expression.

The growing importance of this trend in terms of number of industries and firms that are seeking to engage consumers along the symbolic dimension of exchange can hardly be overlooked any longer by strategy research. They call for developing a deeper understanding of the processes of meaning making in markets, and the role that firms play in these processes. They also call for substantive theorizing about the capabilities required for firms to engage effectively in these processes and to deliver products with symbolic value. This may be a tall order for management research, given its traditional neglect of the consumer side of the value creation process (Ramirez, 1999) and the interpretative, meaning-oriented aspects of market interactions (Rindova and Fombrun, 1999). However, given the momentum that symbolic consumption is gaining in increasingly affluent, technologically-savvy, truly global, and culturally-eclectic markets around the world, we contend that understanding the dynamics of symbolic value creation may well be one of the main challenges facing our field in the twenty-first century. If our field is to preserve its touch with and its relevance to the changing marketplace, where issues of meaning are becoming as important, if not more important than functional and economic benefits, it needs to recognize that all firms producing for consumer markets, not just fashion retailers, movie makes, and publishers and music producers, are in fact in the business of cultural production and the creation of symbolic value.[1]

VALUE CREATION REVISITED

Economic theory defines *value created* as 'the difference between the value that resides in the finished good and the value that is sacrificed to produce the finished good' (Besanko et al., 1996: 447). The sacrificed value is determined by the producers' costs; the value that resides in the finished good is determined by the benefits perceived by final consumers. Besanko et al. (1996: 445) further note that 'competition among firms in a market can be thought of as a process whereby firms, through their prices and product attributes, submit consumer surplus 'bids' to consumers. Consumers then choose the firm that offers the greatest amount of consumer surplus.' In other words, the extent to which firms can create and capture value depends on how consumers perceive their 'bids', i.e. how consumers think and feel about their products.

Despite this recognition of the importance of consumer perceptions, strategy researchers tend to follow the assumptions of economic theory, which views consumer perceptions as idiosyncratic and exogenous, and therefore, generally under very limited control from the firm. Further, to the degree that consumer perceptions are considered, they are understood within a functionalist paradigm, which attributes product demand almost exclusively to functional advantages (see Brown and Eisenhardt, 1995 for a review) and links product advantages almost exclusively to the technological capabilities of firms.

Research in other branches of the social sciences, however, provides ample evidence of the value that consumers place not only on the practical usefulness of products, but also on what they mean to the owner. On the producer side, design scholars recognize that distinct design choices underlie a product's *utility*, that is 'the degree to which designs serve practical purposes and provide affordances or capabilities' (Heskett, 2002: 39), and the product's *significance* (Heskett, 2002). According to design historian John Heskett (2002: 40, italics added):

> 'Significance, as a concept in design, explains how forms assume meaning in the ways they are used, or the roles and meaning assigned to them, often becoming powerful symbols or icons in patterns of habit and ritual. In contrast to the emphasis on efficiency, significance has more to do with *expression* and *meaning*.'

The significance of a particular product to a particular consumer depends on a personal relationship of the latter with the product (Csikszentmihalyi and Rochberg-Halton, 1981). Products help individuals express and manifest their personal identity through the tangible objects they wear, use, or furnish their space with (Belk, 1985). Consumer behaviourists refer to these expected benefits as *self-expressive* (Aaker, 1996). Thus, symbolic value of an object for a particular consumer is determined by the fit between his or her self-concept and the set of meanings associated with the object.

While part of these meanings may be rooted in the users' personal history and experience (Sirgy, 1982), much of the way objects are interpreted depends on the attributes of a product as an object and the meanings that it evokes within a given cultural environment (Sahlins, 1976). As a result of this interplay between an object's form and the web of meanings that constitute a given culture, within which both consumers and producers are embedded, objects differ in their symbolic capacity. Symbolic capacity, we argue, is determined by the set of meanings that are both possible and likely to be ascribed to the product within a culture. Since these meanings in turn derive from the use of objects within a system of social relationships (Sahlins, 1976), the observable practices of product purchase, use, and display convey information to observers about the social identity and status of the product users. The symbolic capacity of a product is therefore defined by the extent to which it conveys meanings related to the social identity or status (McCracken, 1988; Davis, 1992). In sum, while some of the meanings consumers associate with a given product may be private and derived from idiosyncratic life experience (as in the case of products with sentimental value), many of the product's meanings are based on the cultural milieu, in which both consumers and producers are embedded. It is therefore possible, for producers to proactively select meanings that are important to consumers and associate these meanings with their products by strategically redesigning their form, and therefore the consumer experience of them.

Take the case of OtiKids – a line of flashy, colorful hearing aids that are strongly endorsed by several associations of parents of hearing impaired children. Until the advent of OtiKids in the mid nineties, behind-the-ear hearing aids were available only in a flesh color, which, despite the good intentions of designers to blend the device with the human body, had acquired cultural meanings associated with stigma. Far from being concealed against the skin color, the device was widely associated to physical handicap. The bright colors and translucent plastics of OtiKids made the device more visible, but gave it a 'playful character' which seemed to remove the negative cultural connotations. By altering some of the material properties of the object, the new design induced changes in the meaning associated to the object and reduced the psychological burden of its use for young users. While in their functional essence both glasses and hearing aids are devices aimed at compensating for some physical impairment, the design choices that constitute their form interact with the broader webs of cultural meanings in which consumers are embedded. As a result of such design choices, these differently styled and

shaped products acquire different meanings and thereby change their symbolic value to their users.

These examples, and the arguments we advanced so far, suggest that strategy scholars can develop a more comprehensive theory of how firms create value by recognizing that most products have the potential to offer consumers both functional and symbolic value, and that these dimensions may be related. The meanings that products acquire derive from their functions, but through the mediation of socially negotiated and agreed upon meanings that reflect the system of social and class relationships within which object circulate. Functionally equivalent products can have different symbolic capacities, depending on the meanings they evoke. Further, the meanings that products evoke appear to be influenced by the strategic choices of producers, such as design concepts and philosophies. A theory of value creation in management research, then, should address how the strategic choices of producers influence the symbolic capacity of their products, and ultimately their ability to create symbolic value. Table 2.6.1 summarizes the distinction we made in this section between functional and symbolic value creation.

TOWARD A THEORY OF SYMBOLIC VALUE CREATION

Our fundamental assertion is that the creation of symbolic value is a cultural production process (Hatch, 1993). As such, it includes the creation and dissemination of symbols and their assimilation in social practice (Hirschman, 1986) through a set of interrelated processes that link together five communities, among which meanings are created: lead cultures, producers, symbol creation experts (designers and advertisers), institutional intermediaries (media and critics), and consumers. As Figure 2.6.1 illustrates, the set of meanings that are eventually ascribed to an object and determine its symbolic value are collectively constructed in interaction among producers, consumers and other social

Table 2.6.1 Functional vs. symbolic side of products

Functional dimensions	Symbolic dimension
Functionality A set of technical properties of an object that determine its capacity to perform certain functions	**Symbolic capacity** A set of identity-related meanings ascribed to an object within a given cultural context (*semantic space*)
Functional value Congruence between the functionality of an object and a user's practical needs	**Symbolic value** Congruence between the symbolic capacity of an object and a user's self-concept
Functional value creation Rests primarily on technological innovation – i.e. improvements in the underlying technologies or in the way they are combined in product design	**Symbolic value creation** Rests primarily on signification – i.e. the purposeful attempt to imbue objects with meaning through the utterance of material signs (e.g. design) or verbal signs (e.g. advertising)

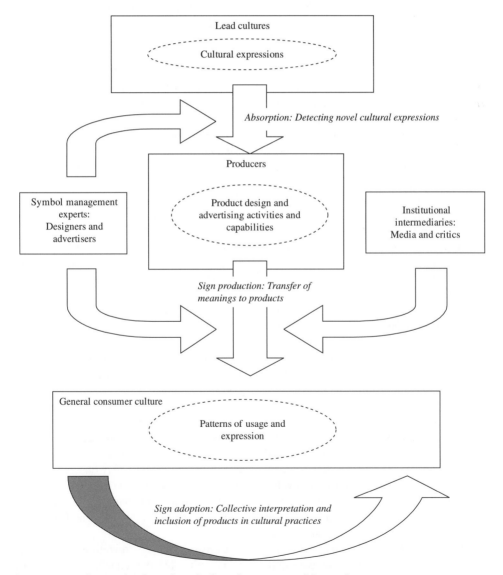

Figure 2.6.1 The production of symbolic value: communities and processes

actors in relation to the larger cultural and discursive context on which they draw to ascribe meanings to the objects they produce and use.

COMMUNITIES

Lead cultures. Lead cultures are subcultures that unite individuals who seek and develop common means to express opposition and/or distancing from the existing structure of social relationships. Examples of such sub-cultures were computer enthusiasts in the early 1970s, punks and Rastafarians in the 1970s (Hebdige, 1979), yuppies in the 1980s (Belk, 1986), skateboarders and surfers in the 1990s (Frank, 1997). Skateboarders, for instance, viewed themselves 'opposing' conservative America, and as persecuted by the police and conservative municipal bodies (Frank, 1997). Computer enthusiasts in the 1970s viewed themselves as opposing corporate America through their opposition to the mainframe computing paradigm.

We refer to these oppositional subcultures as 'lead cultures' because we believe that with regard to symbolic value creation they perform a role similar to that of 'lead users' for technological innovation. 'Lead users' are consumers who experience product needs ahead of the rest of the market and can provide firms with useful suggestions for product development (von Hippel, 1986). In a similar fashion, a lead culture is a community where certain social trends become visible ahead of the rest of the market. In their efforts to express cultural tensions, the members of these subcultures tend to develop a peculiar use of language and objects, the unique usage of which constitutes the subcultural style (Hebdige, 1979). In doing so, lead cultures become a potential source of new symbols, practices, gestures that they develop in order to express a discontinuity, a rupture from an existing culture (McCracken, 1988: 135–136). While many such subcultures exist, few become highly visible and affect general practices and patterns of consumption. Whether a subculture is more or less

prominent depends on the degree to which its interests and oppositional cultural stance come to reflect broader societal concerns with power structures (Holt, 2003, 2004).

Producers and experts. The second community engaged in the production of symbolic value creation is the community of *producers of goods and services*. Conventionally, this community is understood as possessing and using resources that create functional value, and not as a participant in a cultural process of influencing meanings. However, producer activities play an important role in the cultural production process because producers' efforts to offer innovative products with diverse appeals to consumers also generate the impetus for meanings to be revisited and reassigned to physical artifacts. *Product design and advertising* are two producer activities that play a central role in the process of symbolic value creation.

Because producers often lack the requisite capabilities to engage in these activities, they rely on a community of specialists, such as artists, industrial designers, graphic designers, and advertisers, who specialize in the creation of symbols. McCracken refers to these specialists as 'agents who gather ... meaning and accomplish its transfer (McCracken, 1988, 81)'. As experts in the creation and use of symbols, these actors have the ability to convert local, unique cultural forms into widely accepted social practices, and thus to introduce cultural innovations in broader markets (Wernick, 1991).

Although producers assisted by specialists in design and advertising seek to guide consumer choices, it is in the way that consumers choose to integrate products in their activities and to display them in various social interactions that the cultural meanings of products are constituted. As cultural sociologist du Gay observes: '... the processes of production only provide a series of possibilities that have to be realized in and through consumption' (du Gay et al., 1997, 59).

Consumers are therefore, the fourth community that participates in this cultural exchange. As we have observed earlier, consumers frequently use products to communicate identity and status. However, because the meaning of objects is determined within the system of social relationships and continuously renegotiated among consumers, it is only through the practices of consumption that the meaning of products – both new and old – is established and becomes available to other consumers. Therefore, consumers should be viewed as co-creators of symbolic value.

Institutional intermediaries. Finally, a community of critics and journalists intervenes in the cultural production process by affecting both product interpretations and producers' images and reputations (Rindova, et al., 2006), thereby affecting the meanings that are associated with them and their symbolic value. These information intermediaries have expert or institutional power to assert what constitutes value in a given market (Rindova and Fombrun, 1999). Reviews and comments of critics and fashion journalists can enrich or impoverish the symbolic content of goods, as their narratives may influence how the efforts of designers and advertisers are interpreted by consumers who are exposed to them (McCracken, 1986).[2]

PROCESSES

Absorption: Detecting novel cultural expressions. A producer that seeks to create symbolic value needs to develop a keen sense of the web of meanings that constitutes a society's culture. In order to do that, a producer needs to discover sources of new meanings that have the potential to become attractive to consumers as relevant for expressing their individual and social identities. As discussed, the tendency of subcultures to develop unique usage of symbols and artifacts makes of them 'lead cultures' offering a rich source of novel expressive forms (Hebdige, 1979). Further, to the degree that subcultures express tensions that may be more generally shared, their practices of expression – i.e. their style – may become attractive to broader

consumer groups. It is this possibility that producers who seek to increase the symbolic value of their products need to recognize, explore, and engage.

Some firms have access to a lead culture because they are founded by members of a subculture with the goal to produce artifacts that reflect the values of the culture. Nike, for instance, is known to have originated in the runners' culture and its early products were high-performance running shoes. Apple Computers, similarly, originated in the culture of computer enthusiasts in the 1970s and reflected their values, and their wish to give 'computing power to the people' (Belk and Tumbat, 2005). In the more general case, however, producers need to gain deep knowledge of the values, symbols, and practices of such cultures in order to appropriate effectively their expressive forms and meanings.

This is not an easy task, because the distance that subcultures establish from the dominant patterns of social relationships creates a barrier for outsiders, such as producers. Intense interaction with and possibly deep immersion in the subcultural milieu are required in order to truly appreciate its nuances and to recognize cultural changes in a timely fashion. For example, some companies rely on quasi-ethnographic marketing studies, during which marketing researchers 'live' in the lead culture of interest. Other companies engage in what has been termed an intense 'conversation' (Lester et al., 1998) with their customers, by inviting designers, product developers and marketers to plunge in the life and culture of the prospective users of their products. Fashion manufacturers such as Levi's and Diesel have pioneered this trend:

> For Levi's the notion of conversation with the consumer is more than just a metaphor. The company divides the market into age segments and assigns a designer to each segment. The designer is encouraged to become immersed in the segment's culture, to live the life of its members. She goes shopping at the stores where they shop, eats in their restaurants, dances in their clubs, listens to their radio stations, reads their magazines – all in an effort to pick up new trends. The conversation is extended into the company itself through meetings

at which designers discuss what they have seen and what they think it means, comparing developments in the lifestyles of different generations. (Lester et al., 1998: 91)

Designers' expertise in recognizing relationships between form and meaning can improve the ability of a firm to screen and interpret cultural trends and possibilities For example, Alessi, whose catalogue of kitchenware includes objects designed by the most prestigious and innovative architects and industrial designers of the last 30 years, periodically conducts socio-anthropological research coordinated by an internal research center called Centro Studi Alessi. Set up in 1990, Centro Studi Alessi coordinates work with young emerging designers and organizes workshops with industrial designers and social scientists, in collaboration with architecture faculties and schools of arts and design. These workshops are often connected with broader 'meta projects' like *Memory Container* (an anthropological inquiry into the archetypes of food presentation across cultures) or *Family Follows Fiction* (an investigation of the emotional, playful structure of objects). The expected outcome of this process is the acquisition of sufficient familiarity with the symbols of a culture and its practices (Alessi, 2001).

Regardless of the technique used to detect and investigate social and cultural trends, these are processes of deep learning about a society's tapestry of subcultures. We term this process *cultural absorption*. Its outcome is the development of an intended *cultural positioning*, defined as the specific stance an organization takes towards the web of meanings that define what products are and how they are used both functionally and symbolically.

Sign production: Transferring meanings to products. Once novel meanings and cultural expressions are discovered and selected, they need to be integrated with a firm's product. We refer to this process as *sign production* (Eco, 1976) to highlight the need for producers to create products that are going to be used as symbols and signs, i.e. as markers of identity, status, and social position.

As discussed, product design and advertising are two primary activities through which producers create relationships between their products and available cultural meanings.

Product design can be understood as the selection and combination of a number of elements into a whole to achieve a particular sensory effect (Lewalski, 1988). In doing so, it determines the formal properties of new objects and inscribes potential usage patterns on them, thereby enhancing the likelihood that the product will evoke certain meanings. According to du Gay and colleagues:

Design produces meaning through encoding artifacts with symbolic significance; it gives functional artifacts a symbolic form (...) The visual 'look' and tactile 'feel' of a product are crucial means of communicating with consumers, not simply about function of basic 'use' but simultaneously about identity and meaning. (du Gay et al., 1997: 62, 65)

As we illustrated in the OtiKids example above, design can change product meanings by inscribing different possible interactions between the consumers and the product through the use of color, shape, and style.

Like design, *advertising* is aimed at associating a set of meanings with a product and, in the process, at forging identification with certain subculture and lifestyle. Most advertising draws on a pool of existing images and conventions belonging to a collective cultural universe, in order to weave an appealing narrative about a focal product. According to sociologist of culture Andrew Wernick (1991), advertising endows a product with attractive *user imagery* – i.e. a representation of the ideal-typical user of the product – that increases the symbolic gratification gained by the purchase, possession or consumption of the object. Furthermore, advertising attaches meanings to products by providing examples of the *culturally specified social practices*, in which a product should be included, as well as the specific mode of inclusion (e.g. acting youthful when drinking Mountain Dew). While the meanings that can be embodied in a product's form and material texture through design are objectively constrained by the underlying technologies, advertising transfers meanings to products through the more flexible means of discourse about the product. As Wernick notes:

> Advertising transfers meanings on to a product from the outside, through repeated imagistic associations. Through design, on the other hand, that same signification is stamped on to it materially. (Wernick, 1991: 15)

Product design and advertising combine to endow a product with interesting, novel, attractive meanings, and make these meanings available to consumers for their self-expression or social signaling needs. In other words, the products so created become available as new *signs*, which consumers can choose to incorporate in their social interactions, thereby acknowledging that the sign function intended by producers is recognized and is used as such. Therefore, products acquire their 'true' meaning as signs when they are used by consumers as such and influence social relationships accordingly.

Sign adoption: Collective manipulation of the meanings of objects. Objects become effective signs only when actors use them as such and do so collectively. The meaning of objects emerges from the complex interplay of social interactions – spontaneous discovery of new uses, purposeful display of consumption to impress others, etc. – and from the reflection of these processes by various information and cultural intermediaries, such as the media, the works of writers and moviemakers, and the opinion forums of formal and informal opinion leaders.

Consumer behaviorist Elizabeth Hirschman and her colleagues elaborate on the process of social recognition of the product-signs created by producers. These authors argue that the meanings that are ultimately associated with products arise from a combination of purposefully developed texts about products, such as advertising or television programs, and the more tacit meanings embedded in practices grown around the consumption of a particular object in response to historical events such as its adoption by particular social groups (Hirschman et al., 1998). The first release of the Sony Walkman – the first portable tape recorder – for instance, was conceived for shared consumption of music among young consumers, and designed accordingly with two jack sockets for headphones. Early adopters, however, displayed an overwhelming individualistic use of the product as a form of 'escape' – isolating themselves on crowded and noisy public transportation – or 'enhancement' – using it to impose a personal soundtrack to their own environment – by a wider span of users than anticipated. Recognition of these emerging patterns of use brought Sony to reframe the visual imagery and design of the product, emphasizing individual rather than communal uses and trying to appeal to a higher number of potential users, resulting in over 700 different versions produced in the following years (du Gay et al., 1997).

How products are interpreted and evaluated by consumers is strongly influenced by a subset of consumers, known as *opinion leaders*, who by virtue of their visibility, popularity, standing or personal charisma influence trends in culture and lifestyle (Weiman, 1994). In addition, information intermediaries such as journalists and critics, intervene to regulate the exchanges between producers and consumers. McCracken (1988), for instance, highlights the fundamental role of the press in supporting the transfer of meaning from designers to consumers:

> The designer (…) depends on the consumer to supply the final act of association and effect the meaning transfer from world to good. But unlike the [advertising] agency director, the designer does not have the highly managed, rhetorical circumstances of the advertisement to encourage and direct his transfer. The designer cannot inform the consumer of the qualities intended for the good; these qualities must be self-evident in the object, so that the consumer can effect the meaning transfer for him/herself. Therefore it is necessary that the consumer have access to the same sources of information about new fashions in meaning that the designer has. The journalist makes this information available to the consumer so that s/he can identify the cultural significance of the physical properties of the product. (McCracken, 1986: 77)

Similarly, based on an in-depth study of the American fashion industry, strategy scholar Charles Fombrun (1996) concludes:

> Contrary to the romantic image, the establishment of a style involves far more than the creative output of a lone designer working. (…) Success comes to those designers more skillful than the rest at weaving a web of linkages among specialized players in the industry. Good relationships get press; press generates celebrity; celebrity fuels sales.

The reading of product-signs involves considerable degree of social influence. How consumers respond to a producer's products is influenced not only by how interesting, original, or potent expressive means the products offer, but also by the stance that other social actors, especially those with expert or charismatic power, take toward them. For example, sociologists of arts and culture have observed that critics actively influence the cultural inclusion or exclusion, and therefore, position of products framing them as 'in' or 'out', thereby affecting the longevity of their symbolic value (Hirsch, 1972; Becker, 1982; McCracken, 1988: 81–82). Therefore, the processes of social interactions through which product-signs are read are better understood as the co-creation of symbolic value through continuous communication and renegotiation of the meanings associated with products. While this process can be interpreted that the meaning of products is always in flux, and symbolic value is only fleeting, it also points to the possibility of stabilization of meanings and creation of lasting symbolic value around patterns of usage and display that stabilize (e.g. mobile phones as a fashion accessory that is increasingly displayed as watches and other luxury accessories are).

In this section, we described the process of creating symbolic value as a process of cultural production and exchange that unfolds among five communities who are linked by three processes: cultural absorption, production of signs, and adoption of signs. Our core argument is that the creation of symbolic value is a collective process that is outside the scope of activities of a single firm; yet, the activities of firms, and in particular their design and advertising activities play an important role in generating and shaping the process.

TOWARD A RESEARCH AGENDA FOR A CULTURAL PERSPECTIVE ON VALUE CREATION AND EXCHANGE

In this chapter we advanced the argument that while the importance of symbolic consumption is growing in a variety of markets, strategy research appears woefully inattentive to the trend and disinterested in understanding how firms can develop products that are sought after and rewarded by consumers for their symbolic value. We address this problem by proposing that strategy scholars should recognize the role that firms play in the production of meaning, and therefore, culture. In doing so, we believe the strategy filed has the opportunity to rethink and reconceptualize three of its cornerstones, namely conceptualization of value, resources and capabilities, and innovation. We discuss each of these directions next.

Value. The focus of management researchers on technological and economic determinants of value seems to have led them to overlook a significant mechanism through which firms can create and appropriate value – the embodiment of meaning in products and services. Over-reliance on economic frameworks for understanding market dynamics may be partly responsible for this theoretical oversight. As DiMaggio (1997) explains:

> Economics treats tastes as stable, focused on use values, individually formed, and exogenous … Sociology and anthropology view tastes as changeable, focused on symbolic qualities of goods, dependent on perceptions and tastes of others, and intrinsically interesting. (DiMaggio, 1997: 43)

As a result, dominant strategy frameworks for analyzing value creation (Porter, 1980; Moran and Ghoshal, 1999) tend to leave the consumer side out of the value equation, thereby failing to account for the dynamic construction of tastes, preferences, and product demand, as a function of the interplay between producer activities and consumption practices.

Conversely, marketing scholars and consumer behaviorists have widely studied how processes of symbolization take place in the market or at the interface between firms and consumers (e.g. Belk and Acosta, 1998; Goulding, 2000; Peñaloza, 2000). Most marketing research, however, does not offer conceptualizations of the organizational process and capabilities that enable organizations to engage in systematic and purposeful creation of symbolic value as a part of the value creation process of the firm.

Resources and capabilities. In our view, if they want to preserve the relevance of their theories in the face of the increasing centrality of symbolic dynamics in consumer markets, management scholars need to include the study of the organizational and social dynamics of symbolic value production in the research agenda. Some scholars have already begun to explore how firms shape meaning making in markets (Rindova and Fombrun, 1999; Lounsbury and Glynn, 2000; Lawrence and Phillips, 2002; Rindova et al., 2006). The framework we developed in this chapter suggests that this work can be extended to focus on how firms proactively intervene in the constructions of signs and meanings that shape the cultural milieu that surrounds markets. In other words, we argue that firms not only need to use cultural means to improve their positions in markets, but can develop capabilities and activities that shape the cultural environments in which they seek positions.

Another issue regards the relationship between producers and the culture they are embedded in. While the processes that we have described see producers engaged primarily in the decoding of cultural codes and practices, it is not unlikely that some of them might actually attempt to stimulate and nurture the development of 'lead cultures'. In this respect, our framework may be extended and refined by further research to investigate the conditions under which producers enact the very cultural context on which they will later draw in order to infuse their products with significance.

More research seems to be needed also into the strategies and tactics that producers use to enhance the symbolic value of their product. Casual observation indicates that different alternatives exist: while some producers, like Alessi or Bang and Olufsen, rely mainly on the inherent significance of objects, others (e.g. fashion houses) deploy a very wide range of communication devices (advertising, fashion shows, celebrity endorsements, product placement, arts sponsorship). While some of these communication techniques are conventionally viewed as marketing tactics, we urge strategy scholars to explore the strategic implications of incorporating these activities in the strategic planning of a firm's competitive position and advantage, rather than developing them as an afterthought, as a means of selling the technology-driven products firms develop.

Finally, the cultural perspective on value creation we propose suggests the need for strategy and organizational scholars to reconsider how they think about the resources that firms need to develop in order to be able to produce and appropriate value (Moran and Goshal, 1999). While at times tangible resources like financial and physical capital may be critical, recent research highlights the increasing centrality of intangibles in affecting the capacity to create value (e.g. Quinn, 1992; Fombrun, 1996). Management theorists tend to converge on the idea that three broad types of intangible assets exist: intellectual capital (e.g. Quinn, 1992; Nahapiet and Ghoshal, 1998), social capital (e.g. Nahaphiet and Ghoshal, 1998), and reputational capital (e.g. Fombrun, 1996). The conceptual framework emerging from our review of extant literature in sociology and anthropology, however, suggests that symbolic value creation may require additional resources, which are cultural in nature (DiMaggio, 1997). For example, the framework we developed suggests that firms engaged in symbolic value creation need to develop *cultural capital*, which affects the extent to which a firm can grasp and decode cultural meanings, and *institutional capital* – understood as a particular form of social capital embodied in positive relationships with institutional intermediaries. Future research in management may investigate the linkages between organizational processes and these forms of capital, and explore the conditions under which organizations effectively accumulate and deploy them in the production of symbolic value.

Innovation. Finally, our model of cultural production and symbolic production suggests an opportunity and an imperative to reconceptualize extant models of innovation and innovation management. Most strategy research is dominated by a deterministic technological view of innovation and value creation, according to which product improvements arise from technological developments and the abilities of firms to capitalize on them, which in turn depends on their technological search strategies (Katila and Ahuja, 2002) and knowledge recombination capabilities (Helfat and Raubitschek, 2000). In contrast, the perspective that we advance emphasizes that the value of products is determined by how they are interpreted and adopted by consumers. This is not to say that in many industries traditional capabilities and technology-based innovation is becoming or will become marginal to competition. Indeed, the success of companies like Nokia, Apple or Nike seems to lie in their capacity to combine both technological innovation and skillful manipulation of visual and verbal symbols. Future research should explore in greater depth the possible interactions between the technological capabilities of firms and their ability to create objects with high symbolizing potential in order to understand the nature and sources of synergies between these two aspects of value creation.

NOTES

1 The process of cultural production that we discuss here differs from the processes of production of cultural products that take place in the so-called cultural industries (arts, music, television, etc.). The process we are concerned with endows regular material products with symbolizing potential; in contrast, the processes through which cultural products are produced result in products that deliver 'entertainment' or 'experience' (Lampel et al., 2000). Therefore, these are distinct processes and by recognizing them as distinct we can begin to explore similarities and differences among them.

2 It is in this aspect that the process we describe that bears the most similarities with what happens in cultural industries. Because the processes of cultural mediation are relatively well studied by researchers who focus on cultural and creative industries (see Caves, 2000), and because many of the core ideas established in this work apply more generally to symbolic value creation, in our chapter we do not discuss this important process in more detail.

REFERENCES

Aaker, D.R. (1996) *Building Strong Brands*. New York, NY: The Free Press.

Alessi, A. (2001) *The Dream Factory. Alessi Since 1921*. Milano: Electa.

Becker, H.S. (1982) *Art Worlds*. Berkeley, CA: University of California Press.

Belk, R.W. (1985) *Collecting in a Consumer Society*. London: Routledge.

Belk, R.W. (1986) 'Yuppies as arbiters of the emerging consumption style', in Lutz, R. (ed), *Advances in Consumer Research*, vol. 13. Provo, UT: Association for Consumer Research, pp. 514–519.

Belk, R.W. (1988) 'Possession and the extended self'. *Journal of Consumer Research*. 15: 139–168.

Belk, R.W. and Acosta, J.A. (1998) 'The mountain man myth: A contemporary consuming fantasy'. *Journal of Consumer Research*. 25: 218–240.

Belk, R. and Tumbat, G. (2005) 'The cult of Mac'. *Consumption, Markets and Culture*. 8: 205–218.

Besanko, D., Dranove, D. and Shanley, M. (1996) *The Economics of Strategy*. New York, NY: John Wiley.

Bourdieu, P. (1984) *Distinction: A Social Critique of Judgment and Taste*. Cambridge, MA: Harvard University Press.

Brown, S. and Eisenhardt, K. (1995) 'Product development: Past research, present findings, and future directions'. *Academy of Management Review*. 20: 343–378.

Caves, R. (2000) *Creative Industries: Contracts Between Arts and Commerce*. Cambridge, MA: Harvard University Press.

Crane, D. (2000) *Fashion and its Social Agendas. Class, Gender and Identity in Clothing*. Chicago, IL: University of Chicago Press.

Csikszentmihalyi, M. and Rochberg-Halton, E. (1981) *The Meaning of Things: Domestic Symbols and the Self.* Cambridge: Cambridge University Press.

Davis, F. (1992) *Fashion, Culture and Identity.* Chicago, IL: The University of Chicago Press.

DiMaggio, P. (1997) 'Culture and cognition'. *Annual Review of Sociology.* 23: 263–287.

Douglas, M. and Isherwood, B. (1979) *The World of Goods. Towards an Anthropology of Consumption.* New York: Basic Books.

du Gay, P. (ed) (1997) *Production of Culture. Cultures of Production.* London: Sage.

du Gay, P., Hall, S., Janes, L., Mackay, H. and Negus, K. (1997) *Doing Cultural Studies. The Story of the Sony Walkman.* London: Sage.

Eco, U. (1976) *A Theory of Semiotics.* Bloomington, IN: Indiana University Press.

Fombrun, C.J. (1996) *Reputation: Realizing Value from the Corporate Image.* Boston, MA: Harvard Business School Press.

Fombrun, C. and Rindova, V. (2000) 'The road to transparency: Reputation management at Royal Dutch/Shell', in Schultz, M. and Hatch, M.J. (eds) *The Expressive Organization.* Oxford: Oxford University Press.

Frank, T. (1997) *The Conquest of Cool: Business Culture, Counter Culture, and the Rise of Hip Consumerism.* Chicago, IL: The University of Chicago Press.

Gatignon, H. and Xuereb, J.-M. (1997) 'Strategic orientation of the firm new product performance'. *Journal of Marketing Research.* 34: 77–90.

Geertz, C. (1973) *The Interpretation of Cultures.* New York, NY: Basic Books.

Goulding, C. (2000) 'The commodification of the past, postmodern pastiche and the search for authentic experiences at contemporary heritage attractions'. *European Journal of Marketing.* 34: 835–853.

Hall, S. (ed) (1997) *Representation: Cultural Representations and Signifying Practices.* London: Sage.

Hatch, M.J. (1993) 'The dynamics of organizational culture'. *Academy of Management Review.* 18: 657–693.

Hebdige, D. (1979) *Subculture: The Meaning of Style.* London: Methuen.

Helfat, C.E. and Raubitschek, R.S. (2000) 'Product sequencing: Co-evolution of knowledge, capabilities and products'. *Strategic Management Journal.* 21: 961–979.

Henard, D.H. and Szymanski, D.M. (2001) 'Why some new products are more successful than others'. *Journal of Marketing Research.* 38: 362–375.

Heskett, J. (2002) *Toothpicks and Logos. Design in Everyday Life.* Oxford: Oxford University Press.

Hirsch, P. (1972) 'Processing fads and fashions: An organization-set analysis of cultural industry systems'. *American Journal of Sociology.* 77: 639–659.

Hirschman, E.C. (1986) 'The creation of product symbolism'. *Advances in Consumer Research.* 13: 327–331.

Hirschman, E.C. and Holbrook, M.B. (1980) *Symbolic Consumer Behavior.* Ann Arbor, MI: Association for Consumer Research.

Hirschman, E., Scott, L. and Wells, W. (1998) 'A model of product discourse: Linking consumer practice to cultural texts'. *Journal of Advertising.* 27 (1): 33–50.

Holbrook, M.B. and Hirschman, E.C. (1982) 'The experiential aspects of consumption: Consumer fantasies, feelings and fun'. *Journal of Consumer Research.* 9: 132–140.

Holt, D.B. (1998) 'Does cultural capital structure American consumption?' *Journal of Consumer Research.* 25: 1–25.

Holt, D.B. (2003) 'What becomes an icon most?' *Harvard Business Review.* March.

Holt, D.B. (2004) *How Brands Become Icons: The Principles of Cultural Branding.* Boston, MA: Harvard Business School Press.

Hopkinson, G.C. and Pujari, D. (1999) 'A factor analytic study of the sources of meaning in hedonic consumption'. *European Journal of Marketing.* 33: 273–290.

Katila, R. and Ahuja, G. (2002) 'Something old, something new: A longitudinal study of search behavior and new product introduction'. *Academy of Management Journal.* 45 (6): 1183–1194.

König, R. (1973) *À la Mode. On the Social Psychology of Fashion.* New York, NY: Seabury.

Lampel, J., Lant, T. and Shamsie, J. (2000) 'Balancing act: Learning from organizing practices in cultural industries'. *Organization Science.* 11: 263–269.

Lawrence, T. and Phillips, N. (2002) 'Understanding cultural industries'. *Journal of Management Inquiry.*

Lester, R.K., Piore, M.J. and Malek, K.M. (1998) 'Interpretive management: What general managers can learn from design'. *Harvard Business Review.* March–April: 86–96.

Lewalski, Z.M. (1988) *Product Eesthetics: An Interpretation for Designers.* Carson City, NV: Design & Development Engineering Press.

Lounsbury, M. and Glynn, M.A. (2001) 'Cultural entrepreneurship: Stories, legitimacy, and the acquisition of resources'. *Strategic Management Journal.* 22 (6/7): 545.

Marzano, S. (1998) *Creating Value by Design. Thoughts.* London: Lund Humphries.

McCracken, G. (1986) 'Culture and consumption: A theoretical account of the structure and movement of the cultural meaning of consumer goods'. *Journal of Consumer Research.* 13: 71–84.

McCracken, G. (1988) *Culture and Consumption – New Approaches to the Symbolic of Consumer Goods and Activities.* Bloomington, IN: Indiana University Press.

McKendrick, N., Brewer, J. and Plumb, J.H. (1982) *The Birth of a Consumer Society: The Commercialization of Eighteenth-Century England.* Bloomington, IN: Indiana University Press.

Moran, P. and Ghoshal, S. (1999) 'Markets, firms, and the process of economic development'. *Academy of Management Review.* 24: 390–412.

Mukerji, C. (1983) *From Graven Images: Patterns of Modern Materialism.* New York, NY: Columbia University Press.

Nahapiet, J. and Ghoshal, S. (1998) 'Social capital, intellectual capital and the organizational advantage'. *Academy of Management Review.* 23(2): 242–266.

Olins, W. (2000) 'How brands are taking over the corporation', in Schultz, M., Hatch, M.J. and Larsen, M.H. (eds), *The Expressive Organization: Linking Identity, Reputation, and the Corporate Brand.* Oxford: Oxford University Press, pp. 51–65.

Peñaloza, L. (2000) 'The commodification of the American West: Marketers' production of cultural meanings at the trade show'. *Journal of Marketing.* 64: 82–109.

Porter, M. (1980) *Competitive Strategy.* New York, NY: The Free Press.

Quinn, J.B. (1992) *The Intelligent Enterprise.* New York, NY: Wiley.

Ramirez, R. (1999) 'Value co-production: Intellectual origins and implications for practice and research'. *Strategic Management Journal.* 20 (1): 49.

Ravasi, D. and Lojacono, G. (2005) 'Managing design and designers for strategic renewal'. *Long Range Planning.* 38: 51–77.

Rindova, V.P. and Fombrun, C.J. (1999) 'Constructing competitive advantage: The role of firm-constituent interactions'. *Strategic Management Journal.* 20: 691–710.

Rindova, V.P., Pollock, T.G. and Hayward, M.L. (2006) 'Celebrity firms: The social construction of market popularity'. *Academic of Management Review.* 31 (1): 50–71.

Rindova, V.P., Williamson, I.O., Petkova, A.P. and Sever, J.M. (2005) 'Being good or being known: An empirical examination of the dimensions, antecedents, and consequences of organizational reputation'. *Academy of Management Journal.*

Rogers, E.M. (1995) *Diffusion of Innovations,* 4th ed. New York, NY: The Free Press.

Sahlins, M. (1976) *Culture and Practical Reason.* Chicago, IL: The University of Chicago Press.

Schmitt, B. and Simonson, A. (1997) *Marketing Aesthetics: The Strategic Management of Brands, Identity and* Image. New York: Free Press.

Sirgy, J.M. (1982) 'Self-concept in consumer behavior: A critical review'. *Journal of Consumer Research.* 9: 287–300.

Veblen, T. (1899) *The Theory of the Leisure Class.*

von Hippel, E. (1986) 'Lead users: A source of novel product concepts'. *Management Science.* 32 (7): 791–805.

Weiman, G. (1994) *The Influentials: People Who Influence People.* New York, NY: SUNY series.

Wernick, A. (1991) *Promotional Culture. Advertising, Ideology and Symbolic Expression.* London: Sage.

Williams, R.H. (1982) *Dream Worlds: Mass Consumption in Late Nineteenth Century France.* Berkeley, CA: University of California Press.

Wright, N.D., Claiborne, C.B. and Sirgy, M.J. (1992) 'The effects of product symbolism on consumer selfconcept'. *Advances in Consumer Research.* 19: 311–318.

Critically Constructing Constructionism

Dian Marie Hosking

I would like to encourage the continuing development of a critical relational constructionist 'meta theory' (Gergen, 1994) – but not as 'a theory of everything' – and not as a (superior) substitute for other thought styles. Rather, it should be recognized as different from post-positivist approaches to science and different from constructivist theories that discourse persons as individuals with minds constructing knowledge about other people and objects. I use the term Critical Relational Constructionism (CRC) to refer to a very particular discourse that centres ongoing processes in which 'persons and worlds' are constructed as local-historical relational realities. These relational realities include the 'realities' of science and, of course, Critical Relational Constructionism.

Processes of relating go on in multiple, simultaneous inter-acts. Broadly speaking, CRC views inter-action as: (a) a performance; (b) that involves a coming together; (c) of people, objects, statements, facts, events – and, in doing so, (re)constructs person/world relations as (d) relational realities. A few points need to be emphasized. First, whilst inter-action involves conceptual language *at some point*, 'coming together' involves much more than voiced and written texts. Second, persons and worlds are viewed as created in ongoing inter-acts – rather than discoursed as stable, singular, independent entities. In other words, 'the how' of ongoing processes is centred – rather than 'the what' of inputs and outcomes – which leaves open the possibility of multiple and changing constructions as 'content'.

Inter-acts (re)construct multiple Self/Other realities as local ontologies. Ongoing inter-actions can (re)construct stabilized effects such as social conventions, musical forms, organizational and societal structures, Western psychology, and what some language games might call nature, or facts or artefacts. But not all inter-actions will be stabilized e.g. some will go unheard, unseen, unnoticed or unwarranted. The fate of an act/text depends on whether or not it is credited as 'real and good' (Gergen, 1994). As Latour would have it, the fate of a statement depends on others who have to read it, take it up and use it – others have to be 'enrolled' and they have to be 'controlled' (Latour, 1987). CRC takes the view that what is validated or discredited is *local-cultural*, i.e. local to the ongoing practices that (re)construct a particular 'form of life'. Local-cultural is also *local-historical* in that relating both supplements pre-existing acts and has implications for how a process will continue. In other words, the ongoing present reproduces some previously stabilized effect (e.g. the convention of shaking hands) *and* acts in relation to possible and probable futures (e.g. that a greeting will be successfully performed). All acts (texts) supplement other acts (con-texts) *and* are available for possible supplementation and possible (dis)crediting. In the discourse of CRC, inter-actions, and particularly regularly repeated ones, 'make history' so to speak – and history is constantly being re-made.

Continued

Inter-actions can (re)construct hard, soft or indeed minimal Self-Other differentiation. Opening up to the possibility of soft self/other differentiation opens up additional possibilities for relations. Relating can no longer be reduced to *either* 'soft' Humanist *or* 'hard' (factual). Soft differentiation involves both/and ways of relating – ways that allow and support multiplicity, inter-dependence, openness, and appreciation. Soft differentiation (re)constructs 'power to' and 'power with' – when compared with the 'power over' of hard differentiation (Foucault, 1977, 1980). This opens-up possibilities and creates space for multiple, local rationalities – as 'forms of life'. Given these features CRC seems best viewed as a discourse that emphasizes the historical-cultural rather than the natural-scientific. But it is *not* the same as Contextualism – only CRC takes seriously the view that metaphysics, theory, method, and data all are interwoven.

Some necessary developments. Many have argued that an increasingly hard differentiation of self and other has gone together with developments (e.g. in science and technology) that promote vision and visually available actants to the relative neglect of sound and the other senses. Social constructionist inquiries may also be biased in favour of vision and visual acts. For example, constructionism *theorizes* language as action but, in practice, live action often gets reduced to visualized, dead and frozen, interview transcripts of words that can be analysed. Focusing on the written word may promote visual qualities and constructions of solidity, stasis and space – to the relative neglect of other senses, of sound, and of temporal processes. And this may restrict the possibility of soft self/other differentiation. If we wish to explore the latter it seems we may need to amplify our sensitivity to live sound, to the sensuality of live processes and to time and give equal treatment to both human and non-human actants (objects, artefacts, 'nature') as participants in relational processes (Hosking, 2008).

Relatedly, I think we need to explore listening in relation to soft self/other differentiation. This will require letting go over-sharp distinctions between the senses, between the senses and the mind, between the mind and the body, between inside and outside my Self and between self and other. According to Corradi Fiumara it also requires letting go of Western philosophy's one-sided attention to 'the moulding ordering sense of 'saying' i.e. to *logos* and attending more to *legein* (Corradi Fiumara, 1990: 2). It seems that listening (as *legein*) is crucially implicated in soft differentiation – not for 'finding out' (for the purposes of 'moulding' i.e. achieving 'power over' other) – but to enable what Corradi Fiumara (p. 40) called 'the patient labours of co-existence' – labours that seem to need a 'modesty and mildness of language that can exorcise the risk that it (i.e. language) becomes an end in itself'.

REFERENCES

Corradi Fiumara, G. (1990) *The Other Side of Language: A Philosophy of Listening.* London: Routledge.

Foucault, M. (1977, 1980) *Power/knowledge – Selected Interviews and Other Writings.* New York: Pantheon Books.

Gergen, K.J. (1994) *Realities and Relationships: Soundings in Social Construction.* Cambridge: Harvard University Press.

Hosking, D.M. (2008) 'Can constructionism be critical?' in Holstein, J.G. (ed), *Handbook of Constructionist Research.* New York: Guilford Publications.

Latour, B. (1987) *Science in Action.* Milton Keynes: Open University Press.

The Role of Narrative Fiction and Semi-Fiction in Organizational Studies

Gail Whiteman and Nelson Phillips

Organizational scholars are increasingly exploring the usefulness and validity of story-telling and creative narrative in organizational research (e.g. Barry, 1996; Boje, et al., 1996; Czarniawska, 1998, Czarniawska-Joerges and Guillet de Monthoux, 1994; Phillips, 1995; Taylor, 2000; Whiteman, 2004). Phillips (1995), for example, encourages us to use novels, stories, plays, songs, poems, and films as legitimate objects for study and as vehicles to convey valuable organizational knowledge that has the potential to enrich our field. To some degree, these calls have been heeded and the use of narrative fiction in teaching (e.g. Czarniawska-Joerges and Guillet de Monthoux, 1994) and writing about organizations has become increasingly commonplace and accepted. While less common, narrative fiction as a focus of study has also become less of a rarity, with several different forms of fiction now appearing as data in the literature (e.g. Parker et al., 1999; Phillips and Zyglidopoulos, 1999).

At the same time, the use of fictional accounts created by researchers remains highly unusual in management studies, although there are important exceptions (e.g. Hansen et al., 2007; Jermier, 1985; Taylor, 2000). The status of these fictional accounts of organizational life remains unclear and publication is often difficult.[1] The use of semi-fictional, self-authored accounts is even rarer although recent work by Whiteman (2004) suggests that such genres may be particularly provocative for telling ethnographic tales from the field (Van Maanen, 1988).

In this chapter, we contribute to the ongoing discussion of the potential of fiction and semi-fiction by bringing together existing arguments regarding their use, extending these arguments based on our own experiences, and providing examples of their use. In doing so, we make three important contributions. First, we provide a practical introduction and broad review of the literature and bring together discussions of fiction and semi-fiction, which have tended to remain fragmented and disparate. Second, we compare their respective strengths and weaknesses as approaches to the study of organizational phenomenon. While fiction and semi-fiction are similar methods, they have quite different strengths and are useful in very different ways. Finally, we add to existing arguments for the usefulness of fiction and semi-fiction by arguing for the complementarity of the two methods. While both approaches highlight the potential of narrative fiction, they also point to very different opportunities for contributing to organization and management studies.

We begin with an introduction to the existing philosophical discussions around fiction and semi-fiction, define both terms, as well as revisit some of the organizational literature that discusses or uses fiction or semi-fiction. We then discuss some of the ways that fiction and semi-fiction can be used in organizational research focusing on their distinct roles. We conclude with a discussion of future directions for the development of these methods as approaches to the study of organizations.

'ISN'T IT ALL JUST FICTION ANYWAY?'

When one begins to explore the relevant literature, one quickly finds that the division between fiction and non-fiction is no longer fixed. The battle for some sort of strict boundary between truth and fiction has long been lost. While 'fantasy', 'truth', 'reality', and 'fiction' as terms may carry societal meaning, they do not carry any kind of 'objective' status (e.g. Rorty, 1991). Nevertheless, it is clear that this boundary exists in practice and we need to be keenly aware of the societal conventions that shape the usages of these terms in organization studies.

Defining narrative fiction

So what is fiction? From a literary theory perspective, 'the author of fiction invites the reader to engage in a kind of make-believe' (Currie, 1985: 386). Furthermore, fiction is a

linguistic convention in a double sense (Park, 1982: 417–418):

> It is linguistic because it is a convention about language; it is also linguistic because it is a convention concerning a way in which a language in a linguistic product is used. The convention consists in stating that words and sentences in a linguistic product should not be taken as referring to any real things, events, facts, and situations, that is, to the real world. To call *Madame Bovary* and *Alice in Wonderland* 'fiction' is to indicate that the words and sentences in these linguistic products are not used to refer to the real world. If we immediately recognize *Alice in Wonderland* as a fiction that is because the linguistic product indicates itself that what is talked about in it is not real. Fiction is then a linguistic convention about reference. The convention says that the language in a fiction means what it means without its real referent.

Non-fiction, by default, invites the reader to believe in the 'reality' of the referent of the written text – that is, something exists that is not fantasy. The convention of non-fiction is that it refers to something that is not fantasy, but instead something that is 'real'. The hybrid form – semi-fiction – offers a potential way through this interpretive maze and contains characteristics of both fiction and non-fiction. In semi-fiction, the author is making direct claims about its reference to 'reality' and yet at the same time, asking the reader to indulge in make-believe. That is, empirical content is presented in a partial (or total) make-believe form for dramatic communicative effect.

For the purposes of this chapter, we will use the broad term 'narrative' to describe texts that tell a story. In some cases, the authors may describe such a text as fiction, as non-fiction, or as semi-fiction, depending upon how they wish readers to engage with the text. While one can argue that a 'Rose is a rose is a rose is a rose' (Stein, 1922) – that 'it's all just fiction anyway' – we argue that by adopting different textual strategies organizational scholars shape organizational knowledge in different ways. Thus, the relationship between organizational studies and narrative is complex and ambiguous and it is made more ambiguous in that narrative appears in organization studies in several different ways. For example, Czarniawska (1998: 13–14) suggests that 'Narrative enters organizational studies in at least four forms: organizational research that is written in a storylike fashion ("tales from the field", to paraphrase Van Maanen, 1988); organizational research that collects organizational stories (tales of the field); organizational research that conceptualizes organizational life as storymaking and organizational theory as story reading (interpretive approaches); and as a disciplinary reflection that takes the form of literary critique'.

It is interesting to note that there are two different sorts of stories included in Czarniawska's list. On the one hand, there are stories that are produced by organizational members themselves and that are then collected together and studied; on the other hand, there are stories written by others (either fiction authors or organizational researchers) that are used in organizational research in some way. The types of stories we are interested in here are of the latter variety; we are interested in the potential use of narrative fiction and semi-fiction as either data or method. That is, we are interested in stories as potential sources of data that can be analysed to better understand organizational life or as ways of presenting our research results and reflections on organizational life to others.

Narrative fiction in organization studies

The idea of using fiction as data or method has a relatively brief history in organizational studies. At the same time, as we argued above, a growing body of literature attests to the interest in these innovative approaches. As Whiteman (2004: 3) argues, stories are 'a creative means for meaning making and privilege contextualized information and personalized expression'. Nevertheless, using narrative stories in this way lies clearly outside of the mainstream and researchers adopting these approaches face considerable barriers to publication.

The reason for the continued existence of these barriers is somewhat unclear. As Czarniawska (1998: 5) notes: 'there are

no structural differences between fictional and factional narratives, and their respective attraction is not determined by their claim to be fact or fiction'. Entrenched social conventions are likely the causes of such separation within organizational studies (Phillips, 1995). At the crux of the issue is the conventional status and role of organizational 'data'. Stablein (1996) acknowledges that '[a]ll data are representations' and that '[a]s representations, data imply things that are represented, and a process of representing' (p. 511). While there has been considerable debate both about the 'reality' of "The 'Thing' Represented" by data and regarding the representational process, Stablein argues organizational data should – at the very least – be related to the 'empirical world'. But the question remains, how can we do this? We suggest that using the creative techniques of representation without abandoning data in organizational research holds innovative promise. Yet such approaches may face considerable resistance.

Weick (1979, 1995) argues that the standard ways of doing and knowing in an organization (or organizing entity such as academia) tend to follow deeply held schematic approaches to sense-making and that as groups become attached to certain schemas, they actively reinforce the validity of traditional approaches even when this cycle may unduly restrict new ways of knowing. Thus, innovation in sense-making can suffer, and perhaps suffocate, from the very ivory tower which seeks to study and create 'new' knowledge. Other disciplines such as anthropology have also struggled with these issues. For example, Clifford and Marcus argue that 'our sharp separation of form from content – and our fetishizing of form – was, and is, contestable. It is a bias that may well be implicit in modernist "textualism" (Clifford and Marcus, 1986: 21).

Encouragingly, organizational scholars have begun to collapse these artificial boundaries (March, 2006; Phillips, 1995; Whiteman, 2004), and there is a growing stream of research on the process of 'organizational storytelling'. Nevertheless, as organizational scholars, we remain decidedly passive with respect to our own narrative 'play'. While we may be free to study fiction (e.g. March, 2006; Phillips and Zyglidopoulos, 1999), organizational scholars rarely *create* it and even more rarely do they mix fact and fiction into a bricolage of research findings, without carefully footnoting the differences (see Czarniawska, 1998: 63, footnote 2). We remain, resolutely, a collection of serious 'non-fictional' authors.

Yet cognitive processing – the ability to understand, think, and reflect about phenomenon – is not restricted to the realm of 'non-fiction'. For instance, Bruner (1986) differentiates between two modes of cognitive processing: the logico-scientific mode, and the imaginative-narrative mode. Historically, organizational research favours the logico-scientific approach. Journal articles commonly utilize a neutral, objective tone to produce authorial omnipotence (Jeffcut, 1994) and to demonstrate 'plausibility' (Golden-Biddle & Locke, 1993). Editorial preferences for rational academic discourse (Jeffcut, 1994) reinforce our emphasis on logico-scientific approaches to scientific sense-making. In contrast, textual strategies which do not conform to established rhetorical patterns provoke the audience to re-examine their beliefs and suppositions about the world and the meaning of research. Imaginative-narrative texts – such as those presented by Jermier (1985) or more recently by Taylor (2000) and Whiteman (2004) – are examples of what Golden-Biddle and Locke (1993) call the 'criticality' dimension of convincing narrative texts.

In this chapter, we focus on the imaginative-narrative approach to cognitive processing and argue for the use of fiction and semi-fiction in organizational research. While our argumentation style (clearly thus far) follows a logico-scientific approach, we do so in an ironic attempt to argue ourselves (and our colleagues) out of a schematic academic box. The illuminating role of fiction and the subversive role of semi-fiction in organization studies are discussed in the following sections.

THE ILLUMINATING ROLE OF FICTION IN ORGANIZATION STUDIES

The use of narrative fiction has a very long history in social science. Harriet Martineau, for example, was an early proponent of using fiction to teach (O'Donnell, 1989). She began writing her *Illustrations of Political Economy* in 1832 and wrote a total of 18 volumes of fictional stories based on the belief that 'the best way to teach was through stories that gripped the reader's imagination' (O'Donnell, 1989: 315). Fiction has also often been used widely in social science to add colour and life to academic writing with many authors drawing on novels, short stories, plays, and movies to emphasize points and set the stage for more rigorous academic writing. Wittgenstein, for example, drew on detective stories in his lectures on sense data and private experience in 1935.

In organization studies, the use of fiction in teaching is also well accepted (although without quite the same extended history as in economics!). Czarniawska-Joerges and Guillet de Monthoux (1994: 1) in their book on the topic put it succinctly: 'The purpose of this book is to show how good novels can educate better managers'. They then go on to explain why novels are not cases and how they transmit 'tacit knowledge' and present a level of complexity beyond any case which engages and challenges the reader. Similarly, in their article arguing for the use of fiction in teaching business ethics, Kennedy and Lawton (1992) state their case eloquently:

> We undergo an arousal of suspense concerning the nature of that resolution and its ultimate meaning for us. We also take on various roles vicariously through our reading that allow us, through imaginative enactment, to know things otherwise beyond our understanding. This high level of involvement, vicarious role-taking, suspense, conflict, and resolution lead us to new levels of knowing that are both affective and cognitive.

These arguments, and this use of fiction, are well accepted in management teaching with many narrative fictions used in many different classes, suggestions for the use of fiction provided by the authors of textbooks, and various websites and listserv discussions focused on the exchange of suggestions and experiences.

Similarly, the role of narrative fiction as a device in academic articles is also well accepted. A carefully chosen quote from a well-known book adds life and interest to academic articles. Phillips (1995: 637) calls this 'fiction as ambiance' and argues that 'if we can evoke feeling and images appropriate to the discussion, we can effectively clarify and frame an otherwise dry academic piece'. The qualities that make great works of fiction so impactful – their invocation of an alternative reality, the colourfulness of their language, the immediacy of the images they create – are all things that academic writing generally lacks. They are, in fact, all things that academic writing by convention avoids. The use of narrative fiction therefore provides a useful and engaging contrast to academic writing.

But while these two uses of fiction are well accepted in the social sciences generally, and in organization studies in particular, there are two other uses that are much less well established. First, there are an increasing number of researchers who are treating fictional accounts of organizational life as data. For some of these writers, fiction is seen as something that supports and furthers the traditional work of organizational scholars; for others, it is much more than just a supplement to what we have been doing: 'Rather than asking what science fiction can do *for* organization studies, we want to see what it might do *to* organization studies' (Parker et al., 1999: 580).

Narrative fiction thus provides a way to see beyond the world of what has happened into a world that is plausible but goes beyond what we see in our everyday world. In doing so, the discursive practices of narrative fiction challenge us to think differently and perhaps deeper about organizations and management (March, 2006). A recent example of this is given by March who uses 'one of the better known poems by William Butler Yeats, *Easter 1916*,[2] as an illustration of the proposition that poetry is a natural medium for expressing and contemplating doubt, paradox, and contradiction – features of

life, well-known to experienced managers, but normally banished, perhaps with reason, from the public language of management' (p. 70).

Whether one adopts the more or less radical view of the role of fiction as data, what is inescapable is that the use of narrative fiction as data significantly challenges many of the methodological and epistemological principles and assumptions underlying organization studies. The status of the resulting papers is ambiguous and publication is often difficult as reviewers and editors find it impossible to evaluate the contribution and rigour of this kind of work.

An example of this sort of work is Phillips and Zyglidopoulos' (1999) study of Asimov's *Foundation* trilogy. They describe their method as follows:

> [O]ur general approach is to treat works of narrative fiction as intensive qualitative case studies. Structured analysis of these 'thick descriptions' of imaginary worlds allows us to explore issues and ask questions in a different way than is possible using more traditional sources of data. (Phillips and Zyglidopoulos, 1999: 593)

Let's look at an illustrative example. Box 2.7.1 provides an excerpt from *Small World,* a novel written by David Lodge. In the excerpt, the character Persse is attending an academic conference held at a regional university in the UK. The session he is attending is being held in a lecture theatre at the university and Professor Swallow is presenting. The short excerpt encompasses a particular experience of conference attendance in a vivid way. It is also, it is worth noting, used by us in just the way we talked about in the previous paragraphs – as a device to add interest to our paper.

But more than that, we suggest that this fiction could be used by organizational scholars as data. If we adopt Phillips and Zyglidopoulos's method in the preceding example, we are free to treat fictional text like David Lodge's novel *Small World* as a 'intensive case study' of an academic conference. By doing so, we could use this text to develop theoretical insight on the back-stage culture (Goffman, 1959) of conference attendance, including the role of academic boredom in organizational knowledge creation.

Box 2.7.1   An excerpt from David Lodge's *Small World*

Persse yawned and shifted his weight from one buttock to another in his seat at the back of the lecture-room. He could not see the faces of many of his colleagues, but as far as could be judged from their postures, most of them were as disengaged from the discourse as himself. Some were leaning back as far as their seats allowed, staring vacantly at the ceiling, others were slumped forwards onto the desks that separated each row, resting their chins on folded arms, and others again were sprawled sideways over two or three seats, with their legs crossed and arms dangling limply to the floor. In the third row a man was surreptitiously doing *The Times* crossword, and at least three people appeared to be asleep. Someone, a student presumably, had carved into the surface of the desk at which Persse sat, cutting deep into the wood with the force of a man driven to the limits of endurance, the word 'BORING'. Another had scratched the message, 'Swallow is a wanker'. Persse saw no reason to dissent from either of these judgements. (Lodge, 1984: 239–240)

In fact, David Lodge's description of a conference looks quite similar to ethnographic writing in organization such as the work of Rosen (1988, 1985) and we could carry out very similar analysis to uncover the social dynamics that characterize this account of a conference. It may be fictional, yet few who have attended an academic conference would fail to see much that is familiar in this account. It is precisely this ring of truth, growing out of the keen eye and active imagination of a talented writer, that gives this account academic value.

The final role that narrative fiction fulfils in organization studies is much less common and much more radical. It is also the role where narrative has the most potential to contribute to organization studies. This final role is where organization studies researchers use the practices of narrative fiction in order to produce texts that present theoretical insight about organizational phenomena. As Phillips (1995: 641) argues, '[u]sed in this way, fiction provides a way to test the validity of theory'. Fiction allows a complex and nuanced presentation of theory that draws in the reader without the closure and oversimplification of more traditional theory.

Examples of this are quite rare however. Jermier (1985) provides one of the better known examples. In his article he draws on H.G. Wells' short story *When the Sleeper* *Wakes* to contrast different versions of critical theory. Jermier shows first the world as it appears in one theoretical perspective and then tells the same story again but from the perspective of an alternative theoretical frame. The use of narrative fiction provides an excellent way to contrast the two theories and challenge the reader to choose which one rings more true. Note that Calás and Smircich (1996) also use short fictionalized vignettes to highlight different theoretical perspectives on women in management.

Yet, while there are a small number of examples of fiction as method, the approach remains very rare. The reasons for this are threefold. First, writing good fiction is extremely difficult and far from the training and background of most researchers. Second, the barriers of the peer review system are significant for this sort of work. The system rewards conservatism and adherence to the standard practices of representation for academic articles. This obviously creates serious barriers to the publication of fiction in academic journals. Finally, and perhaps most importantly, the methodological tools to produce this sort of work remain underdeveloped. While there are a few examples of this use of fiction in organization studies, the methodological underpinnings remain undiscussed, leaving authors to 'go it alone'.

One interesting recent development has important implications for this last issue. It is the development of semi-fiction as a methodology in organization studies. As we discussed above, semi-fiction refers to both a method of research and a particular kind of text. In the next section we discuss the philosophy and practical considerations of semi-fiction as a method. We believe that semi-fiction provides the necessary theoretical foundation and practical direction to allow much more progress in exploring the potential of narrative fiction as a method in organizational studies.

THE SUBVERSIVE ROLE OF SEMI-FICTION IN ORGANIZATION STUDIES

Agar (1990: 74) offers this definition of semi-fiction: 'when fiction[al] form is laid over a "fact-oriented" research process'. Semi-fictional narrative (also known as 'faction' or creative non-fiction) results when creative licence is taken with the representational form of empirical data. But why put the two types of texts – fiction and non-fiction – together? We argue that semi-fictional narrative can expand the potential meaning of organizational research because 'they provide a space for the reader to enter the story and vicariously experience the events portrayed ... [and] as fictions they are tremendously flexible' (Phillips, 1995: 671). The factual dimension of semi-fictional narrative helps ground textual messages and encourages readers to gain a greater understanding of a variety of 'serious' topics for organization studies. The fictional dimension can increase reader response and help challenge pre-existing assumptions in a creative and subversive way. As such, semi-fictive works may be particularly good at embodying the 'criticality' dimension of convincing texts (Golden-Biddle and Locke, 1993).

Semi-fictional narratives can have a useful and unique place within organizational research precisely because they combine the standard format of both non-fiction *and* fiction in order to provoke readers to re-examine their beliefs and assumptions about research and the world (Whiteman, 2004). This approach is not without a history. For instance, in 1933, the American writer, Gertrude Stein, broke through a linguistic barrier and wrote her own fictive autobiography entitled *The Autobiography of Alice B. Toklas*. In this book, she ostensibly describes her real-life partner Alice's 'real' memories of Stein and other modernists in Paris of the 1920s. At the same time, the paradox between the title and the author give us clues that this may not be non-fiction after all. At the same time, the use of 'real-life' characters in 'real-life' settings gives us clues that this may not be fiction after all. As a hybrid form of fiction and non-fiction, the work has added impact. At the very least in underscoring how language can both imprison and open our minds to new interpretive possibilities.

As a methodological approach, creative non-fiction emerged most concretely from the field of journalism during the 1960s and 1970s. New Journalism (e.g. Wolfe, 1973; Mailer, 1979; Capote, 1965) allows the journalist to place facts in fictional form. New Journalism 'contain[s] strong elements of reportage, which is the anchor and foundation of the highest quality of journalism and of creative nonfiction. The word "creative" refers to the unique and subjective focus, concept, context and point of view in which the information is presented and defined, which may be partially obtained through the writer's own voice, as in a personal essay' (Gutkind, n.d.).

A journalist uses this approach in order to 'convey the immediacy of experience and give it coherence and significance' (Agar 1995: 116), a textual quality that neither technical non-fiction nor creative fiction alone can usually convey. Creative non-fiction typically makes use of some of the following fictional techniques (see Table 2.7.1):

A semi-fictive approach to research may have additional benefits for academic theorizing since this approach helps to reframe data and representational process through

Table 2.7.1   Fictional techniques to help build creative form

Fictional techniques	
The scenic method	The author shows, rather than tells using rich, sensory language to emphasize the immediacy of the experience.
Character development	The story centers on a few characters both real and compiled. The author uses 'internal monologues' to express the characters' subjective point of view, and also switches from different perspectives.
Plot	The author selects and arranges details to build narrative tension and develop a convincing plot.
Authorial presence	The author is present, either in the story or as a voice behind the story.

Source: Agar (1990)

discursive play. Play has been shown to increase organizational creativity and innovation (Dodgson, et al., 2005). With semi-fiction, we suggest that authors may actively try to identify empirical moments that captured, sometimes in a surprising way, interesting aspects of the organizing form under study. The 'strategy of inquiry' (Denzin and Lincoln, 1994) can also focus particular attention on empirical experiences that seem out of context, surprising and/or humorous – a recognizable focal technique of ethnographic work (Hammersley and Atkinson, 1995). Semi-fictive narrative may thus help broaden our understanding of empirical phenomenon by bringing in provocative creative elements to trigger innovative sense-making of empirical data by authors (and readers). '[B]y re-moulding the reality we assume to be objective, art releases to us, realities otherwise hidden…' (Winterson, 1995: 58). In particular we note the value of semi-fictive collage, where meaning builds with the layers of empirical data and narrative imagination which differs from a more linear style of rational composition.

In addition to provoking more creative empirical reflection, semi-fictive approaches to research may have the ability to convey additional (and different) meanings due the choice of the semi-fictional medium which

can convey its own message(s) (McLuhan, 1967). Semi-fictional narrative has the potential to increase reader empathy because it relies upon emotional and intellectual intersubjectivity (Carrithers, 1990) created in part because of the purposive combination of facts and fiction (Whiteman, 2004). The resulting ambiguities may invite greater reader response (March, 2006; Richardson, 1994).

Box 2.7.2 provides an illustrative excerpt of semi-fiction in organization studies. The excerpt is drawn from Whiteman's (2004) paper presenting the results of her dissertation research investigating Traditional Environmental Knowledge among aboriginal Canadians. Rather than present the results of her field research in a traditional format, Whiteman uses semi-fictional methods to present the results in the form of a fictionalized narrative about a doctoral student defending her thesis research in front of a committee of more or less sympathetic academics. The device of semi-fiction allows Whiteman to include dissenting voices and, through a sort of magic realism, include the odd intrusion by the natural world that her character Pip is trying so hard to convey to her committee.

As Whiteman's work so clearly shows, content can be enriched by the choice of form. While some meanings are adequately conveyed through logico-scientific approaches to communication, others are more deeply embedded in sensory and emotional understandings. Such meanings may require alternative frameworks for expression which no longer marginalize emotions, humour, values, and imagination, and yet do not detach completely from empirical experience.

Despite the positive elements of the subversive quality of semi-fictional narrative, we acknowledge the potential difficulties in evaluating the use of semi-fiction in terms of academic validity. Indeed, concern over credibility is the primary issue raised against the legitimacy of creative non-fiction within journalism (Agar, 1990). Agar (1990) suggests that the route forward lies in a simultaneous discussion – and explication – of the

---

Box 2.7.2   Excerpt from *Why are we talking inside?*

'Now Pip, can you please give us an example of TEK (traditional ecological knowledge) in action?' asked a committee member. 'Help us understand what you're talking about'.

'Sure', said Pip. 'I can try. Let's see … The use and value of TEK can best be described by story. In fact, Cree people use story to convey important information about their management approach. Unfortunately, such conversations can easily be marginalized by business executives and management scholars'.

Her supervisor grimaced. Pip continued,

'No, it's true. To illustrate this point, I want to offer a story of my own. Once when I was in James Bay, I was talking with my key informant, a Cree tallyman, who was telling me about his concerns regarding forestry. Freddy had a problem with the way the forestry company was replanting trees. He said to me, 'After clearcutting, when they plant the trees … it's the worst way to do it. Because when they plant a tree, I think it's going to taste different. Like when Porcupine eats it…. It's going to be a different taste'.

Freddy felt that the porcupines needed greater variety than such replanting programs would allow. (Whiteman, 2004: 7)

---

research process itself. That is, a careful discussion of methodology and representative motivation are required. This underscores the importance of an author clearly outlining their own textual guidelines for representation alongside a discussion of the research process (i.e. how data was gathered, analysed, etc.). Agar (1990) stresses the need for in-depth immersion in the phenomenon under study in order to develop a 'factual' or deep experiential understanding of the empirical data. Semi-fiction thus may work well as a qualitative method for exploring empirical reality and pulling together fragments from fieldwork. And it is in this sense that we describe it as a method of data analysis. It is much more than just a way of presenting data, it is a way of working through the data collected by the researcher and developing deep theoretical understandings.

In developing a semi-fictional narrative, the researcher develops a theory of the social context within which the narrative is set. Thus, semi-fictional work has particular relevance for creatively representing qualitative research, especially with ethnographic research (Whiteman, 2004). However, we believe that a semi-fictive text remains somewhat different from an 'impressionistic

tale' from ethnography (Van Maanen, 1988) in that it takes imaginative and fictive licence with form, while an impressionistic tale remains less open to elements of 'make-believe'. In a work of semi-fiction there is no need to be bound by what was seen and heard. What is important is to weave together fragments of social 'data' with the creative licence to make the theoretical insights of the researcher vivid and easily available to the reader.

Non-academic writers like Margaret Atwood agree with the need to clearly outline (for themselves at least) their own textual guide when they write creative historical fiction which becomes similar to semi-fiction (e.g. Alias Grace):

> to be fair, I had to represent all points of view. I devised the following set of guidelines for myself: when there was a solid fact, I could not alter it… Also, every major element in the book had to be suggested by something in the writing about Grace and her times, however dubious such writing might be; but, in the parts left unexplained – the gaps left unfilled – I was free to invent. (1998)

From our own experience, we have found that a semi-fictional approach to research requires a strong empirical focus, and builds upon concrete data and experience (Stablein, 1996).

While semi-fictional text can emerge in a directed way, we also highlight the importance of random aesthetic moments. We suggest that sometimes semi-fiction may not follow a purposive outline and rather text which begins to write itself may add value. Nevertheless, authorial motives remain academic in nature – to capture and reflect upon organizing forms and to engage the reader in this playful yet potentially penetrating activity. We discuss this in more detail below.

SUMMING UP: SEMI-FICTION MEETS DAVID LODGE

The purpose of this chapter is to bring together existing thinking and practice on the use of narrative fiction in organization studies. This topic is one that is of increasing importance and interest among organizational scholars but remains at a very early stage. Consequently, we present both a theoretical and practical discussion of this issue.

The narratives presented in this chapter are two examples of using narrative in organization studies. They are presented in fictive and semi-fiction form by different authors. The questions that remain are: How are these texts different? How are they the same? How does labelling one fiction and the other semi-fiction impact the interpretation of these genres of texts?

With a novelist like David Lodge, we know little about his 'methodology' of writing. The narrative is explicitly presented as a part of a fictional account of life. The intention is not to develop theory, although the author shows deep insight into areas such as the academic world and was, unsurprisingly, an academic himself. Whereas a semi-fiction account is as much about generating insight *in the author* as it is about presenting results in an imaginative way, the work of fiction is focused solely on the presentation of an entertaining and impactful narrative. At the same time, it is indistinguishable in form from the semi-fiction. It is the author's intentions, the attempt to bring fragments of

the real into the narrative, and the context in which the narrative is produced that divides the two.

In contrast, in the excerpt of semi-fiction by Whiteman (2004), the author relied upon 18 months of ethnographic data as well as 'factual' texts like email exchanges, anonymous written reviews from the *Academy of Management Journal*, and actual conversations with living people, which was communicated in the methodology section preceding the semi-fictional account. These concrete elements formed the empirical basis from which she imaginatively explored in a creative form and were explained in her methods section.

The two types of texts are thus related to the extent that they use an imaginative narrative approach to cognitive processing (Bruner, 1986), and as such both demonstrate that organizing forms can be described (and analysed) using more than logico-scientific style. However, aside from notable differences in quality (we can't, unfortunately, all be David Lodge), the production of, and motivation behind, the representation style of fiction and semi-fiction texts may differ. That is, semi-fiction attempts to creatively build upon empirical data grounded in methodological rigour, while fiction makes no claims about data, method or rigour, although is arguably based upon experience (notwithstanding the author's typical note that this work is 'entirely fictitious and not based upon any real people, dead or alive').

We suggest that the labels themselves – of fiction and semi-fiction – may also influence the way the academic reader interprets or consumes the text. In particular, the label 'semi-fiction' signals that this is an imaginative narrative grounded in empirical experience and as such, differs significantly from traditionally accepted academic approaches to research. Semi-fiction attempts to have its cake and eat it too. In this way, semi-fiction acts as a type of Looking Glass, a narrative metaphor, which tests our attachment to entrenched academic traditions surrounding the production, representation and consumption of research. In contrast, a fictional label gives the reader a reflective 'way-out': it's not real so we don't have to take it seriously when we don't want to.

We acknowledge that fiction and semi-fiction remain 'loose' definitions or rough categories of narrative form that require academic experimentation, enactment and further refinement. Such academic sense-making will take time, yet we should not be daunted by this journey of inquiry. Indeed, as Geertz so sagely wrote nearly two decades ago in anthropology: 'It's not clear just what "faction", imaginative writing about real people in real places at real times, exactly comes to beyond a clever coinage; but anthropology is going to have to find out if it is to continue as an intellectual force in contemporary culture' (1988, 141).

We end with a challenge: 'If we admit that language has power over us, not only through what it says but also through what it is, we will be tolerant of literary experiment just as we are tolerant of scientific experiment' (Winterson, 1995: 76). Through fictional and semi-fictional play, a richer understanding of organizations and organizing forms may emerge. But we need more than tolerance; we need continued innovation in fact *and* fiction.

ACKNOWLEDGEMENT

Table 2.7.1 reproduced from Agar, M. (1990) 'Text and fieldwork: Exploring the excluded middle', *Journal of Contemporary Ethnography*, 19 (1): 73–88 with permission from Sage.

NOTES

1 See Hansen et al., 2007 for a useful description of some reactions that might be expected to a narrative fiction submitted to a journal.

2 William, B.Y. (1996) 'Easter 1916', in Jeffares, A.N. (ed), *Yeats's Poems*. London, UK: Macmillan, pp. 287–289.

REFERENCES

Agar, M. (1990) 'Text and fieldwork: Exploring the excluded middle', *Journal of Contemporary Ethnography*, 19(1): 73–88.

Agar, M. (1995) 'Literary journalism as ethnography: Exploring the excluded middle', in J. Van Maanen, (ed.), *Representations in Ethnography*. Thousand Oaks, CA: Sage. pp. 112–142.

Astley, W.G. (1985) 'Administrative science as socially constructed truth', *Administrative Science Quarterly*, 30: 497–513.

Atwood, M. (1998) 'In search of Alias Grace: On writing Canadian historical fiction', *The American Historical Review*, 103(5): 1503–1516.

Barry, D. (1996) 'Artful inquiry: A symbolic constructivist approach to social science research', *Qualitative Inquiry*, 2: 411–438.

Boje, D., Fitgibbons, D.E. and Steingard, D.S. (1996) 'Storytelling at Administrative Science Quarterly: Warding off the postmodern barbarians', in D. Boje, R. Gephart, and T. Joseph, (eds), *Postmodern Management and Organization Theory*. Newberry Park, CA: Sage.

Bruner, J. (1986) *Actual minds, possible worlds*. Cambridge, MA: Harvard University Press.

Calás, M.B. and Smircich, L. (1996) 'From The woman's point of view: Feminist approaches to organization studies', in S.R. Clegg, C. Hardy, and W.R. Nord, (eds), Handbook of Organization Studies: 218–257. London: Sage.

Capote, T. (1965) *In Cold Blood: A True Account of a Multiple Murder and its Consequences*. New York: Random House.

Carrithers, M. (1990) 'Is anthropology art or science?' *Current Anthropology*, 31(3): 263–272.

Carroll, L. (1991) 'Through the looking glass'. Retrieved 17-01-04 from http://www.literature.org/authors/carroll-lewis/through-the-looking-glass/index.html

Clifford, J. and Marcus, G.E. (1986) *Writing Culture: The Poetics and Politics of Ethnography*. Berkeley, CA: University of California Press.

Currie, G. (1985) 'What is fiction?' *The Journal of Aesthetics and Art Criticism*, 43(4): 385–392.

Czarniawska, B. (1998) *A Narrative Approach to Organization Studies*. Thousand Oaks, CA: Sage.

Czarniawska-Joerges, B. and Guillet de Monthoux, P. (1994) *Good Novels, Better Management: Reading Organizational Realities in Fiction*. Chur, Switzerland: Harwood.

Denzin, N.K. and Lincoln, Y.S. (eds) (1994) *Handbook of Qualitative Research*. Thousand Oaks, CA: Sage.

Dodgson, M., Gann, D. and Salter, A. (2005) *Think, Play, Do: Technology, Innovation and Organization*. Oxford: Oxford University Press.

Geertz, C. (1988) *Works and Lives: The Anthropologist as Author*. Stanford, CA: Stanford University Press.

Goffman, E. (1959) *The Presentation of Self in Everyday Life*. New York: Anchor Books.

Golden-Biddle, K., and Locke, K. (1993) 'Appealing work: An investigation of how ethnographic texts convince', *Organization Science*, 4(4): 595–616.

Gutkind, L. (n.d.) 'What's in this name – And what's not. Creative Nonfiction'. Retrieved 17-01-04 from http://www.creativenonfiction.org/thejournal/articles/issue01/01editor.htm

Hammersley, M., and Atkinson, P. (1995) *Ethnography: Principles in Practice*, (2nd ed) London: Routledge.

Hansen, H., Barry, D., Boje. D.M. and Hatch, M.J. (2007) 'Truth or consequences: An improvised collective story construction', *Journal of Management Inquiry*, 16 (2): 112–126.

Jeffcut, P. (1994) From interpretation to representation in organizational analysis: postmodernism, ethnography and organizational symbolism. *Organization Studies*, 15(2): 241–274.

Jermier, J. (1985) 'When the sleeper wakes': A short story extending themes in radical organization theory. *Journal of Management Inquiry*, 11(2): 67–80.

Kennedy, E. and Lawton, L. (1992) 'Business ethics in fiction', *Journal of Business Ethics*, 11: 187–195.

Mailer, N. (1979) *The Executioner's Song*. Boston: Little, Brown.

March, J.G. (2006) 'Poetry and the rhetoric of management: Easter 1916', *Journal of Management Inquiry*, 15: 70–72.

McLuhan, M. (1967) *The Medium is the Message*. New York: Random House.

O'Donnell, M.G. (1989) 'A historical note on the use of fiction to teach principles of economics', *Journal of Economic Education*, 20(3): 314–320.

Park, Y. (1982) 'The function of fiction'. *Philosophy and Phenomenological Research*, 42(3): 416–424.

Parker, M., Higgins, M., Lightfoot, G. and Smith, W. (1999) 'Amazing tales: Organization studies as science fiction'. *Organization*, 6 (4): 579–590.

Phillips, N. (1995) 'Telling organizational tales: On the role of narrative fiction in the study of organizations', *Organization Studies*, 16: 625–649.

Phillips, N. and Zyglidopoulos, S. (1999) 'Learning from Foundation: Asimov's Psychohistory and the Limits of Organization Theory', *Organization*, 6 (4): 591–608.

Richardson, L. (1994) 'Nine poems: Marriage and the family', *Journal of Contemporary Ethnography*, 23 (1): 3–13.

Rorty, R. (1991) 'Inquiry as recontextualization: An anti-dualist account of interpretation', in D.R. Hiley, J.F. Bohman and R. Shusterman, (eds), *The Interpretive Turn*: *Philosophy, Science, Culture*. Ithaca, NY: Cornell University Press. pp. 59–80.

Rosen, M. (1985) 'Breakfast at Spiro's: Dramaturgy and Dominance', *Journal of Management*, 11 (2): 31–48.

Rosen, M. (1988) 'You asked for it: Christmas at the bosses expense', *Journal of Management Studies*, 25 (5): 463–480.

Stablein, R. (1996) 'Data in organization studies', in S.R. Clegg, C. Hardy, and W.R. Nord, (eds), *Handbook of Organization Studies*, Thousand Oaks, CA: Sage. pp. 509–525.

Stein, G. (1922/1995) *Geography and Plays*. Boston, MA: The Four Seas Co.

Stein. G. (1933/2001) *The Autobiography of Alice B. Toklas*. London: Penguin.

Taylor, S. (2000) 'Capitalist pigs at the Academy of Management', *Journal of Management Inquiry* 9: 304–328.

Van Maanen, J. (1988) *Tales of the Field: On Writing Ethnography*. Chicago: University of Chicago Press.

Van Maanen, J. (ed.) (1995) *Representation in Ethnography*. Thousand Oaks, CA: Sage.

Weick, K.E. (1979) *The Social Psychology of Organizing*. Reading: Addison-Wesley.

Weick, K.E. (1995) *Sensemaking in Organizations*. Thousand Oaks, CA: Sage

Whiteman, G. (2004) 'Why are we talking inside? Reflecting on Traditional Ecological Knowledge (TEK) and management research', *Journal of Management Inquiry*, 13 (3): 261–277.

Winterson, J. (1995) *Art objects: Essays on Ecstasy and Effrontery*. Toronto: Knopf.

Wolfe, T. (1973) 'The new journalism', in T. Wolfe and E.W. Johnson, (eds), *The New Journalism*. New York: Harper & Row. pp. 3–52.

Wolcott, H.F. (1995) 'Making a study 'more' ethnographic', in J. Van Maanen, (ed.), *Representation in Ethnography*. Thousand Oaks, CA: Sage. pp. 86–111.

Towards a Critical Engagement with Metaphor in Organization Studies

Cliff Oswick

As Gareth Morgan's work has eloquently demonstrated, metaphors are powerful, vivid and evocative devices (e.g. Morgan, 1996). They illuminate phenomena and they have a generative capacity (i.e. the potential to provide new ways of thinking). It is no wonder that they continue to be popular among organization studies scholars. What is remarkable, however, is the absence of any sustained critical reflection upon the use of metaphors within the field. This is not to say that commentators have not been critical of metaphor-use in organizational analysis, but these concerns seem to operate at two extremes. On the one hand, there is a longstanding view that we need to eschew metaphors on the basis that they act as embellishments and hinder 'scientific inquiry' in organizations studies (e.g. Pinder and Bourgeois, 1982). On the other hand, Cornelissen (2005) has critiqued the dominant 'comparison-based view' of metaphor within organization theory for not going far enough and has advocated the adoption of a 'correspondence view' through a process of conceptual blending which offers insights into both the source domain (the metaphor) and target domain (the organizational object or subject).

In terms of the illuminating potential of metaphor, it would seem that the 'replacement critique' (i.e. eschewing metaphors) posits that they leave us in the dark while the 'expansion critique' (an extended role for metaphor) suggests the light is brighter than we realize. Rather than focusing upon the intensity of the illumination, we might ask questions about the direction in which the 'metaphorical light' is shone. Who shines the light? Who chooses what is illuminated?

What is missing in much of the extant literature on metaphor in organization studies is a political account of the phenomenon. The act of selecting and applying a metaphor is imbued with ideology and involves the exercise of power. Ultimately, it is about privileging a particular discourse (via the process of illumination) and, more importantly, marginalizing alternative ones (i.e. relegating them to the darkness). The hegemony of organizational discourses is well understood, but contributions relating to metaphor are extremely limited. This collective oversight is largely due to the figurative nature of tropes and because metaphors primarily operate in a connotative rather than denotative register (Oswick et al., 2002). Put another way, the fact that metaphors are non-literal and are designed to resonate with, as opposed to directly represent, the phenomenon onto which they are projected makes it difficult to evaluate them meaningfully in literal (or critical) terms. Notwithstanding the problems of analysis, the general prevalence and the considerable purchase of metaphor within organization studies means the dearth of critical work is problematic.

As an illustration of how critical inquiry might be progressed, let us consider the population ecology view of organizations. This taken-for-granted analogue informs a cluster of second-order metaphors, such as the notion of 'corporate predatorship' (Oswick, 2001). The predator metaphor offers rich and vivid image generating potential via the foregrounding of similarities between the behaviour of large corporations and the behaviour of predatory animals. The metaphor cannot be read too literally or in a denotative way (i.e. corporations do not actually eat smaller companies). However, it is possible to develop critical interpretations of the metaphor through connotative connections. To begin with, the predatory behaviour of animals can be perceived of as legitimate insofar as it is natural, instinctive and necessary (i.e. the need to eat to survive). These characteristics are subtly embraced and co-opted by corporations who represent themselves as engaging in activities which are similarly 'natural' and 'necessary'.

When subjected to critical scrutiny, the 'corporate predatorship' metaphor serves particular corporatist ends by reinforcing and legitimating a Darwinian logic of competition and the survival of the fittest. As part of a critical agenda, it is also interesting to ask which metaphors are marginalized by the dominant discourse. In the case of corporate predatorship, it could be argued that juxtaposing counter-ideological metaphors – such as 'corporate theft', 'corporate bullying', and 'corporate rape' – may help to meaningfully capture and illuminate different aspects of the phenomena.

In conclusion, if we are to develop more sophisticated and informative accounts of the role, status and utility of metaphor in organization studies it is important that future research seeks to incorporate a critical dimension. This can be done in two ways. First, through reflexive processes researchers should question their own use of metaphors and ask themselves what their particular choice of metaphor reveals (and obscures) about them and the organizational phenomena onto which is projected. Second, more research which problematizes the dominant metaphors-in-use within the field would also be valuable. In particular, we should address questions, such as: In whose interests, and to what ends, does a given metaphorical construction operate? What underlying political assumptions and ideological connotations are at work? To what extent, and in what ways, can the deployment of salient counter-metaphors aid the generation of richer plurivocal perspectives and alternative conceptualizations of particular phenomena in organization studies?

REFERENCES

Cornelissen, J.P. (2005) 'Beyond compare: Metaphor in organization theory', *Academy of Management Review*, 30: 751–764.

Morgan, G. (1986) *Images of Organization*. Beverly Hills, CA: Sage.

Oswick, C. (2001) 'The etymology of corporate predatorship: A critical commentary', *Tamara: Journal of Critical Postmodern Organization Science*, 1 (2): 21–25.

Oswick, C., Keenoy, T. and Grant, D. (2002) 'Metaphor and analogical reasoning in organization theory: Beyond orthodoxy', *Academy of Management Review*, 27: 294–303.

Pinder, C.C. and Bourgeois, V.W. (1982) 'Controlling tropes in administrative science', *Administrative Science Quarterly*, 27 (4): 641–652.

Routine Dynamics[1]

Martha S. Feldman and Brian T. Pentland

Recently there has been increased interest in organizational routines and particularly how organizational routines relate to organizational change and stability.[2] Two emerging perspectives relate organizational routines and organizational change. We refer to these as routine dynamics and dynamic capabilities respectively. We explore the routine dynamics perspective in this chapter. From this perspective it is important to open the black box of organizational routines and reconceptualize them as being made of interacting parts or aspects (Feldman and Pentland, 2003; Pentland and Feldman, 2005; Levinthal and Rerup, 2006). By contrast, the dynamic capabilities perspective leaves the black box intact and focuses on the routine as a whole (Eisenhart and Martin, 2000; Zollo and Winter, 2002). Each of these emerging perspectives allows us to answer different questions. While the dynamic capabilities perspective is more appropriate for predicting what an organization or an organizational field will be doing from one point in time to another, the routine dynamics perspective is oriented to understanding how stability and change are achieved. This perspective enables us to ask questions about what people can do to promote stability or change and

what people can do to promote sensible innovations on established routines. Routine dynamics is a focus on the internal dynamics of routines and the empirical and conceptual questions that arise from that focus. While much of this work was stimulated by empirical studies demonstrating that routines are not as inertial as once thought,[3] change is not necessarily the outcome of routine dynamics. Indeed, understanding the internal dynamics of routines is as important for understanding organizational stability as it is for understanding organizational change.

The first premise of routine dynamics is that organizational routines are best conceptualized as generative systems rather than treating routines as fixed objects, or black boxes (Feldman and Pentland, 2003; Pentland and Feldman, in press). As generative systems, routines have what we call ostensive and performative aspects. The performative aspects are easy to understand, because they are easy to see: real actions, by real people, in specific times and places. The performative aspects are concrete. The ostensive aspects, on the other hand, are abstract and not so easy to see. They are the patterns formed by the performances; they are what enable us to say that we are engaged in the 'same' performance from one iteration of a routine to another. They are at least partly tacit; they are distributed and partial (in the sense that different points of view allow participants to see different things and also to see the same thing in different ways), they are multiple (both in the sense that different people see different patterns and that the same person may see multiple patterns) and they are often inconsistent or conflicting.

Central to this perspective is our claim that ostensive aspects of an organizational routine are *not* simply 'shared understandings'. Indeed, it is essential to talk about the ostensive in the plural as there are likely to be many ostensive perspectives in any organizational routine. Shared understanding suggests that you and I are doing something for the same reason, that we have the same understanding of why we are engaged in a particular activity. While shared understanding has been used in some instances to explain collective activity, it seems at best to be reasoning by analogy from the individual to the collective and it is clearly not the only way collective activity can occur (see Donnellon et al., 1986 for a simple organizational counterexample). Empirical evidence suggests that people can produce repetitive, recognizable patterns of interdependent action without much in the way of shared understanding (consider the Middle East, for example). Shared or not, the ostensive aspects are invoked as resources for guiding and accounting for action. Indeed some of the interesting dynamics around routines have specifically to do with what pattern we associate with particular actions and how we can legitimate actions by invoking a pattern.

As we conceptualize them, the ostensive aspects of organizational routines pose an exciting challenge: how are the ostensive aspects of an organizational routine created, sustained and modified? The dominant explanation these days would tend to build on theories of structuration (Giddens, 1984) and practice (Bourdieu, 1990). For example, Barley's (1986) study of technological change in two radiology departments uses structuration theory to explain changes in departmental routines. Orlikowski's studies use observations of people performing work routines to show how their actions produce technology-in-practice (1992, 2000). In this view, structure is created and re-created through agency (action). This perspective helps us see the cumulative effect of actions, but leaves open how specific actions come to matter in a specific context. To address this shortcoming, we have found that some simple ideas from actor-network theory provide a useful extension to the structuration perspective.

So, in the brief chapter that follows, we have set out the task of explaining and integrating these emerging perspectives: (1) routines are generative systems, not fixed objects; (2) they have ostensive and performative aspects; and (3) the relationship between ostensive and performative can be expressed through a combination of structuration and 'actor-network'-style explanations.

ORGANIZATIONAL ROUTINES AS GENERATIVE SYSTEMS

An organizational routine can be described as a generative system consisting of performative parts and ostensive parts (Feldman and Pentland, 2003; Pentland and Feldman, 2005). The performative parts are specific actions taken by specific people in specific times and places. The ostensive parts are the abstract pattern, the routine in principle or the narrative of the routine. They are the embodied understandings of the routine that we act out in specific instances. The performative parts of the routine create, maintain and modify the ostensive aspects of the routine. The ostensive parts of the routine guide performances, and are used to account for and refer to performances. Routines change because people adjust their performances and because they select and retain some of these performances in their embodied understandings (the ostensive aspects). People adjust their performances for a variety of reasons (Rerup, 2005; Levinthal and Rerup, 2006). They may need to adjust to contextual variations; they may not be happy with previous outcomes of the routine, or they may have discovered that they can do something that they did not realize before they could do (Feldman, 2000).

We treat standard operating procedures and other artifacts as separate from organizational routines (Pentland and Feldman, 2005). Standard operating procedures are sometimes mistaken either for the routine as a whole or for the ostensive aspects of the routine. When viewing routines as generative systems, however, the standard operating procedure is external though not irrelevant to the system. Standard operating procedures describe or prescribe aspects of the routine, but they are not necessarily followed. A written procedure may be invoked 'as needed', to settle a dispute or justify a course of action. Often, however, written rules and procedures just gather dust.

For the discussion that follows, it is worth elaborating on the ostensive aspects of routines, as we use the term. The ostensive is defined in the Oxford English Dictionary as 'manifestly or directly demonstrative' or 'professedly demonstrative; specious' (1971: 2015). Latour, who has theorized much of actor-network theory, uses the term when he talks about power and society. Ultimately it is the 2nd definition that he is using, though the 1st is also important because power and society (and organization and routine) are constructs that have come to be taken for demonstrable things. He argues that, 'Society is not the referent of an ostensive definition discovered by social scientists despite the ignorance of their informants. Rather it is performed through everyone's efforts to define it' (Latour, 1986: 273). In other words, society (and power, organization, routines, etc.) are not fixed and demonstrable things but, at most, temporarily agreed upon agglomerations.

One of the effects of Latour pointing to the non-demonstrability of 'society' (and other such concepts) is to refocus our attention on performance or what we do to create these ostensive definitions. Latour refers to 'social scientists' as the source of ostensive definitions, but this obscures slightly what is going on. The act that the social scientist engages to produce the ostensive definition is the act of abstraction. Abstracting is not something that only social scientists do, but is what any of us do when we recognize a pattern.

With this minor quibble aside, what Latour draws our attention to is not only the act of creating the ostensive definitions but more importantly the many acts that create associations from which we abstract these ostensive aspects. This perspective also raises some interesting questions. How is it that performances come together to create and sustain the ostensive aspects? What makes one action (e.g. an information session) part of a hiring routine and another action (e.g. an information session) part of a training routine? In this chapter we draw on the actor-network perspective and combine it with a structuration/practice theory perspective to explore how the ostensive aspects form. By doing this we provide a different way of thinking about change in organizational routines.

EXPLAINING ROUTINE DYNAMICS

Our story about change in organizational routines is best understood against the backdrop of more traditional explanations, which may be familiar to some readers. Different explanations emphasize different features of the context and draw our attention to different mechanisms for change. The two most familiar explanations can be called the rational (utility maximizing) and the ecological explanations. In the rational explanation, decisions are made to change routines in order to achieve specific goals. Someone who has 'control' over 'the routine', such as a manager, generally makes such decisions. Control takes many forms, but may consist of specifying performances and creating incentives for particular performances. In this view, routines are changed (from the outside) in response to environmental pressures, as interpreted by managers. The ecological explanation is based on variation and selective retention, and it provides a complementary story. In the ecological view, routines are mostly quite stable (unchanging, like genetic material), except in cases of managerial intervention or incomplete copying, which can be seen as a 'mutation'. The environment selects the more successful (efficient, effective, legitimate) variants. The ecological story goes beyond the simple managerial story by pointing out that environmental changes may wipe out entire populations of routines.

There is no question that managerial intervention changes routines, and that the economic and social environment exerts selection pressures. These explanations draw our attention to exogenous mechanisms of change. Change is imposed from the outside, by managers or by the environment. In these perspectives, the routine itself is treated as black box. These explanations are depicted in Figure 2.8.1 as exogenous change. According to these explanations, to the extent that routines change it is because various pressures push them from the outside.

Exogenous change is only part of the story, of course. Empirical evidence shows that organizational routines exhibit endogenous change (Feldman, 2000, 2004).

Change occurs because the routine is enacted and is integral to the enactment of the routine. Tsoukas and Chia point out that endogenous change is a part of enacting organization as well as enacting organizational routines (2002).

One explanation for endogenous change in organizational routines has its theoretical base in practice theories and theories of structuration (e.g. Bourdieu, 1990; Giddens, 1984). These theories orient us to the interdependence of the structural and the agentic and show how the two are mutually constitutive. Organizational routines, from this perspective, are neither structural nor agentic, but both. They are generative systems in which actions produce and reproduce structures and the structures produced enable and constrain actions. The structuration/practice theory explanation of change in organizational routines is depicted in Figure 2.8.1 as endogenous change. Change occurs because of the interactions between parts of the routine. The routine is still portrayed as an integral entity as in the previous explanations. The entity now has internal dynamics.

While structuration-based explanations draw our attention to the possibility of endogenous change, they are not

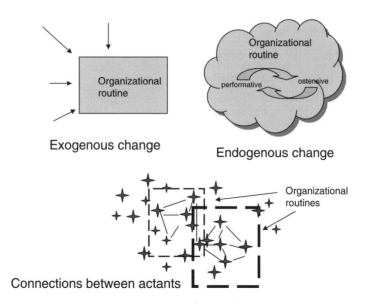

Exogenous change

Endogenous change

Connections between actants

Figure 2.8.1   Images of dynamics in organizational routines

entirely satisfying. The broad category of 'structure', for example, is rather vague. And structures are said to emerge as an unintended consequence of action (Giddens, 1984). This seems rather limited. Structuration-based explanations work especially well for societal-level phenomena, occurring over the decades or centuries, which is where the theory was first articulated. As applied to organizational routines, however, the vocabulary of structuration lacks specificity.

In response to these limitations, actor-network theory (ANT) offers an alternative way to conceptualize both stability and change through variation in networks of associations (Czarniawska and Hernes, 2005; Law and Hassard, 1999). From this perspective, organizational routines consist of 'actants' that are associated through the ostensive aspects of a routine (Feldman and Pentland, 2005). The employment ads, the telephone calls, the applicant files, the committees and their meetings, the interviews, the negotiated offer, the applicants, the interviewers and a host of other actants are connected as the hiring routine. In addition, this network of associations that we call the hiring routine is also associated with other actants and other networks of associations. For instance, it may be associated with other routines, such as the promotion routine or the budget routine. It may also be associated with such things as the status of the organization or with particular notions of professional standards.

From the ANT perspective, change in organizational routines is change in the connections between actants. There is no integral entity that starts out as a routine. Routines are both constructed and fortified by connecting parts. Routines gain or lose strength, stability and legitimacy by their connections. This explanation is depicted in Figure 2.8.1 as connections between actants. The bold stars are actants. The black boxes that define an actor network as an organizational routine are outlines that we impose on a connected set of actants. Strictly speaking, change is not depicted in this part of the Figure. Instead, two routines are depicted,

either of which could change over time and according to the perspectives of various participants or observers.[4] Change occurs as different actants are connected with one another and as we create different outlines to define different organizational routines. The 'we' who create these constructs may be participants or observers as they identify patterns, talk about them and invoke them for various reasons.

The ANT explanation adds three things to the structuration explanation. First, it requires that we include not only performances but also other actants (including non-human actants) in the performative side of the performative-ostensive duality. This emphasizes the distinction between specificity and abstraction (which is also intrinsic to the agency/structure distinction) and allows for the possibility of agency in non-human actants (cf. Latour, 1996). Second, it focuses us on the connections between actants in specific performances and the creation of these connections. Third, it helps us pose a question about how an actor network becomes identified ostensively as an entity that we (who abstract) call a routine.

This reconceptualization of the relationship between performative and ostensive helps us think about the role of agency in the creation and recreation of organizational routines. Agency is an important part of both the structuration and ANT explanations. Agency in the structuration explanation consists of people taking action. This is clearly an important part of the story but not very well defined. The ANT explanation allows us to elaborate this notion of agency not only to taking action but also to creating connections between actions and legitimating (or delegitimating) these connections.

In adopting a view of organizational routines that emphasizes agency and change, there is a risk of slipping into the view that anything goes – that routines are perfectly malleable, and that associations can be created and destroyed at the whim of individual actors. Although organizational routines do change, their defining features are their recognizable patterns of interdependent actions, and while agents can make new and different associations, they often make the same associations. This is, in part, what makes the act of creating associations a political act. To the extent that they become established such patterns signal the dominance of one way of doing things over alternative ways (Doz, 1996; Sydow et al., 2005).

ILLUSTRATION

To illustrate the relative contributions a structuration approach and an actor network theory approach can make to understanding the ostensive aspects of organizational routines, we turn to a provocative case.[5] In this case there is a great deal of pressure to change the established routine in a particular way. As of this writing, the interaction between performative and ostensive has produced relative stability in the part of the routine that is the focus of our attention.

In the decades preceding World War II, the U.S. air force developed a way of thinking about the damage that would be incurred by the bombs that their airplanes could drop. This way of thinking, or frame, was based on a doctrine of precision bombing that assumed that the major damage that a bomb does is caused by blast. This frame carried over to the assessment of nuclear bombs when, shortly after the end of World War II, evaluating what damage would be done by using nuclear weapons became part of the defense analysis. Over the decades between World War II and now, a routine developed for assessing nuclear weapons that was increasingly complex and precise.

The routine, similar to an algorithm, involved calculating the relationship between overpressure ('air pressure above ambient air pressure at sea level' (p. 20)) and the probability of sustaining a designated level of damage (p. 138). This calculation was used to create the Vulnerability Number (VN) scale, which was used to classify structures according to the effect that blast was likely to have on them. This routine, developed in the early 1950s, was further developed over

that decade. By the end of the decade, the VNTK system was developed that also took into account the type of structures (T) and the degree of sensitivity to the duration of the blast wave (K).

As important as this algorithm was, it was not the only outcome of the assessment process. Indeed, the efforts resulted in a whole knowledge system that supported the assessment routine. Eden shows that '… early attempts to predict damage from atomic blast led in the early 1950s to an ambitious research agenda to acquire the specific knowledge necessary to make better predictions and to an expansion of organizational expertise' (p. 8). Research and engineering specialties that provided more knowledge about blast effects thrived and the organizations responsible for providing damage assessments became increasingly rich in knowledge about blast and its effects.

Despite ongoing efforts to improve the routine, it did not and does not include the effects of fire in its assessment. This is particularly strange as the empirical evidence from the nuclear bombs that were dropped during World War II as well as other empirical evidence in more limited testing situations, have shown that fire is an incontrovertible part of the damage that any nuclear weapon would cause. Fire damage was, from the beginning, considered to be unpredictable and research conducted during the 1950s, 60s and 70s supported this idea. During the 1980s researchers in the Defense Nuclear Agency challenged this view and proposed a new damage assessment routine. Throughout the 1990s and into the 2000s support for the inclusion of fire damage continued at a low level. A routine based on fire or on fire and blast never rose to the point of toppling or even co-existing with the blast dominant routine, but it never entirely went away either.

The major question Eden's book poses is why the routine for assessing damage from a nuclear bomb has been based on blast damage rather than fire damage or both kinds of damage. Explanations for this exist at a variety of different levels.

Routine as black box

The preference for blast over fire as a basis for the damage assessment routine could be functional and could have been consciously chosen for its functionality. The following would be one form of that argument. Basing the damage assessment on blast results in smaller damage assessments than basing it on fire or on both fire and blast. There are a variety of reasons that people in a position to choose the damage assessment routine might want to underestimate the damage they do. Underestimation might, for instance, support a case for building more weapons. Alternatively, underestimating might make it seem more reasonable to be contemplating using nuclear weapons at all. This kind of explanation requires a consistency of choice and calculus over a range of organizational actors over several decades. It also requires a connection between the damage assessment routine and other outcomes that may not be warranted. Eden specifically argues against this explanation.

An alternative exogenous explanation involves an ecological preference for predictability. This preference is widely held in society, in the defense community and in the scientific and engineering fields involved in risk assessment. Knowledge-building routines are selected for relevance and results. Routines that appear to build more relevant knowledge and yield replicable predictions are a better fit with this environment than routines that yield less replicable results and are more likely to be selected by this environment. Because the routine based on blast damage appeared to be more predictable, it was more likely to be selected and to 'survive'.

The ecological explanation provides a plausible account of the stability of this routine. The importance of predictability is supported by the evidence in Eden's book. We can safely predict that next year the routine will be the same. But what if we want to try to change the routine? Are there explanations that can help us think about how to do that? For such explanations we need to go inside the black box.

Inside the black box

Going inside the routines helps us understand a little more about why the blast-based routine was so firmly entrenched and why the fire-based routine has not taken hold. A structuration/practice theory explanation suggests that the blast frame as a structure grew through the repeated actions taken that were consistent with it. At the same time, the fire frame was 'starved' by the dearth of actions that were consistent with it. The following details provide information about how this 'growing' and 'starving' took place.

Structuration/practice theory explanation. When damage calculation for nuclear weapons began, the people engaged in it were much better able to predict blast damage than fire damage. The relative inability to predict fire damage at that time came to be understood as fire damage is not predictable. Seeing fire damage as unpredictable resulted in less funding of research on fire damage. Less funding of research resulted in fewer people doing research on fire damage. Fewer people doing research on fire damage resulted in less knowledge. Less knowledge resulted in less predictability. Even some who engaged in fire damage research found it unpredictable. In this way, they also created 'knowledge' that fire damage was not predictable.

A similar, but opposite, dynamic characterized the blast-based routine. The relative ability to predict blast damage came to be understood as 'blast damage is predictable'. Seeing blast damage as predictable resulted in funding of research on blast damage. Funding of research on blast damage resulted in more people doing research on blast damage, and more people doing research on blast damage resulted in more knowledge about blast damage. More knowledge about blast damage provided support for the predictability of blast damage.

These two dynamics worked together to produce a more deeply entrenched blast-based routine and a less and less established fire-based routine. Performances took the form of research, funding for research and explanations of the research. These performances systematically produced patterns of damage assessment. The patterns around blast damage became more powerful while the patterns around fire damage became weaker. We can see, from this explanation, that if we wanted to make fire damage more powerful, we would promote research on fire damage in the hopes of increasing its predictability. Here we run straight into Gidden's paraphrase of Marx that 'Men [let us immediately say human beings] make history, but not in circumstances of their own choosing' (Marx quoted in Giddens, 1984: xxi). We now understand more about why blast damage continues to dominate fire damage, but unless we can change the pattern of research funding we are helpless to change the outcome.

Actor-network explanation. Looking through the lens of actor-network theory helps us to see some of the reasons that the blast damage routine had so much more legitimacy and power than the fire damage routine and provides clues about how to realign associations in ways that could make fire damage assessment more acceptable.

A network of associations legitimized the blast damage routine. Included in this network was the idea of precision bombing, the preferred way of targeting bombs in the U.S. in World War II. The network also included

the ability to calculate damage of specific installations and an ability to predict. Blast damage was associated with organizations that plan wars and was strengthened by association with professional fields (physicists, civil engineers, mathematicians) that had the tools to predict blast damage and had stature in the war planning community. Tools created by these organizations and professional fields, such as the VNTK system for calculating damage, and the understanding of the relationship between overpressure and structural damage, further solidified the legitimacy and power of the blast damage routine.

Figure 2.8.2 shows the network of associations that we have derived based on Eden's historical account which was based on the information provided by a variety of human informants and documents.[6] The various human and non-human actants associated with blast damage are depicted as upward-pointing triangles with positive signs because they are all things that have a positive valence in the domain of nuclear bomb assessment. Not only are all of the actants legitimate in this domain, but they are also all connected to one another. Understanding overpressure, for instance, increased predictability used alone and also fed into the VNTK system, increasing the predictive capacity of that system.

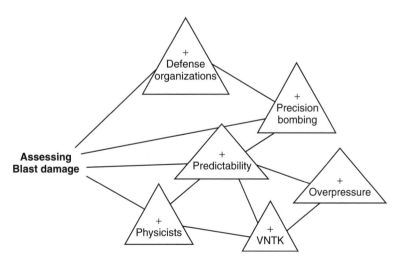

Figure 2.8.2 Network of associations based on Eden's historical account

The fire damage routine, by contrast, was delegitimized by things it was associated with. Fire damage was associated with the area bombing strategy from World War II that was the alternative to precision bombing. Through its association with area bombing, fire damage was connected to indiscriminate damage and all of these are associated with an inability to predict. Fire damage was associated with organizations responsible for civil defense that had little stature in the war planning community and professional fields (chemical engineers, fire protection engineers, foresters) that had neither the disciplinary tools to predict the fires caused by nuclear weapons nor stature in the war planning community.

Figure 2.8.3 indicates that two of the actants in the fire damage network of associations (civil defense organizations and chemical engineers/foresters) were relatively neutral in terms of legitimating this way of doing damage assessment, and three of the actants (those indicated by a downward-pointing traingle and negative sign) were downright negative. Compared with the blast damage network, this network is more loosely connected as well as consisting of actants that did not promote fire damage assessment.

In an interesting turn of events, fire damage was nearly legitimized by gaining associations with physicists, the Defense Nuclear Agency and the VNTK system. In the 1980s

Harold Brode, a respected physicist with support from the Defense Nuclear Agency, developed an algorithm for predicting fire-blast damage. Associations with computer programs that Brode had helped to develop to model blast damage supported this work. These computer programs allowed him to model the flow fields around mass fires, increasing the ability to predict fire damage.

Not only did Brode make an association between fire damage and predictability, but he also connected fire damage to the VNTK system that had become the standard for assessing damage. He did this by using the 'underlying accounting scheme and organizational routines developed in the VNTK system' (Eden, 2004: 225). These efforts to legitimize fire damage by connecting it with predictability and with the VNTK system provides an illustration of the role of agency in developing connections that legitimate the ostensive aspects of routines. Brode could have, for instance, created his own algorithm as an alternative to the VNTK system. Rather than propose a new – way of calculating fire damage, Brode consciously adopted the established algorithm for blast damage and thus associated fire damage with the already legitimated VNTK system.

The nicest part about the invention is that I was able to couch it in precisely the same terms they currently used for the blast VNs by simply changing the VNs to accommodate fire damage, which made it more

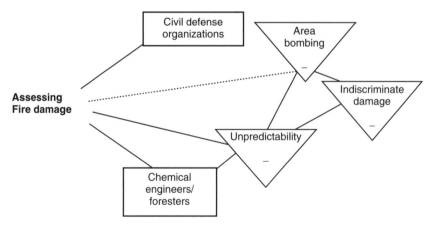

Figure 2.8.3   Network of associations fire damage associations based on Eden's historical account

understandable and more acceptable, both at DIA and JSTPS (Brode, quoted in Eden, 2004: 243)

Figure 2.8.4 maps our best interpretation of the changes Brode was able to bring about in the network of associations connected with fire damage assessment through his effort to use the VNTK system, his identity as a respected physicist and his support from defense organizations. New associations have been created by introducing connections to physicists, defense organizations and the VNTK system. The neutral features from the previous fire damage network (civil defense organizations and chemical engineers/foresters) have been sidelined and replaced by the positive associations indicated by the upward-pointing triangle and positive sign. It appears, however, that several negative associations remain. This figure also indicates that the negative associations may still be much more densely connected than the new positive associations.

Despite Brode's efforts and the creation of more powerful connections surrounding the fire-based damage routine, the routine had not yet achieved the status of the blast-based system that preceded it. Eden writes:

'As of spring 2003, it appears that fire damage has not been incorporated into the U.S. strategic nuclear war plan. According to one well-informed person, every year analysts draw up lists of what they would like to be able to include, but nothing has come of fire damage'. (282).

The figure does not capture the details surrounding this reaction to fire damage, but suggests that additional efforts to alter associations may be necessary before fire damage becomes fully accepted. In particular, creating a denser network of positive associations and disrupting the negative associations may be an important part of the process.

DISCUSSION

In this chapter, we have focused on the question of how actions (performative aspects) and other resources get turned into ostensive aspects. We suggest that understanding the creation of these ostensive aspects is an important part of understanding the dynamics of organizational routines and how organizational routines relate to organizational stability and change.

In the structuration/practice theory explanation, the relation between organizations and their routines and between ostensive aspects of the routine and the performance of it are important. This theory suggests a recursive relationship at these two levels.

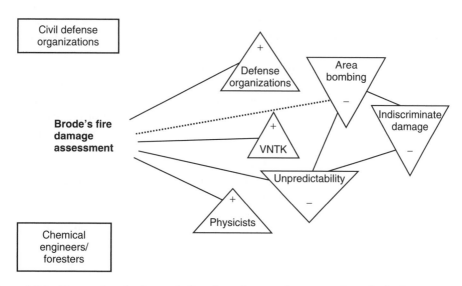

Figure 2.8.4   New network of associations based on our interpretation of Eden's account

Organizations are created and recreated through the performance of routines just as routines are created and recreated through the performance of particular actions that come to be seen as making up the routine.

The actor-network theory explanation helps us understand more about how these performances come to be seen as making up a routine. From this perspective, routines are networks of actants that may be recognized as stable entities in themselves. Focusing attention on the connections between actants enables us to identify the process of making connections as central to creating routines and to point out the often contested nature of this process.

Just as both these explanations open up the black box of organizational routines to help us see the inner workings of these important phenomena, actor network theory helps us open up the black box of the structural or ostensive aspect of organizational routines. Both theories help us to see that agency is an important part of the creation of the ostensive aspects as well as the performative aspects of organizational routines. Agency is intrinsic to the recursive relationship of structuration in which structure is created and recreated through the actions. Thus, research on blast damage and actions to fund research on blast damage produce and reproduce knowledge necessary to assessing nuclear damage. The acts of using that knowledge create and recreate the specific routine of damage assessment.

Actor-network theory and its emphasis on associations helps us go one step further in exploring the nature of the agentic contributions to structure and to the ostensive aspects of organizational routines. We see that the choice to fund and do research on blast damage is not mindless, but based on a pattern of associations that legitimizes and supports this choice. Finding ways to alter that pattern and to create a new and equally legitimate pattern is, from this perspective, fundamental to producing a new damage assessment routine. Brode's efforts show how some of these associations can be changed.

The actor-network perspective also helps us see the distributed nature of the ostensive aspects. The ostensive aspects exist in the connections between actants. That these are different for different participants is evident in the contested nature of the routine described in this chapter. Differences result in efforts to redefine the connections. Although the case we describe here is unusual in content, analyses we do not present here for lack of space show that the dynamics we describe are found in a wide variety of cases and in cases of change as well as in cases that appear to be relatively stable.[7] The main requirement for such analysis is finding cases that have been studied both ethnographically and longitudinally, resulting in the production of evidence that shows the creation of networks of actants and the tug and pull involved in this creation.

The actor-network theory perspective on the ostensive aspects is different from the structuration theory perspective in its inclusion of a broad range of actants, including non-human actants. Structuration theory draws our attention primarily to the recursive relationship between what people do (research on blast damage) and the structures they produce (routines that assess nuclear damage based on blast damage). Actor-network theory takes us inside these structures and draws attention to the associations between human and non-human actants and the ways those associations provide legitimacy to and even a sense of naturalness to the actions (assessing nuclear damage based on blast damage).

In this chapter, we have offered a vision of the ostensive aspects that includes not only the direct content of the work but also the broader set of associations that relate to the work. This perspective extends the vision of other scholars who have noted that path dependency does not necessarily imply inertia (Eden, 2004; Sydow et al., 2005). The inclusion of other actants (including concepts such as 'predictability' and 'indiscriminate damage') in the ostensive aspects creates an interesting opportunity for different actors to enact conflicting visions. If different actors hold different visions for a routine (different actants, different associations), it becomes possible to investigate the ostensive aspects of a routine from a political point of view (Feldman et al., 2006). Which associations will gain legitimacy? Whose vision will become dominant? The view from actor-network theory enables us to articulate and investigate these questions.

Our emerging perspective enables us to think about stability and change in organizational routines not as opposites but as results along a continuum (Weick and Sutcliffe, 2006). These varying results are produced by the same dynamics. Rather than viewing organizational routines as stable because we have defined them as stable, this perspective allows us to investigate the extent of stability and change and to explore the potential for actants to influence stability and change in organizational routines.

We close with a note of irony about our perspective. The first irony is that in writing about these routines we often reify what we try to expose. Though we explain and believe that the ostensive aspects of routines are multiple and distributed, we nonetheless describe routines by identifying a particular ostensive aspect (or in this case two – blast-based and fire-based damage assessment routines) and describing its formation. It is important to remind the reader at this point that these views are constructs variously created by some participants in the routines as well as by researchers. For many participants and observers 'the routine' may be otherwise.

A second irony is that while our primary interest is in process and on focusing attention on the interactions that constitute routines, we often end up talking about entities. In our efforts to describe routines as something other than entities, we have found it necessary to describe parts of routines – the performative and ostensive, and the artifacts that support these parts. These may appear, to some, to be just more entities. From our perspective, their primary importance is to allow us to think about and start to understand the processes that enable us to create routines, but the danger is that these will become additional reified entities. In our efforts to

articulate these parts and to show how they interact in the construction of routines, it may seem that the parts themselves are what is important.

Both of these ironies are on full display in this paper. Though our interest is in routine *dynamics*, we focus much of our attention in this paper on the ostensive aspects of routines. We have tried to overcome the first irony by presenting a case of conflicting ostensive aspects, but as discussed above this does not do justice to either the multiplicity or the distributed nature of the ostensive aspects of routines. We have tried to resist the second irony by opening the black box of the ostensive and exploring alternative perspectives on the processes that create the ostensive aspects and by emphasizing agency as important to these processes.

NOTES

1 Prepared for presentation at the Academy of Management Meetings, August 8, 2005 and for the *Handbook of New and Emerging Approaches to Management*. This chapter is the result of a co-equal collaboration. The authors are grateful for the comments of participants in seminars at the Free University of Berlin, the University of Michigan and the London School of Economics, and to comments by Kathryn Quick, Michael Barzelay, Claus Rerup, David Barry and Hans Hansen.

2 Some of the references include Miner, 1990, 1991; Pentland and Reuter, 1994; Cohen et al., 1996; Adler et al., 1999; Eisenhardt and Martin, 2000; Feldman, 2000; Lazaric, 2000; Lazaric and Denis, 2001; Zollo and Winter, 2002; Hodgson, 2003; Feldman and Pentland, 2003; Howard-Grewville, 2005; Rerup, 2005; Levinthal and Rerup, 2006; Birnholtz et al., 2007; Pentland and Feldman, 2007.

3 Adler et al., 1999; Birnholtz et al., 2007; Feldman, 2000, 2003; Howard-Grewville, 2005; Pentland and Reuter, 1994; Zbaracki, 2007.

4 Our graphic skills are, unfortunately, not up to this challenge.

5 This description is drawn from Eden, 2004. We summarize the very complex argument she makes in her book and apologize for any misrepresentations. All references to page numbers in this section are to Eden, 2004.

6 Our version of the network may differ in both the amount of detail and the specific details from what Eden's or her informants versions would be if they were to create such a network.

7 In writing this chapter, we also analyzed a more mundane case based on Feldman's research about the hiring and training routine in university housing (2000, 2004). In that case, the training and hiring routine changed, resulting in larger changes in the resources the organization had to respond to situations as they arose. Analysis of the budget routine in the same context (Feldman, 2003) displays considerable stability even in the face of pressure from hierarchical superiors to bring about specific changes.

REFERENCES

Adler, P.S., Goldoftas, B. and Levine, D.I. (1999) 'Flexibility versus efficiency? A case study of model changeovers in the Toyota 0production system'. *Organization Science*, 10: 43–68.

Barley, S.R. (1986) 'Technology as an occasion for structuring: Evidence from the observation of CT scanners and the social order of radiology departments', *Administrative Science Quarterly*, 31: 78–108.

Birnholtz, J., Cohen, M.D. and Hoch, S. (2007) 'Organizational character: On the regeneration of Camp Poplar Grove', *Organization Science*, 18: 315–332.

Bourdieu, P. (1990) *The Logic of Practice*. Stanford, CA: Stanford University Press.

Cohen, Michael, D. and Bacdayan, Paul (1994) 'Organizational routines are stored as procedural memory: Evidence from a laboratory study', *Organization Science*, 5 (4): 554–568.

Cohen, M.D., Burkhart, R., Dosi, G., Egidi, M., Marengo, L., Warglien, M. and Winter, S. (1996) 'Routines and other recurring action patterns of organizations: Contemporary research issues'. *Industrial and Corporate Change*, 5: 653–698.

Darr, E., Argote, L. and Epple, D. (1995) 'The acquisition, transfer, and depreciation of knowledge in service organizations: Productivity in franchises'. *Management Science*, 41 (11): 1750–1762.

Donnellon, A., Gray, B. and Bougon, M. (1986) 'Communication, meaning, and organized action', *Administrative Science Quarterly*, 31: 43–55.

Doz, Y.L. (1996) 'The evolution of cooperation in strategic alliances: Initial conditions or learning processes?' *Strategic Management Journal*, 17: 55–83, Special Issue on Evolutional Perspective on Strategy (Summer, 1996).

Eden, Lynn (2004) *Whole World on Fire*. Ithaca, NY: Cornell University Press.

Eisenhardt, K.M., Martin, J.A. (2000) 'Dynamic capabilities: The evolution of resources in dynamic markets'. *Strategic Management Journal*, 21: 1105–1121.

Feldman, M.S. (2000) 'Organizational routines as a source of continuous change'. *Organization Science*, 11: 611–629.

Feldman, M.S. (2003) 'A performative perspective on stability and change in organizational routines'. *Industrial and Corporate Change*, 12 (4): 727–752.

Feldman, M.S. (2004) 'Resources in emerging structures and processes of change'. *Organization Science*, 15 (3): 295–309.

Feldman, M.S., Khademian, A., Ingram, H. and Schneider, A. (2006) 'Ways of knowing and inclusive management practices'. *Public Administration Review*, Volume 66, Special issue on Collaborative Public Management: 89–99.

Feldman, M. and Pentland, B. (2003) 'Reconceptualizing organizational routines as a source of flexibility and change'. *Administrative Science Quarterly*, March 2003, 48: 94–118.

Feldman, M.S. and Pentland, B. (2005) 'Organizational routines and the macro-actor' in B. Czarniawska and T. Hernes (eds), *Actor-Network Theory and Organizing*, Malmö, Sweden; Liber and Copenhagen Business School Press.

Giddens, A. (1984) *The Constitution of Society*. Berkeley, CA: University of California Press.

Hodgson, G.M. (2003) 'The mystery of the routine: The Darwinian destiny of *An Evolutionary Theory of Economic Change*', *Revue Économique*, 54 (2), Mars, pp. 355–384.

Latour, B. (1986) 'The powers of association', in J. Law (ed.), *Power, Action and Belief*. London: Routledge and Kegan Paul. pp. 264–280

Latour, B. (1996) *Aramis: The Love of Technology*. Cambridge, MA: Harvard University Press.

Law, J. and Hassard, J. (eds) (1999) *Actor Network Theory and After*, Oxford: Blackwell.

Lazaric, N. (2000) 'The role of routines, rules and habits in collective learning: Some epistemological and ontological considerations', *European Journal of Economic and Social Systems*, 14 (2): 157–171.

Lazaric, N. and Denis, B. (2001) 'How and why routines change: Some lessons from the articulation of knowledge with ISO 9002 implementation in the Food industry', *Economies et Sociétés*, 6.

Levinthal, D. and Rerup, C. (2006) 'Crossing an apparent chasm: Bridging mindful and less-mindful perspectives on organizational learning'. *Organization Science*, 17 (4): 502–513.

Miner, A.S. (1990) 'Structural evolution through idiosyncratic jobs: The potential for unplanned learning'. *Organization Science*, 1: 195–210.

Miner, A.S. (1991) 'Organizational evolution and the social ecology of jobs'. *American Sociological Review*, 56: 772–785.

Orlikowski, W. (1992) 'The duality of technology: Rethinking the concept of technology in organizations'. *Organization Science*, 3: 398–427.

Orlikowski, W. (2000) 'Using technology and constituting structures: A practice lens for studying technology in organizations'. *Science*, 11: 404–428.

Oxford English Dictionary.

Pentland, B.T. and Feldman, M.S. (2005) 'Organizational routines as a unit of analysis'. *Industrial and Corporate Change* 14 (5): 793–815.

Pentland, B.T. and Feldman, M.S. (in press) 'Empirical field studies of organizational routines', in Markus Becker (ed.), *Handbook of Organizational Routines*. Cheltenham: Edward Elgar Publishing.

Pentland, B.T. and Feldman, M.S. (2007) 'Narrative networks: Patterns of technology and organization', *Organization Science*, 18 (5): 781–795.

Pentland, B.T. and Reuter, H.H. (1994) 'Organizational routines as grammars of action'. *Administrative Science Quarterly*, 39: 484–510.

Rerup, Claus (2005) 'Learning from past experience: Footnotes on mindfulness and habitual entrepreneurship'. Scandinavian Journal of Management, 21: 451–472.

Sydow, Jörg, Schreyögg, Georg and Koch, Jochen. (2005) 'Organizational paths: Path dependency and beyond'. Paper presented at 21st EGOS Colloquium, June 30 – July 2, 2005, Berlin, Germany Subtheme 1: Path Dependence and Creation Processes in the Emergence of Markets, Technologies and Institutions Convenors: Michel Callon, Raghu Garud and Peter Karnøe.

Szulanski, G. (2000) 'Appropriability and the challenge of scope', in Giovanni, Dosi, Richard R. Nelson, Sidney G. Winter (eds), *The Nature and Dynamics of Organizational Capabilities*. Oxford: Oxford University Press.

Tsoukas, H. and Chia, R. (2002) 'On organizational becoming: Rethinking organizational change', *Organization Science,* 13: 567–582.

Weick, K.E. and Sutcliffe, K.M. (2006) 'Mindfulness and the quality of organizational attention', *Organization Science*, 17 (4): 514–524.

Zollo, M. and Winter, S.G. (2002) 'Deliberate learning and the evolution of dynamic capabilities'. *Organization Science*, 13 (3): 339–351.

'Enriching Research on Exploration and Exploitation'

Lori Rosenkopf

Much of the recent research on organization learning makes use of the well-known constructs of exploration and exploitation. The seminal March (1991) paper on these issues has been heavily cited, yet this plethora of research has yielded conflicting theory and results on the antecedents and outcomes of these activities. At the heart of this confusion is the great variety of operationalizations employed by researchers in service of the exploration versus exploitation construct.

March (1991: 71) offers a veritable playground of opportunities for observing these activities:

> Exploration includes things captured by terms such as search, variation, risk taking, experimentation, play, flexibility, discovery, innovation. Exploitation includes such things as refinement, choice, production, efficiency, selection, implementation, execution.

While these terms cut a broad swath, the collections are unified by the general notions of *novelty* for exploration and *routine* for exploitation. Thus, all efforts by researchers to observe exploration and exploitation attempt to distinguish the generation of novelty from more routine activity.

Systematic study of exploration and exploitation via empirical data requires two basic design choices by the researcher. First, the researcher must choose the *context* by which exploration can be distinguished from exploitation. Said differently, a landscape is required which distinguishes 'local' from 'non-local' activity; similarity from distinctiveness; or routine from novelty. Common contexts utilized include geography (nearby or distant), technology (similar or distinctive), organization (internal or external), time (old or new), and social space (previous relationship or new contact).

Having distinguished the context over which an organization explores or exploits, it is necessary to choose the *mechanism* by which the organization may access knowledge. While an ongoing stream of experience-based research in the organization theory domain has suggested that organizations learn from the experience of others as well as their own experience (e.g. Darr et al., 1995), it is silent on the mechanisms by which this learning is accomplished. Strategy scholars' interest in managerial agency, coupled with recent advances in data availability, has motivated analysis of the effects of particular mechanisms that enable or demonstrate learning, such as alliances, mobility, patents and product development.

My contention is that most research on exploration and exploitation limits its focus to one mechanism and one context. Yet constraining the observation of exploration and exploitation to a single context is likely to generate idiosyncratic findings. For example, the strategy literature commonly considers upstream alliances (formed for R&D purposes) exploratory, and downstream alliances (formed for marketing, manufacturing or licensing purposes) exploitative. Contrast this technological context against a social one from the network literature where alliances with new partners are considered exploratory while those with previous partners are considered exploitative. Clearly, the very same alliance might be classified as exploratory in one context and exploitative in the other. Yet the potential antecedents and consequences of exploration and exploitation so defined are the same regardless of this measurement context, suggesting why it is so easy to reach conflicting findings based on design choices and other idiosyncrasies of research settings.

Recent work in this area demonstrates some of these conflicting effects (Lavie and Rosenkopf, 2006). Moreover, it suggests that organizations trade-off exploration of one type against another by demonstrating that software firms decrease technological exploration (upstream alliances) while increasing social exploration (new partners) over time, thereby offsetting the novelty of collaborating with new partners with the more routine activity of re-using existing technologies. Such a finding makes it clear that there is no 'best' way to balance exploration and exploitation across the many mechanisms and contexts where organizations may experience novelty. Even work like this, however, limits its focus to the alliance mechanism and therefore misses a host of opportunities to experience novelty via other mechanisms like acquisitions or internal development.

I conclude with a call for research on exploration and exploitation to integrate more contexts and more mechanisms. Current studies of learning in multinationals, for example, now seek to integrate technological, organizational and geographic contexts. Other studies of industry-wide networks examine multiple mechanisms by analyzing the relative effects of formal relationships (i.e. alliance contracts) and informal relationships (i.e. employee mobility, director interlocks, participation in technical committees) between firms. Only through such multidimensional approaches will we address the variety of ways in which organizations might balance exploration and exploitation across both contexts and mechanisms.

REFERENCES

Darr, E., Argote, L. and Epple, D. (1995) 'The acquisition, transfer and depreciation of knowledge in service organizations: Productivity in franchises', *Management Science*, 41: 1750–1762.

March, J. (1991) 'Exploration and exploitation in organizational learning'. *Organization Science*, 2: 71–87.

Lavie, D. and Rosenkopf, L. (2006) 'Balancing exploration and exploitation in alliance formation'. *Academy of Management Journal*, 49.

The Implications of Aristotle's *Phronēsis* for Organizational Inquiry

George Cairns and Martyna Śliwa

Wasn't the kind of thinkin' you get from workaday university lab scholars, publish-or-perishin' and countin' their pay. The truly original scientist is a free individual. (Haruki Murakami, *Hard-boiled Wonderland and the End of the World.* 1985/1991)

INTRODUCTION

In this chapter, we discuss Aristotle's 'intellectual virtue' of *phronēsis*; generally translated as 'prudence' or 'practical wisdom'. We consider various references to the term in academic literature and its relevance to the area of organizational inquiry. We challenge the dominance of scientific rationality and the search for underlying 'truth' within some organizational research but, at the same time, we find a place for rational thought and for the notion of general 'truths'.

Recently, there has been a growing interest in the concept of *phronēsis* and it has been used to inform academic discussion, not only in the field of philosophy (e.g. Dunne, 1993; Gadamer, 1975; Peters, 1970), but in areas as diverse as medical education (Hilton and Slotnick, 2005), teacher education (Eisner, 2002), fisheries management (Jentoft, 2006), political theory (Ruderman, 1997) and management and organization studies (e.g. Birmingham, 2003; Clegg, 2006; Clegg and Ross-Smith, 2003; Flyvbjerg, 2001, 2003; Hartog and Frame, 2004). Whilst acknowledging the merits of the extant contributions, we identify some confusion and contradiction between interpretations within the various writings. In this chapter, we highlight three key issues arising from the literature that we see as having an impact on the nature of organizational research, namely:

- Relationship and distinction between *epistēmē*, *technē* and *phronēsis*.
- Consideration of *phronēsis* as an intellectual and/or a moral imperative.

- Promotion of the 'phronetic approach' as a method(ology) for organizational inquiry or/and an attitude or state of mind of the organizational researcher.

Through our own resolution of these issues, by reference to contemporary literature and to Aristotle, we discuss one 'phronetic approach' to organizational inquiry. This starts with consideration of the specifics of actors, events and outcomes in a particular context, along with the underlying assumptions, emotions, values and beliefs that impact them. From these, the aim is to develop abstract conceptualizations and theoretical constructs that might inform thinking and acting, both in other particular contexts and at the level of generalization.

The structure of this chapter unfolds as follows: first, we consider the necessary philosophical foundations of *phronēsis*. Second, we engage with a range of contemporary literature in order to explicate the three issues outlined above. Finally, we offer our reflections on the possibilities of broadening the application of phronetic organization inquiry.

PHILOSOPHICAL FOUNDATIONS OF *PHRONĒSIS*

The roots of the term *phronēsis* are to be found in Aristotle's *Nicomachean Ethics*, where it is presented as one of the five 'intellectual virtues' (Aristotle, 2004). (See also Hari Tsoukas' contribution in Chapter 1.12.). The Greek term *phronēsis* has not been subject to adaptation and absorption into contemporary Western language use in the way *epistēmē* and *technē* have been and, in the absence of etymological descendants, *phronēsis* is referred to in English as 'practical knowledge' (Dunne, 1993) or, in translation of the *Ethics*, as 'prudence or practical wisdom' (Aristotle, 2004: 150). Aristotle (2004: 147–154) lists the five intellectual virtues as:

- *epistēmē* – 'science or scientific knowledge ... eternal ... teachable, and its object to be capable of being learnt';

- *technē* – 'art or technical skill ... the study of how to bring into being something that is capable either of being or of not being';
- *phronēsis* – knowledge that is 'reasoned, and capable of (informing) action with regard to things that are good or bad for man';
- *nous* – intuition, or 'the immediate perception of truth';
- *sophia* – wisdom, or 'intuition *and* scientific knowledge: knowledge complete with head (as it were) of the most precious truths'.

For Aristotle, *phronēsis* stands beside and in contrast to epistemological and technological knowledge – to pure and eternal scientific truth, and to knowledge of the productive state – in that it is variable and context-dependent, and is oriented towards action rather than production. However, the variability and contextualism of *phronēsis* should not be read as a counter-movement to, or a denial of epistemological truth, but as a counter-balance to its unifying tendencies.

Despite defining *sophia* as 'the most finished form of knowledge' (2004: 152), Aristotle argues that 'wise' individuals are not necessarily prudent, 'because the objects of their search are not human goods. But prudence is concerned with human goods, i.e. things about which deliberation is possible ... (a)nd the man who is good at deliberation generally is the one who can aim, by the help of his calculation, at the best of the goods attainable by man' (2004: 153–154). Aristotle considers that 'the full performance of man's function depends upon a combination of prudence and moral virtue; virtue ensures the correctness of the end at which we aim, and prudence that of the means towards it' (2004: 163).

Following Aristotle, we posit that, if the proper purpose of organization is to serve the ends of humanity rather than of itself; as if 'organization' exists as some form of non-human organism; and that of management is to ensure the success of organization in achieving this end, then prudence, or *phronēsis*, must be the most important intellectual virtue of the manager. Similarly, if organizational inquiry is to benefit organizations, rather than merely serving the purpose and promotion of the researcher, then the phronetic approach should prevail. So, how do we seek to develop a phronetic understanding of issues affecting organization and management, and what are the key traits required of the phronetic researcher?

CONSTITUTING PHRONETIC ORGANIZATIONAL INQUIRY

In considering *phronēsis* as an 'emerging approach' to organizational inquiry, we contemplate its current status in literature. In seeking to answer the question of whether it is possible for phronetic research to become an attractive and frequently chosen option for significant numbers of researchers and practitioners, we consider what differentiates it from other ways of conducting inquiry. We observe the rapid growth of interest in *phronēsis*, but we also see examples of contradiction and confusion within extant publications. We attempt to clarify these with reference to Aristotle's original discussion of intellectual virtues, and we identify three key issues that we believe must be addressed in developing the phronetic approach.

Distinguishing epistēmē, technē and phronēsis

Whilst Aristotle outlines five intellectual virtues, the boundaries between them are blurred in some contemporary texts, particularly with regard to the distinction between *epistēmē* and *phronēsis*, and between *phronēsis* and *technē*. Aiming to clarify the difference between *epistēmē* and *phronēsis*, and Aristotle's privileging of *phronēsis* over *epistēmē*, Flyvbjerg (2003: 362) employs Aristotle's own illustration of the benefits of eating healthy foods. For Aristotle, the epistemic, or theoretical knowledge that light foods are digestible and wholesome; without knowledge of which foods are light; is of less value than the practical, or phronetic knowledge that chicken is wholesome. To this, we would add the significance of the technical

knowledge of how to prepare and cook the chicken in order to retain this 'lightness'. For us, this simple story provides a practical illustration of the differences between the three types of knowledge.

In the field of organization studies, the relationship between Aristotelian *phronēsis* and other forms of knowledge is discussed by Calori (2002), Birmingham (2003, 2004) and Flyvbjerg (2001, 2003). They consider that, whilst *phronēsis* is concerned with the particular and the context-specifics of knowledge, it is also concerned with a search for some form of generalized knowledge, knowledge that can be applied in analyzing other contexts, and in informing action in these contexts. Calori and Birmingham relate Aristotelian *phronēsis* to the American pragmatist philosophies of James and Dewey. Calori (2002) explicitly states that 'pragmatic epistemology' has its origins in Aristotelian philosophy, and he draws a parallel between Aristotle's notions of *epistēmē* and *phronēsis*, and James's (1950) concepts of 'knowledge about' and 'knowledge of acquaintance', respectively. However, whereas in pragmatic epistemology, Calori sees the ultimate purpose of knowledge of acquaintance in its possibility for 'transform(ation) ... into knowledge about' (Calori, 2002: 878), for Aristotle, the two types of knowledge remain discrete. Flyvbjerg (2003: 362) posits that *phronēsis* 'can only be made scientific in an epistemic sense through the development of a theory of judgment and experience', but such a theory 'is not in sight because judgment and experience cannot be brought into a theoretical formula' (2003: 363). Further, he elaborates that 'Aristotle warns us directly against the type of reductionism that conflates *phronesis* and *episteme*' (2003: 363).

In discussing the relationship between *technē* and *phronēsis*, Kristjánsson (2005) counsels against simplistic differentiation, in which the former 'gives rise to unproblematically codifiable "makings" ... as opposed to the problematic and uncodifiable "doings" which are guided by *phronesis*' (2005: 462–463). He considers that, whilst 'neither *technè*. ... nor *phronesis* are *unproblematically codifiable'* (2005: 464, emphasis in original), the difference between them lies in that the domain of *technē* has an end beyond itself, in the outcome of production, whereas that of *phronēsis* has an end in itself, 'namely good ethical conduct' (2005: 469). In discussing the same relationship, Beckett et al. (2002) posit managers' 'just-in-time training' as an example of phronetic rather than technical activity, on the grounds that it is driven by a purpose. In considering that managers 'justify, both to themselves and others around them, the "whyness" of their "know how"' (2002: 336), these authors see managers' work as inherently phronetic. To Aristotle, however, there is more to *phronēsis* than the mere presence of purpose; he describes it as a state of deliberation about actions, 'with regard to things that are good or bad for man' (Aristotle, 2004: 148). He differentiates prudence both from scientific knowledge, that deals with 'first principles and universals', and from technical knowledge, in that it involves inherently 'good' action, whereas *technē* is not underpinned by any criteria of 'goodness' in relation to action or purpose.

Intellectual and moral characteristics of phronēsis

To Aristotle, ethics and morality constitute an important characteristic of *phronēsis*. He states that *phronēsis* 'is concerned with acts that are just and admirable and good for man ... because the mere possession of knowledge ... (or) training does not make us any more capable of putting our knowledge into practice' (Aristotle, 2004: 162). The ethical dimension of *phronēsis* is recognized in contemporary literature. For example, Waring (2000) highlights that it is the only one of the intellectual virtues that overlaps with the moral virtues. As Aristotle (2004: 166) points out, 'it is not possible to be good in the true sense of the word without prudence, or to be prudent without moral goodness'. To Hilton and Slotnick (2005), *phronēsis* encapsulates the defining characteristics of

professionalism, including: ethical practice, reflection and self-awareness, responsibility and accountability for actions, respect for others ability to work with others and social responsibility.

In the field of education, Birmingham (2003) stresses that *phronēsis* is concerned with ethics and values, in that, being 'situated in morally significant concrete events, (it) incites a moral response' (2003: 192). In developing the concept of 'reflection as phronesis', Birmingham (2003) relates the latter to Dewey's (1933) ethical system of 'reflective morality', whereby every action, through its inter-connectedness with other actions, carries the potential of invoking moral consequences. Birmingham focuses on Dewey's (1932, 1933) conceptualization of 'three virtues of character' which are essential for reflection, namely: wholeheartedness, open-mindedness and responsibility.

In further considering Beckett et al.'s (2002) discussion of the 'phronetic' approach to management training, we see problems in how they frame issues of the 'how' or 'why' of managerial reflection in terms of 'an *organisation's* expectations that making a profit (or whatever) is essential' (2002: 334) (added emphasis). To us, the key to understanding the implications of *phronēsis* as a mode of inquiry lies in that its value-laden nature does not only refer to the particulars of the given context of investigation, such as the organization, but to broader notions of what constitutes 'good' for humanity in general. We see *phronēsis* as an approach to social and organizational inquiry which requires explicit acknowledgement of, and engagement with involved actors' own beliefs and values, along with recognition of notions of subjectivity and emotionality in their interpretations and understandings of what is the 'truth' of any event, and setting this within the wider context of societal wellbeing. However, as Hartog and Frame (2004: 403) point out, whilst for Aristotle the idea of a 'general good' would relate to a largely homogeneous, male citizenry; contemporarily, 'concepts of virtue and community arouse heated debate, not least in a multiracial and multicultural context'. Notwithstanding this limitation, we consider *phronēsis* as requiring both an intellectual engagement with the subject and context of the research, and a critical understanding of moral and ethical implications of decisions and actions beyond the realm of inquiry.

Phronēsis as method(ology) and as attitude/state of mind

In taking account of context and values, a phronetic approach will fall into the category of qualitative or phenomenological method. However, it must be stressed here that not all such methods are phronetic. In extant literature, we find guidelines for undertaking phronetic inquiry, and examples of empirical study which are explicitly stated to be based on the application of *phronēsis*.

Clegg and Ross-Smith (2003: 86) refer to *phronēsis* as challenging management knowledge, which they see as being 'bounded by the great depths of uncertainty and ignorance within which it is constituted'. They propose phronetic knowledge as a form which is 'pragmatic, variable, context dependent, based on practical rationality, leading not to a concern with generating formal lawlike explanations but to building contextual, case-based knowledge'. In their argument, Clegg and Ross-Smith concur with Flyvbjerg (2001, 2003), that contemporary discussion of *phronēsis* cannot take place without consideration of the nature of power, its relationship with the processes of knowledge generation and classification, and of selecting and preferring some knowledge sets over others. In the development of much management knowledge, they see this process of selection as being devoid of moral considerations, where the producers' 'ethic of value freedom places them beyond ethics – it is a kind of ethics that you have when you don't presume any other ethics' (Clegg and Ross-Smith, 2003: 93).

In considering the relationship between researcher and context, Calori (2002) frames discussion of phronetic inquiry in terms of 'real-time/real-space' research, which implies a 'tight connection between action and reflection' (2002: 879). This approach places emphasis on understanding the moral motives, feelings and emotions, intentions and political agendas of and the power relations between organizational actors. In common with Flyvbjerg (2001, 2003), Calori requires the research to take explicit account of the relationships between events over time, the nature of the relevant contexts, and the processes of sense-making of those involved. He identifies three ways of conducting 'real-time/real-space' research: ethnography, action research and enactive research. In ethnography, Calori sees a process that involves engagement, but one where the subjects are not required to reflect on actions, as in the truly phronetic approach. Here, the results may still involve 'second order' interpretation by the researchers; although critical ethnography would appear to address this issue, whereby there is critical reflection on the values and beliefs of the researcher, consideration of the meaning of communication to the thinking subject, and of the impact of power and ideology on the production of 'truth' and theory (cf. Thomas, 1993). Calori also considers action research which, if fully implemented, entails involvement of the researcher in the researched time/space of the subjects (e.g. Eden and Huxham, 1997), engaging with their values and aspirations, but with an intention to draw some generalizations. Finally, the concept of 'enactive research' (Johannisson, 2005) requires the researcher, as author of a theory, to reflect on action on the basis of full participation as practitioner in the action.

For Flyvbjerg (2001: 137), phronetic organization research is seen as 'transcend(ing) dualisms of actor/structure, hermeneutics/structuralism and voluntarism/determinism' which underpin choices of research method(ology). He sees the phronetic researcher as taking any or all of these into account, and exploring the relationships between them in developing contextual research projects which will enable generation of meaning and understanding for involved actors, along with broader implications for society at large. For Flyvbjerg (2001: 166), social science researchers must 'drop the fruitless efforts to emulate natural science's success in producing cumulative and predictive theory … must take up problems that matter to the local, national and global communities in which (they) live … (and) must effectively communicate the results of (their) research to fellow citizens'. Hence, the extrinsic value of the research, in terms of constituting 'practical wisdom' in the broad societal context, must be seen as being at least as important as, if not more so than the intrinsic value to the researcher and the academic community; to publication lists for tenure and promotion, and citation indices for journals that are most likely not read beyond disciplinary boundaries.

Whilst Flyvbjerg (2001) states that *phronēsis* is not a methodological project, he does provide 'methodological guidelines' for phronetic inquiry. He discusses research approaches (Flyvbjerg, 2003) such as anthropological and action research that require the researcher to 'go native'. For him, phronetic research requires that the researcher is part of the phenomenon studied, but still retains a critical detachment that enables multiple perspectives to be addressed. Unlike Calori, he also considers that phronetic research can be undertaken remotely in space and time, for example, through becoming embedded in archives (see his study of the Aalborg project in *Rationality and Power*, Flyvbjerg, 1998).

In outlining his approach to phronetic inquiry, Flyvbjerg (2003), raises four 'value-rational questions', which lead the researcher to consider, within the context of thinking/acting of those involved, where the group is heading, whether proposed developments are desirable, what, if anything, should be done to change direction, and finally, who will gain and who will lose within the process, and by which mechanisms of power. Beyond his initial questions, Flyvbjerg (2001, 2003) goes on to raise further concerns relating to power: what are the power relationships amongst actors?, can they be changed?, is it desirable to do so?, and, what are the power relations amongst those who are asking the questions about the situation?

Assertions in contemporary literature that a phronetic methodology requires application of reflexivity (e.g. Birmingham, 2004; McPherson, 2005) and deliberation on the value-rationalities of self and others (e.g. Flyvbjerg, 2001; Jentoft, 2006) lead us to contemplate whether, as an approach to research, it can be adopted and implemented by every researcher. Because of the link between *phronēsis* and morality, a phronetic researcher needs to be equipped with more than just epistemological knowledge and technological skills and competencies. Aristotle explains that prudence is not identical to 'cleverness', because 'virtue is not merely a state in conformity with the right principle, but one that implies the right principle; and the right principle in moral conduct is prudence' (Aristotle, 2004: 165–166). For Waring (2000; 145–147), 'The goodness of *phronetic* living is intrinsic; it does not aim at an end that is distinct from the activity of living according to virtue … *phronetic* actions do not tend toward *phronesis*, they evince it … *phronetic* application of the moral virtues requires that *the person be in a certain condition when he acts*' (emphasis in original). As Aristotle (2004: 166) reminds us, 'it is not possible to be good in the true sense of the word without prudence, or to be prudent without moral goodness'.

If *phronēsis* is seen, not just as constituting an approach which requires a value-rational consideration of the research context, but as being constituted by the ethics of the researcher, then we suggest the need for particular characteristics of the researcher. These include a moral imperative, but neither one that is underpinned by a deontology which precludes consideration of the situational ethics of the involved actors, nor one of moral relativism which sees all viewpoints as being equally valid.

ADOPTING PHRONETIC APPROACHES TO SOCIAL AND ORGANIZATIONAL INQUIRY

In the previous section, we sought to illustrate that phronetic knowledge is not wholly detached from epistemic or technical knowledge, but must not be conflated with either of them. Also, that it invokes both an intellectual and a moral imperative in the researcher. Finally, we have posited that its application is made demonstrable, not merely through mastery of method(ology), but through a necessary attitude or state of mind that enables the researcher to act in accordance with the moral imperative. Can we identify examples of research and publication which exemplify these characteristics? And, are there examples of research which purports to be 'phronetic', but which fails to meet a necessary threshold of credibility? Below the threshold level, we would place the call for 'just-in-time training' to be termed a 'phronetic activity' (Beckett et al., 2002), on the basis that, whilst it engages with context, actors, values, etc. in organizations, it deals with issues of ethics and morality at a superficial level. In the texts that discuss what we consider to be a truly phronetic approach, we find a variety of emphases with regard to the relevance of *phronēsis* to contemporary society and organizational inquiry. From the writings of three authors (Birmingham, 2003, 2004; Flyvbjerg, 2001, 2003; Jentoft, 2006), we point to illustrations of applications of the concept of *phronēsis*, with particular foci on the ethical dimension, consideration of power relationships, and the complex nature of 'good' in contemporary society, respectively.

In her reflexive paper on experiences of student teachers' work in culturally diverse settings, Birmingham (2003) discusses *phronēsis* in relation to the expectations and actuality of actors, in the context of morality. She argues that teaching and teacher education should be underpinned by synthesis of three concepts, namely: reflective teaching, cultural diversity and moral value. She proposes that 'reflection

is not … a form of knowledge or a thought process, not a rule or principle, but a moral way of being' (2003: 189). Like Aristotle, Birmingham posits that actions and events are not morally neutral. She views *phronēsis* as a necessary 'virtue of the mind' in preparing teachers for complex and ambiguous situations that cannot be managed through the development of teaching techniques and the provision of information alone, but that require effort to develop the personal character of the individual teacher. Moreover, in her later work, Birmingham (2004) proposes *phronēsis* as a valued personal characteristic of teachers, and states that it must encapsulate the ability to critically evaluate instructional goals, and to care for students and ensure fairness for them, their families and colleagues. However, through failure to address issues of power inherent in the teacher/student relationship, and to problematize the underlying assumptions of what is seen as 'moral', 'correct' and 'appropriate', Birmingham's argument might be read as bounded.

Recognition of the student teachers' 'prejudices' and 'preconceptions' is seen as an end in itself, rather than as a way towards challenging their origins, and the socioeconomic structure which underpins them. Although Birmingham (2004: 320) recognizes criticism of virtue-centred ethics as being 'too vague, too subject to interpretation, not easily enough pinned down', she sees this lack of precision as being a strength in reflecting the uncertainties of 'living a moral life'. To her, *phronēsis* is required in order to 'achieve moral goodness, promote excellence in teaching and learning, and advance human flourishing' (2004: 326). Whilst being aware of the simplifications and omissions inherent in Birmingham's argument, we consider the approach to teacher education presented to be much more in line with Aristotle's original writings on *phronēsis*, in that it recognizes the importance of context, ambiguity, and ethical considerations, than those educational models which assume the existence of a 'single best method' in education (e.g. Tyack, 1974).

In contrast to Birmingham, Flyvbjerg (2001, 2003) places consideration of power at the core of how we might seek to construct models for contemporary phronetic research. In his longitudinal study of urban planning and 'sustainable development' in the Danish city of Aalborg, Flyvbjerg (1998, 2001) engages with archival material which records the various documented 'histories' of the project and also interviews involved actors, such that a variety of *post hoc* rationalizations are presented. Out of this study, Flyvbjerg identifies a number of problematic issues. First, he contests the idea that knowledge in the social context is not knowable in an epistemic way. Second, he challenges the notion that power is brought to bear on a problem 'only after we have made ourselves knowledgeable about it' (2001: 143). Third, he calls into question the assumption that democracy is transparent, inclusive and conducive to the realization of the 'common good'. From his analysis of the Aalborg project, he concludes that 'power *defines* what counts as rationality and knowledge and thereby what counts as reality' (Flyvbjerg, 1998: 227, emphasis in original). He also contends that the exercise of power determines not only what problems are brought forward for consideration, but how they are conceived and presented. By reference to examples, he shows that the 'democratic' process can be one of exclusion and the pursuit of self-interest by powerful individuals and bodies. In his text on 'making social science matter', Flyvbjerg (2001) posits that these issues might be surfaced by the application of a phronetic approach, in which the value-rational questions, to which we have referred in the previous section, are posed at the outset, namely:

- Where are we going?
- Is this development desirable?
- What, if anything, should we do about it?
- Who gains and who loses, and by which mechanisms of power? (2001: 60)

Through his deliberations, Flyvbjerg sees that the transition from 'democracy' as practised in the Aalborg context, to a form that will serve the good of society requires genuine transparency and accountability, dialogical communication using all relevant and effective media, and explicit engagement with mediating processes of power and rationality. We see Flyvbjerg as promoting research which aims at development of a contextual understanding of complex social problems, placing involved actors at the centre of considerations and challenging the hegemony of academic, and other power-based discourses.

Drawing upon Flyvbjerg's conceptual framework, Jentoft (2006) highlights the political dimension of issues involving social values and ethics in his call for a phronetic approach to research in the field of 'fisheries management'. He moves beyond consideration of it as being not only a scientific (epistemic) and/or technological endeavour but, in addition, as requiring that political and policy decisions are taken into account, along with their implications in the broader realm of community and society. We see, in Jentoft's text, a resonance with the Aristotelian concern for what is 'good or bad for man'. In the context of contemporary problems, which involve deliberation on social, economic, ecological and other implications of their resolution, he sees the answer to what is 'good' as having to be negotiated within the structures of a democratic society. In acknowledging the problematic nature of defining 'good' in a diverse society, with the existence of conflicting political interests, Jentoft proposes adopting the broader 'governance' perspective, which 'emphasizes the interaction between the state, the market and civil society, recognizing the strengths and weaknesses of each and the need to draw on their respective capacities' (2006: 9). Jentoft sees a role for epistemic or scientific knowledge in this democratic debate, but posits that it must be moderated by the application of phronetic knowledge. Similarly, the application of technological knowledge must not take place without consideration of the implications for involved actors and for society at large. In proposing an inclusive approach to dealing with complex issues, Jentoft sees the concept of governance as 'inviting a more reflexive, deliberative and value-rational methodology than the instrumental, means-end oriented management concept' (2006: 1).

Taking a lead from Jentoft, we propose that a governance-based, rather than a management-based – or any exclusively discipline-based – approach to researching organizations offers scope for developing a truly phronetic engagement with issues.

CONTEMPLATING FUTURE POSSIBILITIES

We consider the major relevance of the phronetic approach to organizational inquiry to be that it is an interpretive approach which places organizational actors at the centre stage, engaging with their values and beliefs, and with their interpretations and understandings of their 'reality'. But, it also seeks to identify general inferences from each context which might inform reflection on options before action in other circumstances. A phronetic approach is focused very clearly on knowledge; that is, fact which has some basis for being considered as such beyond simply being, and beyond self-reference; rather than on mere opinion. However, this knowledge is accepted as being context dependent and value-rational, grounded in the situational ethics of those involved. In considering appropriate methods, we must question the degree to which they require critical reflection on action, deliberation on options for and courses of action and entail informing action rather than just thinking. Nevertheless, as we have stated above, such approaches are not grounded in some moral relativism which accepts all views as equal, but involve making informed judgments which will favor and privilege some options over others. Finally, the phronetic approach is oriented towards what should be done, and reflection on consequences, not to abstract theory on what might be done.

In inviting us to address the future prospects of *phronēsis*, the editors of this text asked us: 'If everyone jumped on the phronetic bandwagon, what would org(anization) studies

look like in the years to come?' We posit that such a situation is not possible. The phronetic approach to organization research sets challenges to the researcher; to abandon the search for a singular 'truth' and 'reality' and for reductive generalized theories, along with the notion that knowledge generation is the privileged domain of the academic. A major challenge is to carve out the time necessary to engage with the domain of thinking/acting of the research subjects in a meaningful way, a way that will allow for multiple iterative cycles of critical reflection. Whilst the central concern of the phronetic approach is that of context and of engagement with the values, beliefs and assumptions of the actors in this context, we must stress that the concern for practice is not, in our view, to view *phronēsis* as a-theoretical and to set up an 'unhelpful false dichotomy' (Feyerabend, 1999) between theory and practice. Like Ruderman (1997), we see *phronēsis* as being informed by '*theoria* (that) can foster flexibility, by helping prudence to gain critical distance on popular but misguided views and to resist the often rigid moralism of the community or regime' (1997: 411). We concur that Aristotle 'does not allow his practical or moral concern for justice to silence the theoretical investigation of what justice is (and cannot be)' (1997: 411).

Adopting phronetic approaches to social and organizational inquiry requires us to engage with actors in their own context of thinking and acting over time, to be able to gain an understanding of events in terms of their origins, emergence, outcomes and implications. This enables us to consider the 'multiple realities' (Beech and Cairns, 2001) of human existence, both those of the subjects of our research and those of the self, the researcher/author. Here, events and actions may have multiple, seemingly contradictory and ambiguous meanings to different actors, or to the same actors at different times, according to context and chronology. However, this form of research engagement is not easily reconciled with the quotidian of academic life, with pressures to 'publish or perish'.

Within the various discussions of the phronetic approach, there is consideration of obstacles to successful inquiry, beyond methodological problems in the nature of engagement in the research time/space. Calori (2002) highlights problems for conducting phronetic research, through pressures of time and the needs of career development, the need to 'perform' for academic progress – publishing in 'A-grade' journals, primarily North American, which lack a history of pragmatic, context-dependent, emotional research, rather than generalized positivist research. These pressures, along with other calls upon limited resources of time, money, etc., make it difficult to contemplate phronetic involvement in complex organizational contexts, engaging with major issues; such as the nature of globalization, of forms of organization outside of the 'developed' world and the impact of management decisions on the lives of those at the far end of the chain of demand and supply. For Flyvbjerg, no researcher can answer all of the relevant questions in complex social science research, but can only offer input into an ongoing dialogue, treading a line between scientific rationality and 'the truth' and breakdown into fragmented nihilism.

REFERENCES

Aristotle (350BC/2004) *The Nicomachean Ethics.* Tr. J.A.K. Thomson, 1953. Rev. H. Tredennick, 1976. London: Penguin Books.

Beckett, D., Zoë A. and Valerie O. (2002) 'Just-in-time training: Techne meets phronesis', *Journal of Workplace Learning*, 14 (8): pp. 332–339.

Beech, N. and George C. (2001) 'Coping with change: the contribution of postdichotomous ontologies', *Human Relations*, 54 (10): 1303–1324.

Birmingham, C. (2003) 'Practicing the virtue of reflection in an unfamiliar cultural context', *Theory into Practice*, 42 (3): 188–194.

Birmingham, C. (2004) 'Phronesis: A model for pedagogical reflection', *Journal of Teacher Education*, 55 (4): 313–324.

Calori, R. (2002) 'Essai: real time/real space research: connecting action and reflection in organization studies', *Organization Studies*, 23 (6): 877–884.

Clegg, S.R. (2006) 'The bounds of rationality: Power/history/imagination', *Critical Perspectives on Accounting*, 17: 847–863.

Clegg, S.R. and Anne R.-S. (2003) 'Revising the boundaries: management education and learning in a postpositivist world', *Academy of Management Learning and Education*, 2 (1): 85–98.

Dewey, J. (1932) *Theory of the Moral Life.* New York: Holt, Rinehart & Winston.

Dewey, J. (1933) *How We Think: A Restatement of the Relation of Reflective Thinking to the Educative Process.* Chicago, IL: Henry Regnery.

Dunne, J. (1993) *Back to the Rough Ground: Practical Judgment and the Lure of Technique.* Notre Dame, IN: University of Notre Dame Press.

Eden, C. and Chris H. (1997) 'Action research for the study of organizations', in S.R. Clegg, C. Hardy and W.R. Nord (eds), *Handbook of Organization Studies.* London: Sage. pp. 526–542.

Eisner, E. (2002) 'From episteme to phronesis to artistry in the study and improvement of teaching', *Teaching and Teacher Education*, 18: 375–385.

Feyerabend, P. (1999) *Conquest of Abundance: A Tale of Abstraction Versus the Richness of Being.* Chicago: The University of Chicago Press.

Flyvbjerg, B. (1998) *Rationality and Power – Democracy in Practice.* Chicago: The University of Chicago Press.

Flyvbjerg, B. (2001) *Making Social Science Matter: Why Social Inquiry Fails and How it Can Succeed Again.* Cambridge: Cambridge University Press.

Flyvbjerg, B. (2003) 'Making organization research matter: Power values and phronesis', in B. Czarniawska and G. Sevón (eds), *The Northern Lights: Organization Theory in Scandinavia.* Copenhagen: Liber Abstrakt – Copenhagen Business School Press. pp. 357–382.

Gadamer, H.-G. (1975) *Truth and Method.* London: Sheid and Ward.

Hartog, M. and Frame, P. (2004) 'Business ethics in the curriculum: Integrating ethics through work experience', *Journal of Business Ethics*, 54: 399–409.

Hilton, S.P. and Slotnick, H.B. (2005) 'Protprofessionalism: How professionalisation occurs across the continuum of medical education', *Medical Education*, 39: 58–65.

James, W. (1950) *The Principles of Psychology.* New York: Dover.

Jentoft, S. (2006) 'Beyond fisheries management: The *phronetic* dimension', *Marine Policy*, 30: 671–680.

Johannisson, B. (2005) *Entreprenörskapets väsen.* Lund: Studentlitteratur.

Kristjánsson, K. (2005) 'Smoothing it: Some Aristotelian misgivings about the *phronesis-praxis* perspective on education', *Educational Philosophy and Theory*, 37 (4): 455–473.

McPherson, I. (2005) 'Refexive learning: Stages towards wisdom with Dreyfus', *Educational Philosophy and Theory*, 37 (5): 705–718.

Peters, F.E. (1970) *Greek Philosophical Terms: A Historical Lexicon*. New York: NYU Press.

Ruderman, R.S. (1997) 'Aristotle and the recovery of political judgment', *American Political Science Review*, 91 (2): 409–420.

Thomas, J. (1993) *Doing Critical Ethnography*. Newbury Park, CA: Sage.

Tyack, D.B. (1974) *The One Best System*. Cambridge, MA: Harvard University Press.

Waring, D. (2000) 'Why the practice of medicine is not a phronetic activity', *Theoretical Medicine and Bioethics*, 21: 139–151.

Philosophy of Management: Instead of a Manifesto

Ole Fogh Kirkeby

The spectre which haunts leading, managing and organizing these days is control by self-control. The enormous increase in knowledge workers, communication workers and consultancy functions at all levels of private and public corporations, demands a totally new attitude towards employees in order to explore their competencies and potentialities properly. The team, and the project, now the rational core of organizing, change the strategies of controlling performances, and the methods of feedback into a dialogical setting, where the emphasis is on recognition and self-evaluation.

Control by self-control demands two things from management: To effectuate and guide 'etho-poiesis', the creation of a 'functional self' both in employees, and in managers; and to develop new codes or even 'languages' of self-control, which are able to recognize and reinforce the proper performance.

What is going on is a multidimensional process of identity-creation in which peculiar and situated demands by the firm to adapted and unique employee-profiles challenge individual claims to personal identities and inner urges to freedom. At the same time, the organization has to balance the sense of rights and duties by its members in order to increase corporate loyalty and democratic responsibility to communities ranging from the corporate world to the global humanity.

The almost explosive rise of 'technologies of intimacy', like the many different types of coaching based on self-rationalization and an often merciless 'cosmo-opticon' in which everybody controls each other, vertically and horizontally, demands new approaches to the chiasm between management and leadership. The intimate control through surveying the employee's mental condition will create new spaces of opposition, spaces that must be filled in by the firm unless the employees transform totally into nomads with loyalty only towards their resumé. Management must, in the capacity of leadership, be able to distinguish between the strategies of controlling self-control through technologies of intimacy, which might lead to further suppression, or to new spaces of freedom.

It must be obvious that these challenges can only be met through a totally new attitude in management, based on a far more reflective mode of leadership, the focus of which is the mastery of normative perspectives, historical and cultural competencies, dialogical capacities, the procedures of legitimization and insights into the limits of strategy. Only one discipline can meet all these claims at the same time, because it contains both a sovereign meta-discourse in relation to different paradigmatic approaches, a set of well-defined and well-tried methods, and a way of being, and this is philosophy.

The real power of philosophy is its ability to unite theory and practice, through the permanent creation of a language, which grows by generalizing over empirical facts and behaviours, and by conceptually anticipating its own goals.

In approaching philosophy, we have to go back to the time before theory and practice were separated, a time where philosophy showed its essence: to create concepts which reflect the challenges of humans to control and identify with their environment, their own

Continued

nature and society. Relative to this, the Greek tradition is a true goldmine of concepts and methods, suggesting the following:

- There exists a direct, lived analogy between society and the human mind.
- It is possible to realize normativity in one's own life through an event-based, experimental, and virtuous application of *the Greek square*, the Good, the Just, the True, and The Beautiful, on the basis of freedom; a process of 'doing virtues' in which these norms are refined and developed further – finally for their own sake.
- There exists a hexis (habitus) of attention, encompassing both attention to a task, attention to other people, and the ability to draw attention to oneself. This hexis can be developed through experience and learning.
- Thinking is a process guided by practice: conceptualizations and wordings create possible worlds which have the possibility to be real if they balance knowledge, emotion, and desire, and are able to develop sustainable, socio-political ideas of the community.
- Thinking must create a bird's-eye view of people, society, and nature, i.e. it must be utterly aware of its own axiomatic background, its attitude towards living life, and must be critical.

Hence, the philosophy of management creates a platform from which every strategic decision can be judged by whether it strengthens the formation, development and quality of personal identity and the core of social relations. It is able to cope with the immense tension between the rationale of the firm as a part of an economic system, and as a social life, and character-forming entity.

Two thousand, five hundred years ago philosophy developed the core of a curriculum for leadership. The Greek cities, especially Athens, formed the place of the creation of executive academies for top leaders, generals, admirals, princes, etc. Such an academy generally taught a group of ten people maximum. The basic attitude was called *protreptics*, which means 'to turn a person towards the real and important issues of someone's life' by urging them to take themselves seriously. The curriculum was built upon four principles which are of immense importance to the development of new practices of leadership:

1. To realise the basic norms or values of one's own life, and hence, the personal signification of one's practice. The subjects dealt with were existential in essence, they related to the concept of happiness as the basis of identity formation. Who am I? What do I want? Who do I want to become? How do I want to act? Which kind of leader do I want to be? Which relation do I want to develop to my community? The answer would concentrate on creating a balance between personal virtues aimed at, and collective virtues mirroring the needs of the community.
2. To be able to communicate this practice of self-reflection to other people, and hence, recreate the settings of the technologies of intimacy in the light of autonomous identity formation and freedom.
3. To learn from one's own experience and from history. To discover history. To enhance and intensify the capacity of attention. To develop a hexis (habitus) of attention which shall create the capacity to control and receive the opportunity of the event. To develop a sense of 'eventing' so as to be able to create history. This constitutes the core of considerate strategy.
4. To be able to choose the best expert advice and the best personal advisers. This means choosing people who dare to contradict you, and who have backgrounds and views of life other than yourself.

The protreptics is a very old discipline of professional and human perfection. It unites professional skills in managers and employees with existential and ethical supremacy. The core of management philosophy is protreptics. It is a learning-programme for life-long learning for all professionals, and hence a principle of 'Bildung'.

In old Danish, to 'lead' has a twofold sense. It both means to 'go in front', and to 'search for', while 'management' comes from the training of horses from the circus. The protreptics underline these capacities in leaders, and hence make the distinction between leaders and managers real.

Doing management philosophy presupposes the capacity to deconstruct the meta-strategic universe in which theories that on the surface seem utterly critical and liberating – like discourse analysis, system theories of 'auto-poiesis', and the Deleuzian dream of transforming the world, by rethinking it, and, of course the programme of deconstruction itself – can be related fundamentally to a sober, existential reflection on the human condition. This means to understand fully the inner tensions of the ultra modern 'etho-poiesis' between functional identity-creation and the need to be the one, you are through becoming the one, you could and ought to be.

Wisdom: A Backdrop for Organizational Studies

David A. Cowan and Lotte Darsoe

Always the beautiful answer who asks a more beautiful question. Joshua Prince Ramus. (McGregor, 2005)

Why is contributing a question often more constructive in the long run than contributing an answer? And why are some questions remarkably better than others? Certain questions embody the capacity to inspire, empower and uplift while others merely sustain or even constrain and distract. For example, what is the difference between asking, 'how can our research agenda be the best IN the world?' and 'How can our research agenda be the best FOR the world' (e.g., Jones, 2001)? Changing one small word alters the entire meaning, refocusing attention and further inquiry. If you look closely at this shift in meaning, it derives from an underlying shift in values. Being best IN the world frames reality as divisive by standing upon values such as self-interest and competition. Being best FOR the world eliminates this boundary by standing upon the values of inclusiveness and integration (e.g., Brown and Isaacs, 2005).

We propose that questions of the second kind serve as indicators of wisdom, more than do questions of the first kind and answers of almost any kind. These questions reflect values of a common good (Sternberg, 2003) that derive from a level of moral development which transcends (but does not ignore) self-interest (Wilber, 1995). Through such values, wisdom promotes systemic and integrative insight that remains intimately connected to context. Wisdom is never neutral, nor is it out of touch with reality. More specifically, wisdom aligns with unique qualities of inclusiveness and synthesis, providing expansive lenses in terms of people and time and insights that connect collective well-being with practical considerations.

Historically, wisdom became arguably subdued around the seventeenth century when scientists began to promote a worldview that enabled them to pull away from the gravity of pervasive religious control. At that time, wisdom had become usurped by religious founders who basically pretended that whatever they proclaimed was wise. Scientists provided leverage to refute the claims of religion but, in doing so, discarded its genuine side. Thus, left-brained, linear thinking arose to offset the longstanding imbalance by favoring objectivity, separation (e.g., of religion and science, subject and object, humanity and nature, mind and heart) and competition. Little by little, and in the name of *progress*, scholarly pursuit became defined only as that which scientists could directly measure, presuming that the measurer was not part of the process. Scientific lenses slowly replaced religious beliefs in the Western world as the driving force of society and a new type of imbalance arose.

What we propose in this chapter is that both the need and opportunity now exist to rejuvenate some of these important values that have been ignored by scientific discourse, and it is our intent to provide a framework that weaves together constructive potentialities of both wisdom and science, as scholars are coming to understand them today (e.g., Kessler and Bailey, 2007). Along the way, we explain why current circumstances provide a unique opportunity for this kind of deep change, what the change involves, and how it may constructively impact current scientific and practical efforts involving organizational life.

Conditions that support the timeliness of this opportunity include accelerated globalization, widespread education, unprecedented access to knowledge, worldwide technological development and emerging networks of near spontaneous communication. On the downside, however, these conditions seem to create an overflow of information, unparalleled complexity, an increasing economic imbalance that favors wealthy peoples and nations and rising tensions between short-term decisions and long-term consequences (Starbuck, 2005). Global turbulence is both reflected in and influenced by organizations. Interestingly, turbulence, apart from disturbing the status quo, provides fertile ground for change (Lewin, 1948) as it offers organizational scholars opportunities to renew their pursuit of integral agendas, sensitive methods and points of practical leverage. We will argue that a backdrop of wisdom enables

inclusive and integrative insights for both researcher and organization.

The goals of this chapter are three. The first is to update the framing of an old topic, wisdom, in a manner that capitalizes on relevant research. Constructively reframing wisdom involves repositioning it from a mysterious, otherworldly realm that only few people attain to an increasingly well-specified potential that many can access. For example, Kessler and Bailey (2007) recently gathered various scholars to help frame wisdom through multiple philosophical lenses – including metaphysics, epistemology, ethics and aesthetics – and multiple levels of analysis – such as individual, team, organizational and global. Our reframing focuses on repositioning wisdom from residing exclusively within single individuals, to residing also in networks of people. From this perspective, various people possess different parts of an overall big picture but no one possesses the entire picture (Surowiecki, 2005). Processes of alignment and synergy come into play as wisdom emerges collectively (e.g., Strogatz, 2003). Speaking toward such phenomena, Margaret Wheatley (2005) suggests that 'we can be wise only together', which may be increasingly true in complex, distributed systems (cf. Waldron, 1995).

Our second goal is to examine wisdom as it moves across such levels of analysis, for example, from leadership and motivation, to organization design and culture and to the design of global communities. In these contexts we address ways in which wisdom manifests both individually and collectively. Our third goal is to offer questions that we believe will motivate researchers to examine and rethink current norms of organizing and organizational studies. We intend to demonstrate that, when framed appropriately for the twenty-first century, wisdom provides more enlightened perspectives for organizational studies, and more inspiring issues for research, practice and the personal development of scholars.

Before we examine more intricately the meaning of wisdom, we want to highlight two values that reside at its core: inclusiveness and integration. As evidence, we provide two examples. One example involves the process of accounting for people who will be affected by an organization's decisions but who are not present when such decisions are being made. Too often it seems that organizations make decisions that do not account for all those who will be affected, which may give rise to negative, systemic consequences. In a compelling Native American story written by Paula Underwood (1991), who uses stories to highlight important values, she describes people who choose a location to live without considering the welfare of native wolves who occupy the region – a story that has direct parallels to organizations that construct new businesses without accounting for all impacted interest groups. After moving into their new location, the people in Underwood's story discover not only that their decision has a negative impact on the wolves, but also that the emergent situation has a negative impact on their own community as the wolves are forced to change their behavior patterns. Realizing the need to employ more inclusive values, these people ultimately decide to move to a more sustainable location that accounts for both sets of interests. From this experience they learn an important principle that they carry forward in the question 'who speaks for wolf?' Through this question, future decision makers are compelled to remember the significance of inclusiveness.

A second example that underscores the importance of inclusiveness and integration comes from the process of bearing witness (e.g., Glassman, 1998). Bearing witness means respecting all other people and their circumstances without judging them as good or bad (e.g., Cowan, 2005a). Most people typically emphasize their own welfare and the welfare of those who possess similar values, while ignoring the welfare of people who possess competing values by numbing sensitivities to their needs, becoming defensive of their own decisions, and so forth. Bearing witness does not necessitate liking or approval, but rather compassion for alternative realities by realizing that any of us,

if we lived in other people's conditions, may have wound up being just like them.

A wisdom perspective seeks synthesis without losing sight of the integrity of differences (cf. Krishnamurti, 1973). As Marco Polo supposedly may have advised Kublai Khan, it is the *arch* that gives a bridge its strength, yet the arch cannot exist without its *individual stones* (Calvino, 1974). In some respects, differences reflect unique positions along developmental continua, such as single-loop to triple-loop (e.g., Agyris, 2002; Argyris and Schon, 1996; Bartunek and Mock, 1987) and archaic to trans-personal (e.g., Wilber, 2003), as increasingly more breadth and depth are taken into account. Each additional loop or level, so to speak, becomes more integrative or strengthens the bridge. Multiple and diverse perspectives co-exist in ways that create opportunity for synergistic actions. Contradictory perspectives that would otherwise be impossible to unite from a backdrop of rationality may become integrated in creative ways when approached from a backdrop of wisdom because wisdom does not reside at the same level of understanding as the conflict.

DEFINING WISDOM

In this section we examine wisdom in more detail by aligning historical foundations with current research in order to increase wisdom's relevance and access in today's world. Our definitional framework consists of an integral structure with four defining patterns (see Figure 2.10.1). We do not pretend that the framework is collectively exhaustive of historical or current literature, but rather that it is representative in ways that are particularly meaningful for organizational contexts in the unfolding twenty-first century.

The integral structure that we believe embodies wisdom is a simple but prominent archetypal symbol present in most cultures throughout history and around the globe: the cross, or perpendicular intersection of axes running horizontally and vertically (e.g., Osho, 1999). The horizontal axis depicts

Figure 2.10.1   Wisdom framework

the experience of life as linear, moving from the past into the future. The vertical axis depicts life experiences from micro to macro in terms of depth and richness (e.g., Emmons, 1999). Life on the horizontal axis evokes typical descriptions of speed, busyness, working against the clock, doing things sequentially, and so forth. On this axis, one is immersed in appearances, material objects, objective measurement, externally defined roles, socially constructed systems, and so forth. Important questions along this axis are mostly pragmatic, time-based and goal-oriented: When will I travel? How much time and money will traveling cost? What work can I get done along the way?

Experiencing life on the vertical axis evokes stillness and depth. Importance is given to reflection, to fully engaging what is here and now, to seeking quality in living, and to letting go of extrinsic agendas as the primary measures of success. Important questions emanating from this axis involve deeper and more systemic issues: Am I realizing my potential? Is this choice healthy and inspiring? How can I contribute my best? Wisdom gains energy and insight from the vertical axis but manifests on the horizontal axis. The horizontal without the vertical is mundane and superficial. The vertical without the horizontal is ethereal and disconnected. In some respects, this structure mirrors the interplay of other integrally interconnected

dimensions of reality, such as form and force, and exploration and exploitation (Augier, 2004; March, 1991).

To appreciate an integral structure of wisdom it helps to complement it with selective defining qualities (e.g., Sternberg, 1998). The first is an intuitive tendency toward wholeness and goodness (e.g., Baltes and Staudinger, 2000; Conger and Hooijberg, 2007). The second quality is a tendency toward a beginner's attitude, which manifests, for example, by continually questioning assumptions and norms (e.g., Weick, 1998). The third quality is a capacity to be fully alive in each present moment, not by being oblivious to the past and future but by drawing both into the present (e.g., Sternberg, 2003; Weick and Roberts, 1993). The fourth quality is a compelling tendency to live life in context, emphasizing what is practical and grounded (e.g., Bigelow, 1992; Locke, 2007). We propose that these qualities intensify along the vertical axis, but also that the point of leverage – where wisdom makes a difference in the world – is only where the axes intersect (e.g., Pfeffer and Sutton, 2000; Sternberg, 1997).

The vertical axis compels people to transcend dualities that comprise ordinary awareness on the horizontal axis. Without the capacity to transcend duality, one stays locked into competing rules, interests, norms and so forth. As Einstein acknowledged long ago, and both Gandhi and Martin Luther King exemplified, we cannot solve problems at the level at which they are created (Einstein, 1954). At that level we do not have sufficient perspective to see integrative possibilities (Churchman, 1971). On the vertical axis, however, the capacity emerges to stand outside the relentless busyness of life and develop a more comprehensive view, for example, by discerning subtle interconnections (e.g., Bateson, 1988; Cowan, 2007a). What you see from a mountaintop is both literally and symbolically more inclusive than what you see from the bottom of the mountain. For wisdom to manifest, the tendency toward wholeness becomes infused with a sense of goodness.

Both the holistic and goodness orientations of the vertical axis increase the capability to question norms. Consciously holding a position of 'not knowing' is a signature of wisdom by comparison to closed attitudes and positions of 'always knowing' (e.g., Chia and Holt, 2007; Meacham, 1983). Depth on the vertical axis makes increasingly apparent the reality that there is always more to see, more to learn, more to the story. Wisdom sustains the freshness of a beginner's attitude by being continually aware, and by frequently questioning, seeking, and changing positions in order to gain more complete perspectives. When the need for choices and actions arises, there is then no doubt or hesitation.

The third quality of wisdom involves the capacity to be fully alive in the present (e.g., Scharmer, 2007; Tolle, 1999), which mirrors Capra's (2002) description of 'heightened aliveness'. Drawing on the wholeness and goodness of the first quality and the quest for understanding of the second quality, the third evokes the energy of aliveness, of fully engaging people and situations here and now. When it is time to plan the future, all of one's knowledge and energy are given to planning the future; yet when it is time to act, all of knowledge and energy are given to acting. Being fully present means being completely engaged with opportunities and responsibilities as they arise. Thus, when interacting with one's fiftieth customer of the day, a wise person still responds as attentively and caringly as with the first.

The fourth quality of wisdom is its tendency to stay grounded in context. This is the primary way that the vertical axis connects with the horizontal. The wholeness/goodness, freshness, and aliveness of the other three qualities must be continually translated into real-life situations (e.g., Cowan, 2005b). Wisdom in this sense stays relevant and vital not only for personal issues, but also for organizational and societal issues (e.g., Bierly et al., 2000). It becomes best not only FOR the world but also IN the world. This practicality brings with it a sense of lightheartedness, rather than anxiety or paralysis, not because life isn't taken seriously but rather because it

becomes apparent that taking life too seriously gets in the way of short-term goodwill and long-term systemic effectiveness (e.g., Dalai Lama and Cutler, 1998). Learning to activate all four qualities simultaneously is certainly not easy (cf. Pascual-Leone, 2000), yet it is perhaps the most exemplary indication of wisdom emerging.

ADDING VALUE TO OTHER FRAMEWORKS

What can the employment of wisdom add to an organizational scholar's repertoire of theories and methods? Alternatively, what aspects of study may be illuminated by a wisdom lens, which other lenses might not include? According to our framework, research guided only by perspectives on the horizontal axis will focus currently and locally – likely in search of 'quantifiable answers'. Research that also brings the vertical axis into play will pay more attention to phenomena that surround and inform current situations. For example, this may include examining subtle premises (e.g., Argyris, 1991) or hidden connections (Capra, 1996, 2002), which all comprise intangible variables. Variables such as these are inevitably less measurable but they are often more valuable for illuminating the bigger picture as an equally integral part of one's work. A backdrop of wisdom challenges scholars to complement explicit measures experienced on the horizontal dimension with measures of depth and aliveness that derive from the vertical dimension. One without the other limits the story told.

Organizations often restrict attention to what they define as problems and opportunities, which are typically framed around self-interest. Similarly, scholars often restrict their own inquiries in order to serve their own interests. Being conscious of the vertical dimension, however, causes a reframing of problems and opportunities at more inclusive levels of inquiry. Each reframing can reveal different motives, concerns, benefits, and questions. In an example to which we later return, the corporation, Aramco, held a meeting 'under the stars of the red sand dunes of one of the most awe-inspiring deserts of the world' (Horvath, in Brown and Isaacs, 2005: 72). The context and process reminded people of their desert heritage and of their obligation to pass on this rich heritage to future generations. Genuinely expanding the depth and breadth of inquiring lenses is often avoided. We suggest, however, that it can reveal a sense of interconnectedness, meaning, and care for the common good that not only invigorates organizations but also inspires more inclusive questions for organizational scholars.

A wisdom lens can also shed more light on personal experiences and growth of both the scholar and the organization involved in a study. Issues that then arise, do so not in opposition of, but as complementary to, mainstream academic training and analytical skills. Qualities such as sensitivity to people and environment (Hall and Hall, 1990), mindfulness (Hanh, 2000), and authenticity (George, 2003) increasingly become signatures of a mature scholar (cf. Feuerstein, 1997), but they do not replace a scholar's scientific capacities. When wisdom becomes part of the equation of scholarly maturity, a 'full professor' may be expected less to maintain quantity publishing expectations (e.g., number of articles) and expected more to model exemplary rich behavior (e.g., through more reflective, integrative writing and apprenticeships). Wisdom as a backdrop can enable scholars to challenge premises that underlie traditional practices on the horizontal dimension, such as suppression of one's identity in reports of scholarly findings.

ORGANIZATIONAL MANIFESTATIONS

For wisdom to become salient as a backdrop for organizational research, it is important to identify ways that it may not only add value to scholarship but also to organizational life (e.g., Barrett, 1998). Toward this end, we address three issues: (1) wisdom's impact on the processes of framing and reframing,

(2) the emergence of collective wisdom, and (3) structures and processes that can increase access to wisdom. Regarding wisdom's access, we also propose a new process that we call 'angel advocacy', which emerged from our rethinking the traditional devil's advocate role. We mention it here because it is an example of our first issue, reframing.

Framing and reframing are processes that can enrich understanding (on the vertical dimension) by shifting familiar cognitive connections (on the horizontal dimension) (e.g., Bolman and Deal, 2003). Because of wisdom's tendencies toward wholeness and freshness, a backdrop of wisdom provides multiple possibilities for reframing (e.g., Zander and Zander, 2000). For example, helping scientists to appreciate the magnitude of their contributions by reframing their work as improving people's lives rather than merely publishing a paper may increase not only the quality of their work but also their self respect and thus the quality of their lives. A backdrop of wisdom does not change their job as much as it positions patterns of constructive meaning around their work (e.g., Wind and Crook, 2005).

Similar situations arise in other work environments when leadership enables employees to see more wholeness and connectedness surrounding their work (e.g., Ray, 2004), evoking a depth of aliveness that leads to quality outcomes previously untapped (Cowan, 1995). Our opening example of Hewlett Packard reframing awareness from being best IN the world to being best FOR the world is a notable example. Using a relevant metaphor, Quinn highlights the power of such reframing:

> Energy that was once held in the form of the acorn gathers new energy from other sources – the soil, the sun, the air, and the rains from the sky – and begins to take form as a tree. People can be like acorns. Our consciousness can unfold, gathering energy from new sources, evolving into something much greater and more life-giving than we presently enjoy. (2000: 84–85)

More expansive reframing of one's own or another's perspectives can significantly enrich work as well as increase organizational vitality (e.g., Koestenbaum, 2002). It can also inspire and invigorate in ways that send constructive ripple effects into other parts of the world (e.g., Dalai Lama, 1999). Beyond reframing a task or situation, wisdom can also promote and sustain full presence in one's work. In this respect, reframing becomes integral to an organization's culture (e.g., Offerman and Phan, 2002; Vaill, 2007). As employees experience one part of work becoming significantly enriched by reframing, it becomes easier to reframe other areas of work (cf. Kotter and Cohen, 2002). A sustained backdrop of wisdom can thereby provide greater awareness of wholeness, connectedness, and aliveness to help sustain engagement in more aspects of work (Csikszentmihalyi, 2003). Employees learn to conceive their tasks as less disconnected from the work of others and from the mission of the organization (e.g., Katzenbach, 1996). What may begin to happen in such cases, we propose, is that more people will get used to seeing and then using wisdom as a vital backdrop to what they do. As a consequence, it is possible that a collective level of wisdom (e.g., Adler, 2007; Srivastva and Cooperrider, 1998) will arise within an organization.

A compelling example of collective wisdom rising, as reportedly observed by a third of the world's population, involves the Live8 gatherings that took place in 10 countries around the world in June of 2005 (e.g., see www.data.org). In order to motivate people around the globe to increase pressure on the G8 countries meeting in Scotland to withdraw their claims of enormous debt from poor African countries, Bob Geldof and U2's Bono arranged 10 concerts with world renowned artists, and held corresponding meetings with presidents and prime ministers to evoke conversations that would raise awareness of and compassionate action toward African debt. These events manifest the power of inclusiveness and integration as an unprecedented peace-time appeal to collective global awareness. At the same time, the appeal attempted to frame leadership action with collective wisdom

instead of within national boundaries of thinking.

An example of a business organization that took a similarly exemplary step in engaging collective wisdom is the Saudi corporation, Aramco, comprising 50,000 employees. In 2003, Aramco arranged a 'World Café' process (Brown and Isaacs, 2005: 71–72) for 700 managers in order to create meaningful conversations about its mission, values and business plan. In a similar gathering held the following year, 'The Shaybah Café', 200 senior managers met under the stars of the Saudi Arabian desert (as mentioned earlier) to build a new business community around meaningful dialogue and learning networks. In both cases, collective wisdom seemingly emerged in line with the structure and qualities that we described above. What do we learn from such examples? We explore this issue in the final section of our chapter.

ORGANIZATION DESIGN AND CULTURE

New ways of communicating and working are increasingly being explored in various countries, as employees move, for example, from land-based phones to email and cell phones, from cubicles to shared space and from centralized and static to more improvisational and spontaneous forms of guidance. As a consequence, changes in physical environments seem insufficient by themselves to understand where organizational changes are heading. If the mentality of employees stays the same, sharing space can have unintended effects that ultimately lead to less flexibility and less sharing. Flexible work environments can increase the potential for inclusiveness and integration, but they alone are not enough to ensure the realization of such potential.

In addition to physical surroundings, we need to consider deeper dimensions such as psychological space, emotional terrain and shared values and assumptions. Similarly, we need to create measures that are sensitive to tacit procedures and processes that connect people and frame communications (e.g., Wheatley and Kellner-Rogers, 1996). Illuminating contexts of such pursuit is vital to understanding organizations in ways and to degrees that keep pace with the times (e.g., Quinn, 2004). Theorizing and measuring must begin to unify physical, emotional, psychological, spiritual, aesthetic, and social spaces – more in the manner that a movie (compared to a journal article) captures lived experience (e.g., Kessler and Bailey, 2007). A wisdom backdrop offers innovative ways to convey the richness of apparent messiness (e.g., Brearley and Darsoe, forthcoming). As such shifts manifest, which we propose they are doing, traditional research premises and methods will need similar rejuvenation. Just as education cannot keep pace with world changes by remaining restricted to classrooms and textbooks, scholarship will likely also need to jettison encumbering traditional rituals such as miring new ideas in long review processes in order to create documents that are then frozen in the pages of a journal.

One organization that appears to be awakening to the potential that wisdom brings is Unilever Faberge in the United Kingdom. In 1999, Unilever top management decided to change its culture, moving from traditional, static norms of obedience and control towards collective, dynamic norms comprising individual initiatives. At Unilever Faberge in London, for example, the chairman initiated a project called 'Catalyst', created and orchestrated by an experienced artist, Alastair Creamer. By employing the Arts and inviting artists to offer workshops on organizational as well as business issues, Unilever Faberge has managed to evolve from a group of self-minded individuals working separately in cubicles, into a cohesive team of inter-minded people working in lively, shared, creative gathering spaces (Darsoe, 2004). Employees have also been given permission to support local communities in a spirited fashion. Thus, while some reach out to help local school children with reading skills, others form alliances with local art directors. Unilever is a good example of working inclusively with structures and processes in order to create a culture of initiatives that touch myriad people in various constructive ways. Another recent study has demonstrated that virtuous organizations outperform less virtuous ones, virtuousness defined as having three key characteristics: moral goodness, human impact and social betterment (Cameron et al., 2004). We believe that organizations such as Unilever are actively increasing access to wisdom by leading the way through experimentation and action.

There are, of course, a great variety of other ways to engage employees and other stakeholders to become committed to meaningful, mutually supportive projects. Within the last couple of decades, new approaches to meetings and conferences have been arising, which are more inspiring than traditional boardroom processes and auditorium lectures. In these instances, collective wisdom may be unfolding more by necessity than from academic prescriptions. Open Space Technology (Owen, 1997), dialogue meetings (Bohm, 1996; Isaacs, 1999), learning conferences (Mirvis et al., 2003), World Cafés (Brown and Isaacs, 2005), and innovative design thinking (Brown, 2005) all provide exemplary structures and processes being triggered more by real needs than by academic theory.

What do such approaches say about emerging organizational and societal development? First of all, they are deeply inclusive, inviting diverse participants to contribute without expectations of top-down control. Second, participants are valued equally – each one's contributions become part of an emergent story or structure, embodying the premise that everybody has important knowledge and experience to share but no one has it all (cf. Wilber, 2003). Third, an indispensable part focuses on unleashing the human spirit through powerful questions that speak to the heart and mind and stimulate creative dialogue (e.g., Wheatley, 2002). Fourth, these approaches provide humane contexts that motivate inspiration, sharing and bonding in ways and to degrees that traditional organizations may have dreamed about but never notably tapped. And fifth, in terms of order but not importance, fluid but cohesive facilitation enables communications to flow and combine in constructive ways.

Finally, we offer a creative idea of our own that we believe can help to facilitate the emergence of wisdom. Our idea stands in contrast to the 'devil's advocate' process, which involves criticizing concepts, procedure, products, and so forth, typically to test and improve them before they enter the marketplace. We suggest, however, that there exists a growing need for an inspirational counterpart, the 'angel's advocate', to illuminate paths of access to wisdom. The role of an 'angel's advocate' is to encourage and energize people by asking transcendent rather than critical questions, such as 'who else could profit from this?', 'who are the unheard but relevant voices?', 'what would make this work more meaningful?' and so forth. An 'angel's advocate' would reframe critical questions, challenge scientific norms of competition, conflict and control, motivate people to think more often of the whole in compassionate ways and remind us to embody the life-sustaining values of inclusion and integration (e.g., Cowan, 2007b). Likewise, an 'angel's advocate' may invoke pauses for reflection and rejuvenation, and create spaces that enable authenticity, presence, and playfulness to infuse work. Returning to our opening example, the time is at hand to energize workers, organizations and scholars alike with questions and challenges that shift values from being best IN the world to being best FOR the world. This is the kind of change that we propose wisdom can provide as a backdrop for organizational studies and practice.

CONCLUSION

In this chapter our intention has been to reframe the concept of wisdom in ways that inspire and provoke more collectively beneficial values to guide research and practice. In some areas of research, wisdom already appears salient to some degree. For example,

Appreciative Inquiry involves constructive framing (Srivastva and Cooperrider, 1999); systemic approaches invite inclusion (Capra, 2002) and integrated processes of development (Cowan, 2005a; Wilber, 2000); and artful approaches engage constructive feelings and enrich consciousness (Darsoe, 2004). Such examples portray a foundation that supports the return of wisdom. We believe that the tide is turning to include mechanical with organic, fragmented and static with holistic and fluid, linear and left-brained with more inclusive, nonlinear, whole-brained (Pink, 2005). Accompanying this change are opportunities for more vital and vibrant reconsiderations of organizational studies.

For this to occur, it is important to generate and study inclusive research questions such as those we indicated throughout our chapter. Inclusive questions offer a new frontier of research challenges that hold the promise of creating a more unified story.

> In both science and poetry, we are remembering a story about life that has creativity and connectedness as its essential themes. As we use this new story to look into our organizational lives, it offers us images of organizations and leaders that are both startling and enticing. It offers us ways of being together where our diversity – our uniqueness – is essential and important. It offers us an arena big enough to embrace the full expression of our infinitely creative human natures. (Wheatley, 2005: 23–24)

In conclusion, we think the most provocative thought we have proposed is not so much employing wisdom as a backdrop for organizational studies, but transcending presumed scientific 'objectivity' to include wisdom. This is not a proposal for 'subjectivity' but rather a reframing and balancing of 'objectivity' in order to integrate the vertical axis of our framework. Similarly we invite fellow scholars to transcend methodological boundaries in bold, unprecedented ways that enable increasingly conscious choices about what is truly worthy of their research efforts. To do so means focusing on how they can make genuine differences in the lives of people involved, and on how they themselves can learn and grow through such processes.

REFERENCES

Adler, N.J. (2007) 'Organizational metaphysics – Global wisdom and the audacity of hope', in E.H. Kessler and J.R. Bailey (eds) *Handbook of Organizational and Managerial Wisdom*. Thousand Oaks, CA: Sage.

Argyris, C. (2002) 'Double loop learning, teaching and research', *The Academy of Management Learning and Education*, 1 (2): 206–218.

Argyris, C. (1991) 'Teaching smart people how to learn', *Harvard Business Review*, 69 (3): 99–101.

Argyris, C. and Schon, D.A. (1996) *Organizational Learning II: Theory, Method, and Practice*. New York: Addison-Wesley.

Augier, M. (2004) 'James March on education, leadership, and Don Quixote: Introduction and overview', *Academy of Management Learning and Education*, 3 (2): 169–177.

Baltes, P.B. and Staudinger, U.M. (2000) 'Wisdom: A metaheuristic (pragmatic) to orchestrate mind and virtue toward excellence', *American Psychologist*, 55 (1): 122–136.

Barrett, R. (1998) *Liberating the Corporate Soul: Building a Visionary Organization*. Boston: Butterworth Heinemann.

Bartunek, J.M. and Mock, M.K. (1987) 'First-order, second-order, and third-order change and organization development interventions: A cognitive approach', *The Journal of Applied Behavioral Science*, 23 (4): 483–500.

Bateson, G. (1988) 'The pattern which connects', in F. Capra (ed.), *Uncommon Wisdom: Conversations with Remarkable People*. New York: Bantam Books. pp. 71–89.

Bierly, P.E. III, Kessler, E.H. and Christensen, E.W. (2000) 'Organizational learning, knowledge, and wisdom', *Journal of Organizational Change Management*, 13 (6): 595–618.

Bigelow, J. (1992) 'Developing managerial wisdom', *Journal of Management Inquiry*, 1 (2): 143–153.

Bluedorn, A.C. (2002) *The Human Organization of Time*. Stanford, CA: Stanford University Press.

Bohm, D. (1996) *On Dialogue*, L. Nichol (ed.). London: Routledge.

Bolman, L.G. and Deal, T.E. (2003) *Reframing Organizations: Artistry, Choice, and Leadership* (3rd edn). San Francisco: Jossey-Bass.

Brearley, L. and Darsoe, L. (forthcoming) 'Vivifying data and Experience through Artful Approaches, Chapter 57, Business Studies', in J.G. Knowles and A.L. Cole (eds), *Handbook of the Arts in Qualitative Research: Perspectives, Methodologies, Examples and Issues*.

Brown, T. (2005) 'Strategy by design', *Fast Company*, June, 52–54.

Brown, J. and Isaacs, D. (2005) *The World Café: Shaping our Futures through Conversations that Matter*. San Francisco: Berrett-Koehler.

Cajete, G. (1994) *Look to the Mountains: An Ecology of Indigenous Education*. Durango, CO: Kivaki.

Calvino, I. (1974; tr. W. Weaver) *Invisible Cities*. New York: Harcourt, Inc.

Cameron, K., Bright, D. and Caza, A. (2004) 'Exploring the relationships between organizational virtuousness and performance', *American Behavioral Scientist*, 47: 766–790.

Capra, F. (1996) *The Web of Life: A New Scientific Understanding of Living Systems*. New York: Anchor Books.

Capra, F. (2002) *The Hidden Connections*. New York: Doubleday.

Chia, R. and Holt, R. (2007) 'Wisdom as learned ignorance: Integrating East-West perspectives', in E.H. Kessler and J.R. Bailey (eds) *Handbook of Organizational and Managerial Wisdom*. Thousand Oaks, CA: Sage.

Churchman, C.W. (1971) *The Design of Inquiring Systems: Basic Concepts of Systems and Organizations*. New York: Basic Books.

Conger, J. and Hooijberg, R. (2007) 'Organizational ethics – Acting wisely while facing ethical dilemmas in leadership', in E.H. Kessler and J.R. Bailey (eds) *Handbook of Organizational and Managerial Wisdom*. Thousand Oaks, CA: Sage.

Cowan, D. (1995) 'Rhythms of learning: Patterns that bridge individuals and organizations', *Journal of Management Inquiry*, 4 (3), September: 222–246.

Cowan, D. (2005a) 'Learning to diversify yourself', *World Futures: The Journal of General Evolution*, 61: 347–369.

Cowan, D. (2005b) 'Translating spiritual intelligence into leadership competencies', *Journal of Management, Spirituality and Religion*, 2 (1): 3–38.

Cowan, D. (2007a) 'Artistic undertones of humanistic leadership education', *Journal of Management Education*, April, 31 (2): 156–180.

Cowan, D. (2007b) 'Don't move until you see it', *Journal of Management Inquiry*, June, 16(2): 174–178.

Csikszentmihalyi, M. (2003) *Good Business. Leadership, Flow and the Making of Meaning*. London: Hodder & Stoughton.

Dalai Lama (1999) *Ethics for the New Millennium*. New York: Riverhead.

Dalai Lama and Cutler, H.C. (1998) *The Art of Happiness: A Handbook for Living*. London: Coronet Books, Hodder & Stoughton.

Darsoe, L. (2001) *Innovation in the Making*. Copenhagen: Samfundslitteratur.

Darsoe, L. (2004) *Artful Creation. Learning-Tales of Arts-in-Business.* Copenhagen: Samfundslitteratur.

Einstein, A. (1954) *Ideas and Opinions.* New York: Crown Publishers.

Emmons, R.A. (1999) *The Psychology of Ultimate Concerns.* New York: The Guilford Press.

Feuerstein, G. (1997) *Lucid Waking: Mindfulness and the Spiritual Potential of Humanity.* Rochester, VT: Inner Traditions International.

George, B. (2003) *Authentic Leadership: Rediscovering the Secrets to Creating Lasting Value.* San Francisco: Jossey-Bass.

Glassman, B. (1998) *Bearing Witness.* New York: Bell Tower.

Hall, E.T. and Hall, M.R. (1990) *Understanding Cultural Differences: Germans, French, and Americans.* Yarmouth: ME: Intercultural Press.

Hanh, T.N. (2000) *The Art of Mindful Living* (compact disk). Boulder, CO: Sounds True.

Isaacs, W. (1999) *Dialogue and the Art of Thinking Together.* New York: Currency.

Jones, D. (2001) *Celebrate What's Right with the World* (dvd). St. Paul, MN: Star Thrower Distribution.

Katzenbach, J.R. (1996) *Real Change Leaders.* New York: Times Business (Random House).

Kessler, E.H. and Bailey, J.R. (eds) (2007) *Handbook of Organizational and Managerial Wisdom.* Thousand Oaks, CA: Sage.

Koestenbaum, P. (2002) *Leadership: The Inner Side of Greatness.* San Francisco: Jossey-Bass.

Kotter, J.P. and Cohen, D.S. (2002) *The Heart of Change.* Boston: Harvard Business School Press.

Krishnamurti, J. (1973) *The Awakening of Intelligence.* New York: HaperCollins.

Lewin, K. [1948] (1973) *Resolving Social Conflicts.* London: Souvenir Press.

Locke, E. (2007) 'Wisdom: Objectivism as the proper philosophy for living on earth', in E.H. Kessler and J.R. Bailey (eds) *Handbook of Organizational and Managerial Wisdom.* Thousand Oaks, CA: Sage.

March, J. (1991) 'Exploration and exploitation in organizational learning', *Organization Science,* 2 (1): 71–87.

McGregor, J. (2005) 'The architect of a different kind of organization', *Fast Company,* June, 66–70.

Meacham, J.A. (1983) 'Wisdom and the context of knowledge: Knowing that one doesn't know', in Basel Karger (ed.), *Contributions to Human Development,* vol. 8: 111–134.

Mirvis, P., Ayas, K. and Roth, G. (2003) *To the Desert and Back: The Story of One of the Most Dramatic Business Transformations on Record.* San Francisco: Jossey-Bass.

Offerman, L.R. and Phan, L.U. (2002) 'Culturally intelligent leadership for a diverse world', in R.E. Riggio, S.E. Murphy and F.J. Pirozzolo (eds), *Multiple Intelligences and Leadership.* Mahwah, NJ: Lawrence Erlbaum. pp. 187–214.

Osho (1999) *Maturity: The Responsibility of Being Oneself.* New York: St. Martin's Griffin.

Owen, H. (1997) *Expanding our Now. The Story of Open Space Technology.* San Francisco: Berrett-Koehler.

Pascual-Leone, J. (2000) 'Mental attention, consciousness, and the progressive emergence of wisdom', *Journal of Adult Development,* 7 (4): 241–254.

Pfeffer, J. and Sutton, R.I. (2000) *The Knowing-Doing Gap: How Smart Companies Turn Knowledge into Action.* Boston: Harvard Business School Press.

Pink, D. (2005) *A Whole New Mind. Moving from the Information Age to the Conceptual Age.* New York: Riverhead Books, a member of Penguin Group (USA), Inc.

Quinn, R.E. (2000) *Change the World: How Ordinary People Can Achieve Extraordinary Results.* San Francisco: Jossey-Bass.

Quinn, R.E. (2004) *Building the Bridge as You Walk on It: A Guide for Leading Change.* San Francisco: Jossey-Bass.

Ray, M. (2004) *The Highest Goal.* San Francisco: Berrett-Koehler.

Scharmer, O. (2007) *Theory U. Leading from the Future as it Emerges.* Cambridge, MA: Society for Organizational Learning.

Srivastva, S. and Cooperrider, D. (1998) *Organizational Wisdom and Executive Courage.* San Francisco: New Lexington Press.

Srivastva, S. and Cooperrider, D. (eds) (1999) *Appreciative Management and Leadership.* Euclid, OH: Williams Custom Publishing.

Starbuck, W.H. (2005) 'Four great conflicts of the twenty-first century', in C.L. Cooper (ed.) *The Twenty-First Century Manager.* Oxford: Oxford University Press. pp. 21–56.

Sternberg, R.J. (1997) *Successful Intelligence.* New York: Plume.

Sternberg, R.J. (1998) 'A balance theory of wisdom', *Review of General Psychology,* 2 (4): 347–365.

Sternberg, R.J. (2003) *Wisdom, Intelligence, and Creativity Synthesized.* New York: Cambridge University Press.

Strogatz, S. (2003) *Sync: The Emerging Science of Spontaneous Order.* Theia Publishing.

Surowiecki, J. (2005) *The Wisdom of Crowds.* New York: Achor Books, Random House.

Tolle, E. (1999) *The Power of Now.* Novato, CA: New World Library.

Underwood, P. (1991) *Who Speaks for Wolf?.* San Anselmo, CA: A Tribe of Two Press.

Underwood, P. (2000) *The Great Hoop of Life, Volume 1: A Traditional Medicine Wheel for Enabling Learning* and for Gathering Wisdom. San Anselma, CA: Tribe of Two Press.

Vaill, P.B. (2007) 'Organizational epistemology – Interpersonal relations in organizations and the emergence of wisdom', in E.H. Kessler and J.R. Bailey (eds) Handbook of Organizational and Managerial Wisdom. Thousand Oaks, CA: Sage.

Waldron, J. (1995) 'The wisdom of the multitude', Political Theory, 23 (4): 563–584.

Weick, K. (1998) 'Improvisation as a mindset for organizational analysis', Organization Science, 9, September-October: 543–555.

Weick, K. and Roberts, K. (1993) 'Collective mind in organizations: Heedful interrelating on flight decks', Administrative Science Quarterly, 38: 357–381.

Wheatley, M. (2002) Turning to One Another: Simple Conversations to Restore Hope to the Future. San Francisco: Berrett-Koehler.

Wheatley, M. (2005) Finding our Way: Leadership for an Uncertain Time. San Francisco: Berrett-Koehler.

Wheatley, M. and Kellner-Rogers, M. (1996) A Simpler Way. San Francisco: Berrett-Koehler.

Wilber, K. (1995) Sex, Ecology, Spirituality: The Spirit of Evolution. Boston: Shambhala.

Wilber, K. (2000) Integral Psychology. Boston: Shambhala.

Wilber, K. (2003) Kosmic Consciousness: The Ken Wilber Sessions (compact disk set). Boulder, CO: Sounds True.

Wind, Y. and Crook, C. (2005) The Power of Impossible Thinking. Upper Saddle River, NJ: Wharton School Publishing.

Zander, R.S. and Zander, B. (2000) The Art of Possibility. Boston: Harvard Business School Press.

Zohar, D. (1997) Rewiring the Corporate Brain: Using the New Science to Rethink How we Structure and Lead Organizations. San Francisco: Berrett-Koehler.

Knowledge in the Absence of Wisdom

David Rooney, Bernard McKenna, Peter Liesch and Kim Boal

In the face of constant change, faddish practices such as Business Process Re-engineering, that promise cure-alls, or easily digested but ephemeral ideas for busy managers in the 'real world', are notorious but irresistible to many. In their place, we argue for wisdom: processes and skills that provide managers with the capacity to distinguish between change as fad or management power game (Zorn et al., 2000) and change that is necessary to adapt to new circumstance.

The world is increasingly beset with a moral, ontological and epistemological malaise. Some call this the postmodern condition in which moral, ontological and epistemological relativism prevails at the expense of certainty, stability and truth. Others see the rise of knowledge-based economies as a response to the 'risk society'. The paradox of the risk society is that the more knowledge we call on to deal with risk, the more we create risks, which leads us to call for more knowledge in an infinite regress. If this thesis is true, and it may well be, this is a path to nowhere.

Imagination, creativity, insight and perspicacity, the transcendent elements of intellection and mind, are capacities we have evolved to make the best of these limits. These transcendent capabilities are at the core of wisdom.

Wisdom is not simply an accumulation of knowledge; it is a way of being and doing. Wise action recognizes the importance not just of rational and systematic intellection (science broadly defined), but also of a transcendent intellection built on a foundation of ethics and character. Wisdom strikes the difficult balance along these three dimensions, thereby bettering the individual and society. We argue, for example, that a fundamental feature of wisdom is that it not be founded only on a great leader. Of course, effective leadership is crucial to organizational success: but an important characteristic of wise and effective leaders is that they create the organizational capacity for wise practice. Many would see the innate tension between the autonomy needed for wise action and the necessary routinization of organizational procedures. Wisdom, though, would see us embrace this tension and work with it rather than deny it.

The practical perils of knowledge without wisdom and of underestimating the transcendent engine of the human mind have long been known. An eighteenth-century Aristotelian, Giambattista Vico, provides a taxonomy of four intellectual types. **The imprudent savant** (*doctus imprudentis*) 'approaches ethics as though it were a manual of propositions to be memorized; makes decisions slowly, is arrogant; and has a lack of persuasive communication'. The savant moves 'in a straight line from general to particular truths' in order to 'burst through the tortuous curves of life' (Miner, 1998: 57). Sometimes successful, they more often fail. **The fool** (*stultus*): 'lacks knowledge of either the general or the particular', and so 'constantly pays for his [or her] rashness' (Miner, 1998: 56). Although the **astute ignoramus** (*illiterates astutus*) knows how to succeed in worldly affairs, s/he lacks reflexive humane wisdom. Thus ignorance of the most important things, as evidenced by constantly preferring utility over what is right, ensures failure in the most important matters (Miner, 1998: 56). **Wise people** (*sapientes*) have practical and theoretical wisdom, 'through all the obliquities and uncertainties of human actions, [they] aim for eternal truth, follow roundabout ways … and execute plans which in the long run are for the best, as far as the nature of things allows' (Miner, 1998: 56). Although written to describe an intellectual process typology, the application to management is obvious.

Caution is also needed: is there a downside to wisdom? Csikszentmihalyi and Rathunde (1990: 44) argue that a disorienting grandiosity and remoteness are dangers that might be associated with the pursuit of wisdom. These can lead to complacency and a lack of humility such as believing that we are smarter than we really are and to believing that we unquestionably know what is best for everyone. Nevertheless, as Csikszentmihalyi and Rathunde (1990: 44) also argue:

> What this suggests to our contemporary way of thinking is that, even under the best conditions, knowledge is dangerous. But then so is ignorance. The point is to understand what are the dangers peculiar to wisdom so that we can reap its benefits while avoiding as much as possible of its negative effects.

Paradoxically, wisdom is a finely balanced, difficult and uncertain thing in itself, and it suggests that we should deal with difficult and uncertain aspects of life by relaxing our urge to resort to rationality for control over human complexity. In other words, we might have more control if we accept less control.

Wisdom is critically dependent on character and the transcendent mind. Wisdom, therefore, is less concerned with how much we know and more with how we apprehend and deploy that knowledge. Moreover, wisdom is a practical way of being in a complex and uncertain world. Thus, wisdom is that which coordinates knowledge and judgments about the '*fundamental* pragmatics of life' (Baltes and Staudinger, 2000: 132).

This note is about explaining what wisdom is to a modern audience because it is a word that has largely evaded the discourse of management (see Boal and Hooijberg, 2000; Kriger and Malan 1993, Malan and Kriger, 1998). We wish to reinvigorate its proper use in daily management and work practice.

REFERENCES

Baltes, P.B. and Staudinger, U.M. (2000) 'A metaheuristic (pragmatic) to orchestrate mind and virtue towards excellence', *American Psychologist*, 55 (1): 122–136.

Boal, K.B. and Hooijber, R. (2000) 'Strategic leadership: Moving on', *Leadership Quarterly*, 11 (4): 515–559.

Campbell, D.T. (1974) 'Evolutionary epistemology', *Language, Development and Culture*. New York, Wiley and Sons. pp. 413–463.

Csikszentmihalyi, M. and Rathunde, K. (1990) 'The psychology of wisdom: An evolutionary interpretation', *Wisdom: Its Nature, Origins, and Development*. Cambridge: Cambridge University Press. pp. 25–51.

Kriger, M.P. and Malan, L.-C. (1993) 'Shifting paradigms: The valuing of personal knowledge, wisdom, and other invisible processes in organizations', *Journal of Management Inquiry*, 2 (4): 391–398.

Malan, L.C. and Kriger, M.P. (1998) 'Making sense of managerial wisdom', *Journal of Management Inquiry*, 7 (3): 242–251.

McKenna, B. (2005) 'Wisdom, ethics and the postmodern organisation', *Handbook on the Knowledge Economy*. D. Rooney, G. Hearn and A. Ninan. Cheltenham, Edward Elgar. pp. 37–53.

Continued

Miner, R.C. (1998) 'Verum-factum and practical wisdom in the early writings of Giambattista Vico', *Journal of the History of Ideas*, 59 (1): 53–73.

Rooney, D. (2005) 'Knowledge, economy, technology and society: the politics of discourse', *Telematics and Informatics*, 22 (3): 405–422.

Zorn, T.E., Page, D.J. et al. (2000) 'Nuts about change: Multiple perspectives on change-oriented communication in a public sector organization'. *Management Communication Quarterly*, 13 (4): 515.

Organization and Management Studies: An End in Itself or a Means Towards a Better Social and Economic life?

Tony Watson

Coming to terms with the unintended consequences of human actions and initiatives is one of the greatest recurring challenges that the human species has faced since it first invented societies. And handling the ways in which *means* tend to subvert *ends* has been a particular issue for the species since it invented bureaucracies. Taking its lead from Max Weber, organization theory has been especially concerned with the issue of means failing to lead to the ends which they were devised to achieve – most notoriously with bureaucracy coming to exist for bureaucracy's sake.

Organization and management studies provide us with powerful resources for understanding the processes whereby means become ends in themselves. They have the potential to inform choices and organizational practices which might lead to more effective links between intentions and effects. But is the potential being realised? Might not organization and management studies be in danger of becoming ends in themselves? I suggest that there is a real danger of this happening. There are several ways in which this might be happening in the business and management schools, the organizations where, for better or worse, organization and management studies have their home.

The very organization of organization and management studies is at the heart of the problem here. There is a complex division of labour at work. This too readily functions more as an end in itself than as a route towards something else. There are divisions of labour which reflect divisions in organizations themselves (marketing, operations management, human resource management, for example). On top of this are divisions which reflect the varying scholarly or disciplinary backgrounds and commitments of teachers and researchers (economics, engineering, psychology, sociology, mathematics). Making all this even more complicated, there are divisions between those who give their work a critical social scientific emphasis and those who give it a more 'applied' emphasis.

At the risk of being accused of intellectual imperialism, I would suggest that organization theory has considerable unrealized potential as a *means* of pulling things together in the application of social science to business and managerial issues. Unfortunately, however, organization theory has tended to become an *end* in itself. The 'academic subject' has become more important to many of its practitioners than its 'subject matter'. After a close examination of a series of recently published books in organization studies (Watson, 2006), I observed what might be characterized as a highly dysfunctional level of dissension among scholars and suggested that these authors might be 'condemning organization studies to a life at the margins of both the academy and the world of practice'. Surely, I suggested in my pain, 'organizational studies can … aspire to be something more than the plaything of disengaged intellectuals disputing with each other over their theories and paradigms in the privacy of their academic playground'.

There are no simple prescriptions that can be offered to bring intellectual means more into line with social ends in the organizational sphere. Some bold suggestions can be ventured, however. At the level of business schools in general, thought needs to be given

Continued

to identifying a common task that can be shared across the divisions and departments. This, I suggest, should be one of *improving our understanding of the organizing and managing of the invention, production and distribution of goods, services, and the administration of public life.* And if organization theory is going to offer itself as a key means towards achieving this end, serious attention needs to be given to calming down the methodological disputes which cripple it. This does not mean developing a bland unified organization theory but working, instead, in a spirit of *pragmatic pluralism.* This would prioritize the analysis of organizational patterns and processes occurring outside the academy, with much greater direct interaction between organizational actors and academic researchers. Theoretical texts and concepts would be treated as means to understanding the organizational world and not as ends in themselves. As long as they are deployed within an epistemologically and ontologically consistent manner within each separate study, concepts from across the social sciences would be drawn upon. But the key criterion for judging the studies which emerge from this activity would be that of how effectively they inform the practices of those who study them in our business schools or read them elsewhere – be those people managers, workers, policy makers or social commentators. Organization and management studies cannot directly improve social and economic life but it can do a great deal more than it currently does to inform the choices that members of society make with regard to organizations and their management.

REFERENCE

Watson, Tony J. (2006) 'The organization and disorganization of organization studies' (review essay), *Journal of Management Studies,* 43 (2): 367–382.

Maternal Organization

Heather Höpfl

Look at any organizational textbook and it is immediately apparent that, with few exceptions, issues of gender are rarely dealt with and, even where they are dealt with, the attention given to the subject is usually scant. Consequently, conventional representations of the organization are patriarchal, masculine and directed by the animus. They reduce the notion of 'organization' to abstract relationships, rational actions and purposive behaviour. In contrast, there are alternative ways in which the organization might be conceived. This chapter on Maternal Organization seeks to explore ways in which it is possible to restore the m/other to the text and thereby, give emphasis to the organization as embodied experience.

PERPETRATORS

It is perhaps ironic to think that the term 'perpetrator' refers to actions, usually outrageous actions, performed or committed by the father (Latin: *per-patrare*).

Some years ago I worked at a very uncongenial university. It was strikingly dominated by men, male attitudes and male thinking.

There was bullying, competitive behaviour and, from time to time, displays of physical strength. Of course not all my male colleagues fitted this mould but those who did not had a difficult time. This university was in a part of the country where 'men were men' as the saying goes. Women were supposed to know their place and to show appropriate respect for aggression and dominance. Despite this testosterone-fuelled atmosphere, almost half of the Heads of School in the university were women: twelve men and ten women. There was one female dean and she had overall responsibility for 'quality assurance' in the university. Then, with the appointment of a new vice-chancellor, the inevitable restructuring was put into effect. The schools were to be amalgamated and there would now be only eleven schools: ten men and one woman and even she was to last only a further eighteen months. The female dean was displaced and left the university. My point here is not to bemoan what for many people in the organization were very distressing experiences; it is, rather, to say that even in organizations which include the notion of 'caring' as part of their declared objectives, it is still possible to encounter quite the opposite – neglect, abuse and disrespect – in practice. Consequently, it might be timely to give some thought to what a maternal organization could offer.

Despite years of theorizing, feminist activism and a generally acknowledged commitment to gender equality, in day-to-day discussions about men and women in organizations the same tired themes seem to emerge. Men are logical and rational. Women are emotional. Men are achievement oriented. Women are community oriented. Men are able to compartmentalize issues and problems. Women cannot separate one life world from another. Men desire order. Women bring disorder. Men are sane. Women are mad. Such notions have a long history. In almost all of these definitions, women are defined by deficiency or lack. Men think. Women feel. Forty years of feminist theorizing has had little effect on practice and, some might say, women today are liberated precisely to be more fully objects of male desire; free to create themselves as commodities for male consumption. This chapter is about the possibility of a maternal organization. It attempts to say what this might be and how it would function in practice. However, this sounds rather naive. In part, this is because any such attempt always and inevitably falls within the province, and I used the word deliberately, of male definitions. Any attempt to describe how a maternal organization might be different in character and form from prevailing forms of organization always requires justification and explanation which derive from paternal styles of organising. Men do not realise the extent to which women live in an alien world. What is normal and taken for granted is a world which is defined, constructed and maintained by notions of male order. In relation to this, women can likewise only be defined, constructed and ordered in relation to patriarchy. That from time to time we forget that this is the state of affairs does not detract from the sense of living in a world which is created out of a paternal notion of order. However, this statement must be read with the caveat that men and women, masculine and feminine,

paternal and maternal, here are used as ciphers for styles of behaviour rather than as a description of gender. Therefore, although this handbook is directed at new approaches to organizations, it is impossible to move to this position without giving some attention to the pervasiveness of male reality definitions and the extent to which these limit the possibility of change.

FOUNDING FATHERS

At the university I have mentioned above, I was a member of the Vice-Chancellor's working group on Fairness and Diversity. We met in the university's boardroom: an impressive, high-ceiled room of heavy, dark wood. One of the strange things about this room was the fact that the chairs were too small for the tables. As a result, it always felt as if the room belonged to much larger people, as if one was infantilized by the furniture. Worse was the fact that every wall surface was covered with huge oil paintings of previous vice-chancellors: all men. This room reminded me of the way Hans Castorp in Thomas Mann's *Magic Mountain* (1927) feels dwarfed by the history of the christening bowl with its listing of father, grand-father, great-grand-father, great-great-grandfather and so on. Here, the history of these 'great' men weighed down on anyone who met under their supervision. So too, in a similar way, when in 1995 in Turku in Finland, I was invited to take over as Chair of SCOS, the Standing Conference on Organizational Symbolism, we held our Board Meeting in a similar room at the university. We were surrounded by the Founding Fathers: they too were all men.

These male spectres establish a powerful presence which may or may not be benevolent but which is certainly intimidating. Such images function to regulate and reinforce a set of values, to remind us of the disciplined regime of the father, to show hierarchy and its rewards, and to show who is to be rewarded and for what. The point is that such images hold a comfortable and implicit notion of male power. This is entirely taken for granted.

There is no malice or conscious intent in these constructions yet they operate nevertheless in a way which reminds all of us of our place and our betters. However, by venerating 'the father' in this way, organizations deprive us of a mother and of the values that remind us of a common humanity, of community and of nurture. When this happens, the organization has to create for itself artificial notions of these lost values which then function as hollow representations of what has been lost. I will say more of this later. Suffice it to say at this point that when the organization ignores the image of the mother it denies the pain of labour. By substituting artificial and representational images of the mother, the organization draws what are perceived as the disordered maternal aspects of organization into the sphere of regulation. That is to say, maternal values become the very means of measuring and controlling organizational processes. An obvious example here is the attempt to define 'quality' or to establish codes of 'ethics', or 'care' or 'customer experience'. It is only when these aspects of an organization are deficient that they are raised to an exalted status, defined and measured. There are many examples of the relationship between definition and taxonomy applied to business practices but perhaps the most obvious ones are to do with the measurement of care, quality, attributes of successful leaders and, of course, culture where such interventions are a means of establishing male order.

CONCEIVING ORGANIZATION

Conventional patriarchal representations of the organization reduce *organization* to mere abstract relationships, rational actions and purposive behaviour. Under these constraints, organization becomes synonymous with regulation and control. This is achieved primarily by the imposition of definition and location. Under such circumstances, organization comes to function in a very specific sense to establish a notion of 'good' order, and to establish what can be taken for granted in administrative and managerial practice.

In contrast, the restoration of the m/other to the organization as embodied presence rather than mere textual representation opens up the possibility of new ways of *conceiving* (as against constructing) organization and, at the same time, permits the possibility of new political interpretations of 'organization'. In other words, in ways where women direct, influence and shape the organization on the basis of the their own embodied experiences rather than being either the instruments of male ordering or being reduced to emblems of the lack of maternal influence. An example of this might be the way in which community is developed, in notions of care which equate to compassion rather than compliance with strategic objectives. It matters little whether this is an essentialist view of women's contribution to organizations. The point is that there is a political opportunity to create a maternal organization whose difference is grasped rather than subsumed. It is always in the interests of patriarchy to subsume difference or else to astutely elevate it in order to deprive it of significance.

In conventional terms, the strategic direction of the organization involves the construction of the organization as a purposive entity with a trajectory towards a desired future state. Consequently, many of the organizational metrics with which we are all so familiar are concerned with the achievement of this future state, the measurement of progress towards this state, and the use of corrective measures to modify and improve deficient performance. There is a privileging of the future over the present. Moreover, the aspirational goals of the trajectory mean that, in the present, we are all deficient relative to the targets which we have to achieve. In such movement into the future, the organization in its actions takes precedence over the individual and, therefore, any ambivalence experienced by the individual about the purpose of the action must be concealed both as the price of membership and as a demonstration of commitment. In the past week I have been involved in precisely this type of situation in my current job. It is a minor illustration as illustrations go but it serves to show how this particular dynamic operates in practice. The university is holding a leadership training course for senior members of staff. It has been very successful particularly in terms of building networks across the university. However, for the final session, participants were told that they would have to produce a five-minute video presentation on the future of the university and that the Vice Chancellor would be arriving during the lunch hour to view the presentations. When I asked who was to benefit from the presentations I was told by the consultant that they would give us the opportunity to view ourselves 'as others see us and to show our passion and commitment'. My point in offering this example is to show how easily we are infantilized. On this occasion, it was in order to show our 'passion and commitment' to the VC, the *father* of the organization. There was no malice in the planning. It was thoughtless. It was taken for granted that we would all like to please the father. And, it goes without saying that I expect some of my colleagues wanted to do just that. Moreover, the consultants themselves had met the Vice Chancellor and wanted to demonstrate their achievement with the staff and that they were worth their fee.

Ironically, even where women are successful and take senior roles in organizations, they cannot become the father. As Kristeva points out 'as woman will only have the choice to live her life either *hyper-abstractly* (original italics) …. in order thus to earn divine grace and homologation with the symbolic order; or merely *different* (original italics), other, fallen….' (Kristeva, 1982; Moi, 1986: 173). To become accepted as a member of an organization, and more so to achieve a leadership position, a woman must either conform to the male projection offered her or else acquire a metaphorical 'member' as the price of entry into 'membership'. Women who do conform are assumed into the body and made homologues of men. However, in order to achieve this status of honorary man, they must accept impotence. They are not and do not possess real members. Such quasi-men cannot become fathers of the organization and have already

resigned themselves to the idea that maternal organization is neither possible nor desirable. True homologues renounce friendship with other women, declare themselves to prefer the company of men and make phallic shows to confirm their membership. In the face of this, to be '*different*, other, fallen ….' to be without members and membership becomes an attractive alternative.

DEFICIENCIES

Here, my intention is to privilege the individual and to valorize the present moment by giving emphasis to what I will call, with appropriate qualification and explanation, 'the maternal organization'. Following Kristeva's (1987) concern to establish a discourse of maternity, it seems appropriate to attempt to present these concerns as an emergent paradigm of organization which gives primacy to embodied present-centred experience.

Of course, there are any number of ways in which the organization constructs itself in textual and representational terms: the explicit use of rhetoric in marketing the products and images of organizations is one such construction. It is also present in the construction of statements, strategies and structures, in its use of representation for regulation. The fundamental characteristic of the organization as a purposive entity is its *directedness* and, clearly, there is a relationship between the direction (as orientation) and direction (as command) of the organization and the rhetorical trajectory. De Certeau (1986) has said that a particular characteristic of rhetoric is that its trajectory is completed by *the other*. That is to say that rhetoric requires something from the audience to which it is directed. It is completed by a response. In a specific sense, the organization as a rhetorical entity *wants something* of the employee, of the customer, the competitor, the supplier and the general public. Ironically, the organization as an abstract entity transfers its own lack to its members who are thereby rendering deficient in relation to the abstract desires of the organization. Of course, the organization requires that its prospective representations – images and texts – are received as convincing by its various audiences. Not surprisingly then, recent years have seen the elaboration of the rhetoric of organizations directed at employees in terms of the pursuit of greater commitment, improved performance, invocations to quality and the construction of ornate narratives of organizational performances. I think of these elaborate representations as enormous erections which serve to regulate the organization by their staying power. However, in producing these elaborate constructions/erections, the organization loses contact with the physical bodies of which it is made up. Without a body, the organization loses any sense of the pain of labour which becomes exiled from the site of production.

In contrast, the maternal organization is concerned with the very ambivalence which is concealed and regulated by the organization as text and phallocentric quest. The notion of the maternal organization thus subverts the dominant social discourse to challenge order, rationality and patriarchal regulation. What this contributes to organizational theory is the capacity to make transparent the effects of the production of meaning, to render explicit the paternalistic quest of the organization and to make problematic the notion of trajectory, strategy and purpose. I would like to start to indicate the possibility of a maternal paradigm by saying something about the matrix.

MATRIX

From Hollywood films, to complex algebra, to organizational structures, the term *matrix* has become familiar to us as a network, a rectilinear construction of cells, as an allocation matrix in operational research, as intersecting lines of responsibility, even as the current craze Sudoku (the word *Sudoku* means 'single number in an allotted place' in Japanese) and so forth. However, it is pertinent to consider the origin of the term. The Latin word *matrix* was formerly used to apply to a female breeding animal. It was only in late Latin that it came to be the term used for the human uterus. Of course, we have largely lost contact with this meaning of the matrix as the various examples used above demonstrate. Hence, in terms of the thrust of phallogocentric discourse, the matrix has been appropriated and transformed into a representational structure for allocation and definition. The capture of the matrix and its conversion into a space of regulation is easily demonstrated by recourse to any management *text*-book. The ubiquitous 2×2 matrix demonstrates how ideas and concepts can be held in place by their location with the cells of the matrix. Such is the power of definition, and it is definition, or at least the power to define, which regulates organizations by the rules which definition imposes. In physical terms, the mastery of the matrix is achieved by the removal of the ovaries which renders the uterus impotent. Likewise, in an organizational sense, the removal of embodied experience is achieved by control of reproduction. Maternal reproduction is then replaced by the reproduction of text and the fertility of the site is surrendered to the fertility of words and regulation. Therefore, the matrix becomes an instrument of management which locates and classifies relationships on the basis of power. In the substitution of words for the natural products of the matrix, the space is regulated, and the reproduction of homologues guaranteed. The paternal matrix can give birth only to sons.

So, the organization constructs itself in diagrams and charts, texts, and metrics which seek to uphold the representation of the feminine, the anima, the body, but which inevitably achieve a cancellation. It is little wonder, therefore, that notions of quality and care, the ubiquitous valorization of staff, have more in them of melancholy abstractions than of physicality. Embodied reproduction is then replaced by the reproduction of concepts and the fertility of the site is given up to the fertility of concepts and theoria. The physical matrix reproduces from itself and matter is made incarnate. The patriarchal matrix, however, deals on the level of the abstract alone. Here, perfection comes from striving. In contrast to the maternal process, the 'patriarchal consciousness' has a preference for rationality and the direction of the will, the 'patriarchal order of society' (Dourley, 1990: 50) and with this comes a commitment to 'sterile perfection in the divine as a hallmark of patriarchal consciousness' (Dourley, 1990: 51) 'which could easily have been avoided by paying attention to the feminine idea of completeness' (Dourley, 1990: 50). Consequently, the matrix gives birth into a world of obsessive reproduction and insatiable desire. Paternal reproduction arises from the sense of lack that only the acknowledgement of the unconscious, of the maternal matrix could satisfy and give a sense of completion. Hence, the patriarchal matrix is concerned with logic and order and rationality, with location and hierarchy, with allocation and definition. The maternal matrix *knows* in embodied experience and this knowledge is sufficient to itself when it finds expression in embodied action.

EFFEMINATE

It is interesting to consider that whereas to *e-masculate* means to castrate, to enfeeble, to weaken by excision, to make powerless and useless, there is no equivalent female term. To render *effeminate*, does not mean to take away a woman's powers. There is no equivalent term. To be effeminate is a term which when applied to men means that they are considered to be unmanly, to lack vigour or to display *unbecoming* female characteristics. Longman's Dictionary lists over twenty-five synonyms for effeminate men all of which are derogatory. However, there is no term which describes the taking away of a woman's power. I am emphatic here because it is striking to realize what this means. Certainly, there are some derogatory or explanatory terms for homosexual women but there is no specific term to describe the *removal* of female power. *To neuter* comes close. This means to remove the ovaries, to make sexless. Kristeva has identified this absence as a primal repression of the mother (Kristeva, 1982: 12).

She argues that it is either possible to *submit* and become the same, in other words to achieve and demonstrate *mastery* of the text, in which case, one becomes a 'man', to become part of the *project* – or, on the other hand, to be other, different and rejected. Organization, dominated as it is by the paternal paradigm, requires that members conform or be cast out. A maternal paradigm does not imply an absence of order; indeed, it does not imply an absence of organization. The maternal paradigm, in contrast to its patriarchal counterpart, seeks to restore the body to the text. Kristeva (1987) has talked about the catastrophic fold of being between the body and the law, between by parity of reasoning, the maternal and the paternal form of organization. This is the site of possibility. The place of the mother.

METROPOLIS

What then might be possible in the place of the Mother? I have been intrigued in recent years and in the time of the TV programme *Sex in the City* to read in glossy magazines of the new sexuality and the behaviour. Advocates of this have been called 'metro-sexuals'. Perhaps it doesn't matter but it does seem strange to speak in terms of new sexual values in terms of the sexuality of the *mother*, for this is precisely what metro-sexual means. In the late nineties, I presented a paper, *The Mystery of the Assumption: Mothers and Measures*, (Höpfl, 2001) in which I tried to examine the two terms which derive from the Greek word meter, that is, *metros*, meaning Mother and *metron*, meaning Measure. So, for example, one might compare, metronome, metronomos as measure/law with metropolis, mother/city. The metropolis is the mother city, the place of the mother, the womb, the locus amoenus. It is the place of polity of process and order. *Polis* is normally rendered city or city state yet, as Heidegger (1953) points out, the term polis means more than this, it is 'the place, the there, wherein and as which the historical being-there *is*' (Heidegger, 1953: 152). It is a coincident word that brings together the body and the law, mother and order: metropolis. The trouble is that organizations have become more metron than metros, more measure than mother and consequently they have not valued the people who work in them. By privileging metrics, maternal values such as care and nurture have been set aside in favour of volume and frequency both of which are primarily patriarchal measures. This can be seen in the obsessive commitment to quantification and taxonomic structures for collecting data on virtually everything. In universities these days the staff are more assessed than the students. Metrics function to regulate behaviour in the present and to guide actions towards specific targets in the future. Yet, it is worse than this. The *representations* of metros produce counterfeit structures, simulated qualities which derive from absence and which have little in common with embodied experience. This inevitably leads to disaffection and a melancholic quality which pervades the task of organizing.

CONCEPTION

By dealing with the *conception* of the organization as maternal, the notion of maternal organization seeks to break the body of the text in order to allow reflections on the mother/motherhood/maternal imagery to enter the text. Thus, the embodied subject speaks of division, separation, rupture, tearing and blood whereas the text of the organization speaks of regulation and representation, of rational argument and rhetorical trajectory. By breaking the text, the implications of 'the sterile perfectionism' of the patriarchal consciousness (Dourley, 1990: 51) is made transparent. So, maternal organization stands against the way in which conventional accounts of management are presented, poses alternative ways of understanding organization and offers insights into the organization as embodied experience.

The very fact that the term is unsettling is evidence enough of its significance. To speak of maternal organization is to invite images of large maternity smocks, pushchairs and all

the paraphernalia of maternity with the fear that the organization might become one large branch of *Mothercare*. At the root of this fear is the problem which impurity poses for the organization and its fear of contamination: as if women might vomit, bleed, urinate or leak the anamnesis of the body into the text. Regulation of the text keeps women within the definitions which regulate textual reproduction and restrict contact with the body.

In this context, it is not surprising that organizations function at variance to the bodies who work in and for them. Consequently, people in organizations are always struggling with issues that arise from the substitution of textual matrices for physical ones. They are rendered abstract by loss of contact with their physicality as organizations reduce them to categories and metrics. But, from the point of view of the feminine, the position is more serious. In the relentless pursuit of future states, organizations as purposive entities seek to construct for themselves the empty emblems of the object of the quest. In part, this is because the purposiveness is without end and, therefore, the notion of any real completion is antithetical to the idea of trajectory. Strategy gives birth to more strategy, rhetoric to more rhetoric, text to more text and so on. The sublime is never attained. The individual in the organization is always constituted in unworthiness, always deficient. But organizations are constructed in such as way as to regard this as the problem of perfectability. This means that for the obsessive commitment to the trajectory to continue, the organization must construct an emblem of what is lost, for example: care, quality, customer service, ethics. These become constructed entities which can be subjected to measurement. This melancholic gesture restores the illusion of completion but, of course, cannot satisfy and is not intended to satisfy.

ALLOCATED AND SAFE

This is rather similar to the idea put forward by Baudrillard in his critique of rationality in which he argues that the reduction of male and female to categories has produced an artificial distinction which objectifies the feminine. By this line of argument, the feminine is now constructed as a category of the masculine and, by implication, the power of the feminine to manifest itself in ambivalence is lost. Baudrillard sees femin-*ism*, per se, as ensnared within the construction of a phallic order (Baudrillard, 1990). In organizational terms, these constructions of the feminine are intended to console like the photograph of an absent loved one whom, secretly, one hopes will never return. The vicarious and representational has more seductive power than the physical and disordered other. These emblems function as an anamnesis to register the loss as representation. For this reason alone, the emblem of loss is melancholic and pervades the organization with melancholy. It cannot offer consolation because ironically it can only recall that there is a loss. So, the emblem of the lost object provides a false reassurance that completion can also arise from a construction. Let me say this more precisely. It cannot reassure because it arises from a mere *erection*. This is only a shadow of the feminine and it is a travesty. It is the feminine constructed in the image of masculine desire to meet the needs of sterile perfectionism and rationality. It is a feminine which in this form is tidy, logical, entirely representation and without power, ambivalence and sexuality. Indeed, it is merely the speculum of the feminine (Irigaray, 1985).

This is apparent in the ways in which organizations seek to re-create the maternal matrix in notions of care and satisfaction: customer care, client satisfaction and emotional intelligence. Harrison's work on 'a strategy for releasing love in the workplace' is a case in point. In a well-intentioned exhortation to be more caring, Harrison argues that service 'will only work if the process *is managed from the heart* (italics added), not just because it is good business, but because it feels right' (Harrison, 1987: 18). It is hard to disagree with the concern for staff which Harrison espouses but behind it is a familiar trajectory.

Consequently, his notion of service seems inevitably to be *in the service of* better business. We can all improve and be improved if we care more, it seems. Sadly, this is a poor substitute. It is emblematic rather than restorative. It does not pose a threat to patriarchal order nor is it dangerous or creative. It keeps the 'proper' order of the polis: patriarchy.

The pain of labour is acknowledged via the restoration of the body to the text of organization. It is threatening because it implicitly rejects the rhetorical trajectory of the patriarchal discourse of organization. This too is a problem but it goes beyond the scope of this discussion to consider it here (Höpfl, 2000a). However, what can be said is that a challenge to the text comes from postmodern characterization. This has political consequence, because it produces 'a marginalization of the reader from a centralized or totalized narrative of selfhood' which renders 'the reading subject-in-process as the figure of the dissident' (Docherty, 1996: 67). This decentring functions in the same way in relation to the exhortationary narratives of organizing. To support this view, Docherty refers to Kristeva's identification of the experimental writer and, as Docherty says, '*crucially*, women' [original italics] as dissident writers. So, the argument runs, what these two 'share is the impetus towards marginalization and indefinition; they are in a condition of "exile" from a centred identity of meaning and its claims to a totalized Law or Truth'. Maternal organizaton, therefore, is dissident since it rejects the trajectory of the patriarchal text. This is one of the reasons why patriarchal order fears maternal organization which it sees as dissident, disorderly and disjunctive. The maternal organization is not seduced by its own constructions, does not put illusions of future satisfactions above the painful experiences of the present; it is not so committed to the notion of perfectibility; is fertile rather than sterile; sensual rather than rational. The notion of maternal organization implicitly threatens the process of de-finition, that is to say, *finalization*, and so intrinsically subverts power relations in the organization. This is the greatest threat. It is what Docherty calls 'indefinition' (Docherty, 1996: 67). Lacoue-Labarthe (1989: 129) indicates what Plato has identified as the major threats to representation as being women and madness and, indeed, women and madness as themes spiral together as surely as hystera (Gk. *womb*) and the psycho*logical* condition of hysteria (as a disturbance of the nervous system thought to be brought about by uterine dysfunction) find a common origin in the function of reproduction. The fear is that the Law will be undermined by the intrusion of the Body.

RESTORING THE MATERNAL

What can the notion of maternal organization contribute to organizational theory? Clearly, from the discussion above, it can be seen that, in part, the challenge to conventional views of the organization are largely to do with boundaries and demarcation. Maternal organization raises concerns about exile and homelessness – both psychological and physical. It is sensual and acknowledges emotion. Here is not the emotion of EQ and the metrics of standards of emotional performance. Metros not metron. Maternal organization values the process towards ends and not just the ends in themselves. Therefore, there is not an exclusive commitment to the future at the expense of the present. The way of being in the present determines the type of futures we will create. Whereas some types of feminism demanded equality with men, the maternal organization presents a different political agenda. It is rooted in the politics of alterity (otherness). It promotes an ethics of alterity. After all, 'What we designate as "feminine", far from being a primeval essence, (is the) "other" without a name' (Kristeva, 1982: 58). Consequently, the notion of maternal organization unhinges a number of continuities. It exiles the *reader* from the security of the continuity of the organizational text. It establishes a metropolitan order, a place of the mother: a

place from which to consider 'the possibility of politics', alterity and ethics. It requires that we take responsibility for our actions. It slows down the frenetic quest for sterile perfection which is 'the hallmark of the patriarchal consciousness' (Dourley, 1990: 51). It restores the body and creates community.

Kristeva offers the best way into the discourse of maternity. Maternity, motherhood and the maternal body figure significantly in her psycho-analytical writing. *Tales of Love* (1987) is perhaps a good place to start. I have pondered the difficulty of writing about maternity and I have tried to write about it in a number of articles, some of which are listed in the references to this chapter. However, it is an extremely difficult topic to deal with. Not only is the imagery of maternity alien to the character of organizations but mothers themselves. Barbara Poggio has written a fascinating piece exploring this theme (Poggio, 2003). Tietze, in her *Metaphors of the Mother*, argues that 'the very essence of being a mother is problematic in modern organizations' (Tietze, 2003: 65). Comparatively, Guillet de Monthoux (2003), has looked at the relationship between managing and the task of the curator in order to re-introduce a notion of *care* into management practice. It seems that there is a desire to restore the body to the text of the organization. In part, this might help to explain why organizations continue to produce only sons. Part of the backlash against feminism in recent years has argued that feminism deprived men of the opportunity for achievement motivated behaviour and some, notably Schwartz (1997b) has looked at the implications for regressive behaviour by both men and women which has resulted from this. This all makes interesting reading but, without resorting to New Age notions of the Gaia principle, if organizations lose sight of the present in the relentless pursuit of the future, the quality of that future – far from being perfection – will be extremely dubious. Endless consumption, endless and insatiable desires prevail. The implications are as devastating as they are obvious. Patriarchal organizations have failed to take care of their staff, resources, ethical principles; have failed to care about exploitation, failed to take responsibility. It is time to see if maternal organization might be able to do better.

REFERENCES

Baudrillard, J. (1990) *Seduction*. London: Macmillan.

de Certeau, M. (1986) *Heterologies, Discourse on the Other*. Manchester: Manchester University Press.

Docherty, T. (1987) *On Modern Authority*. Brighton: The Harvester Press.

Docherty, T. (1996) *Alterities: Criticism, History, Representation*. Oxford: Clarendon Press.

Dourley, J.P. (1990) *The Goddess, Mother of the Trinity*. Lewiston: The Edwin Mellen Press.

Guillet de Monthoux, P. (2003) 'Triptychs of curing: Conversations with mother of the in-betweens', in H.J. Höpfl and M. Kostera (2003) *Interpreting the Maternal Organization*. London: Routledge.

Harrison, R. (1987) *Organization Culture and Quality of Service: a Strategy for Releasing Love in the Workplace*. [1953] London: Association for Management Education and Development (AMED).

Heidegger, M. (1976) *An Introduction to Metaphysics*. New Haven, CT: Yale University Press.

Höpfl, H.J. (2000) 'On being moved', *Studies in Cultures, Organizations and Societies*, 6(1): 15–25.

Höpfl, H.J. (2000a) 'The suffering mother and the miserable son, organising women and organising women's writing, *Gender Work and Organization*, 7(2): 98–106.

Höpfl, H.J. (2001) 'The mystery of the assumption: of mothers and measures, in N. Lee, and R. Monro, *The Consumption of Mass*. Sociological Review Monograph Series. Oxford: Blackwell.

Höpfl, H.J. and Kostera, M. (2003) *Interpreting the Maternal Organization*. London: Routledge.

Irigaray, L. (1985) *Speculum of the Other Woman*, (trans. G. Gill). Ithaca, NJ: Cornell University Press.

Kristeva, J. (1982) *Powers of Horror* (trans. L. Roudiez). New York: Columbia University Press.

Kristeva, J. (1987) *Tales of Love* (trans. L. Roudiez). New York: Columbia University Press.

Lacoue-Labarthe (1989) *Typography*. Stanford: Stanford University Press.

Mann, Thomas (1927) *The Magic Mountain*. London: Secker.

Poggio, B. (2003) *'Who's afraid of mothers?'* in H.J. Höpfl and M. Kostera (2003) *Interpreting the Maternal Organization*. London: Routledge.

Schwartz, Howard S. (1997) *The Power of the Virgin: Psychodynamics of Sexual Politics and the Issue of Women in Combat* (1997a) Part One: *Dimensions fo Sexual Scandal*, (1997b) Part Two: *The Psychodynamics and Power of Feminism*. A paper presented at the SCOC Colloquium in Organizational Psychodynamics, University of Missouri-Columbia, September 1997 at http://www.sba.oakland.edu/faculty/schwartz/POVdr2p1.htm

Tietze, S. (2003) *'Metaphors of the mother'*, in H.J. Höpfl and M. Kostera (2003) *Interpreting the Maternal Organization*. London: Routledge.

Feminist Theorizing: Reforming? Performing? Transforming? the Organizational Subject?

Marta B. Calás and Linda Smircich

Feminist theoretical perspectives have influenced scholarly work in organization studies for more than two decades. Although it is possible to claim that the influence is felt more clearly in the European context than in the US, we are not here to argue about 'more or less'. Rather, our interest is to ask, 'So what'? What difference (if any) have these writings made (other than, perhaps, to proliferate more writings)? Regrettably, we assert that evidence of much difference is hard to find, for little has changed in 'the subject' of our disciplines. Yet we have long thought, and continue to think, that feminist theorizing can contribute significantly to changing the subject of organization studies, and we are not ready to give up now... or at least, not yet.

First, feminist theorizing has indeed changed 'the subject' during this period. While the influence of poststructuralism continues in conversation with contemporary issues in philosophy and social theory, many earlier concerns with language and signification have morphed into questions of the ontological status of the body and the subject. Arguments about the materialization and the materiality of 'the body' figure prominently, and their implications for feminist agency and politics are examined with particular consideration to the context of globalization (e.g. Acker, 2004; Braidotti, 2002; Mohanty, 2003; Moya, 1997; Salih and Butler, 2004).

Second, we suggest these changing concerns in contemporary feminist theorizing also have important implications for the status of 'the subject' in organizational knowledge and action. As scholars in the context of accelerated global change, we *must continually interrogate*: Who/what are 'the subjects' of our knowledge? Who/what do we 'serve'? For whom/for what are we 'good'? The moves in feminist theorizing briefly sketched below help us to 'flesh out' these questions.

Reforming the body (of knowledge). At least since radical feminism articulated its political force- i.e. the personal *is* political (Hanisch, 1970), the body has been central to feminist theorizing, both in its materiality and its symbolism (e.g. Bordo, 1993). From this perspective we argue that organizational scholarship must continue to call into question the ongoing gendering of organizational theories and practices. Consider, whose bodies are still the bodies of our 'knowledge'? Who does 'knowledge' for whom? Who are those visible subjects? And who is being made invisible? For all the Foucaldian, Derridian, Deleuzian and so on and so forth that have been called into critical conversations, there is little evidence that the patriarchs have left space for any 'other' unless the conversation is explictly *about 'the other'*. But where is 'the other' otherwise? Has the representative subject of organization studies changed that much in our, let's say, 'Panoptic' representations? Has the subject changed that much despite all the ink spilled in the name of 'discourse' or 'deconstruction'? Has it changed at all even when hidden behind those exotic 'bodies without organs' or 'becoming-woman'?

Performing the (sexed) body. Contemporary feminist scholarship has gone beyond epistemological arguments regarding *the nature of embodied knowing* to further address

Continued

the body as a category of analysis, and *the body in relationship to the material* or 'corporeal feminism' (Bray and Colebrook, 1998; Fonow and Cook, 2005). The well-known work of Judith Butler and her notion of performativity exemplifies this. Performativity *is not* a social constructionist or ethnomethodological account of what gender is or may be. Butler's ultimate concern is not how gender is 'done' but examining the conditions of possibility for, and the consequences of such 'doings' within norms that delimit acceptable and unacceptable expressions of gender, including desire and sexuality, ordering social and political norms in most societies (e.g. Butler, 1999, 2004).

From this perspective, we must continue to ask: after all is said and done, how is the norm(ed) body performed in organization theories and practices, and with what consequences? Should we not immediately queer the (hetero)normativity of organizational 'actions' and 'contexts' (including the actions and contexts of our writings) regardless of the bodies that perform them?

Transforming (the Western) body. More importantly, perhaps, transnational feminist analyses further argue that the production of knowledge at the (Western) centre is a form of self-fashioning, widely implicated in the constitution and legitimation of imperialism and neocolonialism (e.g. Kaplan et al., 1999; Narayan, 1997). Such works articulate the existence of complex subjectivities and heterogeneous subject positions and relations, produced at the intersections of gender, race, class, ethnicity, sexualities and so on, in the context of specific First-World/Third-World historical *and* contemporary relationships.

These complex subjectivities contribute to rethinking solidarity within and across borders in very material encounters. Their presence refocuses critiques of racism, ethnocentrism, sexism and heteronormativity by committing analyses to subverting simultaneous oppressions, where gender, ethinicity, race, sexuality and class are multiply entangled (e.g. Collins, 1991; Mendoza, 2002). While not always successful, a good amount of this scholarship is intended to cross over the boundaries of the academy and to contribute to actual political action 'in the world'.

What would this mean concretely for organization studies? Areas of analysis would be refocused on the formation of certain actual subjects who are probably the 'truest' contemporary subjects of organization studies. That is, 'transnationalizing' the subject of organization studies is sorely needed, and for that we must articulate areas of analyses where gender, capitalism, and globalization appear to be uniquely intertwined. Acker (2004) has already done so, but much more is needed. How are our theories and our practices complicit in producing the elite masculinities of global capitalism? What gendered, raced, sexed, classed relational practices articulate the restructuring of the world economy? How are we all implicated in the production and reproduction of abject poverty and 'its other' (obscene wealth)? Probably not until our own (academic) bodies hit the ground and bite the dust would we all be able to come down to earth, say what needs to be said ... and do what needs to be done ... perhaps in this volume???

REFERENCES

Acker, J. (2004) 'Gender, capitalism and globalization'. *Critical Sociology*, 30 (1): 17–41.

Bordo, S. (1993) *Unbearable Weight: Feminism, Western Culture and the Body*. Berkeley, CA: University of California Press.

Braidotti, R. (2002) *Metamorphoses: Towards a Materialist Theory of Becoming*. Cambridge: Polity Press.

Bray, A. and Colebrook C. (1998) 'The haunted flesh: corporeal feminism and the politics of (dis)embodiment', *Signs*, 24 (11): 35–67.

Butler, J. (1999) 'Preface from *Gender Trouble* anniversary edition. Reproduced in S. Salih (ed.), with J. Butler (2004) *The Judith Butler Reader*. Malden: Blackwell Publishing. pp. 94–103.

Butler, J. (2004) *Undoing Gender*. New York: Routledge.

Collins, P.H. (1991) *Black Feminist Thought: Knowledge, Consciousness and the Politics of Empowerment*. New York: Routledge.

Fonow, M.M. and Cook, J.A. (2005) 'Feminist methodology: new applications in the academy and public policy', *Signs*, 30 (4): 2211–2236.

Hanisch, C. (1970) 'The personal is political', in, S. Firestone and A. Koedt, (eds), *Notes from the Second Year: Women's Liberation*. N.Y. (out of print). See also http://scholar.alexanderstreet.com/download/attachments/2259/Personal+Is+Pol.pdf?version=1

Kaplan, C., Alarcón, N. and Moallem, M. (eds) (1999) *Between Woman and Nation: Nationalisms, Transnational Feminisms and the State*. Durham: Duke University Press.

Mendoza, B. (2002) 'Transnational feminisms in question', *Feminist Theory*, 3 (3): 295–314.

Mohanty, C.T. (2003) *Feminism Without Borders: Decolonizing Theory, Practicing Solidarity*. Durham: Duke University Press.

Moya, P.M.L. (1997) 'Postmodernism, "realism" and the politics of identity: Cherríe Moraga and Chicana feminism', in J. Alexander and C.T. Mohanty (eds), *Feminist Genealogies, Colonial Legacies, Democratic Futures*. New York: Routledge. pp. 125–150.

Narayan, U. (1997) *Dislocating Cultures: Identities, Traditions, and Third-World Feminism*. New York: Routledge.

Salih, S. and Butler, J. (eds) (2004) *The Judith Butler Reader*. Oxford: Blackwell.

Why Difference Matters in Organizations

Martin N. Davidson

One of my earliest experiences in academia was presenting my early research on the effect of race on conflict styles. I was quite excited about the work; the results were provocative and I felt poised to really make an impact with my presentation. I presented my paper and it was fairly well received, stimulating a flurry of inquiries. And then the discussant for our session began his comments and I remember him pointing out that while my study was quite interesting, the approach I was taking in focusing on race, specifically African Americans and White Americans, was ultimately wrong-headed; that the important organizational phenomena we need to understand would not be uncovered in such a specialized area of study. It was the pursuit of more universal phenomena that should be occupying the time and energy of organizational scholars. I remember being frustrated and discouraged. Clearly, this white American male academic did not understand what I, as a young African American male scholar, was embarking upon. He did not understand the insight I was bringing to the table because my experience didn't fit his paradigm. Yes, I reminded myself, it was racism once again.

Fifteen years later, I've come to realize that this guy was right, albeit for the wrong reasons.

At that stage of my career, I was lost in the trees. I knew there was a forest somewhere, but I was having trouble spotting it. And I didn't even realize I was having any trouble. Research on race in organizations matters deeply. In U.S. organizations, it gives us insight into contradictions within our society that have challenged us for centuries. We espouse a value of fairness and equality for all, no matter how we are different. Yet we live organizational lives that desperately try to ignore any differences whatsoever, as though we could truly be fair to another without understanding what it means to that person to be fair. Race research in organizations also paves the way for research on other kinds of differences within U.S. organizations, such as ethnic, gender, sexual orientation, and national culture differences. While all of this is good, I suspect my discussant would not be persuaded that this was the important 'mainstream' work that management scholars should really focus on, the work that will really further our understanding of organizations.

Here is what he was missing, what I missed until the later stages of my career. Research on race, on gender, on cultural difference doesn't just surface knowledge about people who are marginal; it shines a lot on the very nature of the organizations in which those people reside with their white straight American male counterparts. When I am teaching and consulting with firms trying to leverage difference in their organizations, I share with them the metaphor of the canary in the coalmine. When they are suffering, marginal people in organizations are often simply exhibiting symptoms of a sickness in the organization to which everyone in the organization is susceptible. More mainstream organization members don't show the symptoms as quickly as marginalized people; they can breathe a bit longer because their privilege increases their lung capacity. But they ultimately will and do succumb.

Research on race, gender and other differences is not 'boutique' research. Rather it has profound implications for understanding previously invisible processes in organizations, and for understanding how those processes affect both marginalized and mainstream organization members. These insights have universal application. The future challenge of research on diversity is to pursue an understanding of those who don't fit. This is a mercurial group, shifting in identity depending upon organization, society, nation, time frame. A group that is marginal today may be mainstream in twenty years and another group will hold the label of marginal. We should never abandon our pursuit of understanding the experience of these people in organizations because that is the source of learning about the organization.

Strategy-as-Practice

Paula Jarzabkowski

There is a curious absence of actors and their actions in most academic articles on strategy. While *people* do strategy, strategy theory is populated by multivariate analyses of firm or industry-level effects upon firm performance. Those studies that do incorporate actors focus primarily on top managers, as if only one elite group could act strategically. Even these actors typically are reduced to a set of demographics such as age, tenure and functional background, which can be examined for statistical regularities in relation to some aspect of firm performance. There appears to be little room in mainstream strategy research for living beings whose emotions, motivations and actions shape strategy. This marginalization of the actor is due to the dominant micro-economic foundations of mainstream strategy research. Within the normal science mode of such research, rational actors search for and select optimal solutions in order to maximize profit and asset utility (Hollis and Nell, 1975). Such rational assumptions make the behaviour of strategic actors an uninteresting or unimportant research question. However, increasingly strategy research is being influenced by wider concerns to humanize

management and organization research by bringing the actor back in (Pettigrew et al., 2002; Weick, 1979). The developing field of strategy-as-practice research has taken this concern seriously, bringing actors and their actions and interactions to the centre stage of strategy research. This chapter explains the antecedents of the practice 'turn' in strategy, the core questions and issues for the emerging field of strategy-as-practice, and its implications for strategy research, teaching and practice.

THE PRACTICE TURN IN STRATEGY RESEARCH

The recent practice turn in social theory focuses upon the way that the everyday practices of actors carry, socially construct and transform the social institutions within which those actors live (Ortner, 1984; Reckwitz, 2002; Schatzki et al., 2001). These social theories of practice underpin concerns to humanize management and organization studies (Whittington, 2002). For example, accounting has witnessed a shift from largely normative theories of accounting as a set of rational rules, tools and principles to examining accounting as a social and institutional practice (Hopwood and Miller, 1994), while studies of technology have moved from viewing technology as an organizational structure to technology as a social practice (Orlikowski, 1992, 2000; Orr, 1996; Suchman, 1987). In such practice-based theorizing, accounting and technology are not structural invariants that prescribe action but social practices that may be appropriated by actors to interpret their situations and enact their own interests. The research focus thus shifts from the rule-like properties of accounting and technology to the ways that they are constructed, used and transformed in the daily practice of actors.

The practice turn has also entered the strategy field with the proposition that strategy is not just something that a firm has, a position, but something that multiple actors inside and outside the firm *do*. Strategy-as-practice as a research topic is concerned with the doing of strategy; who does it, what they do, what they use and what implications this has for shaping strategy (e.g. Hendry, 2000; Jarzabkowski, 2004, 2005; Johnson et al., 2003; Whittington, 1996, 2003, 2006). This practice turn in strategy has grown quickly,[1] with its popularity due to a growing dissatisfaction with conventional strategy research, even where this is not explicitly acknowledged. For example, Mir and Watson (2000) note that, despite the dominance of micro-economics approaches, there is a growing social constructionist approach to strategy research that draws on interpretivist theories, such as sense-making (e.g. Gioia and Chittipedi, 1991), and behavioural theories, such as politics (e.g. Pettigrew, 1985) in order to explain phenomena such as strategic change. At the same time, a growing frustration with the normal science straitjacket in strategy research and its narrow norma-tive implications for practice (Bettis, 1991; Ghoshal and Moran, 1996) has led to calls for new approaches that can better capture the complexity of making strategy (Prahalad and Hamel, 1994). Strategy-as-practice captures

the essence of many of these frustrations and concerns with mainstream strategy research, providing a research framework within which to develop more accurate descriptions and richer theoretical understandings of doing strategy.

WHAT IS STRATEGY AS PRACTICE?

An enduring problem for any field of strategy research is defining what strategy is. From a practice perspective (Reckwitz, 2002; Suchman, 1987), strategy is a situated, socially accomplished flow of activity over time. While this definition highlights the importance of situation, being those circum-stances in which activity is shaped, and its social nature, meaning that it involves the actions and interactions of actors, its breadth poses problems for empirical study, as all activity may be considered situated and socially accomplished. Two issues are, therefore, important in studying strategy-as-practice; defining what activity is considered strategic and identifying how situatedness is implicated in its construction. Let us consider each of these in turn.

First, given the all-encompassing nature of practice, how is it possible to isolate some activity as 'strategic'? Much research isolates strategic phenomena by drawing on the dichotomous definitions that characterize strategy research and, indeed, the very language of strategy, such as process versus content, formulation versus implementation and intended versus emergent (Chia, 2004; Clegg et al., 2004; Jarzabkowski, 2005; Johnson et al., 2003). However, strategy as a flow of activity incorporates content and process, intent and emergence, thinking and acting and so on, as reciprocal, intertwined and frequently indistinguishable parts of a whole when they are observed at close range. For example, the content of a firm's strategy is shaped by its process, which feeds back into the content in ongoing mutual construc-tion. Practice research, therefore, does not simply aim to understand how strategy is 'formulated', such as specific decisions that are taken, or the strategy content of the firm in terms of its articulated strategic position. Rather, it aims to understand the practice of constituting some activity as strategic within a specific context. Here, two pragmatic definitions of what activity is strategic are helpful:

- Activity is strategic if it has outcomes that are consequential for the organization and its survival (Johnson et al., 2003); and
- Such activity involves *'the competitive appropriation of value by the organization or its stakeholders'* (Hendry, 2000: 969), which might take the form of revenue or profit, particularly in the private sector, or might constitute some form of social value in the public and not-for-profit sector.

Activity that is associated with defining what constitutes value for a particular organization and its stakeholders, and which enables that organization to appropriate value in ways that are consequential for its survival is thus strategic activity. In focusing upon the micro details of human action involved in constructing activity, research must not lose sight of the strategic nature of that activity if it is to be *strategy*-as-practice research, not simply research into organizational practice. This does not, however, imply that strategy-as-practice research must be concerned with 'the firm' as the level of analysis or 'firm performance' as the outcome of research, as it typical in mainstream strategy research. Rather that, whatever situated level of activity we choose to study, we as researchers are mindful of the consequential nature of that activity for the strategies that organizations pursue.

'Situated' is a key term that populates the practice literature with little or no definition, as if its essential meaning is understood. However, situatedness is a deeply embedded concept comprising multiple layers of meaning, many of which have been sacrificed to the superficial context of interpersonal interactions (Contu and Willmott, 2003). Situated refers to the way that activity both shapes and is shaped by the complex social context within which it occurs. Situation is interpretive and historical, imbuing some ways of acting with meaning whilst discrediting others. As Oakes et al.'s (1998) study of Canadian museums shows, during changes in government funding policy, museums came to adopt an economic rationale for their existence, in the process discrediting some of their initial purposes as cultural custodians and altering the way that museum employees interpreted the historical artifacts that they preserved. For example, Native-American hunting practices began to be explained as examples of entrepreneurial and organizational skills rather than cultural or historical practices (ibid.: 281). Thus, the way that the museum defined value-appropriating activity shifted with changes in policy. The explanation in this study is deeply situated, involving shifts in state policy, reconstruction of the nature and purpose of public organizations, and changes in the daily activity conducted within museums. Strategy-as-practice studies can never be devoid of this complex situatedness since any explanation of strategic activity is meaningful according to the multi-layered social dynamics in which it occurs.

The primary situational focus of a study has implications for the levels of analysis applicable to strategy-as-practice research and the outcomes that may be derived. Mainstream strategy research is concerned with either the firm or the industry as the level of analysis and – a legacy of the micro-economics foundation – with firm performance as the outcome. However, strategy-as-practice research is concerned with strategy as a situated and socially accomplished activity. It therefore wishes to understand how particular situations are associated with particular ways of accomplishing activity and whether and why these are perceived to appropriate value for the organization.

Existing empirical research in the strategy-as-practice field illustrates the implications of primary situational focus for defining levels of analysis, units of analysis, and outcomes in different ways. For example, Vaara et al. (2004) has examined those micro, increasingly taken-for-granted discourses through which airlines and their stakeholders define alliances as a way of appropriating value within the airline industry. The primary level of analysis is institutional while the unit of analysis is discursive practices. The research outcome explains how and why the consequential activity of alliances became the dominant *modus operandi* within the airline industry. In my work (Jarzabkowski, 2005), I have taken a sub-firm level of analysis, examining how streams of activity, such as research, teaching and commercial income, are constructed as strategic within universities. My level of analysis is the specific stream of activity, such as research or teaching, while the unit of analysis is the combination of interactive and administrative practices through which such activities are constructed in different universities. The outcome of the research is an explanation of how streams of strategic activity gain (or do not gain) organizational legitimacy over time. Samra-Fredericks (2003) examines the talk-in-interaction between strategists and how it changes the course of a single strategic decision. Her level of analysis is the decision episode, while the unit of analysis is talk-in-interaction. The research outcome is an explanation of why a firm is committed to a particular course of action. Each of these studies thus uses a different unit and level of analysis to explain the construction of activity that is strategic, albeit that none of them adopts a 'typical' firm level of analysis or firm performance outcome.

While each study has a different situational focus, each is concerned to explain some aspect of strategy as a situated and socially accomplished activity that is consequential for the way organizations define and appropriate value. Strategy-as-practice thus encourages the development of explanatory theory that closely reflects practice rather than the normative theory typical to mainstream strategy. This distinction is not trivial, as 'good' strategy theory is largely considered to be parsimonious, generalizable and, hence, predictive for practice (Hirsch et al., 1988; Langley, 1999; Weick, 1979). However, '*rules of behaviour prescribed by*

economic models, however logical, cannot be normative if managers are not capable of implementing them or if the assumptions on which the models are built do not apply' (Masten, 1993: 127 in Ghoshal and Moran, 1996). As the explanatory theorizing derived from strategy-as-practice research is faithful to the situated and socially accomplished nature of strategy, it is likely to provide a different test of 'good' theory, accuracy (Langley, 1999; Weick, 1979) and, hence, be highly recognizable to practising managers.

STRATEGY-AS-PRACTICE AND OTHER AVENUES OF STRATEGY RESEARCH

Strategy-as-practice is, of course, not the first research agenda to attempt to break through the economics-based dominance over strategy research. Rather, it may be seen as the culmination of broader shifts in strategic management, to which a practice perspective can contribute. This section discusses the intellectual inheritance of strategy process research and the way that this can be extended through a practice perspective on strategy. It then discusses how the strategy-as-practice agenda can contribute to some of the challenges and issues raised in RBV and dynamic capabilities research which, while based in economic theory, aspire to uncover the socially complex foundations of competitive advantage.

Strategy process

The strategy process school introduced a dynamic view of strategy as a *process* in which the role of the managerial actor is problematized. While process research made important steps forward in humanizing strategy research and generating more dynamic theories, from a practice perspective it does not go far enough in two ways. First, while process problematizes the role of top managers, opening the field to other levels and types of actors, it does not carry this through into studying what various actors do.

It thus acknowledges that strategy is socially accomplished but does not pursue the range of actors and interactions involved in that accomplishment. Second, process research is primarily concerned with explanations at the firm level of analysis, necessarily sacrificing more fine-grained analyses of activity construction (Johnson et al., 2003).

The process school is not a consistent body of theory in itself, comprising the Bower-Burgelman (B-B), action and change process veins of research. Beginning with Bower's (1970) influential study of the way that the resource allocation process shapes strategy, the B-B vein of process research counteracted rational choice theories of strategy-making. Building on Bower, Burgelman (1983, 1991, 1996) developed a theory of strategy as an evolutionary process involving multiple actors from the corporate, middle and operational level of the firm. The different roles played by these managers helped to problematize top managers' role as strategy formulators by showing that top managers were prone to inertia while lower level managers provided the initiative and impetus to change strategy. The B-B vein of strategy process thus initiated a dynamic theory of strategy as a multi-level process evolving over time.

However, the agency and influence by which different levels of managers shape the evolution of strategy is less addressed; that is, *how* different managers act and interact remains hollow, leaving a somewhat sterile picture of what people actually do (Johnson et al., 2003; Noda and Bower, 1996; Pettigrew, 1992). This branch of strategy process research thus remains very much at the firm level of explanation, rather than the activity level, negating fine-grained analysis of the everyday actions and interactions involved in shaping strategic activity. This problem is exacerbated by a cautious approach to situatedness, which is deliberately omitted because: '*The problem with situational context, however, is precisely that it is unique to the situation; one can't generalize about it*' (Bower, 1970: 71). Hence, messy situated

aspects of context that are of a '*personal and historical nature*' are omitted and this omission continues to colour the B-B school of research (Noda and Bower, 1996). Strategy-as-practice thus extends the B-B theory of process in two important ways, drawing out the agency involved in managerial actions and interactions and acknowledging the situated nature of activity (see, for example, Regnér, 2003).

The action school defines strategy as '*a pattern in a stream of actions*' (Mintzberg, 1990) because of its emergent rather than intended nature. This school of thought further problematizes concepts of strategy as a top-down process of formulation followed by implementation: '*To assume that the intentions of the leadership are the intentions of the organization may not be justified, since others can act contrary to these intentions*' (Mintzberg and McHugh, 1985: 162). While this emphasizes the situated and social, rather than rational and intended accomplishment of strategy, the action school tends to swing to the other polarity, focusing upon grass roots strategies that emerge within the organization. Although this provides an effective counterpoint to rational choice assumptions, it negates agency in strategy-making as we are left with the messy emergence of strategy that is not populated by actors and that overlooks the complex relationship between intention and emergence in shaping activity (Emirbayer and Mische, 1998; Hendry, 2000). Strategy may indeed emerge from other levels than top managers but its social accomplishment requires attention to the intentions and interests of the multiple actors involved in defining what activity constitutes value for an organization and how this shifts over time.

The change process school focuses upon firm-level change as an outcome of action in context (e.g. Pettigrew, 1985; Johnson, 1987; Van de Ven and Poole, 1990). Pettigrew (1985, 1987, 1990) is perhaps the primary exponent of this method, highlighting the political and cultural aspects of context and their implications for strategic action. Here the actor is clearly instated as a political entity with interest and intent, constrained and enabled by situational features, such as organizational culture. This school thus develops contextual explanations that further problematize rational choice theories and invite us to focus upon strategy as situated managerial action. The change process school of strategy is, therefore, most closely associated with strategy-as-practice. However, this school's absorbing focus is upon the sequence of events involved in change (Van de Ven, 1992). It thus deals with the firm as the level of analysis and the sequence of events within a change as the unit of analysis. By contrast, a practice perspective is concerned with activity at multiple levels of analysis and those actions and interactions that comprise activity as varying units of analysis. This analytical distinction enables a more fine-grained understanding of how activity is constructed without the presupposition of change (Chia, 2004; Johnson et al., 2003; Wilson and Jarzabkowski, 2004).

These distinctions between strategy process and strategy-as-practice in terms of agency, situated action and activity rather than firm-level analysis are a matter of nuance, foregrounding, and focus more than a hard delineation (Johnson et al., 2003). Indeed, a clear intellectual debt is owed to the process field, particularly the latter change scholars. Nonetheless, the distinctions are important for developing a theory of practice, since, as will be shown below, they open further avenues for research that enhance explanatory theorizing of strategy.

Resource-based and dynamic capability theories

Another avenue of strategy research that has developed increasing presence over the last 15 years is the resource-based view (RBV) and its more dynamic 'cousin', dynamic capability theory (Barney, 1991; Helfat, 2000; Teece et al., 1997). While based primarily in an economic paradigm (Conner, 1991), these theoretical developments aim to address and counteract the typical industry levels of analysis in much strategy research by focusing upon competitive advantage as it arises from heterogeneous firm-level resources and capabilities. Heterogeneity implicitly assumes situatedness, as firms must be different because of their unique situational characteristics. Indeed, such theories refer to socially complex forms of competitive advantage that imply both agency and situation. However, this research agenda tends to fall short of its ambitions, resorting to positivistic methods that are too coarse to access deep understandings of how firms differ situationally and, indeed, what difference that makes (Rouse and Daellenbach, 1999). As a result, situation and agency are left within the 'black box', failing to address the very problem that RBV raises (Priem and Butler, 2001).

Dynamic capabilities represent something of a development on the RBV, being in the same broad family of theory, but aiming to go beyond the criticisms of RBV as excessively static and commodified (Scarbrough, 1998; Spender, 1996). Rather than conceiving of resources as something a firm '*has*' that gives it unique advantage, dynamic capabilities are concerned with the learning processes that a firm '*does*'. This is a distinctive contribution from a practice perspective, since it acknowledges more dynamic forms of theorizing. However, despite considerable research, dynamic capabilities still fail to deliver a coherent account of strategy-making; how capabilities are developed and modified over time and what difference that makes to the strategy of the firm (Cockburn et al., 2000). This may be because capability-building theory has also fallen prey to the dominant positivistic traditions in strategy research, and so lacks sufficient fine-grained analysis to furnish a more *dynamic* theory of dynamic capabilities (Regner, 2005). Recent empirical studies illustrate how a strategy-as-practice approach can illuminate the agendas outlined in RBV and dynamic capability theory by focusing on the activities and actions through which dynamic and socially complex resources and capabilities are constituted (e.g. Ambrosini et al., 2006; Salvato, 2003).

IMPLICATIONS FOR RESEARCH: AN INTEGRATIVE CONCEPTUAL FRAMEWORK

The strategy-as-practice research agenda opens a range of potential units of analysis and outcomes that are not typical in other avenues of strategy research. Therefore, a conceptual framework is helpful for identifying and integrating different entry points into the study of strategy-as-practice. Whittington (2006) proposes that strategy-as-practice comprises three discrete but interrelated elements; practice, practices and practitioners (see also Reckwitz, 2002). Building upon these three elements, the conceptual framework, Figure 2.12.1, may be used to identify and integrate different approaches to different strategy-as-practice research problems. As Figure 2.12.1 indicates, these elements are discrete but interrelated, so that it is not possible to study one without also drawing on aspects of the others. A, B and C represent different focal points at the nexus of practice, practices and practitioners, that enable different types of strategy-as-practice explanations. This section briefly defines each element, explains how it has been dealt with

in existing strategy-as-practice research and proposes avenues for taking the research agenda forward.

Strategy-as-practice

Strategy-as-practice is a situated and socially accomplished flow of activity that is consequential for the way an organization defines and appropriates value. The nature of the research question will indicate some levels of situation as more pertinent than others, providing parameters for studying the social accomplishment of activity that might range from quite micro levels of situation, such as specific groups or locales, to its more macro dimensions in institutionalized activity. Existing strategy-as-practice illustrates how these situational levels may be studied empirically and the types of questions that are important to the research agenda.

At the institutionalized levels, strategy is theorized as a powerful and pervasive discourse that may legitimize some courses of activity over others (Knights and Morgan, 1991). The institutional construction of activity may have serious consequences, as the support for 'new economy' strategies such as

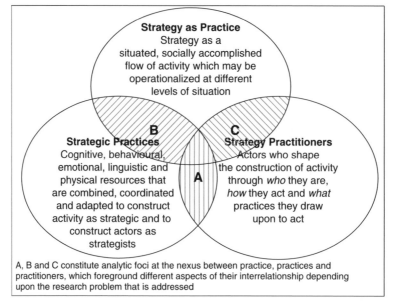

Figure 2.12.1   A conceptual framework for analyzing strategy-as-practice[2]

that of Enron indicates (Whittington et al., 2003). However, despite their influential and potentially damaging consequences, the construction of pervasive strategy discourses and their implications for how firms define and appropriate value is still under-researched, with some noteworthy exceptions (e.g. Oakes et al., 1998; Vaara et al., 2004), providing one significant avenue for research. At the organizational and sub-organizational levels more empirical studies have been conducted, explaining, for example, the transformation of intended strategies as they are enacted in the day-to-day practices of actors (e.g. Balogun and Johnson, 2004, 2005; Rouleau, 2005); how strategic activities emerge and evolve within an organization (Regnér, 2003); and how these activities are legitimized (Jarzabkowski, 2005). There is still, however, need for research into where strategies come from, how they are created (Regnér, 2005), and how different organizational situations provide different legitimacies for what activity is considered strategic (Rouse and Daellenbach, 1999; Wilson and Jarzabkowski, 2004). Relatively few studies have been conducted at more micro levels of situation, albeit that Hendry and Seidl (2003) provide a strong theoretical rationale for examining how the micro-situational characteristics of episodes such as workshops, meetings and away days contribute to stability and change within organizational strategy. While Samra-Fredericks' (2003) study of the implications of talk-in-interaction for decision episodes provides an exception and some recent work is picking up on these concepts (e.g. Hodgkinson et al., 2005; Jarzabkowski and Seidl, 2006; Schwartz, 2004), more research is needed to identify micro-situational characteristics and their implications for strategic activity.

Strategic practitioners

Strategic practitioners are at the heart of strategy-as-practice research, with its concern to reinstate actors and their agency into strategy theory. This raises the question of *who* is a strategist? In the broadest sense, a strategic actor may be considered an actor who shapes the construction of strategic activity. However, most strategy research that does incorporate actors adopts underlying strategic choice assumptions by identifying top managers as strategists, primarily in the process of formulating strategies (e.g. Eisenhardt, 1989). While top managers are important strategic actors, this dominant focus does not accord well with a view of strategy as a situated and socially accomplished activity (Johnson et al., 2003). Practice research thus focuses on the nexus between practitioners and practice (C, Figure 2.12.1), going beyond truncated views of top managers and their role in strategy formulation to examining top managers and other actors as participants in shaping the flow of strategic activity.

A key issue, therefore, is the identification of a broader group of strategic actors, in order that we may gain insights into *who* these actors are, *how* they act and interact, and *what difference* that makes for shaping strategy. Existing practice research has identified and examined the behaviours of a broader group of within-firm actors, such as middle and operational managers, who are influential in shaping strategic activity (e.g. Balogun and Johnson, 2004; Balogun and Johnson, 2005; Mantere, 2005). However, this research can go even further in examining how individuals identify themselves in relation to strategic activity and the associated practices that they appropriate in order to influence that activity. For example, Rouleau's (2005) study of how middle managers enact strategic change illustrates the different gendered practices that people appropriate in their day-to-day actions and how these shape the change process. In her study, *who* a strategist is, is embodied in the gender identity of the individual and *how* s/he acts, as well as embedded within the patriarchal family structures of the society in which the organization is based, influencing the way that actors respond to and interact with each other about the change. The gendered identification and behaviour of strategic actors was consequential for strategic activity because patriarchal patterns of interaction obstructed attempts to develop more open client relationships. A profitable avenue for future research is, therefore, the examination of how strategic actors at all levels identify themselves in association to strategic activity and what difference this makes in shaping that activity.

Additionally, strategy-as-practice research aims to go beyond the firm in identifying strategic actors. Increasingly strategy within organizations is shaped by a range of influential external actors, such as consultants (Schwartz, 2004), consumers (Ambrosini et al., 2006; Lowendahl and Revang, 1998), regulators (Willman et al., 2003) and investors, amongst others. However, there is relatively little research into the strategic influences of these actors who are 'outside' the firm but influential in the way that firms define and appropriate value. Future studies into 'who' a strategist is and 'how' they act might, therefore, adopt a broader definition than simply within-firm actors in order to develop richer and more complex understandings of how strategic practitioners shape strategy.

Strategic practices

In practice theory, strategic practices are those bodily activities, mental activities, 'things' and their use, language, know-how, emotions and motivations that practitioners engage when they are doing strategy (Reckwitz, 2002). Such practices may be strategic in two ways. They may be formally identifiable as strategic practices, such as planning documents, management information, PowerPoint presentations and strategic analyses, which are developed and drawn upon in the formal process of shaping strategy. They may, however, also be strategic because they provide the sources of agency with which to be a 'strategic' actor; that is, to mobilize and pursue an individual's own interests in shaping strategy, even where they do not comprise part of the formal strategy process. These two senses of strategic practices are inter-related, as the practices that are developed and drawn upon in the formal process might also be the practices that an actor appropriates to construct him/herself as

a strategist. However, they indicate different analytic foci within Figure 2.12.1. The first sense of strategic practices refers primarily to B, the nexus between strategic practices and the construction of strategic activity, while the second deals with A, the nexus between practices and practitioners. These different foci have been operationalized in existing strategy-as-practice research to explain different practice phenomena.

The first sense of strategic practices reinstates the formal strategy practices as an object of study, because of the way that these practices may shape strategic activity. These 'rational' practices typically serve the purpose of organizing and coordinating strategy, such as planning mechanisms, budgets, forecasts, control systems, performance indicators and targets. Strategy as a practice is littered with such practices and they comprised an important part of early strategy theory (e.g. Ansoff, 1965). However, following Bower and Burgelman's research into the way resource allocation mechanisms shape strategy and Mintzberg's (1990, 1994) critique of strategic planning and design, such practices have been exposed as not necessarily rational. Therefore, they have, with some exceptions (e.g. Grant, 2003; Langley, 1989), largely disappeared off the research agenda. However, these formal practices persist within organizations and continue to be relevant to practitioners (Hendry, 2000). As such practices are part of the everyday work of doing strategy, strategy-as-practice research has taken them seriously as an object of study. Formal strategic practices are not neutral carriers of strategic intent but historical and cultural artifacts that are both imbued with meaning by the situation in which they occur and which also serve to mediate between the competing interests of different parties involved in shaping strategy. Therefore, existing practice research examines the role of such practices in shaping strategy as a situated and socially accomplished activity. For example, I have studied the situated nature of formal administrative procedures and the way that different groups draw upon them to legitimize their own version of strategic activity within a university context (Jarzabkowski, 2005), while Blackler et al. (2000) explain how ostensibly coherent formal strategy documents may be used differently by different groups, constructing a fragmented and contested concept of organizational strategy. Such research takes B in Figure 2.12.1 as the focal point, explaining how strategic practices are involved in the situated and social accomplishment of strategic activity.

The second sense of strategic practices focuses more upon their nexus with strategic practitioners (A, Figure 2.12.1), studying how actors draw upon a range of practices to construct themselves as strategic actors, able to mobilize their own interests in shaping strategy even where they lack formal strategy roles or access to the formal practices of strategy (Mantere, 2005). From this perspective, strategic practices are more associated with the bodily activities, language, know-how, emotions and motivations that the actor draws upon in order to have influence. For example, Samra-Fredericks (2003) shows how a manager is able to appropriate aspects of the talk between actors to construct greater credibility for his ideas, and so shape the course of a strategic decision. From another angle, Maitlis and Lawrence (2003) explain a failure in strategizing as the inability of key actors to engage the political resources necessary to mobilize other actors within the artistic context of an orchestra. In drawing on these practices, actors are not always consciously constructing themselves as strategists, even so that their actions may be strategically consequential. For example, Regnér (2003) explains how Ericsson entered the mobile telephony market unintentionally, through the technical know-how, market connections and experimentation of actors at the periphery of firms. By drawing on these innate practices associated with their professional expertise, these actors became strategically significant to the firm. The study of strategic practices thus offers different avenues for research, depending upon whether investigators focus upon the nature of the practices themselves and their

implications for strategic activity or the way that actors appropriate strategic practices in order to construct themselves as strategists, intentionally and unintentionally. Both senses of strategic practices are relevant to the strategy-as-practice research agenda.

Figure 2.12.1 thus provides an overarching conceptual framework of three elements: practice, practices and practitioners, that may be used to identify different angles from which to research strategy-as-practice. This framework helps to integrate the diverse units and levels of analysis taken within strategy-as-practice research, by showing inter-relationships between the three elements and providing a point of unification around the concern to explain some aspect of strategy as a situated and socially accomplished activity.

IMPLICATIONS FOR TEACHING

Given the rewards in the academic profession, any perspective typically is judged by its implications for research, somewhat less for its implications for practice and little, if at all, for its teaching implications. However, our classrooms contain the practitioners of the present and future. Currently strategy teaching, as evidenced by the typical content of strategy textbooks, adopts a normative view of strategy as a process of formulation followed by implementation. The dominant focus is on those economics-based models and frameworks through which the formulation part of this process may be understood, such as environmental analyses, resource, competence and capability assessments, and the ubiquitous SWOT to analyse the fit between firm and environment with a view to making strategic recommendations. The case method remains a dominant mode of teaching, focusing upon retrospective analysis of a stylized problem designed to provide students with analytic skills in using typical strategy models and frameworks (Liang and Wang, 2004). While Pascale (1984) exposed the false assumptions of intent, rationality and foresight in much case material with his explanation of Honda's unintentional and emergent penetration of the US motorcycle market, which was in marked contrast to the BCG analysis of Honda's behaviour as a rational analytic approach to dominating a new market segment (Rumelt, 1996; Harvard Honda Case A and B), the dominant case approach persists. Indeed, it is interesting to note that only one case in Liang and Wang's (2004) comparison of 66 popular North American and Chinese case studies reflects strategy as a messy, real-time practice. While this case displays the chaotic, interactive nature of doing strategy in the face of political interests and uncertainty, most cases displayed assumptions of intent, foresight, rationality and perfect information that are far from the 'real business situations' that they purport to describe.

As strategy-as-practice research derives explanatory theory that is closer to practice, it is important that some flow through to teaching that more accurately reflects practice is realized. A strategy-as-practice approach would entail cases based on the real-time unfolding of strategy, in order to illustrate how and why the actions and interactions of multiple actors shape strategy (see, for example, Regnér 2004). Rather than the normative assumptions prevalent in most strategy teaching, such cases would not aim to provide prescriptions for how firms should behave but deep understanding of how actors do behave and the implications this holds for shaping strategy. Indeed, such cases might involve actual practice!

IMPLICATIONS FOR PRACTICE

As noted above, mainstream strategy theories tend to be normative in prescribing to practice, despite the potential fallacy of the assumptions on which they are based (Ghoshal, 2005; Ghoshal and Moran, 1996). Strategy-as-practice is concerned with explanatory theory, endeavouring to reflect actual practice with some accuracy. Explanatory theory has the benefit of familiarity and veracity for practitioners (Weick, 1989). That is,

practitioners will recognise the situations and activity described and explained. While these studies do not have statistical generalizability, they indicate the underlying situational mechanisms involved in human action (Hedstrom and Swedberg, 1998; Tsoukas, 1989) and these are familiar to human actors. Strategy-as-practice theories, therefore, while not prescriptive, provide explanations of activity and its consequences that have sufficient veracity to provoke recognition and reflection. The self-awareness generated by reflection is important in reconstructing and transforming activity (Giddens, 1984; Schon, 1983). Strategy-as-practice theories are, therefore, influential in enabling practitioners to better understand their own actions, to reflect on its strategic implications and, potentially, to reconstruct activity in light of these reflections.

CONCLUSION

Strategy-as-practice research represents a counter position to the normative, economics-dominated theory arising from mainstream strategy research. It is concerned to reinstate the actor within strategy research but not to adopt simplistic notions of top level managerial agency. Rather, it examines multiple sources of agency as they arise within the actions and interactions of the multiple actors involved in shaping strategy as a situated and socially accomplished activity. The practice perspective on strategy draws out the embedded levels of situation from micro episodes to macro institutions within which strategy is accomplished, adopting any of these as a viable level of analysis that may be consequential to the way in which an organization defines and appropriates value. Strategy-as-practice thus raises alternative units and levels of analysis than the firm and industry associations typically found in strategy research, as well as providing alternative outcomes from financial indicators of firm performance.

A common theme in the strategy-as-practice agenda, regardless of the level and unit of analysis, is the desire to surface the 'pixels' of strategy as a social practice through richly evocative descriptions. This does not imply a theoretical void, in which description takes the place of theory, but it does require a different approach than that taken in mainstream strategy research, which is more concerned with the theoretical parsimony of causally related variables. Hence, it is important that we look to other modes of 'doing science' for inspiration, such as anthropology (e.g. Geertz, 1973), ethnomethodology (e.g Garfinkel, 1967) and micro-sociology (e.g. Goffman, 1959). For example, in Whyte's (1943) evocative *Street Corner Society*, or Garfinkel's vivid portrayal of being a transsexual, we gain deep insights into the way that individuals' emotions, bodily actions and speech – indeed the full gamut of their everyday lived experiences – are implicit in the way they make sense of their world and interact with others, in the process shaping the collective activity in which they and others engage. In such fields, thick descriptions support theorizing that is close to the field, explaining the actions and interactions of actors in ways that are faithful to their experiences and situations. These studies do not aim for parsimony but illumination. In this vein, the truly exciting directions for strategy-as-practice research lie in the ability of researchers to evoke the experience of doing strategy from the perspective of the practitioner and to generate explanations of how and why these experiences vary in different situations. Such ambitions for the field involve wider use of methodological resources, greater craft in writing about strategy as a social practice and more receptivity as reviewers in peer appraising such scholarship.

NOTES

1 For example, there are now regular strategy as practice conference tracks at EGOS, EURAM, BAM and SMS, as well as sub-themes, workshops and symposia at ANZAM, AoM and APGOS, as well as a special issue of JMS (2003: 40.1) and a special issue of *Human Relations* (2006), papers in many credible refereed journals, and a website of over 1,200 members – www.strategy-as-practice.org

2 See also Jarzabkowski (2005) and Jarzabkowski et al. (2006) for versions of this diagram.

REFERENCES

Ambrosini, V., Bowman, C. and Burton-Taylor, S. (2006) 'Inter-team coordination activities as a source of customer satisfaction', *Human Relations Special Issue*, 60 (1): 59–98.

Ansoff, H.I. (1965) *Corporate Strategy*. New York: McGraw-Hill.

Balogun, J. and Johnson, G. (2004) 'Organizational restructuring and middle manager sensemaking', *Academy of Management Journal*, 47 (5): 523–549.

Balogun, J. and Johnson, G. (2005) 'From intended strategy to unindented outcomes: The impact of change recipient sensemaking', *Organization Studies*, 26 (11): 1573–1602.

Barney, J. (1991) 'Firm resources and sustained competitive advantage', *Journal of Management*, 17 (1): 99–120.

Bettis, R (1991) 'Strategic management and the straightjacket: An editorial essay'. *Organization Science*, 2 (3): 315–320.

Blackler, F., Crump, N. and McDonald, S. (2000) 'Organizing processes in complex activity network', *Organization*, 7: 277–300.

Bower, J.L. (1970) *Managing the Resource Allocation Process: A Study of Corporate Planning and Investment*. Cambridge, MA: Harvard Business School Press.

Burgelman, R.A. (1983) 'A process model of internal corporate venturing in the diversified major firm', *Administrative Science Quarterly*, 28: 223–244.

Burgelman, R.A. (1991) 'Intraorganizational ecology of strategy making and organizational adaptation: Theory and field research', *Organization Science*, 2 (3): 239–262.

Burgelman, R.A. (1996) 'A process model of strategic business exit: Implications for an evolutionary perspective on strategy', *Strategic Management Journal*, 17: 193–214.

Chia, R. (2004) 'Strategy-as-practice: Reflections on the research agenda', *European Management Review*, 1 (1): 29–34.

Clegg, C., Carter, C. and Kornberger, M. (2004) 'Get up, I feel like being a strategy machine', *European Management Review*, 1 (1): 21–28.

Cockburn, I.M., Henderson, R.M. and Stern, S. (2000) 'Untangling the origins of competitive advantage', *Strategic Management Journal*, 21, 10 (11): 1123–1145.

Conner, K.R. (1991) 'A historical comparison of resource-based theory and five schools of thought within industrial organization economics: Do we have a new theory of the firm'?, *Journal of Management*, 17 (1): 121–154.

Contu, A. and Willmott, H. (2003) 'Re-embedding situatedness: The importance of power relations in learning theory', *Organization Science*, 14 (3): 283–297.

Emirbayer, M. and Mische, A. (1998) 'What is agency?' *American Journal of Sociology*, 103(4): 962–1023.

Eisenhardt, K.M. (1989) 'Making fast strategic decisions in high-velocity environments', *Academy of Management Journal*, 32 (3): 543–576.

Garfinkel, H. (1967) *Studies in Ethnomethodology*. Englewood Cliffs, NJ: Prentice-Hall.

Geertz, C. (1973) *The Interpretation of Cultures*. New York: Basic Books.

Ghoshal, S. and Moran, P. (1996) 'Bad for practice: A critique of the transaction cost theory', *Academy of Management Review*, 21 (1): 13–47.

Ghoshal, S. (2005) 'Bad management theories are destroying good management practices', *Academy of Management Learning and Education*, 4 (1): 75–91.

Ghoshal, S. and Moran, P. (1996) 'Bad for practice: A critique of the transaction cost theory', *Academy of Management Review*, 21 (1): 13–47.

Giddens, A. (1984) *The Constitution of Society*. Cambridge: Polity Press.

Gioia, D.A. and Chittipedi, K. (1991) 'Sensemaking and sensegiving in strategic change initiation', *Strategic Management Journal*, 12: 433–448.

Goffman, E. (1959) *The Presentation of Self in Everyday Life*. New York: Doubleday Books.

Grant, R.M. (2003) 'Strategic planning in a turbulent environment: Evidence from the oil majors', *Strategic Management Journal*, 24 (6): 491–518.

Hedstrom, P. and Swedberg, R. (1998) *Social Mechanisms*. Cambridge: Cambridge University Press.

Helfat, C. (2000) 'Guest editor's introduction to the special issue: The evolution of firm capabilties', *Strategic Management Journal*, 21(10/11): 955–960.

Hendry, J. (2000) 'Strategic decision-making, discourse, and strategy as social practice', *Journal of Management Studies*, 37: 955–977.

Hendry, J. and Seidl, D. (2003) 'The structure and significance of strategic episodes: Social systems theory and the routine practices of strategic change', *Journal of Management Studies*, 40 (1): 175–196.

Hirsch, P., Friedman, R. and Koza, M. (1988) 'Collaboration or paradigm shift?: Caveat emptor and the risk of romance with economic models for strategy and policy research', *Organization Science*, 1 (1): 87–97.

Hodskinson, G., Whittington, R., Johnson, G. and Schwarz, M. (2006). 'The role of strategy workshops in strategy development processes: Formality, communication, co-ordination and inclusion', *Long Range Planning*, 39 (5): 479–496.

Hollis, M. and Nell, E.J. (1975) *Rational Economic Man*. New York: Cambridge University Press.

Hopwood, A.G. and Miller, P. (1994) *Accounting as a Social and Institutional Practice*. Cambridge: Cambridge University Press.

Jarzabkowski, P. (2003) 'Strategic practices: An activity theory perspective on continuity and change', *Journal of Management Studies*, 40 (1): 23–55.

Jarzabkowski, P. (2004) 'Strategy as practice: Recursiveness, adaptation and practices-in-use', *Organization Studies*, 25 (4): 529–560.

Jarzabkowski, P. (2005) *Strategy as Practice: An Activity-Based Approach*. London: Sage.

Jarzabkowski, P., Balogun, J. and Seidl, D. (2006) 'Strategizing: The challenges of a practice perspective', *Human Relations*, forthcoming.

Jarzabkowski, P. and Seidl, D. (2006) 'Meetings as strategizing episodes in the social practice of strategy', *Advanced Institute of Management (AIM) Working Paper* No. 036-March-2006.

Jarzabkowski, P. and Wilson, D.C. (2002) 'Top teams and strategy in a UK university', *Journal of Management Studies*, 39 (3): 357–383.

Johnson, G. (1987) *Strategic Change and the Management Process*. Oxford: Blackwell.

Johnson, G., Melin, L. and Whittington, R. (2003) 'Micro strategy and strategizing: Towards an activity-based view?', *Journal of Management Studies*, 40 (1): 3.

Knights, D. and Morgan, G. (1991) 'Corporate strategy, organizations and subjectivity', *Organizations Studies*, 12: 251–273.

Langley, A. (1999) 'Strategies for theorizing from process data', *Academy of Management Review*, 24 (4): 691–710.

Liang, N. and Wang, J. (2004) 'Implicit mental models in teaching cases: An empirical study of popular MBA cases in the United States and China', *Academy of Management Learning & Education*, 3 (4): 397–413.

Lowendahl, B. and Revang, O. (1998) 'Challenges to existing strategy theory in a post-industrial society', *Strategic Management Journal*, 19 (8): 755–774.

Maitlis, S. and Lawrence, B. (2003) 'Orchestral manoeuvres in the dark: Understanding failure in organizational strategizing', *Journal of Management Studies*, 40 (1): 109–140.

Mantere, S. (2005) 'Strategic practices as enablers and disablers of championing activity', *Strategic Organization!*, 3 (2): 157–284.

Masten, S. (1993) 'Transaction costs, mistakes and performance: Assessing the importance of governance', *Managerial and Decision Economics*, 14: 119–129.

Mintzberg, H. (1990) 'The design school: Reconsidering the basic premises of strategic management', *Strategic Management Journal*, 11: 171–195.

Mintzberg, H. (1994) *The Rise and Fall of Strategic Planning*. New York: Free Press and Prentice-Hall.

Mintzberg, H. and McHugh, A. (1985) 'Strategy formation in an adhocracy', *Administrative Science Quarterly*, 24 (4): 580–589.

Mir, R. and Watson, A. (2000) 'Strategic management and the philosophy of science: The case for a constructivist methodology', *Strategic Management Journal*, 21 (9): 941–954.

Noda, T. and Bower, J. (1996) 'Strategy making as iterated processes of resource allocation', *Strategic Management Journal*, 17: 159–192.

Oakes, L.S., Townley, B. and Cooper, D.J. (1998) 'Business planning as pedagogy: Language and control in a changing institutional field', *Administrative Science Quarterly*, 43: 257–292.

Orlikowski, W. (1992) 'The duality of technology: Rethinking the concept of technology in organizations', *Organization Science*, 3 (3): 398–427.

Orlikowski, W. (2000) 'Using technology and constituting structure: A practice lens for studying technology in organizations', *Organization Science*, 12: 404–428.

Orr, J.E. (1996) *Talking about Machines: An Ethnography of a Modern Job*. New York: Cornell University Press.

Ortner, S. (1984) 'Theory in anthropology since the sixties', *Comparative Studies in Society and History*, 26: 126–166.

Pascale, R.T. (1984) 'Perspectives on strategy: The real story behind Honda's success', *California Management Review*, 26 (3): 47–72.

Pettigrew, A. (1985) *The Awakening Giant: Continuity and Change in ICI*. Oxford: Blackwell.

Pettigrew, A.M. (1987) 'Context and action in the transformation of the firm', *Journal of management Studies*, 24(6): 649–670.

Pettigrew, A. (1990) 'Longitudinal field research on change theory and practice', *Organization Science*, 1 (3): 267–292.

Pettigrew, A. (1992) 'On studying managerial elites', *Strategic Management Journal*, 13: 163–182.

Pettigrew, A., Thomas, H. and Whittington, R. (2002) 'Strategic management: The strengths and limitations of a field', in A. Pettigrew, H. Thomas and R. Whittington (eds), *The Handbook of Strategy and Management*. London: Sage. pp. 3–30.

Prahalad, C.K. and Hamel, G. (1994) Strategy as afield of study; Why search for a new paradigm'?, *Strategic Management Journal*, 15, Special Issue: 5–16.

Priem, R.L. and Butler, J.E. (2001) 'Is the resource-based "view" a useful perspective for strategic management research'?, *Academy of Management Review*, 26 (1): 22–40.

Reckwitz, A. (2002) 'Towards a theory of social practice: A development in cultural theorizing', *European Journal of Social Theory*, 5 (2): 243–263.

Regnér, P. (2003) 'Strategy creation in practice: Adaptive and creative learning dynamics', *Journal of Management Studies*, 40 (1): 57–82.

Regnér, P. (2005) 'Managerial activities and social interactions in evolution: Towards a more dynamic strategy view'. Working Paper 05/01, Institute of International Business, Stockholm School of Economics: Stockholm.

Rouleau, L. (2005) 'Micro-practices of strategic sensemaking and sensegiving: How middle managers interpret and sell strategic change every day', *Journal of Management Studies*, 42, 7.

Rouse, M. and Daellenbach, U.S. (1999) 'Rethinking research methods for the resource-based perspective', *Strategic Management Journal*, 20 (5): 487–494.

Rumelt, R.P. (1996) 'The many faces of Honda', *California Management Review*, 38 (4): 103–111.

Salvato, C. (2003) 'The role of micro-strategies in the engineering of firm evolution', *Journal of Management Studies*, 40 (1): 83–108.

Samra-Fredericks, D. (2003) 'Strategizing as lived experience and strategists' everyday efforts to shape strategic direction', *Journal of Management Studies*, 40: 141–174.

Scarbrough, H. (1998) 'Path(ological) dependency? Core competences from an organisational perspective', *British Journal of Management*, 9 (3): 219–232.

Schwarz, M. (2004) 'Strategy workshops for starategic reviews: Components, practices and roles of actor', Paper delivered at *European Group for Organization Studies*, Ljubljana.

Schwarz, M. (2004) 'Knowing in practice: How consultants work with client to create share and apply knowledge?', *Academy of Management Best Paper Proceedings*, New Orleans.

Schatzki, T.R., Cetina, K.K. and Savigny, E. (2001) '*The Practice Turn in Contemporary Theory*', London: Routledge.

Schon, D.A. (1983) *The Reflective Practitioner*. New York: Arena.

Spender, J.-C. (1996) 'Making knowledge the basis of a dynamic theory of the firm', *Strategic Management Journal*, 17: 45–62.

Suchman, L. (1987) *Plans and Situated Actions.* Cambridge: Cambridge University Press.

Teece, D.J., Pisano, G. and Shuen, A. (1997) 'Dynamic capablities and strategic management', *Strategic Management Journal*, 18: 509–533.

Tsoukas, H. (1989) 'The validity of idiographic research explanations', *Academy of Management Review*, 14 (4): 551–561.

Vaara, E., Kleyman, B. and Seristo, H. (2004) 'Strategies as discursive constructions: The case of airline alliances', *Journal of Management Studies*, 41 (1): 1–35.

Van de Ven, A. (1992) 'Suggestions for studying strategy process: A research note', *Strategic Management Journal*, 13: 169–188.

Van de Ven, A. and Poole, M. (1990) 'Methods for studying innovation development in the Minnesota innovation research program', *Organization Science*, 1 (3): 313–336.

Weick, K. (1979) *The Social Psychology of Organising.* New York: McGraw-Hill.

Weick E. Karl (1989) 'Theory construction as disciplined imagination', *Academy of Management Review*, 14 (4): 516–531.

Whittington, R. (1996). 'Strategy as practice', *Long Range Planning*, 29 (5): 731–735.

Whittington, R. (2002) 'Corporate structure: From policy to practice', in A.M. Pettigrew, H. Thomas and R. Whittington (eds), *The Handbook of Strategy and Management*. London: Sage.

Whittington, R. (2003) 'The work of strategizing and organizing: For a practice perspective', *Strategic Organization*, 1 (1): 119–127.

Whittington, R. (2006) 'Completing the practice turn in strategy research', *Organization Studies* (forthcoming).

Whittington, R., Jarzabkowski, P., Mayer, M., Mounoud, E., Nahapiet, J. and Rouleau, L. (2003) 'Taking strategy seriously: Responsibility and reform for an important social practice', *Journal of Management Inquiry*, 12: 396–409.

Whyte, W.F. (1943) *Street Corner Society: The Social Structure of an Italian Slum*. Chicago: The University of Chicago Press.

Willman, P., Coen, D., Currie, D. and Siner, M. (2003) 'The evolution of regulatory relationships; regulatory institutions and firm behaviour in privatised industries', *Industrial and Corporate Change*, 12 (1): 69–89.

Wilson, D.C. and Jarzabkowski, P. (2004) 'Thinking and acting strategically: New challenges for interrogating strategy', *European Management Review*, 1 (1): 14–20.

A New Focal Point: Interactions, Deliverables and Delivery

Jeffrey D. Ford and Laurie W. Ford

A fundamental model of today's organization architecture is the network, a structure composed of nodes and links. In an organization, the nodes represent people (individuals or groups) doing work; the links between them represent the active and productive communications or handoffs between specific node pairs. Although much is understood about the organizing principles that give networks their topology, little is known about the dynamics that take place along the links (Barabasi, 2003) despite Weick's (1979) observation that interactions are the fundamental unit of organizing.

In a very real sense, the handoffs or deliverables that are passing back and forth between groups are the critical factor in performance, rather than the activities at either end of a link. A deliverable may be a product, service or specific communication that is sent from Node A to Node B. It is the result of the work activities in Node A, which result then travels to Node B (by e-mail, phone, or UPS) and generates new activity there. Deliverables are the heart of an interdependent working relationship and the basis for all understanding of 'performance': i.e. no deliverable, no performance. From this network perspective, the activity that goes on inside a group is of no consequence in the absence of some deliverable that is transmitted to interested recipients elsewhere.

The focus on deliverables as the basis for organization performance suggests that effective (productive) working relationships depend on whether the organization's groups, departments and divisions can successfully transmit the right deliverables. The 'right' deliverable is one that is both 'on time' and 'to specification', where 'on time' means the deliverable arrives when it is wanted and needed by the recipient; and 'to specification' means it meets all the conditions stipulated by the recipient.

A rich area for the design and study of organizations is increased understanding of the *network of deliverables* between groups inside an organization, and between those groups and their external customers, suppliers, and other key relationships for which they are accountable. The challenge is shifting our attention from people as 'doers' to people as 'deliverers'. Recognizing that groups are, above all, in the delivery business, is unfamiliar in most traditional organizations.

The network structure opens new opportunities for examining the ways an organization produces results and creates value for customers, employees and shareholders alike, developing a deeper understanding of the other aspect of an organization's network. What tangible products, services and communications move between people, committees and organizations? Do these deliverables support the organization's mission, vision and strategies? How can we train people to create effective agreements for generating high-value deliverables?

A focus on the links of a network organization does not take away the importance of the human dimension. Shifting attention from what people 'do' to what they 'deliver' helps people look outside themselves in new ways, and learn new skills in listening, negotiation and responsiveness. It adds new dimensions to organizations too, by improving attention to the receiver-customer and discovering the determinants of effective working

Continued

relationships. In an era of increasing attention to networks and network science, it is time for organization design to make a similar shift and focus on the links between nodes rather than the nodes themselves.

REFERENCES

Barabasi, A. (2003) *Linked: How Everything is Connected to Everything Else and What it Means for Business, Science, and Everyday Life*. New York: Plume.
Weick, K. (1979) *The Social Psychology of Organizing*. Reading, MA: Addison-Wesley.

Entrepreneurship and Competition at the Intersection: Maintaining Strategic Resilience

Shaker A. Zahra and R. Isil Yavuz

Profound and persistent changes have challenged companies to explore new arenas in which to compete. Some companies have pursued diversification at home and abroad as a means of changing their competitive landscape. Others have incubated new businesses to broaden their business portfolio. One strategy that has not received as much attention centers on revamping industry boundaries and competing at the intersection of two or more industries, an approach that can ensure organizational agility and resilience in the face of persistent change.

THREE ESSENTIAL INGREDIENTS

Competing at the intersection of multiple industries has three essential ingredients. The first is creating new market arenas by converging two or more existing business fields. Hewlett-Packard's efforts to integrate the printer and PC fields to develop a new industrial landscape are a prominent example of this strategy. This convergence is not always a simple or additive process because technologies and the sciences behind them differ markedly, making their integration difficult (Yoffie et al., 2005). The alchemy of convergence is difficult to decipher and therefore experimentation is necessary to identify the winning formula for success. Experimentation requires imagination, entrepreneurialism and dedicated investments over multiple years, if not decades. The convergence process also demands managerial foresight to envision things to come and how they might shape the evolution of new businesses being developed.

A second essential ingredient is converging different competencies and skills. This convergence could happen naturally or be induced through dedicated investments in building particular, especially new, capabilities. Yet, it is hard to believe that successful convergence could materialize without entrepreneurialism in assembling the resources, conceiving of new uses of existing skills, and developing new capabilities.

Entrepreneurialism manifests itself in uncovering new connections, linking seemingly unrelated competencies in new ways to create new things that hitherto never existed. It could also manifest itself in seeing ways to alter industry structures and corresponding mental models, transforming the competitive arena in radical ways.

A third essential ingredient is the clarity and coherence of strategic vision that, at once, stimulates and balances exploration and exploitation. By competing at the intersection of industries, companies seek to leverage and harvest their existing skills and repertoire of knowledge, shorten the adaptation cycle, reduce the down side risks of unrelated diversification, enhance organizational agility and create new markets where competitors cannot easily imitate their skills. Of course, convergence is not always possible because it requires a combination of scientific, technological, marketing and organizational skills that few companies possess (Kodama, 1995). This combination is unknown *a priori*.

Continued

ENTREPRENEURIALISM AND COMPETITION AT THE INTERSECTION

Given the complexity of and causal ambiguity associated with the convergence approach, success is far from assured. For one thing, companies have to develop unique, portable and dynamic capabilities that could be deployed in multiple arenas. This poses multiple managerial challenges and raises a paradox: companies have to have enduring and sturdy capabilities that are also malleable and portable. Accomplishing this combination requires having multiple and perhaps overlapping capabilities that foster entrepreneurial discovery and exploitation of new opportunities. Further, existing capabilities cannot be migrated into new skills, a factor that can stifle a firm's strategic transformation.

Effective capabilities lead to agility and resilience. Agility is 'the [organizational] ability to detect opportunities for innovation and seize those competitive market opportunities by assembling requisite assets, knowledge and relationships with speed and surprise' (Sambamurthy et al., 2003: 238). As such, agility requires flexible, adaptable and portable skills that enable the company to seize opportunities at the intersection of multiple industries. With persistent change, this agility ensures the firm's resilience – the ability to withstand the challenges of change and the upheaval and crises it might unleash. Dynamic capabilities can help the firm achieve agility and resilience.

Building and deploying dynamic capabilities requires entrepreneurialism (Zahra et al., 2006); so does the creation and maintenance of organizational agility and resilience. Entrepreneurialism gives meaning and substance to managerial foresight and vision, transforming them into possibilities for change. Part of this entrepreneurialism is free wheeling. Other entrepreneurial activities are akin to 'orchestrated improvisation', where executives probe unknown options and learn from the early feedback they receive from the market, employees, suppliers and the competition.

As change continues to pressure companies to reinvent themselves, we believe that more and more executives will recognize the challenges and rewards of focusing their entrepreneurial activities on competing at the intersection of industries. These entrepreneurial activities will help nurture and sustain companies' resilience and allow them to develop new models of competition and even transform the very definition and scope of the competitive landscape.

REFERENCES

Kodama, F. (1995) *Emerging Patterns of Innovation: Sources of Japan's Technological Edge*. Cambridge, MA: Harvard Business School.

Sambamurthy, V., Bharadwaj, A. and Grover, V. (2003) 'Shaping agility through digital options: Reconceptualizing the role of information technology in contemporary firms', *MIS Quarterly*. 27 (2): 237–263.

Yoffie D., Mehta, D. and Sha, R. (2005) 'A note on the convergence between genomics and information technology'. Harvard Business School case (Product Number: 9-705-500), 32 pages.

Zahra, S., Sapienza, H. and Davidsson, P. (2006) 'Entrepreneurship and dynamic capabilities: A review, model and research agenda. *Journal of Management Studies*, 43 (4): 917–955.

Strategic Supply Chain Management: An Emerging Concept

David J. Ketchen, Jr. and G. Tomas M. Hult

Nature abhors a vacuum, and perhaps the same can be said for academic fields. There has long been a tremendous gap between the importance of supply chains to organizations and the amount of attention devoted to supply chains by management researchers. Supply chains are sets of linked organizational units that cooperatively transform raw materials into finished products and distribute them to customers (Handfield and Nichols, 2002). In recent years, a small body of management research has begun to fill this vacuum by examining why some supply chains are more effective than others. Such inquiry reflects not only the potential conceptual value of supply chains, but also their practical value to firms.

Of particular interest is what we label as *strategic supply chain management* – the strategic, operational and technological integration of supply chain participants through relationships, processes and information sharing to provide member organizations a competitive advantage (Hult et al., 2004; Upson et al., 2007). Strategic supply chain management centers on the use of supply chains not merely as a means to create products and move them to where they are needed, but also as a means to enhance key outcomes. The value of strategic supply chain management is reflected in how firms such as Wal-Mart, Toyota, Zara and Dell have used supply chain management as a competitive weapon to gain advantages over peers. Indeed, these corporate titans have redefined the rules of rivalry in their respective industries through their supply chain practices.

Costly supply chain failures by other well-known corporations are equally notable. For example, in 2001 Cisco was forced to write-off $2.25 billion of obsolete inventory due to difficulties with certain supply chain partners. Two years later, Motorola lost many sales when it offered its first camera phone because it was unable to acquire needed parts. More generally, the emergence of a major supply chain problem erodes a firm's market value by an average of 10% (Hendricks and Singhal, 2003). Thus, while effective strategic supply chain management can help firms tremendously, the potential for damage by poor supply chain practices is equally large.

We believe that the emerging concept of strategic supply chain management has much to offer management theory and research. First, as the experiences of the companies mentioned above illustrate, a focus on strategic supply chain management has the potential to shed new light on a central research issue in the strategic management literature – the determinants of organizational performance.

Strategic supply chain management also has implications for organizational behavior research. Pursuing strategic supply chain management forces chain members to think and act strategically, rather than tactically. Members must also build unfamiliar and complex competencies, such as joining or even leading teams that span firm boundaries and guiding continuous improvement processes.

As scholars seek to build knowledge about strategic supply chain management, the related and emerging concept of *cultural competitiveness* is likely to be quite useful. Cultural competitiveness is defined as the degree to which supply chains are predisposed

Continued

to detect and fill gaps between what the customer desires and what is currently offered. Research has shown that cultural competitiveness is positively related to the speed with which a strategic supply chain fulfills its core tasks (Hult et al., 2002). Because a supply chain does not have the formal structure of a traditional organization, alternative mechanisms are needed to bind participants together. Although it is perhaps unrealistic to expect chain members to develop a fully developed culture like those found in organizations, it is clear that a shared spirit centered on meeting and perhaps exceeding customers' expectations can be developed. As such, cultural competitiveness can serve as a key element of efforts to use supply chains as a means to create sustained competitive advantages.

Looking to the future, we expect that competition will become less 'firm vs. firm' and more 'supply chain vs. supply chain' over time. If this prediction is correct, the emerging concept of strategic supply chain management (and the supporting concept of cultural competitiveness) should become increasingly vital to explaining organizational activities and outcomes.

REFERENCES

Handfield, Robert B. and Nichols, Ernest L. (2002) *Supply Chain Redesign*. Upper Saddle River, NJ: Financial Times Prentice-Hall.

Hendricks, Kevin B. and Singhal, Vinod R. (2003) 'The effect of supply chain glitches on shareholder wealth'. *Journal of Operations Management*, 21 (5): 501–522.

Hult, G. Tomas M., Ketchen, David J. and Nichols, Ernest L. (2002) 'An examination of cultural competitiveness and order fulfillment cycle time within supply chains'. *Academy of Management Journal*, 45 (3): 577–586.

Hult, G. Tomas M., Ketchen, David J. and Slater, Stanley F. (2004) 'Information processing, knowledge development, and strategic supply chain performance'. *Academy of Management Journal*, 47 (2): 241–253.

Upson, John W., Ketchen, David J. and Ireland, R. Duane. (2007) 'Managing employee stress: A key to the effectiveness of strategic supply chain management', *Organizational Dynamics*, 36 (1): 78–92.

Improvisation in Organizations

Joao Cunha and Miguel Pina e Cunha

INTRODUCTION

The purpose of this chapter is to use the concept of improvisation to explore the managerial implications of fast-changing competitive environments. We argue that these environments are favorable to companies staffed by complex people improvising around an open organizational design. This design allows employees to bring improvisation to the core of their everyday work, increasing their organization's ability to adapt to changing markets and complex competitive conditions.

To make this point we start by contrasting the approaches to organizational design favored by stable competitive contexts with those favored by complex and dynamic contexts. Managers in stable environments design organizations to ensure employees' compliance with prescribed processes and goals. Managers in complex fast-changing environments provide design resources for employees to improvise local designs to help them deal with competitive challenges as they unfold (Child, 2005).

After establishing this distinction, we present the features of 'complex people' and discuss the three elements of open organizational designs: coordination mechanisms, control mechanisms and resource allocations. We conclude with an outline of the challenges for managers when designing organizations in complex environments.

FROM CLOSED DESIGNS FOR SIMPLE PEOPLE TO OPEN DESIGNS FOR COMPLEX PEOPLE

Throughout their history, management practice and management research have espoused three major views on the nature of the competitive environments surrounding organizations. Each of these views pointed to an approach to organizational design that was best suited to ensure success, or at least survival, in each type of environment. First, organizations were seen as operating in stable contexts. Managers such as Ford (Ford and Crowther, 1926), Barnard (1938) and Fayol (1949), described their markets as providing a steady demand with little if any changes in consumer preferences. Competitors were known and their actions often changed competitive positions in the industry, without changing the fundamentals of production and marketing. Management theory shared these assumptions and was thus turned inwards to the processes and procedures that allowed organizations to address stable markets with increasing efficiency. The assumption was that in competitive contexts where little changes, the chief source of increased profit is reducing costs and increasing speed in the internal functioning of organizations. This led authors such as Taylor (1947) to argue that organizational design was a one-off scientific process that should be carried out by specialists and top managers. The major input for designing organizations in these environments was information about their own internal processes, obtained through time and motion studies and other forms of observation.

This internal orientation worked only as long as competitive environments were stable. As these environments grew in complexity because of increasing competition, changes in customer habits and adverse economic conditions, success and survival demanded an external orientation. Researchers began to pay attention to the differences in rates of change in each industry (e.g. Aldrich, 1979; Burns and Stalker, 1961) and managers addressed their different markets with different product offerings and different competitive strategies (e.g. Sloan, 1964). Instead of assuming one best approach to design the internal process of organizations, researchers and practitioners adopted a contingency approach. Organizations and their processes were designed to allow unit-level managers to fine tune them to match the specific contingencies that they faced in each of their markets. Design was a still a punctuated process but one that required revisions as frequent as competitive dynamics required (Romanelli and Tushman, 1994).

These two approaches differed in the frequency of changes in organizational design, but shared an underlying view on its purpose. This view can be summarized as the 'closed design/simple people' approach. This label is a shorthand for an approach to organizational

design whose purpose was to create organizations whose performance was relatively independent of the talent of its employees. Prescribed roles, rules and procedures were designed to be specific enough to transform any employee in an undifferentiated unit of labor. Organizations needed their employees' hands, but not their brains.

The increasing rate of innovation across a number of industries, together with a number of documented episodes of Schumpeterian 'creative destruction' in a number of sectors, led popular and academic management authors to interpret corporate environments as demanding not only constant adaptation but also constant innovation (Foster and Kaplan, 2001; McGrath, 2001). Companies could no longer rely on a portfolio of products and services that allowed them to hold their competitive positions in each of their markets. Instead companies needed to produce a stream of both incremental and radical innovations to keep ahead of their current competition and survive competitive threats surfacing at the margins of their industries (Eisenhardt and Tabrizi, 1995; Levinthal, 1997). Under these new conditions, managers were told to build their organization's capability for improvisation. Planned innovation and change processes were not agile enough to keep up with changes in competitive dynamics. Organizations needed to respond to market challenges as these unfolded through a set of improvisations – intentional but unplanned deviations from the prescribed processes and procedures that allow organizations to tackle unexpected problems or opportunities (for a review of the literature on this topic see Cunha et al., 1999). This approach to strategy and change had consequences for organizational design. When designing organizations for improvisation, the goal is no longer to create a structure and processes to address environmental challenges. Instead the goal is to rely on talented individuals and teams to move the organization forward through innovation and change (Dougherty and Hardy, 1996).

This does not mean that organizational design is irrelevant in fast changing, complex competitive environments, far from it. With very few exceptions, research argues that creativity, change and innovation do require some level of structure and a sense of direction (Brown and Eisenhardt, 1997; Weick, 1987). Even in creative pursuits that shun structure, such as musical improvisation, there is a minimal level of structure that supports positive deviations (Kamoche and Cunha, 2001). The way this structure is designed differs significantly from the architecture of formal roles and processes that underlie organizations that could thrive in incrementally changing environments.

As a practice, improvisation places an emphasis on people as the determinant factor in an organization's capability to improvise, while underscoring that the right structure can play an important role in how this capability is transformed into action. This literature argues that improvising organizations need complex people working with the help of an open organizational design. In what follows we explore what each of these two conditions implies for managing organizations in fast-changing environments.

Complex people

Improvisation is an outcome of complex people, not a product of crafty complex organizational structures and cleverly prescribed processes. By complex people we mean people that are willing and able to enact the everyday improvisation that organizations need to survive in fast-changing competitive markets. Employees' willingness to improvise is related to their identity. Employees are motivated to improvise when they interpret their ability to address everyday challenges at work as central to their sense of self (e.g. Brown and Duguid, 1991). If employees interpret their identity as only loosely coupled with successfully completing their work tasks, they can engage in a number of practices other than improvisation, such as faking the resolution or ignoring the challenges at hand. Both of these practices can allow employees to earn their bonuses or move up their career ladder, but neither can sustain a positive identity

of professional competence, if employees build that identity on successfully addressing their everyday challenges at work (see Mars, 1983).

This central role of identity in motivating improvisation underscores two important tasks for managers in fast-changing environments. The first is to foster a close link between employees' professional identity and their success in improvising to address their everyday challenges at work (Ibarra, 1999). The second is to create and support practices that keep failures in the course of improvisation from negatively affecting employees' identity (Kondo, 1990).

The first task speaks to the challenge of socialization in complex and dynamic competitive contexts (Pascale, 1985). In such contexts, identification with the organization is no longer a desired output of socialization processes. For the organization, that identification is at odds with the flexibility imposed by dynamic competitive contexts. For employees, the bonds and expectations that identification with an organization create are at odds with the type of careers that dynamic competitive markets favor – a diagonal path that crosses organizations and industries (cf. Ibarra, 2002). The challenge of an organization in dynamic competitive contexts is to shape employees' identity so that successful improvisations become the core resource for identity work (Gagliardi, 1986). When doing so, an organization needs to be careful about its socialization process by also using it as an opportunity to increase the distance between employees' professional identity and the resources they draw on in the course of their everyday work (Orlikowski, 1993). Research has shown that employees tend to draw on these resources when building and maintaining their professional identity (Van Maanen and Barley, 1984). However, research has also shown that through this process, employees crystallize their interpretation of these resources, reducing their ability to improvise (Grafton-Small and Lindstead, 1985).

The second challenge that managers face when attempting to support improvisation in their organization has to do with the identity-related threats of failures in the course of improvisation. If employees' identity hinges on their ability to successfully improvise to address everyday challenges at work, then their failure to do so will constitute a threat to their sense of self (see Goffman, 1967). On the one hand, this dynamic benefits organizational improvisation because the threat of failure will motivate reflective improvisation and drive away any of the thoughtless action often associated with this practice (Miner et al., 2001). On the other hand, the centrality of improvisation for employees' sense of self can make failure such a threat to their professional identity that employees will shun away from it for fear of not being able to keep a positive image of themselves (Weick, 1999). Managers' challenge is thus to enact a set of practices to make failures in the course of improvisation visible so that the organization can learn from them while bracketing such failures in a way that exempts their author from incorporating them in his or her identity.

Employees' ability to improvise hinges on three factors: their level of declarative knowledge, the flexibility of their procedural knowledge and their improvisational skills. Both the popular and the academic management literature argue that open organizational designs are possible because of the increased level of knowledge available in the labor market. Research on organizational improvisation, however, has shown that not all types of knowledge increase employees' ability to improvise when addressing everyday challenges at work. The literature on management improvisation has argued that the complex people that organizations in fast-changing markets need possess a high level of declarative knowledge and a relatively lower level of procedural knowledge (cf. Moorman and Miner, 1998). Declarative knowledge is the knowledge of 'what' and 'why'. This is knowledge about the features and the varieties of experiences, mental maps and resources – the ability to classify the elements of everyday experience at work in a way that fosters action. It is also knowledge about the antecedents,

the process and the outcomes of such elements. Such knowledge allows employees to appropriate the elements of their everyday experience at work in a creative and playful way, which fosters successful improvisation (Turner, 1982). Improvisation, however, is hindered by procedural knowledge – the knowledge of 'how'. This is knowledge about the necessary steps to achieve a certain outcome and knowledge about the standard way of using available resources. Research on organizational improvisation has shown that this type of knowledge hinders creativity and flexibility (Hatch, 1999). Instead, procedural knowledge fosters canonical uses of resources and compliance with implicit or explicit standard procedures. The point, however, is not to argue that employees should keep their procedural knowledge to a minimum. Instead the point is to highlight that employees' ability to improvise depends on the flexibility of their procedural knowledge (cf. Mann and Williams, 1960). Improvisation requires letting go of prescribed uses of resources and prescribed responses to sets of conditions for action, while drawing on these two types of prescribed elements when acting on the complex challenges of everyday work in dynamic competitive environments. There is, however, a type of procedural knowledge that directly strengthens employees' ability to improvise – procedural knowledge about the improvisational process itself (Peplowski, 1998). Accounts of improvisation in jazz, theater and organizations all agree that improvisation is an acquired skill (Vera and Crossan, 2004). Learning how to improvise, however, can only be accomplished through the practice of improvisation. It cannot be learned *in vitro*, away from everyday work. But it does need to be learned. It is not a trait that individuals possess or not. Creative and flexible appropriation of prescribed elements of everyday experience at work is not easily achieved. Training, supervision and reward practices tend to reinforce prescribed work practices. To depart from those practices in a way that successfully deals with the unprescribed elements of everyday challenges at work is not easily learned – and the more unprescribed challenges are, the more difficult it is to depart from the world of prescription to that of improvisation (Weick, 1993a). Complex people are thus not so much a resource that the organization can procure, they are more of an outcome of a set of management processes and practices.

Open designs

Developing and coordinating complex workers, as outlined above, allows and requires organizational designs that are more open than those used to coordinate and control 'simple' employees. We draw on three sets of sources to outline the main design principles that foster an organizational capability to improvise: research on organizational improvisation, research on unprescribed work in organizations and the literature on designing organizations from flexibility and change. Research on organizational improvisation (e.g. Miner et al., 2001) has explained how teams and projects need to be organized to take advantage of the complex skills of expert improvisers. These studies, however, have yet to fully address the design principles that allow organizations themselves to become spaces of improvisation and innovation. The literature on unprescribed work (e.g. Baker et al., 1999; Ezzamel et al., 2001) has documented a number of features that foster improvised practices, but these insights have been limited to the informal side of organizations and has yet to be translated into principles that can be applied to their formal side. These two streams of research thus provide useful insights that can be systematized into an open organizational design that provides complex people the structure they need to improvise when dealing with changing competitive contexts. To articulate the main features of such a design we draw on the principles laid out by theorizing on how to build organizations for flexibility and change (Hedberg et al., 1976; Weick, 1993b). As these authors suggest, the core tenet that organizational design needs to follow when creating flexible organizations is to create open designs that can be improvised on by workers in the course of their everyday work. This is supported by specific design choices when configuring coordination mechanisms, control mechanisms and resource distribution.

COORDINATION MECHANISMS

The literature on coordination suggests that complex people engaging in ambiguous and challenging tasks can only be coordinated through a strong culture that places an emphasis on trust (Ouchi, 1980). The argument is that the ambiguity that such tasks entail can only be overcome by building strong ties among workers anchored on shared values and beliefs. However, research on organizing in dynamic competitive environments has shown that reducing ambiguity at the task level reduces the amount of variety at the organizational level, thus reducing the organization's adaptivity (Church, 1999; Lane and Maxfield, 1996; Perrow, 1986). Studies of coordination in loosely coupled systems suggest an alternative design for coordination mechanisms. This design prescribes a minimal structure that can then be improvised upon by agents, allowing them to take advantage of ambiguity and variety (Kamoche and Cunha, 2001). Choosing this minimal structure requires looking at what is at the core of coordination in each specific type of organization.

Research on new product development in fast-changing, competitive environments suggests that prescribing the temporal structure that grounds everyday work, such as project deadlines and milestones, fosters coordination without limiting flexibility (e.g. Eisenhardt et al., 1995). The goal here is to prescribe outcomes without prescribing their content. Prescribing outcomes limits flexibility because it restricts improvisation to production processes. These studies have found that prescribing milestones at which new product development teams need to reach successive stages towards their final product, fosters coordination and flexibility.

Milestones foster coordination because they force teams to generate an artifact, which can be anything from a sketch of the product to a final prototype (cf. Carlile, 2002). Teams have to bring their ideas and work together into a tangible product. They have no choice but to find ways to integrate their work, even if only temporarily. Milestones foster flexibility because they create a sequence of immediate and important challenges. Research on improvisation in organizations has shown that challenges that are not immediate or important may be addressed in ways that hinder flexibility. Challenges that are important but not immediate can be addressed through prescribed planning processes where flexibility often falls prey to group dynamics and organizational tradition (Dougherty, 1992a). Challenges that are immediate but that are not interpreted as important can be addressed through 'faking' (Hatch, 1999). When faking, employees improvise on the symptoms of challenges, not on challenges themselves, thus creating a façade of success by hiding the presence of problems or opportunities. Challenges that are both immediate and important motivate improvisation because they are interpreted as tightly coupled with employees' interests and because they offer no space from planning to be separated from action (Crossan, 1998). Research on coordination in open-source projects has shown that programming code can be used as a minimal structure to coordinate programmers' efforts (Koch and Schneider, 2002). Open source code can be used effectively as a coordination mechanism without limiting ambiguity and flexibility because it is, at the same time, an open resource and a shared product. Research on open-source software development has shown that programmers interpret code as a flexible resource open to a wide multiplicity of uses through bricolage (Lakhani and von Hippel, 2002). Code can be improvised upon in many creative ways to come up with a variety of solutions to programming challenges. However, code is also a shared product in which all members of an open-source project have a stake and which also has to perform a specified function when compiled. Individual contributions can thus not only be evaluated by peer review but also by actually compiling the code and running it. This allows open source development teams to escape the constraining group dynamics peer review alone would foster.

When improvising, agents draw on minimal structures such as these to engage in organizational design as action unfolds. Agents improvise local coordination practices that allow them to engage in increasingly complex coordination tasks. Bastien and Hostager (1995) and Meyerson et al., (1996) have shown that groups are able to engage in complex coordination tasks without having any prior experience of interaction and even without discussing any processes or rules for interaction. These groups are able to achieve local coordination by growing through a process of mutual adjustment as they engage in tasks of increasing complexity. They follow what Bastien and Hostager (1995) call a 'centering strategy', learning to work together by cooperating in tasks that are increasingly difficult and ambiguous and using this process to learn about how to work with each other and how to work together as a group.

CONTROL MECHANISMS

Control mechanisms are an important element of organizational design because they are channels for information about employees' work and performance. Research on control in organizations has shown that managers use this information for two purposes. One is to prevent, detect and correct deviations from prescribed processes and outcomes (Sallaz, 2002). The other is to learn about their employees' performance, the effectiveness of their organization's strategy and its competitive position (Tyre and von Hippel, 1999).

Although control mechanisms are, in essence, a management tool, they are also used by employees. Research on unprescribed work has shown that employees need information about their own work and the work of others to carry out their everyday tasks (Rosenthal, 2004). Because control systems are designed in accordance with managers' interests, employees need to improvise their own control mechanisms and information systems. This, however, reduces the organization's ability to learn and, consequently, limits its flexibility because these improvised control mechanisms are not available to the organization as a whole. Employees' improvisations are local and isolated phenomena that have little, if any impact on the organization's strategic direction (for an example, see Orlikowski, 1996).

To make information about market challenges available to the whole organization and to diffuse successful improvisations, organizations need to design open control mechanisms. By open control mechanisms we mean control systems that can be improvised upon to suit local conditions while remaining visible to the whole organization. There are two design principles that managers can draw on to achieve this end. The first is to focus on learning. This means designing control systems from an approach that treats the information they produce as an opportunity for learning, not as an opportunity to enforce compliance. The difference between these two approaches hinges in how they address outliers. The 'enforcing' approach treats outliers as an indicator of deviance which needs to be corrected. The 'learning' approach treats outliers as deviations that need to be explored further. Making one of these approaches more salient is, in essence, an outcome of managers' everyday practices (cf. Watson, 2001). However, there are design practices that can support the 'learning' approach. Some examples of these practices include doing away with 'traffic light' systems that signal outliers as red lights and league tables that rank outliers at the bottom of hierarchies based on performance (see Zuboff, 1988).

The second design principle for open control mechanisms is to focus on validity even if at the expense of reliability. What matters in complex markets is quality of information, not consistency of calculation. This means, for example, that the formula for measurements such as sales pipeline needs to be flexible enough to allow salespeople and sales managers to incorporate in it their own tacit knowledge of the market. It also means focusing on a few crucial measurements instead of trying to build a control system that provides a complex array of information. The goal is to give each manager the information that she or he needs to make sense of their market and their organization.

These practices improve the quality of information by trusting employees and their managers to share a commitment to the organization's success. Research has shown that this level of trust can be achieved by giving everyone visibility of everybody else's information (McAllister, 1995; Rindova and Starbuck, 1997; Strickland, 1958). Visibility allows peer-surveillance, motivating employees and managers to think carefully about their information production practices.

As a whole, this approach to control limits managers' ability to differentiate deviation from deviance. The focus on learning requires managers to resist the temptation to enforce compliance because by doing so they would risk pushing adaptive deviations underground, reducing their strategic impact. This, however, is only an apparent limitation. Research on unprescribed work in organizations has consistently shown that formal control systems are vulnerable to employees' improvisations to hide their unprescribed work (e.g. Crozier, 1964; Gouldner, 1954; Lipsky, 1980; Suchman, 1995). Compliance may be more important in the 'enforcing' approach to control than it is for 'learning' approach. However, both approaches' ability to enforce it is equally limited.

RESOURCE ALLOCATION

Open organizational designs need to provide employees with resources that they can use to enact local cooperation and control mechanisms that support improvisation. The literature on improvisation is, at first, of little help in specifying the features of such resources: on the one hand, it describes improvisers as specialists that are skilled in the use of a limited-purpose set of tools (e.g. Barrett, 1998); on the other hand, other studies on this topic describe improvisers as bricoleurs that are able to make do with whatever resources they have at hand (Berry and Irvine, 1986; Weick, 1993a). This paradox is probably related to the low number of empirical studies of improvisation in organizations relative to the high volume of theorizing on this topic (see Cunha et al., 1999). The few empirical studies available show that employees improvise with available tools and resources. Because most of these studies are carried out in new product development processes, available tools and resources are specialized. However, accounts of improvisation in unprescribed work processes suggest that even in new product development, improvisation thrives on resources that are flexible enough to be used in multiple ways (Dougherty, 1992b; von Hippel, 1994). This suggests three design principles for managers that want to draw on complex people to deal with dynamic competitive environments. The first is to seek a minimal level of specialization when defining resources and tools. By minimal specialization we mean maximizing the flexibility of tools and resources. This begins by the criteria for selecting the resources and tools made available for each role and project. The point here is not to focus on customizable or 'radically taylorable resources' (cf. Malone et al., 1992). Research on unprescribed work in factory settings (e.g. Burawoy, 1979) has shown that people with an improvisational disposition are able to make do with even very specialized tools and resources. Instead the point is to seek resources that are simple enough to allow employees to focus all their efforts in the act of improvising, instead of being limited by their level of proficiency with these artifacts (Kamoche et al., 2003). Minimal specialization of resources also includes seeking contractual arrangements that allow the organization to change its resource mix as competitive challenges demand and a set of values and beliefs that foster an interpretation of tools and resources as flexible and open to bricolage.

Second, when designing an organization managers need to grant employees the ability to do their own resource allocation. The material aspect of resources and tools means that they need to be dispersed throughout their organization. Independently of how optimized resource and tool distribution is, the dynamic nature of competitive challenges in fast-changing markets means that at some point in time resources and tools are going to be required in a place other than where they were first allocated. At these times, the organization needs unprescribed cooperation channels through which tools and resources can move to where they are needed (Allen and Cohen, 1969; Krackhardt and Hanson, 1993; Ouchi and Jaeger, 1978). Recent research on unprescribed work has shown that these channels do not need to be supported by personal ties. Instead, organizations can design prescribed communication channels in ways that facilitate their appropriation for unprescribed cooperation (see examples in Heath and Luff, 2000).

Finally, and to fully address the issue of providing resources that support improvisation, it is necessary to go back and think about the materiality of coordination and control processes. The keyword here is visibility. Research has shown that organizations already have control and coordination mechanisms that are used to engage in improvisation (Orlikowski, 1996). However, the resources used to build these systems – post-it notes, paper notebooks and private Microsoft Excel spreadsheets – need a considerable amount of effort to decode and share with others. As the material record of unexpected competitive challenges and the improvisations enacted to deal with remain invisible, so do these challenges and improvisations. The goal is then to provide employees with resources that are 'ready-at-hand' enough to be used to scaffold everyday improvisations which facilitate shared learning by helping making this work visible.

As a whole, the purpose of creating coordination mechanisms, control mechanisms and resource allocations that together constitute an open organizational design is to, as Hedberg et al. (1976) put it, build an 'organizational tent' that employees can setup and change fast enough to keep pace with complex dynamic environments.

CONCLUSION

The purpose of this chapter was to use the concept of improvisation as a scaffold to understand the managerial challenges created by fast-changing competitive environments. The core of our argument was that the high level of improvisational capability that these environments require call for open organizational designs that allow 'complex' employees to respond to competitive challenges as these unfold. This places a number of challenges for managers when designing their organizations and leading their employees, as we outlined above. All of these challenges add up to a specification of the managers' job. Managers need to maintain a high level of improvisation and innovation in their organizations to be able to cope with dynamic markets. These levels of change need people that are willing and able to improvise, people that value and seek change and novelty. However, it is not enough to hold the commitment of this type of employees to the organization. Improvisers and innovators need a structure that they can draw on to create local coordination and control mechanisms and get access to the resources they need to act on environmental threats and opportunities as these unfold. It is in achieving this synthesis between ambiguity and organizing that lies the manager's job.

REFERENCES

Aldrich, H. (1979) *Organizations and Environments*. Englewood Cliffs, NJ: Prentice-Hall.

Allen, T.J. and Cohen, S.I. (1969) 'Information flow in research and development laboratories'. *Administrative Science Quarterly*. 14 (1): 12–19.

Baker, G., Gibbons, R. and Murphy, K.J. (1999) 'Informal authority in organizations'. *Journal of Law Economics & Organization*. 15 (1): 56–73.

Barnard, C. (1938) *The Functions of the Executive*. Cambridge, MA: Harvard University Press.

Barrett, F.J. (1998) 'Coda: Creativity and improvisation in organizations: Implications for organizational learning'. *Organization Science*. 9 (5): 605–622.

Bastien, D.T. and Hostager, T.J. (1995) 'On cooperation: A replication of an experiment in jazz cooperation'. *Comportamento Organizacional e Gestão*. 2 (1): 33–46.

Berry, J.W. and Irvine, S.H. (1986) 'Bricolage: Savages do it daily', in Sternberg, R.J. and Wagner, R.K. (eds), *Practical Intelligence: Nature and Origins of Competence in the Everyday World*. Cambridge: Cambridge University Press, pp. 271–306.

Brown, J.S. and Duguid, P. (1991) 'Organizational learning and communities-of-practice: Toward a unified view of working, learning and innovation'. *Organization Science*. 2 (1): 40–57.

Brown, S.L. and Eisenhardt, K.M. (1997) 'The art of continuous change: Linking complexity theory and time-paced evolution in relentlessly shifting organizations'. *Administrative Science Quarterly*. 42: 1–34.

Burawoy, M. (1979) *Manufacturing Consent: Changes in the Labor Process Under Monopoly Capitalism*. Chicago, IL: University of Chicago Press.

Burns, T. and Stalker, G.M. (1961) *The Management of Innovation*. London: Tavistock.

Carlile, P. (2002) 'A pragmatic view of knowledge and boundaries: Boundary objects in new product development'. *Organization Science*. 13 (4): 442–455.

Child, J. (2005) *Organization*, 2nd ed. London: Blackwell.

Church, M. (1999) 'Organizing simply for complexity: Beyond metaphor towards theory'. *Long Range Planning*, 32 (4): 425–440.

Crossan, M.M. (1998) 'Improvisation in action'. *Organization Science*. 9 (5): 593–599.

Crozier, M. (1964) *The Bureaucratic Phenomenon*. Chicago, IL: University of Chicago Press.

Cunha, M.P., Cunha, J.V. and Kamoche, K. (1999) 'Organizational improvisation: What, when, how and why'. *International Journal of Management Reviews*. 1 (3): 299–341.

Dougherty, D. (1992a) 'Interpretive barriers to successful product innovation in large firms'. *Organization Science*. 3: 179–202.

Dougherty, D. (1992b) 'A practice centered model of organizational renewal through product innovation'. *Strategic Management Journal*. 13: 77–92.

Dougherty, D. and Hardy, C. (1996) 'Sustained product innovation in large mature organizations: Overcoming innovation-to-organization problems'. *Academy of Management Journal*. 39 (5): 1120–1153.

Eisenhardt, K.M. and Tabrizi, B.N. (1995) 'Accelerating adaptive processes: Product innovation in the global computer industry'. *Administrative Science Quarterly*, 40: 84–110.

Ezzamel, M., Willmott, H. and Frank, W. (2001) 'Power, control and resistance in "the factory that time forgot"'. *Journal of Management Studies*, 38 (8): 1053–1079.

Fayol, H. (1949) *General and Industrial Management*. New York, NY: Pitman.

Ford, H. and Crowther, S. (1926) *Today and Tomorrow*. Garden City, NY: Doubleday Page.

Foster, R. and Kaplan, S. (2001) *Creative Destruction: Why Companies that are Built to Last Underperform the Market and How to Successfully Transform Them*. New York, NY: Doubleday Page.

Gagliardi, P. (1986) 'The creation and change of organizational cultures: A conceptual framework'. *Organization Studies*. 7 (2): 117–134.

Goffman, E. (1967) *Interaction Ritual: Essays on Face-to-Face Behavior*. New York, NY: Pantheon Books.

Gouldner, A.W. (1954) *Patterns of Industrial Bureaucracy*. New York, NY: Free Press.

Grafton-Small, R. and Lindstead, S.A. (1985) 'The everyday professional: Skill in the symbolic management of occupational kinship', in Strati, A. (ed.), *The Symbolics of Skill*, Vol. 5, No. 6. Trento, pp. 53–67.

Hatch, M.J. (1999) 'Exploring the empty spaces of organizing: How improvisational jazz helps redescribe organizational structure'. *Organization Studies*. 20 (1): 75–100.

Heath, C. and Luff, P. (2000) *Technology in Action*. Cambridge; New York: Cambridge University Press.

Hedberg, B.L.T., Nystrom, P.C. and Starbuck, W.H. (1976) 'Camping on seesaws: Prescriptions for self-designing organizations'. *Administrative Science Quarterly*. 21: 41–65.

Ibarra, H. (1999) 'Provisional selves: Experimenting with image and identity in professional adaptation'. *Administrative Science Quarterly*. 44: 764–791.

Ibarra, H. (2002) 'How to stay stuck in the wrong career'. *Harvard Business Review*. 80 (12): 40–47.

Kamoche, K. and Cunha, M.P. (2001) 'Minimal structures: From jazz improvisation to product innovation'. *Organization Studies*. 22 (4): 733–764.

Kamoche, K., Cunha, M.P. and Cunha, J. (2003) 'Towards a theory of organizational improvisation: Looking beyond the jazz metaphor'. *Journal of Management Studies*. 40 (8): 2023–2051.

Koch, S. and Schneider, G. (2002) 'Effort, co-operation and co-ordination in an open source software project: GNOME'. *Information Systems Journal*. 12 (1): 27–42.

Kondo, D. (1990) *Crafting Selves: Power, Discourse and Identity in a Japanese Factory*. Chicago, IL: University of Chicago Press.

Krackhardt, D. and Hanson, J.R. (1993) 'Informal networks: The company behind the charts'. *Harvard Business Review*. 71 (4): 104–111.

Lakhani, K. and von Hippel, E. (2002) 'How open source software works: "Free" user-to-user assistance'. *Research Policy*. 32: 923–943.

Lane, D. and Maxfield, R. (1996) 'Strategy under complexity: Fostering generative relationships'. *Long Range Planning*. 29 (2): 215–231.

Levinthal, D.A. (1997) 'Adaptation on rugged landscapes'. *Management Science*. 43 (7): 934–950.

Lipsky, M. (1980) *Street-Level Bureaucracy: Dilemmas of the Individual in Public Services*. New York, NY: Russell Sage Foundation.

McAllister, D.J. (1995) 'Affect and cognition based trust as foundations for interpersonal cooperation in organizations'. *Academy of Management Journal*. 38 (1): 24–59.

McGrath, R.G. (2001) 'Exploratory learning, innovative capacity, and managerial oversight'. *Academy of Management Journal*. 44 (1): 118–131.

Malone, T.W., Lai, K.Y. and Fry, C. (1992) *Experiments with OVAL: A Radically Tailorable Tool for Cooperative Work*. Paper presented at the Proceedings from the conference on computer supported cooperative work, Toronto, Canada.

Mann, F.C. and Williams, L.K. (1960) 'Observations on the dynamics of a change to electronic data-processing equipment'. *Administrative Science Quarterly*. 5: 217–256.

Mars, G. (1983) *Cheats at Work: An Anthropology of Workplace Crime*. London: Unwin Paperbacks.

Meyerson, D., Weick, K.E. and Kramer, R.M. (1996) 'Swift trust and temporary groups', in Kramer, R.M. and Tyler, T.R. (eds), *Trust in Organizations: Frontiers of Theory and Research*. Thousand Oaks, CA: Sage, pp. 166–195.

Miner, A.S., Bassoff, P. and Moorman, C. (2001) 'Organizational improvisation and learning: A field study'. *Administrative Science Quarterly*. 46 (2): 304–337.

Moorman, C. and Miner, A. (1998) 'Organizational improvisation and organizational memory'. *Academy of Management Review*. 23 (4): 698–723.

Orlikowski, W.J. (1993) 'CASE tools as organizational change: Investigating increment'. *MIS Quarterly*. 17 (3): 309–339.

Orlikowski, W.J. (1996) 'Improvising organizational transformation over time: A situated change perspective'. *Information Systems Research*. 7 (1): 63–92.

Ouchi, W.G. (1980) 'Markets, bureaucracies and clans'. *Administrative Science Quarterly*. 25: 129–141.

Ouchi, W.G. and Jaeger, A. (1978) 'Type Z organization: Stability in the midst of mobility'. *Academy of Management Review*. 3: 305–314

Pascale, R.T. (1985) 'The paradox of "corporate culture": Reconciling ourselves with socialization'. *California Management Review.* 27: 26–41.

Peplowski, K. (1998) 'The process of improvisation'. *Organization Science.* 9 (5): 560–561.

Perrow, C. (1986) *Complex Organizations,* 3rd ed. New York, NY: Random House.

Rindova, V.P. and Starbuck, W.H. (1997) 'Distrust in dependence: The ancient challenge of superiorsubordinate relations', in Clark, T. (ed.), *Advancement in Organization Behaviour: Essays in Honour of Derek Pugh.* Brookfield, VT: Ashgate Publishing.

Romanelli, E. and Tushman, M.L. (1994) 'Organizational transformation as punctuated equilibrium: An empirical test'. *Academy of Management Journal.* 37 (5): 1141–1166.

Rosenthal, P. (2004) 'Management control as an employee resource: The case of front-line service workers'. *Journal of Management Studies.* 41 (4): 601–622.

Sallaz, J.J. (2002) 'The house rules: Autonomy and interests among service workers in the contemporary casino industry'. *Work and Occupations.* 29 (4): 394–427.

Sloan, A.P. (1964) *My Years with General Motors.* Garden City, NY: Doubleday Page.

Strickland, L.H. (1958) 'Surveillance and trust'. *Journal of Personality.* 26: 200–215.

Suchman, L.A. (1995) 'Making work visible'. *Communications of the ACM.* 38 (9): 56–61.

Taylor, F.W. (1947) *Scientific Management.* New York, NY: Harper and Row.

Turner, V. (1982) *From Ritual to Theatre: The Human Seriousness of Play.* New York, NY: PAJ Publications.

Tyre, M. and von Hippel, E. (1999) 'The situated nature of adaptive learning in organizations'. *Organization Science.* 8: 71–83.

Van Maanen, J.E. and Barley, S.R. (1984) 'Occupational communities: Culture and control in organizations', in Staw, B.M. and Cummings, L.L. (eds), *Research in Organizational Behavior,* Vol. 6. Greenwich, CT: JAI Press, pp. 287–365.

Vera, D. and Crossan, M.M. (2004) 'Theatrical improvisation: Lessons for organizations'. *Organization Studies.* 25: 727–749.

von Hippel, E. (1994) "'Sticky information" and the locus of problem solving: Implications for innovation'. *Management Science.* 40 (4): 429–439.

Watson, T.J. (2001) *In Search of Management: Culture, Chaos and Control in Managerial Work* (Rev. edn). London: Thomson Learning.

Weick, K.E. (1987) 'Substitutes for strategy', in Teece, D.J. (ed.), *Competitive Challenge.* Cambridge, MA: Ballinger Publishing, pp. 221–233.

Weick, K.E. (1993a) 'The collapse of sensemaking in organizations: The Man Gulch disater'. *Administrative Science Quarterly.* 38: 628–652.

Weick, K.E. (1993b) 'Organizational redesign as improvisation', in Huber, G.P. and Glick, W.H. (eds), *Organizational Change and Redesign.* New York, NY: Oxford University Press, pp. 346–379.

Weick, K.E. (1999) 'The aesthetic of imperfection in organizations'. *Comportamento Organizacional e Gestão.* 5 (1): 5–22.

Zuboff, S. (1988) *In the Age of the Smart Machine.* New York, NY: Basic Books.

Researching the Private–Collective Innovation Model

Georg von Krogh

Innovation benefits firms, economies and societies. An innovation model explains why, and under what conditions, innovation is likely to occur and is, therefore, a central topic in management and organization research. There are currently three major innovation models (von Hippel and von Krogh, 2003). First, in the *private model of innovation*, innovators step forward and invest in process and product innovation if and when they can appropriate the financial returns from these investments. Intellectual property protection mechanisms, such as patents, copyrights and trade secrets, aid the innovator in collecting these benefits. Any uncompensated third-party access to the benefits from the innovation incurs losses for the innovator.

Second, in the *collective-action model of innovation*, innovators contribute to a public good innovation, characterized by the non-rivalry of benefits and non-excludable access to the good. However, since anyone can benefit from a public good, potential innovators may wait for others to step forward and contribute to the innovation. In response to this problem, incentives must be designed so that potential innovators invest, despite the option to free-ride: deflection must be punished and contributions to the public good innovation rewarded. When these incentives are effective, the access for all to the benefits offered by the public good innovation should not represent a loss to the innovator.

Third, drawing upon insights from the previous models, the *private-collective model of innovation* explains under what conditions the innovator's rewards from public good innovation intersect with their rewards from private investment in innovation. The model suggests that the innovator's rewards from the *process* of innovation surpass the rewards available to any free-rider on the public good innovation. While the innovation is freely accessible to all, making a private investment in innovation requires involvement in the innovation process. In turn, process involvement incurs costs and garners rewards for the innovator. The model predicts that public good innovation will occur when process-related rewards exceed process-related costs.

For example, open source software development is now a widespread cultural as well as an economic phenomenon. Instead of the traditional model of software production, where companies hide the details of software code for fear that its value will erode, open source software is generated by the collaboration of thousands of volunteers who agree to share the resulting software product for free. The Internet has enabled these worldwide communities to work together creating, most famously, products such as Linux, an operating system so ubiquitous it runs a fifth of the world's servers.

A puzzle that has triggered research on this phenomenon for several years is this: why should developers release their software product as a public good innovation, rather than applying intellectual property rights to protect it and then profit from licensing it to a third party? According to the private-collective innovation model, open source software developers invest private funds to solve their own technical problems, such as getting an open source software office suite to run on their own computers. However, they benefit from sharing the software with others who test it on their computers, identify, and fix bugs. Compared to software development 'in private', developers save costs in arriving at a well-functioning technical solution to their own problems. When forming a community with others who share common interest in the software product, the developers also enhance their skills and learn about design philosophies, a broader range of technical problems and solutions. Some may find this mode of working stimulating and even benefit from a strong reputation based on their contributions to the community. None of these rewards are available to free-riders who may benefit from the software by using it, but who do not take part in the innovation process.

The private-collective innovation model leads to several exciting research imperatives (von Krogh and von Hippel, 2006). Future studies need to examine in more detail the functioning of the model. It will be important to understand the motives for entrepreneurs to launch innovation projects: while the incentive structure for sustaining the innovation process is known, much less clarity exists regarding the early investment of private funds in public good innovations. Moreover, future research also needs to shed more light on the role of leadership in private-collective innovation. How do leaders emerge and act in innovation communities and what motivates them to contribute their time and effort in the first place? A related issue concerns governance: what are models of project and community governance and how do they impact on the success of a public good innovation? Future work also needs to uncover what factors cause the innovation model to break down. Rapid and unforeseen changes in incentives and market structure, lack of entrepreneurship, ineffective leadership, weak governance, alongside other factors, may contribute to the failure to create public good innovation.

Finally, research needs to examine private-collective innovation beyond open source software, in other industries and fields. Consider a couple of examples where the model flourishes. In the biotechnology industry, firms, universities and scientists increasingly make the tools for life sciences available under 'open-source-like' licences (for example, in agricultural biotechnology). The 'Science Commons' project aims at making public access to scientific results easier in a number of scientific areas, ranging from neuroscience to geography. NASA has adopted open-source principles as part of its Mars mission, asking for volunteers to help draw a map of the Red Planet. ThinkCycle, a Web-based industrial design project, brings together engineers, designers, academics, students and professionals from a variety of disciplines who collaborate in creating a huge variety of technical designs that are made openly accessible to the public. We invite researchers to join us in identifying the plethora of strategies whereby such communities of innovators develop tools and techniques for augmenting rewards and mitigating the cost of public good innovation.

REFERENCES

von Hippel, E. and von Krogh, G. (2003) 'Open source software development and the private-collective innovation model: Issues for organization science'. *Organization Science.* 14 (2): 208–223.
von Krogh, G. and von Hippel, E. (2006) 'The promise of research on open source software'. *Management Science.* 52 (7): 975–983.

PART 3

Acting on Organizations

Performing the Organization: Organization Theatre and Imaginative Life as Physical Presence*

Timothy Clark

INTRODUCTION

The so-called dramaturgical metaphor has been a popular and productive framework within which to analyse organizational and social life for some time. Whilst it has utilized two broad approaches – Kenneth Burke's (1945, 1969a, b) *dramatism*[1] and Erving Goffman's work on *dramaturgy*[2] (1959) – the great majority of this work has drawn on the latter framework with the consequence that the notion of theatre has been used metaphorically. Such a focus has resulted in a general failure to recognize that life is not *like* theatre but that it *is* theatre. The occurrence of drama in everyday life is no longer a matter of metaphor but of form: life is increasingly becoming theatrical and performative in character. In the media we are confronted with a world dominated by idealized images that seek to capture audience attention by creating a spectacular universe of glossy surfaces. Examples include advertising, news stories, celebrity magazines, tourist attractions, political and sporting events, popular music and so-called 'reality' television programmes. Customer service encounters are staged and carefully scripted. The reputations of corporate and political leaders are influenced by their ability to deliver authentic performances. Underpinning all of these examples is a reliance on an ensemble of theatrical practices to create compelling performances and so carefully and strategically manage the impressions of targeted audiences. As Young (1990) has noted, the greater part of our so-called developed world constitutes a *dramaturgical society*. One in which 'the technologies of social science, mass communication, theatre, and the arts are used to manage attitudes, behaviours and feelings of the population' (Young, 1990: 71).

Throughout Western industrialized societies the services of 'expert technicians, research institutes doing surveys, polls and samples, theatrical people, mass communications, are disproportionately available to large-scale organizations' (ibid: 71). The task of these 'functionaries' is to 'use the accoutrements of the theatre, the findings of social science, and the facilities of the mass media to generate an 'informed' public – formed in the image of the purchaser of such services' (ibid: 72).

Whilst the emergence of a dramaturgical society has been acknowledged as part of the more general performative turn within organization studies (Pine and Gilmour, 1999; Thrift, 2000; Mangham, 2001; Mangham and Overington, 1983, 1987), there has been a tendency to focus on the deployment of the techniques of theatre outwardly into the market place to generate attractive experiences/images for consumers. This chapter recognizes that the technology of theatre is increasingly being turned inward to manage employees within the organization. It is therefore concerned with the backstage rather than front stage deployment of theatre. Such a focus shifts our understandings beyond the narrow confines of the metaphorical approach to theatre and refreshes and broadens our conceptions of theatre in organizations by encouraging conceptual and empirical scrutiny of the actual *use* of theatrical techniques and theatre *within* organizations. Building on this focus I begin by discussing theatre as a resource before turning to theatre as technology. I conclude by outlining several potentially fruitful avenues for future research in the area.

THEATRE AS A RESOURCE

There is a burgeoning activity in the use of theatre as a resource to stimulate and enliven training programmes through the deployment of theatrical texts, scenarios, games and activities derived from rehearsal processes. As in arts-based education (Jackson, 1993) the intention is to rupture participants' taken-for-granted assumptions by developing opportunities for imaginative play through the use of alternative, perhaps unusual and tangential ways of seeing. In this way new understanding is created as the conventional is dissolved and re-imagined under the exhilarating and intense spotlight of the extraordinary. One stream of work is concerned with drawing on selective readings of Shakespeare to inform leadership training (Arkin, 2005; Augustine and Adelman, 1999; Burnham, et al., 2001; Corrigan, 2000; Jackson, 2001; Mangham, 2001; Shafritz, 1999; Whitney and Packer, 2000). In these accounts Henry V emerges as the Shakespearean role model for contemporary senior management. Building on the popularity of this analogy, Cranfield School of Management in the UK organized an event created by Richard Olivier (son of the late Lord Olivier) called 'Stepping into Leadership with Henry V'.[3] Such courses intend to create highly adaptive and malleable performance spaces in which audiences are challenged through the presentation of the unexpected or unusual – applying and thinking about Henry V in relation to their working lives. As one delegate at such a course remarked:

> I'd always considered the last act of Henry V a complete waste of time after the action of the earlier acts, but it suddenly got through to me that you can't always be fighting the battle of Agincourt. There's no point unless you learn how to consolidate and build on your victories. I found it a completely new way of looking at issues in leadership and management. (McKee, 1999: 27)

That part of it concerned with the deployment of theatre games and techniques in training sessions is relatively poorly documented, although articles occasionally surface in the press attesting to the benefits of such activities (Ashworth, 1999; Keene, 1999; Kellaway, 2005; Olivier, 2001). In a review of these events Ashworth (1999) gives a number of examples:

> Oxford Stage Company, based in Warwick, ran a workshop for Sainsbury showing how much can be communicated through body language alone … Trade Secrets, another training company, ran a series of communication workshops in Sainsbury's stores to accompany a national tour of Twelfth Night … Body & Soul, based in Gloucestershire, has workers drumming along in harmony – by teaching them Rio Carnival-style samba percussion.

Employees without a musical bone in their body are magically transformed into rhythmic, pulsating beasts. It helps to increase their self-confidence and teaches them to work together ... Other activities from Body & Soul include having one member of a team describe a picture to another who is blindfolded and asking the group to shuffle round to form a perfect circle ... Others rely on variations on conventional training, such as having some poor soul assemble a puzzle blindfolded while team members honk instructions on musical instruments ... Lively Arts, based in London, gets participants to stage their own performances with the help of performers and technical staff drawn from opera, theatre, circus and film. One group of UK business consultants on a 'bonding' trip to Lisbon were given a week in which to create an entire opera – a refreshing variation on the usual team-building games. The effect was exhilarating. One participant said: 'You forget most conferences within two days. We will remember this retreat in detail until we are 85'.

While we might note the apparent absurdity of such events and question their purpose and value, these examples are indicative of the theatrical turn within training. This is no longer a marginal activity. It is not something that can be avoided. Training is increasingly becoming a performative activity in which participants are being asked to step-out of their work roles and adopt another character in the hope that they come to embody some aspect of this role permanently. Thus, in putting on make-up people are afforded the opportunity to change the make-up of their own character in some way. The way in which these events are claimed to work is by making the 'invisible visible', the 'unknown known' and the undiscussable discussable (Thrift, 2000: 680; Barry, 1994: 37) by portraying selected features of the organization to its members in a fun and palatable way. I shall discuss what this might imply for future research later in the chapter.

THEATRE AS TECHNOLOGY

The second emerging approach to the use of theatre in organizations is literally that – the use of theatre in organizations. It is also the one that has perhaps received the least attention. This involves the deployment by an organization of dramatists, actors, directors, set designers, lighting specialists, and musicians to put on performances in front of an audience. In reviewing the present literature on theatre in organizations four forms can be identified: corporate, radical, organizational and situational. Although, as will be explained shortly, these approaches differ in several significant ways, they nevertheless share the idea that theatre can be used to engender change in employees' attitudes and behaviours.

Figure 3.1.1 is a framework that seeks to differentiate between the various forms of organizational theatre that have been identified to date. 'The axes are based on Mangham's' (1990) notion that a theatrical performance is a triadic collusion between the playwright actor and audience and Nissley et al.'s (2004) differentiation between 'control of the role' and 'control of the script' which inturn builds on Schreyogg (2001) and Meisiek (2002). Whoever controls the script establishes the boundaries for the performance but creates an incomplete version of a possible performance. What is seen on the stage is never simply the text, but always an interpretation that is embedded in the performance and realized through it. It is the interaction between the actor and audience that gives a script form and makes it 'come alive'. The axes in the figure emphasize that the types of theatre in organizations imply different roles for the audience and variation in the extent to which a performance is modified either in its prior design or actual playing for the audience who attend.

The first form of theatre as technology Clark and Mangham (2004a) have termed *corporate theatre*. Pineault (1989: 2) offers a broad definition of corporate theatre by suggesting that it is a 'type of production which excites, motivates, and persuades its audience about a company's service, product, and/or slogan through the use of live theatrical performance'. It is informed by the conventions of Broadway, the West End, television and advertising. These are not small-scale events. They are audio-visual extravaganzas utilizing state-of-the-art technology such as revolving stages, hydraulics, lasers, complex lighting rigs, computer programming, back-projection, plasma screens and so forth.

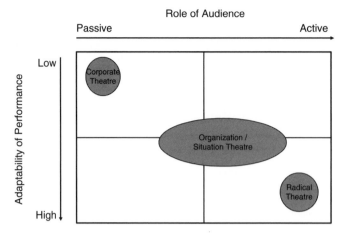

Figure 3.1.1   Typology of theatre in organizations. Based on Mangham (1990) and Nissley et al. (2004: 820–23)

Corporate theatre is located in the top left-hand corner of the figure because such performances involve the delivery of a script determined through consultation between the commissioners of the performance and the organization responsible for overseeing the event. Corporate theatre is not democratic. It is used to contain reflection and to promote the views of a particular group within an organization. The actors do not, indeed are not permitted to improvise. Control of delivery and reception is of critical importance if a single reality is to be sustained. In this form of theatre, the actors and audience are segregated, with the latter observing the former in a 'space which demands uninterrupted scrutiny' (Counsell, 1996). The audience therefore passively receive the message. They are not invited to be involved in the activities being performed. However, corporate theatre does not challenge, rather it seduces. As such it is a 'form of persuasion that entices by touching the right emotional chords, but never threatens or coerces' (Novitz, 1992: 184).

In complete contrast Coopey (1998: 365), drawing heavily upon the ideas and practice of Augusto Boal (1979),[4] puts forward the notion of *radical theatre* which he envisages being used 'directly in furthering the process of discursive exploration, release and political action'. In such an approach the performance

is initially scripted by the professional performers, but the audience, in the role of 'spectactors', are given an opportunity to intervene and become self-directed performers. A key aim of this kind of theatre is to create democratic performance spaces that permit spectators to stop the ongoing activity and become actors. Forum theatre and its associated exercises and activities appear to be designed to provide an opportunity and space for participants to open up, step back, consider the past history of their thoughts and actions, to deliberate and act-out their future thoughts and actions. 'The nature of the performance therefore emerges in consultation with audience members. Through the active participation of the audience a performance has the potential to change from the original intent. In this respect a script initially offers a set of possibilities that the audience are free to accept or reject. As the performance commences they are empowered to take-on the roles of playwright and actor simultaneously and so create something that has meaning and emancipatory possibility for them'.[5]

The final form of theatre Schreyögg terms *organization theatre* (Schreyögg and Dabitz, 1999; Schreyögg, 2001) whereas Meisiek (2002) uses the term *situation theatre*. Both refer to 'the staging of problem-oriented plays in an organizational context' that 'is used to promote problem-awareness and to stimulate a readiness to change' (Meisiek: 50). Working with members of organizations, theatre professionals and social scientists tailor make plays to deal with specific issues within specific organizations. They may use a variety of theatrical approaches – burlesque, melodrama, naturalistic – to realize the resultant drama, but the aim is emancipatory, to 'expose the audience to situations of their daily life, thereby confronting it with hidden conflicts, subconscious behavioural patterns or critical routines' (Schreyögg, 2001: 3). Both Schreyögg and Meisiek imply that the degree of audience participation and the extent of the fluidity of the performance varies. In some cases performances may mirror those of corporate theatre in that a play reflecting the interests of a particular group in the organization may be performed. In other cases, the audience and members of the organization may be involved in both the development of the script and the subsequent performance. Depending on which situation pertains, this form of theatre may fall into any one of the quadrants in Figure 3.1.1. However, existing research suggests that it is most commonly found in the top right-hand quadrant of the figure.

FUTURE DIRECTIONS OF RESEARCH

Scholarly attention to this area of activity has been very limited. A quick perusal of the list of references within this chapter will reveal only a handful of existing studies. This area therefore offers a very fertile opportunity for researchers to make a number of significant novel insights. These divide between developing deeper understandings of the use of theatre and theatrical techniques as an expanding activity within the corporate landscape and, using this site of activity to make broader contributions to debates within management and organization.

In terms of the first area, because of the previous tendency to draw upon case studies of single events or organizations we only have a very partial picture of the different kinds of agents involved in this activity (see Beirne

and Knight, 2007; Clark and Mangham, 2004a, b; Meisiek, 2002; Nissley et al., 2004; Schreyögg, 2001). Broadening our understanding necessitates a move away from an overly micro (performance-by-performance) picture of the field to developing macro mapping of the area. This means ascertaining the number and size of firms offering this type of consultancy service, the nature of the services they offer, and the character of the projects in which they are engaged in different organizations and countries in the world. At the same time there is a requirement to develop a profile of the client organizations and to understand their motivation for using such services. Such research will help to answer questions in relation to some of the following topics:

- **The extent of the activity:** How widespread is the use of theatre within/by organizations? Is it a worldwide phenomenon or restricted to a small number of countries and perhaps certain regions within them? What are the historic trends in its growth?
- **The distinctiveness of the activity:** What is distinctive about the use of theatre in contrast to other forms of consultancy intervention? When and why do organizations use this kind of intervention? What theatrical principles underpin people's approaches to work in this area? What forms of theatre are used and why?
- **The nature of performance development and delivery:** What are the objectives of theatrical assignments (motivating, informing, enlightening, persuading employees, etc.)? How are performances/events developed? Who is involved and at what points in the assignment (actors, writers, designers, senior management, employees, etc.)? What techniques and theatrical accoutrements are used? Where do the performances occur? How are these spaces designed? Who attends them? Who are the actors/performers? What is the role of the actors and the audiences during the performances? What impact do the performances have and why?

Apart from building an expanded and at the same time more nuanced picture of the activities that comprise this phenomenon, future research in this area has the potential to provide insight into broader issues within the management and organization literature. This arises from theatre providing an opportunity to experience 'imaginative life as a physical presence' (Cole, 1975: 5). Cole makes a distinction between what he calls imaginative truth and present truth. Imaginative truth satisfies our longing for coherence, but more often than not it is only something that we envisage, it is not something that is physically manifest. Present truth, on the other hand, surrounds us – it is seeable and graspable – but it lacks the coherence of imaginative form. It has already been noted several times in the chapter, although not in these precise terms, that theatre of all human activities and theatre alone provides an opportunity of experiencing imaginative truth as present truth. 'In theatre, imaginative events take on for a moment the presentness of physical events; in theatre, physical events take on for a moment the perfection of imaginative form' (Cole, 1975: 5). Everything that figures in theatre can be understood in the role that it plays in the manifestation of imaginative life as physical presence. The script is its source, the actor is the one who makes it present and the audience is those to whom the imaginative truth becomes present.

The point here is that drama is potentially liberating because it has the power to reveal the seen but unnoticed by juxtaposing the lived and experienced world with the presentation of an imagined ideal state (i.e., contrast the profane with the sacred). This has been appreciated for some time in that as Lyman and Scott (1975: 2) remind us, for the Greeks the plays that were presented at their festivals were a mimesis of ordinary everyday acting. By seeking to render the everyday 'unhidden' to an audience that was urged to adopt a position of 'wonder, astonishment and naïve puzzlement', theatre was the 'primordial social science'. The essence of this position is picked up in the work of theatrical practitioners and anthropologists, who, in turn have influenced some of those seeking to bring about change in social and organizational behaviour (Cole, 1975; Geertz, 1983; Schechner, 1988). Some, like Victor Turner (1984), an anthropologist with

a deep interest in and knowledge of theatre, acknowledges his debt to the Greeks with his notion that every society needs a form of activity through which its ways of normally perceiving, valuing, feeling and behaving may be reflexively confronted by members of that society:

... any society that hopes to be imperishable must carve out for itself a space and a period of time in which it can look honestly at itself. This honesty is not that of the scientist, who exchanges the honesty of his ego for the objectivity of his gaze. It is, rather akin to the supreme honesty of the creative artist, who, in his presentations on the stage, in the book, on canvas, in marble, in music, or in towers and houses, reserves to himself the privilege to see straight what all cultures build crooked. (Turner, 1984: 40)

This space of performance, and the culturally endorsed reflexivity that distinguishes it, Turner calls a 'liminal' space:

'They are liminal in the sense that they are suspensions of daily reality, occupying privileged spaces where people are allowed to think about how they think about the terms in which they conduct their thinking or to feel about how they feel about daily life ... groups strive to see their own reality in new ways and to generate a language verbal or non-verbal that enables them to talk about what they normally talk'. (Turner, 1984, pp. 22–23)

Theatre is clearly one such privileged space and – as we have indicated above – some working in and around organizations have sought to capitalize upon its potential to provide enlivening opportunities for members of organizations to see straight what has been built crooked. Turner argues that liminality achieves such liberating insight (i.e., thinking differently) because it is characterized by a state of 'betwixt and between'. People experience liminality as a distortion and melding of distinctions. Previous identities and statuses are suspended because people find themselves 'temporarily undefined, beyond the normative social structure. This weakens them, since they have no rights over others. But it also liberates them from structural obligations' (Turner, 1982: 27). Thus at the core of theatre is a paradox; it can make participants both more susceptible to the imagery being portrayed but also liberate them from their pre-existing states. It is in the fuzzy nexus between these two positions that future work in this area has the potential to make a significant contribution. Put more specifically, the critical issue that should inform much research in the area is how and why theatrical interventions support individual and/or organizational change?

The earlier review of various types of theatre in organizations indicates that explanations of the way in which theatrically derived events lead to change are founded on some kind of 'mirroring' process whereby people are offered contrasting experiences of an aspect of their life. In other words, through the creation of the imagined in the present, it is argued that theatre encourages audience members to reflect on their taken-for-granted assumptions and so create new ways of seeing and experiencing the world. This also applies to academic thinking in this area. Schreyögg (2001: 11), drawing on the work of Luhmann (1997), argues that theatre within organizations 'is likely to bring about a *splitting experience*, it divides the reality into two levels, the usual familiar reality view and the theatrical reality (i.e., the reality that appears on stage)'. The suggestion here is that the contrast between the two realities creates discomfort within audience members and detaches them from their 'habituated patterns of behaviour' (Schreyögg, 2001: 12). It is the achievement of relief from this unease that leads to change. Meisiek (2004) stresses the importance of understanding what happens both during and after a theatrical event. In doing so he highlights the notion of catharsis, as well as the ambiguity and uncertainty surrounding its meaning within the literature, and argues that when catharsis does occur it seems to involve a release from an emotional stirring that is brought-on by participating in or witnessing a performance.

If we combine these insights with the previous notion of performances offering liminal spaces, we can see that there are strong parallels with Lewin's (1951) model of change. He proposes a three-stage model of unfreezing (loosening people from

their taken-for-granted assumptions), moving (actions designed to bring about the desired change), and refreezing (reinforcing the desired changes). The implication of our prior discussion is that theatre offers a particularly productive space for inducing some degree of nervous tension within those who attend that makes them more susceptible to change. Indeed, the continuing growth and future popularity of this activity is linked to perceptions amongst those who purchase and participate in these events of the degree to which they are effective at engaging and 'moving' an audience in some way. In these circumstances future research activity needs to be focused on a detailed examination of intricate workings of these events. Researchers need to convey the experience of the event as a performed activity and as an aesthetic/emotional experience. Given that they are intendedly aesthetic experiences, these research efforts can draw upon and contribute to recent research on the aesthetics of organizational life (Strati, 1996; Strati and Guillet de Montoux, 2002; Taylor and Hansen, 2005). Future studies would therefore benefit from using a frame that is as far as possible derived from studies of the theatre. One possible frame is that outlined in Clark and Mangham (2004b) which offers researchers the possibility to organize their description and analysis in a manner that is isomorphic with the activities to which they will be witness. The framework comprises the following components:

1 *Commissioning the Play.* Theatre in organizations – particularly corporate theatre – is an expensive resource and whoever commissions the players has the opportunity to influence both the script and the subsequent performance. For Nissley et al. (2004) control of a piece of organization theatre is an important feature of what they term the 'politics of performance'. When examining a piece of theatre there is therefore a need to pay careful attention to the role of the commissioners in these respects: Who are they? Why have they selected this form of intervention activity? What are their objectives? Is it taken as read that their perspectives will prevail throughout? To what extent (and in what ways) do the commissioners of the events monitor the development of the script and the rehearsals

to ensure that their views of social reality are exclusively promoted? To what extent and in what ways are other perspectives permitted?

2 *The Audience.* In dealing with theatre in organizations it is necessary to consider not only the immediate and later reactions of audiences to the performances, but also their roles during the performances *per se.* Is the audience present simply to be entertained, or is it expected to participate in the proceedings? Does the audience feel itself to be passive, merely watching, or does it sense itself to be part of the action, to have so fully absorbed the impact of the performance as to have broken down the distinction between those on stage and those sitting in the auditorium? In line with reception theory this breaking down of the distinction between performers and audience is likely to be greatly facilitated where the *horizon of expectations* of those involved meet (Hilton, 1987: 131). That is, a circumstance exists in which the beliefs and values of performers and audiences are reasonably close. This means that the composition of the audience may be critical to the success of the performances in terms of the objectives of the consultants and their clients. However, even when audiences are handpicked (as is often the case), it does not follow that there will automatically be a correspondence between the expectations of the performers and audience members involved in an event. As a result, there is a need to identify the other ways in which those involved in preparing and enacting performances attempt to develop a situation in which the audience members' expectations mirror, or at least closely resemble, their own. This will require a longitudinal approach in which the development of each piece of theatre is examined from start to finish.

3 The *Mise en Scene.* The move from a script or text – albeit one that may have been re-written several times – to a performance is no easy matter. What those who attend, see and experience is a finished product. The text is what is heard and the performance is all that is made visible and audible on stage. The audience are party to a performance that is more or less successful, more or less comprehensible, in which the text is only one of several components, others being the space, the setting, the performers, the music, the lighting and the tempo, etc. Pavis (1992: 24), from whom we have taken the term *mise en scene*, defines it 'as the bringing together or confrontation, in a given space and time, of different signifying systems, for an audience'.

He considers the relationship between text and performance to be something more than one of conversion or translation. He prefers to describe it as 'a way of establishing effects or meaning and balance between semiotic systems such as verbal and non-verbal, symbolic and iconic' (ibid: 29). The essence of Pavis' approach is the recognition that the text frames a particular imaginative idea that may be acknowledged, underlined, built upon, undermined, ridiculed or denied by the auditory and visual discourse of the *mise en scene.* In analysing performances researchers will need to examine the relationship between the text and the *mise en scene*, especially in regard to the ways in which an effort is made to establish the 'authenticity' of the performances and thereby succeed in making the 'imaginative truth' the audiences' 'present truth' for the duration of the event.

4 *The impact of the performance.* In examining the impact of the performances it is critical to consider whether the performances motivate, inform or incite audience members to action after they return to their workplaces. One way to do this would be to collect evidence of the immediate *post-hoc* reactions of all the audience members by administering questionnaires on the day of the event. These could ask audience members to record: (1) their overall reactions to the performances; (2) what they think the objectives of the performances were; (3) whether or not they think the performances achieved their objectives and why; and (4) whether they think the performances are likely to lead to any changes in their working life and if so what. Follow-up interviews may generate a more in-depth understanding of their reactions, and establish whether their reactions have changed over time (and if so, why). By linking the audience members' responses to an analysis of both the developmental phases of the assignments and the performances themselves, it might be possible to examine how the performances impact on audience members, and why; and whether or not the performances achieve the commissioners' objectives, and why.

However, these events should not be examined as isolated organizational occurrences. Researchers need to link their use, design and outcomes to broader organizational processes within which they are embedded. In this respect these activities offer a new lens through which to examine a wide range of organizational phenomena. Future research could draw upon and influence such diverse literatures as organizational change, decision making, culture, power and leadership, for example. In each case the critical issues will be both how these factors impinge upon, but are themselves also influenced by theatrical performances.

CONCLUSION

This chapter has argued for a need to lessen our reliance on metaphorical approaches to theatre. This arises because of the increasing use of theatrical techniques and resources to change and control employee attitudes and behaviours. Thus, instead of seeing organizations as theatre we need to investigate the actual use of the technology of theatre within organizations. Whilst attending some kind of theatrical event within an organization may be unusual, it is no longer remarkable. Indeed, new theatrical consultancies have sprung-up to cater for the increased demand within this area. In explaining the factors which might account for this growth it has been argued that theatre is one space where people are offered the opportunity to think about what they think about organizational life. Through engaging experiences participants are encouraged to reflect upon and question taken-for-granted assumptions. In this way theatre, it is claimed, offers a unique opportunity to create individual change. Seen from Lewin's (1951) classic three-fold model of change, theatre offers the possibility of unfreezing and moving participants' ways of thinking. How and whether or not it achieves these grandiose claims is the key area for future research since this activity has prospered without such fundamental assumptions being subject to empirical scrutiny. The chapter has therefore argued for a new research agenda that focuses on developing a broader picture of the range of activities that encompass this area of practice as well as ascertaining how they do, or do not, support individual

change. In the latter respect a framework that encourages organizational performances to be described and analysed in theatrical terms was proposed.

The question remains whether this area of activity will continue to be significant. This is dependent upon at least some of the following factors. First and foremost developing perceptions of its value and success in relation to achieving its claimed aims will be critical. If purchasers begin to view performances as failing to deliver on certain organization related outcomes, or alternative techniques as being better at achieving these outcomes, then demand may decline. It is to debates of this issue that the research agenda outlined in the chapter can most beneficially contribute. In addition, changes to government policy and funding for the arts, which has greatly assisted the emergence of these activities, may also have a detrimental impact on future growth. Finally, the character of the self-discovery zeitgeist may lead to the emergence of other more popular methods of achieving personal change. Theatre within organizations may represent one stop on this ever-changing bandwagon.

NOTES

*The ideas in this chapter draw in part from a programme of work conducted with Iain Mangham. Sadly, Iain passed away in December 2004. This chapter is dedicated to his memory and intended to demonstrate the continuing importance and relevance of studying theatre in organization, an area to which Iain made a series of seminal contributions. I am grateful to Robin Fincham, Eric Guthey and the editors of this volume for their insightful comments on earlier drafts of this chapter.

1 See Mangham and Overington (1983, 1987); Kendall (1993); Pine and Gilmore (1999); Case (2001); Graham-Hill and Grimes (2001); and Walker and Monin (2001) for examples of studies in organizations purporting to derive their method from Burke.

2 See Schlenker (1980); Brissett and Edgley (1990); Gardner (1992); Gardner and Martinko (1988); Giacolone and Rosenfeld (1989); Grove and Fisk (1992); Rosenfeld et al. (1995); Clark and Salaman (1996); Gardner and Avolio (1998) as examples of work in this tradition.

3 More recently, following the Enron and WorldCom scandals Richard Olivier has turned to running workshops on Macbeth (Arkin, 2005).

4 Who, in turn, draws heavily upon notions deriving from both ritual and the practices of the theatre of the ancient Greeks (Boal, 1979).

5 Quoted from private correspondence with Iain Mangham.

REFERENCES

Arkin, A. (2005) 'Power play', *Personnel Management*, 10 March.

Ashworth, J. (1999) 'Dramatic change to art of team building', *The Times*, 6 February, p. 7.

Augustine, N. and Adelman, K. (1999) *Shakespeare in Charge: The Bard's Guide to Leading and Succeeding on the Business Stage*. New York: Miramax Books.

Barry, D. (1994) 'Making the unconscious visible: Symbolic means for surfacing unconscious processes in organizations', *Organizational Development Journal*, 12 (4): 37–48.

Beirne, M. and Knight, S. (2007) 'From community theatre to critical management studies: A dramatic contribution to reflective learning'. *Management Learning*, 38 (5): 591–611.

Boal, A. (1979) *Theatre of the Oppressed*. London: Pluto Press.

Brissett, D. and Edgley, C. (1990) *Life as Theatre: A Dramaturgical Sourcebook* (2nd edn). New York: Aldine de Gruyter.

Burke, K. (1945) *A Grammar of Motives*. Berkeley: University of California Press.

Burke, K. (1969a) *A Rhetoric of Motives*. London: University of California Press.

Burke, K. (1969b) 'Dramatism', in *International Encyclopaedia of the Social Sciences*, Volume VII. New York: Macmillan.

Burnham, J., Augustine, N. and Adelman, K. (2001) *Shakespeare in Charge: The Bard's Guide of Learning and Succeeding on the Business Stage*. New York: Hyperion.

Case, P. (2001) 'Virtual stories on virtual working: Critical reflection on CTI consultancy discourse', in T. Clark, and R. Fincham, (eds), *Critical Consulting: New Perspectives on the Management Advice Industry*. Oxford: Blackwells. pp. 93–114.

Clark, T. and Mangham, I. (2004a) 'Stripping to the undercoat: A review and reflections on a piece of organization theatre', *Organization Studies* (Special Issue on Theatre and Organizations), 25 (5): 841–851.

Clark, T. and Mangham, I. (2004b) 'From dramaturgy to theatre as technology: The case of corporate theatre', *Journal of Management Studies*, 41 (1): 37–59.

Clark, T. and Salaman, G. (1996) 'Creating the 'right' impression: Towards a dramaturgy of management consultancy', *Service Industries Journal*, 18: 18–38.

Cole, D. (1975) *The Theatrical Event: a Mythos, a Vocabulary, a Perspective*. Middleton, CT: Wesleyan University Press.

Coopey, J. (1998) 'Learning to trust and trusting to learn: A role of radical theatre', *Management Learning*, 29 (3): 365–382.

Corrigan, P. (2000) *Shakespeare on Management: Leadership Lessons for Today's Managers*. London: Kogan Page.

Counsell, C. (1996) *Signs of Performance: An Introduction to Twentieth Century Theatre*. London: Routledge.

Gardner, W.L. (1992) 'Lessons in organizational dramaturgy: The art of impression management', *Organization Dynamics*, 21 (1): 33–46.

Gardner, W.L and Avolio, B.J. (1998) 'The charismatic relationship: A dramaturgical perspective', *Academy of Management Review*, 23 (1): 32–58.

Gardner, W.L. and Martinko, M.J. (1988) 'Impression management in organizations', *Journal of Management*, 14: 321–338.

Geertz, C. (1983) *Local Knowledge: Further Essays in Interpretive Anthropology*. Stanford, CA: Stanford University Press.

Giacolone, R.A. and Rosenfeld, P. (1989) *Impression Management in Organizations*. Hillsdale, NJ: Lawrence Erlbaum.

Gibb, S. (2004) 'Arts-based training in management development: The use of improvisational theatre', *Journal of Management Development*, 23 (8): 741–750.

Goffman, E. (1959) *The Presentation of Self in Everyday Life*. New York: Anchor Doubleday.

Graham-Hill, S. and Grimes, A.J. (2001) 'Dramatism as method: the promise of praxis', *Journal of Organizational Change Management*, 14 (3): 280–294.

Grove, S.J. and Fisk, R.P. (1992) 'The service experience as theatre', *Advances in Consumer Research*, 19: 455–461.

Hilton, J. (1987) *Performance*. Basingstoke: Macmillan.

Jackson, B. (2001) 'Art for management's sake? The new literary genre of business book', *Management Communication Quarterly*, 14 (3): 483–490.

Jackson, T. (1993) *Learning through Theatre: New Perspectives on Theatre in Education*. London: Routledge.

Keene, G. (1999) 'How the conference changed its spots', *The Independent on Sunday*, 9 May: 7.

Kellaway, L. (2005) 'Honking for Harvard', *Financial Times*, 25 September.

Kendall, J.E. (1993) 'Good and evil in the chairman's 'boiler plate': An analysis of corporate visions of the 1970's', *Organization Studies*, 14 (4): 148–164.

Lewin, K. (1951) *Field Theory in Social Science*. New York: Harper.

Luhmann, N. (1997) *Die Gesellschaft der Gesellschaft*. Frankfurt/Main: Suhrkamp.

Lyman, S.M. and Scott, M.B. (1975) *The Drama of Social Reality*. New York: Oxford University Press.

McKee, J. (1999) 'Henry V becomes an eye-opener for today's leaders', *The Times*, 6 February, p. 27.

Mangham, I.L. (1990) 'Managing as a performance', *British Journal of Management*, 1 (1): 105–115.

Mangham, I.L. (2001) 'Afterword: Looking for Henry', *Journal of Organizational Change Management*, 14 (3): 295–304.

Mangham, I.L. and Overington, M.A. (1983) 'Dramatism and the theatrical metaphor', in G. Morgan, (ed.), *Beyond Method*. London: Sage: pp. 219–233.

Mangham, I.L. and Overington, M.A. (1987) *Organizations as Theatre: A Social Psychology of Dramatic Appearances*. Chichester: Wiley.

Meisiek, S. (2002) 'Situation drama in change management: Types and effects of a new managerial tool', *International Journal of Arts Management*, 4 (3): 48–55.

Meisiek, S. (2004) 'Which catharsis do they mean? Aristotle, Moreno, Boal and Organization Theatre'. *Organizational Studies*, 24 (5): 797–816.

Miller, P. and Rose, N. (1990) 'Governing economic life', *Economy and Society*, 19: 1–31.

Nissley, N., Taylor, S.S. and Houden, L. (2004) 'The politics of performance in organizational theatre-based training and interventions', *Organization Studies*, 25 (5): 817–839.

Novitz, D. (1992) *The Boundaries of Art*. Philadelphia: Temple University.

Olivier, R. (2001) *Inspirational Leadership: Henry V and the Muse of Fire*. London: Industrial Society.

Pavis, P. (1992) *Theatre at the Crossroads of Culture*, (trans. Loren Kruger). London: Routledge.

Pine, B.J. and Gilmour, J.H. (1999) *The Experience Economy: Work is Theatre and every Business a Stage*. Boston, MA: Harvard Business School Press.

Pineault, W.J. (1989) *Industrial Theatre: The Businessman's Broadway*. PhD dissertation, Bowling Green State University.

Rosenfeld, P., Giacalone, R.A. and Riordan, C.A. (1995) *Impression Management in Organizations: Theory, Measurement, Practice*. London: Routledge.

Schechner, R. (1988) *Performance Theory*. New York: Routledge.

Schlenker, B.R. (1980) *Impression Management: The Self Concept, Social Identity and, Interpersonal Relations*, Monterey, CA: Brooks/cole.

Schreyögg, G. (2001) 'Organizational theatre and organizational change', Discussion Paper No. 13/01, Institute für Management, Freie Universität Berlin.

Schreyögg, G. and Dabitz, R. (1999) *Unternehmentheater: Formen – Erfarungen – erfolgreicher Einsatz*. Wiesbaden: Gabler.

Shafritz, J. (1999) *Shakespeare on Management: Wise Business Counsel from the Bard*. New York: HarperCollins.

Strati, A. (1996) 'Organizations viewed through the lens of aesthetics'. *Organization*, 3 (2): 209–218.

Strati, A. and Guillet de Montoux, P.G. (2002) 'Introduction: Organizing aethetics'. *Human Relations*, 55 (7): 755–766.

Taylor, S.S. and Hansen, H. (2005) 'Finding form: Looking at the field of organizational aesthetics', *Journal of Management Studies*, 42 (6): 1211–1231.

Thrift, N. (2000) 'Performing cultures in the new economy', *Annals of the Association of American Geographers*, 90 (4): 674–692.

Turner, V. (1982) *From Ritual to Theatre: The Human Seriousness at Play*. New York: Performing Arts Journal.

Turner, V. (1984) 'Liminality and performance genres', in J.J. MacAloon (ed.), *Rite, Drama, Festival, Spectacle: Rehearsals Toward a Theory of Performance*. Philadelphia: Institute for the Study of Human Issues.

Walker, R. and Monin, N. (2001) 'The purpose of the picnic: Using Burke's dramatistic pentad to analyse a company event', *Journal of Organizational Change Management*, 14 (3): 266–279.

Whitney, J. and Packer, T. (2000) *Power Plays: Shakespeare's Lessons in Leadership and Management*. New York: Simon & Schuster.

Young, T.R. (1990) *The Drama of Social Life: Essays in Post-Modern Social Psychology*. New Brunswick: Transaction Publishers.

This is Work, This is Play: Artful Interventions and Identity Dynamics

Stefan Meisiek and Mary Jo Hatch

What can art do for business? In much of the world, art and business have long been considered hostile spheres with limited contact occurring mainly through acts of corporate patronage, such as corporate art collecting. But some artists, actors, and musicians have lately been pushing for closer cooperation with businesspeople and their effort is being met by growing demand from managers to learn from the arts. Moving well beyond corporate art collecting and patronage, some managers are asking artists to partner with them to make their organizations more creative, innovative and resourceful. These managers perceive artists as possessing knowledge and capabilities relevant to business life and, together with the artists they consult or commission, they search for ways to effectively translate artistry into business practice (Darsø, 2004). For example, organizational theatre companies offer performances designed to foster organizational change and development (Clark

and Mangham, 2004a, 2004b; Meisiek, 2002, 2004; Nissley et al., 2004; Taylor, 2003) while conductors and jazz musicians introduce managers to musical concepts of rhythm, harmony, and melody to improve leadership, teamwork, management processes and even organizational design (Kao, 1996; Barrett, 1998; Hatch, 1999). In similar ways conceptual artists collaborate with employees to produce works that encourage reflection and self-insight (Harris, 1999; Velthuis, 2005).

For the most part managers bring an instrumental orientation to artful interventions: artists are hired to teach employees how to go about solving problems in a different way. But not all artful interventions have the desired effect of this direct transfer of knowledge and capabilities. Regularly, organizations prove incompatible with artful processes and experience disappointment or outright failure with their artful interventions. The exploration logic of artful processes may prompt questions beyond a narrow instrumental focus and has employees reflect upon who they are as an organization and how they are working.

In this chapter we set forth the proposition that one significant difference between successful and unsuccessful arts-based consulting projects lies in whether or not the intervention taps the dynamics that shape collective identity. We contend that artful interventions require managers and other organizational members to embody and explore aspects of their organization's identity and when they do so, their organizations are opened to change. We will attempt to theorize the link between artful interventions and organizational identity in order to explain why and when artful intervention produces organizational enhancements such as employee resourcefulness, organizational creativity and renewal.

We begin by showing how tearing down the walls between work and play in artful interventions creates the organizational tensions necessary for creative change. That is to say, for an artful intervention to be successful, organizational identity must accommodate play alongside work. We then provide examples from the domains of conceptual art and music to illustrate this tension and introduce ideas about the interrelationships of artful intervention and organizational identity. To help us consider the implications of using our view of work and play for identity theory, we extend Joseph Beuys's notion of the social sculpture to organizations. Equipped with Beuys's perspective, we place artful intervention into the context of a dynamic model of organizational identity change and suggest some advice for those conducting or studying artful interventions, with which we will conclude.

WORK AND PLAY

Beuys claimed that everyone is called to be an artist and live their life in an artful way (Ekstrand, 1998). Thinking and acting like an artist in daily life involves playfully asking questions, posing and confronting problems, tackling new ideas, and developing and using methods, rather than merely representing something (e.g., an object, person, idea, or mood). For Beuys, a finished artwork with its sounds, colors, shapes or words is not what is most interesting about art. This is because the artifact quickly loses touch with the questions and ideas that generated it and instead takes on the questions and ideas that it provokes. If the process of engaging with art is what matters most, we contend that what is needed for artful intervention is a willingness to complement the seriousness of ordinary everyday life with play.

If work is the serious stuff of everyday life in organizations, play becomes a means for employees to step outside their serious work roles, placing them in a position from which they can reflect on those roles and on the organization (Dandridge, 1986). For exactly this reason, however, play has a tainted history in organizations. Employees are supposed to work. That is what they are paid for. When they are playing, according to conventional wisdom, they are only being childish or lazy, wasting corporate time, resources and opportunities for the sake of their private pleasure. Such negative views about play trace back to bureaucratic models of organization and to scientific management. Organizations following these paradigms – in so far as they acknowledge a human necessity for play at all – relegate it to the domains of organizational ritual: Christmas parties, retirement roasts and various sorts of teambuilding exercises (e.g., Dandridge, 1986; Rosen, 1988). In these liminal spaces play can at most only temporarily disrupt the seriousness of work, and at best reaffirm that seriousness by showing the chaos that its absence implies.

Of late play has been making inroads into business, as when employees are asked to engage in 'serious play' – to use their creativity for the benefit of the organization's innovativeness. Rapid prototyping in product development (Schrage, 2000), and artful making as a framework for project development (Austin and Devin, 2003), draw on human playfulness and have been suggested as organizational aids for speeding-up innovation and production processes. Because this type of employee play benefits the organization, its serious ends justify its playful means. But play for the sake of work may not reap all the promised rewards.

Work obliges employees to keep their attention pointed in the direction they need to go to realize strategic aims, to be pragmatic rather than creative. When they focus on the outcome or goal of their work they are less interested in the meaning of the objects surrounding them than in the use that can be made of them (Dandridge, 1986; Tsoukas and Chia, 2002). With such an instrumental state of mind, the direct value of collective self-understandings of organizational purposes is questionable. By contrast, in the artistic process, play turns employees' attention away from practical matters towards reflection and self-understanding, allowing them to obtain appreciation for their reality and giving them the chance to value it. As Bergson noted about artists: 'It is because the artist is less intent on utilizing his perception that he perceives a greater number of things' (quoted in Tsoukas and Chia, 2002: 572).

In the most successful artful interventions, the playfulness of the artistic process is enacted within the context of work, and is designed to help organizational members reflect upon the organization's identity and improve their relationship with it as well as their working conditions. According to Gadamer (1986) the artistic process provides space for imagination, discovery and surprise. It allows playfully exploring and developing self-understanding and organizational identity, phenomena which can never be represented accurately, but can be experienced and expressed as well as reflected upon. At the same time, this playfulness allows for humor, ambiguity and ambivalence without being threatening, which can reduce some of the resistance that normally accompanies organizational change efforts. Playing with identity lets us imagine how it would be to change ourselves, and when the identity we play with is that of the organization, a door

to organizational change opens. Because the artistic process is so intimately related to identity change, we believe that artful intervention provides a path to organizational development. Thus the tensions between work and play, introduced by placing art within business, have the capacity to alter everyday work life.

MIRRORING ORGANIZATIONAL IMAGES AND EXPRESSING ORGANIZATIONAL UNDERSTANDINGS

When commissioned for an artful intervention, artists may play with the impressions they have of an organization, lend them their own interpretations, and express these in finished artifacts or rehearsed performances that are then put on display for organizational members to see and respond to. Showing organization-inspired artworks to audiences of organizational members – as theatrical or musical performances, poetry readings, paintings, sculpture, and so on – offers them opportunities for mirroring organizational images and later reflection about who they are as a company. Employees are typically left to think and converse about the artwork after their encounter and it is hoped that these effects will induce some sort of change. In Gadamer's (1986) observations on art and play, he calls the passive audience of this approach 'Mitspieler' (co-players). While they have no direct influence on the process of art creation, audiences are still feeling and thinking 'as if' they were part of it; this is what makes artwork, even in this constrained context, powerful for many people. Because artworks are deliberately ambiguous and partially undefined, audiences have space in which to play along vicariously and in so doing confront the opportunity for change.

Example 1: Installed by conceptual artist Henrik Schrat in the trading room of the Frankfurt Stock Exchange, *The Appearance of Fantasy* covered 160 square meters of dark wood paneling with 50,000 used candy wrappers (Ventura, 2001). Schrat collected the candy wrappers from visitors to the 120 branches of a bank that operated throughout Germany. Later, part of the installation was sold at auction. Thus by adding artistry to the candy supplied by the bank and consumed by its customers, Schrat converted discarded wrappers – now possessing cultural value – back into money.

For Schrat (2005) 'the candy wrappers on the wall of the stock exchange are by-products that represent the smallest form of luxury. The glittery wrappers offer the lure of satisfaction: On the outside colorful and promising, and inside sweet and short-lived. Because candy has to be consumed to be enjoyed, it creates demand for more candy. Satisfaction begets the desire for more satisfaction (more wants more), so the wrappers are a perfect symbol for capitalism.' The supplement of artistry now carried by the wrappers communicates the notion of value added in an artful way. Thus *The Appearance of Fantasy* offered customers, bank managers, tellers and stock exchange dealers a metaphor for understanding the flows of capital, highlighting the individual transactions in the bank (50,000 candy wrappers standing in for 50,000 bank transactions) and contrasting them to the meta-transactions of the stock exchange. The artwork made invisible flows of money (e.g., from clients to the stock market) visible, and invited stock exchange dealers and bank personnel to mirror their identity in the interconnections between their daily work with numbers and the objects of desire, symbolized by the candy wrappers.

There is one anecdote about the stock exchange installation that beautifully captures the difference between work and play. When the artist told the managers of the bank that he needed 50,000 candy wrappers, they calculated the costs and ordered a batch from a candy producer. The artist shook his head and insisted that the candy wrappers were to be collected one by one. To the managers it seemed a pointless waste of time, money, and resources. They looked at the candy wrappers as raw material used to produce a desired future outcome. The artist,

however, understood that the meaning the wrappers would carry was produced when people picked up a piece of candy, unwrapped and ate it, and placed the wrapper in a box they knew was destined to become an artwork. Once the wrapper had been transported to the stock exchange and mounted above the large screens with the numbers representing stock values, the values of the people who had contributed wrappers could be physically brought into the 'exchange'. It was thus that the installation put play into meaning and meaning into play.

Modern art has long attempted to reduce the distance between artwork and audience, and where employees are involved in the art creation, playing with questions, problems and ideas becomes an active and immediate task for them. Artful interventions that demand active participation permit organizational members to express and address their own questions, perceptions and interpretations, molding this process in ways that pertain to their work lives while being embedded in their cultural self-understandings. Organizational members join actors, musicians and conceptual artists to play with concepts relating to their work environment (e.g., Meisiek, 2004; Velthuis, 2005; Zander and Zander, 2000).

Example 2: Conductor Peter Hanke worked with managers in a financial institution to explore leadership issues via musical representation (Hanke, 2005). This artful intervention was meant to allow the managers to express and reflect on their self-understandings, finding out who they were as leaders based on their own experiences and expressions rather than based on a mirror image. They were asked to play with concepts of rhythm, precision, volume, speed, control and to improvise a musician's expression on the spot to learn about their own leadership style and to develop ideas for how they would like to relate to and interact with their subordinates. Instead of asking how music might be useful in their daily work, they played music as a means to explore their work-related questions, problems and ideas.

In sessions like this one, with up to 24 managers, the conductor presents the curriculum of a co-conductor course to let managers explore music making and the way it resonates with their body while conducting a small orchestra or vocal ensemble. Hanke believes that career experience enables an average senior manager to swap roles with a trained conductor with very little preparation, so long as the music is not too complexly scored. The role of the conductor is offered as an ideal type for leadership and the participants are asked to look for parallels between musical concepts of meaningful sound, and ideas regarding effective leadership. The participants are also encouraged to develop an ear for the coordination of multiple voices. Parallel to the conductor exercises, the participants receive coaching on their posture, appearance, and personal appeal. The exercises used put a heavy emphasis on non-verbal communication and personal style, thus engaging the identities of the participating leaders.

ORGANIZATIONS AS SOCIAL SCULPTURES

We have described play as an emergent process that is an end in itself (Gadamer, 1986) in contrast to work that finds its ends in organizational purposes (Dandridge, 1986), and we have presented two examples of how work and play come together in artful interventions in organizations. Now let us revisit Beuys's call for everyone to be an artist. Beuys's art theory, when extended to organizations, describes a dynamic process that explains how and why artful interventions may act upon organizational identities and allow employees to become more playful, creative and resourceful.

According to Ekstrand (1998), Beuys believed that every human being is called to participate in transforming the conditions, thinking and structures that shape the social sculpture. Beuys developed the concept of social sculpture in the 1970s as an interdisciplinary (combining art, science, and wisdom) and participatory process in which questions, thoughts, and discussions

replace the traditional hard materials of sculpting (e.g., clay, wood or stone). The concept of social sculpture lifts aesthetic consideration from its confines within art, and relocates it within a collective, imaginative work-space in which everybody can see, re-think and re-shape themselves to be in tune with their creative potential (Ekstrand, 1998).

Beuys's notion of social sculpture as applied to organizations seems already embedded in the language of business. For example, a powerful leader 'reshapes' an organization, a marketer 'carves out' a niche, opinions and images are 'molded', employees are said to possess 'soft' and 'hard' skills, and managers who are widely admired are even placed on a 'pedestal' as if they were a sculpture. Within this discourse employees present their organizations as possessing surface and texture, something to be molded, carved and shaped, much as a sculptor would act upon a piece of clay. The concept of social sculpture, because it embodies the notion of sculpting as well as the finished artwork, brings process into the frame ordinarily regarded as strictly structural when the cognate 'social structure' is invoked. To our minds, social sculpture combines the best of the concepts of organizational social structure and culture.

Beuys's notion suggests that artful interventions make the social sculpture of the organization sensible and tangible. Organizational identity is the keystone in this process, because it constitutes how employees perceive themselves as parts of the social sculpture. When employees mirror perceived images or express cultural self-understandings through play, they gain the opportunity to change the social sculpture of their organization and how they work within it.

There are three major implications for organizational identity if we understand an organization as social sculpture (i.e., emerging from ideas and discussions). First, Beuys described the social sculpture as never fixed or finished; it is constantly re-visited and re-shaped and therefore in a process of perpetual becoming

(Ekstrand, 1998). Similarly, organizational identity has been assumed to be fluid in order to provide adaptive capacity (Gioia et al., 2000) and Hatch and Schultz (2002) explicitly described the processes by which organizational identity is created as an ongoing conversation between internal and external stakeholders. According to these researchers, stakeholder images feed into the constant re-construction of organizational identity, and thereby organizational images are often a means to engage the organization in change (cf. Dutton and Dukerich, 1991).

Second, if every employee is an artist working on the organizational social sculpture, then organizations need to be understood as polyphonic (Hazen, 1993). The individual yet different contributions to the social sculpture suggest that organizational identity is distributed across the organization, much as Hatch et al. (2005: 160) claimed when they wrote that:

> organizational identity is socially constructed as it emerges, is maintained and transformed via the distributed awareness (no one person or vantage point contains all the cues needed to define a particular organizational identity) and collective consciousness (organizational identity is indicated by collective reference: 'we' or 'they') of its stakeholders (both internal and external to the organization).

And ever since Kant (1790/1978), an aesthetic experience is said to have the double-sidedness of being ultimately individual, yet aspiring to collective subjectivity. We understand this to mean that each employee would want to know or believe that the others experienced the organizational identity, or the artful intervention that touches it, in a similar (i.e., personally meaningful) way. Employees have differing work identities, and – because the whole is more than the sum of its parts – these distributed understandings, perceptions, and interpretations can be described as the organizational identity.

Third, if a social sculpture is molded on the basis of thoughts and ideas, then the performances and artifacts created in the process are only temporarily relevant.

They are discardable stepping stones on the way to better questions, problems, and ideas. However, it seems that moment-by-moment organizational members need these discardable performances and artifacts to locate themselves and their activities, which they do in a reflexive fashion (e.g., when they ask themselves 'who are we?' or 'what are we trying to accomplish?', Barry, 1994). In this way the artful performance or artifact bridges the gap between work and play. This echoes Beuys's notion that all art is transitory (Ekstrand, 1998). What remains of the artful intervention is the memory of the play; ideas that provide meaning and signal possible changes in the organization's identity dynamics. And if the organizational identity has changed to accommodate play, employees are in a better position to continue shaping the social sculpture that the artful intervention has made tangible for them.

To understand society as a social sculpture was a strategy Beuys developed to liberate creativity from culturally imposed constraints. As such, playfulness can no longer remain just the domain of artists as highly trained specialists, but must become an essential condition of human life (Ekstrand, 1998), i.e., part of each person's identity.

It was through unconstrained dialogue that Beuys wanted to reconcile scientific knowledge with wisdom gained through deeper understanding of our mutual concerns, of who we are, and who we can be (Ekstrand, 1998). Artistic processes spur curiosity about identity and culture, which otherwise remain taken-for-granted in the organization. The desire to create shared meaning through organizational identity finds its expression in the conversations among employees surrounding artful intervention. These conversations might happen immediately, or they might come up over coffee breaks and meetings that follow it (Meisiek and Barry, 2007), as employees seek to reconcile work and play. Considering organizations to be social sculptures that become sensible and tangible through artful interventions enables us to understand the organizational identity conversation as a vehicle for change.

IDENTITY AND ARTISTRY

Artful interventions create images in which organizational members see themselves, and with which they can identify. In regard to this interrelationship between image and identity, Gioia et al. (2000: 67) argued that 'image in its multiple guises provides a catalyst for members' reflexive examination of their organizational self-definition. Image often acts as a destabilizing force on identity, frequently requiring members to revisit and reconstruct their organizational sense of self.' If this dynamic operates as proposed by these theorists, then images of an organization produced by artistic means could influence current interpretations of organizational identity within an organization.

Hatch and Schultz (2002) specified the dynamic by which organizational identity change occurs in terms of a conversation between the organization's internal and external stakeholders; in other words, identity is produced in a continuous arc shifting between feedback (i.e., images) about what the organization is like, provided by its external stakeholders; and internal dialogue about who we are, conducted in the context of organizational culture (see Figure 3.2.1).

When artists make images of their impressions of organizational identity, the gift of their expressiveness augments the communicative power of their message beyond that of most other external stakeholders. In this regard, we observe that artists typically study the organization into which they are to make their artful intervention – attending meetings, talking to employees, and visiting the premises before turning their impressions into an artifact or performance. Following Hatch and Schultz (2002), we claim that the mirrored reflection of the artist's image of the organization enables reactive identity change by setting the organization up for reflection (see arrow 1 in Figure 3.2.1). By this means, employees become co-players in the artistic process.

In the stock exchange example, the social sculpture of the financial market, and therefore the distributed identity, included customers, managers, bank tellers, and stock brokers. We can assume that the artwork led to numerous conversations about the flows of capital and the interconnection of client money, banks, stock brokers and stock holders and to other conversations less easy to guess. The artwork highlighted and made it possible for the people involved, and now for us, to talk about these interconnections and the identities that they communicate.

Similarly, the expression of work issues by employees within an artist assisted artful

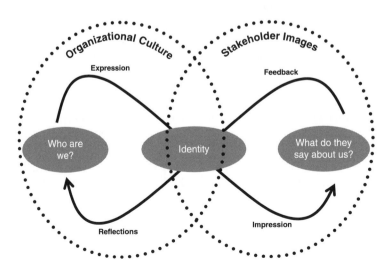

Figure 3.2.1   A model of organizational identity dynamics. Based on Hatch and Schultz (2002)

intervention brings about identity change when organizational members ask and answer their own questions about themselves, their organization, and their work life. For example, with the help of an artist, employees might approximate, distance, abstract, defamiliarize, toggle, or otherwise play with their questions, problems, and ideas (Osborne, 2003) and thus engage their organizational identity dynamic by expressing cultural self-understandings (see arrow 2 in Figure 3.2.1). Because their playfulness enacted in the context of work allows people to act 'as if' and to ask 'what if?' questions, this approach allows employees to reflect upon who they are, how they are working, and what they stand for.

In the conductor example, music's temporary (and temporal) character helped managers explore their roles and promoted their identity as leaders. The ambiguity of music interpretation allowed every manager to find his or her own leadership tune. When they enacted their learning after returning to their everyday work life, they were more likely to carve another aspect into the social sculpture of their organization.

Organizational members must be wary of maintaining too introverted or too extroverted a gaze where identity work is concerned. Hatch and Schultz (2002: 1013) warned that stakeholders will abandon extremely narcissistic organizations (so embedded in organizational culture they cannot take up a self-critical position) and they will mistrust organizations whose identities rest on image alone (so responsive to stakeholder images they lose sight of who they are). We believe that, where the organization needs to be more welcoming of outsider opinions (to avoid narcissism) or to work on its self-esteem (to avoid the loss of culture that over-adaptation can bring), artful intervention can be particularly beneficial.

A narcissistic organization engages in constant cultural navel-gazing in the form of self-absorption and self-seduction. The organization relies completely on expressing and reflecting its cultural self-understandings, and its internal reflections are mistaken for stakeholder images ('we know how others

see us, there is no need to ask'). No attention is paid to stakeholder feedback and the mirroring process is disconnected from the process of organizational self-reflection (Brown, 1997). Hatch and Schultz (2002) argue that the identity conversation needs to be balanced to avoid dysfunctional levels of narcissism. Confrontation with an artistic representation of themselves can serve as a wake-up call for employees in a narcissistic organization. To see themselves, for example, represented in a theatre performance as selfish and compulsive might be more powerful than all the complaints of stakeholder groups. The aesthetic quality and immediacy of artistry might spur employees' curiosity to mirror their identity in the perceived artistic image when they are in denial about stakeholder opinions (e.g., 'that data on stakeholders is nonsense, it was not properly handled'). Another advantage of artful intervention is that its aesthetic and emotional appeal makes it stand out among more mundane images of everyday organizational life such as that presented by graphs and charts.

In hyper-adaptive organizations, by contrast, employees pay too much attention to perceived external images. They are constantly looking in the mirror and thus end up losing an inner sense of who they are. Cultural self-understandings are overwhelmed by constant responsiveness to shifting consumer or shareholder preferences (Alvesson, 1990) such that perceived images replace (rather than combine with) cultural self-understanding in the minds of managers with the result that the culture of the organization begins to atrophy. According to Hatch and Schultz (2002), when images replace cultural substance, organizational identity becomes arbitrary and risks becoming hyper-adaptive. Artful interventions allow employees to explore and represent the present reality they experience in their organizations, rather than requiring that they simulate a desirable future reality for purposes of impression management. Such approaches could bridge the gap between culture and image, helping employees to recover a lost sense of heritage and values (e.g., such as occurs after multiple acquisitions in a growing organization).

The two dysfunctions suggest a reason why artistry is presently gaining popularity in organizations. If organizations in the rapidly transforming global marketplace are under pressures that encourage them to either deny their circumstances or adapt too quickly to every change that appears on the horizon, then there may be an increasing incidence of organizations with identity problems. The dysfunctions also provide us with an idea of the role that artistry might play in identity change as well as a basis for understanding why artful interventions succeed or fail to change the social sculpture of an organization.

CONCLUSIONS

In this chapter we have sought to address how and why artful intervention influences organizational identity and thereby affects organizational change. We have argued that artistic processes allow organizational members to playfully explore cultural self-understandings and stakeholder images of the organization, which in turn lead to identity change and possibly increases employees' creativity, innovativeness, and resourcefulness. This change affects the social sculpture which is the organization, becoming tangible in the process, making it easier to imagine the concrete realities of organizational change.

The present discussion has provided some clues about why, when and how art in business might work. First, employees of narcissistic organizations might choose artful interventions to become aware of how outsiders perceive them. And employees of hyper-adaptive organizations might use artful interventions to explore the substance of their cultural self-understandings and to change them in ways they deem fit. Second, the effects of artful interventions will be limited if focused merely on representation. Artistry draws its power by playing with questions, problems, and ideas, which means it must engage and involve. Third, Beuys's ideas on

social sculpture suggests why artistry might provide organizations with more creativity. In his view, socially sculpting organizations involves employees in the use of their creative resources. When artistry affects organizational identity in the ways we have outlined above, then we believe it is likely that the organization as a whole will enjoy more creativity, innovation, resourcefulness, and motivation.

Based on our discussion of organizational identity we can spot shortcomings in the way some artful interventions are presently conducted. Both the stock market and the conductor examples are incomplete attempts at artful interventions. While they address organizational identity and make the social sculpture tangible, they root themselves in only one side of the organizational identity model (the stock market example hovers over the right side of the model shown in Figure 3.2.1, emphasizing mirrored images; while the conductor example is rooted in the left side, emphasizing reflection and expression). To foster more profound change, these artful interventions would need to take the opposite side of the model into account as well. This might be achieved by further artful interventions, or by other means that continue the identity conversation. We assume that a continued identity conversation between internal and external stakeholders will have a better chance of lasting influence on how employees think and act.

The reader might infer from our chapter that cooperation between artists and organizations is always crowned with success. On the contrary, employees presented with artful intervention might see themselves unable to find anything interesting in the artwork. While a bad portrayal still might spur mirroring of organizational identity, performances or artworks that bore their audiences might not achieve anything. To be successful, artful intervention demands a high level of involvement from employees and artists alike. If employees remain skeptical or uninterested they might not engage in playing with artful means and the reflection on identity will not occur. They might say that acting or painting is definitely not their genre and thus cannot influence how they see themselves. In general, where artistry remains uninspiring and employees overly-distanced, artful intervention in organizational identity change will have little effect.

A further caveat is that if artful interventions are powerful, they are likely to be appropriated by managers for their own goals. While constraints on artistic freedom are inevitable when managers commission artists, these constraints can actually be useful when they stimulate the collaborative efforts that follow. However, if managers attempt to control processes and outcomes in too much detail, the artful interventions are likely to fail. Nissley et al. (2004) point out that managers' attempts at controlling artful interventions frustrate employees and reduce the possibility of a fruitful dialogue. In the long run, employees might start to regard artful intervention as just another management fad (Jackson, 2001). Only if the process is more polyphonic and the organization is understood as a social sculpture, might interesting change begin to happen.

Looking to the future of artful interventions, we might expect to see more of this approach to change as competitive pressures mount and organizational identities face their inevitable crises as a result. At the same time, we can imagine some larger companies making artful interventions a common feature in their organization to underline desired identity change and to balance the identity conversation between the poles of cultural substance and stakeholder images. Spearheading this development are Siemens and Unilever, two companies that have established art programs for their employees (Darsø, 2004). Such programs will, in turn, make it possible for more artists to work in organizations on an ongoing basis. These developments ask for rigorous research on the consequences of artful interventions. We suggest that this research should focus on identity change, which should help in both the conduct and the evaluation of artful interventions by giving these matters a theoretical foundation.

REFERENCES

Alvesson, M. (1990) 'Organization: From substance to image?', *Organization Studies*, 11: 373–394.

Austin, R. and Devin, L. (2003) *Artful Making*. Upper Saddle River, NJ: FT Prentice Hall.

Barrett, F.J. (1998) 'Creativity and improvisation in jazz and organizations: Implications for organizational learning', *Organization Science*, 9: 558–560.

Barry, D. (1994) 'Making the invisible visible: Symbolic means for surfacing unconscious processes in organizations', *Organizational Development Journal*, 12: 37–48.

Brown, A.D. (1997) 'Narcissism, identity, and legitimacy', *Academy of Management Review*, 22: 643–683.

Clarke, T. and Mangham, I. (2004a) 'From dramaturgy to theater as technology: The case of corporate theater', *Journal of Management Studies*, 40: 37–59.

Clark, T. and Mangham, I. (2004b) 'Stripping to the undercoat: A review and reflections on a piece of organization theatre', *Organization Studies*, 25: 841–851.

Dandridge, T.C. (1986) 'Ceremony as an integration of work and play', *Organization Studies*, 7: 159–170.

Darsø, L. (2004) *Artful Creation. Learning-Tales of Arts-in-Business*. Copenhagen: Samfundsliteratur.

Dutton, J.E. and Dukerich, J.M. (1991) 'Keeping an eye on the mirror: Image and identity in organizational adaptation', *Academy of Management Journal*, 14: 517–554.

Ekstrand, L. (1998) *Varje Människa en konstnär*. Bokförlaget Korpen: Göteborg.

Gadamer, H.-G. (1986) *The Relevance of The Beautiful and Other Essays* (Eng. trans. N. Walker, ed. R. Bernasconi). Cambridge: Cambridge University Press.

Gioia, D.A., Schultz, M. and Corley, K.G. (2000) 'Organizational identity, image, and adaptive instability', *Academy of Management Review*, 25: 63–81.

Hanke, P. (2005) 'Kreativitet kan ikke anskaffes – det skal læres', *Ledelse i Dag*, 61: 32–36.

Harris, C. (ed.) (1999) *Art and Innovation: The Xerox PARC Artist-in-residence Program*. Cambridge, MA: MIT Press.

Hatch, M.J. (1999) 'Exploring the empty spaces of organizing: How improvisational jazz helps redescribe organizational structure', *Organization Studies*, 20: 75–100.

Hatch, M.J. and Schultz, M. (2002) 'The dynamics of organizational identity', *Human Relations*, 55: 989–1018.

Hatch, M.J., Kostera, M. and Kozminski, A.K. (2005) *The Three Faces of Leadership: Manager, Artist, Priest*. Oxford: Blackwell Publishing.

Hazen, M.A. (1993) 'Towards polyphonic organization', *Journal of Organizational Change Management*, 6: 15–26.

Jackson, B. (2001) *Management Gurus and Management Fashions: A Dramatistic Inquiry*. London: Routledge.

Kant, I. (1978) *Critique of Judgment*. Oxford: Oxford University Press (first published 1790).

Kao, J. (1996) *Jamming: The Art and Discipline of Business Creativity*. New York: HarperCollins.

Meisiek, S. (2002) 'Situation drama in change management: Types and effects of a new managerial tool', *International Journal of Arts Management*, 4: 48–55.

Meisiek, S. (2004) 'Which catharsis do they mean? Aristotle, Moreno, Boal and Organization Theatre', *Organization Studies*, 25: 797–816.

Meisiek, S. and Barry, D. (2007) 'Through the looking glass of organizational theatre: Analogically mediated inquiry in organizations', *Organization Studies*, 28: 1805–1827.

Nissley, N., Taylor, S.S. and Houden, L. (2004) 'The politics of performance in organizational theatre-based training and interventions', *Organization Studies*, 25: 817–839.

Osborne, T. (2003) 'Against "creativity": A philistine rant', *Economy and Society*, 32: 507–525.

Rosen, M. (1988) 'You asked for it: Christmas at the bosses expense', *Journal of Management Studies*, 25: 463–480.

Schrage, M. (2000) *Serious Play*. Boston, MA: Harvard Business School Press.

Schrat, H. (2005) *Personal Communication*.

Taylor, S. (2003) 'Knowing in your gut and in your head: Doing theater and my underlying epistemology of communication', *Management Communication Quarterly*, 17: 272–279.

Tsoukas, H. and Chia, R. (2002) 'On organizational becoming: Rethinking organizational change', *Organization Science*, 13: 567–582.

Velthuis, O. (2005) *Imaginary Economics: Contemporary Artists and the World of Big Money*. Amsterdam: NAI Publishers.

Ventura, H.K. (2001) *Marion Ermer Preis 2001: Henrik Schrat*. Jena: Marion Ermer Foundation.

Zander, R.S. and Zander, B. (2000) *The Art of Possibility: Transforming Professional and Personal Life*. Cambridge, MA: Harvard Business School Press.

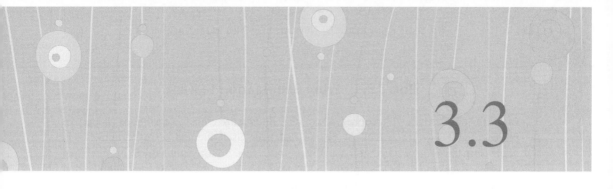

Aesthetic Play as an Organizing Principle

Pierre Guillet de Monthoux
and Matt Statler

Dialogue transcribed by Roxanna Sooudi

Prelude

Matt: All right then, how do we start talking about aesthetic play as an organizing principle?

Pierre: Maybe it seems bizarre, but I think we should start with Immanuel Kant.

Matt: But he's old and forgotten, not new and emerging.

Pierre: Well then, we'd better discuss who the guy is, and why he matters for organization theory today.

Matt: OK, then I'd start by saying that he was the most important philosopher in the Enlightenment, and that he actually laid the groundwork for what we call aesthetic theory today by linking it closely with ethics.

Pierre: And even though few people actually drag themselves through his rather dry and boring texts, it's worth our time to see how he built this bridge. Let me read a passage from his famous *Critique of Judgment*:

> I maintain that the beautiful is the symbol of the morally good; and only because we refer the beautiful to the morally good (we all do so naturally and require all others also to do so, as a duty) does our liking for it include a claim to everyone else's assent, while the mind is also conscious of being ennobled, by this [reference] above a mere receptivity for pleasure derived from sense impressions, and it assesses the value of other people too on the basis of [their having] a similar maxim in their power of judgment. (*Critique of Judgment*, 228)

Here the key is his notion about how the claim that something is beautiful involves a claim to everyone else's assent.

Box 3.3.1   From Baumgarten to Kant

In 1732 the German philosopher Alexander Baumgarten made 'aesthetics' a part of philosophy. This term, which of course had been used far and wide particularly in addressing the issue of whether the arts were truly 'fine' or not, came now to be attributed a special place among the disciplines of the academic sciences. Baumgarten claimed that experiences of beauty could be treated and understood logically, they should for this reason be included as part of philosophy. But it was Immanuel Kant who with his third *Critique* of 1790 made aesthetics a separate chapter in Western enlightenment philosophy. After having described both scientific and ethical knowledge in the first two *Critiques,* Kant reasoned that aesthetics not only has its place in philosophy, it should be seen as a separate form of knowledge with its own rules differing from that which concerns nature and human ethics.

Matt: Exactly. And this claim has normative or ethical dimensions that pertain to the basis for any possible community. Listen to this passage:

> We must [here] take *sensus communis* to mean the idea of a sense *shared* [by all of us], i.e., a power to judge that in reflecting takes account (a priori), in our thought, of everyone else's way of presenting [something], in order *as it were* to compare our own judgment with human reason in general and thus escape the illusion that arises from the ease of mistaking subjective and private conditions for objective ones, an illusion that would have a prejudicial influence on the judgment. (*Critique of Judgment,* 160)

So he means that we are not sharing our individual experiences, but instead, we are sharing something *a priori* behind our individuality.

Pierre: We share experiences because they refer to a fundamental organizational principle.

Matt: So how do different interpretations of this principle lead to different ways of managing?

Pierre: Well that's precisely the question that we should start trying to answer, because depending on how you read Kant, you will develop entirely different ideas about what management is. For example, if you assume that

the judgment of beauty provides only a nice illustration of the transcendental, underlying organizational principle, then art and aesthetics are interesting phenomena, but they're not central to, or necessary for managing and organizing. They are like a decoration that you can either enjoy or cast aside. Like icing on the cake with no real value added.

Matt: And in that case, whatever may be new and emerging about management, we shouldn't spend any time worrying about art and aesthetics, because though it may be nice to have around from time to time, we don't really need it.

Pierre: Right. But we work from a different assumption about Kant, an assumption launched by so-called postmodern philosophers that gives a central role to his *Third Critique*. Let us assume that actually aesthetics and art provide the only possible way of ever engaging with, or having any experience of the organizational principle.

Matt: But if you say it that way, it sounds like social constructionism.

Pierre: No, no! Because social constructionism is basically about texts, words and dialogue, and we are also interested in the embodied

---

Box 3.3.2   Content of Kant's *Critique of Judgment*

Aesthetics can be seen as having two aspects: on the one hand, the beautiful, on the other, the sublime. The beautiful was also light and pleasing; the sublime was dark and overpowering. When one experiences something as beautiful or as magnificently sublime then this is of course an individual feeling. But, and this was Kant's point which later became the focal message of philosophical aesthetics, this individual feeling also signals to us that we are on the trail of something that is a shared and generalized human feeling. What you deem beautiful, and which is in truth worth this designation, should be considered beautiful for all of humanity. It may be that aesthetics begins with a subjective feeling, but its function is to point to something that is objectively and universally true. This is what makes aesthetics a part of philosophy: that it points to something that is objective, i.e., a truth or principle.

---

dimensions of experience brought out by non-verbal visual art.

Matt: The important point is that the 'common ground' cannot necessarily be shared by words only, or known by science alone. Instead, if it can be known at all, it is through embodied experience, including but not limited to the embodied experience of using language. And if it can be shared, it is through doing things together with other people, engaging in practice, taking action. The point about social constructionism is that if we're going to talk about an organizing principle following Kant we cannot slip back into exclusively discursive logics. We have to focus on presentational, aesthetic logics, even if this focus might involve a deliberate rejection of the so-called 'linguistic turn' that dominates a great deal of contemporary organizational theory.

Pierre: Right, making use of aesthetics and art is really a new paradigm taking over after having treated and studied organizations as if they were organized as texts. We want to go for what's new and emerging in organization theory, we don't go for a new twist on semiotics à la Greimas, Derridean deconstruction, or Foucaldian discourse analysis. This new paradigm forces us to leave the idea that we get at social organization by means of some linguistic scientific method; we have to leave scientific management for a new view on organizations as aesthetic play.

Matt: But still, we have to be clearer about what we mean by aesthetic play before we can articulate its importance for management. Why don't you give it a shot?

Rondo

Pierre: Kant's claim is that the aesthetic experience gives a feel of universality, has a claim to universality. And yet he says that aesthetic experience can neither be put into concepts or words, nor argued in the logical ways we are used to when searching for truth.

Matt: Argued, but not proven.

Pierre: Argued, yes, okay – argued, but not proven. And he maintains that although this kind of organizing principle cannot be conceived with logical concepts, it still has a claim to truth, to universal truth.

So art and aesthetics should be taken seriously, and not mistaken as something like personal entertainment, some sort of idle, meaningless pleasure. Instead, aesthetics, because it points at the common ground, is basically a matter of defining the public. It is the only way to discover this kind of common space, common ground, on the basis of which we humans can cooperate and organize.

Matt: As you said, this is, however, a very postmodern way of reading old Kant! The stream of philosophy after Kant that a century later took shape as Anglo-American, analytic philosophy would not agree. The stream of so-called 'Continental' philosophy that includes hermeneutics, phenomenology and critical theory looks upon Kant's *Third Critique* as central to his system, while the analytical philosophers see it as a nice appendix for handling strange 'irrational non-conceptual phenomena' that are difficult to render in the propositional terms associated with rational, conscious human action. Speaking very generally, the analytics tend to ignore aesthetics, studying only what is verbal or propositional, while the Continental philosophers find the non-verbal or presentational much more fruitful as an avenue for philosophical inquiry.

Pierre: Yes, when postmod-Kant insists on aesthetics as fundamental, he means that when we make aesthetic judgments that are by nature subjective, we automatically hook up to an objective, possible public space. So if you make the proposition that, for instance, a landscape is beautiful, or the Niagara Falls are sublime, you assume that everyone must agree with you. This proposition then implies that the landscape gets its beauty through the plan of God, according to Kant. But such a truth

can never be argued, for there are no definite or precise concepts in aesthetics and this is what makes the analytics uneasy. If people disagree with your proposition, you will not end up with a purely rational dialogue, but with a *Streit*, a debate, or even a struggle.

Matt: And as we engage in that fight, Kant insists that we should not let go of our claim and just assume that my taste is mine, and yours is yours, and hey, can't we all just get along…?

Pierre: Peace and love!

Matt: …because in the rare event that peace and love happens, then usually it happens more or less immediately, because if I say 'Beautiful!', and you agree, then there we are in loving peace. This is in tune with Rafael Ramirez' point in *The Beauty of Social Organization* that people choose a place of work for its beauty without ever making this verbally explicit. But if I say 'Beautiful!' and you disagree, what happens then? It could be a fight to the death, or it could be aesthetic play – and in either case, I would argue following Kant that through engagement in practice, we experience the normative and political aspects of the claim to the beautiful, irrespective of whether we then judge these aspects to be moral and pleasing or grounds for war. Maybe we'll get into heated debates about organizations similar to the fights taking place amongst critics in the artworld. Why is the McDonald's brand ugly and Apple's brand beautiful?

Pierre: That's where I think the Schiller developed Kant's thought. He claims specifically that art and the artists can help make this fight about organizational truth somewhat less gruesome precisely by turning it into an aesthetic play. They can actually help us to manage it!

Box 3.3.3   Schiller's Theory of Aesthetic Play

In 1792 the poet Friedrich Schiller began to study Kant's big book. This resulted in a series of letters, later published under the title *On the Aesthetic Education of Man*, in which Schiller created a simplified model of Kant's aesthetics and placed men of his persuasion, i.e., artists, at its center. Schiller asserted that Kant demonstrated how important our ability to make aesthetic judgments (i.e., to discover objective truths through experiences of the beautiful and the sublime) is. If we are not able to make judgments like these we risk ending up either in complete formalism, i.e., becoming locked into logical thinking; or in complete materialism, i.e., only relying on the material aspects of existence. We need, between Form and Matter, to maintain Play, and it is the artist's task to awaken in us the desire to play and remind us always that all is not Form or Matter, or ethics and science. Aesthetics, as Schiller has discovered in Kant's third *Critique,* is a theory that describes a third path.

Allegro

Matt: So you think aesthetic play can help us to develop better ways to manage?

Pierre: Schiller helps us focus on one very important aspect of Kant's aesthetic theory by stating that aesthetic play is a way out of a deadlock between either formalism or materialism or what we might also call the 'ought' and the 'is'. It was as if Kant felt the two to be irreconcilable in practice if unmediated by a third position, i.e., aesthetic play. I think we need to start by looking into this mediation as organizational researchers. I mean, how do people engage in playful practice? Where do we find these artists/managers?

Matt: We could look at emergent organizational phenomena like people gathering in the park to do tai chi, or networks of hackers forming around a shared passion for writing beautiful code. Or we could look at examples of traditional business organizations that engage in play.

Pierre: As well as arts organizations like theaters that produce plays that might ease and unlock the conflict between materialist and idealist positions...

Matt: In any case, Schiller directs our attention to those shared practices through which organization itself takes shape. He shows us how to place theoretical emphasis on the aesthetic dimension of the experience of engaging in such practices.

Pierre: Yes, the aesthetic dimension, for there are other dimensions that Schiller calls 'form' and 'matter', between which this aesthetic play emerges.

Matt: That means that if we're looking for empirical examples of aesthetic play, we cannot afford to look only at organizational forms, or at the content of their strategies and plans. Neither can we assume that we're going to find completely free play that takes place independently of these other dimensions.

Pierre: Aesthetic play is not just about free creativity taking place completely outside of the organizational context. That's a trap that people fall into when they go out on these retreats, have these creativity sessions, and then can't bring it to bear on their everyday life when they come home. For play is something that emerges like a blessing in a problematic situation where we desperately look for formal or material solutions. Aesthetic play can never be 'pure' – it has to be experienced in context to be of any use.

Matt: The old 'Monday morning' syndrome.

Pierre: We're interested in following Schiller toward the aesthetic play that actually emerges, even if it's hiding, in the form and the matter of Monday morning, back at the desk. Organizational aesthetics is something at work and has little meaning as some kind of entertainment enjoyed as leisure or luxury. It has a hell of a bearing on everyday dull and dreary life.

Matt: So then we have to speak both about the playful, aesthetic dimensions of bureaucratic life, as well as about the bureaucratic framing of art in what you call 'art firms'.

Pierre: We can even speak about bureaucracy, and how its ceremonies, rituals, behaviors, and routines might have an aesthetic value. And conversely, we can speak about art that starts up when an institution, like a concert hall, opera house, museum, or theater is filled with something, something like play.

Matt: So following Kant's *Critique of Judgment* the fine arts provide a particularly compelling domain for management research because they are institutions that are deliberately open for playful, aesthetic expression.

Pierre: In these art firms, there are always administrations, wages to be paid, security restrictions, work disciplines, and so on. More importantly, there are traditions and conventions, the expectations of the audience, the career aspirations of the performers, and so on. But within these organizations something happens, and change occurs. In this case, a new form of art. The role of such bureaucracies

is to provide a strict material-formal frame within which artwork can be brought out as the outcome of play.

Matt: And these various constraints and possibilities for innovation become interesting for management theory precisely in the contemporary situation where the 'creative industries' are actually driving the economy.

Pierre: It's in that sense interesting to see how firms increasingly don't produce 'products', i.e., material things. Workers are not even necessarily delivering 'services', i.e., behave according to formal standards. Instead, people put on plays and try to perform like virtuosos.

Matt: Maybe this has always been true for the entertainment business, but today it is also true in other industries, where the bulk of the resources are spent on advertising, media and communications, and marketing. In our 'experience economy', the activity of workers in firms is not a means to the end of producing something, but a playful performance that is an end itself.

Pierre: And the challenge faced by organizations is therefore how to sustain that play, or rather, how they make the show go on within the material-formal frame. This is where we can really learn from looking at how artists and philosophers have mutually inspired each other to keep the aesthetic play going.

Matt: And yet, organizations that draw on this inspiration must also confront the normative or political dimensions of their own performances in practice. Because the play can go well, as in the case of Apple computers and the incredible success that their brand aesthetic has brought them. But it can also go very badly, when an aesthetic principle of organizing comes to appear morally wrong or

---

Box 3.3.4 Philosophers and Artists

With Schiller and Kant leading the way, aesthetics, particularly in German 19th century philosophy, explodes as a theory describing art's capacity for revealing the truth. Artists, of course, love to study aesthetics as it offers a kind of legitimization and explanation for what it is that they are trying to accomplish. This can be seen starting with Richard Wagner's references to Arthur Schopenhauer, in which he is aided by Friedrich Nietzsche; onto how an artist like Hans Haacke converses with the sociologist of art Pierre Bourdieu, or how the American philosopher Arthur Danto teams up with pop artists like Andy Warhol. But starting with Kant and Schiller, philosophers and artists have trod the same ground and joined in creative partnerships. While the artist creates art, the philosopher tries to describe the kind of knowledge or understanding that is created in an audience when confronted with a work of art. In this way, one can say that philosophers and artists together create an aesthetic business, an 'art firm' with a given purpose to create meaning and to keep the third path for knowledge open to traffic.

---

even illegal, like Enron's infamous self-presentation as 'the smartest guys in the room'.

Pierre: Both were creative and spectacular, but why is Apple's performance on the stage a success, while Enron's performance is a scandal?

Matt: Enron's attempt to 'game the energy market' appears in that light as an excess of pure play, free creativity. But Schiller and Kant remind us that aesthetic play has to be connected to form and matter. So Enron played badly by breaking the formal, social constraint of law, as well as by creating material havoc in the case of the California energy crisis and smashing people's retirement plans. And instead of sustaining its own aesthetic play, the organization Enron imploded as a scandal.

Pierre: And by contrast, Apple appears to be playing well, in the sense that they deliver a performance that strengthens the formal, normative force of the community of people who find Apple products aesthetically pleasing. At the same time, what they deliver actually seems to work. So their aesthetic play strikes

a balance between these two other dimensions.

Matt: Aesthetic play is not just about impression management, or creating a sensation. Take Gregory Bateson's definition of aesthetics as 'the pattern that connects'. In Apple's case it worked by connecting the formal and material, but at Enron it blew the balance.

Pierre: So in a business, the formal game must be played according to its ethical rules. And the material game, that is, the technological, scientific part, also has to work. Still, the ethics and the technique depend on the aesthetic play taking part in between them. As if the aesthetic play connected the two and brought them to life, but by its own principle.

Matt: So what kind of management practices do you think the principle of aesthetic play gives rise to?

Pierre: Well Schiller's chicken soup version of Kant explicitly makes artists responsible for keeping the aesthetic play going in society, so I think management based on the principle of aesthetic play is less about control and decision and more about this

---

Box 3.3.5   Artists, Philosophers, Managers

In this spirit, the German artist Joseph Beuys pointed out during the sixties and seventies that art is capital (ART = CAPITAL), that we are all artists when we are subjectively creative and that works of art are in fact social sculptures that give us meaningful, objective, and shared social structures. Through its ability to reveal objective truths, art is one of the most important means for generating public awareness. This was Kant's thesis and it has become a recurring theme in all aesthetics. This is what Nicholas Bourriaud (2001) writes, for example, in an essay that has become as popular among artists of today as Nietzsche and Schopenhauer were at the end of the 19th century. Nietzsche became very popular with Wagner when he held that Wagner's operas revived an aesthetic sense in their audiences. And Bourriaud points to how installations and works by performance artists try and encourage their audiences to playfully initiate relationships among themselves in a way that formally and materially hyper-structured societies have repressed. So both Beuys and Bourriaud emphasize the aesthetic effect of art on organizing.

---

kind of artistic leadership. Managers and engineers have to team up with such leaders providing motivation, inspiration, and passion. That is why people out in industry often look for models of this kind of leadership in various art forms, finding inspiration in directors, conductors, choreographers, and designers. If we regard this kind of leadership from Schiller's Kantian perspective, it is much more about inciting enthusiasm and passion using a kind of playfulness. The effect that this kind of leadership has is more like euphoria or excitement. Just as we can be inspired by art in the opera, the museum, the concert hall, and the festival. To inspire such passion, a leader must be able to charge a situation with aesthetic energy and open up a third aesthetic door where others can only see the two other solutions.

Matt: That breaks away from the traditions of management theory that focus only on those variables that can be known by science.

Pierre: Yes, but it means finding something that can truly motivate. It adds aesthetic value to something that would otherwise work technically and be politically correct, but remain lifeless and unattractive. Rembrandt was certainly a master of technique, but ultimately his mastery as a painter involves something beyond technique. It involves something we may call genius or talent, but from which no method and no rules may be derived.

Matt: That means that in practice, the artist as an aesthetic leader has to balance the industrial engineers and the rational decision-makers.

Pierre: It is precisely the task of balancing these two styles of management that is the role of aesthetic play in organizations. And actually, when you study artists, you are likely to see how they strike this balance in practice.

Matt: On reflection, I wonder whether the aesthetic leader, the industrial engineer and the rational decision-maker have surfaced in this conversation as icons of contemporary organizational practice precisely because they are already engaged in some kind of aesthetic play. The German philosopher Hans-Georg Gadamer seems to make this point when he says:

> We do not learn moral knowledge, nor can we forget it. We do not stand over against it, as if it were something that we can acquire or not, as we can choose to acquire an objective skill... Rather, we are always already in the situation of having to act... (Gadamer, 2002 [1960]: 317)

The point here is that our capacity for aesthetic interpretation is what also enables us to judge situations and act ethically – so our interpretations of aesthetic play in organizations carry significant normative or ethical baggage.

Pierre: For Schiller, the theater was a place where you enjoyed a play, while at the same time aesthetically refining your capacity for ethical judgment. That is why it was important to have court theaters performing for the decision-makers, the prince. The role of these traditional art institutions was to refine the ethical judgment of the societal elites.

Matt: And for Aristotle, one effect of tragedy was to refine the ethical sensibilities not only of the elites, but also of all the citizens in Athenian democracy by providing them with the experience of catharsis.

Pierre: Remember how Nietzsche considered the aesthetic Greek tragedy as the cradle of Western civilization?

Matt: Yes, but if you invoke Nietzsche, then we should also acknowledge that this long historical tradition has to be approached critically and carefully. Our choice of examples makes all the difference, and even choosing to base a management theory on classical examples like Aristotle or Schiller can be deeply ambiguous from a political or moral perspective.

Pierre: That's why I like to talk about how Joseph Beuys, an artist, inspired a political organization – namely, the Green Party in Germany – and a new way of looking upon human creativity as capital, and likewise about how Nicolas Bourriaud claims that relational aesthetics might animate public spaces in ways no urban planners or social worker can do.

Matt: Right, so following Beuys' lead, we should be talking about the fields of flow in management theory and practice.

Pierre: OK, but let's move slowly and carefully.

Andante cantabile

Matt: Well, the first field of flow that I see is between ethics and aesthetics. I think we need to move beyond a notion of ethics as something that has to be based on rules and principles, even though business ethics is dominated by utilitarian and deontological theories.

Pierre: In practice, of course, we seldom have purely utilitarian or deontic situations. It may not be possible to determine the effects of our actions, and it may not be possible to identify a universal rule or maxim to govern our intentions.

Matt: Exactly. That's why if we want to move beyond rules and principles in the flow between ethics and aesthetics, we need to work with a theory, like Aristotle's, that locates moral value not in the intention or the effect, but in the performance of action itself.

Pierre: But what does that have to do with aesthetics?

Matt: Aristotle suggests not only that the virtuous performance of good action is also necessarily beautiful, but that we can only recognize aesthetic beauty if we are ethically virtuous.

Pierre: So that was why Schiller urged decision-makers to attend theater performances, because it would sharpen their eye for the good.

Matt: Yes, Aristotle's conception has influenced the cultivation of the arts throughout Western civilization.

Pierre: So you could say that Kant and company, as well as those advocating aesthetics in management, are reviving this ancient tradition.

Matt: Yes, but the contemporary attempt to revive this tradition within the context of management and organization studies requires two things. First, it requires a more in-depth understanding of the virtues and habits associated with beautiful performance. Second, it requires a greater awareness of the aesthetic dimension of those practices that are considered 'good' management.

Pierre: Do you mean that organizations should have their Schillerian theatres and that business schools should be like classical Greek academies, where cultivation of the arts was as important as the sciences and ethics? Will you become a better manager if you read Homer?

Matt: Not necessarily, but I do think that the widespread, contemporary challenge of 'dealing with complexity' has emerged not necessarily because the world has become more complex, but because two or three generations of managers have been trained to assume that the world should fit within a two-by-two matrix. Instead of working out their strategies on spreadsheets, working out their bodies in the gym and getting their culture fix down at the multiplex cinema, they might be better off if they learned to deal with complexity by engaging in aesthetic play at work.

Pierre: Well, when you talk about inadequate methods of dealing with complexity, it makes me think about the car industry and the 'concept cars' that we know will never be produced

and made available on the market. The car industry feels the need for play and aesthetics, so they ask designers to dream something up. But this industry has developed through technological simplification and capital concentration for almost a century. So now they think play and aesthetics can be introduced as a marketing gimmick in isolation from real production and consumption. This way of isolating aesthetic play turns creative complexity into simple, two-by-two boredom. The concept cars never make it to market, and all the cars that do hit the market end up looking basically the same.

Matt: But surely there are some positive cases in which organizations are exploring the flow between aesthetics and science, no?

Pierre: Well, some people actually claim that successful innovation is frequently inspired by science fiction. Artists like Jules Verne, Ray Bradbury and Arthur C. Clarke have injected aesthetics into science and engineering. And people who have studied software innovation claim that those programmers work as if they were performing artists.

Matt: It seems that right alongside the scientific method, you frequently find playful imagination and bricolage.

Pierre: And the other way around as well: no play is possible without having access to the technological hardware and the ethical framework of the community that sanctions it. This means that you can't outsource aesthetic play – it has to develop within the organization, and it has to re-introduce complexity where it has been squeezed out by the drive to simplify. There are lots of examples of this kind of thing, like the big R&D labs that got squeezed out when project managers moved in and rationalized the corporations.

Matt: Right, and in such cases, the fact that the senior management allowed the source of innovation to be accounted for as a cost may simply mean that they did not appropriately maintain the balance between form and matter through aesthetic play.

Pierre: The result was a simple, 2x2 matrix corporation, one that was less able to deal with complexity of its business.

Matt: So then, the management challenge is how to overcome the tendency to simplify organizational reality in accordance with rules, and reinstate our human capacity to deal with the complexity of our world in ways that are effective, ethical and enjoyable.

Pierre: For complexity can be both beautiful and sublime – it doesn't have to be dangerous and scary. People get nervous about complexity, when actually they could appreciate it, see the potential in it, like you do when you go to a good art show. As Schiller says, artists revive the playful child in us, and art is an invitation to play. Organizational artists become leaders facilitating play and coaching playfulness.

Matt: But since most of us have been taught to think that this playful spirit contradicts the seriousness of adult life, especially when it comes to work, we need Kant, Schiller, and other aesthetic philosophers to help us rediscover a way of thinking and acting that has been effaced by the rise of scientific management and the work ethics associated with it. What we really need is experiential engagement in aesthetically playful practices.

Pierre: The problem, of course, is that since corporations have been built precisely on this misconception, unfortunately, artists don't usually want to join corporations and help develop such practices because they don't feel at home there.

Matt: What's worse, it may be that corporations are seldom perceived as doing good in the world precisely because they lack aesthetic play.

Pierre: As long as that's the case, we have to go to galleries and museums to find what lacks in the corporate world. This in turn may lead us to build corporate art programs and collections to restore the status of play in the organization.

Matt: But this separation reflects an imbalance. If we want to develop practically wise leaders, it's helpful, but not enough to take the board of directors on a gallery tour. We need to integrate aesthetic play into the daily practice of organizational life.

Pierre: Sounds good, but how are we going to do that?

Matt: I guess it would be pretty misguided to think that we've done it already just by talking about it.

Box 3.3.6   Aesthetic Play as an Organizing Principle

When an artist like Rirkrit Tiravanija cooks noodle soup and offers it to guests at a gallery or at the Dokumenta art expo, he wants with this aesthetic play to bring us together in an everyday but nonetheless new way. Bourriaud belongs to the tradition of Schiller by letting the artist become someone who can show the way to a natural rediscovery of playfulness. With Kant in the background, we can realize that this activity, the artistic business of aesthetic play has a far greater purpose than as mere entertainment or as an amusing pastime. It is rather about rediscovering, with the help of the artist and his work, a basic principle that unites us, a basis other than that of form or matter.

Box 3.3.7   Performing Aesthetic Play

Successful Italian artist Michelangelo Pistoletto has founded the Cittadellarte art academy for supporting young artists doing 'socially responsible art'– projects. He sees the great number of artists graduating from art schools as change agents in society. 'You don't have to love the physical art work of every artist but they have a way of approaching problems and engaging in processes that can be extremely helpful' says Michelangelo, whose center has listed more than a hundred websites of artist-driven projects performing aesthetic play to innovate in areas as communication, education, economics, politics, production, and nourishment.

There is no doubt that today's artistry consists in organizing and that the outcomes; i.e., the art-works, often *are* organizations. Post-'68 radical artists explored the world of work and industry; in the 80s artists liked to ironically mirror corporate worlds from a position of outside critique; today, artists, like the ones cooperating with Cittadellarte, enter business organizations and perform art inside the organization, thus staging aesthetic play in organizations. A growing number of artists try to showcase how such aesthetic play can be performed. The Product & Vision show, curated by artists Mari Brellochs and Henrik Schrat at the Kunstfabrik in Berlin 2005, reflects the most recent developments in this direction.

More than 20 attempts to portray one single firm – German publisher Cornelesen – were exposed at the Product & Vision show. The firm had opened its doors for artists to explore its everyday organizational reality; Cornelesen had, so to speak, stripped itself as an artist's model. By confronting its personnel with the installation, a debate on modes of working and communicating was engaged in response to the various 'portraits' on show. For the duration of the show, Kunstfabrik became a stage for an aesthetic play tackling issues important for the firm, issues seldom brought up and almost always overlooked by decision-makers and consultants. Art thus turned from being an 'icing on a successful business-cake', like in most traditional art shows sponsored by corporations, to a way to facilitate aesthetic play in the heart of the organization. This in turn influenced the way to understand the beauty of a firm not as perfection and excellence but as having a 'human face' where success and failure honestly co-habit. Whereas discussions within the firm typically focus on modes of measuring efficiency in organizations, a theme of 'judgment' was softly introduced in the playful discussions. Buzz words like 'knowledge-industry' were dropped as people openly started to speak about the importance of facing and embracing 'ignorance.' Instead of efficiency the concept of 'engagement' came on the agenda. All this signals that an aesthetic play was emerging, and with it process opening to reshaping and reorganizing business from the inside. As the curators/consultants/artists, Brellochs and Schrat (2005) have noted in the reader they published for the show, aesthetic play such as the one staged for Cornelesen in the Kunstfabrik exemplifies how artists and businesspeople can not only meet, but also invent sophisticated survival techniques for organizations.

Pierre: Well, we have to start somewhere.

Matt: I think if we start here by talking about new and emerging management theory, we see that the concept of aesthetic play provides a new ontology of management, a new understanding of what organizing is, or can be.

Pierre: And this new ontology indicates that effective, enjoyable, and ethical organizing can occur whenever the formal and material dimensions of organizational life are balanced, checked and energized through aesthetic play.

Matt: So rather than a metaphysical theory about how many angels can fit on the head of a pin, this new ontology is practical insofar as it encourages managers to develop their own practical wisdom by engaging in play and the arts.

Pierre: And by engaging artists in their organization to safeguard the aesthetic playground. In this sense, aesthetic play is not just a discursive metaphor that portrays organizations as orchestras, it's performed as a kind of organizing.

Matt: Well speaking of performing organizational principles, we've rambled on long enough by now for one chapter don't you think?

Pierre: Probably so. But as for what's new and emerging, shall we go and see what's happening in the kitchen?

Matt: Fine by me.

REFERENCES

Aristotle (1962) *Nicomachean Ethics*. Indianapolis: Bobbs-Merrill.

Bateson, G. (1972) *Steps to an Ecology of Mind*. Northvale: Jason Aronson Inc.

Bourdieu, P. and Hans, H. (1995) *Free Exchange*. Palo Alto: Stanford University Press.

Bourriaud, N. (2001) *Esthetique relationelle*. Dijon: Les presses du reel.

Brellochs, M. and Schrat, H. (2005) *Product Vision Reader; Sophisticated Survival Techniques – Strategies in Art and Economy*. Berlin: Kadmos Kulturverlag.

Gadamer, Hans-Georg (2002 [1960]) *Truth and Method*. New York: Continuum.

Guillet de Monthoux, Pierre, Antonio Strati (eds) (2002) 'Aesthetics and Management – business bridges to art', special issue in *Consumption Markets and Culture*, 5(1), March 2002.

Guillet de Monthoux, Pierre, Antonio Strati (eds) (2002) 'Organizing Aesthetics', special issue in *Human Relations* 55(7), July 2002.

Guillet de Monthoux, Pierre (2004) *The Art Firm: Aesthetic Management and Metaphysical Marketing*. Palo Alto: Stanford University Press.

Guillet de Monthoux, Pierre (2006) *Liedership – a fields of flow musical – CD record*. Stockholm: Arvinius Förlag.

Guillet de Monthoux, Pierre (2006) *Masters of Business Art – a Fields of Flow Movie*. Stockholm: ECAM (pguille@attglobal.net)

Guillet de Monthoux, Pierre, G. Claes and Sjöstrand, Sven-Erik (2007) *Aesthetic Leadership – Managing Fields of Flow in Art and Business*. Houndmills: Palgrave-Macmillan.

Kant, I. (1986) *Critique of Pure Reason*, (trans. Werner S. Pluhar and Patricia Kitcher). Indianapolis: Hackett Press.

Kant, I. (1987) *Critique of Judgment* (trans. Werner S. Pluhar). Indianapolis: Hackett Press.

Kant, I. (2002) *Critique of Practical Reason*, (trans. Werner S. Pluhar). Indianapolis: Hackett Press.

Ramirez, R. (1991) *The Beauty of Social Organization*. Munich: Accedo Verlag.

Schiller, F. (1982) *On the Aesthetic Education of Man* (trans. Elizabeth Wilkinson and L.A. Willoughby). Oxford: Oxford University Press.

3.4

If People are Strange, Does Organization Make Us Normal?

Stewart Clegg

INTRODUCTION

It is possible to write a great deal about organizations without ever addressing the simplest fact that they exhibit: they are premised on relations of power and domination, which may be variably authoritative. It is a possibility whose consummation is rarely achieved in much of the literature which manages to sidestep such self-evidence. Power – and resistance to it – was a theme inscribed in the practical history of organizations at the outset even if it was largely missing in action in many subsequent theorizations. Power is, perhaps, least evident to those whom its relation flatter, seduce, and enroll in its projects; by corollary, it is, perhaps most evident to those whom these relations spurn, estrange, and humiliate. Thus, the crucial relations are those among the person, the organization, and the primal categorization devices of familiar or stranger. Noting that all forms of order face risk, I shall go on to

argue that organizations shape themselves in relation to those strangers society creates – African Americans in the Jazz Age, Islamists today, when the perception is that contemporary organizations are increasingly at risk from a heightened state of insecurity. The strangers whose deviance is used to define organizational normalcy are different–but in different ways. The Jazz Age exists as a case study in how projects of organization power migrate and change socially, which will be indicated by recalling how shifts from policing the body to moral policing occurred. If the southern 'Negro' was the problem in the 1920s, one may say that more recent manifestations of the stranger now capture societal imagination in the West, giving contemporary forms of hypersurveillance a boost, demonstrating that all forms of surveillance and policing produce deviance as the proof of the normal. Finally, a new agenda for researchers is sketched – the impact of societal politics on organizational practices and the need for alertness to the strangers in our midst – some of whom we create through our own practices, others whose strangeness our practices intensify. The overall purpose of the chapter is to highlight the importance of the situational ethics that constitute what it is that organization researchers do and to encourage greater reflexivity toward these practices, and their ethical considerations. In short, good organizational and management research should not accept the tribal wisdom embedded in particular communities of practice as the arbiter of analytic taste. It needs to be reflexive toward that on which it trades.

POWER AS TECHNIQUES OF SOCIAL RELATIONS

Foucault teaches us that, rather than being a resource that can be held or exercised – a capacity inanimate but potential – power is inseparable from its effects. The focus for analysis is the play of techniques, the mundane practices that shape everyday life, structuring particular forms of conduct and more especially structuring the ways in which people choose to fashion their own sense of self, their dispositions and those devices with which, through which, by which, they are shaped and framed. Some representations of the world, which of necessity have a historical specificity (ways of seeing the world are always diachronically shifting and contested language games) become fixed in usage, are normalized, become the common currency of thought and conceptualization. Specific discursive practices become institutionalized and thus have common currency among other discursive practices, even as they are resisted. Thus, in closely related times but in radically disjunctive conjectures of knowledge, justice can be served both by imposing its design on the body or by seeking to discipline the soul (Foucault, 1977).

There are those who know indubitably that their bodies and their souls are dominated, who have power and surveillance exercised over them, and there are those who stand in

hybrid relations to power – partly constituted by it and partly enacting its constitutions. And there are those who move effortlessly through the elite portals of power: they switch effortlessly from boardroom to executive suite, from the Cabinet Office to the corporate headquarters, traversing spaces that are just as designed as the panopticon – but designed to produce *legitimate* asymmetries of authority; asymmetries that the hybrids will want to *desire*, by which they will seek to be *seduced* (Rosen et al., 1990). Still others may be *forced* to accept such relations through *coercion*, while others may be *deceived* as to the intent that resides in these relations and are thus *manipulated*. Different actors may generate power effects through these different modalities. A key role is played by the constitution of the stranger for it is the categories of deviance that define the norm.

THE STRANGER

Bauman (2001: 200) has suggested of societies that they each make their own strangers: the same is true of organizations more specifically.[1]

> All organizations produce strangers; but each kind of organization produces its own kind of strangers, and produces them in its own inimitable way. If strangers are the people who do not fit the cognitive, moral or aesthetic map of the world – one of these maps, two or all three; if they, therefore, by their sheer presence, make obscure what ought to be transparent, confuse what ought to be a straightforward recipe for action, and/or prevent the satisfaction from being fully satisfying, pollute the joy with anxiety while making the forbidden fruit alluring; if in other words, they befog and eclipse the boundary lines which can be clearly seen; if, having done all this, they gestate uncertainty, which in turn breeds discomfort of feeling lost – then each organization produces such strangers, while drawing its borders and charting its cognitive, aesthetic and moral map. It cannot but gestate people who conceal borderlines deemed crucial to its orderly and/or meaningful life and are thus charged with causing the discomfort experienced as the most painful and least bearable.

As Bauman says, 'the stranger carries a threat of wrong classification, but – more horrifying yet – she is a threat to classification as such, to the order of the universe, to the orientation value of social space – to my life-world as such' (Bauman, 1993: 150). Perhaps a critical question for studying organizations relates to how they both create and treat strangers and how strangers are allowed in, or banned. Note that strangers are not necessarily workers from the bottom of the organizational hierarchy: strangers might well sit in boardrooms. (Top) managers can be alienated from their team just as workers from management. That does not mean that we have more sympathy with them, but it stresses the fact that lines of conflict do not follow the organizational chart vertically but emerge rhizomatically throughout the organization. Being a stranger is not a matter of class but, as Bauman writes, 'the stranger is someone of whom one knows little and desires to know even less … [and] … someone of whom one cares little and is prompted to care even less' (Bauman, 1993: 167) yet who might still be in close physical proximity. On this basis, the nature of the strangers created might tell us much about an organization. The problem of modern society and of organizations might be cast as being not how to eliminate strangers, but 'how to live in their constant company' (Bauman, 1993: 159).

Practically, one can imagine the difference of strangers being responded to through one or other of three typical approaches within organizations. First, there is an *anthropophagic* strategy. Organizations devour strangers to annihilate them, making them metaphorically indistinguishable from the body of the existing organization. *This responds to difference, literally, by incorporation.* Some of Goffman's (1961) total institutions, those based on an overarching normative frame, such as boot-camps, barracks, boarding schools, and nunneries, typically seek such annihilation of any difference that pre-exists those that the organization will shape, devising appropriate degradation rituals to achieve this eclipse of identity. Under the spell of instrumental managerialism organizations become culturally, calculably, and contingently totalitarian, sucking the life-worlds

out of their subjects, making them McTeam members incapable of agency or resistance. For management scholars, the issue here is how not to be *sucked in*. Where organizations cannot incorporate through rituals that devour difference, then, once membership prevails, the second, *anthropoemic* strategy can come into play: the organization can vomit strangers out, 'banishing them from the limits of the orderly world and barring them from all communication with those inside' (Bauman, 2001: 201). Excommunication, expunction, and rustication push strangeness outside the orderly inclusive words of an organization that refuses to address some as members, excluding and 'expelling the strangers beyond the frontiers of the managed and manageable territory' (Bauman, 2001: 201–202). *This responds to difference, literally, by dismembering.* The risk is of being *spat out*.

Because identities are in the process of emergence and becoming in different projects, mingling and intercepting with identities already in being, they are oriented to 'conditions of overwhelming and self-perpetuating uncertainty' (Bauman, 2001: 208). Members and deviants, familiars and strangers, are thus the by-products, as well as the means, of production of the incessant and never conclusive process of identity building that organizational discourse, in its different projects, sustains. A key part of the uncertainty relates to how boundaries are blurred and how normal divisions and gaps of complex organization are eclipsed by variable experience in projects that enable people to wander across boundaries, becoming metaphorical strangers in terms of previously fixed organizational identities. Such strangers pose problems for organizations because they actively transgress the boundaries of sensemaking to the extent that management power uses certain legitimated discourses within which strangers cannot be contained. The risks here are neither being *sucked in* nor *spat out* (cf. Parker, 2002) but of *communion*: is one making sense in terms of the range of recognized, institutionalized and powerful ways of making sense to which the organization is host? (Clearly, as the term chosen suggests, these are especially concerns for religious organizations in certain Christian traditions. As cultural commitment begins to take on more and more the elements of religious belief – and as Christian fundamentalism shapes an increasing number of especially US organization members – the aptness of the term should not go unremarked.)

THE JAZZ AGE, STRANGERS WITHIN, AND MORAL PANICS

After the US Civil War, black people left the sharecropper society of the Deep South in droves, fleeing a culture rooted in slavery. And, after hitting Highway 61, they headed for the burgeoning factories of the north, in Chicago and Detroit, in the latter of which Ford began hiring African Americans in large numbers in 1915, paying them the same wages as his white employees. The material basis of the jazz age for the many black people who headed north was working in the factories and assembly plants. By 1923, Ford employed 5,000 Detroit-area black men, far more than in other plants.

The influx of black people into Northern cities and jobs was the occasion for middle-class white anxieties. Indeed, at the time they were a source of what Stanley Cohen (1972: 9) has referred to as a 'moral panic'. A moral panic occurs when some 'episode, condition, person or group of persons' is 'defined as a threat to societal values and interests' because they are 'strangers'. Such moral panics are based on the perception that some individual or group, frequently a *minority*, is dangerously *deviant*, and poses a *menace to society*. They often occur as a result of a fear of a loss of control when adapting to significant changes. Typically, as Cohen suggests, authorities create 'stylized and stereotypical' representations, raise moral fears, and 'pronounce judgment'.

Moral panic fed in to the work of Ford's Sociological Department. They wanted to ensure that the men Ford employed were sober, disciplined men, whose energies would

be conserved and their minds wholly focused on the necessity of being excellent five dollar a day men. They should not be workers who wasted money on booze, dope, and vice, because such were not welcome as Ford employees, as members of the Ford family. Decent white folk knew the type of person most likely to be wasteful of their energies and the kinds of excess in which they would be wasted. African-Americans, jazz, and dope became inexorably intertwined in the popular imagination of, as well as some experience in, black culture. The scapegoating of black cultures, such as jazz, for spreading marijuana usage into white society was emblematic of a deep-seated paranoia (Porter, 2002: 9).

The moral panics that grew in the 1920s and 1930s around 'reefer madness' and 'jazz' were barely coded concerns for the contagion of white society by black bodies and black culture. As Lopes (2005: 1468) suggests, from the Jazz Age of the 1920s 'the sordid world of jazz and the deviant jazz musician became a common trope in the popular press, pulp fiction, and Hollywood film. Jazz in general served as a trope for the darker side of the American urban experience'. Despite the fact that, as its name suggests, marijuana first came into the US from Mexico, jazz and marijuana became inextricably linked with black people and black music in the popular imagination. The first recorded use of marijuana in the US was in Storyville in 1909 (Abel, 1980), which was the red light district of the port of New Orleans and the birthplace of jazz. Foundational jazz musicians, such as Jelly Roll Morton, honing their craft in the bordellos, created incidental accompaniments to the central commerce conducted there. Rather than drink, dope was the preferred drug. Marijuana didn't slow down the reflexes and improvisation the way that alcohol could; also it seemed to heighten the creative impulse.

Jazz and dope were not exactly the stuff of a rationalizing impulse. Thus, having a Sociological Department (as well as employing Pinkerton's to spy on potential trouble makers and unionists and to break up union meetings) seemed a small investment to make to ensure an efficient, reliable, and certain workforce, untroubled by jazz, dope, or booze, or an inability to save, invest and consume. All such irrationalities were to be expected of people who made jazz their culture. It is not surprising that jazz played this role; first, it was associated by respectable white society with unrespectable black society; second, it infused the body with passion, rhythm, movement – a lack of disciplined sobriety. It was wild dance music and its main feature was its exuberant ability to move its fans and musicians to shake their bodies, dance, and beat the rhythm. As Appelrouth (2005: 1497) suggests, 'manners of the body share the potential for becoming a stage on which the struggle for social legitimacy and control is dramatized'. In the body may be seen the larger social order and its struggles to impose good order, taste, and discipline on nature. Pollution of the body is a metaphor for the disruption of the boundaries that shape 'legitimate' society, as Douglas (1966) suggests. Thus, following Appelrouth (2005: 1497) 'we should not be surprised to find anxieties concerning social disruptions expressed through a body-centered discourse. During periods in which challenges are posed to existing social divisions and schemes of classification, attempts to define the body publicly take on heightened significance'. The popular imagination was shaped by a discourse that regarded jazz as disorderly, as Appelrouth notes by citing an article asking: 'Does jazz put the sin in syncopation?' from the *Ladies Home Journal* by Anne Shaw Faulkner (1921), who was the national music chairperson of the General Federation of Women's Clubs, in which she said: 'Jazz disorganizes all regular laws and order; it stimulates to extreme deeds, to a breaking away from all rules and conventions; it is harmful and dangerous, and its influence is wholly bad' (Faulkner, 1921: 16; from Appelrouth, 2005: 1503). Degenerate brains, an inability to follow rules, and a general lack of moral qualities were not what Mr. Ford required in his employees, so the Sociological Department had much to do. The Sociological Department did not last long, but it hardly

mattered: after 1921 it was discontinued and rolled into the notorious Service Department, run by ex-boxer and security chief Harry Bennett, who formed it into a private army of thugs and gangsters to terrorize workers and prevent unionization. Ford's Service Department would grow to be the largest private police force in the world at that time. Its major work was spying – no one who worked for Ford was safe from spies, intent on seeing that the $5 was not being wasted, both literally and metaphorically.

There was increasing societal support for Ford's 'sociological' and 'service' projects: Prohibition, (the doomed attempt to ban alcohol consumption from a number of US states) which started in 1920, also intensified a prohibitory gaze that sought to ensure that employees could resist temptations to vice. In fact, the struggle against liquor was also a struggle against jazz – as they were associated in their licentiousness. Gramsci explicitly made the connection to moral panics:

> The struggle against alcohol, the most danger-ous agent of destruction of laboring power, becomes a function of the state. It is possible for other 'puritanical' struggles as well to become functions of the state if private initiatives of the industrialist prove insufficient or if a moral crisis breaks out among the working masses. (Gramsci, 1971: 303–304)

Moral panic was heightened during the 1930s and extended by the banning of cannabis in seventeen states. The Federal Bureau of Narcotics was established in 1930. In 1937 the Marijuana Tax Act effectively banned cannabis throughout the United States. Power in the organization was now effectively buttressed by power in the wider society; in order to ensure the most efficient routines at work, some control over the type of person that was employed was required. Initially, the new power of surveillance over private life was vested in and an extension of the organization; latterly, as Fordist modernity became characteristic of modernity in general, in workshops large and small, the state took over the functions that private capital had hitherto assumed. Small employers or those new to business could not develop their own

Sociological Departments – but the state, as an ideal total moralist, supplemented the work of surveillance over those in whom the churches and associated temperance movements had not succeeded in instilling a governmental soul. Power shifted its focus from the individual to the collective.

We should understand these innovations as extensions of a panoptical complex. They lacked the specificity of Taylor's (1911) targeting of the body and were more oriented to what Foucault (1977) referred to as bio-power, power oriented to the collective body politic. In accord with Gramsci (1971) we can see these new managerial techniques of Taylorism and Fordism seeking to suppress 'the "animality" of man, training him', as Turner (1984: 100) suggests, 'for the regular disciplines of factory life', in an anatomical politics. Even as the state supplemented 'the private initiatives of the industrialist' in framing the political morality of work (in an era before random drug testing of employees had become widespread), newer, more specifically targeted practices were being shaped in opposition to Taylor's political economy of the body, private initiatives by industrialists, and the state's regulatory bio-power.

At its outset, modern management drilled its practice on the body but with the Jazz Age its attention switched to the collective social body. The panopticon was lodged in the apparatus of engineers and engineering, prior to Ford; with Ford it shifted to the social researcher in the Sociological Department. More recently still, as Townley (1994) and Rose (1989) note, the baton passed to the Human Resources Management staff. In turn, just as Ford's staff made use of the new technologies of social research being pioneered by the Chicago School of sociology of their day, contemporary power is able to draw on new techniques for new strangers.

NEWLY EMERGENT DEVIANT IDENTITIES

For a while, until at least the attack of February 26, 1993 on the World Trade Center,

it might have seemed as if basic matters of identity were hardly of any organizational concern. After the second more successful attack of 9/11 few could think that was still the case. Islamic claims to identity were serving as circuit breakers to existing power relations.

What emerged from the Middle East was not so much a reassertion of pre-modern identities but a positioning of a contemporary identity. It is one that expresses a version of Islam as politically grounded within modern frameworks. Religious thoughts are used as political weapons, alongside modern instruments such as the Internet and video, and with a sophisticated grasp of mass media spectacle. For some in diasporic Muslim communities generally, their hostility is such that their identities in question see nothing that resonates positively in the offerings that the market produces in abundance in the host society. Instead, they see an overly sexualized, narcissistic, and alienating environment. Revolted by what is on offer in the postmodern market – and we in the West are all embraced by this institution now – for some a retreat to the certainties offered by fundamentalism seemed desirable. Here, as Durkheim (2002) would have expected, an excess of social integration can lead to a surplus of altruistic suicide as some people, in some communities, are prepared to kill and die for their beliefs in the appropriateness of identity.

Today, we live not only in a risk society but also in a state of insecurity, a condition that previously characterized societies quite marginal to Western civilization (George and Clegg, 1997). Generalized risk is further amplified by floating signifiers that attract fear and deliver terror. These signifiers can, in reality, be manifest in the destruction of anyone, irrespective of beliefs, ideologies, or identities. At essence they are to do with that most fundamental element of liberal political philosophy – the security of the body of the individual subjects and the security of the body of the polity as a whole. With these new threats, as they are apparent on the streets, skies and subways of Western cities, the risk society is transmuting into a state of uncertainty. Whereas the enemy was eternalized with 9/11 into an Islamic fundamentalism that was situated in failing states supporting network organizations of terrorists, after Britain's 7/7 it suddenly transpired that the enemy was within as well as without.

Today, given the decline of traditional party loyalties, young people in general are less likely to find their identity in a voluntary political process of voting and politics. Thus, there are significant groups of people – particularly amongst the young – who are not fully political or democratic subjects in the normal senses of the word – they do not participate in the formal political process because its meaning is estranged from their own sensemaking. In terms of the sense they make, the major sources of meaning are to be found, as Berger (1990) argues, in transcendent ideas of religiosity. By the twenty-first century a group of young Muslim people in Western democracies were neither involved in the signifiers of a secular society nor the positive polyvalence of the market. Yet, they were not just socially disintegrated, anomic, normless, and meaningless subjects. They were not entirely outside of civility but were building on Sunni notions of civil society that had been nurtured from the most fundamentalist strains in contemporary Islamic thought (Ali, 2002). In the West, in societies with large Muslim populations (most of the major EU countries), where a degree of political alienation is allied with a more general cultural and economic estrangement, then it is hardly surprising if such young people do not become fully aspirational 'normal' economic subjects. Moreover, where they are not greatly involved in consumption – because its narcissism and sexualization is a constant affront to the religious sensibilities they are developing elsewhere – then they will hardly be incorporated as subjects of consumption.

There is an interesting dovetailing of two quite different projects in the estrangement of religious and cultural identities. Throughout the 1980s and into the 1990s the refrain of economic neo-liberalism was that there was no such thing as society. Society could be conceived of simply in terms of individuals making economic choices, using price signals as allocative mechanisms. In the terms of the 'no society' project it was postulated that only individuals should be conceptualized as existentially real. As free subjects they were able to exercise choices in markets, such that consumption became the key to identity. An unanticipated side effect of the project is to whittle down the grounds for identity formation. If you are what you shop to become then identity formation becomes highly contingent on participation in the rituals of a market society. Thus, for those who refused the market and its choices and were estranged politically, economically, and ideologically, there was little or no identity available that could relate to the central projects of the type of society in which they found themselves. For those Muslims with utopian religious worldviews estranged from the dominant orthodoxies, if what is on offer is a reality constructed on narcissism, consumerism, and individualism, then it is not surprising that it should be seen as constituting a hegemon that affronts their existence, faith, and identity. Where utopian ideals turn present-day life into a dystopia, it is hardly surprising if some responses are dysfunctional for the social reality that normalcy constructs.

Where utopian ideology exists in communities that barely interact outside the confines of chosen urban patterns of residence, which, for all the usual reasons are highly concentrated, then dystopian beliefs about identity, the world, and one's place in it as a member of the broader community, can more easily flourish, especially where everything that is needed is found there – food, religion, spouses, culture, and appropriate garb – so there is little need to go outside. Within the embrace of utopianism all faiths develop dystopian groups little involved in the everyday life of a broader society in which they cannot find themselves, where disaffected young people are drawn to radical cliques largely devoid of pluralism, discursively and religiously, because the central role is played by a literalist interpretation of the key text. In such a situation all interpretive politics become condensed into one game of hermeneutics in which those interpretations that seem 'purest' will always attract alienated and anomic individuals.

Finally, as a result of digitalization, individuals have the choice not to be involved in the cultural life of the place where they live, in the larger sense, but are able to participate more vividly in the cultural life of the diasporic community through Al Jazeera and other media, and thus live a reality that, while it is real, is hardly shared at all with the broader context of everyday life. When this reality is treated on the BBC, CNN or France2, let alone FoxNews, it is rarely a personalized but mostly a dehumanized reality – 80 people were blown up by three suicide bombers in Baghdad on the day that I wrote these words – as opposed to the continuing focus on the people who were destroyed in the bombings on one day in London (7/7/2005) or another day in New York (9/11/2001) or Bali (10/12/02).

The electronic panopticon, simulation and the imaginary social collective

Organizations, not just in government, are increasingly making use of available surveillance technologies to seek enhanced supervision and control of all in the name of those perceived as strange, with fundamental Islamism serving as the current candidates. Today, however, the electronic panopticon is going global in an increasingly insecure world, offering opportunities not only for hypersurveillance but also a new kind of organizational simulation, that is hyperreal, a world where we can '*simulate* a space of control, project an indefinite number of courses of action, train for each possibility, and react immediately with preprogrammed responses to the "actual" course of events (which is already over and through a simulacrum)' (Bogard, 1996: 76). Organizations increasingly need neither a political economy of bodies to *handle* power nor to embed it in a moral economy of the soul

through extensive *surveillance*. Instead, they project information in a mode that has been described as 'the purest form of anticipation' (Bogard, 1996: 76).

Almost all large-scale organizations of any sophistication are increasingly premised on work whose doing is simultaneously subject to hypersurveillance of its being done, characteristic of both managerial work and work more generally. The traces of data that all information-laden actions leave automatically as they are enacted become the objects for analysis, for the speeding up of processes, of eradicating porosity through which some effort, time or work might seep, eradicating the gap between the action and its accounts, the work and its record, the deed and the sign. The loop between being, doing, and becoming tightens irrevocably on the terms of those elites that can channel and funnel information, closing down the unaccountable moments in the programmed loop between employees and technologies reporting data that managers have to act on. Such information is not confined to the gathering of data from the physical spaces under control, nor is it premised on crude forms of spying. 'Increasingly virtual realities, artificial intelligence, expert systems, sever us from older forms of control and project that control – refashioned, smoothed and streamlined – onto the plane of simulation ... The god of surveillance is a virtual reality technician's cyborg dream' (Bogard, 1996: 77, 57).

It is not only the security apparatuses and the legislative assemblies that multiply dreams within which identities that are constructs of the profiler, the psychological tester, and the human resources manager, become crucial. All large organizations, equipped with the foresight of simulation, can screen out potential deviance from the organization as easily as the society at large. It is the reality of how, increasingly, organizations use informatics' 'virtual worlds' as they construct identities within which our lives will be lived. Our identity, more than ever, will be a social construction, but not necessarily one made under conditions of our own choosing. Organizations will increasingly adopt bio-surveillance technologies, such as retina, fingerprint, and face scanning, and use this to monitor, restrict, and govern access. Such data, together with those identities that are coded from market-based information, credit records, credit cards, and other forms of transactions, will ensure that some elements of identity become less negotiable. Given the likely direction and speed of development of genetics, organizational capabilities will increasingly be pre-figurative rather than retrospective; as Bogard (1996: 9) puts it, 'genetic technology offers the fantastic possibilities of pre-identification, i.e., identities assigned in advance, profiles that we have seen can be used to target bodies for all kinds of future interventions and diversions'. Potential pathologies for organizations – such as prediction of earlier than required executive demise due to genetic codes or lifestyle triggers – can be problems eliminated in advance. Normalization will no longer be remedial or therapeutic, no longer require the counseling interview as its major device, but will be anticipatory. Bio-psychological screening is becoming ever more closely intertwined with genetic and security screening. Organizational elites will not only be able to reproduce themselves biologically but also to clone themselves socially, with ever more precise simulations (see *Gattaca* – Nicoll, 1997), even as, of course, these projects of normalization face the risk of new deviance that their controls produce (Clegg and Dunkerley, 1980 saw this imperative as a key to the history of organization theory).

CONCLUSION

Organization today increasingly has to deal with a dangerous world of unpredictability. The dispositions of those whom it encounters cannot be guaranteed. Of course, they never could, as the Jazz Age example of Ford demonstrates. Black society was a source of pervasive moral panic for the new industrial organizations. Today, however, the panic is more generalized: simulation and profiling can screen out potential deviance but the social impact of most organizations doing this is substantial. Those that have the resources will be able to do it in a sophisticated way, through hypersurveillance and simulation; those that do not will more readily work through raw prejudices. The results, however, are likely to be the same: the exclusion of whole categories of people from the most promising organizational careers on the basis of their ethnicity, postcode, and religion. The future for organizational power thus looks bleak: we have seen, in the summer of 2005, on the streets of Paris and other major French cities, where such exclusion leads. Power that excludes, that marginalizes, organizationally, ends up stigmatizing socially. And the outcasts have ways of making their presence felt. Organizational security may, indeed, lead to heightened social insecurity.

All of this points to a new agenda for organizational researchers interested in politics and society. We need to be aware that the cumulative effects of organizational practices that seek to ensure the security of the organization may well have a perverse effect. Making organizations more secure may well lessen social security, as screening and profiling techniques find wider purchase. Hence, the concerns of the organization theorist should not stop at the organizations perimeter, its front door or the factory gates. There is always a societal impact, as the Jazz Age case makes clear. Just as jazz, however, is an evolving improvisatory art form, such that the techniques of a Louis Armstrong gave way to those of Dizzy Gillespie, so are organizational practices of power. In Ford's day the new disciplines of sociological field research enabled a degree of social exclusion to occur in constructing the vanguard of organizational employment practices. Today, we are more likely to see electronic and simulation technologies at play. Management and organization theory should be alert to the societal effects that their practices amplify. Organizational researchers need to abandon the shackles of their restricted theory and become socially sensitive in those research questions that they ask. To take at face value the categories that are embedded in the members' usage, in their categorization devices, in their conceptions of what is strange and what is familiar is to surrender analytical autonomy and to accept uncritically the discourse of the tribe. If a field researcher were to come back from Melanesia with a report that reconstituted anthropology in the terms of some primitive categories hitherto strange, it would be a scandal. Such scandals are the norm in that management and organization theory in which the members' categories in use set the terms for debate in such a way that anthropological integrity is routinely compromised. The point is not to accept the categories of the field, in their otherness, but to explicate the possibility and practice of the categories of familiarity and strangeness that the members use.

Also, and this is the moral of the chapter, researchers need to become more reflexive about those strangers that their projects help to create: the deviants of the Jazz Age can too easily be normalized as the problem of diversity and the political nature of what makes the problem problematic be covered over; or, more recently, the enhanced security that post-9/11 organizations espouse can be the occasion for further moral panics with substantial organizational implications. *Organization theorists need to be constantly on guard for those strangers created for them as well those whose deviance they are called on to normalize*: whether it is inner states of motivation or outer practices of spirituality, almost anything can become an occasion for deviance. William Foot Whyte's (1956) *The Organization Man* was a robust critique of earlier urges to conformity; since that time not a great deal of organization theory has chosen to question those familiars – and strangers – it accepts, helps create, sustain, and normalize. To not do so is to practice a peculiarly instrumental blindness. An instrumentally blind organization theory may have its short-term and disposable uses, it can even be profitable, but one thing it can never be is an authentic search for enhanced human freedom because its essential nature is exclusionary and divisive. The most fundamental political act is to define the other as a familiar – or a friend – or as a stranger – or an enemy.

NOTE

1 In the following quote I have substituted 'organization/organizations' for Bauman's 'society/societies'.

REFERENCES

Abel, E.L. (1980) *Marihuana: The First Twelve Thousand Years.* New York: Plenum.

Allen, J. (2003) *Lost Geographies of Power.* Oxford: Blackwell.

Ali, T. (2002) *The Clash of Fundamentalisms: Crusades, Jihads and Modernity.* London: Verso.

Appelrouth, S. (2005) 'Body and soul: Jazz in the 1920s', *American Behavioral Scientist,* 48 (11): 1496–1509.

Bauman, Z. (1993) *Postmodern Ethics.* London: Blackwell.

Bauman, Z. (2001) *The Bauman Reader.* Oxford: Blackwell.

Berger, P. (1990) *The Sacred Canopy: Elements of a Sociological Theory of Religion.* New York: Anchor.

Bogard, W. (1996) *The Simulation of Surveillance: Hypercontrol in Telematic Societies.* Cambridge: Cambridge University Press.

Clegg, S.R. and Dunkerley, D. (1980) *Organization, Class and Control.* London: Routledge & Kegan Paul.

Cohen, S. (1972) *Folk Devils and Moral Panics.* London: Routledge.

Douglas, M. (1966) *Purity and Danger.* London: Routledge & Kegan Paul.

Durkheim, E. (2002) *Suicide: A Study in Sociology* (trans. John A. Spaulding & George Simpson, Introduction George Simpson). London: Routledge.

Faulkner, A.S. (1921) 'Does jazz put the sin in syncopation?' *Ladies Home Journal,* 38: 16–34.

Foucault, M. (1977) *Discipline and Punish: The Birth of the Prison.* London: Allen & Lane.

George, R. and Clegg, S.R. (1997) 'An inside story: Tales from the field – doing organizational research in a state of uncertainty', *Organization Studies,* 18 (6): 1015–1023.

Goffman, I. (1961) *Asylums.* Harmondsworth: Penguin.

Gramsci, A. (1971) *From the Prison Notebooks.* London: Lawrence & Wishart.

Lopes, P. (2005) 'Signifying deviance and transgression: Jazz in the popular imagination', *American Behavioral Scientist*, 48 (11): 1468–1481.

Nicoll, A. (Director) (1997) *Gattaca*. USA: Sony.

Parker, M. (2002) *Against Management: Organisation in the Age of Managerialism*. Cambridge: Polity.

Porter, E. (2002) *What Is This Thing Called Jazz? African American Musicians as Artists, Critics, and Activists*. Berkeley: University of California Press.

Rose, N. (1989) *Governing the Soul*. London: Routledge.

Rosen, M., Orlikowski, W.J. and Schmahmann, K.S. (1990) 'Building buildings and living lives: a critique of bureaucracy, ideology and concrete artifacts', in P. Gagliardi (ed.), *Symbols and Artifacts: Views of the Corporate Landscape*. Berlin: de Gruyter. pp. 69–84.

Taylor, F.W. (1911) *Principles of Scientific Management*. New York: Harper.

Townley, B. (1994) *Reframing Human Resource Management: Power, Ethics and the Subject at Work*. London: Sage.

Turner, B.S. (1984) *The Body and Social Theory*. Oxford: Blackwell.

Whyte, W.F. (1956) *The Organization Man*. New York: Doubleday.

Identity Hijack

Majken Schultz

One of the conceptual pillars of organizational identity is the notion of 'we' – as a group, team or organization embedded in self-referential meaning. As explained by Corley et al. (2006: 3) much of the conceptual debate has concerned how identity is constructed above and beyond its individual members based on the assumption that identity is first and foremost defined by organizational members themselves. In the future I believe that the focus of the debate will shift to a much deeper concern with the other definitional pillar of identity, namely the contextualization of identity. However, contextualization will go beyond impression and mirroring processes with respect to external images, as argued by Hatch and Schultz (2002). Instead we will see a much closer involvement of external stakeholders, which at times will hijack the identity of the organization from its members. This hijack can emerge from emotional attractions, such as consumer communities created to celebrate particular organizational identities; or from an overshadowing of more dominating identities, such as when organizational identities become trapped in national or industrial identities. In both situations, stakeholders considered external to the organization make significant claims to co-define 'who we are as an organization'.

EMBRACED BY STAKEHOLDER DEVOTION

Studies of how consumers relate to brands have showed how some consumers become infatuated and emotionally devoted not only to the products and services offered by the organization, but also to who it is and what it stands for as an organization, i.e., the ideas, beliefs, and claims. In the marketing world, this has been debated as brand-icons or cult-brands, where companies turn customers into what Atkin labels the 'true believers' of the organization, using examples such as Harley riders, iPod owners and members of the Mormon Church (Atkin, 2004). But also without encouragement from companies, consumers and other stakeholders form their own brand communities, supported by on-line media and driven by a shared dedication and attraction to the organization and its identity (Muniz and O'Guinn, 2001). Here they interact, meet on occasion and construct 'who they are' – and start to exchange identity definitions with the organization (Antorini and Andersen, 2005). Drawing upon their community stakeholders can act in a self-defined role as guardians of the heritage of the organizational identity, as when the Adult Fans of LEGO (AFOL's) engaged in a huge revolt against change of the classic colors of the LEGO bricks. More important to the innovation and creativity of organizations, community members can also serve as active co-creators of new and central identity dimensions, as when the AFOL's challenged and expanded the perceptions of play in the LEGO Company, which resulted in a whole new customized digital play concept based in active consumer involvement (LEGO Factory).

Continued

OVERSHADOWED BY STAKEHOLDER RESENTMENT

In contrast to the devoted co-construction of identity within brand communities, the boundaries of organizational identities can also be challenged by external stakeholders enforcing a different categorization of the organization's identity than the one held by organizational members. Such re-categorization can be pursued deliberately by companies, when they seek to transgress the boundaries of an industry identity in the search for new businesses opportunities. However, this may also happen outside the control of the organization in situations where the organizational identity becomes overshadowed by a more dominant identity. For example, when the national or industrial identity that the organization belongs to is confronted with an identity threat or put under pressure, the organizational identity becomes a target of criticism and scrutiny by external stakeholders in ways that encourage organizational members to renegotiate 'who we are' with external stakeholders. One example is how the Danish dairy producer Arla had to renegotiate its organizational identity with central stakeholders in the Muslim world during the crisis in 2006, as its organizational identity became dominated by a negative national identity. Here offensive drawings of the Prophet Muhammed published by a Danish newspaper had thrown Denmark into a severe international crisis resulting in protests, burning down of embassy buildings, flags, etc. in a large number of Muslim countries, where Arla had a leading market position using its Danish identity. As the crisis developed it shifted from an image concern to the company making deliberate efforts to redefine its organizational identity via negotiations with Muslim stakeholders, seeking a clear separation of the organizational and national dimensions of its identity.

THE LOSS OF INNOCENCE OF ORGANIZATIONAL IDENTITY

These examples illustrate in my opinion that future studies of organizational identity will be less concerned with a further sophisticated development of fine-grained conceptual distinctions and methodological issues, and more concerned with the societal circumstances and exchanges with different stakeholders that influence the construction of organizational identity and its inherent dynamic. In that sense organizational identity will lose its theoretical innocence and become a more integrated part of the turmoil of global societies – which will make the concept even more needed and exciting for future studies.

REFERENCES

Antorini, Y.M. and Andersen, K. (2005) 'A communal approach to corporate branding', in M. Schultz, Antorini and Csaba (eds) *Corporate Branding*. Copenhagen: Copenhagen Business School Press.

Atkin, D. (2004) *The Culting of Brands*. New York: Portfolio.

Corley, K. et al. (2006) (in press) 'Guiding organizational identity through aged adolescence', *Journal of Management Inquiry*.

Hatch, M.J. and Schultz, M. (2002) 'Organizational identity dynamics', *Human Relations*, 55: 989–1018.

Muniz, A.M. and O'Guinn, T.C. (2001) 'Brand community', *Journal of Consumer Research*, 27: 412–432.

The Tyranny of Theory

Olav Sorenson

What do I currently see as the biggest impediment to the advancement of a science of management and organizations? Theory – or at least what I will call the 'tyranny of theory'.

The tyranny of theory manifests itself in many forms. It is the editor who rejects a manuscript for its lack of theoretical novelty or for its expected – often referred to as 'obvious' – empirical findings. It is the reviewer who complains that a paper does not have explicit, or (more absurdly) a large enough number of, hypotheses. It is the author who assigns new terminology to existing ideas. It is the reader denigrating a paper for its lack of a 'big idea'.

One can most easily see the consequence of this oppression in what does *not* appear in print in the most influential journals in the field. One rarely sees articles identifying important but unexplained empirical regularities, bringing higher quality or more detailed data to bear on ideas proposed in earlier papers, re-examining the magnitude of effects using more appropriate and sophisticated estimation techniques or identification strategies, or replicating the results of prior studies in new settings or on different data sets. Yet the advancement of any science relies on all of these types of papers.

Where did we go astray? The problem resides not with theory itself. Any improvement in our understanding of the world requires that we iterate between observing, developing models (theory) to explain what we observe, and then scrutinizing their ability to predict behavior in new settings. The problem instead stems from the fact that students of management and organizations have come to worship 'theory' as an idol – somehow superior to the empirical observation and theory testing stages of the scientific endeavor. Though I cannot say when exactly this belief emerged, one can easily see how it persists. Young scholars feel obliged to acquiesce to accumulate the publications necessary to gain tenure, and through the feedback they receive on their own submissions, future reviewers and editors become indoctrinated into the religion that all papers must propose new theory.

In this fetish, we are not alone. To some extent, the idolization of theory pervades the social sciences. So many economists have engaged in model building that in many subfields at least one causal story exists to explain any conceivable empirical observation. And, as in the management literature, sociologists have a penchant for developing new theory tailored to each specific empirical setting. Though one might reprove their relative frequency, theory testing and other forms of more purely empirical research are nonetheless alive and well in both of these disciplines. In the field of management and organizations, however, this imbalance has reached a level verging on monotheism.

As a consequence, knowledge does not accrete. With few notable exceptions – such as organizational ecology or the research on 'structural holes' – we do not engage in research programs. Rather, nearly every paper develops 'novel' theory and uses different measures. We cannot compare results across studies. We cannot say whether most theories apply outside the very narrow contexts in which they have been developed. Trying to understand whether the vast majority of the literature amounts to anything beyond idiosyncratic rationalizations of empirical regularities in specific settings amounts to a Sisyphean task.

Continued

The irony then is that the tyranny of theory has actually stonewalled advancement; despite hundreds of papers detailing thousands of person-years of research, our understanding of management and organizations has advanced surprising little in the last two decades.

A remedy exists. Together we can end this tyranny through individual acts of heresy. Authors can write purely empirical papers – replicating existing results in new settings, re-estimating previous models with new techniques, and simply describing interesting phenomena. Reviewers and editors can evaluate papers on the basis of the quality of their data and analysis rather than on their theoretical novelty and importance. Those intent on engaging in theory can allocate their efforts to reducing the existing menagerie of ideas by identifying equivalencies, redundancies, and special cases.

Ten years down the road, we may have – indeed I hope we will have – matured and look back at the current state of the field with a somewhat fond reminiscence of the foolishness of our floundering. Or we may instead find ourselves facing a field-level mid-life crisis – futilely attempting to relive an adolescence when scholars roamed virgin intellectual territory and thought big thoughts.

That's Important!
Making a Difference with Organizational Research

Adam M. Grant, Jane E. Dutton, and Brent D. Rosso

Organizational scholars care about doing interesting research that captures attention, engages readers, and generates novel insights (Davis, 1971; Bartunek et al., 2006). There is growing concern in our field, however, that interesting research is not necessarily important research. Some have suggested that our research is irrelevant and may even harm managerial practice (Ghoshal, 2005). In response, attention has begun to shift toward conducting research that truly matters, has impact, and makes a social contribution. Despite energy in the field around conducting research that makes a difference, there is little agreement about what 'making a difference' actually means – is it enriching theory, educating students, offering clear direction for managers, or improving public policy and human well-being? Our objective here is to invite deeper consideration of what scholars can do, individually and collectively, to conduct organizational research that makes a difference.

As we examine calls for organizational research that has impact, two questions come to the forefront. First, *for whom* do we want to make a difference (i.e., who are our beneficiaries)? Second, *how* do we want to make a difference (i.e., what forms of impact can we have)? The different audiences we target as beneficiaries of our efforts shape the form that our impact takes. For example, defining fellow academics as beneficiaries implies making a difference primarily by advancing knowledge, while defining students as beneficiaries implies making a difference by sharing this knowledge and making it relevant to students' lives. Defining managers as beneficiaries implies making a difference by making this knowledge practical, while defining communities and societies as beneficiaries implies making a difference by linking the knowledge to policy. Whom do we want to impact? How do we want to make a difference? We propose that deliberate reflection upon these questions is a critical step in enabling difference-making. However, personal reflection alone is not sufficient; we also need to consider the institutional practices that support or undermine our efforts to make a difference. Although many of us are attracted to the field by the prospect of making a difference, achieving these aspirations is much more challenging. We consider three changes in institutional practices that may enable organizational scholars to more effectively make a difference.

First, we propose changes in doctoral education practices. Every organizational scholar faces two charges: producing knowledge and communicating knowledge. Our doctoral training, however, focuses disproportionately on producing knowledge at the expense of communicating it. Suppose we took the communication dimension of scholarship seriously, redefining writing as an art form and public speaking as a performance. We might design courses to provide training in writing, presentation, and public speaking skills to teach doctoral students to communicate their ideas with greater impact and to a broader range of beneficiaries. Such training might better equip scholars to be public intellectuals, with greater access and impact through effective use of a broader range of media. Such training might also aid in capturing the attention of managers and other organizational

Continued

knowledge users, as scholars might be better equipped to make transparent the relevance of organizational research to managers' daily activities.

Second, we suggest changes in academic incentive systems. Current incentive systems reward us for narrowing our questions and can thwart attempts to make a difference beyond our classrooms. Until we reach tenure, we are discouraged from writing books, consulting for organizations, and speaking to public policy. If our aim is to motivate more organizational scholars to seek and create opportunities to make a difference, we need more incentives and rewards for doing so.

Third, we believe that new forms of academic-practitioner dialogues need to be introduced. In current conversations, academics and practitioners often do not occupy the same dialogical or physical space. Designing conferences at which academics and practitioners can share knowledge and ideas on equal ground is one step toward traversing these boundaries. We might also champion and cultivate new communication forums such as interactive websites and blogs for scholars, practitioners, and policymakers to discuss key problems, challenges, and opportunities in organizational life.

These are just a few ideas for how organizational scholars can have a broader and more lasting impact. We encourage organizational scholars to identify other ways to make a difference and reflect on the particular beneficiaries and forms of impact that matter to them – *for whom* and *how* do we want to make a difference? We also encourage organizational scholars to collaborate and innovate in improving doctoral education, incentive systems, and academic-practitioner dialogues. We hope this brief discussion of difference-making will make a difference in how organizational scholars conduct and communicate research, as well as how we structure the institutional practices that undergird our scholarly endeavors.

REFERENCES

Bartunek, J.M., Rynes, S.L. and Ireland, R.D. (2006) 'What makes management research interesting, and why does it matter?', *Academy of Management Journal*, 49: 9–15.

Davis, M.S. (1971) 'That's interesting!: Toward a phenomenology of sociology and a sociology of phenomenology', *Philosophy of Social Science*, 1: 309–344.

Ghoshal, S. (2005) 'Bad management theories are destroying good management practices', *Academy of Management Learning & Education*, 4: 75–91.

Some Thoughts About Trade-Offs

Angelo S. DeNisi

A few years ago, I was asked to participate on a panel that dealt with the trade-offs between relevance and rigor. I thought it would be fun (and it was), but I remembered asking why anyone would consciously choose one over the other. I still wonder why someone would make such a choice, but I realize that much of our research involves some type of trade-off, even if not quite as dramatic as the one discussed at that panel. Yet, I believe that there are some trade-offs we cannot afford to make as a field if we hope to progress. I thought I'd comment on some of these 'non-negotiables'.

I am old enough that, when I was completing my graduate program, most studies employed relatively simple analytical methods. These did not necessarily make these studies better, but it was easier to understand what was actually going on in the study. Statistical techniques have become much more sophisticated and complex. There are many issues, stemming from problems of levels of analysis, that can be addressed by using hierarchical linear modeling, and that would otherwise be difficult to address. Path models help us understand issues of potential causality better than simple regression. Yet, I am concerned that some authors are willing to trade-off clarity for statistical sophistication, and this makes it more difficult for our research to have the impact it should. I am not suggesting that we should abandon more sophisticated statistical techniques, but I do feel that we need to make extra effort to make sure that all our readers understand what we are really saying in our papers.

Another trade-of involving measurement and analysis that we cannot afford to make is between measurement and theory. We use more sophisticated statistical and measurement techniques because they are useful tools to help us address important issues. They are not an end unto themselves, and they cannot replace or compensate for good theory. I often read papers that seem to be more about applying a new technique rather than about answering an important question. Empirical studies still need to be driven by strong theory and construct-valid measures.

The globalization of business has led to a globalization of our field and our research, and this has resulted in another potential trade-off that I don't believe we can afford to make. Some authors seem to believe that unique samples are a good substitute for good theory. Although I see fewer papers that seem to accept this trade-off, the problem persists. Multinational studies require theory as well as do studies employing single samples. The fact that no one ever compared the levels of job commitment among workers in France and those in Nigeria, for example, is not sufficient justification for conducting a study comparing the two. There needs to be some reason why we would expect there to be such differences and some theory for why these differences might be important.

When I participated in that panel, I think I came down hard on the side of rigor. I guess I still would, but I have come to believe that good theory is at least as important as rigor, and therefore, I think our field is harmed by any trade-off involving strong theory. I believe it was Kurt Lewin who said there is nothing so practical as a good theory. I want to close by echoing that sentiment and adding that there is also no substitute for good theory – if we expect to progress as a field.

Abduction

Hans Hansen

Recently, there's been a lot of talk about abduction in organizational studies. In fact, it has become fashionable enough to have reached the status of 'term dropping,' which has raised its profile but also the confusion around it. In the simplest terms, abduction is how we generate hypotheses and is the first (but most neglected) stage in theory building. I will review the concept of abduction introduced by Charles Sanders Peirce (pronounced 'purse') and discuss its importance and place in theory building. I then suggest that we can speak of two types of abduction: weak and creative. The real excitement and challenges surround what I call creative abduction. I use this term to distance and distinguish abduction from induction and sensemaking. It also allows me to make two major contentions. One is that creative abduction is the only way to generate knowledge. A related and more inciteful contention is that all new knowledge begins with a guess.

I will be going so far as to say that it doesn't even matter *what* the guess is. What is important is that we are able to make one at all, and in doing so, we set off an unstoppable march to knowledge construction (and I mean the highly respected Knowledge that pretends

not to come from such meager beginnings as a wild guess). Heresy!

SO WHY ABDUCTION?

We need to develop abduction because it is a crucial part of scientific inquiry. It is also important because we know so little about where what we know comes from, and while we no longer debate that knowledge *is* socially constructed, we don't know *how* it is constructed.

Inquiry consists of observation, explanation, and verification. Organizational studies (trying to live up to the natural sciences) have spent a lot of time on the bookends of these processes. I find it horribly ironic that despite not knowing where explanations come from, we have managed to develop such a fetish for the rules of observation and verification. If we are concerned with theory building, doesn't explanation also deserve attention and a discussion about ways to do it better?

Maybe not. After all, hypotheses seem to be given or 'always available,' so leaving their production a mystery seems harmless enough and doesn't appear to be holding up progress. So science has directed its attention to increasingly sophisticated observation and testing methods, where systematic rules and validation efforts provide more explicit feedback. Kuhn (1962) offers criteria for what new paradigms must achieve to unseat the old, but he focuses more on incommensurability and paradigmatic battles than on the emergence of contenders. Popper's (1959) falsification lays out strict criteria for validation, but leaves hypothesis generation in the black box of 'pure conjecture.'

> The initial stage, the act of conceiving or inventing a theory, seems to me neither a call for logical analysis nor to be susceptible of it. The question of how it happens that a new idea occurs may be of interest to empirical psychology; but it is irrelevant to the logical analysis of scientific knowledge. (Popper, 1959: 20)

Abduction entails a logic of discovery. It involves 'all the operations by which theories and concepts are engendered' (Peirce, 5.590, cited in Fann, 1970). Hanson (1958), a staunch supporter of Peirce, contends that philosophers in Popper's camp are the ones not following a logic of discovery, but merely a logic of testing and validation. 'They begin with the hypothesis as given, as cooking recipes begin with the trout' (Hanson, 1959: 31). The lack of insight regarding how explanations are made remains the 'lock on the door of philosophy' (Peirce, 5.348[1], cited in Davis, 1972: 3).

OK, OK – SO WHERE CAN WE PLACE ABDUCTION?

The person we attach abduction to is Charles Sanders Peirce (1839–1914). The philosophical approach we connect it with is pragmatism. As a logic of discovery, we can contrast it with deduction and induction.

Peirce's pragmatism was rooted in Scottish philosopher Alexander Bain's definition of a belief as 'that upon which one is prepared to act.' From this foundation, Peirce said pragmatism was scarcely more than a corollary, so if he was to be given the moniker 'Father of Pragmatism,'[2] then he thought of

Bain as the grandfather. Peirce's pragmatism was influenced by Kant (Dewey, 1925; Scheffler, 1974), emphasizing pragmatic rules based on, and applicable to, experience. This influence built a predisposition toward the experiential and the rejection of Cartesian thought. These themes are evident across organizational studies, from James' emphasis that all knowing is rooted in experience to Dewey's version of experimentalism that gave rise to action research to Mead's (1934) social influence within pragmatism (Scheffler, 1974) in developing his symbolism and semiotics that has broadly influenced interpretive approaches. Peirce considered abduction 'to be the essence of his pragmatism' (Peirce, 5.196 and cited in Fann, 1970: 5); I would say abduction is the epistemology of pragmatism. Abduction is a process we all engage in as we use our existing mental models to make sense of experiences.

The processes involved in abduction are sensemaking (Weick, 1995), where we attend to and order experience. It is an interpretive process of ordinary everyday life (Peirce, 1955). Take the recent jazz metaphor for organizing (c.f. *Hatch, 1998; Weick, 1998*) as an example of abduction and abductive inquiry. The theoretical gist to jazz as organizing makes the analogy of structure in jazz akin to structure in organizing. In both jazz and organizing, there is a structure that guides the sensemaking of our experience, but that sensemaking in turn influences the guiding structure. Jazz musicians play within a pattern, but their improvisations may become part of the pattern as well. In organizing, we use structures to attend to experience, but in doing so, our sensemaking and improvised actions change our structures. Those structural changes now allow us to capture and explain more diverse experiences in the future. There is also the potential to make sense of experience in ways that force it to fit into the structure we are using to make interpretations.

I use this theoretical stream as an example of abduction because applying jazz improvisation to make sense of 'organizing' was a guess. Using jazz as a metaphor was not arrived at via deduction, or induced from data observed in organizing (though those are later stages of inquiry). The first notion to apply jazz to organizing is an abductive leap. We cast the structure of jazz over 'organizing' and see if it helps to make sense of our experience of organizing. As a result, jazz as a guiding structure allowed us to explain some interesting features of organizing. Our explanation of how organizing happens became richer and revealed some new lines of inquiry, and provided us with some new questions about organizing. Applying the jazz structure changed our sensemaking of organizing, and how we saw it and defined it. We created a representation of the experience 'organizing' by bringing the structure of 'jazz' to bear on it. We couldn't know beforehand that the application of jazz to organizing would reveal anything. There is no way to predict what such a move will reveal, and no expected results can be deduced before application. We are left to try, to take a chance, and only in applying jazz to the context of organizing do we see what happens and what is revealed. So in two senses, there is guesswork involved in abduction. In the first instance, the notion to apply jazz to organization was guessing that nothing about the phenomena of interest (organizing) indicated that jazz could be used to reveal more about it. Secondly, the application to context was the only way to generate inferences. Someone had to make a guess that jazz might help explain organizing, and then try via application to see if it does help.

Inferences are made through an abductive process driven by an experiential context, and tested via application back into context. In formal inquiry, a hypothesis is 'put to the test by forcing it to make verifiable predictions' (Peirce, 5.599 cited in Rescher, 1978), surviving if they account for experience. While abduction shares the falsification (Popper, 1959) assumption that no theory can ever be verified once and for all, they depart regarding inquiry's beginnings. For pragmatists, all knowledge is rooted in experience and inquiry begins with observation, where we are confronted with data that we attempted to explain by generating hypotheses. For Popper, nothing seems to motivate the construction of hypotheses; they are always already present, so science's role is limited to falsify as many of them possible, leaving us with the truth. This subtle difference demarcates a great divide between the constructed realities of pragmatism and Cartesian/rationalist conceptions of reality. Rationalist reality is 'out there' waiting to be discovered, while pragmatism's reality is always in the making (James, 1907).

Peirce's logic of discovery is driven by the experiential and has three stages: abduction, deduction, and induction. Abduction is the first stage of logic that follows observation (perception/experience) and provides a hypothesis regarding some experiential phenomena. We then take that hypothesis and trace out and explicate its consequences by deduction, and then compare those with the results of experiment by induction (Fann, 1970). Deduction develops logical results from hypothesis and induction uses data to validate arguments. Abduction merely suggests that something *may* be, deduction proves that something *must* be, and induction shows that something *actually* is operative (Hanson, 1958).

Because creating an explanation in the first instance occurs only by abduction, the contention is that abduction is the only way to create new knowledge. Deduction merely derives claims based on what is 'already known' (all swans are white...), and induction brings theories to observations, leaving only the work of classifying data. Neither deduction nor induction can ever add even the smallest item to the data of perception (Peirce, 1955). They simply have no role in the first instance of explanation.

> Abduction is the process of forming an explanatory hypothesis. It is the only logical operation that introduces new ideas; for induction does nothing but determine a value, and deduction merely evolves the necessary consequences of a pure hypothesis'. (Peirce 5.171 cited in Fann, 1970: 10)

Induction can verify what is already suggested but can never achieve originality because it is too grounded in our current stocks of knowledge (Carettini, 1983). Induction seeks data;

Table 3.5.1   Abduction compared to induction and deduction

Inference	Stage of inquiry	Process	Level of awareness	School of thought	Application
Abduction	First	Intuitive leap through synthesis or creation of constructs driven by experiential context	Unconscious and conscious	Pragmatism	Uncritical in generation, but reflexive and critical in application back into context
Deduction	Second	Movement from law applied to a case ('top-down')	Conscious	Cartesian	Logical
Induction	Third	Movement from case to produce a law ('bottom up')	Conscious	Empiricism	Experimental

abduction seeks a theory (Fann, 1970). 'The former classifies, the latter explains' (Peirce, 2.636, cited in Fann, 1970). Any synthetic proposition, in so far as it is for the first time entertained as possibly true, is the result of abduction (Davis, 1972).

All this is not to decry induction. While abduction is more of a leap than induction, induction is actually a stronger form of inference. Creating a hypothesis is a risky business that can be wildly wrong. Induction is less often wrong because those inferences are at least based on what is already known, reasoning from facts of the same kind (Davis, 1972). While abduction and induction both move toward the acceptance of a hypothesis based on observation, abduction makes its start from the data without any particular theory in view, and is motivated by the feeling that a theory is needed to explain the surprising fact. Induction already has a theory in mind and seeks confirmation. Abduction is distinguished by a bolder and more perilous step (Peirce, 2.632, cited in Sebeok and Umiker-Sebeok, 1983: 25). In my approach to abduction, you will see that weak abduction certainly touches if not overlaps with induction. I also think there are few differences between weak abduction and sensemaking (Weick, 1995), which should not be surprising given pragmatism's influence on sensemaking.

To summarize, abduction is the creative act of constructing explanations to account for surprising observations in the course of experience (hypothesis generation). Abduction results in a tentative and subjective interpretive synthesis among our sensitizing concepts. Influenced by Kantian synthesis, abduction is concerned with processes of construction where the mind harmonizes into forms what comes to us through our senses. We take disparate elements and place them into relationships that are meaningful for us. Abduction generates hypothesis in the absence of any existing construct to interpret observation. We might arrive at this explanation by creating a new construct, or we may synthesize multiple constructs within our existing stocks of knowledge.

ABDUCTION OPERATIONALIZED: HOW DOES IT WORK?

The things at play during abduction are our knowledge structures and a particular experiential context. Our knowledge structures or 'stocks of knowledge' on hand (Schutz, 1967; Turner, 1987) are made up of sensitizing concepts (Blumer, 1969: 147) and any assumptions and biases we have based on the sense we have made out of previous experiences. These include the construction materials we inevitably use to interpret our world and build representations:

> Schutz noted that an individual approaches the life world with a *stock of knowledge* composed of commonsense constructs and categories that are social in origin. These images, theories, ideas, values,

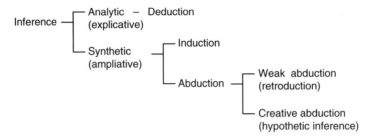

Figure 3.5.1   Inference can be analytic or synthetic. Synthetic reasoning is either inductive or abductive. Abductions can be weak or creative, resulting in a truly innovative idea.

and attitudes are applied to aspects of experience, making them meaningful. Stocks of knowledge are resources with which persons interpret experience, grasp the intentions and motivations of others, achieve intersubjective understandings, and coordinate actions. (Holstein and Gubrium, 1994: 263)

Abduction begins with a perceptual judgment as we move through the stream of experience. 'We live upon the front edge of an advancing wave-crest, and our sense of a determinate direction in falling forward is all we cover of the future of our path' (James, 1909: 68).

Sensations are forced upon us, coming we know not whence. Over their nature, order, and quantity we have as good as no control. They are neither true nor false; they simply are. It is only what we say about them, only the names we give them, our theories of their source, that may be true or not. (James, 1907: 117)

But experience doesn't come ticketed and labeled, we have to discover what it is, capturing what we can (James, 1907). We attend to it with the mass of beliefs of which we find ourselves already possessed, assimilating, rejecting, or rearranging them in different degrees (James, 1907: 42). We engage the world and fling our knowledge structures over experience, hoping to capture it. When experience does not match our subjective reality, we have to account for those inconsistencies.

One key thing to note is that as we are bombarded by experience, our senses allow us to apprehend much more than our minds can assimilate. We take in more than we

can handle, and there are often enigmas that confront us; something poking out of our nets. 'Experience, as we know, has ways of boiling over, and making us correct our present formulas' (James, 1907: 106).

There is some difficulty with this notion that we are compelled to make sense of experience when something we apprehend fails to conform to our knowledge structures. While our stocks of knowledge help us assimilate as we apprehend, they also coerce us (James, 1907), forcing us to make sense of experience in ways we are already familiar with. This means abduction is hard work. Rather than modify our existing stocks of knowledge to fit our observations, we are fond of pretending to see things in such a way that they already fit. The challenge is that given this propensity, it does not seem possible that any experiences would fail to conform to our structures, and if there are parts of experience that are 'independent' from our minds, they seem very hard to find (James, 1907). 'We may glimpse it, but we never grasp it; what we grasp is always some substitute for it which previous human thinking has peptonized and cooked for our consumption' (James, 1907: 119–120). Reality is *always already* interpreted because data merges with theory at the very moment of their genesis (Alvesson and Sköldberg, 2000: 17), '... wherever we find it, it has already been *faked*' (James, 1907: 120, italics in original). Without prior assumptions, there is frequently nothing in our stocks of knowledge that provides experience a basis with which it can 'stick' with us, making it very hard to 'grasp' anything unique as it slides past us.

All this is on top of the fact that we make great efforts at cramming observations into our existing structures, convincing ourselves we saw what we expected to see, reshaping experience rather than our minds. And if we do manage to see something that really surprises us, we are supposed to ignore it altogether! 'Ignore the outliers,' goes the mumbled mantra. This leads to the question: How does this surprising observation that we rely on to kick off the process of abduction ever confront us? Don't we end up missing these enigmas for lack of a conceptual lens with which to see them?

We miss plenty. But there are occasions where enigmas are hard to ignore. We must rely on experience to 'boil over.' It is, after all, only when observations ricochet off of our knowledge structures that we even begin to recognize them as surprising. You can see why experience is so crucial for pragmatists. We not only count on surprising observations to resist us so that we may see them, but also when we attempt to force them into our existing knowledge structures. We count on them to wreck havoc, fighting like cornered beasts when prodded with our stocks of knowledge. We are presented with an enigma which forces us into explanation or *ignorance*. While we can rely on experience to keep boiling over, we can also help. Though many observations stand in stark contrast to what we know, refusing to be ignored, we need to listen for cries of revolution. Being reflexive, we might place ourselves in beautiful conundrums that demand resolution before we can move forward.

Then we are at the moment of the new idea. Abduction is an act of insight, though extremely fallible insight (Peirce, 1955). It is in the instant of assembling an explanation of our experience that an abductive inference is produced. 'The abductive suggestion comes to us like a flash' (Peirce, 1955: 304). 'The mind struggles to grasp a scene and instantly, the connection and harmony becomes apparent. During the period of confusion, all of the data

were already present; all that was lacking was a hypothesis, an interpretation of the data' (Davis, 1972: 47).

We must then find a place for the new concept to reside in our stocks of knowledge. If abduction offers a perfect explanation, but cannot be assimilated, we remain stuck. In attempting to assimilate the new concept, 'we try to preserve the old stocks of knowledge, stretching them just enough to make them admit the novelty' (James, 1907):

> We have a stock of old opinions already, but meet a new experience that puts them to a strain. Somebody contradicts them; or in a reflective moment we discover that they contradict each other; or a desire arises in us that the old ones cease to satisfy. The result is an inward trouble to which our mind till then had been a stranger. We seek to escape by modifying our previous opinions, saving as much as we can, for in this matter we are all extreme conservatives. We try first to change one opinion, and then another, with great resistance, until at last some new idea comes up which can be grafted upon the ancient stock, with a minimum of disturbance to the latter.

But most often, even the most violent revolutions leave most of the old order standing (James, 1907). We preserve as much of our current stocks as we can, rearranging or adding just enough to account for new observations. The new addition then allows us to apprehend and assimilate even more experience, creating more knowledge. If we are successful at assimilating our abductions, they appear to fit into our structures as if they had always been there. The craftsmanship is so fine that repairs are invisible to the mind's eye. Afterward, we may even be perplexed as to why we didn't 'get it' earlier. We might be tempted to trick ourselves into declaring it always has been so, when in fact, we 'made' it so. It is completely synthetic, constructed or created on the fly, but we somehow manage to convince ourselves we have 'found' it. This realist prospect has always been much more comforting than admitting we had been living in the absence of explanation or reason.

What is true then, are those ideas that we can assimilate, validate, corroborate, and verify (James, 1907). A new idea counts as 'true' just in the proportion that it gratifies our desire to assimilate a novel experience into our stocks of knowledge. 'It must solve a problem, leaning on old truth to grasp a new fact' (James, 1907: 36). 'Ideas become true when they carry us prosperously from any one part of our experience to any other part, so far as they help us to get into satisfactory relation with other parts of our experience. New truth is always a go-between, a smooth-over transition between the old stock and new experience and runs them into one another most felicitously and expediently'(James, 1907). The underlying assumption here is that 'truth happens to an idea. It becomes true, is made true by events' (James, 1907: 97). 'Truths emerge from the facts, but they dip forward into facts again and add to them, and so on indefinitely' (James, 1907: 108). Truth is a process, not a state.

WEAK AND CREATIVE ABDUCTION

I would like to distinguish two types of abduction. Both Bonfantini and Proni (1983) and Eco (1983) describe types of abduction ranging from some notion of weak to more creative abduction. For me, weak abduction is close to Peirce's retroduction (which he admits confusing with induction) and the other end of the scale is hypothetic inference in the first instance, or creative abduction.

In weak abduction 'we find ourselves confronted with a phenomenon unlike any we would have expected under the circumstances, we look over their features and notice some remarkable relation among them. At once we recognize them as being characteristic of some conception already stored in our mind' (Peirce, 2.776, cited in Rescher, 1978: 42):

> It is true that different elements of the hypothesis were in our minds before; but it is the idea of putting together what we had never dreamed of putting together which flashes the new suggestion before our contemplation. (Peirce, 1955: 304)

The difference between weak abduction and induction is that the later would have never

suggested a particular concept or synthesis of concepts be applied to this phenomenon. As a result of rearranging or synthesizing our existing constructs, our knowledge structures are extended through weak abduction.

Imagine an inquiry into the distribution of different marbles in a bag. After randomly pulling out over 40 marbles, we begin to feel pretty confident that half of the marbles are yellow and half are red. Then, we pull out a blue marble. We might now bring the category 'blue' to bear on the remaining data, expanding the classification of what we expect in future observations. While the category 'blue' was a concept we were previously familiar with, we had not conceived it would be brought to bear in explaining future data. While weak abduction is a reorganization and expansion of our stocks of knowledge in relation to this particular phenomena, this is construction work done with existing materials. In this putting together of concepts to explain experience, you can see the relation to analogical thinking, conceptual metaphors, bricolage and Koestler's bisociation.

If a more dramatic leap is required to provide explanation, as when our existing knowledge structures contain no material that help us make sense of an experience, we must create an entirely new concept *ex novo* (out of nothing) through creative abduction. It happens on very rare occasions that we are confronted with a surprising observation that we cannot make sense of using our current stocks of knowledge no matter how we combine and recombine them. The data resists classification, perhaps even defying description by the most basic categories such as 'color,' and we must generate a hypothesis in the absence of any referent concepts. With no pre-existing concepts that help us *construct* an explanation, we must *create* one. Creative abduction (hypothetic inference) generates an explanation with something outside of our current stocks. The result resembles nothing that we have ever known before, but the instant it is created, it becomes a new foothold that allows us to push on into experience.

This discussion parallels paradigm growth versus creation, and we can compare weak and creative abduction to Kuhn's (1962) normal and revolutionary science. Just as weak abduction assimilates observations using current stocks of knowledge, normal science hums along nicely solving all the problems it can produce – but *only* the problems it can produce. Revolutionary science results in paradigm change, as rare and radical as creative abduction. Creative abduction and Kuhn's paradigm shift (the decision to ascribe to a new paradigm) both require 'leaps of faith.' Creative abduction challenges us to fit a new concept that has no point of reference, and we may even need to completely reconstruct our stocks around the new concept. In this type of paradigm change, Kuhn demonstrates that there is nothing the members of the new paradigm can say to convince the members of the old paradigm to make the leap. The old and new paradigm are incommensurable, and no matter how eloquent the argument for taking on the new paradigm, it is always made in a language the members of old paradigm simply do not and cannot understand. The old paradigm members simply do not possess the stocks of knowledge that allow them to 'grasp' what the members of the new paradigm are saying. Thus the members of the old paradigm continue along with normal science, assimilating what their stocks of knowledge allow. While weak abduction certainly constitutes valuable scientific progress (the world needs normal science too), it is creative abduction that gives birth to new paradigms.

HERE COMES THE HERESY

The main implication that abduction has for the philosophy of science is that all knowledge begins with a guess. Though Peirce said as much, I go further by claiming that it does even not matter *what* the guess is. At this first stage in the process, the content of the guess is of absolutely no consequence. In fact, it cannot matter. There is no way our hypothesis can give any indication to the 'correctness' of its content, and we have nothing within our existing knowledge structures with which to judge the 'correctness' of the hypotheses.

When we make a creative abduction, we are psychologically incapable of conceiving that it might be true or false (Gaillie, 1966). And furthermore, since the process of abduction is inductively blind (Rescher, 1978), we have no capability to discriminate and absolutely no reason (literally none available) to think any hypothesis is better than another. Remember, it is only in the latter stages of induction that we begin to compare the content of a hypothesis to experience.

Recall Weick's (1987) story of the soldiers lost and stranded in the French Alps. Near defeat, they find a map, and with newfound confidence, use it to make another attempt to find a way out of the mountains. Once to safety, they discover that the map they had relied on was a map of the Pyrenees. Sometimes having something to go by, anything to go by, is often what allows us to move forward. At the point of being seized by a surprising fact, if we can make a guess, any guess, we can make progress. It doesn't matter what the guess is, yet all reality hinges on our ability to make one! But we have seen the challenge in guess*work*, and the cards are stacked against us. It is no easy leap of faith that kicks off the process of theory construction. A guess is the hardest thing you'll ever make.

FOSTERING CREATIVE ABDUCTIONS

It now seems obvious to say that greater leaps result in more progress. Bolder abductions, wilder creative ideas, to the extent that we can assimilate them, result in more truth. Furthermore, if we are able to assimilate the outrageous, it becomes part of a more diverse and complex knowledge structure capable of apprehending more diverse experience. Only our lack of audacity slows scientific progress. If you have not yet warmed up to social construction, then these ideas are likely to further upset your applecart, because what I am saying is that not only is reality constructed, it is downright *guessed* into being. Peirce provides a call to arms: 'We must conquer the truth by guessing or not at all!' (cited in Sebeok and Umiker-Sebeok, 1983: 11).

So how might organizational scholars answer this call? While there can be no hard and fast rules to making abductions, scholars might align their efforts with some currently debated perspectives, such as reflexivity, contextualism, critical theory, and aesthetics. Many of you will have already taken these perspectives on, and sense that many of their assumptions are evident in abduction. While abductive inferences in the first instance are absolutely beyond criticism (Peirce, 1955), they are verified through a critical and reflexive application back in the context which spawned them. Abductions are uncritical, and partially unconscious acts in formulation, yet critical and reflexive in their application back into the context of production.

'We must remember that this whole inquiry into knowing grows up on a reflective level' (James, 1909: 248). Reflexivity is a critical perspective in identifying and challenging one's own underlying assumptions, questioning our use of our current knowledge structures. Though this type of critical reflexivity is still underutilized in organizational research (Calas and Smircich, 1999), it is inherent in abduction. Abductive inquiry deconstructs the current knowledge structures in seeking to bring new sensitizing concepts into our stocks of knowledge. The test of viability by applying an abductive inference back into its context of production is the hallmark of pragmatism.

If in apprehending experience we cannot explain the seed for a new idea, how do we go about getting in touch with the unexplainable? Can we place ourselves in positions that perplex us? We might look to alternate ways of building representations of experience, in hopes that engaging with phenomena in new ways will lead to new ways of seeing them. Aesthetics is concerned with knowledge that is created from our sensory experiences, so it might be useful in dealing with the parts of experience that we apprehend, but are yet to be named, categorized, or assimilated. Peirce (1955) said hypothetic inferences resemble the arising of sensations, and drew a connection between logic and aesthetics.

Eco (1983) also claims aesthetics may play a roll in abduction. Since sensuous knowledge is the purview of aesthetics, the emerging field of organizational aesthetics stands to shed much light on alternative ways of meaning making in organizations (see Taylor and Hansen, 2004 for a recent review).

What might all this mean for organizational studies? Science has spent the last century making a very plausible world. Realizing that knowledge is synthetic, why not push for more interesting and beautiful hypotheses (Weick, 1989) in an attempt to make reality more interesting and beautiful? Interaction and irreverence may be two keys: be irreverent toward your own discipline, and look for material outside of your stocks that you can combine with your stocks. Look to unique experience, and be willing to make weird combinations with diverse stocks of knowledge. While calls for interdisciplinary research are oft-made and seldom done, new efforts might be made in this exploratory sense. As a start, you might consider disciplined imagination (Weick, 1989). Consider yourself an academic artist who roams junkyards looking for strange objects to begin a masterpiece. Incredible realities start with incredulous guesses.

NOTES

1 Much of the material refers to a collection of papers in Peirce, C.S. Collected Papers, Volumes 1–6 edited by C. Hartshorne and P. Weiss, 1935, and Volumes 7–8 edited by A. Burks, 1958. So when I quote Peirce, I try to list an additional published source as well. Peirce, 5.348 indicates volume 5, paragraph number 348 in the paper collection. Peirce (1955), edited by J. Buchler, is more widely available.

2 James gives Peirce full credit for inventing the term, which Peirce derived from Kant's *pragmatisch*, relating to 'definite human purpose' (Reilly, 1970).

REFERENCES

Alvesson, M. and Sköldberg, K. (2000) *Reflexive Methodology: New Vistas for Qualitative Research.* London: Sage.

Blumer, H. (1969) *Symbolic Interactionism: Perspective and Method.* Berkeley: University of California Press.

Bonfantini, M.A. and Proni, G. (1983) 'To guess or not to guess?', in U. Eco and T. Sebeok (eds) *The Sign of Three: Dupin, Holmes, Peirce*. Indianapolis, IN: Indiana University Press. pp. 119–134.

Calas, M.B. and Smircich, L. (1999) 'Past postmodernism? Reflections and tentative directions', *Academy of Management Review*, 24: 649–671.

Carettini, G.P. (1983) Peirce, Holmes, Popper', in U. Eco and T. Sebeok (eds) *The Sign of Three: Dupin, Holmes, Peirce*. Indianapolis, IN: Indiana University Press. pp. 135–153.

Davis, W.H. (1972) *Peirce's Epistemology*. The Hague: Martinus Nijhoff.

Dewey, J. (1925) 'The Development of American pragmatism', in Hickman, L. and Alexander, T. (1998) *The Essential Dewey*. Indiana: Indiana University Press.

Eco, U. (1983) 'Horns, hooves, insteps: Some hypotheses on three types of abduction', in U. Eco and T. Sebeok (eds) *The Sign of Three: Dupin, Holmes, Peirce*. Indianapolis, IN: Indiana University Press. pp. 198–220.

Fann, K.T. (1970) *Peirce's Theory of Abduction*. The Hague: Mertinus Nijhoff.

Gaillie, W.B. (1966) *Peirce and Pragmatism*. Westport, CT: Greenwood Press.

Hanson, N.R. (1958) *Patterns of Discovery: An Inquiry into the Conceptual Foundations of Science*. Cambridge: Cambridge University Press.

Hatch, M.J (1998)'Jazz as a metaphor for organization in the 21st century' Organizational Seience, 9: 556–557.

Hanson, N.R. (1959) 'Is there a logic of scientific discovery?', in H. Feigl and G. Maxwell (eds) *Current Issues in the Philosophy of Science*. New York: Holt, Rinehart and Winston.

Holstein, J.A. and Gubrium, J.F. (1994) 'Phenomenology, ethnomethodology, and interpretive practice, in N.K Denzin and Y.S. Lincoln (eds), *Handbook of Qualitative Research*. Thousand Oaks, CA: Sage. pp. 262–272.

James, W. (1907/1975) 'Pragmatism: A new name for some old ways of thinking', in W. James, *Pragmatism and The Meaning of truth*. Cambridge, MA: Harvard University Press. pp. 1–166.

James, W. (1909/1975) 'The Meaning of Truth: A sequel to "pragmatism" ', in W. James, *Pragmatism and The Meaning of Truth*. Cambridge, MA: Harvard University Press. pp. 167–352.

Kuhn, T. (1962) *The Structure of Scientific Revolutions*. Chicago, IL: University of Chicago Press.

Mead, G.H. (1934) *Mind, Self, and Society: From the Standpoint of a Social Behaviorist*. Chicago: University of Chicago Press.

Peirce, C.S. (1960) *Collected Papers of Charles Sanders Peirce*. C. Hartshorne and P. Weiss (eds). Cambridge, MA: The Belknap Press of Harvard University Press.

Peirce, C.S. (1955) *Philosophical Writings of Peirce*. Justus Buchler (ed.). New York: Dover Publications.

Peirce, C. (1877) 'The fixation of belief', in N. Houser and C. Kloesel (1992) *The Essential Peirce*, Vol 1. Indiana: Indiana University Press.

Peirce, C. (1878) 'How to make our ideas clear', in N. Houser and C. Kloesel (1992) *The Essential Peirce*, Vol 1. Indiana: Indiana University Press.

Popper, K.R. (1959) *The Logic of Scientific Discovery*. New York: Basic Books.

Rescher, N. (1978) *Peirce's Philosophy of Science*. Notre Dame, IN: University of Notre Dame Press.

Reilly, F.E (1970) *Charles Peirce's Theory of Scintific Method*. New York: Fordham University Press.

Schutz, A. (1967) *The Phenomenology of the Social World*. Evanston: Northwestern University Press.

Seheffler, I. (1974) *Four Pragmatists: A Critical Introduction to Peirce, James, Mead, and Dewey*. London: Routledge and Kegan Paul.

Sebeok, T.A. and Umiker-Sebeok, J. (1983) 'You know my method: A juxtaposition of Charles S. Perice and Sherlock Holmes', in U. Eco and T. Sebeok (eds), *The Sign of Three: Dupin, Holmes, Peirce*. Indianapolis, IN: Indiana University Press. pp. 11–54.

Taylor, S. and Hansen, H. (2004) 'Finding form: Looking at the field of organizational aesthetics', *Journal of Management Studies*, 42 (6): 1211–1231.

Turner, J.H. (1987) 'Analytical Theorizing', in A. Giddens and J. Turner (eds), *Social Theory Today*, Stanford: Stanford University Press. pp. 156–194.

Weick, K. (1995) *Sensemaking in Organizations*. Thousand Oaks, CA: Sage.

Weick, K. (1998) 'Improvisation as a mindset for organizational analysis', *Organization Science*, 9 (5): 543–555.

Weick, K.E. (1989) 'Theory Construction as Disciplined Imagination', *Academy of Management Review*, 14: 516–531.

Weick, K. (1987) 'Substitutes for strategy', in J. Teece (ed.) *The Competitive Challenge*. Cambridge, MA: Balinger.

The Dialectics of Propositional and Tacit Knowledge

Daniel G. Spencer

It is not uncommon to encounter statements in our discipline's textbooks such as the following: 'OB *replaces* intuition and gut feeling with a well researched body of theories and systematic guidelines for managing behavior in organizations' (George and Jones, 2005:4). A similar pronouncement was recently made in a *Harvard Business Review* article by Pfeffer and Sutton (2006: 74): 'Evidence-based practice, changes power dynamics, *replacing* formal authority, reputation, and intuition with data'. They hedge in a later statement when they say that 'this means senior leaders – often venerated for their wisdom and decisiveness – may lose some of their stature as their intuitions are *replaced*, *at least at times*, by judgments available to virtually any educated person' (ibid.: 74). Now perhaps statements such as these might be interpreted as merely rhetoric, but I am struck by the utter absurdity of thinking that propositional knowledge can 'replace' intuition or tacit knowledge. The message sent to the discipline's students and to practitioners is that tacit knowledge is virtually worthless – and worse, somehow biased – and must be removed from consideration by management practitioners when confronting organizational problems.

One could take this stance to task, and the positivist epistemological assumptions that underpin it, but this would serve no purpose here. Instead, in the spirit of this note, I will explore one way in which we might begin to address this issue in the future. Obviously, work needs to be done to understand the processes by which practitioners can utilize *both* propositional and tacit knowledge as they grapple with the organizational problems they face. I believe that the key lies in conceptualizing the process in terms of the *dialectical* relationship between propositional and tacit knowledge in practice-based knowledge construction. The underpinnings of such a conceptualization, I argue, can emerge from existing ideas of several theorists: Donald Schon's (1987) work on the epistemology of practice and the role that reflection plays in generating practice-based knowledge; and David Kolb's (1984) work on the structure of knowledge and the role played by dialectical thinking in this process.

Schon has argued that practitioners produce knowledge through an experiential learning process that involves use of intuition, trial and error, and muddling through. More effective practitioners embed 'reflection-in-action' within this process to meta-cognitively take control of their learning and knowledge building. Reflection-in-action is triggered when a person experiences a surprise (a problem) which then surfaces to awareness the person's knowing-in-action (assumptions, tacit knowledge) that may have played a role in creating the surprise. The person then restructures their understanding of the situation: the frame of the problem, the mental representation of what is happening, or the strategy of action employed in addressing the problem. An action strategy is invented for addressing the surprise and implemented in an on-the-spot experiment that either: (1) results in elimination of the surprise and closes the learning cycle, or (2) does not eliminate the surprise but generates new information that kicks off another learning cycle that is now action-based.

According to Schon, the above reflective learning process is largely implicit and, only to a limited extent, occurs in the medium of words. At a later point in time, after reflection-in-action, the person can engage in 'reflection on reflection-in-action' which is largely explicit, and to a greater extent, occurs in the medium of words. Its purpose is to develop deeper understanding of one's learning process and set the stage for more effective future reflection-in-action. It is important to recognize that it is at this point where the person has the opportunity, as well as the ability, to access propositional knowledge that may be relevant to the problematic situation of concern. Certainly, as one encounters problems that cut across broader slices of time and space, the act of reflection-in-action itself becomes more open to explicit analysis and capable of drawing on propositional knowledge relevant to the problem being addressed. Schon does not consider, however, how propositional knowledge and tacit knowledge are juxtaposed and synthesized in the restructuring of understanding and the generation of innovative action strategies. David Kolb's ideas are useful for beginning to understand how to fill this conceptual gap.

Kolb has conceived the meshing of tacit and propositional knowledge as a Hegelian dialectical process. This process is driven by tension between (1) apprehensions generated by concrete involvement in a problematic situation and (2) comprehensions of that situation generated through reflective analytic detachment. Apprehension is of a concrete here-and-now experience in a continuously unfolding present. Comprehension is a record, a representation of the past that seeks to define the future. Kolb feels that 'comprehensions are held provisionally and tested against apprehensions, and vice versa.' While on the right track, Kolb's conceptualization of this dialectic can only be used to partially represent the phenomena present when an individual confronts a learning and knowledge building opportunity. Conceptually, it is limited to intra-psychic inductive and deductive processes that tap a tacit knowing of the particulars of the situation in the sense of Michael Polanyi's 'from-to-knowing' in an action-present. He also fails to incorporate into the process the person's broader tacit knowledge that is a function of previous, sometimes distant, personal experiences. Furthermore, Kolb is a realist in that he sees the dialectic process resulting in a 'higher truth' that transcends apprehension and comprehension. Abstract conceptualizations that result from this process are ultimately viewed as a mirror of nature rather than a creative human construction.

Abduction, I believe, is the essential ingredient for understanding the dialectical thinking embedded in the above human knowledge building process. Simply stated, abduction is a process where existing perspectives (propositional knowledge) are dialectically synthesized with new experience (tacit knowledge) to yield a new perspective.

Only by simultaneously immersing oneself in the phenomena of interest, while holding multiple explicit perspectives, can one set in motion the abductive processes necessary to surface representations that can break the bonds of a deductive overdetermination and generate working hypotheses about the phenomena that are unique to the phenomena. Abduction coupled with the ideas of Schon in particular can be used to conceptualize the role dialectical thinking plays in human problem solving and knowledge construction that is time and context bound. Abductive dialectical synergy between tacit and propositional knowledge occurs, it is argued, within the interpenetrating processes of reflection-in-action and reflection on reflection-in-action resulting in a synthesis of the objective and the relative. Of course future work on this process will need to not only consider building practice-based knowledge from the standpoint of the individual but also from the standpoint of a collection of individuals. Important insights can be drawn from the Pragmatists, especially George Herbert Mead's Symbolic Interactionism, to help examine

Continued

the processes by which meanings are dialectically created, socially negotiated and shared realities constructed.

I strongly believe that management and organization studies must begin to develop an understanding of the meta-cognitive and micro-interactional processes involved in this absolutely important phenomena. Without these understandings, practicing managers, the ultimate target of our knowledge building enterprise in the discipline, are less likely to be able to make sense of their learning and knowledge building processes. Furthermore, they are less likely to be able to take control of their thinking about these processes and attempt to control the actual processes themselves. Currently there is very little concern in the discipline for generating these kinds of understandings. I do not see these issues being holistically addressed in our journals and conferences, and one would certainly never find them addressed in any of our management textbooks. One reason, of course, is that the discipline is dominated by an ontological, epistemological, and methodological stance that simply does not allow investigators to capture the phenomena, let alone generate the conceptual schemes that would sensitize investigators to it. It is indeed unfortunate that these beliefs on the part of teachers and researchers have led our students and practicing managers to believe that their intuitions and tacit knowledge are worthless and must be discarded. The catch, however, is that they cannot be discarded even if one should wish to do so. They are an ever-present influence on the judgments all persons make in every aspect of their life. It is time to (1) recognize this, (2) attempt understand it deeply through alternative ontological, epistemological and methodological stances, and (3) share what is learned about this pervasive phenomena not only with practicing managers but also those practicing the management of life.

REFERENCES

George, J.M. and Jones, G.R. (2005) *Understanding and Managing Organizational Behavior.* Upper Saddle River, NJ: Pearson Prentice-Hall.
Kolb, D.A. (1984) *Experiential Learning: Experience as the Source of Learning and Development.* Englewood Cliffs, NJ: Prentice-Hall.
Pfeffer, J. and Sutton, R.I. (2006) 'Evidence-based management', *Harvard Business Review*, 84 (1): 62–74.
Schon, D.A. (1987) *Educating the Reflective Practitioner.* San Francisco, CA: Jossey-Bass.

700 Sage Words?

Tom Keenoy

One tiresome irony which accompanies any attempt to understand management and management processes through a constructivist epistemology is the issue of 'theorizing'. While grand theory is playing dead and the middle range is for indecisive dissemblers, we social constructivists grub around, 'speculating' in the undergrowth. In pursuit of plausibility we circulate conceptual-theoretic metaphors and attempt to accomplish some variety of – invariably undecidable – 'sensemaking' (and yet, secretly, we desire to convey and carry conviction).

However, the interesting irony here is the presumed distinction between 'sensemaking' and 'theorizing' as discrete activities. Weick (1989) himself adumbrated theory construction as an iterative process involving a 'disciplined imagination' which, quietly, refracts the authors' viewpoints if not interests. Such constraints, it would seem, delimit not only the terrain of any putative 'social science' but also of our very humanity. We do not and cannot 'exist' outside of social values, for the objective eye has long been exposed as a self-delusion. Latterly, Weick (1999), revisiting this issue of how to make sense of theory, exposed the endemic trade-offs to be negotiated by theorists of all persuasions and refined his conclusion to suggest that contemporary 'theorizing' is often conditioned through a process involving 'disciplined reflexivity'. The theorist has, rightly, become a self-conscious input into 'theorizing'. Such a characterization might embolden the social constructivist but, as noted elsewhere, 'Theory thus works by making sense of times and situations for readers and audiences but, because this always involves rhetoric, it is a matter of words, not worlds; of maps, not territories; and of representations, not realities' (van Maanam, 1995: 134).

So, why not just collapse the distinction between 'theorizing' and 'sensemaking' or, even better, abandon the impossible demands of theory-making altogether for the contact-comfort of sensemaking? Even at the level of meaning, etymologically, 'sensemaking' and 'theorizing' may be regarded as Siamese twins – the latter is merely a linguistic formalization of the former. For the real irony in all this is that six of Weick's (1995) seven 'properties' of sensemaking are the routine ingredients of any self-respecting 'theorizing' process.

To wit: theorizing, which privileges the vainglorious quest for ontological security, is the social scientists 'primordial route to *identity construction* (in passing, one should note that this refers both to our own identities as well as the infinitude of social objects and processes we 'see', classify and seek to fix in definition, conceptual abstraction and 'theoretical explanation'). Theory, despite aspiring to prediction, is invariably a historical and *retrospective* artifact; it is processually *enacted* from our myopic (if *sensible*) *environments* and, since it is ever provisional, inevitably inter-subjective, *social* and *ongoing*. And, as such, it is *focused on* and revised in response to all those *extracted clues* our theoretical assumptions direct us to search for. And it is only with Weick's final 'property' that an apparently critical distinction emerges. As a conceptual-analytical approach or – more tellingly – as what Weick calls 'ongoing conversation', sensemaking

Continued

privileges epistemological anxiety and it is for this reason that adherents endeavor to be *plausible* rather than *accurate*.

Of course, all this may be viewed as no more than a speculative word game but – as noted above – word games are all we have to interpose between our sensibilities of the world and our myopic observations of that world. It may be discomfiting, but our theories can never escape beyond those rhetorics, maps and re-presentations. In short, if one dismisses their surface decoration, as reflexive social processes, 'theorizing' is 'sensemaking' and 'sensemaking' is 'theorizing'. This seems plausible to me. Q.E.D.?

REFERENCES

van Maanam, J. (1995) 'Style as theory', *Organization Science*, 6 (1): 133–143.
Weick, K.E. (1989) 'Theory construction as disciplined imagination', *Academy of Management Review*, 14 (4): 516–531.
Weick, K.E. (1995) *Sensemaking in Organizations*. Thousand Oaks, CA: Sage.
Weick, K.E. (1999) 'Theory construction as disciplined reflexivity', *Academy of Management Review*, 24 (4): 797–806.

Corporeal Leaders

Arja Ropo and Erika Sauer

THE MISSING BODY IN LEADERSHIP RESEARCH

Almost like an unwelcome guest, the body of the leader has largely been ignored in leadership and organization studies. Leaders as well as followers do not seem to have concrete, living bodies, but are seen as 'human resources', as something abstracted from their senses, experiences, and gender. Given the emphasis in literature both on the individual and social influence processes between the leader and the followers, one might expect that leadership theories, if any, would take the issue of corporeality seriously. However, although leaders are visible and corporeal as such, very little conceptual attention has been paid on the body and bodily presence of leaders (Ropo et al., 2002). In the following sections, we seek to open up the discussion on the corporeality of leaders in leadership theories and to develop the beginnings of a corporeal leadership theory.

Traditionally, leadership research has a cognitive undertone on human beings. The mainstream leadership theory treats leadership as cognitive, rational, and mindful activity to influence other people.

Leadership is constituted as intellectual knowledge, something that happens based on how we conceptualize the world in our head. In this view, leaders become representations of their positions and roles. They have valuable intellectual knowledge but no corporeal bodies. Leadership is seen as a functional and purposeful guided action that escapes the sensuous body.

Charismatic leadership theories picture the corporeal leader in subtle ways by emphasizing the individual leader and his concrete, physical presence or distance to the followers and different ways of influencing the followers. Also recent shared leadership perspectives allow a relational understanding of corporeal leadership with the emphasis on encounters in the work place and social construction of leadership.

Beyond discussing corporeality within the charismatic and shared leadership theories from the perspective of presence and absence, we develop the argument for a corporeal leadership theory. We find that fundamental part of leadership is about social and physical presence embodied in leaders, which, in turn, has to do with sensory experiences including feelings and emotions. We will discuss how the sensory and emotional understanding of seeing, listening, touching, rhythm, and space are important dimensions to describe corporeal leadership.

The corporeal approach allows another kind of knowledge to become appreciated in leadership. Experiential and sensuous knowledge is needed to foster the subtle social practices and mundane routines that give space for the much-called creativity and innovativeness, especially in professional organizations or teams (Svensson, 1990).

CORPOREALITY THROUGH AESTHETIC EPISTEMOLOGY

The sensory and emotional way of knowing, i.e. aesthetic approach, is how knowledge about corporeal leadership is obtained. During the past ten years aesthetics has grown popular among the front line organization researchers, such as Strati (1989, 1999), Taylor (2000, 2001), Ramirez (1991), and Gagliardi (1996). The fundamental questions are: what do leaders lead, how do they do it, and how can we know about it. Through the aesthetic lenses we aim at building a corporeal leadership theory.

The etymology of 'aesthetics' comes from ancient Greek *aisth* and *aisthanomai*, knowing on the basis of sensible perceptions. It conveys the heuristic action of aesthetics: understanding through physical perception. The verb *aisthanomai* denotes the stimulation of the abilities related to feeling, which means that aesthetics is an active aid to observation (Marquard, 1989). Aesthetics used in the epistemological way emphasizing the sensory faculty differs from the more common understanding of aesthetics as the values of beauty.

Aesthetics differs from rational or cognitive approaches. Aesthetics is a special form of knowing, different from intellectual and rational knowledge. It is heuristic in nature. Aesthetic approach emphasizes that rational analysis neglects important aspects of quotidian organizational practices, not that it chooses to do so, but it cannot grasp or understand their meaning. Aesthetic knowledge is partial, fragmented, and modest. It is not generalizable, universal, or objective; it turns away from the tradition of positivist organization study. Instead, aesthetics enable us to study the subtle, underlying qualities, which we sense, but cannot quite put our finger on (Samier, 2005; Strati, 2000).

Aesthetics allows us to understand bodily knowledge and bodily presence. According to Strati (1999), organizational aesthetics requires a sensory faculty and experience. Experiences are individual in nature: they call for human body. The centrality of body and emotion is crucial in forming aesthetic knowledge (Yancey Martin, 2002). Ropo and Parviainen (2001) have developed the notion of aesthetics of bodily leadership by describing bodily practices of leadership (see e.g., Ropo and Parviainen, 2001; Parviainen 1998). Barnard (1938, cited in Ottensmeyer, 1996) was well ahead of his time when describing the executive process of management as follows:

> The terms pertinent to it are 'feeling', 'judgment', 'sense', 'proportion', 'balance', 'appropriateness'. It is a matter of art rather than science, and is aesthetic rather than logical.

Besides being a cognitive phenomenon, leadership is a sensory experience that occurs in relating to other people. If leadership is understood from this perspective, leaders and subordinates are not abstracted from their concrete living bodies that sense, experience, and reflect with other bodies or artifacts. In contrast, leadership develops and is constructed in and through the bodies as leaders relate to other people in everyday situations. Leadership becomes a corporeal relationship taking place between people. This relationship does not only happen in our intellectual mind but is intertwined with our bodily and aesthetic experiences. This puts leaders and followers into new positions: they become corporeal partners in making leadership.

From linguistic turn to sensory experiences

According to the linguistic approach, such as discourse and narrative analysis, the language itself is considered to be the reality. The text is the world rather than a reflection or means by which something else is described. This marks a shift from objectivity and vision toward subjectivity and voice (Hosking, 1999). Instead of, for example, performing or mimicking experiences, we talk or write about them. The discussion becomes a shared experience where we reconstruct our own experience in relation to the discussed experience. One of the major implications of this is that language, and therefore reality, is ephemeral. Once we have spoken, the reality that was present as we spoke is no longer present.

Aesthetic knowledge is not only verbal, but also visual, gestural, intuitive, and evocative. It depends largely on sensing and feeling, on empathy and intuition and on relating conception to perception (Ramirez, 2005). It poses new challenge to the researchers, when conducting an empirical inquiry: they need to use their own senses and perceptive abilities to produce knowledge. Sensual abilities influence on practices and meanings of organizational life. The tradition of scientific research requires the use of words, even though the sensory nature of aesthetic knowledge would seem to call for more innovative methodologies and ways of reporting the results of the study.

The aesthetic way of experiencing and theorizing upon the world goes further toward subjective experience and experiential knowing. Through senses we experience the world. Aesthetic forms of knowing precede other forms, and shape how these other forms of knowing operate (Damasio, 1999). Senses and emotions are central to knowledge creation. The hands-on experiences, poignant, shaking, heart-felt experiences finally make abstract information to personally absorbed, culturally usable and meaningful knowledge (Sava, 1998: 111).

Paula Yancey Martin states about her ethnographic study in an old people's home:

> By bringing sensate and emotional experiences to the fore, it shows what residential organizations look, smell, sound and feel like to residents, staff and ethnographer. (2002: 865)

Historical and contemporary underpinnings of corporeal leadership

Within leadership research, social constructionism (Berger and Luckmann, 1967) has widened the leadership focus from the individual leader toward the relationship where leadership occurs, i.e. is constructed. Instead of the traditional subject–object or leader – follower/member transaction, we see leadership as a subject–subject relationship. The subject–object view is in line with the historical understanding of work and the class structure. The labor was a burden that had to be done to feed the family, to survive. The managerial view on leadership was emphasized, putting the leader into a conflicting position against the workers.

Today's work needs to convey also symbolic values to build an individual's identity. Besides the salary, the work is expected to provide experiences. As the employee may ask the employer: 'what can you offer me, besides money, to make me work for you?', we need to turn away from the old school oppositional thinking of leaders and followers. The leadership recipe is to be rewritten. The leader is expected to make the work alluring for the employees. The corporeal relationships at the work place become vital. The recent immense interest in the emotion research within organization and leadership studies also speaks for this.

As we aim to contribute to this line of thinking, by no means do we suggest that cognitive knowledge is dispensable. Nor do we say that there is no need for individual, skillful reasoning, rational decision, or organizing structure. What we argue for is, that corporeal, sensuous, and experiential knowledge is needed in leadership theory building.

CORPOREAL PRESENCE AND ABSENCE IN LEADERSHIP

The notion of social distance has been used in the charismatic leadership research (Hunt et al., 2004). In the charismatic leadership research social distance has meant the real, concrete, measurable distance between two people. The focus of interest has been the physical distance of the body of the individual leader to the followers. To examine more closely the notion of corporeality in leadership, it is useful to elaborate the dimension of distance beyond its concrete meaning. As a concept, corporeality is a broader entity than only a physical one. Therefore, we have chosen to talk about both physical and social presence and absence.

The presence or absence of the leader plays a key role in how corporeality within leadership is experienced. In our analysis we develop different kinds of corporeal leadership types through the framework of social and physical presence and absence. We will discuss corporeality in both charismatic leadership theory and shared leadership models and suggest that aesthetic, sensory dimensions of seeing, touching, listening, rhythm, and space are important for corporeal leadership construction.

Presence, either physical or social, is a prerequisite for corporeal leadership to occur. Corporeality is at strongest when a person is both socially and physically present, even though corporeal leadership can also exist when a person is only socially or physically present. If a person is both physically and socially absent we cannot find corporeal leadership.

Physical and social presence can be obtained through many senses, not only by seeing or touching. In the corridor, the smell of the perfume getting stronger when reaching the door of the manager, may tell us that she is around. Through the door we might also hear her voice speaking on the phone. Or, as a theatre director made his presence clear in the theatre building, he played a piano many hours a day in the basement of the theatre. By hearing that, people knew he was there (Sauer, 2005).

CORPOREALITY IN CHARISMATIC LEADERSHIP THEORY

Well-known charismatic leadership theories (e.g., Conger and Canungo, 1998; House, 1977;

Meindl, 1990; Shamir, 1995) describe leaders in terms of certain traits and behaviors, influence processes, and facilitating conditions (Yukl, 1998). According to Shamir and Howell (1999), descriptions of core charismatic behaviors vary somewhat from theory to theory. Conger and Canungo (1987) suggest that charismatic leader behavior includes a compelling vision, unconventional behavior, and sensitivity to follower needs. Image building and impression management have been suggested to be part of charismatic leader identity (e.g., Gardner and Avolio, 1998). Model behavior and imitation is commonly seen as typical charismatic leader behaviors. While most theorists emphasize that charismatic leader is the key power figure, Shamir suggests power sharing as a charismatic leader characteristic (Yukl, 2002).

Also, the processes through which charismatic leader is found to influence followers varies somewhat in different theories. Most theories emphasize personal or social identification, and value internalization. Meindl (1990) has developed the concept of social contagion as a particular type of influence process. According to him, charismatic theories do not explain why charismatic attributions are made by people who do not interact directly with the leader or who have no opportunity to observe the leader. Meindl has offered an explanation that influence processes take place among the followers rather than as a direct influence of the leader toward the followers. This process involves spontaneous spread of emotional and behavioral reactions. Meindl's conception is a social constructionist one and hints toward corporeality by the inclusion of the followers and their mutual interaction, sense-making, and follower experience of the charismatic leader.

Social distance plays an important role in differentiating charismatic leadership (Hunt et al., 2004). Social distance refers to distant and close charismatic leadership. A traditional understanding of charismatic leadership states that psychological distance is required between the leader and the followers. More recent studies show that charisma may emerge also in close-up relationships (ibid.).

Hunt et al. implicitly refer to social and physical distance. They talk about psychological closeness and use a symphony orchestra as an example. However, the physical body of the leader remains conceptually vague or meaningless for knowledge development. The body of the charismatic leader is a black box. What 'physical' and 'social' actually mean in charismatic leadership theories remains obscure.

CORPOREALITY IN SHARED LEADERSHIP MODELS

Pearce and Conger (2003) have defined shared leadership as a dynamic, interactive influence process among individuals in groups for which the objective is to lead one another to the achievement of group or organizational goals. This influence process often involves peer or lateral influence and at other times upward and downward hierarchical influence. The key distinction between shared and traditional models of leadership is that the influence process involves more than just downward influence on subordinates by an appointed or elected leader. Rather, leadership is broadly distributed among individuals instead of a single individual who acts in the role of a superior (ibid.).

There are some early models or movements toward the main idea of shared leadership. Co-leadership, emergent leadership, participative leadership, self-leadership, and empowerment are just a few perspectives mentioned by Pearce and Conger that share the same type of idea of leadership.

According to Lowe (2006: 106), definitions and concepts of shared leadership vary. Shared leadership is seen as distributed and interdependent, embedded in social interaction, as a group level phenomenon, collectively exerted influence, and as lateral influence rather than vertical downward influence.

These definitions and perspectives go beyond the idea of the delegation of tasks, but involve a paradigmatically different conception of leadership (and fellowship) by emphasizing mutuality, social construction, as well as complex, multi-polar influencing

and interaction processes. One might even discern a more experiential understanding of the interaction and influence process where the corporeality of both leaders and followers is in operation.

Corporeality in shared leadership models is explicated in different modes of dialogues suggested by scholars such as Scharmer (2001). These include: presenting, flow, co-creating, politeness, listening, debate, clash, and empathy, among others. Proximity is brought up as a central term in the functioning of R&D teams referring to the physical distance between the leader and the team members (Pearce and Conger, 2003: 60). Corporeality of mutually influencing team members is obvious especially in studies on team diversity, such as gender and racial composition of the team.

We have sought to bring up and investigate the issue of bodily aspect of shared leadership in the context of art and culture organizations (Ropo and Parviainen, 2001; Ropo et al., 2002) where creativity and collaboration are key aspects of work.

We have studied corporeality especially from the perspective of emotions (Sauer, 2005; Sauer and Ropo, 2006) and listening (Koivunen, 2003). Beyond these, our studies suggest that corporeality of leadership involves language practices, gaze, touch, rhythm, and space. Corporeality of leadership may result in feeling insecure, afraid, and unsettled, as well as feeling loved, trusted and free. Corporeality in leadership may be both beautiful and ugly. To us, leadership calls for corporeality and sensuous experience that occur in interaction between people who are willing to put themselves into a process where power positions and roles keep changing, and where the outcome is a result of tensions arising from the bodily nature of the interaction.

CORPOREAL LEADER ILLUSTRATIONS IN CHARISMATIC AND SHARED LEADERSHIP THEORIES

The main distinction on corporeality between shared leadership and charismatic leadership is that shared leadership is not identified as a single person. Rather, it takes place in relationships in a group, it is social in nature, and gets constructed in everyday mundane actions and routines. It demands sharing of authority by the hierarchical leader and acceptance of responsibility by the members of the group. The leader and the followers are in a more dialogical and equal relationship with each other. We illustrate the shared leadership model through an example of the work process of directing a play in theatre. The director of a play can be seen as the formal leader of the ensemble. However, throughout the process, leadership is negotiated in the interaction between the director and the ensemble.

PHYSICALLY AND SOCIALLY PRESENT LEADER(SHIP)

Leader of a sect

In charismatic leadership the physical and social experiences of the distance become meaningful through the presence of an individual leader. The physical and social closeness of the leader are important in leading a sect. The members seek for and even compete about the physical and social closeness of the leader. Hierarchies are built through distance. The most distant subordinates are on the lowest level in the hierarchy whereas the people or groups who share most time close to the leader talking and interacting, are manifestations of social closeness with the leader. A notorious example of physically and socially present leader would be David Koresh, the sect leader, who led the members of his sect, including women and children into their death in 1993 in Waco, Texas.

Ensemble at work

When the social and physical presence is strong, it is possible to build a community, like a theatre ensemble. People learn how to work with each other as they work physically and socially close to each other. Work at a theatre demands opening up to

other people: this is done by staying alert to physical and social impulses coming from others and trying to build on them. The task of the director is to help in creating the way to work where everybody feels safe but also professionally challenged. The basis for trust and reliability and respect toward each others' bodily and social work are formed. The ensemble takes part in making leadership by staying constructive. The danger in this kind of process is that the group becomes self-sufficient and uncritical toward each other's work. Staying both physically and socially close also opens a possibility for a closed entity. The group may lose the ability for self-criticism and become an inverted, closed community (Sauer, 2005).

PHYSICALLY PRESENT, BUT SOCIALLY ABSENT LEADER(SHIP)

Mythical symphony orchestra conductor

A charismatic leader may also be physically close, but socially absent. An example of this is the great conductor Herbert von Karajan, who was said to step in front of the orchestra, physically close, standing on the podium for musicians to see, but as soon as he raised his hands to start, he would close his eyes. The musicians described him being almost in a trance-like state, absorbed completely in himself and the music. They felt like being his marionettes, a medium for him to make his music, not their music. Even though Karajan seemed to ignore the presence of the musicians, they were strongly influenced, even intimidated, by his physical appearance (Lebrecht, 1997: 202).

Attention away from the ensemble

The actors in a theatre have candidly described their annoyance as when in the middle of a rehearsal have noticed that the director does not pay attention to what happens on the stage (Sauer, 2005). Maybe he is writing SMS messages or reading something.

However, from time to time both social as well as physical absence are needed from the director in order to put the work of the group into proportion. Social distance gives a possibility to glimpse the group 'as an outsider'. A danger here is that the 'look of an outsider' gets too critical and unconstructive. If someone takes the right only to criticize and not to participate, soon the others feel that nothing is good enough. The self-esteem of the group may deteriorate.

PHYSICALLY ABSENT, BUT SOCIALLY PRESENT LEADER(SHIP)

Idealized figurehead

An idolized figurehead, sometimes even a rebellious person, cannot or will not be physically close to the followers, but instead, finds a way into their hearts. High political figures are seldom in close physical contact to the people. Organized visits are not natural situations where the leaders and the people could freely interact, but highly orchestrated and scheduled exceptions to the daily routine of both parties. The physical distance is well visualized when we see the figurehead on the balcony waving to the masses below. Despite this, socially s/he may be experienced as close. Princess Diana and Eva Peron were loved by the public, even though most had never seen them. These women are exceptions among their peers, who are typically experienced as distant, and even estranged from the lives of ordinary people. This kind of distant physical but close social relationship between the leader and the followers is typically made through media. Media displays their personal and emotional sides so that people can socially relate to them, no matter how far they are physically or culturally.

Representing the ensemble

Physical absence is often a must in work life. There are meetings and seminars where physical presence of the leader is required for representation. A typical situation for a theatre director is a situation where he is doing PR work for the play. Even though he is physically absent he socially works for the ensemble. Also, some directors describe how hard it is to match family life with the intensive process of play rehearsals, as the thoughts are in the text and in the work of the actors. Sometimes the physical absence of a member may give space and a boost for others to make progress. Solitude following the absence of the leader or a key member of the group may be needed to feed the group with fresh ideas. If the leader or a member of the group is away for long periods, there is a danger that he or she loses touch with the group. Others make progress and simultaneously develop a way to work without the person. It is possible that he or she is not needed any more, no matter how much social presence there had been. The corporeal momentum may be lost.

PHYSICALLY AND SOCIALLY ABSENT LEADER(SHIP)

Paranoid dictator

When talking about charismatic leaders, physical and social absence may seem like a paradox. However, some kind of dark charisma can be found even in the most horrific and paranoid dictators of the world, like Idi Amin and Nicolae Ceausescu. Their charisma may rise from the power they seem to possess over the lives of other people. They separate themselves from the followers by hiding in closed compounds and behind the gatekeepers. They position themselves above criticism leading to social separation from their people. They destroy their enemies without hesitation and put their subordinates under such terror that they cannot do anything else but obey the leader. One would like to call this evil leadership.

Detaching from the ensemble

Where social and physical absence are strongest, there is a danger that shared leadership dissolves. Shared leadership requires both physical and social presence to emerge. If the routines are pertinent, the work is found fruitful and satisfying, and the social bond between people is present, the group may tolerate the physical and social absence of the leader or the member for a while. Needless to say however, shared leadership, both in its close physical and social dimension must be re-established. In the work of a theatre director, detaching is part of the process. As the premiere comes, the director is no longer needed.

BEGINNINGS OF A CORPOREAL LEADERSHIP THEORY

Corporeal leadership is a new way of approaching leadership. It is not another attempt to build on and refine previous leadership theories. It calls for a constructionist ontology and aesthetic epistemology, which lead us away from the objective observations or interpretations of reality that lies out there, away from the people who are observing it. Knowledge formation is sensory and experiential rather than cognitive and intellectual. It goes well beyond the linguistic approach that concentrates on language practices, i.e. how leadership is done in language, what kinds of power structures are built through linguistic means, what kinds of stories are told and metaphors chosen. Methodologically, sensory and experiential knowledge formation calls for expanding our understanding of what research data and analysis may entail. It also invites to look for innovative ways of reporting scholarly work. It encourages readers to participate in knowledge formation through their personal experience.

In addition to traditional individual perspectives that emphasize portrait-like static figures of successful business leaders or relationships understood as cognitive networks, our view of leadership as a sensory and embodied phenomenon enriches the understanding of leading and organizational life. It also points to a different way of theorizing leadership. It opens a path to an aesthetic way of knowing where individual, relational and bodily aspects of leadership are incorporated. It points out the time, history, and context of leadership through the faculties of seeing, touching, listening, rhythm, and space. Corporeal leadership approach appreciates the history of leadership thought but recognizes the need to expand it. Corporeality both links current understandings of leadership but simultaneously breaks the ground for a new line of thinking.

Corporeal leadership seems to be especially important in the communities that seek creativity and innovativeness, such as artistic organizations, research and development teams, and scientific communities. Traditional research practices on corporeal leadership are challenged and researchers are encouraged to use their creativity to answer this call. The suggested dimensions of corporeal leadership call for further analysis in organizational settings. Several guiding questions could be asked, such as: how is leadership understood and done through these dimensions; how does leadership emerge in the process of sharing; how do different rhythms meet; how to construct leadership spatially?

This approach also poses challenges to scholarly practices, such as data collection and reporting. In addition to words, it needs pictures, films, music, and poems which may be better suited to aesthetic knowledge development. While traditional research has emphasized the cool, distanced, and objective forms where the researcher is nowhere to be found, the corporeal leadership theory and aesthetic approach invites a personal touch.

REFERENCES

Berger, P.L. and Luckmann, T. (1967) *The Social Construction of Reality: A Treatise on the Sociology of Knowledge*. London: Penguin.

Brewis, J., Lindstead, S., Boje, D., and O'Shea, T. (eds) (2006) *The Passion of Organizing*. Liber & Copenhagen Business School Press.

Conger, J.A. and Kanungo, R.N. (1998) *Charismatic Leadership in Organizations*. Thousand Oaks, CA: Sage.

Conger, J.A. and Kanungo, R.N. (1987) 'Toward a behavioral theory of charismatic leadership in organizational settings', *Academy of Management Review*, 12: 637–647.

Damasio, A. (1999) *The Feeling of what Happens: Body and Emotion in Making of Consciousness*. New York: Harcourt Brace & Company.

Fineman, S. (2003) *Understanding Emotion at Work*. London: Sage.

Foucault, M. (1967) *Of Other Spaces. Heterotopias*. Translated from French by Jay Miskowiec. Lecture. http://foucault. info/documents/heteroTopia/foucault.heteroTopia.en.html

Gagliardi, P. (1996) 'Exploring the aesthetic side of organizational life', in S.R. Glegg, C. Hardy and W. Nord (eds) *Handbook of Organization Studies*. London: Sage. pp. 565–580.

Gardner, W.L. and Avolio, B.J. (1998) 'The charismatic relationship: A dramaturgical perspective', *Academy of Management Review*, 23 (1): 32–58.

Hosking, D.M. (1999) 'Social construction as process: Some new possibilities for research and development', *Concepts and Transformation*, 4 (2): 117–132.

House, R.J. (1977) 'A theory of charismatic leadership', in J.G. Hunt and L.L. Larson (eds), *Leadership: The Cutting Edge*. Carbondale, IL: Southern Illinois University Press.

Hunt, J. (1991) *Leadership: A New Synthesis*. Newbury Park, CA: Sage.

Hunt, J., Xia, J., Stelluto, G.E. and Ropo, A. (2004) '*Antecendents and consequences of close charisma: An examination of conductor musician relationships in U.S. and Finnish Orchestras*'. Proceedings of the Southern Management Association Conference, 3–6 November, San Antonio.

Koivunen, N. (2003) 'Leadership in symphony orchestras. Discursive and aesthetic practices'. PhD dissertation. Tampere University Press.

Lebrecht, N. (1997) *When the Music Stops … Managers, Maestros and the Corporate Murder of Classical Music*. London: Pocket Books.

Lowe, K.B. (2006) Book Review: Pearce, C.L. and Conger, J.A. 'Shared leadership: Reframing the hows and whys of leadership', *The Leadership Quarterly*, 17 (1): 105–108.

Marquard, O. (1989) *Farewell to Matters of Principle*. Philosophical Studies. Odeon: Oxford University Press.

Meindl, J.R. (1990) 'On leadership: An alternative to the conventional wisdom', *Research in Organizational Behavior*, 12: 159–203.

Meindl, J.R. (1995) 'The romance of leadership as a follower centric-theory: A social constructionist approach', *The Leadership Quarterly*, 6 (3): 328–341.

Ottensmeyer, E. (1996) 'Too strong to stop, too sweet to loose: Aesthetics as a way to know organizations', *Organization*, 3 (2): 189–194.

Parviainen, J. (1998) *Bodies Moving and Moved*. Tampere: Tampere University Press.

Pearce, C.L. and Conger, J.A (2003) 'All those years ago. The historical underpinnings of shared leadership', in C.L. Pearce and J.A. Conger (eds), *Shared Leadership. Reframing the Hows and Whys of Leadership*. Thousand Oaks, CA: Sage.

Ramirez, R. (1991) *The Beauty of Social Organization*. München: ACCEDO.

Ramirez, R. (2005) 'The aesthetics of cooperation', *European Management Review*, 2 (1): 28–35.

Ropo, A. and Parviainen, J. (2001) 'Leadership and bodily knowledge in expert organizations. Epistemological rethinking', *Scandinavian Journal of Management*, 17 (1): 1–18.

Ropo, A., Parviainen, J. and Koivunen, N. (2002) 'Aesthetics in leadership. From absent bodies to social bodily presence', in J. Meindl and K. Parry (eds), *Grounding Leadership Theory and Research: Issues and Perspectives*. Greenwich, CT: Information Age Publishing.

Samier, E. (2005) 'Aesthetic analysis of administration: Foundations, dimensions and critique' and 'The kitsch critique of administration: The new public management and leadership training as high and low kitsch'. In seminar on organizational aesthetics, 23.8.2005, Tampere, Finland.

Sauer, E. (2005) 'Emotions in leadership: Leading a dramatic ensemble'. PhD dissertation, Tampere University Press.

Sauer, E. and Ropo, A. (2006) 'Leadership and the driving force of Shame: A social constructionist analysis of narrative', in W.J. Zerbe, N. Ashkanasy and C. Hartel, (eds), *Research on Emotions in organizations, Volume 2: Individual and Organizational Perspectives on Emotion Management and Display*. Oxford: Elsevier JAI.

Sava, I. (1998) 'Taiteen ja tieteen kietoutuminen tutkimuksessa', M. Bardy (ed.), *Taide tiedon lähteenä*. Helsinki: Stakes.

Scharmer, C.O. (2001) 'Self-transcending knowledge: Organizing around emerging realities', in I. Nonaka, and D. Teece (eds), *Managing Industrial Knowledge: Creation, Transfer and Utilization*. Thousand Oaks, CA: Sage. pp. 68–90.

Shamir, B. (1995) 'Social distance and charisma: Theoretical notes and an exploratory study', *The Leadership Quarterly*, 6 (1): 19–47.

Shamir, B. and Howell, J.M. (1999) Organizational and contextual influences on the emergence and effectiveness of charismatic leadership, *The Leadership Quarterly*, 10: 257–283.

Strati, A. (1989) 'Aesthetics and organizational skill', in B. Turner (ed.), *Organizational Symbolism*. New York: De Gruyter.

Strati, A. (1999) *Organization and Aesthetics*. London: Sage.

Strati, A. (2000) *Theory and Method in Organization Studies: Paradigms and Choices*. London: Sage.

Svensson, L.G. (1990) 'Knowledge as a professional resource: Case studies of psychologists and architects at work', in R. Torstendahl and M. Burrage (eds), *The Formation of Professions: Knowledge, State and Strategy*. London: Sage. pp. 51–70.

Taylor, S.S. (2000) 'Aesthetic knowledge in academia: Capitalist pigs at the Academy of Management', *Journal of Management Inquiry*, 9 (3): 304–328.

Taylor, S.S. (2001) 'A clockwork postmodern', *Journal of Management Inquiry*, 10 (2): 133.

Yancey Martin, P. (2002) 'Sensations, bodies, and the "spirit of a place": Aesthetics in residential organizations for the elderly', *Human Relations*, 55 (7): 861–885.

Yukl, G. (1998, 2002) *Leadership in Organizations*. Upper Saddle River, NJ: Prentice-Hall.

The Future is Now

James G. (Jerry) Hunt

Since receiving my business school major and psychology minor Ph.D. many years ago, I have had a very strong scholarly interest in two aspects of leadership and organizational studies. The first of these has been macro/micro approaches, now mostly subsumed under the label 'contextual'. The second has been temporal emphases, currently reflected by dynamic or processual approaches, or to some extent by the more generic longitudinal perspectives.

These interests are still with me, if anything even more. They are represented by current developments in organizational studies concerned with increasingly common contextual discussions in the field. These discussions cover a wide range of variables such as: national culture; external environment; hierarchical leader level; a wide range of individual, group and organizational characteristics; and leadership mediated by electronic means. They are not simply contingency variables, they provide boundary conditions that influence attempts to understand how such phenomena as leadership emerge and not just the extent to which or how contingencies affect the strength of relationships (Antonakis et al., 2004: 61).

Additionally, the contingencies are represented by increasing emphasis in what are sometimes called third discipline approaches, where the first two disciplines are concerned with experimentation and regression perspectives, respectively (see Hunt and Ropo, 2003). Representative of this third discipline work are complex adaptive system (CAS) perspectives, heavily reliant on computational modeling, focusing on such areas as system dynamics, agency based modeling, and chaos/complexity theory and extend to qualitative dynamic or processual approaches. All these perspectives go beyond more traditional regression-based, cross-sectional and longitudinal approaches and, indeed, have been argued to be part of a longitudinal zeitgeist (tenor of the times) that is currently encouraging both these and third discipline perspectives (see Hunt and Ropo, 2003). Commonalities among the third discipline perspectives are their breaking away from such Newtonian assumptions as: predictable causes and ultimate understanding of physical events one-way linear (proportional) causal relationships and stable predictable linearity with one-way cause and effect. Much of the behavioral science work has followed such assumptions. In stark contrast are third discipline approaches – an attempt to catch reality in flight, explore the dynamic quality of people and organizations, and embed the dynamism over time in various external and internal contextual layers where streams of activity occur (Pettigrew, 1997, as cited in Hunt and Ropo, 2003).

Pettigrew's work is qualitative in nature but in its description is remarkably similar to the CAS perspective. Representative recent CAS work is that of Marion and Uhl-Bien (2001, as cited in Hunt and Ropo, 2003), reviewing CAS leadership literature; Jacobsen and House (2001 as cited in Hunt and Ropo, 2003), and Davis (2006) each covering routinization of charismatic leadership using system dynamics; Black et al. (2006), using an agent based approach to learning; and Osborn et al. (2002), emphasizing context and CAS to stress greater recognition of contextual macro views in four broad

Continued

organizational contexts, which are: stability (a traditional bureaucratic setting); crisis (sudden threats to high priority goals with little response time); dynamic equilibrium (organization in change mode); and edge of chaos (transition zone poised between order and chaos, CAS). Here, leadership is considered to be an emerging social construction embedded in a unique context. These contexts encourage researchers to reconsider temporality, causal relations, units of analysis and dependent variables consistent with the social construction of human agency within a given context.

My argument here, as strongly as I can make it, is that third discipline perspectives need to go beyond even the current longitudinal zeitgeist and be the wave of the future. Such approaches certainly have been emphasized in the natural sciences for a long time. They also have been argued for in the behavioral sciences, on and off, for some 40 years. There are strong internal and external environmental forces supportive of this current CAS wave. Of course as with anything, there are forces against it. Perhaps, for example, first and second discipline approaches will be extended to focus on enough third discipline kinds of issues to slow the discipline's development but the time seems right and I argue that the future is now.

REFERENCES

Antonakis, J., Schriesheim, C.A., Donovan, J.A., Gopalakrishna-Pillai, K., Pellegrini, E. and Rossomme, J.L. (2004) 'Methods for studying leadership', in J. Antonakis, A.T. Cianciolo, and R.J. Sternberg, (eds), *The Nature of Leadership*. pp. 48–70. Thousand Oaks, CA: Sage.

Black, J., Oliver, R.L., Howell, J.P. and King, J.P. (2006) 'A dynamic system simulation of leader and group effects on context for learning', *The Leadership Quarterly*, 17 (1), 39–56.

Davis, J.D. (2006) 'Charisma and its routinization revisited: A system dynamics approach'. Working Paper, Institute for Leadership Research, Texas Tech University, Lubbock, TX.

Hunt, J.G. and Ropo, A. (2003) 'Longitudinal research and the third scientific discipline', *Group and Organization Management*, 23 (3): 315–340.

Osborn, R.N., Hunt, J.G. and Jauch, L.R. (2002) 'Toward a contextual theory of leadership'. *The Leadership Quarterly*, 13 (6): 797–837.

Why Leaders Fail

Robert J. Sternberg

Why do leaders fail? Traditional theories of leadership might tend to view them as failing because of their not having the personality traits associated with successful leadership, or because of behavioral failures, or because of their lacking transformational vision (see summary of theories in Antonakis et al., 2004). I would argue, however, that virtually all leaders who fail do so because they commit a set of cognitive fallacies that eventually does them in (Sternberg, 2003). Failure is *not* the opposite of success. It is of a different nature altogether.

There are six cognitive fallacies failed leaders commit. They illustrate well how the leaders of companies such as Enron, Worldcom, Arthur Andersen, etc., brought down their organizations.

1 *Unrealistic optimism.* The leaders come to believe that, by virtue of their intelligence, power, magnetic personalities, or whatever, they will be able to succeed where others might fail. The invasion of Iraq was an example. President Bush and his colleagues might well have believed that the successful military invasion amounted to a 'mission accomplished'. But they could believe this only by being unrealistically optimistic, and thereby ignoring the likely social, political, and cultural aftermath of the invasion. Andrew Fastow could only have believed that the set of shell companies he created while he was CFO of Enron could continue functioning indefinitely without leading to ruin.

2 *Egocentrism.* Leaders who may, at one time, feel some degree of responsibility to the people they lead, become entirely self-focused, caring exclusively about the enrichment of their finances, power, status, or whatever. Josef Stalin became a cult of arbitrary power, focused only on his own personal whims. Saddam Hussein built palace after palace while his people lived in poverty. In North Korea, Kim Jong Il has followed in the footsteps of his father, building a cult of personality around himself, while his people starve.

3 *Omniscience.* Leaders may come to believe that they are expert not only in the area in which they have acquired expertise, but in all areas. The Kennedy administration spearheaded the disastrous Bay of Pigs invasion based upon very limited information, but believed it had full information (Janis, 1972). More recently, the Bush administration assured the world that Iraq had weapons of mass destruction.

4 *Omnipotence.* Leaders may come to think that they are all-powerful. Bush and Cheney seemed to believe that the US Army was omnipotent and could easily wipe out opposition in Iraq. They were wrong. Kennedy and Johnson believed the same for Vietnam. They were wrong too.

5 *Invulnerability.* Leaders may come to believe that no one can get back at them – that, like Superman, they are invincible. Bill Clinton acted with impunity in his personal life and appears to have perjured himself, or come close to it, in a civil trial, despite his knowledge of the law. Saddam was responsible for many thousands of deaths, and acted with impunity, believing he would never pay the consequences. The leaders of Enron hurt stockholders, customers, employees, and many others, believing the chickens would never come home to roost.

6 *Moral disengagement.* Leaders may become morally disengaged (Bandura, 1999). They simply stop caring about the moral consequences of what they do. Adolph Hitler, Josef Stalin, Pol Pot, and Mao tse-Tung were in a position to recognize the moral turpitude of their acts. They just didn't care.

Continued

Here are three things leaders can do to avoid falling into these traps:

1 *Be a reflective practitioner.* Leaders commit these fallacies because they allow themselves to do so. Seriously evaluate your own behavior, and ask whether you are falling into any of these traps.
2 *Actively seek honest 360-degree feedback.* Leaders become trapped because they do not seek feedback, or seek it only from sycophants. Actively ask others for feedback and use it to improve your performance.
3 *Look at and evaluate the result of your decisions.* Fallacious thinking leads to poor results. Failed leaders shun evaluation of their performance. Excellent ones actively seek it out. Use evaluation to identify errors and improve performance.

REFERENCES

Antonakis, J., Cianciolo, A.T. and Sternberg, R.J. (eds). (2004). *The Nature of Leadership.* Thousand Oaks, CA: Sage Publications.

Bandura, A. (1999) 'Moral disengagement in the perpetration of inhumanities', *Personality and Social Psychology Review,* 3: 193–209.

Janis, I.L. (1972) *Victims of Groupthink.* Boston: Houghton-Mifflin.

Sternberg, R.J. (2003) 'WICS: A model for leadership in organizations', *Academy of Management Learning & Education,* 2, 386–401.

How Can We Make Organizations More Ethical?

Edwin A. Locke

In a previous article (Locke, 2006) I reviewed a number of texts on business ethics. I found that these books mainly discussed theories of ethics which not only contradicted one another but contained numerous weaknesses of their own. This should not be surprising, because Western culture is dominated by skepticism: the doctrine that you can't know anything for certain. This is due mainly to the influence of philosopher Immanuel Kant, the arch enemy of the Enlightenment (Ghate, 2003; Locke and Ghate, 2003; Peikoff, 1982).

So is there an alternative? There is: Ayn Rand's philosophy of Objectivism (Locke and Ghate, 2003; Peikoff, 1991; Rand, 1992). Objectivism holds – and demonstrates – that ethics are objective and that a code of ethics can be based on reason.

Rand argues that the ultimate, objective standard of value in ethics is: life. The issue of value arises only because people are mortal. If they do not take the actions their life requires, they go out of existence. To quote Ayn Rand, 'It is only the concept of "Life" that makes the concept of "Value" possible' (Rand, 1964: 15–16). Life as the standard means the life of each individual, and only individuals exist. A group or society is an abstraction and is composed of individuals.

Objectivism holds that one is the proper beneficiary of one's own actions. Thus Objectivism advocates rational egoism and considers it not condemnatory but morally admirable. Objectivism considers altruism (which does not mean benevolence or good will), that is, sacrifice of the self to others, to be immoral, because it is anti-life and anti-happiness. (One can properly risk one's life for egoistic reasons, e.g., to save one's loved one without whom life would have no meaning. But one would not do it out of Kantian duty.)

The key virtue in Objectivism is rationality, because one gains knowledge through reason and reason is one's main tool of survival. Virtues inherent in rationality are: honesty (the refusal to fake reality); integrity (loyalty to one's rational convictions in action); independence (the use of one's own rational judgment to make decisions and earning one's own living); productivity (creating or earning the material values one's life requires); justice (rationality applied to one's judgment of others and actions toward others which are in accordance with that judgment); and pride (moral ambitiousness, striving to makes oneself morally perfect).

How would one inculcate such a code of ethics or any code) into an organization? First, the CEO would have to have a rational code of ethics and thoroughly understand it. Second, the CEO would have to persuade the top managers and Board of Directors that the code of ethics in question was a good one for the company to practice. Third, one would have to select employees who held the right ethical standards, not just on the basis of motivation and ability.

Fourth, one would have to make the company's code of ethics a key part of the company's training program for new employees, especially managerial employees. The company's code of ethics should also be communicated in print.

Continued

Fifth, the CEO and the top managers must practice the ethics code in their own actions consistently. If they do not serve as role models, their professed views will be seen as hypocritical.

Sixth, the company's moral values should be made an integral part of the performance appraisal system. Reward and punishment (including firing) should be based not just on how one does with respect to the 'numbers' but on moral character (including firing for dishonesty and other moral breaches).

Does any company actually practice what I have been discussing? Yes, BB&T (Branch Banking and Trust), a very financially successful, growing and scandal free banking company located in the mid-Atlantic region. They have shown that you can make money through virtue – if you pick the right virtues!

REFERENCES

Ghate, O. (2003) 'Postmodernism's Kantian roots', in E. Locke (ed.) *Postmodernism and Management: Pros, Cons and the Alternative*. New York: Elsevier.

Locke, E.A. (2006) 'Business ethics: A way out of the morass', *Academy of Management Learning and Education*, 5, 324–332.

Locke, E.A. and Ghate, O. (2003) 'Objectivism: The proper alternative to postmodernism', in E. Locke (ed.) *Postmodernism and Management: Pros, Cons and the Alternative*. New York: Elsevier.

Peikoff, L. (1982) *The Ominous Parallels: The End of Freedom in America*. New York: Stein & Day.

Peikoff, L. (1991) *Objectivism: The Philosophy of Ayn Rand*. New York: Dutton.

Rand, A. (1964) *The Virtue of Selfishness*. New York: Signet.

Rand, A. (1992) *Atlas Shrugged*. New York: Signet.

The Craft and Art of Narrative Inquiry in Organizations

Frances Hancock and David Epston

INTRODUCTION

In this chapter, we explore the application and relevance of narrative forms of inquiry to organizational development practice. We map the journey of an apprenticeship in narrative ideas and practices, showing how one learns and is taught the craft and art of narrative inquiry. In particular, we seek to illuminate some of the measures of a 'good question' and to demonstrate how such inquiry can be harnessed to generate the knowledges of practitioners operating at all levels of organizations to inform organizational change and development, as opposed to exerting outside expert analyses and solutions.

WHY A NARRATIVE APPROACH TO ORGANIZATIONAL INQUIRY?

How do we work with organizations or organizational practitioners in a way that will enable them to find their own solutions rather than impose answers to the challenges and problems they face? A common criticism of 'expert-driven' approaches to organizational development (whether facilitated by internal practitioners or external consultants) is that they fail to generate staff buy-in to or ownership of organizational development initiatives, which can have the effect of hindering implementation and stagnating organizational culture. If staff are included in 'expert-led' reviews, this often happens under the 'pretense of consultation' and with a focus on information-gathering to support expert accounts of organizational problems and recommendations for change.

Narrative inquiry proposes an alternative approach to the patronizing assumptions at work in an expert-orientated manner. Instead, it favors a more respectful and inclusive form of organizational inquiry that 'looks to' and seeks to engage the 'insider knowledges' of practitioners operating at all levels of an organization. Elsewhere, David Epston explains that:

> Insider knowledges are local, particular and at times unique as they often arise from imagination and inspiration, not the usual technologies of scientific knowledge-making. ... Because they are,

in the first instance, the intellectual property or otherwise of the person(s) concerned, outsiders cannot rightly claim either invention or ownership of such knowledges. 'Insider knowledges' are modest and make no claims beyond the person(s) concerned. They do not seek any monopolies of 'knowing' but sponsor many kinds and ways of knowing. 'Insider knowledges' do not provide grand schemes as they are far too humble for that ... and are carried best by and through stories. (Email to Frances Hancock, 5 May 2005)

The narrative inquiry approach proposed in this chapter seeks to apply ideas and practices originated in the field of narrative therapy to the challenge of organizational inquiry. Narrative inquiry seeks to generate insider knowledges through a collaborative (Epston, 1999; Madsen, 1999) and a transparent, reflexive practice (White, 1997, 2000, 2004) in which organizational practitioners are seen as the authorities on their experience and separate from problems (Epston and White, 1992; White and Epston, 1990). In so doing, narrative inquiry highlights and seeks to understand multiple perspectives – 'the many voices of experience' (Sax, 2000) – especially as they take the form of a knowledge.

ST JOHN OF GOD HOSPITALITY PRACTICES PROJECT

In 2003, we (Frances and David) were commissioned to undertake an organizational review for the Australasian Province of the Hospitaller Order of St John of God (SJOG) Brothers, a Catholic religious order sponsoring health, community, and disability services in New Zealand and Australia. The project took place over an 18 month period and focused on the SJOG mission of Hospitality. It generated over 1000 pages of research materials that were reproduced as a book-length document. Hospitality is considered to be the core value, distinguishing characteristic and a kind of spirit permeating SJOG Services. Hospitality not only defines and identifies a SJOG Service but also informs and shapes organizational life and culture. Essentially, it concerns 'who we are', 'what is our purpose', and 'how we do things around here'.

SJOG Services operate in a rapidly changing and competitive environment. They must forge their mission of Hospitality, which dates back to the sixteenth century, in a marketplace driven by competing values and multiple interests. They must meet significant legislative demands and government contractual requirements while managing a diverse workforce. Various forces – professional, cultural and economic – have contributed to changes in the contexts, delivery, and practices of SJOG Services, including a shift from institutional care to community-based settings. The Order and its Services face the ongoing challenge of creating strategies that enable 'finding' and 'nourishing' competent professionals of 'like mind and heart' to exercise leadership at all levels of the organization to carry on its mission of Hospitality. Individual members of the Order have also faced public allegations of sexual abuse that have cast a looming shadow over its Services as those matters have been or are being adjudicated in courts of law. In this maelstrom of organizational enterprise, the Order commissioned a review of its Model of Mission, agreeing to a wide scope of inquiry.

An apprenticeship in narrative inquiry

I (David) welcomed the opportunity to work (as the apprenticer) with Frances (as the apprentice) to explore the application and relevance of narrative therapy enquiries to organizational development work and furthermore to consider how to translate such enquiries into the medium of email conversation, which was central to the project's research design. Could the intimacies of a practice developed in the context of mental health, psychiatry, and psychology be made over and articulated within existing developments in narrative forms of inquiry in organizational development (Boje et al., 1997; Boje et al., 2001; Czarniawska, 2004)? Some essays had already headed in such a direction (Barry, 1997; Barry and Elmes 1997; Sax, 2000).

I (Frances) was eager to learn what constitutes a 'good question' and how to go about making such enquiries in an organizational setting, without sounding like a therapist delving deeply into personal problems. I also brought other concerns: How do I go about generating conversations through which my enquiries summon story-telling rather than information-giving? How do I generate 'storied conversation' for the purposes of an organizational review? Which practices of story-writing do I carry over into email conversations and which conversational practices do I apply? How do I draft questions on the page differently than I might in a face-to-face interview?

A foray into email conversation

For various reasons, we set out to engage primarily with people who had earned the reputation of being 'exemplars' or 'messengers' of SJOG Hospitality – an idea taken from Lawrence-Lightfoot (2000) – and to do so primarily via the medium of email conversation. Initial face-to-face interviews resulted in a 'story-in-text', in which I (Frances) 'wrote up' the conversation of the interview into a 'story' with my conversationalist(s) as protagonists and plotted events along what could be considered as an undercurrent or more formally a 'counterstory' (Nelson, 2001) to that of a prevalent narrative of despair regarding the endurance of the mission of Hospitality in SJOG Services. The stories-in-text were used to seed the email conversations that were to follow.

I (Frances) drafted an early email to an esteemed SJOG exemplar who had agreed reluctantly to participate in the email conversations. Any early attempts at engaging an email conversation were likely to either invite or discourage his continuing participation. I set out to draft a short email with a colloquial tone, conveying genuine interest in our exemplar's ideas but limiting the number of questions so as not to overwhelm him but instead to excite his interest. I also outlined the technicalities of email conversation so that he could learn how to make them work. I asked David to help me to 'freshen up' the questions. I didn't realize it at the time but my language provided a key: a 'good' question is fresh;

it takes a new turn by asking people to think in unfamiliar ways. Below is the draft email with David's revisions in bold.

Dear Exemplar
Thank you for your email. **Indeed, I am grateful for the opportunity to put your mind at rest.** I didn't find your letter rambling at all! In fact you raise a number of ideas that are of very real interest to me and I hope in time to be able to pursue them with you through these email conversations, but for now I will focus on a couple of ideas only.

Please see below my reply. I hope you will excuse the fact that I have 'cut and pasted' quotes from your letter, so as to carry the conversation forward, inserting your name at the front so that when I look back on these emails at a later date I will be clear about who said what. **Let me know if this email etiquette puts you at your ease, 'talking' as though we were together or on the other hand, if it in any way is discomforting for you? Many thanks for your assistance with this 'strange' thing we are doing here!**

EXEMPLAR: Thank you for your letter and your reflection on our time together. It has challenged me to reflect on the source of my ramblings. For me the first source, as a Christian, is the God we worship is primarily a GOD OF HOSPITALITY, a God who not only creates, but invites us to live life and respects the giftedness and limitations of his creatures and invites us into the search.

FRANCES: **Jack (not his real name), can you even hint at** what the 'GOD OF HOSPITALITY' is inviting us to look for? **Your turn of phrase intrigues me as it is so rich in suggestion but I fear I may jump too quickly to my own conclusions. I would appreciate your help here.**

EXEMPLAR: John of God in the sixteenth century, saw himself as a limited person, recognized some personal failures in his life, but showed to the outcasts of Granada a committed love and respect they had never experienced. Those he invited to assist him found their lives being enriched at the same time delivering care and respect to the marginalized.

FRANCES: **Jack, in my journey with St John of God thus far I have come to learn that you are regarded by many as the most venerable Hospitaller, and I am supposing that your years of following in St John of God's footsteps may have you know him longer (and perhaps better) than some others. For that reason among others,** I am fascinated by your idea that St John of God 'invited others to assist him'. **I also confess that I am so far poorly informed regarding the Hospitality of St John of God. My colleague, David, and I made a deliberate choice not to 'find' St John of God in books but to find him out through our exemplars. So I apologize if my enquiries seem naive - I admit they very well may be.**

How did **St John of God** identify particular individuals to help him to carry out his mission of Hospitality? **Were there some particular signs that signaled to him that such a person might be issued his invitation? Or** did people come to him **seeking his invitation**? How, **do you imagine,** he worked out who to 'take on', so to speak? And once he 'took them on', **was there some 'teaching' (using that word in its widest sense) that** he employed to nourish his sense of Hospitality in them? If so what kind of **'teaching'** was that?

Jack, I am grateful you are willing to put your computer skills to work for our research. From now on I will copy our email exchanges to David, who will reply in CAPS so as to distinguish his voice.

Hope all is well with you.
Respectfully
Frances Hancock

The art and craft of schmoozing

I (David) realized in reviewing Frances' draft that I had been tutoring myself over the last few years while working extensively over email in my clinical practice and with the supervision of and consultation to my colleagues. While email conversation is not the usual medium of narrative therapy, I had taken up the practice to accommodate long-distance requests. In speaking to Frances about the intricacies of email conversation, and in particular the craft and art of 'good' questioning, I was bringing it into my own conscious awareness for the first time.

I suggested to Frances that the use of email would not merely be a matter of expedition, but rather it would allow for something of its own making: reflective and deliberately thoughtful replies but in the spirit of lively and animated conversation. I knew from previous experience that email technology engages forms of intimacy and timing that differ from a face-to-face encounter. Such intimacy is combined with thoughts that are externalised into the text which allows arbitrarily taking the time to do what Schon referred to as 'reflection on action' (Schon, 1983). Time, Schon points out, is a prerequisite for such reflection. Frances had yet to learn the 'manners' required in using email technology in order to commingle the rigour and acuteness of research with the congeniality and vivacity of conversation.

I advised Frances to add 'schmoozing' in and around the questions so that they weren't so antiseptic and wouldn't come across as either 'taxing' or 'testing'. I explained that schmoozing is not insincere like sweet talk but rather is a Yiddish term that translates into something like warm, bussy, amiable conversation. In the email above, I indicate an interested tone of voice by textualizing my own intrigue at the exemplar's turn of phrase, seeking his help in assisting me to better appreciate his ideas so as not to jump to my own conclusions. Perhaps 'down the road' when the conversation is running hot, I counseled Frances, you can then ask very 'lean' enquiries as the conversationalist knows where such enquiries are coming from – your own genuine curiosity and vivid interest.

I was also determined to conduct our email conversations in a manner that witnessed the very Hospitality that we had been employed to research. Isn't there such a thing as 'hospitable emailing'? The proof would be the continued engagement of our exemplars in the conversations. The revisions I made to Frances' email assumed that an hospitable approach seeks to put people at their ease and ensure their comfort, even or especially when embarking on the new and 'strange' endeavour of email conversation. How do you put people at ease? By schmoozing!

ENQUIRIES THAT MATTER ARE IRRESISTIBLE

Another matter preyed on my (David's) mind. I was acutely aware of the goodwill of our conversationalists in dedicating their precious time to our study, which, I knew, extended their commitments beyond work hours. I did not want us to take their time for granted. If our emailing was to be hospitable and our practice in tune with the enquiries of narrative therapy, then our questions must generate answers that matter deeply to people and make them wish to 'go on with' the conversation.

Another measure of a 'good' question is its irresistibility. It catches you up in it but you won't let it go without sending it off by way of your response. Early on, Frances asked a nurse manager: Do Hospitallers see the world through the eyes of Hospitality? If so, what world do you see? And what, do you think, would be the effect of putting on dark glasses? The exemplar's reply signalled the irresistibility of these questions:

> You've done it again; made me put my thinking cap on … Your questions take me to places I've not visited too frequently before … I've never seriously had this kind of conversation with too many people before. It is challenging, exciting and uplifting, and in the way that you both are respectful of what I am saying.

Many of our exemplars exchanged with us up to 50 emails over a period of several months, with each exchange deepening each other's understandings. Others also remarked without prompting that these conversations were some of the best of their lives.

Good questions are approachable and go to the crux of the matter

I (David) implored Frances to begin with modest and approachable questions that 'hint' at something larger and more significant. The risk in asking large questions too soon, I counselled, is that your conversationalist may fall through the gap created between the question and their likely response to it. The question must be small enough, so that the person isn't belittled by it, which could have the effect of them walking away from the project on account of a sense of either being overtaxed or humiliated. A small, relatively simple question can comfortably be answered; the depth and magnitude of the question's significance increases proportional to the person's comfort in and desire to continue the conversation.

Small or large, a good question will go to the crux of the matter. Something about the question must seize the imagination of your conversationalist in order for them to treat with indulgence the uncertainty of travelling in the 'unknown lands' that the inquiry leads them toward. The following questions invite an exemplar to not only acknowledge and name her 'private practice review' but also to appreciate its inventiveness; and show the increasing magnitude of significance through a series of inquiries:

> If you were to name it, what would you call what you have been doing for so long now?
>
> How did you know to do this 'private practice review'? Did someone teach this to you? Or did you come to your own discoveries about this?
>
> Although you may not have considered this before, would you now refer to yourself as an 'inventor of practice'?

Situate your enquiries

I (David) also directed Frances to situate her enquiries, that is, to give the reasons for them, so that our conversationalists weren't left wondering about the direction in which she was heading and what were her purposes, ensuring a research conversation based both on transparency and the politics of co-leagueship (Epston, 1999; Madsen, 1999; Maisel et al., 2004). In replying to the questions immediately above, the exemplar expressed disbelief that 'I've invented something all on my own that someone else hasn't thought of'. I responded by making transparent what was implicated in my questions, showing what it means to situate your enquiries (and also to add a little schmoosing at the end to check how the conversation was going):

I (David) am not implying that no one else has ever invented anything similar and you qualify for a patent. What I am implying is that you did this all by yourself. You did not receive instructions, read a book, or go to another common source of 'everyday knowledges'? Or did you? Could you refer to this as 'a petit invention', one that most people don't get any credit for? … I guess that what this research is about is the 'petit inventions' that receive little or no credit because they arise in 'uncommon' places and certainly not the usual ones, for example, scientific laboratories, formal academic research studies and so on. How are we going with this now, after my attempt at an explanation? Let's keep talking, if you have the interest.

Turning the mind inside out to think anew

I (Frances) was beginning to understand that a purpose of narrative inquiry was not to ensnare our conversationalists, by using the wiles of questioning to have them report existing views or our views. A narrative enquirer is not concerned with the objectivist pursuit of testing hypotheses but rather seeks to illuminate rich yet often overlooked or taken for granted storied knowledges, especially of those ranked lower on the hierarchy with textualized organizational knowledges most often at the top.

I was required to turn my mind inside out to think anew. I came to realise that my very questions positioned me and, for that reason, I chose modesty as my mien. Previously I would have asked questions designed to gather information for an outsider expert account that 'arrived' at a tidy list of recommendations. Working closely with David, I was beginning to perceive that such an approach subordinates organizational practitioners as key informants or contributors and assumes that organizational vision is located on a horizon that only the expert can see.

Instead, I was being challenged to assume that a vision was already available but undistinguished among exemplars of the mission. The challenge was to welcome them to distinguish the mission by speaking of and on its behalf. By doing so they were envisioning the future of Hospitality by having the joys and vicissitudes of their everyday practice acknowledged by others.

I had to submit myself to the discipline of 'not knowing all the answers' at the same time as 'knowing how to find things out', in contrast to assuming the professional posture that would arrogate to oneself the presumption of 'knowing all'. I was encouraged to be curious by searching for what our exemplars had to say about what mattered to them about the mission, while at the same disciplining myself to allow people to speak for themselves rather than speak for or about them.

I had to learn how to adopt a reflexive position in order to expose the ideas and assumptions operating within the organization (and myself) and then turn such ideas and assumptions into questions that could be examined thoughtfully and their intended effects deliberated upon, while making myself accountable for any unintended effects. What ideas and assumptions constitute organizational life? Whose ideas are they? How, why, and by whom were such ideas produced? Who benefits from their circulation and whose voices are marginalized?

Perhaps most significantly, I had to think about harnessing narrative forms of inquiry as a work in progress developed through ongoing practice. Narrative inquiry is a learned craft and art. I realised I couldn't 'just do it'; I had 'to learn how' to do it, like learning scales on the piano in order to make music of your own. The challenge was to learn how to ask questions that intrigue, that work the mind, that touch the heart, and that render meanings that can orient people and organizations to new possibilities for organizational change and development by making better use of insider knowledges. I could see in my own enquiries that as I began to develop an ease in the craft of narrative inquiry, I would also develop a flair in its art:

> How has it happened that what you consider as integral to the mission of Hospitality 'has no meaning' to some of your co-workers?

> What is the bedrock on which the SJOG Order and Services should stand and function?

> Who is speaking for a compelling organizational vision and how do they speak about it?

APPRENTICING YOURSELF TO ANOTHER

I (David) suggested to Frances that if she were to apply the ideas and practices of narrative therapy to organizational development, then she must assume that practitioners operating at all levels of organization, including our SJOG exemplars, are 'knowledged'. I referred her to the work of Michael White, who proposes that a narrative practitioner might act according to this assumption:

[W]e can work with [people] to identify the extent that their own lives are 'knowledged'. We can engage people in conversations that are honoring of their knowledges of life, and that trace the history of their knowledgeableness. We can join people in conversations that provide the opportunity for them to build on these knowledges, and that assist people to develop plans for applying this knowledgeableness to those experiences that they find troubling. We can make it our business to work collaboratively with people in identifying those ways

of speaking about their lives that contribute to a sense of personal agency, and that contribute to the experience of being an authority on one's life. (1995: 121–122)

I also recommended the idea of Couze Venne (2000, 2002) 'apprenticeship to another'. Frances, imagine that you are apprenticing yourself to another, in this case to SJOG exemplars, in order to uncover and resurrect their tacit knowledges about the mission of Hospitality so as to inform its future development. Where can your enquiries have your conversationalists go and look for their answers? And how can the sincerity of your abiding interest to learn be infused into the text of the question but be read by its reader as its very gist? For example:

> *Service Manager:* Making a difference in people's lives is a purpose of SJOG Hospitality.

> *David:* What do you intend your Hospitality to do to the lives of those whom you 'touch' with it?

Such enquiries have their provenance in the exemplar's words which are nested in the meanings those words perform. In a manner of speaking, 'the stuff' of the questions will come from them:

> *Social Worker:* Hospitality doesn't read case files!

> *David:* Do you refuse to 'read case files' in the name of Hospitality? If you were to read case files, would that lead to the diminution of the expression of your Hospitality?

Each question follows on from the echoes of the preceding reply of your conversationalist. In narrative inquiry, questions emerge more from within the conversation and less from outside it. This is perhaps what makes such enquiries inherently fascinating.

In the draft email presented earlier in this chapter, I (David) invite the venerable Hospitaller to search his mind for the provenance of his thinking about 'age old' or 'traditional' strategies of recruitment and mentoring. Such questions succeed his previous comments about the life of SJOG and create a text that has a sense of progression. 'Good' questions will provide some sense of direction, pointing to places where your conversationalist might go to look as well as carrying them along to that way. On the one hand you are led by the conversationalist and on the other you lead the conversationalist with your enquiries. This interplay of being led by and leading fosters a sense of parity in the relationship that disavows any temptation to lean on or retreat to the privilege of professional status.

Narrative enquiries implicate persons as actors in matters of dramatic concern

I (David) suggested to Frances that the purpose of narrative inquiry is not to seek ready answers, but rather to guide people to 'live' the questions – to take time over them in order to ferment an answer. Questions often need more enquiries before a person can come to an answer. Answers aren't found as much as found out, or made up through the conversation. As the poet Rainer Maria Rilke, in his Letters to the Young Poet, advises:

> … try to love the questions themselves like locked rooms and like books that are written in a very foreign tongue. Do not now seek the answers, which cannot be given to you because you would not be able to live them. And the point is, to live everything. Live the questions now. Perhaps you will then gradually, without noticing it, live along some distant day into the answer. (1954: 35)

Rilke reminds us that we must enquire in a manner that will implicate persons and organizations as actors in a matter of dramatic concern. 'Good' questions have a dramatic effect. They wake you up. They breathe life into you by revitalizing and inspiriting all your senses. Compare this to the effect of some questions which force the breath out of you with what seems like an unendurable weight, leaving you exhausted even before you broach the question.

Our intention is to foster a conversation that can summon an account or a story of the ways in which SJOG Hospitality is practiced, fostered and passed on within the Services as well as how it is compromised, and to do so for the 'love' of the questions themselves. This demands mustering the 'storied' knowledges that 'live' inside organizational histories, calling them into being by the evocation of the teller's curiosity about him/herself and the 'life' of the organization in which they 'live' part of their lives, and some (in this case, the Brothers of St John of God) almost all of their lives.

As the conversation unfolds, our inquiries serve to fill in the gaps of stories-in-the-making, those indeterminacies, with the aim of having a story re-told so that it becomes more richly and thickly described (White and Epston, 1990: 13). Each party to the conversation remains restive until then. Many of these stories had been constrained from the 'telling' by various circumstances; others had been inadmissible (Cruikshank, 1998: 95). You then face the prospect of representing those accounts as 'a story they [and the Order and its Services] could think with, if they chose to do so' (Cruikshank, 1998: 30).

Leads to externalizing conversations

Aware of the difficulties in generating good questions, I (David) set Frances' mind to work on new streams of inquiry by offering conversational leads to help her to 'see' the possibilities in the remnants of various conversations. Frances provided me with the following comments made to her by different Hospitality practitioners to see how I might pursue an externalizing conversation:

Receptionist: Yes, I believe Hospitality can be inherited.

David: Some vocabulary that 'comes to my mind' – who 'passed' the practice of Hospitality down to you? In a manner of speaking, can you 'infect' others when they are 'touched' by it? Have you ever witnessed this, so that you have been left with an indelible memory?

Nurse of a long-term care facility: We use silliness to lighten the mood and are known to model mistakes.

David: Could that be called something like 'humility on purpose'?

Case Manager: We seek a match between personal values and organizational values and tell job applicants that we have intentionally sought to make it everyday and uncomplicated.

David: By comparison would you say many descriptions of professional practice are arcane and obscure?

Caregiver: Without the SJOG mission of Hospitality the service would be like any other.

David: If you were to join another service, what would be the first thing you would miss about SJOG? After the first two weeks on the job, what would you most keenly regret having left behind at SJOG?

In the questions or 'leads' above, I (David) show Frances how to invite an externalizing conversation (White and Epston, 1990: 38) by conceiving of Hospitality as a social practice with history, legacy, manners, embodiment, organizational culture and managerial practice, rather than something 'essential' to the person. The conversation coheres around this practice in any number of contexts. As much as anything else, externalizing conversations permit one to abstract themselves from their own practices or the discourses in which they are immersed. Such a detachment or de-identification allows for 'reflection on their practice' (Schon, 1983), often to see it anew.

LEARNING TO TRAIN THE SENSES

I (Frances) began to listen more intently to the vocabulary of our conversationalists, taking every opportunity to exploit it for the purpose of our study, even if in doing so I used language that one would not ordinarily expect to hear from an external consultant. I sought to generate metaphors from their vocabulary to tempt them into ongoing and meaningful conversation.

Social Worker: We take apparatus with us when we visit children in their homes; bags, craft colour in sheets, games, reward boxes, stickers, 'Stop, Think, Do' books.

Frances: Could you also describe these resources as the 'apparatuses' or 'tools' of Hospitality?

Social Worker: Yes, that fits well!

I (Frances) often recalled the idea of Lionel Trilling that 'it is in copying that we originate' (Geertz, 1986: 380) and, acting as an apprentice, I took up the practice of copying David's questions. I would type his enquiries into my emails to see what effect they might have on our exemplars. Their responses were often surprising and helped me to 'train my senses', to know what to look for and what to include when drafting a 'good' or 'useful' inquiry.

What I didn't expect, however, was the effect this copying would have on me. The very act of typing David's wide-ranging vocabulary had the effect over time of gradually extending my own. For example, when a Service Manager commented that, 'SJOG polishes the Hospitality you bring', David asked: 'How would you say SJOG has burnished to a high shine the Hospitality you had already been living?' I realized, in copying this question, that David not only extended 'the lead' offered by our conversationalist but also favored the unusual verb 'to burnish' as opposed to using more commonplace alternatives such as 'to enhance' or 'to improve'. The more unusual verb provokes attention whereas a reader's interest will wash over more commonplace vocabulary.

I also became aware of and began to employ, often without immediately noticing, the grammars of an externalizing conversation. When I met a 101-year-old resident of a

SJOG retirement home who had a beautiful complexion, I asked her: 'Is Hospitality good for your skin?' to which she replied: 'It must be; just look at me!' I realized afterwards that I had employed externalizing language, raising the question of whether a social practice, Hospitality, could affect one's body. In reply, David tendered this intriguing inquiry: 'Frances, as you cast your eyes across the faces of those whom we have selected/have selected themselves as exemplars of Hospitality, can you comment about any commonalities? Does Hospitality inscribe itself in the flesh?' If it does, I replied, then it is likely to have the appearance of vitality – a keen look, a lightness of step and a kind of vivacity that leaves one with the impression that SJOG Hospitallers are engaging their passion.

Developing the craft and art of narrative inquiry

As time went on, I (David) began to notice that I was 'reading' the text of Frances' email conversations rather than interpolating alternative enquiries into the text or making any amendments. In the early days of an extended conversation with an exemplar, I interpolated this alternative inquiry for Frances to consider.

> *Exemplar:* [He] was my mentor in the beginning days. [He] is a real people person; someone who engages completely with the person he's with. He gives his total presence to that person no matter how busy he is. He puts the busyness aside and directs his presence totally to the other person.

> *Frances:* What were the characteristics or practices of [his] mentoring that you valued so much?

> *David:* How would you say [your mentor] 'goes about' 'direct[ing] his presence' toward another?

What is different between the two enquiries? Frances' question invites a list by way

of response. I was hoping my question would locate the exemplar as a very observer of his mentor going about his practice so that he might see this in his mind's eye; that perhaps it might suggest a memory of such an incident which he might then bring to mind and into text.

The following passage from the same conversation continues the discussion about the exemplar's relationship with his mentor, who was a highly respected Hospitality practitioner. Frances' purpose in this discussion was to illuminate the possibilities of reinstating a time-honored tradition of mentoring employees into the mission of Hospitality.

> *Exemplar:* [What I valued about his mentoring was his] availability and his time. When he was with me it was as if there were no other pressures. It was as if everything else had stopped as he invited himself to be with me to discover a sense of purpose in relation to what we had to do together. His was a rare presence. He had the time to be with you.

> *Frances:* Was it that [your mentor] 'had the time' or 'took the time' in an otherwise busy schedule?

> *Exemplar:* It was that he took the time.

> *Frances:* What did his 'taking the time' to be with you tell you about how he regarded his relationship with you?

> *Exemplar:* It told me that he valued the relationship very much. It also spoke of his respect for the person.

> *Frances:* What was the provenance of his respect? What, do you think, encouraged [your mentor] to take the time to be with you in the way that he was?

> *Exemplar:* He had a deep appreciation of the John of God Story and the reason why it exists. I could never do it like him.

And later in the conversation …

> *Frances:* I am aware that some people talk about you in the ways that you have been talking about your SJOG mentor. They mention your taking the time to listen; your availability. What comes forward when you hear yourself being talked about in the ways that you talk about your mentor?

> *Exemplar:* It tells me that I'm in good company. I see this guy epitomize the story of St John of God; he holds it and he's an unassuming guy. He is 'being' the story, not simply telling the story. He is it. That's real witness. You don't become aware you are doing it, as it is so much a part of you. It is affirming. A lot of things I can't do; but that's something I can do and do well.

By now Frances' enquiries had a prologue, the consequence of which stimulated our exemplar to comment on himself according to the comments made about him by other colleagues to Frances. You get the sense from her inquiry here that her curiosity regarding the exemplar's practice is now bound up with his about his own practice. After reading the text of the entire conversation I wrote to Frances: 'I wanted to review this again as I realized, on reflection, that I had become so engrossed in the reading of this "text" that I forgot myself. I am sure this is a very good sign to both of us of what a wonderfully seamless and complete interview it was'.

IMPLICATIONS FOR ORGANIZATIONAL DEVELOPMENT

Applying a narrative inquiry approach to the enterprise of organizational development turns on the imperative of asking 'good questions'. Early on I (David) suggested to Frances that 'good questions' implicate the fascination of the questioner, as much as that of the conversationalist. You become so interested that your question conveys your intrigue. You burden yourself with the intrigue of questions, showing a willingness

and a readiness to assist by providing another question pointing in a different direction even if that leads to a dead end from which you are forced to turn back – as if everything goes somewhere. I share the burden of traveling in the unknown but I invest that burden with anticipatory excitement that something is just around the next corner. The practice of professional humility becomes endowed with a wild enthusiasm that both of you should come to know more because such knowledge is there to be found out in the living of the other's life.

The relevance of a narrative inquiry approach is that it 'stirs a response', generating thoughtful deliberation and innovative thinking. Intricate and intimate questions compel people to participate because such enquiries take organizational conversation some place it has never quite been before. People choose to stay in the conversation because they gain something personally *and* professionally from it. They also begin to see how the organization as a whole can benefit. Participants appreciate not only the respect accorded to them and that their contribution matters but also that the way forward is within their and the organization's grasp. In many cases, the solutions to problems are already in use without public and/or formal recognition or, alternatively, the generation of a novel idea may provide an unexpected opportunity that diverse contributors can embrace.

A narrative inquiry approach is flexible enough to shed light on modest consultations, such as to have social workers operating in a social service organization rethink the very purposes of note-taking:

> How could your case-notes contribute to rewriting the stories of the families you work with, as they might wish to have their stories recorded? If families were to read case-notes that gave an account of their acts of resilience against considerable life challenges (however small and inconsequential they might seem to a bystander) as opposed to documenting a litany of failures, what impact might that have (1) on their collective confidence in going forward

together and (2) on how you (and other professionals) regard case-notes?

Or alternatively, to deal with a considerable problematic such as the vexing situation of conflictual relationships between governance and management groups of a community organization:

If you were collectively to develop a story of how you worked together for the benefit of the community and for the long-term sustainability of the organization, what organizational and individual practices would you need to avoid and what professional practices might you actively seek to reinforce and support each other to take up? In reinforcing and taking up such chosen practices are you also likely to grow trust and confidence in the ability of each other (board and management) to perform your particular roles in a professional manner?

In narrative inquiry, illumination comes from the storied knowledges of organizational practitioners rather than the 'know-all expertise' of outside consultants. Such enquiries not only challenge assumptions about what is regarded as acceptable to talk about but also find ways to include those voices not often heard in critical decision-making arenas.

Finally, in this chapter we sought to continue our own experience of an apprenticeship in narrative forms of inquiry. Apprenticeship is an 'age old' tradition of learning that is still actively employed in various professions and trades. Our own experience of apprenticeship demonstrates how inspiriting, mutually beneficial and effective apprenticeship learning can be, provided both parties take the time and are willing to submit to its discipline. The queries of the apprentice 'teach' the apprenticer; they refresh his/her thinking and rescue it from the 'tacit'. Perhaps the most significant benefit of the apprenticeship itself was that once again it 'lived on' in text and could be reflected on, not only 'in action' (Schon, 1983) but 'afterward'.

REFERENCES

Barry, D. (1997) 'Telling changes: From narrative family therapy to organizational change and development', *Journal of Organizational Change Management*, 10 (1): 36–40.

Barry, D. and Elmes, M. (1997) 'Strategy retold: Toward a narrative view of strategic discourse', *Academy of Management Review*, 22 (2): 429–452.

Boje, D.M., Alvarez, R.C. and Schooling, B. (2001) 'Reclaiming story in organization: Narratologies and action sciences', in R. Westwood and S. Linstead (eds), *The Language of Organization*. London: Sage Publications. pp. 132–175.

Boje, D.M., Rosile, G., Dennehy, B. and Summers, D. (1997) 'Restorying reengineering: Some deconstructions and postmodern alternatives', *Special Issue on Throwaway Employees, Journal of Communication Research*, 24 (6): 631–668.

Cruikshank, J. (1998) *The Social Life of Stories: Narrative and Knowledge in the Yukon Territory*. Lincoln: University of Nebraska Press.

Czarniawska, B. (2004) *Narratives in Social Science Research*. London: Sage Publications.

Epston, D. (1999) 'Co-research: The making of an alternative knowledge', in *Narrative Therapy and Community Work: A Conference Collection*. Adelaide, Australia: Dulwich Centre Publications. An extended version can be found at http://www.narrativeapproaches.com/antianorexia%20folder/AAcoresearch.htm. pp. 137–157.

Epston, D. and White, M. (1992) *Experience, Contradiction, Narrative, and Imagination*. Adelaide: Dulwich Centre Publications.

Geertz, C. (1986) 'Making experiences, authoring selves', in V. Turner and E. Bruner (eds) *The Anthology of Experience*. Chicago: University of Illinois Press.

Lawrence-Lightfoot, S. (2000) *Respect: An Exploration*. Cambridge: Perseus Books.

Madsen, B. (1999) *Collaborative Therapy with Multistressed Families: From Old Problems to New Futures*. New York: Guildford.

Maisel, R., Epston, D. and Borden, A. (2004) *Biting The Hand That Starves You: Inspiring Resistance to Anorexia/Bulimia*. New York: W.W. Norton.

Nelson, H.L. (2001) *Damaged Identities, Narrative Repair*. Ithaca, New York: Cornell University Press.

Rilke, R.M. (1954) *Letters to a Young Poet*. New York: W.W. Norton and Company.

Sax, M. (2000) 'Finding common ground between human service seekers, providers and planners: A reauthoring conversations approach'.

PhD dissertation, The Fielding Institute, Santa Barbara. Excerpts of the dissertation are available online: http://www.narrativeapproaches.com/narrative%20papers%20folder/sax.htm.

Schon, D.A. (1983) *The Reflective Practitioner: How Professionals Think in Action*. New York: Basic Books.

Venn, C. (2000) *Occidentalism, Modernity and Subjectivity*. London: Sage Publications.

Venn, C. (2002) 'Refiguring subjectivity after modernity', in V. Walkerdine (ed.), *Challenging Subjects: Critical Psychology for a New Millenium*. Houndsmills: Palgrave.

White, M. (1995) *Re-authoring Lives and Relationships: Essays and Interviews*. Adelaide: Dulwich Centre Publications.

White, M. (1997) *Narratives of Therapists' Lives*. Adelaide: Dulwich Centre Publications.

White, M. (2000) *Reflections on Narrative Practice*. Adelaide: Dulwich Centre Publications.

White, M. (2004) *Narrative Practice and Exotic Lives: Resurrecting Diversity in Everyday Life*. Adelaide: Dulwich Centre Publications.

White, M. and Epston, D. (1990) *Narrative Means to Therapeutic Ends*. New York: W.W. Norton and Company.

The Pragmatics of Resilience

Kathleen M. Sutcliffe and Timothy J. Vogus

Why are some organizations and institutions capable of maintaining function and structure in the face of environmental jolts and other large disruptions? Why do some organizations crumble in the face of high levels of ongoing strain while others thrive and grow more resourceful and poised to tackle future challenges? We argue that answering these questions is increasingly important given that organizations exist in an increasingly tightly coupled and interactively complex world where the unexpected is omnipresent and the speed with which unexpected events can amplify into disaster is ever increasing (Weick and Sutcliffe, 2001). We propose that a theory of organizational resilience must be developed to adequately do so (Sutcliffe and Vogus, 2003). A theory of organizational resilience would provide insight into how organizations continue to achieve desirable outcomes amidst adversity, strain, and significant barriers to adaptation or development. A resilience perspective also would promote insight into the possibility that organizations are more efficacious than some deterministic perspectives in organization theory (e.g., threat-rigidity, Staw et al., 1981) allow. In this brief commentary we map the contours of a theory of organizational resilience by defining resilience, elaborating the mechanisms of resilience, and outlining a potential research agenda.

RESILIENCE DEFINED

We define resilience as the maintenance of positive adjustment under challenging conditions and the capacity to emerge from those conditions strengthened and more resourceful. By 'challenging conditions' we include discrete errors, scandals, crises, and shocks, and disruptions of routines as well as ongoing risks (e.g., competition), stresses, and strain. Adjusting in the face of challenging conditions is thought to strengthen the organization by creating 'a hierarchical integration of behavioral systems whereby earlier structures are incorporated into later structures in increasingly complex forms' (Egeland et al., 1993: 518). In other words, resiling from ongoing strain and discrete jolts implies the presence of latent resources that can be activated, combined and recombined in new situations as challenges arise. As such, resilience implies more than a specific adaptation.

This doesn't mean that competence in one period wholly predicts later competence in a linear deterministic way; rather competence in one period increases the probability of competence in the next. To be resilient is to be vitally prepared for adversity which requires 'improvement in overall capability, i.e., a generalized capacity to investigate, to learn, and to act, without knowing in advance what one will be called to act upon' (Wildavsky, 1991: 70). In this way resilience relies upon past learning and fosters future learning, but exists independently of learning activities in that resilience represents a store of capabilities.

MECHANISMS OF RESILIENCE

Resilience results from processes and dynamics that create or retain resources (cognitive, emotional, relational, or structural) in a form sufficiently flexible, storable, convertible, and malleable, enabling organizations to successfully cope with and learn from the unexpected (Sutcliffe and Vogus, 2003). For example, processes, structures, and practices that promote competence, restore efficacy, and encourage growth endow organizations with capabilities to mediate jolts and strain. These capabilities and associated salutary responses in part are enabled by enlarging informational inputs, loosening control, and reconfiguring resources. Successfully resiling from challenge also initiates a positive feedback loop to an organization's capabilities such that they are strengthened and further resilience in the face of novel events. The recurrent interplay between resilience and its constitutive capabilities also suggests that organizations can continuously bolster and refine their capabilities in a manner that allows them to see more, remain flexible, and avoid the inertial tendencies that traditionally accrue with success. We would also argue that mechanisms of resilience described above both enable and result from a different way of seeing. That is, organizational resilience counteracts tendencies toward threat-rigidity (Staw et al., 1981) as it increases the propensity to better sense, process, interpret, and manage small discrepancies as they emerge, thereby increasing the likelihood that disruptive events and persistent strain will be treated as opportunities rather than threats.

TOWARD A RESEARCH AGENDA

Given the dearth of empirical work exploring resilience in organization theory, many avenues are open for future research. As we have argued, learning is both an input and an outcome of organizational resilience. Resilient organizations seem to employ a superior brand of learning, but more research is needed to understand what specific assets and resources give rise to it. Do resilient organizations deploy more of their financial and cognitive resources in preparation for and response to threat? How do resilient organizations manage to avoid pathological learning cycles (e.g., competency traps)? Do resilient organizations combat competency traps and the perils of success by avoiding simplified interpretations and maintaining a more nuanced picture of organizational operations and the environment? While resilience has been treated as a largely unmitigated good in our commentary, are there boundary conditions on the utility of resilience? Do certain types of environments (hypercompetitive, coarse-grained, fine-grained) make resilience more or less costly than more efficiency-minded strategies?

Understanding how organizations positively adjust under conditions of adversity and emerge more resourceful (i.e., resilience) may serve to answer the most pressing questions facing today's organizations and organization theorists.

REFERENCES

Egeland, B., Carlson, E. and Sroufe, L.A. (1993) 'Resilience as process'. *Development and Psychopathology*, 5: 517–528.

Continued

Staw, B.M., Sandelands, L.E. and Dutton, J.E. (1981) 'Threat-rigidity effects in organizational behavior: A multi-level analysis', *Administrative Science Quarterly*, 26: 501–524.

Sutcliffe, K.M. and Vogus, T.J. (2003) 'Organizing for resilience', in K.M. Cameron, J.E. Dutton and R.E. Quinn (eds) *Positive Organizational Scholarship*. San Francisco: Berrett-Koehler: 94–110.

Weick, K.E. and Sutcliffe, K.M. (2001) *Managing the Unexpected: Assuring High Performance in an Age of Complexity*. San Francisco: Jossey-Bass.

Wildavsky, A. (1991) *Searching for Safety*. New Brunswick: Transaction Books.

A Note on 'The Future of Positive Organizational Scholarship'

Gretchen Spreitzer

Positive Organizational Scholarship (POS) draws on the fields of organizational behavior, psychology, and sociology to better understand the generative dynamics in organizations that promote human strength, resiliency, healing, and restoration. POS assumes that understanding how to enable human excellence in organizations will unlock potential, reveal possibilities, and chart a more positive course of human and organizational functioning. POS draws from a full spectrum of organizational theories to understand, explain, and predict the causes and consequences of positive phenomena. At its core, POS investigates the ways in which organizations and their members flourish and prosper.

POS has blossomed in its first half-decade of life. As part of the Center for POS at the University of Michigan, POS is an important part of my scholarly identity. Not surprisingly, I am pleased to see this new domain of inquiry grow into adolescence with fervor. However, my distinct hope is that POS becomes obsolete before it hits middle age. As scholars continue to explore the positive end of the continuum of organization life and this domain of inquiry becomes commonplace, the call for action to understand the positive domain of organizational studies may become unnecessary and even superfluous. Just as the original mission of the March of Dimes became obsolete as polio was virtually eradicated, the need for POS as a distinct area of inquiry may become obsolete. While I don't expect this obsolescence to come in the near future, my hope and dream is for it to come in the next two decades. To make this point, let me share a couple domains from my own research where I believe a POS focus is transforming the focus on inquiry.

POSITIVE DEVIANCE

At first glance, positive deviance appears to be an oxymoron. Deviance is the label we reserve for society's criminals and outcasts. In organizational behavior, scholars define deviance as intentional behavior that significantly departs from norms (i.e., shared understandings, patterns or expected ways of doing things) – things like sabotage, theft and other negative phenenomena. Yet, the origin of the word 'deviant' comes from two Latin words: *de-* means 'from' and *via* means 'road' – so deviate means off the beaten path. So it is possible to conceive of the notion of positive deviance. Until recently, the positive extreme of the curve – that which focuses on the best of the human condition, the honorable and the extraordinary – has largely been ignored. Positive deviance can thus be defined as intentional behaviors that depart from the norms of a referent group in honorable ways (Spreitzer and Sonenshein, 2004).

Departing from norms in the pharmaceutical industry, Merck made the decision to develop, manufacture and distribute ivermectin (a cure for river-blindness) free to the developing world, costing the company millions of dollars. For example, Kim Cameron and colleagues have a program of research on how organizational virtuousness, a form of positive deviance, enables organizations to recover from trying times in dramatic ways.

Continued

It is beginning to counter the broad literature on corporate ethical lapses. In a similar mode, Jane Dutton and colleagues (in press) have a program of study of compassion at work which shows how organizations can make 'compassionate organizing' part of their systems.

LEVERAGING STRENGTHS IN LEADERSHIP DEVELOPMENT

Leadership development scholars have advocated developing leaders by (1) assessing leadership competencies based on observable indicators of success, and (2) offering developmental challenges to close the gaps. These elements of leadership development are often interpreted and implemented as follows: (1) in the *assessment* of leadership competencies, most energy is focused on identifying performance gaps, and (2) the *challenge* focuses on creating discomfort and hardship to break people out of their comfort zones.

Although these implementation trends have often been associated with successful leadership development, a POS perspective suggests that they reflect an incomplete picture of effective leadership development. They assume a deficit approach to human development; that is, gaps on predetermined areas of generic competence need to be closed, and pain is necessary to prompt leaders to break out of comfort zones to grow. POS research offers a complementary perspective on growing leaders. What if researchers focused on leveraging strengths in assessment? What if researchers study the kinds of positive jolts that energize growth? Clearly, the most impactful leadership development will contain elements of both the traditional and complementary frameworks.

While the short-term future of POS is bright, my hope is that its long term future may be in question. If the growth rate of research continues at this pace, I speculate that POS will not longer be necessary as a distinct field of inquiry.

REFERENCES

Cameron, K., Bright, D. and Caza, A. (2006) 'The amplifying and buffering effects of virtuousness in downsizing organizations', *Journal of Business Ethics*, 69: 249–269.

Dutton, J., Worline, M., Frost, P. and Lilius, J. (2006) 'Explaining compassion organizing', *Administrative Science Quarterly*, 51 (1): 59–96.

Roberts, L.M., Dutton, J., Spreitzer, G., Heaphy, E. and Quinn, R. (2005) 'Composing the reflected best self: Building pathways for becoming extraordinary in work organizations', *Academy of Management Review*, 30 (4): 712–736.

Spreitzer, G. and Sonenshein, S. (2004) 'Toward the construct definition of positive deviance', *American Behavioral Scientist*, 77 (6): 828–847.

Building Community

Natalia Nikolova and Timothy Devinney

INTRODUCTION

That organizations cannot be viewed as uniform and stable cultures or entities but rather as communities of 'loosely constituted overlapping circles of partialled participation' (Blau, 1996: 174) is not a new insight (e.g., Bechky, 2003; Bloor and Dawson, 1994; Dougherty, 1992). To make sense of this world of competing communities, one needs to understand why these subcultures exist, how they form, how they interact – cooperatively and competitively – and how they evolve. In what follows, we address these issues by providing an integrated view of the two theoretical approaches that have built on this thinking: communities of practice (CoP) and critical discourse analysis (CDA). The concept of interpretive communities (ICs), which we propose, builds upon important findings related to both CoP and CDA but overcomes their shortcomings and extends them onto a more general theoretical footing.

Communities of practice, critical discourse analysis and interpretative communities

CoP research claims that different communities exist because individuals are engaged in different activities or practices and knowledge transfer is possible only between individuals within a particular practice (e.g., Brown and Duguid, 1991, 2001; Gherardi and Nicolini, 2002; Lave and Wenger, 2002). Table 3.8.1 summarizes the main assumptions of the CoP view and offers a critical discussion of these assumptions. It shows that the CoP approach does not explain the role of human cognition and power for knowledge transfer and learning. In contrast, the concept of ICs emphasizes that cognition cannot be separated from practice and action and puts stronger emphasis on the connection between power and cognition.

According to CDA, organizations consist of multiple non-neutral and biased discourses that serve as 'sites of power' that influence individuals' interpretations (Mumby and Stohl, 1991: 316).[1] Supporters of CDA analyze how interpretations and perspectives have been 'discursively constructed over time by groups in power aiming to skew social reality and institutionalized [knowledge] to their own advantage' (Heracleous, 2004: 186). Although CDA emphasizes the role of social practices and non-discursive elements for the creation and dissemination of discourses and power (e.g., Fairclough, 2005), the approach does not refer explicitly to the cognitive

Table 3.8.1 Community of practice view: assumptions and shortcomings

	Community of practice view	Shortcomings
Emergence of communities: Explanatory factors	Single factor: engagement within same practice.	Multiple factors: engagement within same practice, educational background, social histories, site-specific or local knowledge.
Origin of knowledge	Practice: 'A theory of situated cognition suggests that activity and perception are importantly and epistemologically prior – at a nonconceptual level – to conceptualization' (Brown et al., 1989: 40).	Practice, i.e., action, together with perception and conception (Bunge, 1983). CoP overemphasizes procedural and pragmatic knowledge and learning as a process of participating and being able to perform the 'practice', ignoring the importance of conceptual knowledge and the possibility of learning through labelling, describing, analyzing, and justifying; i.e., independently of participating in a particular practice (Leinhardt et al., 1995). Cognition and action cannot be divorced from each other (Neisser, 1976).
Nature of knowledge	Knowledge exists independent of individuals; practices/objects as carriers of knowledge.	Individuals as carriers of knowledge; it is individuals' cognitive maps that give meaning to practice, not vice versa (Bunge, 1983). 'The patterns of relating and the cognitive activities encapsulated by the concept "community of practice" are possible in the first place because of the pattern recognition and completion ability of real brains' (Lakomski, 2004: S93).
Types of knowledge	Emphasis on the local contextualization of knowledge.	The existence of generalized knowledge is rejected (Lorenz, 2001); no inquiry into the 'mechanisms that might serve to transmit and diffuse knowledge beyond the confines of particular places and times' (Lorenz, 2001: 318).
Knowledge transfer	Engagement in similar activities (practices) enables knowledge transfer; knowledge transfer outside of CoP not explained; individuals within the same 'practice' transmit and receive information non-problematically.	Collection of workplace narratives is not a sufficient mechanism to provide evidence that CoP are successful in transferring knowledge. Rather, the univocally *interpretation* of activities enables knowledge transfer (Lakomski, 2004).
Power	Power depends on one's position in the CoP (Lave and Wenger, 2002).	Power is located not only in the position of individuals but in social relations; it is relational and diffused throughout society (Clegg, 1989, Scott, 2001). Power issue within CoP approach ignored (e.g., Fox, 2000).

element of discourses. Texts are central to the analysis, not the brains that produce these texts. Thus, 'where do the discourses, narratives, texts and words that are analyzed in organizational discourse come from?' (Marshak et al., 2000: 250) remains an open question.

Following van Dijk's (1993: 251) proposition that cognition is the 'missing link' between discourse and action, it is the contention put forward here that the concept of ICs is the missing theoretical link within CDA.

Furthermore, our discussion outlines the concrete steps by which a particular discourse develops into a dominant position, a key missing component of CDA.

Beginning with the viewpoint that 'a firm is composed of a group of people who all, in varying ways and to varying extents, interpret what they observe and take decisions according to their interpretation' (Loasby, 1983: 357), we argue that individuals with shared interpretive strategies and shared discourses – i.e., who employ a common frame of reference for interpreting their social settings – build an IC (Fish, 1980; Hymes, 1980). In order to get a more complete picture of how knowledge is acquired, created, processed and managed (Bechky, 2003) and who influences this process, we must understand the ongoing process of interaction between members of different communities. Furthermore, because knowledge transfer and learning are inherently political processes, we need to discuss the nature of power as well as the micro processes through which the power – what we call interpretive dominance – of a particular community is developed. Our goal is to present the reader with a multifaceted picture of human cognition and to show important implications for our understanding of power and its role on learning.

ORIGIN AND NATURE OF INTERPRETIVE COMMUNITIES

If knowledge is a product of human cognition (Bunge, 1996; Maturana, 1980; Neisser, 1976), then what characterizes human cognition? Research in neurobiology shows that all cognitive processes are brain processes (e.g., Lakomski, 2004). Therefore, there are 'no ideas in themselves but, instead, ideating brains' (Bunge, 1983: 23; also Lakomski, 2004; Maturana, 1980). At the same time, cognitive processes are in an intensive interaction with individuals' natural and social environment where concepts and symbols – the basis of thinking – are expressed in words that derive their meaning from the way they are used in specific language games or discourses, which themselves are located in distinct social settings (Koppl and Langlois, 2001). Therefore, cognition and discourse are mutually constituted in a process of continuous interaction (Heracleous, 2004). Consequently, context and the embedded existing discourses influence cognition significantly; in other words, cognition is a situated process. Tsoukas and Vladimirou (2001: 977–978) argue that this context can be interpreted as 'a collectively generated and

sustained domain of action' or 'a language-mediated domain of sustained interactions', and 'to engage in collective work is to engage in a discursive practice'. Thus, knowledge is created and transferred within socio-culturally constituted ICs or discursive practices through an ongoing process of interaction between individuals (Bechky, 2003). Cognition is both *embodied*, because people's physical composition determines their thinking, and *embedded*, because the specific context and situations people find themselves determine cognition (Lakomski, 2004).

The two major cognitive processes of perception and conception, together with action, are the sources of knowledge (Bunge, 1996: 76): 'We get to know ideas by thinking of them, and concrete things by perceiving, conceiving, or manipulating them'. When perceiving something, people construct a percept of it with sensations, memories and expectations. They look for similarities and differences, and for patterns. This process, which is referred to as intuiting (Crossan et al., 1999) or sensemaking (Weick, 1979), involves the mapping of an event into one's perceptual system (Bunge, 1983). The resulting cognitive maps are also called schemes. Perceptions themselves do not have a meaning. They can guide the actions of the individual, but they are difficult to share with others because they are non-verbal and subconscious (Crossan et al., 1999). Only through a process of interpreting do individuals assign a meaning to a particular perception (Neisser, 1976). Thus, meanings are the result of thinking processes.

Schemes and their meanings are developed by individual experience. Therefore, 'the same stimulus can evoke different or equivocal meaning for different people' (Crossan et al., 1999: 528). However, research has shown that individuals confronted with similar or the same physical and cultural environment can develop similar schemes and meanings (Neisser, 1976). In other words, the real world, which exists independently of our senses, enables individuals to develop some similar schemes and meanings.[2] Through the course of regular social interaction in the form of communication, participation and problem-solving, individuals begin to favour one interpretation over others and their exchange of experiences leads to the emergence of shared schemes and meaning (Gray et al., 1985; Zelizer, 1993).

Through this process of interaction, individuals with similar interpretive positions build specific worldviews and 'form' a community. As individuals become aware of how their thoughts are guided by such frameworks they can start to choose between them: through their involvement in multiple communities and discourses individuals 'produce a discursive space in which [they] can play one discourse against the other, draw on multiple discourses to create new forms of interdiscursivity, and otherwise move between and across multiple discourses' (Hardy and Phillips, 2004: 304). In this way, different ICs evolve, made up of those who share interpretive frames (Fish, 1980; Hymes, 1980) but who are themselves members of many evolving and potentially overlapping communities (e.g., Reihlen and Ringberg, 2004; Watson, 1982). Over time, individuals establish 'conventions' or 'dominant perspectives' as to how community members can recognize, create, experience and talk about social events and ICs transform into 'communities of memory' (Prahalad and Bettis, 1986; Zelizer, 1993). Therefore, ICs are instantiated both in the actions of their members and in their interpretations and interpretive schemes (Heracleous and Barrett, 2001: 758). They are cognitive communities that are a result of agents' actions and interactions.

An IC builds and expands through the shaping of individuals. As noted by Fish (1980), the thoughts of individuals have their source in some or other IC; thus, they are products of communities. At the same time, actors participating in these communities influence them through their ongoing interpretations and actions. For example, through the interaction with members of other ICs, individuals can introduce changes in a particular IC (Bloor and Dawson, 1994). Therefore, the shared meanings of communities are more or less often transformed (Brown and Duguid, 1991) and large-scale changes in ICs can be caused by large-scale, more-or-less simultaneous frame switches by many independent actors (DiMaggio, 1997). Accordingly, ICs are fluid and evolving rather than unalterable 'fixed systems of positions' (Clegg, 2001: 135; Carley, 1991). Some ICs can be quite durable whereas others are only short-lived; some are broad and expansive while others involve only a restricted number of members.

ICs as discursive practices are maintained at the group level but operate and are manifested through individuals' shared cognitive maps (Harris, 1989). Thus, the selection of environmental elements to be analyzed is likely to be affected by the shared schemes of an IC, and different schemes can lead to dramatically different analysis of the same event or topic (Fish, 1980). Accordingly, members of different ICs may have problems in understanding one another fully 'if knowledge leaks in the direction of shared [meaning], it sticks where [meaning] is not shared' (Brown and Duguid, 2001: 207). Therefore, different communities are often characterized by distinct perspectives rather than by mutual understanding (Gherardi and Nicolini, 2002). Misunderstandings can be expressed in several ways. For example, when looking at the same phenomenon, communities may not only see different solutions to the same problem but may also address quite different problems. Thus, communities may have problems in understanding each other's language, 'where each community maintains its own voice while listening to the voice of the Other, and where communication is both negotiated order and disorder' (Gherardi and Nicolini, 2002: 421). Furthermore, arguments that persuade one's own community convincingly may have little or no weight with other communities (Boland and Tenkasi, 1995). Thus, ICs are characterized by different problem solving logics, which are a main reason for conflicts and communication problems in organizations (Carroll, 1998). Successful cooperation between members of different ICs requires the translation of the different perspectives so that some alignment of meanings is achieved; yet, translation is also a mechanism of power (Clegg, 1989, 2001).

THE POWER OF INTERPRETIVE COMMUNITIES

Because members of ICs are embedded in multiple discourses, they can 'play one discourse against another, draw on multiple discourses to create a new form of interdiscursivity, and otherwise move between and across multiple discourses' (Hardy and Phillips, 2004: 304). Therefore, interactions between ICs are characterized by harmonization, negotiation of meanings and the integration of interpretations as well as by contestations and struggles (Clegg, 1989; Gherardi and Nicolini, 2002), the ultimate goal of which is the establishment of interpretive dominance by one or a combination of communities (Callon, 1986; Meindl et al., 1994). Thus, when ICs interact, power rather than rationality is at work (Bettenhausen and Murnighan, 1985; Flyvbjerg, 1998).

The concept of interpretive dominance examines 'how the field of force in which power is arranged has been fixed, coupled and constituted in such a way that, intentionally or not, certain "nodal points" of practice are privileged in this unstable and shifting terrain' (Clegg, 1989: 17). It is based on the assumption that the power relations amongst groups and actors are dependent on knowledge and institutionalized 'truths' and discourses (e.g., Foucault, 1980). At the same time, actors influence existing power relations and institutionalized discourses through their ongoing interpretations and actions (e.g., Prahalad and Bettis, 1986).

Power and interpretive dominance

Interpretive dominance emerges during agents' interactions as a result of negotiations and translations of meanings. It 'operates through the offering and acceptance of reasons for acting in one way rather than another' (Scott, 2001: 13) and prevents agents from developing and legitimizing

alternative interpretations. It is the result of rhetorical power; power, which is not predetermined by the possession or control of resources but is exercised through a set of 'interpretive frames' (Mumby and Clair, 1997: 184). In its simplest form, rhetorical power rests upon a person's personality and attractiveness to others; i.e., in their charisma (Scott, 2001). However, rhetorical power is rarely the mere result of charisma. Rather, it is the result of cognitive and social processes, in which, 'intrinsically appropriate reasons for action' are constructed and offered to others so that a particular course of action or decision comes to be seen as cognitively, morally, or emotionally appropriate (Scott, 2001). Such a persuasive influence does not depend on rational calculation but on arguments, appeals and reasons that cause individuals to believe that a particular decision or action is more appropriate than another (Scott, 2001). Rhetorical power can operate through cognitive symbols – ideas and representations that lead people to define situations in certain ways. It arises from the attribution of expertise or knowledge to the influencing agent and draws individuals into a particular interpretive framework (Scott, 2001; Somech and Drach-Zahavy, 2002; van Dijk, 1993). Rhetorical power can also operate through the building of value commitments to particular ideas or conditions (Somech and Drach-Zahavy, 2002) and arises when individuals 'defer to the views of those whom they regard as especially fitted to speak on behalf of these values' (Scott, 2001: 15). Therefore, rhetorical power does not imply the mere rhetorical superiority based on a person's charisma but also the power originating in cognitive symbols and arguments and in value commitments.[3]

Existing practices and discourses often advantage particular groups of actors without those groups being clearly connected to the establishing or maintenance of discourses and practices (e.g., Lawrence et al., 2005). Thus, 'some individuals, by virtue of their position in the discourse, will warrant a louder voice than others, while others may warrant no voice at all' (Hardy and Phillips, 1999: 4).

Therefore, agents with some positional power, power that is embedded in existing relations and is based on resources, are better able to influence discourses and to develop interpretive dominance. At the same time, agents without positional power might be 'silenced' (Brown and Coupland, 2005), with less chance to engage in discourses and meaning creation: 'The most effective use of power occurs when those with power are able to get those without power to interpret the world from the former's point of view' (Mumby and Clair, 1997: 184). For example, agents who mediate between different ICs can use their position as a connecting point to enforce their preferred interpretation by translating other perspectives in a manner favourable to them. In the following, we illustrate the process through which interpretive dominance develops and discuss some of the characteristics of the single steps within this process.

The emergence of interpretive dominance

'The notion of interpretive dominance conceptualizes a belief system as an active arena, where interest groups [...] compete to impose their preferred psychological order onto nonbelievers' (Meindl et al., 1994: 291). Through the management of meanings and communication, individuals and ICs can legitimate their interpretive positions and 'institute a form of social control that removes the need to exercise control directly' (Phillips and Brown, 1993: 1551). We illustrate this process by referring to Callon's (1986) four 'moments of translation': problematization, interéssement, enrolment and mobilization.

(1) Problematization
Communication and coordinated action between members of different ICs are often problematic due to their different interpretations of the same issue, to misunderstandings, suspicion and anxiety of disclosure when interactions occur (Czarniawska and Mazza, 2003). Interaction between members of different ICs is successful only when they develop some shared schemes and begin to act and interpret using these (Bettenhausen and Murnighan, 1985), implying that some individuals must change their initial perspective (e.g., Mohammed and Ringseis, 2001). At the foundation of such a change is the attempt by some actors to manage meanings by introducing certain interpretations and establishing certain relations between interpretations (Benford and Snow, 2000; Gray et al., 1985). The goal is to associate the issue at hand with the preferred concept and perspective of these actors (Hardy et al., 2000). Thus, actors need to 'engage' others into their interpretations and discourses.

The first step in this process involves the embedding of the suggested perspective in a larger discursive context so that it would have meaning for the individuals to whom it is directed (Hardy et al., 2000). This process has been called elsewhere 'strategic fitting' or 'recontextualization' (Benford and Snow, 2000; Fairclough, 2005) and encompasses the (intentional) tailoring and fitting of interpretations to the background and experiences of the other party (Benford and Snow, 2000). Next, actors draw the others' attention to certain aspects of their own experience, accenting and highlighting some issues or aspects as being more salient than others. In this way, they impose a pattern of meaning on otherwise ambiguous contexts (Gray et al., 2000). This process of meaning construction involves introducing certain concepts and interpretations, establishing certain relations between concepts, and imparting values as well as the use of a particular language (Gray et al., 1985; Lawrence et al., 2005). Although it is possible to use rhetoric based on inspirational appeals and emotional requests in order to arouse enthusiasm by appealing on the other's values and ideals, persuasions based on the use of logical arguments, factual evidence and existing discourses are the prevalent influence tactics at this stage (Yukl and Falbe, 1990). Thus, at this stage, cognitive persuasion prevails.

If successful, actors establish themselves as 'obligatory passage points' (Callon, 1986) – agents with interpretive authority for others' problems (Zelizer, 1993). These 'nodal points' are pivotal locations within discourses and when institutionalized, represent 'fixed' knowledge domains that are regarded as normal practice. Thus, 'problematization seeks to construct "hegemony" by fixing [obligatory passage points]' (Clegg 1989: 204).[4] It is important to note that actors can engage in such problem formulation unintentionally: they will try to impose their interpretation of an issue because they are embedded in ICs and discourses that influence what they see and how they interpret what they see. However, other actors can also engage in translation and meaning creation by 'counterframing' – by attempting to undermine or neutralize an actor's version and interpretive framework of the problem by creating a competing interpretation (Benford and Snow, 2000: 626). Such counterframing increases the chance for actors to break out of standard, established interpretations and views and to develop novel understandings. However, it is difficult because actors first have to undo all the already existent interpretations (Callon, 1991). In this case, the next three steps of the 'translating' process become even more important.

(2) Interéssement

In the second step of the translation process actors try to lock others into the roles or identities they have defined for them by erecting an interpretation that serves to block or neutralize all potential competing interpretations. One of the goals of this step is to prevent actors from counterframing. Through rhetorical strategies, actors further influence the construction of cognitive maps on the part of others. Actors' rhetoric in this phase often utilizes emotional aspects by stressing that the suggested interpretation leads to a positive future to which the others are attracted and related to, implying that this particular interpretation will take them closer to a desired perspective and action (Ford and Ford, 1995). Thus, the use of symbolic and emotional appeals and, possibly, charisma is more prevalent than in the first phase. A successful 'intéressement' results in the emergence of some 'shared' understandings

and confirms the validity of the suggested interpretation and the proposed role for the involved actors. However, an unsuccessful translation means that the individuals are no longer able to communicate, which will result in disalignment: actors 'reconfigure themselves in separate spaces with no common measure' (Callon, 1991: 145).

(3) Enrolment

If 'intéressement' is successful, a process of multilateral negotiations between actors takes place, coined 'enrolment', which aims at building alliances and coalitions with members of other ICs. The goal is to 'enact' what started as a discourse – to transform the proposed interpretation into new ways of thinking, acting and interacting, into new ways of being and new identities, and, finally, in the materialization of the suggested interpretation, which can take form of new structures, rules, strategies, practices, etc. (Fairclough, 2005). Thus, in this phase, the interpretive schemes that actors started to share in the previous phase are enacted into concrete actions: the enrolled actors build coalitions and alliances and start to act as a cognitively coherent group in regard to the issue at hand.

(4) Mobilization of allies

This phase refers to methods and actions that ensure that interpretations, which were fixed in the previous phases, are widely dispersed through further discourses. It is important to ensure that the already 'enrolled' actors do not betray or undercut the fixed interpretation so established. At this point, individual statements and practices are accumulated and they start to influence the context for future discourse activities, 'as prevailing discourses are contested, displaced, transformed, modified or reinforced' (Hardy et al., 2000: 1236). At the same time, these existing discourses influence the process of dispersion of new interpretations, which makes it to an unpredictable process 'since there are a number of contradictory ways in which knowledge can be consumed, some of which may be quite different from the intentions of the original producers' (Hardy and Phillips, 2004: 370). This is particularly the case when actors reinterpret the original interpretations and/or connect them in different ways to existing discourses.

The role of rhetorical power in knowledge transfer and creation

The rhetorical power that results in the interpretive dominance of particular ICs can have both constraining and enabling effects on learning processes. If the underlying interpretation is based on existing interpretations, rhetorical power is at work that further stabilizes and endorses an existing discourse through the 'locking' of others into established discourses. Such rhetorical power prevents the creation of novel interpretations and knowledge. With a growing dispersion of existing practices the diversity of interpretations decreases as members of ICs are 'disciplined' by existing practices and discourses (Lawrence et al., 2005).

However, rhetorical power does not always have negative effects. For example, the existence of established meanings and interpretive positions can enhance the process of exploitation of existing interpretations and knowledge (Lawrence et al., 2005). On the other hand, if several interpretive views of an issue are legitimate because each of the involved ICs sees different aspects of the issue and generates different solution paths, the involved individuals might not be able to agree on one. In other words, rational decision-making might not be possible. In order to overcome the ambiguity and uncertainty associated with pluralist interpretations and to achieve collective action, it will be necessary for one IC to develop interpretive dominance (Lawrence et al., 2005).

If the generated interpretation is based in a *new* discourse, actors can use their rhetorical power to translate this novel interpretation into a general discourse for similar situations and, in this way, disturb existing discourses and institutionalize new ones. Through further discourses they can achieve a partial fixing of the novel interpretation. Its wide dispersion can lead to the development of new discourses and ICs that can shape other actors' understanding and interpretations.

From this perspective, rhetorical power provides 'the energy that fuels' decision making in a pluralist environment (Lawrence et al., 2005: 188). Power in the knowledge transfer and creation process is not a dysfunctional aspect that needs to be remedied. Rather, it is an intrinsic part of this process that should be appreciated and understood and appropriately leveraged by members of ICs: 'Without it, we face strategic paralysis because we lack a mechanism with which to make change happen' (Hardy, 1996: S3).

CONCLUSION AND DIRECTIONS FOR FUTURE RESEARCH

It is the relationship between knowledge, discourses and power and their role in the development of ICs that is at the heart of this chapter. Through our discussion, we bring cognition back into our understanding of power and learning. We view individuals as members of a number of different ICs and emphasize the unstable, evolving character of human cognition and the importance of the battle between the pluralities of interpretation, putting power in the centre of a discussion of knowledge transfer and learning. In our view, the power of an IC depends on the relevance and importance of its knowledge as well as on its on-going ability to enforce its perspective and persuade others of the superiority of its knowledge (Clegg, 1989, Fox, 2000; Sillence, 2000).

Our approach is multidisciplinary integrating insights from evolutionary economics, organizational learning, cognitive psychology and CDA and aiming at crossing the existing boundaries between different academic disciplines dealing with the same issue but emphasizing only single aspects. In our view, more interdisciplinary research is needed in order to understand and explain the complex nature of human interactions and actions. We see this evolving both theoretically and empirically. Theoretically, we need: (1) insightful interdisciplinary studies that account for the ways in which particular ICs emerge, develop and disappear; and (2) an understanding of the methods by which discursive change and interpretive dominance occur and reshape the power structures between ICs. Empirically, we need to engage in multilevel research that can simultaneously: (1) characterize ICs based upon the cognitive schema of the actors; (2) map the actual process of interpretative dominance development; and (3) reveal the interaction between ICs in the unstable environment of organizations, coalitions and alliances. Ultimately, studies of power and learning should not ignore the connection to cognition. Let us not forget that neither discourses nor power relations and structures would exist without individuals who create, disseminate, institutionalize and destroy them.

NOTES

1 This is the realist version of discourse analysis (Fairclough, 2005; Reed, 2004). According to the main, social constructivist version of discourse analysis, 'organizations exist only in so far as their members create them through discourse' (Mumby and Clair, 1997: 181). In contrast, the realist version stresses that discursive practices are 'constrained by the fact that they inevitably take place within a constituted material reality, with pre-constituted objects and pre-constituted social subjects' (Fairclough, 1992: 60). It forbears from the view that a 'collective identity [is] a linguistically produced object embodied in talk and other forms of text, rather than a set of beliefs [or interpretations] held in members' minds.' (Hardy et al., 2005: 62). Thus, the social constructivist form of discourse analysis is quite similar to the view of practices as carriers of knowledge as suggested by the CoP approach. We show that there is no such thing as convergent linguistic practices without the existence of some shared cognitive maps between the involved individuals.

2 Our approach is based on a realist ontology combined with an epistemological constructivism and epistemic relativism (also Ackroyd and Fleetwood, 2000).

3 In practice, it is difficult to differentiate clearly between these subtypes of rhetorical power as they are closely interwoven (Scott, 2001).

4 Studies of IT consulting projects provide an example how consultants use managerial discourses to establish themselves, i.e. their knowledge and

practices, as an 'obligatory passage point' in the eyes of clients (Bloomfield and Best, 1992). Zelizer (1993) discusses this process in the case of journalists.

REFERENCES

Ackroyd, S. and Fleetwood, S. (2000) 'Realism in contemporary organisation and management studies', in S. Ackroyd and S. Fleetwood (eds), *Realist Perspectives on Management and Organisations.* London: Routledge. pp. 3–25.

Bechky, B. (2003) 'Sharing meaning across occupational communities: The transformation of understanding on a production floor', *Organization Science*, 14 (3): 312–330.

Benford, R. and Snow, D. (2000) 'Framing processes and social movements: An overview and assessment', *Annual Review of Sociology*, 26: 611–639.

Bettenhausen, K. and Murnighan, J. (1985) 'The emergence of norms in competitive decision-making groups', *Administrative Science Quarterly*, 30 (3): 350–372.

Blau, J. (1996) 'Organizations as overlapping jurisdictions: Restoring reason in organizational accounts', *Administrative Science Quarterly*, 41 (1): 172–179.

Bloomfield, B.P. and Best, A. (1992) 'Management consultants: systems development, power and the translation of problems', *The Sociological Review*, 41: 533–560.

Boland, R. and Tenkasi, R. (1995) 'Perspective making and perspective taking in communities of knowing', *Organization Science*, 6 (4): 350–372.

Bloor, G. and Dawson, P. (1994) 'Understanding professional culture in organizational context', *Organization Studies*, 15 (2): 275–295.

Brown, A. and Coupland, C. (2005) 'Sounds of silence: Graduate trainees, hegemony and resistance', *Organization Studies*, 26 (7): 1049–1069.

Brown, J. and Duguid, P. (1991) 'Organizational learning and communities-of-practice: Toward a unified view of working, learning, and innovation', *Organization Science*, 2 (1): 40–57.

Brown, J. and Duguid, P. (2001) 'Knowledge and organization: A social-practice perspective', *Organization Science*, 12 (2): 198–213.

Brown, J., Collins, A. and Duguid, P. (1989) 'Situated cognition and the culture of learning', *Educational Researcher*, 18 (1): 32–42.

Bunge, M. (1983) *Treatise on Basic Philosophy Vol. 5. Epistemology and Methodology I: Exploring the World.* Dordrecht: Kluwer.

Bunge, M. (1996) *Finding Philosophy in Social Science.* New Haven: Yale University Press.

Callon, M. (1986) 'Some elements of a sociology of translation: domestication of the scallops and the fishermen of St Brieuc Bay', in J. Law (ed.), *Power, Action and Belief*. London: Routledge and Kegan Paul. pp. 196–233.

Callon, M. (1991) 'Techno-economic networks and irreversibility', in J. Law (ed.), *A Sociology of Monsters: Essays on Power, Technology and Domination*. London: Routledge. pp. 131–164.

Carley, K. (1991) 'A theory of group stability', *American Sociological Review*, 56 (3): 331–354.

Carroll, J. (1998) 'Organizational learning activities in high-hazard industries: The logics underlying self-analysis', *Journal of Management Studies*, 35 (6): 699–717.

Clegg, S. (1989) *Frameworks of Power*. London: Sage Publications.

Clegg, S. (2001) 'Changing concepts of power, changing concepts of politics', *Administrative Theory and Practice*, 23 (2): 126–150.

Crossan, M., Lane, H. and White, R. (1999) 'An organizational learning framework: From intuition to institution', *Academy of Management Review*, 24 (3): 522–537.

Czarniawska, B. and Mazza, C. (2003) 'Consulting as a liminal space', *Human Relations*, 56 (3): 267–290.

DiMaggio, P. (1997) 'Culture and cognition', *Annual Review of Sociology*, 23: 263–287.

Dougherty, D. (1992) 'Interpretive barriers to successful product innovation in large firms', *Organization Science*, 3 (2): 179–202.

Fairclough, N. (1992) *Discourse and Social Change*. Cambridge: Polity Press.

Fairclough, N. (2005) 'Discourse analysis in organization studies: The case for critical realism', *Organization Studies*, 26 (6): 915–939.

Fish, S. (1980) *Is there a Text in this Class? The Authority of Interpretive Communities*. Cambridge, MA: Harvard University Press.

Flyvbjerg, B. (1998) *Rationality and Power*. Chicago: University of Chicago Press.

Ford, J. and Ford, L. (1995) 'The role of conversations in producing intentional change in organizations', *Academy of Management Review*, 20 (3): 541–570.

Fox, S. (2000) 'Communities of practice, Foucault and actor-network theory', *Journal of Management Studies*, 37 (6): 853–867.

Foucault, M. (1980) *Power/Knowledge: Selected Interviews and Other Writings, 1972–1977*. New York: Pantheon Books.

Gherardi, S. and Nicolini, D. (2002) 'Learning in a constellation of interconnected practices: Canon or dissonance?', *Journal of Management Studies*, 39 (4): 419–436.

Gray, B., Bougon, M. and Donnellon, A. (1985) 'Organizations as constructions and destructions of meaning', *Journal of Management*, 11 (2): 83–98.

Hardy, C. (1996) 'Understanding power: Bringing about strategic change', *British Journal of Management*, 7 (Special issue): S3–S16.

Hardy, C. and Phillips, N. (1999) 'No joking matter: Discursive struggle in the Canadian refugee system', *Organization Studies*, 20 (1): 1–24.

Hardy, C. and Phillips, N. (2004) 'Discourse and power', in D. Grant, C. Hardy, C. Oswick and L. Putnam (eds), *The SAGE Handbook of Organizational Discourse*. Thousand Oaks, CA: Sage. pp. 299–316.

Hardy, C., Palmer, I. and Phillips, N. (2000) 'Discourse as a strategic resource', *Human Relations*, 53 (9): 1227–1248.

Hardy, C., Lawrence, T. and Grant, D. (2005) 'Discourse and collaboration: The role of conversations and collective identity', *Academy of Management Review*, 30 (1): 58–77.

Harris, S. (1989) 'A schema-based perspective on organizational culture', *Academy of Management Proceedings*, 178–182.

Heracleous, L. (2004) 'Interpretivist approaches to organizational discourse', in D. Grant, C. Hardy, C. Oswick and L. Putnam (eds), *The SAGE Handbook of Organizational Discourse*. Thousand Oaks, CA: Sage. pp. 175–192.

Heracleous, L. and Barrett, M. (2001) 'Organizational change as discourse: Communicative actions and deep structures in the context of information technology implementation', *Academy of Management Journal*, 44 (4): 755–778.

Hymes, D. (1980) *Language in Education: Ethnolinguistic Essays*. Washington: Center for Applied Linguistics.

Koppl, R. and Langlois, R. (2001) 'Organizations as language games', *Journal of Management and Governance*, 5 (3/4): 287–305.

Lakomski, G. (2004) 'On knowing in context', *British Journal of Management*, 15 (Special issue): S89–S95.

Lave, J. and Wenger, E. (2002) *Situated Learning. Legitimate Peripheral Participation*. Cambridge: Cambridge University Press.

Lawrence, T., Mauws, M. and Dyck, B. (2005) 'The politics of organizational learning: Integrating power into the 4I framework', *Academy of Management Review*, 30 (1): 180–191.

Leinhardt, G., Young, K. and Merriman, J. (1995) 'Integrating professional knowledge: The theory of practice and the practice of theory', *Learning and Instruction*, 5 (4): 401–408.

Loasby, B. (1983) 'Knowledge, learning and enterprise', in J. Wiseman (ed.), *Beyond Positive Economics?* London: Macmillan. pp. 104–121.

Lorenz, E. (2001) 'Models of cognition, the contextualisation of knowledge and organisational theory', *Journal of Management and Governance*, 5 (4): 307–330.

Marshak, R., Keenoy, T., Oswick, C. and Grant, D. (2000) 'From outer words to inner worlds', *The Journal of Applied Behavioral Science*, 36 (2): 245–258.

Marshall, N. and Rollinson, J. (2004) 'Maybe Bacon had a point: The politics of interpretation in collective sensemaking', *British Journal of Management*, 15 (Special issue): S71–S86.

Martin, J. and Siehl, C. (1983) 'Organizational culture and counterculture: An uneasy symbiosis', *Organizational Dynamics*, 12 (2): 52–64.

Maturana, H. (1980) 'Biology of cognition', in H. Maturana and F. Varela (eds), *Autopoesis and Cognition*. Dordrecht: D. Reidel. pp. 2–62.

Meindl, J., Stubbart, C. and Porac, J. (1994) 'Cognition within and between organizations: Five key questions', *Organization Science*, 5 (3): 289–293.

Mohammed, S. and Ringseis, E. (2001) 'Cognitive diversity and consensus in group decision making: The role of inputs, processes, and outcomes', *Organizational Behavior and Human Decision Processes*, 85 (2): 310–335.

Mumby, D. and Stohl, C. (1991) 'Power and discourse in organization studies: Absence and the dialectic of control', *Discourse and Society*, 2 (3): 313–332.

Mumby, D. and Clair, R. (1997) 'Organizational discourse', in T.A. van Dijk (ed.), *Discourse as Structure and Process: Discourse Studies Vol. 2.* London: Sage. pp. 181–205.

Neisser, U. (1976) *Cognition and Reality*. New York: Freeman.

Phillips, N. and Brown, J. (1993) 'Analyzing communication in and around organizations: A critical hermeneutic approach', *Academy of Management Journal*, 36 (6): 1547–1576.

Prahalad, C. and Bettis, R. (1986) 'The dominant logic: A new linkage between diversity and performance', *Strategic Management Journal*, 7 (6): 485–501.

Reed, M. (2004) 'Getting real about organizational research', in D. Grant, C. Hardy, C. Oswick and L. Putnam (eds), *The SAGE Handbook of Organizational Discourse*. Thousand Oaks, CA: Sage. pp. 413–420.

Reihlen, M. and Ringberg, T. (2004) 'Exploring competing views on knowledge in management studies'. Unpublished working paper, University of Wisconsin-Milwaukee.

Scott, J. (2001) *Power*. Oxford: Blackwell.

Sillince (2000) 'Rhetorical power, accountability and conflict in committees: An argumentation approach', *Journal of Management Studies*, 37 (8): 1125–1156.

Somech, A. and Drach-Zahavy, A. (2002) 'Relative Power and influence strategy: The effects of agent/target organizational power on superiors' choices of influence strategies', *Journal of Organizational Behavior*, 23: 167–179.

Tsoukas, H. and Vladimirou, E. (2001) 'What is organizational knowledge?', *Journal of Management Studies*, 38 (7): 973–993.

Van Dijk, T. (1993) 'Principles of critical discourse analysis', *Discourse and Society*, 4 (2): 249–283.

Watson, T. (1982) 'Group ideologies and organizational change', *Journal of Management Studies*, 19 (3): 259–275.

Weick, K.E. (1979) *The Social Psychology of Organizing*. Reading, MA: Addison-Wesley.

Yukl, G. and Falbe, C. (1990) 'Influence tactics and objectives in upward, downward and lateral influence attempts', *Journal of Applied Psychology*, 75 (2): 132–140.

Zelizer, B. (1993) 'Journalists as interpretive communities', *Critical Studies in Mass Communication*, 10: 219–237.

Shifting Sands in Communities of Scholars

Greg Northcraft

The landscape of academic research and publishing in business schools has endured a subtle but fundamental transformation in the last few decades. It's no longer *authors* who are competing for space in the top journals. Instead, the entity of academic competition is now the authorship *team*. When the top academic business schools first opened their doors, virtually all submissions were single-authored; today the single-authored publication is a rare feat.

And no wonder – the average article length seems to be continually increasing as are the number of citations and the length of methods sections (Schminke and Mitchell, 2003). In other words, it takes a more complex contribution to get published in a top journal today than it used to. A more complex contribution requires more creativity and innovation, and perhaps a more stunning array of skills and expertise. It should not be terribly surprising, then, that the growth of co-authorship has coincided with a technological shrinking of the *de facto* distance among potential collaborators – first by overnight document delivery, then fax, and finally the ubiquitous e-mail. Today e-mail is the vehicle that enables far-flung collaborations, and in doing so may be fueling an escalating 'arms race' of idea complexity in research.

This sounds good for the field, doesn't it? But there is a cloud to this silver lining. Technology that makes it easier to connect with those far away also makes it less necessary to connect with those close by. When I first started my own academic career 25 years ago, we had a *local* community of scholars because that was really the only community that was possible. Long-distance telephones calls were prohibitively expensive, travel budgets were limited, fax machines were a twinkle in someone's eye, and the idea of e-mail – well, that was inconceivable. So I worked with the diverse scholars around me – diverse because most schools can't afford to hire people who do the same thing – and our collaborations provided the glue that held our community of scholars together. A brief read through management journals 25 years ago confirms that at the time, local collaborations were the rule.

Today, e-mail has redefined the reference community of scholars for many of my colleagues. Distant collaborations – certainly cross-country but even cross-national – are now as much the rule as the exception. This raises questions for the future of the local community of scholars, for research, and perhaps for the definition of what it means to be a university faculty member. If your department hires a new addition to its local community of scholars who arrives on the local scene but continues (via technology) to work primary with prior collaborators elsewhere, what have you actually added to the local scholarly community? Technology may make it easy to collaborate with a diverse co-authorship team, but the attractiveness and comfort of similar others (and the start-up costs of working with dissimilar others) suggests that technology may lead scholars to invest primarily in relationships with those like them. Thus, while technology may make it possible to reach a more diverse set of collaborators, in fact it can also be used to maintain contact with a very similar set of collaborators, rather than (without technology) braving local collaboration with dissimilar others.

In a related vein, a few years ago my university began to think that distributed learning models might provide an effective vehicle to fulfill the outreach obligations entailed in its land-grant heritage. Distributed learning allows students who can't be physically present to nevertheless participate, for example by e-commuting into a classroom via the internet. Of course, the perfection of this technology will mean that not only students can e-commute into the classroom – so can their professors! Its one sort of problem if the students are never on campus, but it seems something else together if the faculty aren't. Is that really what the university of the future is supposed to look like? Perhaps I'm a bit 'old school,' but I think a lot of my best collaborations were born of the informal contact of regular social interaction with colleagues – coffee, lunch, 'happy hour' – the kind of informal contact that can't happen over e-mail.

The technological 'shrinking' of the world accomplishes a lot of good – like the possibility of working from home or collaborating with friends overseas – so it's a genie we can't put back in the bottle. What we can do is try to acknowledge, understand, and manage the subtle effects of technological advances. For a local community of scholars, those effects include substituting all those great new things we can do now for all the things we used to have to do – like being at work and talking to the person in the office next door.

REFERENCE

Schminke, M. and Mitchell, M. (2003) 'From the Editors: In the beginning…' *Academy of Management Journal*, 46 (3): 279–282.

Situated Knowledge and Situated Action: What do Practice-Based Studies Promise?

Silvia Gherardi

INTRODUCTION

> 'Knowledge is not something that people possess in their heads, but rather, something that people do together'. (Gergen, 1985: 270)

Since the 1980s, learning and knowing in organizations have been subject to lively and sometimes heated debate in the field of organization studies. More recently there is a form of new convergence around the so-called Practice-Based Studies (PBS) of learning and knowing in organizations. It is natural to enquire as to the reasons for this great interest, and explore how the focus on knowing in practice can contribute to a re-framing of the field.

The success of the theme of PBS in organizations resides, I believe, within that complex and variegated intellectual movement which in the social sciences has exposed the limitations of rationalism (Elster, 2000), and

which in organization studies has dismantled the functionalist paradigm from which the discipline sprang (Tsoukas and Knudsen, 2003). Consider, in fact, how organization theory used to be grounded on an image of the rational organization which privileged decision-making processes, first based on paradigmatic rationality and then on bounded rationality, and strategic planning predicated on *a priori* rationality. The shortcomings of the paradigm became evident as both scholars and practitioners in organizations came increasingly to realize that the theory was unable to account for contingencies and situational rationalities.

The image of an organization guided by the optimization principle was gradually replaced by an image of the organization which proceeds by trial and error, which builds on its own experience and that of others, which extracts maximum value from the knowledge in its possession, which strives after constant improvement, and which networks with other organizations and institutions in order to develop collectively the knowledge that it is unable to produce only on its own. This is an image, therefore, which depicts a more modest rationality of incremental and distributed type. It interprets the spirit of an age which views knowledge as a production factor and the knowledge society as manifesting epochal changes.

I do not wish to argue that study of organizational learning and knowledge in organizations has proceeded homogeneously in an anti-rationalist endeavour; on the contrary, contradictions between *a priori* rationality and incremental rationality, between positivist research and interpretative post-modern research, have traversed the debate. Unquestioning faith in rationality has rendered it into one of the myths most deeply rooted in the Western collective consciousness, and the consequence has been that the mind has been given primacy over the body as the almost exclusive seat of the knowledge-building process. Associated with a mentalist image of knowledge, therefore, is a research methodology which views individual or collective cognitive processes as the appropriate domain in which to investigate the mental schemes and mechanisms by which knowledge is produced and stored. But when knowledge is conceived as a mundane activity, situated in ongoing working and organizing practices, then we need a methodology appropriate to the observation of knowing in practice.

The intention of this chapter is to illustrate the contribution of PBS within a tradition critical of rationalism and cognitivism, doing so on the basis of a complex image of the relationship between working, organizing and knowing. It conceptualizes knowledge in the same manner as those analyses of social and institutional learning which assume the reciprocal constitution of the knower subject and the known object, of knowledge and knowing, and of practice and practising.

What practice-based studies promise to organizational studies is that they will link the study of working practices to the study of organizing, and that they will do so by making knowledge an observable phenomenon (Borzeix, 1998).

HOW TO DEFINE KNOWLEDGE?

Knowledge is not something that people possess in their heads; rather, it is something that people do together (Gergen, 1985: 270). From this perspective we may start our search for a methodology to study knowledge empirically as a situated activity.

As much in everyday life as in work organizations, people and groups create knowledge by negotiating the meanings of words, actions, situations and material artifacts. They all participate in and contribute to a world which is socially and culturally structured and constantly reconstituted by the activities of all those who belong to it. Cognitive and practical activity can thus be pursued only within this world, and through this social and cultural interweaving. Knowledge is not what resides in a person's head or in books or in data banks. To know is to be capable of participating with the requisite competence in the complex web of relationships among people, material artifacts and activities (Gherardi, 2001). On this definition it follows that knowing in practice is always a practical accomplishment.

Knowing is something people do together and it is done in every mundane activity, in organizations when people work together and in academic fields like organization studies, even if we make distinctions between lay, practical and theoretical knowledge. But also the practices of science – like any other social process – are situated in specific contexts of power/knowledge (Knorr-Cetina, 1981). Situated practices are both pre-reflexive (depending on unstated assumptions and shared knowledge for the mutual achievement of sense) and reflexively constitutive of the situated members' contexts from which they arise.

The term 'practice' is a *topos* that connects 'knowing' with 'doing'. It conveys the image of materiality, of fabrication, of handiwork, of the craftsman's skill. Knowledge consequently does not arise from scientific 'discoveries'; rather, it is fabricated by situated practices of knowledge production and reproduction using the technologies of representation and mobilization.

WHERE KNOWLEDGE IS?

We may say that the concept of practice has two important implications:

1 Social action and social knowledge must be regarded as activities inseparably woven together.
2 Knowing cannot be viewed as a conscious activity involving meaningful acts, for it presupposes only presumed or indirect references to norms, meanings and values that it claims to apply or to follow.

Therefore one of the most important directions taken by empirical studies which use the practice-based approach is the study of the practical organization of knowledge, in the form of methods of seeing, reasoning and acting in association of human and non-human elements. In fact, objects and their material world can be construed as materialized knowledge and matter which interrogate humans and interact with them.

Nevertheless, inspection of the literature shows that a unified theory of practice does not exist (Schatzki, 2001), nor does a unified field of practice studies. Rather I see three types of relations established between practices and knowledge:

- a relation of *containment*, in the sense that knowledge is a process that takes place within situated practices. On this view, practices are constituted as objective entities (in that they have been objectified) about which practitioners already have knowledge (i.e. they recognize them as practices) and which comprise bits and pieces of knowledge anchored in the material world and in the normative and aesthetic system that has elaborated them culturally.
- a relation of *mutual constitution*, in the sense that the activities of knowing and practising are not two distinct and separate phenomena; instead, they interact and produce each other.

- a relation of *equivalence*, in the sense that practising is knowing in practice, whether the subject is aware of it or not. Acting as a competent practitioner is synonymous with knowing how to connect successfully with the field of practices thus activated. The equivalence between knowing and practising arises when priority is denied to the knowledge that exists before the moment of its application, so that when applying it something already existent is not performed but the action instead creates the knowledge formed in the action itself and by means of it.

However, the three relations do not exclude each other, and emphasizing one of them does not prejudice the others. We may say that in order to make knowledge observable in its making and un-making we shall focus on working practices as the locus of knowledge production, and reproduction; we shall pay attention to the dynamics between practice as institutionalized knowledge and practising as institutionalizing process, and we shall assume that knowing in practice is synonymous of practising.

KNOWING IN PRACTICE AND KNOWING A PRACTICE

The study of practices by Bourdieu (1972), as well as by Garfinkel (1986) and Giddens (1976), is indebted to Schutz (1962), and to his definition of the social world as constituted by innumerable provinces of meaning viewed as particular sets of experiences, each of them manifesting a specific style and – with respect to this style – not only consistent in itself but also compatible with others. The world of everyday life is a province of meaning dominated and structured by what Schutz calls the 'natural attitude', so that the world is from the outset not the world of the private individual but an intersubjective world, shared by us all, and in which we have not a theoretical but eminently practical interest. However, individuals are usually aware that each of them has a different perception of reality. They are simultaneously aware that they have a sufficient degree of access to the perceptions of others to be able to perform their normal everyday activities. From this point of view, the meanings of our experiences of the outside world are considered for all practical purposes to be 'empirically identical' and thus give rise to the shared meanings indispensable for communication and for that particular 'accent' of reality conferred upon the world of everyday life. On this account, working represents the highest degree of interest in and attention to life, while simultaneously being the means with which individuals are able to alter the external world.

Put briefly, intersubjectivity gives rise not to a matching of meanings, but to the assumption that meanings are shared, or as Garfinkel puts it, to an agreement on methods of understanding. Accordingly, the most significant innovation by ethnomethodology with respect to traditional sociology is its replacement of cognitive categories with the categories of action, and the consequent view of the creation and transmission of knowledge as a socially important practice. Which means that also sociology has taken up Austin's assertion that "knowing is doing in everyday life, and it is doing society' (Giglioli, 1990: 85). In ethnomethodological studies, in fact, the transmission of knowledge as a social practice has been the focus of analysis by studies on work (Garfinkel, 1986). But because these studies have not overtly conceptualized working practice as 'learning', they have been largely ignored in the organizational field; only recently, in fact, has analysis of the social construction of technology and professional cultures by workplace studies resumed a number of ethnomethodological themes (Heath and Button, 2002).

Garfinkel (1967: 4) writes that one can discern the ethnomethodological method for analysis of social as well as working practices:

wherever studies of practical action and practical reasoning are concerned, these consist of the following: (1) the unsatisfied programmatic distinction between and substitutability of objective (context free) for indexical expressions; (2) the 'uninteresting' essential reflexivity of accounts of practical actions; and (3) the analysability of actions-in-context as a practical accomplishment.

The discussion thus far has highlighted three essential features – indexicality, reflexivity and accountability – of the situated practices used by individuals to confer meaning on the social world.

The term 'indexical' was originally used in linguistics to denote expressions that are only completely comprehensible in the concrete context where they are produced and used. In ethnomethodological studies, however, the term has acquired specific connotations. The indexicality of social actions means that actors do not usually have problems in understanding each other, largely because comprehension is a constant and contingent achievement which depends on their interpretive work. Understanding situated practices therefore requires understanding of how individuals successfully use indexical behaviours and expressions whose meanings are constantly negotiated and renegotiated in the course of interaction. One meaning of 'situated' with reference to practices is that their performance depends on the manner in which indexicality is locally resolved. Also social norms are indexical, with the consequence that a rule of behaviour does not have a univocal meaning outside the concrete settings where it is applied. This thesis stresses in particular that the range of application of a rule is always constituted by an *a priori* indefinable number of different situations, so that a norm is always applied 'for another first time' (Garfinkel, 1967: 9)[1] and a work practice is always executed for 'another first time'.

Reflexivity, the second characteristic, is rooted in all order-producing social activities (Garfinkel, 1967: 67). It consists in the practices of accountability, observability, and referability of social action, by which is meant making the world comprehensible to oneself and to the other members of a collectivity. 'Reflexivity refers to the dynamic self-organizational tendency of social interaction to provide for its own constitution through practices of accountability and scenic display' (Flynn, 1991: 28). It is therefore actions themselves that 'reflexively' display their nature as meaningful to social actors. It is this feature that enables the analysis of practices, in that it renders their meanings accessible to 'outsiders' as well, or better, to 'external observers' (Fele, 2002). These observers consequently do not have to rely entirely on what people tell them – a method criticized by Zimmermann and Pollner (1970) because, they maintain, actions speak for themselves. However, this is not to imply that their meanings are abstract or decontextualized; rather, it depends on the fact that they inevitably participate in an organization of activity – they are, that is to say, embedded in a concrete situation.[2]

I finally deal with the notion of accountability. Generally used to denote a 'motive', a 'reason' or an 'explanation', the term is used by Garfinkel (1967: 1) as synonymous with 'observable-reportable, i.e. available to members as situated practices of looking-and-telling', that is, a constantly exhibited and public property of ordinary activities. In other words, accountability evinces the normal, ordinary, comprehensible and natural character of events. Consequently, social actions do not need to be 'baptized' by language for them to be intelligible and indexical to their participants. This signifies that accounts contribute to the setting of which they are part, and that they are interpreted and understood procedurally. 'Accounts, therefore, are not a terminus for social scientific investigation, they are, rather, a point of departure for it' (Heritage, 1987: 250). For that matter, Garfinkel himself maintains that large parts of our actions and interactions are not based on shared agreements but rather on a texture of tacit assumptions, neither explicated nor fully explicable, which are taken for granted. This, therefore, is yet another way to conceptualize tacit knowledge as 'taken for granted' which derives directly from Schulz (1962).

Finally, Garfinkel emphasizes the importance of social action as a moral phenomenon, where 'morality' is tied to patterns of action recognized by the entire community as those most correct, legitimate and adequate in a specific context[3] distinct from others. On this view, the members of society know the moral order when in the actions of others

they recognize those models that represent the 'natural facts of life', not internalized social norms – as Parsons instead argued when he treated social norms as initially 'external' and then integrated into the personality by socialization to take the form of dispositions. This account of morality also views rules as assumed in constitutive function of the intelligibility of concrete actions. Indeed, it is precisely the self-structuring of behaviour in accordance with the prescriptions of a norm which enables the actor to recognize that behaviour as a given type of action.

People engaged in a working practice acknowledge a set of social positions which are interrelated, which make sense, and which are enacted. Practices impart identities and selves that are displayed on appropriate occasions. People's experiences in, with and within practices become incorporated into their identities, the social positions that they occupy, the status that they display while they enact the set of practices, and also when they do not perform it. Professional identities are linked to a set of institutional practices but they are also performed outside their profession.

KNOWING IN PRACTICE AS A SITUATED ACTIVITY

For the time being, we may adopt a methodological perspective which, once the nature of an 'institution of practices' has been established, views analysis of situated 'seeing, saying and doing' as an operational means to give concrete definition to a field of empirical analysis. This methodological approach has already been used with good results by studies of gender as a socially situated practice (Bruni et al., 2004; Martin, 2003; Poggio, 2006), and of learning safety as practical knowledge enacted in appropriate situations (Gherardi, 2006).

However, we should keep in mind the multiple meanings of the term 'situated knowledge' and the multiple uses made of the expression. 'Situated' has a multiplicity of meanings (Gherardi, 2006), all of which are present when we consider the knowing process as embedded with the performance of a working practice:

- *Situated in the body.* The materiality of the knowing subject is primarily anchored in the body, and a body is sexed. The feminist critique of science and feminist work in the sociology of science and technology have helped to show that even 'universal' knowledge is situated, while feminist objectivity simply means bodily-situated knowledge (Fujimura et al., 1987; Harding, 1986; Mol, 1999). The advantage of a 'partial perspective' – the term coined by Donna Haraway (1991) and taken up by Marilyn Strathern (1991) – is that knowledge always has to do with circumscribed domains, not with transcendence and the subject/object dichotomy. Moreover, the material body – the body that works – assumes shape and location within the set of practices that constitute the work setting. The knowledge acquired via the five senses is aesthetic, not mental. It often forms the basis for specific competences. Craft trades required trained bodies – ones, that is, which have incorporated an expertise. It is through the body that 'an eye' (or 'an ear' or 'a nose') for something is acquired, so that aesthetic knowledge (Strati, 2003) also comprises the ability to develop a professional 'vision' in the broad sense.
- *Situated in the dynamics of interactions.* Knowing in practice articulates the emergent – *in situ* – nature of knowledge from interactions. The situation of an action can be defined as the set of resources available to convey the meaning of one's own actions and to interpret those of others (Suchman, 1987). And Latour (1987) suggests that people interact not only with each other but also with the non-human that makes up the remainder of the natural world.
- *Situated in language.* This specification highlights that all expressions change their meanings according to the subject uttering them and according to the context of use. The situation, therefore, not only defines the circumstances of an action, it also produces them through language. I prefer to talk of 'discursive practices', rather than communication or language, in order to emphasize that talking is doing, and to shift attention from the subject that talks and his/her communicative intent to the fact that situated talking practices have a form of their own (*qua* 'practices') and relative independence from the subjects that perform them.
- *Situated in a physical context.* Space is not an empty container for situations, nor is it a passive receptacle for the organized activities of actors-in-situation. On the contrary, subjects actively engage with space and establish relations with it (Kirsh, 1995). An organized space – a workplace – is a 'situational territory' (Goffman, 1971; Suchman, 1996) in which objects remind subjects of what they must do, prevent humans from doing things that may harm them, guide action according to intentions inscribed in their design, and make work and life comfortable, both materially and socially. Because the materiality of situations enters into relations, objects can be conceived as materializations of knowledge, as tangible knowledge which 'steers' and sustains a set of practices.

It is therefore possible to discern various currents of research concerned with 'knowing in practice', bearing in mind that what they have in common is not identification of a particular type of action but rather an endeavour to explain how knowledge organizes action in situation. As Béguin and Clôt (2004) noted, there are different disciplinary 'accents' which articulate three dynamics of this organization of action in situation: *interactionist*, which derives mainly from sociology and stresses interactions mediated by language and draws mainly on Lucy Suchman (1987); *ecological*, which has arisen mainly in psychology and draws on Gibson (1979) and his concept of 'affordance', which shows that some of the organization of action is undertaken by the environment; and *cultural*, which refers to cognitive anthropology and draws on the studies by Norman (1994) on cognitive artifacts and Hutchins (1995) on distributed cognition. Béguin and Clôt point out that these three currents on action and situated cognition seek to establish a relation (in their view an unsatisfactory one) between what is given in the situation and what the actors create in it.

The roots of the intellectual traditions of the study of practice-based studies may be represented as in Figure 3.9.1, where I illustrate its first genealogy as delineated by Conein and Jacopin (1994) in reference to the streams in situated action and activity theory and integrate it with its extension to

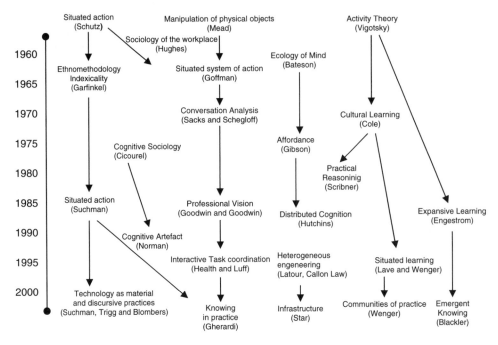

Figure 3.9.1   The streams of practice-based studies

the field of learning and knowing as practical accomplishment (Gherardi, 2000).

A METHODOLOGICAL FRAMEWORK

Once we consider the mutual constitution of practice and practising, and the situatedness of knowing as a practical accomplishment we become able to analyse knowledge as an observable phenomenon and propose a framework that focuses on knowing as a situated practice.

Imagine a work group engaged in everyday work practices which are proceeding smoothly and whose coordination is fluid and unproblematic. In this situation we observe that working is not distinct from organizing activities, and that adjusting them to a context which may change as a result of those same activities is not distinct from habitual knowledge on how to carry out those activities, or from knowing how to modify them contextually. This is therefore a situation in which working, organizing, innovating to adjust to a changing context, situated

learning and prior learning are co-present and co-produced in situation. We may therefore analyse and interpret knowledge in practice as an empirical and observable phenomenon, on the assumption that in order to perform a work practice, the context, the collectivity, the tools and technologies, and language are the resources at hand for purposive action.

It is therefore not necessary to posit the logical primacy of either the actors, or the context, or the material world, or language. Work practice as the successful outcome of the manifestation of practical knowledge in situation is *given and created* by the weaving together of knowledge anchored in the environment and the material and social world to create a texture of practice.

Within this methodological framework the focus will be on the connections-in-action established in the community of practitioners by constant conversation on the practices and the ethical and aesthetic criteria that institutionalize them within that social formation. In fact, this methodological framework proposes a conceptualization of practical activity in which practice coincides neither with routine as an analytical set of activities nor as a doing-in-situation mediated by interactions, language and technologies. The distinctive feature of this view of work practices as social and material accomplishments is the weaving together of resources within a normative conception, constantly produced and reproduced by the practitioners, about what constitutes a 'good practice', and about why one way of doing that practice is more 'attractive' than another. The concept of 'practice' is broader than those of 'activity', 'situated action' and 'routine' because it emphasises, not doing-in-situation but doing-society-in-situation.

The pragmatic dimension of doing is co-present and co-produced together with that of performing situated identities sustained by a normative and aesthetic dimension. The constant conversation that takes place among practitioners in practice and about practice produces coordination in practice and among work practices, as well as ensuring that practices continue to be such – i.e. practised – and reproduced in accordance with the social criteria that sustain them.

CONCLUSIONS: PRACTICE AS AN IN-BETWEEN CONCEPT

When we give priority to practices over mind we contribute to a transformed conception of knowledge, which is no longer possession of mind, which is mediated and propagated both by interactions between people and by the material arrangements in the world, which is discursively constructed, which is diffused, fragmented and distributed as a property of groups working within a situated material environment and within a situated and discursively sustained social world.

Practices, therefore, are modes of ordering which acquire temporal and spatial stability from provisional and unstable agreements in practice. We can say that people share a practice if their actions are appropriately regarded as answerable to norms of correct or incorrect practice, to criteria of aesthetics taste, and to standards of fairness. Therefore when

we look at situated actions in ongoing practices – seeing, saying and doing – we are making 'knowledge observable'. As Yanow (2000) noted, seeing a practice – a set of acts and interactions involving language and objects repeated over time, with patterns and variations – allow the researcher to infer back that a culture of practice is performed. And as Goodwin (1994) illustrated, practitioners learn to see and to sustain a 'professional vision' as a situated activity.

What does the concept of practice promise and why does it do so? I have argued that the 'what and the how' concern making knowledge an empirical and observable phenomenon, and I have outlined a methodological framework for the purpose. As a concluding point I shall address the 'why' question and answer it by stressing the nature of 'practice' as an in-between concept.

The concept of practice may constitute a bridge between antithetical concepts, and for this reason I have defined it elsewhere as an 'in-between concept' (Gherardi, 2003). It lies in-between habit and action in the sense that a practice has habitual features because it is based on the repetition of activities, and it also has the character of a purposeful action. But it is neither a habit nor an action. In the same sense it is an in-between concept between reproduction and production, because in practice the reproduction of society is done day by day, practice after practice, while at the same time practice is productive of its results and effects. The heuristic promise of a concept standing in-between production and reproduction, habit and action resides in its power to account for how society holds together (is reproduced) and changes in being reproduced. While production has been a much-studied phenomenon, reproduction and the endogenous dynamics of reproduction have attracted less interest. The focus is therefore on working practices and on how they are internally changed in being practised, both incrementally through application of situated rationality to the changing resources of the practice at hand, and through the social dynamics stemming from the ongoing conversation of practitioners on the normative standards of the practice. Practice-based studies make a specific contribution to the understanding of how social reproduction and its maintenance is accomplished by means of knowledgeable practices.

NOTES

1 This has two fundamental consequences: the first is that the applicability of a norm necessarily depends on the content of that norm; the second is that norms in themselves are not sufficient to direct human action because they do not exhaustively define the components constituting the behaviour to which they apply, in the sense that it is always possible to find behaviours which are not regulated by any specific rule.

2 However, Garfinkel argues that in no case is the investigation of practical actions undertaken in order that the persons involved might be able to recognize and describe what they are doing in the first place and those conducting the analysis understand the manner in which they are talking about what they are doing. This entails that the actors assume 'the reflexivity of producing, accomplishing, recognizing and demonstrating the rational and wholly practical adequacy of their procedures; they rely upon it, require it, and make use of it' (Fele, 2002: 62).

3 Note that Garfinkel does not view the context as an entity which exists before the action and determines it by means of norms; rather, it self-organizes itself with respect to the intelligible character of its manifestations. In other words, it is constantly reconstituted by actions so that it becomes at once the point of departure and arrival of the selfsame actions that constitute it (Nicotera, 1996: 53).

REFERENCES

Béguin, P. and Clôt, Y. (2004) 'L'Action Située Dans le Development de l'Activité', *@ctivités*, 1 (2): 27–49.

Borzeix, A. (1998) 'Comment Observer l'Interpretation?', in A. Borzeix, A. Bouvier and P. Pharo (eds), *Sociologie et Connaissance*, CNRS edition: Paris.

Bourdieu, P. (1972) *Esquisse d'une théorie de la pratique précédé de trois etudes de ethnologie kabyle*, Switzerland: Librairie Droz S.A. (Engl. trans. *Outline of a Theory of Practice*. Cambridge University Press, 1977).

Bruni, A., Gherardi, S. and Poggio, B. (2004) 'Doing gender, doing entrepreneurship: an ethnographic account of interwined practices', *Gender, Work and Organization*, 11 (4): 406–429.

Conein, B. and Jacopin, E. (1994) 'Action située et cognition: le savoir en place', *Sociologie du Travail*, 94 (4): 475–500.

Elster, J. (2000) *Ulysse Unbound*. Cambridge: Cambridge University Press.

Fele, G. (2002) *Etnometodologia. Introduzione allo studio delle attività ordinarie*. Roma: Carocci.

Flynn, P. (1991) *The Ethnomethodological Movement*. New York: Mouton de Gruyter.

Fujimura, J., Star, S. and Gerson, E. (1987) 'Metode de recherche en sociologie des sciences: travail, pragmatisme et interactionnisme symbolique', *Cahiers de Recherches Sociologique*, 5: 65–85.

Garfinkel, H. (1967) *Studies in Ethnomethodology*. Englewood Cliffs: Prentice-Hall.

Garfinkel, H. (1986) *Ethnomethodological Studies of Work*. London: Routledge & Kegan Paul.

Gergen, K.J. (1985) The Social Constructionist Movement in moderns psychology, American Psychologist, March 1985. pp. 266–275.

Gherardi, S. (2000) 'Practice-based theorizing on learning and knowing in organizations: an introduction', *Organization*, 7 (2): 211–223.

Gherardi, S. (2001) 'From organizational learning to practice-based knowing', *Human Relations*, 54 (1): 131–139.

Gherardi, S. (2003) 'Introduction to the workshop "Practice-based Studies": current trends and future developments'. Trento, November, 6–7.

Gherardi, S. (2006) *Organizational Knowledge: The Texture of Workplace Learning*. Blackwell, Oxford.

Gibson, J.J. (1979) *The Ecological Approach to Visual Perception*. London: Erlbaum Associates.

Giddens, A. (1976) *New Rules of Sociological Method*. London: Hutchinson.

Giglioli, P.P. (1990) *Rituale, Interazione, Vita Quotidiana*. Bologna: Il Mulino.

Goffman, E. (1971) 'The territories of the self', in E. Goffman (ed.), *Relations in Public: Microstudies of the Public Order*. New York: Harper & Row.

Goodwin, C. (1994) 'Professional vision', in *American Anthropologist*, 96 (3): 606–633.

Haraway, D. (1991) 'Situated knowledges: the science question in feminism and the privilege of partial perspectives', in D. Haraway (ed.), *Simians, Cyborgs and Women: the Reinvention of Nature*. London: Free Association Books. pp. 183–202.

Harding, S. (1986) *The Science Question in Feminism*. Ithaca: Cornell University.

Heath, C. and Button, G. (2002) 'Special issue on workplace studies: editorial introduction', *The British Journal of Sociology*, 53 (2): 157–161.

Heritage, J.C. (1987) 'Ethnomethodology', in A. Giddens and J. Turner (eds), *Social Theory Today*. Standford: Standford University Press. pp. 224–272.

Hutchins, E. (1995) *Cognition in the Wild.* Cambridge, MA: The MIT Press.

Kirsh, D. (1995) 'The intelligent use of space', *Artificial Intelligence*, 73: 36–68.

Knorr-Cetina, K. (1981) *The Manufacture of Knowledge. An Essay on the Constructivist and Contextual Nature of Science.* Oxford: Pergamon Press.

Latour, B. (1987) *Science in Action.* Cambridge, MA: Harvard University Press.

Martin, P.Y. (2003) '"Said & done" vs. "Saying & doing". Gendered practices/practising gender at work', *Gender & Society*, 17.

Mol, A. (1999) 'Ontological politics: a word and some questions', in J. Law and J. Hassard (eds), *Actor Network Theory and After.* Oxford: Blackwell.

Nicotera, F. (1996) *Etnometodologia e azione sociale.* Milano: Prometheus.

Norman, D. (1994) 'Les artefacts cognitifs', in B. Conein, N. Dodier, and L. Thévenot (eds), *Les Objects dans l'Action.* Paris: Edition de l'Ecole des Hautes Etudes en Sciences Sociales, 15–34.

Poggio, B. (2006) Introduction to the special issue 'Gender as Social Practice', *Gender, Work, and Organization.*

Schatzki, T.R. (2001) 'Introduction. Practice theory', in T.R. Schatzki, K. Knorr-Cetina and E. von Savigny (eds), *The Practice Turn in Contemporary Theory.* London and New York: Routledge. pp. 1–14.

Schutz, A. (1962) *Collected Papers I. The Problem of Social Reality.* Nijhoff: The Hague.

Strathern, M. (1991) *Partial Connections.* Savage: Rowan and Littlefield.

Strati, A. (2003) 'Knowing in practice: aesthetic understanding and tacit knowledge', in D. Nicolini, S. Gherardi and D. Yanow (eds), *Knowing in Organizations.* Armonk, NY: M.E. Sharpe, pp. 53–75.

Suchman, L. (1987) *Plans and Situated Action: The Problem of Human-Machine Communication.* Cambridge: Cambridge University Press.

Suchman, L. (1996) 'Constituting shared workspaces', in Y. Engestrom and D. Middleton (eds), *Cognition and Communication at Work.* Cambridge: Cambridge University Press.

Tsoukas, H. and Knudsen, C. (2003) 'Introduction: the need for meta-theoretical reflection in organization theory', in H. Tsoukas and C. Knudsen, *The Oxford Handbook of Organization Theory. Meta-theoretical perspectives.* Oxford: Oxford University Press. pp. 1–36.

Zimmermann, D.H. and Pollner, M. (1970) 'The everyday world as a phenomenon', in J.D. Douglas (ed.), *Understanding Everyday Life.* London: Routledge & Kegan Paul. pp. 80–103.

Yanow, D. (2000) 'Seeing organizational learning: a "Cultural" view', *Organization*, 7 (2): 329–348.

W(h)ither Knowledge Management?

Ulrike Schultze

To customize my teaching materials for a class on knowledge management (KM) targeted at executives in the oil and gas industry, I recently asked the CIO of a local petroleum firm what KM solutions were particularly relevant to his industry and which firms were KM leaders in the industry. He replied that KM had been 'hot' in the late 1990s, at which time British Petroleum presented itself as a KM industry leader. Today, however, nobody in his industry was talking about KM any more. KM was passé. Part of the reason for its demise, he explained, was the lack of evidence that KM added value. And, in the absence of credible ROI information, it was difficult to keep investing in solutions that were not only expensive with respect to software and hardware requirements, but also incredibly labor intensive. KM added to employees' workloads by having knowledge workers contribute to discussion boards and lessons-learned databases, as well as search for insights that they could reuse. Whether this KM-related cost paid off was unclear.

This response did not surprise me; instead, it confirmed what I had suspected for a while. Nevertheless, to justify my interest in (and teaching of) this apparently passé topic, I explained that I separated KM as an organizational 'problem' from KM as a 'solution' or organizing vision (Swanson and Ramiller, 1997), that is, 'a vision *for* organizing that embeds and utilizes information technology in organizational structures and processes' (p. 460, emphasis as per original). KM as an organizational 'problem' represents the daily challenges of creating, organizing, sharing and using knowledge in organizations. KM as an organizing vision is a social representation of the organizational implications of using information technologies like groupware, discussion boards and expertise location systems. While KM as a problem remains a significant challenge for the foreseeable future, KM as an organizing vision appears to be dying in the court of practitioner opinion.

The research on the origins of KM highlights that knowledge and efforts to manage it have always been an implicit aspect of all organizational management (Wiig, 1997). In effect, all management is about managing knowledge relevant to the organization. However, the systematic and explicit management of knowledge – and the development of KM as an organizing vision – gained momentum in the 1990s, buoyed by the confluence of ideational/social (e.g., popularization of the knowledge-centric view of the firm, and the end of the re-engineering movement) and technological forces (e.g., commercialization of Lotus Notes, which combined communication, collaboration and content management features).

Envisaging the future of KM, Prusak (2001) identified two alternative career paths. Either, like re-engineering, KM would be hijacked by sloganeers and snake-oil salesmen, and ultimately be discredited as an initiative that did more harm than good. Or, like the quality movement, KM's technologies and practices would become so integrated in everyday work that they would be embedded as an invisible and implicit part of organizing.

Even though Prusak anticipated that by 2006 we would know which path KM was on, there are indications that KM is traveling down both at the same time. For instance, recent research by Haas and Hansen (2005), which highlights that reliance on KM solutions such as systems containing codified information (e.g., best practices databases) can hurt organizational performance, suggests that KM is moving down the former path.

In contrast, praise for KM solutions that 'bake' knowledge into the everyday workflow systems (Davenport and Glaser, 2002), thus making KM part of a just-in-time, on-demand enterprise infrastructure, suggests that KM is moving down the latter career path.

Down which career path do we want KM to go and why? What role can we play in steering KM down that path? How might we shape KM as an organizational problem and an organizing vision?

REFERENCES

Davenport, T.H., and Glaser, J. (2002) 'Just-in-Time delivery comes to knowledge management', *Harvard Business Review*, 80(7): 107–110.

Haas, M.R. and Hansen, M.T. (2005) 'When using knowledge can hurt performance: the value of organizational capabilities in a management consulting company', *Strategic Management Journal*, 26 (1): 1–24.

Prusak, L. (2001) 'Where did Knowledge Management come from?' *IBM Systems Journal*, 40 (4): 1002–1007.

Swanson, E.B. and Ramiller, N.C. (1997) 'The organizing vision in informatin system innovation', *Organization Science*, 8 (5): 458–474.

Wiig, K.M. (1997) 'Knowledge management: where did it come from and where will it go?', *Expert Systems with Applications*, 13 (1): 1–14.

Indigenous Organizing: Enacting and Updating Indigenous Knowledge

Steven J. Finlay

This chapter theorizes indigenization, or how individuals and organizations, profoundly orient themselves to – and enact – indigenous knowledge (IK) in the face of powerful Western ideologies. While there has been much discussion about colonialization and its harmful effects in general, this chapter offers a unique contribution by showing how two indigenous organizations resist Western ideology. I will introduce two communities, one in New Zealand that is fostering their Mäori knowledge (MK) and one in Scotland, the Iona Community which draws from Celtic knowledge (CK). I present the methods that both communities are using to enact an indigenous organization, and outline a working theory of 'indigenous organizing' that describes how indigenous cultures might ensure the survival of their unique holistic cosmologies.

Social phenomenology is ideally suited to theorize how knowledge is used to enable (legitimize) and disable (de-legitimize)

identity, agency and social action (Berger and Luckmann, 1966; Schutz, 1967, 1970, 1973). Knowledge – applied here in its largest form as a holistic cosmology – is defined as finite providences of meaning which 'work' in local contexts, and is socially derived from teachers, parents and local indigenous leaders. Ethno-methods are used to show how members enact indigenous knowledge in everyday ways (Heritage, 1984). The organization is enacted from local histories, rules and purposes within boundaries. Organizing is situated social action, embedded within local conversations, drawing from distinct cultural and ethnic practices (Clegg and Hardy, 1996; Shafritz and Ott, 1987). This theory of indigenization transcends economic bases of relations, describing complicated 'senses of belonging' (Ralston Saul, 2005: 280) thus providing a positive alternative to theories and practices of globalization (Banerjee and Linstead, 2001; Jaya, 2001; Ralston Saul, 2004, 2005).

THE EFFECTS OF WESTERN KNOWLEDGE

Western knowledge refers to complex globalist practices which operate within the colonial encounter (Friedman, 1994a; Prasad, 2003; Ralston Saul, 2005). Globalist practices universally propose Western knowledge systems of economic development as 'what works', devaluing local knowledge and replacing it with knowledge derived from often-hidden American contexts (Jacques, 1996; Ohmae, 1995; Ralston Saul, 2004, 2005). Western knowledge reaches into the nexus of indigenous cultures replacing IK with Western conceptions, products and symbols (Friedman, 1994a). As a result, indigenous knowledge and identity becomes the 'underdeveloped other' of globalist agendas (Dhaouadi, 1994). Table 3.10.1 summaries some of these effects on the indigenous holes this research focused on.

Postcolonial theorists describe how 'imbrication' fragments and devalues IK and identity while constructing Western knowledges as superior (Prasad, 2003; Rattansi, 1997). Repressive authenticity is a strategy of the West where indigenous peoples are deemed 'inauthentic' in 'modern' context by comparing them to a romantic construction produced by the colonial elite. Here IK is rendered valid only in 'traditional' locations, using 'authentic' means. Thus 'Western' superiority over economic and 'modern' domains is maintained (Wolfe, 1999: 173–181). Through these strategies, globalizing practices continue cultural control over indigenous peoples that colonization began (Banerjee and Linstead, 2001, 2004; Prasad, 2003).

INDIGENOUS KNOWLEDGE AND ORGANIZATIONAL IDENTITY

Indigenous knowledge and identity both emerge from 'conceptions of metaphysical balance and a sacred covenantal relationship between individuals and cosmic forces' (Fischer, 1999: 488). These conceptions

Table 3.10.1

Category	WK component	Impact on indigenous people	Mäori Example	Celtic Example
IK:	Rationalism. Language control: English as 'universal language'.	Devalues IK as 'mythology', science and rationality is 'what works'. Language suppressed.	Tohunga Act makes Mäori knowledge experts illegal, Mäori seen as 'savage' in need of English education. Mäori language legislated against until 1970s.	Celts seen as uncivilized 'Barbarian'; 'feckless and dim' and 'the lazy and backwards North' in need of civilizing. Gaelic language legislated against.
Self:	Consumerism; Private self gain.	Self formed in relation to economy as resource or consumer.	Mäori 'taught' greed by early colonial settlers; Mäori 'taonga' or treasures appropriated for colonial gain.	Clan chiefs eschewed clan obligations in favour of new economic orthodoxy of individual wealth.
Community:	Individualism.	Fragments reciprocal ties. Asserts rights and property of individual.	Mäori land resold as individual holdings. Early vote limited to those who 'owned' land. Tribal ownership negated.	Highlands and Islands communal structures replaced with individual smallholdings.
Earth:	Material resource.	Removes ancient connections to land Creates land as commodity.	Land Wars a result of forced land sales. Many tribal lands sold to colonial settlers.	Highland clearances in Mull and elsewhere cleared crofting culture to make way for more profitable options.

contain 'cultural logics' which are 'generative principles expressed through cognitive schemas that promote inter-subjective continuity, (Fischer, 1999: 474). Organizational identity both shapes, and is shaped by, indigenous knowledge held within a holistic cosmology. Celtic knowledge (CK) underpins worship and missionary activities relevant to a Christian community, whereas Mäori knowledge underpins research and education activities relevant to a university. While each case uses their indigenous knowledge differently, they do share similarities in how and why indigenous knowledge is enacted across the organization. The following case histories sketch these dynamics, beginning with The Iona Community.

Celtic Knowledge in Scotland: The Iona Community

St Columba, the Irish Monk, settled on Iona in 563. His missions to the Scottish mainland brought Celtic Christianity, literacy and crofting skills to the Picts and Scotti, the tribal peoples settled in family Kingdoms throughout the Britain of the time. Even then Iona was central to the nascent Scottish imagination (Anderson, 1983). Celtic Christianity is one of the earliest expressions of indigenous British belief systems (Bradley, 1994, 1999). Despite Viking raids, the Dark Ages, the Reformation and later influences of Western knowledge, indigenous knowledge survived in the oral traditions of the outer Isles of Scotland, to be gathered by Carmichael's famous Carmina Gadelica in the 1890s (MacInnes, 1994). The Iona Community has its roots in Govan, Glasgow and the industrial depression of the 1930s. George MacLeod, a parish minister, sought a 'new experiment' in urban mission to the poor. He chose the ruined Benedictine Abbey on Iona in 1938 as a site for this experiment, where newly trained ministers and volunteer workers began rebuilding. This renewal programme extended onto the mainland, where workers were sent to work for justice and peace, rebuilding community in poverty stricken cities often filled with economic migrants from the

highland clearances. The community today has some 200 members and 1400 associates based mostly in Scotland, wider Britain and beyond, all continuing to enact the purposes of 'finding new ways to touch the hearts of all' combining prayer and politics, work and worship within the community concerns. The Island centres of Camas, The MacLeod Centre and Iona Abbey remain places of hospitality and welcome to over 100 guests per week who come for personal reflection, healing or to taste the community life Iona advocates.

In forming the community MacLeod drew from the Celtic imaginary of Columba and the holistic cosmology of Celtic knowledge to underpin the missionary work of a Celtic Christian community, as MacLeod's original language shows:

> how up to date was the enthusiasm of the early Celtic church to infuse with the Christian spirit every department of life; how like the most modern foreign mission station was the early Celtic community with its expert craftsmen, its expert agriculturalist, its educationalist and doctor as well as its Anmchara and presiding minister. How much again, is the world not in need of that sense of Universal Church, which was so profound a belief in our Roman days. (Ferguson, 1988: 60)

MacLeod's vision and strategy sought practical solutions to poverty and urban squalor, while relocating IK in the modern context. He also imparted a profound connection to the land and the sense of the sacredness which was inspired by IK:

> George tried to put a Celtic vision in the 20th century but aligned with a kind of second sight that he had … I think that he loved Scotland, he was empowered by the land and the sacredness of the people, I think that is Celtic. These people [Celtic monks] did that and they've empowered us like his wee group going in 1938 to try and look and see if they could start the rebuilding. (Miller Interview, 2003)

In enacting Celtic knowledge across the organization in everyday ways, the Rule has evolved as a major sense-making device (Heritage, 1984). This is a five-fold set of promises members make and affirm each year. They include: daily prayer and bible-reading; sharing and accounting for the use of money; planning and accounting for the use of time; acting for justice and peace in society, and meeting with and accounting to each other.

The leadership encourages members to understand the Rule as containing the guiding vision of the community, as well as providing accountability: 'the rule is a vision statement; it's not supposed to be an arrival point' (Miller Interview 2003). However, The Iona Community's use of CK, and rotational leadership style is constructed by critics as 'inauthentic':

> [the academics tell us] anything Celtic can only be really claimed through speaking one of the Celtic languages. Also traditional Celtic organizations were very hierarchical. But George MacLeod was educated as a lowlander despite himself coming from a highland tradition. As such he was schooled at Winchester, and was a very public school Victorian gentleman, so the Iona Community has more of the lowland traditions, it tries to be more democratic and egalitarian, with leadership based on open elections and the position held on a rotational seven year term. (Galloway Interview 2003)

Advocates for Celtic knowledge continuities within the community are also aware of challenges to the authenticity of this position:

> when I very consciously began to recover and dig more deeply and appropriate within [the Celtic] tradition, I was aware that one of the misunderstandings and criticisms that we were going to get was that there was no such thing as the Celtic tradition. That it was romanticism. (Newell Interview, 2003)

In 2003 the leadership also carried out a review of strategic priorities. Here the family groups were asked to prioritize aspects of the Community which remained valid. From this Kathy Galloway, the current leader, describes the cohesive function that the Rule plays in the life of the members, suggesting how 'Celtic' or 'Benedictine' accountability structures guide and direct action in the life-projects of the members: 'In our review of strategic priorities the Rule is most central to the life of the members, it is the unifying factor, it is like the spine that holds everything up' (Galloway Interview 2003).

The Rule itself does not adapt. But its application to each context does require the rethinking of how it should apply, indicating at a cognitive level the ongoing and interpretive processes at work between knowledge and context (Heritage, 1984; Holstein and Gubrium, 1994), as Kathy Galloway illustrates: 'The Rule of the community operates in widely divergent contexts, one member is Dean of a University College, others are shop workers or teachers or artists, they take the rule and work it in each context' (Galloway Interview, 2003). The Rule provides the vehicle by which CK directs action in a variety of local contexts, up to and including rebuilding the Scottish national project:

> It has to do with being touched by the possibility of all things being made new and the vision of a better world. People see the life, the structures, the commitment and Rule of the Iona community as a way of being part of that. It has to do with playing a part in reshaping the life of the church and the life of the nation. (Member Interview, 2003)

Mäori Knowledge in New Zealand

Te Wananga o [the University of] Raukawa in Otaki, New Zealand, emerged from a 25 year programme begun in 1975 whose purpose was to rebuild tribal material and spiritual resources. Led by Professor Whatarangi Winiata, the 'Whakatupuranga Rua Mano: Generation 2000' programme sought to reverse Western knowledge effects on Mäori after 150 years of pakeha contact (settler New Zealanders). These effects included: low language (Te Reo) levels; impoverished marae (tribal meeting houses); poor education levels; poor knowledge of Mäori customs and practices in the youth, amongst others.

The university's purpose was also conceived as a new 'experiment': a centre for higher learning dedicated to the recovery and embellishment of Matauranga Mäori (or Mäori knowledge) and the empowerment of the Mäori people of the ART confederation. The university began in 1981 with two students and voluntary staff. Today it has some 1800 + students with 5 certificates, 21 diplomas, 13 degrees, 5 post graduate diplomas, 6 post graduate courses and a PhD programme taught by a mix of full time and voluntary staff on site and at Marae around the region.

The university is a reformulation of an ancient institution, the whare wananga, the most senior of which is Rangiatea (University Charter, 2003: 1). TWoR's original purpose uses MK to enable higher learning for the betterment of the local Mäori communities. Winiata's strategy enables Mäori knowledge:

> a Mäori worldview won't stand still – it will be in a constant state of change, enhancement and refinement ... we find the links and concepts from earlier generations ... a place like this can add to that enrichment and refinement. (Whatarangi Winiata interview, 2003)

As an organizational strategy Mäori knowledge underpins the philosophy and practice of the institution. However, members challenged the validity of Mäori knowledge to operate at the organizational level:

> for a long time Matauranga Mäori [Mäori knowledge] has been ringfenced inside the Marae, and once you start talking about Matauranga Mäori being in an institution like this people start saying 'isn't that stuff just for the Marae' how come you're talking about it here .... (Pakeke Winiata Interview, 2003)

Some members went so far as to insinuate that Western knowledge was more legitimate: 'what use will Matauranga Mäori be to students once they leave the wananga? They need to be taught how to make it in the real world, not just on the Marae' (Member Interview, 2003).

To overcome these challenges and enact the strategy, the leadership encourages actors to use indigenous knowledge in expansive areas. At a leadership hui [meeting] in 2003 Winiata gave each department autonomy to define and select the areas IK underpinned, and to report accordingly. For each department a paper was written in consultation to evidence and describe applications of IK in each context:

> I was asked to write that [paper] last year by Whatarangi Winiata. The paper sets out the fundamental philosophies or values that TWoR ought to have, basically you take a Mäori worldview and it produces a set of kaupapa – principles, values philosophies, out of which grow the operational practices, the methods, the tikanga, the policies, that are aligned to these kaupapa. (Staff interview, 2003)

Members reflects how using MK to explain behaviour expands its domain of application, even if the process of knowledge creation is at times challenging, to maintain authenticity with earlier generations:

> there is no doubt that Mataraunga Mäori is a body of knowledge expanded through creation of explanations, when you have this fairly tenuous attachment to a worldview it does make you a little bit nervous about the prospect of being able to create things and being confident that you are being consistent. (Staff interview, 2003)

Like the Celtic 'Rule', 'tikanga' [Mäori principles] guides how indigenous knowledge is enacted in each context. Most members find this 'directed' freedom within the guidance of 'tikanga' helps strengthen and nourish Mäori knowledge, rather than an imposition of power which limits the functioning of the organization: 'Mäori knowledge has been facilitated greatly by having freedom to develop courses that nurture Matauranga Mäori' (Huia Winiata Interview, 2003). To enact the strategy, 'tikanga' guides how departments themselves account for how MK is enacted across TWoR, in this case ükaipö-tanga [a place of belonging] is evidenced by the following Tikanga:

Tikanga

- arrangements that foster a sense of importance, belonging and contribution;
- work related stress management practices;
- commitment to a higher purpose of the survival of Mäori;
- prioritising stimulating exciting activity;
- maximising student retention and completion. (Guiding Principles of TWoR)

For students at the university, these principles are enacted in life projects to build indigenous community, tribal and national projects:

> attending institutions like this that really keeps your identity, your Mäoritanga that's where I want to end up ... at your iwi [tribe] I think it starts with your family take it to your whanau first from whanau to hapu to iwi then to your other iwi. (Student Interview, 2003)

Table 3.10.2 summaries the Celtic and Mäori indigenous knowledges.

Table 3.10.2

IK	Celtic K (CK)	Māori K (MK)
Conception of personhood: Sacred notions of self, developed in deep relationships to sacred community and land.	'To be creatures in the covenant, to be citizens of heaven, it is not only to be required to be in right relationship with our own human kind, but with the whole creation', (Galloway Sermon, 2003)	'Whakapapa (geneology) links the people together and within Māoridom you can whakapapa back to the land itself … Manaatua, mana whenua, mana tanagata power from God, power from land, power from people, that's all linked in together'. (Staff interviews, 2003)
Conception of land: Stewardship of sacred resources all held within a holistic cosmology which guides action (Fischer, 1999).	'[The Celts held] a conviction of the goodness of the whole creation, not goodness in a moral sense, but ontologically, the goodness of being. All is good, not by virtue of its value to others, or by its resourcefulness or its efficiency, but simply in the fact of its being. Justice is also eco-justice'. (Galloway Sermon, 2003)	'An indigenous person is a person who has the rights and responsibilities of kaitiakitanga and they've acquired that through whakapapa. Kaitiakitanga is guardianship, they don't own it, they just look after it, and enhance it, and pass it on if they can, if not in a better form than they had it, at least not in a worse form for succeeding generation' (Staff Interviews, 2003)
Conception of indigenous: Continuity of guardianship traced back to ancient settlement or deep communion with the land.	'Indigenous has to do with a rootedness to place and to its history… it comes out of people's sense of being grounded in this culture in this place in this time, and feeling for what throbs at the heart of community or at the heart of nature and calls out for expression'. (Bell Interview, 2003)	'Indigenous for me is about our sacred connection to the land … our marae, our Maonga [Mountain] … we say we are 'tangata whenua, the people of the land'… we are the first people here … the people of the land. We're born from the land'. 'I've been told stories of our old people and that they can whakapapa back to the land, to the sacred grasses and rocks of their land … that's what the people of the land is'. (Staff Interviews, 2003)

ENACTING THE INDIGENOUS ORGANIZATION

Indigenous organizing defines how indigenous knowledge is enacted and updated across the organization, overcoming Western knowledge domination. Enacting indigenous knowledge faces ongoing challenges from Western knowledge, carrying implications for organizational and individual identity. In the face of claims of repressive authenticity – often held by indigenous peoples themselves – indigenous organizing is achieved from 'authentic' IK which is the inter-subjective experience of indigenous actors in the face of power relations (Friedman, 1994a, 1994b; Gunew, 1994). Indigenous knowledge continuities thus provide indigenous peoples

with authentic organizational knowledge, recovered as working knowledge in their own historic contexts, and revalidated through expansive application in the current. From the first each organization is permeated by profound connection to indigenous knowledge.

Indigenous organizing as a process enacts indigenous knowledge through each component of the organization, as shown in Fig 3.10.1. Organizational identities are legitimized by having a lineage from historic indigenous institutions. Each organization's agency as purpose directs the expansive use of indigenous knowledge to redress impacts from Western knowledge and build community. Leader's strategies use sensemaking rules to help members enact and account for IK in use across the organization

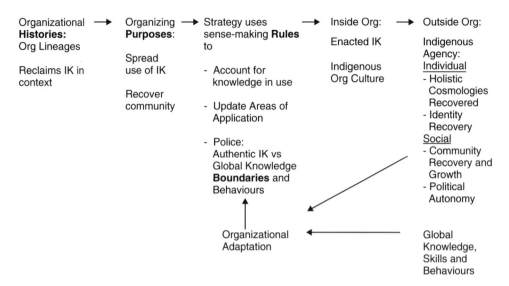

Figure 3.10.1   Enacting the Indigenous Organization

as a whole, fulfilling the purposes in changing contexts as well as building strategic
coherence (Heritage, 1984). IK thus produces
values and philosophies which guide action
and help form collective identity and culture.

Management processes encourage actors to
expand the application of indigenous knowledge to engage with changes in the broader
context. As a result, emerging applications
of indigenous knowledge are proposed. This
autonomy enables members to assess the
validity of IK for themselves, providing
reality definition at local levels and evidencing
the ongoing validity of 'authentic' indigenous
knowledge in the face of Western knowledge
challenges.

Outside the organization purposes are
enacted individually as indigenous agency.
Indigenous knowledge directs the life projects
of individuals, providing stable vehicles for
identity recovery within recovered holistic cosmologies (Friedman, 1994a; Ralston
Saul, 2005). Taken together these projects
rebuild community in the face of Western
knowledge domination, up to and including
projects enabling political autonomy. Within
the broader context WK skills and expertise
are adopted by the organization. However,
sense-making rules police WK and behaviours

which either damage or fragment individual
or organizational identity. This iterative cycle
of organizing is renewed through engagement
with, and feedback from, organizational
members in each context.

RECOVERING INDIGENOUS ORGANIZING

As a theory, indigenous organizing moves
from the ongoing effects of Western knowledge and towards the orientation of local
ancient knowledge, explaining how indigenous knowledge and identity is enacted and
updated. As Table 3.10.3 shows Indigenization encourages the healing and reordering
of identity within holistic cosmologies and
connections rendered separate by Western
knowledge as Table 3.10.3 shows. (Friedman,
1994a).

Indigenous knowledge effects are summarized in Table 3.10.4 at individual,
organizational and social levels, showing
both Western knowledge effects and Celtic
(CK) and Mäori (MK) knowledge responses.
This evidence suggests Western knowledge
remains a pervasive influence, but one
overcome by the international enaction of

Table 3.10.3   Indigenous organizing – Using IK to overcome WK effects

Level	WK Effect	IK Response	Outcome: Enacted IK
Individual	**Identity put downs**	**CK: Belief in people**	**Identity recovery and pride**
Knowledge, Experience and Agency	M: 'When I was at school I was labelled as a troublemaker and told the only thing I'd be good for was prison'.	*MK:* **Whakapapa:** geneology Whakatauaki Kia û ki tôu kâwai tûpuna Kia mâtauria ai I ahu mai koe i whea E anga ana hoki koe ki whea Trace out your ancestral stem So it may be known Where you have come from And in which direction you are going	*CK :* 'It is an experience involving basic issues of identity…'. (Shanks, 1999: 84, 87)
	C: 'Everything I've done is because of Iona… You're never told that on the mainland.. It's just constant put downs…'		*MK:* 'You got to show your identity you can't hide it. That's always going to be a part of your life'.
	Alcohol and drug abuse	*MK:* **Boundaries** 'te kawa te ako is a requirement that students avoid activities which will impede their ability to learn and our ability to teach and you can see that drugs and alcohol do that.'	**Community connection re-established.** IK instils moral and ethical boundaries in context of community. Individual agency works for community growth:
	MK: 'We were beginning to have difficulties with drugs and alcohol'		
	CK: 'Before I came here I thought of Scottish people and Scotland, as like, as a bunch of alkies (alcoholics) and druggies, sort of a bunch of no hopers'		*CK:* 'individual fulfilment is to be discovered only in community… that self development cannot be achieved apart from a concern for one another and the world around us'. (Shanks, 1999:. 84, 87)
	Individualism	CK: **Boundaries** individual discipline and accountability: 'The discipline of chastity in one's private life is not easy. We do expect a kind of chastity from people in our life. The chastity of understanding that our indulgence in sex, or alcohol, or drugs will be seen and noted'	*MK:* 'its given them a link back to their marae. Giving energy back to the marae…'
	M: 'My nephews and nieces next to my kids they're like, they can work hard they can make lots of money but they can't bother to sit down and have, be a whanau and just be…hug each other….'		
	Language loss	*MK:* **Te Reo: Language recovery**	*MK:* **Language recovery and use** 'We've got the reo now and we pass it on to our tamariki [children]'
	M: 'I didn't have much of a Mäori upbringing our parents didn't want us to learn much of that.'	'Each succeeding generation have refined that knowledge-modified it – but the links remain – and the language is an essential part of the link'	
	C: 'Even after Gaelic was banned, it then became the uncivilised language. If you wanted to get on you had to learn English. People would discourage their children from speaking Gaelic'		
Organizational:	**Repressive authenticity**	*MK:* **Aronga Model:** Kaupapa directed by Tikanga: Manaakitanga; Rangatiratanga; Whakawhanaungatanga; etc	**Authentic IK expressed,** and updated in multiple contexts Leadership encourages autonomy which enables members to connect to and learn from context Purposes reworked for changing contexts
Strategy and Management	IK is 'inauthentic' when used in organizational setting.	*CK :* **'The Rule':** incarnational theology; integrated spirituality	
Social:	**Poverty Community and land fragmentation**	**Members Projects:**	**Autonomy within nation state structures**
Agency	Colonial / Imperial Nation State Ongoing IK + identity devaluations	*MK:* Iwi and Hapu development *CK:* Community rebuilding programme	*MK:* Survival of Mäori as people and people as Mäori *CK:* Enabling Scottish community recovery

Table 3.10.4   Indigenization effects

Category	IK	Impact on indigenous peoples
Indigenous Cosmology:	Recovers cosmology as working knowledge.	Worldview regains 'nobility' and pride; encourages language recovery.
Self:	Sacred essence of being in relation to cosmology; community and creation.	Creates ethical and moral framework for behaviour; lessens negative behaviours.
Community:	Source of self identity including family continuity; location of status.	Builds connection to and strength of community.
Earth:	Guardians and stewards of creation. Identity profoundly connected to place.	Relation of self and community held in relation to place and cosmology.

indigenous knowledge, which enables community recovery and growth. Ralston Saul proposes Western knowledge is losing both the power and appeal to explain or predict large scale notions of progress. Instead, new challenges are before us:

> The challenge today may be that we are now not only at the end of the globalism period but also at the end of Western rationalism and its obsession with clear linear structures on every subject. Perhaps we are living the beginnings of a major rebalancing in which other cultures with more complex ideas of what makes up a society are moving to the fore. (Ralston Saul, 2005: 278)

As for the end of globalization, it may be some time yet before the effects of Western knowledge subside in the lives of indigenous peoples. It remains for organizational researchers to examine these competing knowledge claims, and this theory for themselves, but I suggest rich research agendas and journeys of self-discovery await those who do:

> It is a journey that heals and takes us deeply into the treasure that we were born into … the primary image of indigenous is an emerging from within. It is a sort of flowering of what is deeply rooted within us, not what is imposed on the outside. (Newell Interview, 2003)

Given the commitment of indigenous leaders and communities, one may expect this knowledge – and hence these communities – to be around for some time yet, despite the pressures they face. Regardless of whether the grand claims of Western knowledge recede or just change form, indigenous communities can mitigate their worst effects, survive and flourish. Using processes described herein, seeds of ancient knowledge have been nurtured and enacted in many changing contexts so far. For those willing to explore

wider horizons, much indigenous knowledge awaits discovery by us: not as colonial pillagers, but as novices seeking instruction in the many worlds of indigenous organizing.

REFERENCES

Anderson, B. (1983) *Imagined Communities: Reflections on the Origin and Spread of Nationalism.* London: Verso.

Banerjee, S.B., and Linstead, S. (2001) 'Globalization, multiculturalism and other fictions: Colonialism for the new millennium', *Organization,* 8 (4): 683–722.

Banerjee, S. B., and Linstead, S. (2004). 'Masking subversion: Neocolonial embeddedness in anthropological accounts of indigenous management', *Human Relations,* 57 (2): 221–247.

Berger, P. and Luckmann, T. (1966) *The Social Construction of Reality.* Middlesex: Penguin.

Bradley, I. (1994) *The Celtic Way.* London: Pauline Press.

Bradley, I. (1999) *Celtic Christianity: Making Myths and Chasing Dreams.* New York: St Martin's Press.

Clegg, S. and Hardy, C. (1996) 'Introduction', in S. Clegg, C. Hardy and W. Nord (eds), *Handbook of Organization Studies.* London: Sage.

Dhaouadi, M. (1994) 'Capitalism, global humane development and the other underdevelopment', in L. Sklair (ed.), *Capitalism and Development.* London: Routledge. pp. 140–165.

Ferguson, R. (1988) *Chasing the Wild Goose.* London: Collins.

Fischer, E. (1999) 'Cultural logic and Mayan identity', *Current Anthropology,* 40 (4): 473–499.

Friedman, J. (1994a) *Cultural Identity and Global Process.* London: Sage.

Friedman, J. (1994b) *Consumption and Identity.* Chur: Harwood Academic Publishers.

Gunew, S. (1994) *Framing Marginality: Multicultural Literary Studies.* Melbourne: Paul and Co. Pub. Consortium.

Heritage, J. (1984) *Garfinkel and Ethnomethodology.* Oxford: Polity Press.

Holstein, J.A. and Gubrium, J.F. (1994) 'Phenomenology, ethnomethodology, and interpretive practice', in N. Denzin and Y. Lincoln (eds), *Handbook of Qualitative Research.* New York: Sage.

Jacques, R. (1996) *Manufacturing the Employee.* London: Sage.

Jaya, P. (2001) 'Do we really know and profess? Decolonizing management knowledge', *Organization,* 8 (2): 227–233.

Kuhn, T.S. (1996) *The Structure of Scientific Revolutions* (3rd edn). Chicago, IL: University of Chicago Press.

Lincoln, Y. and Guba, E.G. (1985) *Naturalistic Enquiry.* London: Sage.

MacInnes, J. (1994) 'Preface', in A. Carmichael (ed.), *Carmina Gadelica: Hymns and Incantations.* London: Redwood Books.

Ohmae, K. (1995) *The Evolving Global Economy.* Harvard: HBS.

Prasad, A. (2003) *Postcolonial Theory and Organizational Analyses: A Critical Engagement.* New York: Palgrave Macmillan.

Rattansi, A. (1997) Postcolonialism and its discontents. *Economy and Society,* 26 (4): 480–500.

Ralston Saul, J. (2004) 'The collapse of globalism', *Harpers' Magazine, March,* 33–43.

Ralston Saul, J. (2005) *The Collapse of Globalism and the Reinvention of the World.* London: Atlantic.

Schutz, A. (1967) *The Phenomenology of the Social World.* New York: North Western University Press.

Schutz, A. (1970) *On Phenomenology and Social Relations.* Chicago: The University of Chicago Press.

Schutz, A. (1973) *The Structures of the Lifeworld.* London: North Western University Press.

Shafritz, J.M. and Steven Ott, J. (1987) *Classics of Organizational Theory.* Chicago: The Dorsey Press.

Shanks, N. (1999) *Iona – God's Energy: The Spirituality and Vision of the Iona Community.* London: Hodder & Stoughton.

Wineera, A. (2003) *Te Wänanga-o-Raukawa Charter 2003.* Retrieved December 5th 2007 from http://www.twor.ac.nz/docs/pdfs/Charter-English.pdf

Wolfe, P. (1999) *Settler Colonialism and the Transformation of Anthropology.* London: Cassell.

'Organizational' Behavior is Largely Tribal Behavior

Blake E. Ashforth

Much research in the field of organizational behavior focuses on the relationship between the individual and the organization. For example, research regarding organizational commitment and organizational identification focuses on the attachment of the individual to the organization, and research on organizational culture and organizational climate focuses on the milieu within which the individual operates. Such research clearly indicates that the organizational context matters and that individuals are capable of feeling and articulating a connection to that context.

But how does something as abstract as an organization come to be known to the individual? The answer, I argue, is that one's understanding of the abstract is, for the most part, inductively and socially constructed from *grounded* experiences – from concrete events and interactions involving specific people in specific locations at specific times. That understanding becomes visceral and richly nuanced – becomes *real* – through countless episodes over time in localized settings, peopled with familiar faces (Ashforth et al., 2007). In short, the lived experience that informs understanding is essentially and necessarily *tribal* – a term that conveys the primal quality of local attachments. Whether a workgroup, department, occupation, friendship clique, or network, tribes are localized collectives in which one enacts the organization; tribes are not only particularized (comprised of specific individuals with whom one regularly interacts and comes to know reasonably well), but proximal or immediate (vs. the more distal organization), exclusive (vs. inclusive), and concrete (vs. general). These qualities render tribes highly salient and meaningful. Moreover, the impact of the organizational milieu – its cultural initiatives, human resource management practices, senior leadership pronouncements, organizational development interventions, and so on – is largely mediated by one's tribes. It is one's supervisor who enacts many HR prescriptions; it's one's peer group that decides whether an OD intervention is worthwhile or should be sabotaged. Indeed, when an organization's espoused values, beliefs, and norms are contradicted by localized practices, it is the latter that newcomers usually defer to.

Why is all of this so important? So much of our theorizing and empirical work assumes that the primary link is between the individual and the organization rather than individual's tribes. This direct-link assumption leads to misspecified relationships and misleading conclusions. Let me offer two examples. First, research on organizational identification has examined myriad causes and consequences of individuals defining themselves in terms of their organizational membership. And yet research suggests that individuals tend to identify more strongly with their workgroups and occupations than with their organization *per se* (Ashforth and Johnson, 2001). Except under special circumstances (e.g., external threat, unique organizational identity), the visceral tribe resonates more deeply than the abstract organization. Second, most research on psychological contracts in organizational settings assumes that individuals develop 'only one psychological contract – with the organization as a whole' (Shore et al., 2004: 300). As Shore et al. argue, however, individuals develop psychological contracts with their teams and their leaders, begging the question of 'who represents the organization in the EOR [employee-organization relationship]'? (p. 303) It seems likely that the 'organization' is at least partially abstracted from such localized relationships. One's manager may represent and even personify the organization: if the manager breaks the psychological contract, then the organization has broken the psychological contract.

A realization that organizational behavior is largely tribal behavior raises many provocative research questions. For example: how do supervisors and coworkers mediate and moderate the impact of wider organizational dynamics on the individual? To what extent is organizational commitment a pale reflection of more grounded and meaningful attachments? How do individuals socially construct an understanding of the organization as a discrete entity? What kinds of grounded events most strongly shape perceptions of the organization's culture and climate? How do experiences with a particularly salient coworker or supervisor shape impressions of the organization? In short, research needs to examine how localized relationships affect one's relationship with the organization as a whole.

Localized episodes and interactions and the relationships that flow from them are, from the individual's point of view, the essence of the organization (cf. Weick, 1979). Knowing is in the particulars. And as environmental turbulence continues to flatten hierarchies, erode formal job descriptions, and encourage project work and lateral information flows, the individual's locus of interaction – and attention – is likely to continue shifting from the vertical to the horizontal. Although turbulence also means that the membership of the tribes may change frequently, the tribes remain the locus for much of what we mislabel as organizational behavior.

REFERENCES

Ashforth, B.E. and Johnson, S.A. (2001) 'Which hat to wear? The relative salience of multiple identities in organizational contexts', in M.A. Hogg and D.J. Terry (eds), *Social Identity Processes in Organizational Contexts*. Philadelphia: Psychology Press. pp. 31–48.

Ashforth, B.E., Sluss, D.M. and Harrison, S.H. (2007) 'Socialization in organizational contexts', in G.P. Hodgkinson and J.K. Ford (eds), *International Review of Industrial and Organizational Psychology*. Chichester: Wiley. In press.

Shore, L.M., Tetrick, L.E., Taylor, M.S., Coyle Shapiro, J.A.-M., Liden, R.C., McLean Parks, J., Morrison, E.W., Porter, L.W., Robinson, S.L., Roehling, M.V., Rousseau, D.M., Schalk, R., Tsui, A.S., and Van Dyne, L. (2004) 'The employee-organization relationship: A timely concept in a period of transition', in J.J. Martocchio (ed.), *Research in Personnel and Human Resources Management*. Amsterdam: Elsevier. Vol. 23, pp. 291–370.

Weick, K.E. (1979) *The Social Psychology of Organizing*. Reading, MA: Addison-Wesley. (2nd edn).

3.11

Un-gendering Organization

Stephen Linstead and Alison Pullen

INTRODUCTION

Gender is now widely acknowledged as being an important part of our analyses of organization. This is a result of the absorption of a powerful and extensive body of theoretical development, epistemological and political critique, empirical analysis, methodological innovations, and practical social and organizational improvements, influenced in particular by four decades of feminist scholarship. Yet this is a position only recently achieved and still subject to many blindnesses and omissions, particularly in mainstream work. So it may seem paradoxical that we are about to offer an argument, not for completing the process of gendering organization that we celebrate, but for undoing the process, for moving beyond the limitations of existing conceptions of gender towards *ungendering*.

The notion of 'un'doing or 'un'gendering is not new. Burrell (1997) made a similar call for 'un' or 'de' sexing in *Pandemonium*; Brewis and Linstead (2000) argued for a 'heterotics' of organization; Butler (2004) devotes a whole book to the process of *Undoing Gender*; Lorber (2000) calls for a 'feminist degendering movement' which collapses binaries, and Pullen and Knights

(2007: 505) note that 'doing or undoing gender or any other social relation is not particularly new (Game, 1991; Lorraine, 1990)'. But as our argument unfolds, it will be clear that what we are offering is not a rejection of the insights afforded by gender analysis, but a way of realizing their potential at a deeper level, informed by the latest advances in philosophical thought including those of much-misunderstood postfeminism. As such, gender serves as a conceptual ladder that we kick over when we have reached the next elevation – a necessary tool that should not be allowed to become a constraint on future thought.

Mainstream organization theory is typically presented as gender*less* (Linstead, 2000). However, management and organizational life is an inescapably *embodied* and therefore also a *gendered* experience, an experience that is different for men and women. The study of gender difference has highlighted critical flaws in biologically based and essentialist views of the nature of men and women and their effects on how we think and act organizationally. Major developments in social and organizational theory have led to the widespread view of gender as socially constructed (Gherardi, 1995) rather than biologically given. We argue for a move beyond viewing gender as a social construction, but still considering it to be a social process, which is both organized and shapes our sense of social formal and informal organization. As a view of gender, this is too *static* (see also Linstead et al., 2005) because gender emerges and changes in a *dynamic* between a variety of features and forms of masculinity and femininity, which grow alongside each other. A changing and dynamic gender identity transcends its roles in constant becoming: it becomes *genderful* – so expansive and inclusive in its myriad gender alignments that it cannot be aligned or consigned within gender limits, as everything is recognized as a form of gender; or it may become *ungendered*, where gender is dissipated, overlain by and completely absorbed into so many other alignments (i.e. as a dimension of them) that it ceases to function as a category. In staying in motion, in change, it resists those definitions that fix and name it and thus make it one thing or the other. Gender is not the outcome or consequence of a performance but is the *process of the performance* – it's not what you do, it's the way that you do it. Here the 'I' as subject does not possess gender – it acts as a site for gender, which dynamically 'possesses' it (like a haunted house). Yet although gender is no longer seen as the fixed property of individuals, the alternative of viewing it in terms of performativity, where it is the outcome of linguistic and social performances in turn defined by what they achieve (whether agentic or structural, conscious or unconscious) unnecessarily limits the possibilities of thinking multiplicity. We propose something more.

In this chapter we shift from theorizing gender as a social construction that relies on the idea of gender as a dualism to proposing that gender is rhizomatic, an approach which goes beyond binary thinking and regards gender as *multiplicity*. Our retheorizing hinges on one core philosophical and psychological concept understood as the 'motor' for social action – desire – and three core Deleuzian concepts – multiplicity,

becoming, and rhizomes – each of which has a particular and not always obvious acceptance which we will outline briefly before we begin our critique. *Desire* we will discuss in detail shortly. However, in doing this we need to question some of the existing interpretations of terms such as multiplicity and fluidity, redefining them in terms of the thought of Gilles Deleuze and Felix Guattari. *Multiplicity* is conventionally used to indicate multiple units or qualities, identifiable as separate and numerous. This type of multiplicity is extensive, comprising several things that are distinct but may be linked under one category, like the ages of a population. However, there is also an intensive multiplicity which looks at the different processes at work within an apparently integral body. This we might consider, for example, in terms of the different experiences a person has in a day and contains in their emotional memory – happiness, frustration, achievement, love, boredom, pain, motivation – all leaving their immediate mark and remaining without fading away before the other experiences crowd in, leaving a complex often of contradictory feelings. This takes our idea of gender from that of a mode of *being* to recognizing it as a form of *becoming*, to revealing the ultimate implication of the lack of a positive end of the process of becoming as *unbecoming*, and of distinctive gender identity as *gender imperceptibility* which is both corporeal and subjective and yet beyond binary opposition and dialectics (Linstead and Pullen, 2006). But we do offer a health warning – these are radical arguments, and we must proceed gently and with all due caution.

In what follows we consider two alternative ontologies of desire, conceived of as basic social motivation, that can underpin processes of gender identity formation: desire as lack, wish or collection, and desire as force, proliferation, or dispersion. It is desire as lack that has dominated both social and academic formulations of gender, and of organization, and which has led to a privileging of conceptualizations of identity as unity, individuality, molarity, and cohesion. Molarity is a term for processes of aggregation or bringing together disparate elements into structures or institutions – of which gender is one. The terms masculine and feminine each cover a wide variety of tendencies, characteristics and behaviors that are not always compatible. We will then consider two responses to biological essentialism that traverse these forms of desire to be different formulations of multiplicity. First, *multiplicity of sameness,* which still rests on desire as lack and conceives identity as unifying, although it offers a weak social constructionist version of this unity by incorporating difference as varieties of available types of masculinity or femininity. Second, *multiplicity of difference and dispersion*, where play becomes fully ludic and nomadic and the molar boundaries of gender and identity as cohesive concepts are eroded, revealing them as aggregates. It is significant that molar structures, being aggregates, are subject to wearing down, dissolution and instability (Thanem and Linstead, 2006). We then develop Deleuze and Guattari's (1987) concept of the rhizome as a means of representing this multiplicity in action, emphasizing its character as comprising heterogeneous connections between fragments, constantly adding to their connectivity across diverse domains in a proliferation of processes rather than a multiplicity of singularities. The ceaseless connectivity of the rhizome is like the behaviour of particles, and is therefore 'molecular', subject to connection and reconnection with other particles. Before this we will discuss the process of desire in rethinking gender multiplicity.

DESIRE

In this section we analyse the role of desire in rethinking the multiplicity of subjectivity. To do this we take Cooper's (2001: 26–7) discussion of desire as it relates to identity and identity work as being central. Cooper argues that human beings are themselves incomplete – the existence of others in alterity (defined here as otherness – see Czarniawska this volume) confirms this – and that self-image can only persist if it is *recovered* from a remaking process involving human

bodies, their parts and non-human part objects which are the basic raw material for the production and reproduction of society and culture. Desire is an energy which depends on dispersion and loss in order to be renewed – it reassembles identity by collection or recollection and simultaneously disperses self-identity (and recognizes that dispersion) because every moment of differentiation of self from other recognizes a similarity of self-in-other, an alterity that is not radical. Bersani and Dutoit (1993: 75–6) argue that identity is constituted by repetition out of the 'placeless relational mobility' of dispersion, but also that 'there is no moment of self-identification that is not also self-multiplication or dispersal'. Desire then is an autonomous process of collection-dispersion, a play of convertibility from connection to connection, exchange to exchange, a desire for dispersion. Desire as lack, wish, fulfilment or even discourse displays the features of collection, seeking specificity, locatability, meaning, and significance. The form of desire which we describe as proliferation in contrast seeks diffusion, its own generalization by linking itself to others, and the transcendence of the particular. By arguing for desire as proliferation and dispersion, desire as collection/lack does not disappear, as the two processes are irreducible and implicated in each other. Collection/lack circulates in mutuality in the diffuse space of dispersion/proliferation, bricolating the assemblages of identity within the meshworks of the rhizome. We will return to gender as rhizome based on a conceptualization of desire as both collection and dispersal, but first we will discuss our first critique of multiplicity, starting with Braidotti's feminist contribution to thinking multiplicity in gender theorizing which critiques essentialist views of gender and which incorporates Deleuze and Guatarri's thinking to introduce a notion of gender as multiple.

THINKING MULTIPLICITY

Recent studies in sexuality have effectively problematized the traditional binary gender divide. At the social level, there is extensive historical and anthropological evidence for the existence of third and fourth genders in social and cultural groups, recognizing on the one hand that the essential fluidity of gender and sexuality may be labeled in whatever ways a society finds useful and on the other, masculinity and femininity as labels refer to characteristics which may exist side by side and simultaneously in bodies which may be inscribed either male or female.

Identity inscriptions may change through time, space, discourse and interaction at a level as specific as the personal; sexual orientations and choices may be pragmatic, strategic, ephemeral or reversible rather than definitive of such identity; and multiple identities may indeed, as Stone (1995) argues be the human *norm* rather than a pathological form. Poststructuralist informed perspectives enable some movement not only away from unitary, stable categorizations of gendered identities, but also beyond representations of identity as multiplicity and diversity (see Linstead and Thomas, 2002; Kerfoot and Knights, 1998), towards a full recognition of the processual nature of individual subjectivities. Through the work of Deleuze and Guattari gender as rhizomatic can be understood as a plane of immanence, intensity and consistency which always and constantly shifts and realigns – a molecular (particle-d) process characterized by making connections and forging alliances like a multi-armed chain of molecules. Theorizing gender as rhizomatic entails a performance of becoming which is brought together momentarily, interrupted constantly, and dispersed consistently. This has the potential to shift our attention in the field of gender studies away from challenging majoritarian discourses – the dominant, aggregate structures of gender practice and politics which ironically reinforce the gender binary to minoritarian theorizing as illustrated by gender fluidity theory which rests on theorizing the molecular nature of gender. As such, gender may be seen as itself a productive force of becoming rather than simply an outcome of the performativity of social practice and social construction. Gender identity then, is in

constant becoming – rhizomatic, nomadic, a constant journey with no final destination.

To start our thinking beyond binary gender relations, we begin by interrogating *multiplicities of sameness*, characteristic of feminist approaches, based on a notion of desire as lack and the construction of gender identity as collection.

Multiplicities of sameness: feminism

Feminism has made the enormous contribution of enabling the clear recognition of the ontological and social subordination entailed in taking a binary view of gender. Different varieties of feminism have, however, taken different perspectives on resistance to it; to its redress or reversal; to the means of achieving social change; the possibilities of organizing differently and the acceptance or otherwise of gender identifications beyond the customary binary. In our critique of gender multiplicity we see much feminist practice as being problematic which reinforces the feminine, rather than challenges, the gender divide by affirming sexual difference through sexual politics. In our pursuit of a philosophy of becoming, Braidotti's work is illustrative of feminist debates that desire political subjectivity, is loyal to women's history and activism whilst questioning 'the problems of knowledge and epistemological legitimation' (Braidotti, 1994: 159). Moreover, Braidotti usefully reminds us that in order to bring about change, and therefore gender equality, there has to be 'the (unconscious) desire for the new ... [to explore] women's *desire to become*, not a specific model for their becoming' (1994: 160). Grounded in this ontological desire to be, she finds possibilities for change through an emancipatory mode of becoming (Braidotti, 1994: 160; 2006). Although Braidotti starts us moving towards a way of thinking difference, her feminist politics leaves us unsettled, particularly with her level of analysis of the body as neither biological nor sociological, but as an overlap between the physical, symbolic and material. This is a key issue in the feminist struggle for the redefinition of subjectivity. Braidotti questions feminist materiality, offering a *corporeal* or bodily materiality influenced by Deleuze and Guattari (1987) which enables her to go beyond the subject 'woman' as a monolithic essence and appreciate the living concept 'woman' as a site of complex, multiple, contested experiences. However Deleuze and Guattari's radical vision of changing the very image we have of thinking does not fit with her residually feminist politics and there remains an unresolved relationship towards both subjectivity and materialism even in her recent work on nomadic ethics (Braidotti, 2006). That said, Braidotti establishes some fluidity within the gender binary, although the identification of individual gendered identities as same-different does not offer an alternative strategy of resistance that destabilizes the boundaries of the bipolar gender system.

Our task therefore is to think of identity as a site of difference. Rethinking difference then involves, not establishing a reactive pole of a binary opposition between male/female, masculine/feminine, but a multiplicity of possible differences – 'difference as the positivity of differences' (Braidotti, 1994: 164). These ideas lie at the heart of the nomadic vision of subjectivity that takes into account experiences of oppression, exclusion and marginality. The emphasis on *becoming* therefore stands against the static (and inevitably oppressive) nature of *being*. The notion of rhizomes (which we discuss shortly) facilitates the project of challenging gender binaries and is better suited to a nomadic, disjunctive self that evades oppression in avoiding 'being' in any static sense. But although the possession of a penis is no longer the prime determinant of subjectivity, the body stands for the radical materiality of the subject. Rethinking the subject therefore means rethinking the body. Deleuze and Guattari are similarly concerned with the living process of subjective transformation and explore the shifts from what they term the molar, reactive and sedentary based on unity, cohesion and aggregation to the molecular, active and nomadic. They therefore reject a realist ontology and an essentialist account

of the body such as that found in feminism whilst affirming the body's *corporeality*. It is this materialist approach which *post*-feminists find commensurable. Deleuze and Guattari de-essentialize the body, sexuality and sexed identities to move beyond the dualistic oppositions that conjugate the monological discourses of phallogocentrism.

Traditionally feminism has rejected those constructions of desire in which the feminine is constituted as a lack. However, attempts such as Braidotti's to incorporate a more fluid conception of desire as multiplicity, which would break down the binary distinctions that perpetuate oppressive ontologies of desire, fail to go far enough in remaining grounded in desire as phenomenologically subjective. This ontological challenge to dualistic views of gender is critical to our project to constitute gender as process, driven by formless desire beyond binaries and even beyond the multiple identities of individual subjects. *Multiplicities of sameness* are still in much feminism dominated by collection and recollection. Rather than offering a traditional view of sameness 'through a series of hierarchically ordained differences' (Braidotti, 1994: 164) the meshwork of rhizomatics promises a heterarchical difference irreducible to the sameness of repetition. The impasse here seems to be that Braidotti's politicised desire works through a phenomenological subject – the becoming of woman is the working out of the becomings of individual desiring subjects. Though compatible with the feminist desire for emancipation and new social possibilities for becoming woman, this is not consistent with the condition of rhizomatic subjects and nomadic selves who are, as Butler (1999, 2004) notes, not so much desiring subjects but subjects of and subject to desire – or more correctly, desire's desire for the proliferation of desire (O'Shea, 2002). Braidotti (2006: 260) too argues that the desiring impulse to 'get on with it' is the opposite of the political slogan, the requirement to advance a teleologically ordained trajectory – the destination is unknown.

Yet desire as collection/lack does not disappear entirely, the two processes are irreducible and implicated in each other. Collection/lack circulates in mutuality in the diffuse space of dispersion/proliferation, bricolating the assemblages of identity within the meshworks of the rhizome. Multiplicity in this vein which rests on a view of desire as dispersion/proliferation is not a pluralized notion of identity but an ever-changing, non-totalizable collectivity, an assemblage defined, not by its abiding identity or principle of sameness over time, but through its capacity to undergo permutations and transformations, that is, its dimensionality.

In the next section we consider what such rhizomatic thinking entails by exploring *multiplicities of difference and dispersion*. Deleuze and Guattari remind us that molar binaries themselves are *aggregates* rather than unities. As such, they 'cross over into molecular assemblages of a different nature', and become reciprocally dependent. Gender is power, knowledge, work, technology, art and as Deleuze and Guattari emphasize 'the two sexes imply a multiplicity of molecular combinations bringing into play not only the man in the woman and the woman in the man, but the relation of each other to the animal, the plant, etc: *a thousand tiny sexes*', all quotes from (Deleuze and Guattari, 1987: 213).

Multiplicities of difference and dispersion: rhizomatics and fluidity

Deleuze and Guattari's view of the working out of processes that *organize* opposes both the tree metaphor which is a visible emblem of linear, progressive, ordered systems and the root metaphor, which presumes a unity but like the root itself is latent or hidden and may present itself as if were decentered or non-unified. Unlike both these images, rhizomatics are 'an underground – but perfectly manifest – network of multiple branching roots and shoots, with no central axis, no unified point of origin, and no given direction of growth – a proliferating, somewhat chaotic, and diversified system of growths' (Grosz, 1994: 199). De Landa (1999: 120), preferring to eschew the continuity of the horticultural metaphor, calls them *meshworks* which are

a series of middles from which they grow and overspill, rather than having beginnings and ends.

This is a critical point for the understanding of identity, because from this perspective identity is not endogenous to the individual or unit, a positive which is added to the collective, the organization, the culture, the social group, the political party, the nation state, the sexual orientation, the gendered group or even the conversation which enhances and diversifies it. On the contrary, identity is already the result of a *negative* operation which extracts it from the mobile and multidimensional mesh in which it is embedded and is always *less than* its undifferentiated other. Rather than being like a structure, 'defined by a set of points and positions, with binary relations between points and biunivocal relationships between the positions, the rhizome is made only of lines; lines of segmentarity and stratification as its dimensions ... The rhizome operates by variation, expansion, conquest, capture, offshoots ... The rhizome is an acentered, non-hierarchical, non-signifying system' (Deleuze and Guattari, 1987: 21).

The rhizome as based on: *connections* which bring together diverse fragments; *heterogeneity*, as multiple connections which are not only massified linkages but also micro-linkages which bring together diverse domains, levels, dimensions, functions, effects, aims and objects; *multiplicity*, which here does not mean a multiplicity of singularities, of ones, a repetition of the self-same, but a genuine proliferation of processes that are neither ones nor twos; and *ruptures, breaks and discontinuities*, where any one of the rhizome's connections is capable of being severed or disconnected, creating the possibility of the other and different connections (Grosz, 1994: 199–200).

Accordingly rhizomatics has some importance for feminism in the sense that it offers the possibility to critically evaluate the phallocentric discourses, knowledge and representations within which women are marginalized. However, rhizomatics applied to the project of challenging gender binaries and appreciating gender as fluidity has much greater potential. As a decentered set of linkages between things, relations, processes, intensities, speed or slowness and flows, we can read *gender as a rhizome*. This offers possibilities of the other, possibilities of change and transformation, and possibilities for freedom and emancipation that go beyond the constraints of biological sex and socially ascribed genders. This rests on an ontology of desire as a force which is immanent, endless, exuberant and rhizomatic, as distinct from desire as lack (Freud), or desire as wish (Lyotard), which is 'motivated by the perceived lack of something useful, the absence of something which is needed, the urge to generate utility, improve upon our human environment …' (Brewis and Linstead, 2000: 175). This ontology of desire is therefore productive, the desire to give, to contribute, to become part of something creative – desire as excess following Bataille (1991a,b).

We noted earlier in our comments on feminist desire that the interconnection between an ontology of desire as lack and a phenomenological desiring subject, even when proliferated into a multiplicity of identities, might destabilize specific gender positions but it tends to preserve the idea of the boundary by retaining the subject-object dualism and, through reproducing multiple binaries, the binary itself. Rhizomatics requires a view of desire as active and affirmative – excremental (giving, spending, dispersing) rather than incremental (cumulating, accumulating and collecting). It therefore attempts to move us beyond the subject-object dualism, the subject's desire for the 'object (the other) but also the consciousness of the other' or the desire of the other (Hegel cited in Brewis and Linstead, 2000: 175). As such, and consistent with Cooper and Bersani and Dutoit, desire is the ontical urge to proliferate and to be varied. If we read desire as such a creative force into our theorizing on gender then the possibilities of challenging the gender binary become realizable within our social and cultural existence. Desire is a force that *becomes* gendered; as a force desire moves through particular configurations of a rhizome

and where it connects and stabilizes, however temporarily, gender emerges as a plane of consistency, immanence and intensity – one which is changed and transformed through lines of flight as we shift and realign and improvise our gender constantly. But as Deleuze and Guattari argue that desire is arrested by the Body without Organs (Deleuze and Guattari, 1987), so gender flows and intensities become arrested and inscribed.

Deleuze and Guattari are concerned with going beyond the confines of the mind/body dualism. The body, for them, is a 'discontinuous, nontotalised series of processes, organs, flows, energies, corporeal substances and incorporeal events, intensities, and durations' (Grosz, 1994: 193–194). The subject is not an 'entity', or a relation between mind (interior) and body (exterior) but is understood in terms of a series of 'flows, energies, movements, and capacities, a series of fragments or segments capable of being linked together in ways other than those that congeal it into an identity' (Grosz, 1994: 198). The *capabilities* of bodies are more important than their genus and species or their organs and functions. To overcome mind/body dualism Deleuze and Guattari develop Artaud's conception of the Body without Organs (BwO) as 'an interface, a threshold, a field of intersecting material and symbolic forces. The body is a surface where multiple codes (race, sex, class, age, etc.) are inscribed: it is a linguistic construction that capitalises on energies of a heterogeneous, discontinuous, and unconscious nature' (Braidotti, 1994: 169).

The BwO refers to human, animal, textual, socio-cultural and physical bodies. It is a field where desire is produced in new conjunctions (Brewis and Linstead, 2000: 200; Ecstavasia, 1994: 186), intensified through new nodalities and modalities, where desire is immanent, where becomings become (Grosz, 1994: 202–203). It is where we set our bodily characteristics free to pursue new becomings such as becoming-woman and becoming-animal. The ultimate becoming is becoming itself, pure full process, the ability to become context by recognizing it within us, and thus *becoming imperceptible*

(Braidotti, 2006: 259–262). Here identity becomes imperceptibility.

In going beyond the limitations and constraints of the bipolar gender binary, we can bring our discussion of desire, rhizomatics and BwO together to suggest that if *gender is a rhizome* then the possibilities for gender fluidity at an ontological level are actual and real. Moreover if gender is a *productive process* whose productivity is pure, i.e. it rests in the creativity of effulgent desire rather than being defined and delimited by the product it creates (such as gender as a dramaturgical or linguistic performance (Butler, 1990, 1993; Benhabib, 1999), social construction or social practice (Gherardi, 1995)) then our view of gender identity even as conventional multiplicity needs revision. Gender fluidity is not merely movement across a binary boundary (which nevertheless leaves the boundary in place) or across several horizontal boundaries between multiple identities. Identity is motion, fluidity dissolves boundaries and carries them off in its flood.

If gender identity is considered in terms of this molecularity it can be seen as a site within the field of becomings that goes beyond bisexuality and multiple genders; beyond the traversing of gender which may be reversible or irreversible at a physical level and may involve temporary or permanent relocations across the binary divide; beyond the gender performance in both language and action which characterizes itself as gender transient. A truly nomadic gender identity transcends its roles and its transgressive realignments of molar unities as a becoming. It may take several lines of flight: it may, for example, become *genderful* – so expansive and inclusive in its myriad gender alignments that it cannot be aligned or consigned within gender limits, as these limits now contain everything else, themselves a form of gendering; or it may become *ungendered*, where gender is dissipated, overlain by and completely absorbed into so many other alignments that it ceases to function as a category, but remains a minor dimension of all experience. In staying in motion, in change, in becoming other,

it resists those inscriptions that fix and name it and thus allow it to be perceived *as* an identity – it becomes *imperceptible*. This is underscored by our earlier affirmation of an ontology of desire as creative exuberance. The terrain for political praxis is shifted, with this ontological intervention, from the traditional view of gender as property or the performative view of gender as a product of linguistic or social performance to gender as itself *a form of productivity*. Gender is not the construction or outcome of a performance but is immanent within those performances making them productive of new molecular connections in the meshwork of identity.

CONCLUSION: FROM IDENTITY TO IMPERCEPTIBILITY

Deleuze and Guattari's concept of the rhizome offers a means of representing multiplicity in action, emphasizing its character as comprising connections between fragments, constantly adding to their connectivity; the heterogeneity of these connections across diverse domains; multiplicity as a proliferation of processes rather than a multiplicity of singularities; and the creative significance of rupture, breaks and new connections. The end of multiplicity – whether via genderful or ungendering strategies – is not gender identity but gender imperceptibility. As Butler argues: 'If gender is a kind of doing, an incessant activity performed, in part, without one's knowing and without one's willing, it is not for that reason automatic or mechanical ... it is a practice of improvisation within a scene of constraint' (Butler, 2004: 1). Gender identity then, is in constant becoming, a constant journey which must start and end in the middle because 'a rhizome has no beginning and no end: it is always in the middle, between things, interbeing, *intermezzo*'. It has no beginning and end because 'making a clean slate, starting or beginning again from ground zero, seeking a beginning or a foundation – all imply *a false conception of a voyage and movement*'. A similar anti-hodological argument can be found in ten Bos' (2004)

critique of the obsessive study of organizational pathways and the metaphorical
fear of labyrinths, wolves and more literal
wanderings of thought and practice. Linear
or step and stage models of organizational
change; hierarchies of authority; traditional
notions of career but also modern notions
of purposeful networking and the ambitious
accumulation of social capital, all illustrate in
the everyday how this metaphor of the journey
continues to constrain us to pull back from
relationality. But being in the middle is no
easy option and affords lull in the action, no
reflective drop in energy: rather it is the place
where things pick up speed and action, like
a river that undermines its banks and flows
faster in the centre. The rhizome, like gender
identity, is never still, always relational,
always to come, always to connect – 'the
rhizome is uniquely alliance … the rhizome
is the conjunction' (all quotes from Deleuze
and Guattari, 1987: 25). Where there are no
options for incorporation or suppression, there
can be only convertibility and relationality,
a gender dynamics beyond opposition and
dialectics (Baudrillard, 1996: 23).

For Braidotti too, openness, even to difference, means a merging into one's environment
without either dominating that environment or
being dominated by it, where identity involves
being distinguished from that environment.
As she puts it, this marks the beginning of
'a pure process of becoming … the flooding
of the present by possible futures, in a clean
break from the past if by past we mean a
sedimentation of habits, the institutionalized
accumulation of experience whose authority
is sealed by molar or dominant memory
and the identities it engenders' (Braidotti,
2006: 260). Indeed, gender as we know
it is predominantly ascribed through just
these means. Yet becoming-imperceptible,
by blending into the environment, is not a
negation, but 'a sort of transcendence that
plunges us into the impossible, the unheard-of:
an affirmative present' (Braidotti, 2006: 260).
Pure relationality, pure possibility, a slipping
of the bonds with which institutionalized identity forms imprison us is what imperceptibility
delivers. To fully appreciate this relationality

means, we argue, a movement through gender
to *ungendering* organization.

FUTURES

Now that we have begun reconceptualizing
gender in this way we need to rethink the
methodological choices on how genderful or
ungendering practices open up research agendas based on nomadic subjectivity and difference. This involves a desire to undo and think
beyond our existing practices and develop a
practice of multiplicity in gender research.
This project centers on accepting that the
researcher and researched are fractured and
nomadic subjects. At the time of writing this
chapter, three general challenges emerge for
us: validity practices that underpin research;
affective practices that need to be re-embodied
in research; and writing practices themselves.

First, we need to challenge the Same/Other
power binary which appears to be endemic
to virtually all constructions of validity in
research. Existing 'imperial' forms of validity
privilege sameness, marginalizing the other
and multiple differences. New imaginaries
of validity then need to be developed, but
it is contended that this task is difficult
without reproducing practices of the Same.
Transgressing binaries in relation to validity
is to build on work where it is suggested
new possible types of 'transgressive' validity
including rhizomatic validity which involves
creating a 'transformative space in which
a non-dualistic multiplicity (difference) is
cultivated' (Lather, 1993: 686). But we need to
be wary of hubris in proposing 'new' validities
that might end up reproducing the problems
associated with the exclusions of the Same,
behind new masks.

More specifically, rhizomatic thinking,
subversiveness and 'the play of difference',
stems from a willingness to disrupt and
think through multiplicity. We would suggest
that rhizomatic validity undermines stability,
subverts and unsettles from within; it is
a 'vocation', a response to the call of
otherness of any system, its alterity which
actively resists the constraints of mainstream

authority, regularity, and commonsense, and open thought up to creative constructions. Lather suggests that rhizomatic validity:

> unsettles from within, taps underground; generates new locally determined norms of understanding, proliferates open-ended and context-sensitive criteria, works against reinscription of some new regime, some new systematicity; supplements and exceeds the stable and the permanent, Derridean play; works against constraints of authority via relay, multiple openings, networks, complexities of problematics; and puts conventional discursive procedures under erasure, breaches congealed discourses, critical as well as dominant (1993: 686).

Furthermore Lather, quoting Deleuze, argues the '"new"… is not so much about the fashionable as it is the creativity that arises out of social practices, creativity which marks the ability to transform, to break down present practices in favour of future ones (Deleuze, 1997: 163–164)' (ibid.). Methodologically then we need to be reflexive of how gender as rhizomatic influences the research process and how we can encourage mutual reciprocity between research participants. This involves contesting multiple readings of data, text and relationships; interrupting researcher privilege and authority by constructing a 'questioning text' (Williams, 1992a in Lather, 1993: 681) which features tentativeness, partiality, decentering expert authority, practising co-theorizing which remains in tension, untidiness of straddling multiple agendas, letting contradictions remain in tension, to unsettle from within, dissolve interpretations by marking them as temporal, partial, and an investment in transformative praxis' (ibid.: 681). As such, our textual strategies and forms of representation become part of questioning our validity practices and subsequent knowledge claims – a transgression of escape, uncontrollability, messiness, and leakiness. But Lather fails to see the essential *difference* of functioning rhizomatically: it entails not a move from hierarchies to networks, where researchers are interested in the journey 'among intersections, nodes, and regionalizations through a multi-centred complexity' (1993: 680), but a movement within a meshwork *without any centers at all*.

Second, a commitment towards rhizomatic writing which goes beyond the emotionless rationality and writer neutrality of research towards a practice of writing which is affective and corporeal. Writing moves through our bodies and in relationship with other bodies which comprise multiple and moving elements. Probyn (2005) comments how central affects and assemblages are composed and decomposed. Gatens reminds us how affect leads us to 'question commonsense notions of privacy or "integrity" of bodies through exposing the breaches in the borders between self and other evidenced by the contagiousness of "collective" affects' (Gatens, 2000: 14; Probyn, 2005: 141). Experience, affect, writing as a structuring, ordering and sequencing practice then does not impact on the body from the outside, nor does it erupt from the inside; rather, such distinctions are irrelevant. Gatens comments that 'the body in constant interchange with its environment … the body as a nexus of variable interconnections, a multiplicity within a web of other multiplicities' (2000: 7; Probyn, 2005: 141). For Deleuze (1997), it is the affective assemblage of bodies of different orders and elements (Probyn, 2005: 144) – new acts of subjectivity – that goes beyond distinct bodies and explores the relationship between ideas, writing and affects; between thinking and feeling, across mind and body.

Finally, what would such rhizomatic writing look like? For researchers of gender/identity this may feature involvement in projects that we may not have tried before, doing familiar things in unfamiliar ways and vice versa, going into unexpected territories, writing about unforeseen insights, taking different turns and allowing metaphorphoses to take place which would turn text into something different from its beginnings (see Richardson, 1997) for a comparable argument on writing differently). In general, there is a commitment to representing multiple, polymorphous, multifarious realities in a spirit and form which represents multiplicity. Furthermore, rhizomatic writing should use micro cases (the molecular) to disaggregate the molar. So you expose the multiplicitous and ambiguous in specific cases to destabilize the categories of the molar and show how binaries cumulate, coagulate and slide. This is more than deconstruction, because it isn't about overturning binaries to destabilize them. Deconstruction makes the binary its initial focus before it moves into the third space. Rhizomatics arises in the third ... and reveals the 'inner third'.

But none of this is possible without opening up spaces where we don't just shout from the margins for a politics for change, but we endorse a politics of change through a practice of multiplicity. But what ethical and political agendas should we be pursuing with this nomadic vision of subjectivity? And, what do politics based on rhizomatic thinking that goes beyond a politics of gender and identity which rests on a politics of sameness look like? We are not sure, but it rests on a desire to practice difference.

REFERENCES

Bataille, G. (1991a) *The Accursed Share: An Essay on General Economy vol. 1 – Consumption.* New York: Zone Books.

Bataille, G. (1991b) *The Accursed Share: An Essay on General Economy Vol. II – The History of Eroticism/ Vol. III – Sovereignty.* New York: Zone Books.

Baudrillard, J. (1996) *The Perfect Crime* (tr. Chris Turner). Verso: London.

Benhabib, S. (1999) 'Sexual difference and collective identities: The new constellation', in M.A. O'Farrell and L. Vallone (eds), *Virtual Gender: Fantasies of Subjectivity and Embodiment.* Ann Arbor, MI: University of Michigan Press. pp. 217–243.

Bersani, L. and Dutoit, U. (1993) *Arts of Impoverishment: Beckett, Rothko, Resnais.* Cambridge, MA: Harvard University Press.

Braidotti, R. (1994) 'Toward a new nomadism: Feminist Deleuzian tracks; or metaphysics and metabolism', in C. Boundas and D. Olkowski (eds), *Gilles Deleuze and the Theater of Philosophy.* New York: Routledge. pp. 157–186.

Braidotti, R. (2006) *Transpositions.* Cambridge: Polity Press.

Brewis, J. and Linstead, S. (2000) *Sex, Work and Sex Work: Eroticizing Organization.* London: Routledge.

Burrell, G. (1997) *Pandemonium.* London: Sage.

Butler, J. (1990) *Gender Trouble: Feminism and the Subversion of Identity.* New York: Routledge.

Butler, J. (1993) *Bodies that Matter: On the Discursive Limits of Sex.* New York: Routledge.

Butler, J. (1999) *Subjects of Desire: Hegelian Reflections in 20th Century France.* New York: Columbia University Press.

Butler, J. (2004) *Undoing Gender.* London: Routledge.

Cooper, R. (2001) 'Interpreting mass: Collection/ dispersion', in N. Law and R. Munro (eds), *The Consumption of Mass.* Oxford: Blackwell. pp. 16–43.

De Landa, M. (1999) 'Immanence and Transcendence in the Genesis of Form', in I. Buchanan, (ed.) *A Deleuzian Century.* Durham NC: Duke University Press. pp. 119–134.

Deleuze, G. (1997) *Essays Critical and Clinical* (trans. D.W. Smith and M.A. Greco). Minneapolis: University of Minnesota Press.

Deleuze, G. and Guattari, F. (1987) *A Thousand Plateaus.* Minneapolis: Minnesota University Press.

Ecstavasia, A. (1994) 'Fucking (with theory) for Money: towards an introduction of escort prostitution', in E. Amiran and J. Unsworth (eds), *Essays in Postmodern Culture.* Oxford: Oxford University Press. pp. 174–198.

Game, A. (1991) *Undoing the Social.* Buckingham: Open University Press.

Gatens, M. (2000) *Privacy and the Body: The Publicity of Affect.* ASCA Yearbook: The Netherlands.

Gherardi, S. (1995) *Gender, Symbolism and Organizational Culture.* London: Sage.

Grosz, E. (1994) 'A thousand tiny sexes: Feminism and rhizomatics', in C. Boundas and D. Olkowski (eds), *Gilles Deleuze and the Theater of Philosophy.* New York: Routledge. pp. 187–210.

Kerfoot, D. and Knights, D. (1998) 'Managing masculinity in organizational life: A "Man"agerial project', *Organization,* 5 (1): 7–26.

Linstead, A. and Thomas, R. (2002) 'What do you want from me?': A poststructuralist feminist reading of middle managers' Identities', *Culture and Organization,* 8 (1): 1–20.

Linstead, S. (2000) 'Dangerous fluids and the organization-without-organs', in J. Hassard, R. Holliday and H. Willmott (eds), *Body and Organization.* London: Sage. pp. 31–51.

Linstead, S., Linstead, A. and Brewis, J. (2005) 'Gender in change: Gendering change', *Journal of Organizational Change Management,* 18 (4): 542–560.

Linestead, S. and Pullen, A. (2006) Gender as multiplicity: Desire, displacement, difference and dispersion, *Human Relations,* vol 59. no. 9, 1287–1310.

Lorber, J. (2000) 'Using gender to undo gender: A feminist ungendering movement', *Feminist Theory,* 1 (1): 79–95.

Lorraine, T. E. (1990) *Gender, Identity, and the Production of Meaning*. Boulder, CO: Westview Press.

O'Shea, A. (2002) 'Desiring desire: How desire makes us human, all too human', *Sociology*, 36 (4): 925–940.

Probyn, E. (2005) *Blush: Faces of Shame*. Sydney: The University of New South Wales.

Pullen, A. and Knights, D. (2007) 'Undoing Gender', *Gender, Work and Organization*, 14 (6): 505–511.

Richardson, L. (1997) *Fields of Play: Constructing an Academic Life*. New Brunswick: Rutgers University Press.

Stone, A.R. (1995) *The War of Desire and Technology at the Close of the Mechanical Age*. Cambridge, MA: MIT Press.

ten Bos, R. (2004) 'The Fear of Wolves', *Culture and Organization*, 10 (1): 7–24.

Thanem, T. and Linstead, S. (2006) 'The trembling organization: Order, change and the philosophy of the virtual', in M. Fuglsang and B. Meier Sorensen (eds), *Deleuze and the Social*. Edinburgh: University of Edinburgh Press, pp. 39–57.

Gender Inequity and the Need to Study Change

Joanne Martin and Debra Meyerson

Organizational gender research is at once plentiful and severely limited. Many organizational gender studies are 'body counts' that show where in our societies women have attained positions of power, whether they have been rewarded equally for equivalent paid work, and whether work-family policies and, more importantly, practices have created more gender-,equal allocations of responsibility for childcare, elder care, and housework. A second tradition of gender research has gone beyond the limitations of body counts to document the societal level discourses and the subtle processes of cognition and interaction that reproduce gender inequities at work and at home.

We know far less about how to combat gender inequities successfully. In many cases, federal policies demanding more gender equity have been intermittently and incompletely enforced, and have resulted in observable, but relatively slow and small changes. Ely and Meyerson (2000a) explain why so many top-down organizational efforts have failed to produce large-scale, lasting improvements; such efforts often endeavor to 'fix the women' or 'value the traditionally feminine' without changing other aspects of inequitable systems. Meyerson (2001) outlines tactics of incremental change used by individual agents (called 'tempered radicals'), while Ely and Meyerson (2000b) show the effectiveness of a 'small wins' approach that tries carefully selected experiments to demonstrate, within an organization, the possibility of advancing both gender equity and business goals – the so-called dual agenda. We need research that follows up on these incremental approaches to change. Which tempered radical tactics are most effective in producing change? Does this vary by context? What can organizations do to support individuals working for change? Which small wins experiments have the greatest leverage for catalyzing other kinds of change? What can be done to maintain focus on gender goals, given a dual agenda in an organization where business goals are seen as higher priority?

As pragmatic and hopeful as these approaches appear, incremental change efforts driven by individuals offer only piecemeal, small-scale solutions. To effect large-scale change, tempered radicalism requires a full pipeline of women working to advance change. A small win experiment in a single organization may not spread to create other experiments within that organization. In general, deeply rooted, traditional gendered practices can overwhelm individual, incremental, and even dramatic organization-wide efforts to advance equity. Understanding resistance to gender equality is more than just a level-of-intervention problem. Even in countries such as Sweden, Norway and Denmark, that have federal laws requiring equal pay for comparatively equal work, nationally sponsored day care, and a range of other progressive gender equity practices, gender inequalities persist to some degree, particularly in the business sector. In addition, those countries that make societal level efforts to eradicate gender inequalities in such important arenas as pay and elected government representation, have some of the world's most extreme forms of occupational sex segregation, with most women choosing or being relegated to traditionally female, nurturing jobs such as elder care, teaching, and nursing (Blackburn et al., 2000). Studies that challenge the perpetuation of gender inequality and segregation should, we believe, include research on disorganized co-action, where many people in different contexts independently and without awareness of each other, push for similar kinds of changes

(Martin and Meyerson, 1988). Insights from contemporary social movement research can help us analyze the successes and failures of feminist collective action through, for example, the Catholic Church, non-governmental organizations, and the military. We need to evaluate change efforts in those nations where federal laws have required sweeping society-wide changes in gender relations. For example, South Africa tried to couple post-apartheid changes in race relations to changes in gender equity; in the U.S. the telephone company's (A.T.&T.) consent decree changed working conditions for significant numbers of working class men and women. Finally, it is especially important (and difficult) to do systematic comparative international studies.

One reason why gender inequality is so resistant to change stems from institutional interlocks that block wide-scale changes in gender equity (Martin and O'Neill, forthcoming). Institutions are classes of organized entities, like schools, religions, the family, workplaces, courts, federal and state governments. Interlocks occur when change efforts in one institutional context are undermined by other institutions' resistance to change. For example, because women carry a disproportionate share of dependent care responsibilities, what goes on in the family and at school can undermine any gender-related improvement in work settings. Cross-institutional change efforts might be one key to broad-based, lasting change. For example, in New York City, where the federal and state governments do not subsidize universal day care for children, religious authorities, employers in the hospital industry, and employee unions in that industry joined forces to subsidize day care for lower paid workers. What we need is research on which large-scale, cross-institutional innovations like this are effective, and which are not. Then, and this is a crucial step, we need theory so we can go beyond case studies to understand and be able to predict which kinds of cross-institutional planned change efforts are most likely to succeed, and why.

Gender researchers need to go beyond body counts and studies that document discrimination and inequity; we need to refocus our research on change. We need to study change at individual, organizational, institutional, and national levels of analysis – building theories that will help change the inequities that have been so fully documented.

REFERENCES

Blackburn, R., Jarman, J. and Brooks, B. (2000) 'The puzzle of gender segregation and inequality: A cross-national analysis', *European Sociological Review*, 16: 119–135.

Ely, R. and Meyerson, D. (2000a) 'Theories of gender in organizations: A new approach to organizational analysis and change', in B. Staw and R. Sutton (eds), *Research in Organizational Behavior*. Greenwich, CT: JAI Press. pp. 105–153.

Ely, R. and Meyerson, D. (2000b) 'Advancing gender equity in organizations: The challenge and importance of maintaining a gender narrative', *Organization*, 7, 589–608.

Martin, J. and Meyerson, D. (1998) 'Women and power: Conformity, resistance, and dis-organized co-action', in R. Kramer and M. Neale (eds), *Power, Politics, and Influence*, Newbury Park, CA: Sage. pp. 311–348.

Martin, J. and O'Neill, O. (Forthcoming) 'Reconceptualizing resistance to gender equity: A cross-institutional approach'. Stanford University. Manuscript in preparation.

Meyerson, D. (2001) *Tempered Radicals: How People Use Difference to Inspire Change at Work*. Boston, MA: Harvard Business School Press.

Creating Better Understandings of Organizations While Building Better Organizations

Roger L. M. Dunbar, A. Georges, L. Romme and William H. Starbuck

INTRODUCTION

Although people have been organizing themselves for many thousands of years, the number and varieties of organizations increased dramatically during the nineteenth and twentieth centuries, making organization design a central issue in contemporary societies. However, current approaches to organization design rely on static, mechanistic ideas that are often out of touch with changing realities. Specifically, organizations commit to plans that they then use to guide the matching of organization structures and environmental demands. Though environments change and structures evolve, the design process ignores the implications of this evolution. In a changing world, a continued reliance on static and unchanging organization design leads to undesired results and widespread dissatisfaction.

The oldest academic writings about organizations were motivated by desires for improvement (Augier et al., 2005; Dunbar and Starbuck, 2006; Starbuck, 2003). Many writers hoped that more productive organizations would alleviate strife between social classes. A few hoped that bureaucratization, for example, would reduce the dominance of social elites (e.g., Weber, 1972); whereas a much larger number protested that bureaucracies stifle social change (e.g., Popper, 1962). Around the middle of the twentieth century, some academics sought to inject more democracy into organizational processes (e.g., Jaques, 1951; Likert, 1961).

Influential critiques of business school education in the 1950s (Gordon and Howell,

1959; Pierson, 1959) coincided with a change of focus and more emphasis on a science-driven approach to organizational research. In business schools at least, organization research since this time has most often emphasized static description and explanation while largely overlooking ongoing experimentation and exploration processes. Many researchers also paid no attention to issues arising in societies at large and focused instead on developing and testing organization theories that mainly interest academics (Wren, 1994). This turn inward has reduced the contributions and influence of organizational research and has also fostered theories that likely overstate the importance of processes that lead to and sustain organizational stability and conformity and that underestimate the importance of processes to mobilize new organizational developments and potentials.

Although contemporary management texts create an impression that the search for design principles is active and ongoing, this professed interest is in fact more symbolic than real. Most often, management texts refer to descriptive research on organizational structures and designs carried out from the 1950s through the 1970s (Daft, 2006) and teachers and consultants present this material as established, accepted truth. However, many new kinds of organizations have appeared since the 1970s, shifting the focus of design projects to issues that were not important and to organizational properties that were not possible when researchers carried out these earlier studies. For example, current organizational designs must take account of how information and communication technologies have revolutionized organizing processes, how globalization has changed organizational identities, and how staff educational levels, abilities, and expectations have risen rapidly and changed work.

Researchers' neglect of organization design as an active research area limits the effectiveness of organizational research. People and social systems are complex and dynamic. To understand a complex, dynamic system, people must make incremental experiments.

This is because researchers who rely on the passive observation of a complex and dynamic system as they might happen to find it – the research approach most often adopted in recent decades – cannot learn about the potentials that are implicit in such a system. Passive observation is also likely to describe the design options available to such a system incorrectly. As a result, important aspects of organizations will remain not only not understood but also unrecognized. Yet, even if people understand a complex and dynamic system poorly, they may be able to improve it through incremental design experiments.

This chapter seeks to stimulate renewed interest in research about efforts to improve organizational structures and processes – organization design. To build a scientific base for design, research must develop concepts and propositions that suggest opportunities and options for designs and designing. The next section explores relations between social science researchers, their preferred methodologies, and organization design. The ensuing section summarizes and assesses organization design work that has traditionally focused on notions of design 'fit.' The final section explores other approaches to organization design research that may offer benefits to both scholars and practitioners.

INTERACTIONS BETWEEN RESEARCH AND DESIGN

Academic researchers can typically choose what they study and how they study it and most have chosen to work with data that they can easily obtain or observe (Starbuck, 2006). Easily available data are retrospective and theories consistent with retrospective data do not necessarily describe the future or even the present. Because researchers can formulate theories that are consistent with prominent, stylized, retrospective facts, such theories never appear to be utterly ridiculous or inadequate; so many fields tend to retain them as possibly useful ideas. Platt (1964) pointed out that theoretical progress is slow in a research field that consistently cherishes existing lines of thought, and that progress is much faster in a research field that uses definitive experiments to confront theories and to exclude unproductive lines of thought. Because organization research boasts a huge inventory of possibly useful ideas based on retrospective data, and because studies have not tried to rule out unproductive lines of thought, the inventory of organization theories has grown huge even as progress toward useful understandings has been small.

Researchers who rely on retrospective data also tend to develop unrealistically complex theories that have ambiguous implications. Theories become unrealistically complex as they develop elaborate explanations for events that are random or idiosyncratic perturbations from what is normal. Complex theories lack parsimony and 'over fit' the data (Gauch, 2006). Organization designs need theories that make approximate but robust predictions because people can handle on *ad hoc* bases the unique details that always emerge. Pant and Starbuck (1990) showed how simple theories almost always provide better forecasts of future events than complex theories do because complex theories seek to explain non-recurrent events and they do actually produce less accurate forecasts.

Researchers' preferences also reflect the structures of careers in organizational research. Most organization researchers are able to pursue careers of studying organizations because they gain tenure at universities and, to grant tenure, universities require candidates to quickly establish strong research reputations. This means that junior researchers must gain quick recognition from their academic peers, so they often show a strong preference for theories currently fashionable in academic subcultures. Few, however, check out or report how these theories appeal to the people who work in the studied organizations. Researchers also favor research methods where they can gather data quickly (e.g., surveys), or can use accessible data (e.g., online databases) rather than exploring data sources that are more ambiguous and take time to compile (e.g., interviews). To the extent that researchers work in this way, academic views

veer out of touch with local realities. One result is a global community of researchers generating many articles in academic journals that practicing managers deem to be irrelevant to their problems and situations (Starbuck, 2004).

To eliminate unproductive lines of inquiry and to expose the limitations of current organizational research programs, organization researchers and practitioners should use available theories to make predictions and then check whether events match predictions. Organization design is particularly useful because it requires designers to predict the effects of their interventions and it requires researchers to find out which predictions actually proved out in practice. This usefulness is at a price, however, in that researchers usually cannot walk away after collecting sufficient data to write an article. Instead, they have to continue their participation in the design context until satisfactory outcomes have resulted (e.g., Brusoni and Prencipe, 2006).

Although journal editors and reviewers require mainstream research in organizations to meet scientific criteria for theoretical validity, they rarely consider practical usefulness. Organization design research, however, must also consider theories' practical usefulness. That is, the intellectual challenge of organization design research is to link knowledge based on academic research with design ideas that support practical improvements. Worren et al., (2002) suggested that the differing interpretations of *pragmatic validity* by academics and practitioners create problems. As most academics see it, operationally defined constructs, explicit causal propositions, and supportive data analyses establish a basis for prescriptive theory that has pragmatic validity. For managers, in contrast, the demand for precision is not as strong, more ambiguous knowledge still has value, and communication methods rather than research methods are most likely to determine pragmatic validity (Worren et al., 2002). For example, an anecdote may be necessary to illustrate a concept, and a diagram may help people to visualize a model. Organization design research must deal with these validity issues in ways that satisfy both researchers and practitioners.

Whereas retrospective theories describe what did exist, design processes seek to create things that do not exist, at least in specific situations (Simon, 1996). Whereas descriptive and explanatory research can provide knowledge about existing organizational structures, processes and outcomes, the conventional norms about retrospective science provide weak support for 'what should be brought into existence through intention, imagination and innovation' (Nelson and Stolterman, 2003: 31). Design research requires interventions because people and organizations often do not exhibit or even imagine the full range of behaviors of which they can be capable. Rather, on almost all dimensions almost all of the time, people and organizations accept constraints that keep behaviors close to expected equilibria. Thus, the spontaneous behavior that researchers witness leaves almost all potential degrees of freedom unexplored, and researchers cannot know what an organization could do or how it might affect its environments.

Responding to this concern, Schein (1987: 29) asserted that research should begin 'with the assumption that one cannot understand a human system without trying to change it' (also see Glaser 1978; Bronfenbrenner, 1979). This view challenges the more conventional notion, that a designer should understand a system before changing it. A renowned physician told Starbuck that he regarded treatment as an important step toward understanding a medical problem: 'Indeed, the doctor's views, which I later adopted as my own, suggest that to understand a system, one must try to change it and observe how it reacts' (Starbuck, 2004: 1249). Elaborating the logic underlying this approach, this doctor told Starbuck (1993, 2004) that initial medical analyses tend to oversimplify and condense many symptoms into simpler, incomplete diagnoses so that initial treatments often result in surprises. Schein (1987: 64) observed, 'The major implication of this line of reasoning is that all researchers who deal with human systems must have some degree of clinical training, specifically training around

client responsibility and the consequences of data-gathering interventions. The logic of scientific inquiry into organizations must somehow take into account that inquiry itself is an intervention that has implications not only for data validity, but, more important, for the relationship with the people in the organization.' Organization design research that requires researcher involvement facilitates an appreciation of these broader issues. Researchers and practitioners learn that understanding most often builds in iterative cycles of conjecture-intervention-reaction-analysis-conjecture cycles.

To appreciate the full range of organizations' potential actions and reactions, therefore, researchers need to observe how organizations respond to efforts to displace them from equilibrium. They can then learn about the organizations' reactive, adaptive, and proactive capabilities, possibly discovering why equilibriums exist in the first place.

Experimentation offers many benefits as a frame of reference for participants in organization design. People who see themselves as experimenting are more willing to deviate temporarily from practices they consider optimal. They also manage experiments in ways that limit the losses that failed experiments might produce; for instance, they pay careful attention to feedback, and they can investigate more than one alternative at a time. Because they place fewer personal stakes on outcomes looking successful, they evaluate outcomes more objectively, and they are willing to keep on trying for improvements because they know experiments never turn out perfectly. Based on several cases of success and failure in organizational and strategic change, Nystrom and Starbuck (1984) surmised that failures had involved putting 'too many eggs in one basket;' when serious setbacks had occurred the participants had expended their resources and could not pursue alternatives. In successful changes, on the other hand, participants had been ready to discard their previous beliefs about what was best thing to do so they tried some experiments and they watched the results of these experiments with the intention of finding better practices. It is even possible to program experimental searches for better routine practices. Evolutionary operation (EVOP) is a well thought-out method for continual experimentation (Box and Draper, 1969). The basic idea is to run many experiments that entail little risk because each deviates only incrementally from what the experimenters believe to be optimal.

Design projects also offer researchers the possibility of directly selecting the specific dimensions on which changes will occur. From a researcher's perspective, design projects are experiments that are likely to reveal obscure or latent organizational properties. They may also disrupt routines or perspectives and energize organization members to become advocates or opponents of a change. This process may expose differences in the beliefs of overtly similar people, or produce unintended consequences, or uncover symbiotic interactions that define relations between an organization and its environments. All improve organizational understanding.

Organization design projects also have to face the real-life limitations imposed by real people living real lives. Even researchers refuse to become research subjects when participation may threaten their worldviews, their livelihoods or their career prospects (Campbell and Russo, 1998; Riecken and Boruch, 1974; Rivlin and Timpane, 1975). Only design experiments that appear at least initially to offer major benefits and to entail no substantial risks to the organizations studied are feasible to pursue.

As design projects unfold, however, initial predictions of benefits and risks often prove to be inaccurate. For example, Foss (2003) described how the Danish firm Oticon tried to delegate decision making to improve entrepreneurial capabilities and motivation at lower organizational levels. Although upper managers had supposedly made a commitment not to intervene in delegated decision making, upper managers' frequent meddling undercut motivation and caused Oticon to return to a more conventional organizational system. According to Brunsson (1982) and McMaster (1996), designing is especially difficult where key people are trying to

preserve an organization's long-term identity. Where an organization's former identity and power structures interlock, resistance arises to challenge objectives, tasks and situations connected to a new identity (McMaster, 1996). Successful design experiments and interventions depend on being able to analyze how and why people or artifacts resist or help change, and where key resources reside.

THE TRADITIONAL FOCUS ON FIT

Writings about organization design have traditionally assumed that organization designers understand the design context, the goals, and the best organization structures to achieve these goals. Consequently, writers focus on how designers and participants should align organizational components (e.g., Galbraith, 1973, 1995; Nadler and Tushman, 1997). The assumption is that if a design includes appropriate organizational components and if relationships among components support behavior congruent with organizational goals, the design will achieve desired results.

Writings about organization design consistently emphasize ideas about 'alignment,' 'fit', and 'congruence' between design components and environments (e.g., Baligh et al., 1996; Goold and Campbell, 2002). Designers are supposed to create, staff, structure, and relate organizational components so that they can meet future demands and pressures. The assumption is that a design that creates fit will produce efficient and effective achievement of organization goals. Chandler's (1962) claim that firm strategy and structure must fit together illustrates the accepted wisdom expressed by this traditional perspective.

Notions of fit assume that organizations and environments are quite stable and unchanging because unstable conditions make it very difficult for organizations to maintain some alignment between themselves and their environments or among their internal components. If an organization and its environments are changing normally, alignments cannot last long. Notions of fit also assume either that an organization faces a single environment or that its multiple environments require very similar organizational properties. They do not allow for the likelihood that an organization must deal with, and hence fit, multiple environments that imply mutually inconsistent requirements. Moreover, writings on design do not indicate how fit should accommodate the peculiarities of specific situations, and they do not provide useful information about how to maintain a good fit over time. A prescription to match an organization to its environments also does not indicate whether it is better to change the organization or its environments when there is misalignment. Changing only the organization may lead to undeveloped or under-exploited environmental opportunities. Changing only environments may fail to develop or create potentially valuable organizational properties (Dunbar et al., 1996; Porac and Rosa, 1996). As designers can try to alter the properties of the organization and its environments, they possess vast numbers of degrees of freedom, and as they make changes to achieve fits, unanticipated consequences are almost inevitable. Statistical studies intended to describe how organizations achieved fit have come up with results that are difficult to interpret, and what fit may mean seems to shift as a result of analyses (e.g., Russo and Harrison, 2005).

Prescriptions of fit between organizational components or between organizations and environments assume that the participants perceive design contexts accurately. There is convincing evidence, however, that many managers harbor inaccurate perceptions of their organizations' properties and of the properties of their organizations' environments (Mezias and Starbuck, 2003). It is very unclear how people who seriously misperceive the elements they are trying to fit together can achieve the fits that they seek. As well, a very successful consultant observed that managers choosing consultants prefer those whose ideas align most closely with their own, implying that it is very unlikely that such consultants will counteract managers' misperceptions (Rhenman, 1973).

One of the great liabilities of any approach to organization design that assumes excellent prior understanding of the situation, including the 'fit' approach, is that such a perspective vastly amplifies the human and financial costs of change. Believing that they are going to produce optimum organizations, the participants place too-large bets on their current understanding and the stability of the situations, and they make too-small provisions for learning and future developments. For organization design research to yield benefits, it is necessary to abandon the traditional assumptions that imply an all-knowing organization designer working in an essentially static world in which ideas about fit might make sense. Further research in this direction will simply hide the problems organization designers need to solve and can never help researchers or practitioners to understand better how to develop or manage emerging organization designs. Even if it were possible to align organization components, this alignment can only be temporary in a changing world.

RESEARCH THAT MATTERS FOR ORGANIZATION DESIGN

Commonsense and practical experiences suggest that organization design should be an iterative, long-term process rather than a one-time act. Because design projects generate unexpected as well as expected reactions, success requires persistence, designers are likely to discover that they need to revise their beliefs, and the processes involved with designing and taking action intertwine so that reciprocal learning should occur. Furthermore, in recognition that there will be inevitable changes in personnel, routines, resources, and environmental conditions, designs should incorporate elements that will provide continuing support for the exploration of opportunities and the questioning of basic assumptions.

For example, in the software field, where costs and time frames have proven notoriously unpredictable, the Sapient Corporation committed itself to a client-value proposition based on fixed-price, fixed-time-frame contracts (Khurana and Podolny, 2004). To fulfill these contract commitments, Sapient's organization design encouraged employees to become highly mindful of everything related to cost and time issues (Levinthal and Rerup, 2006). The firm asked them to question cost and timing structures and to explore all opportunities to reduce costs and to speed up software development. As a long-term strategy, the firm recruited, trained and rewarded people who helped it meet these commitments, and employees regularly experimented with and modified cost and timing structures in order to make sure projects finished within budget and on time.

Boland and Collopy (2004: 9) observed: 'A design attitude views each project as an opportunity for invention that includes a questioning of basic assumptions and a resolve to leave the world a better place than we found it.' Their observation incorporates three propositions. Firstly, designers should see designing as more than an application of their prior knowledge and instead as an opportunity for inventing new concepts and methods. Secondly, because designers often discover that their prior assumptions were incorrect, they should place low reliance on such assumptions and their design processes should incorporate experiments that help to uncover the errors in these assumptions. Thirdly, by placing design in a broad frame that considers the long-term issues in the surrounding societal context, designers may be able to anticipate the potential impacts of relevant forces that are not immediately apparent in the specific situation that they are aiming to alter.

Imagine a 'normal' organizational state in which everything is functioning well, consistent with past standards of performance. Two deviations from normal can occur. One type of deviation causes performance to fall below historical norms, and so the organization undertakes problem solving to get itself back to normal. The other type of deviation stems from the imaginations of managers who question the assumptions underlying the existing organization and visualize a new organization design that they expect to far exceed past performance levels. To achieve this positive deviation, the organization must develop new concepts and methods and then implement a new organization design. Cameron et al. (2003) called such an imagined improvement an 'abundance gap.' Research studies should investigate how to encourage organization members to imagine new designs that create 'abundance gaps'. Cameron and Lavine's (2006) study of the clean-up of the world's most dangerous nuclear weapons plant affords an example. Reporting that the clean-up was carried out faster and more safely than anyone imagined, they explained, 'The impossible was made possible by adopting an abundance approach to change rather than a deficit approach.' They described this process as amplifying positive consequences and making them self-reinforcing. Garud et al.'s (2006) description of the design of information systems at Infosys also illustrates a design based on 'abundance' gaps. They described how those involved developed new concepts and methods in order to make a new design effective.

The second element of Boland and Collopy's (2004) proposition suggests that designers need to carry out experiments that check the assumptions on which they base their design efforts. Vaast and Levina's (2006) study illustrates what may occur when there is no such experimentation. A newly appointed Chief Information Officer (CIO) decided that his IT department would be the central depository of his firm's IT knowledge and have authority over all IT and IT equipment decisions. He further decided that his IT department could deliver the same level of service as before but at much lower cost if skilled personnel had minimal contact with clients and client relationships channeled through a formalized, web-based information system. The resulting web-based system relied on extensive codification and it enabled client departments to carry out and keep records of many routine tasks. As the CIO had expected, his new design processed requests faster and significantly reduced costs.

Before long, however, powerful client departments began to react. Some client departments had received customized IT services under the former CIO and some clients were struggling with the unfamiliar web-based system. These clients grew increasingly dissatisfied with the new system and its deliverables despite its good performance on objective measures. The CIO did not hear of these frustrations because his redesign allocated all communication with clients to low-level temporary workers; he did not ask the low status temporary workers about client issues and they did not volunteer them. One client department eventually convinced the CEO that the IT department had bungled a particular project, so the CEO allowed this client department to outsource that project to an external vendor. Other client departments learned of this and they too began outsourcing projects. The company then transferred resources from the IT department to the client departments so that they could outsource more. The company reduced the size of the IT department and restricted it to doing simple, routine tasks that easily fitted within the web-based information system. Eventually, it became clear that the company no longer needed a separate IT department and the CEO asked the CIO to resign. In their analysis, Vaast and Levina (2006) noted Tolstoy's view that 'every unhappy family is unhappy in its own way.' Designers should remember that unhappy, possibly unique, design experiences often stem from untested design assumptions.

The third element of Boland and Collopy's (2004) proposition suggests that designers need to take account of long-term influences that could alter their design situations. Madsen et al. (2006), for example, described how two physicians redesigned a pediatric intensive-care unit in a hospital. Unlike many critical care units where physicians make almost all care decisions, this unit involved nurses and support staff in care decisions. These physicians believed that such units should use the most up-to-date information about

critically ill patients, and since nurses and support staff are often the ones who have this information, they should receive training to recognize and report critical signals and to take needed actions. As the unit steadily expanded, its mortality rates declined steadily; it was the source of a steady stream of new care innovations, staff involvement in patient care increased, and turnover declined.

Nevertheless, physicians from other parts of the hospital questioned the autonomy that the new design gave to nurses and staff, which ran against their beliefs and training. Eventually, the two physician designers decided to minimize contact between the unit and the rest of the hospital. Because of the unit's expansion, however, the hospital then hired two new intensivists who thought that the unit's patient-care approach bordered on malpractice. The unit split into camps and physicians outside the unit again voiced concerns. The two physician designers decided to leave and the hospital abandoned the design that had succeeded on so many criteria. Barry and Rerup (2006) described a similar series of developments in a university. Yoo et al. (2006) described how Frank Gehry, the architect, tries to involve all of those who may be affected by his buildings in a continuing dialog in order to encourage long-term acceptance of his often revolutionary-looking buildings.

Expectations have important impacts on design outcomes and King's (1974) field experiment demonstrated such effects. The experiment involved four company plants and appeared to compare the impact of two forms of job design. Plants 1 and 2 experimented with 'job enlargement,' in which machine crews both set up their machines and inspected their own finished work. Plants 3 and 4 experimented with 'job rotation,' where workers shifted from one task to another at scheduled intervals. The director of manufacturing also gave plant managers different reasons for the experiment, creating a further level of difference between the plants. He told the managers of plants 1 and 3 that prior research implied that the job changes should increase productivity, and he told the managers of plants 2 and 4 that research implied that the job changes should improve 'industrial relations'. In the two plants where the plant managers had been told to expect higher productivity, productivity rose 6 percent over the ensuing 12 months; and in the two plants where the plant managers had been told to expect better industrial relations absenteeism declined 12 percent over the ensuing 12 months. However, productivity at the two job-enlargement plants (1 and 2) was only 0.4 percent higher than at the two job-rotation plants (3 and 4), and absenteeism at the two job-enlargement plants differed by less than 1 percent from that at the two job-rotation plants. In this experiment, the changes in workers' actual activities had tiny effects, whereas the differences in the plant managers' expectations had much larger effects. Research needs to develop better understanding of how expectations affect design effectiveness.

Romme and Endenburg (2006) illustrated how designers can use visualizations and narratives to encourage people to imagine new organizational forms. The so-called circular-design process uses a set of straightforward design principles such as 'mistakes must be made' and 'levels in the hierarchy should be double linked'. These principles guide design experiments that test alternative practices and arrangements, and the experimentation uses pictures and stories to clarify the design principles. For example, a Dutch engineering firm applied the circular-design approach to resolve a severe crisis by discussing and implementing strategic measures that an employee had proposed. Ever since, people in the firm have shared repeatedly the story of this dramatic episode (Romme, 1999), and this institutionalized narrative helps newcomers to understand the organizational design processes in this firm. Moreover, the narrative shows them what the possible outcomes of these design processes can be.

CONCLUSION

Research into organization design should seek to understand how designs develop and respond to evolving situations. As design contexts evolve, expectations can create new and contextually relevant responses or insist on adherence to predictions and plans. Our view is that the former is necessary and requires experimentation and the latter is costly and prevents effective design. Since designers do not have complete information as they begin designing, they need to experiment by exploring multiple alternatives in terms of the goals they are trying to achieve and how they are trying to achieve them. Designers also need to recognize that the results of design projects depend not just on the original relationships among the components but also on the processes that are used over time to rearrange, change and adapt these components, and on the motivations of the people who are participating in the design projects and on how all evolve over time. These processes strongly influence how organization members see the current and potential situations, and more specifically, the extent to which they see an articulated organization vision as widely accepted and influential.

REFERENCES

Augier, M., March, J.G. and Sullivan, B. N. (2005) 'Notes on the evolution of a research community: Organization studies in Anglophone North America, 1945–2000', *Organization Science*, 16: 85–95.

Baligh, H.H., Burton, R.M. and Obel, B. (1996) 'Organizational consultant: Creating a useable theory for organizational design', *Management Science*, 42: 1648–1662.

Barry, D. and Rerup, C. (2006) 'Going mobile: Aesthetic design considerations from Calder and the Constructivists', *Organization Science*, 17: 262–276.

Boland, R., Jr. and Collopy, F. (eds) (2004) *Managing as Designing*. Stanford: Stanford University Press.

Box, G.E.P. and Draper, N.R. (1969) *Evolutionary Operation*. New York: Wiley.

Bronfenbrenner, U. (1979) *The Ecology of Human Development: Experiments by Nature and Design*. Cambridge, MA: Harvard University Press.

Brunsson, N. (1982) 'The irrationality of action and action rationality: Decisions, ideologies, and organisational actions', *Journal of Management Studies*, 19: 29–44.

Brusoni, S. and Prencipe, A. (2006) 'Making design rules: A multidomain perspective', *Organization Science*, 17: 179–189.

Cameron, K., Dutton, J.E. and Quinn, R.E. (eds) (2003) *Positive Organizational Scholarship: The Foundations of a New Discipline*. San Francisco, CA: Berrett-Koehler.

Cameron, K. and Lavine, M. (2006) *Making the Impossible Possible: Leading Extraordinary Performance – the Rocky Flats Story*, San Francisco, CA: Berrett-Koehler.

Campbell, D.T. and Russo, M.J. (1998) *Social Experimentation*. London: Sage.

Chandler, A.D., Jr. (1962) *Strategy and Structure*. Boston: MIT Press.

Daft, R.L. (2006) *Organization Theory and Design*. Minneapolis/St Paul, MI: West Publishing.

Dunbar, R.L.M. and Starbuck, W.H. (2006) 'Learning to design organizations and learning from designing them', *Organization Science*, 17: 171–178.

Dunbar, R.L.M., Garud, R. and Raghuram, S. (1996) 'A frame for deframing in strategic analysis', *Journal of Management Inquiry*, 5: 23–34.

Foss, N.J. (2003) 'Selective intervention and internal hybrids: Interpreting and learning from the rise and decline of the Oticon spaghetti organization', *Organization Science*, 14: 331–349.

Galbraith, J.R. (1973) *Organizational Design*. Reading, MA: Addison-Wesley.

Galbraith, J.R. (1995) *Designing Organizations: An Executive Briefing on Strategy, Structure and Process*. San Francisco, CA: Jossey-Bass.

Garud, R., Kumaraswamy, A. and Sambamurthy, V. (2006) 'Emergent by design: Performance and transformation at Infosys Technologies', *Organization Science*, 17: 277–286.

Gauch, H.G. Jr. (2006) 'Winning the accuracy game'. *American Scientist*, 94 (2): March-April 133–141.

Glaser, R. (ed.) (1978) *Research and Development and School Change*. Hillsdale, NJ: Lawrence Erlbaum Associates.

Goold, M. and Campbell, A. (2002) *Designing Effective Organizations: How to Create Structured Networks*. San Francisco, CA: Jossey-Bass.

Gordon, Robert Aaron and Howell, James Edwin (1959) *Higher Education for Busines*. New York: Columbia University Press.

Jaques, E. (1951) *The Changing Culture of a Factory*. London: Tavistock.

Khurana, R. and Podolny, J. (2004) 'Sapient Corporation. HBS Case 9-405-04519', Cambridge, MA: Harvard Business School.

King, A.S. (1974) 'Expectation effects in organizational change', *Administrative Science Quarterly*, 19: 221–230.

Levinthal, D. and Rerup, C. (2006) 'Crossing an apparent chasm: Bridging mindful and less-mindful perspectives on organizational learning', *Organization Science*, 17: 502–513.

Likert, R. (1961) *New Patterns of Management*. New York: McGraw-Hill.

McMaster, M.D. (1996) *The Intelligence Advantage: Organizing for Complexity*. Boston: Butterworth-Heinemann.

Madsen, P., Desai, V., Roberts, K. and Wong, D. (2006) 'Mitigating hazards through continuing design: The birth and evolution of a pediatric intensive care unit', *Organization Science*, 17: 239–248.

Mezias, J.M. and Starbuck, W.H. (2003) 'Studying the accuracy of managers' perceptions: A research odyssey', *British Journal of Management*, 14: 3–17.

Nadler, D.A. and Tushman, M.L. (1997) *Competing by Design: The Power of Organizational Architecture*. New York: Oxford University Press.

Nelson, H.A. and Stolterman, E. (2003) *The Design Way: Intentional Change in an Unpredictable World*. Englewood Cliffs, NJ: Educational Technology Publications.

Nystrom, P.C. and Starbuck, W.H. (1984) 'To avoid organizational crises, unlearn', *Organizational Dynamics*, 12 (4): 53–65.

Pant, P.N. and Starbuck, W.H. (1990) 'Innocents in the forest: Forecasting and research methods', *Journal of Management*, 16: 433–460.

Pierson, Frank, C. (1959) *The Education of American Businessmen*. New York: McGraw-Hill.

Platt, J.R. (1964) 'Strong inference', *Science* 146: 347–353.

Popper, K.R. (1962) *The Open Society and Its Enemies* (fourth edition). London: Routledge and Kegan Paul.

Porac, J.F. and Rosa, J.A. (1996) 'In praise of managerial narrow-mindedness', *Journal of Management Inquiry*, 5: 35–42.

Rhenman, E. (1973) *Organization Theory for Long Range Planning*. London: Wiley.

Riecken, H.W. and Boruch, R.F. (eds) (1974) *Social Experimentation: A Method for Planning and Evaluating Social Intervention*. Written by a committee of the Social Science Research Council. New York: Academic Press.

Rivlin, A.M. and Timpane, P. M. (eds) (1975) *Ethical and Legal Issues of Social Experimentation*. Washington: Brookings Institution.

Romme, A.G.L. (1999) 'Domination, self-determination, and circular organizing', *Organization Studies*, 20: 801–832.

Romme, A.G.L. and Endenburg, G. (2006) 'Construction principles and design rules in the case of circular design', *Organization Science*, 17: 287–297.

Russo, M.V. and Harrison, N.S. (2005) 'Organizational design and environmental performance: Clues from the electronics industry', *Academy of Management Journal*, 48: 582–593.

Schein, E.H. (1987) *The Clinical Perspective in Fieldwork*. London: Sage.

Simon, H.A. (1996) *The Sciences of the Artificial* (third edition). Cambridge, MA: MIT Press.

Starbuck, W.H. (1993) 'Watch where you step!' or Indiana Starbuck amid the perils of Academe (Rated PG). Pages 63–110 in A. Bedeian (ed.), *Management Laureates, Volume 3*. Greenwich, CT: JAI Press.

Starbuck, W.H. (2003) 'The origins of organization theory', in H. Tsoukas and C. Knudsen (eds), *The Oxford Handbook of Organization Theory: Meta-Theoretical Perspectives*. Oxford: Oxford University Press. pp. 143–182.

Starbuck, W.H. (2004) 'Why I stopped trying to understand the *real* world', *Organization Studies*, 25: 1233–1254.

Starbuck, W.H. (2006) *The Production of Knowledge*. Oxford: Oxford University Press.

Vaast, E. and Levina, N. (2006) 'Multiple faces of codification: Organization redesign in an IT organization', *Organization Science*, 17: 190–201.

Weber, M. (1972) *Wirtschaft und Gesellschaft* (ed. by J. Winckelmann) (fifth edition), Tübingen: Mohr.

Worren, N., Moore, K. and Elliott, R. (2002) 'When theories become tools: Toward a framework for pragmatic validity', *Human Relations*, 55: 1227–1250.

Wren, D.A. (1994) *The Evolution of Management Thought*, (fourth edition). New York: Wiley.

Yoo, Y., Boland, R.J., Jr. and Lyytinen, K. (2006) 'From organization design to organization designing', *Organization Science*, 17: 215–229.

The Shape of Things to Come

Raymond E. Miles and Charles C. Snow

A number of years ago, we argued that new forms of organizing arise for two main reasons, one backward-looking and the other forward-looking (Miles et al., 1997). Looking backward, the search for a new organizational form is strongly motivated by efforts to correct the deficiencies of existing organizational forms. Looking forward, the search is often motivated by the belief that current organizational forms will not be able to fully utilize the most critical resources of the foreseeable future.

Using this dual logic, we envision a global economy where knowledge is the key resource used to produce economic wealth. To obtain the full benefit of using knowledge as a resource, many existing organizations will have to be redesigned to increase their capability to innovate. Also, new types of organizations will have to be invented to foster multi-firm collaboration as the key means of creating and applying knowledge. New or redesigned organizations, in turn, will require new management approaches, including a new philosophy of management that emphasizes the human potential for demonstrating positive values and actions instead of the narrow pursuit of self-interest.

A firm may exploit knowledge by tapping into it, acquiring it, or sharing it with its partner firms. Intel, for example, is renowned for its ability to monitor a wide variety of activities and experiments among firms along the industry value chain, and then to access the knowledge and expertise it finds most promising by taking an equity position in those downstream firms which are developing new knowledge. Cisco Systems usually opts for acquiring the upstream firms whose knowledge it believes is potentially most valuable. And, there are countless examples of firms that engage in knowledge transfer through organizational arrangements such as joint ventures in which the resource bases of the partnering firms are complementary.

In the future, we expect to see even more complex pursuits of knowledge assets, especially the joint *creation* and *sharing* of knowledge. Indeed, moving forward, the ability to continuously create and apply knowledge may be the only truly sustainable factor in achieving competitive advantage. Knowledge creation and utilization require the ability to collaborate, both within and across firms, and the concept that we see taking hold in a growing number of business firms and other types of organizations is *collaborative entrepreneurship* – the creation of something of economic value based on new, jointly generated ideas that emerge from the open sharing of information, experiences, and expertise (Miles et al., 2005).

Existing organizational forms, which are geared primarily toward competition – or at most cooperation on specific projects – invariably come up short in facilitating collaboration among firms. Successful inter-firm collaboration is based on deep competence and experience, trust among individuals and organizations, large investments in intellectual and relational capital, and efficient, open sharing of ideas and information. Even the most advanced supply chain organizations, in which a group of firms arrayed along an industry value chain operates as an 'extended enterprise,' are based mostly on a cooperative rather than collaborative model (Miles and Snow, 2007). In a cooperative

Continued

venture, desired outcomes are relatively clear, specific goals and contracts can be defined, and the distribution of future returns can be negotiated ahead of time. Collaboration, on the other hand, may result in positive but unplanned outcomes, and it relies on a joint commitment among participants to the equitable sharing of returns whether or not they can be anticipated.

We are not aware of any complete examples of large-scale inter-firm collaboration in the world today. Therefore, in an attempt to initiate a dialogue about the development of this needed new organizational form, we constructed a hypothetical organization composed of multiple firms working together collaboratively to both create and apply knowledge (Miles et al., 2005). Our fictional organization is able to do what many firms in the global economy are struggling to achieve: the ability to continuously innovate both within and across industries. The notable features of this collaborative network organization include a focus on the creation as opposed to appropriation of economic wealth, mechanisms for bringing together disparate firms to share ideas and approaches, a self-governance system based on broadly defined principles or protocols, and a commitment among all firms in the network to act entrepreneurially but not exploitatively.

Will a futuristic multi-firm organization of the sort we envision emerge someday? We believe such an organization not only can but will appear – and, moreover, it will flourish. Some group of pioneering firms will see the value of this new type of organization and will undertake the risky investments in trust building and collaborative capability required to make it happen. Also, we predict that those pioneering firms will introduce a new philosophy of management, one whose values and practices reflect a sophisticated awareness of social and economic interdependence. Although this philosophy is just beginning to be articulated (Rocha and Ghoshal, 2004), it clearly reflects a view of human nature with the capacity to display as much concern for others as a concern for oneself.

REFERENCES

Miles, R.E., Miles, G. and Snow, C.C. (2005) *Collaborative Entrepreneurship: How Communities of Networked Firms Use Continuous Innovation to Create Economic Wealth*. Stanford, CA: Stanford University Press.

Miles, R.E., Snow, C.C., Mathews, J.A., Miles, G. and Coleman, H.J., Jr. (1997) 'Organizing in the knowledge age: Anticipating the cellular form', *Academy of Management Executive*, 11: 7–20.

Miles, R.E. and Snow, C.C. (2007) Organization theory and supply chain management: An evolving research perspective. *Journal of Operations Management*, 25: 459–463.

Rocha, H.O. and Ghoshal, S. (2004) 'Beyond self-interest: Revisiting the major assumption in economics and management', Working Paper, London Business School.

New Organization Forms – the Career of a Concept

Ian Palmer and Richard Dunford

In the beginning (well, almost the beginning) there was the word – and it belonged to Tom Peters. He spoke to us and let us know that 'in this madcap world, turned-on and theoretically empowered people … will never amount to a hill of beans in the vertically oriented, staff-driven, thick-headquarters corporate structures that still do most of the world's business' (1992: 13). He told us to go forth and make sure 'the arteries are unclogged (the "structure" part), then radically rewired (the "systems" part)' (1992: 13). And so was our attention directed to turn from the old structures, for those were depicted as the way to doom and despair in this high-paced world. Instead, we were told of the need to embrace the new structures, the small, impermanent project-oriented teams which would be able to provide the speed and flexibility needed to survive in this 'madcap world'.

Then followed the cacophony of metaphors competing with each other to describe this new form. Within a very short period of time we were introduced to networks, shamrocks, intelligent structures, boundaryless ones, horizontal and cluster designs, flexible, bi-modal ones, as well as to modular, spinout, spider's webs and starburst structures.

The range of metaphors continued to expand and all clamored for our attention. It was only a matter of time before the question began to be asked: what, if anything, of substance lay behind the battle for semantic supremacy ('my metaphor's better than your metaphor')? Was this burgeoning literature on new forms guiding our way in the face of a fundamental shift in how we should conceive and enact the practice of organizing? How could we tell?

Rather than drowning in this sea of imagery, a few souls stopped to consider a simple question: how strong is the evidence for the emergence of new organizational forms? They discovered that the extant literature was heavily dependent on case studies with a small number of high profile corporations making regular appearances in support of a whole range of different metaphors. How were we to know whether these were a set of interesting experiments on the periphery of mainstream practice – there are always some such experiments occurring – or, as the new forms authors argued, the vanguard of the [necessary] new way of organizing?

Some comfort could be taken from the fact that there was a high degree of consistency in the nature of the organizational practices attributed to these new forms – flattening of structures, decentralization, reduction in functional silos, use of collaborative networks and alliances, outsourcing and the use of project structures were common features. It would have been worrying if, as well as facing the proliferation of images, there had been no commonality regarding the changes purported to be taking place. The challenge was to see how pervasive is this phenomenon of 'new forms' and whether the new forms, to the extent they exist, do so through the replacement of traditional modes of organizing.

What has been found? Virtual organizations, built around horizontal relationships, can exhibit considerable hierarchical tendencies, organizations can combine both bureaucracy

Continued

and flexibility, and increased product modularity does not necessarily lead to less use of hierarchical forms. Transnational organizations may retain hierarchical governance as an overriding feature and it turns out that project-based forms of organizing will '[not become] the paradigmatic replacement for the Chandlerian company in twenty-first capitalism, as some have suggested' (Whitley, 2006: 92).

Formalization is not so bad after all. (Is that a sigh of relief we hear from The Aston School?) It turns out that we still need rules and regulations to reduce risk, especially in high risk environment, to encourage (yes, encourage, not inhibit) innovation and to ensure efficiency and security. Unlikely though it may seem, entrepreneurial start-ups with higher formalization, specialization and administrative intensity outperform those with more organic structures (Sine et al., 2006).

Another previous enemy of flexibility, the villain *centralization,* has been brought in from the cold. It turns out we need it to help with strategic decision-making in uncertain environments, to respond quickly to market intelligence and to reduce the uncertainty and lack of job clarity associated with flatter, decentralized organizations. Through survey based research we have been INNFORMed by Pettigrew and Fenton (2000) that the 'new' organizational practices exist but, very significantly, they do so alongside 'old' practices, a conclusion we also drew (Dunford, Palmer, Benveniste and Crawford, 2007).

Pheeww! Let's take stock – what have we learnt so far from the career of this concept, the new organizational form? There has been a counter-move to the breathless predictions of the demise of organizations as we know them. Reports of the imminent death of the hierarchical organization are much exaggerated. There is a convergence emerging in the findings of empirical research, specifically, that 'old' practices such as formalization and centralization coexist with, rather than are replaced by, new practices even though we need to know much more about how such coexistence works.

However, the field continues to have some unresolved issues in relation to the use of the term 'new organization forms'. First, both the terms 'new' and 'form' can be matters of dispute. Does 'new' mean 'new in time' (the first time we've seen it) or 'new in context' (the first time we've seen it here)? The term 'form' generates its own challenges as there is still ambiguity as to whether it is interchangeable with terms such as 'structure' or 'design.' Authors in this field have experienced this ambiguity in their exchanges with journal reviewers: for some reviewers the distinction is a matter of indifference, for others a matter of fundamental importance.

Second is the issue of complexity. Are new forms simpler or more complex than their previous incarnations? For some writers, new forms are simpler based on them being flatter, knowledge sharing structures; for others they are complex, involving simultaneous juggling of various tensions such as centralized control and decentralized participation and flexibility. Third, what is the driver of new forms? For some writers, managers are the drivers, experimenting with new forms, whereas for others, the environment is the driver, forcing organizations to better fit their environment. Fourth, what is the level of analysis that new form is applied to? Is it descriptive of the whole organization, a section of the organization, or a particular practice which has been newly adopted?

These are yet to be resolved issues associated with the concept 'new organizational form'. Time will tell whether this concept's career is still in the process of maturing, or rather is already approaching a well-deserved retirement.

REFERENCES

Dunford, R., Palmer, I., Benveniste, J. and Crawford, J. (2007) 'Coexistence of "old" and "new" organizational practices: Transitory phenomenon or enduring feature?' *Asia Pacific Journal of Human Resources*, 45 (1): 24–43.

Palmer, I., Benveniste, J. and Dunford, R. (2007) 'New organizational forms: Towards a generative dialogue', *Organization Studies*, 28 (12): 1829–1847.

Peters, T. (1992) *Liberation Management: Necessary Disorganization for the Nanosecond Nineties.* New York: Alfred A. Knopf.

Pettigrew, A. and Fenton, E. (eds) (2000) *The Innovating Organization.* London: Sage.

Sine, W.D., Mitsuhashi, H. and Kirsch, D.A. (2006) 'Revisiting Burns and Stalker: Formal structure and new venture performance in emerging economic sectors', *Academy of Management Journal*, 49: 121–132.

Whitley, R. (2006) 'Project-based firms: new organizational form or variations on a theme?', *Industrial and Corporate Change*, 15: 77–99.

Suppose We Took Organizational Performance Seriously

C. Chet Miller

Students of organizations spend much of their time developing explanations for performance. In so doing, they risk both sanity and professional standing in a chase for the academic equivalent of the biblical Holy Grail. In the memorable words of March and Sutton,

> Scholarly virtue is more a struggle than an achievement, and seeking knowledge about historically ambiguous phenomena such as organizational performance is more a form of disciplined self-flagellation than a pursuit of happiness. (1997: 705)

In this brief essay, I outline the perils of a life devoted to the study organizational performance.

One issue is implied by the term itself. The term 'performance' implies a monolithic phenomenon, or in the academic vernacular a uni-dimensional construct. Indeed, organizational performance is routinely treated as a uni-dimensional construct in theory development (Glick et al., 2005). Moreover, there may be subtle pressure to follow such an approach. In some areas, particularly strategic management, organizational performance seems to serve as a central feature of the professional identity. What is it that we do? We explain organizational performance.

Of course, organizational performance is not monolithic. It is a multi-construct phenomenon comprising a loose assemblage of disparate outcomes. Theory development focused on performance as a generic outcome is necessarily abstract and loose, not to mention counter-productive.

A second issue is the use of simple models, a practice forced on students of organizations by the page limitations of journals and perhaps by the all too human desire for simple explanations. Simple models, however, do not do justice to complex phenomena, which performance most assuredly is. Performance is affected by a multitude of factors interacting in complex ways across multiple levels of analysis. Further, it affects itself. For example, performance above aspirations may result in a decrease in efforts while performance below aspirations may result in strong improvement efforts (see, for example, Cyert and March, 1963). To the extent that such a pattern exists, all firms are involved in a dance where they are attracted to the middle of the distribution.

A third issue corresponds to unattractive measurement options. Although many students of organizations (including journal reviewers) are in the midst of a love affair with archival measures, those measures are hardly without faults. Quoting Carlile and Christensen:

> The data used in many research projects comes from companies' financial statements ... Is this objective? Johnson and Kaplan (1987) showed quite convincingly that the numbers representing revenues, costs, and profits in financial statements are typically the result of processes of estimation, negotiation, debate, and politics that can produce grossly inaccurate reflections of true cost and profit. Even the 'hardest' of numbers ... really are after-the-fact proxy manifestations of the prioritizations, fudging measurements, exaggerations and negotiations that occurred before a number appeared to represent all of those things. (2005: 17)

Key-informant measures (interviews, surveys) also have their problems. If performance is assessed over a long period of time, then simple recall errors can be an issue. If only one informant is used in each organization, then questions of reliability emerge. If interviews and surveys unduly highlight the independent variables under consideration, then naive informant modeling can be an issue. Beyond these well-known drawbacks of informant measures, there are a host of subtle and not so subtle factors to consider. If, for example, a firm is performing well, informants may be biased towards high ratings for any positive variable under their control. This is a form of the well-known self-serving bias from attribution theory.

With the above issues affecting the study of organizational performance, the question becomes – Should we abandon the pursuit of the Holy Grail? Should we abandon attempts to explain performance? Yes and no! Allow me to explain. We should not focus our theory building on a generic construct labeled 'performance.' There is no such thing. Instead, we should focus our attention on specific aspects of this multi-construct phenomenon, aspects that make sense for a given theoretical context. Moreover, we desperately need to develop a comprehensive nomological net connecting various performance constructs and their individual dimensions. Without such a comprehensive mapping of the conceptual domain, we cannot effectively work with 'organizational performance.'

REFERENCES

Carlile, P. and Christensen, C.M. (2005) 'The cycles of theory-building in management research'. Working Paper. Boston: Boston University.

Cyert, R.M. and March, J.G. (1963) *A Behavioral Theory of the Firm.* Englewood Cliffs, NJ: Prentice-Hall.

Glick, W.H., Washburn, N.T. and Miller, C.C. (2005) 'The myth of firm performance', paper presented at the Academy of Management Annual Meeting, Honolulu, Hawaii.

Johnson, H.T. and Kaplan, R. (1987) *Relevance Lost.* Boston, MA: Harvard Business School Press.

March, J.G. and Sutton, R.I. (1997) 'Organizational performance as a dependent variable', *Organization Science,* 8 (6): 698–706.

Managers Who Can Transform Institutions in Their Firms: Activism and the Practices That Stick

Robert Chapman Wood and Liisa Valikangas

Ordinary professionals often don't know their own strength. A powerful yet little-studied way large organizations can innovate is for groups of activist managers and professionals to join together to change routines and alter taken-for-granted ways of thinking. The evidence suggests such activism can be far more powerful than most people – including activists themselves – realize.

Such activism is gaining more attention. Kleiner (1996) wrote an early study. Recent work has documented campaigns in Shell Oil (Hamel, 1999), the World Bank (Wood and Hamel, 2002), and American Telephone & Telegraph (Muller and Valikangas, 2003). Activism has changed basic thought processes. It represents a new way for large, established firms to innovate, quite distinct from strategic planning (Ansoff, 1988), reliance on

'emergent strategy' (Mintzberg, 1990), or the deliberate chief executive decision-making that journalists often celebrate. We argue – drawing principally on data from impactful yet ultimately not fully successful activism at AT&T – that activists who understand the political nature of institutional change can play key roles in enabling firms to meet environmental challenges. This will require, however, knowledge and skills that few activists have adequately demonstrated.

We suggest activists need to draw on recent theory of institutions – the basic, taken-for-granted rules of the game in human systems. First, activists need to understand better the nature of institutions inside their organizations – that they are automatically accepted as part of reality yet ultimately alterable, that they make it possible for activists to perform some vital tasks of renewal while making others enormously difficult. Second, activists need to understand the nature of institutional entrepreneurship. Institutional entrepreneurship theory shows how they can carry out the difficult political tasks of bringing together constituents to support new ways of doing things and then getting people accustomed to ways just different enough to work.

AT&T's Opportunity Discovery Department (ODD) became a hub for a sort of social movement (McAdam and Snow, 1997) in the organization aimed at rejuvenating it. Officially established to examine technology futures and develop tools for scientific strategy-making, its people constantly

promoted change they believed the firm needed to survive. They achieved remarkable, though partial, success. However, the firm's ultimate sale to SBC (which adopted the AT&T name) represented defeat of the venerable, pioneering company that ODD sought to save.

Table 3.13.1 lists lessons from institutional theory and compares them to ODD's behavior and its results. In this chapter we first describe ODD's social movement, its successes, and its ultimate disbandment. Then we briefly consider the definitions of 'institution' and their usefulness for practitioner challenges, suggesting an approach that we believe makes clear the institutional issues

Table 3.13.1   Key lessons of institutionalism for activists

Topic	Literature	ODD Behavior	Results
Nature of institutions	Institutions are rules of the game (North, 1990) that are taken for granted (Berger and Luckmann, 1966) and create logic of appropriateness (March and Olsen, 1989).	ODD knew it was trying to change the rules, but it often took existing rules for granted in ways that hurt its overall project (e.g., acting as a Labs-based support unit, it did not develop strategy for reaching top management).	ODD proved 'right' in retrospect but it did not ultimately succeed in transforming AT&T. Its work had significant impact on some parts, but it never built relationships with the managers most important to its success.
Nature of institutional entrepreneurship	Institutional entrepreneurship is highly political (DiMaggio, 1988).	ODD reveled in being different and using methods that were highly original (including unusual language). ODD was more like a rebellion seeking to awaken than a constitutional movement seeking political and institutional support.	While ODD survived as a movement surprisingly long (perhaps due to its links to Bell Labs), it ultimately dissipated as its position became politically untenable and some of its leaders left.
Process of institutional change	Institutions are formed not so much by deliberate decision as by habitualization, objectification, and sedimentation (Berger and Luckmann, 1966).	ODD was successful in initiating some new management practices (such as scenario planning) but it failed to make these routine practice.	ODD never achieved substantial changes in strategy-making at AT&T as a whole or got core strategy-making efforts to take it, as an R&D unit, seriously as a contributor.
Institutional entrepreneurship skills	Supporters must form 'center or core' supporting new institutions through skillful use of tactics such as agenda-setting and 'goallessness' (Fligstein, 1997).	Some ODD behavior was politically astute, but as it achieved successes it did not develop a political strategy to build on the successes and its large grassroots network to consolidate its support.	Lack of a well-structured coalition and senior executive championing made it easy for enemies to kill ODD after its creator left firm. ODD's revolutionary air may have also felt threatening to the AT&T 'establishment' once ODD became seen as a potentially competent entity.

that activists confront. Finally, we outline what institutional theory could have taught ODD and can teach activists elsewhere – practitioner-oriented understandings of institutions and deliberate institutional change. We compare what institutional theory teaches to ODD's behavior and draw new insights into institutions from ODD's experience.

THE ODD MOVEMENT IN AT&T

Greg Blonder, a physicist and research manager, organized the Opportunity Discovery Department in 1995 in Bell Labs, AT&T's research unit. Senior executives chartered it to analyze large technological trends and develop strategy tools. However, Blonder intended much more – a way to awaken the firm for continuing large-scale strategic change. Ultimately ODD achieved dramatic successes. However, members did not plan how to cement relations with AT&T's most senior executives or deal with opponents. The unit and the movement were eventually disbanded. The account here is based on Muller and Valikangas (2003) and additional interviews, review of AT&T documents, and review of reports in the business press.

AT&T in 1995

When the movement began, Bell Labs was the world's most prestigious private technology laboratory. Created in 1927, it had invented the transistor and the UNIX operating system. When AT&T was a regulated monopoly, its predictable income provided generous support. In 1984, however, the U.S. Justice Department had forced the firm's breakup. It spun off regional phone companies, leaving a smaller firm in the glamorous, less-regulated, but competitive long-distance transmission, telecommunications equipment, and technology services businesses.

The smaller AT&T failed in its efforts to enter new businesses. It lost money selling computers and had great difficulty trying to create new local phone services. The now-independent regional companies,

meanwhile, proved reluctant to continue buying from the former parent as it sought to compete with it. As wireless telephony and the Internet started to undercut core AT&T businesses, professional managers understood the developments far less than many of Bell Labs scientists.

The firm had no effective way of changing its business models. Its Corporate Strategy and Planning (CSP) regularly prepared projections of medium-term trends and required resources, but it had no credible mechanism for thinking in a radical way about large problems. Other firms were imitating AT&T, building high-quality, low-cost networks, and continually reducing prices. AT&T did not seem to understand this as a threat. In fact, in 1996 the firm's chief financial officer said: 'AT&T's strategy is sound. We know that because of the many players in the marketplace with the same strategy' (Muller and Valikangas, 2003: 110).

Later strategy documents recognized the problem as AT&T lost market share. As late as 1998, however, they rarely discussed underlying technical and market dynamics, saying that 'executing well' was the key to success. In 1995 AT&T remained highly profitable and supported more staff than necessary for its businesses. People who understood the technical and regulatory situation suspected, however, that this was unlikely to continue.

The structure of a movement

Blonder's successful technical career had enabled him in 1993 to persuade corporate executives to create the position of chief technical advisor for the firm and give him the job. However, he had achieved little influence over corporate strategy by 1995 when he founded the Scenario Planning and Business Department (as ODD was originally called). It had three people and was to analyze the long-term impact of technology on AT&T and develop or adopt tools (e.g., scenario planning) for more scientific strategy.

Blonder and the staff who joined him saw their real mission to be challenging the status quo so that AT&T could realize its potential. Soon after the launch of the initiative it had to be radically reorganized. Problems in computers and equipment manufacturing forced a second huge spin-off, with AT&T reconstituting NCR Corp (a computer firm it had purchased five years earlier) and creating Lucent Technologies as an independent equipment maker. The Labs were split between AT&T and Lucent, and Blonder appointed Amy Muller, a materials scientist, to head the re-named Opportunity Development Department, which now had eight members.

The unit worked hard to teach scenario planning, then a fairly new technique (see de Geus, 1997). Since many experts saw radical transformation ahead, scenario planning was a strong inducement for more realistic thinking. (Some scenarios were based on the processes that ODD suspected would turn long-distance into a low-cost commodity, for instance. Scenario planning facilitators asked, 'What if [long-distance] minutes were free?')

However, the group pushed aggressively to do more. ODD was soon a small organization in the labs, leading and supporting a corps of active allies among managers and professionals in much of the firm. It organized the Grass-Roots Network of Strategic Thinkers (GNOST), which eventually included 450 managers and professionals. ODD communicated with the network through a newsletter (called 'No Surprises'), a series of meetings called, 'Not Your Usual Research Seminar,' and annual off-site scenario-planning events where issues involving many units of the corporation were discussed. Meetings frequently attracted 50 to 70 professionals. The network put the department in touch with specialist experts on most issues. Rebels within many business units got in touch.

Ideas from strategic planning/scenario-making meetings became part of the people's plans and talking points. The creative ferment eventually encouraged AT&T's largest business units to ask ODD to help them develop strategies although senior corporate executives had not been consulted about ODD's initiatives.

ODD, meanwhile, reveled in being seen as unusual. Its name was chosen with understanding that the acronym would be pronounced 'odd.' It developed offbeat slang. Network members would describe the current state of telecommunications management as a 'confusopoly.' Charts with key information of which the relevant executives were ignorant were called 'ignorance maps.' 'Naked emperors' were misguided executives with delicate egos whom no one was willing to confront.

As a department in the labs, ODD had prestige but was not initially perceived as a threat to power centers. Its direct employees had scientific backgrounds – psychology, chemistry, biology, physics, engineering, materials science. Only one had business management experience – a psychologist with an M.B.A. who had managed parts of a switching system unit. Many outsiders leveraged organizational slack to work on ODD-inspired projects. They rarely seemed to be trying to advance their careers; few showed interest in becoming general managers, and performance appraisal systems did not reward contributions to corporate strategy. Some were inspired by desire to make a difference. But the smart-alecky tone of much ODD work suggests another reason for participation. ODD work was often fun.

Some ODD tactics

Seeking to promote unconventional, skeptical thinking, ODD researched strategic issues such as Internet Protocol version 6, a new standard for how computers should communicate. IPv6's system for 'resource reservation' – ensuring that a continuous data stream such as human speech received what it needed from the Internet – had obvious implications for low-cost human voice transmission in competition with AT&T. Yet corporate strategy people in AT&T knew nothing of the protocol and the firm's established institutions provided no way of ensuring they found out. ODD prepared a paper explaining it.

The movement also sought statistics it could package powerfully. Shocking facts were called 'data bombs.' For instance, it took AT&T 75 years to acquire its first 50 million telephone customers; it took America OnLine just two years to acquire its first 50 million chat users. 'Freight trains' were long-term trends likely to flatten AT&T's business model, the decline in long-distance prices, for instance. Competition and technology had driven prices from above 60 cents a minute in 1985 to 10 cents in 1997.

GNOST members volunteered to 'help' with internal newsletters. ODD saw many up-and-coming executives – M.B.A.s poised to move into general management – as 'empty suits.' It sought to 'infect' them with ODD ideas and measured success by whether it heard them using ODD ideas as their own.

ODD's dialogue with upper management, on the other hand, was sporadic. Most ODDsters were unwilling to fight for time with top managers. ODD had hired one staff member from outside AT&T, however, Anders Fernstadt, a Swedish journalist whom Muller met at a conference. Fernstadt, excited to hear about ODD, had bombarded its staff with thoughtful emails. Deciding that such a zealot might be helpful, they hired him. As hoped, he marketed ODD's ideas with passion. At the end of a trip to Seattle, for instance, Fernstadt called an executive vice president whom he knew had flown there on the corporate jet. Would he mind giving Anders a ride home? Fernstadt gave an intimate executive tutorial on Internet Protocol ver. 6 on the plane.

Corporate Strategy and Planning's annual strategy document – supposed to consolidate strategy work of the past year – became a dramatic 'infection point' for ODD ideas. Lower-level corporate strategy staff did not relish writing it, and it was not widely read. In 1997, however, ODD volunteered to 'help.' The resulting paper clearly articulated AT&T's challenges and ways of dealing with them. It impressed AT&T chief executive Robert Allen, who had a glossy cover created and distributed copies to the board of directors.

A social movement as a response to AT&T's problems

The data above suggests that AT&T was hobbled by institutionalized behavior that prevented it from changing and that the ODDsters represented a genuine social movement promoting transformation. To see a strategy as appropriate because it is the same as other firms' in its industry is common in institutionalized organizational fields (Scott and Meyer, 1991), but inconsistent with success in competitive fields where many firms doing the same thing quickly turn a profitable product into a commodity (Porter, 1980). AT&T's planning resembled systems described in Grant (2003), who notes they help firms adapt to turbulence but rarely support non-incremental innovation.

The response of Blonder, Muller, and their associates embodied each of the elements of McAdam and Snow's (1997) definition of a social movement: '(1) collective or joint action; (2) change-oriented goals; (3) some degree of organization; (4) some degree of temporal continuity; (5) some extrainstitutional collective action.' (We say the work represented extrainstitutional action because it violated both official rules that defined ODD's tasks and informal understandings of what scientists and other low-level professionals did at AT&T.)

For survival, this movement required support inside AT&T's dominant coalition. Senior executives could have fired participants. However, there was good reason for many to support or tolerate the ODDsters' work. Though they had not created means to address them, many senior executives did recognize that the company faced huge challenges. ODDsters, coming from Bell Labs, were given leeway to think about them.

ODD's strengths and weaknesses

By 1997 ODD was making significant contributions. In May executives of AT&T's $26 billion-a-year consumer business asked ODD to help them develop a new strategy. The result called for migrating AT&T home users to AT&T Wireless as the sale of stand-alone long-distance became less viable. AT&T's chief executive, executive council, and board of directors all reacted favorably. They had brought focus to overwhelming problems. They were helping senior executives develop solutions.

However, ODD also had real weaknesses. What exactly was ODD trying to do? It was successfully calling attention to problems. But if the goal was to encourage real business achievement, ODD did not seem to be addressing the whole of the challenge. ODD often seemed to take for granted much of the institutionalized system that marginalized researchers. When the ODDsters referred to a rising executive as an 'empty suit' and sought to 'infect' him, they were thinking like gadflies rather than players. A list of ODDsters' reflections of what they could have done differently included 'avoided us vs. them mentality that may have created some confrontation,' and 'turned down their slight intellectual snobbism' (Muller and Valikangas, 2003: 117). ODDsters never developed a clear and coherent approach to top management or to Corporate Strategy and Planning – although top management would inevitably have to lead the transformation they were seeking, but ODDsters gave little thought to how to deal with challenges to their influence.

The fall of ODD – and AT&T

Building a movement around knowledge of the dangers an organization faces is hazardous. People who understand your message may leave. During 1997, several key movement members left. Departures culminated in November when Greg Blonder left the firm soon after a journalist published his off-the-record thoughts about the future of network evolution. The departures put ODD in a vulnerable position just when it was achieving success that might have led to real power. Neither the head of the labs' research division nor the head of Corporate Strategy and Planning supported ODD's work. The research division head who had approved the ODD's creation had left AT&T soon afterward. His replacement opposed general distribution of ODD analyses.

Skeptics asked why AT&T Labs was funding a unit whose work seemed to duplicate Corporate Strategy and Planning's. ODD members suddenly were asked to explain their achievements in performance reviews in terms of standard lab measures. How many patents had they filed? None. How many technical papers published? Not many. Corporate-level impact was not a criterion. The claim that ODD had been creating a network of strategic thinkers was met with derision. Within eight months of Blonder's departure, ODD was disbanded. Senior executives were unable to solve AT&T's problems, and the firm was merged into SBC and most of its management structures abandoned seven years later.

Dissipated potential for real success?

All the data suggests that ODD's campaign had potential for creating a real ability to innovate. ODD moved strategic thinking in AT&T toward much better cognitive management. It involved the company's best experts in important strategic analysis and brought about careful examination of scenarios. It opened the organization to intelligent consideration of new ideas and creation of credible new strategies for business units that had not had them. Within two years of its founding, it was surprising itself with its influence at the highest levels of the firm. Though opposition proved powerful, ODD clearly had potential to conceive strategic actions if not change them in ways that could have transformed its performance.

However, the data also shows the difficulties of strategic transformation through a social movement. ODD spawned opposition not only from managers who had reason to fear loss of their power but from the new head of Bell Labs who took for granted the existing system. Equally important, the ODD movement suffered from difficulties likely to plague social movements of all kinds, including a lack of sophistication about political management. As mavericks, its members were inexperienced in or unwilling to deal with hierarchical power. They failed to plan for a workable coalition in the organization.

While ODD's achievements were impressive, therefore, the unfulfilled potential of the movement was even greater.

ODD AS AN INSTITUTIONAL CHANGE EFFORT

ODD's story shows the need for activist managers but also the profound difficulty of their task. Institutional theory can help address the challenges. To make it useful, this section discusses how to define 'institution' for practitioners. We also use our definition to show why ODD should be understood as an institutional change effort. This allows the following section to show what the literature on institutions can teach practitioners and how ODD's experience can inform institutional theory.

Defining 'institution' so theory can relate to practice

The study of 'institutions' is notorious for its diversity of definitions.

That said, economics' standard definition is accepted by most institutional economists: 'the underlying rules of the game' (North, 1990). Williamson (2000) shows it works at many levels of analysis. Moreover, to say that AT&T had difficulty because 'underlying rules of the game' failed to support strategic thinking and innovation effectively summarizes key aspects of why AT&T could not innovate. Other definitions could be used, for example Oliver's (1997) actions that 'tend to be enduring, socially accepted, resistant to change, and not directly reliant on rewards or monitoring.' However, while ODD *was* struggling with institutionalized activities as Oliver defines the term, to focus on the fact that strategy processes in AT&T were 'enduring' and 'socially accepted' seems to take us a step away from the issues important to practitioners.

Thus 'the underlying rules of the game' is our definition of 'institution.' But since differing definitions capture different aspects of the underlying reality, we will assume

that the 'underlying rules of the game' in human systems also normally tend to meet Oliver's definition. (They are 'enduring, socially accepted, and resistant to change.') We also hypothesize they fulfill Berger and Luckmann's (1966) definition ('reciprocal typification of habitualized actions by types of actors') and others.

How activist managers should understand the nature of institutions

Changing institutions is difficult because of the very nature of institutions. A first step for managers who wish to learn from institutional theory is to understand that nature. Institutions are not just rules-of-the-game ('regulative structures' in Scott's (2001) terminology). They are also taken-for-granted elements of people's thinking patterns (Berger and Luckmann, 1966). Moreover, they are 'logics of appropriateness' (March and Olsen, 1989) that tell people what to do in certain kinds of situations.

These faces of institutions are powerful sources of inertia that activists need to overcome. People with little or no obviously rational reason to oppose an institutional change (such as the AT&T Labs' leadership in 1997 and 1998) may create overwhelming obstacles just because they take existing ways for granted and deem them appropriate. Moreover, those who seek change can take existing institutions for granted as much as anyone else. The ODDsters' failure to develop politically necessary relationships with senior managers even when their successful annual planning document demonstrated the ODDsters' value, for example, may have derived in part from their tendency to take their institutionalized role as a Labs-based support group as given.

The basic processes of institutional transformation

Managers who understand the problem also need to understand the processes by which they can change institutions. A standard model describes a substantial part of this. New rules of a game become real through a process of first 'habitualization,' then 'objectification,' then 'sedimentation' (Berger and Luckmann, 1966; see also Tolbert and Zucker, 1996). People start doing something a particular way and that way seems to work. So they repeatedly do it that way (habitualization). When activities must be explained to others, particularly to people who join the system, they come to be seen as part of objective reality ('the way things are done around here'). That is objectification. Sedimentation is the completion of the process. The behavior becomes so taken-for-granted that it becomes a standard part of people's mental furniture.

For activists, however, the most difficult challenges occur before anything like 'habitualization' can take place. How does a supporter of institutional change first get an organization to use new ways? DiMaggio (1988) describes the deliberate creation of institutional change as 'institutional entrepreneurship' and each individual effort as an 'institutionalization project.' He argues that successful creation of new institutions 'is a product of the political efforts of actors to accomplish their ends and that the success of an institutionalization project and the form that the resulting institution takes depend on the relative power of the actors who support, oppose, or otherwise strive to influence it.'

To succeed, ODD had to carry out an institutionalization project itself or persuade others, higher in the organization, to do so. DiMaggio portrays the actors in such projects as having a relatively clear idea of changes they want to create, but this may not always be true. Some innovation-supporting institutions seem to emerge because someone improvises one big innovation and then others try to learn from the process, generating a routine (Wood et al., 2004). Whether new institutions are improvised or deliberately chosen, however, DiMaggio argues that goal-oriented struggles create them.

In these political efforts, innovation supporters have to develop a strong coalition for change. Some organized groups always have interest in maintaining institutions as they are. Innovators, moreover, have to overcome institutions' taken-for-granted nature. The ODDsters are examples of activists who probably did not pay enough attention to political processes. Their reflections on what they could have done differently [should have 'sought to address higher audiences in top management in a more systematic manner'] hint at weak political thinking. DiMaggio's argument suggests that activists are inevitably politicians.

Social skills for institutional change

Fligstein (1997) expands on DiMaggio's model. He suggests that creating new institutions is a matter of having the right social skills – the 'ability to motivate cooperation in other actors by providing those actors with common meanings and identities in which actions can be undertaken and justified'. Fligstein focuses on an effort that built new international institutions. However, his analysis is equally relevant to activists in firms.

Fligstein discusses Jacques Delors, the former French finance minister who headed the European Union's governing body in the 1980s. Delors took the job when the Union was in crisis. Its dissolution was being discussed. 'Eurosclerosis' was considered a profound problem, and analysts doubted European firms could compete with Japan and America. Delors and allies among EU officials sought a goal that had much in common with goals of corporate activists: to open Europe to innovation through institutional and market reforms. Moreover, their means had direct parallels with the ODDsters.' Delors and his associates worked to build what Fligstein and Mara-Drita (1996) call an 'elite social movement' – a movement of officials, businesspeople, and others interested in overcoming Europe's problems. Indeed, when Delors joined the EU he joined a movement called 'the Single Market Program' already launched in the EU bureaucracy by officials who, like the ODDsters, saw a need for change. It sought to radically reduce remaining European trade barriers. Delors' political skills invigorated the movement and it succeeded. EU nations agreed to 264 directives in the name of the Single Market Program, eliminating taxes and barriers and harmonizing rules such as health and safety codes. The program went into effect in 1992 and Europeans became habitualized quickly. Moreover, innovation did increase and prosperity returned. The program's success allowed Delors to help create additional new institutions, including European monetary union.

Fligstein builds on this to present a new analysis of how politics can change institutions, which he calls 'the political-cultural approach' (Fligstein, 2001). He describes processes and tactics that institutional entrepreneurs (Delors and the officials who worked with him) can use to remake institutions.

Traditional economics and much political science use rational-actor models of change. They see emergence of new institutions as bargaining. Environmental change makes existing arrangements suboptimal and actors, who have fixed preference functions, bargain to create new arrangements (Shepsle and Bonchek, 1997). These models are not useful to activists, who perceive problems that others do not yet see.

Fligstein, on the other hand, notes that often parties in a problematic situation do not understand each other's positions. Negotiations may be stymied because of their different perceptions. In this situation, institutional entrepreneurs may promote the emergence of a new 'cultural frame' that will cause people's understandings and thus preferences to change. This is how institutional entrepreneurs bring about major change. Existing institutions and organizations 'constrain and enable' actors, structuring what is possible. However, people's interests are not fixed. Institutional entrepreneurs give actors a new sense of their interests and thus support changes in the rules.

They can lead a re-design of areas that are unformed (new technical fields, for instance) or in crisis (like that experienced by Europe's markets in the 1980s). They succeed if they unite the right kind of core group to support something powerful and (to the entrepreneurs) worthwhile. 'Strategic actors must find a way in which to bring together as many groups as possible to form a center or core,' Fligstein (1997) says. By creating an appropriate 'cultural frame,' Delors and EU staff made the Single Market Program appealing.

Fligstein notes actors have to select from 'a small number of tactics' to build a powerful core around an appropriate cultural frame. Among the tactics he discusses are:

- *Agenda-setting*: getting people to agree on what will be talked about.
- *Framing proposed actions:* convincing people to think that what will happen is (a) in their interest, or (b) natural, given values that they accept or should accept.
- *Taking what the system gives*: seizing unplanned opportunities, and seeing opportunities where others see only constraints.
- *'Goallessness:'* appearing open to others' needs, free of values oriented to personal gain, not wedded to a course of action, and therefore an appropriate broker among others.
- *Brokering*: helping people with different attitudes to communicate and reach agreements.[1]

Such tactics can bring together important people in the system to support a new way of thinking, so that a new course of action can be adopted and institutionalized. Delors and his allies built a body politic in all Europe to support a reworking of Europe's market institutions using the tactics Fligstein discusses. He focused on agenda-setting from the beginning, telling European leaders that he would take the presidency of the EU only if they committed to a big project and then quickly concluding after a tour of European capitals that the idea of 'completing the single market' was the most popular alternative. Thereafter he had legitimacy to focus discussion on that. Delors and EU staff framed the project as in the interest of all Europeans. Initially, there was essentially no definition of 'completing the single market,' but the idea of eliminating barriers and harmonizing regulations could be sold as a source of great efficiencies.

The shared belief in 'completing the single market' could then be used to persuade people to support changes they had previously opposed. Delors' relatively goalless attitude when he took the presidency gave him credibility. People believed he would have supported whatever big revitalizing project the leaders of the continent wanted. 'Taking what the system gave,' he allowed the existing European system and the movement that was emerging in support of change to set boundaries. Delors became a well-respected broker, finding aspects of market change that would appeal to each political group.

ODD also used tactics on Fligstein's list, and those tactics contributed to successes. Advocating scenario planning was a way for people with no formal authority to alter agendas. Scenario planning's standardized, non-partisan nature gave the scenario-planning experts an air of goallessness. ODD's willingness to take over activities such as the editing of newsletters was a 'taking what the system gives.'

However, ODD never used these techniques in a coherent approach to the political problem that DiMaggio and Fligstein see as central: creation of a core group powerful enough to truly change the rules. Fligstein never closely examines the EU officials whose role paralleled the ODDsters' – the group that originally conceived the idea of a Single-Market Program. But he seems to imply they always recognized their success required finding major support at higher levels. If ODD had made slightly better use of Fligstein's tactics it still might have failed. But there is every reason to believe there was also a possibility for great success.

CONCLUSION

This analysis shows there is reason to believe that activism and the social movements that activists build in organizations can contribute enormously to change in large firms. The movement that the Opportunity Discovery Department spawned made remarkable progress in encouraging

evolution. It failed to achieve true transformation in part because activists simply did not understand or focus on processes of enrolling senior management in their vision.

Institutional theory provides credible guidance for activists on how to achieve the success that eluded the ODDsters. The challenge is fundamentally political: institutional entrepreneurship. Activists need to bring together strong groups of supporters including top-level executives.

Our knowledge of activism inside organizations remains rudimentary. We especially need case studies that are more theoretically informed than those published to date. Such research is needed because businesses need a better, more theoretically informed practice of activism today, when environmental changes clearly call for dramatic evolution. Business needs more theoretically informed practice on two levels. First is among activists themselves. They need to think through their political roles and tactics. The second, equally important, is among senior managers. If senior managers are to be in charge of evolution of their firms, they need to look to activists to mobilize expertise, articulate possibilities, and play key roles in assembling coalitions. ODD was advocating and making progress toward creating genuinely different ways of thinking about the whole business. Theory provided no guidance to upper management in how to respond.

Activism has the potential to bring about desperately needed institutional changes in large established firms. But much more work is needed by scholars, activists, and senior executives if the promise is to be realized.

ACKNOWLEDGEMENT

The authors wish to express gratitude to Amy Muller, whose help with this chapter was indispensable.

NOTE

1 The other tactics on Fligstein's list are: direct authority (use of existing hierarchical power),

wheeling and anealing (shaking up a situation to see where it ends up), asking for more than you think you can get, maintaining ambiguity, 'trying five things to get one,' aggregating interests, convincing people you hold more cards than you do, making others think they are in control, and faming actions in terms of the dominant groups to gain benefits from the system without disturbing those who are dominant.

REFERENCES

Ansoff, H.I. (1988) *The New Corporate Strategy*. New York: John Wiley. (Original work published 1965).

Berger, P. and Luckmann, T. (1966) *The Social Construction of Reality: A Treatise in the Sociology of Knowledge*. New York: Doubleday, Anchor.

Blonder, G. (2005, searched July 12, 2005) Greg Blonder Bio. www.genuineideas.com/GEBBio/gebbio.html.

de Geus, A. (1997) *The Living Company*. Boston: Harvard Business School Press.

DiMaggio, P.J. (1988) 'Interest and agency in institutional theory', in L.G. Zucker (ed.), *Institutional Patterns and Organizations: Culture and Environment*. Cambridge, MA: Ballinger. pp. 3–21.

Fligstein, N. (1997) 'Social skill and institutional theory', *American Behavioral Scientist*, 40 (4): 397–402.

Fligstein, N. (2001) *The Architecture of Markets: An Economic Sociology of Twenty-First-Century Capitalism*. Princeton: Princeton University Press.

Fligstein, N. and Mara-Drita, I. (1996) 'How to make a market: Reflections on the attempt to create a single market in the European Union', *American Journal of Sociology*, 102 (1): 1–33.

Grant, R.M. (2003) 'Strategic planning in a turbulent environment: Evidence from the oil majors', *Strategic Management Journal*, 24: 491–517.

Hamel, G. (1999, September) 'Bringing Silicon Valley inside', *Harvard Business Review*, p. 70 ff.

Kleiner, A. (1996) *The Age of Heretics*. New York: Doubleday Currency.

March, J.G. Olsen, J.P. (1989) *Rediscovering Institutions: The Organizational Basis of Politics*. New York: The Free Press.

McAdam, D. and Snow, D.A. (1997) *Social Movements: Readings in their Emergence, Mobilization, and Dynamics*. Los Angeles: Roxbury.

Mintzberg, H. (1990) 'The design school: Reconsidering basic premises of strategic management', *Strategic Management Journal*. pp. 171–195.

Muller, A. and Valikangas, L. (2003) 'An "ODD" reaction to strategy failure in America's (once) largest Telco', *European Management Journal*, 21 (1): 109–118.

North, D.C. (1990) 'Institutions, institutional change, and economic performance', (J. Alt and D. North, series eds). *Political Economy of Institutions and Decisions*. Cambridge: Cambridge University Press.

Oliver, C. (1997) 'Sustainable competitive advantage: Combining institutional and resource-based views', *Strategic Management Journal*, 18 (9): 697–713.

Porter, M.E. (1980) *Competitive Strategy*. New York: Free Press.

Scott, W.R. (2001) *Institutions and Organizations. Foundations for Organizational Science*. Thousand Oaks, CA: Sage. (Original work published 1995).

Scott, W.R. and Meyer, J.W. (1991) 'The organization of societal sectors: Propositions and early evidence', in P.J. DiMaggio and W.W. Powell (eds), *The New Institutionalism in Organizations*. Chicago: University of Chicago Press. pp. 108–140. (Original work published 1983).

Shepsle, K.A. and Bonchek, M.S. (1997) *Analyzing Politics: Rationality, Behavior, and Institutions*. New York: W.W. Norton.

Tolbert, P.S. and Zucker, L.G. (1996) 'Institutionalization of institutional theory', in *Handbook of Organization Studies*. London: Sage. pp. 175–190.

Williamson, O. (2000, September) 'New institutional economics: Taking stock, looking ahead', *Journal of Economic Literature*, 38: 595–613.

Wood, R.C. and Hamel, G. (2002, November) 'The World Bank's Innovation Market', *Harvard Business Review*: 104–114.

Wood, R.C., Hatten, K.J. and Williamson, P. (2004) 'The Emergence of Continual Strategic Innovation'. [San Jose State University Department of Organization and Management Working Paper No. 051E].

Is Change on the Outside Like Change on the Inside?

George Roth

In organizational learning and change, there is evidence of high failure rates, estimated at 70% (Beer and Nohria, 2000), but little writing that adequately addresses these low success rates. Collins (2001) examines the performance of the population of 1,435 Fortune 500 companies from 1965 to 1995, and finds only 11 companies that sustained a transition from good to great performance. Why is it that less than 1 percent of companies can attain and sustain great performance? Should not scholars take responsibility for better theorizing that leads to better practice?

Performance and market valuation data provide evidence that a few organizations are more robust and reliable in the ways that they operate, while the companies that hold fast to the core of their traditional ways continue to decline. For example, Asian automotive companies gain market share and profitability, expanding their US operations, while domestic American manufacturers vacillate between giving huge discounts to run their factories full out or shuttering these marquees of mass production. Meanwhile, lean enterprises, like Toyota, continue on a slow but relentless growth path, setting record profits, and achieving market valuations that exceed the sum of those of all their competitors.

What I observe are differences in the learning and change processes in these companies. In the automotive industry, once many of the lean concepts were identified (Womack and Jones, 1994), most domestic manufacturers quickly adopted many of the practices. These companies made some changes, bringing to near parity quality levels and labor content per vehicle. Yet, US companies have not gained relative to Japanese companies. Recent *Business Week* covers provide evidence of the contrasting fate of Toyota and General Motors: On November 17, 2003, the cover was 'Can Anything Stop Toyota? An inside look at how it's reinventing the auto industry,' and on May 9, 2005 it was 'Why GM's plan won't work … and the ugly road ahead.' The difference in performance, and the fate of the company, is whether it can implement lean. An organization that successfully implements lean methods gains benefits in the order of 'needing *half or less* of the human effort, space, tools, time, and overall expense' (Womack and Jones, 1994: 93) to develop, produce, and distribute its products.

Lean enterprises change in different ways from traditional firms. While some aspects of managing change are similar, what differentiates lean enterprises is their abilities to both promote changes internally as well as within their network of suppliers and customers. With respect to Toyota, Honda, and Southwest, Pfeffer and Sutton (2000) note how these firms are able to transfer what they know to their customers and suppliers. For example, Honda's BP program has resulted in productivity increases that averaged 50 percent at its 53 suppliers (MacDuffie and Helper, 1997). Traditional firms send their managers to study these companies' approaches, but fail to be as successful in their own efforts. The challenge is not associated with the intellect, knowledge or capabilities of individuals in traditional firm, but is rooted in the management practices that serve to either enable or constrain capable people in acting on what they know.

Continued

The proposition that follows is that scholars and managers might learn more about change within organizations by examining the practices of firms that manage change effectively outside their organizational boundaries.

Efforts to develop a theory for change across firms began over 20 years ago with studies of transorganizational development (Cummings, 1984), interorganizational networks (Boje and Whetten, 1981), and change in under-organized systems (Brown, 1981). Recent summaries of transorganizational development (Cummings and Worley, 2005) show no new conceptual development and few empirical studies. The cross-organization change writings have followed the same path as organizational development research: a focus on the means has lost sight of the ends. Only a few recent innovations, such as search conferences (Emery and Purser, 1996), large group meetings (Bunker and Alban, 1997), and organization network development (Chisholm, 1998), apply organization development techniques across organizations. Largely analytical practices, such as reengineering, total quality, lean production, action workout and six-sigma improvement efforts, dominate recent cross-organization change in industry. These initiatives are largely from industrial engineering origins, and provide only latent attention to people's social and psychological processes. Based on the authority of their position and their technical or analytic expertise, designated improvement specialists specify changes that the organization then presses its people to implement. The failure rate of these efforts is similar to that of change initiatives, with a half to two-thirds not achieving expectations.

Change across a set of organizations confronts different conditions: there is no central authority, no tight coupling of activities, nor a set structure among units. Most organizations, especially traditional, mass production firms, have a well-defined structure, a close coupling between efforts and outcomes, and a centralized decision-making authority. Enterprises are more like alliances and networks, with an under-organized structure, loosely coupled linkages, and polycentric decision-making. The fact that successful enterprises manage change well within and across their boundaries suggests that, in today's business environment, change on the outside has application for change on the inside of firms. To improve organizational change practices, we should study these cross-organizational transformations and bring the insights that we gain back into the organizational arena.

REFERENCES

Beer M. and N. Nohria (2000) *Breaking the Code of Change*. Boston, MA: Harvard Business School Press.

Boje, D. and D. Whetten (1981) 'Effects of organizational strategies and contextual constraints on centrality and attributions of influence in interorganizational networks', *Administrative Science Quarterly*, 26 (3): 378–395.

Brown, D. (1981) 'Planned change in underorganized systems', in T. Cummings (ed.) *Systems Theory for Organization Development*. New York: John Wiley and Sons.

Bunker, B. and Alban, B. (1997) *Large Group Intervention: Getting the Whole System into the Room*. San Francisco: Jossey-Bass.

Chisholm, R. (1998) *Developing Network Organizations: Learning for Practice and Theory*. Reading, MA: Addison-Wesley.

Collins, J. (2001) *Good to Great: Why Some Companies Make the Leap – and Others Don't*. New York, NY: HarperBusiness.

Cummings, Thomas G. (1984) 'Transorganizational development', in B.M. Staw and L.L. Cummings (eds), *Research in Organizational Behavior*, Vol. 6. Greenwich, CN: JAI Press. pp. 367–422.

Cummings, T. and Worley, C. (2005) *Organization Development and Change* (8th edn), Mason, Ohio: South-Western.

Emery, M. and Purser, R. (1996) *The Search Conference: A Powerful Method for Planning Organizational Change and Community Action.* San Francisco: Jossey-Bass.

MacDuffie, J.P. and Helper, S. (1997) 'Creating lean suppliers: The Honda way', *California Management Review*, 39 (4): 118–151.

Pfeffer, J. and Sutton, R. (2000) *The Knowing-Doing Gap: How Smart Companies Turn Knowledge into Action*, Boston, MA: Harvard Business School Press.

Womack, J. and Jones, D. (1994) 'From lean production to the lean enterprise', *Harvard Business Review*, March-April: 93–103.

Where Are You Going?

Hans Hansen and Daved Barry

> Management at the present time has the blood of new youth coursing through its veins. It is full of new vigor and new enthusiasm. (Sheldon, 1924: ix)

It feels good to use a quote from so many years ago that is as topical as it is dramatic, and one that comes from a fountainhead of management studies. It is tempting to write unobjectionable and inspiring lines like that one, but we will avoid doing so. While immanently quotable, those types of statements never really say anything impactful. Besides, if a statement is impactful, it probably has a short half-life.

Perhaps in closing with our own short note, it is better to leave you with a question, your own chance to answer with a powerful statement, or to decide where you would like to make an impact, perhaps having been influenced by the spirit and tone of our text. The question we would like to ask you involves speculation on your own future research, musings about where you will place your bets on the future, or said another way – 'Where are you going?' The artist Paul Gauguin asked himself the same question in one of his famous paintings 'Where are you going?' The painting depicts a woman in the foreground, and the perspective of the viewer is one shared with the painter.

Gauguin asked himself this question in the middle of a long, strange trip, in what was a strange land, surrounded by people whom others might have called strange. Gauguin spent much of his time chasing exotic places in search of interesting subject matter. He uses this painting to ask himself a reflexive question. Perhaps you too have been in the position to reflect, having found yourself in a far-away place. It seems the context of the far-away somehow fosters such speculation. Perhaps it is at a journey's apex that we reflect about where we have come from and what events bought us to this moment. It is at those moments that we also take time to wonder where we are going in the future. At the time he painted 'where are you going?', Gauguin was experiencing far-away lands that undoubtedly changed his work forever, and he was wondering 'what's next' for him.

Our connection here is that we hope the contributions in our text have taken you to some far-away places and allowed you to explore some new and exotic subject matter. Having done so, we ask you to reflect and speculate about what comes next for you.

We've done the same, and have a few thoughts on the process.

For us, one 'what's next' is that we will make more of an attempt to embrace 'far-away' perspectives that can inform our own work. This, coupled with working with such a diverse set of people on this text, in such a diverse series of places, led to a desire to formalize how working with strangers in strange places on strange topics might be done. Calls for interdisciplinary research are common, but are easier said than done. We want to suggest a way of engaging that might make more of it possible and practical. Appropriately, it involves some speculation and some bets.

First, pick a stranger. You may not have to go far; perhaps there are several within your own department. Sit down together and ask yourselves this question: 'What could we collectively produce together if we both got to say everything we wanted to say and did not have to compromise any of our own ontological and epistemological assumptions?' That is, what if you both got to keep and adhere to all of the assumptions and biases of your own research perspective, and still jointly produced something you both stood by? For example, you might take on a traditional topic, such as structural reorganization. One of you might believe that hierarchies and structures reflect the complexity found in the outside environment that the organization operates in. One of you might believe order is socially constructed and organizations form structures by mimicking well-known organizations so that their business is seen as socially legitimate via the company they keep (or copy, as the case may be).

How would you and your stranger view a particular research context involving a restructuring? We would suggest that at the start, you focus very specifically on the details of a particular context, rather than restructuring in general. This focus will help keep you less bound by the a priori assumptions of your respective research paradigms. Yes, how you see things influences how you explain things, but you might be more open to alternative explanations if the focus is on 'the thing itself', rather than your fields' view of those things.

Next, regarding the particular phenomena, both of you should attempt to lay out 'truth claims', so to speak, about the specific case you are discussing. We are not concerned with validity at this point. When attempting to generate new theory, the value is only revealed much further down the road. What you want at this point are clear statements that explain what is occurring regarding your specific case. Statements are not to be critiqued, especially in light of your parochial perspectives. You should make an effort to improve and tighten each claim or statement, always being respectful of the different perspectives. Questions like, 'Would you say this occurs in other conditions?' and 'Would you say the opposite is true given a seemingly reverse scenario?' or simply asking 'Why?' five times is a good place to start. Both parties can help with the answers, but make sure you are not violating any basic assumptions.

After, and only after, you have made attempts to enhance all of the truth claims, is it time to sort out which ones you would keep on the table, so to speak. If you find two are mutually exclusive, you might remove both from discussion, or you might remove the least objectionable one given both perspectives. Even better, if you reveal an underlying false dichotomy that made the statements appear to be mutually exclusive when they really were not, you might be able to keep both by generating a new assumption or discarding an old one. Whatever the case, you should make every effort to keep as many as you can both tolerate. It should be easy to put truth claims or explanatory statements on the table, and excruciating to take them off. Make every attempt to save them by tweaking them if at all possible, especially if they are statements that seem to conflict with your perspective. Again, do so in a way that allows your partner to retain his or her assumptions.

Then, go about producing the work. Perhaps you will simply describe the new way of looking at the phenomena, or you might review your individual perspectives and describe how combining them allowed you to see the phenomenon in a new way. Outline your contribution by building an argument describing how your explanations reveal new aspects of the phenomena. If you discuss how you combined some unlikely perspectives, identify tensions between them. Use those tensions as an innovative way to look at the phenomena, rather than some conflict to be resolved or eliminated. In fact, try to maintain the tension and carry it forward as you delve deeper into your particular case or move outward to discuss broader phenomena in general.

In closing, we encourage you to explore this method, perhaps by seeking to synthesize your own perspective with one of the new perspectives you have encountered in this text. While we cannot predict what you might reveal about management and organizations, we hope our humble suggestions give you a place to start and encourage the development of future new and emerging topics.

Likewise, we cannot predict what will come of any of the theories or perspectives presented in this text, and it is certainly too early to tell what you might do with the ideas you find here. Kenneth Gergen (1992: 210) tells us that 'theory cannot be evaluated on its capacity to predict ... rather, theory gains its importance from the activities it enables'. Our aim here is to spark new ways to see organizations, hoping those new ways to see will lead to new activities.

So knowing that we cannot make any evaluations, we leave you with the same question that Gauguin was asking himself. 'Where are you going?' And like the subject of that painting, we are also left expecting something to come of all this. Having an uncertain future is certainly no reason to abandon great expectations.

REFERENCES

Gergen, K. (1992) 'Organization theory in the postmodern era', in M. Reed and M. Hughes (eds) *Rethinking Organization.* pp. 207–226. London: Sage.

Sheldon, Oliver (1924) *The Philosophy of Management.* London: Pitman and Sons.

Index

360 degree feedback 482

abduction
    and aesthetics 462
    assimilation 459
    creative 460–1
    definition 454
    and dialectical thinking 465–6
    fostering creativity 461–2
    heresy 461
    operationalization 457–60
    placing 455–7
    reasons for 454–5
    weak 460
absorption, symbolic value creation 276–7
abstraction 304
Abul-Gheit, Ahmed 243
academia 268–9
academic artistry 462
academic institutions, ideology in 242
Academy of Management (AoM) 218–19,
    251–3
Accenture 215
accountability 520
accounting 365
achievement 262
actants 306
action
    dynamics of organization in situation 521
    relational analysis 113
    school of research 368
    and theories 196
actions, and patterns 303
activism 572
    and change 581
    need for understanding 572–3
activist art 34
activity
    and globalization 182
    semiotization 236
    strategic 366
    streams of 367

actor-network theory (ANT) 113, 304, 306–11
    illustrative study 307–11
    routines 309–11, 312–13
actors 364, 371, 372
Adler, Nancy 35
advertising, symbolic value creation 277
aesthetic choices 230–1
aesthetic difference 230
aesthetic discourse 234–6
aesthetic epistemology 470–1
aesthetic knowledge 470
Aesthetic Leadership 35
aesthetic leadership 430
aesthetic play 426–30, 433, 434
aesthetics
    and abduction 462
    as art of organizational sin 230–4
    as common sense 33
    critical 221
    education 232
    and ethics 231–4, 431
    etymology 470
    Friedrich Schiller 426–8
    Immanuel Kant 425–6
    logico-analytical knowledge 236
    mathematics 232–3
    organizational 428
    as organizational inquiry 229
    as organizational power 235–6
    in organizational understanding 43–8
    producing art 222
    as socially constructed 233
    university research 231–4
    visual arts 231–2
affordance 120
Agar, M. 294
agency, actor-network theory 306, 312
agency/structure dilemma 73–5
agents, interaction 196
agility 382
Aguinis, H. 152

Alessi 277
alliances, and strategy 187–8
allomorphism 60–1
alterity
    abstract entities 50
    definitions 49
    IT company 59–60
    maternal 357
    in organizational images 51
    in social sciences 51–2
Alvesson, M. 14
Amsterdam 55
analogies 241
angel's advocate 340
Angwin, D. 190
Ansoff, I. 184, 186, 190
answerability 205
antenarratives 204
anthropoemic separation 438
anthropologists 203–4
anthropology, intersubjective 261
anthropophagic separation 438
Appelrouth, S. 440
Appiah, Kwame Anthony 258
Apple Computers 276, 429
Appreciative Inquiry 206–7, 340
apprehension 465
apprenticeship 491–3, 496
Aquinas, St. Thomas 168
Aramco 336–7, 338
Archer, M. 74, 75
arenas 172
Argyris, C. 121, 132, 133
Aristotle 69, 205, 319, 321, 323, 431
art
    as associative 39
    in business practice 36–9
    as capital 430
    corporate collections 32
    dialogical forms 34
    forums 35
    and management 37
    old versus contemporary 31
    in organizations 33–4
    practice 222
    producing 222
    pullers 33–4
    pushers 34–5
    scribes 35–6
    socially responsible 434
    as training 34
    working definition 32
art management 32
Artaud, Antonin 546

artful interventions 412–13
    appropriation 420
    organizational images and understandings
        414–16
    work and play 413–14
Artful Making 35
article publication 218–19
artifacts
    construction and embodiment of organizational
        knowledge 103–5
    group membership and status 101–3
    and identity 99, 100–1
    methodological approaches 105–7
    movement 104
    occupational jurisdiction 102
    and organizational dynamics 98–9
    photographs 105
    social construction 101
    and social meanings 99
    tracing 106–7
artist-business residencies 34
artistry, and identity 418–20
artists 428–30
arts, and leadership 95
Ashworth, J. 402–3
assimilation 459
associations, in art 39
astute ignoramus 344
asymmetry, of authority 437
AT&T Opportunity Discovery Department (ODD)
    decline 577
    development 574–5
    dissipated potential 577–8
    as hub of social movement 573
    as institutional change effort 578–81
    institutional entrepreneurship 579
    as social movement 576
    strengths and weaknesses 576–7
    tactics 575–6, 581
Athens 56
Atkin, D. 447
Atkinson, Judy 158
Atwood, Margaret 296
audit culture 258
Austin, Rob 35, 36, 37–8, 95, 224
authenticity, of leaders 93–4
authoring 205
authority 102, 437
authors 514–15
Autogena, Lisa 34
automobile industry 188
automorphism 60–1
automotive industry 432, 583
autonomy 257, 258

Bailey, J.R. 333
Bain, Alexander 455
Bakhtin, M 203, 207
Bal, M. 45
Barabási, Albert-László 178, 179
Barcelona 55, 57
Barley, S.R. 303
Barry, Daved 35
Bartlett, C. 187, 189
Bastien, D.T. 390
Bateson, Gregory 429
Baudrillard, J. 355–6
Bauman, Z. 437–8
Baumgarten, A.G. 221, 423
Baxandall, M. 89–90, 91
Bazerman, M. 148
bearing witness 334
beauty 230, 231–4
Beck, N. 116
Beckett, D. and colleagues 321
Bedeian, Arthur 133, 157–8
Béguin, P. 521
behavioral flexibility 93–4
Bellochs, Mari 434–5
benefits, self-expressive 273
Berger, J. 85, 87, 88
Berger, P. 442, 471, 573, 579
Berlin 56
Bersani, L. 542
Besanko, D. and colleagues 273
better management 14
Beuys, Joseph 413, 416, 419, 430, 431
Bhaskar, Roy 73, 74
bias, cognitive 139
Birmingham, C. 321, 324
Blackler, F. and colleagues 373
Blonder, Greg 574
Boal, Augusto 403
body 440, 441, 521, 546
Body without Organs 546–7
Bogard, W. 443, 444
Boland, R. 560–1
Boston Box 192
bottom line, increasing through spirituality 167
boundaries 103, 438
Bourdieu, P. 91, 113, 266–7, 303, 305, 429, 518
Bourriaud, Nicolas 430, 431
Bower-Burgelman theory 368
Bower, J.L. 368
Braidotti, R. 543–4, 548
brand communities 447
Braverman, H. 15
Brearley, Laura 161, 163–4
Brellochs, Mari 34–5

Brewis, J. 540
Brode, Harold 310–11
Brooks, Peter 49
Bruner, Jerome 291
Brunsson, N. 558
Bryson, N. 45
building community and connection 160–2
bureaucracy 428
Burgelman, R.A. 368
Burke, Kenneth 401
Burrell, G. 2, 15, 138, 540
Buruma, Ian 50
business education, standardization 191
business media eye 89
business schools 57–9, 554–5
Butler, Judith 359–60, 540, 544
Byron, K. 110–11

Calder, Alexander 36
Calori, R. 320, 322, 327
Cameron, K. and colleagues 560
capability-building theory 369
Capetta, R. 104
capital, art as 430
care 260, 357
Carlile, Paul 103, 105
Carnegie Report 186
Carnegie School 150
carnival 203
Cartesian approach 42–3, 46, 47
Cartesian dualism, in academic institutions
    268–9
catharsis 407
causal explanation 71–2
cave metaphor (Plato) 68–9, 75, 77
Celtic Christianity 530–1
Celtic knowledge 530–1
Centrale di Latte 56
centralization 189, 568
CEO portraits 88, 89–91
Cetina, Knorr 100
challenges, addressing 390
Chandler, A.D. 140, 184, 188–9, 558
change process school 368–9
changes
    actor-network theory (ANT) perspective 306
    developing theory 584
    rational-actor models 580
    routines 305
    through activism 581
character 51
charisma 507
charismatic leadership 469, 471–2
charismatic leadership theory 472–3

Chmielewski, A. 248
choices, aesthetic 230–1
circular design 562
Cisco 383
Cittadellarte arts academy 434
CityNet 55
civic humanism 256–7
Clark, Timothy 35, 403, 407–9
Clarke, A.E. 172
cleanliness, Stockholm 55
Clegg, S. 2, 15, 322
Clifford, J. 290
closed design/simple people approach 386
Clôt, Y. 521
clothing, symbolism 271
code 390
cognition 505, 510
cognitive fallacies 481–2
cognitive maps 506
cognitive processing 291, 296
cognitive science approach to risk 110
cognitive symbols 507
cognitivism 517
Cohen, Stanley 439
Cohen, William 32
Cole, D. 406
collaboration 514–15, 565–6
collaborative entrepreneurship 565–6
collaborative network organization 566
collective-action model of innovation 396–7
collective wisdom 338
Collins, J. 88, 583
Collopy, F. 560–1
colonialism 50, 529
communicating 338–9
communication, as action 225
communion 438
communities
    brand 447
    of practice (CoPs) 170, 171, 172, 175, 503–4
    symbolic value creation 276–7
competence, cross-cultural 246–50
competitive environments 386
competitiveness, cultural 383–4
complex adaptive system (CAS) perspectives
    479–80
complex people 387–9
complexity 112, 114, 195–8, 432–3, 568
complexity science 113
comprehension 465
concept cars 432
conception 505
    maternal 355
Conein, B. 521

conflicting groups 252–3
Conger, J.A. 472, 473
consciousness 258
constructionism, critical relational 285–6
constructive turmoil 157
consumer perceptions 273
consumers, symbolic value creation 276–7
consummation, story 205
consumption 270, 271, 442
containment, knowledge within practice 518
contamination, by strangers 439
contexts, stable 385–6
continental change 7–9
contingency 70
control mechanisms 390–1
control, of routines 304
control systems 140
convergence 381–2
Cooper, R. 542
cooperation
    conflicting groups 252–3
    spontaneous 197
Cooperrider, D.L. 206–7
Coopey, J. 403
Cornelesen 34–5
corporate agency 75
corporate capitalist eye 89
corporate cultures, as means of control 15
corporate glue 189
corporate life, in-depth study 15
corporate personas 50–1
Corporate Social Responsibility 256
corporate theatre 403–4
corporations, theories of 50
corporeal feminism 359–60
corporeal leadership theory 476
corporeal leadership, underpinnings 471
corporeality
    aesthetic epistemology 470–1
    charismatic leadership theory 472–3
    in leadership 471–2
    leadership research 469–70
    shared leadership 473
counterstories 206
craft 31–2
Creamer, Alistair 339
creation, of knowledge 517
creative action 196
criminality 50
crisis of representation 27
critical antenarratology 204
critical deconstructivism 16
critical discourse analysis 503–4
critical interpretivism 15, 16

critical management studies (CMS)
  anti-CMS features 20
  applications to CMS community 20–1
  appreciation of context 19
  branches of study 16–17
  characteristics 17–20
  definition 13–14
  developing methodologies 21–2
  development and overview 14–16
  mainstream position 17
  methodological approach 18–19
  narrative styles 22–4
  non-managerial studies 17
  objective 19
  theme of study 18
  working definition 18
critical realism 113
  agency/structure dilemma 73–5
  as Aristotelian 69
  causal explanation 71–2
  core arguments 69–75
  historical science 75–7
  implications 75
  intensive research strategy and design 72–3
  retroductive analysis 71
  stratified social ontology 70–1
  transformational model of social action
    (TMSA) 73, 74
critical reflexivity 83
critical relational constructionism 285–6
critical research, definition 13
critical sensemaking 29
critical theory 13, 16, 27
criticism 221
Critique of Judgment 424, 425, 428
cross-fertilization, arts and leadership 95
Csikszentmihalyi, M. 37, 100, 273
cultural absorption 277
cultural capital 281–2
cultural competitiveness 383–4
cultural frame 580
cultural positioning 277
cultural studies 51
cultural-symbolic approach to risk 110–11
culturalism 229, 234
culture
  and globalization 182
  organizational 15
Cummings, S. 186, 190
Cunha, Joao 35
Cunha, Miguel 35
curriculum for leadership 330
cybernetic organization 79
Cyert, Richard 99

Czarniawska, Barbara 60, 205, 289–90
Czarniawska-Joerges, B. 291

Dadirri
  application to organizational life 158
  building community and connection 160–2
  concept of 156
  listening deeply with respect 158–60
  practical application 163–4
  reframing concept of time 162
Danish cartoon crisis 243–6, 448
Danto, Arthur 429
Darsø, Lotte 35
Darwinian organizations 80
dasein 258, 260
data
  deep structure 138
  inferences from 137
  performance and market evaluation 583
  as representations 290
  researchers' choices 555–6
data inference errors 135–6
Davies, Bronwyn 51
de Certeau, M. 352
De Landa, M. 545
De Wit, B. 186
decentralization 189
decision-making 139–40, 141, 146–7
deduction 456
Delebarre, Michael 55
Deleuze, Gilles 51–2, 124, 541–2, 544–5
deliverables, networks 379–80
Delors, Jacques 579–81
democratization 27
denaturalization, critical management studies
    (CMS) 17
Depreciative Inquiry 207
Descartes, René 42–3, 221
design
  circular 562
  interaction with research 555–8
  of products 277
desire 541, 544–5, 546
developmental continua 334
deviance, positive 501–2
deviants 439, 441–4
Devin, Lee 35, 36, 37–8
Dewey, John 321, 455
dialectics, propositional and tacit knowledge
    464–6
Diesel 276–7
difference 230, 362–3, 544
difference scores 143
differentiation, self-other 286

DiMaggio, P. 280, 579
disciplined reflexivity 467
discourse 27, 505
discrimination, in academic institutions 268
distinctiveness 52
distributed learning 515
distributed work 102
diversity, in practice 122
divisions of labour 347
Docherty, T. 356–7
Dougherty, D. 154
Douglas, M. 110
Dourish, P. 117
Dourley, J.P. 354
dramaturgical society 401–2, 406
Drucker, Peter 146
du Gay, P. 276
Dundes, A. 204
Dunkerley, D. 15
Dunne, D. 154
Durkheim, Emile 64, 441
Dutoit, U. 542
dynamic capabilities 302
dynamic capability theories 369
dynamic logic of practice 123–5
dynamics 122, 236
    of networks 379–80
    of routines 304–7
dystopias 442

Eco, U. 462
ecological explanations 304–5
ecological theory 136
ecology 195–8
economics envy 148
Eden, L. 307–8, 309
effectiveness, negative features 18
effeminacy 354
egocentrism 481
Einstein, Albert 335
Elsbach, K. 100–1, 105
email, and collaboration 514–15
email conversation 487–9
emancipation 27, 235–6
embodied experience 425
embodied practice 117
embodiment 117–18
emergence 70
    deviant identities 441–4
    and humanism 258
    interaction of human agents 196
    interpretive dominance 508–10
    as nature of practice 114
    strategy 191

Emirbayer, M. 74
emotional understanding 470
emotions 223, 239–40
employees, and strategy 192
emptiness, organizations 215–16
enactive researcher 322
Endenburg, D. 562
enforcing approach, to control
    systems 391
engagement, levels of 44–7
Enron 429
entrepreneurialism 381, 382
environments, single and multiple 558–9
epistemology 42
    aesthetic 470–1
    Aristotle 319
    enactivist 197
    evolutionary 248
Epston, David 485–6
equality 257
equivalence, knowledge and practice 518
errors 217
essayism 263–4
ethical beauty 231
ethics 322, 325
    and aesthetics 431
    humanism 256–7
    Objectivism 483–4
ethnography, in artifact research 106
ethnomethodology 519
etho-poeisis 329
ethos, of practice 118
Etoy 34
European Academy of Management
    (EURAM) 251, 252, 253
European Group for Organizational Studies
    (EGOS) 251, 253
evaluation, of decisions 482
evolution, design and practice 562
evolutionary epistemology 248
evolutionary operation (EVOP) 558
exemplars 487
existentialism 16
expectations 561–2
experience economy 428
experiences
    embodied 425
    grounded 538–9
    sharing 424
experimentation 381, 557
expert-driven approach 485
experts, symbolic value creation 276
explanations 241
explanatory theory 374

exploitation 316–17
exploration 316–17
expressive verbs 222–6
extensive research strategy and design 72
external goods 118–20

fads 63, 66–7
failure rates, organizational learning and change 583
Fairclough, N. 207
fathers, veneration of 350–1
feelings 222–3
Feldman, M.S. 116, 121, 302, 303
feminism 29, 543–5
feminist studies 15
feminist theorizing 359–60
Fernstadt, Anders 576
Ferraro, F. 148
Feyerabend, Paul 80–1, 247–9
fiction 34
    as data 292
    defining narrative fiction 288–9
    as illumination 291–4
fieldwork 263
financial markets, centrality in decision-making 146–7
fine art 32
Fine, Gary Alan 99
Fiorina, Carly 85–8, 86illus
Fish, S. 506
fit, in design 558–9
Fligstein, N. 579–81
fluidity 543, 545–7
Flyvberg, B. 320, 322–3, 325
folklorists 203–4
Fombrun, Charles 280
fool 344
Ford 439–40, 444
Ford Report 186
formalization 568
forum theatre 403
Foss, N.J. 558
Foucauldianism 16, 17, 52
Foucault, Michel 51, 437, 441
founding fathers 350–1
Fournier, V. 16, 17–18
Fox, Matthew 167
fragility 266–7
fragmentation of study 2
fragmentation, Value Chain 190
fragments, of aesthetic discourse 234–6
Frame, P. 321–2
frames (ways of thinking) 307

framing
    and reframing 337–8
    visual images 87
Frankfurt School 15, 17
Freud, Sigmund 88
Friberg, Maria 59–60
Friends of the Cohort 164
Frost, Peter 133
Fuller, Steve 246–9
Future Forum 243

Gabriel, Y.A. 205
Gadamer, Hans-Georg 414, 430–1
Galbraith, J.R. 139–40
Galloway, Kathy 531
Garfinkel, H. 375, 518, 519, 520
Garud, R. and colleagues 560
Gatens, M. 549
Gauguin, Paul 586, 588
gaze, visual images 87–8
Gehry, Frank 561
gender
    as becoming 541
    expressing 360
    fluidity 543
    future research 548–50
    imperceptibility 547–8
    inequity 552–3
    as multiplicity 541
    as rhizomatic 545–6
    views of 540–1
gender discrimination, perpetrators 349–50
gender fluidity theory 543
gender identity 371
gender imperceptibility 541
gender politics 88
gender stereotypes 350
gender studies 16
General Motors 583
Generic Strategy Matrix (GSM) 187, 188
Generic Value Chain 189–90
genes 242
Gergen, K. 588
gestalt switch 241, 242, 243
Getzels, J.W. 37
Gherardi, S. 115
Ghoshal, S. 148, 187, 189
Gibb, S. 221
Gibson, J. 120, 521
Giddens, Anthony 113, 127, 303, 305–6, 518
Gilani, Shaheed Pervez 244
Gioia, D.A. and colleagues 418
global standardization 189
global terror networks 178–9

globalism 529
globalization 146, 182–3, 536
Goffman, Erving 220, 401, 438
goods 118–20, 270
Goodwin, C. 523
governance and control 75–7
Gramsci, Antonio 15, 440, 441
Grey, C. 16, 17–18
Grosz, E. 545
grounded experience 538–9
Guattari, Felix 541–2, 544–5
Guillet de Monthoux, Pierre 35, 226, 291, 357
Gunditjmara people 157

Haas, M.R. 526–7
habitualization 579
habitus 91
Hamm, Treahna 158, 159–60, 161–2, 163
handbooks, brief history 2–3
Hanke, Peter 39, 415–16, 418
Hansen, Kent 34
Hansen, M.T. 526–7
Haraway, Donna 521
Hardy, C. 2
harmony 175
Harré, Rom 51
Harrison, R. 356
Hartog, M. 321–2
Hatch, Mary Jo 35, 37, 221, 226, 417, 418
Heath, S. 87
Heidegger, M. 113, 118, 258, 260, 354
Hendry, J. 371
Henry V, as leadership model 402
Heskett, John 273
heterogeneity 122
high reliability organizations 36
Hilton, S.P. 321
Hinds, P.J. 102–3
Hirschman, Elizabeth and colleagues 279
historical deletion 242
Hitt, Michael 133
Hjorth, Daniel 35
holons 113
homogeneity 122
Honda 185, 374, 583
Honneth, A. 261–2
horizon of expectations 408
Horn, Kipps 164
Hostager, T.J. 390
Howard-Grenville, J.A. 116
Howell, J.M. 472
humanism 255–6
  autonomy of subject 257
  civic 256–7

development 256
  intersubjectivity 257, 259–61
  and relationship 258–9
  two strands 257–8
humiliation 263
Hunt, J.G. 479
Hunter, J.E. 138, 141–2, 143–4
Hurricane Katrina 266–7
Husserl, E. 113
hyper-adaptivity 418
hypersurveillance 443
hypothesis creation 456, 457
hypothetic inference 460–1

I (Todorov) 260–1
identification technologies 50
identity
  and artifacts 99, 100–1
  and artistry 418–20
  assembling 542
  co-construction 448
  construction 29
  contextualization 447
  creation 329, 417
  defining 66
  deviants 441–4
  as emerging perennial domain 63–4
  expressing through products 271
  as fad 66–7
  fragility of emergent 438
  gender 371, 541
  hijack 447
  and improvisation 387–8
  and indigenous knowledge 529–33
  loss of innocence 448
  as motion 547
  multiplicity 543
  organizational 447–8
  in organizational images 51
  and photographs 84
  play 414
  religious and cultural 442
  as rhizomatic 545
  as site of difference 544
  social construction 443–4
  stakeholder definition 447–8
  tyranny of 49–52
identity/alterity 52
identity/alterity dimensions 56–9
identity continuum 52
identity narratives 58–9
identity paradigm 49–50
ideology 20, 242, 442
ignorance 435

Ikea 272
image-management 208–9
images
　business leadership 89–90
　construction 52
　construction as interplay 52–5
　of European big city (Stockholm) 54–5
　of European capital city (Warsaw) 53–4
　leading European capital city (Rome) 55–6
　of organizations 51, 60–1
　social construction 91
　visual images as sites of social interaction 84
imagination, sociocultural 242
imaginative truth 406
imbrication 529
imperceptibility 547–8
improvisation 124
　as acquired skill 388
　complex people 387–9
　coordination mechanisms 389–90
　employees' ability 388
　and knowledge 388
　management 387–8
　open organizational designs 389, 392
　research 388
　resource allocation 391–3
imprudent savant 344
incommensurability 2, 242
indexicality 519, 520
indigenous knowledge 528
　enacting 533–4
　and organizational identity 529–33
　overcoming Western knowledge 535–6
　recovering 534–6
indigenous management systems 157–60
indigenous organization 533–6
Indigenous Standpoint Theory 156
individuals, and social order 110
induction 456–7
inductivism 139
industrial revolution 158
industries, intersection of 381–2
inequalities 243–6
infantilization 350, 352
inferences from data 137, 456
information feedback 195
information intermediaries 279
information-processing, and data 139–40
information technology, marketing of cities 55
innovation models 396
innovation research 282
inquiry 454–5
insider-outsider studies 134
insight 459

institutional capital 282
institutional change 578, 579–81
institutional entrepreneurship 573, 579, 581
institutional theory 136, 581
institutional transformation 578–9
institutionalization 116
institutions 578
instrumentalities 180
integration, conflicting groups 252
integrity 120
intellectual virtues 319, 320
intellectualocentrism 266–7
intelligent design 248–9
intensity 120
intensive research strategy and design 72–3
intentionality 120–1
inter-action 285–6
inter-firm collaboration 566
inter-practice tensions 121–3
inter-temporal tensions 121–3
interaction 506
　research and design 555–8
interaction effects 152–3
interactions, as situation of knowledge 521
interconnectivity 113
interdependence, negative 252
interdependent reality 168
interdisciplinarity 181
intermediaries, institutional 277
internal goods 118–20
international management 180–1
Internet Protocol version 6 576
interpretation 85
interpretive communities (ICs) 503–5
　enrolment 509
　future research 510–11
　interéssement 509
　mobilization of allies 509–10
　origin and nature 505–7
　power 507–10
　problematization 508–9
interpretive dominance 507–10
interpretive frames 506
intersections of multiple industries 381–2
intersubjective anthropology 261
intersubjectivity 519
　humanism 257, 259–61
intra-practice tensions 121–3
intuition 464–6
inversion 6–7, 38
invulnerability 481
Iona Community 528, 530–1
Irgens, Eirik 38
irony 22, 24, 313

irreverence 462
Islam 441–4
isomorphism 60–1
iteration 559
iterativity 38, 40
I<>thou relationship 263, 264
I<>you relationship 260–1
I<>you<>they relationship 261

Jackall, R. 16
Jacopin, E. 521
James, W. 455, 458, 459, 460
Japanangka 156–7
Jarzablowski, Paula 192, 367, 372–3
jazz
    as metaphor 455–6
    as pollutant 440
Jazz Age 436, 439–41, 444
Jeffcutt, P. 22
Jensen, R.J. 104
Jentoft, S. 325–6
Jermier, J. 293
job interviews 47–8
Johannesburg 53–4
Johannisson, B. 322
Jordan, Mike 164
Jyllands Posten 243

Kant, Immanuel 423–6, 429, 432
Kanungo, R.N. 472
Kennedy, E. 291
Kessler, E.H. 333
Kierkegaard, Soren 247–8
Kieser, A. 116
Kimbell, Lucy 37
King, A.S. 561
Klee, Paul 44–7
Klein, N. 21
Kleinman, Arthur 258–9
Knights, D. 540
knowing 221
    a practice 518–20
    sensory and emotional 470–1
    as situated practice 522–3
knowing-in-action 464
'knowing in practice' 43
knowledge
    absence of wisdom 344–5
    access mechanisms 316
    aesthetic 470
    assumptions 42
    Cartesian approach 42–3
    Celtic 530–1
    collective development 517

declarative 388
defining 517–18
definition 528
elements 259
forms of 319, 320
indigenous 528
interpretive communities (ICs) 505
management 103
Maori 531–3
new 64
objective 247
organization of 518
power dimensions 157
in practice 518–20
of practitioners 491, 496
procedural 388
propositional and tacit 464–6
reforming the body 359
relationship to practice 518
represented by artifacts 102
role of rhetorical power 510
selection 322
situated 520–2
structures 457–8
transfer 104
Western 529
knowledge-based perspective 195–8
knowledge management 154–5, 526–7
Koestler, A. 186
Kolb, David 464
Kosminski, A.K. 221
Kostera, M. 221
Kristeva, Julia 255, 351–2, 354, 357
Kristjánsson, K. 320–1
Kroc, Ray 208
Kuhn, Thomas 80, 138, 149, 241, 242–3,
    246–9, 455
Kuhnian research paradigm 137–9

labour, pain of 351, 356
labour process theorists 16
Lacan, Jacques 88
Lakatos, Imre 80
Lake Condah 157
Lamoreaux, Naomi 51
Langdale, A. 91
language 195–6, 470–1, 493–5, 521
Lather, Patti 157, 549
Latour, B. 113, 285–6, 304, 521
Lave, J. 116, 170–1
Lavine, M. 560
Law of Small Numbers 141–3
Lawrence, B. 373
Lawson, T. 71

Lawton, L. 291
lead cultures, symbolic value creation 276
leaders
  authenticity 93–4
  failure 481–2
leadership 221
  and arts 95
  charismatic 469, 471–2
  corporeality 471–2
  perspectives 479–80
  physically absent but socially present 475
  physically and socially absent 475–6
  physically and socially present 474
  physically present but socially absent 474–5
  shared 469
leadership research 469–70
lean enterprises 583
learning
  about organizations 213–14
  distributed 515
  how to question 490–1
  inhibiting 217
  perspectives of 170–2
  reflexive 464–5
learning approach, to control systems 391
left Weberianism 16
Legge, K. 121
legitimacy, represented by artifacts 102
LEGO 447
Levina, N. 560–1
Levi's 276–7
Lewin, K., three stage model 407, 409
Liang, N. 374
life, as theatre 401
lifeful-ness 6–7
liminal space 406
lines, in paintings 45–6
linguistic approach 470–1
Linstead, S. 540
listening 286
listening deeply with respect 158–60
Live8 338
Lodge, David 292–3
Löfgren, Orvar 57
logical positivism 79
logico-analytical knowledge 236
long-tail economics 190
Lopez, J. 70
Lorber, J. 540
love 261, 426
Lowe, K.B. 473
Luckmann, T. 471, 573, 579
Ludema, J.D. 206–7
Lupton, D. 110

Lutz, C. 88
Lyman, S.M. 406
Lynch, Michael 99

M-form 188–9
MacLeod, George 530
Madsen, P. and colleagues 561
Magic Mountain 350
Maitlis, S. 373
mal-practice 122
male and female, as categories 356
management
  and aesthetic play 429–30
  and art 37
  as distorted communication 14
  philosophy 329–31
  supporting improvisation 387–8
management and organization studies (MOS)
    future 82–3
management scholars, North America/European
    divide 251–3
management studies, as means and ends 347–8
managerialist stories 206
managers
  activist 578
  as ethical models 484
  inferences from data 137
  and strategy 192
Manchester 55
Mangham, I.L. 220, 403, 407–9
Mann, Thomas 350
Maori knowledge (MK) 528, 531–3
Mara-Drita, I. 579
March, J. 67
March, James 2, 99, 121, 146, 148–9, 316
Marcus, G.E. 290
margins, enhancing 188
marijuana 439, 440
market evaluation data 583
marketing and consumption, visual issues 85
marketization, in academic institutions 268–9
Martineau, Harriet 291
Marxism, studies of work organizations 15
Marzano, Stephano 272
maternal organizations 353, 355, 356
maternal, restoring 357–8
Matisse, Henri 45–6
matrices 353–4
matrix 189
MBA, as source of credibility 58
McAdam, D. 576
McCracken, Grant 271, 276, 279
McDonalds 205–6, 208
McHugh, A. 368

McIntyre, A. 118–20
McMaster, M.D. 558
Mead, G.H. 100, 455, 466
meaning 179, 505
  construction 508
  of objects 279–80
meaningful living 167–8
means and ends, organizational and management
    studies 347–8
measurement
  organizational performance 570–1
  scientific emphasis of 333
measurement error 143–4
Meindl, J.R. 472
Meisiek, Stefan 35, 403–4, 407
memes 242
mentalities 180
Merleau-Ponty, M. 45–6, 113, 118
meshworks 545
meta-analysis 141–2
meta-cognition 466
meta theory, critical relational constructionist
    285–6
metaphors 23, 220, 300–1, 567
Metaphors of the Mother 357
metaphysics, profane 256
metapictures 85–7
method acting 223
methodological principles, driving theory 135
methodology
  knowing as situated practice 522–3
  study of artifacts 105–7
Metiu, A. 102
metropolis 354–5
Meyer, Manulani 162
Meyer, R. 186
Meyerson, D. and colleagues 390
Michels, Robert 259
micro-interaction 466
milestones 390
Mill, John Stuart 258
mimesis 51
minimal specialization 392
Mintzberg, Henry 133, 134, 184, 186–7, 368
Mir, R. 365
mirroring 407
Mische, A. 74
mitsein 260
Mitspieler (co-players) 414
models, simple 570
modesty, in enquiry 490–1
Modleski, T. 88
molarity 541–2
monologic stories 206

monophonic stories 206
moral disengagement 481
moral panics 439–41, 444
Morgan, G. 2, 15, 138
Morgan, Gareth 300
Mortenson, M. 102–3
mothers, as ignored figures 350–1
motivation 430
motor racing 118, 119, 120, 121–3
Motorola 383
Mouffe, C. 245
moving 407
Multi-Stylistic Dialogism 207
multiplicity 542–7
  difference and diversion 545–7
  feminism 543–5
  in rhizome 545
  sameness and difference 541–2
  Value Chain 190
Mulvey, L. 88
music 34
mutual constitution, knowledge and practice 518
*Myth, Symbols and Folklore: Expanding the
    Analysis of Organizations* 204

narcissism 418, 419
narrative, as restrictive 205
narrative control 205
narrative fiction 288–9
  in academic articles 292
  defining 288–9
  in organizational studies 290–1
narrative inquiry 485–6
  apprenticeship 486–7
  developing craft and art 494
  email conversation 487–8
  externalizing conversations 492–4
  and organizational development 495–6
  persons as actors 492
  schmoosing 488–9
  St John of God Hospitality Practices
    Project 486
narrative styles 22
  linear 206
  in organizational studies 289–90
narrative therapy 488
narratives, identity 58–9
NASA 397
National Geographic 88
nationalism 50
nature, knowing one's own 257
necessity 70
needs, constructed and met by
    organizations 14

negative interdependence 252
negativity 52
neo-liberalism 256
neo-sociobiology 241
networks
    collaboration 566
    dynamics 379–80
    global terror 178–9
    organizational structures 189
    social spaces 249
    and strategy 187–8
New Journalism 294
new knowledge 64
new managerialism 75
new organizational forms 567–8
new public management 75
New York Times 86–7
niche analysis 144
Nicomachean Ethics 319
Nietzsche, Friedrich 258, 429, 431
Nike 207, 208, 276
Nissley, Nick 35, 407, 420
non-fiction 289
non-performativity, critical management studies
    (CMS) 17
Nord, W.R. 2
nothingness 215
nous 319
novel cultural expressions 276–7
novelty 36, 316
Novo Nordisk 33–4
nuclear weapons 307
Nystrom, P.C. 557

Oakes, L.S. and colleagues 366
objectification 87, 579
objective knowledge 247
Objectivism 483–4
objectivity 340
objects, meanings 279–80
observational methods 105–6, 456
observations 458–9
occupational jurisdiction 102
O'Connor, E. 207
O'Donoghue, Lowitja 160
Olivier, Richard 402
omnipotence 481
omniscience 481
On the Aesthetic Education of Man 427
ontology
    and aesthetics 221
    critical realism 70–1
    local 285
    open world 197

shifting 185
    of substance 115
open control mechanisms 391
open organizational designs 389, 392
open(-plan) fieldwork 259, 263–4
open source code 390
open source software 396–7
opinion leaders 279
optimism 481
organization, as situated social action 528
Organization Science 42
organization studies
    as distinct from economics 148–9
    performative turn 402
Organization Theater 34
organization theatre 403–4
organization theory, updating 146–7
organizational aesthetics 428
organizational culture 15
organizational design
    approaches to 385–9
    closed design/simple people approach 386
    control mechanisms 390–1
    fit 558–9
    research that matters 559–62
    static 554–5
organizational development, and narrative
    inquiry 495–6
organizational folklore 204
organizational identity theory 63–4
organizational learning, approaches to 170–2
organizational portfolio theory 136
organizational research, and recognition 261–3
organizational structures 189
organizational studies
    as means and ends 347–8
    narrative fiction in 290–1
    narrative styles in 289–90
    perspectives 479–80
organizational theatre 35
organizational theory 136
Organizations 146
organizations
    aesthetic nature 220, 221–2
    allocated and safe 355–7
    character and self 51
    conceiving 351–2
    cybernetic 79
    Darwinian 80
    as dynamic 554–5
    emptiness 215–16
    images 51, 60–1
    incorporating aesthetic play 433–4
    as invisible religion 168

organizations (*continued*)
  learning about 213–14
  as living cultures 33
  as living systems 160
  as markets 80–1
  as masculine 349
  maternal 353, 356
  maternal conception 355
  Neo-Carnegie perspective 150–1
  Orwellian 80
  parliamentary democracy 79–80
  patriarchal representations 351
  as positive and negative 14
  restoring the maternal 357–8
  self-construction 352
  size and data management 141–3
  as social sculptures 416–17
  ways of viewing 13
  wider implications 14
Orlikowski, W.J. 43, 101, 303
Orwellian organization 80
Osaka 55
ostensive, definition of 304
Oswick, C. 207, 300
Oticon 558
OtiKids 274, 277
outsourcing 182, 215
Overington, M.A. 220
Øvlisen, Mads 33–4
Owen-Smith, J. 103–4, 105–6

paintings 44–7
panopticon 441, 442–3
papers, writing 514–15
paradigm shift 461
paradigm wars 149
paradigmatic controversies 235
paradigms
  identity 49–50
  masculine and feminine 354
  rival 247
  sociological 15
Park Bei Luc(erne) (Klee) 44–7, 44illus
Park, Y. 289
parliamentary democracy 79–80
Parsons, Talcott 520
participation, in practice 124
partnerships, arts and business 412
Parviainen, J. 470
Pascale, R.T. 373–4
pathos 230, 235
Paton, Doris 158–62
patriarchal consciousness 354
patriarchal representations 351

patterns, and actions 303
Pavis, P. 408
peace and love 426
Pearce, C.L. 473
peer-surveillance 391
Peirce, Charles Sanders 454, 455, 460, 462–3
Pentland, B.T. 116, 121, 302, 303
people 191–2, 387–9
perception 43, 46, 273, 505, 506
performance
  organizational 570–1
  and routine 303
performance data 583
performative perspective 196
performativity 20, 360
  critical management studies (CMS) 17–18
period eye 89–90
personas, corporate 50–1
perspectives
  far away 587
  knowledge-based 195–8
  performative 196
Peters, Tom 567
Peterson, S. 110–11
Pettigrew, A. 368–9
Pfeiffer, J. 583
phenomenology 113
Philips 272
Phillips, N. 288, 292
philosophers, inspired by artists 428–9
philosophy
  analytical 426
  as core competence 79–81
  of management 329–31
  self-knowledge 259
photographs
  in artifact research 105
  as part of identity 84
phronesis 118, 197
  adopting as approach to inquiry 324–6
  distinguishing from episteme and techne
    320–1
  future possibilities 326–7
  growing interest 318
  intellectual and moral characteristics 321–2
  as interpretive approach 326
  key issues 318–19
  as methodology and attitude 322–3
  organizational inquiry 320–3
  philosophical basis 319–20
physical context, as situation of knowledge 521
Picasso, Pablo 64
Pineault, W.J. 403
Pink, Daniel 34

Pistoletto, Michaelangelo 434
Plato 68–9, 75, 77
Platt, J.R. 555
play 38, 295, 413–14, 418, 419, 427, 432–3
pleasure 236
plot 205
pluralism 2–3, 82–3
poetry 34
Poggio, Barbara 357
Polanyi, Michael 465
political values 249
politics
    cave metaphor (Plato) 68–9
    institutional change 572
Pollner, M. 520
pollution, of the body 440
Polyani, Michael 42
polylogic stories 206
polyphonic dialogism 206
polyphonic stories 206
Popper, Karl 79–80, 241, 242–3, 246–9, 455, 554
Porter, M.E. 184, 187
portraits, of CEOs 88, 89–91
positional power 508
positive deviance 501–2
Positive Organizational Scholarship 501–2
post-Hegelianism 51–2
post-industrialism 146
postmodernism 15, 16, 426
poststructuralism 15
Potter, G. 70
power 235–6, 436
    binary 548
    and globalization 182
    interpretive communities (ICs) 507–10
    of organizations 14
    in phronesis 325
    positional 508
    removal 354
    rhetorical 510
    as techniques of social relations 437
practice
    Aristotelian view 118
    arts 222
    as aspect of organization 113
    concept 517–18
    definitions 114–15
    diversity 122
    dynamic logic 123–5
    dynamics 122
    embodied 117
    embodiment 117–18
    emergence 114
    as focus of strategy research 364–5

improvisation 124
integrity, intensity and intentionality 120–1
internal and external goods 118–20
as modes of ordering 523
reconfiguration 125
reflexivity 124
relationship to knowledge 518
repetition 124
research 125–6
routines and rules 115–17
shaping 188–91
situated 519
strategic 372–3
strategy 191
tensions 121–3
in understanding organizations 125–6
practice-based learning 170–2
practice-based studies (PBS) 113, 515
practice theory 303, 305, 308 *see also*
    structuration/practice theory; structuration
    theory
practising 123–4
practitioners
    as knowledged 491
    strategic 371–2
pragmatic-realism 22–3
pragmatic validity 556
pragmatism 113, 172, 175, 320, 455–7, 466
Pratt, M.G. 105
praxeology, poetic 197
praxis 118
pre-identification 444
Pred, Allan 55
present truth 406
press, rights of expression 245
pressure to publish 20–1
Primitive Other 52
principles, methodological 135
prisons, as analogy for organizations 15
private-collective innovation model 396–7
private model of innovation 396
privatization, public services in Rome 56
Probyn, E. 549
process research 367–9
process, strategy 191
processes, symbolic value creation 277–80
producers, symbolic value creation 276
Product and Vision show 434–5
product design 277
production, symbolic 271–3
products, meaning 273
programming code 390
propositional knowledge 464–6
protreptics 330

Prusak, L. 526
publication, criteria 556
Pullen, A. 540
purchasing 270

qualitative methodology 235
quantitive data, inferences from 137
questions
    approachability 489
    as indicators of wisdom 332
    irresistibility 489
    modesty 490–1
    situating 489–90
Quinn, B. 209

Rabelais, François 203
radical humanism 15
radical structuralism 15
radical theatre 403
Rafaeli, A. 105
Ramirez, Rafael 426
Rand, Ayn 483–4
rational-actor models 580
rational choice theories 369
rational explanation 304
rationality 483, 516–17
reality 289
reassignment, symbolic value creation 279–80
Rechwitz, A. 115, 116
recognition, and organizational research 261–3
reconfiguration, of practice 125
reconstructionism, Neo-Carnegie perspective
    150–1
reflection-in-action 464–5, 488
reflexivity 374
    in asking questions 490–1
    critical 83, 462
    critical management studies (CMS) 17
    disciplined 467
    email conversation 488
    job interviews 47
    by leaders 482
    practice 124
    scholars working 133
    situated practices 519–20
    through play 414
    towards strangers 445
reframing 337–8
refreezing 407
Regnér, P. 373
reification 313
relational analysis 113
relationality, Value Chain 190
relationship, and humanism 258–9

relativism 248
reliability 143–4
religious values 245, 246
Rembrandt 430
repetition 124
replication 124
repressive authenticity 529
research
    humanist 262–3
    implications of strategy as practice
        370–3
    of importance to design 559–62
    innovation 282
    intensive strategy and design 72–3
    interaction with design 555–8
    making a difference 451–2
    possible futures 586–8
    practice-centred 125–6
    resources and capabilities 281–2
    into strategy 192
    trade-offs 453
    value 280–1
    value creation and exchange 280–2
research communities, as distinct and
        cooperative 251–3
research outputs 20
research practice 132–3
researchers
    choices 555–6
    inferences from data 137
resilience 382, 498–9
resistance 20
resource allocation 391–3
resource-based view (RBV) 367, 369
resources and capabilities 281–2
respect 164
retailers, speciality 272
retroductive analysis 71
retrospective data 555–6
reward, supervision and training 388
rhetoric 352–3
rhetorical power 507, 510
rhizomatics 545–7
rhizome 541–2, 544, 548
Rilke, Rainer Maria 492
risk 110–11
risk society 344, 441
Rochberg-Halton, E. 100, 273
Rome 55–6
Romme, A.G.L. 562
Ropo, A. 470, 479
Rorty, Richard 51
Rose, Mark 160, 161
Rosenthal, P. 390

Ross-Smith, A. 322
Rouleau, L. 371
routine 316
routine dynamics 302
routines
    actor-network theory explanation 309–11,
        312–13
    as black boxes 308
    change and conservatism 173–4
    changes 303, 305
    control 304
    dynamics 304–7
    as generative systems 303–4
    inside the black box 308–11
    and organizational change 302
    ostensive aspects 302–3, 304
    performative aspects 302–3
    in practice 116
    re-conceptualization 113
    structuration/practice theory explanation
        308–9, 311–12
Ruderman, R.S. 326
Ryle, Gilbert 43

Sahlins, M. 274
Sallaz, J.J. 390
Samra-Fredericks, D. 367, 371, 373
Sapient Corporation 559–60
Saul, Ralston 536
Sayer, A. 71–2, 76
Schatzki, T.R. 115, 116
Schein, E.H. 557
Schiller, Friedrich 426–8, 429, 431–2
Schmidt, Enno 35
Schmidt, F.L. 138, 141–2, 143–4
Schmitt, C. 245–6
schmoosing 488–9
scholars, communities 514–15
Schon, D. 464–5, 488
Schön, D. 121, 132, 133
Schopenhauer, Arthur 428–9
Schrat, Henrik 33, 34–5, 414–15, 434–5
Schreyögg, G. 403–4, 407
Schroeder, J. 85
Schultz, M. 418
Schutz, A. 113, 118, 457–8, 518
Schwartz, H.S. 357
science 333, 461
Science Commons project 397
Scott, Lee 209
Scott, M.B. 406
screening deviance 443
secular fundamentalism 245
sedimentation 579

Seidl, D. 371
selection, of knowledge 322
self-concept 93
self-control 329
self-expressive benefits 273
self-monitoring 93–4
self-organization 113
self-other differentiation 286
self<>other relationship 261
semi-critical studies 15
semi-fiction 288–9
    definition 294
    subversive role 294–7
semiotization of activities 236
Sen, A. 67
Sennett, R. 21
sensemaking 29–30, 455, 457, 467
Sensemaking in Organizations 29
senses
    engagement in storytelling 207
    questioned by art 32
    training 493–5
sensory experience 221
sensory understanding 470
sensus communis 197, 424
September 11th, 2001 110
serious play 413–14
Sevón, Guje 57
Shakespeare, William 220, 402
Shamir, B. 472
shared leadership 469, 473
shared understandings 303
shipping 147
sign production, symbolic value creation
    277–8
significance, of products 273
silence 160
Simon, H.A. 139, 140, 146
situated practices, features 519
situatedness 366, 368
situation theatre 403–4
Slotnick, H.B. 321
small numbers, as sources of error 141
Small World 292–3
Smircich, L. 125
Smith, Kenneth 133
Snow, D.A. 576
Snyder, M. 93–4
social action, transformational model 73, 74
social complexity 114
social constructionism 424, 471
social engineering 241
social interaction, CEO portraits 90
social meanings, and artifacts 99

social membership, and artifacts 101–3
social order, and individuals 110
social phenomenology 528
social pollution 111
social practices 365
social practices, culturally specified 277
social reality, cross-cultural construction 249
social sciences, alterity in 51–2
social sculptures 416–17, 419, 430
social skills, and institutional change 579–81
social values 325
social worlds theory 171, 172–3, 176
socialization 387
society
    health and justice 168–9
    as non-demonstrable 304
socio-cultural theories, of risk 110
socio-political theory, Platonic and Aristotelian
    68–9
sociocultural imagination 242
sociological paradigms 15
software, over-reliance on 207
solidarity 100
Sony Walkman 279
sophia 319
spaces between 157
speciality retailers 272
specialization, minimal 392
speech acts 224
spontaneous cooperation 197
Srivasta, S. 206–7
St John of God Hospitality Practices Project 486
Stablein, R. 290
stakeholders 447, 448
standard operating procedures 304
Stanislavski, C. 220, 223
Starbuck, Bill 251, 557
statistico-organizational theory
    basis 136
    central idea 136, 140–1
    as deductive 139
    focus of attention 138
    Law of Small Numbers 141–3
    measurement error 143–4
    overview 140–4
statistics, in social sciences 137–8
Stein, Gertrude 294
Steyaert, Chris 35
stock market planetarium 34
Stockholm 54–5, 56, 57
stories
    answerability 205
    appropriation 203
    consummation 205

image-management 208–9
    managerialist 206
    restricted by narrative 205
    as retrospective sensemaking 205–6
    textuality and intertextuality 207
    ways of telling 207
story advice books 206
story magic 203
story power 208
story research, possibilities 207–9
story theory, conceptual debates 205–9
storytelling
    as metaphor 220
    technique 222
storytelling organizations 203, 204, 208, 209
strange attractors 179
strangers 436, 437–9
    African-Americans 439–41
    working with 587
Strannegård, Lars 59–60
strategic actors 371
strategic choice 187–8
strategic practices 372–3
strategic practitioners 371–2
strategic supply chain management 383–4
strategic transformation, through social
    movement 577–8
strategic vision 381
strategy
    as academic discipline 199–200
    comes from 186–7
    defining 185–6, 365–6
    employees, managers and students 192
    key personnel 191
    makers 191–2
    margins 188
    people who enact 191–2
    postmodernism 190–1
    practice of 184–8
    research 192
    shaping practice 188–91
    strategic choice 187–8
    underlying assumption 190
    vision and values 190–1
strategy as practice 115
    defining 365–7
    implications for practice 374
    implications for research 370–3
    implications for teaching 373–4
    as research topic 365
strategy of inquiry 295
strategy process research 367–9
strategy research 364–5
Strathern, Marilyn 521

Strati, Antonio 48, 470
stratified social ontology 70–1
Strauss, A. 172, 173
streams of activity 367
Street Corner Society 375
structuralism, radical 15
structuration/practice theory 309–12 *see also*
    practice theory; structuration theory
structuration theory 113, 127, 303, 305–6, 308
    see also practice theory;
    structuration/practice theory
students, and strategy 192
subcultures 503
  symbolic value creation 276–7
subject, autonomy of 257
subjectification 87–8
subjection 235–6
subjectivity 340
subworlds 173, 176
Suchman, Lucy 521
supervision, training and reward 388
supply chain failures 383
supply chain management 383–4
surveillance 442
survival art 36
Sutton, R. 583
SWOT analysis 373
symbolic consumption 271
Symbolic Interactionism 171, 172, 175, 176, 466
symbolic production 271–3
symbolic value 270, 280
symbolic value creation 274–6
  absorption 276–7
  advertising 277
  communities 276–7
  consumers 276–7
  experts 276
  lead cultures 276
  processes 277–80
  producers 276
  reassignment 279–80
  research 280–2
  sign production 277–8
  subcultures 276–7
symbolism, of goods 270
symbolizing potential 273–4
syntactic boundaries 103
Szulanski, G. 104

tacit knowledge 42, 464–6
Tales of Love 357
Tamara 208
Tarde, Gabriel 49, 50
Taussig, Michael 51

Taylor, F.W. 386, 441
Taylor, Steve 37, 38
team dynamics 102
techne 319
technik 257–8
technological frames 101
technologies of intimacy 329
technology 365
telos 118
Ten Bos, R. 547–8
tension
  in art 32
  inter-practice, intra-practice, inter-temporal
    121–3
  and learning 170–2, 175–6
  organizational learning case study 173–5
tensions 114
terrorism 110–11
text positivism 27
textuality and intertextuality 207
The Appearance of Fantasy 414–15
The Art Firm 35
The Beauty of Social Organization 426
the body 359–60
The Nature of Managerial Work 186
The New Art of the Leader 32
The Organization Man 445
theatre 223
  aesthetic judgment 431
  audience 408
  commissioning the play 407–8
  future research 405–9
  impact of the performance 408
  as metaphor for life 401
  mise en scene 408
  as a resource 402–3
  separate realities 407
  as social science 406
  as technology 403–5
themes 6–9
theories
  and action 196
  simple and complex 556
theories of action 132, 133
  as self-fulfilling 148
theorizing 467–8
  feminist 359–60
theory
  driven by methodological principles 135
  tyranny of 449–50
theory of symbolic value creation 274–6
therapy 223
they (Honneth) 261–2
they (Todorov) 261

ThinkCycle 397
Third Critique 424, 426
Thompson, James 31
Thompson, P. 17
Thompson, S. 204
three stage model (Lewin) 407, 409
three virtues of character 321
Tietze, S. 357
'tikanga' 532
time, reframing concept in Dadirri 162
Todorov, T. 259–62
Torbert, B 226
total institutions 438
Total Quality Management 174
Toyota 583
trade-offs, in research 453
tragedy 22
training, supervision and reward 388
training, use of theatre 402–3
transaction cost economics 136, 146
transformation, of Western body 360
transformational model of social action
        (TMSA) 73, 74
translation
    intercultural 250
    sociocultural evolution 242
transnationalism 189
transport systems 53–4, 56
Triavinija, Rirkit 433
tribal behavior 538–9
Trilling, L. 493
trust 104, 391
truth, imaginative and present 406
Tsoukas, H. 42–3, 133, 505
turbulence 333
Turner, B.S. 441
Turner, Victor 406
Twain, Mark 222
tyranny, of theory 449–50
Tyre, M. 390

uncertainty 140
understanding, sensory and emotional 470
Underwood, Paula 334
unfreezing 407
ungendering 540
Ungunmerr, Miriam-Rose 158
Unilever Faberge 339
universality 425
urbanization 50
user imagery 277
utility 273
utility maximizing 304
utopias 442

Vaara, E. and colleagues 366
Vaast, E. 560–1
Vaill, P.B. 220
Valery, P. 181
validity 391, 556
value-added 189–90
Value Chain 189–90
value chimera 190
value commitments 507
value creation 273–4, 280–2
values 190–1
    political 249
    religious 245, 246
    symbolic 270
van Ardenne-van der Hoeven, Agnes 245,
        248–9
Venn, C. 491
verbs, expressive 222–5
Vickery, J. 44
Vico, G. 221, 344–5
virtual companies 215
virtual organizations 239
virtue 323
visibility 391, 392
vision 190–1, 381
visual images
    framing 87
    gaze 87–8
    metapictures 86–7
    objectification 87
    period eye 89–90
    as sites of social interaction 84
    subjectification 87–8
    as tangible 85
visual issues, marketing and
        consumption 85
Vladimirou, E. 505
VNTK system 307, 309, 310–11
voice 263–4
von Hippel, E. 390

Wagner, Richard 428–9
Wal-Mart 208–9
Wang, J. 374
war rooms 208
Warde, A. 115
Warhol, Andy 429
Waring, D. 321
Warsaw 53–4, 56, 57
water quality, Warsaw 54
Watson, A. 365
ways of knowing, spaces between 157
we 447
Weber, Max 259, 554

Wedgwood, Josiah 271
Wedlin, Linda 57–9
Weick, Karl 2, 29, 35, 36, 133–4, 205, 290, 455, 457, 461, 467
Wells, H.G. 293
Wenger, E.C. 116, 170–1
Wernick, Andrew 277–8
West, Errol (Japanangka) 156–7
Western knowledge 529
Wheatley, M. 160, 333
When the Sleeper Wakes 293
White, Michael 491
Whiteman, G. 290, 295
Whittington, R. 115, 116, 187, 370
Whyte, W.F. 375, 445
Williams, R. 91
Willmott, H. 14
Wilson, D. 186
wisdom
    absence from knowledge 344–5
    adding value to other frameworks 336–7
    core values 333–4
    defining 334–6
    downside 345
    framing and reframing 337–8
    and nature of questions 332
    organization design and culture 338–40
    organizational manifestations 337–8
    qualities 335–6
    reframing 333
    as subdued 332–3
    as way of being and doing 344
wisdom lens 336–7
wise people 344–5
Wolin, S. 68–9
women, in organizations 352
work, and play 413–14
work environments 338–9
workplace spirituality 167–9
writing 549
Wunbaya, Alfred 157

Yancey Martin, P. 471
Yanow, D. 523
Young, Carey 39
Young, T.R. 401–2

Zammuto, R. 157–8
Zimmerman, D.H. 520
Zyglidopoulos, S. 292